THE LAWYER'S STYLE GUIDE

A Student and Practitioner Guide

The Lawyer's Style Guide

A Student and Practitioner Guide

Peter Butt

BA, LLM, LLD (Syd)
Emeritus Professor of Law, University of Sydney
Formerly visiting professor of law at Universities of Bristol, Nottingham, Cambridge, Vanderbilt
Former Inns of Court Fellow, Inner Temple, London

• HART •
OXFORD • LONDON • NEW YORK • NEW DELHI • SYDNEY

HART PUBLISHING

Bloomsbury Publishing Plc

Kemp House, Chawley Park, Cumnor Hill, Oxford, OX2 9PH, UK

1385 Broadway, New York, NY 10018, USA

29 Earlsfort Terrace, Dublin 2, Ireland

HART PUBLISHING, the Hart/Stag logo, BLOOMSBURY and the Diana logo are trademarks of Bloomsbury Publishing Plc

First published in Great Britain 2021

A catalogue record for this book is available from the British Library.

Library of Congress Cataloging-in-Publication data

Names: Butt, Peter, author.

Title: The lawyer's style guide / Peter Butt.

Description: Oxford, UK ; New York, NY : Hart Publishing, an imprint of Bloomsbury Publishing, 2021. | Includes bibliographical references and index.

Identifiers: LCCN 2020047682 (print) | LCCN 2020047683 (ebook) | ISBN 9781509936243 (paperback) | ISBN 9781509936267 (pdf) | ISBN 9781509936250 (Epub)

Subjects: LCSH: Legal composition. | Law—Terminology. | Law—United States—Language.

Classification: LCC KF250 .B885 2020 (print) | LCC KF250 (ebook) | DDC 808.06/634—dc23

LC record available at https://lccn.loc.gov/2020047682

LC ebook record available at https://lccn.loc.gov/2020047683

ISBN: PB: 978-1-50993-624-3
ePDF: 978-1-50993-626-7
ePub: 978-1-50993-625-0

Typeset by Compuscript Ltd, Shannon

For Lin

Preface

What are the hallmarks of an effective legal-writing style? Some may say that the question is unhelpful, because the answer is necessarily subjective. To some extent, they are correct: different styles appeal to different readers. Some readers prefer a flowery style, others prefer a dry one; some prefer formality, others informality; some prefer detail, others sparseness. But in my view, to ask whether a legal-writing style is 'effective' goes beyond mere subjective preferences. Rather, it asks whether the writing achieves what it sets out to achieve, in a way that communicates seamlessly to its intended audience. It goes to fundamental principles of communication, many of which are objectively verifiable.

For me, the hallmarks of an effective legal-writing style are encapsulated in three criteria: clarity, brevity, and legal efficacy. *Clarity*—because the meaning of a legal text should be transparent, readily understandable by the intended audience on a first reading. *Brevity*—because the content of a legal text should be as brief as the subject matter allows, with no wasted words or superfluous provisions; the aim should be to communicate, not to impress. *Legal efficacy*—because the purpose of a legal text (even if clear and brief) fails unless it achieves the intended legal outcome. These criteria apply to all kinds of legal writing—including statutes, contracts, deeds, wills, letters, emails, legal advices, and court judgments.

Tested by these criteria, modern legal writing often falls short. Perhaps this is to be expected: few legal education institutions (at least, in Britain and Commonwealth countries) encourage their students to critique legal-writing styles. Indeed, most law students emerge from their educational chrysalis adopting (uncritically) the only legal-writing style they know. And what style is that? It is the style adopted by the role models they encounter in their legal studies—the style of academics, tutors, and judges. But those writers themselves adopted the style of yet-earlier role models—such is the power of precedent in the training of lawyers in the common law world. In this way, conventional legal-writing style passes from one generation to the next, largely unexamined. No wonder, then, that many contemporary lawyers assume that an 'effective' legal-writing style is formal, dense, and academic, packed with passives, archaisms, word strings, and redundancies. Carl Felsenfeld's rebuke says it well:

> 'Lawyers have two main failings. One is that they do not write well. The other is that they think they do.' (Carl Felsenfeld, 'The Plain English Movement in the United States' (1981–82) 6 *Canadian Business Law Journal* 413)

This book aims to help lawyers and law students cast off the fetters of an outmoded style. It urges a better style, one that communicates more readily to a modern readership. It encourages modern legal writers to consider for themselves whether their 'style'—reflected in the structure, tone, and word-choice of their writing—best serves the interests of their readers. Does it draw readers into the text, or does it drive them away, to read no further?

The book follows a 'dictionary' format, with entries arranged in alphabetical order for ease of reference. Entries cover three broad areas:

- **Legal concepts** (headwords in capital letters). These entries cover matters as diverse as ambiguity, deeds, definitions, humour, metaphor, merger clauses, 'fuzzy law', provisos, recitals, simplified outlines, terms of art, tone, and the various principles of legal interpretation.
- **Words and phrases** (headwords in lower case). These entries consider specific legal expressions, particularly ones that non-lawyers find opaque and obscure. The purpose is to convince lawyers and law students that it is usually safe to substitute a plain-English equivalent. To do that, however, it is first necessary to understand the meaning of the original.
- **Practical usage** (headwords usually in upper case, but in lower case where dealing with specific words and phrases). These entries cover usage issues such as abbreviations, acronyms, active and passive voice, brackets, bullet points, citation methods, cross-referencing, fonts, document design, footnotes, gender-neutral language, numbering systems, plain language, punctuation, the use of Latin, structures for legal advices and documents, and techniques for editing and proofreading.

Most entries include examples of style and usage, drawn from judgments, legal documents, and (occasionally) legal textbooks. The sources range across many jurisdictions, including England, Scotland, Ireland, Australia, New Zealand, Singapore, Hong Kong, and South Africa. The book occasionally dips into US legal usage, mostly by way of comparison. Where a style or usage is deficient, the book suggests alternatives, designed to preserve legal nuance while communicating more clearly to modern readers.

Some of the ideas in this book first appeared in *Legal Usage: A Modern Style Guide* (2017), published in Australia and New Zealand only. This present book builds on those ideas, but has been enlarged and rewritten. It is now tailored to a wider UK and Commonwealth readership—in fact, to a readership in any country where English is the language of the law.

My style recommendations unashamedly endorse 'plain English'. Plain English requires more than eliminating archaisms, pruning circumlocutions, and finding alternatives for arcane terms of art. It requires also paying attention to larger matters of audience, structure, and tone. The aim is not to dumb-down communication, but to elevate it; not to deaden writing, but to enliven it; not to discourage elegance, but to enhance it. Nor is the aim to squeeze lawyers into a stylistic straitjacket, devoid of flair and personality. On the contrary, the aim is to show that law can be written in a style that is individual and readable, has punch and panache—and is legally accurate.

My own role models of effective legal style feature regularly in the following pages. They include a number of UK and Commonwealth judges, both current and past. They also include contemporary non-judicial legal writers, such as (in alphabetical order so as not to suggest priority) Mark Adler, Martin Cutts, Robert Eagleson, David Elliott, Bryan Garner, Kevin Gray, Neil James, Joe Kimble, Christine Mowat, and Richard Wydick.

In preparing this book, I have benefited greatly from research at various institutions, over many years. They include the universities of Vanderbilt (USA), Nottingham, Bristol, and Cambridge, and the Centre for Plain Legal Language (University of Sydney, Australia). A period at the Inner Temple, London, as an Inns of Court Fellow, allowed me to examine first-hand the writing styles of barristers, solicitors, legislative drafters, and judges.

On matters of substantive law, I received help in particular from Darryl Browne, David Raphael, and Professor John Stumbles. Mark Campbell, librarian at King & Wood Mallesons, helped gain access to international publications. Professor Nigel Gravells (University of Nottingham) tracked down some notably obscure UK materials.

Others, too, have helped guide the book to completion. Sinead Moloney, of Hart, has been an enthusiastic supporter of the book ever since I first suggested the idea to her. Nick Allen, of Forewords, edited the manuscript with long-suffering patience and an exceptional eye for detail, and Tom Adams expertly guided the page proofs through several iterations. Gill Glen proofread most the manuscript, bringing English- and foreign-language skills to what must have seemed a never-ending task. And my wife, Lin, read the entire manuscript several times, patiently enduring my compulsion to revise, revise, and revise again. Lin is my shrewdest critic and my strongest supporter. To her, I dedicate this book.

The law is stated from materials available to me on 26 January 2021.

Peter Butt

Explanatory Notes

Concepts and Terms

Each entry begins with a headword. Headwords are arranged alphabetically.

Headwords are divided into *concepts* and *terms*:

Concepts are overview topics, dealing with larger aspects of legal style or usage. Most are practical; a few are theoretical. Headwords for concepts are shown in capital letters. For example:

DEFINITIONS
RECITALS
SIMPLER WORDS AND PHRASES

Terms are words or phrases commonly found in legal usage. They range across all areas of legal practice, from the commonplace to the obscure. Headwords for terms are shown in lower case. For example:

ab initio
deem
in the form of

Alternative usages

Where alternative usages (including alternative spellings or capitalisations) exist, the entries in the headword are separated by a forward slash. For example:

Act / act
means / includes
rescind / terminate / end

'See' references

'See' entries refer the reader to the discussion of a concept or term under another entry.

'See also' references

'See also' entries refer the reader to further information about a concept or term.

'Further reading' references

'Further reading' entries refer the reader to other sources discussing the concept or term.

Examples

Many entries include examples, designed to discuss the concept or term. Some examples are hypothetical; other examples are taken from judgments or legal texts. Where a style or usage in an example seems ineffective, archaic, or plainly wrong, then a preferred alternative usage is given in square brackets.

Abbreviations

References to law reports follow standard abbreviation conventions. Thus: AC = Appeal Cases, WLR = Weekly Law Reports, CLR = Commonwealth Law Reports, and so on. Most abbreviations are of standard law reports; but the occasional esoteric ones will be found in any published list of law report abbreviations.

Contents

a (indefinite article)

Singular or plural?

The normal sense of *a* is singular. For example, a covenant restricting the use of land to '*a* private dwellinghouse' limits the use to a *single* dwelling-house only: *Crest Nicholson Residential (South) Ltd v McAllister* [2003] 1 All ER 46, 51; affirmed [2004] 2 All ER 991, [53]. But on occasion, the singular can include the plural—eg, under an interpretation statute, or under an interpretation clause in a contract, or under a principle of interpretation. In such situations, *a* can mean more than one. For example, a person extradited to face trial for '*a* corrupt practice' could be tried for *several* counts of corrupt practice: *R v Riley* (1890) 59 LJMC 122.

Choosing between *a* and *an*

1. Where words begin with a consonant sound, use *a*; where words begin with a vowel sound, use *an*. The sounds control, not the letter: ie, '*a* European Union directive', but '*an* EU directive'.
2. Where *a* precedes the letter *h*, practice varies. The former convention used *an* before *h* (even where pronounced strongly). That convention is disappearing, but is not yet obsolete. The modern convention uses *a* where *h* is pronounced strongly, but *an* where *h* is pronounced lightly. Thus, '*a* hereditament', '*a* hearing', '*a* hypothecation'; but '*an* heir', '*an* honour', '*an* H-bomb'.

Examples

- 'What the judge embarked upon was a determination of *a hypothetical* fact.' [*Van Dal Footwear Ltd v Ryman Ltd* [2009] EWCA Civ 1478, [11]; [2010] 1 WLR 2015 (Lewison LJ)]
- 'It is a unit of property … and is thus *an hereditament* [prefer: *a hereditament*(?)] within the meaning of section 2 of the *Water Charges Act 1976*.' [*South West Water Authority v Rumble's (A Firm)* [1984] 1 WLR 800, 801–02 (Ackner LJ)]
- 'That was relevant to the appellant's reliance upon *an hypothesis* [prefer: *a hypothesis*(?)] of a transfer of DNA from the appellant's hand to Sumner's hand …' [*Fitzgerald v R* [2014] HCA 28, [24]; (2014) 311 ALR 158 (High Court of Australia)]

Repeating for clarity

For clarity, it may be wise to repeat the indefinite article when referring to two or more objects. For example:

> 'The committee chose a secretary and treasurer.' If the organisation's rules allow one person to fill both roles, did the committee choose one person or two? Contrast: 'The committee chose a secretary and a treasurer.'

Used distributively

Sometimes, *a* is used in place of the distributive *per* or *each*. Thus, '12 instalments *a* [ie, in the sense of *each*] year'. Prefer *each*, which carries the sense more immediately:

> '[T]he Civil Service received some 20,000 letters *a* year [prefer: *each* year].' [*Graham v Minister for Immigration and Border Protection* [2017] HCA 33, [142]; (2017) 263 CLR 1 (Edelman J)]

See also **SINGULAR / PLURAL; the.**

a fortiori

Latin: with stronger reason; even more so; more conclusively. Implies that, because a certain conclusion or fact is true, a further conclusion or fact must also be true.

> 'Since the CJEU has been clear in these decisions that unmarried partners do not fall to be treated as direct family members, then *a fortiori* [prefer: *even more so*] there could not be any justification for treating their adult children any differently.' [*Latayan v Secretary of State for Home Department* [2020] EWCA Civ 191, [21] (Peter Jackson LJ)]

The English translation loses nothing of the force of the original—so prefer it.

a posteriori

Latin: from the latter; from what comes after. Refers to reasoning derived from observing facts or from prior experience—ie, inductive reasoning; distinguished from *a priori*, or deductive, reasoning. Although often found, *a posteriori* has not yet become standard English; so, for the benefit of readers untutored in Latin, replace it with standard English. For example:

> 'It is improbable that this reconstruction *a posteriori* [prefer: *after the event*] represents the mental process by which the inventor in fact arrived at his invention …' [*Technograph Printed Circuits Ltd v Mills & Rockley (Electronics) Ltd* [1972] RPC 346, 362 (Lord Diplock)]

See also **a priori**.

a priori

Latin: from what comes before; from what is already known. Refers to reasoning from principles already known—ie, deductive reasoning. Prefer standard English. For example:

> 'One must therefore look to the statute in order to determine what … questions are required to be answered, rather than proceed on *a priori* [prefer: *existing*] assumptions.' [*Perara-Cathart v R* [2017] HCA 9; (2017) 260 CLR 595, [40] (Kiefel, Bell and Keane JJ)]

See also **a posteriori**.

a tempore cuius contrarii memoria non existet

Latin: from a time when there is no memory to the contrary.

See **time out of mind**.

ab agendo

Latin: incapacitated and therefore unable to act in a transaction. An inexcusable Latinism in modern legal usage—and, thankfully, rarely found:

> '[It was not the purpose of the statute] to oust the workman in the matter of compensation for injury under the Act of 1906 from all control of his own affairs, to entitle the Insurance Commissioners to step in and take such control, and to intervene in such matters as though the workman were *ab agendo* [prefer: *legally incapable*] and under their curatory …' [*Gormley v Scottish Iron and Steel Co Ltd* [1918] SLR 667, 671 (Lord Johnston)]

ab ante

Latin: in advance; beforehand. A pedantic Latinism, but still used occasionally (particularly in Scotland, where legal Latin lingers longer). One example is where a court decides *ab ante* a point of law on which other issues stand or fall (so that a decision on that point may avert the need for litigation on other issues). Prefer a plain-English equivalent:

- 'Where accordingly it is *ab ante* [prefer: *at the outset*; *as a preliminary issue*] demonstrable that no actual wrong has been caused or suffered an action thus necessarily for only nominal damages for maintenance will not lie.' [*Neville v London 'Express' Newspaper Limited* [1919] AC 368, 421 (Lord Shaw of Dunfermline)]
- 'Failure to object *ab ante* [prefer: *at the outset*; *early*] to an illegal proceeding cannot convert it into a legal one.' [*Collector of Land Revenue, South West District Penang v Kam Gin Paik* [1986] 1 WLR 412, 417 (PC, Lord Keith)]
- 'Nor do I think it can be said with confidence *ab ante* [prefer: *in advance*] that any evidence about the appeal would be of no relevance to, and would be inadmissible in, the criminal proceedings.' [*The Rangers FC Group Ltd v Stephen* [2017] ScotCS CSOH 85, [12] (Lord Doherty)]

ab antiquo

Latin: from ancient times. Thus, Blackstone uses *ab antiquo* to describe the time at which ecclesiastical jurisdiction began over wills and intestacies: *Commentaries on the Law of England* (1768) book 3, 96. In modern times, however, prefer a plain-English substitute.

ab extra

Latin: from outside; from outside factors. Usually used in relation to the admission of evidence: eg, evidence of a testator's intention might be sought from outside the written terms of the will, or evidence of parliament's intention might be sought from outside the words of a statute. Unless pedantry is prized, prefer a simple English translation. For example:

> 'Traditionally, the amplitude of rights vested in the [owner of land] has been equated with the fullest ultimate rights, subject to any restrictions imposed *ab extra* [prefer: *from external factors*], of use, enjoyment, destruction and alienation known to the common law.' [*Harry v Valuer-General* (1975) 12 SASR 446, 454 (Wells J)]

ab initio

Latin: from the beginning. Usually found as part of a compound term: eg, *rescission ab initio*, *void ab initio*. While having the appearance of a term of art, *ab initio* is easily expressed in plain English with no loss of legal efficacy—so prefer plain English: eg, *rescission ab initio* = 'rescission as from the beginning', or 'rescission from scratch'; *void ab initio* = 'void from the start', or 'void from the outset'. Sometimes, *ab initio* is used alone, as pure affectation—in which case, even more so, prefer plain English: eg, 'The accused could have *ab initio* [prefer: *from the start*] refused to answer any questions.'

abate

To reduce or limit. The term appears in a number of legal contexts; in each, a simpler substitute is available without loss of legal nuance. For example:

- *Legacies*: In a will, if a fund is not sufficient to pay all legacies, each is said to *abate rateably* [prefer: *reduce proportionately*].
- *Nuisance*: In the law of nuisance, a person may have a right to *abate* [prefer: *reduce, limit*] a threatened or existing nuisance.

ABBREVIATIONS

Full stops?

Legal documents use abbreviations in the same way as ordinary prose, unless good reason requires otherwise. However, abbreviation techniques vary between countries.

British and Commonwealth usage

The trend in Britain and most Commonwealth countries is towards 'open punctuation', deleting full stops from:

- initials—J Smith (not J. Smith)
- abbreviations—Co (*not* Co.), eg (*not* e.g. or eg.), ie (*not* i.e. or ie.)
- contractions—Mr (*not* Mr.), Pty Ltd (*not* Pty. Ltd.).

This is now the preferred usage. Formerly, standard usage added a full stop to:

- initials—J. Smith (John Smith)
- abbreviations—Co. (Company), v. (versus), in liq. (in liquidation), e.g. (for example), i.e. (that is).

Usually, modern business entities themselves omit punctuation: 'ABC Electrical Services', 'XYZ Bank Ltd'.

Where punctuation is part of an entity's registered name, it is prudent to retain it in legal documents. This is because, in some jurisdictions, statute requires a contracting party to use its registered name precisely. Failure to do so may cast doubt on the legality of the transaction.

In citations of law reports in most British and Commonwealth countries, abbreviations do not take full stops: eg, 3 Ves & B 79; 35 ER 409 (*not* 3 Ves. & B. 79; 35 E.R. 409); AC (*not* A.C.); All ER (*not* All E.R.); NSWLR (*not* N.S.W.L.R.).

US usage

US legal usage remains more traditional, and still prefers full stops (periods) for abbreviations, including law reports: i.e., e.g., v., S.C., S.W.3d, and so on—eg, *Kane v. Board of Appeals* 390 Md. 145, 164, 887; A.2d. 1060, 1071 (2005), cert. denied, 547 U.S. 1179 (2006).

No apostrophes for plurals

Plural abbreviations do not take apostrophes: NGOs (*not* NGO's), WLRs (*not* WLR's).

Explain clearly

Unless your reader is likely to understand an abbreviation, explain it as if it were a defined term, and as early as possible:

- In a letter or advice: define (explain) the abbreviation when you first use it.
- In a document such as a contract, deed or statute: if you use the abbreviation in one clause only, explain (define) it in that clause; if you use it throughout the document, define it in the dedicated definitions clause.

Always define (explain) the abbreviation, not the full term: if you use 'ADIZ' to mean Air Defence Identification Zone, define (explain) 'ADIZ', not 'Air Defence Identification Zone'.

Having explained or defined an abbreviation, be consistent: do not revert to the full term elsewhere.

See also **ACRONYMS; DEFINITIONS; SHORT NAMES.**

abet

See **aid and abet**.

abeyance

A gap, absence. *Abeyance* appears in highly technical areas of law, so it might appear to be a genuine term of art. But that is not so; *abeyance* can always be replaced with a simpler English equivalent. For example, the classic land law principle, derived from medieval times, that the law abhors an '*abeyance* of seisin', can be restated simply as the law abhors a 'gap in seisin'; or (simpler still), the law abhors a 'vacuum in title': *Ho Young v Bess* [1995] 1 WLR 350, 355 (PC). Other plain-language substitutes include:

- 'The [Home Office] put the Appellant's name on a stop file list of that year. This meant that any passport applications made after that date should have been *held in abeyance* [prefer: *held back*; *suspended*] until the Appellant's identity and entitlement to a passport could be verified.' [*Fayad v Home Office* [2016] EWCA Civ 78, [5] (Jackson LJ)]
- 'Her case was not consolidated with [another case], but *held in abeyance* [prefer: *put on hold*] pending the outcome.' [*Re L* [2013] UKSC 75; [2014] AC 1017, 1029 [9] (Baroness Hale)]
- 'It is of course clear that neither the solicitors, nor [their secretary], had any actual authority from the vendors to make any representation to the purchasers that the vendors' rights would be *kept in abeyance* [prefer: *kept back*; *held in reserve*].' [*Legione v Hateley* (1983) 152 CLR 406, 421 (Gibbs CJ and Murphy J, speaking in the context of estoppel)]

See also **seisin**.

ability / capacity

Ability means the state of being able to do something. *Capacity* means the (legal) power to do something. So a person may *have the ability* (be physically able) to sign a will, but age or dementia may deprive them of the legal *capacity* to make a valid will. The distinction is often blurred, but is worth maintaining. For example:

- '*Bancoult* concerned the *ability* [prefer: *capacity*] of a British court judicially to review an order in council relating to the British Indian Overseas Territory [despite] the *Colonial Laws Validity Act 1865*.' [*Keyu v Secretary of State for Foreign and Commonwealth Affairs* [2015] UKSC 69, [186]; [2015] 3 WLR 1665, 1714 (Lord Mance)]
- 'The availability of insurance depends on the willingness of insurers to enter the particular market, their *ability* to offer affordable premiums, and their *capacity* to pay on the policies entered by employers.' [*A-G for Northern Territory v Chaffey* [2007] HCA 34; (2007) 231 CLR 651, [64] (Heydon J)]
- '[C]ritical to a State's *capacity* to function as a government is its *ability* … to determine the number and identity of those whom it wishes to engage at the higher levels of government [and their] terms and conditions …' [*Re Australian Education Union* (1995) 184 CLR 188, 233 (Mason CJ, Brennan, Deane, Toohey, Gaudron and McHugh JJ)]

See also **capacity**.

abjudge

To take or deprive by judicial decision; the opposite of *adjudge* (to make a judicial decision about a matter).

> 'As a result of the trial a very solemn judgment is pronounced. The land is adjudged to the one party and his heirs, and *abjudged* (*abiudicata*) from the other party and his heirs for ever. Nothing could be more conclusive.' [SFC Milsom (ed), F Pollock and FW Maitland, *The History of English Law before the Time of Edward I*, 2nd edn, reissued (Cambridge University Press, 1968) vol 2, 63, in relation to the writ of right]

Abjudge is now obsolete.

See also **adjudge**.

able and willing

See **ready, able, and willing**.

abode

A person's place of *abode* is the place where they *abide*. In most contexts, the term is sufficiently clear—it is the person's home. But in some contexts it can be ambiguous—it might be the place where they live or where they work:

> 'It is contended that "place of abode" [in s 23 of the *Landlord and Tenant Act* 1927] means the place where the tenant dwelt—his residence in the sense of the place where he slept at night, if nothing more. However, a large number of authorities shows that, at any rate for certain purposes, "residence" or "place of abode" may include a place where the person in question works and has his business.' [*Price v West London Investment Building Society* [1964] 2 All ER 318, 321 (Danckwerts J)]

A person's *abode* might even be their car if they are sleeping rough (as in *R v Bundy* [1977] 2 All ER 382). If *abode* could be ambiguous, consider a more precise word.

about

A word of approximation, the ambit of which varies with the circumstances. When used in the context of measurement, the case law illustrates the word's vagueness: when is a stated measurement *about* the same as the actual measurement? Where possible, specify a precise variation. The following British and Commonwealth examples show the potential for uncertainty:

- Shops—stated frontage of *about* 40 feet not satisfied by actual frontage of 33 feet 2½ inches (vendor entitled to rescind contract for purchaser's objection about deficiency): *Re Cook and Preece's Contract* [1910] VLR 328.
- Wharf—stated river frontage of *about* 60 feet not satisfied by actual frontage of 49 feet 9 inches (purchaser entitled to rescind contract for deficiency): *Re Deptford Creek Bridge Co and Bevan* (1884) 28 Sol J 327.
- Land—stated area of *about* 1,200 square yards not satisfied by actual area of 935 square yards (compensation awarded to purchaser): *Aspinalls to Powell and Scholefield* (1889) 60 LT 595.
- Land—stated area of *about* 5 acres, 0 roods and 26 perches not satisfied by actual area of 4 acres and 3 roods (purchaser entitled to rescind contract): *Jacobs v Revell* [1900] 2 Ch 858.
- Land—stated area of '*about* two and three quarter acres, little more or less' satisfied by actual area of 2 acres, 2 roods and 4 perches: *Denny v Hancock* (1870) 18 WR 566.

- Charterparty—statement that ship capable of '*about* 15.5 knots in moderate weather'; court unable to decree allowable variation as a matter of law, because it depended on matters such as the ship's configuration, size, draft, and trim: *Arab Maritime Petroleum Transport Co v Luxor Trading Corp and Geogas Enterprises SA (The 'Al Bida')* [1987] 1 Lloyd's Rep 124, 129 (Parker LJ).

See also **approximately**; **thereabouts**; **WORDS OF APPROXIMATION**

above / below

Vagueness

Beware of vague references to something being *above* or *below*. Where *above*? Where *below*? If a reader may be puzzled (eg, because there are several possible places *above* or *below*), be specific: eg, 'at p 5 above', 'in clause 10 below'.

Example

> To provide security to the landlord, the tenant granted a charge over property 'as specified in Item 7' of a schedule to the lease. Item 7 (headed 'The Charged Property') was the last item in the schedule, and stated simply 'As above'. Of the prior 6 items, only items 1, 2, and 6 referred to items of property. The reference in item 1 was almost incidental; it set out the tenant's personal details, including his street address. Items 2 and 6 listed items of personal property. Held: the charged property was the property given as the tenant's address in item 1. 'As above' was not to be taken as applying to the item immediately above (item 6), or to all of the items in the schedule. The only way to make commercial common sense of 'As above' was to interpret it as referring to the property listed as the tenant's address in item 1. See *Morris Finance Ltd v Free* [2017] NSWSC 1417; (2017) 18 BPR 37,223 (Ward CJ in Eq).

Archaic variants

Also, avoid antiquated variants of *above* and *below*, which are not merely vague but deaden writing by introducing an archaic tone—eg, 'above-mentioned', 'aforementioned', 'above-specified', 'above-cited'. For example:

> 'The Supreme Court clarified the contract-law principles about consideration. *The above-mentioned court* [prefer: *The court*; or better, *It*] then applied the principles to the facts.'

above-mentioned

See **above / below**.

absent (preposition)

A lawyer's pretentious substitute for *in the absence of* or *without*. Prefer a less pretentious alternative.

> '[T]he clear objective intention of the instrument is that payment should be triggered upon certification … and that there should be no room for defence to such a certification … *absent* [prefer: *in the absence of*] fraud. … The "conclusive evidence" clauses which apply on certification of the amount due under a loan in a loan agreement (*absent* [prefer: *unless there is*; *assuming no*] manifest error) are … designed for a different purpose …' [*Bitumen Invest AS v Richmond Mercantile Ltd FZC* [2016] EWHC 2957 (Comm), [26]–[27] (Sir Jeremy Cooke)]

absente

Latin: being absent; in the absence of. To retain the Latin is pedantic; the English translation is sufficient. For example:

> '[I]t would be outrageous for Your Lordships to find a contempt of the House *absente of* [sic] [prefer: *in the absence of*] contempt of court.' [*Re Lonhro Plc* [1990] 2 AC 154, 162G (in argument)]

In former times, a statement in a law report 'absente [name of judge]' indicated that a judge who was to participate in the hearing was not yet present in court, or (more likely) was present at the hearing but not for the judgment:

- 'absente Holt': *Smith's Case* (1724) Comb 386; 90 ER 544
- 'Held, by Cotton and Fry LJJ (absente Earl of Selborne LC)': *Re Sampson and Wall* (1875) 25 Ch D 482, 483 (headnote).

Modern law reports usually contain a fuller and more helpful statement, along the lines: 'Smith LJ was present at the hearing but did not participate in the judgment.'

absente reo

Latin: the defendant (or accused) being absent. This Latin usage is now inexcusably abstruse, though occasionally still seen:

> 'The decision to arraign Michael in his absence cannot be squared with the language of Rule 43. … Arraignment *absente reo* [prefer: *in the defendant's absence*] was improper.' [*US v Christopher* 700 F 2d 1253, 1262 (US Ct of Appeals, 9th Cir, 1983)]

For non-US examples, see *Horwood v NSW Department of Education* [2007] NSWIRComm 1038 [36]; *Balkar Singh v State of UP* [2007] INUPHC 16134 [5] (High Court of Judicature, Allahabad).

absentia

See **in absentia**.

absolutely void

See **void / voidable**.

absolve (of / from)

Some commentators urge a distinction between *absolve of* and *absolve from*: one is *absolved of* a debt or financial liability, but *absolved from* a crime or wrongdoing (see, eg, Bryan Garner, *Garner's Dictionary of Legal Usage*, 3rd edn (Oxford University Press, 2009) 9). But UK modern legal usage is less nuanced. *Absolved of* and *absolved from* are used interchangeably, with *absolved from* being the more common.

absque

Latin: without. In modern legal usage, pure pedantry. Prefer *without*. Found in combination with other Latinisms, all able to be expressed in plain English:

- *absque aliquo inde reddendo*: without rendering [ie, being required to pay] anything out of it. A phrase found in Crown grants which reserved no feudal services.

- *absque consideratione curiae*: without the consideration of the court; that is, without judgment.
- *absque dubio*: without doubt.
- *absque hoc*: without this. Formerly used in pleadings at common law to introduce the denial of allegations; eg, *Horseman v Waters* (1685) 1 Keb 381; 83 ER 1006.
- *absque impetitione vasti*: without liability for waste: eg, *Abraham v Bubb* (1680) 2 Freem Chy 53; 22 ER 1054. See **without impeachment of waste.**
- *absque tali causa*: without such cause. Part of the larger phrase *de injuria sua propria, absque tali causa* (plural: *de injuriis suis propriis, absque tali causa*) ("of his own wrong, without such cause"), formerly pleaded by a plaintiff in a trespass case to counter the defendant's claim of lawful excuse: eg, *English v Pellitory Tayler & Smith* (1653) Cro Eliz 139; 78 ER 396.

abstract

A summary of a document, particularly in conveyancing law.

See also **abstract of title**.

abstract of title

Sometimes called 'epitome of title'. A summary of the history of a vendor's title to land, tracing the title back to a good root of title of sufficient age; usually in a standard template, honed by centuries of tradition, with up to four levels of indentation to mark off different information: see, eg, J Henry Kelly, *The Draftsman*, 2nd edn (Butterworths, 1881) 45–46. To be a '*proper* abstract of title', the abstract must reproduce the material parts of all documents affecting the title during the period abstracted, and must record all other facts and events relevant to the title during that period, such as births, deaths, marriages, grants of probate, court orders, and bankruptcies. Nowadays, formal abstracts of title are rare. Most modern contracts for the sale of land permit the vendor to provide, in place of the traditional form of abstract of title, a chronological list of documents and events that comprise the title, plus a photocopy of the relevant documents.

Further reading

- *Halsbury's Laws of England*, 'Conveyancing' (Vol 23, 2016), [113] and following
- Peter Butt, *Standard Contract for Sale of Land in New South Wales*, 2nd edn (LBC Information Services, 1998) 868–74 (Commonwealth law)

See also **good root of title**.

abundans cautela non nocet

Latin: extreme caution does no harm.

See **ex abundanti cautela**.

abut

To adjoin; to have a common boundary with. Thus, an advertising hoarding separated from a road by a narrow strip of land did not *abut* the road: *Barnett v Covell* (1903) 20 TLR 134. But meanings vary with context. For example, a landowner whose land was separated from a road by a public reserve 16 feet wide was held liable to pay the local council a betterment tax for road improvements imposed on landowners whose land *abutted* the road: *Krasey v St Boniface City* (1966) 60 DLR (2d) 370.

See also **adjoining**; **adjacent**; **contiguous**.

abuttals

The parts of land that *abut* on neighbouring lands. Land is sometimes described 'by bounds and abuttals'.

See also **abut**; **metes and bounds**.

ACCELERATION CLAUSE

A contractual provision under which a right or liability to pay an amount is brought forward if a stated event occurs. Examples are a clause in a loan agreement that allows the borrower to repay early on agreed terms; or a clause in a mortgage that provides for the whole amount outstanding to fall due immediately if the mortgagor fails to pay a monthly instalment.

accession

A term of art, found in two different areas of law.

Property law

1. The blending of items owned by different persons, with ownership normally passing to the owner of the principal item. Thus: bricks built into a wall become part of the wall; thread stitched into a coat becomes part of the coat; planks, nails, and pitch worked into a ship become part of the ship: *Appleby v Myers* (1867) LR 2 CP 651, 659, 660. But if the blending creates a new item (as where wine is made out of grapes, or bread out of flour), the new item belongs to the person who produced it: Sir William Blackstone, *Commentaries on the Laws of England* (Clarendon, 1766) book 2, 404.
2. The principle under which natural or artificial additions to a corporeal substance belong to the owner of the principal item. Examples are additions flowing from the pregnancy of animals or the growth of vegetables, or the legally recognised shift in land boundaries.

International law

The process by which a state becomes a party to a treaty that is already in force between other states.

See also **admix**.

accessory

As an adjective, additional [to] or incidental [to]. For example, in planning law, an *accessory use* is a use that is incidental to a main use.

As a noun, a person who helps another to do something—particularly (but not exclusively) to commit a crime:

- *accessory after the fact*: a person who knows that a crime has been committed and who helps the offender evade arrest or prosecution. In most jurisdictions, a person (A) commits an offence if A knows that another (B) has committed an offence, and A intentionally does something to impede B's arrest or prosecution.
- *accessory before the fact*: a person who helps or encourages another to commit a crime but is not present when the crime is actually committed. (Most jurisdictions now treat such a person as a principal offender.)

accident

A word with a plain dictionary meaning—ie, an unfortunate incident that happens unexpectedly. That plain meaning is often seen in law: eg, industrial *accident*, *accidental* injury, motor vehicle *accident*. In Lord Macnaghten's oft-quoted words, an accident is 'an unlooked-for mishap or an untoward event which is not expected or designed': *Fenton v Thorley & Co Ltd* [1903] AC 443, 448. On that basis, for example, an *accident* occurred where a portable step unexpectedly moved while a passenger was disembarking an aircraft (*Air Link Pty Ltd v Paterson* [2009] NSWCA 251; (2009) 75 NSWLR 354); but no *accident* occurred where a person became deaf because of cabin pressure changes during flight (*Air France v Saks* [1985] USSC 43; 470 US 392 (1985)); nor where a person developed deep-vein thrombosis during long-haul flights (*Re Deep Vein Thrombosis and Air Travel Group Litigation* [2005] UKHL 72; [2006] 1 AC 495; *Povey v Qantas Airways Limited* [2005] HCA 33; (2005) 223 CLR 189).

However, as with most words, the meaning of *accident* is context-dependent. It must be interpreted

> 'in its setting, in the context, and in the light of the purpose which appears from the [document] itself. … [People] have taken the liberty of using it, as they use so many other words, not in any exact sense but in a somewhat confused way, or rather in a variety of ways. … In short, the common meaning of this word is ruled neither by logic nor by etymology, but by custom, and no formula will precisely express its usage for all cases.' [*Trim Joint District School Board of Management v Kelly* [1914] AC 667, 680–81 (Earl Loreburn)]

In line with this context-dependent meaning, an event has been held to be an 'accident' even where it resulted from conduct whose consequences might have been expected:

- Within the context of a disability insurance policy, there was an *accident* where a person injured his spine doing very heavy work: *Australian Casualty Co Ltd v Frederico* (1986) 160 CLR 513.
- Within the context of a policy insuring an employer against the negligence of employees, there was an *accident* where an employee carelessly loaded a truck, which was then damaged when he attempted to drive under a rail bridge: *Hammersley v National Transport Insurance* [2015] TASFC 5; (2015) 25 Tas R 194.

If the meaning of *accident* in the particular context could be uncertain, use another word—or at least define what constitutes an *accident* for the purposes of the document.

See also **LITIGATED WORDS AND PHRASES**.

accommodate

To *accommodate* means to provide lodgings for someone ('this hostel *accommodates* homeless people') or to fit in with someone's needs ('we try to *accommodate* your wishes'). However, in the law of easements, *accommodate* carries a finely nuanced meaning of 'benefit'. Thus, an easement is said to *accommodate* land if it is connected with the normal enjoyment of the land (as distinct from a being mere personal benefit to the owner of the land): *Re Ellenborough Park* [1956] Ch 131, 173–75.

accord / accordance

In accord [with] means 'in agreement [with]': eg, 'Our decision *is in accord with* the decisions of other courts on this point.' *In accordance [with]* means 'in compliance [with]': eg, 'We reach this decision *in accordance with* the doctrine of precedent.'

accord and satisfaction

A lawyer's pairing, in which (unusually for pairings in law) each word carries a distinct meaning. The concept is of an agreement for value to discharge an obligation: A agrees to accept from B some payment or benefit, in return for which A releases B from a cause of action that A has against B. The *accord* is the agreement that discharges the obligation; the *satisfaction* is the consideration that makes the agreement enforceable in contract law: *British Russian Gazette and Trade Outlook Ltd v Associated Newspapers Ltd* [1933] 2 KB 616, 643 (Scrutton LJ).

Accord and satisfaction appears in both contracts and statutes. However, the term is likely to be incomprehensible to non-legal readers. If you feel you must use it when addressing a reader who is not a lawyer, explain the term, as in the first of the following examples. Otherwise, find a substitute term—eg, 'agreement for value to release an obligation'. Other context-relevant substitutes are suggested in the second and third examples.

1. 'Accord and satisfaction (the former being the agreement or consent to accept the latter) requires acceptance of something in place of the full remedy to which the recipient is entitled, coupled with provision of the consideration agreed upon.' [*Thompson v Australian Capital Television Pty Ltd* [1996] HCA 38; 186 CLR 574, 610 (Gummow J)]
2. '[This] case is one of valid compromise involving consideration on both sides. Put another way, there was an accord and satisfaction in respect of the mutual claims and cross-claims under and arising from [prefer: a binding agreement to give up the mutual claims and cross-claims under] the settlement agreement.' [*Simantob v Shavleyan* [2018] EWHC 2005 (QB), [142] (Kerr J)]
3. 'The difficulty is that the agreement was performed, in the sense that there was not merely an accord [prefer: an agreement], but an accord and satisfaction [prefer: an agreement that had become binding]. All policy claims were thus not just agreed to be settled, but they actually were settled.' ['*The Alexandros T*' [2013] UKSC 70 [154]; [2014] 1 All ER 590 (Lord Mance)]

See also **WORD PAIRINGS**.

acknowledge and agree

See **agree and acknowledge**.

ACRONYMS

Uses, and alternatives

You can reduce wordiness by using an acronym in place of a longer term. Acronyms are generally formed by the initial letters of key words of the full name: eg, Plain English Commission becomes 'PEC'.

If an acronym is in common use, there is generally no problem in using it:

> 'Mr Holden's car failed its MOT because of corrosion to its underside.' [*R & S Pilling v UK Insurance Ltd* [2019] UKSC 16, [2]; [2019] 2 WLR 1015, [2] (Lord Hodge JSC). There is no need to explain 'MOT' to a UK reader.]

But if an acronym is unfamiliar, define it. Failure to define it can cause a contract to fail for uncertainty: see, eg, *Durunna v Air Canada* (2013) 555 Alberta Reports 367, [54].

Sometimes an abbreviation or short name may be clearer than an acronym:

Not this:

> This Agreement is made between Acme Constructions (Great Britain) Ltd (**ACGB**) as vendor of the one part and Superior Scottish Homes and Gardens (Scotland) Ltd **(SSHGS)** as purchaser of the other part.

But this:

> This Agreement is made between Acme Constructions (Great Britain) Ltd (**Acme**) as vendor of the one part and Superior Homes and Gardens (Scotland) Ltd (**Superior Homes**) as purchaser of the other part.

In a contract, it may be clearer to avoid acronyms or short names altogether, and instead refer to parties by their role in the transaction:

> This Agreement is made between Acme Constructions (Great Britain) Ltd **(Vendor)** of the one part and Superior Homes and Gardens (Scotland) Ltd (**Purchaser**) of the other part.

Format

Legal usage generally highlights the first appearance of an acronym in **bold**, to help it stand out to the reader: thus, 'Zero Music Company Ltd (**ZMC**)'. However, there are alternatives: some writers use italics (*ZMC*), or bold italics (***ZMC***), or no formatting at all (ZMC). Some writers include the acronym in **bold** and within quotation marks ('**ZMC**'), but this is excessive and unnecessary.

Plurals and possessives

- For the plural of an acronym, add s (lower case) but no apostrophe: REITs, EISs.
- For the possessive, add an apostrophe as for normal text: 'the REIT's approach'. But if this seems unidiomatic, consider using the longer form instead of the possessive: 'the approach of the REIT'.

Defining acronyms

When defining an acronym, two techniques are common (and equally acceptable). The first technique merely lists the acronym, without expanding the letters into the fuller term, and refers the reader to the definition of the fuller term:

> **VAT**: see **Value Added Tax**.

The second technique includes the acronym in the definition of the fuller term:

> **Value Added Tax** or **VAT** means …

Acronyms as irritants

Acronyms can irritate readers, on at least three bases.

1. Unfamiliar acronyms

Unless an acronym is in common use, consider whether you really need it, particularly if the reader may find it intrusive.

> 'To assist specialists in the field, who may perform computer searches by acronyms, we note that the case involves thc CWA, specifically WLA's established as part of the TMDL's issued by

the EPA pursuant to a WQS, which are implemented in NPDES permits. The opinion is written in words rather than acronyms to make it easier to read.' [*Longview Fibre Co v Rasmussen* 980 F 2d 1307, 1308, n 1 (9th Cir, 1992), with intended irony.]

2. Superfluous acronyms

An acronym is superfluous if readers cannot misunderstand it. For example:

A document refers to the *Law of Property Act 1925*, but to no other Act. It is pointless to name the Act and then create the acronym '**LPA**'. In later references, simply call it 'the Act'.

3. Humour-inducing acronyms

Do not allow acronyms to become an unintended source of humour:

A contract for the construction of a power station used the acronym 'BOO' to mean the building, owning and operating of the power station. This led to obligations such as 'the Project Entity shall BOO the Power Station'. See *Regional Power Corporation v Pacific Hydro Group Two Pty Ltd* [2013] WASC 356, [18]; (2013) 46 WAR 281.

See also **ABBREVIATIONS**; **DEFINITIONS**; **HUMOUR**; **POSSESSIVES**; **SHORT NAMES.**

Act (legislation)

When referring to a statute, the convention is *Act* (upper-case *A*). Journalists sometimes lapse into *act* when referring to legislation; so also do some judges:

'The Registrar of Titles refused to register the transfer [because] the relevant *act* [prefer: *Act*] did not permit a registered proprietor to deal with land …' [*Primewest (Mandurah) Pty Ltd v Ryom Pty Ltd* [2014] WASCA 28, [76] (Martin CJ)]

See also **CITATION OF LEGISLATION**; **enactment**.

act (something done)

General meaning

An *act* (lower-case *a*) is a general term for an action taken or thing done. As with all words, its meaning is context-dependent. This makes *act* a candidate for litigation about meaning. Case law demonstrates in particular two problem areas—both of which an adept drafter will foresee and avoid:

- *Does a series of activities constitute a single act*? Sometimes yes, sometimes no. For example, in *O'Connor v Bar Standards Board* [2017] UKSC 78; [2017] 1 WLR 4833 the conduct of the Bar Standards Board in bringing and pursuing disciplinary proceedings against a barrister was held to be a single 'act' for the purposes of the *Human Rights Act 1998*.
- *Can an 'act' include an omission*? Sometimes yes, sometimes no. For example, in *R v Miller* (1983) 77 Cr App R 17; [1983] 1 All ER 978 (HL), a failure to extinguish a fire was an *act* constituting the crime of arson, because it was part of the continuing activity begun when the accused fell asleep while smoking. But in *R v Ahmad* (1987) 84 Cr App R 64 failure to complete renovations to a flat was not an *act* calculated to interfere with the peace or comfort of the tenant, because the work had started but then ceased for more than a year. Drafters commonly overcome this 'act vs omission' quandary by defining *act* to include 'omission'.

'acts and omissions'

A common pairing—eg, in tort law a person is said to be liable for their 'acts and omissions' (ie, for what they do and for what they fail to do). In contracts, a covenant not to do an act is sometimes drafted as a covenant 'not to do or omit to do' the act. The intent is clear enough, but the drafting is ungainly (and read literally, a nonsense). Instead, add a few words to express the meaning more clearly: 'not to do the act, and not to omit to do anything that would prevent the act from occurring'.

See also **act of God**; **TERMS OF ART**; **WORD PAIRINGS**.

act of God

An event that occurs by force of nature (ie, without human intervention) and that is unforeseeable (or, if foreseeable, cannot reasonably be guarded against), such as a storm or earthquake. *Halsbury* defines the term in this way:

> '[An act of God may be defined as] an accident (1) due to natural causes, directly and exclusively without human intervention; and (2) which could not by any amount of ability have been foreseen, or, if foreseen, could not by any amount of human care and skill have been resisted. … It must … be something overwhelming, and not merely an ordinary accidental circumstance.' [*Halsbury's Laws of England*, 'Contract' (vol 22, 2019) [269]]

Lord Esher MR explained it this way:

> 'In the older, simpler days I have myself never had any doubt but that [the expression *act of God*] did not mean the act of God in the ecclesiastical and biblical sense, according to which almost everything is said to be the act of God, but that in a mercantile sense it meant an extraordinary circumstance which could not be foreseen, and which could not be guarded against. But in this case there cannot possibly be any foundation [to suggest that] this gnawing of a pipe by rats and letting in sea-water is … the act of God.' (*Pandorf & Co v Hamilton, Fraser & Co* (1886) 17 QB 670, 675, Lord Esher MR)

Being unforeseeable, damage or loss caused by 'act of God' is generally uncompensable (reflecting the maxim, *actus Dei nemini facit injuriam*: an act of God does a wrong to no one).

Although quaint to rationalist ears, *act of God* is unlikely to be replaced by non-theistic equivalents. Suggested alternatives such as 'irresistible force' (compare *force majeure*), or 'inevitable occurrence', do not reflect the requirement of *natural* forces. A substitute might be: 'an accident of nature that cannot reasonably be guarded against'.

Further reading

Halsbury's Laws of England, 'Contract' (vol 22, 2019) [269] (case law on 'act of God')

See also **force majeure**; **TERMS OF ART**.

actio personalis moritur cum persona

Latin: a person's right of action dies with the person. The maxim expresses a common-law principle that is no longer universally true, because statutes now allow certain causes of action to survive the claimant's death. But regardless of whether the maxim remains relevant, its expression in Latin does not. The English translation adequately captures the legal meaning, making the Latin redundant. For example:

- 'The legislature [in the *Law Reform (Miscellaneous Provisions) Act 1934*] had particularly in mind causes of action in tort which used to fall with the death of either party under the old common law maxim *actio personalis moritur cum persona* [better: add a translation—*a person's cause of action dies with them*].' [*Sugden v Sugden* [1957] P 120, 134 (Lord Denning MR)]

- 'Prior to the [legislation], the common law maxim *actio personalis moritur cum persona* provided that a cause of action in tort died with the person in whom it was vested.' [*WorkCover Queensland v Amaca Pty Ltd* [2010] HCA 34, [34], (2010) 241 CLR 420, 434 (High Court of Australia, supplying an explanation—thus making the Latin superfluous)]

action or proceeding

Rarely, if ever, is this doublet needed when referring to *court* actions. All (court) *actions* are *proceedings*, and all (court) *proceedings* are *actions*; so one word suffices.

See also **WORD PAIRINGS**.

ACTIVE VOICE / PASSIVE VOICE

Identifying active voice and passive voice

A sentence in the *active voice* states who did/does what to whom:

Subject (agent)	**Verb (action)**	**Object (affected)**
John	hit	Jack.
The judge	decided	the case.

The sentence is *active* because the subject performs the action.

In the *passive voice*, the subject does not perform the action but is affected by it ('passive' carrying the sense of 'suffering' or 'enduring'):

Subject (affected)	**Verb (action)**	**(Agent)**
Jack	was hit	by John
The case	was decided	by the judge.

A passive construction requires both the verb 'to be' (in any form) and a past participle:

His car *was* ramm*ed* from behind.

The accused *was* defend*ed by* Mr Smith.

In a passive construction, the word *by* is often (but not necessarily) present:

A meeting must be called *by* the directors.

Sometimes, the passive omits the actor altogether:

The fees are *to be recalculated* each month. [By whom?]

Prefer the active voice

Generally, prefer the active voice over the passive, for at least three reasons.

1. Active-voice sentences are usually shorter than passive-voice sentences, at least where they mention both subject and object. Compare 'The case was decided by a new judge' (8 words) and 'A new judge decided the case' (6 words). The saving might seem minuscule (2 words); but it is 25% of the sentence—and in a long document with many passive sentences, a saving of 25% per sentence is worthwhile. The savings

multiply where sentences contain a number of passive constructions. Compare 'The repairs were ordered by the judge to be carried out by the tenant' (14 words) and 'The judge ordered the tenant to carry out the repairs' (10 words).

2. Active-voice sentences mirror the normal form of speech. The active is the natural construction; the passive requires the reader to invert the sentence for meaning, interposing an impediment to comprehension.
3. The tone of active-voice sentences is more direct and less bureaucratic than the tone of passive-voice sentences. The active voice enlivens the text; the passive deadens it. That is why George Orwell wrote, 'Never use the passive voice where you can use the active': 'Politics and the English Language' (1946), reprinted in George Orwell, *Why I Write* (Penguin, 2004) 119.

Beware of slipping into the habitual passive—particularly in the (misplaced) belief that legal writing necessarily requires a formal tone. Almost always you can make your point in the active voice—politely but firmly.

Rewriting passive to active

To redraft the passive into the active is usually straightforward:

Passive	Active
The case was decided by Judge Judy.	Judge Judy decided the case.
A meeting must be called.	[Someone] must call a meeting.

One way may be to recast a passive verb as an adjective:

Passive	Active
A summons that is undelivered is invalid.	An undelivered summons is invalid.
The justice system is not served well by cases that remain undecided.	Undecided cases do not serve the justice system well.

Beneficial uses of the passive

The admonition is to *prefer* the active, not to banish the passive entirely. The danger lies in the habitual use of the passive. When used deliberately, rather than habitually, the passive can have advantages. Here are some:

To leave the actor unstated

The passive can mask the identity of the 'doer' of an action. It emphasises the action, but can leave the actor unstated. For example:

- Jack was hit. [By whom? You may not wish to state.]
- The necessary repairs were made. [By whom? The repairer's identity may be unimportant; or for good reason you may wish not to identify the repairer.]
- The application was rejected [by whom?] and then a decision to appeal was made [by whom?].

Leaving the actor unstated can be useful, as in examples 1 and 2 below:

1. Parties to a prospective commercial deal want to sign up as quickly as possible. They have agreed to hold joint monthly meetings, but they have not yet worked out the mechanics of the meetings (who is to call them, at what time of the day, at what location, and so on). The passive voice is the ideal vehicle. The Heads of Agreement can simply record: 'A meeting is to be called each month.'

2. Regulations require prospectuses to be in plain language. The regulator's concern is with the end product, not with the identity of the drafter. The regulation can safely state: 'Prospectuses must be in plain English.'

But leaving the actor unstated can also be a trap, if it fails to allocate important responsibility, as in example 3:

3. A sandmining agreement provided for royalty payments to '*be reassessed* annually' based on cost-of-living increases. The passive voice left unstated who was to initiate the reassessment—the landowner or the sandmining company? This required court proceedings to clarify: *Birdon Contracting Pty Ltd v Hawkesbury City Council* (2009) 167 LGERA 178; [2009] NSWLEC 91. An active-voice sentence would have identified *who* was to initiate the reassessment.

To appear less 'accusing'

The passive voice can soften the bluntness of an active sentence:

- The wrong form of writ was lodged. [*Instead of*: You lodged the wrong form of writ.]
- My client's car was damaged by your client's negligence. [*Instead of*: Your client's negligence damaged my client's car.]
- The leading case was not cited. [*Instead of*: Counsel failed to cite the leading case.]

To improve sentence structure

A good writer makes sentences flow. One technique is to use parallel structures, keeping the same item as subject. This may require an occasional passive:

> Ms Jones is an excellent public speaker. *She was coached by* a famous judge. [*Not*: A famous judge coached her.]

To add punch at sentence-end

Many writers consider that the natural 'stress point' of a sentence lies at its end. For that reason, they seek to place important words or phrases at sentence-end. This may require a passive construction. Compare:

- The judge, not the jury, decides whether evidence is hearsay. [Active]
- Whether evidence is hearsay is decided not by the jury but by the judge. [Passive]

The first sentence emphasises the hearsay issue; the second sentence emphasises the decision-maker.

Further reading

Robert C Farrell, 'Why Grammar Matters: Conjugating Verbs in Modern Legal Opinions' (2008) 40 *Loyola University Chicago Law Journal* 1, 13–19 (reviewing US cases where the result turned on the active/passive distinction)

See also **SENTENCE STRUCTURE**.

actual

As a descriptor, *actual* rarely adds anything. For example: there is no difference between 'the *actual* terms' of a radio interview and 'the terms' of a radio interview, or between 'the *actual* language' of a letter and 'the language' of a letter: *Minister for Immigration v Jia Legeng* [2001] HCA 17; (2001) 205 CLR 507, [144], [149] (Kirby J). Nor is there a difference between a person's 'actual circumstances' and their 'circumstances': *Re W* [2016] EWCA Civ 804, [15] (Macur LJ).

However, for some legal purposes, *actual* may add important information. Examples include:

- *actual possession* (as distinct from *constructive* possession—where a person is treated as being in possession despite not being in physical possession)
- *actual notice* (as distinct from *constructive* notice—where a person is treated as knowing of a fact despite not actually knowing of it)
- *actual fraud* (as distinct from *imputed* fraud or *constructive* fraud)
- *actual military service* (as distinct from being on leave at home).

Also, *actual* may bear a specialised meaning in certain contexts. For example, the House of Lords held that, in the context of the law of reinsurance, a reinsurer's obligation to indemnify an insurer against sums 'actually paid' in settlement of losses, meant not sums in fact (already) paid, but rather sums 'when finally ascertained'—ie, the words supplied a yardstick for calculating the amount of the reinsurer's obligation, not a temporal precondition on recovery: *Charter Reinsurance Co Ltd v Fagan* [1997] AC 313.

actual notice

See **notice / knowledge**.

actus Dei

Latin: act of God.

See **act of God**.

actus Dei nemini facit injuriam

Latin: an act of God does a wrong to no one.

See **act of God**.

actus non facit reum, nisi mens sit rea

Latin: an act does not make a person guilty unless their mind is guilty.

See **actus reus**.

actus reus

Latin: a wrongful act. Usually seen in tandem with another Latin scrap, *mens rea*: a guilty mind. Together, the *actus reus* and the *mens rea* constitute the key elements of a criminal offence—the physical element and the mental element: David C Ormerod (ed), *Smith and Hogan's Criminal Law*, 12th edn (Oxford University Press, 2008) 42. They are seen combined in the maxim *actus non facit reum, nisi mens sit rea*, usually translated as 'an act does not make a person guilty unless his or her mind is guilty'—or better and time-honoured, 'The intent and the act must both concur to constitute the crime': *Fowler v Padget* (1798) 7 TR 509, 514; 101 ER 1103, 1106 (Lord Kenyon). Lord Diplock, for one, preferred to dispense with the Latin:

> '[I]t would I think be conducive to clarity of analysis of the ingredients of a crime that is created by statute ... if we were to avoid bad Latin and instead to think and speak ... about the conduct of the accused and his state of mind at the time of that conduct, instead of speaking of *actus reus* and *mens rea*.' [*R v Miller* [1983] 2 AC 161, 174]

Further reading

Halsbury's Laws of England, 'Criminal Law' (vol 25, 2016) [5]

See also **mens rea**.

ad colligenda bona defuncti

Latin: for collecting the goods of the deceased person; often shortened to *ad colligenda bona*. Used in probate law to describe a temporary grant of administration for the purpose of protecting the whole or part of the deceased's estate, where the delay in obtaining a normal grant would endanger the assets and an immediate grant can protect them: *Whitehead v Palmer* [1908] 1 KB 156; *Re Cohen (dec'd)* [1975] VR 187. The grant can also be for a limited act (eg, the discharge of a mortgage), where the estate may be endangered by a delay in carrying it out.

Many probate lawyers seem unwilling to give up their Latin—but they could at least explain the meaning of the term. In the first example below, the judge does so; in the other examples, the judges do not.

- 'This is the plaintiff's motion for a grant of administration *ad colligenda bona defuncti*. Literally translated that means the plaintiff is seeking a form of limited administration "to collect the deceased's goods".' [*Fazio v Naso* [2016] WASC 385, [1] (Sanderson M, with translation)]
- 'On 2 February 2002 the claimant was granted administration *ad colligenda bona* [add explanation: *ie, for the limited purpose of collecting and preserving the estate*]out of the Winchester District Probate Registry.' [*Al-Bassam v Al-Bassam* [2004] EWCA Civ 857, [4] (Chadwick LJ)]
- '[T]he claimants asked for directions as to distribution of the estate on the footing that the will was validly executed. … But I note … that in any event only one of the claimants is a personal representative; they are both grantees *ad colligenda bona* [explain: *for the purpose of collecting the assets*] (which however does not entitle them to distribute).' [*Vucicevic v Aleksic* [2017] EWHC 2335 (Ch), [47] (Judge Paul Matthews)]

ad diem

Latin: at (on) the appointed day. Nothing is served by retaining the Latin; prefer the English.

> 'The expression "periodically as required" should be taken to refer to a substantial adherence to a period specified in the instrument of separation but not necessarily to strict payment *ad diem* [prefer: *on the appointed day*; *on the precise date*].' [*Ogston v Ogston* (1935) 53 CLR 526, 530 (Rich J, in the context of late payments of alimony)]

ad hoc

Latin: for this (purpose), in the sense of 'for a special purpose or occasion'. Hence, 'ad hoc committee'—a committee set up temporarily to consider a particular matter; 'ad hoc argument'—an argument for a particular occasion. This Latinism has become standard English, at least in business and commerce, and is therefore no longer italicised.

See further, **LATIN**.

ad hominem

Latin: at the man (person). Used to describe an argument directed at an opponent's character—*argumentum ad hominem*—rather than against the principle the opponent is espousing. The stand-alone phrase 'ad hominem' may have become sufficiently accepted as standard English to no longer need italics.

See further, **LATIN**.

ad idem

See **consensus ad idem**.

ad interim

Latin: in the meantime. The English expression *in the interim* mirrors the Latin nicely.

ad litem

Latin: as regards the action (court case); for the purpose of the action (court case). For example, a 'guardian ad litem' is a guardian appointed for the purpose of a court action. The English translation serves perfectly well. Some court rules substitute 'litigation friend'—eg, *Civil Procedure Rules 1999*—which to the uninitiated may be as puzzling as the Latin.

See also **guardian ad litem**.

ad longum

Latin: at length (ie, in contrast to a summary or précis). An unnecessary Latinism, given the adequacy (and guessability) of the English translation.

> 'Since the judgment of the Court of Justice is fully reported I do not find it necessary to repeat it *ad longum* [prefer: *at length*; *in full*].' [*Shevill v Presse Alliance SA* [1996] AC 959, 981 (Lord Jauncey)]

ad medium filum

Latin: to the middle line. A term denoting the boundary of a property that adjoins a road or river—the title extends to the middle line of the road or river. Fuller versions are:

- *ad medium filum viae* (to the centre of the road)
- *ad medium filum aquae / fluminis* (to the centre of the water / stream).

In each case, the English translation suffices . Writers wedded to the Latin should at least add an explanation (as in the first of the following examples):

- 'The judge held that the eastern boundary of Fiveacres is the centre line of Clay Lane. He arrived at this conclusion by the application of the archaically termed presumption *usque ad medium filum viae*, the presumption that the owner of land bordering a right of way is the owner of the land subject to the right of way (public or private) to the mid-point of the way.' [*Gilks v Hodgson* [2015] EWCA Civ 5, [12] (Sir Stanley Burnton)]
- 'No *ad medium filum* [prefer: *middle line*] analogy is available [in establishing boundaries between colonies].' [*New South Wales v Commonwealth* (1975) 135 CLR 337, 368 (Barwick CJ)]

Further reading

Kevin Gray and Susan Francis Gray, *Elements of Land Law*, 5th edn (Oxford University Press, 2009) [1.2.4], [1.2.7]

ad referendum

Latin: for further consideration; subject to finalisation of details. A term found particularly in treaties or similar documents, where a party may sign while reserving their position subject to agreement by government or others:

> 'I know [this was the purpose of the Convention] because I signed it on behalf of HM's Government (*ad referendum*).' [*Tyne Improvement Commissioners v Armement Anversois Société Anonyme (The Brabo)* [1947] 2 All ER 363, 370 (Scott LJ)]

The continued use of the Latin term in treaties may be excused on the ground that the language of treaties remains peculiarly formulaic. But in other contexts there seems no purpose in preferring the Latin over the English. No one today would (or should) speak of having signed an '*ad referendum* agreement' (cf correspondence cited in *Re North West Argentine Railway Co* [1900] 2 Ch 882, 885).

ad rem

Latin: to the matter at hand (literally: 'to the thing'). An argument *ad rem* (*argumentum ad rem*) attacks the opponent's points, in contrast to an argument *ad hominem*, which attacks the opponent's character. *Ad rem* is probably less common in English usage than *ad hominem*, and so remains italicised.

See also **ad hominem**.

ad summam

Latin: in short, in summary. Even though the meaning of the Latin is eminently guessable, only a pedant would prefer the Latin over the plain-English translation.

> '*Ad summam* [prefer: *In summary*], I would observe that Mr Tregonning's reinstatement will likely provide for him the one final opportunity to achieve his ambition of becoming a police officer.' [*Police Association of New South Wales on behalf of Adam Tregonning, and New South Wales Police Service* [2000] NSWIRComm 14, [166] (Sams DP)]

ad testificandum

Latin: for testifying. To be sought *ad testificandum* (sometimes shortened to *ad test*) is to be sought to appear as a witness. Unless court forms or court rules require use of the Latin, prefer the English translation.

See also **subpoena**; **WOOLF REFORMS**.

ad valorem

Latin: according to value; in proportion to value. Used especially in relation to taxes and stamp duties calculated as a proportion of the value of the property being taxed: the higher the value, the higher the tax or duty. Although Latinisms are generally to be avoided—unless the reader is learned in Latin—this term is now normal English usage, and is no longer italicised.

See also **LATIN**.

add that ...

The prefatory lead-in 'I/we might add that ...' or similar, is a weak introduction. If something really needs to be added, then simply add it. Similarly with openers such as 'It is interesting to point out that ...': if it is indeed interesting, make it more so by deleting the vacuous introduction.

See also **THROAT-CLEARING PHRASES**.

ADDRESSING CORRESPONDENCE

See **CORRESPONDENCE (LETTERS AND EMAILS)**.

adduce / educe

Adduce means *offer as proof*: eg, 'The plaintiff failed to *adduce* evidence of the defendant's negligence.' *Educe* (now rare) means *draw out*: eg, 'The cross-examination *educed* information about the plaintiff's claim.'

adeem

Latin: *adimere* to remove, take away; noun, *ademption* (Latin, *ademptio* = a taking away). By the doctrine of *ademption*, a specific gift in a will fails if the testator disposes of that property in his or her lifetime. The reason for the disposition is generally irrelevant: see, eg, *Re Slater* [1907] 1 Ch 665 (resumption).

Adeem (verb) and *ademption* (noun) are terms of art, difficult to convey precisely in plain English. When writing for non-lawyers, the plainer-English *extinguish* (verb) and *extinction* (noun) should suffice:

> 'The word "ademption" when applied to specific legacies of stock or of money ... must be considered as synonymous with the word "extinction".' RS Donnison Roper and Henry Hopley White, *A Treatise on the Law of Legacies*, 4th edn (usually cited as *Roper on Legacies*) (London, Butterworth, 1847) vol 1, 329.

Unless the context requires the precise elements of the doctrine of ademption to be stated, a plainer-English term causes no uncertainty:

> 'The deceased's last will had made specific legacies of No 7 to the Hart claimants, and of No 43 to the Samways claimants. As a result of the sales of these properties, these gifts were *adeemed* [prefer: *extinguished*].' [*Hart v Burbidge* [2014] EWCA Civ 992, [3] (Vos LJ)]

adhuc sub judice lis est

Latin: the case (or issue) is still under consideration (ie, has not yet been decided). The Latinism is now almost lost to the law:

- 'And from [that case], there is an appeal, and it is *adhuc sub judice*.' [*Fanshaw v Rotheram* (1758–59) 1 Eden 276, 280–81; 28 ER 691, 692]
- 'As to the jurisdiction of [the US Supreme Court] over [State courts], *adhuc sub judice lis est*.' [*Camden v Doremus* [1845] USSC 16, [73]; 44 US 515]

Nowadays, only a pedant would prefer the Latin over the English translation.

See also **sub judice**.

adjacent

Does *adjacent to* mean *next to* (ie, contiguous), or merely *nearby*? Both interpretations are found in case law; hence, a prudent drafter will clarify the intended meaning.

> '*Adjacent* is not a word to which a precise and uniform meaning is attached by ordinary usage. It is not confined to places adjoining, and it includes places close to or near. What degree of proximity would justify the application of the word is entirely a question of circumstances.' [*Wellington Corp v Lower Hutt Corp* [1904] AC 773, 775–76 (PC), holding that a council district was 'adjacent' to another council district, even though they were six miles apart and three other council districts lay between them.]

See also **adjoining**.

adjoining

As with *adjacent*, the meaning of *adjoining* varies with context, as the following examples show. A careful writer will clarify the intended meaning. Unless contiguity is intended, *neighbouring* may be preferable.

Examples of meaning of 'adjoining'

- 'conterminous': *New Plymouth BC v Taranaki Electric-Power Board* [1933] AC 680, 682
- 'having a common boundary with': *Solomon v Licensing Court of New South Wales* (2009) 52 NSWLR 31
- 'touching'—ie, being in physical contact with: *White v Harrow* (1902) 86 LT 4, 5–6; *Re Ecclesiastical Commissioners for England's Conveyance* [1936] Ch 430
- 'nearby though not touching': *Lightbound v Higher Bebington Local Board* (1885) 16 QBD 577, 584, Bowen LJ
- land on either side of a passageway 10 feet wide: *Foster v Lyons & Co Ltd* [1927] Ch 219
- land on either side of a road: *Auckland Lai v Warringah Shire Council* (1985) 58 LGRA 276
- land within the same subdivision: *Break O'Day Council v Resource Management and Planning Appeal Tribunal* [2009] TASSC 59; (2009) 19 Tas R 94.

See also **abut**; **adjacent**; **contiguous**.

adjudge

To make a judicial decision about a matter. The word must seem quaint to non-lawyer readers. Prefer a plain-language equivalent:

> '[I]f it is *adjudged* [prefer: *judged*; *decided*; *found*] that aggravated damages should be payable, [he has agreed] to pay them on that basis.' [*Ashley v Chief Constable of Sussex Police* [2008] UKHL 25; [2008] 1 AC 962, [74] (Lord Carswell)]

See also **abjudge**.

admeasurement

An archaism for *measurement*. It is still sometimes used in surveyors' metes and bounds descriptions of properties, from there finding its way into deeds of conveyance and mortgage ('containing by admeasurement [X] acres'). Prefer *measurement*. For example:

> '[T]he specification of the land merely as "part of Lot 11 d.p. 3725" together with the *admeasurements* [prefer: *measurements*] which appeared … did not permit of this being done.' [*Cooney v Ku-Ring-Gai Municipal Council* (1963) 114 CLR 582, 594 (Taylor J)]

See also **metes and bounds**.

administrator / administratrix

The person appointed to administer a deceased estate. Modern gender-neutral language favours *administrator* for both male and female appointees. The female form, *administratrix* (plural: *administratrixes*, or the more Latin-bound *administratrices*) is falling into disuse.

See further, **executor / executrix**; **GENDER-NEUTRAL LANGUAGE**; **testator / testatrix**.

admix

To mix with something else. The noun is *admixture*. Technically, an *admixture* is a physical mixing of items, each of which retains its original nature (although now mixed with other items); so, *admixture* is not strictly apposite to describe an entirely new substance that results from combining a number of items. For example, hydrogen and oxygen may combine to form water (H_2O), but water is not properly described as an *admixture* of hydrogen and water: *Gledhall v Dalton Main Collieries Ltd* (1934) 27 BWCC 181. In everyday use and most legal uses, *admix* means simply *mix with*—in which case, prefer *mix with* (verb) and *mixture* (noun):

- '[I]t appears likely … that the insulating material used by the laggers was *an admixture* [prefer: *a mixture*; *a combination of materials*] containing fiberized asbestos, and was therefore "asbestos" as defined by the Regulations.' [*McDonald v National Grid Electricity Transmission Plc* [2014] UKSC 53; [2015] AC 1128, [152] (Lord Reed)]
- '[T]he terms of the Deed, although widely drawn, did not authorise the *admixture* [prefer: *mixing*] of trust funds.' [*Commissioner of Taxation v Bargwanna* [2012] HCA 11; (2012) 244 CLR 655, [10] (French CJ, Gummow, Hayne, and Crennan JJ)]
- '[The appellant's Outline of Argument] contains *an admixture of* [prefer: *mixture of*] grounds and argument.' [*Velissaris v Fitzgerald* [2014] VSCA 139, [11] (Ashley JA)]

adoption

A word with three distinct meanings in law:

1. The process of 'adopting' a child, so that the child becomes the child of the adopting parent and the adopting parent becomes the parent of the child.
2. In contract law, the continued acceptance of a contract as binding on both parties, although the circumstances might otherwise entitle the wronged party to repudiate it.
3. The formal acceptance of a proposal, finding, resolution or amendment.

Context will almost certainly clarify the intended meaning.

adumbrate

A verb with multiple meanings, depending on context. Meanings include 'to list', 'to outline', or 'to trace' (in the sense of 'to set out the development of'). The following examples show different uses of the word. If the intended meaning could be unclear, prefer a clearer (and plainer) alternative.

- 'A large part of [the] difficulty stems from the lack of empirical evidence to support any of the feared outcomes such as have been *adumbrated* [prefer (depending on intended meaning): *outlined*; *listed*; *considered one by one*] in [certain cases].' [*Michael v Chief Constable of South Wales Police* [2015] UKSC 2, [184]; [2015] AC 1732, 1782 (Lord Kerr)]

- 'The history of the development of the doctrine *adumbrated* [prefer: *propounded*; *traced*?] by the Court of Appeal in the present case.' [Heading in *National Provincial Bank Ltd v Ainsworth* [1965] AC 1175, 1184]
- 'Considered together the two agreements seem to *adumbrate* [prefer: *foreshadow; set out*?] a scheme to avoid taxation by manipulation of the depreciation provisions of the Act.' [*Ferling v Federal Commissioner of Taxation* (1966) 115 CLR 603, 621 (Windeyer J)]
- 'His Honour [in his judgment] *adumbrates* [prefer: *lists*; or *considers one by one*] seven issues that have been the subject of argument before the Court of Appeal.' [*Macedonian Orthodox Community Church St Petka Inc v Metropolitan Petar* [2013] NSWCA 223, [237] (Emmett JA)]
- 'It is important to *adumbrate* [prefer: *collate* (?)] the statistics into meaningful numbers … to understand the import of the other studies …' [*King v Western Sydney Local Health Network* [2013] NSWCA 162, [192] (Ward JA)]

ADVERBS

See **MODIFIERS**.

adverse possession

See **prescription / adverse possession**.

adversely affect

A term often found in commercial contracts—eg, where a contracting party is given the right to rescind if a state of affairs is found to 'adversely affect' that party's rights under the contract. Although often used, the term is inherently vague. For example:

- what degree of affectation is required before it can be described as 'adverse'?
- must the affectation be direct, or is indirect affectation sufficient?
- is the affectation to be tested subjectively or objectively?

A careful drafter will foresee these issues and clarify accordingly. A careful drafter will also avoid spelling mistakes:

> '[Such an order] is likely to have a very significant *averse effect* [correct to: *adverse effect*] on the children.' [*Secretary of State for Home Department v Khafif* [2015] UKAITUR IA493492014, [40] (Judge O'Ryan)]

advice / advise

Advice is the noun; *advise* is the verb: 'The lawyer *advised* the client in a written *advice*.'

See also **ADVICE (FORM OF)**; **judgment (and variants)**.

ADVICE (FORM OF)

Forms of advice

Written legal advices take many forms and have many different audiences. Some advices are written by lawyers for non-lawyer clients; others are written by lawyers for lawyers (eg, a barrister's advice to a solicitor). Some advices are internal office memoranda. Some are for company boards, or for government ministers and their departments. Some audiences will know the subject matter, others will not; some will have legal backgrounds, others will not; some will have good readership skills, others will not; and some will be keenly interested, others will not. In more modern times, some advices will be by formal letter; others will be by email.

As a result, there is no single, ideal form of written advice. Each advice must be tailored to its audience.

Structure

All advices benefit from close attention to the way in which information is structured.

Traditional structure

Traditionally, legal advices followed a standard pattern, doubtless adopted from the structure of legal judgments:

1. The issue
2. The facts
3. The relevant law
4. Application of the law to the facts
5. Conclusion (including what steps the client should take next).

Many legal writers still follow this structure. But although hallowed by time and convention, the structure is not ideal for readers. It mirrors the writer's process as he or she wrestles through the legal issue to arrive at a conclusion: first, isolate the issue; then master the facts; then research the law; then apply the law to the facts; and then reach a conclusion. But why put readers through the same process? Most readers probably expect—or at least hope—that their question will be answered early, not postponed to the end of the document. So, having gone through the process as a writer, why not cut-and-paste the material to meet the reader's expectation or hope?

Modern structure

A more modern structure seeks to cater for the reader's expectation—or hope—by 'front-loading' the material the reader is most likely to be seeking. It therefore begins by briefly framing the issue (without which the conclusion may lack context), and then proceeds immediately to the *conclusion* (reversing the traditional approach):

1. Issue (stated briefly)
2. Conclusion (including what steps the client should next take)
3. Key legal reasons for the conclusion
4. Background (including the facts and any necessary amplification of the key legal reasons)
5. Restatement of the conclusion (optional).

Notice that the key legal reasons for the conclusion (step 3) come before the detailed statement of the facts. Also, preferably, the key legal reasons should avoid excessive detail. The details of the facts and legal reasons can come in step 4. This structure is deliberate: reasons are more persuasive if laid bare, undiluted by too much detail. It frees readers from having to 'hunt for truffles' buried in the document (to adapt *United States v Dunkel* 927 F 2d 955, 956 (7th Cir, 1991).

If the advice deals with a number of issues, the format may need tweaking:

1. Issues, listed one by one
2. Conclusions, listed in the same order as the issues and including what steps the client should take next in response to each conclusion
3. Key legal reasons for each conclusion, listed in the same order as the conclusions

4. Background, including the facts and any necessary amplification of the key legal reasons
5. Restatement of the conclusions (optional).

Order reasons logically

Where there are several reasons, rank them in order of importance, with the most important first. That way, the reasons also reflect the front-loading technique, presenting the reader with the key points before descending to less important ones.

Executive summary?

This modern structure renders an executive summary strictly unnecessary. A briefly stated issue and conclusion serve the same purpose. However, some readers, particularly in business and government, expect executive summaries. If they are required, executive summaries must be brief. They should start with a brief statement of the issue (ideally, no more than one or two sentences), followed by a brief statement of the conclusion, and then a brief statement of the reasons. Any further elaboration belongs in the body of the advice, not in the executive summary.

Other matters to consider

A well-thought-out advice format will consider also the following matters.

Table of contents

In an advice of any length, include a table of contents. (You can usually create it automatically from the headings.) The table not only gives the reader an overview of the text (and facilitates 'dipping into' parts of the text of particular interest), but also helps the writer ensure that the topics follow logically.

Numbered headings

It is useful to number headings. The benefit is as much for the writer as for the reader, because the process of numbering helps ensure a logical flow of ideas.

Legal writers have their preferred numbering systems. All start with main headings numbered 1, 2, 3, and so on; but different writers then favour different lower-level headings. The main systems are:

- Arabic/Roman
- decimal
- combination of Arabic/Roman and decimal.

For examples, see discussion under **NUMBERING SYSTEMS**. Logically, where an advice contains headings and subheadings (and possibly sub-subheadings), a decimal numbering system is better. This is because each number is complete in itself; no 'part' numbers accompany the text. Readers know instantly where they are in the hierarchy of headings—and the discipline of decimal numberings encourages writers to place subtopics under their appropriate main heading.

Example

2. Validity of the lease

2.1 Is the duration certain?
2.2 Is the description of the premises certain?
2.3 Are the legislative requirements for validity satisfied?

3. **Termination**
    - 3.1 Has the tenant breached the lease?
    - 3.2 Has the landlord waived the breach?
    - 3.3 Has the landlord given the proper notice?

[Headings from legal advice considering whether a lease is valid, and (if so) whether the landlord has effectively terminated it.]

Numbered paragraphs

If an advice is short (say, up to two pages), there is little benefit in numbering the paragraphs. But if the advice is longer, it may be useful to number the paragraphs for ease of later reference.

Where headings use decimal numbering, paragraph numbers should reflect that system. Where a paragraph stands alone under a heading, it needs no number. To illustrate these points (to continue the previous example):

2. **Validity of the lease**
    - 2.1 Is the duration certain?
        - 2.1.1 [text]
        - 2.1.2 [text]
    - 2.2 Is the description of the premises certain?
      [text—this is the only paragraph under 2.2]
    - 2.3 Are the legislative requirements for validity satisfied?
        - 2.3.1 [text]
        - 2.3.2 [text]

Some writers simply number paragraphs consecutively (ie, without descending to decimal subnumbering), starting at 1 and continuing to the end of the advice. Where this is done, some design experts suggest making the paragraph numbers less 'noisy', by reducing font size and using grey rather than black: eg, '10' not '10'.

Recommendations or 'next steps'

Where an advice recommends further action or 'next steps', state the recommendations and steps clearly and in a logical location. The most logical location is often up-front, as part of the conclusion. If it is necessary to expand the discussion, do so in a separate section of the advice.

Weaknesses in the reasons

If you can see weaknesses in the reasons, chances are that your reader too will see them. It is better to acknowledge the weaknesses—and then refute them if possible. To leave them unmentioned invites criticism and weakens the strength of the valid reasons.

Insipid beginnings and endings

Get straight to the point. An insipid opening wastes the reader's time and dilutes the writer's efforts to make the advice compelling and persuasive. Avoid openings like: 'I refer to previous correspondence in this matter', or 'I refer to your telephone conversation of last Monday'.

Similarly, avoid insipid endings. A wimpish ending dilutes the force of a well-structured argument. Refrain from endings such as: 'Please let me know if you need further clarification of the matters I have discussed' or 'If I can be any further assistance, please telephone me'. These not only make the writer seem insincere, but also imply that the advice is not as clear and targeted as it could be.

Design

Attention to structure and language goes only so far. Design and layout (the 'look' and 'feel' of a document) are also important if an advice is to engage the reader. Consider such matters as font, use of white space, line length, line spacing.

For an example of a bold approach to design matters of this kind—including the innovative use of colour—see the award-winning design of a legal advice at www.corrs.com.au/news/2012/07/corrs-incisive-advice-honoured-at-australian-international-design-awards (noted in (2019) 98 *Michigan Bar Journal* (Sept) 42).

Barristers' advices

Barristers' advices tend to be more formulaic than solicitors' advices, favouring more traditional structure, language and design. There is no justification for this conservatism, except tradition. As with solicitors' advices, so too barristers' advices benefit from the techniques discussed above.

Email advices

Many modern advices are given not by formal document but by email. The language of emails tends to be more relaxed than that of formal advices (which is evidence, if any were needed, that a relaxed tone can be as precise as a formal tone). However, even assuming a more relaxed tone, email advices too benefit from attention to 'structure'—eg, by starting with a brief statement of the issue, then moving immediately to the answer (the conclusion), then giving the reasons, and only finally traversing the background facts.

'Before' and 'after' examples

The following 'before' and 'after' examples illustrate these points. Both examples are solicitors' letters of advice to non-lawyer clients, who (let us assume) are unfamiliar with legal terms of art and the traditional structure of legal advices.

Example 1

Before

To: XY client

The issue

You have instructed us that you own a parcel of land (Lot 1) which adjoins a parcel of land (Lot 2) owned by your neighbour, Mr Jones. Your land has no street frontage of its own, but it has a registered right of way across Mr Jones' land. This provides your only means of access to the nearest street (Temple Street). You have told us that Mr Jones plans to erect a gate across the entrance to the right of way where it exits into Temple Street. Mr Jones apparently fears that pedestrians using Temple Street may assume that the right of way is a public laneway, and someone might walk down the right of way, find themselves alongside his house, and break into his house. So he plans to forestall that threat by installing a steel gate across the entrance to the right of way, secured with a padlock. This will inconvenience your use of the right of way.

The facts

The right of way was created in 1950, when your lot (Lot 1) was subdivided from the rest of a larger parcel of land (which became Lot 2). At the time of the subdivision, a right of way was created to give Lot 1 access across Lot 2 to reach Temple Street. This is the right of way you currently enjoy. The right of way is in a fairly standard form: specifically, it gives the owner of Lot 1 the right to 'pass and repass, at any time of the day or night, without or without vehicles' across Lot 2. It says nothing about any right to install a gate where the right of way exits into Temple Street.

The law

The owner of land burdened by an easement remains the freehold owner of the land, with all the rights of a freehold owner, consistent with the existence of the easement. Normally, of course, an owner of land can install a gate on his or her land. But under the law of easements, the owner of land burdened by an easement cannot 'unreasonably' interfere with the rights of the owner of the land benefited by the easement. The key word is 'unreasonably'. Some interference is permitted in exercise of the normal rights of ownership; in other words, the owner of the benefited land must be prepared to suffer some interference. The question is whether the interference can be described as 'unreasonable'.

The issue of gates across rights of way has arisen in a number of court cases. While each case depends on its own facts, the general thrust of the case law is that the owner of the burdened land is entitled to install a gate on his or her land at the exit point of a right of way, and is entitled to attach a padlock, as long as they give a key to the owner of the benefited land. The existence of a lockable gate may well cause some interference in the benefited owner's use of the right of way; but it is an interference which the benefited owner must endure.

Application of the law to the facts

Mr Jones, as the owner of the burdened land (Lot 2), is entitled to secure his land from threats of trespass or theft. This entitlement includes securing the land by installing a gate where the right of way exits into Temple Street. This will cause you some inconvenience, and doubtless some exasperation. Instead of driving or walking straight out into Temple Street, you may have to stop and unlock the gate; and you may have to repeat the process when you return to your property. However, the law says that the owner of the burdened land is within his or her rights to install a locked gate—as long as they provide the owner of the benefited land with a key.

Conclusion

In our view, Mr Jones can erect a gate across the entrance to the right of way where it opens out into Temple Street, and can put a padlock on the gate, as long as he provides you with a key.

After (version 1)

To: XY client

The issue

Can your neighbour, Mr Jones, install a locked gate where your right of way exits into Temple Street?

Answer

Yes, he can, as long as he gives you a key to the gate.

Reasons

Mr Jones' land is burdened by a right of way in favour of your land. Mr Jones must respect that right of way. However, Mr Jones is also entitled to protect his land and property against threats of trespass or theft, including by erecting a fence and gate where his land fronts the street. But he cannot do anything that will unreasonably interfere with your right of way. The key word is 'unreasonably'. The law permits *some* interference, in exercise of normal rights of ownership—the question is whether the interference is 'unreasonable'.

The question of gates across rights of way has arisen in a number of court cases. While each case depends on its own facts, the general principle is that the owner of the burdened land (Mr Jones) has the right to install a gate on the land at the exit point of a right of way, and has the right to attach a padlock, as long as they give a key to the owner of the benefited land (you). The existence of a lockable gate may well cause *some* interference in the use of the right of way; but the law regards it as an interference which the benefited owner (you) must put up with.

Background facts

The right of way was created in 1950, when your lot (Lot 1) was subdivided from the rest of a larger parcel of land (which became Lot 2). At that time, a registered right of way was created to give Lot 1 access across Lot 2 to reach Temple Street. The right of way is in a fairly standard form, and gives the owner of Lot 1 the right to 'pass and repass, at any time of the day or night, without or without vehicles' across Lot 2. It says nothing about any right to install a gate where the right of way exits into Temple Street. For that reason, it is necessary to fall back on the common law to find the answer. We base our conclusion and reasons on the common law's approach to resolving issues of this kind.

After (version 2—shorter, but may be all that the client requires)

To: XY client

The issue

Can your neighbour, Mr Jones, install a locked gate where your right of way exits into Temple Street?

Answer

Yes, he can, as long as he gives you a key to the gate.

Reasons

Mr Jones has the right to protect his property against threats of trespass or theft. This means he can erect a fence and gate on his street frontage, even though this impedes your use of your right of way. However, the fence and gate must not *unreasonably* interfere with your use of the right of way. The key word is *unreasonably*. The courts have ruled that, as long as you are given a key, the inconvenience of a locked gate is not an *unreasonable* interference with your use of the right of way.

[end]

[**Note**. This version omits *Background*. While the legal adviser needs to master the background facts, the reader already knows them. Hence the writer can explain the legal position without reciting the background facts. Note also the absence of paragraph numbering in all three versions; while numbering might have been useful in the original version, both revised versions are short enough to dispense with numbering.]

Example 2

Before

Ms X
Chief Executive Officer
ABC Ltd

RE: RESTRICTIVE COVENANT ON ABC LTD'S PROPERTY

Your company, ABC Ltd ('the Company'), owns a property in a subdivision in Smithtown. The title is subject to a restrictive covenant, which prohibits certain materials being used in any building on the land. You have told us that ABC Ltd has recently constructed new factory premises on the land, using materials that are common in modern factories but that do not comply with the covenant. You are concerned that this breach of covenant may result in neighbouring owners seeking to compel the Company to demolish the addition.

Our title searches show that there are 56 lots in the subdivision. The subdivision was created in 1910. The developer imposed a covenant in identical terms on each lot as it was sold off. Each covenant is expressed to burden the lot being sold and to benefit every other lot in the subdivision. That means that there are 55 other properties in the subdivision that are technically benefited by the covenant that binds your title.

Given that the Company does not wish to demolish the factory, then the Company's options are either: (1) to take steps to extinguish the covenant or to have it modified to permit the building to remain; or (2) to simply do nothing and put the onus on any complaining neighbours to enforce the covenant against the Company.

As to extinguishing or modifying the covenant: two options are available. One is by obtaining a signed agreement between the Company and the owners of the other 55 lots in the subdivision to release or modify the covenant. However, such a solution is impractical. The Company would need the signatures of the owners of all 55 lots, and the trouble and expense in achieving this would be considerable (and of course some owners might not agree).

As to applying to a court or tribunal: the purpose would be to get a court order modifying or extinguishing the covenant. But that would also involve considerable expense in preparing the application, preparing affidavits from the Company, and inviting the participation of all or most other owners in the subdivision regarding the use of unauthorised building materials in the subdivision. The Company would have to pay its own legal costs, and probably the legal costs of other owners who participate in the proceedings. In our view, the costs would far outweigh any benefit to the Company.

That leaves the option of simply doing nothing, and putting the onus on neighbours to enforce the covenant against the Company. You have told us that most other properties in the subdivision use materials that would breach the covenant. This indicates that most other owners in the subdivision have 'waived' compliance with the covenant. Also, you have told us, most modern buildings of this type in the UK use materials prohibited by the covenant. This indicates that the terms of the covenant bear little relevance to the building materials used today—ie, that the covenant is obsolete. On both grounds, we are confident that no one in the subdivision could enforce the covenant against the Company. In our view, it is therefore quite safe to sit back and do nothing.

However, should the Company come to sell the property, we suggest that you should draw the breach of covenant to the attention of the solicitors preparing the contract, so that the breach can be disclosed in the contract, thereby ensuring that a purchaser cannot use the breach to avoid his or her obligations as purchaser under the contract.

After you have had the opportunity to read this letter and consider its contents, may we suggest you contact Mr Laws of this firm and advise us of the Company's wishes in this matter. If there is any other aspect of the covenant, as it relates to the property, that you would like us to further clarify, please do not hesitate to contact us.

[End of letter]

After

Ms X
Chief Executive Officer
ABC Ltd

Restrictive covenant on ABC Ltd's property

1. **Issue**

   Should ABC Ltd ('ABC') be concerned that its factory in Smithtown is built of materials that breach the covenant on the land?

2. **Answer**

   No. (But note point 6 below about future sale of the land.)

3. **Reasons for the answer**

   3.1 **So many other owners in the subdivision have breached the covenant that no one can enforce it against ABC.** The covenant that affects ABC burdens all 56 lots in the subdivision. It also benefits all 56 lots. That is, every owner can enforce the covenant against every other owner. But so many of the owners have breached the covenant that a court or tribunal would rule that they had given up ('waived') the right to enforce it. Realistically, no one could enforce the covenant against ABC.

   3.2 **Changes in building materials since the covenant was created mean that it is now obsolete.** The covenant has become so outmoded by changes in building materials that it no longer serves any useful purpose. On that basis, a court or tribunal would almost certainly rule that the covenant is obsolete and can no longer be enforced. So it would be pointless for anyone to take the Company to court about the breach.

4. Other options (but in our view, not worth pursuing)

4.1 *Try to get all the other owners in the subdivision to agree to extinguish or modify the covenant.* But that would mean getting the owners of all 55 other lots to agree, which is both unlikely and expensive. And because they probably cannot enforce the covenant (for reasons discussed above), there would be no point.

4.2 *Ask a tribunal or court to modify or extinguish the covenant.* That too would require notifying the owners of all 55 other lots, which would involve considerable legal and court costs. Here also, because no one probably can enforce the covenant, there would be no point.

5. Background

The covenant was created in 1910, shortly after the creation of the subdivision of 56 lots. The covenant prohibits the use of certain building materials. When the Company built its factory, it used materials that the covenant prohibits. The prohibited materials are now common in modern building practices.

6. Caution: disclosure on future sale

If in the future the Company decides to sell the factory, it should disclose the breach in the contract for sale. The disclosure should prevent the purchaser from getting out of the contract on the technicality that the covenant has been breached.

[End of letter]

Notes about this *After* example:

- The main heading—**Restrictive covenant on ABC Ltd's property**—is centred. Headings are better left-aligned (because the eye defaults to that position, at least in English-language text); but here, given that all the following headings are left-aligned, the centred location helps the main heading stand out.
- Each introductory sentence of the Reasons is highlighted in **bold**. So too is the key answer (in 2). The purpose is to enable a busy reader (here, the CEO) to understand the gist of the advice by scanning the bold material (and, if they wish, skipping the more detailed explanations).
- The *Background* is not crucial, because the CEO can be assumed to know the facts. However, it is included here because the advice might be circulated to other readers (eg, Board members, or shareholders), less familiar with the facts.

Further reading

- Peter Butt, 'Judgment Writing: An Antipodean Response' (2013) 129 *Law Quarterly Review* 7
- Robert Eagleson, 'Drafting Matters—Letters of Advice' (2007) 58 *Clarity* 23; reprinted (2014) 71 *Clarity* 55; also at www.clarity-international.net/clarity-journal/archives/
- Joseph Kimble, 'First Things First: The Lost Art of Summarizing' (2001–2002) 8 *Scribes Journal of Legal Writing* 103; reprinted in Joseph Kimble, *Lifting the Fog of Legalese: Essays on Plain Language* (Carolina Academic Press, 2006) 73

See also **AUDIENCE; CORRESPONDENCE (LETTERS AND EMAILS); DOCUMENT DESIGN; DOCUMENT STRUCTURE; EXECUTIVE SUMMARY; FONTS; NUMBERING SYSTEMS.**

adviser / advisor

Preferred spelling is *adviser*, although even senior judges slip between the *-or* and *-er* spellings:

'[9] The panel … were assisted by an HR *adviser* from the Schools Education Advisory Team ("SEAT"). The head teacher … was assisted by a SEAT HR *adviser*. The head teacher presented

> the management case and she was assisted by a SEAT HR *adviser*. … [72] [T]he child protection officer was questioned by the disciplinary panel and their head teacher's *advisor* …' [*R v Governors of X School* [2011] UKSC 30; [2011] 3 WLR 237, [9], [72] (Lord Dyson)]

However, the adjective is *advisory*. And in commercial terminology, *advisor* is increasingly seen: eg, 'financial *advisor*', 'business *advisor*'.

aedificatum solo[,] solo cedit

Latin: that which is built on land becomes part of the land; whatever is built on land becomes part of it. A maxim used in the law of fixtures. The ready availability of a clear translation makes continued use of the Latin unnecessary.

See also **fixtures and fittings**.

affd / aff'd

Abbreviation for *affirmed*—denoting that the appeal court upheld or confirmed the decision under appeal.

affect / effect / impact

Affect is a verb, meaning 'to influence' or 'to act on': eg, 'Lack of a witness did not *affect* the validity of the document.'

Effect may be either a noun or a verb:

- *effect* (noun) means 'result': eg, 'Lack of a witness has no *effect* on the validity of a document.'
- *effect* (verb) means 'to bring about' in the sense of achieving a result: eg, 'You can *effect* service of the notice personally.' (Better: 'You can serve the notice personally.')

Affect can be a useful generality where the precise extent of the *effect* of an action need not be exhaustively delineated: eg, 'Nothing in clause 5 *affects* clause 10.'

Impact has become a modern catch-all for *affect* and *effect*, possibly because writers imagine that *impact* enlivens the prose, or perhaps because they are unsure how to choose between *affect* or *effect*. Whatever the reason, always prefer *affect* or *effect* over *impact*, unless you really need to stress the power of the action: eg,

> Lack of a witness did not *impact* [prefer: *affect*] the validity of the document.
>
> Lack of a witness had no *impact* [prefer: *effect*] on the validity of the document.

Sometimes also, *impact* shows the writer's lack of verbal awareness:

> Car crashes *impact* [prefer: *affect*; *hinder*] traffic flow.

See also **adversely affect**; **VERBAL AWARENESS (LACK OF)**.

aforesaid

Something already mentioned: eg, 'the *aforesaid* contract'. As with the briefer 'said', it is often superfluous, because the context will clarify which item is meant. But where it is necessary to retain the idea of 'already mentioned', prefer a modern, standard English word or phrase: eg, 'the contract already mentioned' or 'the contract referred to previously'.

Apart from its archaic overtones, *aforesaid* introduces ambiguity where there are a number of possible referents. Where it is unclear to which antecedent *aforesaid* might refer, it is usually taken to refer to the immediately preceding antecedent: *Peake v Screech* (1845) 7 QB 603, 610; 115 ER 616, 620 (Lord Denman CJ). However, this is no more than a rule of thumb, applicable only as a last resort. It does not always resolve the ambiguity. For example:

- Section 32 of a railways statute authorised railway companies to take and use land for a number of specified 'purposes', and authorised the companies to carry out works on the land 'for the purposes *aforesaid*'. Earlier sections in the statute also referred to 'purposes'. Did *aforesaid* refer to those purposes also? Held, no; 'aforesaid purposes' referred only to the purposes in s 32: *Fenwick v East London Railway Co* (1875) 20 Eq 544 (Jessel MR).
- A US court struck down for uncertainty a clause containing a surfeit of *aforesaids*, because it was impossible to discern to which of a number of earlier items each *aforesaid* referred: *Sanders v Ashland Oil Inc* 696 So 2d 1031, 1037 [13] (La Ct App, 1st Cir, 1997).

It is much better to use clearer drafting to avoid the ambiguity.

See also **LAST-ANTECEDENT RULE; said.**

after (a date)

General principle

In calculating a period of time *after* a specified day, that day is normally not counted—ie, counting starts with the next day: *The Goldsmiths' Co v West Metropolitan Railway Co* [1904] 1 KB 1, 5 (Mathew LJ). So, '5 days *after* 1 December' is 6 December.

'shortly after'

How soon is 'shortly after'? The answer depends on the context in which the term is used—which makes the meaning objectively uncertain. For example:

> Legislation governing the admissibility of evidence allowed evidence of a statement made by a person who had since died, if the deceased had made the statement 'shortly after' the event in question. The purpose was to ensure the reliability of recollections that could fade over time. Held, a statement made 5 days after the event was admissible: *R v Ryan* [2013] NTSC 54; (2013) 33 NTLR 123. But in another case, a statement made 5–6 days after the event, was not made 'shortly after' the event: *Williams v The Queen* [2000] FCA 1868; (2000) 119 A Crim R 490.

See also **beginning with / beginning from**; **from (a date)**; **TIME**.

age

When attained

In normal usage, a person attains a specified age on the anniversary of the day of their birth: eg, if born on 1 January, their age increases by one year on each succeeding 1 January. However, in strict legal usage, a person attains a specified age on the day *preceding* that anniversary. So a person born on 22 July 1891 attained the age of 25 on 21 July 1916: *Re Shurey* [1918] 1 Ch 263. In some jurisdictions for some purposes, statute has amended this legal usage to bring it into line with normal usage—so that a person attains a specified age at the start of the anniversary of the date of their birth.

> '[A] rule [of the common law] is fixed inveterately that during the whole of the day preceding the twenty-first anniversary of his birth a man is of full age. One might have supposed that it is only on the expiry of that day that twenty-one calendar years are fulfilled. But the law will have none of this. All day long he is of full age.' [*Prowse v McIntyre* (1961) 111 CLR 264, 270 (Dixon CJ)]

'over' an age

A person is *over* a specified age as of the first day on which they attain that age. For example, where an insurance policy excluded from benefits a person '*over* the age of 65 years', it excluded a person aged 65 years and 7 months (otherwise, 'over the age of 65 years' would mean 'when the 66th birthday is attained'): *Lloyds Bank Ltd v Eagle Star Insurance Co Ltd* [1951] 1 TLR 803.

Stating an age

When stating an age, use numerals, even if the number is below 10: 'He is 5 years old.' If an age is expressed as an adjective before a noun, or as a substitute for a noun, use hyphens: 'The book is for 5-year-olds', 'She is a 4-year-old girl'.

See also **NUMBERS**.

agenda / agendum

Latin: *agenda*, things to be done; items to be dealt with at a meeting. Etymologically, *agenda* is the plural of *agendum*: one *agendum*, many *agenda*. But in practice *agenda* has become the singular—eg, 'Today's agenda is …'—with *agendas* the plural.

agree and acknowledge

Two words with different meanings: *agree* imposes a contractual obligation to do something ('I *agree* to pay you $100'), while *acknowledge* records a state of facts ('I *acknowledge* that you have paid me $100'). However, the two words are often paired: thus, a party *agrees and acknowledges* that a certain state of affairs exists. In this context, one word alone generally suffices—either *agree* or *acknowledge*.

See also **agree and declare; agree and warrant**; **WORD PAIRINGS**.

agree and declare

A common pairing in contracts: eg, 'The Parties *agree and declare* as follows.' An *agreement* is an arrangement or contract establishing a legal relationship between parties. A *declaration* is a formal statement about an existing state of affairs; it is not itself an arrangement or contract, though it may have legal consequences (such as creating a warranty or setting up an estoppel). Despite their different meanings, the two words often appear in combination as if they were synonyms. Almost always, one can be deleted.

See also **agree and acknowledge; agree and warrant**; **condition / warranty**; **WORD PAIRINGS**.

agree and warrant

A companion pairing in contracts—as where a party 'agrees and warrants' that a state of affairs exists. Almost always, either word—*agrees* or *warrants*—suffices. The only exception is where the drafter consciously intends *warrant* to carry the sense of a promise (a *warranty*), breach of which gives only a right to damages, not a right to terminate.

See also **agree and acknowledge**; **agree and declare**; **WORD PAIRINGS**.

AGREEMENT / DEED

See **DEED (document)**.

aid and abet

As a legal pairing, *aid and abet* is entrenched in the language of the criminal law. It sometimes appears as part of a longer expression, *aid, abet, counsel, and [or] procure*. *Aid* has the general meaning of help or assist. *Abet* has an overlapping meaning of helping or assisting as an accomplice. In criminal law, the distinction between *aid and abet* and *counsel and procure* lies in whether the defendant was present (but not participating) or absent: an act that amounts to *aiding and abetting* if done while present at the crime, amounts to *counselling and procuring* if done while absent: JC Smith, 'Aid, Abet, Counsel or Procure' in PR Glazebrook (ed), *Reshaping the Criminal Law: Essays in Honour of Glanville Williams* (Stevens & Sons, 1978) 120, 127. But the distinction is rarely drawn, and the word string *aids, abets, counsels, and [or] procures* is taken to encompass all the means employed to bring about an offence: *R v Ready* [1942] VLR 85, 88–89; *R v B* (2012) 114 SASR 170, [13].

In some contexts it may be necessary to retain the entire word string (eg, when referring to the statutory offence itself). Otherwise, prefer more idiomatic phrases such as 'being knowingly involved in' the commission of an offence, or 'helping or encouraging' the commission of an offence.

Further reading

'Aid and Abet', in *Law Words* (Centre for Plain Legal Language, University of Sydney, 1995) 10; link at www.clarity-international.net/plain-language-resources/general-resources/

See also **WORD PAIRINGS; WORD STRINGS**.

alibi

Strictly, the defence of being somewhere other than the place of the crime; colloquially, an excuse for wrongdoing.

alien

Latin: *alienus*—belonging to another. In general usage, *alien* suggests an element of threat or danger, or at least undesirability. But in legal usage *alien* means simply a person who is a non-citizen of the country concerned; such a person has the status of *alienage*. For that reason, even in legal usage, prefer *non-citizen* or *foreigner* (or similar).

alienate

To dispose of something, usually for value; noun, *alienation*. In legal usage, *to alienate* carries no nuance of *to estrange* (although the Latin root *alienare* is common to both meanings). Alternative legal descriptors include *transfer* (particularly for land covered by land-registration systems), *convey* (particularly for land under pre-land-registration systems), and *dispose of* (a generic term).

alienation

See **alienate**.

alike

A legal archaism, meaning *equally* or *in equal shares*:

> 'The word *alike* is the same as the word *equally*': *Loveacres d Mudge v Blight* (1775) 1 Cowp 352, 357, 98 ER 1125, 1128 (Lord Mansfield CJ).

Alike sometimes appeared in wills, as where property was given 'to A and B *share and share alike*'—which meant (and still means) 'to A and B *in equal shares*'. There is no reason to preserve the archaism.

aliquot

Latin: some; so many. In law, *aliquot* indicates a proportionate part of the whole: thus, co-owners who are tenants in common are said to have *aliquot* shares in the land. The term can apply to unequal holdings: eg, two tenants in common of a property, one holding 1/100th and the other 99/100ths, are still properly described as having *aliquot* shares.

Aliquot is likely to be meaningless to most readers—in which case, use *proportionate.*

See also **joint tenant / tenant in common**.

aliter

Latin: otherwise (usually in the sense of 'it is otherwise if …'). To retain the Latin is pure affectation.

- '[T]he legislation here in question clearly places the primary duty of care upon the driver rather than the passenger. *Aliter* [prefer: *It is otherwise*; *The contrary applies*] under seat belt law.' [*Madden v Quirk* [1989] 1 WLR 702, 708 (Simon Brown J)]
- '[I]f incompetence or unfitness is not an element in the accident, the lack of a licence or certificate is incidental and irrelevant; *aliter* [prefer: *it is otherwise*; *the opposite applies*] if unfitness or incompetence is a contributing cause.' [*John Pfeiffer Pty Ltd v Canny* (1981) 148 CLR 218, 230 (Mason J)]

aliunde

Latin: outside; from some other source. This is not a legal term of art, but merely a Latin affectation. The English translation serves the purpose as well as the Latin, even if it takes a few more words.

- '[O]n the face of it [the notice] appears to be good and it is only on proof of facts *aliunde* [prefer: *external to the notice*] that the notice is shown to be bad.' [*Miller-Mead v Minister of Housing and Local Government* [1963] 2 QB 196, 226 (Upjohn LJ)]
- 'Consequently, despite such concerns as there may have been about the reliability of the statutory declaration, in the end the judge's decision was based upon proof *aliunde* [prefer: *by another means*] of the existence of the express trust.' [*Schweitzer v Schweitzer* [2012] VSCA 260, [44] (Nettle JA)]

all

All can have shades of meaning, depending on context.

- Normally, *all* means 'the whole quantity of' or 'the entirety of'—as in 'deny *all* liability', 'take *all* responsibility', or 'prove beyond *all* reasonable doubt'.
- But *all* can mean *any* (in the sense of 'any or all'), to include also the situation where there may be none. For example, a reference to *all* non-native title rights meant *if any exist*: *Griffiths v Minister for Lands, Planning and Environment* [2008] HCA 20; (2008) 235 CLR 232, [4], [49].

all and every / all and any

The single word *all* is sufficient, because *all* necessarily includes *every* and *any*:

> 'The proper way of construing a word like *all* [in the phrase "A has *all* the powers of B"], is to say that it means *all*, and does not mean *some*, unless one finds a compelling context which forces one to place some limitation on the word.' [*Re Wellsted's Will Trusts* [1949] Ch 296, 306 (Lord Greene MR)]

To add after *all* the words *and every*, or *and any*, is redundant. For example:

- '[T]he claimants have not, in their latest evidence, provided full and complete disclosure of *all and every aspect* [prefer: *all aspects*; *every aspect*] of the circumstances in which they acted for E-Clear.' [*E-Clear (UK) plc v Elia* [2012] EWHC 1195, [15] (Judge Mackie QC)]
- 'An employer is not liable for *all and every* [prefer: *every*] injury suffered by an employee … caused in some way by engagement in the employment duties.' [*Oram v BHP Mitsui Coal Pty Ltd* [2014] QSC 230, [45] (McMeekin J)]

all and singular

An irredeemably quaint expression. Prune to *all*.

all of

Generally, *of* is superfluous. If so, delete it:

- 'I convey *all of* [prefer: *all*] my interest in the land.'
- '[A]n inquiry whether, on *all of* [prefer: *all*] the evidence, the verdict was unreasonable must entail a consideration of *all of* [prefer: *all*] the evidence that was before the [trial judge].' [*RP v The Queen* [2016] HCA 53; (2016) 259 CLR 641, [23], plurality of High Court of Australia)]

not all / all … not

The negative forms—*not all* and *all … not*—can be ambiguous: do they mean *none*, or *less than all* (but allowing for some)? For example:

- 'Not all lawyers write well.' Does this mean: (1) no lawyers write well; or (2) some lawyers write well but some do not? Probably (2), but it is not entirely clear.
- A contract allowed a party to rescind 'if *all* of the [c]onditions have *not* been discharged' by a certain date. Did this mean that a party could rescind: (1) if *any* of the conditions had not been discharged by that date; or (2) if *none* of the conditions had been discharged by that date? Held, both meanings were open, but (1) seemed more likely to have been intended: *Dooba Developments Ltd v McLagan Investments Ltd* [2016] EWHC 2944 (Ch).

all reasonable endeavours

See **best endeavours / reasonable endeavours.**

ALLITERATION

Alliteration is the repetition of the same letter or sound at the start of words in a series. Careful alliteration can aid communication by drawing attention to words and concepts. But alliteration done purely for show can impede communication by drawing attention to its own banality:

> 'All acknowledge the art of alliteration is of ancient ancestry; but propensity for this peculiar phrasing is the predilection of particular persons and plenty of people profess positive prejudice against the practice.' [*Megdal v Oregon State Board of Dental Examiners* 605 P 2d 273, fn 1 (Oregon 1980)]

Beware also of alliteration that unwittingly draws a chuckle, as in the following statutory definition:

> '**Reshippers**—Persons who transship shucked shellfish in original containers, or shellstock, from certified shellfish shippers.' [Source: *25 Tex Admin Code* § 241.21 (repealed); quoted in (1992) 25 *Clarity* 16; see www.clarity-international.net/clarity-journal/archives/]

See also **CADENCE; LATIN; LITERARY ALLUSIONS.**

allow / permit

In general usage, to *allow* is to *permit*; both words carry the same meaning. So, for example, in the pairing *allow and permit* (eg, 'The landlord will *allow and permit* the tenant to remain open after normal business hours'), it seems tolerably clear as a matter of English that either *allow* or *permit* will suffice. However, all words take their meaning from context, and it may be, as several cases have suggested, that in some contexts *allow* is wider than *permit*: *Barton v Reed* [1932] 1 Ch 362, 375 (Luxmoore J); *De Kupyer v Crafter* [1942] SASR 238, 243–44.

When drafting a prohibition against doing something, lawyers often add a prohibition against *allowing or permitting* it to be done: eg, 'The tenant must not damage the premises or *allow or permit* them to be damaged.' An instinctive response is to say that one word (either *allow* or *permit*) suffices. However, the doubling-up is doubtless intended to rebut any argument that a prohibition against doing something is not a prohibition against allowing someone else to do it. While such a strained interpretation seems unlikely, commercial contracts often forestall it with a catch-all interpretation provision along the lines that 'A prohibition on an activity includes a prohibition on permitting or allowing that activity'.

See also **cause (to be done)**; **permit**; **suffer**.

alternate / alternative

Alternate (noun or adjective) means a substitute:

> 'They were alternates on the Board'; 'He was an *alternate* director.'

Alternative (noun or adjective) means a choice between two or more possibilities:

> 'The judge had the *alternative* options of imposing a fine or imprisonment.'

Similarly with the adverbs *alternately* and *alternatively*: *alternately* means *in turn* or *one after the other*, while *alternatively* involves making a choice. For example:

> 'The judge gave counsel a choice in the jury selection: either question the potential jurors *alternately*, or *alternatively* reject them all immediately and start again with a fresh panel.'

The two words are often confused in pleadings (where *alternatively* is generally meant):

> [The defendant] seeks the following orders:
>
> (1) An order that the whole or *alternatively* part of the claim ... be dismissed ...
>
> (2) Further to paragraph 1, an order that ...
>
> (3) *Alternately* [prefer: *alternatively*] to paragraph 2, an order that the proceeding be transferred to [another court].
>
> (4) Further and *alternatively* to paragraph 1, an order that the whole proceeding be transferred to [another court].
>
> [Pleadings in *Overall v Permanent Trustee Co Ltd* [1999] FCA 1385]

am / pm

Omit the full stops? Practice varies, but the trend is towards omitting them:

> Office hours: 9 am–5 pm [*not* 9 a.m.–5 p.m.] (Note the use of the en dash, not the hyphen.)

Space after the number? Practice also varies: eg, 9am/9 am; 10pm/10 pm. Some legal publishers insert a space; others omit it.

See also **ABBREVIATIONS; NUMBERS; TIME.**

AMBIGUITY

'Ambiguity' explained

Ambiguity occurs where a word, phrase, or sentence is equivocal, in the sense of having two or more possible meanings. Ambiguity may be *patent* (open; obvious) or *latent* (obscured; apparent only in the light of surrounding circumstances). But in either case, it is the lawyer's curse.

Ambiguity distinguished from vagueness

Always distinguish ambiguity from *vagueness*. Some legal terms or concepts are inherently vague. But vagueness need not always be shunned. In some circumstances it can be a virtue, by allowing elasticity in specifying or identifying rights and obligations. For example:

- a criminal statute may require evidence to be excluded if it is 'unfair' to the accused
- a limitations statute may allow proceedings to be brought out of time if justified by 'reasonable cause'
- a contract may require a party to act 'with all convenient speed', or to perform an obligation 'within a reasonable time', or to use 'reasonable endeavours' to achieve a result.

The meaning of each of these formulations is context-dependent, and the inherent vagueness can give rise to argument. But none is strictly ambiguous: 'a term is not rendered ambiguous merely because its meaning may vary according to the circumstances': *Horace Mann Insurance v Stark* 987 F Supp 562, 567 (Michigan, 1997, McKeague J, discussing the term 'resident').

Ambiguity and contronyms

Contronyms (words with contradictory meanings) can cause ambiguity: which meaning does the writer intend? Examples in law are: *sanction* (support; punishment); *licence* (permission; freedom to act without needing permission); *enjoin* (encourage; seek to stop); *exemplary* (excellent; punishing to set an example, as in *exemplary* damages); *oversight* (supervision; neglect); *peruse* (read closely; skim lightly). Usually, context resolves the ambiguity—but if in doubt, choose another word.

Possible excuses for ambiguity

Very occasionally, ambiguity may be tolerated in legal writing. Examples include where:

- time is pressing and the ambiguity is minor—so that commercial reality trumps professional pride
- the time needed to negotiate an ambiguity-free text would make the deal uncommercial
- the document is of a kind where parties deliberately prefer ambiguity over clarity so as to leave wriggle-room—such as international treaties
- one party sees the ambiguity but is content to take a commercial risk that the other party will overlook it.

Syntactic ambiguity

A common problem

The most common ambiguity in legal writing is syntactic ambiguity—ie, ambiguity arising from the location of words or phrases within a sentence. An example is the following fictional case:

> A testator bequeathed 'to Matthew Stradling, gent, all my black and white horses'. The testator died leaving 6 white horses, 6 black horses, and 6 pied horses [ie, part black, part white].' To which horses was Matthew Stradling entitled? [Source: *Stradling v Styles* (satirical law report; fictional law reporter, Martinus Scriblerius), in Jonathan Swift, *Collected Works* (London, 1744) vol IV, 259; answer not given.]

More seriously, in the following (genuine) cases the drafters were presumably too close to their writing to notice the syntactic ambiguity.

1. Court Rules provided that 'a writ for service on a defendant *within the jurisdiction*' did not have to be served personally, but could be served by putting a copy in the defendant's letter box. Did *within the jurisdiction* refer to: (1) the writ and its service, or (2) the defendant? The Court of Appeal held that the words referred to (1), not (2). However, on appeal the House of Lords held that the words referred to (2), not (1). See *Barclay's Bank of Switzerland v Hahn* [1989] 1 WLR 13 (CA); [1989] 1 WLR 506 (HL). (The question arose because, when the plaintiff put a copy of the writ in the defendant's letter box, the defendant was out of the jurisdiction.)
2. Sir Roger Casement was charged with treason, for which the penalty was death by hanging. The statute 25 Edw 3 defined treason as being 'adherent to the King's enemies in his realm, giving to them aid and comfort in the realm, or elsewhere'. Casement had been 'adherent to the King's enemies' abroad. Did this make him guilty of treason? Held, yes, because 'or elsewhere' governed not only 'aid and comfort in the realm' but also 'adherent to the King's enemies in his realm'. See *R v Casement* [1917] 1 KB 98. The decision prompted Lord Diplock's comment, 'it has been said that Roger Casement was hanged by a comma': *Town Investments Ltd v Department of the Environment* [1978] AC 359, 385.

3. A statute establishing a Commission stated that the Commission 'may … cause … a proceeding to be begun and carried on' in another person's name. The Commission sought to take over and continue (ie, 'carry on') proceedings begun by someone else. Did the Commission have the power to do this? Held, no—the statute merely gave the Commission power to carry on proceedings that *it* had begun. That is, 'may cause' was not to be read distributively: *Carey v Australian Securities and Investments Commission* [2008] FCA 963; (2008) 169 FCR 311 (Finkelstein J).
4. Court rules provided for leave (permission) to serve a person outside Australia if a proposed court action was 'for the recovery of taxes … which have been imposed or become due on or in respect of property situate [sic] within' Western Australia. Did this rule authorise service outside Australia for the recovery of (1) *any* taxes that had been imposed, or (2) only those imposed on property situated in Western Australia? Held, it authorised service for the recovery of *any* taxes, regardless of whether they were imposed on property within Western Australia. That is, 'recovery of taxes' was to be read distributively. See *Deputy Commissioner of Taxation v Dunn* [2012] WASC 500; (2012) 91 ATR 665.

Adjectives qualifying two or more nouns

Syntactic ambiguity often arises where an adjective (or an adjectival phrase) precedes or follows a series of nouns. Does the adjective (or phrase) qualify all the nouns in the series, or only one of them? The following hypothetical example shows the problem:

> An education regulation provides: 'No pupil shall be excluded from any school, college or hostel *provided by a council*.' Does the phrase *provided by a council* refer only to *hostel*, or does it refer also to *school* and *college*? (Example based on Sir Alison Russell, *Legislative Drafting and Forms* (Butterworths, 1938) 102.)

Examples from case law are legion:

1. Tax legislation gave tax relief for 'fixed plant or machinery'. Did 'fixed' qualify both 'plant' and 'machinery', or only 'plant'? Held, it qualified both, so that relief was not available to movable machinery (ie, motor vehicles): *Williams v Evans* [1982] BTC 155 (Nourse J).
2. Where land was compulsorily acquired, the amount of compensation to which landowners were entitled depended on whether there was a 'general demand and market' for the land. Did 'general' qualify both 'demand' and 'market', or only 'demand'? Held, it qualified only 'demand': *Harrison & Hetherington Ltd v Cumbria County Council* (1985) 50 P & CR 396 (HL).
3. A regulation provided:

   > 'No person shall … remove … any fencing, gangway, gear, ladder, hatch-covering … or other thing whatsoever *required by these regulations to be provided*.'

   Did the italicised words qualify all the items in the list, or only the words 'other thing whatsoever'? The Court of Appeal (reversing the trial judge) held that the words qualified all the items in the list: *Cockerill v William Cory & Son Ltd* [1959] 2 QB 194.
4. A will authorised the testator's trustees to distribute her property to any 'charitable institutions and organisations'. Did 'charitable' qualify both 'institutions' and 'organisations', or only 'institutions' (so that, taken literally, the trustees could distribute to non-charitable organisations)? Held, 'charitable' qualified both 'institutions' and 'organisations': *Re Griffiths* [1926] VLR 212, 219.
5. A contract for the sale of land promised that there would be 'no *unsatisfied* judgment, order or writ of execution' at the time of completion. Did 'unsatisfied' qualify each of 'judgment', 'order' and 'writ', or only 'judgment'? Held, it qualified each: *Robina Syndicate Pty Ltd v RPA Properties Pty Ltd* [2011] QCA 151.
6. Under the terms of a restrictive covenant over land, the owner covenanted

   > 'not to erect any structure … or grow trees or vegetation … of a height in excess of [X metres]'.

Did this preclude the erection of *any structure* at all, or only structures in excess of X metres? Held, it precluded the erection of *any structure* at all, regardless of height: *Panton v Owners of Survey Strata Plan 46838* [2013] WASC 35.

Rule of last antecedent

Under the so-called 'rule of the last antecedent', courts assume that a qualifying word or phrase that follows a series of nouns applies only to the last item in the series. This can only be—at best—a rebuttable presumption (unless context shows that the drafter intended some such rule to apply). However, some courts apply the 'rule'—either instinctively or deliberately—as a last resort to resolve the ambiguity. This is particularly so in the United States:

> A statute prescribed a mandatory 10-year sentence for a crime, if the accused had been previously convicted of a crime relating to 'aggravated sexual abuse, sexual abuse, or abusive sexual conduct *involving a minor*'. Did 'involving a minor' qualify all the listed crimes or only the last one? Held, it qualified only the last one, under the 'rule of the last antecedent': *Lockhart v United States* (USSC, 1 March 2016; 135 S Ct 2350; see www.supremecourtreview.com/case/14-8358).

(See further discussion, under **LAST-ANTECEDENT RULE.**)

Transitive or intransitive verbs

Another cause of ambiguity lies in the use of verbs which could (in the context) be either transitive or intransitive. A transitive verb transfers its action to an object (a person or thing); an intransitive verb requires no object on which to operate. If the context fails to clarify whether a verb operates transitively or intransitively, readers are left unsure:

> An employment contract gave employees the right to a share of profits. The agreement provided, 'If the employee *ceases* employment [with the employer], any retained profit share allocation that has not vested to them will be forfeited.' Was *ceases* making a statement of fact ('the employment has ceased') or did it require an act by the employee (giving notice to cease the employment) or by the employer (giving notice to terminate the employment). Held, *ceases* was neutral as to who brought the employment to an end; the question simply was whether it had come to an end: *Byrne v Macquarie Group Services Australia Pty Ltd* [2011] NSWCA 68, [43]–[55] (Whealy JA).

Further reading

- JS Ammon, 'Ambiguous Drafting and the 12-Pound Cat' (2011) 90 (July) *Michigan Bar Journal* 56
- Anthony Aust, *Modern Treaty Law and Practice*, 2nd edn (Cambridge University Press, 2007), ch 23 (on the language peculiarities and deliberate vagueness of international treaties)
- Jeffrey Barnes, 'When "Plain Language" Legislation Is Ambiguous—Sources of Doubt and Lessons for the Plain Language Movement' (2010) 34 *Melbourne University Law Review* 671
- Peter Butt, *Modern Legal Drafting*, 3rd edn (Cambridge University Press, 2013) 196–98
- P Conway, 'Syntactic Ambiguity' (Law and Justice Foundation of NSW, 2002), at www.lawfoundation.net.au/ljf/site/articleIDs/63B6C5E2ABB6A511CA25714C000CFF37/$file/syntactic.pdf
- WA Wilson, 'Questions of Interpretation' (1987) 8 *Statute Law Review* 142

See also **COMMAS; GENERALITY; LAST-ANTECEDENT RULE; MODIFIERS; VAGUENESS.**

ambulance chaser

Also hyphenated: *ambulance-chaser*. A derogatory term for a lawyer who actively seeks out as potential clients people injured in accidents, often car accidents. Ironically, *ambulance* derives from the Latin *ambulare* (to walk).

AMENDING TEXT

See **TEXTUAL AMENDMENTS; DELETIONS.**

amendment (reference to)

Legal documents often include a boilerplate interpretation provision to the effect that a reference to a document or to legislation includes a reference to that document or legislation 'as amended'. But what is an 'amendment'? Is the novation of a document an amendment? Is the repeal, and later re-enactment, of a statute an amendment? To overcome uncertainty, some documents add a boilerplate provision along these lines:

> '**amendment** includes a supplement, variation, novation, extension, re-enactment or replacement'

See also **AMENDMENTS TO LEGISLATION (INTERPRETATION CLAUSE).**

AMENDMENTS TO LEGISLATION (INTERPRETATION CLAUSE)

The issue

Difficulties of interpretation can arise where a statute (statute A) refers to another statute (statute B), and statute B is later amended or re-enacted. Is the reference in statute A limited to statute B in its form at that date, or does it extend to its form as later amended or re-enacted?

The same issue arises when interpreting documents other than statutes. Where a document (eg, a contract or deed) refers to a statute, is the reference to the statute in its form at the date of the document, or in its form as later amended or re-enacted?

The solution: (1) references in statutes

Standard interpretation legislation in most jurisdictions specifies that the reference to a particular statute includes that statute as amended: eg, *Interpretation Act 1978*, s 20. Some go further and specify that the reference to a particular statute includes that statute as re-enacted, with or without modification: eg, the Australian *Acts Interpretation Act 1901* (Cth), s 10. This can pose problems of interpretation: when is a statute a 're-enactment' of an earlier statute, particularly where later statute has a different title?

The solution: (2) references in documents

What is the position where private-sector legal documents refer to statutes that are later amended or repealed? Here, the parties must rely on the common law, or seek to cover the situation by express agreement.

The common law

English courts hold that there is no starting presumption about whether a reference to a statute is a reference to the statute as in force when the document was signed or as in force from time to time: *William Hare Ltd v Shepherd Construction Ltd* [2009] EWHC 1603, [30] (affirmed on other grounds, [2010] EWCA Civ 227). It is simply a question of interpreting the document: did the parties intend their agreement to be governed by the legislation as in force at the time of their agreement, or be affected by later forms of the legislation?

However, this may not be the view in some other jurisdictions. For example, in Australia the starting presumption seems to be that a reference in a document to legislation is a reference to the legislation's form at the time the document came into operation: *Re Universal Distributing Co Ltd* (1933) 48 CLR 171, 173 (Dixon J).

Express agreement: the need

The uncertainty at common law makes it prudent for contracting parties to include an express provision clarifying their intention. Failure to do so can leave their contract open to unexpected interpretations, as in the following two examples:

1. An agreement provided for certain consequences on 'insolvency'. The legislation governing insolvency was later amended. Held, the agreement did not capture the statutory changes in the meaning of 'insolvency': *William Hare Ltd v Shepherd Construction Ltd* [2010] EWCA Civ 283.
2. A retail shop lease calculated rent by reference to turnover—ie, the price paid by customers. When the lease was granted, that price included an amount for a statutory 'purchase tax'; strictly, that tax was payable by the wholesaler, but the wholesaler passed it on to the retailer, who was reimbursed at the point of sale by passing it on to the customer. Later, that tax was replaced by VAT, which was payable by customers. The price paid by customers included the VAT, but the retailer had to remit the VAT to the government; so the turnover now included an amount for VAT which the retailer could not keep. Nevertheless, held: the VAT amount was to be included in the turnover, and so was to be reflected in the rent: *Debenhams Retail plc v Sun Alliance and London Assurance Co Ltd* [2005] EWCA Civ 868.

As these examples show, some kind of 'statute-updating' provision is necessary to protect against changes in the statutory regime regulating a commercial transaction. Otherwise, the parties may be saddled with a commercial framework that is frozen in time and no longer reflects their expectations.

Express agreement: standard clauses

Standard 'boilerplate' clauses providing for automatic updating of references to legislation adopt the pattern of the following provision:

References to legislation

A reference to legislation includes a reference to:

(1) that legislation as amended, extended, or applied by or under any other legislation made before or after the date of this document; and

(2) any legislation which that legislation re-enacts with or without modification; and

(3) any subordinate legislation made before or after date of this document under that legislation, including (where applicable) that subordinate legislation as amended, extended or applied as described in (1), or under any legislation which it re-enacts as described in (2).

But provisions of this kind can also introduce uncertainty. For example, clause (2) refers to legislation that 're-enacts' the relevant legislation 'with modification'. While this language reflects the standard legislative language, its limits are unclear. When is a statute a 're-enactment' of an earlier one? What is a 'modification'? To include such a wide-ranging interpretative provision may invite more problems than it solves.

See also **amendment; CITATION OF LEGISLATION.**

amicus curiae

Meaning

Latin: friend of the court; sometimes abbreviated to *amicus*; plural *amici curiae*. A person appointed by the court to help the court where a party is unable or unwilling to obtain legal representation, or to help the court resolve an important point of law.

> 'The Latin, *amicus curiae*, emphasises the nature of the appearance only as a friend of the Court. No party has a right to be heard as *amicus curiae*. The *amicus curie* [sic] appears to assist the Court. The common circumstance in which a Court will grant leave to a person to address as *amicus curiae* is where one of the parties is unable or unwilling to arrange for legal representation, or where there may be no contradictor to bring a particular argument to the attention of the Court. An *amicus curiae* does not become a party to the proceedings and may not appeal.' [*Perdaman Chemicals and Fertilisers Pty Ltd v The Griffin Coal Mining Co Pty Ltd (No 7)* [2012] WASC 502, [106] (Edelman J)]

In US legal English, pleadings (plural) lodged by friends of the courts are *amicus briefs* (not *amici briefs*).

Replacing the Latin

Some may regard this Latin term as too well-entrenched to be replaced by an English translation. However, the Latinism is a late intruder: from the late 1700s until about 1900, *friend of the court* was more frequent in print than *amicus curiae*: *Black's Law Dictionary*, 10th edn (Thomson Reuters, 2014). No misunderstanding can arise from using the English translation. The terms *friend of the court*, or *advocate to the court* (favoured in modern English Court Rules), carry the sense perfectly, as shown in the first example below.

- 'Subsequently, a request was made for an *amicus curiae* or 'advocate to the court' to be appointed and [X] fulfilled that role with excellent written submissions and helpful oral argument.' [*Bishop v Chhokar* [2015] EWCA Civ 24, [23] (Aikens LJ), offering both Latin and English]
- '[A]s the applicant is self-represented, I informed the parties that I considered the Court would be assisted at the hearing by the appointment of *amicus curiae* [prefer: *a friend of the court*] to provide written and oral submissions.' [*Bandara v District Court of New South Wales* [2016] NSWCA 14, [13] (Gleeson JA)]

See also **WOOLF REFORMS**.

among / amongst

The meanings are the same, but *amongst* carries a hint of archaism—so prefer *among*. For example:

- '[Counsel] helpfully refers us, *amongst* [prefer: *among*] other authorities, to the case of *Re H* ...' [*Re B (Child)* [2017] EWCA Civ 264, [30] (Black LJ)]
- 'When the division of opinion *amongst* [prefer: *among*] its members is not equal, the majoritarian decision-making rule [applies].' [*Perara-Cathart v R* [2017] HCA 9; (2017) 260 CLR 595, [79] (Gageler J)]

among / between

See **between**.

amove

To remove a person from a position or office, used particularly of judges. If the reader might be puzzled by *amove*, then *remove* would do just as well.

ampersand (&)

In normal usage, the ampersand (&) often replaces *and*. In formal prose, however, the ampersand is generally avoided, and it is still rare in legal usage, except where part of a formal name: eg, 'Smith & Jones Pty Ltd'.

anchor tenant

The key tenant in a development. For example, in a shopping centre comprising a supermarket and smaller speciality stores, the supermarket is generally the anchor tenant.

ancient lights

A quaint legalism, meaning the right to light acquired by prescription. A plain-language equivalent would be 'right to light acquired by long use'.

See also **prescription / adverse possession**.

ancillary

Usually meaning 'subordinate' or 'subservient'. But depending on context, it may also mean 'allied with' or 'in conjunction with', without connotations of a subsidiary nature. For example, in contract law, an agreement that is 'ancillary to' another agreement 'may well involve some variation of that [other] agreement and thus, in one sense, a measure of conflict with it': *R v Her Majesty's Treasury* [1985] QB 657, 673–74 (Slade LJ, speaking of international treaties). In planning law, the general UK position seems to be that 'ancillary' connotes a relationship of subservience: ie, for Lot A to be 'ancillary' to Lot B implies that Lot B has the primary role—so, for example, an airport terminal is 'ancillary' to runways and infrastructure (not vice versa), because aircraft movements are the raison d'être of the airport: *R v Environment Secretary* [2020] EWHC 959 (Admin); [2020] 3 WLR 597, [133]–[134] (Holgate J). However, that approach is not necessarily taken elsewhere. For example, in Australian planning law it has been said that an 'ancillary' land use is not necessarily one that is subordinate or subservient to another land use; thus, for example, the patient-care aspect of a university-run hospital can be 'ancillary to' the hospital's use as a clinical teaching facility: *Macquarie International Health Clinic Pty Ltd v University of Sydney* (1998) 98 LGERA 218, 223–24.

If doubt could arise over the meaning of 'ancillary', always clarify.

and

Meaning—and potential ambiguity

And denotes conjunction: ie, *A and B* means both A and B. That much is clear.

However, some usages of *and* may be ambiguous:

Example 1

'A *and* B may sign the document.' This could mean:

- A and B together may sign.
- Each of A and B may sign, and both A and B together may sign.
- A and B as a single entity (eg, as a joint party to a contract) may sign.

The risk of ambiguity is also present in a series of *ands*, particularly where the serial comma (or 'Oxford comma') is omitted, as in Examples 2 and 3.

Example 2

> 'I give my library to A and B and C shall have my music.' This could mean:
> - A and B get the library, and C gets the music.
> - A gets the library, and B and C get the music.

Example 3

> By her will, the testatrix gave to her children 'all my real and personal estate whatsoever and wheresoever *and* over which I shall have any disposing power at the time of my decease'. In addition to her own property, the testatrix had a special power of appointment over property which was part of her deceased father's estate. Was this a gift to her children:
>
> (1) of her own property only; or
>
> (2) of her own property plus ['and'] the property over which she had the power of appointment?
>
> Interpretation (1) would treat *and* as merely introducing an explanation of the earlier words 'all my property'—ie, 'all my property' is property 'over which I [have] disposing power at the time of my decease'. Interpretation (2) would strain the language of the gift, but would give effect to *and* as a word of conjunction, adding new material. The court adopted interpretation (2), reading *and* in its 'normal … conjunctive meaning'. The court then held that the words after *and* constituted an effective exercise of the power of appointment: *Re Welford's Will Trusts* [1946] 1 All ER 23, 25 (Romer J).

The risk of ambiguity is heightened when *and* and *or* are used in series, as in Example 4.

Example 4

> 'If the purchaser defaults, the vendor may retain the deposit and terminate or sue for damages.' This could mean that, if the purchaser defaults, the vendor may either:
> - [retain the deposit] *and* [terminate or sue for damages]; or
> - [retain the deposit and terminate] *or* [sue for damages].

Can *and* mean *or*?

As a matter of ordinary English, *and* does not mean *or*, and *or* does not mean *and*. The two words serve different purposes: *and* for conjunction, *or* for disjunction. The two words will normally carry their ordinary meaning. But all words take their meaning from context. This has emboldened courts sometimes to conclude that, viewed in the particular context, drafters used *and* when they meant *or*, and *or* when they meant *and*. The context required interpreting the words in ways contrary to their normal meaning.

> 'There is certainly no doubt that generally it is assumed that *or* is intended to be used disjunctively and the word *and* conjunctively. Nevertheless, it is equally well settled that if so to construe those words leads to an unintelligible or absurd result, the courts will read the word *or* conjunctively and *and* disjunctively, as the case may be; or, to put it another way, substitute the one word for the other. This principle has been applied time and again …' [*Federal Steam Navigation Co v Department of Trade and Industry* [1974] 1 WLR 505, 523–24 (Lord Salmon)]

Examples where *and* meant *or*

- The Preamble to the *Statute of Charitable Uses 1601* lists as one of the Act's purposes the 'relief of aged, impotent, *and* poor people'. By long-accepted judicial interpretation, *and* here means *or*. That is, the words 'aged, impotent, and poor' are to be read disjunctively, not cumulatively. For example, relief of the aged may be charitable independently of impotence and poverty. See, eg, *Re Glyn's Will Trusts* [1950] 2 All ER 1150 (note) (Danckwerts J); *City of Hawthorn v Victorian Welfare Association* [1970] VR 205, 208–09.

- The *Official Secrets Act 1920*, s 7, punished '[a]ny person who attempts to commit any offence under [certain Acts] … *or* aids *or* abets *and* does any act preparatory to the commission of an offence under [those Acts]'. Did the Act create a separate offence of doing an act preparatory to the commission of an offence? Held, yes; to read *and* literally would make the statute unintelligible for a number of reasons, including that it would be an offence for a person to do an act preparatory to their own attempting to commit an offence. Hence, *and* here meant *or*: *R v Oakes* [1959] 2 QB 350.
- A testator directed his trustees to use income and capital 'for the education *and* welfare of Bahamian children and young people'. Held, *and* here meant *or*: *Attorney-General of the Bahamas v Royal Trust Co* [1986] 1 WLR 1001 (PC).
- A theatrical association included the following object in its memorandum of association: to present plays that are 'classical, artistic, cultural *and* educational dramatic works'. Held, *and* here meant *or*; ie, the works could be classical *or* artistic *or* cultural *or* educational, or any combination: *Associated Artists Ltd v Inland Revenue Commissioners* [1956] 1 WLR 752.
- A priority deed defined 'security' to mean a stipulated mortgage '*and* any other security'. Held, *and* here meant *or*: *Home Building Society Ltd v Pourzland* [2005] WASCA 242.

Examples where *or* meant *and*

- A statute imposed criminal liability on the 'owner *or* master' of a ship if the ship discharged oil into the sea. The owner was convicted of an offence. Could the master also be prosecuted? Held, yes, because *or* here meant *and*: *Federal Steam Navigation Co v Department of Trade* [1974] 1 WLR 505 (HL). Contrast *The Banco* [1971] P 137, where a statute permitted the Admiralty jurisdiction to be invoked against an offending ship *or* another ship in the same ownership. Held, despite *or*, that once the jurisdiction was invoked against one ship, it could not invoked against another.
- A contract for sale defined 'completion date' as (a) 14 days after the seller gives the buyer a certain note, *or* (b) 30 days after the contract date. Held, *or* here meant *and*; ie, (a) and (b) were a composite provision producing one completion date, not distributively producing two dates (either of which could be the completion date): *Sunbay Projects Pty Ltd v Naughton* [2010] QCA 247.

The above cases show that it can be difficult to determine whether the drafter has used *and* to mean *or*, and vice versa. Different judges may disagree, even within the same case:

> A statute gave victims of nervous shock the right to compensation 'if the symptoms *and* disability persist for more than 6 weeks'. Held (by the New South Wales Court of Appeal), *and* here meant *or*: *Victims Compensation Fund v Brown* (2002) 54 NSWLR 668. But held (on appeal to the High Court of Australia), *and* here meant *and*: *Victims Compensation Fund v Brown* (2003) 77 ALJR 1797.

Consistency of use a guide

Where it is unclear whether, in a particular place in a document, the drafter used *and* and *or* in their ordinary meanings, a relevant factor is whether elsewhere in the document the drafter used the words in their ordinary meanings. In an Australian case, the judge was satisfied that the drafter had generally used *and* and *or* in their ordinary meanings throughout the document. This meant that, in using *and* to introduce a particular (and problematic) subclause, the drafter had probably meant the conjunctive *and*: *Oxanda Childcare Pty Ltd v MAAG Developments Pty Ltd* [2018] VSC 370, [41], [47] (Croft J). The decision was reversed on appeal on the ground that the subclause was so inconsistent with the commercial purpose of the parties' deal that 'something has gone wrong with the language': *MAAG Developments Pty Ltd v Oxanda Childcare Pty Ltd* [2018] VSCA 289, adopting the words of Lord Hoffmann in *Chartbrook Ltd v Persimmon Homes Ltd* [2009] UKHL 38; [2009] 1 AC 1101, 1114 [25]. The appeal court therefore rejected as surplusage the entire subclause, including the introductory *and.*

Avoiding misinterpretation

A drafter who fears judicial potential for misconstruing *and* as *or*, and vice versa, can minimise the risk by adding appropriate lead-in words, such as *both* or *either.*

Original	Better
The landlord has the right to sue for damages *and* to terminate the lease.	The landlord has the right *both* to sue for damages *and* to terminate the lease.
The landlord may sue for damages *or* terminate the lease.	The landlord may *either* sue for damages *or* terminate the lease [and if still room for doubt, add *but may not do both*].
The landlord has the right to: (a) sue for damages; *or* (b) terminate the lease; *or* (c) re-lease the premises.	The landlord has the right *to do any one or more* of the following: (a) sue for damages; (b) terminate the lease; (c) re-lease the premises. [Or, if it is intended to give one only of the listed rights:] The landlord has the right to do *one only* of the following: (a) sue for damages; (b) terminate the lease; (c) re-lease the premises.

Further reading

Dennis C Pearce and Robert S Geddes, *Statutory Interpretation in Australia*, 9th edn (LexisNexis, 2019) [2.46]–[2.51] (judicial decisions on 'and')

See also **and / or; or; COMMAS; CONJUNCTIONS.**

and/or

Use in legal writing

The expression *and/or* is increasingly common in legal writing, reflecting its increasing use in writing generally. Its intrusion into legal writing is not new. Examples can be found in commercial documents at least as far back as the mid-19th century:

- *Young v Turing* (1841) 2 M & G 593, 593; 133 ER 883, 884 (rendered as $\frac{\textit{and}}{\textit{or}}$)
- *Oliverson v Brightman* (1844) 1 Car & K 358, 361:174 ER 846, 847 (insurance cover for goods being carried 'by land and/or water').

By 1932, Scrutton LJ described the use of *and/or* in the document before him as liberally sprinkled 'as if from a pepper-pot': *Gurney v Grimmer* (1932) 44 Lloyds L Rep 189, 194.

In 1965, Lord Reid said that *and/or* was not yet part of the English language: *John G Stein & Co Ltd v O'Hanlon* [1965] AC 890, 904. Nowadays, it probably is.

Judicial condemnation

For many years, the use of *and/or* in legal writing has received strident judicial condemnation in a number of countries. Examples follow:

UK

- an 'unfortunate expression which I have not met before and which, I hope, I may never meet again': *Re Lewis* [1942] 2 All ER 364, 365 (Farwell J)
- 'the bastard conjunction … which has, I fear, become the commercial court's contribution to basic English': *Bonitto v Fuerst Bros & Co Ltd* [1944] AC 75, 82 (Viscount Simon LC)
- 'the expression and/or is not a happy one and, if occurring in a simple gift, might give rise to a serious problem of construction': *Neame v Neame's Trustees* [1956] SLT 57, 64 (Lord Sorn).

Australia

- 'an elliptical and embarrassing expression which endangers accuracy for the sake of brevity': *Fadden v Deputy Commissioner of Taxation* (1943) 68 CLR 76, 82 (Williams J)
- a 'common and deplorable affection … inviting trouble': *Millen v Grove* [1945] VLR 259, 260 (speaking of its use in a notice to quit).

US

- 'one of those inexcusable barbarisms which was sired by indolence and damned by indifference, and has no more place in legal terminology than the vernacular of Uncle Remus has in Holy Writ': *Cochrane v Florida East Coast Ry Co* 145 So 217, 218 (Flo, 1932)
- 'that Janus-faced verbal monstrosity, neither word nor phrase, the child of the brain of someone too lazy or too dull to express his precise meaning, or too dull to know what he did mean, now commonly used by lawyers in drafting legal documents, through carelessness or ignorance or as a cunning device to conceal rather than express meaning with view to furthering the interest of their clients': *Employers' Mutual Liability Insurance Co v Tollefsen* 263 NW 376, 377 (Wis 1935)
- 'the abominable invention … as devoid of meaning as it is incapable of classification by the rules of grammar and syntax': *American General Insurance Co v Webster* 118 SW 2d 1084, 1084 (Tex, 1938)
- 'a much-condemned conjunctive-disjunctive crutch of sloppy thinkers': *Raine v Drasin* 621 SW 2d 895, 905 (Ky, 1981).

The assumption behind these condemnations seems to be that *and/or* is too compressed; it forces the reader to tease out all possible combinations of meanings. For example, if a statute states that an offender is liable to 'a fine *and/or* imprisonment', the meaning is 'a fine, *or* imprisonment, *or both* a fine *and* imprisonment'. For some readers, it is assumed, *and/or* may obscure these possibilities.

Often clear

In many situations, however, the meaning of *and/or* is tolerably clear. Judges themselves have said so: eg, 'the meaning is clear': *Big River Timbers Pty Ltd v Stewart* (1999) 9 BPR 16,605, 16,608 (Mason P). Scrutton LJ once said that, if a charterparty were to state that the ship was to proceed to 'Rotterdam *and/or* Antwerp' at the charterer's option, the charterer could send the ship: (1) to Rotterdam alone; or (2) to Antwerp alone; or (3) to both Rotterdam and Antwerp. There would be no room for confusion: *Gurney v Grimmer* (1932) 44 Lloyds' LR 181, 194.

And/or also supplies conciseness, which is normally a boon in legal writing. The Ontario Court of Appeal has said when 'properly used [*and/or*] can serve as a convenient abbreviation to avoid clumsy circumlocution': *Higgins v Orion Insurance Co Ltd* (1985) 17 DLR (4th) 90, 108. A US court pointed out that *and/or* 'can anticipate alternative possibilities without the cumbersome itemization of each one': *Re Bell* 122 P 2d 22, 29 (Cal, 1942). And the Australian High Court saw the advantage of brevity (with no risk of ambiguity) in describing a plaintiff 'at risk of being targeted by the Sri Lankan Government *and/or* military groups in Sri Lanka': *Plaintiff M47/2012 v Director General of Security* [2012] HCA 46; (2012) 251 CLR 1, [5].

In the following examples, the meaning of *and/or* was tolerably clear. The examples come from such diverse areas of law as contract, landlord and tenant, wills, trust deeds, pleadings, and patent applications.

- A contract to ship 'a cargo of sugar, molasses, *and/or* other lawful produce' is briefer than 'a cargo of sugar and molasses, *or* of other lawful produce, *or* a cargo of sugar and molasses *and* other lawful produce', and was not suggested to be inherently uncertain: *Cuthbert v Cummings* (1855) 10 Ex 809, 814; 156 ER 668, 670 (Alderson B).
- A contract specified that goods were to be shipped during the months of 'March *and/or* April'. This was a briefer description than 'during March, *or* during April, *or* during *both* March and April'. The more concise *and/or* version did not appear to strike the court as inherently uncertain: *Bowes v Shand* (1877) 46 LJQB 564 (HL).
- A landlord's notice to quit served on a tenant listed six grounds separated by *and/or*. Held, the notice clearly stated each of the grounds, and the landlord needed only to prove any one of them. The tenant would not have been in any uncertainty about the grounds: *Looke v Parbury Henty & Co Pty* Ltd [1950] VLR 94, 98.
- A will gave property 'to A *and/or* B'. A and B were husband and wife. Held, the gift was sufficiently clear—namely, that A and B took as joint tenants, and that if A had predeceased the testator, then B would have taken absolutely: *Re Lewis* [1942] 2 All ER 364.
- A deed gave a widow a power to appoint property 'to the children of the marriage *and/or* their issue'. Held (by majority), this meant 'the children of the marriage *and* their issue' as a composite class—the widow could select between them as she wished: *Neame v Neame's Trustees* 1956 SLT 57.
- Pleadings alleged conversations between Mr Rubin and 'the Fourth Defendant *and/or* the Fifth Defendant'. Held, this sufficiently identified the parties to the conversation as Mr Rubin and the fourth defendant, or Mr Rubin and the fifth defendant, or Mr Rubin and the fourth and fifth defendants: *Bli Bli # 1 Pty Ltd v Kimlin Investments Pty Ltd* [2010] QCA 136, [25].
- The plaintiff in a patent claim for isotretinoin stated that 'the isotretinoin is partially in suspension *and/or* partly in solution'. The defendants claimed that *and/or* rendered the term indefinite. Held, the claim was not indefinite, and covered products in which the isotretinoun was (1) partially in suspension, (2) partially in solution, and (3) partially in suspension and partially in solution: *Cipher Pharmaceuticals Inc v Actavis Labs FL Inc* 99 F Supp 3d 508 (NJ, 2015).

Judicial use

Some senior judges themselves use *and/or*, unapologetically—and with clarity. Recent examples include:

- '[A] party is normally entitled to a trial where he and his witnesses can give evidence, and he can test the reliability of the other party *and/or* her witnesses by cross-examination.' [*Gohil v Gohil* [2015] UKSC 61; [2015] 3 WLR 1085, [50] (Lord Neuberger)]

- 'A contractual relationship may create the occasion for and give rise to a tortious duty of care owed by one contracting party to the other *and/or* to a third party.' [*Badenach v Calvert* [2016] HCA 18; (2016) 257 CLR 440, [23] (French CJ, Kiefel and Keane JJ)]
- '[T]he respondents claimed for loss of income *and/or* profits as a consequence of the compulsory acquisition of the Yabtree Street land.' [*Health Administration Corp v George D Angus Pty Ltd* [2014] NSWCA 352; (2014) 88 NSWLR 752, [25] (Tobias AJA)]
- '[The client's liability to pay the solicitor's costs] was established because the costs had been agreed *and/or* paid.' [*Blavo v Law Society* [2018] EWCA Civ 2250; [2019] 1 WLR 1977 [43] (Moylan LJ). The conjunction *and/or* appears 16 times in this judgment, including (at [38]) in combination with *whether/when*, to produce a puzzling series of possibilities: 'An issue developed ... about *whether/when* [the bills for the solicitor's costs] had been agreed *and/or* paid by the [client].']

Lazy *and/or*

Even though *and/or* may be acceptable in appropriate circumstances, some lawyers use it lazily. Sometimes they mean simply *and*; at other times they mean simply *or*. By using *and/or*, the writer burdens the reader with the task of deciding whether one word would have sufficed—and if so, which word—or whether the writer intended all possible combinations.

Examples

- A sporting organisation engaged an agent to find sponsors. The agency contract entitled the agent to a commission where a sponsor was 'located *and/or* introduced by [the agent] *and/or* the agreement [was] negotiated *and/or* concluded by [the agent]'. Did this require the agent to locate *and* introduce *and* negotiate *and* conclude, or was it sufficient to locate *or* introduce *or* negotiate *or* conclude? Held, in the context of the contract, it was sufficient to do one only of those things: *Edmunds-Jones Pty Ltd v Australian Women's Hockey Association Inc* [1999] NSWSC 1014 (Santow J). Better drafting would have avoided litigation.
- Plaintiffs in a class action alleged they were 'patrons of the Cartersville public school system *and/or* taxpayers of the City of Cartersville'. Held, *and/or* did not sufficiently state to which category (class) the plaintiffs belonged: *Shadden v Cowan* 96 SE 2d 608 (Georgia, 1937).

Sometimes indeed, *and/or* is not merely lazy, but indicates that the writer did not understand the underlying legal issues: *Looke v Parbury, Henty & Co Pty Ltd* [1950] VLR 94, 98 (Barry J).

Examples

- A jury's verdict assessing the defendant's punishment a 'a fine of $100.00 *and/or* confinement in the county jail of 30 days', later reflected in the court's verdict, was ineffective for failing to specify *which* punishment: *Allen v State* 136 SW 2d 232 (Tex, 1940).
- A judgment in favour of a landlord described as 'Charles JR Sproule *and/or* the Fidelity Life Insurance Company' was void for uncertainty, for failing to designate with sufficient certainty in whose favour it was given: *Sproule v Taffe* 13 NE 2d 827 (1938, Ill).
- An entity (A) purported to exercise an option 'for itself *and/or* its related entity B'. (The option had been originally granted to A, which had then assigned it to B.) Held: the purported exercise was ineffective, for failing to identify *who* was exercising the option. The use of *and/or* suggested three possibilities: (1) A exercised the option for itself; or (2) A exercised the option for itself and B; or (3) A exercised the option for B only. See *Burwood Project Management Pty Ltd v Polar Technologies International Pty Ltd* (1999) 9 BPR 17,355.

The lesson is clear: where the single word *and* or *or* will suffice, use the single word.

Before	**After**
You must obey all statutes *and/or* regulations.	You must obey all statutes *and* regulations. [*Or* might suggest a choice.]
No food *and/or* drink is allowed on the premises.	No food *or* drink is allowed on the premises. [No one could argue that this leaves you free to bring *both* food *and* drink.]

And/or in series

While a single *and/or* may be clear, multiple *and/or*s may not be. The reader must unpack an escalating number of possibilities. For a short series, this may be tolerable: for example, 'The defendant is liable in circumstances A, B, and/or C' means 'The defendant is liable in circumstances A or B or C, or any combination', and a reader should be be able to tease out the possible permutations. But the longer the series, the greater the number of possibilities. Ultimately, this leads to undesirable vagueness, as in the following examples:

- A charterparty specified 'a full and complete cargo of wheat *and/or* maize *and/or* other lawful merchandise'. The drafter failed to recognise the flexibility allowed by the multiple *and/or* provisions. Devlin J said: '[T]he first question which would occur to a lawyer would be to ask … why the parties bothered to refer to wheat or maize if they meant that the cargo might be anything from chalk to cheese, including turpentine': *Chandris v Isbrandtsen-Moller Co Inc* [1951] 1 KB 240, 246.
- Pleadings alleged a breach of duty by a law firm's partners 'A *and/or* B *and/or* C *and/or* D *and/or* E'. The court struck out the pleadings for failing to express precisely the foundation of the proceedings: *Re Moage Ltd* (1998) 153 ALR 711 (Burchett J).
- Pleadings alleged liability for a helicopter crash caused by the 'negligence *and/or* breach of duty of care of the first defendant *and/or* the second defendant *and/or* third defendant *and/or* fourth defendant *and/or* fifth defendant'. The court decried the multiple *and/or*s, saying that the aim of pleadings is to clarify and concentrate the issues; here, the pleading 'ranges from alleging that one defendant of the five is liable to all defendants being liable': *St Clair v Timtalla Pty Ltd (No 2)* [2010] QSC 480, [14] (Martin J).

Further reading

- Anon, 'In Defense of *And/Or* (1936) 45 *Yale Law Journal* 918
- Liam Boyle, '*And/Or* in the Law: Condemnations, Uses and Misuses' (2013) 87 *Australian Law Journal* 349
- Maurice B Kirk, 'Legal Drafting: The Ambiguity of "And" and "Or"' (1971) *2 Texas Tech Law Review* 235 (asserting at 237 that while the 'Andorians' have lost to the 'Anti-Andorians', the uncertainties inherent in *and* and *or* are more complex than those inherent in *and/or*)
- Sir Robert Megarry, *A New Miscellany-at-Law*, ed Bryan Garner (Hart, 2005) ch 14 ('Andorandorand')
- Ira P Robbins, '"And/Or" and the Proper Use of Legal Language' (2018) 77 *Maryland Law Review* 311 (favouring the careful use of *and/or* as an effective way of expressing an 'inclusive disjunction')

See also **and**; **or**; **COMMAS**; **CONJUNCTIONS**.

animus / animo

Latin: *animus*, mind, usually translated in legal contexts as 'intention'; *animo*, with a mind to, usually translated in legal contexts as 'with intent to'. These Latinisms appear in many legal terms, all of which can be translated into plain English without loss of meaning. For example:

animo cancellandi—with intent to cancel
animo capiendi—with intent to take
animo custodiendi—with intent to take care of
animo derelinquendi—with intent to abandon
animo donandi—with intent to give as a gift
animo furandi—with intent to steal
animo injuriandi—with intent to harm
animo lucrandi—with intent to profit
animo manendi—with intent to remain
animo morandi—with intent to delay
animo possidendi—with intent to possess
animo remanendi—with intent to stay away
animo revertendi—with intent to return
animo revocandi—with intent to revoke
animo testandi—with intent to make a will
sine animo remanendi—without the intention of staying away (ie, intending to return)
sine animo revertendi—without the intention of returning (ie, intending to stay away)
solo animo—by the mind alone (ie, by mere intention, not coupled with an act carrying out the intention)
uno animo—with one mind.

ANNEXURES

Purpose

It is sometimes necessary or convenient to attach a document to another document (the main document). Two drafting issues commonly arise:

1. Is a reference in the main document to an annexure a reference to the particular annexure to the document? The answer is self-evidently 'yes', although some drafters make it express ('A reference to an annexure is a reference to the annexure to this document').
2. Is the annexure part of the binding agreement contained in the main document, or is it included merely for information? Here the answer is not so clear, although the context and the nature of the information in the annexure may help. If necessary, always clarify.

If the main document includes a table of contents, include the annexure(s) in the table.

Terminology: annexure/appendix/schedule

The usage of these three words vary:

- Lawyers tend to use *annexure* and *appendix* interchangeably, though *annexure* is now more common.

- Some lawyers also use *annexure* and *schedule* interchangeably. But in strict legal usage, *annexure* (or *appendix*) is best reserved for material inserted after the place in the main document where the parties sign, while *schedule* is best reserved for material that is inserted before the place where the parties sign. In practice, however, those distinctions are often ignored.

See also **APPENDIX; SCHEDULES.**

Anshun estoppel

A form of estoppel that precludes a party from raising in subsequent proceedings a cause of action or issues which it was unreasonable for them not to have raised in the former proceedings. The term is used particularly in Australia and New Zealand, and takes its name from the Australian case *Port of Melbourne Authority v Anshun Pty Ltd* (1981) 147 CLR 589. Australian lawyers have even coined the verb 'to be *Anshun* estopped': eg, *Champerslife Pty Ltd v Manojlovski* [2010] NSWCA 33; (2010) 75 NSWLR 245, [58], [69], [71], [90] (Giles JA).

However, in truth the term reflects a long-standing principle of English law, often called 'the principle in *Henderson v Henderson*', or 'cause of action estoppel'. Under this principle, parties who have litigated a matter cannot later litigate other matters which they could have brought forward in the first litigation, but failed to do so 'by negligence, inadvertence, or even accident': *Henderson v Henderson* (1843) 3 Hare 100, 115; 67 ER 313, 391 (Sir James Wigram V-C).

As with many shorthand descriptions derived from case names, the term is inscrutable to non-lawyers. Therefore, when addressing non-lawyers, prefer a plain-language explanation (ending, if you wish, so as to reassure legally trained readers: 'ie, *Anshun* estoppel or cause of action estoppel').

Further reading

Halsbury's Laws of England, 'Civil Procedure' (vol 12A, 2015), [1605], [1611]

See also **estoppel**.

answerable

In normal usage, *answerable* carries the sense of 'responsible for/to'. But in legal usage, *answerable* is often used with the more intense meaning of 'liable for/to'. If that is the legal usage, to avoid misunderstanding, prefer *liable for* or *liable to*, which lays bare the meaning.

Examples

- 'Further, the injunction … is founded upon the proposition that Topshop is *answerable for* [prefer: *liable for*] a misrepresentation by omission …' [*Fenty v Arcadia Group Brands Ltd* [2015] EWCA Civ 3, [26]; [2015] 1 WLR 3291, 3299 (Kitchin LJ)]
- '[The legislation] expressly provides that an agent or trustee "shall be *answerable* as taxpayer … *for* the payment of tax" on income, profits or gains derived by him or her in his or her representative capacity. This language creates a personal liability in an agent or trustee to pay tax …' [*Commissioner of Taxation v Australian Building Systems Pty Ltd* [2015] HCA 48; (2015) 326 ALR 590, [104] (Keane J, explaining the meaning)]

anti money laundering

When used as a compound adjective—eg, 'anti money laundering law'—to hyphenate or not? Given that compound adjectives ought to be hyphenated (*money-laundering* law), and that *anti* is normally hyphenated to the word it precedes (*anti-stress* pills), then preferred usage should be: *anti-money-laundering law*. But standard usage is *anti-money laundering law*. This seems counter-intuitive, because the prohibition is against laundering *money*, not against laundering *anti-money*.

See also **HYPHENS**; **money laundering**.

ANTI-AMENDMENT CLAUSE

See **'NO VARIATION' CLAUSE**.

anti-assignment provision

See **'NO ASSIGNMENT' CLAUSE**.

Anton Piller order

An order allowing the plaintiff to search the defendant's premises, so that the plaintiff may seek out and remove material relevant to the plaintiff's case; named after *Anton Piller KG v Manufacturing Processes Ltd* [1976] Ch 55. Now known in many common-law jurisdictions as *search orders* following the lead set by the *Woolf Reforms* to use plain-language tags. Sometimes misspelt *Anton Pillar*, as in the following examples:

- 'A copy of the disputed email was found on the hard drive of the appellant's computer when an Anton Pillar [sic] order was executed at his home …' [*Wright v Ryan* [2005] NSWCA 368, [11] (Handley JA)]
- 'That, after all, is the justification for the grant of freezing (*Mareva*) or search (*Anton Pillar*) [sic] orders without notice.' [*Re A (A Child)* [2016] EWCA Civ 572; [2016] 4 WLR 111, [61] (Sir James Munby P)]

See also **WOOLF REFORMS**.

any

Meaning *all*

Any, when used to mean *all*, contains no inherent limitations. A requirement 'You must produce *any* documents in your possession' means 'You must produce *all* documents in your possession'. The following cases illustrate this interpretation.

- A right to allow *any* friend to use a property for sport includes friends in general, not merely one friend: *Gardiner v Colyer* (1864) 10 LT 715, 715.
- A prohibition against leasing *any part* of premises includes a prohibition against leasing the *whole* of the premises, since *any part* necessarily includes *every part*: *Field v Barkworth* [1986] 1 All ER 362, 364.
- A statutory power to control the price of *any goods* includes *all* goods: *Victorian Chamber of Manufacturers v Commonwealth of Australia* (1943) 67 CLR 335, 346.

Possible ambiguity

Sometimes, *any* can be ambiguous. Clarity may require replacing *any* with 'a', 'an', or 'all', depending on what the context requires:

- 'The landowner must consult with *any* adjoining owner before lodging a development application.' Is this satisfied by consulting with *one* adjoining owner, or must *all* be consulted? (As a matter of English, *any* here probably means *all* or *every*; but clearer drafting would clarify.)

- 'Before making an industrial training order the Minister shall consult *any* organisation [representing employers] engaging in the activities concerned …' Did this statutory provision require the Minister to consult *every* organisation of the specified kind, or only *some*? Held, the Minister must consult *every* organisation: *Agricultural, Horticultural and Forestry Industry Training Board v Aylesbury Mushrooms Ltd* [1972] 1 All ER 280.

See also **all**; **any and all**.

any and all

Because *any* normally includes all, the added *or all* is redundant. Delete it: *any ~~and all.~~*

See **all**.

anything / any thing

Usually one word: *anything*. But when contrasted to 'any person', then two words: *any thing*. For example:

- This warrant allows the police to seize *anything* in the premises.
- This warrant applies to any person or *any thing* found on the premises.

However, fine distinctions may be required. In the following statutory example, the use of two words in subsection (3) is justified on the ground that it parallels the (correct) use of two words in subsection (1):

(1) *Any thing* liable to forfeiture … may be seized …

(2) …

(3) Where the person seizing or detaining *any thing* … is a constable …

[*Customs and Excise Management Act 1979*, s 139]

apparent

A word with two different meanings, and therefore potentially ambiguous. One meaning suggests conclusiveness: ie, *clear*, *obvious*. The other meaning suggests likelihood only: ie, *probable* (but not beyond argument), *likely*. Always clarify:

- It was *apparent* [meaning: *clear*] that the son was the beneficiary of the family trust.
- The son was the *apparent* [meaning: *probable*] beneficiary of the family trust.

apparent paradox

See **paradox**.

appeal

A surprisingly ambiguous term, especially in legislation. What kind of appeal? There are at least six possibilities:

- appeal to supervisory jurisdiction (judicial review)
- appeal on questions of law only
- appeal after a trial before judge and jury
- appeal from a judge to a higher court
- appeal from a judge by way of rehearing
- appeal involving a hearing *de novo*.

[See *Applications A1 and A2 v Brouwer* [2007] VSCA 139; (2007) 16 VR 612, [7].]

A prudent drafter, alert to the ambiguity, will clarify the nature of the intended 'appeal'.

appeal / appeal against

Conventionally, in British English one 'appeals *against* a decision'; in contrast, in US English one 'appeals a decision'. However, the US usage is becoming acceptable in British and Commonwealth English also. Examples follow:

UK

- 'Mr Smith now seeks *to appeal that* decision.' [*R v Land Registry* [2010] 3 WLR 1223, 1226 (Arden LJ)]
- 'The appellant sought permission to *appeal the orders* made by the trial judge.' [*Re S-W (Children)* [2015] EWCA Civ 27, [2]]
- 'Mrs Waring also *appeals the costs order* that the judge made.' [*Cocking v Eacott* [2016] EWCA Civ 140, [2]; [2016] 3 WLR 125, 127 (Vos LJ)]

Australia

- 'These proceedings ... include an application for leave to *appeal a judgment of* de Jersey CJ.' [*Burns v Queensland* [2006] QCA 235, [1]]
- 'An application to *appeal that decision* was dismissed by the Privy Council.' [*Alcan (NT) Alumina Pty Ltd v Commissioner of Taxes* (2007) 19 NTLR 153, 181 [92]]

New Zealand

- '[The appellant] seeks leave to *appeal a decision* of the Court of Appeal.' [*Caie v A-G* [2006] 3 NZLR 289 [2006] NZSC 7, [1]]

Canada

- 'The appellant accused *appeals a decision* of the Ontario Court of Appeal.' [*Courville v The Queen* [1985] 1 SCR 847, [1]]
- A and B 'appealed the Commission's findings'. [*Re Cartaway Resources Corp* [2004] 1 SCR 672, [31]]

See also **de novo**.

appealable / appellable

The conventional usage is *appealable*, not *appellable*—even though the party who lodges an appeal is the *appellant* and the court is the *appellate* court.

APPENDIX

An *appendix* (preferred plural, *appendices*) is the appropriate place for material that is supplementary to the main text. Do not relegate important material to an appendix. If important material is so complex that it would threaten the flow of the main text, consider moving it to a schedule (rather than an appendix).

If a document contains a table of contents, include appendices in the table.

See also **ANNEXURES**; **SCHEDULES**; **TABLE OF CONTENTS**.

appertaining to

Meaning 'belonging to' (*Barlow v Rhodes* (1833) 1 Cr & M 439, 447, 149 ER 471, 475, Lord Lyndhurst), 'relating to', 'about'. In modern usage, *appertaining to* seems overly quaint.

The noun *appurtenance* (adjective *appurtenant*) carries a similar sense of *belonging to*, but is generally a term of art and therefore not so easily dismissed as quaint. For example, an easement is properly described as *appurtenant* to the land it benefits. To use the plainer *belonging to* (that land), or *relating to* (that land), might not adequately carry the sense of inherent connection with the land—a connection so close that the benefit of the easement automatically travels with the land on sale or lease.

applicable

Applicable, while sometimes useful, can be redundant. In the first example below, 'applicable' is useful; in the second and third examples, it is redundant.

- 'The vendor must hand to the purchaser on completion all paintings, jewellery, vintage cars, and garden furniture on the property, plus all *applicable* insurance policies.' [Useful; means insurance policies for the listed items.]
- 'The vendor must pay in full all *applicable* property taxes.' [Redundant; can the vendor be required to pay *inapplicable* taxes?]
- 'In holding an auction sale, the auctioneer must not breach any *applicable* laws'. [Redundant; can the auctioneer breach an *inapplicable* law?]

approbate and reprobate

Literally, approve (*approbate*) and reject (*reprobate*). In the form of a colourful brocard ('one cannot approbate and reprobate'), the pairing is used in the law of election to hold a person to a choice between two inconsistent rights: having chosen one, the person cannot later choose the other: *Scarfe v Jardine* (1882) 7 AC 345; *Kammins Ballrooms Co Ltd v Zenith Investments (Torquay) Ltd* [1971] AC 850. For example, the vendor's breach of a contract for the sale of land may entitle the purchaser to terminate the contract. But the purchaser is equally entitled to continue with (affirm) the contract. Having chosen one course (eg, to affirm, despite the breach), the purchaser cannot later choose the other (to terminate for the breach): *Sargent v ASL Developments Ltd* (1974) 131 CLR 634. Again, under a lease, the tenant's breach may give the landlord the right either to terminate the lease or affirm it; having chosen one course (eg, to affirm it, by accepting rent), the landlord cannot later choose the other: *Matthews v Smallwood* [1910] 1 Ch 777.

> '[I]t seems that the phrase "you may not approbate and reprobate", or the Latin "quod approbo non reprobo", ... is no more than a picturesque synonym for the ancient equitable doctrine of election, originally derived from the civil law, which finds its place in our records as early as the reign of Queen Elizabeth.' [*Lissenden v CAV Bosch Ltd* [1940] AC 412, 418 (Lord Maugham)]

The brocard's alluring symmetry makes it as irresistible to lawyers as it is mystifying to clients; but it is merely the lawyerly equivalent of 'you cannot have your cake and eat it too'.

Further reading

Halsbury's Laws of England, 'Estoppel' (vol 47, 2014) [312]

See also **brocard**; **waiver**.

approximately

An inherently uncertain term. Its comparative formality when set against vernacular counterparts such as *about* or *roughly* might suggest certainty; but this is not so.

Approximately is irredeemably prone to litigation: when is A *approximately* B? Much will turn on the particular circumstances. For example, if a contract for sale warrants that the frontage of a London city property is 'approximately' 20 yards, a shortfall of a few inches might not be excused; but on the sale of a large farm, it probably would be.

It is always better, where possible, to state the permissible variation—eg, 10%. Otherwise litigation may follow. The following examples from British and Commonwealth courts show the importance of context:

- Contract to ship wheat—stated weight of 10,069 tons was *approximately* 10,400 tons: *Louis Dreyfus v Parnaso Cia Naviera SA* [1960] 2 QB 49.
- Sale of house on residential estate—stated garden length of 36 feet was not *approximately* 40 feet: *Bellotti v Chequers Developments Ltd* [1936] 1 All ER 89.
- Sale of industrial property—stated area of 2,360 square yards was not *approximately* 3,920 square yards: *Watson v Burton* [1957] 1 WLR 19.
- Sale of a suburban terrace house—stated frontage of 12 feet 10¾ was not *approximately* 15 feet 6 inches: *Stephens v Selsey Renovations Pty Ltd* [1974] 1 NSWLR 273.
- Sale of farm—stated area of 3,728 acres was not *approximately* 3,832 acres: *Owmist Pty Ltd v Twynam Pastoral Co Pty Ltd* (1985) NSW ConvR 55-221.

See also **about**; **thereabouts**; **WORDS OF APPROXIMATION**.

appurtenance

See **appertaining to**.

arbiter / arbitrator

Arbitrator is generally reserved for a person who has been formally appointed to decide a dispute, while *arbiter* is used more generally to mean simply 'one who decides'. (In Scotland, however, *arbiter* often is used in the formal sense of an appointed *arbitrator*.)

> 'I accept that a purpose of [certain provisions of the Act] is in some circumstances to make [approved medical specialists], rather than judges or *arbitrators*, the final *arbiters* of "medical disputes" as defined by section 319.' [*Riviera Wines Pty Ltd v Registrar of Workers Compensation Commission of NSW* [2007] NSWCA 149, [84] (Campbell JA)]

ARCHAISMS

Archaisms have no place in modern legal writing. They give legal writing a stilted, pompous appearance, adding nothing of substance. Always choose a modern, idiomatic alternative. Examples are:

- *aforesaid* (prefer: *the*; never *said*)
- *chattels* (prefer: *goods*)
- *hereto* (prefer: *to this …*)
- *indenture* (prefer: *deed*)
- *instrument* (prefer: *document*)
- *situate at* (prefer: *located at*; or just state the address).

See **SIMPLER WORDS AND PHRASES**.

arguendo

Latin: in argument; sometimes *in arguendo* (although *in* is strictly redundant). Sometimes (particularly in the US) meaning 'for the sake of argument' (eg, 'Let us consider, *arguendo*, whether is is correct'). But in UK legal usage, indicating that a statement was made in the course of argument before the court, and therefore if made by a judge carries no binding force of precedent. In this sense, the meaning of the Latin may be guessable—but why force readers to guess, when the English *during argument*, or *in the course of argument*, is a good translation?

- 'I would not accept that Lord Brougham's statement, which was after all only made *arguendo* [prefer: *in the course of argument in the case*], is correct today.' [*R v Chaytor* [2010] UKSC 52, [132]–[133]; [2011] 1 AC 684, 729–30 (Lord Clarke)]
- 'As his Honour put it to counsel *in arguendo* [prefer: *in the course of argument*] ...' [*Shannon v Commonwealth Bank of Australia* [2014] FCAFC 108; (2014) 318 ALR 420, [60] (Logan J)]

argumentum ad hominem

See **ad hominem**.

argumentum ad rem

See **ad rem**.

arising from / out of / under

All these variants imply a causal connection, but leave open the precise degree of connection. The generally accepted legal interpretation is that 'arising from' requires *some* causal connection between the event and the consequence, but it is a less proximate relationship than required by 'caused by': see, eg, *GIO (NSW) v R J Green & Lloyd Pty Ltd* (1966) 114 CLR 437, 443 (Barwick CJ), 445 (Menzies J), 447 (Windeyer J).

Arising *out of* and *arising under* are sometimes synonymous: if X *arises out of* Y it also *arises under* Y. But context may require otherwise. For example, in building industry legislation, a dispute *arising out of* a building contract may be a wider concept than a dispute *arising under* a building contract: see, eg, *Grave v Blazevic Holdings Pty Ltd* (2010) 79 NSWLR 132; [2010] NSWCA 324. But context is a hard taskmaster, as the many decisions on these phrases attest (some are reviewed in *Comandate Marine Corp v Pan Australian Shipping Pty Ltd* (2006) 157 FCR 45, [169]–[176]). In the process of forensic dissection, courts are prone to scrutinise prepositional phrases more closely than the drafter may have expected. So, if context could possibly cloud the ambit of an '*arising* ...' phrase, clarify the meaning or consider another expression.

See also **consequence of**; **in connection with**; **under (and ...)**.

arm's length

Where used to modify a noun, hyphenated: eg, *arm's-length transaction*, *arm's-length relationship*. An *arm's-length transaction* is one negotiated between parties who are acting independently of each other and in their own self-interest; and parties are in an *arm's-length relationship* if they are genuinely independent and acting in their own self-interest. Being at 'arm's length', the parties owe each other no special duty or obligation which might otherwise colour the terms of their transaction (*Australian Trade Commission v WA Meat Exports Pty Ltd* (1987) 75 ALR 287, 291).

Arm's length is used in law, but it is not a term of art. Drafters using it must be alert to two distinctions in the case law. The first is that the courts may treat parties who are *not* at arm's length (eg, related corporate entities) as having entered into a transaction that *is* at arm's length, if the facts support that view. The second (and converse) is that the courts may treat parties who *are* normally at arm's length (eg, independent retailers and customers) as having entered into a transaction that is *not* at arm's length, if the facts support that result: see *AXA Asia Pacific Holdings Ltd v Commissioner of Taxation* [2009] FCA 1427; [2009] ATC 20-151, [98].

arrangement

A protean word, of broad and vague meaning. In normal English, *arrangement* means a way of doing things, usually in an agreed or predictable fashion. It is not a legal term of art, so it bears the same meaning in legal English also: *Re British Slag Ltd's Application* [1963] 1 WLR 727, 739 (Wilmer LJ). The breadth of meaning inherent in *arrangement* allows flexibility, which may have advantages for the adept drafter. It can include activities mutually undertaken by parties, despite the absence of any direct communication between them, or any direct contractual relationship: *Office of Fair Trading v Lloyds TSB Bank plc* [2004] EWHC 2600 (Comm), [23]–[25]; [2005] 1 All ER 843 (Gloster J; 'arrangement' between credit card issuers and suppliers). Its breadth makes *arrangement* a favoured word in tax-avoidance provisions. For example, the *Finance Act 2013* negates tax advantages arising from abusive tax 'arrangements' (s 206). The word 'arrangements' necessarily casts the net widely; but for more abundant caution, the Act defines 'arrangement' to include 'any agreement, understanding, scheme, transaction or series of transactions (whether or not legally enforceable)' (s 214). Australian income tax legislation defines 'arrangement' even more broadly, to include: (a) any agreement, arrangement, understanding, promise or undertaking, whether express or implied, and whether or not enforceable, or intended to be enforceable, by legal proceedings; and (b) any scheme, plan, proposal, action, course of action, or course of conduct whether unilateral or otherwise: *Income Tax Assessment Act 1936* (Cth), s 159GE.

However, its inherent vagueness means that legal writers must use *arrangement* with care. For example:

- A lease of premises in a shopping centre states that tenants must comply with any security *arrangements* the landlord makes with a security company. Is an informal understanding between the landlord and the security company an 'arrangement'?
- A testator directs his trustees 'to honour existing *arrangements* I have made with charities'. What kind of promises to, or dealings with, charities are 'arrangements'?

arrears

Standard usage is *arrears*, in preference to *arrear*; eg, a payment is said to be *in arrears* (rather than *in arrear*). The term *in arrears* can have different meanings, leading to possible misunderstanding. They include the following:

1. *Owing and unpaid*—ie, overdue: *Coulson v Austin Motor Co Ltd* (1927) 43 TLR 493, 494, 495. For example:
    - 'This is a claim for rent *in arrear* [meaning: *overdue*].' [*Good v Parry* [1963] 2 QB 418, 421 (Lord Denning MR)]

- 'Mr and Mrs White owned and lived in a house, but it was subject to a mortgage which was *in arrears* [meaning: *overdue*] ...' [*Superstrike Ltd v Rodrigues* [2013] 1 WLR 3848; [2013] EWCA Civ 669, [31] (Lloyd LJ)]

2. *As yet unpaid*—as in *Re Springbok Agricultural Estates Ltd* [1920] 1 Ch 563, where 'arrears of dividends' payable on a winding-up meant dividends that would have been paid out of profits, had profits been available to declare.
3. *After the date*—a statement of fact, with no overtones of default: eg, rent payable *in arrears* is rent that is payable after each rental interval (as distinct from rent payable in advance). For example:
   - '[A]t common law rent (whether payable in advance or *in arrear* [meaning: *at the end of the rental period*]) is not apportionable in respect of time ...' [*Pillar Denton Ltd v Jervis* [2015] 1 Ch 87; [2014] EWCA Civ 180, [7] (Lewison LJ)]
   - 'The facility agreement provided for payment of interest at the rate of 11.25% per annum, accruing daily but payable three monthly *in arrears* [meaning: *at the end of each 3-month period*].' [*Tael One Partners Ltd v Morgan Stanley & Co International plc* [2015] UKSC 12; [2015] 4 All ER 545, [4] (Lord Reed)]

ARTICLE

See **a (indefinite article)**; **the**.

articles

The clauses or paragraphs in formal or legal documents, particularly (but not exclusively) constitutions, conventions and treaties: eg, *articles of association* of a company. In statutes, usually called *sections*; in contracts or deeds, usually called *clauses*.

artificial person

An entity that is not a human being but that the law treats for some purposes as having powers and duties similar to those of a human being—eg, a corporation.

See **person**.

as

See **because**.

as amended

A phrase (sometimes more fully 'as amended from time to time') indicating that a reference to a statute or instrument is a reference to the statute or instrument in its form as amended from time to time, and not merely in its initial form. In statutory drafting, standard Acts-interpretation legislation now supplies an 'as amended' reference without the need for express mention: see, eg, *Interpretation Act 1978*, s 17(2)(a); *Acts Interpretation Act 1901* (Cth), s 10. But the standard Acts-interpretation statutes generally apply only to statutes and regulatory instruments. They do not apply to documents such as contracts, deeds, wills, and the like; and so it is common to insert into such documents an equivalent interpretation provision to the effect that a reference in the document to a statute or regulatory instrument is a reference to the statute or instrument in its form as amended or re-enacted from time to time.

See **CITATION OF LEGISLATION**.

as and when

A lawyer's subconscious pairing—eg, 'A must pay B *as and when* called upon to do so'. *When* (alone) suffices.

as he (she) then was

A polite concession to the fact the person referred to—usually a judge—later held (or now holds) a higher rank. The words usually appear in parenthesis, as an aside. They are unnecessary:

> '*As he then was* is another irritating phrase, referring to a barrister or judge who has risen to a higher sphere. Readers who already know that will not find the information useful; those who do not already know it will not find it of much interest.' [Staughton LJ, in 'Courtly Language', *Counsel*, May 1988]

Almost certainly no impoliteness is intended, or offence taken, if the promotion is left unstated. The statement, or aside, can be deleted, as shown in the following examples:

- 'This statement was made by Denning J ~~(as his Lordship then was)~~.' [Denning J later became, successively, Denning LJ, Lord Denning (in the House of Lords), and Lord Denning MR.]
- 'This statement was made by French J ~~(as his Honour then was)~~.' [French J later became French CJ.]

as nearly as may be

A minor, but unnecessary, eccentricity—as in 'the procedure in this court is to follow *as nearly as may be* the procedure in [another court]'. It means simply 'as nearly as possible', or 'as closely as possible', or 'as nearly as reasonably practicable': *Schipp v Herfords Pty Ltd* [1975] 1 NSWLR 412, 420 (Samuels JA). Use a simpler—and more idiomatic—equivalent.

as of right

See **right (as of)**.

as soon as possible / as soon as practicable

These two terms are elastic, but not so elastic as to be void for uncertainty. Precisely how soon is *possible* or *practicable* is a question of fact, varying with the circumstances. If case law is any guide, the two terms may not always convey the degree of urgency the drafter intended. Where possible (or practicable), specify a more precise time—eg, 'within [X] days' or similar.

as soon as possible

To do something *as soon as possible* means to do it 'within a reasonable time, [but] with an understanding to do it in the shortest practicable time': *Hydraulic Engineering Co Ltd v McHaffie, Goslett and Co* (1878) 4 QBD 670, 673 (Bramwell LJ). That is, *as soon as possible* does not require the greatest speed humanly possible, but rather requires reasonable expedition. A manufacturer who promises to fill an order *as soon as possible* need not discard all other work to make the promised item, and a tailor need not put down a half-made item to begin another order: customers should realise that the manufacturer or tailor may have other orders on hand: *Hydraulic Engineering*, above, 673 (Bramwell LJ). The factual context will be key.

Example

> A statute required drivers to report motor vehicle accidents to the police 'as soon as possible'. On the day of the accident, the driver arranged with a police officer to report it three days later. Held, taking this circumstance into account, a delay of three days complied with the requirement to report 'as soon as possible': *Emirhussein v Radovanovic* [2012] VSC 136; (2012) 221 A Crim R 41.

A senior Australian judge has said that *as soon as possible* means merely 'within a reasonable time' having regard to the party's ability to perform the task: *Bowes v Chaleyer* (1923) 32 CLR 159, 193 (Starke J). However, that probably understates the required degree of urgency. Other judges have taken a more robust approach, particularly where the context includes factors which themselves suggest urgency (eg, 'by return fax'): *SWV Pty Ltd v Spiroc Pty Ltd* [2006] NSWSC 668; (2006) 201 FLR 238, 249 (Barrett J). Less helpfully perhaps, yet another judge said that *as soon as possible* means as soon as possible in the circumstances that, to the parties' knowledge, could affect the time for performance: *Amann Aviation Pty Ltd v Commonwealth* (1990) 22 FCR 527, 558 (Burchett J).

as soon as practicable

To do something *as soon as practicable* may imply less urgency than *as soon as possible*, because *practicable* suggests a greater allowance for pragmatism or commercial reality. But it requires more promptness than 'at the promisor's convenience'; and so a contract to ship a cargo of oil *as soon as practicable* was breached where the promisor had a ship available but chose to use it for another purpose first: *Anglo-American Oil Co Ltd v Port of London Authority* [1914] 1 KB 14.

as soon as reasonably practicable

If every word in a phrase counts, the variant 'as soon as *reasonably* practicable' should allow some leeway. However, it still requires the matter to be done 'without delay once the circumstances, objectively assessed, render it reasonably practicable to do so': *Santhirarajah v Attorney-General* [2012] FCA 940; (2012) 206 FCR 494, [74] (North J).

See also **forthwith**; **immediately**; **practical / practicable**.

as the case may be

A phrase often inserted in the belief that precision requires it. But almost always *as the case may be* means merely 'respectively'; and almost always the meaning is clear without it—in which case, delete it. The following examples show the deletions.

- 'The [reasons for decision] should enable disappointed developers to assess their prospects of obtaining some alternative development permission, or~~, as the case may be,~~ their unsuccessful opponents to understand how the policy or approach underlying the grant of permission may impact upon future such applications.' [*South Bucks District Council v Porter (No 2)* [2004] UKHL 33; [2004] 1 WLR 1953, [36] (Lord Brown)]
- '[It] is clear that any misuse of the power to authorise or confirm or search will expose the authorising officer, the Secretary of State or the constable~~, as the case may be,~~ to corrective legal action.' [*R v Commissioner of Police of the Metropolis* [2006] UKHL 12; [2006] 2 AC 307, [14] (Lord Bingham)]
- Section 22 of the Australian *Quarantine Charges (Collection) Act 2014* (Cth):

  (1) This section applies in relation to a vessel if:

  (a) the owner or operator of the vessel is liable to pay a quarantine charge or a late payment fee ...

(2) A charge is created on the vessel by force of this section to secure the payment of the quarantine charge or late payment fee ~~(as the case may be)~~.

Occasionally, courts have invoked the drafter's use of 'as the case may be' to help separate the consequences that attach to one or more courses of action. An example is *Bluston & Bramley Ltd v Leigh* [1950] 2 KB 548, where the structure was 'if A or B, then C or D *as the case may be*'. But the structure could have been more simply cast as 'if A, then C; if B, then D'.

as the crow flies

Not an expression one would expect to find in a formal document—but if it is used, it simply means 'in a straight line' as distinct from (for example) by road or footpath: *Stokes v Grissell* (1854) 14 CB 678, 689; 139 ER 279, 283 (Maule J). Even without the expression, the rule for measuring distance is 'by a straight line on a map'—so, for example, where a person promises not to open a competing business within a stated distance from named premises, the distance is measured in a straight line on the map, without regard to any extra distance that would need to be covered by road or path, and regardless of distance added by hilly topography: *Mouflet v Cole* (1872) LR 8 Exch 32. Further, if precise measurement between two buildings is necessary, the distance is taken from the nearest point of the one to the nearest point of the other, without regard to where the doors are situated (ibid, 36).

See also **distance**.

as to

Do not let *as to* intrude unnecessarily into sentences. It is often a harbinger of wordiness more generally; if so, delete it (and sometimes rewrite the sentence). For example:

Before	**After**
The decision was rigorous *as to* legal principle.	The decision applied legal principle rigorously.
The jury has no concern *as to* the rules of evidence.	The jury is not concerned with rules of evidence.
The judge was in two minds *as to whether* to impose a severe punishment.	The judge was in two minds *whether* to impose a severe punishment.

However, *as to* may be useful at the start of a sentence to introduce a fresh subject: '*As to* punishment, I want to discuss the latest cases.'

See also **whether**.

ascertain

'To find out', usually with the added implication 'for certain'. But how 'certain'? The accepted legal interpretation seems to be that 'ascertain' is concerned not so much with objective correctness—ie, with one uniquely correct answer—as with whether the enquirer, acting in good faith, was satisfied that the information was correct. For example, an architect or surveyor engaged 'to ascertain' the loss suffered from breach of a building contract needs to be satisfied about the amount of the loss, but need not be 'certain': *Walter Lilly & Co Ltd v Mackay* [2012] EWHC 1773 (TCC); (2012) 143 Con LR 79.

And a person engaged 'to ascertain' the cost of completing a building is entitled to exercise personal judgement and discretion, and to rely on the expert advice of a quantity surveyor: *Dura (Australia) Constructions Pty Ltd v HUE Boutique Living Pty Ltd* [2013] VSCA 179; (2013) 41 VR 636.

asset lending

Sometimes rendered as 'asset-based lending'. Lending based on the value of the property taken as security, rather than the borrower's capacity to repay. It is not a legal term of art.

> '"Asset lending" is not a label or a legal frame of reference. It is a convenient expression, used in [certain decisions] to describe a form of lending where the lender has little, if any, regard for the capacity of the borrower to repay and rests satisfied with the security to protect itself.' [*Fast Fix Loans Pty Ltd v Samardzic* [2011] NSWCA 260, [43]; 15 BPR 29,445 (Allsop P)]

Where used as a compound adjective, add a hyphen: *asset-lending principles*.

assign / assignee (noun)

As a noun, *assign* means the person to whom something is assigned. However, that usage is now dated (though still correct); the more common and idiomatic noun is *assignee*.

> 'Thus the *assign* [prefer: *assignee*] could not stand in any better position than the assignor ...' [*Re Modular Design Group Pty Ltd* (1994) 35 NSWLR 96, 104 (Santow J)]

Strictly speaking, an *assign* (or *assignee*) takes title by deliberate act (eg, a purchaser to whom property is assigned in return for paying the purchase price), not merely by operation of law (eg, a trustee in bankruptcy, who takes title by operation of statute). Also strictly, *assign* (or *assignee*) means only a 'legal' assign (ie, one who takes a legal title, not a mere equitable title). But these distinctions are often ignored, and in any case are subject to contrary intention in the particular document or statute.

assign / transfer (verb)

General meaning

To assign is to *give*, or *hand over*, or *make over*, particularly in relation to property: eg, 'I *assign* [give/hand over/make over] my rights to you.' *To transfer* has the same meaning but with a wider import: *transfer* is the one of 'widest terms' to indicate the process by which persons divest or move property, and includes not only a positive act of transfer, but also one occurring by operation of law, such as on bankruptcy or under a court order: *Gathercole v Smith* (1881) 17 Ch D 1, 7 (James LJ).

In land law and related areas, *assign* is used particularly for conveying interests in land held under unregistered title (commonly called 'old system' title, or 'common law' title). For land held under registered title (in Australia and many other Commonwealth countries, 'Torrens' title), the more appropriate verb is now *transfer*. In either case, however, the pairing *assign and transfer* (or *transfer and assign*) is a redundancy: choose the particular verb—*assign* or *transfer*—and use it alone.

Subsidiary meaning of 'assign': allocate

In some contexts, *assign* may mean merely 'allocate'—ie, to set apart for, but not transfer or convey to:

> 'The minister may *assign* water rights to farmers on the basis of the areas of their farms'. Here, *assign* means *allocate to*—the minister does not personally convey the water rights: *Zander v Minister for Sustainability, Environment and Conservation* (2013) 118 SASR 1; [2013] SASC 149).

Further reading

'Transfer and Assign', in *Law Words*, Centre for Plain Legal Language, University of Sydney (1995) 89; link at www.clarity-international.net/plain-language-resources/general-resources/

See also **assign / assignee (noun); conveyance; novation / assignment; transfer (noun); 'NO ASSIGNMENT' CLAUSE; transfer (noun).**

assignation

In standard English, a clandestine meeting. In Scots law (more prosaically), an assignment of an interest in property.

assignment / novation

See **novation / assignment.**

assignment / sublease

General usage sometimes blurs the differences between an *assignment* of a lease and a *sublease*. But legal usage observes them strictly. In legal usage:

- An *assignment* of a lease is a transfer of the whole of the tenant's interest in the lease (ie, the whole of the unexpired term of the lease). It does not create a new lease, but merely transfers the assignor's existing interest.
- In contrast, a *sublease* is the creation of a lease out of a lease—a carving-out of a new interest—by a transfer of less than the whole of the tenant's interest in the lease. For this reason, a *sublease* (or *underlease*) is necessarily shorter in duration than the lease out of which it is carved—eg, less one month, or less one day.

Drafters ignore these differences at their peril. For example:

- A purported 'assignment' of less than the remaining term of a lease necessarily results in a sublease: *409 Lonsdale Pty Ltd v Carra* [1974] VR 887.
- A purported sublease for longer than the remaining term of a lease necessarily results in an assignment: *Milmo v Carreras* [1946] KB 306; *Olympic Corporation Ltd v Orcatory Road Properties Ltd* [1990] 2 NZLR 519; *Lee v Ferno Holdings Pty Ltd* (1993) 33 NSWLR 404, 407, 410–11.

The differences between *assignment* and *sublease* are also reflected in the interpretation of covenants in leases. For example:

- A covenant against 'assigning' does not prohibit a sublease: *Church v Brown* (1808) 15 Ves Jun 258, 265; 33 ER 752, 755; *Sweet & Maxwell Ltd v Universal News Service Ltd* [1964] 2 QB 699. (Whether a covenant against 'subleasing' prohibits an assignment is not so clear: *Marks v Warren* [1979] 1 All ER 29, 31.)

- A covenant against both assigning and subleasing does not prohibit parting with possession under a revocable licence: *Stoyles v Job* (1954) 73 WN (NSW) 41.
- A covenant 'not to underlet or part with possession' prohibits an assignment, at least where the assignment involves parting with possession: *Marks v Warren* [1979] 1 All ER 29, 31.

Drafters who successfully navigate these shoals must also watch for another danger, namely that courts interpret covenants against assigning or subleasing as prima facie applying only to transactions effective *at law*: *Gentle v Faulkiner* [1900] 2 QB 267, 274, 276–77. For example:

- A covenant against 'assigning' is not breached by an assignment of an equitable interest only (*MacDonald v Robins* (1954) 90 CLR 515, 520) or by a declaration of trust (*Gentle v Faulkner* [1900] 2 QB 267).
- A covenant against 'assigning' is not breached by entry into a mere *agreement* to assign, since an agreement to assign creates an equitable interest only: *Brown & Root Technology Ltd v Sun Alliance and London Assurance Co Ltd* [2001] Ch 733, 742; *Australian Mutual Provident Society v 400 St Kilda Road Pty Ltd* [1990] VR 646 (affirmed, [1991] 2 VR 417).

These prima facie interpretations yield to contrary context, but clear words are required to overturn them. For example, in *Old Papa's Franchise Systems Pty Ltd v Camisa Nominees Pty Ltd* [2003] WASCA 11, [43]–[45] the prima facie interpretation was not overturned by a covenant against assigning the lease 'or any estate or interest therein'.

Therefore, while brevity is a desirable attribute in legal drafting, a prudent drafter may need to add wording that forbids 'assignment or sublease whether at law or in equity or by way of a declaration of trust'.

Further reading

- S Bridge, E Cooke, and M Dixon (eds), *Megarry & Wade's Law of Real Property*, 9th edn (Sweet & Maxwell, 2019) [16-141]–[16-145], [18-126]
- Brendan Edgeworth (ed), *Butt's Land Law*, 7th edn (Lawbook, 2017) [7.980]–[7.1050] (on Commonwealth law)

See also **assign / transfer (verb); sublease / underlease**.

assume / presume

Both words mean to accept something as true, usually without proof. The difference between them is a matter of emphasis—to *presume* that a fact is true implies more confidence than to *assume* it is true. Hence, many principles of law are termed *presumptions* (*presumption* of innocence, *presumption* of regularity, *presumption* of vesting), not *assumptions*.

See also **PRESUMPTIONS**.

assure / ensure / insure

assure

In normal usage, *to assure* (noun, *assurance*) means to convince or to provide confirmation: 'Let me *assure* you of that.' In legal usage, *to assure* (noun, *assurance*) more usually means to convey or transfer: 'I will *assure* the policy to you tomorrow.' 'I promise to complete the sale of the property by executing a deed of *assurance*.'

ensure

Ensure means 'make sure' (ie, that something happens), and is generally used in the active voice: eg, 'I will *ensure* that this happens.' It has no particular legal meaning.

insure

Insure means protect by insurance: eg, 'We *insured* our house.' Where the subject matter is a person's life, conventional British and Commonwealth usage is *life assurance*, while US usage is *life insurance*. However, British and Commonwealth usage is moving inexorably to *life insurance*.

Unidiomatically, the insurance fund established by land registration systems in many Commonwealth countries—notably the Torrens system of land registration—is called the *Assurance Fund*. Its purpose is to compensate owners who are deprived of their registered interests in land by fraud or departmental error. See, eg, *Real Property Act 1900* (NSW), s 134.

See also **ensure (that something be done)**.

at any time

Courts give *at any time* an unrestricted meaning, unless the context requires otherwise. For example:

- A one-year charterparty gave the shipowners the right to substitute another vessel *at any time*. Held, they could do so not only at the time of their choosing, but also more than once: *SA Maritime et Commerciale of Geneva v Anglo-Iranian Oil Co Ltd* [1954] 1 WLR 492 (CA). (However, Birkett LJ thought the meaning might be different where only one voyage was contemplated.)
- A statute allowed a party to a building contract to require an adjudication *at any time*. Held, this gave the right to require the adjudication at any time into the future, even after the normal limitation period had expired: *Connex South Eastern Ltd v M J Building Services Group plc* [2005] EWCA Crim 1092; [2005] 1 WLR 3323 (CA).

Often, *at any time* is superfluous. For example, where a lease provides that the tenant 'may *at any time* sublease the premises', the words *at any time* serve a purpose only if it could be argued that the right to sublease is a right to sublease once only. If such an argument is open, the additional words are justified; if not, they are not.

at least (time)

General meaning

A period of *at least* a stated period generally means a *clear* period, as the following cases show:

- A requirement that blood-alcohol samples be taken '*at least* 15 minutes [apart]' means a minimum of 15 clear minutes: *R v Davis* (1977) 35 CCC (2d) 224; [1978] 1 WWR 381.
- A requirement that an applicant for a licence give '*at least* 21 days' notice', requires 21 clear days' notice: *Ayers v Chacos* (1972) 19 FLR 468.
- A period of '*at least* [X] days' means 'at a minimum, [X] clear days': *Forster v Jododex Australia Pty Ltd* (1972) 127 CLR 421, 444–45 (Gibbs J, adding that the same interpretation is given to 'not less than').
- A requirement under a company's by-laws to give notice of '*at least* 15 days' to call a meeting, requires a minimum of 15 clear days: *Ashton v Powers* (1921) 51 OLR 309; 67 DLR 222.

Statutory meaning

In some jurisdictions, the general meaning (above) is enshrined as a rule of statutory interpretation: eg, in Australia, s 36(1) of the *Acts Interpretation Act 1901* (Cth):

> Where in an Act any period of time, dating from a given day, act, or event, is prescribed or allowed for any purpose, the time shall, unless the contrary intention appears, be reckoned exclusive of such day or of the day of such act or event.

Choose a different expression?

Meaning always varies with context. It is possible that Parliament, or the parties to a document, intended to give a different meaning to 'at least' in the particular context: see, eg, *Timmerman v Central Guaranty Trust Co* (1992) 8 OR (3d) 669 (citing conflicting decisions on whether a statutory requirement that a mortgagee's notice of proposed sale be '*at least* 35 days' required 35 clear days). Therefore, to avoid the need for litigation, specify a particular date or the expiry of a stated number of 'clear days'.

See also **clear day; not less than (time)**.

at once

Normally, a requirement to do something *at once* requires it to be done immediately or without delay. However, meaning varies with context, and in some situations *at once* may imply less urgency: eg, *R v Rogers* (1877) 3 QBD 28, 33, where an employee's obligation to remit money *at once* was held to mean *within a reasonable time*. Where possible, specify a particular time-span: eg, 'within 2 days'.

See also **forthwith**; **immediately**.

at the present time

See **present time (at the)**.

attach

The meaning of *attach* may change with context. Generally, a legal requirement to *attach* something to something else—eg, to attach a document to another document—requires physical connection by joinder, fastening, stapling, or similar: *MNM Developments Pty Ltd v Gerrard* [2005] QCA 230; [2005] 2 Qd R 515. But in some contexts the meaning is looser—more like 'accompanying' or 'associated with': *Bosaid v Andrey* [1963] VR 465, 473. For rating purposes, heavy machinery that is integral to the use of the rateable land on which it stands, but that is kept in place solely by its own weight, may as a matter of ordinary English be described as 'attached' to the land: *Tyne Boiler Works Ltd v Longbenton Overseers* (1886) 18 QBD 81, 91 (Lindley LJ). An adept drafter will anticipate any uncertainty and clarify.

attempt

If syllable-count matters (as it should), *attempt* can usually be shortened to *try*. Even more so can *make an attempt* be shortened to *try*.

- She *attempted* [prefer: *tried*] to file the summons.
- She made an attempt [prefer: *tried*] to file the summons.

Sometimes, however, substituting *try* does not work:

He *made an attempt* on his own life.

See also **PLAIN LANGUAGE; SIMPLER WORDS AND PHRASES.**

attendee

Most *-ee* endings denote someone who receives a benefit: eg, *lessee* (one to whom a lease is granted—ie, a tenant), *mortgagee* (one to whom a mortgage is granted), *trustee* (one to whom property is entrusted), *grantee* (one to whom property is granted). The sense is implicitly passive. But *attendee* carries the active sense of 'one who attends (a meeting)'—as if the word were *attendor*. If ambiguity is feared, vary the formulation: eg, *not* 'there were three attendees', *but* 'three people attended'.

See also ***-ee* / *-or* endings.**

attest

Legal meaning

In standard English, to *attest* means to affirm the truth of something: eg, 'I can *attest* to that'. That meaning carries over into legal usage, but with a nuance: *attest* means to bear witness to the thing itself, not merely to affirm a belief in its truth. So, to *attest* a person's signature is to bear witness to the fact that the person has signed. Preferred spelling for 'a person who attests' is *attestor* (not 'attester').

Older case law suggests that an attestor (A) could *attest* B's signature without A also having to sign; it was enough that A was present when B signed. But more recent case law treats *attesting* as requiring *both* being present *and* indicating that presence by signing: see, eg, *Re Selby-Bigge* [1950] 1 All ER 1009, 1011 (Hodson J); *Netglory Pty Ltd v Caratti* [2013] WASC 364, [127]–[147] (Edelman J). Further, the attesting (including by signing) must be contemporaneous with the signature witnessed—and so, for example, it is not sufficient that the witness (B) was present when the party (A) signed but added his or her signature later: *Netglory*, [148]–[169]; *Brown v Tavern Operator Pty Ltd* [2018] NSWSC 1290, [496] (Ward CJ in Eq); contra *Deacon v Auckland District Land Registrar* (1910) 30 NZLR 369. However, where nothing on the face of the document suggests that the attesting witness was not present when the document-maker signed, the document-maker may be estopped from raising non-presence as a defence to an action on the document: *Shah v Shah* [2002] QB 35 (CA) (but distinguished in *Briggs v Gleeds* [2015] Ch 212, and *Brown v Tavern Operator Pty Ltd* [2018] NSWSC 1290, [496], on the basis that estoppel cannot overcome a complete absence of attesting signatures).

Statutory requirements

Statute may require one or more *attesting* witnesses to certain documents. Thus, in many jurisdictions a deed must be *attested* by at least one witness (who must not be a party to the deed): see, eg, *Law of Property (Miscellaneous Provisions) Act 1989*, s 1(3). Again, in most jurisdictions a will must be *attested* by two or more witnesses, present at the time the testator signed: eg, *Wills Act 1837*, s 9.

Further reading

- Martin Dockray, 'Deeds Speak Louder than Words. Attesting Time for Deeds?' (2013) 77 *Conveyancer and Property Lawyer* 298
- Brian Sloan, 'Testing Times for Attestation' (2019) 83 *Conveyancer and Property Lawyer* 182

See also **ATTESTATION CLAUSE; execute (a document); TESTING CLAUSE.**

ATTESTATION CLAUSE

A clause by which a person attests another's signature. (In Scottish usage, called *testing clause.*) A non-deed (ie, a 'mere' agreement) needs no formal attestation clause—usually, it is enough for the witness (if indeed a witness is needed at all) to sign their name. The conventional form is:

Signed by [the document maker] ....
in the presence of:
  witness name ....
  witness signature ....

However, a deed needs a formal attestation clause. Historically, a deed's attestation clause had two components:

1. The testimonium, starting with 'in witness whereof …' and then authenticating the instrument and prefacing the maker's signature.
2. The attestation itself, starting with 'sealed and delivered in the presence of …' to introduce the signature of the witnesses certifying the deed-maker's signature.

Example (now archaic)

In witness whereof [the deed-maker] has hereunto subscribed his name and affixed his seal:
Signed, sealed and delivered by [the deed maker] ....
in the presence of:
  witness (1) name and signature ....
  witness (2) name and signature ....

Modern attestation clauses for deeds are briefer and use plainer language. The modern form of clause usually states 'Executed as a deed', followed by the signatures of the makers and the witnesses.

Where corporations sign (or 'execute') documents under common seal, a 'signature block' is often used, with places for affixing the seal (if used) and for the relevant company officers to sign.

Further reading

Nicholas Seddon, *Seddon on Deeds* (Federation Press, 2015) [2.9]

See also **attest; execute; in witness whereof (the parties have signed); signed, sealed and delivered; testimonium; TESTING CLAUSE.**

attorney

A word carrying two meanings:

1. *A person who acts on behalf of another*, most commonly under a 'power of attorney'. See further, **power of attorney**.

2. *A lawyer*. This meaning has a long history in British law. The *Oxford English Dictionary* traces its use back to the 15th century. At first, *attorney* denoted a practitioner in the common-law courts, and *solicitor* denoted a practitioner in the Court of Chancery. (A third category, *proctor*, denoted a practitioner in the Court of Probate, in the Court for Divorce and Matrimonial Causes, in the High Court of Admiralty, and in the ecclesiastical courts.) In time, *solicitor* began to supersede *attorney*, as legal practitioners increasingly took on work in both common law and equity. The *Supreme Court of Judicature Act* 1873 rounded out this gradual change in terminology, by specifying that all solicitors, attorneys, and proctors became *solicitors* of the Supreme Court.

In US usage, *attorney* remains a general term for 'lawyer'. British/Commonwealth usage prefers *legal practitioner* as the general term, and *barrister* and *solicitor* as the role-specific terms. However, the inexorable spread of US English is making *attorney* more acceptable in British/Commonwealth usage.

See also **power of attorney**.

attorney-general

In British/Commonwealth usage, conventionally hyphenated. Plural: *attorneys-general* (not 'attorney-generals'), because *general* is the adjective, and *attorney* is the noun. In US usage, two separate words and unhyphenated ('attorney general', 'attorneys general'). British/Commonwealth usage is sliding towards US usage, with some English and Australian dictionaries and law reports now dropping the hyphen.

attornment

Historically, a feudal landowner's transference of his or her homage and service to a new lord (from the Old French, *atournement*). Modern law retains the word (and echoes its historical origins) in the procedure following a sale of leased property, where the tenant 'attorns tenant' to the purchaser—ie, acknowledges the purchaser as landlord: *Cornish v Searell* (1828) 8 B & C 471; 108 ER 1118. In most jurisdictions, statute has removed the requirement for strict attornment of this kind; instead, the purchaser simply notifies the tenant of the sale and directs the tenant to pay all future rent to the purchaser as landlord: eg, *Law of Property Act 1925*, s 151.

attributable to

An inherently vague term: it connotes connection, but how direct? Not necessarily very direct, according to three senior Australian judges:

> 'It seems clear that the expression "attributable to" [in certain decisions] involved an element of causation. The cause need not be the sole or dominant cause: it is sufficient to show "attributability" if the cause is one of a number of causes provided it is a contributing cause.' [*Repatriation Commission v Law* [1980] FCA 92; (1980) 31 ALR 140, 151 (Bowen CJ, Brennan and Lockhart JJ)]

If direct causal connection is intended, always prefer a more precise term, such as 'caused by', 'because of', or similar.

See also **cause (noun, verb); in consequence of; novus actus interveniens**.

audi alteram partem

Latin: hear the other side. A maxim encapsulating a principle of natural justice that a court or tribunal should not reach a decision without giving parties the opportunity to be heard. It can be translated as 'each party has a right to be heard'—and should be so translated for readers unaccustomed to Latin. For example:

- 'Although the matter is in the end one for the discretion of the judge, *audi [alteram] partem* [prefer: *the right of each party to be heard*] is a salutary and important principle.' [*National Commercial Bank Jamaica Ltd v Olint Corporation Ltd* [2009] 1 WLR 1405, 1408 [13] (Lord Hoffmann)]
- '[The sections of the Act] alter, or at least would allow the Tribunal to depart from the *audi alteram partem rule* [prefer: *the rule that a party has the right to be heard*]. Their effect is to enable the Tribunal to use against a party evidence and findings which it has had no opportunity of testing or controverting.' [*BHP Billiton Ltd v Schutz* [2004] HCA 61; (2004) 221 CLR 400, 491 [253] (Callinan J)]

AUDIENCE

Taking audience into account

All effective writing takes account of the intended audience. The writer crafts both language and style to be as accessible as possible to that audience. The aim is text that a reasonably motivated audience-member can read, understand, and act on after a single reading. Legal writing should have a similar aim.

The centrality of audience means that legal language and style may need to vary depending on the intended audience. For a sophisticated legal audience, the language may properly include terms of art and legal abbreviations, and the style may assume a familiarity with legal-document structure. But that approach would be unsuitable for a consumer audience, where the same language skills and knowledge base cannot be assumed.

Who is the audience?

The audience for legal writing may be obvious: eg, the client who seeks the legal advice, or the seller and buyer who sign the contract for sale, or 'the consumer' who must sign standard terms and conditions.

Sometimes, the immediate audience is small, but has the potential to become larger as the document is circulated to increasingly widening audiences. For example:

1. **Who is the 'audience' for a judge's decision?** The immediate audience is the parties personally, who are unlikely to be legally trained and therefore unlikely to understand terms of art, legal shorthand and the traditional structure of judgments (where the reader is not told the result until the end). In line with this view, the Court of Appeal has recently said that the primary audience for a judge's sentencing remarks is the offender. The judge's remarks must therefore be directed to the offender, not with 'the eye to the Court of Appeal'. Specifically, the remarks must be in language that the offender can understand, explaining what sentence has been passed, why it has been passed, what it means, and what might happen if the offender fails to comply: *R v Chin-Charles* [2019] EWCA Crim 1140 (Practice Note), [6]–[7].

   Another audience is the parties' legal advisers. They will understand terms of art, legal shorthand and traditional judgment structure. Another (potential) audience is a higher appellate court, to which one or both parties might appeal. That court will be familiar with terms of art, legal shorthand and traditional judgment structure.

Widening the circle, another audience might be lawyers needing to advise clients in future disputes dealing with similar subject matter. And finally, another audience might be law students, who must read the decision as part of their studies.

In this way, the audience for a single decision may multiply from several readers, to dozens of readers, and finally to thousands of readers, with diverse backgrounds and expertise, yet all having to wrestle with the same document.

2. **Who is the audience for a legal advice?** The immediate audience is the 'client'. If the client is a single person or sole trader, the writer can address that audience directly. But what if the client is a large corporation or entity? The immediate reader is the officer who sought the advice. That person may or may not be legally trained. But that person may then forward the advice to in-house counsel, who will be legally trained. In-house counsel may then recommend that the advice be circulated to the Board, who may or may not be legally trained. In this way, too, the advice reaches an ever-widening circle of readers, some legally trained and some not.

This audience-multiplicity might give legal writers cause for pause: should I cater for my immediate audience, or should I try to cater for the potentially wider and more disparate readership? These issues can complicate 'writing for the audience'. Nevertheless, all legal writers can *lessen* the complexity for *all* audiences by using standard plain-language techniques. These include short sentences (instead of long), active voice (instead of passive), verbs (instead of nouns or noun phrases), ambiguity-free writing, and in particular front-loading key information. (For these and similar techniques, see cross-references under 'See also' at the end of this topic.)

Further reading

- Rabeea Assy, 'Can the Law Speak Directly to its Subjects—The Limitation of Plain Language' (2011) 38 *Journal of Law and Society* 376 (arguing that plain language of itself is not sufficient for lay readers to understand complex legal issues)
- RP Charrow and VR Charrow, 'Making Legal Language Understandable: A Psycholinguistic Study of Jury Instructions' (1979) 79 *Columbia Law Review* 1306
- Peter McClellan, 'Looking Inside the Jury Room' (5 March 2011), at www.supremecourt.justice.nsw.gov.au/Pages/SCO2_publications/SCO2_judicialspeeches/sco2_speeches_pastjudges.aspx#mcclellan (reviewing the literature on the extent to which juries understand directions from the judge)
- Robert Waller et al, 'Cooperation through Clarity: Designing Simplified Contracts' (2016) 2 *Journal of Strategic Contracting and Negotiation* 48 (on designing a document for Canadian Aboriginal readers)

See also **ACTIVE VOICE / PASSIVE VOICE; CLAUSE STRUCTURE; DOCUMENT DESIGN; DOCUMENT STRUCTURE; DOCUMENT TESTING; NOUNS / VERBS; PLAIN LANGUAGE; READABLILITY TESTS; SENTENCE LENGTH; SENTENCE STRUCTURE; SIMPLER WORDS AND PHRASES.**

automatically

Often, the adverb *automatically* adds no meaning to a phrase or sentence—if so, delete it. For example:

> 'The period of notice *automatically* lapses at midnight on 1 June.' Here, *automatically* is superfluous: the period simply lapses.

However, sometimes *automatically* is necessary for meaning—in which case, retain it. For example:

> 'If the purchaser fails to complete on time, this contract *automatically* terminates'. Here, *automatically* is not superfluous. On the contrary, it usefully indicates that termination is self-executing and requires no further action by the vendor (such as serving a notice of termination).

See also **terminate by notice of [stated period]**.

autrefois

Law French: on another occasion, formerly; used in criminal law in the terms *autrefois acquit* (ie, previously acquitted [of this offence]) and *autrefois convict* (ie, previously convicted [of this offence]). The usages are technical, but for most purposes can be dispensed with: it is enough to say (in plain English) that a person who has been acquitted or convicted of an offence cannot be tried again for the same offence.

> '[The principle is] that a man should not be tried for a crime in respect of which he has previously been acquitted or convicted (autrefois acquit and autrefois convict).' [*R v Lama* [2014] EWCA Crim 1729; [2017] 3 WLR 469, [109] (Hallett LJ, using plain English but adding the technical term so as not to be misunderstood)]

avizandum

Latin: being looked into; being considered. A term used in Scots law to indicate that the court is considering its decision. The equivalent Latinism in English law is *curia advisari vult* (the court wishes to be advised).

See also **curia advisari vult.**

avoid

In common usage, *to avoid* means *to keep away from* or *to escape* or *to evade*. In legal usage, however, *to avoid* means *to render void*, in the sense of *to terminate* or *to bring to an end* or *to set aside*. The legal usage is not always instructive, because (in the absence of more information) it fails to identify the ground for the avoiding. Was it for breach of contract (in which case, damages would flow)? Was it for a vitiating factor in the formation of the contract, such as mistake or innocent misrepresentation (in which case, damages would normally not flow)? Was it under a statutory right (in which case, damages may or may not flow, depending on the intent of the statute)? It may be helpful to explain the ground for the avoiding.

See also **rescind / terminate / end**.

avoidance of doubt

See **for the avoidance of doubt**.

BACKGROUND

See **RECITALS**.

backhand rent

A Scots law term, indicating that rent is payable in arrears (ie, after each rental period), as distinct from *forehand rent*, which is payable in advance.

See also **arrears**.

BACK-REFERENCES

See **CROSS-REFERENCES.**

BACKSHEET

See **COVERSHEET.**

balance / remainder

In financial contexts, *balance* generally means 'the rest of'—eg, the *balance* of a debt that is still to be paid, or the *balance* of a bank account that has not been spent. *Remainder* can mean the same thing—the *remainder* (balance) of a debt, or the *remainder* (balance) of a bank account.

In the context of land law, a *remainder* is a particular interest in property. It arises where an owner of property disposes of the whole of his or her interest in the property, but does so in two or more 'slices' to take effect consecutively. The second and subsequent slices are *remainder* interests (or, more shortly, *remainders*).

See also **remainder / reversion.**

balloon payment

The largest repayment in a loan that is otherwise repaid by smaller instalments over the loan period; usually paid at the start or at the end of the loan period.

Compare **bullet repayment.**

banco

See **in banco.**

bank holiday

A day declared under legislation to be a holiday for all banks within the jurisdiction: *Banking and Financial Dealings Act 1971*, Sch 1. *Bank holiday* is not the same as *public holiday*, although dates for the two may overlap.

Contractual interpretation clauses generally provide for what is to happen if a day on which something is to be done turns out to be a bank holiday. These clauses can pose issues where contractual rights and obligations involve multiple parties in different jurisdictions, and a day on which something is to be done is a bank holiday in one jurisdiction but not in the other. See, eg, *Griffin Energy Group Pty Ltd v ICICI Bank Ltd* [2015] NSWCA 29; (2015) 317 ALR 395 (for facts, see **business day**).

See also **business day**; **public holiday.**

basis

Beware of *basis*-phrases, such as 'on a … basis', or 'on the basis that'—they almost always harbour verbosity. Prune wherever possible:

- The government funds the courts *on a continuing basis* [prefer: *continuously*; *permanently*; *annually* (if that is the meaning)].
- Retired judges offer their services *on a consultancy basis* [prefer: *as consultants*].

- Retired judges hear cases on a part-time basis [prefer: part-time; as part-time judges].
- Reducing legal aid *on the basis of reducing* [prefer: *to reduce*] cost is not good policy.

'be' verbs

The English language has eight forms of the verb 'to be': *am, are, is, was, were, be, being, been*. All are useful. However, overuse of the verb *to be*, particularly as a sentence-opener and in passive constructions, can produce wordy sentences. Recasting the sentence to eliminate the 'be' verb almost always reduces word-count. It may also improve sentence structure, including by ending the sentence more forcefully.

Before	**After**
There are three reasons why this should *be* done by courts. [10 words]	Courts should do this for three reasons. [7 words]
This is one important factor that all courts place emphasis upon. [11 words]	All courts emphasise this one important factor. [7 words]
This was not the kind of decision the parties *were* expecting *to be* given by the court. [17 words]	The parties did not expect the court to give this kind of decision. [13 words]
There were two aspects of this reasoning upon which reliance *was placed by* the parties. [15 words. Source: *Trives v Hornsby Shire Council* [2015] NSWCA 158, [38]; (2015) 89 NSWLR 268, 278 (Basten JA)]	The parties relied on two aspects of this reasoning. [9 words]

See also **ACTIVE / PASSIVE; being (participle); PROLIXITY; SENTENCE STRUCTURE; TENSE; was.**

bearing date

An archaism for *dated*; eg, 'bearing date 1 January 2018'. To describe something as *bearing date* is now mere affectation; prefer 'dated 1 January 2018'. Even more affected is 'bearing even date herewith'; prefer 'dated today'.

because

Avoid weaker substitutes

When denoting a cause–effect relationship, prefer *because* over weaker subsitutes.

'since'

One such weaker substitute is *since*: 'The trial plaintiff disliked the defendant *since* [prefer: *because*] he complained to the police.'

Also, *since* can be ambiguous: does it denote cause or time? 'The trial plaintiff disliked the defendant *since* he complained to the police.' Does this mean '*because* he complained to the police' or '*since the time* that he complained to the police'?

'as'

Another weak substitute is *as*. Prefer *because*, which carries more immediately the sense of cause or reason: 'The judge dismissed the case *as* [prefer: *because*] the accused was clearly innocent.'

Avoid wordy substitutes

Avoid wordy substitutes for *because*—eg, 'for the reason that', 'due to the fact that', 'on the ground that'. For example:

- 'I would refer first to contracts for the sale of goods ... *for the reason that* [prefer: *because*] one of the remedies provided to the seller ... is an action for the price.' [*White and Carter (Councils) Ltd v McGregor* [1962] AC 413, 437 (Lord Keith)]
- '[The Tribunal's decision] was criticised *on the ground that* [prefer: *because*] it gave inadequate weight to certain considerations and undue weight to others.' [*Minister for Immigration v Eshetu* (1999) 197 CLR 611, 628 [45] (Gleeson CJ and McHugh J)]
- 'A difficulty arose at the outset *due to the fact that* [prefer: *because*] whereas Mrs Williams and Mrs Campbell were desirous of selling Mr Scahill did not wish to do so.' [*Federal Commissioner of Taxation v Williams* (1972) 127 CLR 226, 228–29 (Stephen J). *Better still*: 'A difficulty arose at the outset because Mrs Williams and Mrs Campbell wished to sell but Mr Scahill did not.' (29 words reduced to 20)]

Ambiguity at sentence-end

Beware of possible ambiguity when ending a sentence with a '*because* ...' clause: 'The vendor cannot terminate the contract *because of* hardship.' This could mean:

- Hardship on the vendor precludes the vendor from terminating the contract.
- Hardship on the purchaser precludes the vendor from terminating the contract.
- Hardship is not a justification for terminating the contract.

Punctuation

General

Usually, *because* needs no preceding comma. In all the examples considered so far, to insert a comma before *because* would be unnecessary.

However, a comma can be useful to echo natural speech patterns—as where the speaker would pause before *because*. For example:

> 'The judge had a difficult task in controlling opposing counsel in yesterday's murder trial at the Old Bailey, *because* passions were running high.'

Avoiding ambiguity

Also, *because* sometimes needs a comma to avoid ambiguity, particularly in a *not ... because* formulation. For example:

> 'I'm not going to sue you *because* you're a judge.' This could mean:
>
> (1) 'I am not going to sue you. Your position as a judge means that suing you would be pointless.'
>
> (2) 'I am going to sue you. However, that is not because you are a judge, but [for some other reason].'

Context might clarify the intended meaning. But to clearly indicate meaning (1) an adept writer will add a comma or dash before *because*: 'I'm not going to sue you, because you're a judge.' Or, 'I'm not going to sue you—because you're a judge.'

Sometimes, rewriting is the better option:

'We will not forgive the debt *because* you are in financial difficulty.' Depending on the intended meaning, this could be rewritten in two ways:

- 'Even if you are in financial difficulty, we will not forgive the debt.'
- 'The reason for not forgiving the debt has nothing to do with your financial difficulty, but ...'

Starting sentences

No grammar 'rule' proscribes starting sentences with *because*. Many leading judges do so.

See also **since**.

because of

See **by reason of**; **cause (noun / verb)**; **in consequence of**.

before

The general meaning is clear—'earlier than' or 'sooner than', but not 'on' or 'after'. However, meaning can vary with context, opening up avenues for ambiguity:

- Where something is to be done *before* a ship loads, it is too late to do it *at the start of the loading*: *Maxine Footwear Co Ltd v Canadian Government Merchant Marine* [1959] AC 589, 603 (PC).
- Where a compensation right was expressed to accrue *before* a date, it was enough that it accrued *on but not after* that date: *Thornton's Executrix v Angus & Sons' Trustee* 1934 SC 279, 290.
- Where property rights were to be determined by the use to which spouses put the property *before* their marital separation, the relevant date was *previously to* the separation or *up to the time of* the separation: *Evers v Evers* [1985] 2 NZLR 209, 211 (NZCA).

Also, *before* does not, of itself, indicate 'how long before'. On that basis, where a statute required a buyer to sign a warning statement *before* signing a contract to purchase a property, signing any time before sufficed—it did not have to be immediately before: *Doolan v Rothmont Projects Pty Ltd* [2010] QSC 193; [2010] Q ConvR 54-736.

beginning with / beginning from

beginning with

In calculating a period *beginning with* a stated day, counting starts on that day: *Hare v Goucher* [1962] 2 QB 641. The same applies to equivalent expressions such as *starting with* and *commencing with* a day—counting starts on that day: *Darwin Broadcasters Pty Ltd v Australian Broadcasting Tribunal* (1990) 21 FCR 524 (Beaumont J). So a period of '5 days *beginning with* [or *starting with*, or *commencing with*] 1 December' ends on 5 December.

beginning from

However, in calculating a period *beginning from* (or *beginning after*) a stated date, that date is excluded, and counting starts from the next day: *Trow v Ind Coope (West Midlands) Ltd* [1967] 2 All ER 900, 913 (Salmond LJ). The same applies to equivalent expressions such as *commencing from* (or *after*) or *starting from* (or *after*).

See also **after (a date)**; **by (a date)**; **from (a date)**; **on (a date)**; **TIME**; **within (a period) from**.

being (participle)

Try to avoid using *being* as a participle; as a formula, it is clumsy. It is found in two main situations: joining relative clauses and imposing an obligation.

Joining relative clauses

The construction 'a person *being* …', though often seen in legal writing, is ungainly when used to join relative clauses. It unnecessarily interrupts the flow of the sentence. Revise the sentence to avoid the construction.

Before	After
If served with a summons, a person, *being* a tenant or trespasser, must vacate the premises immediately.	A tenant or trespasser who is served with a summons must vacate the premises immediately.
A trespasser who is in occupation of a building, *being* a residential property, cannot acquire a possessory title.	A trespasser who is in occupation of [*or*: A trespasser occupying] a residential building cannot acquire a possessory title.

Imposing an obligation

Under an antiquated style of drafting, *being* can impose an obligation. Prefer a simpler style, as in the following example:

> A tenant covenanted to keep various parts of the premises in repair, 'the same *being previously put in repair by*' the landlord. Held, *being previously put in repair by* the landlord was a covenant by the landlord to repair: *Cannock v Jones* (1849) 3 Exch 233, 238; 154 ER 829, 831 (Parke B). A clearer draft would be: 'The landlord must put the premises into repair, after which the tenant must keep them in repair.'

See also **'be' verbs**.

believe / suspect

To *believe* that a state of affairs exists is to be confident that it exists. To *suspect* that a state of affairs exists is to accept that it could exist, but with a still-open mind that it might not: 'I suspect but I cannot prove': *Hussien v Chong Fook Kam* [1970] AC 942, 948 (Lord Devlin).

But suspicion is more than 'idle wondering' whether a state of affairs exists. Rather, it

> 'is a positive feeling of actual apprehension or mistrust, amounting to "a slight opinion, but without sufficient evidence", as *Chambers's* [sic] *Dictionary* expresses it. Consequently, a reason to suspect that a fact exists is more than a reason to consider or look into the possibility of its existence.' [*Queensland Bacon Pty Ltd v Rees* (1966) 115 CLR 266, 303 (Kitto J)]

Of course, context may require varied shades of meaning. As a general proposition, however, whether a person *believes* something imposes a more stringent test than whether a person *suspects* something. And so where a statute uses both terms—*believe* and *suspect*, or their noun forms *belief* and *suspicion*—courts assume that the drafter intended each word to carry a distinct meaning: *George v Rockett* (1990) 170 CLR 104, 116.

below

See **above / below**.

bencher

A senior member of one of the Inns of Court, chosen by the existing benchers from those members of the Inn who are judges, QCs, or other barristers of high standing in the legal profession. Often termed *Master of the Bench*. An honorary bencher is a person chosen as a bencher from outside the membership of the Inns of Court, on the basis of a distinguished career, usually (but not necessarily) in the law.

See also **Inns of Court**.

beneficial

The general meaning is clear: *of benefit to*. But in legal usage—particularly in the terms *beneficial interest* and *beneficial ownership*—*beneficial* carries a different and specific meaning, for which a plain-English equivalent is difficult to find. The origin of *beneficial* lies in the way in which the English legal system allows the ownership of property to be split into *legal* and *equitable* interests—*legal* interests being those traditionally recognised by the courts of common law, and *equitable* interests being those traditionally recognised by courts of equity.

The most common example is where property is subject to a trust. The common law recognised only the trustee's interest (thus, a *legal* interest). It fell to courts of equity to recognise and protect the beneficiaries' interests (thus, *equitable* interests). The interests of beneficiaries under the trust are called *beneficial* interests. Confusingly, even where there is no trust over a property, it is still correct to describe its owner as the *beneficial owner*—because no one else has rights of ownership over it.

Further reading

- John McGhee (ed), *Snell's Equity*, 33rd edn (ThomsonReuters, 2015) ch 2
- *Halsbury's Laws of Australia*, 'Equity', [185-175]–[185-195] (Commonwealth law on equitable property interests)

bequeath

See **give, devise and bequeath**.

best endeavours / reasonable endeavours

Contracting parties commonly promise to use *best endeavours* or *reasonable endeavours* to carry out a particular act. The parties may be content to use the terms believing that each term has been litigated on many occasions and therefore offers the security of a formula 'tried and tested'. But this belief (if it exists) is only partly true: yes, the terms have been heavily litigated, but only because their meaning is always context-dependent. And because their measure always varies with circumstances, they in fact possess little certainty. Their context-dependency ought to discourage their use, not encourage it.

'best endeavours'

Although hallowed by use, *best endeavours* remains inherently vague. Goff J once asked rhetorically whether anything could be less specific or more uncertain than an exhortation to use *best endeavours*: *Bower v Bantam Investments Ltd* [1972] 3 All ER 349, 355.

Some cases hold that *best endeavours* imposes an onerous obligation:

- *Best endeavours* 'means what it says—it does not mean second-best endeavours. … [The promisor] must, broadly speaking, leave no stone unturned …': *Sheffield District Railway Co v Great Central Railway Co* (1911) 27 TLR 451, 452.
- *Best endeavours* 'requires the party to apply itself conscientiously to the task … with the vigour which would be expected if it were prudently attempting to secure its own interests': *Hawkins v Pender Bros Pty Ltd* [1990] 1 Qd R 135, 150.

But other cases hold that *best endeavours* requires little or no more than 'reasonable endeavours':

- *Best endeavours* requires no more than doing what can reasonably be done in the circumstances: *Terrell v Mabie Todd & Co Ltd* [1952] 2 TLR 574.
- *Best endeavours* does not require endeavours 'beyond the bounds of reason': *Hospital Products Ltd v United States Surgical Corp* (1984) 156 CLR 41, 64 (Gibbs CJ).
- *Best endeavours* requires doing what is reasonable in the circumstances, having regard to the nature, capacity, qualifications, and responsibilities of the promisor viewed in the light of the particular contract: *Transfield Pty Ltd v Arlo International Ltd* (1980) 144 CLR 83, 101 (Mason J).

'reasonable endeavours'

The same vagueness inherent in *best endeavours* is present in *reasonable endeavours*—as where a party promises to use *reasonable endeavours* to achieve a stated result. The extent of the obligation is always context-dependent, making decisions on the phrase of little precedential value in other cases.

Some decisions observe the semantic distinction between *reasonable* and *best*. They hold that an obligation to use *reasonable endeavours* is generally less onerous than an obligation to use *best endeavours*: see Kim Lewison, *The Interpretation of Contracts*, 6th edn (Sweet & Maxwell, 2015) [16.07]. Australian judges occasionally take this view also: ie, an obligation to use *reasonable endeavours* is not as onerous as one to use *all reasonable endeavours* or *best endeavours*: *Stepping Stones Child Care Centre (ACT) Pty Ltd v Early Learning Services Ltd* [2013] ATCSC 173, [274]–[300].

But (as discussed above) other decisions hold that there is no substantial difference between *best endeavours* and *reasonable endeavours*. Both require doing only what is 'reasonable' in the circumstances. See, eg, *Electricity Generation Corp v Woodside Energy Ltd* [2014] HCA 7; (2014) 251 CLR 640, [41]. The Singapore Court of Appeal has said that the gap between *best endeavours* and *all reasonable endeavours*—if, conceptually, it exists at all—is a small one: *KS Energy Services Ltd v BR Energy (M) Sdn Bhd* [2014] SGCA 16, [89].

Limits of obligation

Neither *best endeavours* nor *reasonable endeavours* requires the promisor to sacrifice its own commercial interests: *CPC Group Ltd v Qatari Diar Real Estate Investment Co* [2010] EWHC 1535 (Ch), [250]–[252]; *Electricity Generation Corp v Woodside Energy Ltd* [2014] HCA 7; (2014) 251 CLR 640, [41]. But just how far the promisor must go depends on the nature and terms of the contract in question. In some cases, the promisor may have to do a great deal (*Jet2.com Ltd v Blackpool Airport Ltd* [2012] EWCA Civ 417; [2012] 2 All ER (Comm) 1053); but in others, it can put its own business interests first (*Electricity Generation Corp v Woodside Energy Ltd* [2014] HCA 7; (2014) 251 CLR 640, [40]–[43]). Also, an obligation to use *best endeavours* or *reasonable endeavours* to achieve a stated result in an ongoing commercial arrangement may allow the promisor to look after its own interests more than is permissible in a one-off deal. An example is a vendor's obligation in a contract for the sale of land to use *best endeavours* to obtain planning permission, without which the sale cannot proceed: *IBM United Kingdom Ltd v Rockware Glass Ltd* [1980] FSR 333, 343 (Buckley LJ); *Paltara Pty Ltd v Dempster* (1991) 6 WAR 85, 89 (Malcolm CJ and Pidgeon J).

Tested objectively

Whether a person (the promisor) has used *reasonable endeavours* or *best endeavours* is tested objectively, not subjectively. That is, the test is what steps a reasonable bystander would consider the promisor should take, not what steps the promisor personally considers they should take: *Electricity Generation Corporation v Woodside Energy Ltd* [2014] HCA 7; (2014) 251 CLR 640, [56] (Gageler J). In applying the objective test, relevant circumstances include the commercial context of the promise, and the promisor's age, intelligence, wealth, and business contacts: *Transfield Pty Ltd v Arlo International Ltd* (1980) 144 CLR 83, 101 (Mason J).

Variants

Occasional variants of *reasonable endeavours* and *best endeavours* are seen. Doubtless the parties intend these variants to suggest subtle differences, but it is doubtful whether any variant makes a significant difference. The following are common variants:

- ***best reasonable endeavours***. At first sight, this might suggest something more onerous than *reasonable endeavours*: *Foster v Hall* [2012] NSWCA 122, [33] (Macfarlan JA). However, the difference is minimal, particularly if *best endeavours* requires little more than doing what is reasonable (see discussion, above).
- ***all reasonable endeavours***. UK and Singapore cases generally hold this to be more onerous than (mere) *reasonable endeavours*: *MacTaggart & Mickel Homes Ltd v Hunter* [2010] CSOH 130; *EDI Central Ltd v National Car Parks* [2012] Scot CS CSIH 6, [28]. These cases hold that *all reasonable endeavours* is on a par with *best endeavours*: *Rhodia International Holdings Ltd v Huntsman International LLC* [2007] EWHC 292 (Comm), [33]. This is because *reasonable endeavours* might require the obligor to take only *one* reasonable course of action, but *not all* reasonable courses of action: *Rhodi International Holdings Ltd v Huntsman International LLC*, above, [33]; *KS Energy Services Ltd v BR Energy (M) Sdn Bhd* [2014] SGCA 16, [63]. But as with other expressions, the meaning of *all reasonable endeavours* is context-dependent. For example, Australian courts have held that whether *all reasonable steps* have been taken to find a witness is commensurate with the importance of the witness's evidence: *ZL v The Queen* (2010) 208 A Crim R 325, [32] (Nettle JA), applied in *R v TI (No 2)* [2015] ACTSC 208; (2015) 11 ACTLR 58, [49] (Penfold J).
- ***reasonable commercial endeavours***. The addition of 'commercial' implies that the promisor must take commercially realistic steps to achieve the stated result, including (in the

particular context) seeking to persuade a related entity to undertake contractual obligations: *Cypjayne Pty Ltd v Babcock & Brown International Pty Ltd* [2011] NSWCA 173, [68]–[70].

Vagueness: some issues

The inherent vagueness of *best endeavours* and *reasonable endeavours*, and their variants, means that it is always preferable to indicate precisely what must be done. Otherwise, obligations are left uncertain. For example:

- Do *reasonable endeavours* or *best endeavours* require the promisor to expend large sums of money to achieve the desired end?
- Do *best endeavours* require the promisor to appeal against an initial rejection by an administrative decision-maker? See *IBM United Kingdom Ltd v Rockware Glass Ltd* [1980] FSR 335 (Buckley LJ: probably yes).
- Do *best endeavours* require the promisor to press on with securing necessary approvals until all reasonable prospects of appeal are exhausted (*Hawkins v Pender Bros Pty Ltd* [1990] 1 Qd R 135), or seek to enter into agreements with relevant authorities to achieve the desired end (*Joseph Street Pty Ltd v Tan* [2012] VCA 113)?
- Do *reasonable endeavours* or *best endeavours* excuse a promisor who has done *their* best but has been let down by the actions of their agents, contractors or specialist advisers (*Masters v Belpate Pty Ltd* (2001) 10 BPR 18,527, [60]–[65])?
- Do *reasonable endeavours* require the promisor to keep trying, over and over again, to achieve the desired end? Answer: maybe, depending on events as they unfold, including extraordinary events: *Yewbelle Ltd v London Green Developments Ltd* [2006] EWHC 3166 (Ch), [123] (Lewison J), affirmed [2007] EWCA Civ 475, [29], [33], [122], [124].

Further reading

- Kenneth A Adams, *A Manual of Style for Contract Drafting*, 4th edn (ABA, 2017) ch 8 (preferring *reasonable* over *best* (because a court may interpret *best* as requiring extraordinary measures), and preferring *efforts* over *endeavours*)
- Kim Lewison, *The Interpretation of Contracts*, 6th edn (Sweet & Maxwell, 2015) [16.07]

between

Two items only?

Etymologically, *between* (Old English *bi-*) suggests a relationship between two things only. This is reflected in some case law, holding that a choice *between* items assumes two items only:

- A gift by will 'to be divided *between* A and the children of B' was a gift of one-half to A and one-half to the children of B: *Re Walbran* [1906] 1 Ch 64 (B had 4 children).
- A gift to be divided 'equally *between* all of our nephews and nieces on my wife's side and my niece'—there being 22 nephews and nieces on the wife's side—was a gift to the testator's niece of ½, not 1/23rd: *Lefeavre v Pennington* 230 SW 2d 46 (Ark, 1950).

As a matter of preferred usage, '*between* expresses one-to-one relations of two or more things, while *among* expresses collective and undefined relations of three or more' (Bryan Garner, *The Elements of Legal Style*, 2nd edn (Oxford University Press, 2002) 103). Nevertheless, the question is always what the parties meant by *between*, not what the preferred usage or etymology suggests. Thus, if a document dividing property indicates that drafter intended *between* to mean a division into three or more parts, the court must interpret accordingly. On this basis, a gift to be divided *between* 'A and the children of B' may well intend a division by headcount: see, eg, *Re Harper* [1914] 1 Ch 70; *Re Ninnes* [1920] SALR 480; *Re Cossentine* [1933] Ch 119; *Re Alcock* [1945] Ch 264.

between / among

Faced with a choice of *between* or *among*, some writers prefer *among* to indicate a division or choice between more than two things or people. So, some would say: 'A and B agreed *between* [not *among*] themselves', but 'A, B, and C agreed *among* [not *between*] themselves'.

> 'But where there is no agreement *between* or *among* co-owners which provides for the termination of the co-ownership[,] or where an agreement *between* or *among* co-owners would prevent the termination of the co-ownership, it would be contrary to the policy of the [legislation] to deny the remedies they afford.' [*Nullagine Investments Pty Ltd v Western Australian Club Inc* (1993) 177 CLR 635, 651 (Brennan J). The context shows that Brennan J used *between* to indicate two co-owners, and *among* to indicate more than two.]

between A *and* [*or*?] B

Where a choice is to be made between two parties (A, B), the appropriate formula is 'between A *and* B' (*not* 'between A *or* B').

between (dates)

When something is to be done '*between* [date A] and [date B]', the first and last days are generally excluded. For example, the period '*between* 1 July and 1 August' excludes both 1 July and 1 August. However, as with all expressions, context may suggest otherwise. If in doubt, amplify to 'after [date A] and before [date B]'; or if still in doubt, 'after, but excluding, [date A] and before, but excluding, [date B]'.

beyond reasonable doubt

The onus of proof borne by the prosecution in criminal proceedings: *Woolmington v DPP* [1935] AC 462, 481. Although the term trips off the tongue, its meaning is difficult to pin down. Proof 'beyond [a] reasonable doubt' does not mean proof to a scientific certainty (*R v Bracewell* (1978) 68 Cr App Rep 44, 49)—but beyond that, it is difficult to be more precise. Australian courts say (rather unhelpfully) that *beyond reasonable doubt* is 'plain English' (*Hanlon v R* [2018] VSCA 81, [13]) and that the expression 'means what it says' (*R v Dookheea* [2017] HCA 36, [41]; (2017) 262 CLR 402). In both England and Australia, appeal courts say that trial judges should not attempt an explanation, ostensibly for fear of confusing juries: *R v Stephens* [2002] EWCA Crim 1529, [14]–[15] (Keene LJ); *Thomas v R* (1960) 102 CLR 584, 595, 604; *Dawson v R* (1961) 106 CLR 1, 18. Similarly, US courts say that trial judges should not attempt to explain 'beyond reasonable doubt' to juries, because: (1) the judge may get it wrong, leading to a right of appeal; and (2) different judges may give different explanations, leading to a loss of uniformity in jury directions: *People v Redd* (1999) 698 NYS 2d 214.

Further reading

- *Halsbury's Laws of England*, 'Criminal Procedure' (vol 28, 2015) [452]
- Martin CJ, 'Beyond Reasonable Doubt' (2010) 1 NTLR 225

biannual / biennial

Biannual means twice-yearly; six-monthly. *Biennial* means two-yearly; every two years. The terms are often confused (as in *Luen Fook Tong Inc v Lowe* [2011] NSWSC 1004, [55], where a requirement in an association's constitution for 'biannual' general meetings was an error for 'biennial' meetings).

Blackacre

The name given to a parcel of land in hypothetical examples, as in: 'Assume that A conveys Blackacre to B'. Where the example involves more than one parcel of land, each is given a distinguishing colour, such as Redacre, Whiteacre, Greenacre.

black-letter books

Books published between 1482 and 1679 containing transcriptions of cases from the Year Books; called black-letter books because of their heavy Gothic typeface. FW Maitland considered that the transcriptions contained many inaccuracies, being full of 'mere, sheer nonsense': 'Introduction', *Year Books Series, 1 & 2 Ed II* (Selden Society, 1903) vol 17, xxi. To be distinguished from the 'Black Books', which were the records of Lincoln's Inn, dating back to 1422.

See also **black-letter law**; **Year Books**.

black-letter cases

Cases (ie, judicial decisions) found in the black-letter books.

See **black-letter books**.

black-letter law

Fundamental legal principles, usually in core legal subjects such as property, contract, and tort; sometimes distinguished from 'soft law', which focuses less on rules and more on legal and social policy. By extension, a 'black-letter lawyer' is one who considers that the law should be immune from social policy, or who is more comfortable with technical legal rules than with the social forces that affect them. In some circles, 'black-letter lawyer' is a pejorative term, suggesting a lack of awareness of the social context in which law operates; in other circles, it is a term of admiration, acknowledging mastery of detailed principle.

BLANKS (IN DOCUMENTS)

Leaving blanks unfilled in documents may have more consequences than mere embarrassment. If the missing information is important, and the meaning is not clear from other parts of the document or from admissible extrinsic evidence, a court may decline to fill the blank:

- A building contract penalised the builder for late completion, but the parties left the completion date blank. There was oral evidence that the parties had agreed on a completion date, but (the court concluded) there remained some dispute about the date. Given the consequences of imposing a penalty, the court declined to insert a date: *Kemp v Rose* (1858) 1 Giff 258; 65 ER 910.

- But compare: a will named an executor as 'Percival ___ of Brighton, the father'. The court filled in the blank surname, because (in the case of wills) extrinsic evidence is admissible to show what a testator meant by the words he or she used: *In the Goods of De Rosaz* (1877) 2 PD 66, 69.

Unfilled blanks do not necessarily invalidate an agreement. The question is whether the omissions are important terms: *Brogden v Metropolitan Railway Co* (1877) 2 App Cas 666, 674; *Empirnall Holdings Pty Ltd v Machon Paull Partners Pty Ltd* (1988) 14 NSWLR 523, 530. Also, statute may authorise a tribunal or court to fill a blank by recourse to evidence specified in the statute (as in *Mears v Safecar Security Ltd* [1983] 1 QB 54, 80).

Where the date of a deed is left blank, the deed is presumed to operate from the date of its delivery, because delivery is the final act in bringing a deed into operation: *Glebe Administration Board v Tifan* [1968] 3 NSWR 455. (See further, **delivery (of deed)**.)

blind-eye knowledge

Sometimes, 'shut-eye knowledge'. A term with Nelsonian overtones, denoting a conscious decision not to enquire into something for fear of learning the truth: *Manifest Shipping Co Ltd v Uni-Polaris Shipping Co Ltd* [2001] UKHL 1; [2003] 1 AC 469, [3], [116]. It involves a suspicion that relevant facts exist, plus a deliberate decision to avoid confirming their existence. A person with 'blind-eye knowledge' of facts cannot claim ignorance of them. The legal usage is not quite the same as the general usage 'turning a blind eye', where the nuance is more 'avoiding the consequences of having to deal with the situation' (eg, where a person sees someone shoplifting but 'turns a blind eye').

See also **Nelsonian knowledge**; **shut-eye knowledge**.

BLOCK TEXT

See **CAPITALS**; **LISTS AND ENUMERATIONS**; **QUOTATIONS**.

boarder / lodger

In general usage, *boarder* and *lodger* are used interchangeably. In legal usage, it is possible to distinguish between them. A *boarder* is a person for whom the landlord provides lodging and meals: *Otter v Norman* [1989] AC 129; *Noblett & Mansfield v Manley* [1952] SASR 155, 158; *Roberts v Waverley Municipal Council* (1988) 14 NSWLR 423, 430. Providing one meal per day was enough to meet a UK statutory definition: *Otter v Norman*, above, 145–46 (continental breakfast sufficient, but not a mere 'early morning cup of tea'). A *lodger* is a person who occupies premises owned by someone else, with the owner retaining control over (and usually residing on) the premises: eg, a guest in a hotel or inn, or a longer-term occupant of a room in a house or serviced accommodation: *Allen v Liverpool Overseers* (1874) LR 9 QB 180; *Luganda v Service Hotels Ltd* [1969] 2 Ch 209. The key common characteristic of *boarder* and *lodger* is that the occupant lacks the legal right to exclusive possession: *Antoniades v Villiers* [1990] AC 417, 459 (Lord Templeman), 467 (Lord Oliver); *Commissioner for Fair Trading v Voulon* [2005] WASC 229, [59], [82].

For most modern legal purposes, it is not necessary to distinguish between *boarder* and *lodger*. Rather, the key issue is whether the person is (1) a boarder or lodger, *or* (2) a tenant. That is because, until fairly recently, residential tenancy legislation protected only 'tenants' (ie, occupants with exclusive possession), not boarders and lodgers. This encouraged extravagant drafting devices seeking to categorise occupants as mere boarders or lodgers: see, eg, *Street v Mountford* [1985] AC 809; *Radaich v Smith* (1959) 101 CLR 209. But yet more modern residential tenancy legislation extends protection to all occupants, regardless of whether they have 'exclusive possession'.

Further reading

Kevin Gray and Susan Francis Gray, *Elements of Land Law*, 5th edn (Oxford University Press, 2009) [4.1.88]–[4.1.90]

See also **tenant**.

body corporate

An entity with a legal personality, with enforceable rights and obligations, and having an existence independently of its members. The plural is *bodies corporate*, despite occasional lapses into *body corporates* by barristers (eg, *J H Rayner (Mincing Lane) Ltd v Department of Trade and Industry* [1989] Ch 72, 87) and judges (eg, *Paudel v Minister for Immigration* [2014] FCCA 665, [20]).

boilerplate

Occasionally hyphenated: *boiler-plate*; contractual language that is fixed or standardised. The term describes 'the clauses, common to nearly all commercial contracts, which deal with the way in which the contract itself operates, as opposed to the rights of the parties under the particular transaction that they have agreed upon and embodied in the substantive clauses': R Christou, *Boilerplate: Practical Clauses*, 7th edn (Thomson Reuter, 2015) [1-002].

In some contexts, *boilerplate* has pejorative overtones: 'Oh, that's just boilerplate—take no notice of it.' That is because, in practice, boilerplate provisions are standard, covering predictable subject matter, and often included out of habit or retained out of indolence. However, boilerplate in a contract is as contractually binding as any bespoke provision. And, properly used—and updated as circumstances require—boilerplate is a useful time-saver:

> 'The best boilerplate … is hammered out by the lawyer himself after a succession of attempts. It is done by preserving drafts that deal with recurrent problems and by improving those drafts, usually on a piecemeal basis, as the occasion suggests. Boilerplate need not and should not remain frozen while significant improvement is possible. A provision may have to go through many generations of change before it matures into a reliable, top-grade module of prefabricated law.' [Reed Dickerson, 'Electronic Aids to the Drafting of Legal Instruments' (1970) 1 *Rutgers Journal of Computers and the Law* 76]

Examples of topics commonly covered by boilerplate clauses:

- **Arbitration / Alternative dispute resolution**—the procedures for resolving disputes between the parties
- **Assignment**—whether a party may assign rights, and whether the other party's consent is required
- **Business days**—where the day for doing something is not a business day, performance is postponed until the next business day
- **Confidentiality**—the steps the parties must take to maintain the confidentiality of information

- **Costs**—who bears the costs of the agreement
- **Counterparts**—a contract that is in two more parts or documents is read as a single contract
- **Entire agreement**—the written agreement is the sole source of the terms which bind the parties
- **Force majeure**—a party's obligations to perform are excused by circumstances beyond the party's control
- **Further assurance**—a party must do whatever is required to ensure that the other party receives the full benefit of the contract
- **Governing law**—specifying the law of which country or state/province governs the contract
- **No partnership**—the arrangement between the parties does not constitute a partnership (thus excluding the application of partnership law)
- **Notices**—the ways in which notices are to be given
- **Severability**—if a part of the contract is found to be unenforceable, the rest of the contract continues to apply
- **Variation**—how the contract can be varied (usually, only in writing)
- **Waiver**—whether a party may waive rights and obligations (usually, only in writing).

(See separate entries for each of these topics.)

bona fide

Latin (adverb, adjective): in good faith, honestly; sometimes in the sense of 'genuine'. Older usage sometimes hyphenated the term, *bona-fide*.

Meaning: in good faith

Where the meaning is *in good faith*, no sound reason exists for retaining the Latin, which carries no more precision than the English. Thus, 'John acted *bona fide*' means no more and no less than 'John acted in good faith' or 'John acted honestly'.

Meaning: genuine

Sometimes, *bona fide* is used to mean 'genuine'. In the following examples, *genuine* carries the intended meaning more than 'in good faith' or 'honestly':

- A '*bona fide* traveller' means a salesperson who does in fact travel about soliciting orders: *Killick v Graham* [1896] 2 QB 196, 201.
- The '*bona fide* use' of a trade mark means the open and genuine use of the trade mark: *Baume & Co Ltd v AH Moore Ltd* [1958] Ch 907, 921.
- A '*bona fide* occupant' of premises is a person whose occupation is substantial and genuine: *Morgan v Davis* [1962] NSWR 1013, 1017.

See also **honestly**; **in good faith**.

bona fides

Latin (noun): good faith; honest intent. As with *bona fide*, no good reason exists for retaining the Latin. Thus, 'John displayed *bona fides*' means 'John showed good faith' or 'John acted with honest intent'.

See also **in good faith**.

bona vacantia

Latin: vacant (ie, ownerless) goods. The term is used in modern law mainly to describe the legal status of two kinds of property:

1. The property of a person who dies without a will (ie, intestate) and with no one entitled to inherit (in which case the property vests in the Crown as 'bona vacantia'). Historically, the term was not applied to the intestate's real estate, which 'escheated' to the Crown (ie, reverted to the Crown, which had always been the underlying feudal owner); but escheat was abolished in 1925 (*Administration of Estates Act 1925*, s 45), and real estate now vests in the Crown as 'bona vacantia'.
2. The property of a company that has been dissolved (in which case, the property vests in the Crown as 'bona vacantia': *Companies Act 2006*, s 1012).

To lawyers, the Latin implies in some contexts not merely that the property is (or appears to be) ownerless, but how it became so. That nuance is lost in a plain-English translation such as 'ownerless property' or 'property without an apparent owner'. Nevertheless, for the needs of most readers, a plain-English translation will suffice. Also—as if to demonstrate that *bona vacantia* is not a true term of art—some modern statutes dispense with the term completely: eg, 'If an intestate dies leaving no person who is entitled to the intestate estate, the State is entitled to the whole of the intestate estate' (*Succession Act 2006* (NSW), s 136).

See also **escheat**.

bondsman

Historically, a serf or villein (also termed *bondman*). In modern times, the person providing a performance bond. There is no settled gender-neutral term.

bracket principle

The principle that a valuer is not negligent in providing a valuation that miscalculates the value of property, as long as the valuation falls within a 10% (or sometimes 15%) band from the actual value. Also termed *margin-of-error principle*. The principle probably derives from *Singer & Friedlander Ltd v John Wood & Co* [1977] EG 569. Although termed a 'principle', it would be better termed a 'rebuttable presumption': if an error is within the band, the *starting* presumption is that the valuer was not negligent, but a party may be able to reverse the presumption and show that the valuer was in fact negligent: *Adwell Holdings Pty Ltd v Smith* [2003] NSWCA 103, [9] (Meagher JA).

BRACKETS

Terminology

In British and Commonwealth legal usage:

- the paired symbols ( ) are called variously brackets, round brackets or parentheses
- the paired symbols [ ] are usually called *square brackets*.

This differs from US legal usage, which prefers *parentheses* ( ) and *brackets* [ ].

This book follows British and Commonwealth usage.

Usage: round brackets

To mark off explanatory material

In standard usage, brackets ( ) often mark off material that is explanatory. This technique is used widely in statutes, consigning to history Lord Esher's aphorism that 'in an Act of Parliament there are no such things as brackets any more than there are such things as stops': *Duke of Devonshire v O'Connor* (1890) 24 QBD 468, 478.

Example

> 'This section has effect only for the purpose of preventing the title of a disponee being questioned (and so does not affect the lawfulness of a disposition)': *Land Registration Act 2002*, s 26(3).

Here, the material in brackets helps clarify the preceding statement. Instead of brackets, the drafter *could* have inserted a comma to introduce the text that follows—but that would have given each part of the sentence equal weight, obscuring the chiefly explanatory nature of the second half of the sentence.

Of course, this usage is not peculiar to statutory drafting. Contractual documents also commonly use brackets to mark off explanatory material:

- (including ...)
- (such as ...)
- (whether or not ...).

At other times, the bracketed material, while still explanatory, carves out exceptions:

- (but not ...)
- (except for ...).

Always omit explanatory material (whether bracketed or not) that is so self-evident as to be otiose: *Investors Compensation Scheme Ltd v West Bromwich Building Society* [1998] 1 WLR 896, 904 (Lord Lloyd).

To mark off subsidiary material

In standard usage, brackets also mark off material that is subsidiary. In legal writing, this poses a potential issue of interpretation: do you give the marked-off material the same weight as the surrounding text? And of course a busy reader may skip bracketed material, considering it less important than the surrounding material: *Investors Compensation Scheme Ltd v West Bromwich Building Society*, above, 902–03 (Lord Lloyd).

The case law suggests that courts do not usually treat legal text as less important merely because it is enclosed within brackets.

Examples

- A statute required a notice to include a statement about inspecting a company's articles of association. The included statement had to specify 'a place (in England or Wales) at which the articles of association may be inspected'; it also had to specify inspection times 'of at least two hours on each of at least three days (including a Saturday or Sunday or both) ...' Held, the brackets did not render the bracketed words optional: *Elim Court RTM Co Ltd v Avon Freeholds Ltd* [2017] EWCA Civ 89; [2017] 3 WLR 876, [37]–[38].
- A contract for the sale of land required the buyer to notify the seller of two matters. The first matter was to be notified '(within 10 Business Days)' [ie, brackets] and the second matter was to be notified 'within 5 Business Days' [no brackets]. Held, the use of

brackets did not characterise the first period as a mere 'aspirational goal', devoid of legal effect: *Mentech Resources Pty Ltd v MCG Resources Pty Ltd* [2013] QCA 79, [68]–[71] (Gotterson JA).

To replace commas

Consider using brackets to replace a pair of commas, to aid the readability of a sentence otherwise overloaded with commas.

Before	After
The tenant must, unless excused by the landlord, pay rent on time and must notify the landlord, or the landlord's agent, that payment has been made.	The tenant must (unless excused by the landlord) pay rent on time and must notify the landlord (or the landlord's agent) that payment has been made.

However, as with excessive commas, too many brackets can weigh a sentence down:

> 'This is not (subject to an exception, below) how I would see your case (ie, the one presently in court), because the principles of interpretation (as set out in court decisions) require courts (but not mediators) to apply settled approaches (which are not strictly rules).'

To enclose defined terms or acronyms

Brackets are used to enclose defined terms or acronyms.

> The parties to this contract ('the parties') are Mr Jones and Approachable Barristers Chambers Ltd ('ABC').

Often, to help catch the eye, the enclosed material is in bold, and either with or without quotation marks.

- The parties to this contract (**'the parties'**) are Mr Jones and Approachable Barristers Chambers Ltd (**'ABC'**).
- The parties to this contract (**the parties**) are Mr Jones and Approachable Barristers Chambers Ltd (**ABC**).

Strictly, the brackets themselves should not be in bold—they mark off the enclosed material but are not part of it. However, no confusion arises if this subtlety is overlooked.

Usage: square brackets

To indicate interpolated material

Square brackets [ ] indicate that the author has interpolated material of his or her own—sometimes to provide information or explanation, and sometimes to indicate surprise or to point out an error in the original.

Examples

- 'The judge said that he was *completely* [emphasis in original] surprised by this tactic.' (Square brackets added to explain use of italics.)
- 'Judge Judy said that her approach to judging was normal [*sic*], and that no defendant had ever protested about it before.' (Square brackets around *sic* to indicate the author's surprise.)
- 'The defendant said that the name of his son [stepson] was John.' (Square brackets indicating error in original—he said *son*, but meant *stepson*.)

The use of square brackets to indicate interpolated material is so conventional that to use round brackets for this purpose is apt to confuse the reader, and may even attract judicial opprobrium:

> '[T]he Court notes, with some considerable dismay, that plaintiff's addendum inserts material ... in such a way as to make it appear that the material was in the original, by using parenthesis rather than brackets. In legal writing, it is commonly accepted that matter added editorially is bracketed, not surrounded by parentheses, as plaintiff's counsel apparently knows from having done it thus in other quotations.' [*Walsh v Avalon Aviation Inc* 125 F Supp 2d 726, 728 (D Md, 2001). Being a US case, this quotation uses *parenthesis* [but note the singular] to mean 'round brackets', and *brackets* to mean 'square brackets'.]

To indicate material excised, rewritten, or repunctuated

Square brackets also indicate that the author has altered the quoted text by removing portions, rewriting portions, or repunctuating. For example:

Original text

> 'It is also clear that in circumstances where persons provide the purchase price for a property in unequal shares, equity presumes that they intend to hold in shares proportionate to their contributions.'

Variant	Explanation
Variant 1 '[I]n circumstances where persons provide the purchase price for a property in unequal shares, equity presumes that they intend to hold in shares proportionate to their contributions.'	Square brackets indicate that the original sentence did not begin with *In*, but rather that the quoted material starts part-way into the original sentence.
Variant 2 '[Where] persons provide the purchase price for a property in unequal shares, equity presumes that they intend to hold in shares proportionate to their contributions.'	Square brackets indicate that the original sentence did not begin with *Where*, and that the quoted material starts part-way into the original sentence.
Variant 3 '[Where] persons provide the purchase price for a property in unequal shares, equity presumes that they intend to hold in [proportionate shares].'	Square brackets at the start indicate that the original sentence did not begin with *Where*, and that the quoted material starts part-way into the original sentence. Square brackets at the end indicate a restatement of the original concluding words.

A caution: go easy

Square brackets intrude into the text. The reader may find them irritating. Sometimes they can be removed easily, as in the second of these examples:

1. The judge said that '[t]his is not the way to write clearly'.
2. The judge said: 'This is not the way to write clearly.'

Usage: law reports

Publishers of law reports generally distinguish between round brackets and square brackets when referring to cases. *Square brackets* indicate that the reports are organised by year; *round brackets* indicate that the reports are organised by volume number. See discussion under **CITATION OF CASES, Citing law reports.**

Punctuation issues

Whole sentence / part sentence

If a whole sentence is within brackets (whether round or square), put the full stop inside the closing bracket:

(This is a whole sentence, so the full stop appears inside the closing bracket.)

If part only of the sentence is within brackets, put the full stop outside the closing bracket:

Not a whole sentence (as anyone will tell you).

Commas around brackets

Do not insert commas on either side of brackets (though it may be necessary to retain a comma after the closing bracket).

Example 1

'The judge commented, (as was his custom), on the barrister's rumpled jacket.'

Both commas are unnecessary. Prefer:

'The judge commented (as was his custom) on the barrister's rumpled jacket.'

Example 2

'Hence, it is submitted, (and would appear to be the case), if there were an application for subdivision it would need to deal with …': *Finlay Stonemasonry Pty Ltd v JD & Sons Nominees Pty Ltd* (2011) 28 NTLR 183, 187 (Blokland J).

Delete the comma before the bracket, but retain the comma after the bracket:

'Hence, it is submitted (and would appear to be the case), if there were an application for subdivision it would need to deal with …'

Brackets within brackets

Brackets within brackets can appear clumsy. Consider commas or dashes instead of the internal brackets:

Before	After
The court (which was sitting in chambers (clearly of a temporary nature) in a side street) felt aggrieved at the lack of suitable accommodation.	The court (which was sitting in chambers—clearly of a temporary nature—in a side street) felt aggrieved at the lack of suitable accommodation.

Stylistic issues

Keep bracketed material short, omitting redundancies:

Not

(the court stated that this was not always the case)

but rather

(this was not always the case)

Also, for material within brackets, prefer a parallel structure:

Not

The requirements for continuing education are complex (solicitors must undergo monthly continuing education, barristers are required to undergo annual continuing education, magistrates should undergo two-yearly continuing education, judges are exempt from continuing education).

but rather

The requirements for continuing education are complex (solicitors must undergo monthly continuing education, barristers must undergo annual continuing education, magistrates must undergo two-yearly continuing education, and judges are exempt from continuing education).

or (if the context is clear)

The requirements for continuing education are complex (solicitors—monthly; barristers—annually; magistrates—two-yearly; judges—exempt).

Brackets and ambiguity

Misplaced brackets: words

A misplaced bracket can change the meaning of a phrase or sentence. For example:

Under a deed between investors and a statutory compensation entity, the investors assigned to the entity their right to recover money from certain third parties. However, under an exception, the investors were free to seek to recover '[a]ny claim (whether sounding in rescission for undue influence or otherwise)' they might have against the third parties. Held, the meaning was 'any claim sounding in rescission (whether for undue influence or otherwise)'; ie, the parties had misplaced the brackets, and the words were to be read as the parties intended, not as written: *Investors Compensation Scheme Ltd v West Bromwich Building Society* [1998] 1 WLR 896 (HL).

Misplaced brackets: formulas

A misplaced bracket in a formula can be disastrous.

Examples

1. A formula in a land development contract for calculating a profit (P) expressed as 'P = A – B – C' is not the same as 'P = A – (B – C)'. [Example based on *Chartbrook Ltd v Persimmon Homes Ltd* [2009] UKHL 38; [2009] 1 AC 1101—one calculation produced a profit of about £897,000, the other produced a profit of about £4,500,000. The formulas pinpointed the parties' contrasting claims; the original document used words, not figures.]
2. Assume that the actual cost of a development project (A) exceeds the budgeted cost (B). An agreement to pay '25% of the actual cost in excess of the budgeted cost', read literally, could be expressed as '¼(A–B)' or as '(¼A)–B'; but the latter would be 'commercial nonsense': *Chartbrook Ltd v Persimmon Homes Ltd*, above, example given by Lord Walker.
3. A formula in a lease for calculating the annual rent (AR) expressed as 'AR = HLR2 – (HLR1 × ½) + rent for the previous year' is not the same as 'AR = (HLR2 – HLR1) × ½ + rent for the previous year': *Leahy v Austwin Management Services Pty Ltd* [2011] QCA 186.

See also **ACRONYMS; CITATION OF CASES; DEFINITIONS; PUNCTUATION; sic.**

break costs

The cost to a lender (usually a bank) when a borrower repays a loan before the repayment date. The costs are usually calculated on: (1) the cost to the lender of relending the money on the open market; plus (2) the lender's internal costs of processing the early repayment. The loan agreement between lender and borrower usually allows the lender to pass the break costs on to the borrower.

brevi manu

Latin: with a short hand (ie, by direct action, without court proceedings). The Latinism is preserved particularly (but not exclusively) in contract law, where a person is said to rescind or terminate a contract *brevi manu*. An appropriate plain-English translation suffices, with no loss of legal precision:

- '[A vendor] may not use the power of rescission to get out of a sale *brevi manu* [prefer: *summarily*], since by doing so he makes a nullity of the whole elaborate and protracted transaction.' [*Selkirk v Romar Investments Ltd* [1963] 1 WLR 1415, 1422 (Viscount Radcliffe)]
- 'These are necessary conditions for the exercise of this [power to punish for contempt of court], whatever the type of contempt against which it is exercised and whether in exercising it the court is described as acting *brevi manu*, or immediately, or instanter, or of its own motion, or summarily.' [*Balogh v St Albans Crown Court* [1975] QB 73, 89 (Stephenson LJ, with translations and near-synonyms)]
- 'The case was dealt with *brevi manu* [prefer: *summarily*]. Lord Halsbury said that the point taken was unarguable.' [*McQuarrie v James* (1954) 92 CLR 262, 298 (Fullagar J)]

brevitatis causa

Latin: for the sake of brevity; in the interests of brevity. A woefully pedantic Latinism in the face of a plain-English translation:

> 'The measure of the proper award to a widow (who is generally the main dependant and to whom alone I refer, *brevitatis causa* [prefer: *in the interests of brevity*]) is a sum which, prudently invested, would provide her with an annuity equal in amount to the support that she has probably lost through the death of her husband …' [*Cookson v Knowles* [1979] AC 556, 576 (Lord Fraser of Tullybelton)]

BREVITY

Aim for brevity in legal writing (as in business and technical writing generally). If you can say something in fewer words, do so. If you can remove a redundancy, do so. If you can shorten a sentence, do so. If you can remove embedded (nested) information, do so. But brevity is not an end in itself. Brevity that leads to obscurity is misplaced:

> 'The purpose of the [*Animals Act 1971*] was to simplify the law. … Section 2 contains provisions relating to liability for damage done by dangerous animals. Unfortunately the language of section 2(2) is itself opaque. In this instance the parliamentary draftsman's zeal for brevity has led to obscurity.' [*Mirvahedy v Henley* [2003] 2 AC 491, [9] (Lord Nicholls)]

And so in addition to brevity, legal writing requires clarity. Never prune at the expense of clarity. As expressed by Justice Michael Kirby:

> 'Brevity, simplicity and clarity. These are the hallmarks of good judgment writing. But the greatest of these is clarity.' ['On the Writing of Judgments' (1990) 64 *Australian Law Journal* 691, 704]

See also **EMBEDDED (NESTED) INFORMATION; PROLIXITY; SENTENCE LENGTH; SESQUIPEDALIANISM; SIMPLER WORDS AND PHRASES; SURPLUSAGE (PRESUMPTION AGAINST); WORD STRINGS; WORD PAIRINGS.**

brief (noun)

From Latin *brevis* ('short') and Anglo-Norman *bref* (a letter or dispatch, or a writ or summons). In England and Commonwealth countries, written instructions which a solicitor gives to a barrister—eg, 'brief to appear [in court]', 'brief to advise', 'brief on evidence'; hence 'to brief'—ie, to instruct a barrister to appear in court. In US legal usage, a brief is a written outline of argument prepared for the court.

brocard

An elementary legal maxim or saying, usually derived from Latin or the early common law.

- 'In the system of law in which I was brought up, that was expressed by one of those *brocards* of which perhaps we have been too fond, but which often express very neatly what is wanted: "Certum est quod certum reddi potest".' [*May & Butcher Ltd v R* [1934] 2 KB 17, 21 (Viscount Dunedin)].
- 'Plainly, the source for these remarks was the well-known Latin brocard *cuius est solum, eius est usque ad coelum et ad inferos*.' [*Star Energy Weald Basin Ltd v Bocardo SA* [2011] AC 380; [2010] UKSC 35, [10] (Lord Hope)]

See also **certum est quod certum reddi potest**; **cuius est solum**; **maxim**.

brown land site

Sometimes *brownland* (single word): eg, *brownland site*. Land that has already been used or developed.

See also **green field site**.

brutum fulmen

Latin: literally, an insensible thunderbolt. Used in the sense of 'an empty threat', one that cannot be carried into effect; sometimes used in the sense of 'a pointless exercise'. Unless readers are likely to know Latin, prefer an English translation.

- 'The court should guard against slipping into playing the role of King Canute. Even though an order may be desirable for the protection of privacy, and may be made in accordance with the principles currently being applied by the courts, there may come a point where it would simply serve no useful purpose and would merely be characterised, in the traditional terminology, as a *brutum fulmen* [prefer: *pointless exercise*]. It is inappropriate for the court to make vain gestures.' [*Mosley v News Group Newspapers Ltd* [2008] EWHC 687 (QB), [34] (Eady J). Eady J's own expression 'serve no useful purpose' would have been sufficient, needing no elaboration in Latin.]
- '[I]f the conveyance … purports to convey land beyond the pre-existing boundary, then it is to that extent *a brutum fulmen* [prefer: an *empty exercise*; or *worthless*]. The seller cannot convey that to which he has no title.' [*Parmar v Upton* [2015] EWCA Civ 795, [13] (Briggs LJ)]

building

A word that is notoriously difficult to define. There are two main issues:

Substantial structure?

How permanent or substantial need a structure be to qualify as a *building*? The general concept is said to be a structure of brick or stone and covered with a roof: *Moir v Williams* [1892] 1 QB 264, 270 (Lord Esher MR). However, modern construction techniques employ building materials well beyond brick or stone, and clearly some structures can be 'buildings' even though not roofed-over. The term has been heavily litigated and is clearly context-dependent, as the following examples show:

- A screen erected to preclude a neighbour acquiring a prescriptive right to light was not a building: *Paddington Corporation v A-G* [1906] AC 1.
- An advertising hoarding may be a building (*Nussey v Provincial Bill Posting Co* [1909] 1 Ch 734) or may not be a building (*Foster v Fraser* [1893] 3 Ch 158).
- A subway was a building: *Schweder v Worthing Gas Light & Coke Co* [1912] 1 Ch 83.
- A concrete driveway was a building for the purposes of legislation regulating neighbours' rights over encroaching 'buildings': *Clarke v Wilkie* (1977) 17 SASR 134; *Ward v Griffiths* (1987) 9 NSWLR 458.
- Model houses in a miniature village were buildings: *Buckinghamshire County Council v Callingham* [1952] 1 All ER 1166.
- A tennis court with a fence was not a building (because 'building' implies a structure with a roof): *Hilderbrandt v Stephen* [1964] NSWSR 740.

The only lesson to draw from cases such as these is that, where possible, indicate what kinds of structures you mean by *building*.

Non-structure?

Case law indicates that, depending on context, 'building' may include areas that are not confined within a structure. For example:

- For the purposes of rating law, 'building' included the land on which a building stood: *City of Vancouver v Bishop of Vancouver Island* [1921] 2 AC 384.
- For the purposes of compulsory acquisition law, 'building' included the gardens ancillary to a house: *Governors of St Thomas's Hospital v Charing Cross Railway Co* (1861) 1 J & H 400; (1861) 70 ER 802.
- For the purposes of leasehold enfranchisement law, 'building' included the airspace above the structure and the subsoil beneath it: *LM Homes Ltd v Queen Court Freehold Co Ltd* [2020] EWCA Civ 371; [2020] 2 WLR 1135.

Cases such as these point up the importance of context when interpreting *building*. If your meaning could be open to doubt, always clarify.

See also **structure / structural**.

BULLET POINTS

Use bullet points to break up information-strings, even in formal writing. A bulleted list helps catch the reader's eye in a way that run-on text can never do.

Points of style

Approaches to the use of bullet points vary. However, the following conventions are fairly well settled in legal writing.

Sentence fragments

Where each bullet point is a sentence fragment (not a complete sentence), style bullet points by:

- using a colon after the lead-in statement
- making the bullet points flow grammatically from the lead-in, using a parallel structure
- starting each bullet point (including the first) with a lower-case letter (unless the word is a proper noun)

- omitting conjunctions ('and', 'or') between bullet points
- omitting punctuation at the end of bullet points (except the last one)
- putting a full stop at the end of the last bullet point.

Occasionally, for idiomatic flow, it may be necessary to depart from one or more of these conventions. See, for example, the bullet list under **lien**. There, each bullet point ends with a full stop, even though most bullet points in the list are mere sentence fragments. This is because *some* bullet points include full sentences. To end them without full stops would be grammatically perverse; but equally perverse would be to end some bullet points with full stops and others without—hence the addition of full stops to all bullet points. Likewise, see the bullet list under **more or less**; there, each bullet point takes the form of a compressed sentence, beginning with a capital letter—and therefore logically ends with a full stop.

Complete sentences

Where each bullet point is a complete sentence:

- Follow the conventions for sentences—ie, start each bullet point with a capital letter, and end each bullet point with a full stop.
- If useful, you can include more than one sentence per bullet point.

Do not mix sentence fragments and complete sentences

Avoid mixing sentence fragments with complete sentences. A bullet list should be *all* sentence fragments or *all* complete sentences.

No numbers for bullet points

Bullet points are not numbered. This may be problematic in long lists, if you later need to refer to items in the list: eg, 'Refer to the 10th item in the list.' In such a case, consider using a numbered list.

Hanging indents

Use hanging indents for bullet points, to help demarcate each bullet point clearly from its neighbours.

See also **LISTS AND ENUMERATIONS**; **PUNCTUATION**.

bullet repayment

A single repayment of a loan at the end of the loan period.

Compare **balloon payment**.

Bullock order

A court order that an unsuccessful defendant pay the costs of a successful defendant, where the plaintiff had joined both defendants because of doubts over which was the proper defendant: *Bullock v London General Omnibus Co* [1907] 1 KB 264; *Gould v Vaggelas* (1984) 157 CLR 215. Needless to say, this legal shorthand will mean nothing to a non-lawyer.

business day

Meaning

A day on which business is transacted. Definitions may narrow or widen that meaning for particular purposes.

In statutes

Standard interpretation legislation in most jurisdictions defines 'business day' when used in statutes to mean a day that is not a Saturday, Sunday, or a public holiday in the place concerned: eg, in Australia, *Acts Interpretation Act 1901* (Cth), s 2B. In the UK, the comparable statutory term is 'working day', defined to mean (in the case of corporations) 'a day that is not a Saturday or Sunday, [is not] Christmas Day, [is not] Good Friday or [is not] any day that is a bank holiday under the Banking and Financial Dealings Act 1971 (c 80) in the part of the United Kingdom where the company is registered': *Companies Act 2006*, s 1173(1).

However, variations are found—and sometimes lead to litigation. For example, legislation in an Australian state declared a day to be a *non*-business day for the whole of the state if the day was declared a non-business day in any part of the state: *R v Macdessie* [2014] TASSC 64; (2104) 24 Tas R 311 (public holiday declared for two (small) parts of a state disqualified the day as a 'business day' everywhere in the state).

In contracts and other documents

Most commercial contracts define 'business day' as a day that is not a Saturday, Sunday, or a public holiday in the place where the contract was entered into or where it is to be performed. Generally, these definitions are straightforward. But difficulties can arise where a contract is to be performed in several jurisdictions, and a 'business day' in one jurisdiction is not a 'business day' in another.

Example

> A contract for the sale of shares defined 'business day' to mean any day except a Saturday, Sunday, or public holiday in Perth, Western Australia. The contract also provided that if the date for completion fell on a day that was not a 'business day', it was extended to the next available business day. The contract called for completion on 1 March, which was a Sunday. The next day, Monday 2 March, was a public holiday in Perth. Therefore, the day for completion (ie, the next available business day after 1 March) was Tuesday 3 March. The purchaser intended to finance the purchase with letters of credit provided by a Singaporean bank. The letters of credit defined 'business day' to mean any day (except a Saturday or Sunday) on which banks were open for general business in (relevantly) Australia, also with automatic extension to the next available business day. The letters of credit were due to expire on Sunday 1 March. Because that was a non-business day, the expiration was extended to the next business day. That day was Monday 2 March, **not** Tuesday 3 March, because (the Court held) banks were open for general business in Australia on that day (only in Perth were banks closed for general business on 2 March). The financier declined to extend the letters of credit beyond the Monday, leaving the purchaser with no finance on Tuesday 3 March. This caused the purchaser to default under the contract for the sale of shares. See *Griffin Energy Group Pty Ltd v ICICI Bank Ltd* [2015] NSWCA 29; (2015) 317 ALR 395.

Where no definition

Where the statute or the document contains no definition of *business day*, the meaning becomes a matter of interpretation in the particular context. Probably, *business day* does not mean simply 'working day' (in the sense of a day on which the parties themselves are working). Rather, it probably means a day on which business activities of the kind relevant to the particular context, are generally carried on. For example, *business day* (undefined) in a building construction contract would not include Saturdays, Sundays and public holidays, if builders in the industry do not normally work on those days; but it would (unless the contract indicated otherwise) include other days of the week, even though, for some reason, the particular builder does not work on those other days: *PPK Willoughby Pty Ltd v Eighty Eight Construction Pty Ltd* [2014] NSWSC 760, [108]–[111] (McDougall J).

Performance on non-business day

Must perform early?

Contracts sometimes provide that if the day on which something falls to be done is not a business day, it must be done on or by the *preceding* business day. Such provisions merely reflect the common law: *Mardorf Peach & Co Ltd v Attica Sea Carriers Corp of Liberia (The Laconia)* [1977] AC 850.

May perform later?

In some jurisdictions, statute allows performance on the *next* business day: eg, in some jurisdictions, a bill of exchange falling due on a non-business day is payable on the next business day. But unless an exception can be found, the promisor must perform earlier, not later.

Also, the precise terms of a 'may perform later' provision are important. The indulgence is no wider than the contractual terms allow.

Examples

- Assume that a credit facility agreement is expressed to 'expire' on a stated date. That date turns out to be a Saturday (a non-business day). Also assume that the 'business day' clause allows acts that fall to be *performed* on a non-business day to be *performed* on the next available business day. That of itself does not extend the credit until the next available business day—the letters of credit do not in terms *require* the funds to be made available on a Saturday, but merely state that the letters of credit *expire* on the Saturday. See (by analogy) *Minister for Immigration and Border Protection v Kumar* [2017] HCA 11; (2017) 260 CLR 367.
- A contractual provision allowed 'completion' of a contract for sale of land to be postponed from a Saturday, Sunday, or public holiday to the next business day. But that did not allow a corresponding extension of time for exercising an option to purchase the land, because exercising an option is not 'completion' of a contract to purchase: *Wilbow Corporation Pty Ltd v Mailli* [2001] QSC 213; [2002] 1 Qd R 574.

See also **day**; **public holiday**.

but

As sentence-opener

No grammatical 'rule' bans *but* as a sentence-opener. The law reports are full of instances where senior judges start sentences (indeed, even paragraphs) with *but*. Even statutory drafters start sentences with *but*:

> *Perpetuities and Accumulations Act 2009*, s 14
>
> (1) This section applies to an instrument to the extent that it provides for property to be held on trust for charitable purposes.
>
> (2) *But* it does not apply where the provision is made by a court or the Charity Commission for England and Wales.

An inflexible no-*buts* rule is at best a personal preference and at worst a lost opportunity.

Example

> Suppose you plan to write two sentences on the subject of precedent. The first will make a statement about the binding force of precedent. The second will qualify the statement. You could write:
>
> > 'All judgments are binding in some way. Judgments at a lower level of court, however, cannot bind a higher court.'

The reader does not glimpse the qualifying purpose of the second sentence until part-way through the sentence—until the word *however*. It would be better to immediately alert the reader to the qualification. One way is by moving *however* to the start of the second sentence:

> 'All judgments are binding in some way. However, judgments at a lower level of court cannot bind a higher court.'

But a shorter word has more punch than a longer one. So, sharpen the qualification by starting the second sentence with *But*:

> 'All judgments are binding in some way. But those at a lower level of court cannot bind a higher court.'

Some cautions

To start all contradicting or qualifying sentences with *But* would deaden the punch. So, vary the opening word. But don't ban *But*.

Also, unless you want the reader to pause, avoid a comma after *But*. While *But* speeds up the prose, the comma slows it down. Compare:

- But, with due respect to judges, litigants find court procedures intimidating.
- But with due respect to judges, litigants find court procedures intimidating.

'but for' test

In the law of negligence, a test for determining whether the negligence of one party caused the injury of another: 'Would the plaintiff have suffered the injury *but for* the negligence of the defendant?' Although lawyers are likely to understand the shorthand, non-lawyers are not. Explain it to them.

but so that

A standard, but clumsy, way of introducing a qualification. For example:

> 'I leave my property to my children, *but so that* if my children predecease me, any children who survive them are to take their parent's share.' Prefer: 'I leave my property to my children. *However* [or *But*] if my children predecease me ...'

Morton LJ treated the words *but so that* as equivalent to *provided that* or *provided always that*: *Re Litt* [1946] Ch 154, 161. But they too are ungainly substitutes for *however* or *but*.

See also **but; PROVISOS.**

buy-back

As a noun or adjective, preferably hyphenated:

- noun: 'the company undertook a *buy-back* of its shares'; 'the company entered into a *buy-back*'
- adjective: 'the company entered into a *buy-back arrangement*'.

Where used as a verb, the hyphen is less common ('I promise to *buy back* the shares'), unless implying participation in a buy-back arrangement ('I promise to *buy-back* the shares').

by [a date]

Unless context requires otherwise, when something is to be done *by* a stated date it can be done *on or before* that date: *Eastaugh v Macpherson* [1954] 3 All ER 214, 215 (Lord Evershed MR). For example:

- A tenant who is given a notice to quit the premises '*by* 31 July' has until the end of 31 July to vacate: *J H Munroe Ltd v Vancouver Properties Ltd* [1940] 3 WWR 26.
- A court submission that must by lodged '*by* 7 April' can be lodged on 7 April: *Murragong Nominees Pty Ltd v MMBW* (1985) 60 LGRA 210.

See also **from [a date]**.

by and between [persons]

Prefer *between*. An agreement made '*by and between* A and B' is made '*between* A and B'.

See also **between**.

by reason [of]

By reason of implies a close connection of cause and effect. Unless context requires otherwise, the connection must be direct, and is closer than the connection implied in 'by reference to': *Republic of Croatia v Snedden* [2010] HCA 14; (2010) 241 CLR 461, [22]–[25]. In most contexts, *by reason of* means simply *because [of]* (ibid, [69]), which (being one word, not two) is marginally preferable. However, *by reason of* is always better than the egregiously long-winded *by reason of the fact that*:

- 'However, there are bound to be other people … who are denied the automatic right to citizenship *by reason of the fact that* [prefer: *because*] their British father was not married to their non-British mother at the time of their birth.' [*R v Secretary of State for the Home Department* [2016] UKSC 56, [36] (Lady Hale)]
- 'But the question mark over the reliability of the assertion *by reason of the fact that* [prefer: *because*] it was made by an accomplice is not answered by pointing to the unlikelihood that [X's] memory of events had faded.' [*Sio v R* [2016] HCA 32; (2016) 259 CLR 47, [66] (High Court of Australia)]

by reason of the fact that

See **by reason [of]**.

by right

See **right (as of)**.

bylaw

Variants are *by-law*, *byelaw*, *bye-law*. However, *bylaw* is now the standard usage.

cadit quaestio

Latin: the question falls, the argument lapses (ie, there is nothing left to discuss). Unless the reader is likely to understand the Latin, prefer an English translation, eg:

> 'If the Bank beneficially owned the £875,000 …, *cadit quaestio* [prefer: *that is the end of the matter*] so far as the Bank's subrogation to the Lien is concerned …' [*Bank of Cyprus UK Ltd v Menelaou* [2015] UKSC 66; [2016] AC 176, [103] (Lord Neuberger)]

CADENCE

Most legal writing has a utilitarian purpose—to communicate information. But a utilitarian purpose can rise above a mundane style. Legal writing can have zest and panache, and still serve its purpose to communicate. A compelling cadence draws the reader onwards, helping the meaning flow logically. To paraphrase Justice Holmes, a carefully constructed sentence should be felt, not merely read: *United States v Johnson*, 221 US 488, 496 (1911). Good writers, including good legal writers, know this instinctively. Techniques include word choice, alliteration, literary allusions, clause structure and sentence length.

See also **ALLITERATION; ACTIVE VOICE / PASSIVE VOICE; LITERARY ALLUSIONS; SENTENCE LENGTH; SENTENCE STRUCTURE; SIMPLER WORDS AND PHRASES**.

cæteris paribus

See **ceteris paribus**.

calculated (to ...)

This inherently ambiguous term can mean (1) 'intended (to ...)', or (2) 'likely (to ...)'. Meaning (1) looks to subjective intent; meaning (2) looks to objective effect. Drafters sometimes fail to indicate which meaning they have in mind. For example, a statute may create an offence of doing something '*calculated to* offend a bystander'; or a contract may mandate compensation for an act '*calculated to* harm a party to the contract'. In each case, does 'calculated to' impose a subjective test (what did the person intend?) or an objective test (what would a reasonable bystander regard as the likely result of the conduct?).

Courts in many jurisdictions have had to wrestle with the term: see, eg, *R v Kopyto* (1987) 47 DLR (4th) 213, 257, 298–99; *Nationwide News Pty Ltd v Wills* (1992) 177 CLR 1, 24; *Secretary for Justice v Choy Bing Wing* [2011] HKEC 63, [37]; *Dhooharuika v DPP* [2014] UKPC 11; [2014] 3 WLR 1081, [42]. Where the meaning is in doubt, courts generally favour the objectively leaning 'likely to' as the intended meaning:

- Wearing clothing so closely resembling that of a police officer as to be *calculated to* deceive, meant *likely to* deceive: *Turner v Shearer* [1972] 1 WLR 1387.
- Demanding money in a manner *calculated to* cause distress, meant demanding money in a manner *likely to* cause distress (and not demanding money with the subjective intent of causing distress): *Norweb plc v Dixon* [1995] 3 All ER 952.
- Inducements *calculated to* influence voters, meant inducements *likely to* influence voters: *Crafter v Webster* (1980) 23 SASR 321.
- Actions *calculated to* cause loss, meant actions *likely to* cause loss: *Customglass Boats Ltd v Salthouse Bros Ltd* [1976] 1 NZLR 36.

An adept drafter will clarify the intended meaning of 'calculated to'—or better still, will choose another term.

Further reading

Hood Phillips, 'Calculated to Confuse' (1973) 89 *Law Quarterly Review* 175 (arguing that drafters should avoid *calculated to* and prefer language that better conveys the intended meaning)

See also **likely to**.

Calderbank letter

A letter sent by one litigating party to the other party, offering to settle the litigation, but on terms that the letter is not to be disclosed to the court except on the question of costs. Sometimes called *Calderbank offer*. Named after *Calderbank v Calderbank* [1976] Fam 93, where the practice was judicially endorsed; in England and Wales now termed a 'Part 36 letter', under Pt 36 of the *Civil Procedure Rules 1999*. Both terms ('Calderbank letter' and 'Part 36 letter') will mystify a non-lawyer reader—so explain.

calendar month

See **month**.

call option

An agreement between parties (A and B) that permits (but does not compel) one party (A) to require B to deal with property that B owns, in specified ways (eg, that B sell to A, or that B grant a lease to A).

Compare **put option**.

camera

See **in camera**.

can

can / may

In ordinary speech, *can* is often used as a synonym for *may*. But careful writers distinguish the two words: they use *can* to convey the sense of 'has the ability to', and *may* to convey the sense of 'has permission to'. For example, a child 'can' dive into a pool, even if the child 'may not' (ie, does not have permission to do so).

In legal usage, the distinction is slightly different. While *may* still connotes 'has permission to', *can* connotes rather 'has the legal power or right to'. For example:

- Where a statute lists activities in which a corporation *can* engage, it means activities in which the corporation has a legal power to engage.
- Where a statute states that a contract for the sale of land *can* only be made in writing, it means that there is no legal power to do so except in writing: *Law of Property (Miscellaneous Provisions) Act 1989*, s 2(1).
- Where a lease states that the tenant *can* trade from the premises during normal business hours, it means that the tenant has the legal right to do so.

However, even while understanding the distinction between *may* and *can*, many drafters regard *can* as too vernacular and prefer *may*. This is unlikely to cause ambiguity. Thus, in the last example above, *may* would cause no ambiguity:

> 'The tenant *may* [meaning, *has the legal right to*] trade from the premises during normal business hours.'

cannot

What of the negative form, *cannot*? Consider the following example: 'The tenant *cannot* dispose of tea leaves down the sink.' Read literally, this does not match the intended sense.

In reality, the tenant *can* (ie, is physically able to) dispose of tea leaves down the sink. Rather, it means that the tenant *must not* do so. Nevertheless, to say that the tenant *cannot* do so will not cause misunderstanding—the meaning is clear enough (*cannot* = *must not*). However, in other situations the distinction may be less clear, as in the following examples:

- A statute provides that a creditor bound by a deed of arrangement *cannot* file a summons to wind up the company. Held, while a creditor may in fact file a summons, it has has no legal standing to do so: *Torsir Pty Ltd v Maxgrow Developments Pty Ltd (No 2)* (1995) 7 BPR 14,392, 14,395.
- A statute provides that a corporation *must not* exercise certain powers and *cannot* exercise other powers. The corporation purports to exercise both kinds of powers. Held, the purported exercise of a power that *must not* be exercised may nevertheless be valid (though subject to criminal proceedings, or requiring later ratification), but the purported exercise of a power that *cannot* be exercised is always ineffectual. See *2 Elizabeth Bay Road Pty Ltd v Owners Strata Plan No 73943* [2014] NSWCA 409, [34]–[37]; (2014) 88 NSWLR 488, 496–97 (Barrett JA). (The legislation, similar in purpose to the *Commonhold and Leasehold Reform Act 2002*, placed obligations (*must*), prohibitions (*must not*), powers (*can*), and limitations (*cannot*), on the management of commonly owned buildings.)

See also **may; may not; shall / must; shall be lawful for.**

cannot

See **can**; **may not**; **shall / must**.

CANONS OF CONSTRUCTION (INTERPRETATION)

Over centuries, courts have developed guidelines to help interpret documents. These guidelines are given varying descriptions: eg, 'principles', 'presumptions', 'rules', 'canons'. Whatever description they carry, they are never ends in themselves, but merely guidelines to help glean the intentions of the parties. Nevertheless, the doctrine of precedent encourages their hardening from guidelines into dogma. Yet their essential malleability remains. For almost every canon of construction there exists a countervailing canon, leaving the court free to choose which (in the court's view) best helps elucidate the parties' intentions. The following table illustrates the point.

Canon	**Countervailing canon**
If language is plain and unambiguous, it must be given effect.	Not where a literal interpretation would lead to absurd or mischievous results or thwart the parties' manifest purpose.
Words and phrases that have received judicial interpretation to be understood according to that interpretation.	Not where the document indicates that the parties intended the words or phrases to have a different meaning.
Words are to be taken in their ordinary meanings unless they are technical words or terms of art.	Not where the document indicates that the parties intended otherwise. In this way, a popular word may bear a technical meaning, and a technical word may bear a popular meaning.
Every word must be given effect.	Not where the word is inadvertent or repugnant to the rest of the document (and so can be rejected as surplusage).

(continued)

(Continued)

Canon	Countervailing canon
The same language used repeatedly in the same context is presumed to bear the same meaning throughout the document.	Not where the parties clearly intended otherwise (allowing different meanings to be assigned to make the document consistent).
Words are interpreted according to the proper grammatical effect of their arrangement.	Not where strict adherence to rules of grammar would defeat the parties' evident purpose.
General terms receive a general interpretation.	Not where the general words are limited by specific terms or by the scope and purpose of the document.
Where general words follow an enumeration, the general words apply only to things of the same general kind as those enumerated (ie, the *eiusdem generis* principle).	Not where *eiusdem generis* would confine the operation of a clause more narrowly than the parties intended.
Qualifying or limiting words or clauses are taken to refer to the immediately preceding antecedent.	Not where evidence, sense, and meaning require a different interpretation.
Punctuation is relevant to interpretation.	Punctuation does not control the plain and evident meaning of language.
Permissive words (eg, 'may') are to be distinguished from mandatory words (eg, 'shall', 'must').	Permissive words may be read as mandatory words, and vice versa, when necessary to reflect the parties' intention.
A proviso qualifies the provision immediately preceding it.	Not where the proviso is clearly intended to have a wider scope.

Further reading

Karl Llewellyn, 'Remarks on the Theory of Appellate Decisions and the Rules or Canons about How Statutes Are To Be Construed' (1950) 3 *Vanderbilt Law Review* 401

See also **construction (of documents); eiusdem generis; interpretation / construction; MAXIMS; may; shall / must.**

capacity

In legal usage, means more than possessing the *mere* ability to do something ('Mary is *able* to sign a will'), but rather possessing the *legal* ability to do something ('Mary is *capable* of signing a will'). So, a person may be *able to* sign a contract or commit a crime, but lack the *capacity* to do so. The ungainly adjective *capacitous*—as in a person who is vulnerable but 'capacitous': *R v Kurtz* [2018] EWCA Crim 2743; [2019] QB 1195, passim—seems not yet to have reached standard dictionaries.

See also **ability / capacity**.

CAPITALS

Overuse of capitals

Overuse of capital letters is a hallmark of traditional legal writing. Well into the 19th century, some judges commonly used capitals for nouns: eg, *Howgrave v Cartier*

(1814) 3 Ves & B 79; 35 ER 409. So too did some statutory drafters: eg, *Merchandise Marks Act 1862*. Document drafters conventionally used capital letters for whole words to break up blocks of text and give the appearance (though not the reality) of sentence breaks; examples included WHEREAS, TOGETHER WITH, PROVIDED THAT, ALL THAT.

Readability studies suggest that text in capitals slows reading speeds by up to 20%, even for simple sentences: see, eg, Karen A Schriver, *Dynamics in Document Design: Creating text for readers* (Wiley, New York, 1997). Test it for yourself in the following example:

> TEXT IN ALL-CAPITALS REDUCES READABILITY. READERS TYPICALLY RECOGNISE WORDS BY SHAPES, USING THE ASCENDERS AND DESCENDERS AS DISTINGUISHING IDENTIFIERS. THE OVERUSE OF CAPITALS NEGATES THIS BENEFIT BY SQUEEZING WORDS INTO AN UNFAMILIAR SHAPE, REQUIRING READERS TO PROCESS THEM LETTER-BY-LETTER.

Capitals for emphasis

Before the days of modern word-processing programs, legal writers sometimes used capitals for emphasis—for example, to ensure that a contractual provision was not overlooked or misunderstood. This practice has continued to some extent into the modern era. Thus, the English Court of Appeal took note of the use of capitals in a clause which gave a party an 'EITHER … OR' choice; in the court's view, the capitals made it abundantly clear that these were true alternatives: *BMBF (No 12) Ltd v Harland and Wolff Shipbuilding and Heavy Industries Ltd* [2001] EWCA Civ 862, [82] (Nourse LJ). But that decision does not dictate that capitals are the *only* legally effective method of emphasis. And writers who use capitals for emphasis may not appreciate the increased difficulty of reading block text in capitals (which may in fact encourage readers to skip the material entirely). Nowadays, emphasis is better achieved by other techniques, particularly by using **bold**.

United States practice

In US legal documents the practice has survived of capitalising whole words or sentences—or even whole paragraphs—for emphasis. This is seen especially in exemption clauses, disclaimers, and limitations of warranty. The apparent purpose is to make the terms 'conspicuous'—conspicuity being a common statutory requirement to bring material to the reader's attention, particularly in consumer documents (eg, *Uniform Commercial Code* §2-316(2)). But the purpose is misguided:

> 'Lawyers who think their caps lock keys are instant "make conspicuous" buttons are deluded. … A term that appears in capitals can still be inconspicuous if it is hidden on the back of a contract in small type [or] buried deep within a long paragraph in capitals …' [*American General Finance Inc v Bassett* 285 F 3d 882, 887 (9th Cir 2002)].

As a matter of law, text can be 'conspicuous' without being in capitals. Unless a statute requires otherwise (as in Arizona Revised Statutes §12-1366(C), requiring *both* capitals and bold), conspicuity can be achieved by a number of means—eg, by using capitals for the heading (only) of the clause; or by using a larger (lower-case) font than the rest of the document; or by using the same font as the rest of the document but printed in bold (*American Eagle Ins Co v United Technologies Corp* 51 F 3d 468 (5th Cir 1995)). This is because, in determining conspicuity, US courts consider the entire document. The question is whether a reasonable person in the consumer's position would have been surprised to find the clause in the contract, taking account of the reader's sophistication and the circumstances in which the contract was negotiated and signed: see discussion in 67A Am Jur 2d, *Sales* §781.

Indeed, conspicuity may sometimes be achieved simply by clause order—eg, by placing the relevant clause (lower case) first in the document (and ensuring that no aspect of its formatting or appearance makes it less visible or difficult to read).

Further reading

- Martin Cutts and Chrissie Maher, *Writing Plain English* (Plain English Campaign, 1980) 21
- *Guidelines for Document Designers* (American Institutes for Research, 1981) 87–88
- National Consumer Council, *Plain English for Lawyers* (London, 1984) 25

See also **DOCUMENT DESIGN; FONTS; SENTENCE LENGTH.**

case

Formulations containing *case*—eg, *in case of, in the case of*—are usually innately wordy. Prune, and rework the sentence as required.

Before	**After**
In a case to which clause 2 applies …	*If* [or *Where*] clause 2 applies …
In the case of Jones v Smith …	*In* Jones v Smith …
(1) *In a case to which* clause 2 applies … (2) *In any other case*, …	(1) *If* [or *Where*] clause 2 applies … (2) Otherwise, …
In case of the judge getting it wrong, we will appeal.	*If* the judge gets it wrong, we will appeal.
A Class X licence is required *in the case of* manual-driven vehicles.	A Class X licence is required *for* manual-driven vehicles.
The quality of judges in appellate courts is higher than *is the case with* lower courts.	The quality of judges in appellate courts is higher than *in* lower courts.
Judges usually come from the ranks of barristers, *in many cases* out of touch with the street-front practice of law.	Judges usually come from the ranks of barristers, *often* out of touch with the street-front practice of law.

Similar wordiness can infect formulations containing *instance*.

See also **instance**.

case law / caselaw

British and Commonwealth usage prefers two words: *case law*. However, modern US usage tends to prefer *caselaw* (one word), a preference now spreading to some other countries. When using as an adjective, hyphenate: eg, 'Most law school teach by the *case-law* method.' But the hyphenated noun form—'I am researching *case-law*'—is obsolete.

casebook method

Also *case method*. A method of instructing law students in legal principles by close analysis of judicial decisions, said to have been initiated at Harvard Law School by Dean Christopher Columbus Langdell, using his book *A Selection of Cases on the Law of Contracts* (1871).

casus omissus

Latin: a case omitted (in the sense of a situation which the law or a statute has overlooked). Though hallowed by legal usage, the Latin is not a true term of art but merely an affectation. The English equivalent *oversight* (or *omission*) will suffice. For example:

- 'It is most unlikely that [the document] was not intended to cover early retirement in ill health … and the commissioner accordingly took it to be an inadvertent *casus omissus* [prefer: *oversight*].' [*Venables v Hornby* [2003] UKHL 65; [2003] 1 WLR 3022, [20] (Lord Millett)]
- 'This may either be a *casus omissus* [prefer: *omission*], overlooked by the drafter, or there may be no gap in the statutory scheme …' [*Chief Commissioner of State Revenue v Platinum Investment Management Ltd* [2011] NSWCA 48, [62]; (2011) 80 NSWLR 240, 251 (Handley AJA)]

causa causans

Latin: the 'causing cause'; the core reason; the immediate cause. In the context of breach of a duty, the effective or proximate cause of the harm or loss. As with many other Latin tags, *causa causans* suggests more precision than it deserves. To use an appropriate English translation would encourage closer scrutiny, as Lord Wright observed:

> 'I cannot help deprecating the use of Latin or so-called Latin phrases in this way. They only distract the mind from the true problem which is to apply the principles of English law to the realities of the case. *Causa causans* is supposed to mean a cause which causes, while *causa sine quâ non* means, I suppose, a cause which does not, in the sense material to the particular case, cause, but is merely an incident which precedes in the history or narrative of events, but as a cause is not in at the death, and hence is irrelevant. English law can furnish in its own language expressions which will more fitly state the problem in any case of this type.' [*Smith, Hogg & Co Ltd v Black Sea and Baltic General Insurance Co Ltd* [1940] AC 997, 1003]

In Australia, Windeyer J also disapproved of this Latin tag:

> '[S]ignposts in Latin do not really make [the path of establishing causation] easy. … An examination of such cases as I have been able to discover … in which the expression *causa causans* was used makes me think that either it has no certain meaning for legal purposes or, if it has, that its use in some cases was catachrestic.' [*National Insurance Co of New Zealand Ltd v Espagne* (1961) 105 CLR 569, 590]

But judges still use the Latin formulation, as in the following examples:

- 'The master's employment of the servant was only a *causa sine qua non* of the injury [prefer: *an event without which the injury would not have occurred*]: it was not the *causa causans* [prefer: *immediate cause*]. It was not "foreseeable" by the master that his employment of the servant would cause injury to the person who sustained it.' [*Morris v CW Martin & Sons Ltd* [1966] 1 QB 716, 733–34 (Diplock LJ)]

- '[T]he words "by reason" suggest to my mind that is the real reason, the core reason, the *causa causans*, the motive for the treatment complained of[,] that must be identified.' [*Chief Constable of West Yorkshire Police v Khan* [2001] UKHL 48; [2001] 1 WLR 1947, [77] (Lord Scott, reducing the Latin to English synonyms)]

See also **causa sine qua non**.

causa sine qua non

Latin: the indispensable cause, without which an event (such as an injury) would not have happened. No magic resides in the Latin; the English translation is perfectly adequate.

See also **causa causans**; **sine qua non**.

cause (noun, verb)

Causation is inherently complex. Lord Shaw of Dunfermline once said:

> 'Causes are spoken of as if they were as distinct from one another as beads in a row or links in the chain, but … it is not wholly so. The chain of causation is a handy expression, but the figure is inadequate. Causation is not a chain, but a net. At each point influences, forces, events, precedent and simultaneous, meet: and the radiation from each point extends infinitely.' [*Leyland Shipping Co Ltd v Norwich Union Fire Insurance Society Ltd* [1918] AC 350, 369]

Or, as Lord Salmon later put it:

> 'It seems to me that, giving the word 'cause' its ordinary and natural meaning, anyone may cause something to happen intentionally or negligently or inadvertently without negligence and without intention. For example, a man may deliberately smash a porcelain vase; he may handle it so negligently that he drops and smashes it; or he may without negligence slip or stumble against it and smash it. In each of these examples, no less in the last than in the other two, he has caused the destruction of the vase.' [*Alphacell Ltd v Woodward* [1972] AC 824, 847]

To ask whether a person's acts or omissions *caused* an event implies deeper enquiry: do we mean *directly* caused, or *indirectly* caused, or *negligently* caused, or *deliberately* caused, or *inadvertently* caused? Also, do we mean the sole cause, or one of a number of causes? If the meaning is left unclarified, a court is likely to interpret *cause* broadly. For example, legislation in many jurisdictions gives compensation to injury or damage 'caused by' an aircraft in flight. The Australian High Court has said that whether an injury is 'caused by' an aircraft in flight is 'a question of fact to be answered by reference to commonsense and experience' and includes 'considerations of policy and value judgments', and that there can be 'multiple causes of the one damage': *ACQ Pty Limited v Cook* [2009] HCA 28; (2009) 237 CLR 656, [25]–[27]. Such a broad meaning is unlikely to promote certainty of outcome.

Drafters sometimes overlook (or choose to ignore) the complexities inherent in 'caused by'. Sometimes they use other 'causation' terms such as 'attributable to', 'by reference to', 'in consequence of'. But these also leave unclear the precise connection between cause and effect.

See also **allow**; **cause (to be done)**; **directly**; **in consequence of**; **novus actus interveniens**; **suffer**.

cause (litigation)

In the context of litigation, a generic term meaning an action, suit, or proceeding between parties. It is mostly used in the context of civil proceedings, but is appropriate also for criminal proceedings: eg, '*cause* means any action or any criminal proceedings' (*Senior Courts Act 1981*, s 151(1)).

cause (to be done)

Almost always, this formula is superfluous. To *cause* something to be done almost always simply means to do it (including by having someone else do it). For example:

- 'The company *must cause* an apology *to be published*' means simply 'The company *must publish* an apology'.
- 'The tenant *must cause* the premises *to be repaired*' means simply 'The tenant *must repair* the premises'. To say that 'The tenant must repair' does not require the tenant to carry out the repairs *personally* (unless, exceptionally, the tenant is a builder and the evidence shows that the parties intended personal compliance; but in that case, the original formulation—'The tenant must *cause* the premises to be repaired'—is also deficient).
- 'The landlord shall *cause* the premises to be cleaned' means simply that the landlord must take steps to have them cleaned: *Stiles v Galinski* [1904] 1 KB 615, 622 (Lord Alverstone CJ). That in turn is sufficiently expressed by saying: 'The landlord must clean the premises.' (As with the previous example, it would be difficult to argue that 'The landlord must clean …' requires the landlord to personally clean the premises, rather than have someone else do the work.)

See also **ensure (that something be done)**.

cause of action estoppel

See ***Anshun* estoppel**; **estoppel**.

caution

In English and Commonwealth law, a warning; a record lodged on title to warn of an interest in or claim to land.

Also, in Scots law, a security for a deed or for a debt:

> '[We argue that] (1) *caution* is not required in the interests of justice; and, separately, (2) if required, the level of *caution* sought is excessive.' [Scots pleading, quoted in *Albert Bartlett & Sons (Airdrie) Ltd v Gilchrist & Lynn Ltd* [2007] CSOH 140, [3]]

See also **caveat**.

cav

See **curia advisari vult**.

cave

Latin [pronounced *car-vay*]: beware. The Latin serves no purpose. Prefer standard English. (See Megarry J's use of *cave uxorem*, under **HUMOUR**.)

See also **caveat**.

caveat

Latin: let [X] beware. In law, *caveat* can be a noun (a document) or a verb (warning against action). As a noun, a *caveat* is a document aimed at preventing action by the person to whom it is directed (eg, a caveat lodged with a land registry office to prevent registration of dealings with land). As a verb, used in combination with other Latinisms, *caveat* warns people about potential liability in their activities: eg, *caveat emptor* (buyer beware), *caveat fabricator* (manufacturer beware), *caveat subscriptor* (signatory beware), *caveat venditor* (seller beware).

Occasionally, attempts to add *caveat* to an English word produces a linguistic solecism. For example:

> 'Just as in the case of a purchaser of a business the rule is *caveat emptor*, so in the case of the lease of property the rule is *caveat lessee*; he must take the property as he finds it.' [*Erskine v Adeane* (1873) LR 8 Ch App 756, 761 (Mellish LJ). The intended meaning—'let the lessee beware'—is guessable but etymologically errant.]

See also **caveat emptor**; **LATIN**.

caveat emptor

Latin: let the buyer beware (ie, let the buyer make their own enquiries to protect their own interests). As used in law, the Latinism implies more than its English translation, because the implication is not merely that the buyer should make their own enquiries, but that there is no legal obligation on the seller (vendor) to tell (eg, that a house is termite-infested). For that reason—and despite the usual advice to avoid Latinisms—it may be prudent to retain the Latin, but of course to add English translation or explanation. For example, a lawyer's advice to a prospective purchaser of a house might state:

> 'As to the condition of the property, the principle *caveat emptor* (let the buyer beware) applies.'

Caveat emptor has spawned variants that are witty but grammatically embarrassing, as in the following article titles:

- Heather Conway, '*Cadaver emptor* and the Vendor's Duty of Disclosure' (2004) 78 *Australian Law Journal* 430 (discussing whether a vendor must tell the purchaser that the property had been the site of a murder)
- Lynden Griggs, 'The Duty of Disclosure by Vendors in a Conveyance: If *Caveat Vendor*, Are We Allowing the Camel's Nose of Unrestrained Irrationality Admission to the Tent' (1999) *7 Australian Property Law Journal* 76 (using *vendor* instead of the correct Latin *venditor*)

Further reading

Walton H Hamilton, 'The Ancient Maxim Caveat Emptor' (1931) 40 *Yale Law Journal* 1133

See also **caveat**; **LATIN**.

caveator / caveatrix

One who lodges a caveat. Contemporary legal writing prefers the gender-neutral *caveator*. But where the caveator is female, *caveatrix* is still seen:

> 'On [date] the deceased's sister, Ms Jennings ('the *caveatrix*'), filed grounds of objection to the application. … As the paternal aunt of the deceased's children, the *caveatrix* sought an order appointing her as the guardian of the children. … The *caveatrix's* parents and two siblings are

alive. However, the *caveatrix* asserts that, to the best of her knowledge, her parents do not wish to obtain a grant of representation in the estate of the deceased.' [*Re Gleeson* [2019] VSC 589, [5] (McMillan J)]

In modern usage, however, no purpose is served by retaining *caveatrix*.

See also **caveat**; **executor / executrix**; **GENDER-NEUTRAL LANGUAGE**; **testator / testatrix**.

cease and desist

A lawyer's pairing, meaning no more than 'stop'. Therefore, prefer 'stop'.

See also **WORD PAIRINGS**.

ceiling

An upper limit, as in 'debt ceiling'. Sometimes a ceiling is said to be *increased* or *decreased*, but prefer *raised* or *lowered*.

certificates

See **conclusive certificates**.

certiorari

Latin: to be informed. Historically, the name given to a process by which a superior court supervises the jurisdiction of a lower court or tribunal. It enables the superior court to 'quash' (set aside) the order of the lower court or tribunal on one or more established grounds, such as jurisdictional error, failure to observe procedural fairness, fraud, or error of law on the face of the record. In many common-law jurisdictions, writs of certiorari are no longer available, but court rules allow applications 'in the nature of certiorari'. For all except hardened lawyers, *certiorari* will be meaningless. For non-lawyers, prefer a modern equivalent: eg, *not* 'We will seek an order in the nature of certiorari', *but* 'We will ask the court to review the decision'.

See also **mandamus**; **quash**; **WOOLF REFORMS**.

certum est quod certum reddi potest

Latin: that is certain which is capable of being made certain; more prosaically, 'if something can be made certain, then it is certain'. The rhythm of the Latin is alluring—but allure is a poor substitute for communication. Unless the reader knows Latin, it is best to translate, as Rix LJ does in the first example below:

- 'Any of these three solutions would do justice to the parties' agreement, as working out a detail of it. The applicable legal motto is: that is certain which can be rendered certain (*id certum est quod certum reddi potest*).' [*Scammell v Dicker* [2005] EWCA Civ 405, [39]; [2005] 3 All ER 838, 848 (Rix LJ)]
- 'Such a lease would be valid, for if the machinery for fixing the rent should fail, the court's machinery will be available to fix it: *certum est quod certum reddi potest* [prefer: *if something can be made certain, then it is certain*].' [*Booker Industries Pty Ltd v Wilson Parking (Qld) Pty Ltd* (1982) 149 CLR 600, 617 (Brennan J)]

cessante ratione legis, cessat lex ipsa

Latin: when the reason for a law ceases, the law itself ceases. This Latin maxim may have a certain cadence, but cadence does not justify use for an audience untutored in Latin—even more so when cadence can be carried into the translation:

> 'The judges created the [advocate's immunity from liability for negligence] and the judges should say that the grounds for maintaining it no longer exist. *Cessante ratione legis, cessat lex ipsa* [restate: *When the reason for a law ceases, the law itself should cease*].' [*Arthur J Hall & Co v Simons* [2000] UKHL 38; [2002] 1 AC 615, 705 (Lord Hoffmann)]

In any case, the Latin overstates the legal position. Judges are not necessarily free to discard a principle merely because the underlying reasons for the principle no longer exist, as the High Court of Australia has explained:

> 'The maxim *cessante ratione* cannot be read literally and "in its widest signification, is erroneous and misleading". It goes no further than to reflect the process of legal reasoning whereby previous authority may be distinguished or restricted in its operation. That is to say, it may afford a useful guide in the making of a permissible choice; it does not create the choice itself. The maxim "is not a licence to courts to change the law if it appears to them that the circumstances in which it was framed have changed".' [*Lamb v Cotogno* (1987) 164 CLR 1, 11, citations omitted]

cestui que trust

Meaning

Law French: beneficiary. The term had its origins in the 'use' of land, the progenitor of the modern concept of 'trust'. Land would be conveyed to a trustworthy person (the 'feoffee to uses'), who was to hold it not for personal benefit but for the underlying benefit of ('to the use of') another person. The person for whose underlying benefit the land was conveyed—in modern language, the beneficiary—was the 'cestui que use', from the law French 'cestui a que use le feoffment fuit fait' ('the person for whose use the feoffment was made'). With the demise of the use and the rise of the modern trust, the term became *cestui que trust*. In modern times, *beneficiary* carries the meaning perfectly.

Plural

Grammatically, the plural is *cestuis que trust*. However, the variant *cestuis que trustent* sometimes appears in the law reports: eg, *Re Whiting's Settlement* [1905] 1 Ch 96, 101 (Byrne J); *Prescott v Birmingham Corporation* [1955] Ch 210, 235 (Jenkins LJ); *Australia and New Zealand Banking Group Ltd v National Mutual Life Nominees Ltd* (1977) 137 CLR 252, 264 (Jacobs J). This variant Charles Sweet described as 'hopelessly wrong' (see (1910) 26 *Law Quarterly Review* 196), because *trust* here is not a verb. The English plural *beneficiaries* carries the meaning perfectly, and avoids grammatical embarrassment.

Further reading

SFC Milsom (ed), F Pollock and FW Maitland, *The History of English Law before the Time of Edward I*, 2nd edn, reissued (Cambridge University Press, 1968) vol 2, 233–39

ceteris paribus

Latin: other things being equal. The English translation is perfectly adequate. To retain the Latin is pedantic:

- '[T]here would appear to be—*ceteris paribus* [prefer: *all things being equal*]—a strong case for allowing the Plaintiffs to continue with their action here.' [*Black-Clauson International Ltd v Papierwerke Waldhof-Aschaffenburg AG* [1975] AC 591, 634 (Lord Wilberforce)]
- '[I]n the context of multi-party proceedings, there appears, *ceteris paribus* [prefer: *all things being equal*], to be no reason why the court's power … should be curtailed.' [*Navigator Investment Services Ltd v Acclaim Insurance Brokers Pte Ltd* [2010] 1 SLR 25, [58]]
- 'Similar contraventions should incur similar penalties, *ceteris paribus* [prefer: *all things being equal*], albeit that other things are rarely equal.' [*Australian Energy Regulator v Snowy Hydro Ltd (No 2)* [2015] FCA 58, [121] (Beach J); indeed, the suggested translation adds a symmetry that the Latin lacks.]

cf

Abbreviation for *confer* (Latin), meaning *compare*. In Latin, it carries the sense of an order to be obeyed; in English, it is more of an invitation. In some countries (particularly the US), the abbreviation retains a full stop; in most countries, however, the full stop is now omitted, in line with the practice for abbreviations generally.

chapeau

The introductory words to a provision. For example:

> '[T]he language of the *chapeau* of subs (2) is the same as the *chapeau* of subs (2A), namely, "[f]or the purpose of exercising its functions".' [*Woollahra Municipal Council v Minister for Local Government* [2016] NSWCA 380, [76] (Beazley P)]

Although the term is familiar in the context of treaties, its use to describe the introductory words to provisions in statutes and documents is relatively recent, dating from the 1990s. As of 2020, this meaning had not appeared in the *Oxford English Dictionary*. Unless the reader is likely to know the meaning, prefer 'introductory words' or similar.

charity

In normal usage, *charity*—and its adjectival form *charitable* ('charitable purpose', '*charitable* organisation')—means 'designed to help the needy or disadvantaged'. But in legal usage, *charity* (and its adjectival forms) has a much narrower meaning, developed over centuries of case law since the *Statute of Charitable Uses*, 1601.

> '[T]he legal meaning and the popular meaning of the word "charitable" are so far apart that it is necessary almost to dismiss the popular meaning from the mind as misleading before setting out to determine whether a gift is charitable within the legal meaning.' [*Verge v Somerville* [1924] AC 496, 502 (PC)]

In legal usage, *charity* is a term of art, meaning (in short) activity falling into one or more of four categories: (1) trusts for relieving poverty; (2) trusts for advancing education; (3) trusts for advancing religion; and (4) trusts for other purposes 'beneficial to the community', not falling under any of the preceding heads: *Commissioners for Special Purposes of Income Tax v Pemsel* [1891] AC 531, 583 (Lord Macnaghten). So settled are these meanings that courts assume that legal drafters who use the word *charity* or *charitable* intend this term-of-art meaning.

Further reading

Halsbury's Laws of England, 'Charities' (vol 8, 2019) [1]–[6]

See also **TERMS OF ART**.

charterparty

Preferred spelling in legal usage is *charterparty* (one word). Variants are *charter-party* (hyphenated, and preferred by the *Oxford English Dictionary*) and *charter party* (two words).

chattel

See **chattel real; goods and chattels; moveable / immoveable**.

chattel real

Personal property (*chattel*) that relates to, or exhibits the characteristics of, *real* property; plural, *chattels real*.

The only modern example is the lease of land, which derives from the historical circumstance that the common law regarded leases of land as personal contracts between landlord and tenant, standing outside the system of freehold estates and tenures. Their connection with land gave rise to the hybrid description *chattels real*. The term is a genuine term of art, difficult to express in any other way. But its inscrutability is unlikely to pose practical problems, given that its use in modern law is largely limited to student texts and legal treatises.

See also **goods and chattels**.

child

Meaning

Legitimate only?

Historically, *child* denoted a *legitimate* child, ie, a child born in wedlock: *Hill v Crook* (1873) LR 6 HL 265. More recently, statute law in most jurisdictions has extended this original meaning to include ex-nuptial children, stepchildren, adopted children, and children born by surrogacy or artificial conception.

Further, quite apart from statutory extension, context may show that *child* means natural child, stepchild (*Warton v Yeo* [2015] NSWCA 115), illegitimate child, and adopted child (*Harris v Ashdown* (1985) 3 NSWLR 193, 197–200, Kirby P). This is particularly (though not exclusively) the case in the law of wills, where the 'armchair' principle admits extrinsic evidence to explain the meaning of words and expressions used in a will, the purpose being to find the testator's intentions from the words used in the context in which the testator understood and used them (FV Hawkins and EC Ryder, *The Construction of Wills*, 3rd edn (Sweet & Maxwell, 1965) 12–21). Two examples follow:

- A will contained a gift 'to my children'. The testator had no children, but he had stepchildren, whom he treated as his children. Held, 'my children' meant the stepchildren: *Re Estate of Nies* [2014] SASC 93.

- A will contained a gift 'to my grandchildren'. The testator had grandchildren; and in addition, one of the testator's children had two stepchildren. The testator drew no distinction between his 'natural' grandchildren and the stepchildren. Held, 'grandchildren' included the stepchildren: *Re Staughton* [2017] VSC 359.

Age

At what age does a person cease to be a child? The common law sets no specific age, and much depends on the context. For example, a girl of 14 was a *child* for the purpose of legislation which required children to be billeted during wartime: *Rodger v Varey* [1942] 1 KB 508. However, 'somewhere between 16 and 17' was the upper limit of *childhood* for the purpose of educational courses funded by school boards: *R v Cockerton* [1901] 1 QB 322, 340–41).

A statute may prescribe a maximum age for a *child* governed by its provisions. For example, in an Australian statute regulating the care of children, *child* is a person under 16 (*Children and Young Persons (Care and Protection) Act 1998* (NSW), s 3(1)); and in a statute regulating criminal proceedings against children, *child* is a person under 18 (*Children (Criminal Proceedings) Act 1987* (NSW), s 3(1)).

Unborn child

For some purposes (such as in gifts by will), a person may come within the description *child* where conceived but not yet born—a child *en ventre sa mère*.

'child of the marriage'

The term *child of the marriage* may narrow down a person's qualification as a *child*. *Re Wicks' Marriage Settlement* [1940] Ch 475 held that a person, who was born before his parents married, was not a *child of the marriage* (despite being a child of the two prospective spouses).

First generation only?

Normally, *child* denotes the first generation of progeny, not succeeding generations. Therefore, a disposition to *children* does not include *grandchildren*: *Re Atkinson* [1918] 2 Ch 138, 144; *Re Williams* [1950] Qd St R 148, 196 (Macrossan CJ). However, context may extend the meaning to *grandchildren*, particularly in wills (as in *Re Smith* (1887) 35 Ch D 558, 560).

See also **en ventre sa mère; issue (offspring); parent**.

choate

Now used to mean 'complete', as if it were the opposite of *inchoate* ('incomplete'). But it is a false opposite, because it assumes (wrongly) that the *in-* of *inchoate* is a negative form: 'You know that there is no such word as *choate*, but *choate* is to *inchoate* as *sult* is to *insult*' (Scalia J, in oral argument in *Internal Revenue Service v McDermott*, 7 December 1992; 1992 WL 687881 (US), 35). However, the acceptance of *choate* seems too firm to overturn, as in the following examples:

- 'The difficulty created by the terseness of the [judge's direction to the jury] is that the appellant answered an allegation of attempted robbery and his only conviction for the *choate* offence (robbery) was 13 years earlier.' [*R v Harty* [2016] EWCA Crim 345, [23] (Rafferty LJ)]

- 'Although the conspiracy was not likely to materialise into a *choate* offence, because of the identity of the other participants, that was not known to the respondent at the time.' [*R v DW* [2012] NSWCCA 66, [41] (Basten JA)]

See also **inchoate / incohate**.

'CHOICE OF LAW' CLAUSE

A clause under which the parties to a contract or deed agree that the law of a particular state or country is to apply to their document. Usually seen in tandem with a 'jurisdiction clause'—ie, that the courts of the same state or country are to have jurisdiction to decide disputes arising under the document.

At common law, courts will uphold a choice of law clause, as long as the choice does not contradict public policy: see, eg, *Vita Food Products Inc v Unus Shipping Co Ltd* [1939] AC 277, 289–90; *James Miller & Partners Ltd v Whitworth Street Estates (Manchester) Ltd* [1970] AC 583, 603.

For more abundant caution, some 'choice of law' clauses add a qualification that the chosen law is not to include that law's choice-of-law rules; the aim is to ensure that those rules do not subject the dispute to the laws of yet another jurisdiction. But even absent an express qualification to that effect, the courts will probably imply it—at least, US courts have so held: *Chan v Society Expeditions Inc* 123 F 3d 1287, 1297 (9th Cir, 1997).

See also **GOVERNING LAW; JURISDICTION CLAUSE.**

chose in action

Chose (French) = thing. An intangible personal property right that can be claimed or enforced only by court action, not by taking physical possession: *Torkington v Magee* [1902] 2 KB 427, 430 (Channell J). The term can mean the right enforceable *by* action, and the right *of* action itself. Examples are the right to payment under a contract, the right to payment under a bill of exchange, rights under a trust, copyright, and a cause of action in tort.

Chose in action is a term of art, not easily translatable into concise, plain English. If you feel you must use it even for readers unlikely to understand it, add an explanation.

See **TERMS OF ART**.

circa

Latin: about. Usually in relation to a date: eg, 'circa 1990'. Generally not italicised, having become standard English. Usually abbreviated to 'c' (eg, 'c 1990') or in the US 'c.' (eg, 'c. 1990', in line with the general US preference for preserving full stops for abbreviations).

CITATION OF BOOKS AND JOURNAL ARTICLES

How much information?

Citation methods for books and journal articles vary. When writing for a particular publisher, follow their style guide. However, so far is it possible to generalise, there are two basic approaches: (1) provide as much information as possible; or (2) provide enough information to enable the reader to find the source, but no more. Approach (2) is sufficient for most legal writing, but academic style guides often require approach (1). The following table shows some of the main differences:

Nature of information	**Approach (1)—full information**	**Approach (2)—sufficient information**
Author's name	Full name as appears on title page, including titles such as 'Sir', 'Dame', peerage titles	Surname only
Book title	Full title, including any subtitle, both in italics	Title in italics; lengthy subtitle omitted
Book publisher and place of publication	Full name of publisher and place of publication	Short name of publisher (sufficient to identify); place of publication omitted (unless different editions published in different places)
Year and edition	Year and edition	Year and edition
Journal title	Full title (italics): eg, *Cambridge Law Journal*	Abbreviated title (not italics): eg, CLJ
Journal article	Full title and any subtitle, in single quotes	Full title only (no subtitle), in single quotes
Book example	Kevin Gray and Susan Francis Gray, *Elements of Land Law*, 5th edn (Oxford, Oxford University Press, 2009)	Gray and Gray, *Elements of Land Law*, 5th edn (OUP, 2009)
Journal example	Harry Hobbs, Andrew Lynch and George Williams, 'The High Court under Chief Justice Robert French' (2017) 91 *Australian Law Journal* 53	Hobbs, Lynch and Williams, 'The High Court under Chief Justice Robert French' (2017) 91 ALJ 53

Pinpoint references

Pinpoint references take the reader to details such as chapter, page, or paragraph. Pinpoint reference styles also vary between publishers, but generally divide into two groups: (1) provide as much information as possible; (2) provide sufficient information to enable the reader to find the source, but no more. Also, modern practice favours an economy of style, and so often omits a comma after the publication details, and eschews markers such as *p* [page] or *para* [paragraph].

Full information	**Sufficient information**
Sir Frederick Pollock and Frederick William Maitland, *The History of English Law Before the Time of Edward 1*, 2nd edn (SFC Milsom) (Cambridge, Cambridge University Press, 1968) vol 2, 80	Pollock and Maitland, *History of English Law*, 2nd edn (CUP, 1968) vol 2, 80

Where a pinpoint reference is to a page that also carries paragraph numbers, there are two approaches: (1) specify both page and paragraph number; (2) specify paragraph number only, if that is sufficient to identify the passage. This book generally follows approach (2).

Full information	Sufficient information
Peter Butt, *Land Law*, 6th edn (Lawbook Co, 2010), 95 [5.19]	Butt, *Land Law*, 6th edn (Lawbook, 2010), [5.19]

CITATION OF CASES

The methods for citing cases vary from country to country, from court to court, and from publisher to publisher. Subject to any formal requirements of court or publisher, the two key principles are: (1) adopt an efficient method—ie, one that allows readers to find the cases quickly and accurately; and (2) be consistent. This book generally follows the citation conventions adopted by the *Oxford University Standard for the Citation of Legal Authorities* (OSCOLA), 4th edn, which is the norm for UK academic use. But occasionally it departs from that guide for reasons of efficiency, logic, or space.

The parties' names

General

- Cite the parties' names, in *italics*.
- Where there are multiple parties, cite only the first-named plaintiff and the first-named defendant. Omit references to 'and Ors', 'and others', or similar.

Where parties are individuals

Omit the parties' initials and given names.

Where parties are corporations or businesses

- Use the relevant abbreviation (no full stops) *Ltd*, *Pty Ltd*, *Co*, *Corp*, *Inc* (but note jurisdictional variations, such as *Pte* in Singapore).
- Where *The* is part of the name, include it.
- Where a party is in liquidation or similar, standard tags include *in liq* (in liquidation), *in prov liq* (in provisional liquidation), *admin apptd* (administrator appointed), *mgr apptd* (manager appointed), *rec apptd* (receiver appointed). Some legal writers include these tags in the case citation, for completeness; others omit them on the ground that readers do not need them to identify the case. This book omits them.
- Omit trading names (*t/as*, *trading as*).

Where Commonwealth, a State or a Territory is a party

Give only the name (minus 'State of', 'Territory of')—eg, *New South Wales v Commonwealth*.

The Crown

- Where the Crown is the first-named party, abbreviate to *R* (for *Rex* or *Regina*).
- Where the Crown is the respondent, some citation guides specify *The King* or *The Queen* (as appropriate). This book abbreviates to *R*, because that sufficiently identifies the Crown.

Public and governmental entities

Where a public or governmental entity has an accepted short name, use it rather than its fuller name (eg, *Shire of Smithville*, **not** *Mayor and Councillors of the Borough of Smithville*;

Federal Commissioner of Taxation, **not** *Commissioner of Taxation of the Commonwealth of Australia*)

Attorney-General and Director of Public Prosecutions

In the main text of a discussion, use *Attorney-General* and (in relevant jurisdictions) *Director of Public Prosecutions* in full. In footnotes, however, abbreviate to *A-G* and *DPP*.

Multiple proceedings between parties

To distinguish multiple proceedings between the same parties, courts allocate each case a separate number. When citing a case, include the number of the decision—by convention, in square brackets: *Bahr v Nicolay [No 2]*. The square brackets, though perhaps quaint to non-legal eyes, prove useful where round brackets also appear in the case name, as where a litigant is a corporation and its registered name includes a number: *Brand v Product X Pty Ltd (No 2) [No 5]*.

Procedural tags: shorter is better

Procedural tags help mark out the form of court proceedings. The tags may be important to the parties and to the court; but rarely, if ever, are they important to readers seeking to find the decision in case reports or other media. For that reason, many legal writers and publishers shorten the tags, giving sufficient information to find the decision, but no more. However, some court rules and publishers' citation guides still require the longer form.

Traditional longer form	**Acceptable shorter form**
In re / In the matter of	*Re*
Jones versus Smith	*Jones v Smith*
Smith at the suit of Jones [This cites the case from the defendant's perspective: ie, *Jones v Smith* becomes *Smith ats Jones*. The parties' legal advisers generally use the tag in correspondence; but it is not used in formal citations of the case.]	*Smith ats Jones*
Re Smith; Allsop v Barry [The case is brought by Allsop against Barry, in relation to some act of Smith. For example, Smith may have created a trust, and Allsop and Barry are disputing their rights under the trust.]	*Re Smith*
Ex parte Jones; Re Hudson [The case is an *ex parte* application brought by Jones, challenging the acts of Hudson.]	*Ex parte Jones* [*Ex parte* is not abbreviated.]
R v Smith; Ex parte Jones [The case is an application for a prerogative writ.]	*R v Smith*
Attorney-General (NSW) ex rel Jones v Victoria [The case is a relator action—*ex rel* introduces the relator's name.]	*Attorney-General (NSW) v Victoria*
The Bounty [This is an Admiralty case involving the ship itself (an action *in rem*).] *Jones v Smith; 'The Bounty'* [This is an Admiralty case between parties in relation to the ship (a personal action—*in personam*), with the parties' names preceding the ship's name.]	*The Bounty* [Use for actions *in rem* and for actions *in personam*.]

Citing law reports

Abbreviations

Cite law reports by their accepted abbreviations (not italicised): AC, not Appeal Cases; WLR, not Weekly Law Reports; All ER, not All England Law Reports; CLR, not Commonwealth Law Reports. The accepted abbreviation is generally given in the opening pages of each volume of the law reports themselves. Modern British and Commonwealth usage for abbreviations omits full stops.

Where authorised report

Where a case is reported in an authorised series of law reports, cite that report in preference to a report in an unauthorised series. 'Authorised' reports are published by official law reporting councils, which give judges the opportunity to review and revise their judgments before publication. All other series are 'unauthorised'. In practice, judges rarely make changes when revising for publication, rendering the concept of an 'authorised' report more fictitious than real, but the convention lives on in court rules and legal publishing houses.

Where no authorised report

A case may be reported in one or more unauthorised series of law reports. Where an unauthorised series is generalist (eg, All England Reports, or Weekly Law Reports) and one or more series is subject-specific (eg, Intellectual Property Reports), the convention is to cite the generalist series in preference to the subject-specific series. But there are exceptions where:

- the particular publisher prefers to cite the series it publishes, in preference to a competing publisher's series
- for readers' convenience, it is logical to cite a subject-specific series; eg, for property lawyers, a specialist property law series such as Property and Conveyancing Reports (P & CR) for English property lawyers, or Butterworths' Property Reports (BPR) for Australian property lawyers.

Year and volume

When referring to the year of a court decision, published law reports conventionally distinguish between round brackets and square brackets. Square brackets indicate that the reports are organised by year: the year is key to finding the report. Round brackets indicate that the reports are organised by volume number: the volume number is key, with the year being incidental to finding the report. Examples follow. Some law publishers have been known to start with one convention and then change to another (as in the third example).

Examples

- *Marshall v Cottingham* [1982] 1 Ch 82—year crucial for finding case; report is in volume 1 of Chancery Reports for 1982.
- *Smart Hardware Co Ltd v Town of Melfort* (1917) 32 DLR 552—volume crucial for finding case; year is for information only.
- *Clark v Esanda Ltd* [1984] 3 NSWLR 1 (year crucial); *Mirror Newspapers Ltd v Waller* (1985) 1 NSWLR 1 (volume crucial)—publisher changed convention.

The distinctions between round and square brackets are apparent when a case appears in different law reports. Thus:

> *Lancaster v London Passenger Transport Board* [1948] WN 419; [1949] LJR 94; [1948] 2 All ER 796—all organised by year

but

Lancaster v London Passenger Transport Board (1948) 64 TLR 584; (1948) 112 JP 460; (1948) 92 SJ 704; (1948) 46 LGR 1—same case, but organised by volume number.

Neutral citations

All courts now reference their decisions with a citation that is *neutral* (sometimes called *medium neutral* or *media neutral*)—*neutral* because the citation does not depend on a publisher for identification. For example, *FMX Food Merchants Import Export Co Ltd v Revenue and Customs* [2020] UKSC 1 indicates that the decision is the first Supreme Court decision of 2020. The decision can be found on the Supreme Court's website, and on internet collections of decisions (such as www.bailii.org) without needing a published law report reference.

Different courts began allocating medium neutral citations at different times—eg, in 2001, the House of Lords, Privy Council, Court of Appeal, and Administrative Court; in 2002, all other divisions of the High Court. In jurisdictions with many courts, the dates vary extensively: eg, in Australia, the High Court of Australia (HCA) in 1998, the Federal Court of Australia (FCA) in 1999, the Federal Court of Australia Full Court (FCAFC) in 2002, and the Supreme Court of South Australia Full Court (SASCFC) in 2010.

Where a decision has a neutral citation and can also be cited by reference to a published series of law reports, most (but not all) court rules and citation guides require *both* citations to be provided—with, as above, an authorised report being preferred over an unauthorised. Where both citations are provided, practice varies over whether the neutral citation comes before the law report citation or follows it. Some court rules and style guides require one practice, others require the opposite. In this book, the neutral citation is usually given before the law report citation.

Unreported decisions

Where a decision is unreported, but has a neutral citation, use that neutral citation; there is no need to add 'unreported'.

Where a decision predates neutral citations for the court in question, and is unreported, the convention is to give the name of the case, followed by (in brackets) the court and/or the name of the judge(s), and the date of the judgment: eg, *Ward v Gregory* (CA, 7 March 2000); *Huthwaite Printing Company Ltd v Wade* (Slade J, 24 July 1978). Some legal publishers add 'unreported' (some with lower-case 'u', others with upper-case 'U'), but many omit it. This book generally omits it, because it is obvious from the lack of reference to a report.

In Commonwealth countries, styles for citing unreported decisions vary, but all provide the same basic information. For example, the most recent edition of a leading Australian academic style guide omits 'unreported', but otherwise includes information similar to UK practice: eg, *El Cheikh v Gratsis* (New South Wales Supreme Court, Hamilton J, 4 July 1997) (see *Australian Guide to Legal Citation* (Melbourne University Law Review Association, 4th edn, 2018) [2.3.2]).

Retrospective neutral citations

Some internet publishers have allocated neutral citations to cases decided before the courts began the practice. While this makes the cases easier to find on the internet, these retrospectively allocated citations have no formal standing. For that reason, some legal practitioners and publishers refrain from using them, as does this book.

Pinpoint references

Pages and paragraphs

Pinpoint references take varying styles. Some styles are sparse; some are fuller. Which style to adopt is a matter of personal preference, unless dictated by a compulsory style guide or by court rules. This book adopts a sparse style.

Some usage guides and court rules require pinpoint references to include both the page and paragraph number. Others require the page number only, with the paragraph number being optional. Yet others require the paragraph number only, because that is sufficient to find the passage. This book generally cites the paragraph number only.

The following table shows the main differences between the styles. Notice that (regardless of whether the style is sparse or fuller) citations omit the words *page* and *paragraph* as well as their abbreviations *p* and *para*.

Reference	Fuller style	Sparser style
Page	*Secretary of State for Health v Servier Laboratories Ltd* [2020] 2 WLR 149 at 153 *R v Holmes* [1946] 1 All ER 524 at 524 [pinpoint reference is to a statement on the first page of the report]	*Secretary of State for Health v Servier Laboratories Ltd* [2020] 2 WLR 149, 153 *R v Holmes* [1946] 1 All ER 524, 524.
Paragraph	*Secretary of State for Health v Servier Laboratories Ltd* [2020] 2 WLR 149 at [7]	*Secretary of State for Health v Servier Laboratories Ltd* [2020] 2 WLR 149 [7] **or** insert a comma between page and para, thus: [2020] 2 WLR 149, [7]
Page and paragraph	*Secretary of State for Health v Servier Laboratories Ltd* [2020] 2 WLR 149 at 153 [7]	*Secretary of State for Health v Servier Laboratories Ltd* [2020] 2 WLR 149 [7] **or** insert a comma between page and para, thus: [2020] 2 WLR 149, [7]

Spans

Page and paragraph spans are properly indicated by a non-spaced en dash: eg, *Secretary of State for Health v Servier Laboratories Ltd* [2020] 2 WLR 149, 153–55, [7]–[18]. In practice, however, many legal documents use a hyphen in place of an en dash.

Some publishers and legal style guides seek to save space by using as few numbers as possible when indicating page spans, although most retain at least two for the final number in the span: eg, 2–5, 12–18, 31–36, 121–22, 1685–86, 1685–760. While understandable, these exhortations are rarely heeded in legal practice, where full numbers are usually given. See also **NUMBERS (Number spans)**.

Older law reports (no paragraph references)

Older series of law reports did not allocate numbers to paragraphs. However, some publishers printed capital letters (A, B, C, etc) in the margin, making it possible to pinpoint a place on the page: eg, *Webb v Frank Bevis Ltd* [1940] 1 All ER 247, 250G.

'In-text' citations?

When referring to a case by name in the text, is it better to include the citation reference there (in the text) or relegate it to a footnote? (This assumes the need to refer to the case name or the citation at all; some readers have no need of case names, and many find legal citations meaningless.) Both practices are found, and there are arguments in favour of each. See discussion in **FOOTNOTES**.

Further reading

RE Megarry, *A Second Miscellany-at-Law* (Stevens, 1973) 117–33 (on the variable quality of early law reports)

See also **FICTITIOUS LAW REPORTS**; **FOOTNOTES**; **in personam**; **in re**; **in rem**.

CITATION OF LEGISLATION

Different jurisdictions adopt different conventions for citing legislation. In choosing a convention, the key issue is whether it enables the reader to understand the citation and find the provision. The following conventions are now reasonably standard.

Statutes: primary legislation

UK statutes

Cite statutes by short title and date: eg, *Law of Property Act 1925* (no comma before the year). Some style guides recommend roman (ie, non-italics)—Law of Property Act 1925—but this book prefers italics, being the more usual style in professional legal writing in Britain and in Commonwealth countries.

(Publishers outside the UK usually add '(UK)' after the name and year of a 'British' statute, even though the statute in fact may apply only to England and Wales: eg, '*Law of Property Act 1925* (UK)'. Publishers within the UK leave it to the reader to identify (or surmise) the jurisdiction.)

Conventions for citing legislation from Wales, Scotland, and Northern Ireland follow the same basic pattern, but with some differences: see *Oxford University Standard for the Citation of Legal Authorities* ('OSCOLA'), 4th edn, [2.4.6]–[2.4.8].

Strictly, until 1963 statutes were properly cited by regnal year and chapter number. For example, the *Law of Property Act* was Act number 20 of the 15th year of the reign of King George V, and would be cited 15 Geo V c 20. The common abbreviations for regnal citations are:

Hen	(Henry)	Jas	(James)
Edw	(Edward)	Cha	(Charles)
Rich	(Richard)	Wm & M	(William & Mary)
M	(Mary)	Wm	(William)
Ph & M	(Phillip & Mary)	Vic	(Victoria)
Eliz	(Elizabeth)	Anne	(Anne)

(Note that modern usage omits full stops after these abbreviations.)

Do not add 'as amended', and do not add a date span—even where the Act has been amended since enactment:

- *Law of Property Act 1925* ~~(as amended)~~
- *Law of Property Act 1925*~~–2020~~.

In some jurisdictions, statutory-interpretation legislation expressly abolishes any need for these descriptors; but even without legislative intervention, the same convention has developed.

Imperial statutes

For UK legislation intended to apply to a colony, the convention is to add '(Imp)' for 'Imperial': eg, *Australian Courts Act 1828* (Imp).

Statutes: Commonwealth primary legislation

When citing non-UK statutes, conventions vary from jurisdiction to jurisdiction. The variants are too numerous to list here. But, for example, in Australia the standard information is: short title (in italics), year of enactment (italics), and jurisdiction (brackets, abbreviated, not italics).

- *Conveyancing Act 1919* (NSW)
- *Corporations Act 2001* (Cth) ['Cth' being the accepted abbreviation for statutes of the Commonwealth of Australia, in contrast to statutes of a State or Territory].

In Canada, the standard information is: short title (usually italics), statute volume (jurisdiction—including whether part of a statutory consolidation—and year), and chapter number:

- *Adult Guardianship and Trustee Act*, SA [Statutes of Alberta] 2008, c A-4.2
- *Garage Keepers' Lien Act*, RSA [Revised Statutes of Alberta] 2000, c G-2
- *Indian Act*, RSC [Revised Statutes of Canada] 1985, c I-5.

Pinpoint references

Sections

1. When starting a sentence, spell out 'Section' (no italics) in full.
2. In other places, abbreviate 'section' to 's' (no full stop, no italics) followed by a space: eg, s 5.
3. Abbreviate 'sections' (plural) to 'ss' (no full stop, no italics, and usually followed by a space [but see point 6, below]): eg, ss 5–7 (complete span); ss 5, 7, 13 (span not consecutive).
4. Cite the statute first, followed by the section number: eg, *Law of Property Act 1925*, s 21. Note the comma after the year, and the space after 's'.
5. However, the usage in 4 is not universal. Other conventions are:
   - omit the comma: eg, *Law of Property Act 1925* s 21
   - reverse the order: eg, s 21 of the *Law of Property Act 1925* [note 'of the'—*not* s 21 *Law of Property Act 1925*].
6. Spacing practices are not uniform. Some style guides, legal publishers and parliamentary drafters omit the space: eg, 's74C', 'ss74–77'. This mirrors the practice of generally omitting spaces between references to paragraphs and subparagraphs: eg, 's74(1)(b)(iii)'. A space always follows the full word 'section': 'section 5' [*not* 'section5'].

Subsections, paragraphs, subparagraphs

Paragraph is sometimes abbreviated, sometimes not; when abbreviated, the usual abbreviation is *para*, but *par* is occasionally seen. *Subsection* and *subparagraph* are sometimes hyphenated (*sub-section*, *sub-paragraph*), sometimes not; and they are sometimes abbreviated (and hyphenated), sometimes not (*subs/sub-s*; *subpara/sub-para*). Unless dictated by a compulsory style guide or court rule, these are matters of personal preference. The only 'rule' is to be consistent.

When citing subsidiary parts of sections (subsections, paragraphs, subparagraphs), state the 'highest level' first, not the 'lowest level'. This is simpler, and likely to mirror the reader's thought processes.

Highest level first (better)	**Lowest level first (poor; poorer)**
s 12(1)	subs 12(1); subs (1) of s 12
s 12(1)(a)	para 12(1)(a); para (a) of s 12(1);
s 12(1)(a)(ii)	subpara 12(1)(a)(ii); subpara (a)(ii) of s 12(1) [or worse: subpara (a)(ii) of subs (1) of s 12]

Delegated legislation

Generally, cite the short titles of delegated legislation (regulations, orders, rules) in the same way as you cite legislation. Thus:

1. If you italicise the titles of statutes, then logically you should italicise the titles of delegated legislation. However, practice varies. Some lawyers and publishers italicise the titles of all delegated legislation; some italicise the titles of regulations but not of orders; and some—even those who italicise the titles of statutes—italicise none. This book, in line with general practice in many Commonwealth countries, italicises the titles of regulations and rules, but not of orders. Thus:

   Grants to the Churches Conservation Trust Order 2020.

   Some style guides require the SI number also: thus, '*Grants to the Churches Conservation Trust Order 2020*, SI 2020/403'. However, other guides omit that information, because the title sufficiently identifies the document.
2. Cite parts within delegated legislation following the conventions for citing parts within legislation, with these abbreviations:

regulation / regulations	reg / regs [lower case; no full stop; no italics]
rule / rules	r / rr [lower case; no full stop; no italics]
article / articles	art / arts [lower case; no full stop; no italics]
order / orders	o [or, ord] / orders [or, oo—but ungainly]

   To illustrate:

   - *Land Registration Rules 2003*, r 15—or, r 15 of the *Land Registration Rules 2003*
3. Cite the Civil Procedure Rules and the County Court Rules, using these abbreviations:
   - CPR 3 (or, if pinpointing subrule, CPR 3.1)
   - CCR Ord 2, r 4.

Bills

1. In citing Bills, follow the conventions for citing statutes. However, in the UK and in most Commonwealth countries, it is common **not** to italicise Bill titles.
2. Provisions of Bills are 'clauses'; abbreviation 'cl' (singular), 'cll' (plural), with no full stop and no italics.

References to later-amended statutes

Where a statute (statute A) refers to another statute (statute B), and statute B is later amended or re-enacted, the reference in statute A is taken to be a reference to statute B in its amended or re-enacted form. This is the effect of statutory-interpretation legislation in most jurisdictions: eg, *Interpretation Act 1978*, s 17; *Acts Interpretation Act 1901* (Cth), s 10 (Australia).

See also **AMENDMENTS TO LEGISLATION (INTERPRETATION CLAUSE); SHORT TITLES.**

CITATION SYMBOLS

The need

In legal writing, as in other technical fields, readers expect writers to cite authority for their propositions. The authority may be, for example, a case, a statute, or a textbook. Where an authority directly supports the proposition stated, it needs no introductory explanation: it can be cited directly after the proposition. Sometimes, however, a writer needs to cite an authority for a purpose more nuanced—for example, to qualify the proposition, or to mention other writers' views about the proposition, or even to contradict the proposition.

The symbols

In both legal and academic writing, convention pairs certain introductory words—'symbols'—with particular citation tasks. The following table lists the main symbols. In British/Commonwealth legal usage, the symbols are not generally italicised.

Symbol (word or phrase)	**Meaning**
See	The authority implicitly supports the proposition. (Where the authority explicitly supports the proposition, 'see' is not needed.)
See especially (*or* See esp)	The authority strongly supports the proposition.
See, eg, [note commas]	The authority supports the proposition and gives examples of its use.
See also	The authority gives additional support for the proposition—but sometimes less directly than 'see' or 'see especially'. US usage prefers *accord*.
See generally	The authority gives useful background material to the proposition.
But see	The authority provides a contrary perspective to the proposition; it may or may not contradict it directly.
Cf [prefer: Compare]	(*Cf* = Latin *confer*, compare.) The authority provides a useful comparison with the proposition, or supports it by analogy.
But cf [prefer: But compare]	The authority supports a contrary position to the proposition.
Contra	The authority contradicts the proposition.

CJ

Abbreviation for *Chief Justice*. In some jurisdictions, also abbreviation for *Chief Judge* of a separate division of a court—eg, Jones CJ in Equity, Smith CJ at Common Law.

claim

A word particularly susceptible to litigation over meaning, usually over the content and/or formality required for a request or demand to constitute a *claim*. Case law throws up many examples. In some, *claim* required substantial content and formality; in others it did not. Seek to forestall argument by being more specific. To illustrate:

- In court rules, *claim* normally means the 'assertion of a cause of action'. Thus:
  - A *claim* to recover for damage to a motor vehicle means a demand made formally through a court: *Khiaban v Beard* [2003] 1 WLR 1626, 1630 (Dyson LJ).
  - A defence that a deed (under which one party had covenanted not to libel the other party) was void, was not a '*claim* in respect of libel': *Shordiche-Churchward v Corle* [1959] 1 WLR 351 (CA).
- A *claim* for indemnity under an insurance policy requires an assertion of the amount claimed: *Metcash Trading* Ltd *v Credit Guarantee Insurance Corporation of Africa Ltd* [2004] ZASCA 9; [2004] 2 All SA 484 (SCA), [16] (following a long line of South African cases).
- A landlord's insurance policy covered the landlord against *claims* by the tenant. Held, a tenant's letter to the landlord's estate agent alleging defects in the property and requesting compensation, was a *claim* against the landlord: *Livesay v Hawkins* [2012] QSC 122.
- A note on a company's annual accounts, submitted to a tax inspector, that its profits were 'subject to group relief', was a *claim* for group tax relief. To qualify as a *claim*, it was not necessary to identify the individual companies or the amount of the relief that each one surrendered: *Gallic Leasing Ltd v Coburn* [1991] 1 WLR 1399 (HL).

See also **complaint**.

Clapham omnibus

The London public bus on which rides 'the reasonable man' (or, as we would now say, 'the reasonable person'). The first reported usage is by Collins MR in *McQuire v Western Morning News* [1903] 2 KB 100, 109, attributing the term to Lord Bowen in 1871. A number of London buses serve destinations in or around Clapham, so it is unclear which particular bus carries this hypothetical person with their reasoned, balanced, and unbiased approach to life.

The expression is too well entrenched to be abandoned, but not all judges embrace it:

> 'God forbid that the standard of manners should be taken from the man on the Clapham omnibus. Besides which, if I may say so with great respect to the learned Lord Justice who first used it, that is a most unfortunate phrase from any point of view.' [*Lea v Justice of the Peace Ltd*, unreported, 14 March 1947, King's Bench Division, Hilbery J in argument, reproduced in *Privacy and the Press*, ed H Montgomery (Butterworth, 1947) 156]

The expression has encouraged many variants, some tongue-in-cheek: eg, 'the man who takes the magazines at home, and in the evening pushes the lawn mower in his shirt sleeves': *Hall v Brooklands Auto Racing Club* [1933] 1 KB 205, 224 (Greer LJ, quoting an American usage).

Judges outside the UK occasionally invoke similar reasonable passengers on their own transport systems. This has spawned colourful counterparts:

- *Australia*: the person on the Bondi tram: *Papatonakis v Australian Telecommunications Commission* (1984) 156 CLR 7, 36 (Deane J); or the person on the Bourke Street tram: *Re Pandos and the Commonwealth of Australia* [1991] AATA 18, [88].

- *Hong Kong*: the 'man on the Shaukiwan tram': *Ng Chiu Miu and others v Securities and Futures Commission*, [2009] Securities and Futures Appeals Tribunal (HK) Nos 7, 8 and 9 of 2007, [95] (Stone J).
- *Canada*: 'Clapham', but with the passenger more snugly ensconced, 'the man *in* the Clapham omnibus': *Beloit Canada Ltée Ltd v Oy* (1986) 8 CPR (3d) 289, [17].

clause

In normal usage, *clause* means a grammatical unit with a subject and predicate. In legal usage, however, *clause* can mean any of the following: a paragraph containing a number of sentences; a single sentence; a part-sentence; or part only of a part-sentence. It can even mean a mere snippet of words, making no sense if taken alone. For example, a testator made a gift by will to 'Elizabeth Ely, her heirs and assigns for ever'; later, the testator crossed out 'her heirs and assigns for ever'; by crossing out these words, the testator was revoking a *clause* in his will: *Swinton v Bailey* (1878) 4 App Cas 70, 77 (Lord Cairns LC).

CLAUSE STRUCTURE

Benefits of a careful structure

Legal documents conventionally divide information into clauses. Each clause deals with a separate topic or subtopic. Clauses can themselves be divided into subclauses, which can be further divided into paragraphs, subparagraphs, and so on. Careful division into these information segments improves understanding—not merely by breaking down the information into shorter 'bites', but also by showing the relationship between items of information.

Move from general to particular

When drafting, it is usually better to start with the general, before moving to the particular. The general gives the context for the particular; to start with the particular complicates the reader's task. Within that framework—general to particular—different options are possible. The following table outlines a suggested clause structure (though not all clauses will require all steps).

Structure—step by step	Example (simplified for illustration)
1. General (or introductory) material.	1. This clause sets out the landlord's obligation to provide quiet enjoyment.
2. The basic principle.	2. The landlord agrees to provide quiet enjoyment to the tenant.
3. First exception to the basic principle.	3. However, the landlord's promise in (2) is conditional on the tenant paying rent on time.
4. Qualification to the first exception.	4. If a date for rent payment falls on a public holiday, the payment is not late if the tenant pays it on the next business day.
5. Second exception to the basic principle.	5. The landlord's promise in (2) is also conditional on the tenant keeping the premises in repair.
6. Qualification to the second exception.	6. There is no breach of (5) merely by failing to repair fair wear and tear.

One main concept per clause

For readers' convenience, try to limit each clause to a single, core concept. Combining two or more core concepts in the same clause can add unnecessary complexity. For example, leases formerly combined the demise (ie, the formal grant of the lease) with the reddendum (ie, the obligation to pay rent); but a modern reader would better understand the transaction if the grant of the lease and the rent obligations were in separate clauses.

More than one sentence per clause?

There is no 'one-clause-one-sentence' *rule*. While legal drafters usually *prefer* 'one-clause-one-sentence', it is sometimes useful to include a second sentence in a clause. Examples are: (1) to show the close relationship between the ideas in each sentence (a relationship that could be lost by separating the sentences into different clauses); and (2) conversely, to show that the idea in the second sentence is merely subsidiary (a subtlety that could be lost if the second sentence were elevated to a separate clause).

However, beware of single clauses that combine full sentences with sentence fragments. The practice may be convenient for the drafter, but it can be grammatically ungainly.

Example

Poor

The Law Society may issue a licence to practise that:

- (a) limits the fields of law permitted by the licence. The fields may be civil law or criminal law, or both; and
- (b) specifies the maximum hourly charge-out rate for each field of law. The Law Society must review the rates annually.

Better

The Law Society may issue a licence to practise that:

- (a) limits the permitted fields of law to civil law or criminal law, or both; and
- (b) specifies the maximum hourly charge-out rate (which the Law Society must review annually) for each field of law.

Better still (moving the charge-out rate provision into a separate clause)

1. The Law Society may issue a licence to practise that:
   - (a) limits the permitted fields of law to civil law or criminal law, or both; and
   - (b) specifies the maximum hourly charge-out rate for each field of law.
2. The Law Society must review the maximum charge-out rate annually.

Paragraphing conventions

When to paragraph

Paragraphing is useful for separating items or information that would otherwise appear in run-on lists. The technique helps the reader to assimilate information, and helps the writer to ensure that nothing is omitted. Factors in deciding whether to paragraph include: the number of items in the list; whether the items can be listed in a parallel structure; and whether a paragraph structure will improve clarity and reduce ambiguity. The process of paragraphing may add words—as in Examples 2 and 3, below—but that is no bad thing if it increases readability.

Example 1 (dividing into paragraphs)

Before

If the mortgagor defaults, the mortgagee may take possession of the land for as long as the mortgagee considers appropriate, and may sell the land or any part of it including by subdividing it into lots, by public auction or by private sale, or may grant a lease of the land for such period as the mortgagee considers appropriate, without being liable for any loss.

[65 words. Problems include:

- too many items in list;
- items are complicated by qualifications;
- ambiguity over whether the final words—'without being liable for any loss'—qualify only the grant of a lease.]

After

If the mortgagor defaults, the mortgagee may (without being liable for any loss):

(a) take possession of the land for as long as the mortgagee considers appropriate;

(b) sell the land or any part of it (including by subdividing it into lots) by public auction or by private sale;

(c) grant a lease of the land for any period the mortgagee considers appropriate.

[63 words]

Example 2 (dividing into more complex paragraphs)

Before

The landlord may grant the tenant consent to assign the lease if the tenant submits a request for consent that is signed and witnessed by two persons, accompanied by a certificate from an accountant about the proposed assignee's creditworthiness and financial acumen, and a statement from the assignee's bank manager certifying the balance of funds in the assignee's bank account and the assignee's current liabilities, and is sent by registered post or certified mail.

[74 words; too much information in single sentence]

After: version 1

The landlord may grant the tenant consent to assign the lease if the tenant submits a request for consent that is:

(a) signed and witnessed by two persons;

(b) accompanied by:

  (i) a certificate from an accountant about the proposed assignee's creditworthiness and financial acumen; and

  (ii) a statement from the assignee's bank manager certifying the balance of funds in the assignee's bank account, and the assignee's current liabilities; and

(c) sent by registered post or certified mail.

[78 words]

After: version 2 (better)

[Collapsing the clause into two elements: (1) the need to request; and (2) the procedure for, and contents of, the request.]

(1) If the tenant requests, the landlord may grant the tenant consent to assign the lease.

(2) The request must be:

  (a) sent to the landlord by registered post or certified mail;

  (b) signed and witnessed by two persons; and

(c) accompanied by:
   (i) a certificate from an accountant about the proposed assignee's creditworthiness and financial acumen; and
   (ii) a statement from the assignee's bank manager certifying:
      - the balance of funds in the assignee's bank account, and
      - the assignee's current liabilities.

[82 words; longer, but clearer]

Example 3 (improving existing paragraphing)

Before

If the amount the landlord pays for outgoings for the premises:

(a) is more than the amount the tenant has paid in advance to the landlord on account of anticipated outgoings, the tenant must pay the shortfall to the landlord within 10 business days of the landlord requesting payment; or

(b) is less than the amount the tenant has paid in advance to the landlord on account of anticipated outgoings, the landlord must pay the excess to the tenant within 10 business days of the tenant requesting payment.

[89 words; existing division into (a) and (b) is better than no division, but is unnecessarily complex.]

After

(1) This clause applies where the amount the landlord pays for outgoings for the premises differs from the amount the tenant has paid in advance to the landlord on account of anticipated outgoings.

(2) If the amount paid by the landlord is more than the amount paid by the tenant, the tenant must pay the difference to the landlord.

(3) If the amount paid by the landlord is less than the amount paid by the tenant, the landlord must pay the difference to the tenant.

(4) A party must make the payment within 10 business days of the other party requesting it.

[103 words; longer than original, but clearer]

Paragraph-formatting conventions

1. Do not create a paragraph for a single item.

Poor	**Better**
If the tenant fails to: (a) keep the premises open for trade, the landlord may terminate the lease.	If the tenant fails to keep the premises open for trade, the landlord may terminate the lease.

2. Make each paragraph flow grammatically from the lead-in.

Poor	**Better**
The landlord may terminate the lease if the tenant fails: (a) to keep the premises open for trade; or (b) unless the landlord agrees otherwise, to keep the premises clean.	The landlord may terminate the lease if the tenant fails: (a) to keep the premises open for trade; or (b) to keep the premises clean (unless the landlord agrees otherwise).

3. Make paragraphs grammatically parallel.

Poor	**Better**
The tenant may assign the lease: (a) if the proposed assignee has appropriate business experience; and (b) after giving at least 21 days prior notice to the landlord.	The tenant may assign the lease if: (a) the proposed assignee has appropriate business experience; and (b) the tenant has given at least 21 days prior notice to the landlord.

4. A paragraph may refer to items in an earlier paragraph (even though the lead-in does not mention them).

The Law Society may issue a licence to practise that: (a) limits the fields of law permitted by the licence; and (b) specifies the maximum hourly charge-out rate for each field.

Indenting

Indenting is a powerful tool for conveying meaning. Here are some of its benefits:

To prevent ambiguity

Indenting paragraphs or text can help prevent ambiguity. In the following examples, taken from Australian legislation, appropriate indenting would have avoided litigation over meaning.

Example 1 (no paragraphing in original)

Section 10(1) of the *Motor Car Act 1909* (Vic):

> [It is an offence to drive] a motor car on a public highway **recklessly** or **negligently** or **at a speed or in a manner which is dangerous to the public** having regard to all the circumstances of the case including the nature condition and use of the highway and to the amount of traffic which actually is at the time or which might reasonably be expected to be on the highway. [Bold and underlining added for illustration.]

Which of the words or phrases in **bold** were qualified by the words underlined? Two interpretations were open:

Interpretation 1	**Interpretation 2**
[It is an offence to drive] a motor car on a public highway: • recklessly, or • negligently, or • at a speed or in a manner which is dangerous to the public, having regard to all the circumstances of the case including the nature condition and use of the highway and to the amount of traffic which actually is at the time or which might reasonably be expected to be on the highway. [Interpretation adopted in *Chammen v Gilmore* [1914] VLR 455]	[It is an offence to drive] a motor car on a public highway: • recklessly, or • negligently, or • at a speed or in a manner which is dangerous to the public having regard to all the circumstances of the case including the nature condition and use of the highway and to the amount of traffic which actually is at the time or which might reasonably be expected to be on the highway. [Interpretation adopted in *Kane v Dureau* [1911] VLR 293]

Example 2 (ambiguity caused by *and*)

Section 13 of the *Fair Trading Act 1987* (WA):

13. False representations categorised

(1) [A] statement shall be taken to be a false representation if—

(a) it is false, or deceives, or if it or any information thereby provided is materially inaccurate *and* that statement is intended [to achieve certain purposes]. [Italics added for illustration.]

The placement of *and* created two possible meanings:

Meaning 1	**Meaning 2**
A statement is taken to be a false representation if: • it is false, or • it deceives, or • it or any information thereby provided is materially inaccurate *and* that statement is intended [to achieve certain purposes].	A statement is taken to be a false representation if: (a) (i) it is false, or (ii) it deceives, or (iii) it or any information thereby provided is materially inaccurate, *and* (b) it is intended [to achieve certain purposes].

A magistrate decided in favour of meaning (2). On appeal, the Supreme Court decided in favour of meaning (1), given that court's view of the provision's perceived policy. (The facts are from *Landers v G & M Giorgiante Nominees Pty Ltd* [2006] WASC 32; (2006) 31 WAR 563.)

To show relationship between parts

Careful indenting can show the relationship between parts of a provision.

Example 1

Before

This clause applies to members and directors, but does not apply to associate members unless they are spouses of members, or partners of members who are engaged to be married and of good character.

After

(1) This clause applies to members and directors.

(2) But it does not apply to associate members, unless they are:

(a) a member's spouse, or

(b) a member's partner, who is engaged to the member and of good character.

Example 2

A lease contained the following clause, laid out in the following way (text simplified for illustration):

11 If during the term of the lease the premises are destroyed or damaged, then

(a) Either the lessor or the lessee may terminate the lease without compensation to the other.

(b) The termination will not affect the rights of either party in relation to earlier matters.

(c) On the happening of the damage or destruction, the rent abates proportionately.

(d) If the lessor wants to demolish or rebuild, the lessor can give six months' notice to terminate the lease.

Was the landlord's power to terminate under para (d) controlled by the opening words of clause 11—ie, exercisable only if the premises were destroyed or damaged—or was it a stand-alone power exercisable at any time? The two meanings can be illustrated with indenting and clause numbering:

Meaning 1 (only if premises destroyed or damaged)	**Meaning 2 (stand-alone power)**
11 If during the term of the lease the premises are destroyed or damaged, then (a) either the lessor or the lessee may terminate the lease without compensation to the other; (b) the termination will not affect the rights of either party in relation to earlier matters; (c) on the happening of the damage or destruction, the rent abates proportionately; and (d) if the lessor wants to demolish or rebuild, the lessor can give six months' notice to terminate the lease.	11 If during the term of the lease the premises are destroyed or damaged, then (a) either the lessor or the lessee may terminate the lease without compensation to the other; (b) the termination will not affect the rights of either party in relation to earlier matters; and (c) on the happening of the damage or destruction, the rent abates proportionately. 12 If the lessor wants to demolish or rebuild, the lessor can give six months' notice to terminate the lease.

The court held in favour of meaning (1): the lessor's power under cl 11(d) was controlled by the opening words of cl 11. That is, the power existed only where the premises were destroyed or damaged; para (d) was *not* a stand-alone right to require the tenant to vacate. Presumably the result would have been different had the drafter made para (d) an entirely independent clause, divorced from the opening words of cl 11 (as in meaning (2)). See *Spathis v Hanave Investment Co Pty Ltd* [2001] NSWSC 265; (2001) NSW ConvR 55-983.

Judicial approaches to indenting

Judges give due weight to indenting as a guide to meaning. Lord Donovan once said that he never understood why some conveyancers regarded it as beneath their dignity to use paragraphing techniques to make their meaning plain; and that, had that been done on the facts of the case before him, 'much trouble and expense would have been avoided': *Re Gulbenkian's Settlement* [1970] AC 508, 526. Australian judges, too, give effect to deliberate paragraph indenting: see, eg, *Clerk v Equity Trustees Executors & Agency Co Ltd* (1913) 15 CLR 625, 628 (Griffiths CJ), 634 (Isaacs J).

Example

> A clause in a charterparty stated that time lost as a result of 'all or any of the causes hereunder' was not to be counted as laytime. There followed a list of nine causes (eg, accident, interruptions on railways or port), ending with:
>
> > (ix) Any cause of whatsoever kind or nature, *beyond the control of Seller*, preventing cargo preparation, loading or berthing of the vessel. (Italics added.)
>
> Held, the words 'beyond the control of Seller' applied only to cause (ix), and could not be read back into the preceding causes (i) to (viii): *Emeraldian Ltd Partnership v Wellmix Shipping Ltd* [2010] EWHC 1411 (Comm); [2011] 1 Lloyd's Rep 301.

However, a court will not allow poor indenting or paragraphing to compel a meaning that (in the court's view) the parties did not intend. For example:

- An English judge declined to allow the erroneous indentation of text, giving the appearance of a subclause, to obscure the clause's intended status as a freestanding provision—even though the drafters had ample opportunity to review the wording and layout: *BP Exploration Operating Co Ltd v Kvaerner Oilfield Products Ltd* [2004] EWHC 999 (Comm), [95].
- A Canadian appellate court held that a stand-alone sentence that followed immediately after clause 10(ii) and was indented to the same extent as clause 10(ii), in fact applied to the

preceding clause 10(i) also: *Moffat Tank Co v Canadian Indemnity Co* [1974] 1 WWR 688; 42 DLR (3d) 280.

In this way, judges in effect re-paragraph in the way they consider more clearly reflects the drafter's intention: for other examples, see, eg, *Re AB* [1950] VLR 1; *Marine Board of Strahan v Kirkpatrick* [1967] Tas SR 179.

Avoid over-division

Sometimes, the desire to mark out information clearly can lead to over-division of text, complicating information rather than clarifying it and slowing both writer and reader. The solution may be to redesign the structure.

Example

Poor (over-division)

The mortgagee may take proceedings for orders:

(a) permitting a sale, which may be:
- (i) by private sale, or
- (ii) by auction, after
  - (A) appropriate advertising, and
  - (B) obtaining a valuation, by
    - (1) a licensed real estate agent, or
    - (2) a registered valuer; or

(b) requiring a mediation between:
- (i) the parties; and
- (ii) their legal representatives, who may be:
  - (A) barristers, or
  - (B) solicitors, who are:
    - (1) on the roll of solicitors, and
    - (2) of at least 5 years' standing.

[87 words]

Better (restructured; longer but clearer)

1. The mortgagee may take proceedings for orders:
   - (a) permitting a sale, or
   - (b) requiring a mediation between the parties and their legal representatives.
2. The sale may be by private sale or by auction.
3. If by auction, the mortgagor must first:
   - (a) arrange appropriate advertising, and
   - (b) obtain a valuation, by
     - (i) a licensed real estate agent, or
     - (ii) a registered valuer.
4. If the court orders a mediation, the parties' legal representatives may be:
   - (a) barristers, or
   - (b) solicitors who are on the roll of solicitors and of at least 5 years' standing.

[100 words]

Reduce cross-references

Where possible, eliminate cross-references. In particular, where in-clause cross-references are self-evident, do not complicate the drafting by making them express. Thus:

Instead of this	Try this (cross-references removed)
(1) A mortgage over land must be registered with the Registrar-General.	(1) A mortgage over land must be registered with the Registrar-General. [unchanged]
(2) An application for registration under subsection (1) must be lodged with the Registrar-General.	(2) An application for registration must be lodged with the Registrar-General.
(3) On receiving an application for registration under subsection (1), the Registrar-General must notify all interested parties of the intention to register.	(3) On receiving the application, the Registrar-General must notify all interested parties of the intention to register.
(4) On registration following an application under subsection (1), the mortgagee has all the powers of a registered mortgagee.	(4) On registration, the mortgagee has all the powers of a registered mortgagee.

Avoid 'sandwich' constructions

A 'sandwich' construction starts with an introductory statement, then drops to the next line for one or more indented paragraphs, and then (on a new line) reverts to the margin to pick up where the introductory statement left off. Sandwich constructions require the reader to mentally hold the introductory statement while processing the indented paragraphs, before returning to the main theme. Try re-constructing the presentation, by promoting the final statement to follow directly after the introductory statement—rearranging the sandwich, as it were.

Example 1 (lease)

Before	After
The landlord may do any of the following: • close the access points, • direct the tenant to leave, • forcibly remove the tenant and the tenant's customers, if a fire breaks out in the common areas.	The landlord may do any of the following if a fire breaks out in the common areas: • close the access points • direct the tenant to leave • forcibly remove the tenant and the tenant's customers.

Example 2 (judgment)

Before	After
'In case of anyone: (a) over 70; (b) being cared for by someone; (c) who resides in a nursing home or similar facility; or (d) about whom for any other reason the solicitor might have concern about capacity, the solicitor should ask the client and their carer whether there is any reason to be concerned about capacity …' [Source: *Ryan v Dalton* [2017] NSWSC 1007, [107] (Kunc J)]	The solicitor should ask the client and their carer whether there is any reason to be concerned about capacity, where the person— (a) is over 70; or (b) is being cared for by someone; or (c) resides in a nursing home or similar facility; or (d) is someone for whom, for any other reason, the solicitor might have concern about capacity.

Two-slice sandwiches are bad enough. Even worse are three-slice ('club') sandwiches; always try to simplify their structure.

Before	**After**
If any of the following occur: (a) fire breaks out in the common areas; (b) the police advise of a terrorist threat; (c) an emergency authority orders the premises to be closed off to the general public, the landlord may do any of the following: (d) close the access points, (e) direct the tenant to leave, (f) forcibly remove the tenant and the tenant's customers, without having to give the tenant prior notice.	(1) If any of the events in clause (2) occurs, the landlord may take any of the steps in clause (3) without having to give the tenant prior notice. (2) The events are: (a) fire breaks out in the common areas; (b) the police advise of a terrorist threat; (c) an emergency authority orders the premises to be closed off to the general public. (3) The permitted steps are: (a) close the access points; (b) direct the tenant to leave; (c) forcibly remove the tenant and the tenant's customers.

Referring to subclauses and paragraphs

The most efficient way to refer to a subsidiary part of a clause, such as a subclause or paragraph, is to start with the highest level and move towards the lowest. For example:

- 'clause 10(1)' [*not* 'subclause 10(1)'; *not* 'subclause (1) of clause 10']
- 'clause 10(1)(a)' [*not* 'paragraph 10(1)(a)'; *not* 'paragraph (a) of clause 10(1)'; *not* 'paragraph (a) of subclause (1) of clause 10'].

See also **CROSS-REFERENCES; DOCUMENT STRUCTURE.**

clean hands

See **unclean hands.**

clear day

Meaning

A *clear day* is a whole day within a specified period. The first and last days of the period are excluded: *Armstrong v Great Southern Gold Mining Co (NL)* (1911) 12 CLR 382. Counting does not start until the following day (and ignores fractions of a day). For example:

- Where a contract specifies a notice period of '3 *clear* days' before one party can require the other to pay money, a notice given on Monday cannot require payment before Friday.
- A car hiring arrangement made on Monday, providing a car 'for 3 *clear* days', allows its use for all of Tuesday, Wednesday and Thursday.
- Where something is to be done within '10 *clear* days' of 1 June, time runs until the last moment of 11 June.

Is *clear* superfluous?

As a matter of ordinary English, a stipulated interval between two events is a *clear* interval. Thus, where an 'interval of two days' must elapse between event A and event B, it means 2 *clear* days: *Re Railway Sleepers Supply Co* (1885) 29 Ch D 204, 208 (Chitty J). Again:

> '[W]hen you talk of doing a thing within a period of a certain number of days, it is quite clear that the end of the last day is the furthest limit. It is impossible to say that a thing required to be done within seven days is done within seven days if done on the eighth day, and it is impossible to make any alteration of the limit by adding the word "clear".' [*Armstrong v Great Southern Gold Mining Co* (1911) 12 CLR 382, 388 (Griffith CJ)]

Hence, *clear* is often superfluous. It may also be unwise. Consider the following example:

> A landlord gives a notice to a tenant: 'You have 5 *clear* days to vacate the premises.' The sentence means simply 'You have 5 *days* to vacate the premises.' *Clear* adds no extra meaning. Indeed, to include it may introduce uncertainty elsewhere. Suppose the notice also says: 'You can keep the keys for 5 days.' Could this be construed as *not* clear days—so that the keys must be returned on day 5, not on day 6?

See also **at least**; **day**; **not less than (a period)**; **within**.

clearly / obviously

Often superfluous: if something is '*clearly* true' or '*obviously* true', it is simply 'true'. Indeed, to add *clearly* or *obviously* may hint at disingenuity or bias, thereby undermining the statement. For example, to say 'Lord Diplock was *obviously* a better judge than Lord Denning' implies that Lord Diplock knew the law better than Lord Denning, which in turn may suggest (to some readers) a bias in favour of black-letter lawyers over lawyers who put subjective fairness above settled precedent.

Also, beware of juxtaposing *clearly* or *obviously* in ways that create temporary miscues:

- The judge was *clearly* uncertain about the argument.
- *Obviously*, the argument is vague.

Unless you genuinely need *clearly* or *obviously* for emphasis, omit it, as in the following examples:

- The trial judge ~~clearly~~ thought otherwise.
- The plaintiff's argument is ~~obviously~~ overstated.

CLICHÉS

Avoid clichés. A cliché is 'a phrase whose aptness in a particular context when it was first invented has won it such popularity that it has become hackneyed, and is used without thought in contexts where it is no longer apt': Ernest Gower, *The Complete Plain Words*, Sidney Greenbaum and Janet Whitcut (eds), 3rd edn (Penguin, 1987) 86. Clichéd terms in common use include: 'silver bullet', 'perfect storm', 'ground zero', 'going forward', 'reach out to', 'avoid like the plague', 'at the end of the day', 'space' (eg, 'I work in the taxation space'), 'thin end of the wedge', 'silver lining'. A leading US judge has said:

> 'Clichés ... deaden our senses to the nuances of language so often critical to our common law tradition. ... The problem of clichés as a substitute for rational analysis is particularly acute in the legal profession, where our style of writing is often deservedly the subject of ridicule.' [*Eminence Capital LLC v Aspeon Inc* 316 F 3d 1048, 1054 (Reinhardt J) (9th Cir 2003), lamenting the trial judge's clichéd 'three bites at the apple'.]

Even the best legal writers sometimes descend to clichés: 'The proof of the pudding is in the eating' (*R v Greater London Council* [1976] 1 WLR 550, 556, Lord Denning MR). However, distinguish clichés from metaphors. Clichés deaden writing; imaginative metaphors enliven it.

See also **METAPHORS**.

clog on the equity of redemption

A restriction on a mortgagor's right to recover the mortgaged property free of encumbrances or restrictions despite repaying the debt or performing the obligations which the mortgage secures. Generally, a *clog* (or 'fetter') of this kind is unenforceable. For example, a mortgagee cannot, as part and parcel of the mortgage transaction, take an option to purchase the property, because if exercised it would allow the mortgagee effectively to preclude the mortgagor from regaining the property even after repaying the debt: *Samuel v Jarrah Timber and Wood Paving Co Ltd* [1904] AC 323. Lawyers will be (or should be) familiar with this term of art. But non-lawyers will find it mystifying—so explain it to them.

Further reading

S Bridge, E Cooke and M Dixon (eds), *Megarry & Wade's Law of Real Property*, 9th edn (Sweet & Maxwell, 2019) [24-085]–[24-098]

See also **equity of redemption**.

close proximity

Almost always tautologous: if something is in *proximity*, it is close. Also, *proximity* is almost always a puffed-up substitute for 'near [to]'—in which case, prefer *near* [to]. For example:

- 'She was *in very close proximity to* [prefer: *very close to*; *very near*] Williams at that moment …' [*Robinson v Chief Constable of West Yorkshire Police* [2018] UKSC 4; [2018] AC 736, [12] (Lord Reed)
- 'We have been addressed on … the way in which Ms Hill was questioned about the CCTV cameras that were *in close proximity to* [prefer: *close to*; *near*] the events on 1 June 2012 …' [*R v Gorman* [2019] EWCA Crim 2271, [61] (Fulford LJ)]

co- words

Some words with the prefix *co-* always take a hyphen, others never do, and yet others may or may not. In this, legal usage follows standard usage. For some words, the hyphen is useful to avoid a temporary miscue: eg, *co-respondent* (compare *correspondent*), *co-worker* (compare *cow worker*), *co-op* (compare *coop*). For others, the hyphen helps differentiate between successive vowels: eg, *co-adjutant*, *co-executor*, *co-institution*, *co-user*. *Co-* words commonly encountered in law include the following.

co-operate / cooperate

The increasing tendency is to omit the hyphen: *cooperate*; *cooperative*; *cooperation*. Despite this tendency, the hyphen helps show the sense of the word—*co-operate* = work together—and is retained in recent legislation: eg, *Co-operative and Community Benefit Societies Act 2014*; *Co-operatives National Law* (Australia). And a hyphen is still useful to distinguish between a co-operative store (*co-op*) and a chicken enclosure (*coop*).

co-owner / coowner

The word is almost always hyphenated. Instances of the non-hyphenated form *coowner* are seen, but they are aberrations. For example:

- 'Mr Hendricks's interest as *coowner* [prefer: *co-owner*] had been charged to the bank.' [*Barclays Bank plc v Hendricks* [1996] 1 FLR 258, 263 (Laddie J)]
- '[I]t is plain that Mr Edwards wishes to continue to live in the premises … and I shall assume that Mrs Edwards, the other *coowner* [prefer: *co-owner*], does so as well.' [*Edwards v Edwards* [2010] EWHC 652 (Ch), [31] (Trower QC)]

co-partner / copartner

The hyphenated version is more common, although both versions are seen. But is 'co' needed? A partner must be a partner with another partner. For example: 'A is co-partner with B' means simply 'A is a partner with B' (or better: 'A and B are partners').

co-payment / copayment

The hyphenated version is the norm, although both versions are seen.

co-worker / coworker

A word that benefits from a hyphen, particularly where context may cause an initial miscue: eg, where an employment award in the dairy industry distinguishes between employees working alone and *coworkers*. Nevertheless, the unhyphenated form is sometimes seen:

- 'Partners or *coworkers* [prefer: co-workers] as jurors' [Heading to *Juries Act* 1967 (Tas), s 15]
- '[In] *Took Leng How v PP* [2006] 2 SLR 70, [the] appellant had killed a child of a *coworker* [prefer: *co-worker*] by smothering her …' [Stanley Yeo, *Criminal Law*, (2006) 7 *Singapore Academy of Law Annual Review* [11.9]. Notably, the court itself in *Took Leng How* hyphenated *co-worker*.]

See also **HYPHENS**.

codefendant / co-defendant

Preferably hyphenated (to prevent a miscue, even only temporarily, for *code*). However, non-hyphenated versions are sometimes seen:

> 'The claimant and his *codefendant* [prefer: *co-defendant*] got on at Camberwell and sat two rows behind them. … When the victim's two friends got off the bus, the claimant and his *codefendant* [prefer: *co-defendant*] began to raise their voices …' [*C v Balham Youth Court* [2003] EWHC 1332 (Admin), [4] (Scott Baker LJ)]

codify / consolidate

A *codifying* statute collates and states authoritatively the existing law (usually case law) on a particular topic. A *consolidating* statute collects all previous statutes and amendments on a particular topic, and re-enacts them as a single, up-to-date statute.

coemployee / co-employee

Preferably hyphenated:

> '[Close] relationships may exist between employer and employee and *co-employees* ...' [*Tame v New South Wales* [2002] HCA 35, [366], (2002) 211 CLR 317, 439 (Callinan J)]

COGNATE TERMS

See **DEFINITIONS**.

collateral

Used as an adjective, means *subsidiary*, *alongside*, or *in conjunction with*. Examples are *collateral damage*; *collateral debt*; *collateral security*; *collateral contract*; and (in the US) *collateral estoppel*. Used as a noun, is shorthand for 'collateral security'—eg, a bank may require 'collateral' over a property as security for a loan.

COLLATERAL CONTRACT

A contract made 'alongside' another contract (the main contract). Collateral contracts are of two kinds:

1. A contract between A and B in which one or both agree to do or refrain from doing an act that pertains to the main contract between them. In practice usually called a 'side agreement' or 'side deal'.

   Example

   A lease (the main contract) requires the tenant to pay rent each month, but by a collateral contract the landlord agrees to excuse the tenant from having to pay rent for the first six months.

2. A contract under which a person agrees to enter into a contract with another person (the main contract). For example, C and B may agree (the collateral contract) that B will enter into a contract with A (the main contract) on terms that benefit C.

   Examples

   - A car repairer (C) contracts with an insurance company (B) that under B's insurance policies (the main contract) with its customers (A), B will nominate C as the preferred repairer. [Example based on *Charnock v Liverpool Corporation* [1968] 1 WLR 1498 (CA).]
   - A credit card company (C) contracts with a service station proprietor (B) that C will honour the credit card when a customer (A) purchases petrol from B (the main contract) using the card. [Example based on *Re Charge Card Services Ltd* [1989] Ch 497 (CA).]

Context should easily clarify which meaning of 'collateral contract' is intended. In particular, meaning (1) can apply only where the parties to each contract (the 'collateral contract' and the 'main contract') are identical.

Further reading

Halsbury's Laws of England, 'Contract' (vol 22, 2019) [133]

See also **side deal**.

COLON PLUS DASH (SYMBOL)

See **DASHES**.

COLONS

Uses

A colon is a punctuation mark leading into information that is about to follow. It tells the reader: 'now, here comes the detail'. For example:

> The road rules cover the following matters: vehicular speed, traffic lights, driver training, and police powers.

Some more traditional legal writers indicate a lead-in by using, not a mere colon, but a colon plus a dash. Of these traditionalists, some prefer a short [en] dash (:–), others a long [em] dash (:—). But regardless of the length of the dash, a 'colon plus dash' adds nothing to a colon alone, and is disappearing from current usage.

Abuses

Do not use a colon in the following circumstances:

- *After a preposition*: 'He excelled *in* [no colon needed] advocacy, drafting, and interviewing.'
- *After a verb, where the colon would separate the verb from its object*: 'He liked to [no colon needed] research carefully and argue strongly.'
- *After words that inherently introduce a list*: 'She liked to research all possible sources, *including* [no colon needed] case law, statutes and academic articles.'

See also **DASHES; PUNCTUATION**.

COLUMNS

See **DOCUMENT DESIGN**.

COMMA SPLICE

See **however (Avoiding comma splice)**.

COMMAS

To aid understanding

Use commas in legal writing as in ordinary prose—to aid understanding. The presence and placement of a comma can significantly alter the meaning of a sentence, as the following examples show.

Version 1	**Version 2**
The court said Sir Owen Dixon lacked legal expertise.	The court, said Sir Owen Dixon, lacked legal expertise.
The judge put his wig on quickly, deciding to enter court.	The judge put his wig on, quickly deciding to enter court.
The [purpose] … is to facilitate the just, quick and cheap resolution of the real issues. [*Civil Procedure Act 2005* (NSW), s 56(1)]	The [purpose] … is to facilitate the just quick and cheap resolution of the real issues …
The court may order the defendant to serve a prison term or pay a fine and pay compensation.	The court may order the defendant to serve a prison term, or pay a fine and pay compensation. [That is, *either* (1) prison term, *or* (2) both a fine and compensation.] The court may order the defendant to serve a prison term or pay a fine, and pay compensation. [That is, (1) either prison term or fine, *and* (2) pay compensation.]
'[The trustees may revoke] the trusts terms and conditions contained in [a certain document].' [Clause in trust deed considered in *Mercanti v Mercanti* [2016] WASCA 206; (2016) 50 WAR 495]	'[The trustees may revoke] the terms and conditions of the trust contained [in a certain document].' Or '[The trustees may revoke] the trusts, terms[,] and conditions contained in [a certain document].' (Held to be intended meaning.)

Some legal writers use commas sparingly, perhaps to minimise the visual clutter of too many commas. But multiple commas are a blessing, not a curse, if they ensure clarity. In the following example, commas would have avoided litigation over meaning.

> An employer took out workers' compensation insurance to cover injuries to employees engaged in the employer's business. The policy described the employer's business as 'Fuel Carrying and Repairing' [no commas]. (The description had been carried over from the proposal form completed by the employer or its agent.) An employee was injured when driving the employer's vehicle carrying bricks. Was carrying bricks within the description 'Fuel Carrying and Repairing'? The New South Wales Court of Appeal held that it was, overruling the trial judge on this point. The evidence showed that the employer's business was three-fold: (1) supplying petroleum and transporting it in fuel trucks; (2) general carrying (including of bricks); and (3) repairing lawn mowers and chain saws. The Court interpreted the policy as if 'fuel' and 'carrying' and 'repairing' were three separate heads. Had the wording included commas ('Fuel, Carrying, and Repairing'), litigation would have been avoided. See *Manufacturers' Mutual Insurance Ltd v Withers* (1988) 5 ANZ Insurance Cases 60-853.

To mark off independent clauses

Even where a comma does not change meaning, it can aid understanding by making the sentence construction more apparent, particularly in long sentences. The following two examples illustrate the point. In the first example, adding a comma—indicated by [,]—would clarify meaning by showing the parallel structure of the sentence. In the second example, adding commas—also indicated by [,]—would more clearly mark off explanatory information.

1. 'Under s 43, a compensation notice … must be in a prescribed form, must notify the owner that the land has been compulsorily acquired, must state that the owner is entitled to compensation, must offer to pay a specified amount of compensation as determined by the Valuer-General and be accompanied by a form of deed of release and indemnity[,] and must inform the owner of the right to object to the amount offered.' [*Golden Mile Property Investments Pty Ltd v Cudgegong Australia Pty Ltd* [2015] NSWCA 100, [15] (Emmett JA)]
2. 'The circumstances which would decide the balance of convenience against the extension of the caveat[,] where the consequence of failing to do so is effectively to defeat the caveator's claim[,] are not closed.' [*McInnes v Davies* [2014] SASC 184; (2014) 121 SASR 219, [20] (Stanley J)]

In short sentences commas are less necessary to mark off independent clauses, unless for effect or emphasis. Compare:

- The trial stopped and then started again. [comma unnecessary]
- The trial stopped, and then started again. [comma added for effect, to reflect the stop-start nature of the trial]

To mark off subsidiary information

Commas often mark off subsidiary material, in the same way as brackets (parentheses). For example:

> A and B agreed to appoint as an insurance adjuster, 'Mr [X], of [ABC Co], or if he is not available [then Mr Y].' (Note the commas.) Mr X later left ABC Co for a different employer. The court held that the commas marking-off 'of [ABC Co]' indicated that the reference to Mr X's employer was subsidiary; they were words describing Mr X personally, not Mr X in his capacity as an employee of ABC Co. Those words therefore did not limit Mr X's qualification to act: *Plymouth Mutual Life Insurance Co v Illinois Mid-Continental Life Ins Co* 378 F 2d 389 (3rd Cir, 1967).

However, this usage of commas as equating to parentheses must yield to context. For example:

> Statute entitled a receiver appointed by mortgagees to claim commission on the gross amount collected, at the rate specified in the instrument of appointment (but not exceeding 5%), 'and if no rate is so specified, then at the rate of five per centum on that gross amount, or at such other rate as the court thinks fit to allow, on application made by him for that purpose'. Could a receiver claim 5% without having to apply to the court? Held, yes; in effect the statute allowed a claim to either (1) 5%, or (2) another rate allowed by the court on application: *Marshall v Cunningham* [1982] Ch 82. In Megarry J's view, no rule required words enclosed by a pair of commas to be treated as merely parenthetical (at 88).

Judicial recognition of commas

Grammatical use normally assumed

Judges usually assume that drafters know how to use commas to help clarify meaning, and interpret documents accordingly. Many cases demonstrate the importance that judges place on the presence or absence of commas. For example:

- The 'Due Process Clause' of the US Fourteenth Amendment states: 'nor shall any State deprive any person of life, liberty, or property, without due process of law.' Held, the comma following 'property' indicated that the qualifying clause 'without due process of law' applied to all three terms: life, liberty, and property: *Kane v Board of Appeals* 390 Md 145, 164, 887 A 2d 1060, 1071 (2005), cert denied, 547 US 1179 (2006).

- A statute described the duties of delivery drivers as follows: 'The … packing for shipping [*no comma*] or distribution of [certain products]'. This description could mean: (1) a single activity of 'packing for shipping or distribution'; or (2) two separate sub-activities, being (a) packing for shipping, and (b) distribution. A comma after 'shipping' would have made that clearer, but there was no comma. Held, the text was ambiguous, and it was impossible to discern definitively whether the legislature intended meaning (1) or meaning (2). However, meaning (1) better reflected the court's view of the legislative policy: *O'Connor v Oakhurst Dairy* 851 F 3d 69 (US Court of Appeals, 1st Cir, 2017); discussed in Joseph Kimble, 'Deep in the Weeds of Textualism' (2018) 21 *Green Bag* 2D 297; at www.ssrn.com/abstract=3270367.
- A regulation prohibited the long-term parking of 'any motor vehicle [*no comma*] camper, trailer, farm implement and/or non-motorized vehicle'. Did the regulation apply to pick-up trucks? Held, no. The absence of a comma between 'motor vehicle' and 'camper' indicated a single item (motor vehicle camper) not two items (motor vehicle, camper). Nor was such an interpretation absurd, because other legislation in the same US state recognised camping vehicles. See *Village of West Jefferson v Cammelleri* 2015 WL 3824456 (Ohio Court of Appeals, 2015).

Consistent use assumed

Be consistent in the use of commas. If the use varies, a court may read purpose into the variation—just as it may read purpose into a variation of terminology. Indeed, a court may deduce from the consistent use of commas throughout a document that the *absence* of a comma in a particular place is deliberate.

Example

> A clause in a professionally drawn 25-year lease gave the landlord the right 'to enter upon the Premises … to inspect … the same [*no comma*] to view the state of repair and condition thereof [*no comma*] and [to document certain matters]'. The premises had been used as a garage with underground fuel tanks. The landlord sought to enter to test for contamination; this would involve drilling boreholes and cordoning-off the area under investigation. Did the clause give the landlord that right? The court held that it did not. In the court's view, the wording conferred only a limited right of entry—namely, a right to enter and inspect the premises to view their state of repair (and to document the matters mentioned). It did not give the right to interfere with the tenant's possession by undertaking interruptive works of the kind the landlord sought. Punctuation supported this conclusion: throughout the lease, the drafter had not generally omitted commas and other punctuation marks. Here, the *absence* of a comma after 'the same' suggested that the drafter intended the landlord to have the limited right only. (Other factors were: (1) the absence of a covenant by the landlord to repair any damage caused by work of the kind proposed (such a provision would be expected in a professionally drawn lease); and (2) the word 'view' implied matters observable on the surface, not matters requiring core samples.) See *Possfund Custodial Trustee Ltd v Kwik-Fit Properties Ltd* [2008] CSIH 65 (Extra Division, Inner House, Court of Session).

Poor grammar excused?

The judicial focus on punctuation techniques assumes, of course, that the writer knows how to use commas. Inferences from the presence or absence of commas are harder to draw where drafters are careless with punctuation—either because they obviously do not know the conventions, or because they *should* know the conventions but are careless in their use.

Examples

1. A clause in a home-drawn ('holograph') will was to be interpreted *as if* a comma were present, because that better reflected the intention of a testator who was semi-literate and unfamiliar with the role of commas: *Re Steel* [1979] Ch 218 (Megarry V-C).
2. The absence of a comma did not control the meaning of a provision in an Australian industrial award, which '[was] plainly not drafted with the degree of precision that would permit punctuation to govern its construction': *R v Australian Teachers' Union* [1993] FCA 209, [18].
3. The absence of a comma in an exclusion clause in an insurance policy was irrelevant because the drafting was 'haphazard': *Chalmers Leask Underwriting Agencies v Mayne Nickless Ltd* (1983) 155 CLR 279, 286.
4. The location of commas was no guide to meaning in a commercial contract which had been translated from French into English and was 'littered with grammatical errors': *Mainteck Services Pty Ltd v Stein Heurtey SA* [2014] NSWCA 184; (2014) 89 NSWLR 633, [106] (Leeming JA).

In short, inconsistency in the use of commas will not override the meaning which the court considers to have been the parties' meaning: *Wood v Sureterm Direct Ltd* [2015] EWCA Civ 839, [50] (Clarke LJ).

Serial (Oxford) comma

Some drafters seem reluctant to use the so-called 'serial' or 'Oxford' comma. The reluctance may derive from a dimly remembered 'rule' from schooldays that *and* and *or* do not take a comma. But there is no such grammatical rule, and the serial comma can help clarify meaning. Example 1 is a simple hypothetical illustration; examples 2 and 3 are taken from US cases.

1. 'In this court you will find the President, a senior judge[,] and expert in the field.' Does the President sit alone?
2. A Texas law entitled a successful defendant to payment of his 'court costs, reasonable attorney's fees, [comma] and other expenses [no comma] incurred in defending against the legal action as *justice and equity* may require' (italics added). A successful defendant incurred $67,000 in attorney's fees, but the trial court awarded him only $6,500, on the basis that 'justice and equity' justified only that lower amount. On appeal, the Texas Supreme Court awarded $67,000 because:
   - the *absence* of a comma after 'and other expenses' suggested that the following phrase modified only 'other expenses'; and
   - the *presence* of a comma (the Oxford comma) before 'and other expenses' suggested the same (ie, that only the last of the three items in the list was modified by 'as justice and equity may require'.

   See *Sullivan v Abraham* 488 SW 3d 294 (Texas Supreme Court, 2016).
3. A New York Law made it an offence to deprive an animal 'of necessary sustenance, food [no comma] or drink …' The accused had deprived an animal of medical treatment. Held, the absence of a serial comma after 'food' indicated that 'necessary sustenance' meant 'food or drink'. The accused had not deprived the animal of food or drink—therefore, no offence was committed: *People v Walsh* 2008 WL 724724 (NY Crim Ct, Jan 2008). (To illustrate the importance of the serial comma, the judge cited the example of an author's dedication 'to my parents, the Pope and Mother Teresa': the absence of a comma after 'Pope' implies that the author's parents are the Pope and Mother Teresa.)

The serial comma is particularly useful where a word at the start of a series of words suggests a negative (as in example 4).

4. 'The court criticised the lawyers for their lack of empathy and arrogance.' Was the criticism for the lawyers' arrogance or their lack of arrogance? Perhaps the context would clarify the meaning—but so too would a comma: 'The court criticised the lawyers for their lack of empathy, and [for their] arrogance.'

Alternatives to commas

'Stronger' punctuation

Sometimes, a punctuation mark 'stronger' than a comma enhances readability by marking off clauses that need clear separation. Examples include an em dash or a semicolon—or even a full stop.

Comma	**Stronger punctuation mark**
The trial stopped, and then started again.	The trial stopped—and then started again. [Em dash emphasises the stop-start nature of the trial.]
The judge called for the accused to be brought into the courtroom, and the accused's counsel then asked to approach the bench.	The judge called for the accused to be brought into the courtroom; the accused's counsel then asked to approach the bench. [Semicolon shows more separation than comma; note the deliberate omission of 'and'.] *Or, for yet stronger separation*: The judge called for the accused to be brought into the courtroom. The accused's counsel then asked to approach the bench. [Full stop stronger than semicolon.]

Brackets

While commas are useful for breaking up text into manageable bites, in long sentences their use can become puzzling. Multiple commas may cause the reader to miscue: 'how does the information between these commas relate to other information in this comma-strewn sentence?' To prevent confusion from multiple commas, try using dashes or brackets (or both).

Example

Original

But there are occasions, particularly in relation to contracts of a simple, frequently used type, such as contracts for sale, where the context in which the words are used, and the conduct of the parties at the time when the contract is made, tells you as much, or even more, about the essential terms of the bargain than do the words themselves. [Source: *Devani v Wells* [2019] 2 WLR 617, [59] (Lord Briggs)]

[62 words; 1 sentence; commas only]

Revision

But there are occasions—particularly in relation to contracts of a simple, frequently used type (such as contracts for sale)—where the context in which the words are used, and the conduct of the parties at the time when the contract is made, tells you as much (or even more) about the essential terms of the bargain than do the words themselves.

[62 words; 1 sentence; commas, dashes and brackets]

Better still: divide into separate sentences

But there are occasions where the context in which the words are used, and the conduct of the parties at the time when the contract is made, tells you as much (or even more) about the essential terms of the bargain than do the words themselves. This happens particularly in relation to contracts of a simple, frequently used type, such as contracts for sale.]

[64 words; 2 sentences; commas and brackets

Further reading

- Kenneth A Adams, 'Bamboozled by a Comma' (2015) 16 *Scribes Journal of Legal Writing* 45
- Susan J Hankin, 'Statutory Interpretation in the Age of Grammatical Permissiveness: An Object Lesson for Teaching why Grammar Matters', at www.ssrn.com. abstract=1516382 (reviews US cases on punctuation, including the serial comma)
- David A Marcello, 'The Case of the Serial Comma: what can plain-language drafting tell legislative drafters?' (2020) 19 *The Scribes Journal of Legal Writing* 127

See also **AMBIGUITY; however (avoiding comma splice); LAST-ANTECEDENT RULE; PUNCTUATION; SEMICOLONS.**

commence

A stilted substitute for *start*. Where possible, prefer the vernacular *start*: eg, 'This lease ~~commences~~ starts on 1 January next.'

In at least two situations, however, *start* may not be appropriate.

1. *Where a prescribed form uses 'commence'.* A land registry form of lease may have a space on the cover page for inserting the 'commencement date' of the lease. It may not be possible to change that description on the cover page. This effectively mandates using the same term ('commencement date') throughout the lease; to change to 'starting date' after the cover page could create ambiguity, given the presumption that a change in terminology heralds a change in meaning. You could define 'starting date' to mean 'the commencement date stipulated on the cover page'; but drafting by definition is rarely ideal, particularly for readers unaccustomed to the technique.
2. *Where referring to the 'commencement' of a statute.* Statutory-interpretation legislation invariably uses the term 'commencement' for the starting date of a statute: see, eg, *Interpretation Act 1978*, s 4 (headed 'Time of commencement').

See also **CONSISTENCY OF TERMINOLOGY.**

commencing with / commencing from

See **beginning with / beginning from.**

common / mutual

Common means shared (by two or more); *mutual* means reciprocal, in the sense of directed by one to another. Hence:

- '*common* knowledge' differs from '*mutual* knowledge'
- co-owners of land are 'tenants *in common*', not '*mutual* tenants'

- in the context of rescinding a contract for mistake, the preferred term is '*common* mistake', not '*mutual* mistake'
- parties make '*mutual* wills', not '*common* wills'.

See also **mirror wills / mutual wills; mutual.**

common land

In normal usage, land that is open for public use. Legal usage carries the same meaning, though with an overlay of 'rights of common', a term of art with no easy translation into plain language. In England, there were four categories of rights of common: (1) the common of pasture (ie, the right to graze cattle, horses, sheep, and other animals); (2) the common of estovers (ie, the right to take wood to build and maintain houses and fences, and for fuel and other agricultural purposes); (3) the common of piscary (ie, the right to fish); and (4) the common of turbary (ie, the right to dig peat).

In many British colonies (such as Australia), early Governors created commons to ensure a reliable stock of grazing land, but without the historical overlay of 'rights of common'. Later, commons were set apart by the Crown and created by grant or dedication under various statutes, again without the overlay of rights of common.

Today, most commons—even those based on common law—are also subject to statutory regulation.

Further reading

- S Bridge, E Cooke, and M Dixon (eds), *Megarry & Wade's Law of Real Property*, 9th edn (Sweet & Maxwell, 2019) [26-051]–[26-054], [26-058]–[28-063]
- Enid Campbell, 'Rights of Common in New South Wales: A History' (2007) 11 *Legal History* 243 (colonial experiences with 'common land')

common property

See **common property / joint property**.

common property / joint property

Property held in common (*common property*) is held by two or more persons in separate, though physically undivided, shares. For example, if A, B, and C are owners in common [technically, *tenants in common*], each may dispose of their share as they wish. So, if A dies, A's share passes under A's will (or, if A has no will, on intestacy), leaving B's and C's shares unaffected. Then, if B later dies, B's share passes under B's will (or on intestacy), leaving C's share unaffected. In contrast, property held jointly (*joint property*) is held by two or more persons as joint tenants, with right of survivorship. For example, if A, B, and C are *joint* owners [technically, *joint tenants*] of land, and A dies, then B and C together own the whole property—A's will cannot affect that result. Then, if B dies, C owns the whole property—B's will cannot affect that result.

However, the clear distinction between these two meanings is sometimes blurred, with *joint* property being used (loosely) for property that is strictly held *in common*:

> 'There is now an accepted distinction between "joint property" and "common property". But while a consistent nomenclature may now be expected it has to be noticed that the terms may be interchangeably used in older texts.' [*Clydesdale Bank Plc v Davidson*, unreported, [1997] UKHL 55 (Lord Clyde)]

See also **joint tenant / tenant in common; ius accrescendi; tenant.**

commorientes

Latin: those dying together. Used particularly to describe persons who perish apparently simultaneously in a calamity, and where it is not possible to tell who survived whom. Hence:

- *commorientes rule*—the statutory rule that where it is impossible to tell who survived whom, a younger person is presumed to have survived an older
- *commorientes clause*—a clause declaring that a beneficiary's gift under a will is contingent on the beneficiary surviving the testator by a stated period.

Commorientes is useful shorthand for lawyers, but can always be replaced with an appropriate English translation. For example:

> 'In the ordinary case there is no difficulty in ascertaining which of two persons died first. But in the vicissitudes of human life there occur instances in which, owing to the absence of any positive evidence, … the matter is left in uncertainty. The most familiar case is where two or more persons meet their death in a common calamity, the case of *commorientes* [prefer: *persons dying at the same time*], as lawyers designate it.' [*Hickman v Peacey* [1945] AC 304, 320 (Lord Macmillan)]

communis error facit jus

Latin: a general (commonly accepted) error makes the law. A maxim to the effect that although a long-accepted legal principle is (or may be) based on an error, it remains the law until corrected by the courts or parliament. As with many Latin maxims, it is little more than a truism, reflecting a commonsense principle favouring predictability over uncertainty. And as with many Latin maxims, it can be expressed in standard English without loss of meaning:

> 'It may be that such a development [of the law of false imprisonment] was erroneous or at least founded on an erroneous premise but, if so, *Communis error facit jus* [prefer: *a commonly accepted error remains the law*; [or] *it remains the law despite the error*].' [*R v Voller* [1996] 1 VR 95, 179 (Ormiston J)]

compear

A Scots law term, meaning to appear as a party in court, in person or by counsel or agent. It is not used in other Commonwealth countries. Etymologically equivalent to 'compeer' in English (archaic term for a person of equal rank or standing).

complaint

In general usage, a *complaint* is an expression of censure, resentment, or discontent, which may or may not be in writing. In legal usage, in civil litigation, a *complaint* is the process by which proceedings are started; in criminal law, a *complaint* is information in written form giving details of an alleged offence.

But meaning can vary with context, and so in some legal contexts *complaint* can carry its general-usage meaning. For example:

> A statute enabled a person to make a *complaint* about a liquidator's conduct. Held, a *complaint* was sufficiently made by a party's barrister making submissions to the court critical of the liquidator's conduct. In the context, *complaint* did not require a formal request to inquire into the liquidator's conduct: *Hall v Poolman* [2009] NSWCA 64; (2009) 75 NSWLR 99, [94]–[97] (contra, [101]).

See also **claim**.

complement / compliment

To complement is to add to in a way that enhances or improves; *to compliment* is to congratulate or praise politely:

> The judge *complimented* the litigants for *complementing* the pleadings with further material.

Planning regulations often confuse the words:

> 'New development must *compliment* [prefer: *complement*] the physical form of existing development in the neighbourhood.' [Source: standard formula in Australian planning codes.]

Even senior judges (or their typists) sometimes get it wrong:

- 'I am satisfied that the respondents' instruction to pursue maximum efficient production in the factory from the outset, whilst maintaining the full *compliment* [prefer: *complement*] of employees …, was foolhardy.' [*Timbs v Birrell Management (Australia) Pty Ltd* [1990] FCA 102, [91] (Von Doussa J)]
- 'The applicant submitted that the evidence contained in each statement *complimented* [prefer: *complemented*] the other and provided a more holistic picture of the drug operation.' [*R v OS* [2016] QCA 278, [39] (Atkinson J)]

comply

To *comply* with an obligation or duty means to act in accordance with it, or obey it, or be bound by it. Persons who contractually promise to *comply with* a document may be bound by its provisions even though they have not signed it. For example:

> Parties undertook to execute documents which would add them as parties to a certain deed. They agreed that, until that happened, they would 'comply with' the deed. Held, their agreement to 'comply with' the deed meant that they were to be treated as if bound by it immediately, even though they had not yet signed it: *Oswal v Yara Australia Pty Ltd (No 3)* [2011] WASC 255, [376]–[378].

compos mentis

Latin: of sound mind (ie, competent to enter into legal transactions).

See also **non compos mentis**.

COMPOSITE EXPRESSIONS

When seeking the meaning of composite expressions, be aware that the meaning of the composite whole is not necessarily the meaning of the sum of its parts. For example, the meaning of 'family violence' is not necessarily discerned by considering the separate meanings of 'family' and 'violence'—because 'family violence' (as the term is generally used) may encompass acts within a relationship that is not strictly 'family', and involve coercion or emotional abuse that does not involve (physical) violence. The crucial issue is always the context in which the expression is used: compare *Yemshaw v Hounslow London Borough Council* [2011] UKSC 3; [2011] 1 WLR 433, [27]–[28] ('domestic *violence*' may include emotional pressure), and *Jones v First Tier Tribunal* [2013] UKSC 19; [2013] 2 AC 48 ('crime of violence' requires physical force).

See also **DEFINITIONS (Multi-word definitions)**.

compound

A word that takes various meanings and grammatical forms. It can be a noun (a chemical *compound*), an adjective (*compound* interest, *compound* word), or a verb (meaning to mix or combine, or to complicate—eg, *compound* a mistake). In legal usage, it also carries two other meanings:

- to come to terms with (*compound* a difference; *compound* the amount of a debt)
- to accept money or some other advantage for not reporting a felony (*compound* a felony).

Context should resolve any ambiguity over the intended meaning; but if in doubt, clarify.

COMPOUND PREPOSITIONS

See **PREPOSITIONS**.

comprise / composed of

In conventional usage, the whole *comprises* the parts, and the parts *compose* the whole: eg, 'The bench *comprises* five judges', 'The bench *is composed of* [not *is comprised of*] five judges.' (See RD Burchfield (ed), *Fowler's Modern English Usage*, 3rd edn (Oxford University Press, 1998) 167–68.)

However, that usage is changing, and *compose / comprised of* are now found where *comprise / composed of* respectively would formerly have been used. Most style guides acknowledge the change and concede that it is now too late to resist. The change is reflected in modern legal usage, where (depending on context) 'comprise' can mean 'consists of', 'is made up of', 'is composed of', or 'is constituted by': *General Clutch Corporation v Spriggs Pty Ltd* (1997) 38 IPR 359, 373–76 (Lindgren J, expounding at length on 'comprising' in a patent application). 'Comprise' can also mean 'includes': *Walker Corporation Pty Limited v Director-General Department of Environment, Climate, Change and Water* [2012] NSWCCA 210; (2012) 82 NSWLR 12, [33] (in the context of habitat-protection legislation, so as not to exclude other types of vegetation). For the careful writer, the only rule is to be consistent.

You can sidestep the issue by choosing another word or phrase. The result may be tighter writing, which is always a benefit. For example:

- The judges hearing this case *comprise* [prefer: *are*] three of the most senior in the court.
- This clause applies to all residences *comprised in* [prefer: *forming part of*] mixed-use buildings.
- The decision of *those comprising the majority of* [prefer: *the majority of*] shareholders binds the company.
- The regulation affects all wind generators *in the area comprised within* [prefer: *within*] 1 km of farms.

compromise

Latin: *compromissum*, a mutual promise to abide by a decision. Originally in legal usage, a *compromise* was an agreement between disputing parties to abide by the decision of an arbiter. Now, however, a *compromise* (or *compromise agreement*) is any binding agreement between disputing parties to settle their differences by mutual giving-and-taking: *Re Guardian Assurance Co* [1917] 1 Ch 431, 442 (Younger J).

The giving-and-taking must be genuine—otherwise, there is no *compromise* in this legal sense. This appears from the following examples:

- A bank was not bound by a *compromise* to give up its right to fixtures on mortgaged premises, where its 'agreement' to give up the right had been made under a mistake about the facts: *Huddersfield Banking Co Ltd v Henry Lister & Son Ltd* [1895] 2 Ch 285.
- There was no *compromise* where a company entered into a property swap with another company, but in the absence of any real dispute on foot between the companies: *Mercantile Investment and General Trust Co v International Company of Mexico* (1891) [1893] 1 Ch 484n, 491 (CA).
- There was no *compromise* between two contracting parties where one, exercising its overwhelming majority vote, 'expropriated' the rights of the other. This was because *compromise* 'implies some element of accommodation on each side. It is not apt to describe total surrender': *Re NFU Development Trust Ltd* [1973] 1 All ER 135, 140 (Brightman J).

The scope of a compromise agreement is a matter of interpretation of the words used in the agreement. In principle, a party can agree to give up rights of which he or she was unaware at the time—but the law requires clear words to that effect: *Bank of Credit and Commerce International SA v Ali* [2002] 1 AC 251.

concerned in

When is a person *concerned in* specified activity? For example, when is a person *concerned in* activity proscribed by a criminal statute? Or when is a person *concerned in* a business—as where a contract for the sale of a business forbids the seller from being *concerned in* similar kinds of business (eg, does it extend to lending money to a competing business, or holding shares in a competing company)? The decided cases are legion. About all that can be said with certainty is that *concerned in* is so vague and context-dependent that it is best avoided. Instead, clarify precisely what conduct is covered.

conclusive certificate

Contracts sometimes provide that a certificate of the amount that one party owes to the other is 'conclusive'. For example, a mortgage may state that the lender's certificate stating the amount owing is 'conclusive'. Contractual provisions of this kind are usually upheld: *Bache & Co (London) v Banque Vernes et Commerciale de Paris* [1973] 2 Lloyd's Rep 437 (CA); *Dobbs v National Bank of Australasia Ltd* (1935) 53 CLR 643, 651–54; *Julong Pty Ltd v Fenn* [2003] Q ConvR ¶54-586; [2002] QCA 529. There are some exceptions: for example, a creditor cannot rely on a certificate that contains a 'manifest error' (*North Shore Ventures Ltd v Anstead Holdings Inc* [2011] 3 WLR 628, CA), nor, probably, one prepared without due care (*Shomat Pty Ltd v Rubenstein* (1995) 24 FLR 284, 289). Also, unfair-contracts legislation may strike down a 'conclusive certificate' clause as unjust: *Cook v Bank of New South Wales* (1982) 2 BPR 9580, 9587. And where parties are of unequal bargaining power, the stronger party's reliance on a 'conclusive certificate' clause in the face of genuine dispute over the amount owing may be unfair or unconscionable: eg, *Toscano v Holland Securities Pty Ltd* (1985) 1 NSWLR 145, 151.

Further reading

Halsbury's Laws of England, 'Building Contracts' (vol 6, 2018) [331] (certificates under building contracts); 'Financial Instruments and Transactions' (vol 49, 2015) [717] (certificates in financial transactions)

See also **final and conclusive**.

concurrent lease

A lease granted to operate concurrently with an existing lease. It arises where a landlord (L) grants a lease to a tenant (A) and then, while that lease is current, grants a lease of the same land to another person (B). B cannot usurp A's right to possession while A's lease lasts; but the legal effect of the concurrent lease is to interpose B as A's landlord, supplanting the landlord and tenant relationship between L and A. Unless the lease between L and A precludes L from granting a concurrent lease, A is powerless to prevent it. The 'device' of the concurrent lease lay relatively dormant until revived in the mid-20th century as a way of circumventing rent-control legislation, and (yet more recently) to enable leases to be 'securitised'.

Further reading

S Bridge, E Cooke, and M Dixon (eds), *Megarry & Wade's Law of Real Property*, 9th edn (Sweet & Maxwell, 2019) [16-133]–[16-137]

condescendence

A Scots law term meaning a statement of fact by the pursuer (ie, the plaintiff or complainant) in civil proceedings. It is not used in other Commonwealth countries.

condition

Condition carries two distinct meanings in law.

A contractual provision giving the right to terminate for breach

In the technical language of contract law, a *condition* is a contractual promise, breach of which (no matter how minor the breach, and regardless of whether it is later remedied) gives rise to a right to terminate the performance of the contract and sue for damages: *Wickman Machine Tool Sales Ltd v L Schuler AG* [1972] 1 WLR 840, 851 (Lord Denning MR). A legal drafter, alert to this meaning, should choose *condition* only when intending a breach to have that consequence. However, drafters sometimes use *condition*, not in this draconian sense, but in the more general sense of a term of the contract, in which case the court will give effect to that less draconian intent. For example, in *L Schuler AG v Wickman Machine Tool Sales Ltd* [1974] AC 235, the majority of the House of Lords held that breach of a term, described as a *condition*, was intended to give a right to terminate only if the breach remained unremedied after a demand to remedy it.

An intent to give the innocent party a right to terminate the contract for breach of a term (no matter how minor the term and how minor the breach) is best achieved by an express statement in the document that the term is 'fundamental' or 'essential': *Shevill v Builders Licensing Board* (1982) 149 CLR 620, 627; *AMEV-UDC Finance Ltd v Austin* (1986) 162 CLR 170, 185; *Gumland Property Holdings Pty Ltd v Duffy Bros Fruit Market (Campbelltown) Pty Ltd* (2008) 234 CLR 237, 259 [58]).

A generic term of a contract

Often, *condition* is used not in its technical sense (above), but simply to mean a provision in a contract. For example, a clause that states 'This contract is subject to our standard *conditions* of sale' tells nothing about the relative importance of any particular 'condition'. It is merely a catch-all description. Indeed, *term* could be used instead of *condition*. Further, in the composite expression *terms and conditions*—'This contract is subject to our standard *terms and conditions* of sale'—*conditions* is almost always superfluous; the single word *terms* would suffice.

See also **condition precedent / condition subsequent; condition / warranty; CONDITIONAL CLAUSES; terms and conditions.**

condition / warranty

In the technical language of contract law, a *condition* is a contractual promise whose breach (no matter how minor the breach, and regardless of whether it is later remedied) entitles the innocent party to terminate the contract and sue for damages: see **condition** (first meaning). In contrast, a *warranty* is a contractual promise whose breach (no matter how serious) entitles the innocent party to damages only, with no right to terminate the contract.

A term's self-description as a *warranty* is a strong factor in characterising it as such: eg, *R G Grain Trade LLP v Feed Factors International Ltd* [2011] EWHC 1889 (Comm), [41]; [2011] 2 Lloyd's Rep 433. But it is not necessarily conclusive, just as a term's self-description as a *condition* is not necessarily conclusive—as in the generic 'terms and *conditions* of sale'.

Further reading

- JW Carter, *Carter on Contract* (LexisNexis) [14-020]–[14-040]
- *Halsbury's Laws of England*, 'Contract' (vol 22, 2019) [348]–[349] (distinguishing between conditions and warranties)

See also **condition; innominate term; terms and conditions.**

condition precedent / condition subsequent

Condition precedent

Meaning

A 'condition'—or stipulation—that must be fulfilled before a legal state of affairs comes into existence; plural, 'conditions precedent'. In contract law, there are two categories of condition precedent:

1. *Where no contract is yet in existence*: a condition on which formation of the contract depends.
2. *Where a contract is already in existence*: a condition on which further performance under the contract depends.

To illustrate these two categories: assume that it is unlawful to sell part of a parcel of land without planning consent to subdivision of the land. A landowner and a prospective purchaser enter into a 'contract' for sale of part of the land 'on condition that' (meaning 'if') the planning authority consents to a subdivision within the next three months: that would be category (1). Or they enter into a contract for sale of the part immediately, but 'on condition that' the authority consents to a subdivision within the next three months (with a right to rescind if consent is denied): that would be category (2).

Where possible, courts prefer to hold that a condition comes within category (2): ie, the condition is precedent to performance of an obligation under a contract already in existence, rather than precedent to the contract coming into existence (*Perri v Coolangatta Investments Pty Ltd* (1982) 149 CLR 537, 552, Mason J). This means that a drafter wishing to ensure that a condition falls within category (1) should say so unequivocally:

> 'This agreement does not come into effect unless and until [the condition is performed].'

Pronunciation of 'precedent'

Traditionally, lawyers stressed the second syllable—prec*ed*ent. However, more recent usage stresses the first syllable—*pre*cedent.

Condition subsequent

A 'condition'—or stipulation—that the occurrence of a stated event ends the obligation of one or more parties to perform the contract or a provision of it. An example is a provision that neither party need complete a contract for the sale of land if the relevant authority refuses consent to subdivision. A condition subsequent necessarily operates on a contract that is already in existence.

Difference can depend on drafting

Conditions precedent and subsequent are conceptually distinct. In particular, different consequences attend their breach. For example, if a person's right to property depends on the performance or occurrence of a condition precedent, no right 'vests' in that person until the condition is performed or occurs. But a condition subsequent operates on property already 'vested', causing the interest to 'divest' if the condition is breached. Adept drafting can help discern the difference, as shown in the following examples:

Condition precedent	Condition subsequent
I give my property to A *on condition that* [or *if*] A qualifies as a lawyer. [If A does not become a lawyer, then I give the property to B.]	I give my property to A, *but if* A fails to become a lawyer [then I give the property to B].
I agree to sell you this property *on condition that* the council gives subdivision consent.	Completion of this contract is *conditional on* the council giving subdivision consent.

See also **condition / warranty**; **terms and conditions**.

CONDITIONAL CLAUSES

Structure of conditional clauses

Traditional structure: condition before substantive provision

Where a sentence or clause contains a condition that qualifies a substantive right or obligation, what do you state first: the condition, or the substantive right or obligation? The traditional style of legal drafting states the condition first. This style goes back at least to the writings of George Coode: *On Legislative Expression* (London, William Benning & Co, 1845) 9–45. Coode divided legislative provisions into four elements:

- *the legal subject*—the person or entity to whom the provision is directed
- *the legal action*—what the law allows or prohibits
- *the case*—the circumstances in which the law is intended to operate
- *the conditions*—any preconditions that need to be satisfied before the law operates (typically starting with *if*).

In Coode's view, the ideal provision proceeds in the order: (1) case, (2) conditions, (3) legal subject, (4) legal action. In practice, this places qualifying statements (case and condition) before substantive statements (legal subject and legal action).

Modern structure: substantive provision before condition

Coode's structure runs contrary to modern understandings of readability, which favour an 'up-front' statement of the main idea, with qualifications placed after, not before. Modern studies suggest that to start a sentence with a conditional clause hinders comprehension. (See Dennis Kurzon, 'Clarity and Word Order in Legislation' (1985) 5 *Oxford Journal of Legal Studies* 269, 270; AC Lovgren, 'The Place of Case in Legislative Sentences' [1986] *Statute Law Review* 23, 27.) While Coode's structure promotes consistency of approach (which is not necessarily a bad thing), it hinders comprehension.

It is true that readability may not be compromised where 'up-front' conditions are brief and few:

> *If* [or *When*] the vendor has obtained development consent [first condition] and established a good title [second condition], the purchaser must pay the purchase price.

But for more complex provisions, Coode's recommended order is problematic. Readers must hold the case and condition in their mind as they search for the legal subject (perhaps themselves) and the legal action (what they can or cannot do). That is why modern drafting turns Coode's order on its head: it prefers to state the legal subject and legal action first, and only later moves to case and condition. In summary, it states the main point before stating the conditions that qualify its application.

Example

Assume that a contract for the sale of land requires the purchaser to pay the purchase price, but not until the vendor has satisfied three agreed conditions. The Coode-sanctioned structure would take the following form [*if* clause + *if* clause + *if* clause + obligation]:

> *If* [or *When*] the vendor has
> (a) obtained development consent; and
> (b) established a good title; and
> (c) paid all outstanding rates,
> then the purchaser must pay the purchase price.

This order may seem logical to the legal drafter, who is familiar with these kinds of conditions precedent to the obligation to pay the purchase price. But it is counter-intuitive for many non-lawyers, who lack a context in which to interpret the conditions until they reach the end of the clause. The structure also suffers from a 'sandwich' construction (see **CLAUSE STRUCTURE**), which forces the reader to hold the opening line in mind while consuming the 'filling', before reaching the end of the clause.

The non-legal reader is better served if the main obligation appears up-front, before the conditions (ie, obligation + *if* clause + *if* clause + *if* clause):

> The purchaser must pay the purchase price *if* [or *when*] the vendor has complied with the following conditions:
> (a) obtained development consent; and
> (b) established a good title; and
> (c) paid all outstanding rates.

Stand-alone conditional clause

Usefulness

Where conditions are complex, it may be clearer to separate them into a stand-alone clause, rather than combine them with the substantive obligation in a single lengthy clause or sentence. For example:

Before

If a ratepayer, having been served with a default notice, *fails* within 30 days to pay the amount levied for road improvements, *or fails* within 30 days to notify the Council that it cannot afford to pay the amount levied, *then* the Council may take proceedings to recover the amount. [emphasis added to show structure: if + if + if + obligation]

After

(a) The Council may take proceedings to recover unpaid levies for road improvements *if* [or *only if*] the Council complies with the conditions in paragraph (b).

(b) The conditions are:

  (i) the Council has served on the ratepayer a default notice specifying the unpaid amount; and

  (ii) the ratepayer has failed within 30 days either to pay the amount or to notify the Council that it cannot afford to pay.

Location

When adopting the 'stand-alone conditional clause' technique it may sometimes be logical—despite the general exhortation to depart from the Coode-structure—to place the conditional clause first. An up-front conditional clause may give the reader a useful context for the obligation: 'why must I do this?'

Example 1 (contract for sale of land)

Before

Buyer's election to proceed

If:

  (a) the vendor breaches an essential term of the contract; and

  (b) the buyer could terminate the contract for that breach; and

  (c) the buyer wishes to proceed with the contract and recover damages rather than terminate the contract,

then the buyer must advise the vendor of the wish to proceed with the contract, and must specify the amount of damages it seeks to recover.

After

Buyer's election to proceed despite vendor's essential breach

(a) This clause applies if, despite the vendor's breach of an essential term of the contract, the buyer wishes to proceed with the contract and recover damages, rather than to terminate the contract.

(b) The buyer must advise the vendor of the wish to proceed with the contract, and must specify the amount of damages it seeks to recover.

[Note the changed heading, helping reveal the logic behind the restructure.]

Example 2 (statute)

Before

'Where a conveyance or grant executed in pursuance of this Chapter is of a dwelling-house situated in a National Park, or an area designated under section 87 of the National Parks and Access to the Countryside Act 1949 as an area of outstanding natural beauty, or an area designated by order of the Secretary of State as a rural area, and it is executed by a local authority (as denned in section 50 of this Act), a county council, the Development Board for Rural Wales or a housing association ("the landlord") the conveyance or grant may contain a covenant limiting the freedom of the tenant and his successors in title to dispose of the dwelling-house in the manner specified below.'

[Source: *Housing Act 1980*, s 19(1), now repealed. I am indebted to Dr Duncan Berry for drawing this provision to my attention.]

After

(1) This section applies to a conveyance or grant of a dwelling-house executed in pursuance of this Chapter where two conditions are satisfied.
  - (a) First, the dwelling-house is situated in any of the following areas:
    - (i) a National Park
    - (ii) an area designated under section 87 of the *National Parks and Access to the Countryside Act 1949* as an area of outstanding natural beauty
    - (iii) an area designated by order of the Secretary of State as a rural area.
  - (b) Second, the conveyance or grant is executed by any of the following:
    - (i) a local authority (as defined in section 50 of this Act)
    - (ii) a county council
    - (iii) the Development Board for Rural Wales
    - (iv) a housing association.

(2) The conveyance or grant may contain a covenant limiting the freedom of the tenant and his successors in title to dispose of the dwelling-house in the manner specified below.

'Method' form for multiple conditions

For multiple conditions, the 'method' form of statement is becoming more popular. This states up-front the substantive right or obligation and then steps the reader through the conditions one-by-one.

Example 1 (lease)

Tenant's right to renew lease

The tenant is entitled to renew the lease for a further 5 years if the tenant meets each of conditions A to D.

- A: the tenant has paid all rent up to the end of the lease.
- B: the tenant has complied with its repairing obligations under the lease.
- C: the tenant has given the landlord 6 months' prior written notice of intention to renew the lease.
- D: the tenant pays all the landlord's legal costs for granting the new lease, as well as stamp duty and registration fees.

Example 2 (statute)

4B Deprivation of liberty necessary for life-sustaining treatment or vital act

(1) If Conditions 1 to 4 are met, D is authorised to take steps which deprive P of liberty.

(2) Condition 1 is that the steps—

(a) are wholly or partly for the purpose of giving P life-sustaining treatment or doing any vital act, or

(b) consist wholly or partly of giving P life-sustaining treatment or doing any vital act.

(3) A vital act is any act which the person doing it reasonably believes to be necessary to prevent a serious deterioration in P's condition.

(4) Condition 2 is that the steps are necessary in order to give the life-sustaining treatment or do the vital act.

(5) Condition 3 is that D reasonably believes that P lacks capacity to consent to D taking the steps.

(6) Condition 4 is that—

(a) subsection (7) applies, or

(b) there is an emergency.

(7)–(9) [omitted]

[*Mental Capacity Act 2005*, s 4B]

Commas after lead-in

Where a sentence is short (like this one) no comma is needed after the lead-in condition. However, it is different where the sentence is longer—and particularly where the lead-in condition itself is long or where there are several lead-in conditions. Then a comma after the lead-in condition (or after the last of the lead-in conditions) can help the reader follow the sense. The comma indicates the end of the introductory words.

Example

> 'If you fail to pay rent, taxes and outgoings, and [if you] fail to keep the premises in good condition and repair, the landlord can evict you.'

The comma after 'repair' signals the end of the introductory *if* clauses and the start of the substantive material. (Even better: after the comma, add 'then'. See **if … then**.)

Concealed conditions

Unmask concealed conditions. Concealment often results from an unnecessarily complex sentence construction; if so, simplify the construction to reveal the condition. Unless you deliberately intend to conceal conditions (always a doubtful purpose), lay them bare to the reader.

Example 1 (concealed condition in contract for sale of land)

Original

The vendor's failure to complete this transaction on time does not prevent the vendor from terminating the contract for the purchaser's default.

Better

If the vendor fails to complete this transaction on time, the vendor may still terminate the contract for the purchaser's default.

Better still (stating substantive right first)

The vendor may terminate the contract for the purchaser's default *even if the vendor fails to complete this transaction on time.*

Example 2 (concealed condition in statute)

Original

(1) A person will not be regarded as having survived an intestate unless:
- (a) the person is born before the intestate's death and survives the intestate by at least 30 days, or
- (b) the person is born after the intestate's death after a period of gestation in the uterus that commenced before the intestate's death and survives the intestate for at least 30 days after birth.

[*Succession Act 2006* (NSW), s 107(1)]

Better

(1) A person will not be regarded as having survived an intestate unless:
- (a) *if born before the intestate's death*—the person survives the intestate by at least 30 days, or
- (b) *if born after the intestate's death*—the period of gestation in the uterus commenced before the intestate's death and the person survives the intestate for at least 30 days after birth.

Dispersed conditions

If conditions are dispersed throughout a clause or document, consider consolidating them into one place. At the same time, lay bare all 'hidden' conditions (as recommended above). Both techniques help readers process the information more efficiently.

Example

Original

Types of court-imposed conditions

(1) When granting relief against forfeiture, the court may impose conditions requiring the doing of any specified thing or the refraining from doing any specified thing.

(2) Without limiting subsection (1), the following are examples of types of conditions that the court may impose:
- (a) that the landlord give the tenant a new set of keys;
- (b) that the landlord publicise the fact that the tenant has the right to return to possession;
- (c) that the tenant arrange to pay future rent by direct debit;
- (d) that the tenant undertake not to breach the lease in the future.

(3) A condition may require the tenant to enter into one or more security agreements to ensure compliance with the conditions.

(4) A condition may require that the tenant provide character references.

(5) A character reference is a reference, provided by a person who knows the tenant, stating that the tenant is likely to comply with the conditions.

[Fictional statutory provision; 159 words]

Consolidated version

Types of court-imposed conditions

(1) When granting relief against forfeiture, the court may impose conditions requiring one or more specified acts to be done or not done.

(2) For example, a condition may require:
- (a) the landlord to give the tenant a new set of keys;
- (b) the landlord to publicise the tenant's right to return to possession;
- (c) the tenant to arrange to pay future rent by direct debit;

(d) the tenant to undertake not to breach the lease in the future;
(e) the tenant to enter into one or more security agreements to ensure compliance with the conditions;
(f) the tenant to provide character references from someone who knows the tenant, stating that the tenant is likely to comply with the conditions.

[124 words; note in particular the consolidation of the former (4) and (5) into the new (2)(f)]

Conditions framed as relative clauses

Sometimes, a condition masquerades as a relative clause. If so, reframe the sentence to reveal the condition.

Original	Better
A landlord who considers that the tenant has traded unprofitably may ask the tenant to provide sales and turnover details.	**Version 1 (substantive provision before condition)** The landlord may ask the tenant to provide sales and turnover details, *if the landlord considers that the tenant has traded unprofitably*. ***Or* Version 2 (condition first)** *If the landlord considers that the tenant has traded unprofitably*, the landlord may ask the tenant to provide sales and turnover details.

Has the condition been fulfilled?

A practical issue with drafting conditional clauses is providing a mechanism by which parties are to know if or when the condition is fulfilled. Should the document provide some kind of notification procedure?

Example

> A contract provides for the sale of a lot in a subdivision that is yet to be approved by the planning authority. The contract as drafted requires the purchaser to complete within 10 days of the approval being granted, but does not require the vendor to notify the purchaser of the approval. How is the purchaser to know whether or when the approval has been granted? A more practical clause would state that the 10-day period starts to run from the date when the vendor notifies the purchaser of the approval.

See also **condition / warranty**; **EXCEPTIONS**; **if … then**.

conjunct and several

A Scots law equivalent of the English law term *joint and several*.

See **joint and several**.

CONJUNCTIONS

As sentence-starters

No 'rule' of grammar forbids conjunctions at the start of sentences. Even the briefest dip into the law reports reveals innumerable instances of learned judges starting sentences with conjunctions; many even start paragraphs with conjunctions.

An appropriate sentence-starting conjunction has immediacy and punch. For example:

- *And* immediately and concisely shows the link with the previous sentence.

- *But* provides an immediate and concise (shorter than *However*) contrast to what went before.
- *So* shows a logical sequitur.

So do not hesitate to start sentences (and paragraphs) with *and*, *but*, *however*, *so*, and the like. All the best writers do so.

Qualifications

There are two important qualifications to conjunctions as sentence-starters:

1. Do not overuse the technique. If overdone, the conjunctions will lose their punch. They may also give the writing a kindergarten feel.
2. Take care not to create sentence fragments (unless you do it deliberately, for effect). For example:

   'The judge worked late into the night to ensure that the judgment would be ready by morning. But couldn't sleep for worrying about punctuation.' A single run-on sentence would have worked: '… ready by morning, but couldn't sleep …' The attempted division into two sentences has left a sentence fragment.

See also **and**; **and / or**; **but**; **or**; **LISTS AND ENUMERATIONS**; **PUNCTUATION**.

connected with

See **in connection with**.

consensus ad idem

Latin: agreement on the same thing. In contract law, *consensus ad idem* implies a meeting of minds on the necessary elements for a binding contract (though it does not tell *what* elements are necessary). The term is merely a convenient shorthand—for which an English translation such as 'of one mind' usually suffices.

Examples

- 'A contract will not be concluded unless the parties are agreed as to its material terms. There must be *consensus ad idem* [prefer: *agreement on those terms*]. Whether the parties have reached agreement on the terms is … in large measure, determined by making an objective appraisal of the exchanges between the parties.' [*Shogun Finance Ltd v Hudson* [2003] UKHL 62; [2004] 1 AC 919, 964 [123] (Lord Phillips)]
- 'Furthermore, the parties' pleaded cases were *ad idem* [prefer: *at one*] on the question whether [B] should have possession of the caravan.' [*Grace v Black Horse Ltd* [2014] EWCA Civ 1413, [48] (Briggs LJ)]
- 'His Honour concluded, in our view correctly, that there had been nothing to prevent a *consensus ad idem* [prefer: *meeting of minds*; *binding agreement*].' [*Bank of South Australia Ltd v Ferguson* [1998] HCA 12, [18]; (1998) 192 CLR 248, 258 (High Court of Australia)]

Sometimes, the shorter *ad idem* is seen, without the contract law overtones—in which case 'at one' suffices.

consensus in idem

The Scots law equivalent of *consensus ad idem*.

See **consensus ad idem**.

consequence of

Connotes a causal relation: eg, a loss occurs 'in consequence of' an accident, or benefits accrue 'as a consequence of' a decision. But how direct a causal relation? Some consequences of an act or omission are foreseeable, others are unforeseeable; some consequences are direct, others are remote, and yet others result from intervening acts. In some contexts, 'in consequence of' may connote no element of causation at all, but mean merely 'in light of': eg, *Re Kay* [1965] 1 WLR 1463, 1467 (Russell LJ). Further (to state the obvious), '*a* consequence of' (ie, one of a number of possible consequences) does not carry the same meaning as '*the* consequence of' (ie, the sole consequence).

A drafter who intends rights or obligations to accrue 'in consequence of' an act or omission should seek to specify the intended degree of causation. This may help avoid litigation to clarify meaning. Litigated examples include:

- *Preston v Norfolk County Council* [1947] KB 775: when does a tenant vacate premises 'in consequence of' a notice to quit?
- *Iron and Steel Holding and Realisation Agencies v Compensation Appeal Tribunal* [1966] 1 WLR 480: when is employment lost 'in consequence of' sale of the employer's business?
- *Parker v Registrar-General* [1977] 1 NSWLR 22: when is an owner deprived of land 'in consequence of' fraud?

See also **cause (noun, verb); novus actus interveniens**; **result of**.

consequential loss

Conventional view

English courts give *consequential loss* a technical meaning, viewed in the prism of the leading case of *Hadley v Baxendale* (1854) 9 Exch 341; 156 ER 145. That case divided damages for breach of contract into two 'limbs' (ie, categories). Under the 'first limb', a party has a right to damages for loss that flows naturally—ie, 'according to the usual course of things'—from the breach. Under the second 'limb', a party has a right to damages that the contracting parties may reasonably be supposed to have contemplated, at the time they made the contract, as the probable result of its breach. English courts hold that a clause excluding liability for 'consequential loss' excludes liability only for loss falling within the *second* limb of *Hadley v Baxendale*; it does not exclude liability for loss falling within the first limb. Other terms meaning the same as *consequential loss* in this sense are 'special loss' and 'indirect loss'.

- '[A]uthority dictates that the line between direct and indirect or consequential losses is drawn along the boundary between the first and second limbs of *Hadley v Baxendale*.' [*Hotel Services Ltd v Hilton International Hotels (UK) Ltd* [2000] EWCA Civ 74, [19]; [2000] 1 All ER (Comm) 750 (Sedley LJ, approving a statement of Rix J)]
- 'The result of [the] decisions is to make it clear that there is no difference between the terms *special*, *indirect* or *consequential* loss, and that they all equate to losses falling within the second limb of the rule in *Hadley v Baxendale*.' [R Christou, *Boilerplate: Practical Clauses*, 7th edn (Sweet & Maxwell, 2015) para 7-116]

Wider view

Courts in some other jurisdictions—Australia in particular—give *consequential loss* a wider meaning, not limited to loss falling within the second limb of *Hadley v Baxendale*.

They hold that *consequential loss* connotes everything beyond the 'normal' measure of damages. The rationale is that a court should give words in a commercial contract the meaning that commercial people would give them in the circumstances of the particular case—and that meaning is not necessarily the same as legal precedent from past eras might give those words. This (courts have held) is particularly important when interpreting exclusion clauses. A clause that excludes liability for *consequential loss* is now to be taken at face value. On that rationale, 'consequential' simply means 'following from'; hence, the clause excludes liability for everything beyond the 'normal' measure of damages: see, eg, *Alstom Ltd v Yokogawa Australia Pty Ltd (No 7)* [2012] SASC 49, [281] (Bleby J); *Patersons Securities Ltd v Financial Ombudsman Service Ltd* [2015] WASC 321, [127]–[128] (Mitchell J).

The future?

To date, courts elsewhere seem reluctant to follow this wider view: see, eg, *PH Hydraulics & Engineering Pte Ltd v Airtrust (Hong Kong) Ltd* [2017] SGCA 26, [153] (where, however, the judgment records that the parties 'accepted' the conventional English position). Nevertheless, several fairly recent English decisions may point to a more flexible approach. In *Star Polaris LLC v HHIC-Phil Inc* [2016] EWHC 2941, the court found that, in the circumstances, 'consequential loss' was not to be understood in its *Hadley v Baxendale* meaning (ie, as legal shorthand for the second limb of *Hadley v Baxendale*), but rather in 'a cause and effect sense'. More recently, the Court of Appeal has questioned whether some of the 'consequential loss' decisions would be decided differently today, when 'courts are more willing to recognise that words take their meaning from their particular context and that the same word or phrase may mean different things in different documents': *Transocean Drilling UK Ltd v Providence Resources Plc* [2016] EWCA Civ 372, [15]; [2016] 2 Lloyd's Rep 51.

Further reading

JW Carter, 'Exclusion of Liability for Consequential Loss' (2009) *Journal of Contract Law* 118

See also **Hadley v Baxendale ('limbs' of)**; **in consequence of**; **LITIGATED WORDS AND PHRASES**.

consider

In legal usage, a verb having three possible meanings:

1. *deliberate* (with a view to making a decision), *reflect on*, *take note of*: eg, 'The court must *consider* the submissions before making its decision.'
2. *determine*, *decide*: eg, 'Where the tribunal *considers* that the appellant's argument is preferable, it must award costs to the appellant.'
3. *treat as* (in the sense of *deem*): eg, 'If interest is paid, late payments are to be *considered* as being paid on time.'

As with other words with varying meanings, be careful to use the word consistently throughout the document.

See also **deem**.

consideration

Meaning

In ordinary English, the meanings of *consideration* include: make allowance for (eg, 'take into consideration'); be kind to (eg, 'show consideration towards'); weigh up an argument (eg, 'on further consideration', 'on no consideration'). But in law, *consideration* carries the technical meaning of a *quid pro quo* for a promise:

> 'Valuable consideration has been defined as some right, interest, profit, or benefit accruing to the one party, or some forbearance, detriment, loss, or responsibility given, suffered, or undertaken by the other at his request. It is not necessary that the promisor should benefit by the consideration. It is sufficient if the promisee does some act from which a third person benefits, and which he would not have done but for the promise.' [*Halsbury's Laws of England*, 'Contract' (vol 22, 2019) [110], citations omitted]

Consideration (in its legal meaning) must have some value, but need not equal the value of the promise for which it is given. Variant descriptions include (in diminishing monetary value) '*valuable* consideration', '*good* consideration', '*adequate* consideration', and '*nominal* consideration'. Even a nominal amount such as £10 generally suffices to render a promise binding.

Use a different word?

Although the existence of consideration (as a concept) is central to the formation of a binding contract, the word *consideration* is not. A plain-language equivalent will suffice. In a document to be read only by lawyers, to use *consideration* is justifiable; but in a document intended for non-lawyers, alternatives are available. One is to use another term; another is to delete any reference to the notion of consideration, because whether consideration has been given is a question of fact, not of statement.

Examples

Before	After
In consideration of $100 paid by A to B, B agrees to ...	*In return for* $100 paid by A to B, B agrees to ...
In consideration of advances to be made by the Bank to the Customer, the Customer agrees to ...	*In return for* advances to be made by the Bank to the Customer, the Customer agrees to ...
G gives this guarantee *in consideration of* the Bank's advances to G Ltd.	G *guarantees* the Bank's advances to G Ltd.

See also **executory**.

CONSISTENCY OF TERMINOLOGY

The drafter's golden rule

The first principle of legal drafting is this: 'Never change your language unless you wish to change your meaning, and always change your language if you wish to change your meaning.': Jeremy Bentham, *The Works of Jeremy Bentham* (Edinburgh, William Tait, 1859) vol 8, 'Essay on Language', Rule III, 315. This has been a cardinal legal-drafting principle for centuries: '[N]ever ... change the form of words unless you are going to change their meaning': *Hadley v Perks* (1866) LR 1 QB 444, 457 (Blackburn J). As Lord Diplock famously said:

> '[T]he habit of a legal draftsman is to eschew synonyms. He uses the same words throughout the document to express the same thing or concept, and consequently if he uses different words the presumption is that he means a different thing or concept.' [*Prestcold (Central) Ltd v Minister of Labour* [1969] 1 WLR 89, 97 (CA)]

Examples

- Do not vary the description of premises in a lease—eg, *leased premises* in one place, *demised premises* in another place, and *leased property* in yet another place.
- Do not describe the objects of gifts in a will as *legatees* in one place and *beneficiaries* in another.
- Do not describe the right to bring a contract to an end for default as *termination* in one part of the contract, but *rescission* in another part.

Courts assume that legal drafters understand this principle, and interpret documents accordingly. This leaves little room in legal drafting for so-called 'elegant variation'. A change in words is taken to herald a change in meaning: *Craig Williamson Pty Ltd v Barrowcliff* [1915] VLR 450, 452; *Interactive Investor Trading Ltd v City Index Ltd* [2011] EWCA Civ 837, [29]. In the United States, this is sometimes called the 'presumption of uniformity':

> 'There is a presumption that a given term is used to mean the same thing throughout a [document], [and the] presumption [is] surely at its most vigorous when a term is repeated within a given sentence.' [*Brown v Gardner* 513 US 115, 118 (1994)]

A senior Australian judge has described the presumption as 'weak': *Fitness First Australia Pty Ltd v Fenshaw Pty Ltd* [2016] NSWCA 207, [43] (Leeming JA, speaking of the phrase *in respect of*, used a number of times in the one document with slightly different connotations each time). However, drafters would be unwise to expect leniency for their lack of consistency.

Examples

- A statute used the standard modern terminology of *may* to indicate discretion and *must* to indicate compulsion. In one provision, however, to interpret *may* as indicating discretion could possibly produce an unexpected result. Nevertheless, the court assumed that the drafter used *may* in that provision also to indicate discretion, not compulsion. See *Cain v New South Wales Land and Housing Corporation* [2014] NSWCA 28; (2014) 86 NSWLR 1, [24]–[25].
- Clause 44 of a building contract required the supervisor to 'ascertain' the cost of completing the building work following the contractor's default. Did 'ascertain' require absolute certainty, or could the supervisor rely on matters of estimation and approximation? Another clause of the contract required the supervisor to 'ascertain' amounts in a context where estimation and approximation were clearly part of the process. Held, 'ascertain' had the same meaning in clause 44 also (ie, allowing estimation and approximation): *Dura (Australia) Constructions Pty Ltd v Hue Boutique Living Pty Ltd* [2013] VSCA 179; (2013) 41 VR 636, [26]–[29].

Judicial leniency

General

Courts recognise that writers err. The overarching purpose of interpretation is to discern the parties' intentions. Sometimes this requires overlooking the drafter's imperfect technique. And so even though the drafter has given the same word different meanings, or given different words the same meaning, the court may absolve the drafter's sloppiness (as in *Watson v Haggitt* [1928] AC 127 (PC); *Murphy v Farmer* (1988) 165 CLR 19, 27; *Spring House (Freehold) Ltd v Mount Cook Land Ltd* [2002] 2 All ER 822, [28]).

Examples

- A contract defined *Completion* (capital C) to mean, in effect, the date when payment was made under a binding agreement. It also used the term *consummated*. Held, despite the consistency-of-terminology presumption, the drafter intended the two terms to mean the same—ie, when the sale is '*Completed*' meant the same as when the sale is '*consummated*': *African Minerals Ltd v Renaissance Capital Ltd* [2015] EWCA Civ 448.
- Court rules, dealing with proceedings, used the terms 'commenced', 'started' and 'begun'. Held, it was 'impossible to divine any sensible differentiation' between the terms; they meant the same thing: *Harrison v University Hospitals NHS Trust* [2017] EWCA Civ 792; [2017] 1 WLR 4456, [59] (Davis LJ).

Specific situations

Judicial rescue from the effects of the presumption is more likely in two particular circumstances:

1. Where the document is self-evidently poorly drafted, or is the product of an inexperienced drafter. On this basis it has been said that lapses may be excused more easily in regulations than in statutes, because those who draft regulations may be less experienced than those who draft statutes: *Environment Protection Authority v Schon G Condon as liquidator for Orchard Holdings (NSW) Pty Ltd (in liq)* [2014] NSWCA 149, [44].
2. Where the document is the product of a number of drafters, or the collation of a number of precedents: *Shop Distributive & Allied Employees' Association v Woolworths Ltd* (2006) 151 FCR 513, [26].

These are but illustrations of the principle that a court may 'correct' a drafter's errors when needed to give effect to the parties' intentions. However, this is not always an easy task. In particular, it may be difficult to distinguish an 'error' from a careful and deliberate discrimination in language. The drafter may have intended subtle distinctions.

Example

A rent review provision in a lease used two similar, but different, terms. One term was 'current annual *market rental*'; the other was 'current annual *market rental value*'. The court assumed the difference to be intentional: both terms had accepted industry meanings. In its view, the drafter intended *market rental* to mean 'face rent'—ie, the rent actually payable; and intended *market rental value* to mean 'effective rent'—ie, the rent after taking into account matters such as incentives to the tenant. See *Eureka Funds Management Ltd v Freehills Services Pty Ltd* [2008] VSCA 156, [52]; (2008) 19 VR 676, 692 (leave to appeal to High Court refused, *Freehills Services Pty Ltd v Eureka Funds Management Ltd* [2009] HCATrans 115).

Further reading

- Peter Butt, *Modern Legal Drafting*, 3rd edn (Cambridge University Press, 2013) 192–93
- Keith Mason, 'The Intent of Legislators: How Judges Discern It and What They Do if They Find It' (2006) 27 *Australian Bar Review* 253, 257–58
- Dennis C Pearce and Robert S Geddes, *Statutory Interpretation in Australia*, 9th edn (LexisNexis, 2019) [4.6]–[4.10]

See also **CORRECTIONS (BY COURT); DEFINITIONS; ELEGANT VARIATION; INCONSISTENT PROVISIONS; LITIGATED WORDS AND PHRASES; Mitsui principle; STANDARD FORMS; TERMS OF ART**.

consortium

Latin: a community; a fellowship. (The Latin plural *consortia* is occasionally used, but the preferred English plural is *consortiums*.) In legal and commercial usage, a *consortium* is an association of persons or entities formed for a business purpose.

Consortium is also the association and fellowship between husband and wife. In standard English, this usage is rare, but was seen in the husband's cause of action for damages for 'loss of consortium' (now abolished: *Administration of Justice Act 1982*, s 2).

constat

Latin: it follows; it is agreed. More often seen in the opposite, *non constat*.

See **non constat**.

constrain

The meaning has varied over time, from 'compel' to 'restrain'. Both meanings are found in law, though the more common now (since it reflects modern ordinary usage) is 'restrain'. An example of each meaning follows:

- 'Mr Hill QC was *constrained* [ie, *compelled*] to accept [a certain argument] …' [*Alize 1954* v *Allianz Elementar Versicherungs AG* [2020] EWCA Civ 293, [60] (Flaux LJ)]
- 'Electoral choice thereby constitutes the principal *constraint* [ie, *restraint*; *restriction*] on the constitutional exercise by the Parliament of the legislative power of the Commonwealth …' [*McCloy v New South Wales* [2015] HCA 34; (2015) 257 CLR 178, [111] (Gageler J)]

construction (of documents)

Most non-lawyers would instinctively assume that *construction* has to do with the erection of buildings, not the meaning of words. But in the context of legal documents, *construction* carries the sense of 'interpretation'. Some judges distinguish between 'construction' and 'interpretation' (see **interpretation / construction**). But in almost all contexts the generally accepted word is *interpretation*. Therefore, when writing for non-lawyers, prefer *interpretation* over *construction*.

See also **CANONS OF CONSTRUCTION (INTERPRETATION)**; **interpretation / construction (of documents)**.

constructive notice

See **notice / knowledge**.

constructive trust

A trust arising by operation of law when the circumstances make it unconscionable for the owner of property or an interest in property to assert their own interest and deny the beneficial interest of another. The term may be a true term of art, making it difficult to substitute a concise plain-English term.

Further reading

Halsbury's Laws of England, 'Trusts and Powers' (vol 98, 2019) [114]–[121]

See further, **beneficial**; **TERMS OF ART**.

consult

A requirement to *consult* opens up questions of degree. What level of consultation—peremptory or detailed? Need the consultor await a response? Need the consultor explain solutions already considered but rejected?

The case law on *consult* suggests that, unless context requires otherwise:

- An obligation to *consult* requires a genuine invitation for feedback: *Agricultural, Horticultural and Forestry Industry Board v Aylesbury Mushrooms Ltd* [1971] 2 WLR 190.
- The consultee must be given sufficient time to respond: *R v Secretary of State for Social Services* [1986] 1 WLR 1.
- Failure adequately to *consult* and allow feedback may invalidate a decision, either generally or at least as it affects the consultee: *Lee v Napier* [2013] FCA 236; (2013) 301 ALR 663.

contemnor

Also (rarely) spelled *contemner*: person who commits a contempt, such as contempt of Parliament, contempt of commissions, or contempt of court.

See also **contempt**.

contemporanea expositio est optima et fortissima in lege

Latin: a contemporaneous exposition is the best and most powerful in law. That is, the best way to understand a document is to interpret it as it would have been understood when made. See RH Kersley (ed), *Broom's Legal Maxims*, 10th edn (Sweet & Maxwell, 1939) 463.

contempt

In general usage, disrespect or scorn. In legal use, particularly disrespect or scorn of a judicial or quasi-judicial body, as in the following.

Contempt of commissions

Obstructing or bringing into disrepute, or tending to obstruct or bring into disrepute, the proceedings of a commission, such as a royal commission of inquiry. Because commissions are not courts (and therefore lack inherent power to punish for contempt), they require statutory power to prosecute or punish for contempt.

Contempt of court

Conduct that tends to bring the authority and administration of the law into disrespect, or that tends to impede the administration of justice.

> 'Contempt of court may take many forms. It may consist of what is somewhat archaically called contempt in the face of the court, for example, by disrupting the proceedings of a court in session or by improperly refusing to answer questions when giving evidence. It may, in a criminal case, consist of prejudicing a fair trial by publishing material likely to influence a jury. It may, as in the present case, consist of refusing to obey an order of the court. These are only a few of the many examples that could be given of contempt.' [*Jennison v Baker* [1972] 2 QB 52, 61 (Salmon LJ)]

Varieties of contempt of court include:

- *civil contempt*—the failure to obey a judgment or court order made for another party's benefit
- *contempt in the face of the court*—words said or acts done in court, or in the precincts of the court, that obstruct or interfere with, or tend to obstruct or interfere with, the administration of justice
- *consequential contempt*—contempt that falls short of gross insolence or direct opposition to the courts, but plainly tends to create universal disregard of their authority
- *criminal contempt*—words or acts that obstruct, or tend to obstruct, the administration of justice, usually by impairing confidence in or respect for the courts or their judgments (sometimes called *common-law contempt*)
- *direct contempt*—contempt that openly insults or resists the power of courts or the judges who preside in them
- *sub judice contempt*—contempt of court committed by publishing words that have a real and definite tendency to prejudice the fair trial of cases that are pending or in progress
- *technical contempt*—a contempt of court which, though proven, the court chooses to leave unpunished because of the particular circumstances (such as the contemnor's lack of wilfulness): *Hunt v Clarke* (1889) 58 LJ QB 490; *Bell v Stewart* (1920) 28 CLR 419.

Contempt of Parliament

Conduct or words that obstruct or impede Parliament (or, in bicameral jurisdictions, either House of Parliament) in the performance of its powers and duties—such as defiance of parliamentary rules or orders, misconduct in the House, or deceiving Parliament. Judicial discussions include: *Speaker of the Legislative Assembly of Victoria v Glass* (1871) LR 3 PC 560; *R v Richards; Ex parte Fitzpatrick* (1955) 92 CLR 157.

See also **embracery; sub judice**.

conterminous

Sharing a common boundary. Sometimes means 'co-extensive with'. Variants include *coterminous* and *co-terminous*.

Examples

- 'The claim was for breach of contractual and/or *conterminous* tortious duties to exercise reasonable skill and care.' [*Aspect Contracts (Asbestos) Ltd v Higgins Construction Plc* [2015] UKSC 38; [2015] 1 WLR 2961, [3] (Lord Mance; but using *coterminous* at [22])]
- '[The second possibility is that] the right under HRA should be *coterminous* with the temporal jurisdiction of the ECtHR.' [*R v Secretary of State for Foreign and Commonwealth Affairs* [2015] UKSC 69; [2015] 3 WLR 1665, [243] (Lord Kerr; similarly at [252])]
- 'But the duty of the employee being co-extensive, or *co-terminous*, with that of the employer there was … no room for apportionment.' [*Nicol v Allyacht Spars Pty Ltd* (1987) 163 CLR 611, 623 (Dawson J)]

contiguous

Latin *contiguus*: touching; sharing a common boundary with. The normal meaning is 'touching', not merely 'neighbouring': *Spillers Limited v Cardiff (Borough) Assessment Committee* [1931] 2 KB 21, 43; *Hunter's Hill Council v Minister for Local Government*

[2017] NSWCA 188 (land separated by river spanned by bridge not 'single area of *contiguous* land').

However, meaning yields to context, which may indicate a broader meaning, such as:

- 'nearby' but not actually touching: *Waihi Grand Junction Gold-Mining Co Ltd* (1909) 29 NZLR 499, 505
- 'on the other side of the street': *Haynes v King* [1893] 3 Ch 439

If the context makes *contiguous* open to doubt, clarify it.

See also **abut**; **adjacent**; **adjoining**.

continual / continuous

Continual denotes happening again and again, over a long time: eg, 'The time-pressure on judges is *continual*.' *Continuous* denotes unbroken, without interruption: eg, 'To acquire a possessory title, your adverse possession must be *continuous*.'

contra bonos mores

Latin: against good (decent) moral standards; contrary to accepted decent behaviour. Blackstone, in discussing the ancient powers of magistrates to bind over offenders for good behaviour, distinguished between matters contrary to morality (*contra bonos mores*) and matters contrary to law and order (*contra pacem*—'against the peace', in the sense of against the King's/Queen's peace): *Commentaries on the Laws of England* (Clarendon, 1769) book 4, ch 18.

Despite its long use in law, *contra bonos mores* is irredeemably obscure. What is good (decent), and by whose standard, and at what period in history (given that concepts of decency change over time)? It is best to drop the Latin and choose an English translation that reflects the intended meaning, as in the following examples:

- 'When Lord Mansfield … said that the Court of King's Bench was the *custos morum* [prefer: *moral custodian*] of the people and had the superintendency of offences *contra bonos mores* [prefer: *against decency*; *against good morals*], he was asserting, as I now assert, that there is in that Court a residual power, where no statute has yet intervened to supersede the common law, to superintend those offences which are prejudicial to the public welfare.' [*Shaw v Director of Public Prosecutions* [1962] AC 220, 268 (Viscount Simonds)]
- '[W]hat may be injurious [to the public] at one time or under one set of circumstances may not be so at another time and under different circumstances. … In my opinion it is not *contra bonos mores* [prefer: *against public decency*] to retain … such a specimen [ie, the body of a malformed baby] unburied.' [*Doodeward v Spence* (1908) 6 CLR 406, 413–14 (Griffith CJ)]

contra pacem

Latin: against the peace (ie, against public law and order).

See **contra bones mores**.

contra proferentem

The conventional shorthand version of the Latin maxim, *verba chartarum fortius accipiuntur contra proferentem*: the words of an instrument are taken most strongly against the party employing them. (To similar effect: *ambiguitas contra stipulatorem est*: an ambiguity is taken against the party using it.)

Principle of interpretation

Under the *contra proferentem* principle, if ambiguity in a provision cannot be resolved in any other way, the provision is interpreted against the interests of the person who put it forward. The rationale is that the person who put it forward (the 'profferor') had the opportunity to protect his or her own interests in clear terms—and having failed to do so, must accept an unfavourable interpretation.

Examples

- In an insurance policy, an ambiguous provision (one possible construction favouring the insurer and another favouring the insured) is interpreted in favour of the insured: *Rowlett, Leakey & Co v Scottish Provident Institution* [1927] 1 Ch 55, 69 (Warrington LJ); *Major Engineering Pty Ltd v CGU Insurance Ltd* [2011] VSCA 226; (2011) 35 VR 458; *European Film Bonds AS v Lotus Holdings LLC* [2020] EWHC 1115 (Ch), [63]. This includes, for example, an exclusion clause: *Nissho Iwai Australia Ltd v Malaysian International Shipping Corp* (1989) 167 CLR 219, 227.
- In a lease, an ambiguous provision imposing obligations on the tenant, or creating rights in favour of the tenant, is interpreted in favour of the tenant: *John Lee & Son (Grantham) Ltd v Railway Executive* [1949] 2 All ER 581 (CA); *Spring House (Freehold) Ltd v Mount Cook Land Ltd* [2001] EWCA Civ 1833; [2002] 2 All ER 822, [52]; *World Best Holdings Ltd v Sarker* [2010] NSWCA 24; (2010) 14 BPR 27,549.
- In a contract for the sale of land, an ambiguous provision is interpreted in favour of the purchaser: *Savill Brothers Ltd v Bethell* [1902] 2 Ch 523, 537–38.
- In a guarantee, an ambiguous provision is interpreted in favour of the guarantor: *Eastern Counties Building Society v Russell* [1947] 1 All ER 500, 503; affirmed [1947] 2 All ER 734, 736 (CA).
- In an indemnity, an ambiguous provision is interpreted in favour of the person providing the indemnity (ie, against the party seeking to rely on the indemnity): *Andar Transport Pty Ltd v Brambles Ltd* (2004) 217 CLR 242, [117]. However, it may be otherwise if the party giving the indemnity also drafted it: *Gardiner v Agricultural and Rural Finance Pty Ltd* [2007] NSWCA 235, [21] (Spigelman CJ).
- In a grant of land, an ambiguous provision is interpreted in favour of the grantee: *Halsbury's Laws of England*, 'Deeds and other Instruments' (vol 32, 2019) [378]. But it is otherwise if the grantor is the Crown; there, the ambiguity is interpreted in favour of the Crown: *Viscountess Rhondda's Claim* [1922] 2 AC 339, 353; *Minister for Natural Resources v Brantag Pty Ltd* (1997) 8 BPR 15,815, 15,821–22 (NSWCA).
- In a loan agreement, an ambiguous provision is interpreted in favour of the borrower: *Budget Stationery Supplies Pty Ltd v National Australia Bank Ltd* (1996) 7 BPR 14,891.

Unclear ambit

Despite the principle's antiquity, difficulties attend many aspects of its operation. Even how best to formulate the principle is disputed, as the following variants show:

- The court asks who introduced the particular (ambiguous) provision into the contract, and interprets the provision against that party, regardless of which party 'proffered' the document as a whole: *Bartlett & Partners Ltd v Meller* [1961] 1 Lloyds Rep 487, 494; *Lobb v Phoenix Assurance Co Ltd* [1988] 1 NZLR 285, 288, 289, 291.
- Where a party has overall responsibility for drafting the document, an ambiguous provision is interpreted against that party even though the other party had some involvement in the drafting: *Halford v Price* (1960) 105 CLR 23, 30 (Dixon CJ), 34 (Fullagar J).
- The court asks who is to be taken to be 'saying' the ambiguous words, and then interprets the words against that person: *Amax International Ltd v Custodian Holdings Ltd* [1986] 2 EGLR 111, 112 (Hoffmann J—in interpreting an ambiguous rent clause, the tenant is the covenantor and therefore technically the *proferens*).

- The ambiguous provision is interpreted against the person for whose 'benefit' it is inserted: *Burton v English* (1883) 12 QBD 218, 220 (Brett MR), 222, 224 (Bowen LJ); *J Fenwick & Co Pty Ltd v Federal Steam Navigation Co Ltd* (1943) 44 SR (NSW) 1, 5–6 (Jordan CJ).
- Where the party responsible for the drafting inserted the ambiguous provision for the benefit of the other party, it is interpreted against the interests of that other party: *Electric Life Pty Ltd v Unison Finance Group Pty Ltd* [2015] NSWCA 394 (provision in equipment lease inserted by owner of equipment for benefit of renter, interpreted against renter).

Last resort only

As with other principles of interpretation, courts apply the *contra proferentem* maxim only where they cannot resolve the ambiguity by any other legitimate means: *St Edmundsbury and Ipswich Diocesan Board of Finance v Clark (No 2)* [1975] 1 WLR 468, 477; *Darlington Futures Ltd v Delco Australia Pty Ltd* (1986) 161 CLR 500, 510. If they can resolve the ambiguity in another way, the maxim has no room to operate. In that sense, it is a principle of last resort: *The Sabrewing* [2007] EWHC 2482 (Comm); [2008] 1 Lloyd's Rep 286, [15] (Gloster J); *Rava v Logan Wines* [2007] NSWCA 62, [55] (Campbell JA); *Chubb Insurance Co of Australia Ltd v Robinson* [2016] FCAFC 17; (2016) 239 FCR 300, [167].

No place in commercial contracts?

Courts have suggested that the maxim is rarely useful in interpreting commercial contracts: *K/S Victoria Street v House of Fraser (Stores Management) Ltd* [2011] EWCA Civ 904, [68]; [2012] Ch 497. In particular, there may be little scope for the maxim where both parties are commercially astute and experienced, where both have had the benefit of legal advice, and where both have roughly equal bargaining power: *Rayford Homes Ltd v Bank of Scotland Plc* [2011] EWHC 1948 (Ch), [72]; *Rich v CGU Insurance Ltd* (2005) 79 ALJR 856, 859–60 (Kirby J). In such cases, the words used, the commercial sense, and the context should normally be enough to determine the meaning: *Transocean Drilling UK Ltd v Providence Resources plc* [2016] EWCA Civ 372; [2016] 2 Lloyd's Rep 51; *Persimmon Homes Ltd v Ove Arup & Partners Ltd* [2017] EWCA Civ 373.

Nevertheless, courts still occasionally invoke the *contra proferentem* maxim in commercial contracts. Examples include:

- In a 99-year lease of an office block, the description of 'premises' in a clause forbidding the tenant from placing goods 'outside the premises' was interpreted in favour of the tenant, although 'very much as the last resort': *Spring House (Freehold) Ltd v Mount Cook Land Ltd* [2002] 2 All ER 822, [52] (Ward and Rix LJJ).
- In a lease of premises in a food court, an approved use clause was interpreted *contra proferentem* the landlord (again, as a last resort): *World Best Holdings Ltd v Sarker* [2010] NSWCA 24; (2010) 14 BPR 27,549.
- In a fee agreement between an investment bank and client, and drafted by the bank, ambiguities about the bank's entitlement to a fee were interpreted against the interests of the bank: *JP Morgan Australia Ltd v Consolidated Minerals Pty Ltd* [2011] NSWCA 3.

Contracting out

Parties can agree that the *contra proferentem* principle is not to apply to the interpretation of their document. For example:

> 'Nothing is to be interpreted adversely to a Party merely because that Party put forward this contract or the relevant part of this contract.'

Subject to vitiating factors such as undue influence or misrepresentation, courts give effect to that agreement: *GL Nederland (Asia) Pty Ltd v Expertise Events Pty Ltd* [1999] NSWCA 62, [26].

Further reading

- *Halsbury's Laws of England*, 'Deeds and other Instruments' (vol 32, 2019) [378]–[379]
- Peter Butt, *Modern Legal Drafting*, 3rd edn (Cambridge University Press, 2013) 66–69
- Kim Lewison, *The Interpretation of Contracts*, 6th edn (Sweet & Maxwell, 2015) [7.08], [12.05]
- Joanna McCunn, 'The *Contra Proferentem* Rule: Contract Law's Great Survivor' (2019) 39 *Oxford Journal of Legal Studies* 483

CONTRACTIONS

In general writing

Contractions—eg, *won't, don't, can't, I'll, we'll*—are increasingly common in modern prose. One study finds that authors before 1800 averaged 0.6 apostrophes (including apostrophes to indicate contractions) per 100 words, while those after 1920 averaged 2.2: Wayne A Danielson and Dominic L Larosa, 'A New Readability Formula Based on the Stylistic Age of Novels' (1989) 33 *Journal of Reading* 194.

In legal writing

Many lawyers unhesitatingly use contractions in emails: eg, '*We'd* like to discuss this with you.' Some are more hesitant in using contractions in correspondence: eg, 'We *wouldn't* recommend that course of action.' Most probably feel uncomfortable in using contractions in formal documents, such as leases ('The tenant *mustn't* damage the premises') or wills ('The executor *musn't* sell my house to pay my debts'). For them, informality of this kind in documents is a step too far.

But no *legal* reason precludes the use of contractions in formal legal contexts. The only barrier is the lawyer's ingrained reluctance to appear casual. But if that reluctance can be overcome, and as long as no ambiguity arises, the use of contractions is acceptable. The only requirement is to be consistent: don't switch between contractions and no-contractions, at least without self-evident logic. Also, having chosen to use contractions, have the strength of your convictions:

> An Australian statute used a contraction in a section heading: 'What happens if you *don't* comply' (*Income Tax Assessment Act 1997* (Cth), s 900.185). However, as if to step back from the brink, the text of the section used the formal 'do not': 'If you *do not* comply with a notice for a particular expense, you cannot deduct the expense.'

CONTRADICTORY EXPRESSIONS

See **INCONSISTENT PROVISIONS.**

contravene

Usually, *contravene* implies a positive act—doing something that breaches an obligation or a law. But depending on context, *contravene* can include passively omitting to do something: eg, omitting to report an accident that the law requires to be reported. Thus, in legal usage, *contravene* can include breach by omission:

> 'The word "contravention" [in the Act] is quite apt to include a disobedience which consists merely in abstaining from doing an act, [and covers] a failure to perform a positive requirement as well as disobedience of a negative command.' [*R v Commonwealth Court of Conciliation and Arbitration* (1953) 89 CLR 636, 649 (Dixon CJ, Webb, Fullagar and Kitto JJ)]

CONTRONYM

A word with two contradictory meanings: examples in law are *sanction* (support; punishment); *licence* (permission; freedom to act without needing permission); *enjoin* (encourage; seek to stop); *exemplary* (excellent; punishing to set an example—eg, *exemplary* damages); *oversight* (supervision; neglect); *peruse* (read closely; skim lightly). Usually, context shows the intended meaning; but if in doubt, clarify.

See further, **AMBIGUITY**.

contumacy

Perverse and stubborn opposition to authority (adjective: *contumacious*). The word has a certain quaintness, which may attract lawyers but probably bemuses non-lawyers. When addressing non-lawyers, prefer an alternative:

> '[D]isobedience to the order of a court constitutes criminal contempt when the disobedience is *contumacious* [prefer: *defiant*].' [*Witham v Holloway* (1995) 183 CLR 525, 538–39 (McHugh J)]

Contumacy and *contumacious* are sometimes paired with 'defiant' (eg, 'defiant *or* contumaceous') or 'wilful' (eg, 'wilful *and* contumaceous'). However, because contumacy involves defiance, and because both *wilful* and *contumacious* carry the sense of deliberate act, these pairings can be replaced with *defiant*, as in the following example (strike-through added):

> 'Failure to obey an injunction is not a criminal offence unless the failure to comply is defiant ~~or contumacious~~ [delete]. The contempt alleged in this case is a criminal contempt. It is alleged that CFMEU is guilty of *wilful and contumacious* [delete and substitute: *defiant*] disobedience of an injunction.' [*Construction, Forestry, Mining and Energy Union v Boral Resources (Vic) Pty Ltd* [2015] HCA 21, [65]–[66] (Nettle J)]

contumely

Insolent reproach or abuse; insulting or contemptuous language (adjective: *contumelious*). Although not a specifically legal term, its calculated quaintness seems at home in formal legal prose—which is a good reason to avoid it and substitute a normal English word, or (as in the third example below) to explain it. For the adjective (*contumelious*), substitutes are *insolent, wanton, reprehensible*. For example:

- 'To behave in such a way is in my judgement to treat the court with intolerable *contumely* [prefer: *scorn*; *disdain*].' [*Janov v Morris* [1981] 1 WLR 1389, 1395 (Watkins LJ)]
- 'Take a common case: a man is assaulted, or his land is trespassed upon, with accompanying circumstances of insolence or *contumely* [prefer: *reprehensibility*; *abuse*].' [*Cassell & Co Ltd v Broome* [1972] AC 1027, 1115 (Lord Wilberforce)]
- '[Exemplary] damages … can apply only where the conduct of the defendant merits punishment, which is only considered to be so where his conduct is wanton, as where it discloses fraud, malice, violence, cruelty, insolence or the like, or, as it is sometimes put, where he acts in *contumelious* [add explanation:—*ie, blatant or insolent*—] disregard of the plaintiff's rights.' [*Uren v John Fairfax & Sons Pty Ltd* (1966) 117 CLR 118, 122 (McTiernan J, quoting from *Mayne & McGregor on Damages*, 12th edn (1961) 196)]

convenant

A common typographical error for *covenant*:

> 'The Declaration may be compared to a restrictive *convenant* [correct to: *covenant*].' [*Commonwealth v Western Australia* (1999) 196 CLR 392, 488 [282] (Callinan J)]

convenient

A vague word, with potential for ambiguity. When is it *convenient* to do something? How fast is 'with all *convenient* speed'? Is the meaning determined by objective or subjective standards? Even to pose the questions indicates the need for clarification. The potential for vagueness is demonstrated by a series of Australian cases on whether it is 'not *convenient*' to have trial by jury: see, eg, *Lawsen v Jensen* [2017] TASSC 34; (2017) 29 Tas R 196 (answer: when the complexity of documents, or of medical or scientific evidence, would be beyond the competence of jurors).

conveyance

The transfer of property (usually land) by one person to another; also, the document by which property is transferred. The term *conveyance* properly applies only in the context of unregistered land (ie, land under 'old system title' or 'common law title'). For registered land, the appropriate term is *transfer*.

Some statutes widen the meaning of *conveyance* beyond land, to any 'assurance of property': eg, *Law of Property Act 1925*, s 205(1)(ii). This can result in esoteric transactions being treated as *conveyances*: eg, the vesting of a chose in action in newly appointed trustees: *Commissioner of State Taxation (SA) v Cyril Henschke Pty Ltd* [2010] HCA 43; (2010) 242 CLR 508.

See also **assign / transfer (verb)**; **transfer (noun)**.

conviction

In criminal law, a word with two meanings, related but different: (1) a finding of guilt, regardless of whether a penalty is imposed; (2) a finding of guilt, including the imposition of a penalty. Context will determine whether meaning (1) or (2) is intended: *S v Recorder of Manchester* [1971] AC 481, 502–03; *R v Vanek* [1944] OR 428; *Della Patrona v DPP (No 2)* (1993) 38 NSWLR 257, 263–66.

cool-off / cool off

When used in the sense of changing one's mind, *cool-off* normally takes a hyphen, whether used as a verb ('a consumer's right to *cool-off*') or as an adjective ('a consumer's *cooling-off* right'). For example:

> 'Parliament's purpose was ... to ensure that all consumers should have the "safety net" of a *cooling-off* period.' [*Swift v Robertson* [2014] 1 WLR 3438, 3449 (Lord Kerr)]

However, in line with the modern trend towards dropping hyphens, a hyphen-less form is increasingly seen:

> '[T]here is to be a *cooling off* [prefer: *cooling-off*] period for every contract for the sale of residential property ...' [*Conveyancing Act 1919* (NSW), s 66S(1)]

See also **HYPHENS**.

copy (of document)

In former times, when documents were copied by hand or printed by printing press, it may have been difficult to distinguish the 'original' from a 'copy'. For a time, after the advent of the typewriter, it became easier to distinguish the original from the copy, because the copy was invariably produced by carbon paper. In modern times, printers and photocopiers have made it more difficult again, for they can produce multiple 'copies' of a document, each looking like an original, and each, as a matter of ordinary English, being called a 'copy'; indeed, there may be no easily identified single original. These developments have affected the legal understanding of 'copy'. For example:

- A statutory requirement to serve a *copy* of a document was satisfied by serving either the original or a photocopy: *Emhill Pty Ltd v Bonsoc Pty Ltd* [2005] VSCA 239; (2005) 12 VR 129.
- A statutory requirement to serve a copy of an affidavit was satisfied by serving two versions, each incomplete but together reproducing the full version of the original: *Medeco Group Pty Ltd v Cripps* [2009] NSWSC 927; (2009) 27 ACLC 1404.

coram

General

Latin: in the presence of; sometimes abbreviated to *cor* (no full stop). In law, used especially in the context of 'in the presence of' a particular judge, or 'in the court presided over by' a particular judge: thus *coram Smith J*, or *cor Smith J*. The English translation will do just fine.

Variants include the following:

coram judice

Latin: in the presence of a judge. Used more expansively to mean 'within jurisdiction'. Thus, a judge who acts *coram judice* cannot be sued for errors in the judgment: *Sirros v Moore* [1975] QB 118, 139 (Buckley LJ). Prefer the English 'within jurisdiction' or 'within power'.

coram non judice

Latin: in the presence of one who is not a judge (ie, a person lacking jurisdiction). Prefer the English 'lacking jurisdiction' or similar. For example:

- '[W]hether a court or other tribunal of limited jurisdiction has acted without jurisdiction (*coram non judice*) can be determined by considering whether at the outset of the proceedings that court had jurisdiction to entertain the proceedings at all.' [*Re McC* [1985] AC 528, 536 (Lord Bridge—prioritising the English over the Latin)]
- '[T]he questions of immigrant and immigration were really decided *coram non judice*, before a person who had no jurisdiction to entertain them.' [*Wall v R (No 1)* (1927) 39 CLR 245, 265 (Higgins J; having given a translation, he could have excised the Latin)]

coram populo

Latin: in the presence of the public, publicly; sometimes rendered *coram populi*. For example: the normal rule of English law is that 'legal proceedings must be *coram populo*': *Schooley v Nye* [1950] 1 KB 335, 338 (in argument). The pedantry-free English *in public* is perfectly adequate.

corporation

A body of persons (a *corporation aggregate*) or an office (a *corporation sole*) which the law recognises as having a personality distinct from the separate personalities of the members of the body or the personality of the holder for the time being of the office.

corporation aggregate

Plural, *corporations aggregate*. A corporation composed of a number of persons, in contrast to a *corporation sole*, which comprises one person only. Sometimes, corporations aggregate are incorporated by Act of Parliament or Royal Charter, and given specific rights and duties; examples include the mayor and aldermen of a council; a joint stock company; and (in the Established Church) the dean and chapter of a cathedral. However, the term *corporation aggregate* is also used more generally to mean any corporation other than a corporation sole.

corporation sole

Plural, *corporations sole*. A corporation that comprises one person only and his or her successors in a particular office, and having a perpetual existence. Statutes establishing public authorities or high offices of state often declare them to be corporations sole. At common law, the Crown is a corporation sole; so also are bishops and some other clergy in the Established Church.

It is the *office* that is incorporated, not the individual holder from time to time, and that office continues despite the lack of a particular incumbent at any particular time: *Crouch v Commissioner for Railways (Qld)* (1985) 159 CLR 22, 35. Successive office-holders enjoy property vested in a corporation sole without the need for conveyance to them.

Further reading

Halsbury's Laws of England, 'Corporations' (vol 24, 2019) [412]–[415]

corporeal / incorporeal

In normal usage, *corporeal* means 'material', 'tangible'; *incorporeal* means 'having no material substance', 'intangible'. Legal usage reflects these meanings, particularly as applied to interests in property (usually, though not exclusively, property in land). Early English lawyers adopted the terms *corporeal* and *incorporeal* from Roman law. They classified land—being a tangible 'thing'—as *corporeal*; and they classifed interests *in* land, such as easements—being intangible—as *incorporeal*. Today, legal philosophers would see the *corporeal/incorporeal* distinction as unsatisfactory and would classify both land and interests in land as 'rights', or 'bundles of rights', rather than 'things'.

Further reading

Kevin Gray and Susan Francis Gray, *Elements of Land Law*, 5th edn (Oxford University Press, 2009) ch 5.1 (on the nature of property in land)

corporeal hereditament

A tangible (corporeal) property interest that is 'heritable'—ie, capable of passing on death by will or intestacy—such as land. The usage is rare; more often seen is its opposite, *incorporeal hereditament*.

See also **corporeal / incorporeal; incorporeal hereditament**.

corpus

Latin: body. Commonly used to refer to the body of property that is held in a trust (eg, 'the corpus of the estate'), or the principal sum on which interest is earned (eg, 'the corpus of the investment'). The *Oxford English Dictionary* gives the Latin-based *corpora* as the only plural. In legal usage, however, *corpuses* is sometimes seen. An early example is the plural for the writ of habeas corpus: *Wood's Case* (1799) 3 Wils KB 172, 175; 95 ER 996, 997 (de Grey CJ, 'habeas corpuses'). But more recent examples exist:

- 'Assets would not be subject to attachment, however, where there are two separate *corpuses* which chance to be held by the same trustee corporation.' [*Re The Land Conservancy of British Columbia Inc* [2014] 7 WWR 122, [177] (Fitzpatrick J)]
- 'These rules governing the treatment of trust *corpuses* and payments out of trusts do not apply universally.' [*Maine Pooled Disability Trust v Hamilton* 927 F 3d 52, 56 (US Ct of Appeal, 1st Cir, 2019)]

corpus delicti

Latin: the body of the crime, in the sense of the body of evidence proving that the crime has been committed. In criminal proceedings, the prosecution must 'prove the *corpus delicti*, the body of the offence': *A-G of Jersey v Norton* [1967] 1 AC 464, 465 (in argument). The accused's proven motives are part of the *corpus delicti*: *Plomp v R* (1963) 110 CLR 234, 247–50 (Menzies J).

Corpus delicti does not mean the 'dead body'. In a murder, for example, a jury may be entitled to convict on proof of death, despite the absence of a body: *R v Onufrejczyk* [1955] 1 QB 388, 393 (Lord Goddard CJ).

In practice, *corpus delicti* is used almost exclusively in criminal law. However, the expression can mean more generally 'the body of (or evidence for) the wrong' in torts law. Thus, in a torts case where the plaintiff sued a garment manufacturer after suffering a rash: 'The *corpus delicti* was a pair of underpants. Had they been washed before use, no ill-effects would have resulted': *Haseldine v C A Daw and Son Ltd* [1941] 2 KB 343, 376–77 (Goddard LJ, speaking of *Grant v Australian Knitting Mills Ltd* [1936] AC 85).

Despite its long-accepted use, this Latin term is mere legal shorthand, apt more to cloud than clarify. An appropriate English translation—such as 'the facts establishing the crime', or 'the evidence showing that the wrong occurred'—would communicate more effectively.

See also **actus reus; mens rea.**

CORRECTIONS (BY COURT)

A court may 'correct' obvious drafting errors to give effect to what it sees as the parties' true intentions. This is an aspect of interpretation, not 'rectification' in any formal sense; rectification is unnecessary where the parties' true meaning can be ascertained on the face of the document without needing to resort to extrinsic material.

No self-respecting drafter would rely on judicial intervention to correct drafting errors, but it may be a handy backstop. In the following examples, the court corrected the drafter's slip:

- 'John' meant 'Mary': *Wilson v Wilson* (1854) 5 HLC 40, 67; (1854) 10 ER 811, 822 (Lord St Leonards)
- 'coloured blue' meant 'coloured blue and red': *St Edmundsbury Board of Finance v Clark* [1973] 1 WLR 1572, 1585 (Megarry J)
- 'inconsistent' meant 'consistent': *Fitzgerald v Masters* (1956) 95 CLR 420, 427
- 'shorter' meant 'longer': *Saxby Soft Drinks Pty Ltd v George Saxby Beverages Pty Ltd* [2009] NSWSC 1486; (2009) 14 BPR 27,213 (Brereton J).

See further **CONSISTENCY OF TERMINOLOGY; EDITING; ELEGANT VARIATION; INCONSISTENT PROVISIONS; LEGALESE; PROOFREADING.**

CORRESPONDENCE (LETTERS AND EMAILS)

Techniques for effective correspondence

Overview

Effective correspondence—whether letters, faxes or emails—uses the same techniques as other forms of effective writing. In particular, it:

- puts the main points as early as possible
- uses language that is as simple as the subject matter allows
- uses short sentences
- prefers the active voice over the passive
- prefers verbs over nouns and noun phrases.

The opening

Always tell readers up-front why they should read what you are writing: start with the key points. For example, in a letter of advice, start with the question being asked and then move straight to the answer, including any steps the reader should take; any necessary detailed discussion of the law and the facts can come later. In a letter that seeks action from an official or department, start by stating what you seek.

Make the first sentence powerful, not wimpish. That means avoiding standard recitations such as 'I refer to previous correspondence' or 'I refer to your telephone message of 1 May'; they are formulaic and lifeless. (If you really do need to refer to previous correspondence or telephone messages, postpone that until you have made your key points.) Also, avoid sentences that later turn out to be superfluous—as in a letter that starts (weakly): 'I refer to your application for membership of the club' and then proceeds (verbosely) 'We are pleased to advise that we have granted your application for membership of the club.'

The ending

Avoid stock-standard endings such as 'Please advise if we can be of any further assistance' or 'If you have any questions, please feel free to contact the undersigned.' Such endings draw out the writing unnecessarily—and may even appear insincere. In any case, they are unlikely to add anything, because a reader who wants to get back in touch will do so without needing the invitation. When you have finished saying what you want to say, just sign off.

Addressing correspondence

Conventions for addressing letters, faxes and emails vary. They are usually less formal than in earlier times, particularly in electronic communications. The following are guidelines only.

Name block for recipient

- *Female*: 'Ms [no full stop] Joan Smith' (unless you know that the addressee prefers *Mrs* or *Miss*).
- *Male*: 'Mr [no full stop] John Smith' (*not* 'John Smith Esquire'; *not* 'John Smith Esq'; *not* 'John Smith', unless you know him well).
- *Title*: Dr, Professor, Senator, etc, plus the addressee's given name and surname.

- *Firm*: direct name, without a prefix: 'Sly and Muddle' (*not* 'Messrs Sly and Muddle').
- *Officer or department*: any of the following:

Title plus individual's full name	Title but no individual's name	Department, no person in particular
Mr Simon Hayes[,] Chief Executive and Chief Land Registrar[,] HM Land Registry [Postal address]	Chief Executive and Chief Land Registrar[,] HM Land Registry [Postal address]	HM Land Registry [Postal address]

Salutations

Salutations to individuals

- Recipient's name not known, but gender known: 'Dear Sir' or 'Dear Madam'; if gender unknown, 'Dear Sir or Madam'.
- Recipient's surname known: 'Dear Mr Smith' or 'Dear Ms Jones'.
- Recipient's given name known: whether to use it depends on how well you know them, and their seniority within the organisation (for senior recipients, familiarity may be inappropriate).
- Less formal: recipient's first name: 'Dear John' or 'Dear Joan'.
- No comma after the salutation.

Salutations to entities or groups

- Recipient a law firm or entity: no salutation.
- Recipient a small group: all their names: 'Dear Ms Jones, Mrs Smith and Mr Black'.
- Recipients the directors of a company: 'Dear Board Members'.
- Recipient a group comprising both sexes: 'Dear Sirs and Mesdames' (but many today would consider this too formal).

Salutations in memos and internal emails

A less formal style is acceptable (although the relationship between writer and reader may dictate otherwise). Generally omit courtesy titles (eg, 'Mr', 'Ms'). If appropriate, omit the opening salutation (eg, 'Dear Bill', 'Bill') and go straight into the text.

Subject line

The older style, underlined, is now becoming rare: <u>Re Your Will</u>. Modern correspondence drops 'Re' ('in the matter of') and states the subject matter directly, in bold, not underlined: **Your will**.

Sign-offs

Style and content depend on the nature of the correspondence, and on the relationship between writer and reader.

Letters and faxes

The conventional sign-offs are:

- Addressee named in person (ie, 'Dear Mr', 'Dear Ms'; 'Dear John', 'Dear Joan'): 'Yours sincerely'.
- Addressee a firm or organisation: 'Yours faithfully'.
- No comma after the sign-off.

However, these conventional forms are disappearing, under the influence of the less formal sign-offs used in emails.

Memos and internal emails

- Recipient an external person or body where formality is appropriate: 'Yours faithfully' or 'Yours sincerely'.
- Otherwise: 'Regards' [often no comma] *or* 'Kind regards' [often no comma].

See also **ADVICE (FORM OF); DOCUMENT DESIGN; DOCUMENT STRUCTURE; FONT**.

corresponding-date rule

Rarely hyphenated, though logically it should be, given that 'corresponding date' here is a phrasal adjective ('corresponding-date rule').

The rule

Application

A rule (strictly, a principle of interpretation), deriving from *Dodds v Walker* [1981] 2 All ER 609 (HL), that in calculating a period '*[x] months of* [or *from*, or *after*]' a stated date, the period ends on the day of the month corresponding with the day on which time started. For example, if an act is to be done 'within 12 months of the date of the contract', and the contract is dated 30 January, the time for doing the act expires on 30 January the following year.

Examples

- A period of 'not more than 4 months after' 30 September 1978 expired on 30 January 1979: *Dodds v Walker* [1981] 2 All ER 609 (HL).
- A right to apply for a review of a criminal conviction 'within 6 *months after* the date of' the conviction, where the accused was convicted on 6 October, expired on 6 April (not 7 April): *Talbot v Lane* (1994) 75 A Crim R 115, 124 (Malcolm CJ).

However, not all judges apply the corresponding-date rule remorselessly. Some adjust the rule by coupling with it the principle that if something is to be done 'within x days/months *after*' a date, counting does not start until the following day. For example:

- The completion date for a contract for the sale of land was '12 months *after*' 20 June 2006. Held: the completion date was 21 June 2007 (*not* 20 June 2007). The logic was that when calculating the 12-month period, counting starts on the first full day after 20 June, namely 21 June 2006, and the 12-month period does not expire until 21 June 2007. Under a strict application of the corresponding-date rule, the date ought to have been 20 June 2007. See *Proctor v Chahi* [2009] ANZ Conv R 9-004; [2008] NSWSC 1252 (Ward J).

- Under a contract for the sale of land, an act was to be done on 'the date being six months *after* the Completion Date'. The Completion Date was 3 December 2012. Held: counting start on 4 December, with 'six months after the Completion Date' being 4 June 2014. See *Lactalis Jindi Pty Ltd v Jindi Cheese Pty Ltd (No 2)* [2013] VSC 699.

Ending at midnight?

Does the period expire at midnight on the last day, or at the close of business hours on that day? The House of Lords in *Dodds v Walker* [1981] 2 All ER 609 assumed that it ends at midnight, but courts elsewhere have left the question open: see, eg, *Carr v Keys-Arenas* (1982) NSW ConvR 55-069 (NSWCA).

Qualification: 'starting with …'

The corresponding-date rule assumes that the period is expressed to start *from* or *of* or *after* (or similar expression) a date: eg, a period of 2 months *from* 3 September ends on 3 November. That is consistent with the principle that when calculating a period *from* or *of* or *after* a date, the first day is excluded. But if a period is expressed as 2 months *starting with* 3 September, the first day (3 September) is included, and (it is said) the period ends on 2 November: *R v City of Westminster Magistrates' Court* [2011] 1 WLR 994, [15]–[16].

> 'The time limit expires on the eve of the corresponding date. All that the person concerned has to do having determined from the statutory language that the day of the occurrence is included is mark in his diary the eve of the corresponding date.' (ibid, [17]).

Likewise, a period of '12 months *beginning with* the date of this agreement' starts on the date of the agreement: *Zoan v Rouamba* [2000] 1 WLR 1509, 1516–17 (Chadwick LJ).

A 'simple' rule?

In *Dodds v Walker* (at 610–11), Lord Diplock said that the corresponding-date rule is 'simple … and easy of application [and that] all that the calculator has to do is to mark in his diary the corresponding date in the appropriate subsequent month'. In truth, the rule has inherent complexities. For example:

- A period of '*1 month of/from/after*' necessarily varies according to the length of the relevant month. Notices given in a 31-day month allow more days than notices given in a 30-day month.
- The rule cannot apply literally where the month in which the period expires is too short to have a corresponding date. In that case, the rule operates as analogously as possible, and the period ends on the last day of that (short) month. Thus, a 3-month notice given on 31 March expires on 30 June; and a 4-month notice given on 31 October expires on 28 February (or 29 February in a leap year).

Not limited to 'months'

Dodds v Walker [1981] 2 All ER 609 strictly concerned corresponding 'months'. But the principle has been held to apply by analogy to weeks:

> A statute allowed an application to be made 'within 6 weeks' of a court order. The court order was made on Tuesday 18 June. Held, the application could be made up until (and including) Tuesday 30 July: *Okolo v Secretary of State for the Environment* [1997] 2 All ER 911.

Boilerplate provision

A standard provision in commercial contracts deals with the possibility that a corresponding date might not be a business day. The provision is to the effect that: (1) if there is no numerically corresponding day in the end-month, the period ends on the last business day in that month; and (2) if the period starts on the last business day of a month, it ends on the last business day in the corresponding month.

See also **after**; **beginning with / beginning from**; **boilerplate**; **business day**; **day**; **from**; **HYPHENS**.

corrigendum

Latin: to be corrected; plural *corrigenda*. Indicates errors that are to be corrected, such as spellings or omitted words.

See also **erratum**.

costs

Meaning

In general usage, 'costs' are outgoings or expenses. In legal usage, more specifically, 'costs' are the fees and disbursements due to a lawyer for performing legal work. There are two main categories:

1. *Solicitor and own client costs* (or more simply, 'solicitor–client' costs): the costs and disbursements a person must pay their lawyer for professional services. The liability arises under a contract between solicitor and client.
2. *Party and party costs*: costs payable following proceedings before a court or tribunal. The purpose is to indemnify (in practice, only partially indemnify) the winning party for their legal fees incurred in the proceedings. The liability arises under the order of a court or tribunal.

The process of challenging legal costs is conventionally called 'taxation of costs'. Some jurisdictions have adopted the plainer-language 'assessment of costs' (or in England and Wales, 'detailed assessment').

'costs follow the event'

A traditional lawyerism, meaning 'the loser pays the winner's costs' (or more bluntly, 'loser pays'). The principle derives from the Civil law, expressed in the Latin maxim, *in expensarum causa victus victori condemnandus est*'. In English law, this principle developed from the 13th century onwards: Sir William Holdsworth, *A History of English Law*, 3rd edn (Sweet and Maxwell, 1966) vol 4, 536.

For most practical purposes, 'costs follow the event' suffices, though it hides a number of complexities. For example, 'the event' may not simply be the general outcome of the case (one party wins and the other loses) but rather the outcome on each of various issues in the case, requiring the costs to be apportioned between the parties.

Further reading

- *Halsbury's Laws of England*, 'Civil Procedure' (vol 12A, 2015), [1707]
- *Civil Procedure Rules*, Pt 44: 'General Rules about Costs'

council / counsel

Two words easily confused.

council (body)

A *council* (plural *councils*) is a formally constituted body of people, acting in an administrative or advisory capacity; or a local authority. *Council* may take a definite article (eg, 'We intend to approach *the* council about …') or an indefinite article ('We intend to approach *a* council about …'), or no article at all ('We intend to approach council about …').

counsel (legal adviser)

Counsel (plural *counsel*, never *counsels*) is a legal adviser—in British and Commonwealth usage, usually a barrister or advocate (as disinct from a solicitor). *Counsel* takes no article: 'We intend to brief *counsel* about …' (not '*a* counsel'; not '*the* counsel'). To 'brief counsel' or 'instruct counsel' is to engage a barrister.

Where a reader may be unfamiliar with *counsel*, or may confuse *counsel* with *council*, consider substituting 'barrister', as in the following examples:

- Judge speaking to unrepresented litigant: 'You should consider *instructing counsel* [prefer: *hiring a barrister*].'
- Solicitor speaking or writing to client: 'We should warn you that the *Council's counsel* is very experienced.' [Prefer: 'We should warn you that the *Council's barrister* is very experienced.']

See also **junior counsel; Queen's Counsel; senior counsel**.

counsel (noun)

See **council / counsel**.

counsellor / counselor

British and Commonwealth spelling is *counsellor*; US spelling is *counselor*.

counterfeit / forge

These words overlap, but have sufficiently distinct meanings. To *counterfeit* is to produce a copy of something, in breach of law. For example, a person may *counterfeit* a product in breach of patent legislation, or may *counterfeit* banknotes in breach of currency laws. However, a person *forges* a document or a signature.

See also **forgery**.

COUNTERPARTS

Commercial agreements are sometimes produced in *counterpart*, each printed as if it were an original, and with each party receiving a version signed by the other party (or parties, if more than one other). In such cases, the agreement usually includes a 'counterparts clause', clarifying that each counterpart is to be treated as a binding copy for enforcement purposes.

Example 1: standard clause

> **Counterparts**
>
> This Agreement may consist of a number of copies each signed by one or more parties to the Agreement. If so, the signed copies are treated as making up the one document.

Example 2: Better

Counterparts

If this Agreement consists of a number of copies each signed by one or more parties to the Agreement, then the signed copies make up the one document.

Note that the wording in these two examples leaves open whether the Agreement in fact consists of a number of copies. To clarify, prefer an even better formula (assuming it reflects the parties' intentions), along these lines:

Example 3: Better still

Counterparts

This Agreement consists of a number of copies each signed by one or more parties to the Agreement. The signed copies together make up the one document.

court / Court

Whether to use upper- or lower-case 'C' depends on context:

- When referring to courts in general, use lower-case *c*: 'Citizens respect the *courts* of the land.' And be consistent:

  '[T]he "common law" [is] the body of law which the *courts* [preferred usage] create and define ... [But] the Parliament cannot exercise the powers of the *Courts* [prefer: *courts*] [and] the *Courts* [prefer: *courts*] cannot exercise the powers of the Parliament.' [*Western Australia v Commonwealth* (1995) 183 CLR 373, 485]

- When first mentioning a particular court, use upper-case *C*: 'the Supreme Court', 'the High Court'. For later mentions, most writers retain the upper case: 'The Court then said ...' However, some modern style guides prefer lower case when referring to a specific court previously mentioned. For example: 'The High Court sat all day. The court then adjourned until the next day.'
- When referring to the court in which you are appearing, use upper-case *C*: 'May it please the Court', 'This Court normally ignores antipodean authorities.'

court-martial

The hyphen is customary in British and Commonwealth usage (though *court martial* is also seen—eg, *Court Martial Act 2007* (NZ); *Li v Chief of Army* [2013] HCA 49; (2013) 250 CLR 328 (passim). The plural is *courts-martial*, not *court martials*—unless the reference is not to multiple courts-martial, but to multiple trials, each by a separate court-martial (as in the second example below).

- '*Courts-martial* ... are as truly entrusted with the exercise of the judicial power of the state as are civil courts.' [*Attorney-General v British Broadcasting Corporation* [1981] AC 303, 360 (Lord Scarman)]
- 'The judge referred to two US *court martials* ... and found that in relation to Captain Maynulet, the circumstances bore a certain degree of similarity.' [*R v Blackman* [2014] EWCA Crim 1029; [2015] 1 WLR 1900, 1913 (Lord Thomas CJ)]

cousin

In legal usage, *cousin* usually means first cousin. Context may extend the meaning to a wider class—eg, to second cousins—but that is not the prima facie meaning: *Re Cullen* [1946] VLR 47, 50.

covenant

Strictly, a promise made under seal (ie, in a deed). That strict meaning is useful to distinguish promises made in less solemn written form (eg, in 'mere' writing, not in the form of a deed) or promises made verbally without supporting writing. However, *covenant* is often used to mean more broadly promises in any kind of agreement, regardless of whether by deed, and regardless of whether in writing: eg, in *Leahy v Canavan* [1970] Qd R 224.

covenant and agree

A lawyer's pairing, usually tautologous despite technical differences between a *covenant* and an *agreement*. A *covenant* is a promise made in a deed; an *agreement* can be made in any written form (deed or non-deed), or (if the law permits) without any writing at all. In this technical sense, to *covenant* is always to *agree*; but to *agree* is not always to *covenant*. In practice, however, unless there is a particular need to distinguish between a promise made by deed and a promise made in some other way, *agree* is sufficient.

See also **covenant**.

COVERSHEET

The practice

Formerly, it was common practice to attach a *backsheet* to a legal document. As its name suggests, a backsheet was attached to the back of the document. It recited the nature of the document (eg, deed of conveyance) and the parties and date. The sheet was attached with typing facing outward; and if the document was to be folded lengthwise for filing, the typing would be restricted to one side of the page, so that it could be read when folded.

While this practice is still sometimes seen, modern document-production methods—especially word processing and easy printing—have led to the use of coversheets and (for lengthy documents) ring binders. The information on the coversheet tends to be the same as on the old-style backsheet, but now spread across the page.

Information on backsheet or coversheet

If the description of the document on the backsheet or coversheet conflicts with the description in the formal part of the document, which prevails? The answer is unclear. In the UK, it has been said that a judge may take account of the contents of a backsheet: *Meadfield Properties Ltd v Secretary of State for the Environment* [1995] 1 EGLR 39, 41 (Warner J). In Australia, an appellate court treated a backsheet as irrelevant in deciding whether a document was in law a deed—even though the backsheet described the document as a 'deed'. This was because (1) the backsheet was carelessly drawn, and (2) it was unclear whether the backsheet had been attached before or after the document was executed: *Interchase Corporation Ltd v Commissioner of Stamp Duties (Qld)* [1993] QCA 485; (1993) 27 ATR 154, 156. Also in Australia, the High Court disregarded information on a backsheet to a document creating an encumbrance over land, where the backsheet pointed to the existence of a common building scheme (which, if enforceable, would bind a purchaser of the land to comply with restrictive covenants affecting the land). This was because, under the Torrens system of land registration, the backsheet was not part of the formal title register on which title restrictions had to be notified: *Deguisa v Lynn* [2020] HCA 39.

coverture

The former legal status of a woman while married, ie, when under the authority and protection of her husband. Under that (former) position, the legal status of a wife was assimilated to that of her husband:

> '[T]he very being or legal existence of the woman is suspended during the marriage, or at least is incorporated and consolidated into that of the husband: under whose wing, protection, and *cover*, she performs everything.' [W Blackstone, *Commentaries on the Laws of England* (1765) book 1, ch 15, 430 (emphasis in original)]

The word survives in older legislation, especially when dealing with wills and land. Otherwise, it is obsolete.

crave

To earnestly request. As used in legal pleadings or submissions ('I *crave* the court's leave to …'), it seems to modern ears self-consciously servile—even craven. Replace it with *ask*, *request*, or similar: eg, 'I ask the court's permission to …'; or more formally, 'I seek leave to …'

See also **leave**.

criteria / criterion

Criteria is plural; *criterion* is singular. The plural version is often used incorrectly for the singular. The following examples use the terms correctly:

- 'While accepting that the first and third *Hodgson criteria* have been satisfied, nevertheless I must still determine if the second *Hodgson criterion* is also made out.' [*Public Prosecutor v Aniza bte Essa* [2008] SGHC 61, [53] (Chan Seng Onn J, discussing the three sentencing criteria in *R v Hodgson* (1968) 52 Cr App R 113)]
- '[The court] … relied on the explanatory note … to demonstrate satisfaction of each of the *criteria* identified by Brennan J in *Gerhardy*, including, in relation to the third *criterion*, the existence of consultation.' [*Maloney v R* [2013] HCA 28; (2013) 252 CLR 168, [315] (Gageler J)]

cross-

Cross- words in law are usually hyphenated, with good reason. For example:

- *cross-action* (not *cross action*—an action taken in anger).
- *cross-claim* (not *cross claim*—a claim made in anger)
- *cross-examination* (not *cross examination*—an examination by someone who is angry—eg, a cross cross-examiner).

See also **CROSS-REFERENCES**.

CROSS-REFERENCES

The need

Sometimes it is necessary for one provision in a document to refer ('cross-refer') to another. This may be to indicate that one is subject to the other, or that one complements the other, or that one qualifies the other.

Where the provisions are near each other, their relationship may be clear without the need for express cross-reference. But where they are distant from each other, a person reading one provision may be unaware of the other provision (despite the principle that a document is to be read and interpreted as a whole). It therefore becomes necessary—or at least useful—to warn the reader to take note also of the other provision. This is done by cross-referencing one provision to the other.

The terminology: 'subject to'

Conventionally, cross-references are heralded by the words *subject to*: thus, a section or clause is *subject to* another section or clause. But the meaning of *subject to* is not always clear.

Example

'Clause A is subject to clause B.'

This could mean one of more of the following:

- Where clause B applies, clause A does not apply.
- Clause B sets out in more detail how clause A operates (as in *Forrest v Nix* [2012] NSWSC 493, [36]).
- Clause B sets out conditions for the operation of clause A.
- Clause B sets out different scenarios for the operation of clause A in particular circumstances.
- Clause B sets out exceptions to clause A.

Seek to reduce cross-referencing

Cross-referencing increases reading difficulty. The writer compels the reader to consult other provisions in order to fully understand the current provision. This can complicate communication, as in the following egregious example:

> For purposes of paragraph (3), an organization described in paragraph (2) shall be deemed to include an organization described in section 501(c)(4), (5), or (6) which would be described in paragraph (2) if it were an organization described in section 501(c)(3). [Source: US *Internal Revenue Code*, s 509(a), final sentence]

So, where possible, try to minimise cross-referencing. In particular, where the cross-referenced provisions are close to each other—especially where they are subclauses of the same clause, or immediately succeeding clauses—it may be possible to incorporate what is in reality a cross-reference without invoking *subject to*.

Example 1

Before	**After**
Rent	**Rent**
(1) *Subject to* clause (2), the tenant must pay rent each month of the lease.	(1) The tenant must pay rent each month of the lease.
(2) No rent is payable for the first month of the lease.	(2) However, [*or* But] no rent is payable for the first month of the lease.

Example 2

Before (cross-references shown in italics)	**After (showing deletions)**
(1) The tenant may apply to the landlord for consent to assign the lease.	(1) The tenant may apply to the landlord for consent to assign the lease.
(2) An application *under clause (1)* must be accompanied by proof of the assignee's trading experience and ability to pay the rent.	(2) The application ~~*under clause (1)*~~ must be accompanied by proof of the assignee's trading experience and ability to pay the rent.
(3) When considering an application *under clause (1)*, the landlord may take into account any matters the landlord considers relevant.	(3) When considering the application ~~*under clause (1)*~~, the landlord may take into account any matters the landlord considers relevant.
(4) The landlord must notify the tenant of the decision made in response to the application *under clause (1)* within 2 weeks of making the application *under clause (1)*.	(4) The landlord must notify the tenant of the decision made in response to the application ~~*under clause (1)*~~ within 2 weeks of the application ~~*under clause (1)*~~.

Parenthetical descriptions in cross-references

Where you simply cannot avoid inserting a cross-reference to another provision, consider adding (in brackets) the text of the heading of that other provision. This may save the reader from needing to jump immediately to the other provision—the gist of the provision may be all that the reader needs at present. For example:

> Subject to clause 11 ('Early Possession by Purchaser'), …

If the referred-to clause has no heading, then a brief statement of its content may help:

> Subject to clause 11 (which deals with early possession by the Purchaser), …

Accuracy of cross-references

Ensure that cross-references are accurate. This is not merely a matter of reader convenience. Where a clause ('the referring clause') erroneously cross-refers to another clause, the error may make the referring clause void for uncertainty.

Example

> An arbitration clause (the 'referring clause') in a building contract specified that a party wishing to initiate an arbitration had to give a notice under clause 12(b). There was no clause 12(b), nor was there any other clause that the parties could be taken to have intended by the reference to clause 12(b). Held, the referring clause was void for uncertainty: *Hardesty and Hanover International LLC v Abigroup Contractors Pty Ltd* [2010] SASC 44 (Full Court).

Also, ensure that cross-references are in fact inserted, to avoid automatically generated statements such as 'Error! Reference source not found' (as occurred in *Cohen v Tesco Properties Ltd* [2014] EWHC 2442, an error that '[n]o-one appears to have noticed or bothered about' (ibid, [28]).

See also **CLAUSE STRUCTURE**.

Crown

In modern legal usage, references to 'the Crown' are usually a shorthand way of referring to the executive government. Although the formal head is the monarch, 'the Crown' is for most purposes the collection of individuals and institutions (including ministers, public servants, and Cabinet) exercising the executive functions of government.

In former colonial jurisdictions operating under a federal system with separate states or provinces, 'the Crown' is a shorthand reference to the executive power of the Crown exercised by ('in right of') the federal government (or the 'Commonwealth' government in countries such as Australia) or the government of the state or province.

cta

See **cum testamento annexo**.

cui bono

Latin: for whose benefit? It seems hard to justify the Latin in the face of such a simple translation. For example:

> 'Modern defamation statutes ... provide for many defences. *Cui bono* [Prefer: *For whose benefit*]? Whom does the modern law of defamation assist?' [*Papaconstuntinos v Holmes à Court* [2012] HCA 53; (2012) 249 CLR 534, [53] (Heydon J)]

cuius est solum

Shorthand for the Latin maxim: *cuius est solum, eius est usque ad coelum et ad inferos*—the person who owns the surface [of land] owns also to the heavens above and down to the centre of the earth. The maxim is of great antiquity: see (1931) 47 *Law Quarterly Review* 14; (1978) 52 *Australian Law Journal* 160. It may have been adequate in times before aircraft and deep drilling, but now is fanciful. Sir Percy Winfield described it as 'an unfortunate scrap of Latin' that had clogged the law's development: *Winfield on Tort*, 1st edn (1937) 339. The Privy Council said that 'so sweeping, unscientific and unpractical a doctrine is unlikely to appeal to the common law mind': *Commissioner for Railways v Valuer-General* [1974] AC 328, 351. Modern case law limits the maxim's literal application, at least in its operation heavenwards, for otherwise a satellite would trespass when passing over a suburban garden: *Bernstein of Leigh (Baron) v Skyviews & General Ltd* [1978] QB 479, 487. The maxim's fall from grace is almost complete. The English Court of Appeal has described it as 'not part of English law': *Bocardo SA v Star Energy Onshore Ltd* [2010] Ch 100, [59].

Further reading

Kevin Gray and Susan Francis Gray, *Elements of Land Law*, 5th edn (Oxford University Press, 2009) [1.2.15]–[1.2.32]

culpa lata

Latin: gross negligence (cf *culpa levis*—a lighter degree of negligence). A term used more in Scots law than in English law; always translatable as *gross negligence*, as in the following example:

> 'The position under Scottish law was clear: as a matter of general principle it was not possible for a trust deed to exclude liability for *culpa lata*, that is for gross negligence. ... Guernsey customary law would have followed the Scottish model, based as it was on the civilian law maxim

culpa lata dolo aequiparatur (gross negligence is equivalent to fraud) and because Guernsey had a mixed legal system like Scotland, with civilian and common law origins.' [*Spread Trustee Co Ltd v Hutcheson* [2012] 2 AC 194, [11] (Lord Clarke, supplying his own translations)]

cum testamento annexo

Latin: with the will annexed; usually abbreviated to *cta*. A term used in the grant of letters of administration, often in conjunction with *de bonis non administratis* (abbreviation *dbn*). There seems little justification for retaining the Latin in the face of an adequate English translation. And what little justification might remain disappears if abbreviations alone are used: who (except hardened probate lawyers) would understand the meaning of 'a grant of administration *dbn cta*'?

See also **de bonis non administratis**.

'CUMULATIVE REMEDIES' CLAUSE

A provision in a contract to the effect that a party's remedies under the document are in addition to, rather than in substitution for, the party's remedies at common law. The purpose is to ensure that contractual remedies granted in the document are not read as exhaustive.

curia advisari vult

Latin: the court wishes to be advised. Abbreviation: *cur ad vult*, or *cav* (or *c.a.v.*), sometimes capitalised (*CAV* or *C.A.V.*). Used in law reports at the end of the reported arguments to indicate that the court took time to consider its decision ('reserved its decision'), before handing it down—ie, that the decision was not given *ex tempore*.

See also **avizandum**; **ex tempore**.

currency (money)

Commercial documents commonly provide that a reference to an amount is a reference to the amount in the currency of a particular country: eg, a reference to pounds means English pounds, and a reference to dollars means United States dollars, and so on. In most contexts this is probably superfluous. For example, where a contract is entered into in England, between English residents, for the sale of products manufactured in England, could anyone seriously argue that a reference to 'pounds' was not to English pounds? But it does no harm to include it, if only to avoid argument about the applicability of the common-law presumption that a contract requires payment in the currency of the place where payment is to be made: *Auckland Corporation v Alliance Assurance Co Ltd* [1937] AC 587, 606 (PC).

However, a further provision that a reference is to '*lawful* currency'—as in 'a reference to English pounds … is a reference to the lawful currency of England'—is unnecessarily cautious.

curtilage / curtilege

Meaning

An area of land integral to the enjoyment of a house or other building; for example, a house's courtyard or garden, or its garden shed or garage, or its driveway or pathways.

The area and nature of land that qualifies as *curtilage* varies with the character of the land under consideration. In one case, an area of 100 acres was too large to be within the curtilage of a country mansion (*Skerritts of Nottingham Ltd v Secretary of State for Environment, Transport and Region* [2001] QB 346), but in another case an area of 40 hectares formed the curtilage of a farm (*Public Trustee v O'Donnell* (2008) 101 SASR 228). The *curtilage* of an airport terminal may be quite large: *R v Environment Secretary* [2020] EWHC 959 (Admin); [2020] 3 WLR 597, [74]–[100], [125]–[127], [144]–[148] (Holgate J, reviewing a multitude of cases on 'curtilage'). Where the property is a suburban block of land, the curtilage is generally the whole parcel: *Lee v Osborn* (1993) 15 *Adelaide Law Review* 254 (on the facts, including a tennis court). The variability of the circumstances makes the ambit of *curtilage* almost always uncertain. If it is necessary to refer to ancillary areas of this kind, list them specifically rather than risk the vagaries of *curtilage*.

Spelling

The correct spelling is *curtilage*, though the variant *curtilege* is seen. For example:

- '[T]he consistory court did not have the power … to allow the alienation of *curtilege* [substitute: *curtilage*] of church land …' [*Re St Peter and St Paul, Scrayingham* [1992] 1WLR 187 (headnote)]
- 'Any boundary alteration which would reduce the *curtilege* [substitute: *curtilage*] of house No. 118 could be expected to have adverse affects on the value of Lot 100.' [*Brown v Brown* [1999] NSWSC 383, [30] (Bryson J)]

See also **messuage**.

cy-près

Norman French, *cy-près comme possible*, 'as near as possible'. Used mostly in the law of trusts and wills. Under the *cy-près doctrine*, where literal effect cannot be given to the settlor's or testator's intentions under a charitable gift or bequest, the court allows the funds to be applied as nearly as possible to the intended purposes, under a *cy-près scheme* (literally, 'as-near-as-possible scheme'). In modern times, courts have (tentatively) extended the *cy-près doctrine* to areas beyond trusts and wills. One such area is class actions: where it is impracticable to pay out some or all of the proceeds of a class action to class members, a court may authorise payment to a charity with purposes that relate to the subject matter of the action.

Cy-près is a term of art. A mere translation ('as near as possible') does not capture the legal nuances. For readers unaccustomed to legal terminology, an explanation is better than a mere translation.

Further reading

Halsbury's Laws of England, 'Charities' (vol 8, 2019) [207]–[214]

damnify

A quaint lawyerism for 'suffer financial damage'. In modern legal usage, *damnify* is used almost exclusively in the passive voice: eg, 'The plaintiff was *damnified* by the defendant's conduct', not 'The defendant's conduct *damnified* the plaintiff.'

Although old-fashioned, *damnify* still finds its way into modern legislation and judgments. However, a more idiomatic, plain-language alternative is always available:

- 'We would accept … that if a defendant intends to cause harm to the members of a particular class, but in fact only some suffer harm, then those actually *damnified* [prefer: *harmed*] can sue.' [*Air Canada v Emerald Supplies Ltd* [2015] EWCA Civ 1024; [2016] Bus LR 145, [168] (CA)—though, to give the Court its due, it had in mind Lord Lindley's use of *damnified* in a similar context in *Quinn v Leathem* [1901] AC 495, 535.]

- 'Likewise, if [defendants] consider they have a good defence, why should they be *damnified* [prefer: *penalised*] for failing to embrace the potential additional costs of ensuring that proceedings … advance to a trial?' [*Millerick v Minister for Finance* [2016] IEHCA 206, [38] (Irvine J)]
- '[A] person *damnified by* [prefer: *who suffers financial loss from*] the [mortgagee's] breach of duty has a remedy in damages against the mortgagee …' [*Law of Property Act 1974* (Qld), s 85(3)]

damnum sine (absque) injuria

Latin: loss or damage (*damnum*) without legal wrong. The implication is that the loss or damage is therefore not compensable. Sometimes this implication is made explicit by adding the words *esse potest* ('there can be') after *injuria*: the full version then becomes *damnum sine injuria esse potest* ('damage or loss may be suffered without any act being done which the law regards as an injury').

The Latinism is entrenched in law. But it is apt to mislead readers unfamiliar with Latin, who are likely to assume that *injuria* means 'injury' (which makes the maxim nonsensical—'damage without injury'). The English translation—'damage suffered but without legal wrong', or similar—serves perfectly. For example:

- 'The majority of the court [considered] that the plaintiff's privilege of voting was not a matter of property or profit, so that the hindrance of it was merely *damnum sine injuria* [prefer: *loss without legal wrong*].' [*Watkins v Secretary of State for Home Department* [2006] 2 AC 395, 416 (Lord Rodger)]
- 'If there was *damnum sine injuria*, that is to say a breach but no damage flowing therefrom, then the appellants would receive only nominal damages.' [*Waribay Pty Ltd v Minter Ellison* [1991] 2 VR 391, 405 (Murphy J, providing a translation)]

See also **injuria**.

DASHES

Two kinds: em dash and en dash

An *em dash* (or *em-dash*, or *em rule*)—colloquially, a *long dash*—is sometimes said to reflect the length of the letter *m*. More precisely, however, the em dash harks back to the days of hot metal type and represents the height (top to bottom) of a piece of type. Typewriter keyboards lacked (and still lack) an em dash, so the convention was to substitute two hyphens side-by-side. Modern computer keyboard-shortcuts can insert the em dash symbol.

An *en dash* (or *en-dash*, or *en rule*)—a short dash—is said to reflect the length of the letter *n*, but more correctly is half the length of an em-dash.

The hyphen is smaller still.

Em dash

Five main uses

Em dashes have five main uses.

1. To mark off mid-sentence material in a way that adds more punch than brackets (parentheses) or commas.

Parentheses, comma	Em dash
The court of appeal considered that the trial judge (who had great experience in this kind of case) on this occasion misunderstood the law. The court of appeal considered that the trial judge, who had great experience in this kind of case, on this occasion misunderstood the law.	The court of appeal considered that the trial judge—who had great experience in this kind of case—on this occasion misunderstood the law. [Notice the extra emphasis.]

2. To emphasise end-sentence material more effectively than brackets or a comma.

Parentheses, comma	Em dash
All lawyers can write clearly (if only they would try). All lawyers can write clearly, if only they would try.	All lawyers can write clearly—if only they would try. [Notice the extra emphasis.]

3. To minimise comma-confusion.

Comma	Em dash
The court, which sits every day, and which has stretched resources, limited court space, and limited judicial time, should be able to hear the case soon.	The court—which sits every day, and which has stretched resources, limited court space, and limited judicial time—should be able to hear the case soon.

4. To lead into a list or series, in the much the same way as a colon, and with more emphasis than a comma.

Colon	Em dash
The judge made a number of mistakes in his reasons: including rejecting the plaintiff's evidence and misapplying the legal principles.	The judge made a number of mistakes in his reasons—including rejecting the plaintiff's evidence and misapplying the legal principles.

5. To indicate the key action that follows a lengthy lead-in, where a comma would not so clearly isolate the action.

Comma	Em dash
In return for the vendor providing: (a) the Services, the purchaser will pay $1 million by 30 June; (b) the Additional Services, the purchaser will pay $500,000 by 30 July.	In return for the vendor providing: (a) the Services—the purchaser will pay $1 million by 30 June; (b) the Additional Services—the purchaser will pay $500,000 by 30 July.

Don't overdo it

Limit the number of dashes (whether used in pairs or singly) in a sentence. Too many will confuse the reader.

> Judges—who are after all the dispensers of justice—which should be for everyone—should not accept bribes—which serve only to corrupt the legal system.

En dash

En dashes have three main uses:

1. To mark off a range of values or numbers: eg, 'pages 27–35'; '1901–1925'. (But where the range starts with *from*, use *to*, not an en dash: eg, 'from pages 27 to 35', 'from 1901 to 1925'. And where the range starts with *between*, use *and*, not an en dash: eg, 'between 1901 and 1925'.)
2. To join items of equal weight: eg, attorney–client privilege; landlord–tenant relationship.
3. To denote a connection, comparison or contrast between pairs of words: eg, London–Paris flight; east–west relations; Commonwealth–State disputes. But take care when the connection is between expressions that are themselves hyphenated. The resulting text may then appear to the eye as a hyphen string: eg, 'This body has quasi-administrative–quasi-judicial powers.' It will be better to redraft: eg, 'This body has powers that are both quasi-administrative and quasi-judicial.'

Variant uses

In practice, the uses of em dashes and en dashes vary. Practice is far from universal. In particular:

- Some publishers and lawyers avoid the em dash, using only the en dash.
- Some lawyers use neither the em dash nor en dash; instead, they use only the hyphen. This they do for speed and convenience, because it avoids the need to hunt for the special dash 'symbols'. While purists may condemn the practice, in reality it is unlikely to confuse readers.

Spacing dashes

Here too practice varies. Some publishers leave em dashes unspaced—like this—but others prefer to space them. Publishers who substitute en dashes for em dashes, prefer to space the en dash – like this. This book—which carefully chooses its em dashes from its en dashes—leaves all unspaced.

Colon plus dash

Older legal drafting used a hybrid mark, combining both colon and dash (or, for convenience, colon and hyphen):

> In this Lease, the following expressions have the following meanings:—[*or*:-]

This usage is disappearing in favour of *either* a colon *or* a dash (or hyphen), but not both.

See also **HYPHENS**.

data / datum

In Latin, *data* is plural and *datum* is singular. However, modern English usage accepts *data* for both singular ('one piece of *data*') and plural ('various pieces of *data*'). To insist on *datum* for the singular is unidiomatic (unless in the sense of *datum line*).

Being treated as singular, *data* also takes the singular verb form and singular pronouns. For example:

- 'Thank you for this one item of *data*. I will keep *it* safe.'
- 'Thank you for your company's abundant *data*. I will keep *it* safe.'

DATES

In Britain and most Commonwealth countries, the conventional style is:

- 1 March 2020 [day, month, year, no punctuation]; *not* March 1, 2020; *not* March 1st, 2020; *not* 1st March 2020
- 1/3/2020 [= 1 March 2020]; *not* 3/1/2020; and therefore 11/9/2001 (11 September 2001), *not* 9/11/2001
- from 1980 to 2020
- between 1980 and 2020
- 1990–2000; 2014–16
- the 1990s (no apostrophe)
- 20th century (no superscript); *or* 20th century (superscript, sometimes compelled by style guides).

US conventions differ: March 1, 2020 [month, day, comma, year]; 9/11/2001 [= September 11, 2001].

day

General meaning

Day can carry at least three meanings in law: (1) the period beginning with one midnight and ending with the next; (2) any period of 24 hours; (3) the period between sunrise and sunset.

Examples

- In a tax statute giving favoured treatment to taxpayers who spent more than 30 *days* abroad, *days* meant calendar days—ie, the entire period between 12 am and 12 midnight: *Hoye v Forsdyke* [1981] 1 WLR 1442.
- In an insurance policy, *day* meant any period of 24 hours; thus, a period of 'thirty days' meant 30 consecutive periods of 24 hours: *Cornfoot v Royal Exchange Assurance Corp* [1904] 1 KB 40.
- In the common law of distress (the landlord's right to sell the tenant's goods to recover rent arrears), *day* meant the period between sunrise and sunset: *Tutton v Darke* (1860) 5 H & N 647; 157 ER 1338.

By agreement or conduct, parties may establish their own meaning of *day*: see, eg, *Goodridge v Macquarie Bank Ltd* [2010] FCA 67, [131], 265 ALR 170, 202–03 (parties waiving the right to insist on *day* being a full period of 24 hours).

Up to midnight?

Where something is to be done on or by a stated day, then prima facie it can be done up to midnight on that day. This has been the accepted position for over 150 years: *Startup v Macdonald* (1843) 6 Man & G 593; 134 ER 1029, and has been confirmed authoritatively in more recent times: *Afovos Shipping Co SA v Pagnan* [1982] 3 All ER 18, CCA, [1983] 1 All ER 449 (HL); *Ex parte Robertson* [1983] 1 Qd R 526.

However, the 'up-to-midnight' principle yields to context, as in the following examples:

- In England in conveyancing transactions, by convention an act to be done on or by a certain day is to be done by the end of *business hours* on that day: *Commodities and Services International SA v Clemence Properties (Grays Inn) Ltd* (unreported, High Court, Walton J, 1986; noted [1991] Conv 476).
- In Australia in conveyancing transactions, while in principle a person has until midnight to perform an obligation, a conveyancer is not required to keep their office open after normal business hours just in case the obligor turns up unannounced to perform the obligation: *Raco v Grove Homes Pty Ltd* (1974) 2 BPR 9411.

To resolve uncertainties about whether a 'day' ends at close-of-business or at midnight, commercial contracts commonly provide that (1) if something must be done on a day, it must be done by close-of-business hours on that day, and (2) notices given after close-of-business hours on a business day are treated as given on the next business day.

Fractions of a day

The law normally takes no account of fractions of a day: *Fitzhugh v Dennington* (1704) 2 Lord Raym 1094, 1095; 92 ER 225, 226; *Forster v Jododex Aust Pty Ltd* (1972) 127 CLR 421, 449, 452–53. Therefore, in the absence of express provision or commercial convention, the time 'within' which something is to be done does not start running until the very end of the starting day and does not expire until the very end of the finishing day: *Lester v Garland* (1808) 15 Ves 248; 33 ER 748; *Cartwright v MacCormack* [1963] 1 All ER 11, 15; *Mission Corp Ltd v Telecom Auckland Ltd* [1994] 2 NZLR 357, 360. For example:

- By statute, a 'consent to adoption' form bound the mother who signed it only if the child was less than 10 days old when the mother signed. The child was born at 5.15 am on 12 June. The mother signed the form between 9 am and 10 am on 22 June. Held: the form did not bind the mother, because counting did not begin until the very start of 13 June, and the 10 days did not expire until the very end of 22 June: *T v J* [2000] 2 NZLR 236.
- An offer for settlement was open for seven days. The offer was received at 2.41 pm on 22 February (in a non-leap year) and was accepted at 5.42 pm on 1 March. Held: it was accepted within time, because the whole of 22 February was excluded. The offer could be accepted at any time within seven full days after its receipt—ie, at any time up until midnight on 1 March: *Ford v La Forrest* [2001] QCA 455; [2002] 2 Qd R 44.

See also **business day**; **clear day**; **not later than**; **within**.

dbn

See **de bonis non administratis**.

de bene esse

Latin: as being good. Usually indicating (widening its literal translation) 'provisionally' or 'acceptable for now'—as in an action or procedure that suffices for now but may later be replaced by something more persuasive or appropriate. As with many foreign expressions in law, the Latin infuses with false certainty a term that is inherently vague: 'There is no satisfactory translation [of *de bene esse*]. Views differ as to its meaning': John Gray,

Lawyers' Latin: A Vade Mecum, 2nd edn (Robert Hale, London, 2006) 46. Nevertheless, 'provisionally' or 'for now' usually suffices:

> '[The Court] considered these materials in the course of the hearing of the appeal *de bene esse* [prefer: *provisionally*] without deciding whether they should be admitted.' [*Pora v The Queen* [2015] UKPC 9, [22] (Lord Kerr)]

See also **FOREIGN (NON-ENGLISH) WORDS AND PHRASES.**

de bonis asportatis

Latin: concerning goods taken away. Now obsolete, but historically used in a form of trespass—*trespass de bonis asportatis*—to recover damages for goods wrongfully taken. Being obsolete, a plain-language substitute is unlikely to be needed.

de bonis non administratis

Latin: for (because) the estate is not administered. Often shortened to *de bonis non* and abbreviated to *dbn*. Used in probate law to describe the situation where the court appoints an administrator of a deceased estate because the nominated administrator (or last survivor of a number of nominated administrators) has died without having fully administered the estate. The English translation—'unadministered estate'—is perfectly sufficient, making it hard to justify retaining the Latin; but traditions die hard in probate law and practice.

de bonis propriis

Latin: from (out of; affecting) his or her own goods; out of his or her own pocket. In the law of succession and trusts, an executor, administrator or trustee who has misapplied funds or negligently administered estate or trust property may be ordered to pay back the deficiency or loss from his or her own pocket (*de bonis propriis*). Given the adequacy of the English translation, it seems time to give up the Latin.

de die in diem

Latin: from day to day; daily. No benefit derives from retaining the Latin; even the alliteration can be echoed in the English *from day to day*. For example:

- '[The] charterer's liability for demurrage accrues *de die in diem* [prefer: *daily*] from the moment when … the detention of the ship by him begins.' [*President of India v Lips Maritime Corp* [1988] AC 395, 422 (Lord Brandon)]
- 'Difficulties sometimes arise in deciding whether [expenditures] are to be viewed as payments of a lump sum purchase price by instalments or as recurrent payments accruing *de die in diem* [prefer: *from day to day*] or at other intervals.' [*AusNet Transmission Group Pty Ltd v Federal Commissioner of Taxation* [2015] HCA 25; (2015) 255 CLR 439, [143] (Nettle J)]

de facto

Latin: in fact; actually. Often used in contrast to *de jure* (in law; in right) to indicate the appearance of legality but not its reality. While some readers will know the meaning of *de facto*, others will welcome a translation:

- '[There has subsequently been an evolution towards the complete *de facto* [prefer: *actual*] and *de jure* [prefer: *legal*] abolition of the death penalty within the member states of the Council of Europe.' [*Elgizouli v Secretary of State for the Home Department* [2020] UKSC 10, [110] (Lord Kerr, quoting from *Al-Saadoon v United Kingdom* (2010) 51 EHRR 9, [116])]

- 'It is usually easy to tell if a person is a director [of a company] if he has been duly appointed as such by the company (and is then a *de jure* director or "director in law"), but much less easy if he has not been even purportedly appointed as a director but has simply acted as a director on occasions (when he might be a *de facto* director or director "in fact") or if he has persuaded the directors to act in a particular way (when he might be a "shadow" director).' [*Smithton Ltd v Naggar* [2014] EWCA Civ 939, [16]; [2015] 1 WLR 189 (Arden LJ, providing translations)]
- 'When the matrimonial relation has for that period ceased to exist *de facto* [prefer: *in fact*], it should, unless there are special reasons to the contrary, cease to exist *de jure* [prefer: *in law*] also.' [*Pearlow v Pearlow* (1953) 90 CLR 70, 78 (Dixon CJ)]

See also **de jure**.

de integro

Latin: afresh; as from the start. The English translation is perfectly adequate. For example:

> '[The issue is] whether the court … must determine the matter *de integro* [prefer: *afresh*; *from scratch*], or whether it is entitled and bound to take into account [later events].' [*Re Waymouth Guarantee* ((1975) 10 SASR 407, 426 (Wells J))]

de jure

Latin: by law; by right; legal. As with its comparator *de facto*, many readers will welcome a translation.

> 'The object of the Convention is to provide refuge for those groups who, having lost the *de jure* [prefer: *legal*] or *de facto* [prefer: *actual*] protection of their governments, are unwilling to return to the countries of their nationality.' [*Minister for Immigration and Multicultural Affairs v Ibrahim* [2000] HCA 55, [68]; (2000) 204 CLR 1 (McHugh J)]

See also **de facto**.

de minimis

Latin: concerning minor (ie, insignificant) matters. Usually found in the longer maxim: *de minimis non curat lex*—the law does not concern itself with trifling matters. Sometimes rendered (wrongly) *de minimus*: *Universal 1919 Pty Ltd v 122 Pitt Street Pty Ltd* [2020] NSWCA 50, [26].

Although lawyers may bemoan the loss of a Latin favourite, an appropriate English translation suffices. For example:

- 'Evidence that those [physical] changes are not felt … and may never be felt tells in favour of the damage coming within the principle of *de minimis non curat lex* [prefer: *the law does not concern itself with trifling matters*].' [*Cartledge v E Jopling & Sons Ltd* [1963] AC 758, 779 (Lord Pearce)]
- 'But the first respondent … submitted that s 471.12 does not "effectively burden" the freedom of political communication because its effect could be described as *de minimis*, insubstantial, slight or unrealistic.' [*Monis v The Queen* [2013] HCA 4; (2013) 249 CLR 92, [92] (Hayne J, providing his own translation and rendering the Latin superfluous)]

An alternative version, less commonly seen, is *de minimis non curat praetor*—the judge is not concerned with trifling matters. Here too, an English translation suffices:

> 'If the prospects [of medical treatment for cancer] were speculative or illusory, the law will ignore them. *De minimis non curat Praetor* [prefer: *A judge is not concerned with trifling matters*]. But if they were significant the appellant is entitled to feel that he has lost something ...' [*Gregg v Scott* [2005] UKHL 2; [2005] 2 AC 176, 207 [116] (Lord Hope)]

Further reading

Max L Veech & Charles R Moon, 'De Minimis Non Curat Lex' (1947) 45 *Michigan Law Review* 537 (tracing the history of the maxim in English law and noting US applications)

See also **trifle**.

de momento in momentum

Latin: from moment to moment; moment by moment (in the sense of 'with strict attention to every passing moment'). A pointless Latinism in the face of an adequate and similarly alliterative English translation:

> 'The [document] required was executed upon July 12 following, about seven in the evening. Computing the time *de momento in momentum* [prefer: *moment by moment*], six calendar months had not elapsed ...' [*Lester v Garland* (1808) 15 Ves Jun 248, 253; 33 ER 748, 252 (Sir William Grant MR)]

de novo

Latin: afresh, anew, from the start; a matter heard *de novo* is heard over again from the beginning. *De novo* may have different connotations in different contexts. For example, in some contexts a court or tribunal hearing a case *de novo* is confined to the evidence or materials presented to the original decision-maker; in other contexts, it may make a decision based on its own view of the law and the facts as presented to it at a fresh hearing. An 'appeal by way of rehearing' is usually conducted on the basis of the materials before the first instance body, although with power in some circumstances to hear new evidence. Any English translation of *de novo* must be context-conscious, so as not to conflate these different meanings. But once the context is determined, a translation or explanation is not difficult:

> 'One would ordinarily expect such a re-determination [under s 458 of a certain statute] to be by way of a hearing *de novo*—that is to say, a fresh hearing at which witnesses give evidence and are cross-examined, and documents may be tendered.' [*Boland v Boxall* [2016] TASSC 30; (2016) Tas R 444, [5] (Blow CJ, using the Latin but explaining its meaning)]

See also **appeal**.

de proprio motu

See **proprio motu**.

de son tort

Law French: of (by) his (or her) own wrong. Sometimes, those who interfere without authority ('intermeddle') in the affairs of others may find themselves saddled with continuing obligations and liabilities. For example, those who intermeddle in the affairs of a trust may find themselves declared a trustee *de son tort*, with the obligations and liabilities of a trustee; or those who intermeddle in the administration of a deceased estate may find themselves declared an executor *de son tort*, with the obligations and liabilities of an executor. The terminology *de son tort* is unlikely to mean anything to non-lawyers. Therefore, provide a translation or explanation. For example:

> '[T]he appellant took upon himself to act, and did act just as if he was [a legally appointed manager of the company]. The question, therefore, is, whether a person who is thus a manager *de son tort*—a manager in his own wrong—whether he can protect himself from the liability cast upon a manager under [the Act], by saying, "I am not manager *de jure*". I think he cannot.' [*Gibson v Barton* (1875) LR 10 QB 329, 337–38 (Blackburn J, translating *de son tort* but not *de jure*)]

See also **de jure**; **executor de son tort**; **intermeddle**; **trustee de son tort**.

debitum in praesenti solvendum in futuro

Latin: a debt due now [but] payable in the future (ie, not payable until a future date); plural: *debita in praesenti solvenda in futuro*. While the Latin encapsulates the principle, the English translation loses none of the legal nuance—so prefer the English translation. For example:

- '[R]ent is not a simple debt. It is the consideration for the right to remain in possession. The tenant's liability to pay future rent is not *debitum in praesenti solvendum in futuro* [prefer: *a present debt, but payable in the future*]. Its existence depends upon future events. Rent in respect of a future rental period may never become payable at all.' [*Christopher Moran Holdings Ltd v Bairstow* [1999] UKHL 2; [2000] 2 AC 172, 187 (Lord Millett)]
- 'If [the clause] was read in isolation, it might create a present debt for the entire rental, although it would allow the lessee the indulgence of paying the sum due by instalments, provided the payments were duly and punctually made. In other words, there might then be *debitum in praesenti* [prefer: *a presently owing debt*], although *selvendum* [sic] *in futuro* [prefer: *to be paid in the future*], and, if so, [certain results would follow].' [*O'Dea v Allstates Leasing System (WA) Pty Ltd* (1983) 152 CLR, 368–69 (Gibbs CJ)]

See also **penalty**.

deceased estate

A counter-intuitive term: the deceased is the *person*, not the *estate*. Logically, the term should be *estate of a deceased person*, but long use has normalised the solecism.

decedent

In US legal usage, a deceased person. The term is rare in British/Commonwealth usage, where the preferred term is *deceased*:

> 'Section 62 provides that the Commissioner is to have the same power to assess the executor or administrator as he would have had against the *decedent* [prefer: *deceased*] if alive.' [*Commissioner of Stamps (WA) v West Australian Trustee Executor and Agency Co Ltd* (1925) 36 CLR 98, 108 (Isaacs and Rich JJ; s 62 did not use *decedent*)]

decennial loan

A loan irredeemable for 10 years, and repayable at the end of the 10 years: see, eg, the loan in *Dimes v Scott* (1828) 4 Russ 195; 38 ER 778. A loan of this kind would have trouble circumventing modern consumer-protection laws and rules against clogs on the equity of redemption.

See also **clog on the equity of redemption**.

deceptively

A word that is deceptively ambiguous. It denotes that something is not what it appears to be—but is often open to misunderstanding. For example:

- 'The barrister's argument was deceptively good.' Does this mean it was bad (ie, it appeared to be good, but it was not), or that it was unexpectedly good, or that it was very good? Context might clarify: eg, if the next sentence were to read: 'She spoke only briefly, but covered all the main points.' But it would be better to make the meaning immediately apparent.
- 'The accused's behaviour was deceptively dangerous.' Does this mean the behaviour was very dangerous, or not dangerous at all? Again, context might clarify: eg, if the next sentence were to read: 'He smiled often, but carried a concealed gun.' Here too, it would be better to make the meaning immediately apparent.

decision

In normal usage, a *decision* is a conclusion or resolution reached after considering an issue. In legal usage, it carries that same general meaning, but the context in which the word appears may create uncertainty over its precise meaning. For example, courts have considered whether 'decision' includes the following:

- a preliminary ruling: *Loade v DPP* [1989] 3 WLR 1281 (no)
- an interlocutory order: *R v Lands Tribunal* [1982] 1 WLR 258 (no)
- a refusal to extend time for an appeal: *Lawrence v European Credit Co Ltd* [1992] BCC 792 (yes)
- a refusal to adjourn an application: *Southwark LBC v H* [1985] 1 WLR 861 (yes)
- a minister's refusal to adjourn a planning enquiry: *Co-operative Retail Services v Secretary of State for the Environment* [1980] 1 WLR 271 (no)
- a refusal to extend time for an appeal in bankruptcy proceedings: *Podberry v Peak* [1981] 1 All ER 699 (no).

If doubt over meaning is possible, always clarify.

decision-making

Always hyphenate when used as a phrasal adjective: eg, 'the decision-making panel'.

> 'Mr Scott … chose to speak to [Mr McCullagh] and make a factual statement which was designed to influence the *decision making processes* [prefer: *decision-making processes*] of Mr McCullagh.' [*McCullagh v Lane Fox & Partners Ltd* [1995] EWCA Civ 8; [1996] PNLR 205, 234D (Hobhouse LJ)]

Also, ideally, hyphenate when used as a noun: 'The panel did not like decision-making.'

> 'The third and broadest level of *decision-making* is that required by s 27.' [*R v London Borough of Hackney* [2020] EWCA Civ 518, [40] (Bean LJ)]

See also **HYPHENS**.

decree

See **judgment (and variants)**.

decree nisi

See **nisi**.

DEED (document)

Definition

According to Norton's classic early-20th century definition, at common law a deed is 'a writing (i) on paper, vellum or parchment, (ii) sealed and (iii) delivered, whereby an interest, right, or property passes, or an obligation binding on some person is created, or which is in affirmance of some act whereby an interest, right, or property has passed': Robert F Norton, *A Treatise on Deeds*, 2nd edn (Sweet & Maxwell, 1928) 3. Statutes in most common-law jurisdictions have amended the common-law requirements in a number of ways. These include: relaxing the need for paper, vellum or parchment; adding a requirement of signature and attestation by witnesses; and removing or qualifying the requirement for sealing. The requirement for delivery has generally remained. In addition, since 1991 in England and Wales an instrument is not a deed unless it is clear on its face that the person or persons making it intended it to be a deed—eg, by describing it as a deed or by expressing it to be executed or signed as a deed: *Law of Property (Miscellaneous Provisions) Act 1989*, s 2(a).

Categories of deeds

The common law recognises two categories of deeds: *indentures* and *deeds poll*. An indenture is a deed to which there are two or more parties. A deed poll is a deed to which there is only one party (though two or more people together may constitute that party).

Formal parts of deeds

A deed usually consists of the following formal parts, in this order:

1. Words describing the instrument (eg, conveyance, guarantee, mortgage, release, settlement)
2. Date
3. Parties' names
4. Recitals
5. Testatum—containing the operative provisions, and historically introduced by 'witnesseth that …'
6. Testimonium—stating that the parties have 'signed, sealed and delivered' the deed in the presence of witnesses, who also have signed. In modern times, the 'signed, sealed and delivered' formula is often shortened to 'executed as a deed'.

However, this order is not sacrosanct: a change in the order does not invalidate the deed. Nor does the absence of one or more of the formal parts invalidate the deed, unless statute requires otherwise (eg, that deeds be signed, or delivered, or witnessed).

When is a deed necessary?

The circumstances in which an instrument *must* take the form of a deed vary from jurisdiction to jurisdiction. They include:

- **Where consideration is absent.** The rationale is that the parties to a deed—which is the most solemn form of document possible—are estopped from alleging that their contract is a bare promise, unenforceable because made without consideration: *Halsbury's Laws of England*, 'Deeds and Other Instruments' (vol 32, 2019), [259];

Leonard v Booth (1954) 91 CLR 452, 474. But this is a rule of the common law; a court of equity may decline to enforce a deed that lacks consideration (eg, in an action for specific performance or rectification): *Jefferys v Jefferys* (1841) Cr & Ph 138, 141; 41 ER 443, 444; *Re Earl of Lucan* (1880) 45 Ch D 470, 475; *Minister Administering National Parks and Wildlife Act 1974 v Halloran* [2004] NSWCA 118, [94] (Bryson JA).

- **Where statute requires it**. Examples are:
  - to create or convey a legal interest in land (*Law of Property Act 1925*, s 52)
  - to create a settlement of land (*Settled Land Act 1925*, s 4(1))
  - to enlarge a long-term lease into a fee simple (*Law of Property Act 1925*, s 153)
  - where a trustee is to retire or be appointed (*Trustee Act 1925*, s 39; *Trusts of Land and Appointment of Trustees Act 1996*, s 19(4))
  - to create a power of attorney (*Powers of Attorney Act 1971*, s 1(1))
  - to give mortgagees statutory powers of sale (*Law of Property Act 1925*, s 101(1)).
- **To take advantage of an extended limitation period.** The limitation period for enforcing rights under a deed is usually 12 years; for non-deeds the period is usually 6 years. See, eg, *Limitation Act 1980*, ss 5, 8.
- **To vary an existing deed.** See, eg, *West v Blakeway* (1841) 2 Man & G 751; 133 ER 940. However, if consideration is given, equity may well specifically enforce a (non-deed) contract to amend a deed, or at least preclude the parties from denying that they had amended the deed: *ING Funds Management Ltd v ANZ Nominees Ltd* [2009] NSWSC 243, [72]–[77]; (2009) 228 FLR 444. But estoppel can work only for a deed which has two or more parties; variation of a deed poll (one party only) always requires a deed: *ING Funds Management Ltd v ANZ Nominees Ltd*, above, [76]–[77]. See also **TEXTUAL AMENDMENTS (A deed to amend a deed?)**.
- **To authorise the execution of a deed.** See, eg, *Steiglitz v Egginton* (1815) Holt NP 141, 142; 171 ER 193; *Hibblewhite v McMorine* (1840) 6 M & W 200, 214; 151 ER 380, 387; *Powell v London & Provincial Bank* [1893] 2 Ch 555, 563; but cf *Longman v Viscount Chelsea* (1989) 58 P & CR 189, 198–99.
- **To authorise the delivery of a deed.** See, eg, *Re Seymour* [1913] 1 Ch 475, 481. This common-law principle no longer exists in some jurisdictions: eg, *Law of Property (Miscellaneous Provisions) Act 1989*, s 1(1)(c). However, it survives in some other Commonwealth jurisdictions.
- **To release an accrued cause of action.** See *Halsbury's Laws of England*, 'Deeds and other Instruments' (vol 32, 2019), [212]; *McDermott v Black* (1940) 63 CLR 161, 176; *Scaffidi v Perpetual Trustees Victoria Ltd* [2011] WASCA 159, [14].

Use a deed only when necessary

Some documents take the form of a deed where that form is not strictly needed. For example, a 'guarantee' conventionally takes the form of a deed ('deed of guarantee') even where consideration is given (making the use of a deed strictly unnecessary).

Conversely, certain types of documents have come to be called 'deeds' though they are not in fact deeds. For example, a 'deed of arrangement' or a 'deed of company arrangement' often takes the name, but not the form, of a deed. It follows that such 'deeds' need not be executed in the way required by the law of deeds: *MYT Engineering Pty Ltd v Mulcon Pty Ltd* (1999) 195 CLR 636 [13]–[14].

However, unless the law, or strongly settled convention, requires a deed, think carefully before casting a transaction in the form of a deed. This is so for two main reasons.

First, deeds have formalities for 'execution' that are stricter than the formalities for non-deeds. Second, deeds must be 'delivered' (see **signed, sealed and delivered**). Until delivered, a deed has no effect; conversely, once delivered, a deed can bind a party in circumstances where a mere agreement may not have bound them.

Distinguishing deeds from non-deeds

Whether an instrument is a deed depends on whether the parties intended it to be a deed when they executed it. In discerning the parties' intention, objective factors are paramount: in particular, does the document reflect the phraseology and structure commonly found in deeds, and is it cast in the most solemn form of documentation appropriate for that particular transaction? In jurisdictions where sealing is no longer necessary for a deed (eg, under s 1 of the *Law of Property (Miscellaneous Provisions) Act 1989*), a document that bears no seal can be a deed as long as the parties who executed it intended it to be a deed: *Liberty Partnership Ltd v Tancred* [2018] EWHC 2707 (Comm); [2019] QB 903. Conversely, a document is not a deed merely because it is executed under seal (a principle given statutory force under the *Law of Property (Miscellaneous Provisions) Act 1989*, s 2A).

A relevant factor is whether the instrument describes itself as a 'deed'. However, self-description is not decisive: an instrument describing itself as an agreement may be a deed (as in *Re Wilsons' Settlements* [1972] NZLR 13), and an instrument describing itself as a deed may be a mere agreement (as in *FJ Richards Pty Ltd v Mills Pty Ltd* (unreported, Queensland Supreme Court, Kelly SPJ, 14 September 1990)).

Questions of 'deed' or 'non-deed' have been heavily litigated in antipodean courts: see, eg, *Re Wilsons' Settlements* [1972] NZLR 13, 22–24; *Manton v Parabolic Pty Ltd* (1985) 2 NSWLR 361, 368–69; *Comptroller of Stamps v Associated Broadcasting Services Ltd* [1990] VR 335; *Dean v Lloyd* (1991) 3 WAR 235; *Farrow Mortgage Services Pty Ltd v Hogg* (1995) 64 SASR 450. The antipodean cases allow some role for subjective factors: did the parties (subjectively) intend the document to be a deed? These cases hold that, while subjective factors are irrelevant when interpreting the meaning of the parties' words, they are relevant when deducing the nature of the document the parties intended to create: see, eg, Nicholas Seddon, *Seddon on Deeds* (Federation Press, 2015) [2.5]; *Electricity Meter Manufacturing Co Ltd v Manufacturers' Products Pty Ltd* (1930) 30 SR (NSW) 422, 426; *Rose v Commissioner of Stamps* (1979) 22 SASR 84, 87–88; but cf R Vann, 'To Deed or Not to Deed' (1980) 54 *Australian Law Journal* 424. Also, in all jurisdictions, extrinsic evidence has always been admissible in determining whether the parties, when executing the instrument, intended it to be a deed: eg, *Xenos v Wickham* (1867) LR 2 HL 296, 312; *Wardley Australia Ltd v McPharlin* (1984) 3 BPR 9500; *Ansett Transport Industries (Operations) Pty Ltd v Comptroller of Stamps* [1985] VR 70; *Dean v Lloyd* (1991) 3 WAR 235, 252.

Date of deed

Where a deed bears a date, it is presumed to operate from that date: *Styles v Wardle* (1825) 4 B & C 908; 107 ER 1297; *JLF Corporation Pty Ltd v Mount Petrie Developments Pty Ltd* [2004] 2 Qd R 267. Where it bears no date, or where the date it bears would defeat the parties' evident intentions, it is presumed to operate from the date of its delivery (because delivery is the final act in bringing a deed into operation): *Glebe Administration Board v Tifan* [1968] 3 NSWR 455.

Defective 'deed' taking effect as a contract

Where a document purporting to be a deed is not executed in the way required by the law of deeds, it may still take effect as a contract if signed in the manner required for a 'non-deed' contract (and assuming that the transaction is not one that requires a deed): Nicholas Seddon, *Seddon on Deeds* (Federation Press, 2015) [2.29[–[2.34]; *Australia and New Zealand Banking Group Ltd v Fairfield City Council* [2016] NSWSC 668, [21]–[22] (Emmett AJA).

Further reading

- Peter Butt, *Modern Legal Drafting*, 3rd edn (Cambridge University Press, 2013) 135–43 (on the nature of deeds, execution requirements for deeds, binding effect of deeds, delivery of deeds, and the formal parts of deeds)
- Graham McBain, 'Abolishing Deeds, Specialties and Seals' (2006) 20(1) *Commercial Law Quarterly* 15 (Part 1); (2006) 20(2) *Commercial Law Quarterly* 3 (Part 2)
- Nicholas Seddon, *Seddon on Deeds* (Federation Press, 2015)

See also **DEED POLL; escrow; execute; indenture; in witness whereof (the parties have signed); signed, sealed and delivered; specialty; testatum; testimonium.**

DEED OF RELEASE

A deed releasing a party from a liability or a cause of action. Deeds of release are often prolix. This may be a drafting response to four key principles the courts apply when interpreting them:

1. **Courts interpret general words in a release in the context of the disputes existing between the parties at the time the release is given.** This means, therefore, that courts read the words in the context of the kinds of matters that the parties would have had in mind when executing the deed of release. Because the release would have been given in the context of competing claims, it is logical to limit general words in a release 'to that thing or those things which were specially in the contemplation of the parties at the time when the release was given': *London & South Western Railway Co v Blackmore* (1870) LR 4 HL 610, 623 (Lord Westbury).
2. **In addition to (1), courts presume that a release does not apply to claims of which the releasor was ignorant at the time of the deed.** This principle was developed in courts of equity, which look to the releasor's subjective knowledge, and applies regardless of why the releasor did not know of the claims (including that the law only came to recognise such claims at a later date): *Lyall v Edwards* (1861) 6 H & N 337; 158 ER 139; *Grant v John Grant & Sons Pty Ltd* (1954) 91 CLR 112, 129–130; *Burness v Hill* [2019] VSCA 94, [81].
3. **Principles (1) and (2) do not necessarily preclude a deed of release from effectively releasing all conceivable further disputes.** The question is whether the wording is unambiguously wide enough to cover all such disputes, and (further) whether it is unconscionable in the circumstances to rely on it. With appropriate wording and in appropriate circumstances, a release may well be effective if it is clear that the parties, at arm's length and properly advised, intended their general words of release to encompass all conceivable further disputes, including even those not known at the time: *Doggett v Commonwealth Bank of Australia* [2015] VSCA 351; (2015) 47 VR 302, [63].
4. **The *contra proferentem* principle** may help resolve ambiguity against the interests of the person who proffered the deed.

Sadly, principles (1), (2) and (3) often encourage verbosity. Plain-language drafters may want to prune the verbosity, but they will need to be wary when drafting deeds of release that are intended to range widely.

Further reading

Joseph Kimble, *Seeing Through Legalese: More Essays on Plain Language* (Carolina Academic Press, 2017), 133–40 (essay on redrafting US deed of release into plain language)

See also **contra proferentem**; **DEED (document)**; **DEED POLL**.

DEED POLL

Preferred plural form, *deeds poll*—although *deed polls* is sometimes seen in judgments (eg, *Katara Hospitality v Guez* [2018] EWHC 3063 (Comm), [49] (Moulder J); *Bell Group Ltd v Westpac* (2008) 39 WAR 1; [2008] WASC 239, [3359] (Owen J)) and in learned texts (eg, Graham McBain, 'Abolishing Deeds, Specialties and Seals: Part 1' (2006) 20(1) *Commercial Law Quarterly* 15, passim). The term *poll* reflects a time when the paper or parchment on which this kind of deed was written was 'polled' (ie, trimmed evenly, as distinct from an *indenture*, where the top or sides were cut in a zigzag fashion).

In general usage, *deed poll* has come to mean a deed by which a person changes his or her name. But in legal usage the meaning is far wider: a *deed poll* is any deed to which there is only one party (with an exception, mentioned below). This distinguishes a *deed poll* from an *indenture*, which is a deed made between two or more parties.

While an indenture is enforceable only by the parties to it, a deed poll may be enforceable by persons who are not parties to it: Robert F Norton, *A Treatise on Deeds*, 2nd edn (Sweet & Maxwell, 1928) 29; *Jones v Bartlett* (2000) 205 CLR 166, [141]. The persons need only be named or sufficiently identified (even if only by implication) in the deed poll as entitled to sue on it: *Cooker v Child* (1673) 2 Lev 74; 83 ER 456; *Chelsea and Walham Green Building Society v Armstrong* [1951] Ch 853; *Tipperary Developments Pty Ltd v Western Australia* [2009] WASCA 126; (2009) 38 WAR 488, [253]–[254]. An example is a declaration of trust: the beneficiaries can enforce the trustee's obligations although they are not parties to the deed: *Oakes v Commissioner of Stamp Duties* [1954] AC 57. Another example is a deed of guarantee—creditors can enforce the guarantor's obligations even though they are not parties to the deed: *Moody v Condor Insurance Ltd* [2006] 1 WLR 1847, [15].

The presence of more than one signatory does not of itself disqualify a deed as a deed poll. The question is whether in the deed:

- the signatories make promises to each other, in which case it is an indenture, and only the parties to the deed may sue on it: *Accordent Pty Ltd v Bresimark Nominees Pty Ltd* (2008) 101 SASR 286; or
- all of the signatories together make a promise to a non-party, in which case it is a deed poll, and the non-party may sue on it: *Re A & K Holdings Pty Ltd* [1964] VR 257.

Further reading

Nicholas Seddon, *Seddon on Deeds* (Federation Press, 2015) [6.4], [6.9]–[6.10] (the nature and enforcement of deeds poll)

See also **DEED (document)**; **indenture**.

deem

A quaint word: choose another

Lawyers use *deem* for many purposes. The word has a long pedigree. Some lawyers find *deem* appealing, unaware that it suffocates their writing with archaism, formality, and solemnity. Always prefer a plain-language equivalent.

To find the appropriate plain-language equivalent requires unpacking *deem*'s purpose in the particular context. There are three possible purposes.

'Deem' means 'consider' or 'treat as'

Deem is often an archaic substitute for *consider* or *treat as*. If so, replace it with *consider* or *treat as*:

- 'The bank may appoint any valuer it *deems* [prefer: *considers*] appropriate.'
- 'The bank may *deem late payment to be* [prefer: *treat late payment as*] a default.'

'Deem' confirms a fact

Deem sometimes merely confirms a fact, putting it beyond argument. If so, replace *deem* with the statement of fact. For example:

- A contract for sale states that the purchaser 'is *deemed* to be in default' if the deposit is not paid on time. It simply means that the purchaser *is* in default.
- An agreement states that a notice 'is *deemed* to be validly served' if sent by registered post. It simply means that it *is* validly served if sent by that process.

In reality, *deem* serves no purpose in these cases. On the contrary, it complicates what could be a direct statement of fact ('is'): *Barclays Bank Ltd v Inland Revenue Commissioner* [1961] AC 509, 541 (Lord Denning).

'Deem' creates a legal fiction

Sometimes, a thing is *deemed* to be something that it is not, or an event is *deemed* to have occurred even though it has not. For example:

- A statute states that it is *deemed* to have come into operation retroactively: eg, a statute enacted on 30 June 2020 is '*deemed* to have come into operation on 1 January 2017'. This creates a legal fiction of commencement, backdating the statute's operation.
- A statute states that service of a notice is *deemed* to have occurred three days after posting. This creates a legal fiction of valid service, even though the intended recipient may never have received it.
- A contract states that a party is *deemed* not to have made any representations or warranties. This creates a legal fiction of 'no liability for representations or warranties', even though one party has made representations or warranties and the other has relied on them (as in *Trident Turboprop (Dublin) Ltd v First Flight Couriers Ltd* s; [2008] 2 Lloyd's Rep 581).
- A statute *deems* the date of registration of a trade mark to be the date on which it was lodged for registration. This creates a legal fiction of the registration date, regardless of the actual registration date: *Hunter Douglas Australia Pty Ltd v Perma Blinds* (1970) 122 CLR 49, 65–66 (Windeyer J).

This form of *deeming* is highly artificial, requiring a finding in the face of facts that show otherwise. It can usually be replaced with *treated as*. However, *treated as* will not always help the reader very much, because the change is cosmetic only. The real problem lies in the inherent complexity of the deeming, not the absence of the word *deem*. Consider the following example, where *treated as* is not enough:

> 'For the purposes of this Part of this Schedule a person over pensionable age, not being an insured person, *shall be treated as* an employed person if he would be an insured person were he under pensionable age and would be an employed person were he an insured person.' [*National Insurance Act 1965*, Sch 1, Pt 2, final para (as originally enacted); derided in Robert Megarry, *A New Miscellany-at-Law*, ed Bryan A Garner (Hart, 2005) 192.]

Occasionally, the fictional result sought by 'deeming' is so artificial that courts simply cannot take it seriously. For example:

> A provision in a company's articles *deemed* retiring directors to be re-elected. Held, this result was 'repugnant to common sense' and could not be applied: *Robert Batcheller & Sons Ltd v Batcheller* [1945] Ch 169, 175, 176 (Romer J).

The courts' task is made more difficult where two or more 'deeming' provisions apply to the same circumstances. For example, in *Barclays Wealth Trustees (Jersey) Ltd v Revenue and Customs Commissioners* [2017] EWCA Civ 1512 one statutory provision *deemed* persons to be domiciled in the UK when in fact they were not, and another provision *deemed* their property to remain in their hands when in fact it did not.

Nor, of course, can a court give effect to a 'deemed' state of affairs in the face of a statutory prohibition. For example:

> A statute declared early claims for payment under building contracts to be invalid. Held, a provision in a building contract 'deeming' a claim to be made later than it was actually made could not negate the invalidity: *All Seasons Air Pty Ltd v Regal Consulting Services* [2017] NSWCA 289.

Extent of deeming

If a statute or document 'deems' a state of affairs to exist, is the deeming limited to that statute or document, or does it extend to other statutes or documents dealing with the same subject matter? In statutes, the deeming is carried as far as is necessary to achieve the statutory purpose, but no further: *DEG-Deutsche Investitions-und Entiwicklungsgesellschaft mbH v Koshy* [2001] EWCA Civ 79; [2001] 3 All ER 878, [16] (Robert Walker LJ). On that basis, for example, where a statute deems specified property to be income of a trust, it is not deemed to be income for the purposes of trust law generally: *Gilchrist v Revenue and Customs Commissioners* [2014] UKUT 169 (TCC); [2015] Ch 183.

Presumably, the same principle applies in other kinds of legal documents. For example, if a deed between A and B in relation to a particular business enterprise were to 'deem' their relationship not to be a partnership, that deeming would not necessarily carry over to later deeds between A and B.

Conclusive deeming?

Generally, courts treat a *deeming* provision as conclusive: what is deemed to be is conclusively deemed to be: *Starmark Enterprises Ltd v CPL Distribution Ltd* [2001] EWCA Civ 1252; [2002] Ch 306. However, in some contexts *deemed* can mean 'until the contrary is shown': ie, what is deemed to be is merely rebuttably deemed to be (as in *Carne v Debono* [1988] 1 WLR 1107, where *deemed* service was held not conclusive). If you must resort to 'deeming', always state whether it is rebuttable or irrebuttable. For example:

> Under s 7 of the *Interpretation Act 1978*, 'unless the contrary intention appears', service of a notice by post is *deemed* to be effected by properly addressing, pre-paying, and posting it; and

'unless the contrary is proved', service is *deemed* to occur at the time it would be delivered in the ordinary course of post. Each *deeming* is expressly rebuttable; unless rebutted, the *deemed* consequences apply: *Anixter Ltd v Secretary of State for Transport* [2020] EWCA Civ 43; [2020] 1 WLR 2547.

Further reading

- Dennis C Pearce and Robert S Geddes, *Statutory Interpretation in Australia*, 9th edn (LexisNexis, 2019) [4.57]–[4.58] (judicial approaches to *deem* in statutes)
- 'Deemed', in *Law Words* (Centre for Plain Legal Language, University of Sydney (1995) 13; at www.clarity-international.net/plain-language-resources/general-resources/

defence / defense

In British and Commonwealth usage, the spelling is defence (and offence). US spelling is defense (and offense).

defender

In Scottish legal usage, the person against whom a civil action is taken. In English legal usage, the *defendant*.

DEFINITIONS

Purpose of definitions

Definitions may be needed to give meaning to words and phrases. For example, the word or phrase:

- may be new—a neologism coined for the document—and therefore needs defining
- may be inherently vague—and therefore needs clarifying
- may have an expansive meaning—and therefore needs narrowing
- may have a limited meaning—and therefore needs expanding.

To be contrasted with definitions are 'interpretation' provisions. These give general directions about how the document is to be interpreted rather than specific directions about the meaning of words. See **INTERPRETATION CLAUSES**.

How to apply definitions

The conventional way of applying a definition is to insert it into the relevant provision and then to interpret that provision. To interpret the definition in isolation from the relevant provision invites error about the meaning of the provision: *Kelly v R* (2004) 218 CLR 216; [2004] HCA 12, [103] (McHugh J). This is so even with a definition inserted generically by an interpretation statute: '[T]he meaning of the definitions [in the interpretation statute] draw their content from the context of the statute into which they are inserted': *Commissioner of State Revenue v WestNet Rail Holdings No 1 Pty Ltd* [2013] WASCA 110; (2013) 45 WAR 140, [102] (McLure P).

However, it may be different where the definition itself is unclear. It will then be necessary to seek to give it some meaning before reading its words into the relevant provision (as in *Tovir Investments Pty Ltd v Waverley Council* [2014] NSWCA 379, [13]–[16], Basten JA).

Using definitions to shorten documents

Definitions can help reduce a document's length, by standing in for wordy expressions that would otherwise need repeating in the document. To illustrate, consider the before-and-after versions of a clause from a traditionally worded mortgage:

Original

The mortgagee, for himself, *his heirs, executors, administrators and assigns*, covenants with the mortgagor, *his heirs, executors, administrators and assigns*, that if the mortgagor, *his heirs, executors, administrators and assigns*, pays on time all instalments of interest and observes all the covenants to be performed by the mortgagor, *his heirs, executors, administrators and assigns*, then the mortgagee, *his heirs, executors, administrators and assigns* will not call up the principal sum until [date]; and it is also agreed that the mortgagor, *his heirs, executors, administrators and assigns*, will not call upon the mortgagee, *his heirs, executors, administrators and assigns*, to accept repayment of the principal sum until [date].
[Total words 107; italics added to show repetition]

After (version 1)—using definitions (but leaving other aspects largely unchanged)

Definitions

Mortgagor includes the mortgagor's heirs, executors, administrators and assigns.
Mortgagee includes the mortgagee's heirs, executors, administrators and assigns.

Repayment date

The mortgagee covenants with the mortgagor that if the mortgagor pays on time all instalments of interest and observes all the covenants to be performed by the mortgagor, then the mortgagee will not call up the principal sum until [date]; and it is also agreed that the mortgagor will not call upon the mortgagee to accept repayment of the principal sum until [date].
[Total words: 84]

After (version 2)—improving other aspects of original

Definitions

Mortgagor includes the mortgagor's heirs, executors, administrators and assigns.
Mortgagee includes the mortgagee's heirs, executors, administrators and assigns.

Repayment date

- If the mortgagor pays all instalments of interest on time and observes all the mortgagor's covenants, the mortgagee will not call up the principal sum until [date].
- The mortgagor will not require the mortgagee to accept repayment of the principal sum until [date].

[Total words: 66]

Over-defining

Do not define more than is necessary. In at least three situations definitions are generally unnecessary:

- **Where the expression is an ordinary English expression and can safely be left to its ordinary meaning**. Words that carry well-understood meanings need no defining. To define ordinary English expressions places unnecessary burdens on readers. Readers cannot be expected easily to cast off ordinary meanings—and so may feel compelled to keep returning to the definitions to guard against unconventional meanings.

Also, there is no need to define ordinary words merely because they appear in association with words that need defining:

> A statute regulated 'retail shops'. The word 'retail' needed to be defined (eg, to determine whether it included 'trade' sales or internet sales), but 'shop' could be left to take its ordinary meaning: *Manly Council v Malouf* [2004] NSWCA 299; (2004) 61 NSWLR 394, [8].

Exceptionally, an ordinary word may need defining to negate vagueness at its margins. To illustrate:

> Assume a statute allows lawyers to witness declarations. Can a person who has graduated with a university law degree, but who does not practise law, witness declarations? To clarify, you may need to define 'lawyer': eg, '***lawyer*** means a lawyer who holds a current practising certificate issued by the Law Society'.

- **Where the meaning can be readily deduced from context**. All words take their meaning from context, and the particular context may make the meaning obvious. If so, a definition is unnecessary. Indeed, 'The primary goal for drafters is to use words in their ordinary sense so that they do not need to be defined' (Law Reform Commission of Victoria, *Plain English and the Law: Drafting Manual* (1987) para 104).
- **Where the expression is a technical term and the reader will know the technical meaning**. If the reader has the expertise to know the meaning of a technical word or phrase—and if there is nothing in the context to suggest that the word might not carry that technical meaning—there is no point in defining it.

Choosing the definitional 'label'

Make it meaningful

Choose a definitional 'label' that helps convey the concept being defined, not an anodyne label that gives the reader no hint. Often that can be done by choosing as the label a key word or phrase in the definition. For example:

- in a deed appointing an administrator, 'the company under administration' is a more helpful label than 'the company'
- in a mortgage requiring monthly payment to a bank account, 'monthly bank payments' is more helpful than 'payments'.

Relevance to interpretation

Courts sometimes use the definitional 'label' to help clarify potential ambiguities in a definition or in a provision where the definition is to be applied. Lord Hoffmann put it this way:

> '[T]he contract does not use algebraic symbols [for the defined terms *total land value* and *minimum guaranteed residential unit value*]. It uses labels. The words used as labels are seldom arbitrary. They are usually chosen as a distillation of the meaning or purpose of a concept intended to be more precisely stated in the definition. In such cases the language of the defined expression may help to elucidate ambiguities in the definition or other parts of the agreement.' [*Chartbrook Ltd v Persimmon Homes Ltd* [2009] UKHL 38, [17]; [2009] AC 1101, 1112–13]

The Australian High Court followed this approach to conclude that the definitional label 'MBM area' indicated that the definition referred to a *physical area* of land rather than to abstract *rights over* land: *Mount Bruce Mining Pty Ltd v Wright Prospecting Pty Ltd* [2015] HCA 37l; (2015) 256 CLR 104.

'Labels don't count'

These (or similar) judicial pronouncements have prompted some drafters to add an interpretation provision discounting the importance of definitional 'labels'. For example:

> 'Labels used for definitions are for convenience only and do not affect interpretation.'

The aim is to protect the parties against the possibility that a court will use the definitional label to give the definition a meaning that the parties did not intend. But the aim seems counter-productive. Definitional labels normally reflect what was in the drafter's mind when drafting the definition. To say to the court, 'When interpreting the definition, read the text but ignore the label which heads it', is unhelpful. And where the drafting is seriously inept, to ignore the definitional label may make the meaning impossible to discern (as in *Tovir Investments Pty Ltd v Waverley Council* [2014] NSWCA 379, where the court relied on the definitional label 'backpackers accommodation' to help decide whether premises fell within the definition).

Definitions masquerading as substantive obligations

A definition should define—and only define. To include a substantive provision in a definition goes beyond the definition's proper function. Reed Dickerson called these kinds of definitions 'stuffed'—ie, stuffed with an operative element: *Fundamentals of Legal Drafting* (Little, Brown & Co, 1965) 151.

Example

> A contract for the sale of land defines 'Completion date' in these terms:
>
> > 'Completion date' means 30 June 2021, and on that date the purchaser must pay the purchase price and relieve the vendor of liability for all rates and taxes payable on the property.'
>
> This goes further than defining the term 'Completion date'. In the guise of a definition, it imposes contractual obligations.

A stuffed definition almost certainly 'works' to impose the obligation buried in the definition. For example, in *AIB Group (UK) Ltd v Martin* [2002] 1 WLR 94 (HL), a definition of 'mortgagor' successfully imposed joint and several liability on each of several mortgagors. But the technique complicates the task of the reader, who justifiably assumes that a definition merely allocates meaning, not substantive rights and obligations: *Gibb v Federal Commissioner of Taxation* (1966) 118 CLR 638.

'Read-as-you-go' definitions

Where legal text is intended to be read from start to finish in a single step (eg, a letter of advice, or a simple contract), definitions can be inserted into the text as they appear, suitably tagged. For example, a legal advice could begin:

> 'This advice considers the rights of a second mortgagee of registered land (***the mortgagee***) following default by a corporate mortgagor that has gone into liquidation (***the mortgagor***).'
>
> [But note that the definitions would be unnecessary if the advice deals only with a particular mortgagee and mortgagor—because references to *the mortgagee* and *the mortgagor* could only mean the particular parties.]

However, this technique assumes that readers will read the document from beginning to end, rather than dip into particular parts only. Hence the technique does not work so well for lengthy contracts. Nor does it work for statutes: Office of Parliamentary Counsel (Commonwealth of Australia), *Results of the 2010 Legislation Users Survey* (2010) 51.

Narrative definitions

Sometimes readability is aided by a 'narrative' definition—one that defines a term by folding it into the 'story' of how it operates.

Example

(1) This clause applies where the vendor terminates the contract for the purchaser's default.

(2) Where this clause applies, …

Here, para (1) is, in effect, a definition of *terminate*: '*terminate* means terminate the contract for the purchaser's default'. It serves both as a definition and as an introduction to the purpose of the clause, making it more accessible than a normal definition.

For another example, see **REDRAFTING IN PLAIN ENGLISH** (**'Sense-bites' approach**, Example 5, Steps 1, 2 and 3).

Different meanings for different contexts

In long documents, some drafters find it efficient to give the same term different meanings in different parts of the document. While this practice is not ideal for the reader (it would be better to choose a different word), it can be useful, as in the following example:

claim:

(a) in relation to arbitral proceedings—see clause10;

(b) in relation to mediations—see clause 20;

(c) in relation to court proceedings—see clause 30.

Definitions incorporating other definitions

In the same document

Sometimes a definition (the subsidiary definition) serves the sole purpose of helping define another definition (the main definition) in the same document. Rather than wrap the subsidiary definition into the main definition, the drafter leaves that task to the reader. The technique may ease the drafter's burden, but it can complicate the reader's task—all the more so where the two definitions are alphabetically distant. For example:

An insurance policy defines ***Vehicle*** to include ***Car***. It separately defines ***Car*** to include a motorised buggy. The two definitions should be combined: ie, '***Vehicle*** includes a car and a motorised buggy'.

Sometimes a definition not only does its own work but also helps define another defined term. This too can complicate the reader's task.

Example

A lease contains the following definitions (arranged alphabetically):

Landlord's Works means …

Premises means …

Tenant's Works means so much of the ***Works*** on the ***Premises*** as are not ***Landlord's Works***

Works means …

To understand *Tenant's Works*, the reader must incorporate the meaning of each of the other defined terms: *Landlord's Works*, *Premises*, and *Works*. To do so requires referring to each of those other definitions—each of which does its own independent work as well as helping to fill out the meaning of *Tenant's Works*. The imposition on the reader makes this technique less than ideal, although in practice it may be difficult to avoid.

From other documents

Sometimes a document (document A) incorporates terms as defined in another document (document B). This 'incorporation by reference' may save paper; but it may also frustrate the reader—particularly where the reader does not have the other document to hand. Farwell LJ described the practice as 'pernicious': *Chislett v Macbeth & Co* [1909] 2 KB 811, 815. A senior Hong Kong judge described the practice in legislation as 'anti-democratic', because at the Bill stage legislators find it difficult 'to follow [the] inferential details': Bokhary PJ, 'Legislative Drafting: A Judicial Perspective' [2010] *The Loophole* (January) 26, 38.

However, reader-frustration is not the only issue with this practice. There are at least three others, illustrated in the following three examples. In each example, assume that document A incorporates a definition from document B.

- The standard wording is: 'In this [document A], the term ***X** has the meaning given* in [document B].' The drafter probably assumes that the definition in document B is to the effect that '***X** means* ...' and is unambiguous. But if the definition in document B takes the form '***X** includes* ...' or '***X** does not include* ...', or if it is ambiguous, any doubts over meaning will be carried over into document A.
- Does document A merely incorporate the defined term, divorced from its actual role in document B? Or does document A incorporate the defined term as interpreted in the *context* of document B? If the latter, the defined term may bear a nuance that is not apparent when read in isolation. There is authority that a definition in statute A 'borrowed' from statute B cannot be interpreted without regard to its use in statute B, because its use in statute B is integral to its meaning: *Producers' Co-operative Distributing Society Ltd v Commissioner of Taxation* (NSW) [1948] AC 210, 213; *Certain Lloyd's Underwriters v Cross* [2012] HCA 56; (2012) 248 CLR 378, [31]. Presumably the same applies in private-sector document drafting: a definition in document A borrowed from document B cannot simply be lifted and treated as an anodyne, stand-alone word or phrase, but must be read as used in the context of document B.
- What happens if document B is later amended to alter the definitions in it? Are the altered meanings carried across to document A, or are the meanings in document A frozen at the time document A came into operation?

From unnamed sources

More difficult again is the technique of incorporating the meaning of a term from a source which is known to the cognoscenti but almost certainly not known (or even knowable) to the average reader.

> A statute prohibited dispositions of property intended to *defraud* creditors. Did this include dispositions intended to *delay or hinder* creditors? Held, yes; earlier versions of the statute, extending back to Elizabethan times, used *defraud* to include 'delay or hinder', and so in the present statute, *defraud* meant 'delay, hinder, or otherwise defraud': *Marcolongo v Chen* [2011] HCA 3; (2011) 242 CLR 546, [19]–[21]. But only readers who know the history of the Elizabethan statute could anticipate that interpretation.

From stand-alone definitions document

Some transactions involve a number of related documents using terms in common. In such cases, it can be useful to collect all the definitions in a separate, stand-alone 'definitions document'. The other documents then incorporate the definitions from that stand-alone document. This is seen, for example, in complex commercial transactions comprising a suite of documents: all use the same defined terms, sourced from a stand-alone definitions document. The technique sidesteps the issue (discussed earlier) whether a borrowed definition is to be read as used in the context of the source document.

Consistency across document 'suites'

Where a transaction involves a number of interrelated documents, ensure that the definitions are consistent across the suite of documents. For example, ensure that the definition of 'Business Day' is consistent across all documents—otherwise, a day for the performance of a key obligation may turn out to be a 'Business Day' under one document but not another (as occurred in *Griffin Energy Group Pty Ltd v ICICI Bank Ltd* [2015] NSWCA 29; (2015) 317 ALR 395).

Usage issues with definitions

Once-only definitions

You are unlikely to need a stand-alone definition for a term used only once. It is usually better to wrap the meaning into the text of the relevant provision. For example:

> Parties to a contract agree that they will submit their differences to arbitration, but that the arbitrator must have professional qualifications. The contract could add a definition of *arbitrator* to mean 'an arbitrator who has professional qualifications'. But it would be simpler to dispense with the definition and merely state that the parties agree to submit their differences to 'an arbitrator who has professional qualifications'.

Consistency in using defined terms

Having defined a term, always use it when referring to the item defined. For example, if in a document regulating school attendance you define schoolchildren as *pupils*, always use *pupils*. To switch to *children*, or *attendees*, or *students* will at best puzzle the reader, and at worst introduce ambiguity.

'Shall' in definitions

Shall has no proper role in definitions (just as it has no proper role in modern legal drafting more generally). Replace it with a plain-language equivalent. For example:

Traditional phrase	Plain-language equivalent
X shall mean Y	X means Y
X shall mean and refer to Y	X means Y
X shall have the meaning that …	X means that …

Self-referential definitions

Try to avoid definitions that include the word being defined. To say '*dwellings* means dwellings used for residential purposes' is not particularly enlightening. Better to say: '*dwellings* means premises used for residential purposes', or similar.

Unpronounceable definitions

If a definition is likely to be read aloud, try to make it easily pronounceable. For example:

> Section 73 of an Act defined a company by the abbreviation 'a RTM company'. Lewison LJ described the definition as 'unfortunately … unpronounceable': *Elim Court RTM Co Ltd v Avon Freeholds Ltd* [2017] EWCA Civ 89; [2017] 3 WLR 876, [17].

Multi-word expressions

When interpreting a multi-word expression, bear in mind that the meaning lies in the expression as a whole. It is generally impermissible to sever the individual words and then interpret the entire expression merely by interpreting the separate, severed words. For example:

- Was the trade name *Exxon* an 'original literary work'? The Court of Appeal held that it was 'original', and 'literary' in the sense of comprising written letters, and a 'work' in the sense that time and effort had been used in inventing it. But it was not an 'original literary work', because that expression was a composite expression, not merely the sum of its component words: *Exxon Corporation v Exxon Insurance Consultants International Ltd* [1982] Ch 119.
- A statute defined the composite term 'proprietary maritime claim', but not the component word 'proprietary'. Held, in interpreting the composite term, it was impermissible to consult separately the dictionary meaning of 'proprietary': *Owners of Shin Kobe Maru v Empire Shipping Co Inc (The Shin Kobe Maru)* (1994) 181 CLR 404, 419.
- A research institute collected and disseminated information of public interest. It applied for information under a freedom of information statute. 'Educational institutions' paid reduced application fees. The institute claimed to be an 'educational institution'. Held, 'educational institution' was to be read as a whole, and meant, in effect, a school; the term was not to be interpreted by reference solely to its individual words to encompass any body ('institution') that disseminated information ('education'): *National Security Archive v US Dept of Defense* 880 F 2d 1381 (DC Cir, 1989).

Separate long definitions and short definitions

In complex documents, it may be useful to collect shorter definitions in one group and longer definitions in another. This allows the reader to process the shorter definitions without (yet) having to master the longer ones. For an example, see the Australian *Personal Property Securities Act 2009* (Cth), s 10 (shorter definitions) and s 12 (entitled 'Concepts relating to security interests and personal property'). If a definition is very long, consider moving it to its own stand-alone provision—but alert the reader by a reference in the main definitions clause (eg, '**Related entity**—see clause 5').

Definition design protocols

General

Definition clauses follow settled design protocols:

- Definitions are arranged alphabetically.
- Definitions are not numbered.
- Definitions take an initial capital letter ('**Design**'). If a defined term contains more than one word, each main word takes an initial capital letter ('**Design of Equipment**').

Usually (but not universally), where a defined term is a proper noun that takes the definite article, 'the' is omitted ('**Company** means …', *not* '**The Company** means …').

Punctuation

Punctuation practices vary. Some drafters insert a full stop at the end of each definition; others insert a semicolon; others leave the end of each definition punctuation-free.

Formatting

- Generally, defined terms (but not the text of the definitions) appear in bold (**Design**) or bold italics (***Design***).
- Sometimes, quotation marks are inserted (**'Design'**), sometimes not (**Design**). Where quotation marks are used, they also are generally in bold (**'Design'**).

Location of definitions

At the start?

Conventional practice is to place definitions at the start of the document. Most lawyers and business readers expect to find definitions there. However, that location is not necessarily ideal for readers unaccustomed to legal documents. For them, up-front definitions may make the document appear more intimidating than is necessary, because they consider that they must read (and master) legal documents in a linear fashion, starting at the front and moving through the document clause by clause. In contrast, lawyers and experienced business readers—familiar with the conventional up-front placement—are likely to cursorily scan the definitions and proceed directly to the substantive provisions, returning to the relevant definitions to fill out meaning only when necessary.

At the end?

Another practice is to place definitions at the end of the document. Readers begin with the substantive provisions, coming to the definitions later, by which time they have gained some feeling for the document's substance. They can always jump ahead to the definitions when necessary. This end-location has long been used in some UK statutes (eg, *Law of Property Act 1925*). It gained popularity in some Commonwealth countries in the 1980s and 1990s, as private-sector and statutory drafters experimented with plain-English techniques to make legal documents more accessible to non-lawyers. (Commonwealth statutory drafters often titled the collected, at-end definitions, 'Dictionary'.)

However, many drafters have now abandoned this reader-centred experiment with at-end definitions and have reverted to up-front definitions. This location, of course, makes the definitions easier to find, for lawyers and non-lawyers alike—particularly in documents with annexures or schedules (because the definitions are then somewhere in the middle of the document). Even parliamentary drafters, long practised in at-end definitions, generally prefer the convenience of up-front definitions: see, eg, IML Turnbull, 'Clear Legislative Drafting: New Approaches in Australia' (1990) 11 *Statute Law Review* 161.

A 'table of contents' compromise?

Another practice—still rare, but with much to commend it—aims for a middle course. It lists the defined terms (in alphabetical order) at the start of the document, and at the same time refers to reader to the specific place in the document where each definition appears in full. That specific place may be document-end, or it may be in the text of the section that uses the defined term. This 'table-of-contents' technique sometimes appears in legislation; examples are the *Inquiries Act 2005* and the Australian *Native Title Act 1993* (Cth). It allows the reader to move reasonably directly to the substantive provisions, forewarned that certain words and phrases have defined meanings, but not yet burdened with the detail of those meanings.

One-clause definitions

A definition may be relevant to one clause only, or to one part only, of the document. Should the definition appear in the general list of defined terms, or only in the clause or part to which it relates? Practice varies, and arguments exist for both approaches.

- Some readers expect to find all definitions collected in one place. By placing the definition in the general definitions clause, you affirm that expectation and therefore help the reader negotiate the document.

- A lengthy definitions clause can be intimidating. Moving the definition to the clause for which it is most relevant shortens the dedicated definitions clause, providing some relief from what might otherwise appear a daunting list. This technique is improved by listing the definition alphabetically in the main definitions section and then adding a 'signpost' to its location (eg, '**Termination**—see clause X')—hence the term 'signpost definition'.

Just-in-time definitions

Another convention is to define a term when the reader first meets it. (This is akin to 'read-as-you go' definitions, discussed earlier.) The logic is that readers do not need the definition until they meet it—hence the tag 'just in time'. This is not ideal in long documents, where the reader is unlikely to read the entire text in a linear fashion but rather dip into different parts as required. However, this problem is overcome by listing the definition alphabetically in the main definitions section (eg, '**Termination**—see clause X').

Definitions in recitals

A practical issue arises where a defined term is used in a recital, ahead of the main body of definitions. Is it best to define the term there (in the recitals), or postpone the definition until the main definitions clause? Practice varies: some drafters define the term immediately in the recital; others (having highlighted the term in the recital to indicate that it is a defined term) postpone the definition to the main definitions clause. The key factors are (or should be) 'audience' and consistency: adopt the practice that is likely to be more useful for the intended reader(s) of the document, and having adopted that practice, apply it uniformly. (See also **'Read-as-you-go' definitions**, above.)

Highlighting (flagging) defined terms

To highlight or not to highlight?

The practice of highlighting (flagging) defined terms helps readers by warning them that particular words have particular meanings. Despite this help, legislative drafters have long tended not to highlight (flag) defined terms, but to leave readers to work out for themselves whether a term has a defined meaning. As long ago as 1845, George Coode criticised this lack of advance notice: *On Legislative Expression* (William Benning, 1845) 62, fn. Some modern legislative drafters have at last taken the criticism to heart.

Drafters of private-sector legal documents always highlight (flag) defined terms, warning readers that the terms have special meanings.

Initial capital letter(s)

Private-sector legal drafters generally highlight a defined term by capitalising the initial letter of the word—eg, *Design*. If the term comprises more than one word, they highlight the initial letter of each main word—eg, *Design of Equipment*. However, although hallowed by convention, the technique is less than perfect:

- Does the reader understand the technique—or will the reader assume, for example, that the capital letter is a typographical error, thus missing the point?
- What if a defined word appears at the start of a sentence or at the start of a heading? The first letter of words in these positions is always capitalised. Is the word then being used in its defined sense?

Examples

- Claimants brought proceedings against defendants for alleged breaches of several contracts between the claimants and the defendants. The contracts contained provisions about protecting 'Confidential Information' (defined). A heading in the claimants' pleadings stated: 'Further misuse of … Confidential Information'. In fact, the body of that pleading made no reference to confidential information, creating a mismatch between heading and content. But also (more relevant to this discussion), the pleadings elsewhere used 'confidential information' (lower case). The judge was prepared to assume that the pleadings meant 'Confidential Information' (defined term), but said that 'pleading[s] should not leave it to the reader to resolve this sort of question': *Gamatronic (UK) Ltd v Hamilton* [2013] EWHC 328, [37] (Andrew Smith J; for a number of reasons, the judge struck out the pleadings).
- A lease contained the defined term 'Equipment'. Clause 26 of a lease was headed 'Equipment' (upper-case 'E'), but the text of clause 26 required the tenant to repair 'plant and equipment' (lower-case 'e'). Did the clause require the tenant to repair 'Equipment' (as defined) or 'equipment' generally? Held, the context of the clause as a whole indicated that the text meant 'equipment' generally rather than 'Equipment': *R A & K Becker Pty Ltd v Cariste Pty Ltd* [2001] NSWSC 663, [28]–[30]; (2001) 11 BPR 20,111 (Austin J).
- A lease used two similar terms: 'Commencement Date' (defined) and 'date of commencement of the lease' (undefined). The tenant exercised an option to renew the lease. The lease granted on exercise of the option also used both terms. It contained a clause imposing repair obligations calculated by reference to the condition of the premises 'as at the date of commencement of the lease'. Did this mean (1) at the Commencement Date (of the new lease), or (2) at the 'date of commencement' of the earlier lease? Held, (2), though not without considerable judicial debate: *Agtan Pty Ltd v Caltex Australia Petroleum Pty Ltd* [2018] VSCA 169.

Documents that use the 'we/you' style usually define 'We' and 'You' adopting the convention of initial capital letters: '**We**' means …', '**You**' means …' But after the definition, there is no need to continue capitalising throughout the rest of the document. To do so would introduce an air of formalism, when the drafter is clearly aiming for a lighter tone. Provided there is only one possible *we* and only one possible *you*, no uncertainty can arise.

Other options

The convention of initial capital letters is well entrenched in common-law usage. But other techniques exist, although none is perfect. They include:

- italics (eg, *design*)—but (for readers unaccustomed to the technique) this may suggest *emphasis*, not defined meanings
- bold (eg, **design**)—this also may suggest emphasis, not defined meanings; and the bold type may appear to jump off the page, distracting readers from the message
- an asterisk, preceding or following (eg, *design, or design*). This technique is used in some Australian legislation (eg, *A New Tax System (Goods and Services Tax) Act 1999* (Cth)). However, research shows that readers find asterisks puzzling when a term comprises two or more words. For example, consider '*design of equipment'; does the definition relate to one word (*design*), or the combined term (*design of equipment*)? (For issues with asterisks, see discussions by Office of Parliamentary Counsel (Commonwealth of Australia), 'Drafting Manual' (edn 3.2, July 2019) [69]–[71], at www.opc.gov.au/drafting-resources/drafting manuals), and *Results of the 2010 Legislation Users Survey* (2010) 42–46.)

Caution: is a highlighted (defined) term used in its general (non-defined) sense?

Beware of defining an ordinary English word, and then using the word also in its ordinary (non-defined) sense. Even though the drafter may be careful in flagging defined terms (eg, by initial capital letters), readers may be puzzled: 'This word is not flagged; is this deliberate, or has the drafter erred?'

Example

> A software company enters into a contract to sell the software program 'XYZ' to a buyer. The company also sells software programs generally. Clauses 1 and 2 of the contract provide:
>
> 1. [definition] 'Software' means the XYZ program.
> 2. [substantive provision] You must not make unauthorised copies of software programs you buy from us.
>
> Does clause 2 relate only to copies of the program XYZ, or software programs generally? That is, is *software* in clause 2 a typographical error for *Software*?

Redundant definitions

Some definitions found in legal documents are strictly redundant, because statute supplies them. For example, under s 61 of the *Law of Property Act 1925*:

- *month* means calendar month
- *person* includes a corporation
- the masculine includes the feminine and vice versa
- the singular includes the plural and vice versa.

Similar provisions exist in most other Commonwealth jurisdictions. To repeat the effect of these provisions in a document is legally superfluous. Again, legislation in many Commonwealth jurisdictions provides that the benefit of a covenant made with two or more persons is joint and several (eg, s 81 of the *Law of Property Act 1925*). To state this in the document is superfluous.

However, readers who are not lawyers are unlikely to know these statutory provisions. A document ought to be as comprehensible as possible for its readers. Therefore, where the statutory definitions are relevant to the content of the document, it may be useful to set them out in the document.

Self-evident definitions

Avoid definitions that are self-evident. They parody the law and insult the reader, as in the following Australian examples:

- 'unsolicited goods' means goods sent to a person without any request made by or on behalf of that person: *Fair Trading Act 1985* (Vic), s 5(1) [repealed]
- 'unmarried person' means 'a person who is not a married person': *Social Services Consolidation Act 1947* (Cth), s 18 [repealed]
- 'forest' means an area containing trees: *Forest Practices Act 1985* (Tas), s 3(1).

Counter-intuitive definitions

Avoid definitions that stretch a word's core meaning to mean or include the unexpected. This is so whether the word is an ordinary English word or a technical term. For example, it is unhelpful to define 'cat' (an ordinary word) to include 'dog', or to define 'real property' (a technical term) to include 'bonds'. Where a definition is counter-intuitive, the reader is unlikely to be able to discard completely the word's expected meaning. It is 'psychologically impossible for a reader, even when fully and explicitly warned, abruptly to shift from an established meaning to a radically new one': Reed Dickerson, *Fundamentals of Legal Drafting* (Little, Brown & Co, 1965) 13. Indeed, courts recognise this reality and do not normally interpret a definition 'without regard to the normal meaning of the word defined': *Hastings Co-Operative Ltd v Port Macquarie Hastings Council* [2009] NSWCA 400; (2009) 171 LGERA 152, [17] (Basten JA, on the meaning of 'shop' as defined in planning law).

Some definitions stretch meaning beyond the unexpected to the bizarre, greatly complicating the reader's task:

- 'insurmountable obstacles' means 'significant difficulties' (ie, less than insurmountable): *R v Home Secretary* [2017] UKSC 11; [2017] 1 WLR 823, [44]
- 'personal estate' includes 'real estate': *Administration of Estates Act 1925*, s 30(4))
- 'real property' includes 'personal property' and 'any contractual right ... in relation to land': *A New Tax System (Goods and Services Tax) Act 1999* (Cth), s 195.1 (Australia)
- 'day-old poultry' means 'poultry up to 72 hours-old': *Poultry Act 1968* (NZ), s 2(1) [repealed]
- 'September 16, 1940' means 'June 27, 1950': cited in Reed Dickerson, *Fundamentals of Legal Drafting* (Little, Brown & Co, 1965) 101
- 'fish' includes 'beachworm': *Fisheries Management Act 1994* (NSW), s 5
- 'fingerprint' includes 'toeprint': *Crimes Act 1958* (Vic), s 464
- 'egg' includes 'citrus fruit': *Marketing of Primary Products Act 1958* (Cth), s 35H(a) [repealed]
- 'appointed day' means 'four o'clock' on the day before the proclaimed day': *Accident Compensation Act 1985* (Vic), s 5(1)
- 'foreign resident' (in an Australian tax statute) means 'a person who is not a resident of Australia': *Income Tax Assessment Act 1997* (Cth), s 995.1(1) (intuitively, one might expect 'foreign resident' to mean a person of foreign origins who *is* a resident).

Derivatives of definitions (cognate terms)

Whether the meaning of a defined term extends to terms derived from it ('cognate terms') is a question of interpretation. The test is whether the extension from defined term to derivative term 'works harmoniously': *Genders v Ajax Insurance Company Ltd* (1950) CLR 470, 482. If it 'works harmoniously', then the parties (or, for legislation, parliament) can be taken to intend the term to extend its cognates. On this basis, for example, the definition of 'repair' (noun) extended to a party's obligation 'to repair' (verb), and the definition of 'owner' (noun) extended to 'own' (verb): *Genders*, above.

However, the answer is not always clear. To ensure that nothing is left to chance (or to the vagaries of judicial interpretation), standard practice is to add an interpretation provision along the following lines:

- 'Where a word or expression is defined, other forms of the word or expression have corresponding meanings.'
- 'Where a word or phrase has a defined meaning, other parts of speech and grammatical forms of that word or phrase have corresponding meanings.'
- 'A word that is derived from a defined word has a corresponding meaning.'

Courts pay close attention to the precise wording of such provisions. The result may be to give the clause a narrower interpretation than the drafter intended:

Examples

- An interpretation provision stated that defined meanings extended to 'derivatives' of the defined term. Held, this did not require the definition of 'occupier' (noun) to apply to 'occupied' and 'unoccupied', which were not derivatives of the noun but past participles of the verb 'to occupy': *Redland Shire Council v Stradbroke Rutile Pty Ltd* 133 CLR 641, 665 (Stephen J).

- An interpretation provision stated that defined meanings extended to words that were 'other parts of speech and grammatical forms' of the defined term. Held, the definition of 'driving' did not flow through to 'driver', because (1) both were the *same* part of speech (a noun), and (2) 'driving' was not a *grammatical* form of 'driver': *Transport Accident Commission v Treloar* [1992] 1 VR 447, 463–64.
- An interpretation provision stated that defined meanings extended to other 'grammatical forms' of the same word. A first-instance court held that 'non-dependent child' was not a grammatical variant of 'dependent child', because the negative of a word or phrase is not a different grammatical form of that word or phrase: *Jankovic v Minister for Immigration and Ethnic Affairs* [1994] FCA 1316, [21] (Moore J). However, an appeal court held that it would be 'artificial' to ignore the defined meaning of 'dependent' when interpreting the negative form 'non-dependent': *Jankovic v Minister for Immigration & Ethnic Affairs* (1995) 56 FCR 474, 479.

'Subject to context'

Definition clauses commonly add a qualification 'unless the context requires otherwise' or similar. Confident drafters should not require this safety net—but even they find old habits hard to break. See further, **unless the context otherwise requires**.

Further reading

- *R v Ojibway* (1965–66) 8 *Criminal Law Quarterly* 137 (definition of 'small bird' includes a pony with a feather pillow on its back; hypothetical)
- Robert Eagleson, 'Legislative Lexicography', *The Loophole*, March 1989, article #6 (at www.calc.ngo/publications/loopholes#loophole-table-1989), recommending applying lexicographical techniques to drafting statutory definitions
- Louise Finucane, 'Definitions—A Powerful Tool for Keeping an Effective Statute Book', *The Loophole*, Feb 2017, 15
- Daniel Greenberg, 'Is it a Bird? Is it a Plane? Well it Certainly Isn't Legislation' (2015) 36 *Statute Law Review* v–vi (criticising a statute's failure to define terms such as 'acting heroically')
- Bilika H Simamba, 'The Placing and Other Handling of Definitions' (2006) 27 *Statute Law Review* 73

See also **CONSISTENCY OF TERMINOLOGY; DOCUMENT DESIGN; GLOSSARIES; INTERPRETATION CLAUSES; means / includes; RECITALS; shall; TONE; unless the context otherwise requires; we / you.**

dehors

French: outside; beyond. Often used to describe rights or terms outside of (ie, not included within the express terms of) a contract. The French adds nothing to the English—so unless the reader will know the meaning of the French, prefer the English. For example:

- '[The respondent] prefers that we should infer the tenancy from month to month from factors *dehors* [prefer: *beyond*] the agreement …' [*Berrisford v Mexfield Housing Co-Operative Ltd* [2010] EWCA Civ 811; [2011] 2 Ch 244, [31] (Wilson LJ)]
- '[T]he wife's reliance on evidence *dehors* [prefer: *outside*] the terms of the Trust itself gives plausibility to what the other parties claimed.' [*Kennon v Spry* [2008] HCA 56; (2008) 238 CLR 366, [181] (Heydon J)]

delegatus non potest delegare

Latin: a person with delegated authority cannot (further) delegate. Sometimes rendered *delegata potestas non potest delegari*: delegated power cannot be further delegated. The maxim appears in the law of agency (an agent cannot delegate the authority to another person) and administrative law (an official with delegated authority cannot delegate the authority to someone else). It trips off the tongue, its attractiveness heightened by rhythm and alliteration. But in Bentham's view, the 'music of the maxim [has] drowned the … dictates of common sense': Jeremy Bentham, *An Introduction to the Principles of Morals and Legislation* (1823 edn) vol 1, 23, n 1. An appropriate English translation does just as well: eg, 'a delegate cannot sub-delegate'. For example:

- 'The District Judge referred to the principle that a delegate cannot delegate further: delegatus non potest *delegare*.' [*Financial Ombudsman Service v Heather Moor & Edgecomb Ltd (Rev 1)* [2008] EWCA Civ 643; [2009] 1 All ER 328, [42] (Burnton LJ, the alliterative explanation making the Latin superfluous)]
- 'The maxim "*delegatus non potest delegare*" reflects the general proposition that delegates to whom a power has been delegated must, generally speaking, exercise that power themselves.' [*Mills v Hendriksen* [2008] WASC 79; (2008) 184 A Crim R 212, [57] (Hasluck J, explaining the maxim in terms that made the Latin unnecessary)]

DELETIONS

Admissible as aids to interpretation?

Formerly, courts ignored deleted (ie, struck through) words or clauses when interpreting contracts. The task was to interpret what the parties had agreed, not what they had *not* agreed. The striking-out indicated that the words formed no part of the parties' agreement, and so were to be disregarded: *Inglis v Buttery* (1878) 3 App Cas 552, 569, 571. It was 'as if the deleted words had never formed part of the print': *Sasoon (MA) & Sons Ltd v International Banking Corporation* [1927] AC 711, 721 (Viscount Sumner).

However, the modern approach is more flexible. It allows recourse to deleted material in at least two situations:

1. **Where the text remaining after the deletion is ambiguous.** The deletion may help clarify what the parties meant by what remains. This approach has substantial judicial support: eg, *Mottram Consultants Ltd v Bernard Sunley & Sons* [1975] 2 Lloyd's Rep 197, 209 (Lord Cross); *Team Services Plc v Kier Management and Design Ltd* (1993) 63 BLR 76 (Lloyd LJ); *NZI Capital Corporation Pty Ltd v Child* (1991) 23 NSWLR 481; *Sanko Steamship Co Ltd v Sumitomo Australia Ltd* [No 2] (1996) 63 FCR 227, 256–58; *Ecosse Property Holdings Pty Ltd v Gee Dee Nominees Pty Ltd* (2017) 261 CLR 544; [2017] HCA 12, [9], [85].

   Example

   > A landowner wished to sell part of its land to a purchaser. Planning law prevented a sale of part only of the land, but did not prevent a lease of part only of the land. Accordingly, instead of a sale, the owner granted a 99-year lease of the relevant part. Under clause 4 of the lease, the tenant was to pay 'all rates taxes assessments and outgoings whatsoever ~~excepting land tax~~ … payable by the ~~Landlord or~~ tenant' [striking-out in original]. On its face, this was ambiguous: it could require the tenant to pay all rates (etc); or it could require the tenant to pay only those rates (etc) normally payable by a tenant (which would exclude rates (etc) which the law levies on landords). The Victorian Court of Appeal held (by majority) that the struck-out words indicated that the parties had rejected the meaning that the tenant should pay rates (etc) normally payable by landowners/landlords; these therefore remained the landlord's responsibility: *Gee Dee Nominees Pty Ltd v Ecosse Property Holdings Pty Ltd* [2016] VSCA 23. On appeal, the High Court

reversed this decision, holding that clause 4 was to be read in the context of the parties' commercial purpose, which was to re-create in a lease (as far as possible) the conditions on a sale. The parties therefore had intended the tenant to pay all the rates (etc), including those normally levied on landowners: *Ecosse Property Holdings Pty Ltd v Gee Dee Nominees Pty Ltd* [2017] HCA 12; (2017) 261 CLR 544.

2. **To negate the implication of a term.** A term cannot be implied into a contract if the parties in fact turned their mind to the subject matter and decided not to provide for it. Struck-out words may indicate not only that the parties turned their mind to the matter, but also that they agreed *not* to provide for it. This negates the implication of a term that might otherwise be implied: *Narandas-Girdhar v Bradstock* [2016] EWCA Civ 88; [2016] 1 WLR 2366, [20] (Briggs LJ).

   Examples

   - The parties to a standard-form loan agreement deleted the repayment clause. If a loan agreement is silent about repayment, the law implies a term that the borrower is personally liable to repay the loan. Held, the deletion indicated that the parties had agreed that the borrowers were not liable personally to repay: *NZI Capital Corp Pty Ltd v Child* (1991) 23 NSWLR 481.
   - A lease to two joint lessees contained an option to renew. At common law, joint lessees together must exercise any option to renew, unless the lease document allows one only to exercise the option. The parties had deleted wording that would have allowed only one of the joint lessees to exercise the option. Held, the deletion indicated that the parties intended that both lessees must join in exercising the option: *Brennan v Kinjella* (1993) 6 BPR 13,168, 13,172 (Young J).

However, these approaches to deletions must be treated with care. For example, the evidence may show that the parties deleted the words believing they added nothing to the document, or believing that the words were inconsistent with what was already in the document. The evidence may even show that the deletions were a mistake. See generally, *Narandas-Girdhar v Bradstock* [2016] EWCA Civ 88; [2016] 1 WLR 2366, [19] (Briggs LJ), citing *Keating on Construction Contracts* (8th ed, 2006) 3-007. Also, if what remains is ambiguous, it is illogical to adopt an interpretation that mirrors what was deleted: *Walker Group Constructions Pty Ltd v Tzaneros Investments Pty Ltd* [2017] NSWCA 27, [114]–[119] (Bathurst CJ).

Make a 'clean' copy

It is always prudent to print a 'clean' copy for parties to sign. In past times, practical considerations may have dictated leaving struck-out material in the text of a document; to prepare a 'clean' copy may have required the entire document to be re-engrossed, a time-consuming and costly procedure in days of handwriting or typewriting. But modern office equipment has changed this. It is now relatively easy to prepare a 'clean' copy for parties to sign. Doing so is more than a mere matter of tidiness: residual struck-through text may suggest avenues for litigation that would pass unnoticed in clean text.

See also **engross**.

deliberate / deliberative

Deliberate means intentional, fully considered (not impulsive)—eg, a *deliberate* act. *Deliberative* means for the purpose of debate—eg, Parliament's *deliberative* function. The two are sometimes confused:

> '[T]he areas studied *deliberately* [correct usage] focused on those in which organised hunting actively takes place, rather than rural communities in general. … Methods involving guns probably account for the greater part of those foxes which are *deliberatively* [sic: *deliberately*]

> killed, but there are marked regional variations.' [Extracts from *Burns Report on Hunting*, quoted in *R v Attorney-General* [2006] EWCA Civ 817; [2007] QB 305]

Sometimes, the writer's meaning is not immediately apparent:

> '[The section in the 1975 Act allowing the court to award reasonable financial provision] represents a *deliberative* [sic: *deliberate?*] legislative choice ...' [*Ubbi v Ubbi* [2018] EWHC 1396, [14] (Shuman M)]

At other times the writer simply chooses the wrong word:

> 'His evidence about past events has been under-researched by him and, at times, his approach has been *deliberatively* [sic: *deliberately*] obstructive.' [*Hart v Hart* [2018] EWHC 549 (Fam), [3] (Judge Wildblood QC, quoting from his 2015 judgment involving the same parties)]

delivery (of deed)

The final step in the coming into effect of a deed, demonstrated by any act or words sufficiently showing that the deed-maker regards the deed as presently binding: *Xenos v Wickam* (1866) LR 2 HL 296, 312; *Alan Estates Ltd v WG Stores Ltd* [1982] Ch 511, 526. Delivery must be the last step in the deed-making process. A deed purportedly 'delivered' before signing must be redelivered before it can take effect: *Tupper v Foulkes* (1861) 9 CB (NS) 797; 142 ER 314; *Powell v London and Provincial Bank Ltd* [1893] 2 Ch 555.

Delivery may be conditional on some future event occurring. Such a deed is called an 'escrow'. Although the deed-maker can no longer resile from the deed, it does not come fully into operation until that event occurs. When the event occurs, the deed takes effect retroactively to the date on which it was (conditionally) delivered: *Hooper v Ramsbottom* (1815) 6 Taunt 12; 128 ER 936; *Federal Commissioner of Taxation v Taylor* (1929) 42 CLR 80; cf Phillip Kenny, 'Dating an Escrow' [1982] *Conveyancer and Property Lawyer* 409 (arguing that an escrow operates retrospectively only where necessary to give efficacy to the transaction).

Where only one party executes a multi-party deed, it is a question of fact whether that one delivered it unconditionally then and there (making it immediately binding on that party), or conditionally with the intent that it should not become binding until all other parties also execute it: *Federal Commissioner of Taxation v Taylor* (1929) 42 CLR 80, 87; *Naas v Westminster Bank Ltd* [1940] AC 366.

See also **DEED (document)**; **escrow**; **execute (a document)**; **signed, sealed and delivered**.

delivery up

A *delivery up* clause (better: '*delivery-up* clause') requires a party to the contract to hand over or return material to the other party when the contract expires. For example, a distribution agreement may require the *delivery-up* of customer lists, or a confidentiality agreement may require the *delivery-up* of product information, at the expiration or earlier termination of the contract.

demise

As a noun: in standard usage, a death; in strict legal meaning, a lease operative at common law—a 'legal lease' (as distinct from an 'equitable lease', operative only in equity). As a verb (*to demise*): to grant such a lease. Historically, a demise (lease) was ineffective unless created by deed, because only a deed could pass a legal interest in land. Under modern land registration statutes, a demise—now simply called a lease—is created by completing and registering prescribed forms. These statutes have heralded the demise of *demise*: the word *lease* is both pervasive and sufficient.

Indeed, to retain *demise* (lease) would in most modern contexts seem quaint and a parody of legalese: 'We enclose the documents for your demise' [solicitor's letter to landlord client]. There was a time when the use of *demise* indicated the intent to grant a legal lease (effective immediately) rather than a mere agreement to grant a lease: *Bicknell v Hood* (1839) 5 M & W 104, 108; 151 ER 45, 47; *Truro Diocesan Board of Finance v Foley* [2009] 1 WLR 2218. But the disappearance of *demise* from the normal legal lexicon makes this distinction less convincing today.

dependant / dependent

In British and Commonwealth English, the preferred usage is *dependant* (noun) for the person, and *dependent* (adjective) for the person's description. So, a parent may have three *dependants*, each being a *dependent* child. However, that usage is slowly sliding towards the US preference for *dependent* for both noun and adjective.

dependent / interdependent

In contract law, words describing the nature of the promises the parties must perform if each is to hold the other to the bargain. For example, in a contract for the sale of land, the vendor cannot require the purchaser to pay the purchase price unless the vendor is able to transfer the title, and the purchaser cannot require the vendor to transfer the title unless the purchaser is able to pay the purchase price. Neither promise is enforceable without performance of the other, so the promises are said to be *dependent* or *interdependent*. Each word is correct in that context—but *interdependent* is preferable, because it more clearly expresses the intertwined relationship between the obligations.

deposit

Latin: *depositum*, that which is laid down or committed for safe keeping. In law, *deposit* carries that sense, but with nuances that may make *deposit* a term of art. For example, by long-accepted authority, a deposit paid under a contract for sale serves two purposes. The first is as a security for the purchaser's performance: if the vendor becomes entitled to terminate the contract for the purchaser's default, the vendor can keep ('forfeit') the deposit. It is 'an earnest to bind the bargain', a function that deposits have served since Roman times: *Howe v Smith* (1884) 27 Ch D 89, 101 (Fry LJ). The second is as part payment of the purchase price: if the contract proceeds to completion, the deposit is applied to the balance of money payable under the contract. (On both these purposes, see, eg, *Howe v Smith* (1884) 27 Ch D 89; *Soper v Arnold* (1889) 14 App Cas 429; *Brien v Dwyer* (1978) 141 CLR 378.) These dual aspects of *deposit* are not readily apparent from the word itself. Nor are other matters, such as the principles that limit the 'usual' deposit to 10% of the purchase price, and may entitle to the purchaser to relief against the loss of the deposit in certain circumstances. So, for a non-lawyer audience, consider giving a brief explanation.

Further reading

- *Halsbury's Laws of England*, 'Conveyancing' (vol 23, 2016) [57] (the nature of deposits), [452] (relief against loss of deposits)
- S Bridge, E Cooke and M Dixon (eds), *Megarry & Wade's Law of Real Property*, 9th edn (Sweet & Maxwell, 2019) [14-105]–[14-109] (deposits under contracts for the sale of land)

See also **forfeit**.

deprecate / depreciate

To *deprecate* is to disparage, express disapproval of. To *depreciate* is to reduce in value, although it is sometimes also used in the sense of to reduce the value of an argument (and so akin to *deprecate*). The following examples illustrate correct usage:

- 'Our sole obligation is to consider whether a conviction is unsafe. We would *deprecate* resort to undue technicality.' [*R v Graham* [1997] 1 Cr App R 302, 309 (Lord Bingham)]
- 'Such analysis was, in essence, designed to extol the reasoning of the Upper Tribunal and to *depreciate* the reasoning of the statement of reasons.' [*R v Attorney General* [2013] EWHC 1960 (Admin); [2013] 3 WLR 1631, [92] (Davis LJ)]

derivative action

An action brought by a person who relies on, and seeks to enforce, a cause of action belonging to someone else. An example is an action brought by a shareholder to enforce a corporation's right against a third party, where the corporation has failed to pursue the right.

descendants

A word that can mean: (1) *direct* descendants ad infinitum—children and their children and their children, and so on; or (2) more widely, descendants ad infinitum of any degree (ie, not merely direct). Courts generally favour meaning (2), which can make *descendants* a dangerous term—particularly if the drafter intended only direct children of the first generation. For example:

- '*Descendants* means children and their children and their children to any degree, and it is difficult to conceive any context by which the word "descendants" could be limited to mean children only.' [*Ralph v Carrick* (1879) 11 Ch D 873, 883 (James LJ)]
- '[*D*]*escendants* means, in its ordinary sense, issue of every degree.' [*Estate of Auerbach* [1974] 1 NSWLR 57, 63–64 (Mahoney J)]

desire (verb)

Some lawyers crave *desire*, when all they need is *wish* or *want* or similar. For example:

- 'If the tenant *desires* [prefer: *wishes*] to assign the lease, she must obtain the landlord's prior consent.'
- 'If the tenant *is desirous of* [prefer: *wants*; *wishes to take*] a further lease after the present lease expires, she must give at least 3 months' prior notice to the landlord.'
- 'If the tenant *shall desire* [prefer: *intends*] to take a renewed lease … [the tenant] shall give to the Landlord notice in writing of *such desire* [prefer: *that intent*] …' [extract from lease in *Suiga Pty Ltd v Hamden Properties Pty Ltd* [1997] NSWSC 104]

A cautious drafter may prefer *wishes to* over *wants*, surmising that *wants* is too colloquial. But even statutory drafters use *wants*: eg, in the UK, *Stalking Protection Act 2019*, s 4(2)(b) (court must hear any chief police officer 'who *wants* to be heard'); in Australia, *Corporations Act 2001* (Cth), s 553C ('a person who *wants* to have a debt or claim admitted').

See also **need / want**.

despite anything else in this agreement, …

This formula is acceptable as a shorthand precedence provision—but only if used once. If used twice or more in a document, confusion is inevitable: which *despite* provision prevails?

See also **PRECEDENCE CLAUSE.**

determine

A word with two meanings: *decide* and *bring to an end*. Context will generally resolve any ambiguity, but careless collocations may leave the reader bemused. For example:

> 'The landlord *determined* [prefer: *decided*] to *determine* the lease [prefer: *bring the lease to an end*; *terminate the lease*].' Or even worse: 'The landlord *determined* to *determine* the lease *term*.'

devil

To do research (usually for a lawyer), often for low pay and as a way of gaining experience in the law. For example:

> '[The junior barrister] *devilled* one piece of work for a member of the chambers … who paid her £150.' [*Edmonds v Lawson* [2000] QB 501, 508 (Lord Bingham CJ)]

devise

To leave by will.

See **give, devise and bequeath**.

devisee / devisor / divisor

A *devisee* is a person to whom property is devised (ie, left by will). The *devisor* is the person who makes the gift (ie, the testator). In law, *devisee* remains common, but *devisor* is now rare. A different word altogether is *deviser*—ie, a person who contrives or invents.

A *divisor* is the number by which another number is divided. *Divisor* and *devisor* are easily confused, as in this example:

> '[In law] the standard unit of measurement of time is six minutes; a unit explicable only as a convenient *devisor* [substitute: *divisor*] of the unit of time of one hour and not otherwise having any logical correlation with the way in which legal services are usually provided.' [*Universal 1919 Pty Ltd v Barraket Stanton Lawyers Pty Ltd* [2015] NSWSC 540, [32] (McCallum J)]

dicta

See **dictum**.

DICTIONARIES

Use in law

Judges commonly cite dictionaries as a guide to meaning. An early example is *Matthew v Purchins* (1608) Cro Jac 203; 79 ER 177. Normally, the most appropriate dictionaries are those published in the country of the document or statute being interpreted. This usually gives judges a number of choices, from which they can (and do) choose the entry that best suits their view of the meaning of the word or phrase.

Courts outside the UK increasingly favour dictionaries that preference local meanings over British meanings. To illustrate:

- Australian courts prefer the *Macquarie Dictionary*: *Provincial Insurance Australia Pty Ltd v Consolidated Wood Products Pty Ltd* (1991) 25 NSWLR 541, 553 (Kirby P), 560–61 (Mahoney JA); *House of Peace Pty Ltd v Bankstown City Council* (2000) 48 NSWLR 498, 504–05 (Mason P).
- Canadian understandings of words such as 'fall' (season) and 'bonnet' (car) are not reflected in dictionaries printed for UK readers: *Ontario Mushroom Co v Learie* (1977) 76 DLR (3d) 431.

But this does not preclude a judge from applying a meaning given in an 'overseas' dictionary, nor from applying an 'overseas' meaning given in a local dictionary: *Kuzmanovski v New South Wales Lotteries Corporation* [2010] FCA 876; (2010) 270 ALR 65, [37] (giving 'bathe' a meaning that an Australian dictionary qualified as 'chiefly British'). Also, contemporary dictionaries may not be ideal when interpreting the text of documents or statutes of yesteryear. For example, a US court took pains to identify four suitable dictionaries (published between 1760 and 1806) for interpreting the text of the US Constitution in its first few decades: *Baca v Colorado Department of State* 935 F 3d 887, 934–44 and nn 24, 25 (10th Cir 2019).

Judges can cast their enquiries more widely than dictionaries. For example, to discern technical meanings, judges are entitled to consult technical publications: *Shore v Wilson* (1842) 9 Cl & F 355; 8 ER 450 (HL); *Association of British Travel Agents Ltd v British Airways Plc* [2000] 2 Lloyd's Rep 209 (glossary of terms used in airline industry). How far judges go in this search for meaning is up to them, of course. For example, in interpreting the meaning of 'limousine' in a tax statute, an Australian appellate court declined to consult the Australian Design Rules relating to the subject: *Dreamtech International Pty Ltd v Commissioner of Taxation* [2010] FCAFC 103; (2010) 187 FCR 352, [28]–[29].

And of course judges can ignore dictionaries and rely on their own understanding of a word. For example, in an Australian case a senior judge considered it unnecessary to rely on the dictionary meaning of 'sponge' in deciding whether 'sponge' was 'cake' or 'pastry', because the meaning of 'sponge' was 'one of the few things that every schoolboy knows': *Herbert Adams Pty Ltd v Federal Commissioner of Taxation* (1932) 47 CLR 222, 230 (Evatt J).

Dangers

There are at least four dangers in using dictionaries to discern the meaning of legal terms.

1. A dictionary may supply different shades of meaning for a term, and multiple dictionaries may compound this problem. Which meaning prevails?

Example

A life insurance policy excluded cover where the insured died 'by his own act'. The insured died by self-inflicted gunshot. He was delusional at the time. The court adopted the primary meaning of 'act' in Murray's *New English Dictionary*, namely, 'a deed, a performance of an intelligent mind'. In doing so, it did not cite another meaning in the same dictionary, namely, an act not necessarily directed by the conscious will of a sane person (as in the 'act of a madman'): *Ballantyne v The Mutual Life Insurance Co of New York* [1891] 17 VLR 520, 536 (Higinbotham CJ). See Peter Gilliver, *The Making of the Oxford English Dictionary* (OUP, 2016), 223.

2. The issue always is what the word means in the particular document, not what it means in the dictionary. Dictionaries illustrate usage in general, but a document or statute has its own context. For this reason (as Learned Hand J famously said), readers—including courts—should not make 'a fortress out of the dictionary': *Cabell v Markham* (1945) 148 F 2d 737, 739. More prosaically, as an Australian appellate judge said:

   'Dictionary definitions may assist in identifying the range of possible meanings a word may bear in various contexts, but will not assist in ascertaining the precise meaning the word bears in a particular context. … [D]ictionaries are no substitute for the interpretative process.' [*TAL Life Ltd v Shuetrim* (2016) 91 NSWLR 439, 457; [2016] NSWCA 68, [80] (Leeming JA). To similar effect, see *Provincial Insurance Australia Pty Ltd v Consolidated Wood Products Pty Ltd* (1991) 25 NSWLR 541, 560–61.]

   Example

   A statute prohibited 'mutilation' of female genitalia. The dictionary meaning of 'mutilate' is to cut off or destroy. Held, however, in the context of female genital mutilation, 'mutilate' meant 'injure to any extent', including by nicking or cutting in a way that leaves no visible scarring: *R v A2* [2019] HCA 35; (2019) 93 ALJR 1106.

3. Where a dictionary suggests synonymous expressions as a guide to meaning, to focus on the synonym risks diverting attention from the meaning of the original expression.

   '[W]e have been warned time and again not to substitute other words for the words of a statute. And there is very good reason for that. Few words have exact synonyms. The overtones are almost always different': *Brutus v Cozens* [1973] AC 854, 861 (Lord Reid). To the same effect, see *Norrie v New South Wales Registrar of Births, Deaths and Marriages* [2013] NSWCA 145; (2013) 84 NSWLR 697, [85] (Beazley ACJ).

4. The meaning of a compound term is not necessarily determined by the meaning of one or more of its component parts. For example, the term 'extreme hardship' is not understood merely by consulting the separate dictionary definitions of 'extreme' and 'hardship': *Kumar v Minister for Immigration and Ethnic Affairs* (1997) 144 ALR 441. Nor is 'insulting behaviour' understood merely by consulting the dictionary meaning of 'insult': *Brutus v Cozens* [1973] AC 854. (On this, see also **DEFINITIONS, Definitions of phrases**.)

dictum

Latin: word, remark. Often used (loosely) in the plural, *dicta*, when referring to one word or remark only: eg, 'I would categorise the judge's comment as mere dicta.' In legal usage, *dictum* (*dicta*) carries more than the general sense of a word spoken or remark made. It has come to mean a judge's expression of opinion that is not essential to the decision—and therefore has no binding force under the doctrine of judicial precedent—and is often seen in its longer manifestations, *obiter dictum* and *obiter dicta*.

See **obiter dictum**.

dies non

Latin: a day that does not count. Sometimes used as an abbreviation for *dies non juridicus* (a day on which the court does not sit), and sometimes used more generally to mean a day that does not count for particular purposes. In either case, to retain the Latin is unpalatable pedantry. For example:

- '[W]hen a time is prescribed by a statute for doing any act, and that act can only be done if the court office is open … then, if it turns out … that the day is a Sunday or other *dies non* [prefer: *day when the court office is closed*], the time is extended until the next day on which the court office is open.' [*Pritam Kaur v S Russell and Sons Ltd* [1973] 1 QB 336, 349 (Lord Denning MR)]
- '[The question is whether] a schoolteacher can with impunity have sexual intercourse with a pupil on a *pedagogical dies non* [prefer: *non-school day*]. The issue presented to the jury on the trial of the present applicant was whether the day of the incident was a *dies non* [prefer: *non-school day*].' [*R v Howes* [2000] VSCA 159, [61]; (2000) 2 VR 141]

See also **dies non juridicus**.

dies non juridicus

Latin: a day not for litigation (ie, a day on which the court does not sit). Prefer an appropriate English translation:

> 'The first point taken by [counsel] … is that Sunday is a *dies non juridicus* [prefer: *day on which courts do not sit*; *non-court day*] upon which no judicial act can lawfully be done …' [*Re N* [1967] Ch 512, 523 (Stamp J)]

See also **dies non**.

direct (causation)

Direct, in the context of causation ('a *direct* cause', '*directly* caused') is inherently vague: when is something the *direct* cause of something else? Context may provide an answer; but unless context (or express provision) requires otherwise:

- An act may be the 'direct' cause of an event ('the consequence') even though there are steps between the act and the consequence: *Boiler Inspection and Insurance Co of Canada v Sherwin-Williams Co of Canada Ltd* [1951] AC 319, 333–34.
- The consequence need not be 'solely due' to the event: *Weld-Blundell v Stephens* [1920] AC 956, 983.
- The consequence need not follow immediately after the event. The looked-for connection is sequential rather than time-based: *Best v R* [2015] VSCA 15, [78]–[79].

See also **cause (noun, verb)**.

discharge

A word with many meanings in law. In its verb form, its meanings include:

- to fulfil or perform an obligation
- to carry out a function

- to sack (fire) an employee
- to dismiss a court case
- to dismiss a jury
- to release a prisoner from custody or imprisonment.

Context usually resolves any ambiguity over which meaning is intended. But if not, clarify.

discovery

The process by which a party to litigation discloses relevant documents to another party. This legal usage differs from the word's normal usage of 'finding something that has been lost'. In some jurisdictions, such as England and Wales, *discovery* has been replaced with *disclosure*, bringing legal usage more into line with normal usage.

See also **WOOLF REFORMS**.

discreet / discrete

Discreet means circumspect or unobtrusive; *discrete* means separate. The two should not be confused:

> '[W]here more than one injury is occasioned by an incident, then there are separate and *discreet* [substitute: *discrete*] liabilities in respect of each injury. … If there are separate incidents leading to *discreet* [substitute: *discrete*] injuries, each injury generates a separate liability …' [*Canute v Comcare* [2004] AATA 627, [79]]

disinterested / uninterested

Disinterested mean unbiased by personal interest; *uninterested* means not interested. Do not confuse the meanings. For example, a New Zealand appeal judge (properly) corrected a trial judge who had said that he was 'singularly *disinterested*' in taking a procedural step, when he meant that he was *uninterested* in taking that step: *McKay v District Court* [2008] 1 NZLR 133, [15] (Priestley J). Correct usage is reflected in the following example:

> 'I found [the social worker] to be totally *disinterested* in relation to this case—*disinterest* is the correct word, not *uninterested*—and that she has put forward very strongly her views.' [*Miller & Brass* [2008] FamCA 944, [14] (Bell J)]

dispone

In Scots law, to convey land. Hence also *disponer* (vendor, grantor); *disponee* (purchaser, grantee); *disponible* (capable of being conveyed); *disposition* (the document by which property is disponed). For example:

> '[A]s between *disponer* and *disponee* the transfer of all the former's interest is at once complete upon the delivery of the *disposition*.' [*Sharp v Thomson*, 1997 SC (HL) 66, 73 (Lord Jauncey)]

disposition (of property)

Meaning

Disposition is a broad term which, at common law, encompasses any method by which property passes, whether by act of the owner or by act of law: *Duke of Northumberland v Attorney-General* [1905] AC 406, 410–11 (Lord Macnaghten). Besides the common-law understanding of the term, statute often defines 'disposition' in broad, sweeping terms, to catch up transactions that otherwise might escape the net of taxation or duties. About the only limitation is that *disposition* must involve the act of disposing of an interest, so that (for example) the mere making of a will is not a disposition (because no property can pass until after the testator dies), nor is exercise of a statutory ministerial power to withdraw land from someone's ownership or control (eg, *Valuer-General (NSW) v New South Wales Golf Club* [2012] NSWCA 355, [42]).

Dispositive clause

The clause in a document by which property is disposed of (transferred), as in the following examples:

- 'The relevant part of the *dispositive clause* left assets to "my trustee" on trust for various purposes.' [*Marley v Rawlings* [2012] EWCA Civ 61; [2013] Ch 271, 287 [64] (Black LJ)]
- 'The *dispositive clause* of the will is clear and definite. It is an immediate gift, and provides for the complete and final distribution of the testator's real and personal property.' [*National Trustees, Executors and Agency Co of Australasia Ltd v O'Connor* (1919) 27 CLR 60, 69 (Rich J)]

disregard (verb)

To pay no attention to. Often used in law in the passive construction 'X *is to be disregarded*'. Though common enough in legal writing, this passive construction may introduce a degree of conceptual complexity. The reader must imagine the state of affairs that is to be disregarded, and then disregard it—for a thing cannot be disregarded until it is first regarded. Prefer substitutes such as *does not count* or *is to be ignored*; they are blunter and may ease the mental gymnastics.

Before	After
In reviewing the rent, improvements the tenant has made to the property *are to be disregarded* by the valuer.	In reviewing the rent, the valuer is to *ignore* improvements the tenant has made to the property. [Or, recast as directions to the valuer: 'In reviewing the rent, *ignore* improvements the tenant has made to the property.']

dissentiente

Latin: dissenting. Nothing is gained by preserving this scrap of Latin. Prefer English. For example:

> 'In the High Court, Taylor, Windeyer and Owen JJ (*dissentiente* Barwick CJ and Kitto J [prefer: Barwick CJ and Kitto J *dissenting*]) held that they were so entitled.' [*Ogden Industries Pty Ltd v Lucas* [1970] AC 113, 123 (Lord Upjohn)]

See also **nemine contradicente / nemine dissentiente**.

distance

Is distance measured by straight line ('as the crow flies'); and if so, is it measured along a horizontal plane, or by following the curvature of the earth? Or is distance measured by road (or footpath); if so, is it by the nearest available road (or footpath) or the nearest reasonably passable road (or footpath)? Context may provide the answer: see the discussion in *Stokes v Grissell* (1854) 14 CB 678, 688–89; 139 ER 279, 283. But if precise measurements are important, it is prudent to specify. General interpretation legislation often prescribes whether distances are to be measured by road or by straight line for the purposes of statutes: see, eg, *Interpretation Act 1978*, s 8 (straight line on a horizontal plane).

See also **as the crow flies**.

distrain / distress

To *distrain* (verb) is to exercise the right of *distress* (noun), which is a landlord's right at common law to enter leased premises to seize and sell the tenant's chattels to satisfy arrears of rent. The right of distress has been abolished in the UK and many other countries.

Further reading

- *Halsbury's Laws of England*, 'Landlord and Tenant' (vol 62, 2016) [282] (abolition of distress as remedy for arrears of rent)
- *Hill and Redman's Guide to Landlord and Tenant Law* (Butterworths, 1999) ch 9 ('Distress')
- P Walton, 'Landlord's Distress—Past its Sell by Date? [2000] *Conveyancer and Property Lawyer* 508

ditto

Ditto means 'the same as stated above or as before', indicating that the word, figure, or phrase above is to be repeated. In older usage, it was often abbreviated to *do* (or with a full stop, *do.*) or indicated by two short lines similar to double quotation marks (").

divide between

If property is to be 'divided *between* A and the children of B', and B has three children, does A take one-half or one-quarter? The older view was that A takes one-half, on the ground that the etymological derivation of *between* (*bi-*) suggests a division into two parts: *Re Walbran* [1906] 1 Ch 64. But later cases discount the etymological derivation and conclude that the drafter probably intends a division on headcount: *Re Cossentine* [1933] Ch 119.

A direction in a will that property be 'divided' between named beneficiaries creates a tenancy in common, not a joint tenancy. If one beneficiary dies, that person's 'share' passes under his or her will or intestacy; it does not go to the surviving named beneficiaries. See *Halsbury's Laws of England*, 'Wills and Intestacy' (vol 102, 2016) [395].

See also **among / between**; **between**; **joint tenant / tenant in common**.

Division

When denoting a component of an Act, *Division* conventionally took an initial capital; lower-case *division* was never seen. This usage is changing, and some style guides now recommend lower case—*division*. However, this is not yet the norm. Unless compelled by a style guide, prefer upper-case *Division*. Likewise, prefer upper-case *Part*.

See also **HEADINGS (Part and Division headings); Part**.

do / don't

The logical plural forms are *dos / don'ts*—not *do's / don't's*—because plurals generally take no apostrophes.

- 'The topics [in the handout for English teachers] include the ... *dos and don'ts* of a speaking test[,] and reducing test stress.' [*Oise Ltd v Revenue & Customs (Value Added Tax – Exemption)* [2016] UKFTT 749 (TC) 749, [151] (Judge Nicholas Paines QC); correct usage]
- 'At times, the Judge might have been perceived to be intent on giving Ms Winsor a stern lecture on the *do's* [prefer: *dos*] and *don'ts* [correct usage] of cross-examination.' [*M&P Enterprises (London) Ltd v Norfolk Square (Northern Section) Ltd* [2018] EWHC 2665 (Ch), [210] (Hildyard J)]

docket

A schedule of cases allocated to a judge, usually as part of a case management system. The term derives from US legal usage, and is now used in many British and Commonwealth court systems. For example:

- 'In the present case, the *docketed* judge decided that ... the provision for automatic striking out ... did not apply.' [*Super Industrial Services Ltd v National Gas Company of Trinidad and Tobago Ltd* [2018] UKPC 17, [1] (Lord Briggs); appeal from Trinidad & Tobago]
- 'In the Court of which I am Chief Justice [the Federal Court of Australia], a *docket* system has been in place since 1997. Like the concept of caseflow management itself, the *docket* system is an American innovation. ... Each judge is responsible for the matters in his or her *docket*.' [Allsop CJ, 'Judicial case management and the problem of costs' [2014] *Federal Judicial Scholarship* 16; www.austlii.edu.au/au/journals/FedJSchol/2014/16.html]

document

Document is particularly appropriate to denote something written on paper. But *document* is not limited to paper. Historically, a *document* was something written on parchment; and before parchment, something written on stone, marble, clay, or even metal: *R v Daye* [1908] 2 KB 333, 340 (Darling J). Today, in line with modern technology, *document* may, depending on context or statutory definition, include anything on which, or in which, information is kept and from which it can be retrieved. Examples of 'documents' in this sense include the following:

- a computer database: *Derby & Co Ltd v Weldon (No 9)* [1991] 1 WLR 652; *R v Revenue and Customs Commissioners* [2011] 1 WLR 1964
- information on a computer hard disk drive: *R v Misic* [2001] NZCA 128; [2001] 3 NZLR 1
- a Word document on a laptop computer: *Re Estate of Michael* [2016] SASC 164; (2016) 126 SASR 299; *Re White* [2018] VSC 16; *D'Angelo v Coleiro* [2020] SASC 99
- a tape recording: *Snow v Hawthorne* [1969] NZLR 776; *Beneficial Finance Corp Ltd v Conway* [1970] VR 321
- information on a mobile phone: *Palavi v Queensland Newspapers Pty Ltd* [2012] NSWCA 182; *Re Yu* [2013] QSC 322; *Re Estate of Russell* [2016] SASC 56; *Re Quinn* [2019] QSC 99
- a text message on a mobile phone: *Re Nichol* [2017] QSC 220, [41]
- a video tape: *Cassie v Koumans* [2007] NSWSC 481
- 'footage' on closed-circuit television: *Wade v R* [2014] VSCA 13; (2014) 41 VR 434
- a DVD recording: *Re Estate of Wilden* (2015) 121 SASR 516.

DOCUMENT (READABILITY OF)

See **READABILITY TESTS.**

DOCUMENT DESIGN

Overview

Design principles play an important role in effective legal documents. A well-designed and clearly laid out document draws readers into the text; a poorly designed document deters them. The following discussion considers some key aspects of document design.

But first, several warnings:

- Do not overuse the design techniques at your disposal. Exuberant design that attracts attention to itself is self-defeating, because it diverts the reader from the message.
- Do not use techniques that may be lost in transit between writer and reader—as where a document formatted with sophisticated word-processing capabilities is transmitted to a device with limited formatting options.

Also, do not use design options to conceal important material. For example, an exclusion clause might be camouflaged by wily layout—but that could render the clause unenforceable.

Examples (concealed material)

- A South African court refused to enforce an exclusion clause printed on the back of a rental-car agreement. The document was printed in small type and its layout did 'everything to discourage anyone from reading it and becoming aware of' the exclusion clause: *Fourie v Hansen* [2000] 1 All SA 510 (W), 517.
- An American court refused to enforce a 'condition' under which a party waived all rights and authorised the other party to sign judgment against them. The condition was in small print in a five-page contract, and was 'buried' on the reverse side of a page; and the document's physical characteristics meant that readers were likely to ignore the reverse sides: *Cutler Corp v Latshaw* 97 A 2d 234, 237 (Pen SC, 1953).

Fonts

For the relevance of fonts in document design, see **FONTS**.

Single-column vs two-column

Single-column format is standard for most legal documents. But some documents—particularly consumer documents—can benefit from a two-column format. A two-column format:

- can appear less intimidatingly 'legal' than a single-column format
- produces a shorter line length, aiding readability
- saves paper, because headings and paragraph endings take only half a line, not a full line (see below, under **Line length**).

On the other hand, indents may need to be narrower than in a single-column format, to prevent cramped line lengths. And narrower indents may give the page a denser, more cramped look, impeding the appearance (even if not the reality) of accessibility.

Also, a two-column format generally benefits from a smaller font size than a single-column format. A more standard font size may appear disproportionately large.

A three-column format generally does not work for legal text, unless printed in landscape orientation.

Headings

Headings are key markers in legal documents. They are crucial signposts for readers. Here we discuss the document-design aspects of headings. For other aspects of headings, see **FONTS**; **HEADINGS**.

Visibility

Make headings stand out from the body of the text. Techniques include **bolding**, *italics*, or a larger font—or a combination of these. Never underline a heading. Also, consider using a font that differs from the text font, but not so different as to make the text appear fussy. If the text is *serif*, consider using *sans serif* for headings—to visually separate headings from the body of the text.

Alignment

Align headings flush-left, not centred. In languages where writing runs left to right, the reader's eyes look for a vertical axis at the left of the page. Centred headings disappoint that expectation and impede brain–eye connection: NSW Parliamentary Counsel's Office & Centre for Plain Legal Language, *Review and Design of NSW Legislation* (1994) [2.3.7]. Use centred headings only when readers will genuinely expect them to be centred and where that focal point will not interrupt the flow of the text—eg, top-level headings such as book titles, document descriptions, or chapter headings.

Lower case

Make headings lower case, not upper case (except where readers will genuinely expect upper case, such as for book titles and document descriptions). Research shows that lower case is easier to read than upper case (see **CAPITALS**). But of course use upper case for the initial letter of the first word, and for the initial letters of defined terms (if you follow that convention for 'flagging' defined terms—see **DEFINITIONS**).

Spacing and position

Allocate generous spacing before and after headings. But do not leave headings to 'float' between paragraphs. Where a heading sits between paragraphs of text, allow less space after the heading than before it, so that the heading 'links' visually with the text to which it relates.

Also, do not 'orphan' headings by stranding them at the foot of the page, separated by page-turn from the text to which they relate.

White space

'White space' makes a page less cluttered, which in turn makes it more approachable, encouraging readers into the text. To generate white space:

- break up long slabs of text (logically, not arbitrarily)
- allow generous spacing between clauses
- allow ample margins all round, including at the top and bottom of the page.

Line spacing

Inter-line spacing is critical to readability. Double-spacing (ie, a blank space equal to the full height of a line of text between the rows of words) is useful for draft documents, facilitating mark-up. But otherwise double-spacing can obscure the structure of paragraphing. It can also impede readability, because the eye too easily skips a line. At the other extreme, single spacing can be hard to read, particularly if the font is small. Research shows that the ideal line spacing is between 1.2 and 1.45 (see www.practicaltypography.com/line-spacing.html). For practicality, many drafters prefer the compromise of 1.5 spacing.

Line length

Long lines are not reader-friendly. They tend to slow the reading process, because readers can lose their place on the line. Long lines also reduce margin-width, making pages appear cramped.

Line lengths of 60 mm–120 mm (and ideally 80 mm–110 mm) are said to be the most efficient. This translates to 35–72 characters per line, depending on type size, style and leading: *Review and Redesign of NSW Legislation*, Discussion Paper, Parliamentary Counsel's Office and Centre for Plain Legal Language (1994) [2.3.2].

Justified / unjustified text

Left-justified text aligns the left margin vertically, but leaves the right margin to end where the words naturally end; this makes the right margin uneven (or 'ragged'). Fully justified text aligns both left and right margins vertically.

Many document drafters prefer fully justified text because (in their view) it looks more businesslike, while (again in their view) text with a ragged right edge looks more casual and informal. But fully justified text can open 'rivers of space' on the page—a problem exacerbated where lines are short—although professional printing programs can help (as can hyphenation options in standard word-processing programs). Most publishers prefer justified text because it looks neater—and their sophisticated typesetting techniques allow them to avoid uneven gaps and rivers of space.

Ultimately, the choice between fully justified and right-ragged is a matter of subjective preference. Readability research on the pros and cons of each seems inconclusive. Some researchers conclude that justified text promotes readability more than right-ragged does; others conclude that readers with poor literacy skills find right-ragged text easier to read (because they are less likely to lose their place on the page), but that other readers find it makes no difference.

Further reading

- American Institutes for Research, *Guidelines for Document Designers* (1981)
- Matthew Butterick, *Typography for Lawyers* (Jones McLure, 2010)
- Centre for Plain Legal Language, Discussion Paper: *Review and Redesign of NSW Legislation* (1994)
- Martin Cutts, *Oxford Guide to Plain English*, 5th edn (Oxford, 2020) ch 30
- James Hartley, *Designing Instructional Text*, 3rd edn (Kogan Page, 1994)
- Karen Schriver, *Dynamics in Document Design* (Wiley, 1997)
- Robert Waller et al, 'Cooperation through Clarity: Designing Simplified Contracts' (2016) 2 *Journal of Strategic Contracting and Negotiation* 48 (on designing a document for Canadian Aboriginal readers)
- Colin Wheildon, *Communicating: or Just Making Pretty Shapes* (1986; study for Newspaper Advertising Bureau of Australia)

See also **CAPITALS; DOCUMENT STRUCTURE; FONTS; HEADINGS.**

DOCUMENT STRUCTURE

Order of provisions

The 'structure' of a document is the way in which its contents are organised. What is the best way to organise the contents of a legal document? The answer is as open-ended as the question. To require all legal documents to follow a standard structure would exasperate the writer and fail the reader. Each transaction has its own key elements, and each client is different.

However, legal drafters who give some thought to the structure of their documents tend to use one of three basic structures. It is likely that one—or a variation of one—will suit most transactions.

The following discussion uses a commercial contract as its example. But the principles apply equally to most kinds of legal documents, including statutes.

Front-loaded structure

This structure puts key concepts before subsidiary ones. It front-loads the most important elements. Crucially, it allocates concepts as 'key' from the standpoint of the reader, not of the writer.

Example: front-loaded structure

1. Start with introductory provisions (title, parties, date, overview of document).
2. Next, move straight to the key commercial information (the 'heart of the deal').
3. Next, move to material that is less 'key' but still important for carrying out the deal—including the important machinery provisions.
4. End with functional and procedural material, including boilerplate (eg, choice of law, service of notices, basic interpretation principles).

This structure aims to reflect the reader's expectation (or hope) that important material will be prioritised. It also takes account of the reality that, at least for long documents, the reader's concentration may wane—and so it places the key material up-front, to be read while powers of concentration remain strong.

Some commercial documents achieve the same practical effect as a front-loaded structure by incorporating a 'Term Sheet' at the start of the document. For example, a Term Sheet for a commercial lease may set out in table form key details such as the premises, duration, rent, whether there is an option to renew, the tenant's proportion of outgoings, and the like, with cross-references to relevant clause numbers in the lease. This allows readers to access key points immediately.

Topic-based structure

This structure deals with each main subject area, one after another. It does not attempt to front-load the 'heart of the deal'. Rather, it takes each main topic and presents all the material relevant to it; then it moves on to the next main topic and presents all the material relevant to it; and so on. Only after completing the main subject areas does it reach the boilerplate.

Example: topic-based structure

1. Start with introductory provisions (title, parties, date, overview of document, etc).
2. Next: main topic one.
3. Next: main topic two.
4. Next: main topic three; then further main topics.
5. Finally, functional and procedural material, including boilerplate (eg, choice of law, service of notices, basic interpretation principles).

To illustrate, consider a lease. Logically, a lease starts with the grant of lease and the description of the premises. It could then deal with all of the lessor's powers, both important and insignificant. After that, it could deal with all of the lessee's obligations, both important and insignificant. And so on.

A topic-based structure helps the drafter to group related material, which promotes ease of both drafting and reading. A front-loading structure would break this mould, by separating key information from less-key (but related) information.

Chronological structure

A chronological structure mirrors the order of steps in the transaction. It would suit, for example, a contract for the sale of land, where one step follows another in time-honoured order—like a 'stately saraband': *Re Stone and Saville's Contract* [1962] 1 WLR 460, 465 (Buckley J). To cut and paste the settled conveyancing progression into a front-loaded or topic-based order could impede understanding rather than aid it.

Example: chronological structure (contract for sale of land)

1. Cover page: key details of the transaction (eg, parties, property, amount of purchase price and deposit, contract date and completion date).
2. Deposit (payment; remedies for non-payment; payment by bank guarantee).
3. Requisitions and objections on title; compensation for errors and misdescription.
4. Liabilities arising between entry into contract and completion.
5. Obligations on completion (including calculating balance remaining, and adjustments for rates, etc).
6. Notices to complete.
7. Remedies for failure to complete; post-completion remedies.
8. Boilerplate (serving of notices, merger, interpretation).

Table of contents

In a document of any length, add a table of contents. The table eases the reader's path by providing an overview of the document structure. It also helps the writer ensure a logical grouping of topics. See discussion under **TABLE OF CONTENTS**.

Further reading

- Peter Butt, *Modern Legal Drafting*, 3rd edn (Cambridge University Press, 2013) 129–35
- Neil James, *Writing at Work* (Allen & Unwin, 2007) ch 3

See also **CROSS-REFERENCES; DOCUMENT DESIGN; FONTS; TABLE OF CONTENTS.**

DOCUMENT TESTING

Usefulness

The best way to determine whether a document communicates effectively with its intended audience is to 'test' it against that audience. This is so for all legal documents; but it is particularly so for standard-form documents intended to be used widely (eg, residential leases and mortgages), and for consumer documents intended to advise or bind members of the public generally. The drafter may have followed accepted guidelines about form and structure, and may have applied established techniques for writing in modern, standard English, but the document may nevertheless fail to communicate. Perhaps the writer did not understand the needs of the particular readership or the context in which the document was to operate. Testing the document may be the only sure way of knowing whether the intended readers can interpret and apply it.

Methods

Testing of legal documents is now an established skill, supported by many empirical studies. Two main types of testing are common, reflecting document-testing methods more generally.

- *Focus groups* aim to test what readers 'feel' about a document—what they find to be difficult, easy, superfluous, helpful, or unhelpful. The results are particularly useful before embarking on a substantial redraft of a standard document, and as a follow-up when comparing the redraft against the existing document.

- *Usability testing* (or *protocol testing*) aims to test what readers think the document means. Readers are asked to read the document, usually in successive portions, and are then questioned on each portion.

Timing

Ideally, testing occurs at various stages of a document's preparation:

- *Before preparation*: if a document is to replace an existing document, preliminary testing helps uncover what readers find difficult in the existing document.
- *During preparation*: testing at this stage can save much time at later stages.
- *Post-completion (but before release)*: testing after completion, but before releasing the document, gives one last chance to test the document's effectiveness.

Further reading

- D Berry, 'Techniques for Evaluating the Quality of draft Legislation', *The Loophole* (March 1997) 31–47 (at www.calc.ngo/publications/loopholes#loophole-table-1997)
- M Cutts, *Lucid Law* (Plain Language Commission, 2004) 22–28
- M Duckworth and G Mills, *Organising a Plain Language Project* (Federation Press, 1996) 18–19, 63
- JS Dumas and JC Redish, *A Practical Guide to Usability Testing* (Intellect Ltd, 1999)
- DI Huron, 'Testing Plain Language Texts with Adult Learners' (2004) 51 *Clarity* 24 (at www.clarity-international.net/clarity-journal/archives/)
- Paul Salembier, 'Testing Client Policy: The Emperor's Clothes', *Loophole* (August 2011) 44 (on 'road-testing' proposed legislation)
- W Schiess, 'The Texas Pattern Jury Charges Plain-Language Project: The Writing Consultant's View' (2008) 60 *Clarity* 23 (at www.clarity-international.net/clarity-journal/archives/)
- Anita Wright, 'The Value of Usability Testing in Document Design' (1994) 30 *Clarity* 24 (at www.clarity-international.net/clarity-journal/archives/)

See also **READABILITY TESTS**.

DOCUMENT TITLES

Ideally, a document's title should reflect its purpose: eg, *Agreement for Sale of Land*, *Sale of Shares*, *Deed of Indemnity*, *Mortgage*. Resist the temptation to give the document a title that is catchy but uninformative. Private-sector legal drafters generally have control over the titles of their documents. Parliamentary drafters may have less control, sometimes being commanded by their political masters to use titles that are politically coloured and self-serving.

Where the nature of a transaction seems unclear, the title the parties give their document may shed light on their intentions. For example:

- The title 'debenture' was relevant in holding an instrument to be a debenture (rather than a promissory note) for stamp duty purposes: *British India Steam Navigation Co v Commissioners of Inland Revenue* (1881) 7 QBD 165.
- The title 'contract of employment' may be relevant in holding a person to be an employee rather than an independent contractor: *Massey* v *Crown Life Insurance Co* [1978] 1 WLR 676.
- The title 'policy of insurance' was relevant in holding an instrument to be an insurance policy and not a loan: *NM Superannuation Pty Ltd v Young* (1993) 41 FCR 182; 7 ANZIC 61–163.

However, there are limits to reliance on document titles to help determine their nature and effect. A document that is a 'sham'—in the sense of being cast in one form as a pretence to cloak its true nature—is no less a sham despite its title. On this basis, for example, a document deliberately cast in the form of a licence to disguise its true nature as a lease remains a lease despite being titled 'Licence': *Radaich v Smith* (1959) 101 CLR 209; *Street v Mountford* [1985] AC 809; *AG Securities v Vaughan* [1990] 1 AC 417; *Bruton v London & Quadrant Housing Trust* [2000] 1 AC 406.

Further reading

Paul O'Brien, 'Legislative Titles—What's in a Name?', *The Loophole* (Nov 2012) 17

See also **sham**.

does not include

See **means / includes**.

doli incapax

Latin: incapable of committing a crime, in the sense of having no legal capacity to do so. Given the adequacy of the English translation, to retain the Latin seems pedantic.

- 'Section 34, rather unusually, uses the Latin *doli incapax* in the heading and then, in the section itself, refers to the rebuttable presumption that a child aged 10 or over is "incapable of committing an offence". Incapacity of committing an offence is as good a translation of *doli incapax* as any.' [*R v T* [2009] UKHL 20, [8]; [2009] 1 AC 1310, 1329 (Lord Phillips, providing a translation)]
- '[T]here is a rebuttable presumption that a child aged between 10 and 14 is *doli incapax* [prefer: *legally incapable of committing a crime*].' [*PGA v R* [2012] HCA 21, [124]; (2012) 245 CLR 355, 40 (Heydon J)]

domicile / residence

A person's *domicile* is the place where they have, or are treated by the law as having, their permanent home. It is where they live 'with the intention of remaining there for ever, unless some circumstance should occur to alter [their] intention': *Whicker v Hume* (1858) 7 HL Cas 124, 164; 11 ER 50, 66 (Lord Wensleydale). The common law presumes every person to have a *domicile* in this sense. A person's *domicile* is not necessarily their *residence*; a person can *reside* at many different places over the years, but retain only one *domicile*.

Further reading

Halsbury's Laws of England, 'Conflict of Laws' (vol 19, 2011) [336]–[338 (the law of 'domicile')

dominant tenement / servient tenement

The *dominant tenement* is the land (tenement) benefited by an easement or servitude, and (less precisely, but sufficiently unambiguously) the land benefited by a covenant. The reciprocal land is the *servient tenement* (burdened land). Nothing is lost, in principle or practice, by using modern, plain-language equivalents for *dominant* and *servient* ('benefited' and 'burdened'), and *tenement* ('land'). For example:

- 'It is well established that an easement (that is, a right in favour of the so-called *dominant* [prefer: *benefited*] land over the so-called *servient* [prefer: *burdened*] land, such as a right of way, a right to light, a right of support, or a right of drainage) can be acquired by prescription as well as by express grant.' [*Coventry v Lawrence* [2014] UKSC 13; [2014] 1 AC 822, [29] (Lord Neuberger, half-helping readers by substituting *land* for *tenement*, but retaining *dominant* and *servient*)]

- '[In that case], a grant of a right of way "for all purposes" across the *servient tenement* [prefer: *burdened land*] did not plainly identify any *dominant tenement* [prefer: *benefited land*], and from there travelling to some further property.' [*Westfield Management Ltd v Perpetual Trustee Co Ltd* [2007] HCA 45; (2007) 233 CLR 528, [21] (High Court of Australia)]

See also **servitude; tenement**.

domitae naturae

Latin: tamed, domesticated; used to describe animals that are tamed (as distinct from animals that are untamed: *ferae naturae*). Prefer plain English over the Latin.

See also **ferae naturae**.

donatio mortis causa

Latin: a gift made in contemplation of death; plural, *donationes mortis causa*. The Latin tag encapsulates an ancient doctrine under which a person, who fears imminent death, can make an effective gift to operate on death despite the absence of a formal will.

As with many other Latin tags in law, *donatio mortis causa* does not fill out the detail of the doctrine it encapsulates, namely (i) the donor's fear of *imminent* death, and (ii) the donor's intention that the gift is to take effect only when and if death in fact occurs. Because the doctrine bypasses the normal requirements for a valid will, courts scrutinise the circumstances in which the gift was made: *King v Dubrey* [2016] 2 WLR 1 (CA). The English translation ('gift made in contemplation of death') mirrors the meaning of the Latin, but shares the Latin's shortcomings in failing to fill out the detail of the doctrine. For that reason, a thoughtful writer may wish to give the reader both a translation and an explanation.

> '[T]he courts will examine any case of alleged *donatio mortis causa* [prefer: *gift in anticipation of death*] and reject it if in truth what is alleged as a *donatio* [prefer: *gift*] is an attempt to make a ... will ... not complying with the forms required by the Wills Act.' [*Birch v Treasury Solicitor* [1951] Ch 298, 307–08 (Lord Evershed MR)]

Further reading

Halsbury's Laws of England, 'Gifts' (vol 52, 2014) [271]–[277] (gifts *mortis causa*)

DOUBLE NEGATIVES

See **POSITIVES / NEGATIVES**.

DOUBLETS

See **REDUNDANCIES; WORD PAIRINGS**.

doubt (avoidance of)

See **for the avoidance of doubt**.

drafter / draftsman / draughtsman

The preferred modern usage is *drafter*—avoiding the gender-specific *draftsman* and the clunky *draftsperson*. The spelling *draughts-* ('draughtsman', 'draughtsperson') is obsolescent. Having chosen one spelling, be consistent throughout the document: cf *Lennard v Jessica Estates Pty Ltd* [2008] NSWCA 121 (Tobias JA), using *draftsperson* at [43], [45], but *draughtsperson*, [52], [55], [56] and [64].

dubitante

Latin: doubting; expressing doubt. Used particularly to indicate that a judge expresses reservations about, or does not wish to commit to, a decision on a point of law or fact. The English translation is clear, rendering the Latin redundant. For example:

> '[T]he Court of Queen's Bench held, Fitzgerald J *dubitante* [prefer: *doubting; expressing doubt*], that the plea was good.' [*R v Chief Constable of Gloucestershire* [2006] UKHL 55; [2007] 2 AC 105, 145 [97] (Lord Carswell)]

due

See **may be due**.

due and payable

A pairing commonly found in commercial documents. Rarely is a debt said to be merely *due* [on 1 June], or merely *payable* [on 1 June]; instead, it is said to be *due and payable* [on 1 June]. Are the two words synonymous? In everyday usage, probably yes—if an amount is *due* it is also *payable*; therefore, either word should suffice. But in legal usage, context may require otherwise. For example:

- In some contexts, a debt may be 'due' without yet being 'payable'. That is, *due* denotes the existence of liability, while *payable* denotes the date for discharging the liability. In such a case, regardless of when the debt is *due*, the obligation to pay does not arise until the debt is *payable*: see, eg, *Ex parte Sturt & Co* (1871) LR 13 Eq 309, 311 (Bacon CJ); *Re Stockton Malleable Iron Co* (1875) 2 Ch D 101, 103 (Jessel MR). To cite a Latin maxim, *debitum in praesenti* [but] *solvendum in futuro*—ie, the debt is *due* (in the sense of existing now) but not *payable* until a future date: eg, *Ex parte Kemp* (1874) LR 9 Ch App 383, 388 (Mellish LJ); *Re Mendonaca* (1969) 15 FLR 256, 259 (Gibbs J). For example, tax legislation may decree that a tax liability is 'due' when an event occurs but is not 'payable' until the tax authorities issue a notice of assessment (as in *Federal Commissioner of Taxation v Australian Building Systems Pty Ltd* [2015] HCA 48; 257 CLR 544). Or payment under a contract may be 'due' on a stated date, but if that date is not a 'business day' and the 'business day' clause defers payment until the next available 'business day', then it is not 'payable' until that next day (as in *Griffin Energy Group Pty Ltd v ICICI Bank Ltd* [2015] NSWCA 29; (2015) 317 ALR 395).
- In other (though rarer) contexts, a debt may be 'payable' without yet being 'due'. For example, a long-term ground lease may require the tenant to 'pay' the rent annually, but legislation may defer the rent from being 'due' until the landlord has given the tenant the appropriate notice: *Cheerupmate2 Ltd v Calce* [2018] EWCA Civ 2230; [2019] 1 WLR 1813.

Further reading

Andrew Marshall, 'Is "Due and Payable" a Magic Phrase?' (2007) 15 *Insolvency Law Journal* 100

See also **business day**; **debitum in praesenti solvendum in futuro**; **may be due**.

due diligence

Literally, 'appropriate care'. *Due diligence* is used in law in at least three senses.

1. *Due diligence towards others*: in particular, the obligation to 'exercise reasonable care' for the safety of others: *Riverstone Meat Co Pty Ltd v Lancashire Shipping Co Ltd* [1960] 1 QB 536, 581 (Willmer LJ). For example, workplace legislation may require employers to exercise *due diligence* in providing a safe system of work: *Bibby-Cheshire v Golden Wonder Ltd* [1972] 1 WLR 1487.
2. *Due diligence towards self*: the standard of care a person needs to take in commercial or property transactions to ensure self-protection against adverse factors—eg, by making careful enquiry into the conduct and accounts of a business being purchased, or the condition of a property being purchased. Hence, 'due diligence room', where lawyers are closeted to review confidential records of a business's holdings and activities.
3. *Due diligence in the conduct of affairs*: the speed, efficiency or care with which rights must be exercised or obligations must be performed. For example, a building contract may require the builder to act with *due diligence* in constructing the building; in this context, *due diligence* requires not merely personal industriousness, but reasonable efficiency in managing and organising the works: *Hooker* [or *Hooper*] *Constructions Pty Ltd v Chris's Engineering Contracting Co* [1970] ALR 821, 823 (Blackburn J). Or legislation may require *due diligence* in protecting a patent from threatened infringement: *Johnson v Edge* [1892] 2 Ch 1. Or yet again, the law may require an executor to exercise *due diligence* in paying the deceased's debts: *Re Tankard* [1942] Ch 69.

due expedition

An inherently vague term—if something is to be done with *due expedition*, how quickly must it be done? Usually, *due* here means *proper* or *adequate*: *R v Coleman* (1992) 95 Cr App R 345. So, to proceed with *due expedition* is to proceed with speed that is appropriate in the circumstances: *Churnin v Pilot Developments Pty Ltd* [2003] NSWCA 391; 11 BPR 21,603, [70] (Santow JA). But that is vague; it is much better, if the subject matter allows, to state precisely how soon the thing is to be done.

due to the fact that

An inexcusably wordy expression, always reducible to *because* or similar. For example:

- '[T]his was *due to the fact that* [prefer: *because*] Gillette had recently introduced a new Fusion razor blade.' [*Davis & Dann Ltd v Commissioners for Her Majesty's Revenue and Customs* [2016] EWCA Civ 142, [36] (Arden LJ)]
- 'The legislature dispensed with these requirements *due to the fact that* [prefer: *because*] the opportunity for objections and public submissions … had been conferred through other legislation.' [*Mandurah Enterprises Pty Ltd v Western Australian Planning Commission* [2010] HCA 2; (2010) 240 CLR 409, [33] (French CJ, Gummow, Crennan and Bell JJ)]

See also **because**.

duly

A much-overused word. In law, rarely are things merely *done*; rather, they are *duly done*. For example, a person is not merely *authorised*, but *duly authorised*; a notice is not merely *served*, but *duly served*; a document is not merely *signed*, but *duly signed*. In phrases such as these, *duly* is usually a lawyer's uncritical reflex, adding nothing. For example:

> A lease gave the tenant the right to buy the landlord's interest in the property, but only if the tenant had '*duly* paid' the rent. Held, the tenant could buy even though he had paid the rent late—'*duly* paid' meant simply 'paid', not 'paid on time': *Starkey v Barton* [1908] 1 Ch 284, 289 (Parker J).

Occasionally, however, *duly* serves a purpose: namely, to clarify not merely that a thing must be done, but that it must be done in accordance with prescribed time limits or formalities. In such a case, it is useful. For example:

- A cheque was not '*duly* stamped' where the stamp it bore had been affixed by a person not authorised by law to affix stamps: *Hobbs v Cathie* (1890) 6 TLR 292.
- A lease was not '*duly* attested' where the alleged witness had not been present when the lease was signed: *Freshfield v Reed* (1842) 11 LJ Ex 193.

So the lesson is not necessarily to discard *duly*, but to reserve it for circumstances where it plays a genuine role, as in the following case:

> A party's submission to an adjudicator included material which, under the relevant statute, should not have been included. Held, the submission was not *duly* made: *Broad Construction Services (NSW) Pty Ltd v Vadasz* [2008] NSWSC 1057; (2008) 73 NSWLR 149.

DUPLICATED WORDS

See **REDUNDANCIES; WORD PAIRINGS; WORD STRINGS.**

durante

Latin: during. Usually found in combination with other Latin words or phrases—all of which can be expressed in standard English. Always prefer the standard English.

durante absentia

Latin: during absence (in the sense of being out of the court's jurisdiction). Used in probate law to describe a grant of administration of a deceased estate while the nominated executor (or, in an intestacy, the next of kin) is out of the jurisdiction: *Re Suarez* [1897] P 82. Prefer the English translation 'while out of the jurisdiction'.

durante dementia

Latin: during dementia; while suffering from unsoundness of mind. Used in probate law to describe the situation where the person entitled to a grant of probate or administration is incapable of administering the estate because of mental or physical incapacity. The court may then grant administration to another person, limited to the period of the incapacity. The English translation suffices, so prefer it.

durante minore aetate

Latin: during minority; while still a minor. Found often in probate law, in relation to the administration of deceased estates. A grant of probate or administration cannot be made to a minor, and so the court may make a grant to the minor's guardian during the minority. No reason—except tradition—exists for retaining the Latin; the English translation is precise and accurate (although tradition and Latin live long in probate law and practice):

> 'If a person appoints a minor as his or her executor, the court makes a *grant durante minore aetate* [prefer: *a grant during minority*] and then makes a final grant when the minor comes of age.' [*Ackerley v Felton* [2012] NSWSC 1468 (Young AJ)]

durante viduitate

Latin: during widowhood. Now obsolete; prefer the English translation.

during

Often used ambiguously—and if case law is any guide, by drafters who fail to notice the ambiguity.

1. *During* can mean *for the whole duration of*: eg, 'I will keep my office open *during* normal business hours.' For example:
   - A pauper's claim under the Poor Laws turned on whether he had been a resident of a village *during* certain years. Held, *during* required residence for the whole of those years: *R v Inhabitants of Anderson* (1846) 9 QB 663, 668; 115 ER 1428, 1430 (Lord Denman CJ, expressing the view that this was the 'strict and proper legal sense' of *during*).
   - A promised to pay B an annuity '*during* A's lifetime'. B predeceased A. Held, A must continue to pay the annuity to B's legal representatives, for as long as A lived: *Reid v Coggans* [1944] AC 9.
   - A tax statute applied if the taxpayer held shares '*during* the period of ten years ending with the disposal' of the shares. Held, this required a continuous holding during the entire 10-year period: *Davenport v Hasslacher* [1975] 3 All ER 396.
2. *During* can mean at any time within the period. For example:
   - 'An offender may be sent back to prison for an offence committed *during* probation.'
   - The time for bringing action could be extended if a party to a contract was out of the jurisdiction '*during*' a 6-month period. Held, the extension applied if the party was out of the jurisdiction at any time within the 6-month period: *Austin v Olsen* (1868) LR 3 QB 208.
   - Under Canadian income tax legislation, a person's liability to tax turned on whether the person was ordinarily resident in Canada '*during*' the tax year. Held, during meant 'at any time within' the year, and not 'for the whole of' the year: *Thomson v Minister of National Revenue* [1946] SCR 209—distinguishing *R v Inhabitants of Anderson* (above) on the basis that the tax statute and the Poor Laws had different purposes.

A prescient drafter will foresee the possibility of ambiguity, and clarify which meaning of *during* is intended.

Dutch auction

An auction where property is sold by decreasing bids. The auctioneer announces a starting price and decreases that price until someone makes a bid. The first person to bid becomes the purchaser: *Carroll v Soloman* (1930) 33 WALR 82. The term is said to originate in the practice of selling tulips in 17th-century Holland, where this bidding system ensured quick sales (one bid only) at the buyer's highest price.

duty

In law, a *duty* is not always obligatory. Courts draw a terminologically difficult distinction between an 'imperative' (or 'mandatory') duty on the one hand, and a 'directory' duty on the other hand. The distinction is applied, for example, in deciding whether a decision-maker's failure to comply with a statutory 'duty' invalidates exercise of the decision-making power:

> 'Lawyers speak of statutory provisions as *imperative* when any want of strict compliance with them means that the resulting act, be it a statute, a contract or what you will, is null and void. They speak of them as *directory* when they mean that although they are legal requirements which it is unlawful to disregard, yet failure to fulfil them does not mean that the resulting act is wholly ineffective, is null and void.' [*Clayton v Heffron* (1960) 105 CLR 214, 247 (Dixon CJ, McTiernan, Taylor and Windeyer JJ)]

See also **has a duty to (do something)**; **shall / must**.

dwelling-house / dwelling house / dwellinghouse

To hyphenate or not? The preferred usage is *dwelling-house*, reflecting the compound nature of the term. However, *dwelling house* (two words) and *dwellinghouse* (one word) are becoming common, reflecting the gradual disappearance of hyphens from standard English usage. Normally, of course, either *dwelling* or *house* is sufficient.

Further reading

Daniel Greenberg (ed), *Stroud's Judicial Dictionary*, 9th edn (Sweet & Maxwell, 2017) title 'dwelling house' (myriad cases on the meaning of 'dwelling-house')

See also **HYPHENS**.

e converso

Latin: conversely. This Latinism appears to have all but disappeared from present-day legal usage. Resist its re-emergence. Prefer the English:

- 'In [that decision] Lord Ellenborough *e converso* [prefer: *to the contrary*] fortified his ruling, that a *de facto* enjoyment for above twenty years of support gave the right to it ...' [*Dalton v Angus* (1881) LR 6 App Cas 740, 757 (Field J)]
- 'The absence of a certificate ... is not the cause [of the accident]. And *e converso* [prefer: *conversely*] the cause is still incompetent driving, even if he has a certificate.' [*Leask Timber and Hardware Pty Ltd v Thorne* (1961) 106 CLR 33, 45 (Kitto J)]

each and every

A pairing often seen in traditional legal drafting. The two words are closely related: *each* derives from the Old English *aelc*, and *every* from the Old English *aefre*. In almost all circumstances, however, it is sufficient to use either *each* or *every*.

The qualification 'almost all' is added, because sometimes the pairing may be useful for emphasis: 'You must carry out *each and every* one of these promises.' Here, *each and every* drives home the point—you must not merely do *each* of them, but *every one* of them. However, this (rare) circumstance does not justify pairing *each and every* out of habit.

See also **every**.

earlier in time

To say that event A is *earlier in time* than event B is tautologous: if A is *earlier*, it must be *earlier in time*. Yet the tautology is often seen. For example:

- 'But Mr Samaroo's equitable interest, being *earlier in time* [prefer: *earlier*], has priority over all these equitable interests of Mr Sookraj.' [*Sookraj v Samaroo* [2004] UKPC 50, [15] (Lord Scott)]
- 'He said that *earlier in time* [prefer: *earlier*] at the Federal Magistrates' Court he told the deceased she could have what she wanted but to leave the house. … *Earlier in time* [prefer: *earlier*] the deceased … informed the appellant of her wish to be divorced.' [*Bayram v R* [2011] VSCA 6, [9], [14] (Warren CJ)]

earnest (noun)

Money or some tangible thing given when a contract is made, as a guarantee ('deposit') that the party who gives it will fulfil the contract: *Howe v Smith* (1884) 27 Ch D 89, 101 (Fry LJ); *Farr Smith & Co Ltd v Messers Ltd* [1928] 1 KB 397.

See also **deposit**.

easement

A right attached to land owned by one person to use land owned by another person in a particular way (a positive easement) or to prevent the owner of other land from using that land in a particular way (a negative easement). Examples are rights of way (positive easements) and easements for light (negative easements). An easement does not permit taking any part of the soil or produce of the land; a right of that kind is a profit à prendre.

Further reading

S Bridge, E Cooke, and M Dixon (eds), *Megarry & Wade's Law of Real Property*, 9th edn (Sweet & Maxwell, 2019) [26-001] and following (the nature of, and requirements for, easements)

See also **dominant tenement / servient tenement**; **incorporeal hereditament**; **profit à prendre**; **servitude**.

easements rights and privileges

A tripartite term often found in conveyances of land: the conveyance is expressed to include all 'easements rights and privileges'. It is usually unpunctuated, reflecting the lamentable lack of punctuation in traditional legal writing. At the least, it should be punctuated thus: 'easements, rights and privileges'—or better still, using the serial comma: 'easements, rights, and privileges'. But matters of punctuation aside, it is unnecessarily wordy. This is because an *easement* is a *right* (over land), and both *easements* and *rights* are *privileges* (Latin *privilegium*, from *privus*: private; and *lex*: law). Unless the context requires the three concepts to be individually identified (which seems unlikely), *right* suffices for all three.

See also **COMMAS**; **privilege**; **PUNCTUATION**; **WORD PAIRINGS.**

eavesdrop

A word with two distinct meanings: (1) to secretly listen to a conversation; (2) to allow water to fall from the eaves of a property onto a neighbouring property (sometimes *eavesdrip*). Meaning (1) is more common than meaning (2). From meaning (2) comes 'easement for eavesdrop' (or in Scots law, the servitude of *stillicide*)—a right to insist that property A accept water dropping from eaves on the neighbouring property B.

See also **servitude**.

EDITING

Need for editing

All writing benefits from editing, and all editing benefits from further editing. Legal writing is no different. Busy lawyers may begrudge the time for editing; but lack of editing can have serious consequences. In a US case, a lawyer was suspended from practice for 60 days for filing a brief which the court described as 'virtually incomprehensible' and as 'little more than fifteen unclear and ungrammatical sentences, slapped together as two pages of unedited text with an unintelligible message': *Kentucky Bar Association v Brown* 14 SW 3d 916 (Kentucky, 2000) 917–18.

Editing techniques

Few writers can edit adequately on a single run-through of the text. Effective editing is done in stages, moving from higher level (general) to more particular (specific). It starts with high-level matters of structure and tone, then narrows to matters at paragraph and sentence level, and then narrows further to matters at word and punctuation level. If time is short, prioritise higher-level tasks over lower-level tasks.

Suggested steps (moving from high level to specific)

1. *Document structure*: is the structure the most logical for the document (ie, logical from the reader's perspective, not the writer's)?
2. *Tone and voice*: does the writing strike the right 'tone'? Is it approachable and professional? Or is it impersonal and condescending, patronising and sexist? Is the 'voice' professional yet direct (eg, using the 'we/you' style), or is it unduly formal ('the client', 'the company') or (at the other extreme) too familiar?
3. *Paragraph structure*: does the writing follow the principle 'one paragraph, one main idea'? Is the topic sentence placed first in the paragraph?
4. *Sentence-level*: are the sentences reasonably short? Do they flow logically one to another?
5. *Excessive verbiage*: is there scope to trim unnecessary words and phrases?
6. *Jargon and terms of art*: will any legal jargon and technical terms puzzle the reader? (And if they will, can you delete them, or at least explain them?)
7. *Active / passive verbs, and noun phrases*: can active verbs replace passive verbs, and can verbs replace nouns and noun phrases?
8. *Spelling and punctuation*: is spelling correct and punctuation accurate?

Further reading

- Joan Ames Magat, *The Lawyer's Editing Manual* (Carolina Academic Press, 2009)
- Timothy Perrin, *Better Writing for Lawyers* (Law Society of Upper Canada, 1990) chs 8–12

See also **DOCUMENT STRUCTURE; JARGON; NOUNS / VERBS; PROOFREADING; PUNCTUATION; SENTENCE LENGTH; TERMS OF ART; TONE.**

educe

See **adduce / educe.**

-ee / -or endings

Many law-related terms end in *-ee* or *-or*. In this, they reflect general English usage:

- *-ee* endings normally (but not universally) denote someone who receives something: eg, *lessee* (one to whom a lease is granted), *mortgagee* (one to whom a mortgage is granted), *trustee* (one to whom property is entrusted), *grantee* (one to whom property is granted). The sense is implicitly passive.
- *-or* endings normally denote someone who grants something: *lessor, mortgagor, grantor*. The sense is implicitly active.

Lawyers familiar with words that end in *-ee* and *-or* should have no problem distinguishing their meanings. But it may be different for non-lawyers. Because the words are usually distinguished *only* by the different endings, non-lawyers may find them confusing. For example, non-lawyers may well ponder:

- mortgagor / mortgagee: who is the lender and who is the borrower?
- lessor / lessee: who is the landlord and who is the tenant?
- chargor / chargee: who gives (bears) the charge and who receives (benefits from) it?
- encumbrancer / encumbrancee: who gives the encumbrance and who receives it?
- lienor / lienee: who gives the lien and who receives it?
- covenantor / covenantee: who gives (bears the burden of) the covenant and who receives its benefit?

If in doubt about the reader's capacity to discern the difference, choose a substitute term—eg, *landlord / tenant* (instead of *lessor / lessee*). However, take care where (rarely) legal efficacy may *demand* the *-ee / -or* words. For example, to use *borrower / lender* instead of *mortgagor / mortgagee* may raise doubts about the nature of the parties' relationship—is it a mortgage, with all the incidents of a mortgage (security over the property, power of sale), or is it merely a personal loan? Again, to use *grantor / recipient* instead of *lienor / lienee* may create doubts about the kind of security granted. In these (and other) cases, it may be necessary to use the *-ee / -or* terms, but coupled with an explanation—after which it may be possible to move to simpler substitutes.

See also **REDRAFTING IN PLAIN ENGLISH.**

effect

See **affect / effect.**

effective date

A lawyer's shorthand for the date on which a document or statute comes into operation. For example, the *effective date* of a contract is the date on which the contract becomes binding (which may differ from the date on which a party signs it). The *effective date* of a statute (also called the 'commencement date') is the date on which the statute comes into operation (which may differ from the date on which it is enacted).

effeiring to

A term in Scots law to denote *relating to*, *pertaining to*—often applied to ancillary rights transferred with a property. For example:

> 'Increases in ground rent reflected the increasing cost of providing and maintaining the rights *effeiring to* [prefer: *pertaining to*; *attached to*] the tenancy-at-will such as rights to draw water and to gain access to the site.' [*Wright v Shoreline Management Ltd* [2009] ScotSC 14, [12] (Dunlop QC)]

effluxion of time

A lawyer's consciously formulaic paraphrase for 'expiry of time' or 'passage of time'. For example, when a lease for a fixed term has run its full course, it is said to have expired 'by effluxion of time'—which means simply that it has expired. Often the phrase can simply be deleted as superfluous (as in the first two examples below). Otherwise, a plain-English substitute is always available (as in the third example).

- '[I]f a Purchase Order is placed for work specified to take over six months, on 29th December 2011, it would not be invalidated by the expiry of the Enabling Agreement ~~*by effluxion of time*~~ [delete as superfluous] two days later.' [*Northrop Grumman Missions Systems Europe Ltd v BAE Systems (Al Diriyah C41) Ltd* [2015] EWCA Civ 844, [14] (Briggs LJ)]
- '[E]ach visa constitutes a permission … to remain in Australia which continues until it *expires* ~~*by effluxion of time*~~ [delete as superfluous] or is consciously revoked.' [*Minister for Immigration and Multicultural and Indigenous Affairs v Nystrom* [2006] HCA 50; (2006) 228 CLR 566, [40] (Gummow and Hayne JJ)]
- '[T]he … basis for these applications was that by reason of the *effluxion of time* [prefer: *passing of time*] since 1965, for the defendants a fair trial was not possible.' [*Batistatos v Roads and Traffic Authority of NSW* [2006] HCA 27; (2006) 228 CLR 566, [31] (Gleeson CJ, Gummow, Hayne and Crennan JJ)]

eg / e.g.

Abbreviation for Latin *exempli gratia* = 'for example'. When used at the start of a list, indicates that the list is illustrative but incomplete. British usage now generally omits the full stops (*eg*), but US usage generally retains them. In both usages, italics are now disappearing: 'eg', not '*eg*'.

British/Commonwealth usage generally inserts a comma before *eg*; practice varies over whether to insert a comma after:

- This will require more resources, eg, money.
- This will require more resources, eg money.

US usage generally inserts a comma both before and after:

> This will require more resources, e.g., money.

See also **exempli gratia**.

eggshell

The foundational word in two colourful legal expressions—neither of which is a true term of art, and each of which is inherently vague:

- *eggshell lease*: A lease that extends only to the internal skin of the building (ie, excluding the external structures of the building): *Pumperninks Ltd v Land Securities plc* [2002] 3 WLR 898 (an 'eggshell tenancy'); *Field v Freehold Properties 250 Ltd* [2020] EWHC 792 (Ch); [2020] 3 WLR 233 (although not using the expression).
- *eggshell skull*: The principle of tort law that defendants take plaintiffs as they find them. Thus, if a defendant negligently injures a plaintiff, it is no defence that the plaintiff would have suffered less injury, or no injury at all, had he or she not possessed 'an unusually thin skull or an unusually weak heart': *Dulieu v White* [1901] 2 KB 669 at 679 (Kennedy J).

either

Generally, *either* means *one or the other*, but not *both*. The qualification 'generally' is added because context can indicate a different meaning. In particular, *either* can mean 'each of two'—in effect, *both*. Thus, 'you can take *either* side' (ie, both sides, if you like), or 'the river overflowed on either side' (ie, on both sides): examples from *Currie v Glen* (1936) 54 CLR 445, 453 (Starke J). Indeed, the law reports contain many examples where (in the court's view) *either* meant *both*:

- A bequest of furniture in *either* of two houses allowed the beneficiary to choose from *both*: *Re Wavertree* [1933] Ch 837.
- A gift by will to A, to take effect on the death of *either B or C*, meant on the death of *each of B and C*: *Currie v Glen* (1936) 54 CLR 445.
- A testator's direction that her property be divided between her two sisters, but that if *either* of them should predecease her, their children should take the parent's share, included the situation where *both* sisters predeceased her: *Re Fyfe* [1946] ALR 344.
- An employment contract allowing *either* party to give notice of termination to the other allowed *both* to give notice to each other: *Adventure World Travel Pty Ltd v Newsom* (2014) 86 NSWLR 515 (although one party's act in giving notice would exhaust the right to terminate by notice, making a later notice by the other party ineffective).

The lesson is obvious. If any doubt could arise about the meaning of *either*, clarify it. It may be necessary to add a few words: eg, 'either A or B, but not both'.

See also **either … or**.

either … or

A formula expressing alternatives more emphatically than simply 'or'. The formula is useful where the writer fears that a court may (mis)interpret an unadorned *or* as *and*. While that seems unlikely, it is not impossible—as witness the many cases where judges have read 'or' to mean 'and', and 'and' to mean 'or'. So, while judges or readers might interpret 'A *or* B' to mean 'A *and* B', it is much harder to interpret '*either* A *or* B' to mean

'A *and* B'. Prudence may dictate the extra words. Sometimes, however, prudence bites back, as in the following case:

> A will gave property to A for life, and after A's death, to B and C in equal shares, but if *either* B *or* C predeceased A, then to X. Both B and C predeceased A. Held, the gift to X failed, because the event on which it was conditioned—the death of *either* B *or* C—was not fulfilled by the death of *both* A *and* B: *Re Pickworth* [1899] 1 Ch 642.

When using *either … or*, take care to place *either* in the most appropriate position. Careless positioning can lead to arguments over meaning. For example, the Australian High Court found it necessary to 'correct' a statutory drafter's positioning of *either* in the following provision: '[T]he Supreme Court shall, if it allows an appeal against conviction, ~~either~~ quash the conviction and either direct a judgment and verdict of acquittal to be entered or … order a new trial': *DPP (Nauru) v Fowler* (1984) 154 CLR 627 (original position indicated by strikethrough; new position indicated by underlining).

See also **and**; **either**; **or**.

eiusdem generis

Latin: of the same class (kind). Sometimes spelled with *j*—*ejusdem generis*.

Statement of the principle

The principle of interpretation that where a list of specific items belonging to the same 'genus' (ie, group or class) is followed by general words, a court interprets the general words as confined to the same class. The rationale is said to be that, in compiling the list, the drafter's attention was focused on that class of item, and by adding the catch-all *other*, the drafter meant not to stray from that class, but merely to bring within the class items omitted through oversight or for brevity: *Quazi v Quazi* [1980] AC 744, 807–08 (Lord Diplock).

Examples

- In matrimonial proceedings, a wife sought an order for inspection of cheques and paying-in slips relating to her husband's bank account, under a statute that allowed inspection of 'ledgers, day books, cash books, account books *and other records* used in the ordinary business of the bank'. Held, cheques and paying-in slips were not *other records*, because they did not fall within the same class as the listed items: *Williams v Williams* [1988] QB 161 (CA).
- A statute required a licence to sell 'meat, fish, poultry, vegetables, fruit, *and other provisions*'. Held, a licence was not required to sell bread and confectionery. The list 'meat, fish, poultry, vegetables, fruit' pointed to a class of natural products; bread and confectionery were manufactured items, and so outside the class: *Hy Whittle Ltd v Stalybridge Corporation* (1967) 65 LGR 344.
- A statute made it an offence to cause a traffic obstruction 'by speaking, shouting, singing, playing upon, operating or sounding any musical or noisy instrument *or doing anything whatsoever*'. The accused caused a traffic obstruction by gesticulating silently, dressed in a gorilla suit. Held, he was not guilty, because '*doing anything whatsoever*' was to be read down by reference to the class inherent in the list of specific activities—namely, activities that generated noise: *Hughes v Winter* [1955] SASR 238.
- A statute made it an offence to threaten a person 'by letter, telegram, telephone, cable, radio, *or otherwise*'. Held, 'or otherwise' did not extend the offence to purely oral threats, made face-to-face: *R v Nabis* (1974) 48 DLR (3d) 543 (SC of Canada—though strictly not on the ground of *eiusdem generis*, but rather that, given the history of similar provisions, Parliament could not have intended to create an offence of oral threats).

- A statute created the offence of obstructing a federal investigation by destroying 'any record, document, *or tangible object*'. A professional fisherman threw undersized fish into the water to escape prosecution. Held, *tangible object* was to be read *eiusdem generis* with *record* and *document*. It referred to items used to record information, such as computer hard drives, but not fish: *Yates v United States* 135 S Ct 1074 (2015).
- A clause in a bill of lading exonerated a ship's master from liability for refusing to take the ship into port, if the master deemed entry into the port 'unsafe in consequence of war [or] disturbance *or any other cause*'. The master considered the port unsafe because of sea-ice. Held, icing-up of the sea was not within the class of events characterised by 'war [or] disturbance'; therefore, the clause did not exonerate the master: *S S Knutsford Ltd v Tillmanns & Co* [1908] AC 406, HL.
- A prosecution against an employer for injury to a worker could only be brought within a two-year limitation period. A court could extend that period for 'delay in the onset or manifestation of an injury ... or a condition of defect of any kind, *or any other relevant factor or circumstance*'. Delay occurred because the prosecution was brought against the wrong employer. Held, an oversight of this kind was not within *any other relevant factor or circumstance*, because the 'genus' in the preceding list was the manifestation of some injury or disease: *Gelzinis v T & R (Murray Bridge) PtyLtd* [2009] SASC 61; (2009) 103 SASR 194.

Need for a 'class'

The *eiusdem generis* principle applies only where the specific words belong to a *genus* (ie, class). In the absence of a class, the principle has no scope to operate.

Examples

- A charterparty stated that hiring charges would cease 'in the event of loss of time from deficiency of men or owners' stores, breakdown of machinery, or damage to hull *or other accident*'. The ship ran aground accidentally. Held, the list formed no particular class, so that *accident* was not to be read down: *S S Magnhild v McIntyre Brothers and Co* [1920] 3 KB 321
- The list 'any food, toy *or other product*' contained no common and dominant feature of food and toys which could limit 'other product': *Hawkins v Van Heerden* [2014] WASC 127.

Single instance class?

Can a 'class' be found in a single instance? Almost certainly, no. For example, where a statute required a company receiver to pay 'the rent *or other amounts*' payable by the company, the court held that 'rent' formed no genus, and therefore did not restrict the meaning of 'other amounts payable': *Rapid Metal Developments (Aust) Pty Ltd v Rildean Pty Ltd (No 3)* [2010] NSWSC 7. One case points otherwise:

> Building legislation required one month's prior notice before taking proceedings against 'any district-surveyor or *other person*'. Held, *other person* was read *euisdem generis* with *district-surveyor*, and did not include a tradesman working for a building owner: *Williams v Golding* (1865) LR 1 CP 69.

The result in *Williams v Golding* seems out of accord with the decisions on the *eiusdem generis* principle (although perhaps justifiable under the *noscitur a sociis* principle).

Excluding the principle

Like other principles of interpretation, the *eiusdem generis* principle is a principle of common law. It can be excluded, either expressly or by implication. Courts have acknowledged this for over a century: see, eg, *Thorman v Dowgate Steamship Co Ltd* [1910] 1 KB 410, 419. The principle can be excluded in at least four ways.

1. **Reverse the order and add an inclusionary statement**. That is, start with the general words and then introduce the specifics with a phrase such as *including without limitation*, or *including (but not limited to)*: eg, 'provisions, *including (but not limited to)* meat, fish, poultry, vegetables, and fruit.' Strictly, of course, the parenthetical (*but not limited to*) is tautologous, because *including* imports *is not limited to*. But the extra words should deter any judicial temptation to apply the *eiusdem generis* principle. A variant, used in some Australian legislation, is '*including, for example, ...*'

   It may be enough merely to reverse the order (ie, without the additional *including without limitation* or similar). There is some authority to this effect: *Inland Revenue Commissioners v Parker* [1966] AC 141, 161, 173. However, the additional words put it beyond argument.
2. **Expand the list, so as to cast the 'class' as widely as possible**. The general words then embrace more. But the technique is less than ideal, because to widen the class in this way encourages wordy drafting, with overlong lists of specifics. And it may not be judge-proof, for as long as a 'class'—no matter how broad—is apparent, the *eiusdem generis* principle remains potentially applicable.
3. **Add an expansionary word or phrase such as 'whatever', 'of whatever kind', or similar**. (See examples discussed at **whatever / whatsoever**.) However, this does not always work—see, eg, *Hughes v Winter*, above, where '*anything whatsoever*' failed to oust the principle.
4. **State that the principle is not to apply**. Commercial documents increasingly include a provision to the effect that the *eiusdem generis* principle is not to apply when interpreting the document. Sometimes this is done by express reference to the principle: eg, 'The *eiusdem generis* principle is not to apply.' Sometimes it is done less directly, by stating the principle's effect: eg, 'The principle that ... is not to apply.' Sometimes it is done by a combination of both approaches, as in the following suggested wording:

   > 'Where an example is given of a general statement, that example is not to limit the general statement. In other words, the *eiusdem generis* principle is not to apply to this document.' [Paul Clark, 'When drafting goes wrong' (2018) 82 *Conveyancer and Property Lawyer* 109, 111]

Further reading

- *Halsbury's Laws of England*, 'Statutes and Legislative Process' (vol 96, 2018) [815], [819]
- Peter Butt, *Modern Legal Drafting*, 3rd edn (Cambridge University Press, 2013) 60–64
- Joseph Kimble, '*Eiusdem Generis*: What Is it Good For?' (2016) 100(2) *Judicature* 49
- Dennis C Pearce and Robert S Geddes, *Statutory Interpretation in Australia*, 9th edn (LexisNexis, 2019) [4.34]–[4.42] (*eiusdem generis* in statutory interpretation)
- Glanville Williams, 'The Origin and Logical Implications of the *Ejusdem Generis* Rule' [1943] *Conveyancer and Property Lawyer (New Series)* 120

See also **including (but not limited to)**; **noscitur a sociis**; **whatever / whatsoever**.

election

The act of choosing one of several inconsistent remedies. Having chosen one remedy, the elector cannot later choose the other(s). For example, a purchaser may have the right to rescind a contract on some ground; but if, knowing of that right, the purchaser takes steps towards completing the contract, the purchaser will be found to have *elected* to go on with the contract, and cannot thereafter rescind on that same ground: *Scarf v Jardine* (1882) 7 App Cas 345; *Sargent v ASL Developments Ltd* (1974) 131 CLR 634.

Further reading

Halsbury's Laws of England, 'Estoppel' (vol 47, 2014) [312]

See also **approbate and reprobate; estoppel; waiver.**

eleemosynary

Greek, to Latin 'eleemosynarius', to English 'alms'. An adjective describing the purpose of an organisation (eg, *eleemosynary* charity, or *eleemosynary* corporation), namely the perpetual distribution of the founder's alms for the poor. The word's obscurity suggests that it is a term of art, but in truth it is not:

> 'The particular term "eleemosynary charity" is not a term of art with a judicially established definition. … [It] covers all charities directed to the relief of individual distress, whether due to poverty, age, sickness or other similar individual afflictions.' [*Re Armitage* [1972] Ch 438, 444–45 (Goulding J)]

Unless your readers know the meaning of *eleemosynary*, or (perhaps) unless you want the court to be in no doubt that you intend to sweep-up the case law on the meaning of *eleemosynary* in its various contexts, prefer a simpler English word. *Alms* and *alms-giving* may seem quaint. *Charitable* suffices for most purposes—but remembering that, etymologically, *eleemosnynary* looks more to the source of the money (ie, given by the founder for perpetual alms) while *charitable* looks more to the use to which the money is put. Hence it is said that *charitable* purposes might be broader than, and do not necessarily coincide with, *eleemosynary* purposes: *City of Mandurah v Australian Flying Corps* [2016] WASCA 185; (2016) 50 WAR, [50]–[51] (Buss P). But that distinction is unlikely to be important in most contexts; almost always, the simpler *charitable* suffices.

See also **SIMPLER WORDS AND PHRASES.**

ELEGANT VARIATION

The substitution of a word (usually a noun or a verb) for another earlier word (noun or verb) in the interests of variety, as a device to tease the reader's interest. Occasionally, it is true, writing would benefit from the practice, as in the following extract:

> '[T]he role of custom and its *proof* from time immemorial *proves*, once again, how legal history has a habit of *proving* the need to have some knowledge of the origins of the law.' [Michael White, 'Time Immemorial', in *Table Talk of the Selden Society in Queensland* (Supreme Court Queensland Library, 2004) 1, 14 (emphasis added)]

But often writers pursue the practice without sufficiently understanding its effect on readers. The Fowler brothers condemned it as 'cheap ornament', attracting more attention than the monotony it seeks to avoid: HW Fowler and FG Fowler, *The King's English*, 3rd edn (Oxford, Clarendon Press, 1931) 184. HW Fowler later condemned it as a 'literary vice, alluring chiefly to second-rate writers, those intent rather on expressing themselves prettily than on conveying their meaning clearly': HW Fowler, *Modern English Usage* (OUP, 1952) 130. In his view, 'the effect is to set readers wondering what the significance of the change is, only to conclude disappointedly that it has none' (*Modern English Usage*, 131).

Legal writers should think carefully before practising 'elegant variation', particularly given the principle of legal interpretation that a change in terminology signifies a change in meaning.

See **CONSISTENCY OF TERMINOLOGY; DEFINITIONS.**

ELLIPSES

Function

A series of three dots (points), indicating the omission of material; plural *ellipses*. Its most common use is to indicate omissions from quotations. In typewriter days, lawyers would insert the closest typewriter equivalent, a row of three full stops. Nowadays, word-processing programs have an ellipsis special character (three non-breaking dots), and some automatically convert a row of three full stops into an ellipsis.

Spacing

1. Where an ellipsis indicates words missing in the middle quoted text, insert a space before and after: 'The judge … said that he was not at all impressed with the evidence presented to the court.' (Original in full: 'The judge, who was pressed for time, said that he was not at all impressed with the evidence presented to the court.')
2. Where an ellipsis indicates words missing from the end of quoted text, insert a space before. On whether to insert a space after the ellipsis, practice varies: see discussion under **QUOTATIONS**.
3. Where an ellipsis indicates words missing between quoted sentences, follow the full stop at the end of the first sentence with: (1) a space, (2) the ellipsis, (3) an additional space, (4) the next sentence: 'The judge, who was pressed for time, said that he was not all impressed with the evidence presented to the court. … The court then adjourned.'

Quantity of omitted content

An ellipsis indicates only that content is omitted; it does not disclose the *quantity* of content omitted. The omission might be of a few words, or many words; and (as in point 3 under 'Spacing'), the omission might be of one sentence, or many sentences, or even one or more paragraphs. Readers wanting to know the quantity of omitted material must consult the original.

Further reading

Matthew Butterick, *Typography for Lawyers* (Jones McLure, 2010) 53–54

See also **QUOTATIONS**.

EM DASH

See **DASHES**.

email

The spelling has morphed from *electronic mail*, to *e-mail*, to *email*. Current preferred usage is *email*.

EMAILS

See **CORRESPONDENCE (LETTERS AND EMAILS)**.

EMBEDDED (NESTED) INFORMATION

The problem

A sure-fire way to hinder readers' understanding is to cram too much information into sentences. This is particularly so where the cramming embeds—or 'nests'—subsidiary material between the key parts of the sentence, severing the links between *subject-verb-object*. Readers must then hold the key information in their minds while they navigate the embedded information, only later returning to the sense of the sentence. They must 'keep track of the initial part of the construction until the nested item has been absorbed and the balance of the construction is revealed': Susan Krongold, 'Writing Laws: Making Them Easier to Understand' (1992) 24 *Ottawa Law Review* 495, 517.

Resolving the problem

Generally it is not difficult to excise embedded information and move it to a separate sentence. However, take care to preserve the logical connection between what has been moved and what remains. This may require adding a linking word or phrase, such as *therefore*, *because*, *as a result*, or similar.

Examples

Original	**Redraft**
The original form, with its fine print, broken sections, long sentences, passive verbs and nominalisations, was very hard to read. [1 sentence]	The original form was very hard to read. It [*Or, to show link*: This was because it] had fine print, broken sections, long sentences, passive verbs and nominalisations. [2 sentences]
The rule in *Bain v Fothergill*, which limits the damages that a purchaser may recover against a vendor who is unable to make title through no fault of the vendor, and which many courts condemned as inappropriate in modern conveyancing conditions, has been repealed by legislation. [1 sentence]	Legislation has repealed the rule in *Bain v Fothergill*. That rule limited the damages that a purchaser may recover against a vendor who is unable to make title through no fault of the vendor. Many courts condemned the rule as inappropriate in modern conveyancing conditions. [3 sentences]
Unless a poll is demanded a declaration by the Chairman that a resolution has on a show of hands been carried or carried unanimously, or by a particular majority, or lost, and an entry to that effect in the book containing the minutes of the proceedings of the Association shall be conclusive evidence of the fact without further proof of the number or proportion of the votes recorded in favour of or against the resolution. [1 clause]	(1) The Chairman may declare that a resolution has been carried or lost: • on a show of hands; or • unanimously; or • by a particular majority. (2) An entry of the Chairman's declaration in the Association's minute book is conclusive evidence of the fact, without further proof of the number or proportion of the votes recorded in favour of or against the resolution. (3) Clauses (1) and (2) do not apply if a poll is demanded. [3 clauses]

Judicial examples

Justice Cardozo wrote that a sentence 'may be so overcrowded with all possible qualifications that it will tumble down under its own weight': Benjamin N Cardozo, 'Law and Literature' (1939) 52 *Harvard Law Review* 472, 474. Some judges could do well to heed this advice. Two examples follow.

Example 1

Original

'The question which arises for consideration on the present appeal from a Judgment delivered by Cole J (as his Honour then was) on 1 May 1991 in proceedings which had been brought by the Appellant seeking to recover from the Respondents as Guarantors damages for the failure by a company known as Penrado Pty Limited ('Penrado') to comply with the terms of a form of Memorandum of Lease into which it had entered on 29 June 1990, is whether, by reason of the provisions of clause 10 of the Memorandum of Lease, which clause I will set out in extenso below, the Respondents were liable to the Appellant under the Guarantee notwithstanding that at the time of Penrado's vacating the premises the subject of the Memorandum of Lease and of the Appellant's re-entry into those premises, the form of Memorandum of Lease which was for a term of 5 years had not been registered pursuant to the provisions of the *Real Property Act 1900*.'

[*Telado Pty Ltd v Vincent* [1996] NSWSC 286 (NSWCA, 19 July 1996); (1996) 7 BPR 14,874 (Powell JA). Underlining added to help show sentence structure.]

[164 words; 1 sentence.]

Redraft version 1: breaking up the sentence

The question which arises for consideration on the present appeal is whether the Respondents were liable to the Appellant under the Guarantee. The appeal comes to us from a Judgment delivered by Cole J (as his Honour then was) on 1 May 1991. The Appellant had sought to recover from the Respondents as Guarantors damages for the failure by a company known as Penrado Pty Limited ('Penrado') to comply with the terms of clause 10 of a form of Memorandum of Lease into which it had entered on 29 June 1990. (I will set out clause 10 in extenso below.) The lease was for 5 years. The issue was that at the time of Penrado's vacating the premises the subject of the Memorandum of Lease and of the Appellant's re-entry into those premises, the form of Memorandum of Lease had not been registered pursuant to the provisions of the *Real Property Act 1900*.

[153 words; 6 sentences]

Redraft version 2: further revision

The question in this appeal is whether the Respondents were liable to the Appellant under the Guarantee. The appeal is from a decision of Cole J on 1 May 1991. The Appellant had sought to recover from the Respondents as Guarantors damages for the failure by Penrado Pty Limited ('Penrado') to comply with clause 10 of its lease. (I will set out clause 10 in detail below.) The lease was dated 29 June 1990 and was for 5 years. The question arises because when Penrado vacated the leased premises and the Appellant re-entered the premises, the lease had not been registered under the *Real Property Act 1900*.

[107 words; 6 sentences]

Example 2

Original

'The Court indicated at the hearing that it would not consider it appropriate, in the event that the appeal were to succeed, to proceed to consider the issue raised in the notice of contention (that being as to whether, even if the *Retail Leases Act* does apply, ss 31 and 32 do not apply in this case because the rent for the relevant renewed term had already been determined and agreed by the parties in accordance with the process provided for under the lease such that there was no scope for the operation of those statutory provisions) since that issue, though raised before the Tribunal and the Appeal Panel, was not determined by either.'

[*Pyrmont Point Pty Ltd v Westacott* [2016] NSWCA 33, [7]; (2016) 91 NSWLR 170, 172]

[114 words; 1 sentence]

Redraft version 1: breaking up the sentence

The Court indicated at the hearing that it would not consider it appropriate, in the event that the appeal were to succeed, to proceed to consider the issue raised in the notice of contention. That issue was as to whether, even if the *Retail Leases Act* does apply, ss 31 and 32 do not apply in this case because the rent for the relevant renewed term had already been determined and agreed by the parties in accordance with the process provided for under the lease. This would mean that that there was no scope for the operation of those statutory provisions. That issue, though raised before the Tribunal and the Appeal Panel, was not determined by either.

[117 words; 4 sentences]

Redraft version 2: further revision

We indicated at the hearing that, even if the appeal were to succeed, we would not consider the issue raised in the notice of contention. That issue was whether, even if the *Retail Leases Act* does apply, ss 31 and 32 do not apply in this case. Those sections could not apply if the rent for the renewed term had already been determined under the lease provisions and the parties had agreed on it. That issue was raised before the Tribunal and the Appeal Panel, but neither body decided it.

[90 words; 4 sentences]

One clause, one sentence?

Some drafters follow the convention that a provision (such as a section, paragraph or subparagraph) should contain only one sentence; and conversely, that each new sentence demands a new provision. The convention can impede readability, because the writer feels compelled to include all the relevant information in a single sentence. However, this convention has never been a 'rule': no 'rule' precludes a multi-sentence provision or clause. Indeed, you can often improve readability by dividing a lengthy clause into several sentences—provided you do not fracture the clear relationship between closely linked subject matters.

Further reading

Edwin Tanner, 'The Sanctity of the Single Legal Rule/Single Sentence Structure' (2006) 26 *Monash University Law Review* 203

See also **SENTENCE LENGTH**.

embracery

The quaintly named common-law offence of attempting to corrupt or influence a juror by such means as money, promises, threats, or persuasions. The offence is said to be obsolescent, because the same conduct comes under other, better known, offences, such as contempt of court, or conspiracy to pervert the course of justice: *R v Owen* [1976] 1 WLR 840, 841 (Lawton LJ).

See also **contempt**.

emigrate / immigrate

To *emigrate* is to leave a country permanently; to *immigrate* is to come to a country to live permanently.

EMOJI

See **EMOTICONS / EMOJI**.

EMOTICONS / EMOJI

An emoticon (from 'emotional icon') is a pictorial representation of a facial expression, using basic punctuation marks, numbers and letters, and can be created from a keyboard—such as ':)'. An emoji (plural *emoji* or *emojis*) is a digital image or icon, used to express an idea or emotion; it usually takes the form of a face, object or symbol. Both kinds of symbols are now used in electronic communications to express a person's mood. It now seems reasonably clear that an emoticon or emoji is (in an appropriate context) capable of defaming someone: eg, *Burrows v Houda* [2020] NSWDC 485.

Is there a role for emojis and emoticons in serious legal writing? Probably not. The main problem is that senders and recipients might attach different (and objectively reasonable) meanings to the same emojis or emoticons, creating misunderstanding. On that ground, a US judge refused to take judicial notice of an emoticon's meaning, except to comment that it supposedly expressed 'some form of sadness': *People v George* 2018 WL 1100942, [3] (Cal App Ct, 1 March 2018). Similarly, at least one English judge declined to find any fixed message in an emoji:

> 'The mother left a message in the caravan. … The message said that the family would be back on 3 August. It has a ☺ beside the date. [The police] found the message and say that the ☺ is winking, meaning that the mother knew they wouldn't be coming back. I don't agree that the ☺ is winking. It is just a ☺.' [*Lancashire County Council v M* [2016] EWFC 9, [13] (Peter Jackson J)]

An Australian court accepted as a valid will a draft text message (SMS) containing a 'smiley face': *Nichol v Nichol* [2017] QSC 220—though it is unclear whether the smiley face was part of the will admitted to probate in solemn form.

Further reading

Eric Goldman, 'Emojis and the Law' (2018) 93 *Washington Law Review* 1227

EMOTIONAL LANGUAGE

Good legal style does not play overtly on the reader's feelings. It does not need the prop of emotional language. Wit, yes; direct and forceful argument, yes; but emotional language, no. Research shows that US judges regard emotional language in briefs (written arguments to the court) as undermining credibility—and therefore less likely to persuade the court to accept the arguments propounded: Ryan C Black, Matthew EK Hall, Ryan J Owens, Eve M Ringsmuth, 'The Role of Emotional Language in Briefs before the US Supreme Court' (2016) 4 *Journal of Law and Courts* 377.

See also **EXAGGERATION AND HYPERBOLE**.

empanel / impanel

To swear-in a jury to try a case. *Empanel* seems now the preferred form:

> 'It is now submitted that the way in which the jury was *empanelled* was wrong in law because it contravened [the *Juries Act 1974*].' [*R v AM* [2012] EWCA Crim 2056; [2013] 1 WLR 958, [6] (Lord Judge CJ)]

However, *impanel* is still seen:

> 'No judgment after verdict in any trial by jury in any court shall be stayed or reversed by reason: (a) that the provisions of this Act about the summoning or *impanelling* of jurors … have not been complied with …' [*Juries Act 1974*, s 18(1)(a)]

EMPHASIS

In modern legal writing, the key formatting techniques for emphasis are **bold**, *italics*, or a ***combination*** of both:

> [The Departmental officers] should be in a position to demonstrate with clarity that ***this*** applicant (that is, the ***particular*** person to be removed) has been afforded a ***full and reasonable*** opportunity to seek an injunction to prevent his removal.' [*Moana v Minister for Immigration and Border Protection* [2019] FCA 659, [47] (Allsop CJ, original emphasis), in a case where immigration authorities had deported the applicant despite the currency of court proceedings which may ultimately have established his right to remain in the country.]

In typewriter times, emphasis was achieved by underlining or CAPITALS (or BOTH). However, modern word-processing facilities have rendered these techniques archaic. The only possible exception is where a page of text already contains large amounts of italics or bold (eg, because it contains a lengthy quotation from a source that contained large amounts of italics or bold), necessitating a different technique for emphasis. But that would be unusual.

The technique of **bold and underlining**, though sometimes seen, is unnecessary. **Bold** is sufficient.

See also **CAPITALS**; **FONTS**.

EN DASH

See **DASHES**.

en passant

French: in passing; by the way. No purpose except pedantry is served by preferencing this scrap of French over a plain-English translation. For example:

- 'It may be that the judge could have mentioned it to the jury *en passant* [prefer: *as an aside*; *incidentally*] …' [*R v Wilson* [2014] QB 704, [23] (Gross LJ)]
- 'Curiously enough he made no reference to observations made, *en passant* [prefer: *in passing*], by the Full Court in the Emerald-Hill Case …' [*Attorney General for Victoria v City of Knox* [1979] VR 513, 527 (McInerney J)]

en ventre sa mère

Law French: in the mother's womb—conceived but not born. The term is found most commonly in the context of the rule against perpetuities, to indicate that the life of a person conceived but not yet born is counted when deciding who qualifies as a 'life in being' or as a beneficiary under a gift. To retain the French today seems pretentious. Prefer an appropriate English translation, such as 'conceived but not yet born' or 'as-yet-unborn':

> 'Since the infant plaintiff was at the time of the accident *en ventre sa mère* [prefer: *as-yet-unborn*; *not yet born*] she was not then a person … and in fact she had no separate existence apart from her mother.' [*Watt v Rama* [1972] VR 353, 355 (Winneke CJ and Pape J)]

Further reading

Rosalind Atherton, 'Between a Fridge and a Hard Place: The Case of the Frozen Embryos, or Children en Ventre sa Frigidaire' (1998) 6 *Australian Property Law Journal* 53

enactment

A generic term for a statute, or a regulation or bylaw made under a statute. It can mean the whole of a statute (or regulation or bylaw), or part only of the whole (such as a section or Division of an Act): *Wakefield and District Light Railways Co v Wakefield Corporation* [1906] 2 KB 140, 145–46 (affirmed [1907] 2 KB 256 (CA), [1908] AC 293 (HL)). 'Any provision, long or short, which achieves a distinct objective may be an enactment': *John Lyons Charity v London Shepardi Trust* [2017] EWCA Civ 846; [2018] 2 WLR 1016, [39] (Briggs LJ; brief saving provision an 'enactment').

However, as with all words, the meaning of *enactment* can vary with context. This may call for fine distinctions. An example is the case law whether a decision is made or an action is taken 'under an *enactment*':

- enactment includes a regulation: *Allsop v North Tyneside Metropolitan Borough Council* [1992] ICR 639, 648 (Parker LJ)
- *enactment* does not include a regulation: *Rathbone v Bundock* [1962] 2 QB 260; *Ex parte Berkeley* [1963] SR (NSW) 741; *Deeley v Butcher* [1976] 1 NSWLR 1
- *enactment* does not include a rule, regulation, bylaw, or local council ordinance: *Birdon Contracting Pty Ltd v Hawkesbury City Council* [2009] NSWLEC 91; (2009) 167 LGERA 178.

Adept drafters, sensing possible doubt over the meaning of *enactment*, will clarify it. For example, a standard boilerplate clause in commercial contracts provides that a reference in the contract to an 'enactment' includes regulations, bylaws (and so on as required) made under the enactment.

See also **Act / act**.

enclosed / inclosed

Spelling

The normal spelling is *enclosed*. However, statutes in some jurisdictions have long employed the variant *inclosed*: see, eg, *Vagrancy Act 1824*; *Inclosed Lands Act 1854* (NSW).

Meaning

Like other words, *enclosed* (or *inclosed*) takes its meaning from context. The meaning is not always predictable, as the following examples show:

- In a Scottish vagrancy statute aimed at preventing unauthorised intrusion into '*enclosed* areas', a car park walled on three sides, with the entrance on the fourth side, was not 'enclosed': *Baecker v Gray* 1973 SLT (Notes) 31
- In an English vagrancy statute, an office within a university building was not an '*enclosed* area'—the term denoted an outdoor (enclosed) area, not an area within a building: *Talbot v DPP* [2000] 1 WLR 1102.
- In an Australian vagrancy statute, the fenced grounds of a university college were not an '*enclosed* area'. To be *enclosed*, the grounds would need a 'barrier of some kind' indicating exclusion of the public: *Webb v Epstein* [1955] ALR 154, 161.

- In a statute exempting landowners from the need for a licence to hunt on their '*enclosed* land', *enclosed* meant farmland enclosed by hedges, in contrast to open moorland: *Jemmison v Priddle* [1972] 1 All ER 539.

encompassing

A word of problematic extent. For example, in *Todd v Alterra at Lloyd's Ltd* [2016] FCAFC 15; (2016) 239 FCR 12 an insurance policy covered a financial adviser against claims alleging an act, error or omission 'in the performance of financial planning *encompassing* advice on approved investment products'. The court split on whether *encompassing* meant:

- 'containing'—so that if an advice dealt with both approved products and non-approved products, insurance cover would apply only to the advice about approved products (Allsop CJ and Gleeson J, [65]), or
- 'including'—so that if an advice dealt with both approved products and non-approved products, cover would extend to the advice about both kinds of products (Beach J, [83]).

encroach / encroachment

To 'encroach' (noun, 'encroachment') usually involves physical entry onto another's land or physical interference with another's rights: eg, a person *encroaches* onto a neighbour's property, or *encroaches* upon another's privacy. In land law (as in ordinary usage), an *encroachment* need not involve physical interference: eg, blocking a neighbour's access to light may constitute an *encroachment* against their property (as in *Metropolitan Housing Trust Ltd v RMC FH Co Ltd* [2017] EWHC 2609; [2018] 2 WLR 432).

encumber

See **encumbrance**.

encumbrance

Sometimes spelled *incumbrance*. A word of wide import, and not always of precise meaning. Meanings include the following:

- A mortgage, charge, lien, or similar right, over property, securing a debt or obligation.
- More generally, any proprietary right that binds other property; eg, an easement or covenant.
- Perhaps, a lease—eg, where a vendor covenants to sell land 'free of *encumbrances*' (*Caballero v Henty* (1874) 9 Ch App 447), or where a settlement precludes a married woman from 'encumbering' the property (*Baggett v Meux* (1844) 13 LJ Ch 228). But this meaning is not accepted in all jurisdictions. For example, in Australia, a lease is not an *encumbrance*: eg, *Wallace v Love* (1922) 31 CLR 156, 172; *Commissioner of State Revenue (Vic) v Bradney Pty Ltd* (1996) 34 ATR 233; *Trust Co of Australia Ltd v Valuer-General* [2008] SASC 169; (2008) 101 SASR 110.

encumbrancee / encumbrancer

The *encumbrancee* is the person having the benefit of an encumbrance; the *encumbrancer* is the person who grants the encumbrance. For example, in a mortgage, the mortgagor (borrower) is the *encumbrancer*, and the mortgagee (lender) is the *encumbrancee* (see discussion in *Cambridge Credit Corp Ltd v Lombard Australia Ltd* (1977)

136 CLR 608, 615–16). However, even legislative drafters sometimes get the terms confused. For example:

- 'Licences will automatically terminate ... if and when ... an administrator, receiver, administrative receiver or other *encumbrancer* [sic: *encumbrancee*] takes possession of ... the assets of a Licensee.' [*Copyright (Certification of Licensing Scheme for Educational Recording of Broadcasts) (Educational Recording Agency Limited) Order 2007*, cl 21]
- 'Property held upon the "statutory trust for partition" shall be held upon trust—(a) with the consent of the *incumbrancer* [sic: *encumbrancee*] of the entirety (if any) to partition the property ...' [*Conveyancing Act 1919* (NSW), s 66F(3)]

See also ***-ee* / *-or* endings**.

end

See **expiration / expiry / end**; **rescind / terminate / end**.

endorse / indorse

In normal usage, *endorse* has largely superseded *indorse*: you *endorse* a political candidate, or *endorse* an argument. However, in legal usage *indorse* is still seen in the sense of 'writing on the face of' (or 'on the back of')—eg, *indorsing* a cheque; but there too, *endorsing* is gaining ground.

engross

To produce a version of a deed or other legal document in its final form, ready for signature; hence, *engrossment*.

enjoin

A word with two distinct meanings, creating possible ambiguity. The distinction is between *enjoin to* and *enjoin from*, as in these examples:

- The court *enjoined* [meaning: *required*] the parties *to* negotiate towards a solution.
- The court *enjoined* [meaning: *stopped* (by injunction or similar order)] the parties *from* negotiating towards a solution.

enjoy

In normal usage, to *enjoy* something is to take pleasure or delight in it. In legal usage, *enjoy* carries the much more pedestrian sense of *entitled to* or *own*; pleasure or delight, actual or hoped-for, is irrelevant. When used in a pairing, *enjoy* is often redundant; for example, *enjoy* is redundant in the common pairing *use and enjoy* (as in 'I give you all the property which I currently *use and enjoy*').

See also **use and enjoy**.

enquire / inquire

In general British and Commonwealth usage:

- *enquire / enquiry* is preferred for a question: 'May I *enquire* about your health?'

- *inquire / inquiry* is preferred for an investigation: 'The police *inquiry* will establish guilt'; 'The government will establish a commission of *inquiry*.'

However, legal usage often ignores these distinctions and treats the two words as interchangeable:

- '[It] does not seem to me that it was perverse of the reviewing officer not to *inquire* further into the difficulties of travel to and from the old school. ... But conscientiously I cannot say that the Recorder was wrong in law to conclude ... that this was not a case where it was incumbent upon the local authority to *enquire* further.' [*Williams v Birmingham City Council* [2007] EWCA Civ 691, [20] (Ward LJ)]
- 'It is helpful to consider the ordinary meaning of *enquire* and *enquiring*. We were referred to various dictionary definitions. The words are synonymous with *inquire* and *inquiring* and it is clear to us that in the context [the word *enquire*] must mean "examine", "investigate" or "make an investigation into". Another synonym would be "scrutinise".' [*Portland Gas Storage Ltd v Revenue and Customs Commissioners* [2014] UKUT 270 (TCC); [2014] STC 2589, [42], on the meaning of a power to *enquire* into a claim for repayment of tax.]

US preference is *inquire* in all contexts.

ensure (that something be done)

To *ensure* that something be done is simply to *make sure* that it is done: *Reliance Permanent Building Society v Harwood-Stamper* [1944] Ch 362, 373. Thus, a promise 'to *ensure* [*make sure*] that something is done' is merely a promise that it will be done. This has two consequences. First, liability for breach of the promise may arise even without personal fault by the promisor; that is, the liability may be non-delegable: *TNT Australia Pty Ltd v Christie* [2003] NSWCA 47, [45]–[47]; (2003) 65 NSWLR 1. Second, the promise may amount to a guarantee that it will be done, and therefore be subject to the principles governing the law of guarantees—including that a variation of the underlying contract may discharge the guarantee: *Associated British Ports v Ferryways NV* [2009] EWCA Civ 189; [2009] 1 Lloyd's Rep 595.

However, regardless of these technicalities, always consider replacing the more formal *ensure* with the less formal—but no less precise—*make sure*.

See also **assure / ensure / insure**; **cause (to be done)**; **procure (that something be done)**.

entailed interest

See **fee tail**.

'ENTIRE AGREEMENT' CLAUSE

Purpose

A clause (sometimes called a 'whole agreement clause') that specifies that the parties' written agreement is the entire agreement between them.

> 'The purpose of an entire agreement clause is to preclude a party to a written agreement from thrashing through the undergrowth and finding, in the course of negotiations, some (chance) remark or statement (often long-forgotten or difficult to recall or explain) upon which to found a claim ... to the existence of a collateral warranty.' [*Inntrepreneur Pub Co (GL) v East Crown Ltd* [2000] Lloyd's Rep 611, 614 (Lightman J)]

The precise terms of 'entire agreement' clauses vary. Many are to this effect:

> 'This agreement constitutes the entire agreement between the parties as to its subject matter, and has effect to the exclusion of any other agreement or understanding between the parties in relation to that subject matter.'

Other clauses merely state that any prior representations or statements about the subject matter merge into the written terms. Yet others state that no prior representations have been made, or if made have not been relied on—more a 'no reliance' clause than an 'entire agreement' clause. But in all cases, the purpose is to preclude parties from invoking claims based on matters outside the four corners of the document.

Interpretation

Parties are generally free to insert in their contract whatever provisions they wish. This includes 'entire agreement' clauses, which courts will enforce according to their terms: *Hope v RCA Photophone of Australia Pty Ltd* (1937) 59 CLR 348. But as with all contractual provisions, the ambit of an 'entire agreement' clause depends on its precise terms; and case law shows that courts tend to interpret such clauses strictly, allowing them no wider operation than their wording requires. Hence, drafters who intend their clause to be wide-ranging must not be mealy-mouthed (*Thomas Witter Ltd v TBP Industries Ltd* [1996] 2 All ER 573, 596 (Jacob J)), particularly where the clause may be interpreted *contra proferentem.*

Examples of restrictive interpretation

1. An 'entire agreement' clause which states that the written agreement supersedes any prior *representations* may not prevent claims based on *mis*representations: *Axa Sun Life Services plc v Campbell Martin Ltd* [2011] EWCA Civ 133; [2012] 1 All ER (Comm) 268, [92]–[94] (Rix LJ).
2. An 'entire agreement' clause which states that the written agreement supersedes all agreements or understandings *preceding* the written agreement does not preclude reliance on agreements that are *contemporaneous* with the written agreement: *Cheverny Consulting Ltd v Whitehead Mann Ltd* [2007] EWHC 3130 (Ch); [2007] 3 WLR 317 (entire agreement clause not precluding collateral contract contained in a side letter).
3. An 'entire agreement' clause does not preclude reliance on extrinsic evidence aimed at illuminating the contractual language, because that is not to contradict or vary that language but to explain it: *Zurich Insurance (Singapore) Pte Ltd v B-Gold Interior Design & Construction Pte Ltd* [2008] 3 SLR(R) 1029, [113], [122]–[123]; *Scotia Homes (South) Ltd v McLean* [2012] ScotSC 111, [38] ('entire agreement' clause not precluding evidence to supplement property description); *Taluja v Australian International Academy of Education Ltd* [2011] NSWCA 416, [67]; (2011) 16 BPR 30,319 ('entire agreement' clause not precluding extrinsic evidence to identify the property being leased).
4. An 'entire agreement' clause does not preclude reliance on implied terms, because implied terms are part (albeit unexpressed) of the contract itself: *Harrison v Shepherd Homes Ltd* [2011] EWHC 1811 (TCC); *Servcorp WA Pty Ltd v Perron Investments Pty Ltd* [2016] WASCA 79, [88].
5. An 'entire agreement' clause does not preclude claims based on equitable principles, which trump reliance on contractual provisions such as 'entire contract': *Saleh v Romanous* [2010] NSWCA 274, [57]. One such principle is rectification. Thus, rectification trumps an 'entire agreement clause', because rectification seeks to enforce the terms of the parties' actual agreement: *Surgicraft Ltd v Paradigm Biodevices Inc* [2010] EWHC 1291 (Ch) ('entire agreement' clause not precluding re-instatement of a compensation clause which by mistake had dropped out of the final, signed, version of the agreement); *Macdonald v Shinko Australia Pty Ltd* [1999] 2 Qd R 152 ('entire agreement' clause not precluding rectification of an incorrect property description).

6. An 'entire agreement' clause might not preclude reliance on an estoppel arising from conduct or negotiations, whether pre-contract (*Franklins Pty Ltd v Metcash Trading Pty Ltd* [2009] NSWCA 407; (2009) 76 NSWLR 603, [33], [554]; *Caringbah Investments Pty Ltd v Caringbah Business and Sports Club Ltd* [2016] NSWCA 165, [73]), or post-contract (*Lloyd v MGL (Rugby) Ltd* [2007] EWCA Civ 153).
7. An 'entire agreement' clause might not preclude claims based on:
   - fraud (*HIH Casualty and General Insurance Ltd v Chase Manhattan Bank* [2003] UKHL 6; [2003] 2 Lloyds Rep 61; but query whether it may protect against claims based on an agent's fraud); or
   - statutory rights, such as claims for misleading and deceptive conduct (*IOOF Australia Trustees (NSW) Ltd v Tantipech* [1998] FCA 924; (1998) 156 ALR 470) and claims under 'unfair terms' legislation.

Further reading

- R Christou, *Boilerplate: Practical Clauses*, 7th edn (Sweet & Maxwell, 2015) ch 10
- IM Jackman, 'Some Judicial Fallacies Concerning Entire Agreement Clauses' (2015) 89 *Australian Law Journal* 91
- David McLauchlan, 'The Entire Agreement Clause: Conclusive or a Question of Weight?' (2012) 128 *Law Quarterly Review* 521
- Elisabeth Peden and JW Carter, 'Entire Agreement—and Similar—Clauses' (2006) 22 *Journal of Contract Law* 1

See also **contra proferentem**; **'NO RELIANCE' CLAUSE**.

entitled to

See **is entitled to**; **shall / must**.

enumeratio unius

See **expressio unius**.

ENUMERATIONS

See **LISTS AND ENUMERATIONS**.

enure / inure

To enure is to belong to or be available to, with the sense of continuing in force: eg, 'This easement enures for the benefit of Lot 1.' *Inure* means 'to habituate' (usually someone to something), or to 'harden' or 'toughen'. In the passive form with *to* (as more commonly found), it means 'to be accustomed to', or 'to put up with', something unpleasant: eg, 'He became *inured to* harship.'

The distinction between *enure* and *inure* is sometimes difficult to draw, particularly in describing a hardship that a person endures for a long time. The following example is correct usage:

> 'The equitable doctrine concerning detriment is concerned with the consequences that would *enure* to the disadvantage of a person who has been induced to change his or her position …' [*Australian Financial Services and Leasing Pty Ltd v Hills Industries Ltd* [2014] HCA 14; (2014) 253 CLR 560, [84] (Hayne, Crennan, Kiefel, Bell and Keane JJ)]

eo die

Latin: on that day; on the same day. The usage is more common in Scots law, where the civil law background tends to encourage the survival of Latinisms. However, regardless of the jurisdiction, this Latinism serves no purpose in the face of a clear English translation:

> 'On 5th December 1978 the respondent and his family were evicted from 16 Welsh Drive. *Eo die* [prefer: *On that day*] the respondent applied to the appellants for accommodation.' [*Brown v Hamilton District Council* 1983 SLT 397, 411 (Lord Dunpark)]

eo nomine

Latin: (called) by that name; properly so-called. Thus, payment of rent *eo nomine* (by that name) points towards the existence of a tenancy: *Arnold v Mann* (1957) 99 CLR 462, 489. The adequacy of the English translation renders this Latinism redundant:

- '[T]he information will only be protected if it can properly be classed as a trade secret [or if it requires] the same protection as a trade secret *eo nomine* [prefer: *properly so-called*].' [*Faccenda Chicken Ltd v Fowler* [1987] Ch 117, 137 (McNeil LJ)]
- 'However, while they did not hold him out as a director *eo nomine* [prefer: *as such*; *by that name*], they clearly authorised him on occasion to perform functions such as would lead a reasonable third party dealing with him to believe he was acting as a director …' [*Grimaldi v Chameleon Mining NL (No 2)* [2012] FCAFC 6; (2012) 200 FCR 296, 336 [133] (Finn, Stone and Perram JJ)]

epitome

A summary, as in *epitome of mortgage* (a summary of the main provisions of a mortgage). However, *epitome* is rarely seen in common usage, and carries no particular legal nuance; so prefer *summary* or *keypoints*.

epitome of title

See **abstract of title**.

equitable right to redeem

The mortgagor's right to redeem (ie, clear, pay off) a mortgage, even after the stipulated date for repayment has passed: *Gurfinkel v Bentley Pty Ltd* (1966) 116 CLR 98. To exercise this right, the mortgagor must usually give six months' notice of intention to redeem, or else pay six months' interest in place of notice: *Smith v Smith* [1891] 3 Ch 550. The right is lost after the mortgagee forecloses. It is a true term of art, better explained than replaced.

Further reading

S Bridge, E Cooke and M Dixon (eds), *Megarry & Wade's Law of Real Property*, 9th edn (Sweet & Maxwell, 2019) [24-106]

See also **equity of redemption**; **foreclosure**.

equity

Meaning

The word *equity* (plural *equities*) carries a range of meanings. They include:

- the principles and doctrines applied by courts of equity (as distinct from those applied by courts of common law)

- the courts of equity themselves ('Equity courts')
- general concepts of fairness and justice
- an obligation binding on a person's conscience
- an interest in property of a kind recognised by the courts of equity (as distinct from those recognised by the courts of common law)—eg, the mortgagor's 'equity of redemption' in the mortgaged property, and the purchaser's 'equitable interest' in the land being purchased
- the rights and obligations to which an assignee of property is subject (ie, an assignee takes subject to the 'equities' binding the assignor).

For lawyers, the context will show which meaning of 'equity' is intended. For non-legal readers, however, context is unlikely to illuminate the meaning; therefore, explain it.

Lower case or upper case?

The inexorable trend is towards *equity* (lower-case *e*), paralleling the use of lower-case initial letters in *common law*. However, in some contexts upper-case *E* (*Equity*) is still seen. In the following examples, the struck-through versions (upper case) are not strictly 'wrong', but they are no longer preferred style.

- The essence of *equity* [~~Equity~~] is the power to do *equity* [~~Equity~~].
- Various courts of *equity* [~~Equity~~] administer the principles of *equity* [~~Equity~~].
  [But compare: Jones CJ in *Eq* [abbreviation for Jones, Chief Judge in *Equity*, in jurisdictions where the courts have a separate Equity Division—always upper case *E*].
- The principles of *equity* [~~Equity~~] traditionally temper the principles of the common law.
- The court said that *equity* [~~Equity~~] follows the *law* [~~Law~~].
- A key maxim is that '*equity* [~~Equity~~] will not assist a volunteer'.
- Under the doctrine of *equitable* [~~Equitable~~] estoppel, the promisor's conduct gives rise to an *equity* [~~Equity~~] in favour of the promisee.
- Time is not of the essence in *equity* [~~Equity~~].
- Rectification is an *equitable* [~~Equitable~~] remedy.
- Priority between *equitable* [~~Equitable~~] interests is normally determined by the 'first in time' principle.
- As between rival claimants, the enquiry is who has the better *equity* [~~Equity~~].
- This case is within the *equity* [~~Equity~~] of the statute.
- The courts distinguish between an *equitable* [~~Equitable~~] interest and a mere *equity* [~~Equity~~].

equity of redemption

The mortgagor's interest in the property remaining after granting a mortgage: *Duchess of Hamilton v Countess of Dirlton* (1654) 1 Ch R 165, 167; 21 ER 539; *Kreglinger v New Patagonia Meat and Cold Storage Co Ltd* [1914] AC 25. As with *equitable right to redeem*, a true of art; when addressing non-lawyers, it is better explained than replaced.

Further reading

- Kevin Gray and Susan Francis Gray, *Elements of Land Law*, 5th edn (Oxford University Press, 2009) [6.2.6]–[6.2.10]
- S Bridge, E Cooke and M Dixon (eds), *Megarry & Wade's Law of Real Property*, 9th edn (Sweet & Maxwell, 2019) [24-083]–[24-089]

See also **clog on the equity of redemption**.

equity's darling

A colourful tag for a bona fide purchaser of a legal estate in land, who (at the time of purchasing) had no notice of an existing equitable interest in the land. A court administering equitable jurisdiction allows such a purchaser to take free of the equitable interest—hence, 'equity's darling'. For a twist, see www.equitysdarling.co.uk/.

erratum

Latin: an error; plural *errata*. Used to indicate an error, usually in writing or printing. Sometimes used interchangeably with *corrigendum* ('to be corrected').

See also **corrigendum**.

errors and misdescriptions

A compendious term from conveyancing law, covering the kinds of matters for which a purchaser may have a remedy against the vendor in compensation, rescission, or termination. The term is hallowed by convention, but its meaning is difficult to pin down. The concept is of an omission to disclose, or a misstatement about, a matter of fact or title that makes the property different from that which the purchaser contracted to purchase.

Further reading

- *Halsbury's Laws of England*, 'Conveyancing' (vol 23, 2016) [456] (remedies for misdescription)
- Peter Butt, *Standard Contract for the Sale of Land in New South Wales*, 2nd edn (LBC Information Services, 1998) [6.8]–[6.10] (detailed case law on errors and misdescriptions)

ESCALATION CLAUSE

A contractual provision by which the price increases according to a set formula, or according to market fluctuations, or according to rises in the consumer price index. Examples are found in leases (eg, tying rent increases to an external index) and in building contracts (tying increases to industry-wide price increases, or wages growth).

See also **RATCHET CLAUSE**.

escheat

Law French: expire, come to an end. A feudal common-law doctrine under which an estate in land reverted to the lord of whom it was held. Escheat occurred in two main situations:

1. Escheat *propter delictum tenentis* ('for the tenant's [ie, owner's] crime'), where the landholder was attainted (that is, convicted and sentenced to death) for felony.
2. Escheat *propter defectum sanguinis* ('for failure of blood'), where the landholder died without leaving an heir.

Escheat could occur in other situations also, but they were rare: see T Cyprian Williams, 'The Fundamental Principles of the Present Law of Ownership of Land' (1931) 75 *Solicitors' Journal* 843.

Where the land was held of an intermediate ('mesne') lord, it escheated to that lord; otherwise, it escheated to the Crown. The lord did not take the land by succession or inheritance. Rather, the holder's estate having come to an end, 'the lord is in by his own right': *Attorney-General of Ontario v Mercer* (1883) 8 App Cas 767, 772 (PC).

For most practical purposes, escheat has been abolished and its function superseded by statute. Escheat *propter delictum tenentis* has been replaced by a statutory forfeiture regime (beginning with the *Forfeiture Act 1870*). Escheat *propter defectum sanguinis* was abolished in relation to estates of persons dying after 1925 (*Administration of Estates Act 1925*, s 45(1)(d)). A process akin to escheat still occurs where property is disclaimed by a liquidator (*Companies Act 2006*, s 1013) or by a trustee in bankruptcy (*Insolvency Act 1986*, ss 178, 315).

'Escheat' is a term of art, rarely used and even more rarely understood. Unless there is good reason to use it, prefer a plain-English equivalent. To write that property 'escheats' to the Crown would, to most modern readers, seem inscrutably obscure. Prefer 'reverts to' the Crown, or 'vests in' the Crown.

See also **bona vacantia**.

escrow

Pronunciation

In the US, pronounced *es-kroh*. In Britain, traditionally pronounced *es-krau*, but the British pronunciation is slowly being overwhelmed by the US.

Meaning: in law of deeds

In British and Commonwealth legal usage, an escrow is a specific form of document: namely, a deed that has been 'delivered' subject to a condition that must be fulfilled before the deed comes into full effect. Lawyers commonly speak of delivery 'in escrow', but more precise usage is delivery 'as an escrow': but cf *Bolton Metropolitan Borough Council v Torkington* [2004] Ch 66 (Peter Gibson LJ, using 'in escrow' and 'as an escrow' interchangeably).

The condition imposed on delivery may be express (eg, when a specified date arrives, or when another party to the transaction does some act), or it may be implied (eg, where a vendor delivers deed of conveyance on the implied condition that title is not to pass until the purchaser pays the purchase price: *Walker v The Ware (etc) Railway Co* (1865) 35 Beav 52, 58; 55 ER 813, 816). If the condition never occurs, the deed never becomes operative; if and when the condition occurs, the deed operates retrospectively from the date of delivery.

Whether delivery is conditional or unconditional is a question of what the parties intended. That intention can be gathered from the parties' words or conduct before or when executing the deed, or from post-execution events to the extent that they evidence the parties' intention at the time of execution: *Bowker v Burdekin* (1843) 11 M & W 128, 147; 152 ER 744, 751; *Naas (Lady) v Westminster Bank Ltd* [1940] AC 366; *Federal Commissioner of Taxation v Taylor* (1929) 42 CLR 80, 87; *Mirzikinian v Tom & Bill Waterhouse Pty Ltd* [2009] NSWCA 296, [39]–[48].

The kinds of conditions that parties can impose on delivery are many and varied. However, there are two limitations: (1) a deed cannot be delivered on a condition that it is to bind the deed-maker only when *that* person does some future act (for that would negate its binding effect on the deed-maker); (2) a deed cannot be delivered on a condition that it is to become effective when the deed-maker dies (for then it is a testamentary disposition, requiring the formalities for a will): *Foundling Hospital v Crane* [1911] 2 KB 367, 375, 379; *Re Carile* [1920] VLR 427.

Meaning: generally

In commercial vernacular, *escrow* has expanded beyond the law of deeds to mean something (often a document) held on trust until a condition is fulfilled. Hence the verb 'to escrow'. This usage still reflects the concept of 'conditional delivery'—in the sense that the thing is held by a third party until the condition is fulfilled—but otherwise any nexus with the law of deeds has disappeared. Thus, stock exchange listing rules commonly provide that restricted securities cannot be dealt with for a specified 'escrow period'; or that the holder of certificates must give them to a bank or recognised trustee to hold 'in escrow' (akin to holding 'on trust').

More recently, *escrow* has expanded even further, to include the more general sense of funds or property 'held back' for certain purposes. Although *Black's Law Dictionary* once labelled this usage a 'perversion' (4th edn, 1951; not repeated in the current edn), it is now widely accepted.

Examples of general meaning

- **Building and construction industry**: a developer may enter into an 'escrow arrangement' with a building contractor, under which the developer deposits funds into an 'escrow account', to be held by a trustee. The purpose is to ensure that the contractor is paid for work done. See www.citysolicitors.org.uk/clls/clls-precedent-documents/construction-law-escrow-agreement/.
- **Mergers and acquisitions**: a party may deposit assets (such as cash or stock) into an 'escrow account', to be held by a trustee (the 'escrow agent') pending satisfaction of a contractual contingency or condition. For example, buyers may require a portion of the purchase price to be placed 'in escrow' to secure the seller's post-closing obligations, such as purchase price adjustments and indemnification obligations.
- **Information technology**: a source code may be stored by an 'escrow agent', on terms to release the code when specified events occur.

Plain-language alternatives

There is no magic in *escrow*. If the reader of a document or statute is unlikely to understand it, plain-language equivalents are not hard to find. For example:

- **In the context of a conditional deed**: 'This deed comes into operation only when X [condition] is performed.'
- **In the context of a third party holding a document (or property) in escrow**: 'A holds this deed (or property) on trust until X [condition] is fulfilled.'

Further reading

- 'Escrow', in *Law Words* (Centre for Plain Legal Language, University of Sydney, 1995) 16; at www.clarity-international.net/plain-language-resources/general-resources
- Nicholas Seddon, *Seddon on Deeds* (Federation Press, 2015) ch 3

See also **DEED (document)**; **delivery (of deeds)**; **in escrow**; **signed, sealed and delivered**.

escrow period

The period during which a deed or document remains conditional: *Monarch Petroleum NL v Citco Australia Petroleum Ltd* [1986] WAR 310, 356.

See also **escrow**.

essential term (of contract)

See **condition**.

estate or interest

A lawyer's conventional pairing, exhibiting the familiar tendency of using multiple words where one may well suffice.

What is an 'estate'?

As a term of art in relation to land, *estate* reflects—historically, at least—the landholder's 'status' in relation to the land. In medieval legal theory, a land 'owner' owned merely an *estate in* the land, not the land itself (which was owned by the Crown, and which the estate 'owner' merely 'held of the Crown'). English law recognised three 'estates' in land, distinguished by their potential duration: the life estate, the estate in fee tail, and the estate in fee simple.

Non-technically, *estate* is also used loosely to mean 'property', which may in turn be real property (land) or personal property (non-land), or both. Thus, a will may say: 'I leave all of my *estate* [ie, everything I own] to Jane.'

What is an 'interest'?

An *interest* is any kind of right. The term is normally used of property (eg, 'my interest in my house; 'my business interests'), but can extend to rights more generally (eg, 'a legal interest in a fair trial'). In the context of *estate or interest* in land, an 'estate' is always an 'interest', although an 'interest' is not necessarily an 'estate'.

Do you need both 'estate' and 'interest'?

It was once said that a drafter who uses the expression *estate or interest* must intend to distinguish *estate* from *interest*—otherwise, why use both terms?: *Re Thomas* (1896) 33 Ch D 166, 171 (Kay J). But in reality, most legal drafters use the pairing *estate or interest* out of habit, as a single, composite expression, not intending any technical distinction between the two words. Nor do they necessarily use the composite expression consistently. For example, in an Australian statute, the drafter used (apparently interchangeably), 'estate', 'interest', 'estate or interest', and 'estate and interest': *Mining Act 1978* (WA).

Except in the rarest of technical circumstances, the pairing *estate or interest* (and its variant, *estate and interest*) is unnecessary. Almost always, *interest* (alone) suffices, because an *estate or interest* (in land) is sufficiently described as an *interest* (in land): *R (Flynn) v Communities and Local Government Secretary* [2014] EWHC 390 (Admin), [34]–[35]; [2014] 1 WLR 3270. Exceptionally, it is sometimes necessary to distinguish between an *estate* (in land) and an *interest* (in land): eg, *Law of Property Act 1925*, s 1, which separately specifies the only *estates* in land that are capable of existing and the only *interests* in land that are capable of existing. But that is no justification for preserving the pairings *estate or interest* and *estate and interest* in everyday legal parlance. In some jurisdictions, standard Acts-interpretation legislation achieves the desired end (ie, one word suffices) by defining *estate* to mean (in effect) 'any estate or interest', allowing drafters confidently to use *estate* (not *interest*, and not the pairing) in statutes: eg, in Australia, *Acts Interpretation Act 1901* (Cth), s 2B.

The following example removes the unnecessary pairing:

Original	Better	Better still
I give to my wife my *estate or interest* in my house in X Street.	I give to my wife my *interest* in my house in X street.	I give my wife my house in X Street.

Further reading

'Estate or Interest', in *Law Words* (Centre for Plain Legal Language, University of Sydney, 1995), 19; see at www.clarity-international.net/plain-language-resources/general-resources/

See also **fee simple**; **fee tail**; **life estate**; **personal estate**.

estoppel

Law French, *estoupail*, bung or cork. Few legal doctrines are more complex than estoppel. Variant forms include issue estoppel, conventional estoppel, estoppel per rem judicatum, estoppel by deed, estoppel by conduct, estoppel in pais, estoppel by acquiescence, promissory estoppel, proprietary estoppel, and (mainly in the US) collateral estoppel. The concept underlying them all is that persons may be prevented ('estopped') by conduct or conscience, or both, from taking a course of action.

All *estoppel* variants are terms of art, with multiple limitations and qualifications. To encapsulate the full meaning of any of them in a concise, plain-English phrase is probably impossible. In dealings between lawyers—who can be expected to know legal terms of art—it is, of course, acceptable to use *estoppel* in any of its variant forms. But when addressing non-lawyers, unless the technical term *estoppel* must for some (rare) reason be used, it is usually unnecessary to attempt a detailed exposition. Its sense is adequately conveyed by the simpler, non-technical, *stopped* or *prevented*. To illustrate (assuming that the writer is addressing a non-legal audience):

- 'In the *High Trees* case, Lord Denning held that the landlord was *estopped* [prefer: *prevented*] from increasing the rent.'
- 'A court may rule that a person's conduct *estops* [prefer: *stops*, *prevents*] them from denying the force of their representation.'
- 'A person who has chosen to enforce one of two competing rights is *estopped* [prefer: *precluded*] from later enforcing the other.'

Further reading

Halsbury's Laws of England, 'Estoppel' (vol 47, 2014) [301]–[311]

See also ***Anshun*** **estoppel**; **election**; **issue estoppel**; **res judicata / res adjudicata**; **waiver**.

et al

Latin: abbreviation for 'and others'. US usage often retains the full stop (*et al.*), but British legal usage now drops it (*et al*). The usage *et. al* is always wrong. Unabbreviated forms, rarely now seen, are *et alii* (masculine), *et aliae* (feminine), *et alia* (neuter).

See **also etc**.

et cetera

See **etc**.

et seq

Latin: abbreviation for *et sequens* ('and following') or *et sequentes paginae* ('and the following pages'). In modern British and Commonwealth usage, *seq* takes no full stop (*et seq*), but US usage generally retains it (*et seq.*). The plural form is *et seqq* (in the US, *et seqq.*).

Although *et seq* and its variants are unlikely to disappear, their English substitutes sufficiently carry their meanings. For example:

- *See p 5 et seq*: this refers the reader to page 5 and the immediately following page, ie, page 6. Prefer: *See pages 5 and 6.*
- *See p 5 et seqq* (or *See pp 5 et seqq*): this refers the reader to page 5 and the following pages, but without specifying how many following pages (except that it is more than 1). Prefer: *See pages 5 and following.* Better still, add the page span: *See pages 5–9.*

In practice, many legal authors ignore the distinction between *seq* (singular) and *seqq* (plural), and use *seq* for both singular ('page following') and plural ('pages following')—leaving careful readers perplexed. This makes the English ('page' vs 'pages') even more preferable.

See also **ff**.

etc

Latin: abbreviation for *et cetera* (and other things; the rest). US usage often retains the full stop ('etc.'), but more recent British usage omits it ('etc'). Italics are not used, because the expression is fully anglicised. 'Etc' is not appropriate for 'other people', but only for 'other things'. (If wedded to Latin, use *et al* for people: 'The guests were John, Joan, Jeremy, *et al*.' Better still, prefer 'and others'; or rewrite, 'The guests included John, Joan, and Jeremy.')

Although often used, 'etc' is a lazy expression—whether in its full form (*et cetera*), or abbreviated form ('etc'), or symbol ('&c'). This is because it is inherently vague. What 'other things'? Do they not matter? If they do matter, is the writer too lazy or indifferent to bother identifying them? Regardless of the answer, 'etc' transfers the burden of identification from writer to reader. It should have no place in legal writing. Nevertheless, it finds its way into legal advices and contracts, and even into the title of statutes (eg, *Health and Safety at Work etc. Act 1974*).

When faced with 'etc' in legal documents, judges must try to give it *some* meaning, as in the following examples:

- In a gift by will of 'the whole of my property and effects, that is to say, my box, clothes, bedding, &c., &c.', the symbols meant 'and all other things': *Gover v Davis* (1860) 29 Beav 222, 225; 54 ER 612, 613 (Romilly MR).
- In a contract for the sale of land, together with 'buildings, material, &c.' the symbol referred to 'material' (on the facts, bricks), not a right of way: *Re Walmsley and Shaw's Contract* [1917] 1 Ch 93.
- In a will, the testatrix directed her trustees 'to divide the residue of my estate among various charities, Nursing Associations, Infirmaries, *etc.*, to be selected by them.' Held, *etc.* was to be read *eiusdem generis* with the preceding associations, all of which were charitable: *Milne's Trustees v Davidson* 1956 SLT 34.
- In a charterparty, an exclusion clause applied if the vessel was detained 'by causes over which the charterers have no control, viz, quarantine, ice, hurricanes, blockade, … *etc*.' Held, *etc* meant 'all the rest'; that is, the listed items (ending with *etc*) were examples of 'causes over which the charterers have no control', but did not reduce the width of those words: *Ambatielos v Anton Jurgens Margarine Works* [1923] AC 175.

See also **euisdem generis**; **et al**.

EUPHEMISMS

There is a place in legal writing, as in literature generally, for euphemisms. But a euphemism cannot replace legal precision, and it may be necessary sometimes to sacrifice the politeness of euphemism for the bluntness of facts, no matter how tasteless it may seem. Thus, a court set aside a woman's conviction for 'walking with a member of [Cambridge] University', because there was no such criminal offence; the expression was a euphemism for soliciting for an immoral purpose—but the charge did not use that wording: *Ex parte Daisy Hopkins* (1891) 61 LJ KB 240.

event of default

Legal shorthand for an occurrence that triggers a party's remedies. Commercial documents often define or list agreed 'events of default'. These defined or listed events sometimes include occurrences that are not strictly defaults (in the sense of failure to perform an obligation)—eg, if a creditor presents a winding-up petition—but that the parties have agreed to treat as if they were defaults.

See also **fail (to do something)**.

every

Does *every* mean *all*? Not necessarily. Depending on context, *every* can mean *each one* (individually). So, in *Brown v Jarvis* (1860) 29 LJ Ch 595 a testator gave property to A and B, and then 'after the decease of *every* of them', to A's children. Lord Campbell LC held that *every* meant *each one of them*, not *all of them*, so that as each died his or her share went to A's children.

See also **each and every**.

ex abundanti cautela

Latin: for more abundant caution—in the sense of, 'to be on the safe side', 'to make it perfectly clear'. Variants are: *ex abundantiori cautela*, 'to be even more on the safe side'; *per majorem cautelam*, 'for greater caution'. The Latin is unlikely to communicate to most readers—so prefer an English translation. For example:

- 'My Lords, such inference as to the ambit of enacting words that can be derived from the presence of a proviso or the exception is notoriously a weak one, since the proviso or exception may have been inserted *per majorem cautelam* [prefer: *for greater caution*].' [*R v Goodchild (No 2)* [1978] 1 WLR 578, 583 (Lord Diplock)]
- 'I can think of no other purpose for the addition of this subsection [in the statute] than *ex abundanti cautela* [prefer: *for additional caution*] to counteract any argument, however ill-founded, that a way which runs, for instance, through a ford, is not a way "upon or over land".' [*A-G v Brotherton* [1992] 1 AC 425, 438 (Lord Oliver of Aylmerton)]
- 'Dixon J appeared to treat the additional words as having been added merely *ex abundanti cautela* [prefer: *for more abundant caution; to make the point perfectly clear*].' [*Crouch v Commissioner for Railways* (1985) 159 CLR 22, 41 (Mason, Wilson, Brennan, Deane and Dawson JJ)]

See also **for the avoidance of doubt**.

ex adverso

Latin: opposite to (especially when describing the location of land or buildings in relation to other land or buildings). The phrase survives mainly in Scottish law, and in the judgments of Scottish-trained judges. There seems no point in retaining the Latin, in the face of the clear, standard English translation, particularly as the Latin is apt to mislead most readers by suggesting the meaning 'adversely'. For example:

> 'Counsel submitted that the easement [entitled] the appellants to take vehicles across the sidewalk between their lots and the roadway … in order to park on the lots, and was incompatible with the current use of the roadway *ex adverso* [prefer: *opposite*] the lots for parking.' [*J & O Operations Ltd v The Kingston and Saint Andrew Corp* [2012] UKPC 7, [12] (Lord Reed)]

ex contractu

Latin: from the contract; eg, liability arises '*ex contractu* or *ex delicto*' ('from the contract or from the law of tort'). The Latin *ex contractu* carries no more meaning than the English 'from [the] contract' or 'by [the] contract', so prefer the English:

- '[A] director's duty of care and skill … arises from a particular relationship, brought about by lawfully permitted acts, which generates mutual rights and obligations *quasi ex contractu* [prefer: *as if by contract*] though not in fact by contract.' [*O'Keefe v Caner* [2017] EWHC 1105 (Ch), [113] (HH Judge Keyser QC)]
- '[I]n my opinion, the resulting cause of action is tortious and in no sense arises *ex contractu* [prefer: *from the contract*] …' [*Mutual Life & Citizens' Assurance Co Ltd v Evatt* (1968) 122 CLR 556, 570 (Barwick CJ)]

See also **ex delicto**; **quasi**.

ex curia

Latin: out of court; in a non-judicial context. Used in two main senses:

1. To mean simply 'out of court': eg, 'I propose an *ex curia* settlement'. Prefer the plain English, *out of court*: 'I propose an out-of-court settlement'.
2. To refer to a judge's utterances made elsewhere than in a judgment—'out of court' in that sense—for example, in a seminar paper or legal journal. Statements made *ex curia* lack the precedential force they would have if made in a judgment (although they are accorded due deference, particularly if the judge is an expert in the field). The Latin carries no more meaning than an appropriate English translation, so prefer the English. For example:
    - 'McHugh J, writing *ex curia* [prefer: *in a non-judicial context*; *in a non-judicial capacity*] predicted that neither [proximity nor reliance] would last forever as universal *indicia* for a duty of care at common law.' [*Pyrenees Shire Council v Day* [1998] HCA 3; (1998) 192 CLR 330, [238] (Kirby J)]
    - 'Here, I would refer to an *ex curia* opinion [prefer: an opinion expressed out of court; an opinion expressed in a law review article] of Lord Halsbury on this subject. His Lordship said …' [*Wee Soon Kim Anthony v Law Society of Singapore* [1988] SGHC 44; [1988] SLR 510, [22] (Chan Sek Keong JC)]

ex debito justitiae

Latin: out of the obligation of justice (ie, 'as of right'; 'because justice necessarily demands it'). There is no magic in the Latin; an appropriate English translation always suffices. For example:

- 'But if the letter [serving the summons] is returned undelivered, and nevertheless, notwithstanding its return, a judgment or order by default should afterwards be obtained, it is irregular and will be set aside *ex debito justitiae* [prefer: *because justice demands it*].' [*R v London County Quarter Sessions Appeals Committee* [1956] QB 682, 694 (Denning LJ)]
- 'The right to wind up a company is by statute a discretionary right. Yet the books and authorities point out that in many cases as against the company an unpaid creditor on a winding-up petition is entitled to a winding up order *ex debito justitiae* [prefer: *as of right*; *automatically*]. This means no more than that, in accordance with settled practice, the court can only exercise its discretion in one way, namely, by granting the order sought.' [*Re Pritchard* [1963] 1 Ch 502, 520–21 (Upjohn LJ)]

ex delicto

Latin: arising out of a tort; as a result of a tort. The English translation always suffices.

See also **ex contractu**.

ex dolo malo non oritur actio

Latin: a right of action does not arise from fraud. An early use appears in Lord Mansfield's judgment in *Holman v Johnson*:

> 'The principle of public policy is this: *ex dolo malo non oritur actio*. No Court will lend its aid to a man who founds his cause of action upon an immoral or an illegal act.' [*Holman v Johnson* (1775) 1 Cowp 341, 343; 98 ER 1120, 1121 (Lord Mansfield, providing a useful translation)]

Despite this impeccable pedigree, an English translation—in fact, along the lines suggested by Lord Mansfield himself in the quoted extract—will do just fine.

See also **ex turpi causa non oritur actio**.

ex facie

Latin: on the face of it; at face value. The English translation is perfectly adequate:

> '[The cited decision] seemed to me to be *ex facie* [prefer: *at face value*] helpful to [the litigant] on the first of the two points, ... [But] as regards the second point, ... it seemed to me increasingly quite difficult to see why it was not both *ex facie* [prefer: *at face value*] helpful to [the litigant] and possibly correct as a matter of Russian law.' [*Enka Insaat Ve Sanayi AS v OOO 'Insurance Company Chubb'* [2019] EWHC 3568 (Comm); [2020] Bus LR 463, [106] (Baker J)]

ex gratia

Latin: out of grace; as a matter of grace; often in contrast to *ex lege* ('as a matter of legal compulsion'). A payment made as a favour, not as a legal obligation (*ex debito justitiae*). The Latinism is no better than its English translation, so prefer the translation.

See also **ex debito justitiae**; **ex lege**.

ex lege

Latin: according to law; as a matter of law. Sometimes (as in the following extracts) with the sense of 'compelled by law'; sometimes italicised, sometimes not. There is no benefit in retaining the Latin; prefer an English translation:

- '[T]he Crown having legally taken [the land], is it bound to pay compensation *ex lege* [prefer: *compelled by law*] or is the offer to pay compensation ex gratia ...?' [*Attorney-General v De Keyser's Royal Hotel Ltd* [1920] AC 508, 523 (Lord Dunedin); on the facts, the Crown took the land by statutory authority. In the report, 'ex lege' is not italicised.]
- 'The relations [between the Crown and the policeman] arose out of the Act and *ex lege* [prefer: *were compelled by law*]: the Crown and the policeman were not master and servant in the legal sense ...' [*Attorney-General for NSW v Perpetual Trustee Co Ltd* (1952) 85 CLR 237, 255 (McTiernan J). In the report, 'ex lege' is italicised.]

See also **ex gratia**.

ex mero motu

Latin: of one's own free will; of his or her own motion (usually in the context of a judge deciding on a course of action in a trial). An appropriate English translation captures the Latin perfectly—so discard the Latin. For example:

- 'I agree, and in order not to fall behind my learned brethren in Latinity, I express my conclusion in this way: that the injuries sustained by the respondent were due to a course which he adopted *ex mero motu* [prefer: *of his own free will*; *willingly*].' [*Cutler v United Dairies (London) Ltd* [1933] 2 KB 297, 307 (Eve J)]
- 'The principal justifications *for proceeding ex mero motu* [prefer: *for the judge to proceed without being prompted*] are to protect the respective interests of the child and of the administration of justice.' [*Re M (a minor) (Contempt of court: Committal of Court's Own Motion* [1999] Fam 263, [40] (Ward LJ)]
- 'In all cases of contempt, the Court has power to act not only summarily but *ex mero motu* [prefer: *of its own motion*; *unprompted*].' [*R v Fletcher* [1935] HCA 1; (1935) 52 CLR 248, 258 (Evatt J)]

ex nudo pacto non oritur actio

Latin: no right of action arises from a bare promise (ie, a promise unsupported by valuable consideration). The Latin carries no more legal meaning than the English, so prefer the English.

See also **nudum pactum**.

ex officio

Latin: by virtue of office; by reason only of holding the office. While the English translation captures the meaning of the Latin—which is generally sufficient reason to prefer the English—this particular Latinism is now standard English, at least in commerical and administrative contexts. Being standard English, it is not italicised.

ex parte

Latin: from one side; ie, in the absence of the other party. Used in the context of applications heard in the absence of the party against whom the order is sort (eg, for reasons of urgency, or where the purpose of the application would be frustrated if the other party knew of the proceedings); hence, '*ex parte* hearing' or '*ex parte* proceedings'. An explanation, longer than a literal translation, would be 'without notice being given to the other party'. In England and Wales, *ex parte* has yielded to *without notice* (as part of the Woolf Reforms); hence, 'proceedings without notice'.

See also **inter partes**; **WOOLF REFORMS**.

ex post facto

Latin: after the event; after the deed is done; retrospectively. Thus, a law may be expressed to operate *ex post facto* to validate an act that was unlawful when committed. As with many other Latin terms in law, the English translation captures the Latin meaning—which generally justifies preferring the English. But for many readers, this Latin term will have become standard English; if so, no harm results from using it when addressing them.

ex proprio motu

See **proprio motu**.

ex tempore

Latin: from time; extemporaneously (ie, without needing more time). Sometimes one word: *extempore*. In court usage, generally referring to a judgment given immediately after hearing argument (or very shortly afterwards), and usually orally, without the judge taking further time to reflect and to put reasons in writing—that is, without 'reserving' the decision. The English translations 'extemporaneously', 'immediately', or 'without taking further time to consider', adequately capture the meaning. So too does 'unreserved'—although to non-lawyers that may carry the misleading sense of 'completely endorsing' rather than 'without needing further time' [to reach a decision]. For example:

- 'The judge then gave an *extempore* [prefer: *immediate*; *extemporaneous*] judgment.' [*Vallee v Birchwood* [2014] Ch 271; [2013] EWHC 1449 (Ch), [10] (Jonathan Gaunt QC)]
- '[The party's] application was dismissed by Jagot J, who delivered an *ex tempore* [*immediate*; *unreserved*] judgment on 17 October 2012.' [*Wellington Capital Ltd v Australian Securities and Investments Commission* [2014] HCA 43, [4]; (2014) 254 CLR 288, 296 (French CJ, Crennan, Kieffel and Bell JJ)]

ex turpi causa non oritur actio

Latin: no cause of action arises out of illegality. Often abbreviated to *ex turpi causa*. Generally used in the context where A claims a right against B, and B's defence is that A's claim arises out of A's own illegal act. The rationale is not so much to protect B as to protect the public, by precluding litigants from using the courts to enforce rights arising from illegal acts: *Holman v Johnson* (1775) 1 Cowp 341, 343; 98 ER 1120, 1121 (Lord Mansfield); *Chai Sau Yin v Liew Kwee Sam* [1962] AC 304, 311 (PC). The English translation carries the sense perfectly, making the Latin redundant. Indeed, as with many Latin maxims in law, the Latin injects an unwarranted sense of precision into a principle that is inherently problematic. So much so, that the doctrine of illegality has been described as 'among the most heavily litigated rules of common law, and by the end of the twentieth century it had become encrusted with an incoherent mass of inconsistent authority': *Bilta (UK) Ltd v Nazir (No 2)* [2015] UKSC 23; [2015] 2 WLR 1168, [61] (Lord Sumption).

Further reading

Michael Poulsom, 'Acquiring Property Rights Ex Turpi Causa' (2019) 83 *Conveyancing and Property Lawyer* 149 (discussing conflicting case law)

See also **ex dolo malo non oritur actio**.

EXAGGERATION AND HYPERBOLE

Deliberate exaggeration and hyperbole are rarely appropriate in legal writing. Let your arguments speak for themselves, free from embellished facts or extravagant statements. For example, overwrought prose, such as in the following extract, has no place in judgments:

> 'The law should represent the truth at all times. Fiction should be for the novelists and fantasy for the clairvoyants. Labyrinthian and sophistical explanations should be for superannuated philosophers resting in the shade of melancholy maples as the sun of reality disappears into the mystic darkness of conjecture and superstition.' [*Meisel v Little* 180 A 2d 772, 781 (Pa 1962) (Musmanno J). For other hyperbolic outbursts of this judge, see Robert Megarry, *A New Miscellany-at-Law*, ed Bryan A Garner, Hart, 2005) 205–09.]

A US appeal court criticised (and reversed) a trial judge who described an employer's increase in overtime demands as having '*shot up* from an average of about 50 hours per week for the preceding two months to a *whopping* 201 hours', when in fact, averaged over the number of employees, it amounted to less than 1 hour per week per employee: *Midwest Stock Exchange Inc v National Labour Relations Board* 635 F 2d 1255, 1260 (7th Cir 1980, emphasis added).

This is not to deny a role for (appropriate) emphasis. For example, a statute may authorise a tribunal to certify that a claim is '*totally* without merit'. Here, *totally* provides emphasis, but does not constitute exaggeration (and in fact means 'bound to fail', or 'hopeless', or '[having] no rational basis': *R v Secretary of State for the Home Department* [2016] EWCA Civ 82; [2016] 1 WLR 2793, [17]). But a defendant's argument that the plaintiff's claim is '*totally* without merit' may be inappropriate exaggeration—'without merit' would suffice.

Exaggeration and hyperbole are not merely unseemly; they can be counter-productive. Their overwrought nature suggests to the audience, 'you need not take this seriously'—which is a less-than-ideal way to seek to persuade. And there is always the potential embarrassment that an opponent's argument, so extravagantly derided, may turn out to be correct:

> 'There are good reasons not to call an opponent's argument "ridiculous," which is what [the defendant] calls [the plaintiff's] principal argument here. The reasons include civility; the near-certainty that overstatement will only push the reader away ...; [and here, that] the argument that [the defendant] derides as ridiculous is instead correct.' [*Bennett v State Farm Mutual Automotive Insurance Co* 731 F 3d 584, 584–85 (6th Cir, 2013)]

See also **EMOTIONAL LANGUAGE**.

EXAMPLES

See **NOTES AND EXAMPLES**.

excambion

In Scots law, an exchange of one piece of land for another. For example:

> 'It is obviously possible for house builders to structure a transaction as a true "land swap", or in other words a form of *excambion*, with the two parts of the transaction dependent on each other.' [*Persimmon Homes Ltd v Bellway Homes Ltd* [2011] CSOH 149, [8] (Lord Drummond Young)]

except (as / when / where)

Variants of *except*—'except as', 'except when', 'except where'—can often be shortened to *unless*. If so, shorten them. For example:

- '*Except as* [prefer: *Unless*] required by the judge, male jurors need not wear a coat and tie.'
- 'The judge said that jurors need not wear a coat and tie *except when* [prefer: *unless*] in court.'
- 'Long quotations are unacceptable *except where* [prefer: *unless*] you need to focus on the precise words.'

See also **save / save for / save and except for**.

excepting and reserving

A lawyer's pairing, often misused. The pairing commonly heralds a qualification to the transfer of a property, intoned as if the words were synonyms. However, their meanings differ. An *exception* is an exclusion of part of the property from the transfer; the part excluded never passes to the transferee: *Cooper v Stuart* (1889) 14 App Cas 286, 289–90 (PC); *Commissioner of State Revenue (Vic) v Pioneer Concrete (Vic) Pty Ltd* (2002) 209 CLR 651, 665 (Gleeson CJ, Gummow, Kirby, and Hayne JJ). In contrast, a *reservation* is a re-grant out of the property of something not previously existing, such as an easement: *Jones v Consolidated Anthracite Collieries Ltd* [1916] KB 123, 135. So, for example, if an owner sells part of a property and wishes to retain a right of way over the part being sold, the appropriate term is *reservation* of the right of way (in effect, the purchaser grants the right of way to the vendor), not *exception* of the right of way (as if somehow the property being transferred were a fee simple minus a right of way).

Indiscriminate pairing of the terms manifests the drafter's ignorance of the distinction between them. Nevertheless, the distinction is so often blurred that courts sometimes deliberately overlook the drafter's confusion, so as to give effect to the parties' obvious intentions. This is seen, for example, in Australian case law interpreting 'reservations and exceptions' in Crown grants of land: see, eg, *Wade v New South Wales Rutile Mining Co Pty Ltd* (1969) 121 CLR 177, 194; *Perilya Broken Hill Ltd v Valuer-General* [2015] NSWCA 400, [82]. It is said that US courts 'wisely disregard' the distinction, preferring instead to carry out the parties' perceived intention: Jon W Bruce and James W Ely, *The Law of Easements and Licenses in Land* (2019 US edn, Thomson Reuters) §3.7.

Further reading

Halsbury's Laws of England, 'Deeds and other Instruments' (vol 32, 2019) [438]–[440] (distinctions between 'exceptions' and 'reservations')

See also **WORD PAIRINGS.**

exceptio probat regulam

Latin: the exception proves the rule. The meaning (commonly misunderstood) of 'exception' here is 'the action of excepting', not 'that which is excepted'; ie, by specifying what is excepted, the rule's application over other matters is strengthened. Regardless of how the writer understands the meaning, using the Latin will complicate, not clarify. Prefer standard English:

> 'This exception, being founded on a special reason, so far from derogating from the general rule [against perpetuities], in truth establishes and confirms it, according to the maxim, *exceptio probat regulam* [prefer: *the exception proves the rule*].' [*Lee v Lee* (1860) 1 Dr & Sm 85, 87; 62 ER 310, 311 (Kindersley V-C)]

exceptional circumstances

A drafter's saviour—and nightmare. Saviour, because the phrase sidesteps the need for close analysis: 'This applies unless there are exceptional circumstances.' Nightmare, because it leaves open for debate (and litigation) the meaning of 'exceptional'. As the following extract shows, courts are prone to explain 'exceptional' by invoking near synonyms—but at the risk of diverting focus from the original word, which remains vague.

> 'We must construe "exceptional" as an ordinary, familiar English adjective, and not as a term of art. It describes a circumstance which is such as to form an exception, which is out of the ordinary course, or unusual, or special, or uncommon. To be exceptional a circumstance need not be unique, or unprecedented, or very rare; but it cannot be one that is regularly, or routinely, or normally encountered.' [*R v Kelly* [2000] QB 198, 208 (Lord Bingham)]

The following paragraphs (a)–(e) summarise the case law on the meaning of 'exceptional circumstances'. The summary (by an Australian appellate judge) indicates the term's inherent vagueness, and the prudence of seeking a clearer alternative if the circumstances permit:

> (a) Exceptional circumstances are out of the ordinary course or unusual, or special, or uncommon. They need not be unique, or unprecedented, or very rare, but they cannot be circumstances that are regularly, routinely or normally encountered.
>
> (b) Exceptional circumstances can exist not only by reference to quantitative matters concerning relative frequency of occurrence, but also by reference to qualitative factors.
>
> (c) Exceptional circumstances can include a single exceptional matter, a combination of exceptional factors, or a combination of ordinary factors which, although individually of no particular significance, when taken together are seen as exceptional.
>
> (d) In deciding whether circumstances are exceptional within the meaning of a particular statutory provision, one must keep in mind the rationale of that particular statutory provision.
>
> (e) Beyond these general guidelines, whether exceptional circumstances exist depends upon a careful consideration of the facts of the individual case.
>
> [*Yacoub v Pilkington (Australia) Ltd* [2007] NSWCA 290, [66] (Campbell JA); citations omitted]

EXCEPTIONS

Order of stating exceptions

Where a proposition is subject to an exception or qualification, try to state the proposition before stating the exception or qualification. Readers find it more logical to meet the main message before meeting the exception or qualification to it. This order in fact reflects the modern practice for conditional clauses, namely, stating the substantive provision before stating the condition (reversing the traditional order of 'condition before substantive provision').

Before	After
Except for notices under s 10, notices must be served in person.	Notices must be served in person, except for notices under s 10.

This is all the more so for multiple exceptions or qualifications, as in the following example.

Before	After
Except for disputes over arrears of rent, breaches of repair obligations, and failure to keep the premises clean, the parties must refer all disputes to an independent arbitrator.	The parties must refer all disputes to an independent arbitrator, except for disputes over arrears of rent, breaches of repair obligations, and failure to keep the premises clean. [*Better still*, list the exceptions in bullet points] The parties must refer all disputes to an independent arbitrator, except for disputes over: • arrears of rent • breaches of repair obligations • failure to keep the premises clean.

Combine exception into main concept?

Where an exception or qualification is brief, it may be possible to improve readability by wrapping the exception or qualification into the main subject, rather than isolating it.

Before	After
All judges *except* those who hold positions as appellate judges must retire at 72.	All non-appellate judges must retire at 72.

See also **CONDITIONAL CLAUSES.**

EXCLAMATION MARKS

Exclamation marks add emotion to writing. Perhaps for that reason, they are rarely found in legal writing, which favours an emotion-free style. But exceptions can be cited. For example, some old statutes included exclamation marks in the closing line of forms of proclamations, as in 'God save the King!' (see *Tinker Tailor Pty Ltd v Commissioner for Main Roads* (1960) 105 CLR 334, 342). And Lord Northington LC, speaking tongue-in-cheek of the need for a 'supreme seer' to fathom the meaning of a poorly drafted deed of settlement, exclaimed: 'Thank God, it is not this court!': *Le Rousseau v Rede* (1761) 2 Eden 1, 4–5; 28 ER 795, 796.

However, examples such as these rare. Indeed, judges have been known to censure lawyers (and fellow judges) for using exclamation marks:

- A US appeal court observed that counsel's repeated use of exclamation marks (and hyperbolic terms such as 'ridiculous' and 'ludicrous') to describe opposing counsel's arguments, were inappropriate in an appellate brief, though not sufficient to warrant punishing the offending lawyer: *In the Marriage of Sykes* 596 NE 2d 1226, 1233 (Illinois Appellate Court, 1992).

- Another US appeal court chided a trial judge for including an exclamation mark in his written answer to a jury's question about the admissibility of evidence ('The answer to the … question is yes!'); but the appeal court also held that the exclamation mark was not an improper comment on the weight of the evidence, and so did not give rise to appealable error: *George Pharis Chevrolet Inc v Polk* 661 SW 2d 314, 317 (Texas Ct Appeals, 1983).

In reality, warnings such as these are not normally needed. Most legal drafters see no role for exclamation marks in formal legal writing. They prefer formatting techniques such as **bold** or *italics* to supply more subtle avenues for emphasis.

See also **EMOTIONAL LANGUAGE.**

EXCLUSION CLAUSE

A clause that limits or excludes a party's liability for breach of contract; sometimes called an *exemption clause.*

Operation

Courts interpret exclusion clauses using the same principles they apply when interpreting other contractual provisions: *Photo Production Ltd v Securicor Ltd* [1980] AC 827; *Mitchell (George) (Chesterhall) Ltd v Finney Lock Seeds Ltd* [1983] 2 AC 803; *Darlington Futures Ltd v Delco Australia Pty Ltd* (1986) 161 CLR 500, 510. They focus not merely on the words of the exclusion clause, but on the clause's role in the context of the contract as a whole: *Selected Seeds Pty Ltd v QBEMM Pty Ltd* [2010] HCA 37, [29]; (2010) 242 CLR 336.

In principle, nothing precludes an appropriately worded exclusion clause from ranging widely, excluding even liability for fundamental breach of contract: *Photo Production Ltd v Securicor Transport Ltd* [1980] AC 827; *Spread Trustee Co Ltd v Hutcheson* [2011] UKPC 13; [2012] 2 AC 194. Indeed, it seems that appropriate wording can exclude even the normal principle of interpretation that persons are not entitled to take advantage of their own wrong: *Mickelfied v SAC Technology Ltd* [1990] 1 WLR 1002, applying *Alghussein Establishment v Eton College* [1988] 1 WLR 587, 595 (Lord Jauncey).

However, judges in fact read exclusion clauses closely and, where ambiguous, *contra proferentem*. The clause must clearly extend to the liability sought to be excluded. For example:

- An exclusion clause sought to exempt a bus company from liability for injury to passengers. The clause excluded liability: 'Where the passenger *occupies a motorcoach seat* fitted with a safety belt …' (emphasis added). Held, this wording did not exclude liability for injury to passengers who were standing and moving around the bus: *Insight Vacations Pty Ltd v Young* [2011] HCA 16; (2011) 243 CLR 149.
- A catering supplier contracted with X to provide catering services to X. An exclusion clause provided that the supplier would have 'no liability whatsoever' for any loss suffered by X 'in relation to this Agreement'. The supplier repudiated the agreement by abandoning it. Held, the words 'in relation to this Agreement' applied only to the performance of tasks under the agreement, not to a repudiation of it; and so the exemption did not protect the supplier from liability for X's loss: *Kudos Catering (UK) Ltd v Manchester Central Convention Complex Ltd* [2013] EWCA Civ 38; [2013] 2 Lloyds Rep 270.
- A building company took out insurance cover against liability incurred by the acts or omissions of its executives. An exclusion clause denied cover for acts or omissions in rendering 'professional services' to third parties. An executive wrongly authenticated a progress claim submitted to a third party. Held, this was not the supply of 'professional services'—the term meant services of a professional nature involving the application of skill and judgment, not the mere supply of information: *Chubb Insurance Co of Australia Ltd v Robinson* [2016] FCAFC 17; (2016) 239 FCR 300.

Liability in negligence

This strict interpretation is seen also in attempts to exclude liability for negligence. The starting point is that a contracting party (A) is unlikely to intend to absolve the other contracting party (B) from loss caused by B's negligence: *The Raphael* [1982] 2 Lloyd's Law Reports 42, 50–51 (Stephenson LJ). Therefore, liability for negligence is excluded only where stated clearly. The clearest way is by expressly excluding liability for 'negligence', but specific mention of 'negligence' is not necessary where the intent to exclude liability for negligence is clear. The test is whether the words, read in context, clearly imply that liability for negligence is being excluded: *Canadian Steamship Lines Ltd v R* [1952] AC 192 (PC); *Hollier v Rambler Motors (AMC) Ltd* [1972] 2 QB 71 (Salmon LJ); *Smith v South Wales Switchgear Co Ltd* [1978] 1WLR 165 (HL). For example:

- Effective wording to exclude liability in negligence might be 'any loss under any circumstances whatever', or 'any other cause whatever', because although not mentioning negligence specifically, the wording necessarily encompasses loss resulting from negligence: *G L Nederland (Asia) Pty Ltd v Expertise Events Pty Ltd* [1999] NSWCA 62, [22]–[23]; *Glenmont Investments Pty Ltd v O'Loughlin [No 2]* (2000) 79 SASR 185, 244–47.
- But where A engaged B to carry out building work, an exemption clause stating that A 'bears the sole risk of loss from fire' was not sufficient to exclude B's liability for negligence when a fire damaged the premises: *Casson v Ostley PJ Ltd* [2001] EWCA Civ 1013; (2001) 85 Con LR 18.

See also **contra proferentem**; **DEED OF RELEASE.**

EXCLUSIVE JURISDICTION CLAUSE

See **JURISDICTION CLAUSE.**

execute (a document)

Meaning

Although lawyers freely use *execute*, the word may puzzle non-lawyers. To *execute* a document is not to kill it, but rather to do what the law requires to bring it to life. Lawyers talk of 'executing' many kinds of documents: eg, wills, deeds, conveyances, transfers. Sometimes this results in unintended humour, as in the following example from a lawyer's letter:

> 'We refer to your letter … with a proposed contract attached *for our client's execution* [prefer: *for our client to sign*]'. [Lawyer's letter, quoted in *Melham v Katter* [2013] NSWDC 203, [6].]

Non-deeds

Where the document is not a deed, 'execute' is unnecessarily formal. 'Sign' usually suffices, because signing is usually sufficient to bring the document into operation. Sometimes, however, statute requires witnessing as an additional aspect of 'executing' a document: eg, wills, statutory declarations, enduring powers of attorney.

Deeds

A deed requires more for its *execution* than mere signing. In the time-honoured phrase, a deed must be 'signed, sealed and delivered'. A more modern formulation is 'executed as a deed', a wording intended to encapsulate all that is required to bring a deed into effect.

When is a document 'executed'?

Non-deeds

For most purposes, an agreement embodied in a document that is not in the form of a deed (a 'non-deed') is *executed* when it is signed. The document comes into operation when it is signed, unless the parties agree otherwise.

Deeds

In contrast (as already mentioned), a deed is *executed* when it is 'signed, sealed and delivered'. These steps may take place almost simultaneously (with delivery being the last step); but if they do not, the deed is not *executed* until all three steps are completed (again, with delivery being the last step). This makes 'execution' of a deed a process rather than a single step at a single instant of time: *Terrapin International Ltd v Inland Revenue Commissioners* [1976] 1 WLR 665, 670 (Walton J). (For the requirement of 'delivery', see **delivery (of deed)**.)

Execution clauses

The *execution clause* (usually at the end of a document) indicates where the parties sign and the capacity in which they sign. (Although called a 'clause', it may be a few words, lacking any formal grammatical structure.) In a traditional form of deed executed by a natural person, the execution clause invariably states '*signed, sealed and delivered by …*', with provision for one or more witnesses to attest the signature. This formula reflects the legal requirements for executing deeds. In a document executed by a corporation, the traditional execution clause records that the common seal was affixed in the presence of (and signed by) one or more of the company's directors, or one or more of its office-bearers. In modern forms of deeds, the execution clause often states, more simply, '*executed as a deed*', a formula intended to update the traditional wording but still to confirm that the putative deed has gone through the formalities (including, presumably, delivery) for a valid deed.

Electronic execution

Modern legislation increasingly allows documents (including deeds) to be executed by electronic means.

Further reading

- 'Execute', in *Law Words* (Centre for Plain Legal Language, University of Sydney, 1995) 21; at www.clarity-international.net/plain-language-resources/general-resources/
- *Halsbury's Laws of England*, 'Deeds and other Instruments' (vol 32, 2019) [227]–[256] (execution of deeds)
- Law Commission, *Electronic Execution of Documents* (Law Com No 386, 2019)
- Diccon Loxton, 'Not Worth the Paper They're Not Written On? Executing Documents (Including Deeds) under Electronic Documentation Platforms', Parts A and B (2017) 91 *Australian Law Journal* 133 and 205
- Nicholas Seddon, *Seddon on Deeds* (Federation Press, 2015) ch 2

See also **attest**; **DEED (document)**; **delivery (of deed)**; **escrow**; **execute**; **in witness whereof (the parties have signed)**; **sign / signature**; **signed, sealed and delivered**.

execute (verb)

To carry out, bring into force. The ordinary meanings of *to execute* include (depending on context) 'to fulfil' (eg, an obligation), 'to put into effect' (eg, a search warrant), 'to put to death', 'to give effect to a court decision' (eg, execute a judgment), 'to carry out the duties of an executor of a will' (a rare meaning). Context usually determines the relevant meaning. Usually, the 'ordinary meaning' carries the legal meaning clearly and without loss of legal nuance.

executed as a deed

See **execute (a document)**; **signed, sealed and delivered.**

EXECUTION CLAUSE

See **execute (a document)**.

EXECUTIVE SUMMARY

Purpose

Executive summaries (or merely 'summaries') are common in business documents and reports. They have a place in legal writing also.

An executive summary should:

- briefly explain what the document is about;
- summarise the most important contents of the document;
- list the main recommendations (if any) the document makes;
- indicate where the points in the summary are amplified in the body of the document.

Effectiveness

An effective executive summary meets three key objectives:

1. **Brevity**. It must be a *summary*—ie, it must be brief.
2. **Structure**. It should place the conclusion up-front—ie, it should not argue *towards* the conclusion. In a legal advice containing an executive summary, that means stating the answer as soon as possible; in a report, it means stating the key recommendations as soon as possible.
3. **Location**. It should appear first in the document. An executive summary at the end of the document is better than no summary at all, but its location reduces its effectiveness.

For documents with multiple parts or sections, it is useful to begin each part or section with its own executive summary. This will help all readers, but particularly those who dip into one or more parts only.

Summaries in court judgments

Executive summaries would be helpful in court judgments, but are rarely seen. The traditional form of judgment follows a standard pattern: (1) the facts; (2) the law; (3) applying the law to the facts; (4) the court's conclusion. But most readers of judgments would find the text easier to navigate if given at the start a summary of what is to follow. In recent times, some judges have become alert to the benefits of an up-front summary, and are beginning their judgments with one (even if not headed 'Summary'). Others begin with an up-front statement of the issues, but (less effectively) postpone the answer to the end.

Examples of up-front summaries

- *Lee v Cardiff County Council* [2016] EWCA Civ 1034; [2017] 1 WLR 1751, [1] (Arden LJ)
- *Annettes v Adeleye* [2018] EWCA Civ 555; [2018] 1 WLR 4539, [1]–[7] (Arden LJ)
- *Northern Territory v Griffiths* [2019] HCA 7; (2019) 93 ALJR 803, [1]–[4] (Kiefel CJ, Bell, Keane, Nettle and Gordon JJ; excellent summary of complex issues and decision)
- *Zurich Australian Insurance Ltd v Metals & Minerals Insurance Pte Ltd* [2009] HCA 50; (2009) 240 CLR 391, [1] (French CJ, Gummow and Crennan JJ)
- *BVD17 v Minister for Immigration* [2019] HCA 34; (2019) 93 ALJR 1091, [2] (plurality of High Court of Australia: 'The short answer is … The short reason is …')
- *Nassif v Caminer* [2009] NSWCA 45; (2009) 74 NSWLR 276, [3]–[4] (Macfarlan JA)
- *Joseph Street Pty Ltd v Tan* [2012] VSCA 113; (2012) 38 VR 241, [1] (CA).

Examples of less effective summaries

- *Inplayer Ltd v Thorogood* [2014] EWCA Civ 1511, [58]–[62] (Jackson LJ) (summary at end)
- *Lee v Ashers Baking Co Ltd* [2018] UKSC 49; [2020] AC 413, [1]–[8] (Baroness Hale; too long)
- *SK & K Monk v Newbigin* [2017] UKSC 14; [2017] 1 WLR 851 (up-front summary of issue, but answer deferred until end; likewise, *Gilham v Ministry of Justice* [2019] UKSC 44; [2019] 1 WLR 5905)
- *R v Lord Chancellor* [2015] EWHC 402 (Admin); [2015] 1 WLR 4497 (starting with a summary, headed 'Introduction: issue and conclusion', running for 2,414 words—too long for a summary).

Further reading

- Peter Butt, 'Judgment Writing: An Antipodean Response' (2013) 129 *Law Quarterly Review* 7
- Joseph Kimble, 'First Things First: The Lost Art of Summarising' (2001–2002) 8 *Scribes Journal of Legal Writing* 103; reprinted in Joseph Kimble, *Lifting the Fog of Legalese: Essays on Plain Language* (Carolina Academic Press, 2006) 73

See also **ADVICE (FORM OF); DOCUMENT STRUCTURE**.

executor / executrix

Traditionally, *executor* means a male executor, *executrix* (plural *executrices*) a female. In modern times, though *executrix* is sometimes used, *executor* has become the standard, gender-neutral term for both sexes, as in the following examples:

- 'The applicant is *Mrs* Florence Ann Williams, the *executor* and sole beneficiary of the will of the late Arnold William Seals.' [*Williams v Seals* [2014] EWHC 3708 (Ch), [2] (Richards J)]
- 'Accordingly, I will order that [the sale proceeds be paid into a trust account] on trust for the plaintiff Suzanne Claire Pontifex in *her* office as *executor* of the will of John Arthur Street, deceased …' [*Pontifex v Kittelty* [2013] WASC 296, [23] (EM Heenan J)]

See also **GENDER-NEUTRAL LANGUAGE**.

executor de son tort

Law French: executor 'by his [her] own wrongdoing'. A person who, though not actually appointed as an executor, nevertheless purports to act as one, and whom the law then treats as responsible as if properly appointed. There need be no conscious wrongdoing; for example, a person whose appointment as executor is vitiated by a formal defect in the appointment process may, by acting as executor, become an executor *de son tort*, despite believing that the appointment was valid. For that reason, a plain-language substitute would be 'executor by his [her] own act' or 'self-appointed executor'.

See also **de son tort**; **vitiate**.

executory

Yet to be carried into effect. In law, the term appears as an adjective, adding to its associated noun the sense of 'not yet in effect'. Examples include:

- *executory consideration*: consideration in the form of an as-yet-unfulfilled promise to do something or to refrain from doing something, in return for the other party's promise
- *executory contract*: a contract as-yet-unperformed, in whole or in part
- *executory devise*: an interest in land created by a will, but not yet in effect (eg, because the beneficiary is yet to attain the specified age)
- *executory interest*: an interest to arise in the future
- *executory trust*: a trust in which the interests of the trustees and beneficiaries are not 'perfected' because (for example) the trust documents have yet to be executed or (in the case of certain land) yet to be registered.

executry

A Scots law term for the process of winding up the estate of a deceased person in accordance with the will or the law of intestate succession.

exemplary

Usually meaning 'setting a good example'—eg, 'the defendant's conduct was *exemplary*'. But in the law of damages, it can imply the opposite—namely, where conduct is so bad that the court must 'set an example' by exacting additional punishment or awarding additional damages. Thus, a court may award 'exemplary damages' where the defendant has acted in complete disregard of the plaintiff's rights; or it may impose additional penalties on an accused to signify its abhorrence of the accused's conduct or to create a deterrent for the wider community. Also called 'punitive damages' and retributive damages'.

Further reading

Halsbury's Laws of England, 'Damages' (vol 29, 2019) [325]–[333].

exempli gratia

Latin: by way of example; for example. In modern usage, generally abbreviated to 'eg' (not italicised). The older unabbreviated Latin usage (*exempli gratia*) is sometimes seen, but it is rare—and in any case, for the unabbreviated form prefer the English *for example*.

- 'The court is entitled to be credited with a knowledge of the ordinary use of the English language, and has a duty to apply such knowledge. *Exempli gratia* [Prefer: *For example*],

I should think that war savings certificates ... might well be considered as covered by the ordinary use ... of the word "money".' [*Perrin v Morgan* [1943] AC 399, 418 (Lord Thankerton)]

- '[Taxes unnecessarily paid to the Crown] cannot be recovered from the Crown ... unless the circumstances were such that they would be recoverable as between subject and subject, *exempli gratia* [prefer: *for example*] as involuntary payments or payments made under a mistake of fact.' [*Mason v State of New South Wales* (1959) 102 CLR 108, 117 (Dixon CJ)]

See also **eg / e.g.**

EXEMPTION CLAUSE

See **EXCLUSION CLAUSE.**

exist / subsist

These words have different nuances: to *exist* is *to be*, while to *subsist* is to *continue to be*. In practice, however, *subsist* is rarely used, and may seem stilted. If the nuance of continuity is required, prefer a more idiomatic expression such as 'continues to exist' or (more simply) 'continues'. For example, 'during the *subsistence* of the marriage' means simply 'while the marriage *continues to exist*': *Waters v Waters* [1968] P 401, 409 (Lane J); or, more simply, 'while the marriage *continues*'; or indeed, 'while the marriage *exists*' (because if something *exists*, it continues to exist). To take another example:

> 'Non-repair for six years does not result in the repairing obligation becoming statute-barred while the tenancy still *subsists* [prefer: *exists*; *continues*].' [*Bell v Peter Browne & Co* [1990] 2 QB 495, 501 (Nicholls LJ]

existing

Take care with *existing*—'existing when'? Depending on context, *existing* may be anchored to a point in time or may be ambulant. For example, planning laws that allow '*existing* uses' to continue despite a change in zoning, look to uses that existed when the change came into operation. But a power in a trust deed to appoint new trustees to replace *existing* trustees looks to the situation from time to time (not to the situation at the date when the trust deed came into operation).

existing use

See **use (verb)**.

expect (to happen)

A notoriously open-ended term: when is something 'expected' to happen? How soon? How firm an expectation? Sometimes, open-ended terms are useful in legal writing. Usually, though, they are problematic, for courts are driven to invoke synonyms or near-synonyms, a practice which then focuses attention on the substitute term rather than the original.

Example

> An institution held funds in the capacity of 'stakeholder'. It sought directions from the court as to how it should pay the funds. The Rules of Court enabled stakeholders to seek directions where competing claims to the funds were 'expected' to be made. Held: 'expected' required a

'real foundation for the expectation'; but it did not require that a claim should already have been asserted, or that necessary steps prior to making a claim should already have been taken; and a claim could be 'expected' even where it possibly might not be made at all. See *Global Currency Exchange Network Ltd v Osage 1 Ltd* [2019] EWHC 1375 (Comm); [2019] 1 WLR 5865, [87], [92].

See also **expectancy**; **stakeholder**.

expectancy

An expectation or hope of benefiting by receiving property in the future, but with no current entitlement to receive it at that future time. For example, a child's expectation or hope to inherit his or her parent's land on the parent's future death is no more than an 'expectancy'—because, for example, the child may predecease the parent, or the parent may give the land to someone else. For that reason, an expectancy is not strictly an existing property right, and common-law courts declined to recognise it as one.

However, courts of equity did recognise expectancies. For example, a court of equity would recognise an assignment of an expectancy, if given for value: *Re Lind* [1915] 2 Ch 345 (expectant share as next of kin). In modern times, legislation allows an expectancy to be conveyed or disposed of even at common law: eg, *Law of Property Act 1925*, s 4(2); *Conveyancing Act 1919* (NSW), s 50(1).

Further reading

Halsbury's Laws of England, 'Equitable Jurisdiction' (vol 47, 2014) [219]

See also **expect (to happen)**.

expectorate

An over-genteelism for *spit*. Prefer the bluntness of *spit*. Readers are unlikely to be shocked:

- 'At that time she was very breathless, was *expectorating* [prefer: *spitting*; *coughing-up*] dirty coloured sputum and complaining of severe chest and shoulder pains.' [*Re T (Adult: Refusal of Treatment)* [1992] 3 WLR 782, 788 (Lord Donaldson MR)]
- 'The incident occurred when he stood on a trunk near the window to *expectorate* [prefer: *spit*] but over-balanced, falling to the ground below.' [*Roncevich v Repatriation Commission* [2005] HCA40; (2005) 222 CLR 115, [34] (Kirby J)]

expedient

A time-honoured term in legal writing, meaning simply beneficial, worthwhile, or advantageous. It is not a term of art, and takes its colour from its context. For example, in the context of police powers to stop and search vehicles where *expedient* to prevent terrorism, *expedient* means simply 'advantageous': *R v Metropolitan Police Commissioner* [2004] EWCA Civ 1067; [2005] QB 388, [31] (Lord Woolf CJ); affirmed [2006] 2 AC 307, with the added comment that *expedient* here does not mean 'necessary' (at [14], Lord Bingham). In the context of charities law—eg, the power to vary a charitable trust if 'expedient' to do so—*expedient* carries its ordinary meaning of 'advantageous', 'desirable', and 'suitable to the circumstances' (*Riddle v Riddle* (1952) 85 CLR 202, 222), and its opposite *inexpedient* carries the meaning 'disadvantageous', 'undesirable', or 'not suitable to the circumstances' (*Knowles v Attorney-General* [2016] TASSC 25; (2016) 26 Tas R 19, [14]–[16]).

So, beware of the inherent open-endedness of *expedient* and *inexpedient*. For example: 'The court may make any order it considers *expedient*.' *Expedient* to whom? What degree of *expedience*—slight, overwhelming? *Expedient* from the standpoint of finance, or emotion, or politics? Take care to clarify.

expiration / expiry / end

General

Expiration and *expiry* are interchangeable: 'before the *expiration* of this agreement' = 'before the *expiry* of this agreement'. In line with plain-language principles, where possible the verbal form '*to expire*' is better: eg, 'This lease *expires* on 31 December.' (Not: 'The *expiry* date [or *expiration* date] of this lease is 31 December.')

In many legal contexts, even better than *expire*, is *end*: eg, 'This lease *ends* on 31 December.' This is because a shorter word usually communicates more immediately than a longer word. Similarly:

> 'A member may be reappointed *on the expiration of* [prefer: *at the end of*] their initial term.'

Or better:

> 'A member may be reappointed when their initial term *ends*.'

Qualifications

End is not always the ideal word to describe what happens when a right or agreement concludes for reasons other than the passage of time. For example, a party may *terminate* an agreement for the other party's default, or may *rescind* it for a reason associated with its formation (such as mistake or misrepresentation). In such situations, *end*—while shorter and more idiomatic—obscures the legal reason *why* the right or agreement has ended.

Nor is *end* ideal where a statute, regulation, or official form prompts another word. For example, a land registry form of lease may require the parties to specify the 'Expiry date'. Assuming that there is no power to change that expression, for the parties to use *end date* in later clauses could cause ambiguity: is the *end date* the same as the *Expiry date*?

See also **commence**; **rescind / terminate / end**.

expose

In Scottish law, to put up for sale by auction. For example:

> '[T]he pursuer undertook, on behalf of the defender, to *expose* the table for sale by auction …'
> [*Lyon & Turnbull Ltd v Sabine* [2012] CSOH 178, [2] (Lord Brodie)]

express notice

See **notice / knowledge**.

expressio unius

A fragment of the fuller Latin maxim, *expressio unius est exclusio alterius*: the expression of one thing is the exclusion of the other. Sometimes rendered *inclusio unius est exclusio alterius* (the inclusion of one is the exclusion of the other). The maxim embodies a principle of interpretation under which express reference to one matter is taken to indicate that other matters are intentionally excluded. For example, where a document lists specific matters but omits others that a reader might otherwise have thought to be relevant, the omission is taken to be deliberate. The maxim should unsettle the lawyerly habit of long lists; indeed, the longer and more exhaustive the list, the greater the maxim's potential for operation.

Examples of the maxim's application are found in the case law on powers of attorney. Traditionally drafted powers of attorney listed exhaustively the powers given to the attorney (the donee of the power); lists sometimes ran to many pages. The courts adopted the common-sense principle that a power not included in an extensive list must have been deliberately omitted: *Bryant v Banque du Peuple* [1893] AC 170, 177; *Re Dowson and Jenkins* [1904] 2 Ch 219, 224. But the principle is not limited to powers of attorney. It applies in other legal contexts as well. Examples include lists of exclusions in insurance policies (as in *McCann v Switzerland Insurance Australia Ltd* (2000) 203 CLR 579, [78]) and lists of decision-making tribunals in statutes (as in *Director of Investigation and Research v Newfoundland Telephone Company* [1987] 2 SCR 466, 483–84). In all such cases, omissions from the lists are presumed to be intentional.

As with other principles of interpretation, the purpose of *expressio unius* is to discern intention, not to supply it. And so, ironically perhaps, drafting that is clearly substandard or time-pressured may escape the principle's application. This is not to excuse sloppy drafting, but to reflect the court's wish to discern the parties' true intentions. Examples include:

- Commercial documents poorly drafted by inexperienced drafters. See, for example:
  - the pension fund deed in *National Grid Co Plc v Mayes* [2001] 1 WLR 864, described by Lord Hoffmann at [55] as a 'patchwork document'
  - the commercial lease in *Australia Pacific Airports (Melbourne) Pty Ltd v Nuance Group (Aust) Pty Ltd* [2005] VSCA 133, described by Nettle JA at [31] as one in which 'very little thought has been given to consistency in drafting'.
- Statutes bearing the hallmarks of pressures under which parliamentary drafters labour. See, eg, *Ryland Brothers (Australia) Ltd v Morgan* (1926) 27 SR (NSW) 161, 168–69; *Bruce v Cole* (1998) 45 NSWLR 163, 173 (Spigelman CJ).

Further reading

- *Halsbury's Laws of England*, 'Statutes and Legislative Process' (vol 96, 2018) [818] (expressing one thing excludes another)
- John Mark Keyes, '*Expressio Unius*: The Expression that Proves the Rule' (1989) 10 *Statute Law Review* 1
- Dennis C Pearce and Robert S Geddes, *Statutory Interpretation in Australia*, 9th edn (LexisNexis, 2019) [4.43]–[4.45]

EXPRESSIONS OF TIME

See **TIME**.

expressum facit cessare tacitum

Latin: that … which is express puts an end to (literally, 'causes to cease') that which is implied; an express provision leaves no room for implication. A principle of interpretation by which the express mention of certain things excludes things not mentioned. Its operation is similar to the *expressio unius* principle.

Further reading

Halsbury's Laws of England, 'Statutes and Legislative Process' (vol 96, 2018) [817] (Statement ends implication)

See also **expressio unius**.

extempore

See **ex tempore**.

extent

A writ to recover debts due to the Crown; now archaic. The term often appeared in old forms of deeds of release, which customarily listed at length the various causes of action given up under the deed. For an example, see the Deed of Release reproduced under **WORD STRINGS**.

f / ff

Abbreviation for 'following' (plural, 'ff'), when referring to following pages. Prefer an English equivalent:

- *p 5f* (ie, pages 5 and 6): prefer *pages 5–6*
- *pp 5ff* (ie, pages 5 and [more than one] following: prefer *pages 5 and following* (or better, give the precise span—*pages 5–12*).

Also abbreviation for 'folio' (plural, 'folios').

See also **et seq**.

facsimile

Latin *facere* (to make) and *simile* (the same): an exact copy; plural *facsimiles*. The former hyphenated form, *fac-simile*—eg, in *Clinton v Peabody* (1844) 7 Man & G 399, 401; 135 ER 166, 168—is long obsolete.

In general use, *facsimile* (unabbreviated) means an exact copy—as where a museum makes a *facsimile* of an ancient book, or a UK corporation uses a *facsimile* of its seal in overseas operations (*Companies Act 2006*, s 49).

In more general usage, including modern law and practice, *facsimile* is mostly used in its shortened form (*fax*) to mean the process by which an exact reproduction of a document is sent by electronic means: 'sent by *facsimile*', 'sent by *fax*'. In this usage, *fax* has become a verb (*to fax* a document), an adjective (*fax* machine), and a noun ('I'll send you a *fax*' / 'I'll send you some *faxes*'). There is no need to retain the longer (and more formal) *facsimile* or *facsimile transmission*: 'I will send this by facsimile transmission' = 'I will send this by fax'. Many legislative drafters now use the shortened form:

- *Civil Procedure Rules*, Practice Direction 6A, para 4.1, allowing service of proceedings by 'fax' or other electronic means
- *Navigation Act 2012* (Cth), s 28(1), allowing inspectors to apply for a warrant by 'fax' or other electronic means (Australia).

facta probantia

Latin: the facts adduced to prove or disprove that ultimate fact. To be distinguished from the *factum probandum* (the ultimate fact in issue): *Hayes v Federal Commissioner of Taxation* (1956) 96 CLR 47, 51.

fail (to do something)

To '*fail to* do' (something) can mean a number of things:

- simply not doing it, irrespective of reasons
- not doing it as a result of carelessness or oversight
- intentionally not doing it.

In most contexts, the first meaning is the most likely (and usually encompasses the second and third meanings anyway). For example, a lease may provide: 'If the tenant *fails to* pay rent, the landlord may terminate the lease.' The meaning is that the landlord can terminate for any failure to pay, whether caused by oversight, by carelessness, or by intent. (In most legal systems, the reason for the failure may be relevant to the tenant's claim for relief against forfeiture.)

However, it is wise to avoid argument by more carefully defining whether *fail to* covers all cases of non-fulfilment, or only non-fulfilment arising from certain causes (to paraphrase Mahoney JA in *CBS Productions Pty Ltd v O'Neill* (1985) 1 NSWLR 601, 615–16). If the intent is to cover only failure that is deliberate or wrongful, it is prudent to say so (as in *Grand Junction Waterworks Co v Rodocanachi* [1904] 2 KB 230: 'wrongfully fails'). Otherwise, litigation may ensue, as in the following case:

> A statute stated: 'A taxpayer who *fails to* furnish specified information under the legislation, commits an offence.' Held, there is no offence unless the taxpayer deliberately or carelessly fails to furnish the information: *Deputy Commissioner of Taxation v Ganke* [1975] 1 NSWLR 252.

failing agreement between the parties

A contract may provide for a consequence if the parties 'fail to agree on' something. For example, a lease may provide that, if landlord and tenant 'fail to agree on' a revised rent, an arbitrator is to fix the revised rent. However, a 'fail to agree' provision can be ambiguous, having two possible meanings:

1. it could be merely a statement of objective fact—the parties do not agree; or
2. it could require, by implication, that the parties must first have tried to agree—ie, the 'fail to agree' consequence follows only if there has been an unsuccessful attempt to agree.

The preferred view seems to be possibility (1): 'failing agreement' means simply 'if not settled by agreement', rather than there must have been an unsuccessful attempt to agree: *Hogg v Vickers* (1921) 14 BWCC 229, 234 (Lord Sterndale MR). If parties mean more than that, they should stipulate it expressly.

fair and reasonable

A notoriously vague phrase: 'fair and reasonable' to whom? When used in a contract, unless the parties have given to someone (eg, an arbitrator) the power to determine whether a specified requirement is 'fair and reasonable', the decision is left to the court (as in *Re Stuart* [1893] 2 QB 201, on whether the terms of an agreement with a solicitor were 'fair and reasonable'). And even the court may be unwilling or unable to clarify whether something is 'fair and reasonable', leaving the contract too vague to be enforced.

See also **reasonable**.

fair wear and tear

See **wear and tear**.

fait accompli

French: something accomplished and not now changeable. Plural = *faits accomplis.*

fallen from

A lawyer's affectation for 'spoken by': eg, a judge may say, 'I agree with what has *fallen from* my brother Jones.' The expression is consciously archaic and pedantic. Alternatives are not difficult to find:

> 'I agree with *what has fallen from Dillon LJ* [prefer: *Dillon LJ's judgment*; *what Dillon LJ has said*].' [*Abu Dhabi Helicopters Ltd v International Aeradio plc* [1986] 1 All ER 395, 399 (Sir George Waller)]

falsa demonstratio non nocet

Latin, in full: *falsa demonstratio non nocet cum de corpore constat*: 'a false description does not vitiate, if there be sufficient certainty as to the object': RH Kersley (ed), *Broom's Legal Maxims*, 10th edn (Sweet & Maxwell, 1939) 426. A maxim of interpretation under which, if a document describes a person or thing in two or more ways, and one description is correct but one (or more) is incorrect, a court ignores the incorrect, leaving the correct to prevail: *Watcham v East Africa Protectorate* [1919] AC 533, 541. It is irrelevant whether the correct description appears first, or last, or somewhere in the middle of a number of descriptions: *Cowen v Truefitt Ltd* [1899] 2 Ch 309.

Examples

- A deed of conveyance of a farm described the property in four ways: (1) by name; (2) by area; (3) by the names of the occupants; and (4) by attached plan. At issue was whether the deed conveyed an area of land not specifically referred to in it. Of the four descriptions, the first three were of no help (the name was incorrect, the area was imprecise, and the occupants' names were wrong). But the disputed area of land was within the land described in the attached plan. Held, the first three descriptions were to be disregarded, leaving the disputed area to pass under the fourth: *Eastwood v Ashton* [1915] AC 900.

- A contract for the sale of a home unit described the property as 'lot 117 … 25th level'. In fact, lot 117 was on the 24th level (there being no 13th level). Held, the subject matter of the sale was lot 117; the court rejected the erroneous level number as *falsa demonstratio*: *Dainford Ltd v Tari Nominees Pty Ltd* (1985) Q ConvR 54-162.

FALSE NEGATIVES

See **POSITIVES / NEGATIVES.**

farther / further

These terms have long been used interchangeably: in Middle English, 'farther' and 'further' (and 'ferther') were variants of the same word. In modern usage, 'further' is more common, but usage varies with context and idiom:

- When used as an adjective, 'further' is more idiomatic: 'I have one *further* point, your Honour'; 'this requires *further* analysis'; 'without *further* delay'.
- When used with connotations of figurative distance, 'further' is more idiomatic: 'I am no *further* advanced in my legal research'. But when used with connotations of actual distance, 'farther' is preferred: 'to the *farther* edges of space'.
- When used as an adverb, either is acceptable: 'I can walk no *further / farther*'; 'In my view, the court can go no '*further / farther*.'

In two situations, *further* is the only appropriate word:

- When used to mean 'moreover' or similar: '*Further*, this argument means that …'
- When used as a verb ('to further'): 'This book *furthers* your use of good style.'

fax

See **facsimile**.

fee simple

Usage

Plural: *fees simple* (not 'fee simples'). More fully, *estate in fee simple*. The word *fee* denotes an interest that can be sold or passed to descendants by will or intestacy; the word *simple* denotes that the interest is not curtailed in the way as some other interests (eg, the fee tail). Older usage sometimes inserted *of* for *in*—an 'estate *of* fee simple'. Older usage also sometimes hyphenated the term (*fee-simple*): eg, *Earl Howe v Earl of Litchfield* (1866) 35 Beav 370, 374; 55 ER 939, 941 (Lord Romilly MR); however, current usage has settled uniformly on the unhyphenated *fee simple*.

Nature of fee simple

The fee simple is the largest estate known to the law: *Amodu Tijani v Secretary, Southern Nigeria* [1921] 2 AC 399, 403. Of the three 'freehold' estates—the fee simple, the fee tail, and the life estate—the fee simple is the 'most extensive in quantum, and the most absolute in respect to the rights which it confers': *Challis's Law of Real Property*, 3rd edn (Butterworths, 1911) 218. Ownership of an 'estate in fee simple' is as close as the common law gets to ownership of the land itself, consonant with the feudal principle of tenure (in those places where that principle remains in force) and with modern statutory restrictions on landowners' rights.

A plain-language alternative—'freehold'

Fee simple is a genuine term of art, difficult to express concisely in any other way. However, unless statute compels using *fee simple*, for most purposes *freehold* carries the meaning with sufficient precision. It is true that *freehold* lacks the feudal overtones of *fee simple*—but those overtones survive only in the theory of the law, not in its modern practical application. For all practical purposes, to describe persons as owning the *freehold* means that they own the estate in fee simple.

The use of 'freehold' in this way has strong judicial support, going back many years.

Examples

- 'There is no person literally entitled upon the determination of the *freehold* to take except the Crown. If a *freehold* estate comes to an end by death without an heir, or by attainder, it goes back to the Crown on the principle that all *freehold* estate originally came from the Crown, and that where there is no one entitled to the *freehold* estate by law it reverts to the Crown.' [*Re Mercer and Moore* (1880) 14 Ch D 287, 295 (Jessel MR, in the context of land escheating to the Crown)]
- '[A series of 19th-century cases established that statutes vesting highways in local authorities] operated in a much more limited way than would a simple conveyance or transfer of the *freehold*. First, it was a determinable, rather than absolute, *fee simple*, which would end automatically if the body responsible for its repair ceased to be so responsible (eg, if the road ceased to be a public highway).' [*London Borough of Southwark v Transport for London* [2018] UKSC 63, [8]; [2018] 3 WLR 2059 (Lord Briggs, using *freehold* and *fee simple* interchangeably)]

Further reading

- *Halsbury's Laws of England*, 'Real Property and Registration' (vol 87, 2017) [66]–[70] (nature and incidents of a fee simple)
- S Bridge, E Cooke and M Dixon (eds), *Megarry & Wade's Law of Real Property*, 9th edn (Sweet & Maxwell, 2019) [3-011] and following

See also **escheat**; **estate or interest**; **fee tail**; **life estate**; **seisin / seizin**; **words of limitation**; **words of purchase**.

fee tail

Nature of fee tail

Plural: *fees tail*. A fee tail (or *entail*) is an estate in land that continues for as long as the original holder lives and is survived by lineal descendants. Other terms used to describe the fee tail are *estate tail*, *entail*, and *entailed interest* (strictly, an entail of an equitable interest). Medieval land law characterised the fee tail as a lesser interest than the fee simple, because (unlike a fee tail) a fee simple continued for as long as the original holder lived and was survived by heirs of any degree (not merely lineal descendants).

The succession to a fee tail could be limited within bounds narrower than lineal descendants at large. For example, there could be an estate in *tail male*, descending only to male descendants and males tracing their descent through male descendants. Or there could be an estate in *tail female*, devolving to female descendants only. Or there could be an estate in *special tail*, devolving only to the holder's descendants by a named husband or wife. Or indeed, the *special tail* could be further restricted to male or female descendants. These various types of estates tail could be combined in a series of limitations by way of remainder, with each successive limitation broadening out on failure of the preceding one.

Terminology

Fee tail is a genuine term of art, with no plain-language equivalent. However, the term is rare in most modern common-law jurisdictions, except in historical or technical treatises. This is because, almost everywhere, estates tail have been legislatively phased out, converted into estates in fee simple (although they occasionally still surface, as in *Stilbo Pty Ltd v MCC Pty Ltd* [2003] TASSC 6; (2003) 11 Tas R 63). On that basis, a plain-language equivalent is unlikely to be needed.

Further reading

- S Bridge, E Cooke and M Dixon (eds), *Megarry & Wade's Law of Real Property*, 9th edn (Sweet & Maxwell, 2019) [3-046]–[3-059]
- Brendan Edgeworth (ed), *Butt's Land Law*, 7th edn (Lawbook, 2017) [3.220]–[3.230] (use, and phasing out, in former colonial jurisdictions)

See also **estate or interest**; **fee simple**; **life estate**; **remainder**; **words of limitation**; **words of procreation**.

ferae naturae

Latin: of a wild nature; used to describe animals that are untamed, as distinct from animals that are tamed (*domitae naturae*, or *mansuetae naturae*). In all cases, to preserve the Latin seems pedantic; but if for some reason the Latin is preferred (eg, for fear of losing existing judicial exegesis), then at least offer readers an explanation, as in the following examples:

- 'The [*Animals Act 1971* (UK)] addressed (inter alia) three rules of the common law; first, the rule imposing strict liability on the keeper of an animal *ferae naturae*, ie wild, for damage caused by the animal; second, the rule imposing strict liability on the keeper of an animal *mansuetae naturae*, ie tame, for damage caused by the animal attributable to a vicious, mischievous or fierce propensity which the keeper knew the animal possessed (the so-called scienter rule); and, third, …' [*Mirvahedy v Henley* [2003] 2 AC 491, 519 [82] (Lord Scott)]
- 'The common law divides animals into two categories, harmless or domestic (*mansuetae naturae*) and those which are dangerous or wild by nature (*ferae naturae*). The distinction is significant.' [*Yanner v Eaton* (1999) 201 CLR 551, 574 [80] (Gummow J)]

feu

In Scots legal usage, land held by a vassal (*feuar*) who pays a *feuduty* (a perpetual rent) and is the effective owner of the land, provided he or she observes the conditions attached to the feu. The closest English term is *fee*, as in *fee simple*.

See also **fee simple**.

fewer / less

The general conventions are:

- *fewer* relates to numbers of items that can be counted as individual units, and *less* relates to quantity or degree of something that is indivisible; and
- *fewer* takes plural nouns, and *less* takes singular or collective nouns.

Examples

- '*Fewer* judges sit today.'
- 'Judges have *less* opportunity than in the past.'
- '*Fewer* judges means *less* opportunity [but: *fewer* opportunities] for promotion.'

However, *less* is also used with units of time or of measurement: eg, '*less* than 10 days', '*less* than 10 kilos'.

Sometimes, the choice between *fewer* and *less* is difficult: '*fewer* than 25% of the lawyers were experts' (because *lawyers* is a plural noun); or '*less* than 25% of the bar were experts' (because the reference is to a collective noun—the *bar*). Where the choice could go either way, prefer *less*, as more idiomatic in modern use. And of course eliminate redundancies such as 'a *lesser* number than' (simply, '*fewer* than'), and 'fewer in number' (simply, '*fewer*').

fiat justitia ruat caelum

Latin (sometimes *coelum*): let justice be done though the heavens fall; ie, let justice be done regardless of the consequences. A grand, if hyperbolic, sentiment—described by Jeremy Bentham 'as full of extravagance as it is of harmony': *An Introduction to the Principles of Morals and Legislation* (1823 edn) vol 1, 23–24, n 1. But it is no less grand and hyperbolic when expressed in English, so prefer the English. For example:

- 'The short answer to this is that if the practice is unlawful, expedience will not make it lawful. *Fiat justitia ruat coelum* [prefer: *Let justice be done though the heavens may fall*].' [*R v Gateshead Justices* [1981] QB 470, 479 (Donaldson LJ)]
- 'As [counsel] might have said: "*fiat justitia, ruat caelum*" [prefer: *Let justice be done regardless of the consequences*].' [*Walton v Scottish Ministers* [2012] UKSC 44, [106]; 2012 SLT 1211, 1226 (Lord Carnwath)]
- 'It may sound pompous to cite the old Latin tag *fiat Justitia ruat caelum* (let justice be done though the heavens fall) but a court that works on any other principle and does so for fear of the consequences is betraying the trust that the public reposes in it.' [*Erlam v Rahman* [2015] EWHC 1215 (QB), [527] (Richard Mawrey QC, providing a translation)]

FICTITIOUS LAW REPORTS

Some 'reported' cases appear genuine but are in fact concocted. To cite them as genuine cases will destroy your credibility.

Examples

- *Regina v Ojibway* (1965–66) 8 *Criminal Law Quarterly* 137—Canadian statutory definition of a 'small bird' includes a pony with a feather pillow on its back.
- *Grenouille v National Union of Seamen* ('reported' in *Not-yet-the-Times* newspaper, August 1979)—frog has legal standing to prevent trade union from picketing its pond. (Recounted in Lord Denning, *The Family Story* (Butterworths, 1981) 219–20.)
- *C v B* (1935–38) 1 *Res Judicatae* 302—nature of common law rights to possession of land. (Reasoned 'decision' of the 'Court of Appeal of the Law Students' Society of Victoria'.)
- *Stradling v Styles* (fictional law reporter, Martinus Scriblerius), in Jonathan Swift, *Collected Works* (London, 1744) vol IV, 259—what property passes under a bequest of 'all my black and white horses', where at his death the testator has 6 white horses, 6 black horses, and 6 pied horses. (The 'decision' found its way into the US case of *Wilkins v Taylor* (1799) Wythe 338, 351–52 (cited with some scepticism—'if indeed the case ever existed'), thence

into Professor Reed Dickerson's redoubtable *Materials on Legal Drafting* (West, 1981) 239 as if a genuine case.)

See also **CITATION OF CASES.**

fiduciary

Pertaining to a relationship of trust. Used as both a noun and an adjective: a trustee is a *fiduciary*, and all trustees have *fiduciary* obligations.

FIGURES

See **WORDS AND FIGURES.**

filius nullius

Latin: a son of no one; a bastard; an illegitimate person. Used mainly in the context of inheritance—in English law, such a person could not be an heir, and no one could inherit through him. The Latin tag lingers in law—but it is not a term of art, so prefer an appropriate translation:

- 'It has often been laid down that a bastard is *filius nullius* [prefer: *legally unrecognised; in legal terms, the child of no one*]. Of that expression it is sufficient to say that it is as true in a legal as it is untrue in a natural sense.' [*Clarke v Carfin Coal Co* [1891] AC 412, 420 (Lord Watson)]
- 'At least until the second half of the eighteenth century, a child born to unmarried parents, called "illegitimate", was regarded by the common law as *filius nullius* [prefer: *a child of no one*]. Consequently such a child was under the legal guardianship of nobody.' [*AMS v AIF* [1999] HCA 26; (1999) 199 CLR 160, [136] (Kirby J)]

The concept was taken to its logical absurdity in the apocryphal *Gules v Saltire*, to hold that a *filius nullius*, being the son of no one, could not in law bequeath property to 'my father': Justice Darling, *Scintillae Juris* (Stevens & Haynes, 1914) 13.

final and conclusive

A lawyer's pairing for *final*—or for *conclusive*. Choose either, but not both.

See also **conclusive certificates; WORD PAIRINGS.**

find / hold

By accepted legal usage, a court *finds* facts and *holds* a conclusion of law: eg, 'The court *held*, having *found* the facts, that the mortgagee breached its duty of care.' However, the distinction is often ignored, and no loss of meaning results: eg, 'In *Jones v Smith*, the court *found* that mortgagees owe a duty of care.'

fine

In both standard usage and legal usage, an amount payable as the penalty for an offence. However, in legal usage *fine* also carries two other meanings:

- A medieval form of conveyance.

- An amount payable 'up front' for the grant or renewal of a lease; also called a 'premium'. (See, eg, definition of 'fine' in *Law of Property Act 1925*, s 205(1)(xxiii).) Some jurisdictions outlaw payments of this kind.

These meanings are unlikely to communicate to non-lawyers (nor, indeed, to many lawyers). An explanation may be required.

Further reading

- AWB Simpson, *A History of the Land Law*, 2nd edn (Oxford University Press, 1986) 122–25 (on the 'fine' as a medieval form of conveyance)
- *Hill and Redman's Guide to Landlord and Tenant Law* (Butterworths, 1999) [2.77] (on the meaning of *fine* in the law of leases)

finis litium

Latin: an end to litigation. Usually seen as part of a longer maxim, *interest reipublicae ut sit finis litium*, which can be translated: 'it is in the interests of the State that there be an end to litigation'. But whether alone or as part of a longer maxim, the translation is sufficient, making the Latin redundant.

first instance court

The court in which a case is first heard, as distinct from a court that hears an appeal (*appellate court*).

first refusal (right of)

A right to have the first choice of acquiring an interest in property if and when the owner decides to deal with the property in a given way. Examples are a right of first refusal to purchase, if and when the owner decides to sell; and a right of first refusal to take a lease, if and when the owner decides to grant a lease. In reality, the owner makes a negative promise: 'I will not sell [or lease] my property without first offering it to you.' *First refusal* is a somewhat inapt term, because the offeree wants the opportunity to *accept* an offer, not to *refuse* an offer: *Woodroffe v Box* (1954) 92 CLR 245, 257 (Fullagar and Kitto JJ).

first, secondly, thirdly, ...

The convention in legal and formal writing is *first* [not *firstly*] / *secondly* / *thirdly* (and so on). But though long practised, this convention is illogical, ungrammatical, and for large numbers ungainly (*thirteenthly*, *twentiethly*). The grammatically correct and idiomatically favoured style is *first* / *second* / *third* (and so on). But ingrained habits are hard to break, as the following examples show.

Conventional usage

- '[I]n a number of respects VAT is in a different category from either income or corporation tax ... *First*, ... *Secondly*, ... *Thirdly*, ... *Fourthly*, ...' [*R v Harvey* [2015] UKSC 73, [25]–[29]; [2017] AC 105 (Lords Neuberger and Reed)]
- '*First*, I consider that ... *Secondly*, ... *Thirdly*, ... *Fourthly*, ...' [*The Creative Foundation v Dreamland Leisure Ltd* [2015] EWHC 2556 (Ch), [55]–[58]; [2015] 3 WLR 1814, 1826 (Arnold J)]

- 'There are a number of reasons to prefer [this] construction. *First, ... Secondly, ... Thirdly, ... Fourthly, ... Fifthly, ... Sixthly, ...*' [*Northern Australian Aboriginal Justice Agency Ltd v Northern Territory* [2015] HCA 41; (2015) 256 CLR 569, [215]–[224] (Nettle and Gordon JJ)]

Preferred usage

- 'Historically, there have been three main reasons for this. The *first* is that ... *Second, ... Third, ...*' [*Geys v Société Générale, London Branch* [2012] UKSC 63, [119]; [2013] 1 AC 523, 567 (Lord Sumption)]
- 'Three points may be made about s 708A. *First, ... Second, ... Third, ...*' [*Kuczborski v Queensland* [2014] HCA 46; (2014) 254 CLR 51, [83] (Hayne J)]

Aberrant usage

- 'In the *first* place, it is axiomatic that ... *Secondly*, a transfer of this kind will ordinarily be unnecessary ... *Third*, so far as ...' [*Prest v Petrodel Resources Ltd* [2013] UKSC 34, [40]; [2013] 2 AC 415, 490 (Lord Sumption)]

fit and proper

A lawyer's familiar pairing: eg, '*fit and proper* remedy', '*fit and proper* person'.

'fit and proper' remedy

A '*fit and proper* remedy' is simply a remedy that is appropriate in the circumstances. There is no legal reason to continue with the pairing; prefer *appropriate*.

'fit and proper' person

General

Judges have said that *fit and proper* (person) has no settled legal meaning, but draws its meaning from context: *Australian Broadcasting Tribunal v Bond* (1990) 170 CLR 321, 380 (Toohey and Gaudron JJ). Thus, the content of 'fit and proper' will vary with the circumstances. For example:

- Whether a schoolteacher is a 'fit and proper person' includes considerations of moral integrity, honesty, and character, and not necessarily physical ability: *Teachers Registration Board of South Australia v Edwards* [2013] SAFCFC 80; (2013) 117 SASR 246.
- Whether a tax agent is a 'fit and proper person' includes considerations of honesty and technical knowledge of tax and accounting: *Re Toohey and Tax Agents' Board* [2008] AATA 262; [2008] 70 ATR 939.

Fitness for office

To be *fit* for an office requires acting with honesty in the office, knowing what is required to be done, and having the ability to do it: *Hughes and Vale Pty Ltd v State of New South Wales (No 2)* (1955) 93 CLR 127, 156. To be *proper* for an office simply means to be suitable for it. Therefore, *proper* is almost always superfluous: a person who is *fit* for an office is also *proper* (appropriate, suitable) for the office.

In employment law, prefer the sole word *fit*; but if you want to fill it out a little, prefer substitutes such as *suitable* or *appropriately qualified*. Some may feel that these substitutes are vague and subjective; indeed they are—but no more so than *fit and proper*.

Further reading

'Fit and Proper', in *Law Words* (Centre for Plain Legal Language, University of Sydney, 1995) 24; www.clarity-international.net/plain-language-resources/general-resources/

fit out (noun, verb)

As a noun, items installed to make premises fit for their intended use—eg, in retail premises, partitions, service conduits, shelving, and counters. As a verb, to install such items in premises. Hyphenation depends on whether the term is a noun or a verb:

- as a noun: eg, 'You must install *fit-out*.'
- as a verb: eg, 'You must *fit out* the premises.'

fittings

See **fixtures and fittings**.

fixed charge

A specific charge given over an asset to secure a loan.

Compare **floating charge**.

fixed term

Legal shorthand for 'specified period'. Thus, a lease for a *fixed term* is a lease for a specified duration (eg, 3 years), rather than for an indeterminate duration (eg, 'at will' or 'from year to year').

See also **tenancy for a term of years**; **term (of lease)**.

fixtures and fittings

A pairing common in property law. *Fixtures* (from the late Latin, *fixura*) are things that have become so attached to land that the law regards them as forming part of the land. *Fittings* are things that are fitted (to something else); in non-technical usage, *fittings* are items that have been attached (and so usually are *fixtures*) but remain essentially removable, such as fitted carpets, kitchen racks, and bathroom cabinets. Judges rarely seek to separate the two words; if anything, judicial distinctions are not between fixtures and *fittings*, but between fixtures and *chattels* (*Elitestone Ltd v Morris* [1997] 1 WLR 687). Lawyers generally assume that the two words are synonyms—which is a self-evident reason to excise one of them. Prefer *fixtures*, because case law illuminates its meaning (in comparison, there is little case law on the meaning of *fittings*).

Further reading

S Bridge, E Cooke and M Dixon (eds), *Megarry & Wade's Law of Real Property*, 9th edn (Sweet & Maxwell, 2019) [22-00]–[22-011] (the law of fixtures)

See also **goods and chattels**; **WORD PAIRINGS.**

flagrante delicto

See **in flagrante delicto**.

flammable / inflammable

These two words have the same meaning. The prefix *in-* here is an intensifier, not a negative. The opposite is *non-flammable*.

flat

Whether premises are a *flat* depends on the context in which the issue arises. Premises may be a *flat* in one context but not in another. Mere recourse to the dictionary meaning—'a floor or storey in a house' or 'a suite of rooms on one floor, forming a complete residence' (meanings given in the *Oxford English Dictionary*)—may be a guide but will not always provide the answer. Judicial definitions include:

- 'a separate self-contained dwelling': *Murgatroyd v Tresarden* [1947] KB 316, 320 (Somervell LJ), in the context of the Rent Acts
- areas within a building in the process of renovation, which have reached 'a stage of construction to be suitable for use for the purposes of a dwelling': *Alford House Freehold Ltd v Grosvenor (Mayfair) Estate* [2019] EWCA Civ 1848; [2020] 2 WLR 116, [36] (Lewison LJ), in the context of leasehold enfranchisement legislation.

FLESCH READING EASE FORMULA

A readability tool that measures, in a sample of 100 words, the number of syllables and number of words per sentence.

See **READABILITY TESTS.**

FLESCH–KINCAID GRADE LEVEL FORMULA

A readability tool that measures the same variables as the Flesch Reading Ease Formula, but then converts them to a school grade-level calculation.

See **READABILITY TESTS.**

floating charge

A charge that 'floats' above the assets over which it is given, allowing the assets to be used in the normal course of business until an event of default occurs, at which time the charge crystallises (becomes fixed) over the assets then existing.

Compare **fixed charge**.

FLOW CHARTS

Flow charts are relatively rare in legal documents. They are more likely to be found in subsidiary documents, intended to be read *with* the primary legal document but not *part of* its substantive text. Yet there is no legal reason to consign flow charts to a purely explanatory status. They can be part of the text itself.

A flow chart allows readers to make a series of sequential steps without needing to remember the previous step in the sequence. This liberates them from the memory feats often needed to navigate the same steps in dense text. In this way, for example, a flow chart can lead readers through the steps in a complex transaction, or illustrate visually the relationship between entities in a partnership or joint venture.

Statutory drafters are more at ease with experimental techniques than are their private-practice counterparts. The use of flow charts is an example. Two statutory examples follow.

Example 1: identifying relevant entity

Diagram of the rules for making invitations

(5) This diagram shows when, under section 203A and this section, invitations can be made ... for applications for recognition as the representative body for a particular area.

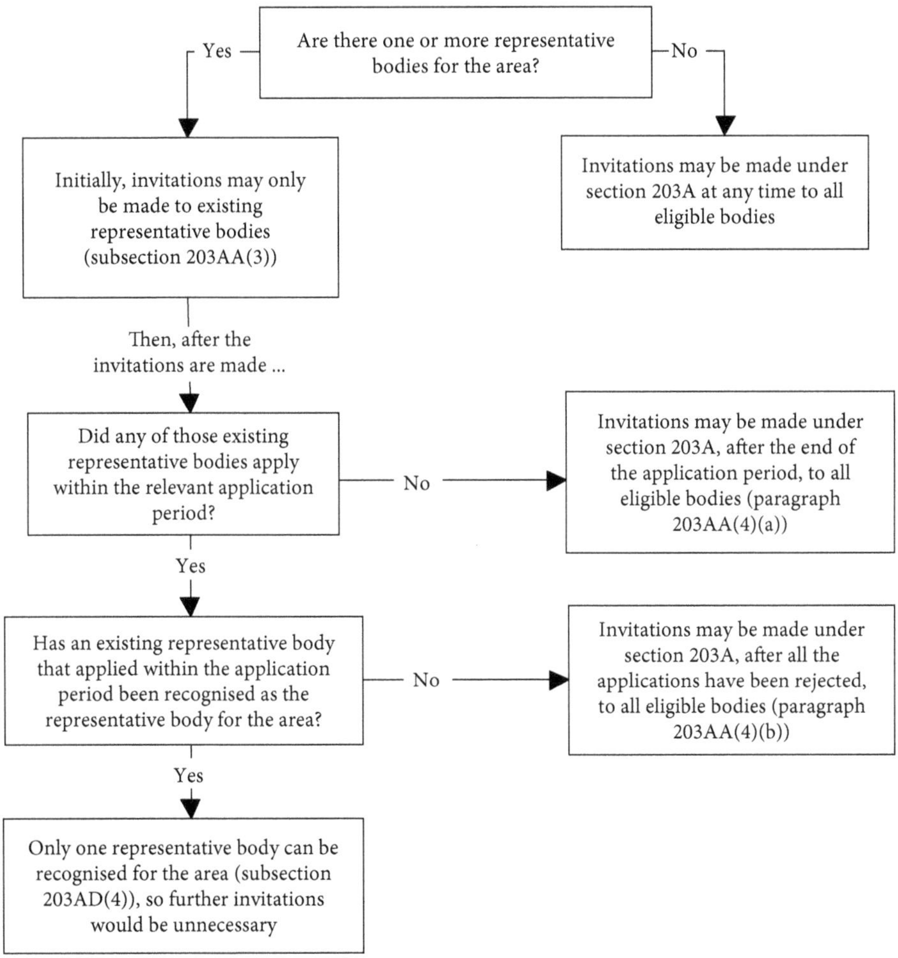

[Source: *Native Title Act 1993* (Cth), s 203AA(5) (Australia) [repealed]]

Example 2: admissibility of evidence

The following diagram shows how this Chapter applies to particular evidence:

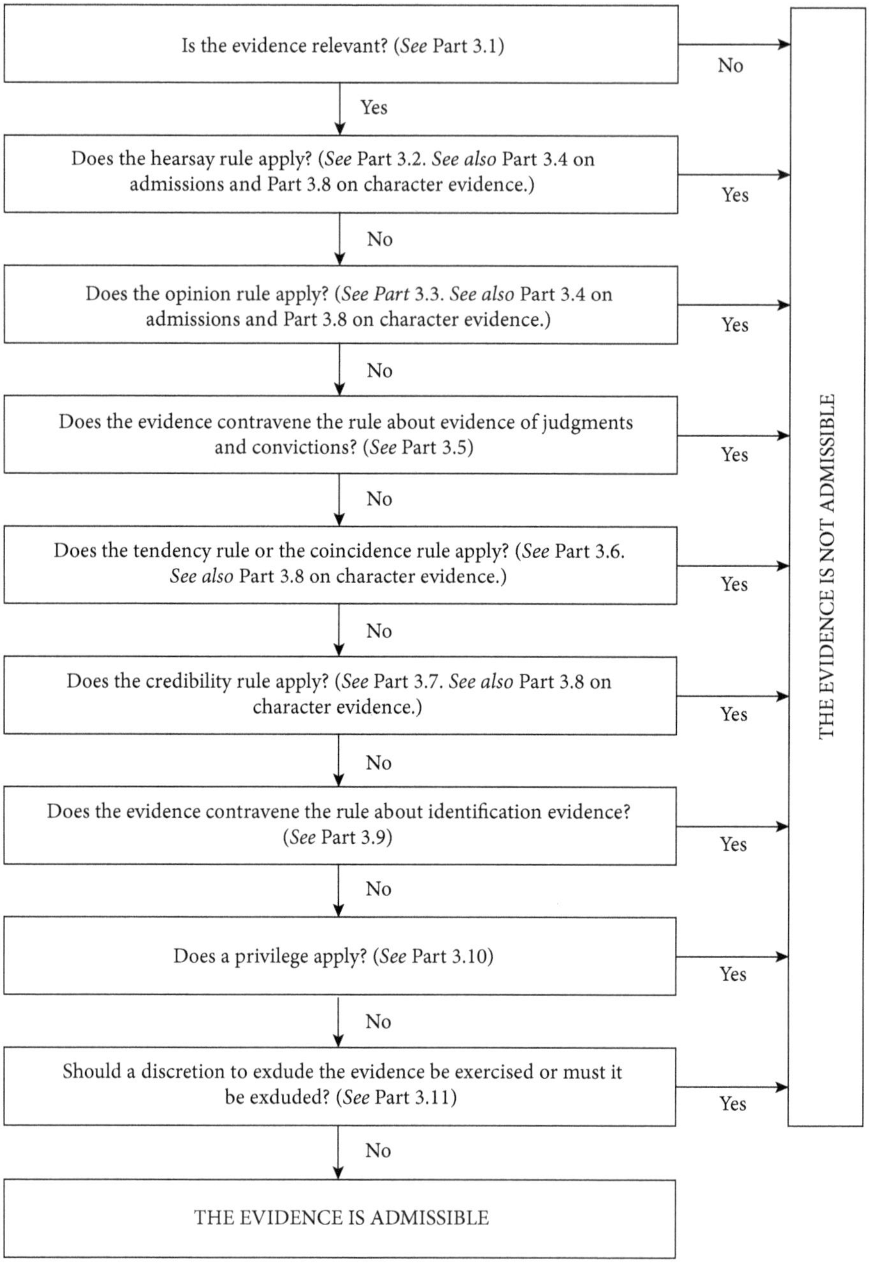

[Source: Introductory Note to Part 3 of the *Evidence Act 1995* (NSW)]

Further reading

PC Wason, 'The Drafting of Rules' [1968] *New Law Journal* 548 (an early discussion of the usefulness of flow charts in setting out complex legal information)

See also **MAPS AND DIAGRAMS**; **PLANS**.

fn

Abbreviation for *footnote*.

See **FOOTNOTES**.

FOG INDEX

A readability tool that measures, in a sample of 100 words, the average number of words per sentence and the number of words of more than two syllables.

See **READABILITY TESTS**.

folio

A page or sheet of paper (Latin: folium); commonly used in two main contexts:

- *official records*—eg, a *folio* (page) of the titles register allocated to a parcel of land
- *legal costs*—historically, a word-counting measure. Lawyers would charge by the 'folio' for reviewing ('perusing') or drafting documents. In common-law proceedings, a folio was 72 words; in exchequer proceedings, 80 words; in chancery proceedings, 90 words.

following

Where meaning *after*, prefer *after*: it is shorter than *following*, and means the same.

fons et origo

Latin: the source, the origin (literally, the source *and* origin); the foundation of; the basis for. A colourful phrase that means no more than an English translation. Unless your readers are Latin scholars, prefer the English. For example:

- 'The *fons et origo* [prefer: *the source and origin*; more idiomatically, *the origin*] of this doctrine is to be found in the decision of the European Court in *Soering v United Kingdom*.' [*United States of America v Barnette* [2004] UKHL 37, [22]; reported as *Government of the United States of America v Montgomery (No 2)* [2004] 4 All ER 289, 299 (Lord Carswell)]
- '[The transaction] constituted *fons et origo* [prefer: *the foundation*] of all that occurred.' [*Federal Commissioner of Taxation v John* (1987) 16 FCR 188, 194 (Bowen CJ)]

FONTS

serif / sans serif

The difference

Typeface falls into two broad categories: (1) with serifs, and (2) without serifs (*sans serif*, or *sans-serif*, or *sanserif*). Serif fonts have extenders or flourishes (the serifs) at the ends of the main strokes. Sans serif lacks these extenders or flourishes—or at least, uses them sparingly.

Serif fonts tend to have stronger italics, which helps legal citations stand out. Of serif fonts, Times Roman and Times New Roman have long been popular, not only because of their serifs, but also because of their 'weight', which makes them more suitable for multiple copying or faxing. However, many writers and publishers now see these fonts as conservative and boring; they prefer other serif fonts such as Georgia and Palatino Linotype; and for sans serif, they prefer a font such as Calibri. (In reality, Calibri's popularity may depend more on MS Word's choice as its default font than on writers' choice as their favoured font.)

A common modern font is Arial. While some recommend it for screen-based text, general expert consensus is against it for printed text. Matthew Butterick writes:

> 'As a system font, Arial has achieved ubiquity akin to Times New Roman. And like Times New Roman, Arial is permanently associated with the work of people who will never care about typography.' [*Typography for Lawyers* (Jones McLure, 2010) 84]

Which is better?

Studies suggest generally (though not unanimously) that a serif font is more readable on paper than a sans serif font. Because serifs are horizontal, they are thought to help the eye move horizontally across the page (unless they are so thin—'hair serifs'—as to serve no readability purpose). For on-screen reading, however, sans serif is generally considered more readable. And for both paper and screen, much depends on the actual font used—for fonts vary widely.

Studies favouring serif font

- Centre for Plain Legal Language, *Review and redesign of NSW legislation*, Discussion Paper, Parliamentary Counsel's Office and Centre for Plain Legal Language (1994) 14 (but favouring sans serif for headings)
- C Wheildon, *Communicating: or Just Making Pretty Shapes* (1986; a study for the Newspaper Advertising Bureau of Australia Ltd) 16, 17.

Studies less favourable to serif font

- James Hartley, *Designing Instructional Text*, 3rd edn (Kogan Page, 1994) ch 4
- Alex Poole, 'Which Are More Legible: Serif or Sans Serif Typefaces?' (2012), accessed at www.alexpoole.info/blog/which-are-more-legible-serif-or-sans-serif-typefaces/

Font size and 'leading'

For ease of reading, use a generous font size with adequate 'leading' (ie, spacing between lines). ('Leading' gets its name from the strips of lead that were used to separate lines of type, in the days of hot metal typesetting.) As a general rule, leading value should be between 1.25 and 1.5 times greater than the font size.

Different fonts have different sizes: for example, Arial 11 point appears larger than Palatino Linotype 11 point, which in turn appears larger than Times New Roman 11 point. The literature on typography and design agrees that a type size of between 9 and 12 point is the most legible for general reading purposes. This book uses Minion, with main text 10 point (leading 11 point), and examples 9 point (leading 10 point).

Selected studies on font sizes

- Parliamentary Counsel's Office and Centre for Plain Legal Language, *Review and redesign of NSW legislation* (Discussion Paper, 1994), 16–17
- James Hartley, *Designing Instructional Text*, 3rd edn (Kogan Page, 1994) 23–24
- *Guidelines for Document Designers* (American Institutes for Research, 1981) 77–78.

Here are some common fonts illustrated (10 point):

Times New Roman	Readability research indicates generally (though not universally) that readers find a serif font easier to read than a non-serif (*sans serif*). Serif fonts have extenders or flourishes at the ends of the main strokes.
Georgia	Readability research indicates generally (though not universally) that readers find a serif font easier to read than a non-serif (*sans serif*). Serif fonts have extenders or flourishes at the ends of the main strokes.
Palatino Linotype	Readability research indicates generally (though not universally) that readers find a serif font easier to read than a non-serif (*sans serif*). Serif fonts have extenders or flourishes at the ends of the main strokes.
Calibri	Readability research indicates generally (though not universally) that readers find a serif font easier to read than a non-serif (*sans serif*). Serif fonts have extenders or flourishes at the ends of the main strokes.
Arial	Readability research indicates generally (though not universally) that readers find a serif font easier to read than a non-serif (*sans serif*). Serif fonts have extenders or flourishes at the ends of the main strokes.

Distinguish headings from text

To make headings stand out, consider using a different font from the one for the body of the text. This book uses different fonts and font sizes for the various levels of headings:

- Heading Level 1 = Minion Pro-Bold – 14 pt (leading 16 pt)
- Heading Level 2 = Minion Pro-Bold – 12 pt (leading 14 pt)
- Heading Level 3 = Minion Pro-Bold – 10 pt (leading 12 pt)
- Heading Level 4 = Minion Pro-Regular – 10 pt (leading 12 pt)

Although a serif font may be best for text, a sans serif may provide a useful contrast for headings. Printed statutes in some jurisdictions follow this practice.

Resist the temptation to use 'fancy' fonts—whether for headings or text. By drawing attention to themselves, they divert attention from the content.

For further discussion, see **HEADINGS (Hierarchy of headings)**.

Judicial attitudes to font size

Font size generally irrelevant

Subject to three qualifications (see below), font size plays no part in legal interpretation. The common law generally holds parties bound by what they sign, regardless of the font in which it is printed: *Lezam Pty Ltd v Seabridge Australia Pty Ltd* (1992) 35 FCR 535. Judges have sometimes condemned the use of too-small type sizes in legal documents: see, eg, *Goldsbrough v Ford Credit Aust Ltd* (1989) ASC 55-946, 58,584; *George T Collings*

(Aust) Pty Ltd v H F Stevenson (1991) ASC 56-051. But judicial displeasure does not necessarily translate into an enforceable remedy.

Examples

- The Privy Council declined to place importance on fonts when interpreting an insurance policy. The policy incorporated the proposal form, which (their Lordships said) used up to 10 different fonts: 'The appellants use a proposal form which is printed in at least ten different founts of type. This no doubt diversifies its appearance, but for purposes of construction founts of type have no legal meaning.' [*Yorkshire Insurance Co Ltd v Campbell* [1917] AC 218, 222 (Lord Sumner). The fonts are not reproduced in the AC report, nor in reports of the case in the courts below at (1914) 19 CLR 166 and (1913) 15 WALR 122.]
- The Australian High Court saw no reason to deny force to a 'Romalpa' clause printed on the back of a form merely because the note on the front of the form drawing the reader's attention to the clause was in tiny type: *Associated Alloys Pty Limited v ACN 001 452 106 Pty Limited* [2000] HCA 25; (2000) 202 CLR 588, [71] (reproducing exactly the font and size).

Qualification (1): prescribed font sizes

Statute may prescribe minimum font sizes for text. The consequence of failure to comply will then depend on the specified consequences (if any) for breach.

Example

In New South Wales (Australia) vendors of land must attach a cooling-off statement to the contract for sale of the land. The statement must follow a prescribed form, with certain words to be printed 'in bold face capital letters at least 14 point', and the rest to be printed 'in bold face figures and letters at least 10 point'. Failure to comply entitles the purchaser to rescind the contract. [*Conveyancing (Sale of Land) Regulation 2017* (NSW), regs 12, 17]

In the UK, a Bill to regulate the font size in contracts in England and Wales was not enacted: see Small Print Bill 2008, at www.publications.parliament.uk/pa/cm200708/cmbills/076/08076.i-i.html

Qualification (2): consumer-protection legislation

Modern consumer-protection legislation often requires contract terms to be 'fair' or 'transparent'. Some stipulate font size as a factor in determining 'fairness' or 'transparency'. But even without express stipulation, courts may treat font size as a relevant factor in deciding whether the statuory protections have been breached. Antipodean courts in particular have been ready to do so:

- *Australian Competition and Consumer Commission v Chrisco Hampers Australia Ltd* [2015] FCA 1204, [90]; (2015) 239 FCR 33 (Edelman J: a 'densely packed page of small print terms and conditions')
- Australian Competition and Consumer Commission v JJ Richards & Sons Pty Ltd [2017] FCA 1224, [60] (font size 'very small')
- *Commerce Commission v Home Direct Limited* [2019] NZHC 2943, [53]–[54] ('small font in a condensed box towards the bottom of the page' and 'very small font … at the bottom of the page following a large number of other closely typed clauses').

Notably in these cases, the small font size obscured the importance of the information being conveyed.

Qualification (3): exemption clauses

Judges have occasionally taken small font size into account in holding exemption clauses unenforceable. Examples exist in a number of countries:

- **England**: *J Spurling Ltd v Bradshaw* [1956] 1 WLR 461, 468 (Denning LJ): 'Some clauses which I have seen would need to be printed in red ink on the face of the document with a red hand pointing to it before the notice could be held to be sufficient.'

- **Canada**: *Aurora TV and Radio Ltd v Gelco Express Ltd* (1990) 65 Man R (2d) 145 (limitation of liability clause on reverse side of bill of lading, in very small print, buried amongst other words under a heading that did not indicate a limitation clause; also, wording of the clause 'neither plain nor unambiguous,' 'unclear', and 'quite simply, legal gobbledygook').
- **Australia**: *Australian Competition and Consumer Commission v Henry Kaye* [2004] FCA 1363 (advertisement by property developer promising to select from those who attended seminars one to become a millionaire, qualified by fine print; held to constitute misleading and deceptive conduct in breach of trade practices legislation).
- **South Africa**: *Fourie v Hansen* [2000] JOL 5993 (W).
- **United States of America**: *Henningsen v Bloomfield Motors Inc* 32 NJ 358; 161 A 2d 69 (1960, NJ).

Further reading

- Matthew Butterick, *Typography for Lawyers* (Jones McLure, 2010) 135–37, 146–47
- Martin Cutts, *Oxford Guide to Plain English*, 5th edn (Oxford, 2020) ch 30
- Mark Sableman, 'Typographic Legibility: Delivering Your Message Effectively' (2016–2017) 17 *Scribes Journal of Legal Writing* 9
- Karen Schriver, *Dynamics in Document Design* (Wiley Computer Publishing,1997) chs 5 and 6
- Colin Wheildon, *Type & Layout* (Stathmoor Press, 1981)

See also **CAPITALS; DOCUMENT DESIGN; EMPHASIS; HEADINGS; READABILITY TESTS.**

FOOTNOTES

Be sparse with them

Do you really need footnotes? Perhaps you do, to convey ancillary information. In legal writing, that information might include case citations or statutory references. Usually, however, material that is important enough to include is important enough to embody in the main text, not consigned to footnotes. Too often, footnotes include material that is merely tangential to the main discussion—a repository of information proudly displayed, as if excessive detail were proof of deep analysis. In reality, excessive footnoting may betray an underlying insecurity with the subject matter: writers confident in their knowledge do not need the prop of voluminous footnotes. Indeed, busy readers learn to ignore footnotes of excessive length and detail, in the process perhaps missing nuggets buried in dross.

In judgments

Historically, footnotes in judgments were limited to providing case references, and occasional citations in support of propositions stated. With the advent of word processors, however, judgments began to use footnotes to comment on ancillary points and debate alternative perspectives—a practice now settled, and one that judges in past eras would have considered unnecessary distractions from the main task. The first United Kingdom appellate decision to use footnotes seems to have been *Corr v IBC Vehicles*, where Sedley LJ added 11 footnotes (strictly, endnotes): see [2006] EWCA Civ 331. Notably, as if to resist this development, the authorised report ([2007] 1 QB 46) incorporated the footnotes into the body of the text, giving the judgment a footnote-free appearance. But since then, footnotes have become commonplace in judgments. The practice provoked a commentator to liken judgments with footnotes to fish with feathers: R Munday, 'Fish with Feathers: English Judgments with Footnotes' (2006) 170 *Justice of the Peace* 444.

The precedential significance of footnotes in judgments remains an open question: *New South Wales Land and Housing Corp v Quinn* [2016] NSWCA 338, [61] (Ward JA). This is particularly so where the footnote purports to decide a point of law (as in *Farah Constructions Pty Ltd v Say-Dee Pty Ltd* [2007] HCA 22; (2007) 230 CLR 89, [125] fn 170).

Style issues

Conventions

For footnote numbers ('citational footnotes'), the following conventions are reasonably settled.

1. Insert the number immediately after the text to which it relates.
2. Use superscript.
3. Place the number directly after any relevant punctuation, as in Example 1:

   Example 1

   In *Jones v Smith*,[1] the court refused to overrule *Harris v Scarfe*[2]—a long standing case—because of the reputation of the judges who comprised the court.[3]

   [1] [2016] 1 All ER 27.
   [2] [1980] 1 All ER 99.
   [3] Lord Denning MR, Russell and Harman LJJ.

4. Some Commonwealth jurisdictions depart from conventions 2 and 3. For example, the High Court of Australia in more recent times:
   - in judgments as issued by the Court, prints footnote numbers in superscript, with the numbers *before* any relevant punctuation
   - in judgments as published in the authorised reports (ie, the Commonwealth Law Reports), puts footnote numbers in normal font inside brackets, with the numbers *after* any relevant punctuation.

   These usages appear in Example 2, taken from *R v Independent Broad-Based Anti-Corruption Commissioner* (2016), [53].

   Example 2

   Judgment as issued by High Court of Australia, [2016] HCA 8:

   > 'Thus, in *Sorby v The Commonwealth*[35], Gibbs CJ referred to *R v Boyes*[36], where it was said …'

   Judgment as published, (2016) 256 CLR 459:

   > 'Thus, in *Sorby v The Commonwealth* (35), Gibbs CJ referred to *R v Boyes* (36), where it was said …'

For the body of the footnotes:

1. Where a footnote contains multiple references, separate them with semicolons.
2. Otherwise, use normal punctuation within the body of a footnote, including ending with a full stop or other appropriate punctuation (such as a question mark).
3. For pinpoint references, follow the style for pinpoint references generally.

In text or at foot of page?

Should you keep footnotes 'in text', following immediately after the material to which they relate? Or should you move them to the foot of the page (hence, '*foot*note')? Both practices are found, and there are arguments in favour of each. To leave the material 'in text' suits readers who are interested in the authority for a proposition; but it interrupts the flow for those who are not. On the other hand, to move the material to the foot of the page helps readers who have no interest in that detail; but it interrupts the flow for those who have—for they must look down to the foot of the page, read the material, and then find their place again in the main text. Best practice may therefore be a matter of audience.

The use of '*end*notes'—whether at the end of a passage, or of a chapter, or of the book—seriously interferes with the flow for those interested in the endnoted material.

Further reading

- Arthur D Austin, 'Footnotes as Product Differentiation' (1987) 40 *Vanderbilt Law Review* 1131
- Bryan Garner, 'The Citational Footnote' (2000) 7 *Scribes Journal of Legal Writing* 97 (advocating footnotes for citations only)
- Ross Guberman, *Point Taken* (OUP, 2015) 147–53 (advocating four kinds of footnotes in judicial opinions: (1) to cite cases to show that a principle is well established; (2) to distinguish authorities; (3) to counter objections; and (4) to buttress a point)
- Joseph Kimble, *Seeing Through Legalese: More essays on Plain Language* (Carolina Academic Press, 2017), 187–92 (essay on where to put footnotes)
- Charles R Mayer, 'The Infernal Footnote' (1984) 70 *American Bar Association Journal* 93 (lamenting the legal writer's incurable addiction to footnotes—or 'Ping-Pong Ocular Syndrome')
- Abner Mikva, 'Goodbye to Footnotes' (1985) 56 *University of Colorado Law Review* 647 (advocating abolishing footnotes from judicial opinions)

See also **AUDIENCE; CITATION OF CASES.**

for the avoidance of doubt

Purpose

The purpose of *for the avoidance of doubt* (or simpler, *to avoid doubt*, or *to clarify*) is plain enough. It is to make clear to the reader something that might otherwise seem unclear, or to emphasise that the text does mean what it seems to be saying—'yes, dear reader, I really did mean to say that'. One situation might be where, taken at face value, a provision seems uncommercial. A statement added 'for the avoidance of doubt' may help negate the general principle of interpretation that courts prefer to interpret contracts in a commercially realistic ('business-like') way—because parties are able, if they wish, to enter into *un*commercial contracts. Another (more usual) situation is to give an example to reinforce a proposition, to ensure that the reader understands it. *Panochini v Jude* [2002] 2 Qd R 322, [15].

Arguments for and against

For

For the avoidance of doubt (or a simplified equivalent) can be useful where a provision might otherwise be puzzling or counter-intuitive. For example:

> 'It is hereby declared *for the avoidance of doubt* that, in relation to registered land, each of the following—
>
> (a) an equity by estoppel, and
>
> (b) a mere equity,
>
> has effect from the time the equity arises as an interest capable of binding successors in title ...' [*Land Registration Act 2002*, s 116]

The introductory *for the avoidance of doubt* helps put at rest any doubts over a point that might otherwise be puzzling. The proposition that the 'equities' specified in (a) and (b) are capable of binding successors in title may startle hardened land lawyers, or at least be sufficiently doubtful to require clarification—because long-accepted case law suggests otherwise.

Courts have found *for the avoidance of doubt* relevant in interpretation:

- A statement in a landlord's break notice to the tenant that *for the avoidance of all doubt* the landlord would be closing the premises on 24 October, clarified that the notice expired on 24 October and not (as might otherwise have been arguable) on 25 October: *Trafford MBC v Total Fitness (UK) Ltd* [2003] 2 P & CR 2, [53].
- A provision in a *Police Act* that, *to avoid doubt*, the existence of a criminal charge against an officer did not prevent the Commissioner from instituting disciplinary proceedings against the officer, clarified that the Commissioner could sack the officer before the charge was heard: *Commissioner of Police v Ferguson* [2019] WASCA 14; (2019) 54 WAR 177.

Against

There are two main arguments against *for the avoidance of doubt*. First, if a statement is clear, it needs no amplification to avoid doubt. This is particularly so in legislation, where a provision enacts what its words provide, regardless of any additional 'to avoid doubt ...' Logically, in legislation the expression adds no meaning: *Allen v Feather Products Pty Ltd* (2008) 72 NSWLR 597; [2008] NSWSC 259, [24]–[29]. Second, *for the avoidance of doubt* may *raise* doubts—for it may prompt the reader, otherwise in no doubt, to seek a reason for the words.

ex abundanti cautela

Some writers revert to the Latin original: *ex abundanti cautela*—for more abundant caution. The arguments for and against *for the avoidance of doubt* apply also to the Latin variant. However, the Latin poses the obvious problem that few readers will understand it. Prefer the plain English.

See also **ex abundanti cautela**.

for the purpose of

When used with the active participle of a verb, *for the purpose of* means simply *for*. So, trim it to *for*. Better still, where possible avoid the participle and substitute the verb: eg, *for the purpose of obtaining* a benefit = *to obtain* a benefit.

But take care in one situation. Where *for the purpose of* is intended to denote intent (*purpose*) rather than merely result, to substitute *for* may subtly change the meaning. For example, employees who do something which in fact *results* in personal advantage, but which they did not do *for that purpose*, may not be using their position *for the purpose of* gaining personal advantage: *Chew v The Queen* (1992) 173 CLR 626.

for the purposes of identification only

A phrase sometimes found in conveyances, leases, or other documents dealing with land, to limit the role of an attached plan that delineates the property. Where a plan described as 'for the purposes of identification only' conflicts with a written description of the land, the written description prevails: *Hopgood v Brown* [1955] 1 WLR 213, 228 (CA); *Johnson v Shaw* [2004] 1 P & CR 10, 133, 138 (CA). The self-abnegating formula 'for the purposes of identification *only*' deprives the plan of conclusive effect: *Strachey v Ramage* [2008] EWCA Civ 384, [39].

Variants include 'for the purposes of identification only[,] more particularly delineated' or 'for identification more particularly described'. Megarry J criticised the former phrase as self-contradictory (*Neilson v Poole* (1969) 20 P & CR 909, 916); Lord Hoffmann described it as 'fairly inconclusive' (*Alan Wibberley Building Ltd v Insley* [1999] 1 WLR 894, 899).

See also **PLANS**.

for the reason that

Prefer the shorter *because*.

See **because**.

for the time being

See **from time to time / for the time being**.

forbid / forbade

The past tense is 'forbade'—but it is sometimes misspelled 'forbad', perhaps because it rhymes with 'had'.

- '[The paragraph] needed to be clear on its face as to precisely what it meant, and precisely what it *forbad* [prefer: *forbade*] both the appellant and the respondent from doing.' [*S-C v H-C* [2010] EWCA Civ 21; [2010] WLR 1311, [17] (Wall LJ)]
- '[The] United States Supreme Court decided, in *Roper v Simmons*, that the Eighth and Fourteenth amendments of the United States Constitution *forbad* [prefer: *forbids*] the imposition of the death penalty upon offenders who were under 18 when the offence was committed.' [*R v Secretary of State for Home Department* [2005] UKHL 51; [2006] AC 159, [23] (Baroness Hale)]

force majeure

Law French: a major force; a higher force; an irresistible force; in law, a force so beyond a party's control that it excuses the party from performing a contractual obligation. Though often used, the term is inherently vague:

> '[T]he precise meaning of [*force majeure*] if it has one, has eluded lawyers for years.' [*Thomas Borthwick (Glasgow) Ltd v Faure Fairclough Ltd* [1968] 1 Lloyd's Rep 16, 28 (Donaldson J)]

For example, how strong must the force be? When is it beyond a party's reasonable control? All case law on these questions is necessarily context-dependent, giving an answer for the particular case but for few others. Where possible, list the specific events that will excuse performance—but remembering that sweep-up language at the end of a list of specifics might be read down under the *eiusdem generis* principle of interpretation.

Further reading

- *Halsbury's Laws of England*, 'Contract' (vol 22, 2019), [268] (force majeure clauses)
- 'Force Majeure', in *Law Words* (Centre for Plain Legal Language, University of Sydney,1995) 27; www.clarity-international.net/plain-language-resources/general-resources/ (plain language alternatives)
- David Yates, 'Drafting Force Majeure and Related Clauses' (1991) 3 *Journal of Contract Law* 186

See also **act (something done)**; **eiusdem generis**.

foreclosure

One of the mortgagee's remedies for the mortgagor's default. Foreclosure extinguishes the equity of redemption, making the mortgagee the absolute owner of the property (usually land): *Heath v Pugh* (1881) 6 QBD 345, 360. To be distinguished from *sale*, where the mortgagee sells the property and recoups the debt from the proceeds of sale. In some jurisdictions (notably the US), *foreclosure* is also used in the sense of *sale*; but English and Commonwealth usage generally preserves the distinction.

Further reading

S Bridge, E Cooke and M Dixon (eds), *Megarry & Wade's Law of Real Property*, 9th edn (Sweet & Maxwell, 2019) [24-006]–[24-012]

See also **equity of redemption**.

forego / forgo

To *forego* means to go before (a *foregone* conclusion); to *forgo* means to give up (a *forgone* debt). The two are often confused, eg:

- 'Discovering the reasons why a particular landlord came to lose or to *forego* [substitute: *forgo*] public funding … [is not always] a difficult task.' [*Birmingham City Council v Secretary of State for Work and Pensions* [2016] EWCA Civ 1211, [41] (Lindblom LJ)]
- '[T]he Senior Financiers will *forego* [substitute: *forgo*] their debt …' [*JP Morgan Chase Bank NA v Australia and New Zealand Banking Group Ltd* [2011] NSWSC 1359, [51] (Barrett J)]

forehand rent

See **backhand rent**.

FOREIGN (NON-ENGLISH) WORDS AND PHRASES

History

Legal English reflects the mixture of languages that produced the English language generally. The main sources are French and Latin. The French influence came chiefly from the Norman Conquest of 1066. The invaders spoke Norman French—a dialect form of French. For nearly 300 years after the Norman Conquest, French was the language of legal proceedings, which is why many words in current legal use have their roots in this period.

However, during this 300-year period Latin remained the language of formal records and statutes: Pollock and Maitland, *The History of English Law Before the Time of Edward I*, 2nd edn (Cambridge University Press, 1968) vol 1, 82, 86. Statutes were in Latin until about 1300, then in French until 1485, then in English alongside French for a short time, and in English alone from 1489: Baugh and Cable, *A History of the English Language*, 5th edn (Routledge, 2002) 153, 154.

Whether to use foreign terms

Lawyers today continue to use terms drawn from Latin or French. Should they do so? The answer depends on the term's acceptance into standard English. Where a foreign word or phrase has entered standard, modern English, there is no harm in using it. Examples from Latin in standard use, and familiar to many readers, include *ad hoc* (temporary), *et cetera* (and the rest), *inter alia* (among other things). Examples from Norman French in standard use, and familiar to many readers, include *chattel, possession, property*.

But many foreign-sourced legal words or phrases have not been accepted into standard, modern English. Examples from Norman French, familiar to lawyers but meaningless to non-lawyers, are *seisin*, *voir dire*, and *cestui que trust*. Where foreign-sourced terms have not become standard English, lawyers should consider avoiding them, for four reasons:

1. The reader may not understand them—and what is the point of text that readers do not understand?
2. The reader may consider the writer to be pompous.
3. The foreign origin may convey a sense of precision and technical significance that the terms do not possess.
4. Most are not true legal terms of art, so there is little risk in discarding them for a modern English substitute.

The difficulties are exacerbated where lawyers quote slabs of text from non-English-language sources. An extreme example, quoted by judges more than once, is the prayer of Ajax, rendered in Classical Greek.

Example 1

> 'Courts … should recall the prayer of Ajax:
>
> Ζεῦ πάτερ, ἀλλὰ σὺ ῥῦσαι ὑπ ' ἠέρος υἷας'Αχαιῶν,
> ποίησσν δ ' αἴθρην, δὸς δ' ὀφθαλμοῖσιν ἰδέσθαι·
> ἐν δὲφάει καὶ ὄλεσσον, ἐπεί νύ τοι εὔαδεν οὕτως.
>
> [This] is a supplication that must have occurred to many who have considered recent decisions on the subject of the duty of care: "[S]ave us from this fog and give us a clear sky, so that we can use our eyes."' [*Graham Barclay Oysters Pty Ltd v Ryan* [2002] HCA 54; (2002) 211 CLR 540, 616 [211] (Kirby J), by way of footnote acknowledging the source and offering a summary translation: Homer, *The Iliad*, trans EV Rieu (Penguin,1956) 333.]

Example 2

> 'The prayer of Ajax—"Eν δε Φαει και ολεσσον"—has been heard before in your Lordships' House, but I think its appeal is even stronger when obscurity is created by deliberate legislation than when it arises from the less wilful confusions of the common law.' [*St Aubyn v Attorney-General* [1952] AC 15, 45 (Lord Radcliffe), offering no translation]

Whether to italicise

The general convention is to italicise foreign words and phrases, unless by familiarity they have become standard English (eg, ad nauseam, alias, alibi, bona fide, prima facie). However, some writers and publishers no longer italicise any foreign words and phrases, no matter how common in standard English; and this practice is sufficiently standard not to be considered 'wrong'.

Further reading

- 'The French Connection', *Law Words* (Centre for Plain Legal Language, University of Sydney, 1995) 7; www.clarity-international.net/plain-language-resources/general-resources tracing the use of Law French in English law, and counselling against its continued use except where necessary and always adding an explanation in standard English)
- Theobald Mathew, 'Law-French' (1938) 54 *Law Quarterly Review* 358 (tracing the history of Law French in England)

- Roderick Munday, 'Lawyers and Latin' (2004) 168 *Justice of the Peace* 775 (arguing for the use of Latin in law, at least between lawyers)

See also **LATIN**.

forfeit

Used in law in the contrasting senses of *lose* and *take*. A person who loses something is said to *forfeit* it; thus, a defaulting purchaser *forfeits* (loses) the deposit, and a defaulting tenant *forfeits* (loses) the lease. This meaning is also seen in, for example, the '*forfeiture* rule'—ie, the public policy rule precluding a person who has unlawfully killed another from benefiting from the killing (as in the *Forfeiture Act* 1982)—and the equitable principle of 'relief against *forfeiture*'. But a person who takes away something under legal right is also said to *forfeit* it; thus, a vendor *forfeits* (takes) a defaulting purchaser's deposit, and a landlord *forfeits* (takes) a defaulting tenant's lease.

This contrasting usage, though well-known to lawyers, is apt to confound non-lawyers. Sometimes, there may be no choice but to use *forfeit* or *forfeiture*—eg, in a landlord's statutory notice to a tenant 'forfeiting' the lease, or a tenant's counter-notice seeking 'relief against forfeiture'. Otherwise, however, prefer a self-evident alternative. For example:

- '[The Lease] included, in clause 5, a right for the landlords to *forfeit* [prefer: *confiscate*; *terminate*] the Lease for non-payment of rent or other breach of covenant by the tenant.' [*Marks and Spencer plc v BNP Paribas Securities Services Trust Company (Jersey) Ltd* [2015] UKSC 72; [2016] AC 742, [7] (Lord Neuberger)]
- 'A long line of authority establishes that if an insured makes a fraudulently inflated claim under the policy he *forfeits* [prefer: *loses the right to*] any lesser claim which he could properly have made.' [*Versloot Dredging BV v HDI Gerling Industrie Versicherung AG* [2014] EWCA Civ 1349; [2015] 2 WLR 1063, [75] (Clarke LJ)]

See also **deposit**.

forge (verb)

To fraudulently imitate something else, as where A forges B's signature to a document. In legal terminology, 'forgery' is said to be used in two senses: (1) the 'strict' sense, where A forges B's signature as if it were B's own; and (2) the 'looser' sense, where A executes a document purportedly 'on behalf of' B, but without B's authority—eg, where a company director attaches the genuine company seal to a document and signs as director, but has no authority to bind the company to the document: see *Caratti v Mammoth Investments Pty Ltd* (2016) 50 WAR 84, 201–02; [2016] WASCA 84, [541]–[542].

Further reading

Halsbury's Laws of England, 'Criminal Law' (vol 25, 2016) [405] and cross-references to forgery-related offences.

See also **counterfeit / forge**.

form of

See **in the form of**.

FORMATTING

See **DOCUMENT DESIGN; EMPHASIS; FONTS**.

former / latter

It is usually better to repeat words or phrases than rely on the shorthand *former* or *latter*. The writer, having produced the text, will know which referred-to matter is *former* and which is *latter*, but the reader may have to look back to identify which is which. The reader's difficulty is compounded where the content of each *former* and *latter* matter is complex, as in the following examples:

- 'The essential issue between the parties is whether the regulation 2(a) covered only the asbestos industry and was concerned with asbestos in its raw unprocessed condition, as submitted on behalf of the appellant, or whether it extended to processed asbestos products, as contended on behalf of the respondent. In powerful judgments, Lord Reed espouses the *former* view, whereas Lord Kerr espouses the *latter*.' [*McDonald v National Grid Electricity Transmission Plc* [2014] UKSC 53, [115]; [2015] 1 AC 1128 (Lord Clarke)]
- 'A distinction is to be drawn between any place which is, and any place which is not, occupied, managed or controlled by the accused and the location of the drug must, for the purposes of the section, properly be ascribable to the *former*, not the *latter*.' [*Symes v Lawler* [1995] 1 Qd R 226, 228 (Fitzgerald P and Cullinane J)]

formulae

The Latin plural of *formula*. Modern legal usage accepts *formulas*.

FORMULAS

Their uses

Properly used, mathematical formulas can replace words—reducing length, aiding comprehension, and averting ambiguity. Judges encourage their appropriate use in legal documents. Sometimes judges themselves take the initiative (as in example 2).

Examples

1. In negotiations for a lease, the parties' surveyors prepared an agreed rent-review formula. The parties' lawyers then attempted to put the formula into words. The formula was relatively simple, but the words were tortuous—so much so that no one noticed that the words differed from the formula. Lord Hoffmann said:

   'I doubt whether the mistakes which gave rise to this litigation would have happened if the surveyors' formula had been expressed algebraically instead of verbally. … Rent formulae can often be expressed more simply and unambiguously in algebraic form and this case shows that a very modest degree of numeracy can save a great deal of money.' [*London Regional Transport v Wimpey Group Services Ltd* (1986) 280 EG 898, 900; (1987) 53 P & CR 356]

2. A statute imposed stamp duty on transactions by 'land rich' companies. The statute used words to define 'land rich'. The court transformed the words into a formula, as follows:

   'A taxpayer is "land rich" if (at the relevant date):

   $$\frac{L}{P} \times \frac{100}{1} \geq 60\%$$

   where L is the value of the land owned by [the taxpayer], and P is the value of all of [the taxpayer's] property (including the land).'

   [*Commissioner of State Revenue v Snowy Hydro Ltd* [2012] VSCA 145; (2012) 43 VR 110, [5]. The medium neutral (internet) version does not reproduce the formula accurately.]

Prefer simplicity (where possible)

Will the reader understand the formula? Some formulas assume a detailed knowledge of mathematics and scientific symbols. Unless the reader has that knowledge, a complex formula communicates no more effectively than a complex sentence.

Choose helpful symbols

When drafting formulas, choose symbols that intuitively relate to the subject matter of the formula. To illustrate, consider the obligation of a tenant of premises in a shopping centre to pay a proportion of the total outgoings for the centre, based on proportionate floor area. The obligation could be expressed:

$$\text{Proportion of outgoings} = \frac{\text{Tenant's floor area}}{\text{Centre's floor area}}$$

where:

'**Proportion of outgoings**' means ...

'**Tenant's floor area**' means ...

'**Centre's floor area**' means ...

That can be recast as:

$$A = \frac{B}{C}$$

where:

A is the proportion of outgoings payable by the Tenant

B is the floor area of the Tenant's premises

C is the floor area of the Centre.

However, the symbols (letters) A, B, C are not helpful. It would be better to choose symbols (letters) that more self-evidently reflect the concepts which are the subject of the formula. Thus, a more reader-friendly formula would be:

$$P = \frac{T}{C}$$

where:

P is the proportion of outgoings payable by the Tenant

T is the floor area of the Tenant's premises

C is the floor area of the Centre.

Calculations by steps

In some contexts, an alternative to a formula is a 'step' procedure, which leads the reader step-by-step through the process of calculation.

Example

A lease of a premises in a shopping centre requires the tenant to pay a proportion of the outgoings for the entire centre, based on proportionate floor area. The calculation can be expressed by steps, as follows:

(1) The Tenant must pay as outgoings an amount that bears the same proportion of the total outgoings for the Centre as the floor area of the Tenant's premises bears to the floor area of the Centre. [*Or simpler*: The Tenant must pay a proportion of the total outgoings for the Centre based on floor area.]

(2) To calculate the amount:

(a) first, work out the floor area of the Tenant's premises;
(b) second, work out the floor area of the Centre;
(c) third, calculate the area in (a) as a proportion of the area in (b);
(d) finally, apply that proportion to the total outgoings for the Centre.

The resulting amount is the amount the Tenant must pay.

The explanation takes more space than a formula, but some readers might find it easier to follow.

Need for accuracy

Of course, formulas (whether expressed in symbols or steps) must be accurate. Loosely drafted formulas can wreak as much havoc as loosely drafted words, as in the following examples:

- A formula for calculating the price that a landowner was to pay a developer on the sale of flats in the development omitted a component ('+E'). Although the omission was to one party's (the developer's) significant disadvantage, the court refused rectification: *George Wimpey UK Ltd v VI Construction Ltd* [or *VI Components Ltd*] [2005] EWCA Civ 77.
- A charterparty escalation clause, designed to provide for a base figure to be increased by reference to Italian inflation, stated the base figure in US dollars. The figure should have been in Italian lire. The court refused rectification: *Agip SpA v Navigazione Alta Italia SpA (The Nai Genova)* [1984] 1 Lloyds Rep 353.
- The formula 'x% of A in excess of B' is ambiguous. It can mean '(x/100×A)−B', or it can mean 'x/100(A−B)': *Chartbrook Ltd v Persimmon Homes Ltd* [2009] UKHL 38; [2009] 1 AC 1101, [86] (example by Lord Walker).

Worked examples

If there is any doubt about how a formula operates, include a worked example. Of course, the worked example must be correct: the drafter's mistake in applying the formula undermines the correctness of the formula itself. As a precaution against error, drafters commonly include a qualification that if an example conflicts with the text, the text prevails; this qualification may undermine confidence in the drafter's skill, but at least precludes argument over which prevails.

Further reading

- Nicky Armstrong, 'Mathematics in Legislation', *Loophole* (Jan 2018) 4, at www.calc.ngo/publications/loopholes#loophole-table-2018 (recommending formulas—figures only, not words and figures—for all except the simplest calculations)
- Peter Butt, *Modern Legal Drafting*, 3rd edn (Cambridge University Press, 2013) 159–61
- M Casen and J M Steiner, 'Mathematical Functions and Legal Drafting' (1986) 102 *Law Quarterly Review* 585

See also **BRACKETS**; **FRACTIONS**; **NOTES AND EXAMPLES**; **NUMBERS**.

foro

See **in foro**.

forthwith

An archaism popular with lawyers, but inherently vague and open-ended. If something is to be done *forthwith*, how quickly must it be done? Context might clarify—but then, it might not. *Forthwith* can imply a range of degrees of urgency:

- immediately
- with as little delay as possible: *Hill v Sidney* [1991] 2 Qd R 547
- in the shortest practicable time having regard to the surrounding circumstances: *Hudson v Hill* (1874) 43 LJ CP 273, 280 (Grove J); *Chesham v Wright* [1970] NZLR 247, 251 (Beattie J); *Scott v Ministry of Transport* [1983] NZLR 234, 236 (Cooke J)
- within a reasonable time: *Measures v McFadyen* (1910) 11 CLR 723, 729 (Griffith CJ); *Hillingdon London Borough Council v Cutler* [1968] 1 QB 124, 135 (Harman LJ).

Examples

- Delivery within 14 days could be delivery *forthwith*: *Staunton v Wood* (1851) SC 15 Jur 1123.
- Delivery delayed one hour was not delivery *forthwith*: *Bontex Knitting Works Ltd v St John's Garage* [1943] 2 All ER 690.
- Action delayed for almost 3 years was (in the circumstances) carried out *forthwith*: *Brown v Bonnyrigg Magistrates*, 1936 SC 258.

Wherever possible, specify the date or time within which something is to be done. But if that is not possible, consider substituting for the quaint *forthwith* more modern equivalents such as *at once*, *immediately*, *straight away*, *without delay*.

Further reading

Kim Lewison, *The Interpretation of Contracts*, 6th edn (Sweet & Maxwell, 2015) [15.10]

See also **as soon as possible / as soon as practicable**; **immediately**; **promptly**.

forum non conveniens

Latin: a court or tribunal that is inconvenient. A maxim expressing the principle that courts have a discretion to decline jurisdiction when justice and the parties' convenience would be better served by taking the dispute to the courts of another jurisdiction. For lawyers, the Latin may capture the extensive case law on whether a forum is 'inappropriate'. However, except in technical contexts, an English translation would better inform most readers—eg, 'inconvenient forum' or 'inappropriate forum'. For those lawyers who feel umbilically joined to the Latin, one option is to retain the term but explain it (as in the first two extracts below). But a better option is to have the strength of conviction to ditch the Latin, as in the third extract.

- '[An] English court has power to order a stay of proceedings on the basis that England is an inappropriate forum (*forum non conveniens*) ...' [Dicey, Morris and Collins, *The Conflict of Laws*, 15th edn (Sweet & Maxwell, 2012) Rule 38(2)—stating the principle, then adding the Latin tag]
- '[An earlier case] considered the impact of article 2 [of the *Brussels Regulation*] on the ability of the English court to stay proceedings in its discretion on the grounds of *forum non conveniens*, that is to say that it would be more appropriate for a court in a jurisdiction outside the European Union to resolve the dispute.' [*Plaza BV v The Law Debenture Trust Corporation Plc* [2015] EWHC 43 (Ch), [59] (Proudman J)—retaining the Latin but adding an explanation]
- 'It is surely better to use English language when attempting to explain English law. In the *Spiliada* case Lord Goff observed ... that "appropriate" was a better translation of the Latin word "*conveniens*" than "convenient". The Latin word "*forum*", however, has also become an English word. So, in what follows, I will refer to the principle as being that of the less appropriate forum.' [[2020] UKSC 30; [2020] 3 WLR 171, [28] (Lord Wilson)]

See also **'CHOICE OF LAW' CLAUSE**; **JURISDICTION CLAUSE**.

FORWARD SLASH

The forward slash (/)—sometimes called the *virgule* or the *solidus*—is increasingly seen in legal writing. Sometimes it simply means *each* or *per* (eg, *20 words/minute*). Usually, though, it indicates a relationship between concepts or between people: eg, 'the law/equity distinction' (shorthand for 'the distinction between common law and equity'), or 'the landlord/tenant relationship' (shorthand for 'the relationship between landlord and tenant'). The relationships can also be represented (and perhaps more clearly) with an en dash (eg, 'law–equity', 'landlord–tenant').

The forward slash is also used as a substitute for *and/or*: eg, 'You can sue in tort/contract.' But the meaning of the slash in such constructions is not always self-evident, requiring readers to deduce meaning from the writer's shorthand.

Example

> '[Regardless of whether the reference extends to] claims based on *estoppel/misleading [etc] conduct*, [the clauses] are predicated on an amount [owing], … and if there is an arguable defence that [no sum was owing] at the date demand was made of the borrower, then there is no *right/liability* upon which the [clauses] can operate.' [*O'Brien v Bank of Western Australia Ltd* [2013] NSWCA 71; (2013) 16 BPR 31,705, [94] (Ward JA)]
>
> The first slash seems to invite the meaning: 'claims based on estoppel *and/or* claims based on misleading [etc] conduct'. This could be expressed more briefly: 'claims based on estoppel *or* on misleading [etc] conduct', because (as a matter of ordinary English, in this context) claims based on 'A *or* B' include claims based on 'A *and* B'. The second slash seems to invite the meaning: 'there is no right *and/or* liability upon which the clauses can operate'. This also could be expressed as 'no right *or* liability'. In the result, the sentence could be recast more simply:
>
> '[Regardless of whether the reference extends to] claims based on *estoppel or misleading [etc] conduct*, [the clauses] are predicated on an amount [owing], … and if there is an arguable defence that [no sum was owing] at the date demand was made of the borrower, then there is no *right or liability* upon which the [clauses] can operate.'

See also **and / or**; **DASHES**.

FRACTIONS

Standard conventions

- Prefer fraction-symbols, not Arabic numbers separated by a slash—eg, 5½ (*not* 51/2; *not* 5 1/2)—unless perhaps there is a risk that the fraction symbols might disappear when importing or reformatting the document.
- Where a simple fraction stands alone, use hyphenated words: eg, one-half (*not* ½), one-quarter, three-quarters.
- Where a non-decimal fraction has a denominator greater than 10, use Arabic numerals: eg, $^{11}/_{12}$ or $^{25}/_{27}$.
- Where a fraction symbol may detract from readability, spell it out in full: 'the first half of the year' (*not* 'the first ½ of the year').

Most writers decimalise fractions that have exact decimal equivalents: eg, 10.25 (*not* 10¼). But this is a matter of personal preference; the only rule is to be consistent throughout the document.

See also **FORMULAS**; **NUMBERS**.

FRACTIONS OF DAY

See **day**.

fraud / fraudulent / fraudulently

General meaning

Beware of ambiguity inherent in *fraud*, and in its grammatical variants as an adjective (*fraudulent*) and adverb (*fraudulently*). The word (and its variants) can pose many potential issues. For example:

> A uses B's money to purchase an item for A's own use. Is A guilty of the crime of '*fraudulently* using' B's money where:
>
> - A believes he is using his own (A's) money?
> - A believes he has B's authority to spend the money?
> - A believes that B would give authority if B knew the circumstances?
> - A believes that the use of B's money would not harm B?
> - A intends to pay back the money?
>
> The term '*fraudulently* using' of itself does not answer these questions.
>
> [Source: Bernard MacKenna, 'The Undefined Adverb in Criminal Statutes' [1966] *Criminal Law Review* 548, 549]

Special meanings

Fraud (and its grammatical variants) has a special meaning in certain contexts, where case law has resolved some of the ambiguities inherent in the general meaning. Examples include:

- **Fraud on a power**. An equitable doctrine prohibiting the exercise of a power for a purpose or with an intention beyond the scope of the instrument creating the power: *Vatcher v Paull* [1915] AC 372, 378. *Fraud* here does not connote dishonest intent, but merely acting beyond the scope of the power.
- **Fraud on the minority**. A company law principle rendering invalid a majority decision altering the company's articles to allow expropriation of a minority holder's shares or rights attaching to those shares. Here also *fraud* does not require dishonest intent; rather, the question is whether the power was exercised for an improper purpose or operates oppressively on the minority.
- **Fraudulent conveyance**. A disposition of property made with intent to put the property beyond the reach of creditors. Here, *fraud* requires dishonest intent, but the disposition is valid if the transferee purchased for value and did not know of the fraudulent intent. See (1571) 13 Eliz I c 5 entitled 'An Act against Fraudulent Deeds, Gifts, Alienations, etc'; replaced by *Law of Property Act 1925*, s 172; in turn replaced by *Insolvency Act 1986*, ss 423–25.
- **Fraudulent misrepresentation**. A representation made either with dishonest intent or without caring whether it was true or false (ie, with 'reckless indifference' about its truth or falsity).

free and clear

An unnecessary pairing: *free* and *clear* mean the same thing. For example, if a land title is *free* (in the sense of 'free from encumbrances'), it is also *clear*; if it is *clear*, it is also *free*. Using both words is pure legalism. So, in conveyancing documents a vendor may warrant that the title is 'free and clear', or even 'free, clear, and unencumbered'; but it is sufficient to warrant that it is 'clear' or that it is 'free' or that it is 'unencumbered'—the longer, composite versions offer no additional protection: *Kohlbrand v Ranieri* 823 NE 2d 76 (Ohio, 2005) (Painter J).

See also **encumbrance**; **WORD PAIRINGS**.

free and uninterrupted

A lawyer's pairing, often found in the grant of property rights such as easements, where the grantee is given 'the free and uninterrupted' right of passage through the grantor's land. Here, *free* means 'unhindered'—which might not always mean the same as 'uninterrupted', and so the two words might not be synonyms. But when joined in a legal context they mean essentially the same thing: passage will not be impeded. Indeed, usually *both* words can be discarded: eg, 'the ~~free and uninterrupted~~ right of passage through the grantor's land'.

See also **full and free**; **WORD PAIRINGS**.

free rein

Thus spelled, not 'free reign'. The expression's heritage is equestrian, not royal.

> 'I propose to deal with this application on the basis which is artificially favourable from the claimant's prospective [sic] that he has *a free reign* [prefer: *free rein*] to seek to argue what he chooses before this court …' [*R v Association of Chartered Certified Accountants* [2017] EWHC 2383 (Admin), [14] (Kay J)]

freed and discharged

A lawyer's standard word pairing: eg, in security documents, a person is 'freed and discharged' from a debt; or in conveyancing documents, land is conveyed 'freed and discharged' of [ie, from] encumbrances. In law, *charge* can have many meanings—a criminal accusation; a judge's instruction to the jury; expenses; an encumbrance on property to secure payment of a debt. But *dis*charge always carries the sense of unloading, unburdening, or freeing. So in the pairing, *freed* and *discharged* are synonyms; one word will suffice.

See also **WORD PAIRINGS**.

freehold

In relation to land, the equivalent of a fee simple. A *freehold* owner has the same rights and duties as the owner of an estate in fee simple: *Glasgow v Hall* [2007] QCA 19.

See **fee simple**.

freely and voluntarily

A lawyer's habitual pairing, found in a number of areas of law: eg, criminal law (consent 'freely and voluntarily' given) and wills (testator's consent 'freely and voluntarily' given). Despite the considerable case law around the term (surveyed at length in *Tonkiss v Graham* [2002] NSWSC 891), in most circumstances either *freely* or *voluntarily* will suffice—there is no need for both.

See also **WORD PAIRINGS**.

freezing order

The modern, plain-language synonym for 'Mareva injunction' (so-named after the decision in *Mareva Compania Naviera SA v International Bulkcarriers SA* [1995] 2 Lloyd's Rep 509). The synonym was introduced with the Woolf Reforms. A freezing order prevents defendants from transferring assets beyond the reach of the judicial process: *Mercedes Benz AG v Leiduck* [1996] AC 284, 306; *Cardile v LED Builders Pty Ltd* (1998) 195 CLR 1.

See also **WOOLF REFORMS**.

FRI lease

In UK usage, a lease under which the tenant agrees to keep the premises in full repair and to insure them—hence Full Repair and Insure—or to reimburse the landlord for doing so.

from (time)

from … (a date)

Usual meaning

When time is expressed to start *from* a stated day, that day is excluded. So, in calculating the period of '7 days *from* today', the period begins tomorrow. A week's notice '*from* now' [early afternoon on 15 July] starts to run on the next day [16 July]: *West v Kneels* [1987] ICR 146. Case law supplies many examples:

- An insurance policy, issued at 11.45 am on 2 December, was expressed to be valid for '15 days *from* the commencement date'. Held, the policy started at midnight on 2/3 December (ie, at the end of, and so not counting, the first day), and therefore was still current at 5.45 pm on 17 December: *Cartwright be MacCormack* [1963] 1 WLR 18.
- A shareholder was entitled, by notice to the company, to convert his preference shares to ordinary shares. The shares would become ordinary shares '*from*' the date of delivery of the notice. Held, the conversion took effect on the day following the day of delivery of the notice: *Associated Beauty Aids Pty Ltd v Federal Commissioner of Taxation* (1965) 113 CLR 662.
- A contract for sale allowed the vendor to serve on the purchaser a notice requiring completion '14 days *from*'1 March. The vendor served a notice requiring completion on 15 March. Held, the notice was too short; it allowed only 13 (clear) days: *Velik v Steingold* [2013] NSWCA 303, [53]–[59].
- A mortgage stipulated for interest to be paid '*from* 1 July'. Held, the obligation to pay began on 2 July (ie, no interest was payable for 1 July): *Re Serafino* (1989) 86 ALR 283.

Subject to context

However, this 'usual' meaning of *from*—as with all words and phrases—varies with context. The circumstances may show that *from* (a date) is used in an inclusive way, with that date included in the counting. For example:

- A contract of employment starting *from* 15 October started *on* that day: *Wilkinson v Gaston* (1846) 9 QB 137; 115 ER 1227.
- In a deed, 'twenty-one years *from* the date of [this deed]' included the day *on which* the deed was executed: *English v Cliff* [1914] 2 Ch 376.
- In a bankruptcy notice specifying the 'date *from*' which interest under a judgment debt is claimed, interest can be claimed from the actual day of the judgment (not the following day): *Ashworth v Metcash Food & Grocery Pty Ltd* [2015] FCA 292; (2015) 231 FCR 567.

Is there a 'usual meaning' at all?

So many cases hold that *from* can carry either an exclusive or an inclusive sense, that it may be doubted whether any 'usual' meaning exists. Rather, it may simply be a matter of finding the meaning from the context: *Ackland v Lutley* (1839) 9 Ad & E 879; 112 ER 1446; *Meggeson v Groves* [1917] 1 Ch 158; *West v Barr* [1945] 1 WWR 337; *Hughes v NM Superannuation Pty Ltd* (1993) 29 NSWLR 653; *Chief Commissioner of Land Tax v Macary Manufacturing Pty Ltd* (1999) 48 NSWLR 299.

Thus, the starting date of a lease 'to commence *from* 1 January' may be the same as a lease 'to commence *on* 1 January'—ie, 1 January is day 1 of the lease: *Pugh v Duke of Leeds* (1777) 2 Cowp 714; 98 ER 1323; *Sidebotham v Holland* [1895] 1 Ch 378, 384 (Lindley LJ). This may be particularly so where the lease stipulates that the first payment of rent is due on 1 January: *Ladyman v Wirral Estates Ltd* [1968] 2 All ER 197. But the cases are not easily reconcilable: in *Meggeson v Groves* [1917] 1 Ch 158, a tenancy granted *from* 25 March was held to commence at midnight of 25/26 March (ie, counting was postponed until 26 March).

Variants

from and after (a date)

When time is expressed to start *from and after* a stated day, that day is excluded. The addition of *and after* reinforces the 'usual' meaning of *from*.

from ... until (a date)

The introduction of 'until' introduces a possible ambiguity. Consider: 'The premises are available *from* 1 June *until* [or *to*] 1 July.' Are they available *on* 1 June, and are they available for the *whole of* 1 July? It is much better to state, for example:

> 'The premises are available from 1 June until 1 July, both days included.'
>
> Or:
>
> 'The premises are available from 1 June until 1 July, both days excluded.'

from ... (an event)

Meaning

Where time is expressed to start *from* an event—such as *from* the giving of notice or consent—the computation starts at the moment the event occurs, and not on the next day (as would be the case where time runs simply *from* a day): *Howard's case* (1699) 2 Salk 625; 91 ER 528. For example, if insurance cover starts '15 days *from commencement of risk*', it starts at the actual time on the actual day on which the risk commenced, which is earlier than '15 days *from the date of commencement of risk*' (which normally starts on the following day): *Cartwright v MacCormack* [1963] 1 WLR 18; [1963] 1 All ER 11 (CA). To counter the possibility of a court invoking the principle against recognising fractions of a day, specify the hour of the day from which time is to run—eg, '15 days commencing at 4 pm on 3 October and ending at 4 pm on 18 October'.

Variant: from and after (an event)

In some contexts, 'from and after' (an event) points not to a date span but to a condition—ie, not *from* but *subject to*. Consider the following example:

> A testator devises property 'to my widow for her life, and *from and after* her death, to my nephews'. Here, *from and after* could mean either of two things:
>
> 1. The nephews take immediate interests, but *payment* to them must await the widow's death (as in *Rhodes v Rhodes* (1882) 7 App Cas 192).
> 2. The nephews acquire no interest until the widow dies (and only if they survive the widow); that is, the phrase introduces a condition precedent (as in *Re Jobson* (1889) 14 Ch D 154).

Further reading

Elizabeth Cooke, '"Touching the Time for the Beginning of a Lease for Yeares"' [1993] *Conveyancer and Property Lawyer* 206 (the quotation is from Lord Coke).

See also **after (a date)**; **by (a date)**; **beginning with / beginning from**; **condition precedent**; **corresponding-date rule**; **day**;TIME; **until (a date)**.

from the beginning of the world

An expression found in some deeds of release: eg, 'I release you from all claims ... *from the beginning of the world* to the date of this deed.' In times before the first general statute of limitation (*Limitation Act* 1623), the expression may have served some purpose. But it survived the enactment of that Act (see the deed of release in *Wood v Barker* (1865) LR 1 Eq 139), and although now self-evident nonsense, is still found in some modern deeds of release (see, eg, the deed of release reproduced in **WORD STRINGS**).

from time to time / for the time being

Meanings

From time to time: an adverbial phrase, indicating that a power can be exercised, or an obligation must be performed, more than once. It means 'as occasion may require' (*Bryan v Arthur* (1839) 11 Ad & El 108, 117; 113 ER 354, 358, Williams J), or 'at any time' (*McNeil v McNeil* (1942) 59 WN (NSW) 202, 203–04, Jordan CJ). For example, 'The trustees may *from time to time* mortgage trust property.'

For the time being: an adjectival phrase, indicating that a provision applies to whoever holds a particular office at the relevant time: eg, 'The trustees *for the time being* may mortgage trust property.'

Sometimes unnecessary

The two phrases often appear in combination: eg, 'The trustees *for the time being* may *from time to time* mortgage trust property.' While the meaning is clear, the combination is unnecessarily repetitive. Unless context requires otherwise, there is no apparent difference between the following two examples:

1. 'The trustees *for the time being* may *from time to time* mortgage trust property.'
2. 'The trustees may mortgage trust property.'

The formulation in (2) clearly refers to the trustees at the time of mortgaging the property (whoever they may be), so 'for the time being' is superfluous. And the only possible reason for retaining *from time to time* would be to preclude any argument that the trustees, having exercised a power once, have discharged the function and cannot exercise it again: *Lawrie v Lees* (1881) 7 App Cas 19, 29 (Lord Penzance). That seems an unlikely meaning.

In statutes, argument over the matter is resolved by s 12 of the *Interpretation Act 1978*:

> **12 Continuity of powers and duties**
>
> (1) Where an Act confers a power or imposes a duty it is implied, unless the contrary intention appears, that the power may be exercised, or the duty is to be performed, from time to time as occasion requires.
>
> (2) Where an Act confers a power or imposes a duty on the holder of an office as such, it is implied, unless the contrary intention appears, that the power may be exercised, or the duty is to be performed, by the holder for the time being of the office.

Sometimes ambiguous

Be aware of potential ambiguity in *from time to time* or *for the time being*. For example:

> A testator appoints as his executor 'the priest *for the time being* at the parish of X'. Does this mean: (1) the person who is the priest at the time of making the will; or (2) the person who is the priest at the time of the testator's death; or (3) the persons who, successively, are the priests at the parish (a shifting executorship)? See *Estate of Chomiak* (2012) 112 SASR 245; [2012] SASC 27.

fructus

Latin: fruit; produce of land. In legal usage, generally found as part of longer terms. Key examples are:

- *Fructus industriales* (industrial fruits); ie, 'fruits of industry'—namely, agricultural crops or produce, requiring periodic labour for their production. By legal convention, *fructus industriales* are limited to annual crops, such as wheat (*Mayfield v Wadsley* (1824) 3 B & C 357; 107 ER 766), corn (*Jones v Flint* (1839) 10 A & E 753; 113 ER 285) and potatoes (*Evans v Roberts* (1826) 5 B & C 829; 108 ER 309).
- *Fructus naturales*: crops and trees that are the natural produce of the soil. *Fructus naturales* also include the produce of crops and trees that may require attention when planted but do not require it each year to produce a crop. Examples are:
  - fruit trees and their fruit (pears on trees: *Rodwell v Phillips* (1842) 9 M & W 501; 152 ER 212; cherries on trees: *Saunders v Pilcher* [1949] 2 All ER 1077)
  - turf: *Carrington v Roots* (1837) 2 M & W 248; 150 ER 748
  - grapevines and their grapes: *Carrington v Roots* (1837) 2 M & W 248; 150 ER 748.
- Other variants:
  - *fructus pecudum* (produce of a flock, such as wool)
  - *fructus pendentes* (hanging fruit, unpicked fruit)
  - *fructus percepti* or *fructus separati* (produce which has been gathered or picked)
  - *fructus rei alienae* (produce from another's property).

As with most Latinisms in law, prefer a plain-language alternative; or, if you fear losing some legal nuance in translation, explain the meaning.

See also **profit à prendre**.

frustration

In normal usage, *frustration* denotes annoyance, irritation, or vexation. Legal usage is different: *frustration* denotes the discharge of a contract by circumstances so fundamentally unanticipated that the parties would never have entered into the contract had they known what would happen: *Morgan v Manser* [1948] 1 KB 184, 191. The parties to a contract may indeed be *frustrated* (annoyed, irritated, or vexed) by the changed circumstances, but in law that is not enough to *frustrate* their contract. The change in circumstances must strike at the root of the contract as a whole, and be so far beyond what the parties had contemplated, that to hold them to the contract would be to hold them to a contract to which they would never have agreed: *Re Badische* [1921] 2 Ch 331, 379 (Russell J).

Further reading

Halsbury's Laws of England, 'Contract' (vol 22, 2019) [259]–[281]

See also **act of God**; **force majeure**.

full and free

A pairing often found in property law, as where a person is granted a '*full and free* right of way' over land. *Full* here means 'unlimited'; *free* here means 'without interruption'. Thus, in the context of property law the phrase is usually tautologous: if a right of way is *full*, it is *free*; if it is *free*, it is *full*. It would be better to drop the pairing and substitute *unrestricted*: eg, 'I grant you an *unrestricted* right of way over my land'.

In other contexts, however, both words may be needed: eg, 'the accused made a *full* [complete] and *free* [without duress] confession'.

See also **free and uninterrupted**; **WORD PAIRINGS**.

full and sufficient

See **indemnify (variants of)**.

Full Bench

A court consisting of more judges than the normal quorum for hearing appeals. Most appellate courts have a quorum of three judges to hear appeals; and so a Full Bench is five or seven or nine (depending on the local custom).

full force and effect

Typical legal prolixity. If something is *in full force and effect*, it is enough to say that it is *in force*, or that it is *in effect*. Prune the wordiness.

fulsome

Fulsome means 'abundant to excess'; it implies more put-down than praise. To heap 'fulsome praise' on someone is to over-egg the flattery. However, *fulsome* has evolved to mean simply 'generous', and it is unlikely that the evolutionary process can be reversed. Nevertheless, if you mean 'generous' or 'plentiful', say so—and avoid *fulsome*.

- '[The defendant solicitor] has received, as was shown to the Tribunal and has been shown to us, *fulsome* [prefer: *generous*] testimonials as to both her honesty and conscientiousness by colleagues and clients.' [*Shuttari v The Law Society* [2007] EWHC 1484 (Admin), [3] (Mitting LJ)]
- 'The facts were not in dispute. They are set out *more fulsomely* [prefer: *in more detail*] in the reasons of the learned primary judge which I gratefully adopt.' [*Burton v Commissioner of Taxation* [2019] FCAFC 141, [98] (Steward J)]

functus officio

Latin: 'having discharged one's official duty'. Used, for example, where a judge has handed down the decision in a case, or a public official has completed a duty assigned by statute. The Latin term has come into standard business and administrative language, where it may now be idiomatic English. Nevertheless, an English translation is easy to formulate, and is superior in contexts where readers are unaccustomed to official or business language. For example:

- 'Any convicted defendant has the right to appeal to the Court of Appeal (Criminal Division) if he can show an arguable case that his conviction is not safe. If that fails, a defendant cannot mount a second appeal, because *the court is functus officio* [prefer: *the court has exhausted its role*].' [*R v Chief Constable of Suffolk Constabulary* [2014] UKSC 37; [2014] 4 All ER 21, [20] (Lord Hughes)]
- '[A]n order for the removal of the Arbitrator would serve no meaningful purpose *now that he was functus officio* [prefer: *now that he had exhausted his office*; *now that he had finished his task*] having rendered his final award …' [*PT Central Investando v Franciscus Wongso* [2014] SLR 978, [3] (Belinda Ang Saw Ean J)]
- 'Upon so doing [the taxation officer] *became functus officio* [prefer: *had exhausted his role*] and no longer had power to modify his taxation upon consideration of objections.' [*Australian Coal & Shale Employees' Federation v Commonwealth* (1953) 94 CLR 621, 624 (Kitto J)]

fundamental term (of contract)

See **condition**.

fungibles

Personal property that can be substituted for money or other things. Historically in Scottish law (derived from the civil law), personal property (ie, chattels, not land) intended for consumption, and usually estimated by weight or volume (eg, coal: *Simpson v Annker* (1792) 3 Paton (HL)).

furnish

Almost always means simply *give*, or *provide*; eg, to *furnish* information means no more than to *give information*—so prefer the plainer *give*.

further

See **farther / further**.

'FURTHER ASSURANCE' CLAUSE

A clause by which the promisor undertakes to do what is required to give full effect to the transaction. The precise extent of the obligation depends on the wording: eg, it might be an obligation to do whatever is 'necessary' to give effect to the transaction, or it might be an obligation merely to take 'reasonable steps' to give effect to the transaction. To avoid argument, it is prudent to specify the key specific steps that may be required, such as obtaining consents (and whether to appeal against refusal of consents), completing blanks in documents, and signing documents.

'Further assurance' clauses are often needlessly verbose, particularly in land transactions. For example, the standard 'covenant for further assurance' used in deeds of conveyance usually adopts a statutory form (one sentence, 223 words) reproducing almost verbatim a precedent drafted by Sir Orlando Bridgman in the 1660s: see, eg, *Law of Property Act 1925*, s 76 and sch 2; *Conveyancing Act 1919* (NSW), s 78(1)(A).

See also **best endeavours / reasonable endeavours**; **REDRAFTING IN PLAIN ENGLISH.**

FUZZY LAW

The 'fuzzy law' style of drafting prefers general statements of principle over detailed regulation ('fussy law'). It has the benefit of simplicity, but may leave some aspects unclear or unstated. The traditional common-law style of drafting prefers detailed regulation.

'Fuzzy law' may be more appropriate for legislation than for private-sector legal documents. This is because general statements in legislation can be filled out later with regulations and bylaws; only rarely do drafters of private-sector legal documents have access to these backstops. The following examples are drawn from legislation.

Example 1 (Hong Kong)

Section 3 of the *Protection of the Harbour Ordinance* Cap 531 (HK) provides:

3. Presumption against reclamation in the harbour

(1) The harbour is to be protected and preserved as a special public asset and a natural heritage of Hong Kong people, and for that purpose there shall be a presumption against reclamation in the harbour.

(2) All public officers and public bodies shall have regard to the principle stated in subsection (1) for guidance in the exercise of any powers vested in them.

Note the 'fuzzy' generality of the directions in subs (1): the harbour 'is to be protected and preserved'. That fuzziness is underscored by the direction in subsection (2) that public officers and bodies 'have regard to' the directions, but only 'for guidance'.

Example 2 (Australia)

Section 52 of the *Trade Practices Act 1974* (Cth), s 52 (repealed) stated:

52. Misleading or deceptive conduct.

(1) A corporation shall not, in trade or commerce, engage in conduct that is misleading or deceptive.

(2) Nothing in the succeeding provisions of this Division shall be taken as limiting by implication the generality of sub-section (1).

A commentator on s 52 noted:

'It took several years before judges came to accept that this thin provision was designed to drag them brutally away from their comfort zone. It compelled them to apply a radical, widely intrusive provision in situations where neither Parliament nor parliamentary counsel had provided many clues. As we know, judicial grumbling on this account has led to a cluster of later fussier provisions surrounding and partially qualifying the core enactment in s 52.' [Keith Mason, 'The intent of legislators: How judges discern it and what they do to find it' (2006) 27 *Australian Bar Review* 253, 259]

Further reading

- P Bayne, 'Fuzzy Drafting and the Interpretation of Statutes in the Administrative State' (1992) 66 *Australian Law Journal* 523

- Lisbeth Campbell, 'Legal Drafting Styles: Fuzzy or Fussy?' (1996) 3(2) *Murdoch University Electronic Journal of Law*; see www5.austlii.edu.au/au/journals/MurUEJL/1996/17.html
- John M Green, ' "Fuzzy Law"—A better way to stop "snouts in the trough"?' (1991) 9 *Companies and Securities Law Journal* 144

gaming and wagering

A compendious term, generally denoting gambling on an uncertain outcome in return for a prize of money or money's worth. Unless statute requires the compendious term, use the less consciously quaint *gambling*.

As a standalone term, 'game' implies a contest between two or more players; similarly, 'game of chance'. However, context may require different nuances. For example, for statutory purposes, a spot-the-ball competition (in which entrants placed a cross where they thought the ball might be) was a 'game of chance' despite the absence of inter-player interaction: *IFX Investment Co Ltd v Revenue and Customs Commissioners* [2016] EWCA Civ 436; [2016] 1 WLR 3592.

See also **wager**.

gazumping

The practice of a seller who, having accepted from a buyer an offer that is not yet legally binding (eg, because no formal contract has been signed), demands a higher offer, or accepts a higher offer from someone else; described as 'a practice as unattractive as its name': *Mulhall v Haren* [1981] IR 364, 378. The origin of *gazump* is unknown; suggestions include Yiddish (*gezumph*, to cheat or to overcharge), 1960s car-sales slang, or West Country (England, Yeovil area) dialect ('to go one better').

Compare **gazundering**.

gazundering

The practice of a buyer who, having made an offer which the seller has accepted but that is not yet legally binding (eg, because no formal contract has been signed), retracts the offer and makes a lower one.

Compare **gazumping**.

geared rent

Rent payable by a tenant to a landlord, calculated as a proportion of the rent that the tenant receives (or is entitled to receive) from subtenants.

GENDER-NEUTRAL LANGUAGE

The issue

Lawyers have long used the masculine pronoun to include the feminine. In this, they were not alone: it was a convention common to most writers. The first grammarian to record the convention seems to have been Ann Fisher, in *A Practical New Grammar with Exercises of Bad English* (1st ed, c 1745): 'The Masculine Person answers to the general Name, which comprehends both Male and Female: [eg,] Any Person who knows what he says, etc.' [quotation from 7th ed, 1778, amended title, *A New Grammar of the English Language with Exercises of Bad English* (amended title) 106, footnote].

Sometimes, drafters of contracts and statutes would add an interpretative rider to the effect that 'masculine includes feminine'; and even if they did not, Parliament eventually achieved the same end by enacting an interpretive backstop that in all documents the 'masculine includes feminine'. However, that artifice had loopholes. For example:

1. Taken literally, the reverse did not apply: ie, the feminine did not include the masculine. On that basis, a statutory provision allowing the 'wife' of an Aboriginal person to live on a reserve with her non-Aboriginal husband did not allow a non-Aboriginal husband to live on the reserve with his Aboriginal wife: *Ogilvie v Lowe* [1963] VR 225. This could be overcome, of course, by a more wide-ranging provision to the following effect—which would address the immediate issue, but not the underlying convention of male-pronoun drafting:
   - The masculine includes the feminine and vice versa.
   - A reference to a gender includes every other gender.
   - Words that are gender-specific include each gender.
2. Depending on precise wording, a provision to the effect that 'masculine includes feminine' might not apply to a status or relationship, rather than a gender. Thus, a reference in an insurance policy to 'the insured or his wife' did not extend (in the case of a female insured) to 'the insured or her husband': *Automobile Fire and General Insurance Co of Australia Ltd v Davey* (1936) 54 CLR 534.

Changing attitudes

The movement to gender-neutrality was not without difficulty. As late as 1985 a leading Australian barrister and judge advised lawyers to 'spare the Bench your gender neutrality': JP Bryson, 'How to Draft an Affidavit' (1985) 1 *Australian Bar Review* 250, 256. Even today, senior judges sometimes lapse into the generic masculine:

- '[Even if an agent] has … no obligation to disclose the actual amount of commission *he* is paid when *his* principal knows *he* is being paid …, it does not advance the matter to say that, because *he* is a fiduciary, *he* must disclose the actual amount *he* is being paid.' [*Medsted Associates Ltd v Canaccord Genuity Wealth Ltd* [2019] EWCA Civ 83; [2019] 1 WLR 4481, 4495 (Longmore LJ)]
- 'A solicitor … remains responsible for the conduct of anyone to whom *he* subcontracts work that *he* (the solicitor) is retained to do. That is particularly so where the subcontractor … does not *himself* owe an independent duty to the court.' [*Bamrah v Gempride Ltd* [2018] EWCA Civ 1367; [2019] 1 WLR 1545, [26] (Hickinbottom LJ)]

But that attitude (and style) is now generally regarded as outmoded. Nor is it considered acceptable any longer to fudge the issue by invoking the interpretative backstop that 'the masculine includes the feminine'. Modern legal writers avoid the exclusive use of the male pronoun, and consciously adopt a gender-neutral (or 'gender-silent') approach.

Suggested techniques

Many techniques exist to ensure that legal writing is gender-neutral. The only overarching requirement is that the writing be idiomatic. Text that is *un*idiomatic—even in pursuit of a noble cause—draws attention to itself, impeding communication. Here are some suggested techniques.

Technique	**Before (gender-specific)**	**After (gender-neutral)**
Omit the pronoun.	A trustee may resign *his* office if …	A trustee may resign office if …
Repeat the noun.	A trustee may resign *his* office if …	A trustee may resign the office of trustee if …
Use the plural	A trustee may resign *his* office if …	Trustees may resign their office if …
Convert to a verb.	The trustee must give *his* consent to an application if *he* is satisfied …	The trustee must consent to an application if satisfied …
Replace a possessive with a definite article.	The trustee must state *his* reasons for *his* decision not to distribute the estate.	The trustee must state reasons for *the* decision not to distribute the estate.
Use a relative clause.	Where a trustee considers it appropriate to advance capital to a beneficiary, *he* may …	A trustee who considers it appropriate to advance capital to a beneficiary may …
Use *they* as a singular pronoun.	See separate discussion below.	

'he or she'

The *he or she* pairing is well established in legislative drafting. An example now almost 200 years old is the *Vagrancy Act 1824*. Section 3 deems a person to be idle and disorderly for failing to 'maintain *himself or herself*, or *his or her* Family'; and s 5 deems a person to be an 'Incorrigible Rogue' if (amongst other things) '*he or she*' escapes from prison, or resists a police officer apprehending '*him or her*'

The *he or she* technique is fine for occasional use, but becomes ungainly if overdone:

> 'A decision-maker falls into jurisdictional error if *he or she* misunderstands the nature of the jurisdiction to be exercised, misconceives *his or her* duty, fails to apply *himself or herself* to the question to be decided or misunderstands the nature of the opinion which *he or she* is to form.' [*Re Patterson; Ex parte Taylor* [2001] HCA 51; (2001) 207 CLR 391, [82]–[83] (Gaudron J), emphasis added]

A variant is to use *he* and *she* alternately throughout (even in the same sentence). This too may be acceptable for an occasional sentence, but grates if overdone:

> '[This question] depends partly on whether one's perception of the average [bank] customer … is that *he* is spendthrift and improvident, or that *she* is disadvantaged and finding it hard to make ends meet.' [*Office of Fair Trading v Abbey National plc* [2009] UKSC 6, [2]; [2010] 1 AC 696 (Lord Walker)]

Another variant is to use *she* throughout. This, too, may be acceptable where used sparingly. But if overdone, it will seem strained—and even paternalistic, as in the following two-paragraph example, where the discussion assumes both male and female observers, but the text refers only to female:

> 'The observer who is fair-minded is the sort of person who always reserves judgment on every point until *she* has seen and fully understood both sides of the argument. *She* is not unduly sensitive or suspicious. … *Her* approach must not be confused with that of the person who has brought the complaint. But *she* is not complacent either. *She* knows that fairness requires that a judge must be … unbiased. *She* knows that judges, like anybody else, have their weaknesses. …
>
> Then there is the attribute that the observer is "informed". It makes the point that, before *she* takes a balanced approach to any information *she* is given, *she* will take the trouble to inform *herself* on all matters that are relevant. *She* is the sort of person who takes the trouble to read the

text of an article as well as the headlines. *She* is able to put whatever *she* had read or seen into [context]. *She* is fair-minded, so she will appreciate that the context forms an important part of the material which *she* must consider before passing judgment.'

[*Helow v Home Secretary* [2008] UKHL 62; [2008] 1 WLR 2416, 2418 [2]–[3] (Lord Hope of Craighead), emphasis added]

'Slash' alternatives

Some writers seek gender-neutrality by resort to 'slash' alternatives, with the slash implying 'or':

- he/she
- she/he
- s/he
- s/he/it.

While these are increasingly seen, and their meaning is clear, they are unpronounceable. Better techniques exist.

Issues with gender-neutral terms

While most writers now consciously adopt a gender-neutral approach, some issues still arise. For example:

1. Some words have both a gender-specific form and a gender-neutral form. When referring to a person known to be of a particular gender, do you use the gender-specific form? For example, if the person is female, do you use *testatrix* (not *testator*), *administratrix* (not *administrator*), *caveatrix* (not *caveator*), *executrix* (not *executor*), *prosecutrix* (not *prosecutor*), *tutrix* (not *tutor*)? Some writers do so. However, most prefer the gender-neutral term at all times, regardless of the particular person's gender.

   Wills are mostly written by solicitors in Main Street for clients in Struggle Street. What do solicitors in Main St and clients on Struggle St make of words like 'testatrix', 'executrix', 'administratrix' and 'caveatrix' ...? These are words redolent of different times and different thinking. ... A legitimate question is ... 'If courts continue with this practice, how removed from common language and ready understanding will the law become?' [Darryl Browne, 'Let's Exorcise Some Wordy Ghosts' (2019) 31 *Judicial Officers' Bulletin* (April) 25, 27–28]

2. Some legal terms have—as yet—no gender-neutral equivalents. An example is *remainderman*—there is no equivalent such as *remainderperson*. (Long-winded possible alternatives are *remainder holder* or *holder of a remainder interest*.)
3. Some gender-neutral substitutes appear precious to some readers. This is particularly so for words containing the suffix '-person'. Whether to use them may call for fine judgement. Time often fosters acceptance. The following examples have become accepted, despite earlier resistance.

Gender-specific terms	Gender-neutral terms
businessman; businesswoman	executive; businessperson
chairman	chair; chairperson
craftsman	artisan
forefather	ancestor
foreman	supervisor
fireman	fire officer; firefighter
headmaster, headmistress	principal

(continued)

(Continued)

Gender-specific terms	Gender-neutral terms
layman	layperson; non-professional; non-specialist
man-hours	work hours
mankind	humanity; human race ['humankind' seems forced]; people
man-made	artificial; synthetic; manufactured
manpower	work force; staff; labour
policeman, policewoman	police officer
postman, postmistress	postal officer; postal worker
spokesman, spokeswoman	official; representative; spokesperson
sportsman, sportswoman	athlete; player
stewardess	flight attendant
workman	worker
workmanlike	competent; skilful

They as singular pronoun

The technique

One technique for avoiding gender-specific language is to use *they* and its variants as a singular pronoun. This usage is found in both private-sector legal documents and in statutes. It is not new—the *Oxford English Dictionary* traces its ancestry to the *Rolls of Parliament* of 1464. Leading judges use it:

> 'It is not to be assumed in every case that *a franchisee* wishes to be relieved of *their* bargain.' [*Master Education Services Pty Ltd v Ketchell* [2008] HCA 38; (2008) 236 CLR 101, [39] (Gummow ACJ, Kirby, Hayne, Crennan and Kiefel JJ), emphasis added]

Some writers oppose this use of *they* on the ground that (in their view) it is both ungrammatical and unidiomatic. The strength of the opposition at one time persuaded the Office of Parliamentary Counsel to posit that *they* as a singular pronoun 'is best avoided': *Drafting Guidance*, 20 March 2014, [2.3.15]. However, the Office's updated guidelines have grudgingly accepted it (*Drafting Guidance*, June 2020, [2.1.16]–[2.1.18]), and more recent British statutes now use it:

Example

> **1. Sale of corrosive products to persons under 18**
>
> (1) A person commits an offence if *they* sell a corrosive product to a person who is under the age of 18.
>
> (2) [I]t is a defence for a person charged … to prove that *they* took all reasonable precautions …
>
> [*Offensive Weapons Act 2019*, s 1]

Many drafters now use the singular *they*. The key requirement is to be idiomatic: *they* must sit naturally in the sentence, without drawing attention to itself. If *they* diverts the reader's attention, it detracts from smooth communication between writer and reader. But if it flows idiomatically, the reader will not even notice.

The following are examples of *they* as a singular pronoun.

Idiomatic examples

- '[The legislation recognises that] *a* solicitor might be involved in a business which is distinct from *their* practice': *Blavo v Law Society* [2018] EWCA Civ 2250; [2019] 1 WLR 1977, [98] (Moylan LJ, using this technique nine times in the judgment).

- 'Such a claim is concerned with the personal obligations of *the registered proprietor* rather than with the sanctity of *their* title': *Regal Castings Ltd v Lightbody* [2009] 2 NZLR 433; [2008] NZSC 87, [148] (Tipping J).
- 'If *a staff member* cannot personally settle the grievance *they* may refer the grievance to *their* supervisor': Staff Grievance Policy, V1.2, Australian College of Physical Education, cl 3.1.2.

Unidiomatic examples

- '"consumer" means *any person* who … desires to acquire the tobacco for use or consumption by *themself* or other persons …' [Ontario *Tobacco Tax Act*, s 1, definition of 'consumer'. A more idiomatic expression would be: 'for their own, or another's, use or consumption'.]
- 'His Honour dealt first with the situation where a person purchases property … in the name of *themself* and another jointly.' [*Ong v Lottwo* [2013] SASCFC 57; (2013) 116 SASR 280, [34] (Nicholson J). A more idiomatic expression would be: 'in their own and another's name jointly'.]

Beware of ambiguity

When using *they* as a singular pronoun, beware of ambiguity—as with any pronoun.

Example

'When the vendor notifies the purchaser of the amount of the rates, *they* must pay *them* immediately.' Does *they* refer to the vendor or to the purchaser? Does *them* refer to the vendor, or to the purchaser, or to the rates?

Further reading

- British Columbia Law Institute, *Gender-Free Legal Writing: Managing the Personal Pronouns* (1998) www.bcli.org
- Julian Burnside, 'She–He–They' (1999) 110 *Victorian Bar News* (Spring) 53
- Brad Charles and Thomas Myers, 'Evolving *They*' (2018–19) 18 *Scribes Journal of Legal Writing* 81 (US law and literature on the singular '*they*')
- Corporations Law Simplification Program, *Drafting issues: A Singular Use of THEY* (Simplification Task Force, Australian Commonwealth Attorney-General's Department, September 1995)
- Robert D Eagleson, 'A Singular Use of "They"' (1994–95) *Scribes Journal of Legal Writing* 87; reprinted in (1996) 34 *Clarity* 29, and also in (2014) 71 *Clarity* 19; www.clarity-international.net/clarity-journal/archives/
- New Zealand Law Commission, Report No 35, *Legislation Manual—Structure and Style* (Wellington, 1996) 47
- Office of Parliamentary Counsel, *Drafting Guidelines* (2014), 'Gender Neutrality' 28–32 (with suggested techniques); (2020) [2.1.1]–[2.1.33]
- Sandra Petersson, 'Gender Neutral Drafting: Historical Perspective' (1998) 19 *Statute Law Review* 93 Sandra Petersson, 'Gender-Neutral Drafting: Recent Commonwealth Developments' (1999) 20 *Statute Law Review* 35
- Donald L Revell, Cornelia Schuh and Michel Moisan, '"Themself" and Nonsexist Style in Canadian Legislative Drafting' (1994) 10(1) *English Today* 10; reproduced, (1994) 31 *Clarity* 27; see www.clarity-international.net/clarity-journal/archives/
- Donald L Revell and Jessica Vapnek, 'Gender-Silent Legislative Drafting in a Non-binary World' (2020) 48 *Capital University Law Review* 103 (the history and techniques of gender-neutral drafting)
- Paul Salembier, 'Is Bad Grammar Good Policy? Legislative Use of the Singular "they"' (2015) 36 *Statute Law Review* 175 (arguing against the singular *they* in legislation)
- Jocelyn Scutt, 'Sexism in Legal Language' (1985) 59 *Australian Law Journal* 163

- Christopher Williams, 'The End of the "Masculine Rule"? Gender-Neutral Legislative Drafting in the United Kingdom and Ireland' (2008) 29 *Statute Law Review* 139

See also **GRAMMAR**.

general partner

A partner whose liability to contribute to the partnership's debts and obligations is not limited by the capital that he or she has contributed to the firm.

Compare **limited partner**.

general rule / principle

To describe a rule, or a principle, as *general* can be ambiguous. It could mean that the rule (principle) applies either: (1) always; or (2) usually but not always. Sometimes context supplies the answer, but a careful writer clarifies.

Mostly, to say that a rule is *general* means *mostly but not always*: *Bablu Holdings Pty Ltd v Capital Finance Australia Ltd* [2011] NSWCA 39; (2011) 279 ALR 166, [57]–[71] (Campbell JA, the context being the 'general rule' that a mortgagor who seeks to restrain the mortgagee from exercising power of sale must offer to pay into court the amount owing under the mortgage).

generalia specialibus non derogant

Latin: general terms do not control special ones. A principle of interpretation by which, if a general provision in a contract conflicts with a specific provision, the general yields to the specific (*Yarm Road Ltd v Hewden Tower Cranes Ltd* [2003] EWCA Civ 1127, [41], Laws LJ); or, which amounts to the same thing, the particular prevails over the general (*Golden Fleece Maritime Inc v ST Shipping And Transport Inc* [2008] EWCA Civ 584, [23]; [2008] 2 Lloyd's Rep 119, Longmore LJ). Sometimes expressed differently, but with the same result: *generalibus specialia derogant* (or *specialia generalibus derogant*)—specific things control general things. A common example is where a special condition, added to a standard form of contract, conflicts with a provision in the standard form; in such a case, the special condition prevails: *The Babrant* [1967] 1 QB 588, 601; *Hobbs Bell Pty Ltd v Pola* (1995) 7 BPR 14,761. By similar logic, a handwritten variation to a standard form prevails over an inconsistent provision in the standard form: *Glynn v Margetson & Co* [1893] AC 351, 358.

Further reading

Dennis C Pearce and Robert S Geddes, *Statutory Interpretation in Australia*, 9th edn (LexisNexis, 2019) [4.51]–[4.53] (how courts apply the principle in statutory interpretation)

See also **INCONSISTENT PROVISIONS**.

GENERALITY

Generality of expression in legal writing is not necessarily to be feared. Sometimes, lawyers have no option but to use generalities; detail may not be possible. For example, in heads of agreement parties may wish to bind themselves contractually without waiting for their lawyers to work through the fine detail; usually, this does not create legal uncertainty.

Generality is to be condemned only where it produces text that is ambiguous—ie, text that is open to two or more contrasting meanings.

See also **AMBIGUITY; HEADS OF AGREEMENT; VAGUENESS.**

gentlemen's agreement

An agreement that lacks the formal requirements for enforceability (such as writing in the case of an agreement to sell land) but relies on the parties' good faith. There is, as yet, no gender-specific equivalent, except the longer 'agreement binding morally but not legally'.

GERUNDS

A gerund is a verbal noun, typically formed by adding *ing* to the base form of the verb. Being a noun, a gerund can be the subject of a sentence: 'Writing is good fun.' It can also be the object of a sentence: 'I enjoy writing.' Its function as a noun was important in the following case:

> A property insurance policy excluded cover for damage caused by '[f]lood, surface water, waves, tides, tidal waters, *overflowing of any body of water*, or their spray'. The insured claimed for damage to his property caused by a hurricane. The trial judge held that 'overflowing of any body of water' qualified the preceding nouns (flood, surface water, waves, tides, tidal waters), and that because on the facts none of the damage was caused by water that burst its banks (overflowing water), the exclusion clause did not apply. That is, although he did not use the term, it was a participle that limited the previous nouns. The appeal court reversed that ruling, holding that *overflowing of any body of water* was a verbal noun, operating as an independent item in the list of nouns. It did not qualify the previous nouns. Therefore, the exclusion applied: *Transcontinental Insurance Co v RBMW Inc* 551 SE 2d 313 (Va 2001).

Further reading

Robert C Farrell, 'Why Grammar Matters: Conjugating verbs in modern legal opinions' (2008) 40 *Loyola University Chicago Law Journal* 1, 33–42 (reviewing US cases on the importance of distinguishing gerunds from participles)

See also **POSSESSIVES.**

get / got

Usage

Some writers baulk at the vernacular *get* or *got* (eg, 'X *got* a benefit from the contract with Y'), and prefer instead a more refined word such as *obtained* or *received*. At least one Australian appellate judge has flinched at the statutory use of *get*: see *Gillett v Burke* [1997] 1 VR 81, 100, where Ormiston J said that, in using *get* in a statute, Parliament had 'descended in a notably imprecise way into the vernacular'. But *get* and *got* appear regularly in modern statutes, and are so much a part of accepted usage as normally to pass unnoticed (see, eg, *Federal Commissioner of Taxation v Unit Trend Services Pty Ltd* [2013] HCA 16; (2013) 250 CLR 523). Judges themselves have long used *get* in judgments: see, eg, *Liverpool Borough Bank v Turner* (1860) 2 De GF & J 502, 508; 45 ER 715, 718: 'It is the duty of Courts of Justice to try to *get* at the real intention of the Legislature …' (Lord Campbell LC).

'gotten'

More controversial is the past participle form, *gotten*. Though once familiar in medieval English, its use became peculiar to American English. But such is the gravitational pull of American English in modern times that *gotten* now peppers spoken English usage in Britain and the wider Commonwealth. However, it is still rare in serious prose outside of the US, except in compounds such as *forgotten*, *begotten*, and *ill-gotten*. Exceptionally, it was used in the *Petroleum (Production) Act 1918*, ss 1 and 2, dealing with petroleum '*gotten*' from land.

give (a notice)

See **serve / give**.

give, devise and bequeath

Give, devise and bequeath has come down to modern law as a hallowed trilogy. Rarely do testators *give* (alone); nor do they *devise* (alone) or *bequeath* (alone). Instead they *give, devise and bequeath*, sometimes minus all commas, and almost always minus the serial comma (*give, devise, and bequeath*)—though logically the serial comma is useful to clearly demarcate the three (separate) terms.

Give has always been a general term for disposing of property by gift. But in the context of disposing of property by will, for centuries lawyers allocated specific terms for the two main classes of property, real and personal. They allocated *devise* for disposing of land (real property) and *bequeath* for disposing of personal property (eg, money or goods). Precisely why, or when, this allocation developed is unclear. Writing in 1590, Henry Swinburne spoke of '*bequeathing or devising* landes, tenementes, and hereditaments': *A Brief Treatise on Testaments and Last Wills* (1st edn, 1590; reprint Garland Publishing, 1978) 69. But by 1628, Blackstone was using *devise* for land and *bequeath* for personal property: Sir William Blackstone, *Commentaries on the Laws of England* (1st edn, 1628) book 2, chs 23 and 32.

Regardless of the history, case law since at least the 1850s makes it clear beyond argument that *bequeath* is effective to dispose of real estate: *Whicker v Hume* (1851) 14 Beav 509, 518; 51 ER 381, 385 (Romilly MR); *Re Galligan* (1913) 13 SR (NSW) 291, 293–94 (Harvey J).

More recent case law also makes it clear beyond argument that *give* (alone) covers all three words:

> 'Even amongst lawyers, let alone lay people, the subtleties of any historical differences between the words *devise* and *bequeath* have generally been lost to view, and both have been overshadowed by the more general word *give*. Each of the words *give* and *bequeath* is capable of embracing a testamentary gift of real estate.' [*Anderson v Dupain* [2013] NSWSC 108, [30] (Lindsay J)]

In modern will drafting there is no justification for retaining the trilogy. It is better to *give* than *devise*, and it is better to *give* than *bequeath*.

Further reading

'Give, Devise and Bequeath', in *Law Words* (Centre for Plain Legal Language, University of Sydney, 1995) 31; www.clarity-international.net/plain-language-resources/general-resources/

See also **COMMAS**.

GLOSSARIES

Glossaries are rare in legal documents—but they need not be. Properly used, glossaries can play a useful role in helping readers understand unfamiliar concepts. This is not to supplant the role of definitions. Glossaries *explain* terms; they do not *define* terms.

When using glossaries in legal documents, it is prudent to clarify their intended role—eg, by stating that they are a non-binding aid to understanding. In this way, no consequence (except embarrassment) follows if a glossary is vague or even wrong.

Example

> Suppose a clause in a contract for the sale of land uses the term *time of the essence*:
>
> > 'The purchaser must complete on 1 December 2020, time of the essence.'
>
> *Time of the essence* carries a wealth of learning. To attempt to *define* it would be difficult (even foolhardy). But to *explain* it in a non-binding glossary would be easier, while still helping the reader understand the concept:
>
> '*Time of the essence*. This indicates that the date is crucial. If the purchaser does not complete on that date, the vendor can terminate the contract, keep the deposit, and sue the purchaser for damages.'

See also **DEFINITIONS; time of the essence**.

gobbledegook / gobbledygook

Language that is contorted, pretentious, long-winded, and often abounding in technical jargon, making it unintelligible to most readers. As coined in the US, the spelling was *gobbledygook*, but many dictionaries now give *gobbledegook* as the preferred spelling.

good / goods

Goods are items of moveable personal property, especially (but not exclusively) merchandise used in trade and commerce and requiring carriage from one place to another. The plural form *goods* is preferred, even for a single item; eg, the sale of a single car is a 'sale of *goods*'. However, usage is changing, and the singular *good* is sometimes seen. The singular has intruded even into judgments: see, eg, *Gammasonics Institute for Medical Research Pty Ltd v Comrad Medical Systems Pty Ltd* [2010] NSWSC 267; (2010) 77 NSWLR 479 (but using inverted commas—'good'—as if to suggest that it remains unidiomatic).

See also **goods and chattels**.

good faith

See **in good faith**.

good marketable title

A title which, though technically defective, is of sufficient quality to discharge the seller's obligations to the buyer: *Barclays Bank plc v Weeks, Legg & Dean* [1999] QB 309. Usually, *marketable title* will suffice: if a title is *marketable*, it is *good* enough for a court to force on the buyer.

good reason

What is a 'good reason' for doing, or not doing, something? The answer is intractably context-dependent. The reported case law is replete with examples:

- what is a 'good reason' for seeking an extension of time in court proceedings (eg, *Tower Hamlets London Borough Council v Al Ahmed* [2020] EWCA Civ 51; [2020] 1 WLR 1546)?
- what is a 'good reason' for possessing a dangerous weapon?
- what is a 'good reason' for making a particular administrative decision, or for refusing to make a decision?
- what is a 'good reason' for appointing a provisional liquidator?

If possible, always specify the acceptable reason; do not leave it to the vagaries of 'good reason'.

good root of title

An acceptable documentary starting point for proof of title to land under common law ('old system') title—ie, unregistered land. The classic definition of a 'good root of title' is by TC Williams:

> '[A good root of title is an] instrument of disposition dealing with or proving on the face of it (without the aid of extrinsic evidence) the ownership of the whole legal and equitable estate in the property sold, containing a description by which the property can be identified, and showing nothing to cast any doubt on the title of the disposing parties.' [TC Williams, *Vendor and Purchaser*, 4th edn (Sweet & Maxwell, 1936) 124]

By conveyancing convention (accepted by the courts), a good root of title was a document at least 60 years old at the date of the (present) dealing with the land. Most jurisdictions eventually reduced that period—in England and Wales, successively to 40 years, 30 years, and now to 15 years: *Law of Property Act* 1925, s 44(1). Instruments of sufficient age satisfying the definition include a conveyance for value of the whole legal and equitable interest in the land, a first (legal) mortgage, and (possibly) a sale by a mortgagee exercising power of sale. Instruments not satisfying the definition include a conveyance of the equity of redemption, a will, and a deed exercising a power of appointment. An instrument that by statute conveys a fee simple free of encumbrances and cuts off all previous interests, is a good root of title (eg, a statutory sale by a rating authority for unpaid rates).

Further reading

- *Halsbury's Laws of England*, 'Conveyancing' (vol 23, 2016) [113] and following
- Peter Butt, *The Standard Contract for Sale of Land in New South Wales*, 2nd edn (LBC Information Services, 1998) 879–81 (includes Commonwealth case law)
- S Bridge, E Cooke and M Dixon (eds), *Megarry & Wade's Law of Real Property*, 9th edn (Sweet & Maxwell, 2019) [14-075]–[14-077]

goods and chattels

Meaning

A common legal pairing. *Goods* (from the old English, *god*) are items of moveable personal property, often (but not exclusively) merchandise sold in trade and commerce and requiring carriage from one place to another. Legislation governing 'sale of goods' generally defines *goods* to mean tangible or moveable personal property.

Chattels (from Old French *chatel*) are also items of moveable personal property. A chattel can be any kind of personal property: *Robinson v Jenkins* (1890) 24 QBD 275, 279 (Fry LJ). The common law divides chattels into *chattels real* (ie, leases) and *chattels personal.* It further divides chattels personal into *corporeal chattels* (items of physical property) and *incorporeal chattels* (items of intangible property, such as intellectual property).

A plainer alternative?

As a matter of strict definition, *goods* and *chattels* do not entirely overlap in meaning. *Chattels* is the wider term; some *goods* might not be *chattels*. But as a matter of practice, the pairing *goods and chattels* is habitually used in contexts where one word would suffice—preferably *goods*, because it lacks the incipient archaism of *chattels.*

Further reading

'Goods and Chattels', in *Law Words* (Centre for Plain Legal Language, University of Sydney, 1995) 34; www.clarity-international.net/plain-language-resources/general-resources/

See also **chattel real**; **good / goods**.

got / gotten

See **get / got**.

GOVERNING LAW

In contract law, the law (of the country) that governs rights and obligations under the contract. In the absence of a contractual provision, that law is determined by the principles of private international law. To obviate argument, most commercial agreements include a 'governing law' or 'choice of law' clause, under which the parties agree that their contract is to be governed by the law of a particular jurisdiction. Most 'governing law' clauses also contain a 'jurisdiction clause' indicating which jurisdiction's courts are to decide disputes.

Example

> **Governing law**
>
> This contract is governed by the law in force in [Scotland].
>
> **Jurisdiction**
>
> In any proceedings in relation to this Agreement, each Party submits to the jurisdiction of the courts of [Scotland] and the courts competent to hear appeals from those courts.

See also **'CHOICE OF LAW' CLAUSE; JURISDICTION CLAUSE.**

government

Use lower-case 'g', unless part of a formal title. For example:

- The newspapers yesterday praised all government ministers.
- On average, Scottish governments are elected every three years.
- You should contact the Welsh Government's legislative drafters.

Governor-General

Hyphenated (despite occasional lapses by colonial Parliamentary drafters—as in *Governor General's Residence (Grant) Act 1945* (NSW)). The plural is *Governors-General.*

GRAMMAR

Relevance to interpretation

Unless writing is so poorly constructed that the writer was clearly ignorant of basic grammar, courts start the process of interpretation by assuming that the writer has followed grammatical conventions. Indeed, courts must start this way, for otherwise what yardstick are they to apply when discerning meaning from a sentence? The US Supreme Court has stated that it 'naturally does not review congressional enactments as a panel of grammarians; but neither [does it] regard ordinary principles of English prose as irrelevant to a construction of those enactments' [*Flora v United States* 362 US 145, 150 (1960)]. Thus, good legal writing should follow the conventions of grammar—not as an end in itself, but to ensure accurate communication between writer and reader.

Nevertheless, courts caution against making a fortress out of grammatical conventions. This is for three reasons:

1. Some writers do not understand the conventions:

   > '[E]xperience shows that insurance documents in the London market are rarely drawn with the precision of language needed for grammatical contrasts to be a reliable guide to intention.' [*Touche Ross & Co v Baker* [1992] 2 Ll R 207, 213, Lord Mustill]

2. The conventions are not universally accepted. For example, views differ over the importance of the *that / which* distinction, and over the use of the 'serial comma'.
3. Courts should not allow the drafter's grammatical infelicities to thwart the parties' intended meaning. See, eg, *Technology Holdings Ltd v IAG NZ* [2008] NZHC 1228; (2009) 15 ANZIC 61-786 (inconsistent and missing prepositions).

Relevance to readers' perceptions of writers

Writers should not assume that readers will dismiss grammatical lapses as unimportant. Quite the opposite: research shows that readers think less of writers who make grammatical mistakes (see *Further reading*, below). This of itself should persuade legal writers to be careful with their grammar.

Further reading

- April Bleske-Rechek et al, 'Grammar Matters: The Tainting Effect of Grammar Usage Errors on Judgments [sic] of Competence and Character' (2019) 141 *Personality and Individual Differences* 47
- Robert C Farrell, 'Why Grammar Matters: Conjugating Verbs in Modern Legal Opinions' (2008) 40 *Loyola University Chicago Law Journal* 1 (discussing court cases where grammatical analysis determined the outcome)

See also **COMMAS**; **CONSISTENCY OF TERMINOLOGY**; **NOUNS / VERBS**; **POSSESSIVES**; **SPLIT INFINITIVES**; **SUBJECT–VERB AGREEMENT**; **that / which**.

grandchild

In appropriate circumstances, 'grandchild' can mean a stepchild of a person's (natural) child.

See **child**.

grandfather clause

A clause that preserves existing rights in the face of a change in the law. The term is vague, because it does not of itself explain the nature, extent, or duration of the rights preserved; but it has become an accepted part of the popular and professional lexicon. As yet, there is no gender-neutral equivalent.

grantor / granter

The person who makes a grant (usually of land, or of an interest in land such as an easement or servitude). English and common-law usage favours *grantor*. Scots law prefers *granter*, as do some Scottish-trained lawyers (as in the following examples):

- '[The rules] are founded upon the principle that a *granter* may not derogate from his grant …' [*Sovmots Ltd v Secretary of State for the Environment* [1979] AC 144, 183 (Lord Keith of Kinkel)]
- 'The *granter's* signature in the 2006 disposition had been forged.' [*McAuley v Chalmers* [2015] CSIH 75, [16] (Lady Paton)]

grassum

In Scots law, a single payment in addition to, or in place of, periodic payments; in particular, a lump sum payment made in return for the grant of a lease. For example:

> '[The quoted passage] … deals with … whether at review the prime rental values in Glasgow city centre should be ascertained by reference to the "headline" rents, or whether those "headline" rents should be adjusted for the effect of *grassum*, reverse premiums, etc.' [*Legal Services Centre Ltd v Peter Samuel LLP* [2009] CSOH 141, [162] (Lord Glinnie)]

The term is unique to Scots law. The English or common-law equivalent is *premium* or *key-money*.

See also **key-money**.

gratuitous

Without payment of money or other consideration. In legal usage, the word carries none of the menace implied in standard English usages (eg, 'a gratuitous threat'). Thus, a *gratuitous promise* is simply a promise made without receiving money or other consideration in return; and a *gratuitous conveyance* is a conveyance made without receiving money or other consideration in return.

Great Britain

In strict legal usage, the combined lands and territorial waters of England, Wales, and Scotland (but not Northern Ireland): see *Union With Scotland Act 1706*, Preamble and Article 1; and *Interpretation Act 1978*, s 22(1). This usage, as with all legal usages, may give way to a different meaning where context or statute requires.

See also **United Kingdom**.

greater / lesser of

Correct usage is 'the greater / lesser of A *and* B' (not 'A *or* B').

See **lesser of**.

green field site

Sometimes *greenfield* [one word] *site*. Land that has not previously been developed or used (except perhaps for agricultural or recreational use).

See also **brown land site**.

gremio

See **in gremio**.

grossing-up clause

A clause under which a party agrees to increase ('gross-up') a payment by an amount equivalent to any tax or other charge that will be deducted from the payment in the hands of the recipient.

ground rent

Literally, a rent payable for the value of the 'ground' alone, without buildings on it. From that usage: the rent payable under a lease of land on which the tenant is to erect a building: *Bartlett v Salmon* (1855) 6 De GM & G 33, 41; 43 ER 1142, 1145. More generally, a nominal rent payable under a long-term lease, especially where the lease is granted in return for an upfront payment (a 'premium').

guarantee (noun)

See **guarantee / indemnity / warranty**.

guarantee (verb)

The verb *to guarantee* can mean: (1) 'to give a guarantee' (eg, 'I *guarantee* payment of A's debt to B'); or (2) to promise firmly that something will be done (eg, 'I *guarantee* to pay you back tomorrow'). Within meaning (2), *guarantee* need not have the nuance of a promise so fundamental as to be a 'condition' (properly so called) rather than a mere 'warranty'. So, a statement in a company prospectus that the company would pay a *guaranteed* bonus was merely a 'warranty' that it would do so: *Re Commonwealth Homes and Investment Co Ltd* [1943] SASR 211, 219 (Mayo J).

See also **guarantee / indemnity / warranty**.

guarantee / indemnity / warranty

A *guarantee* is a binding promise by the guarantor (G) to perform an obligation which a person (A) owes to another person (B): as where A owes money to B, and G *guarantees* to B that G will pay if A fails to pay.

An *indemnity* is a binding promise to keep the promisee free from loss if something occurs. Almost always, an indemnity involves an obligation to compensate for specified loss or damage. For example, an insurance company agrees to *indemnify* a house owner against loss if the property is damaged by fire, or a builder agrees to *indemnify* a client against loss the client might suffer if the building work is faulty.

A *warranty* is a binding promise to do something, breach of which justifies an action for damages (for breach of contract). For example, A (a builder) *warrants* to X that B (a subcontractor) will carry out work on X's property in accordance with approved plans.

The differences between the terms are important. For example:

- Under a *guarantee*, the guarantor assumes a secondary liability—ie, the guarantor promises to answer for another person's obligation. Under an *indemnity*, the liability is direct—ie, the indemnifier assumes a primary liability: *Associated British Ports v Ferryways NV* [2009] EWCA Civ 189, [1]; [2009] 1 Lloyd's Rep 595, [1] (Kay LJ).
- An *indemnity* may be easier to enforce than a *warranty*, because, if drafted appropriately, an indemnity can sidestep issues about remoteness of damage and the duty to mitigate, both of which can limit recovery of damages for breach of warranty. See R Christou, *Boilerplate: Practical Clauses*, 7th edn (Thomson Reuters, 2015), [6-077].

See also **condition / warranty**; **guaranty**; **indemnify (variants of)**; **warrants and represents**.

guaranty

Guarantee is the preferred spelling in modern British English for both verb ('I *guarantee to* …') and noun ('this deed of *guarantee*'). The spelling *guaranty* (noun) was once common and has survived in occasional (but rare) British and Commonwealth legal usage: eg, *Longulf Trading (UK) Ltd v Niyazi Onen Gida San As* [2019] EWHC 1573, [10] (Christopher Hancock QC, sitting as High Court judge, describing a company as the 'guaranty' [meaning 'guarantor'] of a person); *Richard Brady Franks Ltd v Price* (1937) 58 CLR 112, 144 (Dixon J). In the US, *guaranty* is common as a noun.

See also **guarantee / indemnity / warranty**.

guardian ad litem

A person appointed as a person's guardian for the purpose of a court case. In some common-law jurisdictions, called *litigation friend* (eg, in the modified court terms introduced as part of the Woolf Reforms in England and Wales).

See also **ad litem**; **WOOLF REFORMS**.

guidelines

How closely must *guidelines* be followed? Are they: (1) merely suggestions; or (2) matters that should be considered but accorded whatever weight (including none at all) the decision-maker considers appropriate; or (3) matters fundamental to the validity of the decision? In the absence of helpful context, *guidelines* connotes 'suggested action' or 'recommended action', not 'mandatory requirements'; ie, *guidelines* provide information and point the way to a particular conclusion, without dictating that conclusion. Or (to vary the language slightly), *guidance* is advisory, helping the decision-maker but not compelling a particular outcome; while *rules* are mandatory, compelling the decision-maker to reach a particular result: *R v Secretary of State for the Home Department* [2012] UKSC 33; [2012] 1 WLR 2208, [210] (Lord Clarke). But context may show otherwise: eg, *Smoker v Pharmacy Restructuring Authority* (1994) 125 ALR 577 ('guidelines' held to be 'rules).

A careful writer, attuned to potential disputes over meaning, will indicate the intended status of 'guidelines' (or similar). Consider the following Australian examples:

- '[C]odes of practice [established under this Act] are in the nature of guidelines and compliance is not mandatory.' [*Cemeteries and Crematoria Act 2013* (NSW), s 29(1)]
- 'The following guidelines must be followed' (in reaching a decision)—eg, *Safety, Rehabilitation and Compensation Act 1988* (Cth), s 41(2).

See also **have regard to**; **rule of thumb**.

habendum

Sometimes *habendum clause* (although *clause* is strictly redundant), or *to-have-and-to-hold clause*. The part of a deed that marks out the extent of the interest granted—eg, a fee simple, or life estate, or lease. The *habendum* also mentions any liabilities or incidents subject to which the grant is made (and which will be imposed contractually elsewhere in the deed). The existence of an *habendum* is not necessary to a deed's validity, as long as the deed contains the information that would be found in one: *Goodtitle d Dodwell v Gibbs* (1826) 5 B & C 709, 717; 108 ER 264, 267.

habile

Latin: *habilis*, manageable, suitable; hence *modus habilis* (a competent method), *habile modo* (in a competent way). In legal usage, *habile* now seems limited to Scots law, where it is used in the sense of 'competent for a legal purpose', 'admissible', 'valid'. There seems no benefit in retaining the word, given that a modern, standard English term will suffice. For example:

- 'Lord Johnston said [in a Scottish case] that the word "behaviour" was all embracing and *habile* [prefer: *effective*] to cover not only any form of conduct but also the making or issuing of statements.' [*DS v Her Majesty's Advocate* [2007] UKPC D1; 2007 SC (PC) 1, [45] (Lord Hope)]
- 'The broad words of [the section] … which might be thought *habile* [prefer: *sufficient*] to cover any steps taken by the Commission …. must … be read in the context of the particular relationship …' [*R v Secretary of State for Employment* [1995] 1 AC 1, 13 (Lord Jauncey)]

habitable / inhabitable

The meanings are the same—able to be lived in. The *in-* is an intensifier, not a negative.

Hadley v Baxendale ('limbs' of)

A reference to 'the limbs' of *Hadley v Baxendale* (1854) 9 Exch 341; 156 ER 145 is a reference to Alderson B's discussion in that case of the two categories of damages for breach of contract:

> 'Where two parties have made a contract which one of them has broken, the damages which the other party ought to receive in respect of such a breach of contract should be [*first limb*] such as may fairly and reasonably be considered either arising naturally, i.e., according to the usual course of things, from such breach of contract itself, or [*second limb*] such as may reasonably be supposed to have been in the contemplation of both parties, at the time they made the contract, as the probable result of the breach of it.' [ibid 354; 151 (words in square brackets added)]

The principles outlined in that quotation have been applied consistently in UK and Commonwealth cases ever since 1854 (see, eg, *A-G Virgin Islands v Global Water Associates Ltd* [2020] UKPC 18; [2020] 3 WLR 585).

See also **consequential loss**.

hanged / hung

A picture is *hung*; so too is a parliament (when no single party has a majority) and a jury (when the jurors cannot agree on the verdict). A person may also be *hung*: thus, Mussolini was killed and his body *hung* upside down in a Milan plaza. But in the law of sentencing, a person is *hanged*—as in the phrase 'sentenced to be *hanged* by the neck until dead'. In medieval times, convicted traitors were sentenced to be '*hung*, drawn, and quartered'; there, *hung* was correct usage, because convicted traitors were to be taken down from the scaffold *before* they died, then disembowelled, beheaded, and their body divided into four pieces.

In former times, before the modern systematisation of spelling, variants could be excused. For example, Samuel Pepys wrote of seeing people 'hanged' and 'hanged, drawn and quartered': *The Diary of Samuel Pepys*, ed Richard Le Gaillienne (Modern Library edn, 2003) entries for 13 and 15 October 1660. But preferred modern usage keeps the distinctions clear.

has a duty to (do something)

Has a duty to [do something] usually means simply *must* [do something]. If so, prefer *must*: eg, instead of 'a trustee *has a duty to* prioritise the interests of the beneficiaries' prefer 'a trustee *must* prioritise the interests of the beneficiaries'. Both formulations, however, may leave the consequences of failure (to do it) unstated. It then becomes a question of interpretation: what consequences follow? A prescient drafter will foresee the gap. For example:

> Under s 6 of an animal welfare statute, a person in charge of an animal 'has a duty to' take all reasonable precautions to ensure the animal's welfare. The section was simply a statement: it did not set out any consequences for failure to ensure the animal's welfare. However, other sections in the statute imposed specific obligations towards animals with specific consequences for breach. Held, s 6 imposed a duty whose breach could be the subject of a prosecution under the other sections, depending on the consequences of the breach: *Mitchell v Marshall* [2014] TASSC 43; (2014) 27 Tas R 1, [5], [27] (Blow CJ).

See also **duty**; **shall / must**.

hatched

A description of cross-drawn lines on a plan or map: eg, 'The purchaser agrees to buy the land shown *hatched* in the attached plan.' An occasional variant is *hachured* (noun *hachure*, sometimes misspelled *hatchure*), as in 'The purchaser agrees to buy the land shown *ha[t]chured* in the attached plan'; but this is more correctly a cartographical term indicating the steepness of a slope by the closeness and thickness of lines.

have regard to

To *have regard to* something is to take it into account, or to consider it. The law often uses the expression: eg, a criminal statute may require a judge to *have regard to* the victim's feelings before passing sentence; or a rent review provision in a lease may require a valuer to *have regard to* rents of comparable properties.

However, the formula 'have regard to' is inherently vague:

> '[T]he term "have regard" is almost of necessity bound to create difficulties. How much regard is to be had, and what weight is to be attached to the regard when it has been had?' [*English Exporters (London) Ltd v Eldonwall Ltd* [1973] 2 WLR 435, 444 (Megarry J)]

This vagueness has produced two distinct lines of authority about the force of 'have regard to':

1. The matters to which the decision-maker is to 'have regard' are fundamental to the decision-making exercise: see, eg, *Singh v Minister for Immigration and Multicultural Affairs* [2001] FCA 389; (2001) 109 FCR 152, [54] (Sackville J). That is, the matters are to be the focal point of the decision-making process: *Zhang v Canterbury City Council* [2001] NSWCA 167; (2001) 51 NSWLR 589, [71]–[73] (Spigelman CJ).

2. The decision-maker has a discretion to decide how much weight, if any, to give to the matters. He or she must 'tick-off' having considered the matters, but need not give them any particular level of attention. The decision-maker may also consider additional matters: *Rathborne v Abel* (1964) 38 ALJR 293, 295 (Barwick CJ), 301 (Kitto J). Even a direction to *have particular regard to* certain matters does not require that those matters receive extra weight, but only that they be considered specifically and separately from other matters: *Ashdown v Telegraph Group Ltd* [2001] 2 All ER 370, 383 (Morrit V-C).

An adept drafter will foresee the inherent uncertainty in *have regard to*, and specify more precisely the weight the decision-maker must give to the specified matters.

See also **guidelines**.

haver

Pronounced 'havver'. A person who holds a document required as evidence in court proceedings. The term is found only in Scots law, eg:

> '[The Court of Session in Scotland has the power] to grant warrant for the citation of witnesses and *havers* to give evidence or to produce documents before the panel …' [*Health and Social Care Act 2008*, s 106(4)(b)(i)]

head up (verb)

Prefer *head*: eg, 'She was appointed to *head ~~up~~* the committee.'

HEADINGS

Usefulness

All forms of legal writing benefit from meaningful headings. It is true that in generations past, headings were rare in legal documents: they were almost never seen in wills, deeds of conveyance, leases, letters of advice—or even court judgments. But the lack of headings deprived readers of useful signposts. For that reason, most modern legal writers seek to include headings, and many also include subheadings.

The move towards using headings in legal documents was largely voluntary, as lawyers began to see the value of headings. Sometimes, however, it needed official encouragement, for example by mandating headings in pleadings (as in the *California Rules of Court 2019*, Rule 8.204). Some statutes now insist on headings in consumer documents, as part of the requirements for 'plain language'.

What is a heading?

Headings are usually allocated a separate line and printed in a distinctive font (**bold**, or *italics*, or similar). This clearly distinguishes them from the text to which they relate. Occasionally, lower-level headings are in 'run-on' form, marked out in bold or italics (or similar), leading immediately into the text to which they relate.

Sometimes it is not clear whether material is a heading or normal text. This can complicate interpretation, particularly where the document contains a 'headings do not count' stipulation (as to which, see later). This occurred in the following case:

> A contract for the sale of a home unit 'off the plan' generally adopted the normal convention of short headings, printed in bold font, with related text starting on a new line, non-bold.

However, one multi-sentence clause took a different form: it started with a complete sentence in bold, followed (on a new line) by other sentences also in bold:

> **39. This agreement is conditional on Apartment 211 being built as per the attached layout and plans.**
>
> **Should the joinery line be re-enstated [sic] as per September 2004 resource consent, the developer shall notify the purchaser. The purchaser shall then have the right to withdraw from this agreement or renegotiate with the developer a new pricing structure, which will reflect the difference in total area.**

Held: this layout and font indicated that the first sentence was not a heading, but rather part of the text of the substantive provision itself. So also (in the judge's view) did the full stop at the end of the first sentence: *Love v Auburn Apartments Ltd* [2012] NZCA 34, [23]; [2012] ANZ ConvR 12-005.

Hierarchy of headings

Make it obvious

Make the hierarchy of headings apparent, so that readers know at a glance how the heading they are reading fits into the scheme of the document as a whole. This can be done by appropriate typography and formatting, with descending heading levels marked by a shift from larger font to smaller font, from bold roman to light italics, from flush left to indented, and so on.

Example (formatting indicates hierarchy)

> **Level 1 heading**
>
> **Level 2 heading**
>
> *Level 3 heading*

Another—and clearer—method of indicating hierarchy is the decimal numbering system (as in the following example). The decimal points can clearly mark out descending levels of heading. And because the numbering system itself reflects the hierarchy, a decimal system does not require different formatting techniques (font size, bold, italics, etc)—although they can be used if the drafter prefers (as in the following example). Nor does a decimal system require indenting to demarcate different levels of headings (although indenting can be used, as shown in the right-hand column, if the drafter prefers).

Example: decimal numbering in lease

Not indented	**Indented**
2 **Dealings with lease**	2 **Dealings with lease**
2.1 **Assignments**	**2.1 Assignments**
2.1.1 *When permitted*	2.1.1 *When permitted*
2.2 **Subleases**	**2.2 Subleases**
2.2.1 *When permitted*	2.2.1 *When permitted*

The following example shows the use of decimal headings in a will. The main headings (Part 1, Part 2, etc) are in bold, and subheadings are given decimal numbers.

Example: decimal numbering in will

Part 1 **Declarations**

1.1 My will
1.2 Appointment of executors and trustees

Part 2 **Payment of funeral and administrative expenses, debts and taxes**

2.1 Funeral and administrative expenses
2.2 Debts
2.3 Taxes

Part 3 **Specific gifts**

3.1 Personal property to my wife
3.2 If my wife predeceases me, personal property to my children
3.3 Resolution of disputes

Part 4 **Disposition of my residuary estate**

4.1 Beneficiaries
4.2 Creation of trust
4.3 Powers of trustees
4.4 Investing principal
4.5 Use of income and principal
4.6 Time limit on residuary trust

[Source: Based on Joseph Kimble, *Drafting Documents in Plain Language* (Business Forms Management Association, circa 1993), 17]

Section and clause headings

Make the main heading stand out, preferably in **bold**. (If you insert headings for lower-level divisions of the text, use a heading style that reflects the lower level: see discussion under **FONTS**.) If you then indent intelligently, the readers will know exactly where they are in the clause.

Part and Division headings

In both statutes and private-sector legal documents, Parts and Divisions are numbered using Arabic numbers. The former convention of Roman capitals (*Part I*, *Part V*, *Part VIII*) is now rarely seen. Part and Division headings are usually centred, to distinguish them from section headings (flush left).

Example

Part 1

Creation of Department

Division 1—Appointment of CEO

Be generous

As a practical matter, try ensure that every page contains at least one heading (if that is possible without unduly fracturing the text). That way, readers know at a glance where they are in the document. Headings also provide psychological relief—a heading-less page always seems more daunting than a page with headings.

Not too many heading-levels

Do not introduce too many levels of headings. Up to three levels—main, sub, sub-sub—should be enough. Any further levels—sub-sub-sub, and so on—may fracture the subject matter, making the document appear more complex than it is. See example under **NUMBERING SYSTEMS (Indentation)**.

Running headers

In a document of any length, running headers help readers know where they are in a document. Because the eye finds the top of the page before it finds the foot of the page, headers are more useful than footers.

Legal status of headings: statutes

Judicial approaches

Formerly, courts took the view that headings are not part of a statute: see, eg, *R v Hare* [1934] 1 KB 354, 355 (Avory J, CCA). But this ignored the reality that headings are physically part of the text of a statute and therefore, logically, part of the material to which a court may advert when interpreting the statute. The modern view, now well established, is that section headings are relevant when interpreting the sections to which they relate. (See generally, *Halsbury's Laws of England*, 'Statutes and Legislative Process' (vol 96, 2018), [728].)

However, that is not to say that headings in statutes are decisive. Their status is always subsidiary, as explained in *R v Schildkamp* [1971] AC 1:

- headings are not of equal weight with the words of the Act (Lord Reid, 10)
- headings are merely a guide, and are not to control the operation of the enacting words (Viscount Dilhorne, 20)
- the weight to be given to headings depends on the circumstances of each case, and it is not possible to lay down any rules (Lord Upjohn, 28).

Nevertheless, courts now routinely consult headings as a guide to the meaning of statutory provisions.

Examples

- A section was headed 'Power to require proper maintenance of waste land, etc'. Held, this was relevant to deciding whether an area of land, fenced but not built on, was 'open land' within the meaning of the section: *Stephens v Cuckfield Royal District Council* [1960] 2 QB 373, 383 (answer: it was not 'open land').
- In a statute amending the statute of limitations, a marginal note stated 'as respects personal injury actions'. Held, this was relevant to deciding whether the amended statute of limitations (allowing an extension of time for suing) applied to an action for breach of contract: *Akbar v CF Green & Co Ltd* [1975] QB 582, 585 (answer: it did not apply to an action for breach of contract).
- Section 3 of a statute lacked its own heading. However, the section was one of a group of sections (ss 2–7) headed 'Dispositions by Mercantile Agents'. The section stated that 'a pledge of the documents of title to goods shall be deemed to be a pledge of the [actual] goods'. The section made no reference to the legal capacity of the pledgor. Held, the group heading indicated that s 3 dealt only with pledges by mercantile agents; therefore, a pledge of the documents of title by the owner of the goods was ineffective as a pledge of the goods themselves: *Inglis v Robertson* [1898] AC 616.

Statutory qualifications

Legislation in some Commonwealth jurisdictions expressly limits the relevance of headings when interpreting the text to which they relate. The legislation varies considerably. In Australia, for example, headings in Commonwealth (ie, Federal) statutes are part of the text of an Act (*Acts Interpretation Act 1901* (Cth), s 13), but in some States they are not (eg, *Interpretation Act 1987* (NSW), s 35). Again, in some Australian States, Chapter headings, Part headings, Division headings, and Subdivision headings are part of an Act, but section headings are not (eg, *Acts Interpretation Act 1915* (SA), s 19). However, Australian courts have held that headings are not necessarily deprived of all function merely because an interpretation statute excludes them from the text of an Act; for example, headings remain 'extrinsic' material to which courts may look to resolve ambiguity: see, eg, *Re Kierath* [2000] WASCA 156; (2000) 22 WAR 342, 359 [62] (Wheeler J; Wallwork J agreeing); *Carey v Australian Securities and Investments Commission* [2008] FCA 963, [10]; (2008) 169 FCR 311 (Finkelstein J). Indeed, some Australian interpretation statutes now expressly recognise this possibility (eg, *Interpretation Act 1987* (NSW), s 34).

Headings added by publishers and others

Of course, headings that find their way into statutes independently of parliamentary sanction are not part of the text of the statute, and therefore are not relevant to interpretation. For example, headings added by private-sector publishers for the convenience of their subscribers are irrelevant to interpretation: *People v Avanessian* 76 Cal App 4th 635, 641–42, 90 Cal Rptr 2d 367, 371 (California, 1999). Again, headings added by parliamentary officers or printers after an Act has passed through the legislature are irrelevant to interpretation: *The Ombudsman v Moroney* [1983] 1 NSWLR 317, 324–25 (Street CJ); *Sea Shepherd Australia Ltd v Western Australia* [2014] WASC 66; (2014) 313 ALR 184, [115] (Edelman J).

Legal status of headings: non-statutes

In non-statutory materials, headings are part of the text and relevant in interpreting the text. The courts allow headings to inform the meaning of the text to which they relate.

Examples

- A two-sentence clause in a document granting an option was headed 'Exercise of Option'. The first sentence specified that notice of exercise was to be in writing and posted; the second sentence specified that the notice was to be accompanied by payment of 1% of the purchase price. The optionee argued that another clause in the document allowed the 1% to be paid *after* exercise of the option. Held, the heading 'Exercise of Option' applied to both sentences in the clause, indicating that payment must accompany the exercise: *George v Cluning* (1979) 28 ALR 57, 61–62 (Mason J).
- Recitals in a contract were headed 'Background'. This indicated that the parties did not intend the recitals to create contractual obligations: *Equable Life Resorts Ltd v Monte Vista RVS Ltd* [2006] NZHC 1588.

However, two further points are relevant: (1) a heading is almost certainly subsidiary, and cannot override the plain meaning of the text; and (2) a vituperative or deceptive heading gravely reduces its usefulness. The following cases illustrate these points.

- A clause in a charterparty provided that delays caused by 'hindrances' were not to count as laytime. The clause was headed 'Force Majeure'. Held: the heading did not narrow the meaning of the word 'hindrances' to occurrences that were unpredictable and avoidable. Rather, the drafter had used 'Force Majeure' as an omnibus description for a variety of different causes: *Navrom v Callitsis Ship Management SA* [1988] 2 Lloyd's Rep 416 (CA). For another example, see *Cott UK Ltd v FE Barber Ltd* [1997] 3 All ER 540, 545G.

- Claimants brought proceedings against defendants for alleged breaches of several contracts between the claimants and the defendants. Two items of the claimants' pleadings were headed 'Improperly claimed expenses and stolen laptops'. But the text of the pleadings merely alleged, more blandly, that the defendants had failed to return laptops, with no allegations of theft or dishonesty. The judge struck out the headings and ordered them to be replaced with 'neutral headings': *Gamatronic (UK) Ltd v Hamilton* [2013] EWHC 328, [28]–[29] (Andrew Smith J; for a number of reasons, the judge struck out the whole of the pleadings).

'Headings do not affect interpretation'

Most non-legislative drafters include in their documents a standard clause to the effect that 'headings do not count'. Wording varies, but it generally takes a form such as:

- 'Headings do not affect interpretation.'
- 'Headings are for convenience only and do not affect meaning.'

For drafters who give careful thought to their headings, it is difficult to see the purpose behind this standard clause—but some authors strongly recommend it: eg, R Christou, *Boilerplate: Practical Clauses*, 7th edn (Sweet & Maxwell, 2015) [2-077].

Where such a clause is used, judges usually give effect to it, on the basis that courts should respect what the parties have agreed: *Gregory Projects (Halifax) Ltd v Tenpin (Halifax) Ltd* [2009] EWHC 2639 (Ch), [28] (Lewison J); *Orleans Investments Pty Ltd v Mindshare Communications Ltd* (2009) 254 ALR 81; [2009] NSWCA 40, [68]; *Franklins Pty Ltd v Metcash Trading Ltd* (2009) 76 NSWLR 603; [2009] NSWCA 407, [348].

However, depending on its precise wording, the provision may not deter courts from consulting headings for limited purposes. For example:

- A statement that headings are 'for convenience only' (or similar) allows recourse to the headings for the 'convenience' they are designed to provide, namely telling the reader 'at a glance' what a clause is about: *SBJ Stephenson Ltd v Mandy* [2000] FSR 286, 297; *Doughty Hanson & Co Ltd v Roe* [2007] EWHC 2212 (Ch), [71].
- A prohibition against using headings for 'interpretation' may not prohibit consulting a heading to help identify the contracting parties to the document: *Green v CGU Insurance Ltd* [2005] NSWSC 254, [31]; (2005) 215 ALR 612.

Forms of headings

Headings take many forms. Conventionally, they are short and direct—'topic headings'—pointing the reader to the subject matter of the clause but conveying little information about the detailed content of the clause. However, to make headings more useful for readers, three alternative forms of headings are increasingly used: question headings, direction headings, and message (or 'information-rich') headings.

Question headings

This form of heading aims to focus the reader's attention by mirroring a question that may be in the reader's mind. For example, in a lease, the conventional form of heading for a clause dealing with rental obligations would be the single word *Rent*—which tells the reader nothing except 'here is where you will find details about the rent'. In contrast, the question-form would draw the reader to the kinds of questions the reader is likely to be asking: eg, *When is rent payable?* or *What payment methods are accepted?*

However, headings forced into question-form purely for effect may appear strained—and any device that draws attention to itself diminishes effective communication. Also, research shows that some experienced readers of legislation find the question-format patronising: Office of Parliamentary Counsel (Commonwealth of Australia), *Results of the 2010 Legislation Users Survey* (2010) 55.

Direction headings

This form of heading tells the reader not merely 'this is the subject matter of this clause', but rather 'this is what you must do about the subject matter'. This form is seen increasingly in consumer documents. For example, headings in a consumer mortgage might read:

Pay the instalments on time (clause requiring payment on specified dates)

Paint the premises every three years (clause requiring three-yearly painting)

Notify any change of address for service of notices (clause requiring parties to keep their address-for-service details up to date).

Message ('information-rich') headings

This technique seeks to summarise the contents of the clause to which it relates. The purpose is to give the reader not merely a statement of the subject matter, but rather an overview or snapshot of the content. A busy reader can then get the sense of the provision merely by reading the heading. This form of heading could be appropriate for many kinds of legal documents, including judgments. To illustrate:

- **The primary judge's reasons were not inadequate**
- **The agreements were also vitiated by unconscionable conduct**

[Headings in *Thorne v Kennedy* [2017] HCA 49; (2017) 263 CLR 85, 111 (HCA, Full Court)]

Contrast the following headings in a recent UK Supreme Court decisions. The headings in the left-hand column are taken from the actual judgment. The headings in the right-hand column are suggested 'information-rich' alternatives.

Heading in judgment	**Suggested information-rich alternative**
The appeal to the Court of Appeal	Court of Appeal allowed appeal, by majority
Was there a binding contract?	Parties reached binding contract
Implied term	No need for implied term about obligation to pay commission on completion (but if needed, term could be implied to same effect)
Scancarriers	Scancarriers and other decisions do not preclude finding of binding contract
The Estate Agents Act 1979	On facts, breach of Estate Agents Act 1979 does not preclude claim to (reduced) commission

[*Source:* selected headings from *Devani v Wells* [2019] UKSC 4; [2019] 2 WLR 617 (Lord Kitchin JSC); in the judgment, headings appeared in italics.]

However, there are at least two potential drawbacks with message (information-rich) headings:

1. They are almost always longer than conventional headings. This offends those legal drafters who aim for brevity in headings.
2. They encourage repetition. To illustrate, consider a message heading *Tenant must pay rent on first day of each month.* The substantive provision will inevitably repeat that (or similar) wording when imposing the obligation to pay rent on the first day of each month.

Forms of headings compared

The following table illustrates the various techniques discussed above. The headings are taken from a commercial lease.

Conventional heading	Question heading	Direction heading	Message (information-rich) heading
Rent	When is rent payable?	Pay rent each month	Tenant must pay rent monthly [*or*, if payment date is crucial] Tenant must pay rent on first day of each month [*or*, if both date and payment method are crucial] Tenant must pay rent on first day of each month by bank transfer
Repair	What are the tenant's repair obligations?	Keep premises in repair	Tenant must keep premises in repair
Mediation	When must parties mediate?	Before suing, attempt mediation	Parties must attempt to mediate before starting court proceedings

Be consistent with forms of headings

Seek to keep heading-forms consistent across a document; do not move from one form to another. In the following headings from a commercial lease, the mix of heading-forms lacks discipline.

Fit-out [conventional form]

Tenant must keep premises clean [direction form]

What are the Tenant's repair obligations? [question form]

Either party can terminate the lease for the other party's breach of essential term [message ('information-rich') form]

Spacing between headings and text

Some document designers caution against headings that 'float'—ie, headings with equal spacing between the end of the text that precedes them and the start of the text that follows them. They prefer headings to be visually 'tied' more closely to the text they introduce than the text they follow. For example:

Floating	Preferred
xxxxxxxxxx [end text] **Heading** xxxxxx [start text]	xxxxxxxxxx [end text] **Heading** xxxxxx [start text]

Modern word-processing programs, with style sheet facilities, make this spacing relatively easy to achieve.

Punctuation in headings

Punctuation in headings generally follows standard usage. However, there are some qualifications:

No full stop

Do not end headings with a full stop (even for message headings). A heading that ends with a full stop may puzzle the reader: is this a heading, or it is a substantive statement? (See, eg, *Love v Auburn Apartments Ltd*, discussed above under **What is a heading**?)

Limited capitalisation

Capitalise only the initial letter of the first word in a heading, eg, 'Cleaning obligations', *not* 'Cleaning Obligations'. Breach this rule only when second or later words in the heading are proper nouns or defined terms: eg, in a lease, 'Cleaning and Maintenance obligations of Landlord' (where 'Maintenance' and 'Landlord' are defined terms).

Be careful when the initial word of a heading is itself a defined term. The reader may be left wondering: is this word used in its defined sense or not? To illustrate: in the preceding example, is 'Cleaning' a defined term? If it is, consider shuffling the order of words: eg, 'Landlord's Cleaning and Maintenance obligations'. The amended version removes the doubt (accepting that *Landlord* is always a defined term in a lease). (For an example where this issue surfaced, see *R A & K Becker Pty Ltd v Cariste Pty Ltd* [2001] NSWSC 663.)

Subject line in letters and emails

The former convention was to introduce the subject-line heading with *Re* (Latin: in the matter of): eg, 'Re your recent accident'. Modern usage omits *Re* and gets straight to the point: eg, **Your recent accident** (no full stop; no italics; no quotation marks; and preferably in **bold**).

Further reading

- Plain Language Action and Information Network, 'Effective Headings', at www.plainlanguage.gov/guidelines/organize/effective-headings/
- *Guidelines for Document Designers* (American Institutes for Research, 1981) 118–20
- Michele van Eck, 'Ignore this Heading. It Will Not Influence Your Interpretation of this Article … Or Will it?' (2019) 52 *De Jure Law Journal* 447 (South African approach to headings)
- Nick Horn, 'Legislative Section Headings: Drafting Techniques, Plain Language, and Redundancy' (2012) *The Loophole* (April 2012) 7; see www.calc.ngo/publications/loopholes#loophole-table-2012

See also **DOCUMENT DESIGN**; **FONTS**; **PLAIN LANGUAGE**; **PUNCTUATION**.

headings are for convenience only

See **HEADINGS.**

headlease

Occasionally spelled *head-lease* or *head lease*. A lease from a landlord to a tenant, out of which the tenant then grants one or more subleases. For example, where the owner of the freehold (L) grants a lease to a tenant (T), who then grants a sublease to a subtenant (ST), the lease from L to T is the *headlease*. Were ST then to grant a sublease (strictly, a sub-sublease) to ST2, the sublease from T to ST would be the headlease in relation to the sub-sublease.

headline rent

The rent as published, rather than the rent as paid. For example, a lease may stipulate a rent of $X per year, but other provisions in the lease or in side documents may allow deductions or concessions which reduce the actual rent; the *headline rent* is $X per year.

HEADS OF AGREEMENT

Meaning

Also called 'Heads of Terms', 'Memorandum of Understanding', 'Letter of Intent', 'Preliminary Agreement'. A document that records the parties' agreement on basic points of principle and serves as the basis for a later, more formal and complete, agreement.

Enforceability

Beware of entitling a document 'Heads of Agreement' without also giving thought to whether the document is meant to be contractually binding. Not every document entitled 'Heads of Agreement' is binding. For example:

- Its terms may be too uncertain to be enforceable under general principles of contract law.
- The matters left open for further negotiation may be so fundamental that the document is no more than a general statement of intention or an 'agreement to agree'.
- Although the parties have negotiated all key terms, they may not intend to be bound unless and until a formal document is drawn up and signed.

However, it is different where the agreed key terms are sufficiently certain, where any further points to be negotiated will fit into the framework of the agreed key terms, and where the drawing up of a formal document is merely to restate the parties' already-concluded agreement in fuller or more precise terms.

- '[A]s soon as the fact is established of the final mutual assent of the parties so that those who draw up the formal agreement have not the power to vary the terms already settled, I think the contract is completed.' [*Rossiter v Miller* (1878) 3 App Cas 1124, 1151 (Lord Blackburn)]
- '[T]he mere use of the words "subject to more complete documentation" [in a document titled *Heads of Agreement*] does not ... prevent the agreement having binding effect if on the overall agreement, it is clear that it is intended to have some contractual force.' [*Beta Investment SA v Transmedia Europe Inc* [2003] EWHC 3066 (Ch), [43] (Fenwick QC, Deputy HC Judge)]

To avoid arguments over enforceability, always indicate expressly whether the heads of agreement are intended to be binding.

Further reading

- JW Carter, *Carter on Contract* (LexisNexis, online) 'Preliminary Agreements' [04–030]
- Michael Furmston, 'Letters of Intent and Other Preliminary Agreements' (2009) 25 *Journal of Contract Law* 95

See also **LOCK-UP CLAUSES**.

heir

Technical meaning

A person who succeeds by right of blood to his or her ancestor's real estate. Historically, identifying a person's *heir* could be difficult, as the answer depended on medieval principles governing the devolution of title to land. In outline, those principles were as follows ('A' being the deceased):

1. A's issue were preferred to A's collaterals (brothers and sisters).
2. Within A's issue, males were preferred to females.
3. The eldest male was preferred to the younger male(s) (ie, 'primogeniture'); but if no males survived, then the females took equally.
4. Where a person (B) inherited in accordance with rules 1–3 and then died intestate leaving issue, the property descended to B's issue (who themselves were preferred among themselves in accordance with rules 1–3).
5. If B died intestate without leaving issue, the property descended to the person next entitled among A's issue. For example, if B was A's eldest son, the property descended to A's second son and that son's heirs; and if A had no other issue, then the property descended to A's collaterals (brothers and sisters).

Relevance of context

In formal documents, courts gave *heir* its technical meaning—in line with the general presumption that terms of art carry their legal meaning. But there was an exception in the law of wills, where courts gave (and still give) effect to the testator's idiosyncratic language if that better carried out the testator's intentions. (This is the so-called 'testator's armchair principle', which admits extrinsic evidence to explain the meaning of words and expressions in a will: *Boyes v Cook* (1880) 14 Ch D 53, 56 (James LJ); FV Hawkins and EC Ryder, *The Construction of Wills*, 3rd edn (Sweet & Maxwell, 1965) 12–21.) On this basis, *heirs* could mean (for example) immediate children only: eg, *Milroy v Milroy* (1844) 14 Sim 48, 54–55; 60 ER 274, 277 (Shadwell V-C).

Modern meaning

Modern legislation dealing with rights to intestate property has rendered the common-law meaning of *heir* largely irrelevant. Property now devolves according to rules that no longer follow the common law devolution to 'heirs'. Also, courts now usually treat a disposition 'to my heirs' as meaning 'to my next-of-kin': eg, *Re Hinkson* [1959] VR 686, 689.

See also **heir-at-law**; **intestacy / intestate**; **issue (offspring)**; **next-of-kin**; **TERMS OF ART**.

heir-at-law

Strictly, the words '*at-law*' are superfluous, as there is no concept of *heir-in-equity*; but *heir-at-law* is the accepted term—preferably hyphenated, to reflect the terms's composite nature (although *heir at law* is also seen).

- 'Mary Ellen died intestate in 1967 and a grant of Letters of Administration to her estate was issued to Roger, her *heir-at-law*.' [*Higgs v Leshel Maryas Investment Co Ltd* [2009] UKPC 47, [7] (Lord Scott)]
- '"Hereditament" is a somewhat archaic conveyancing term which as a matter of ordinary legal terminology refers to any species of real property which would descend upon intestacy to the *heirs at law*.' [*Woolway v Mazars* [2015] UKSC 53; [2015] 1 All ER 299, [4] (Lord Sumption)]

See also **heir**.

heirs, executors, administrators, successors, and assigns

Sometimes (sadly) minus commas: *heirs executors administrators successors and assigns*. This word string is often found in contractual provisions that define a party to include the party's 'heirs, executors, administrators, successors, and assigns' (or some in that list). But the effect of such provisions is limited. A definition cannot convert a non-party into a party. It is true that some or all of a party's heirs, executors, successors, and assigns may become liable under the contract—eg, under the principles that govern succession on death, or that bind a party's executors to an obligation, or that allow easements or covenants to bind land in the hands of successors in title. But that is because various legal principles produce that result, not because a clause seeks by definition to bind non-parties. Indeed, to define a party to include their 'assigns' may have unintentional consequences, such as implying that the contract is inherently assignable: *Tolhurst v Associated Portland Cement Manufacturers Pty Ltd* [1903] AC 414.

Further reading

'Heirs, Executors, Administrators, Successors, and Assigns', in *Law Words* (Centre for Plain Legal Language, University of Sydney, 1995) 38; www.clarity-international.net/plain-language-resources/general-resources/

HENDIADYS

A figure of speech in which a single complex idea is expressed by two words connected by a conjunction (usually *and*). For example:

- 'The vendor must *co-operatively help* the purchaser' becomes (as a hendiadys) 'The vendor must *co-operate with and help* the purchaser'.
- 'The claimant must *furnish a completed* statement' becomes (as a hendiadys) 'The claimant must *complete and furnish* a statement'.

By separating-out the elements of a concept, a hendiadys can add clarity. But in legal contexts a hendiadys can also create ambiguity, because of the 'presumption against surplusage', under which every word is presumed to have a role: specifically, is there a single (combined) action or two separate actions?

Examples

- An insurer promised 'to *co-operate with* [a committee] *and assist* [the committee] to carry out its duties'. Was this a composite (single) obligation or two distinct obligations? Held, it was a composite (single) obligation—to *co-operate with* the committee in carrying out its duties: *Traders Prudent Insurance Co Ltd v Registrar of Workers Compensation Commission of New South Wales* [1971] 2 NSWLR 513.
- Legislation allowed damages for nervous shock where '*symptoms and disability*' persisted for six weeks. Was this a hendiadys (ie, meaning that *disability symptoms* must persist for six weeks) or did it require that *each* of disability and symptoms must persist for six weeks? Held, it required each to persist for six weeks: *Victims Compensation Fund Corp v Brown* [2003] HCA 54; (2003) 201 ALR 260.
- A statute defined 'organised crime offence' as involving (amongst other matters) '*systemic and continuing* criminal activity'. Held, 'systemic and continuing' was a hendiadys. It was a 'composite adjectival expression modifying the compound noun *criminal activity*'. Each adjective in the composite expression complemented the other: *McLeod-Dryden v Supreme Court of Victoria* [2017] VSCA 60, [25].
- But compare: employers proposed obtaining background reports on job applicants. Legislation required the employers to provide the applicants with '*clear and conspicuous*

> *disclosure*' that they intended to obtain the reports. Was this one requirement or two? Held, it was two requirements. *Clear* meant 'reasonably understandable', and *conspicuous* meant 'readily noticeable to the consumer'. Satisfaction of one requirement was insufficient. On the facts, the disclosure was conspicuous, but not clear. See *Gilberg v California Check Cashing Stores Inc* 913 F 3d 1169, 1176–77 (9th Cir 2019).

Further reading

Samuel L Bray, '"Necessary and Proper" and "Cruel and Unusual": Hendiadys in the Constitution' (2016) 102 *Virginia Law Review* 687

See also **SURPLUSAGE (PRESUMPTION AGAINST)**.

'HENRY VIII' CLAUSE

A legislative provision allowing a statute to be amended or repealed by subordinate legislation (or sometimes ministerial fiat); so called because of Henry VIII's power under the *Statute of Proclamations 1539* to issue proclamations having the status of legislation—in effect, empowering him to change the law by public announcement. By convention (though not by legal compulsion), modern parliaments usually limit Henry VIII clauses to mechanical matters, such as amending financial limits, bringing lists up to date, or altering details within a narrowly defined field. However, occasionally parliaments ignore these self-imposed limits: eg, *European Union (Withdrawal) Act 2018*, giving ministers wide powers to regulate how retained EU law is to operate in the UK.

The constitutionality of Henry VIII clauses rests on the premise that parliament, in the exercise of its plenary power, can empower another body or person to make legislation. As a practical matter, if a provision conferring Henry VIII powers is at all ambiguous, the courts interpret it restrictively: *R v Secretary of Social Security* [1991] 1 WLR 198, 203 (Lord Keith).

Further reading

- Dennis Morris, 'Henry VIII Clauses: Their Birth, a Later 20th Century Renaissance and a Possible 21st Century Metamorphosis' (2007) *The Loophole* (March, 2007) 14; see www.calc.ngo/publications/loopholes#loophole-table-2007
- JM Keyes, *Executive Legislation*, 2nd edn (Canada, LexisNexis, 2010) 110–11, 362–65

here- words

Most *here*-words are archaic. Replace them with modern equivalents that carry the same meaning, minus the musty legalism. For example:

Instead of this	**Try this**
hereafter	below; in clause X; in the future
herein	in this clause; in this document
hereinafter	in clause X; below
hereinafter referred to as	called in the rest of this document; called in clause X
hereinbefore	called in clause X; called above
hereof	of [this agreement]; of it
hereto	to this [agreement]
hereunto	[do not use]
herewith	with [this agreement / letter]; I / we enclose ...

Occasionally, *here-* words confound even lawyers. For example, the drafter of the lease in *Creer v P & O Lines of Australia Pty Ltd* (1971) 125 CLR 84 muddled *hereinafter* with *hereinbefore*. And in the following extract from a US judgment, the paired *here-* words, prefaced with a *there-* word, would confound even the most experienced lawyer:

> '[Proper notice was published in a newspaper] as fully appears from the affidavit of the publisher thereof heretofore herein filed.' [*Penn v Pensacola-Escambia Governmental Center Authority* 311 So 2d 97, 102 (Fla 1975) (Roberts J, quoting from judgment of the trial judge)]

See also **hereby**; **SIMPLER WORDS AND PHRASES**; ***there-* words**.

hereafter

A word favoured by lawyers, but often obscure: where, exactly, after? For example, if a provision in a contract or statute begins with 'subject as *hereafter* provided', does that mean (1) subject as provided in the later parts of *this* provision, or (2) subject as provided in some *later* part of the document (and if so, where)? Context does not always help. In *English Sewing Cotton Co Ltd v Inland Revenue Commissioners* [1947] 1 All ER 679, the trial judge held (1), but the Court of Appeal held (2).

See also ***here-* words**; **SIMPLER WORDS AND PHRASES.**

hereby

Almost never needed

Some legal writers add *hereby* for legal 'feel'; others add it out of habit. Rarely, however, does *hereby* serve any legal purpose. To say that something is '*hereby* done' means simply that it is 'done'.

To indicate a dispositive act?

Some legal writers add *hereby* to indicate that what is being done is a dispositive act, not a mere statement of existing fact. But this use seems doubtful. Consider this statement in a statute: 'The Department of Justice is established.' No reader would take this as a statement of existing fact—namely (as if the reader were unaware) that there exists a Department of Justice. Rather, the reader would take it as a statement that the statute itself establishes the department; to say 'is *hereby* established' would be redundant. Nevertheless, several acknowledged experts on legal writing see benefit in using *hereby* to mark such a distinction:

- Bryan Garner, *Garner's Dictionary of Legal Usage*, 3rd edn (Oxford University Press, 2011) 407: 'I [*hereby*] name you as my successor.' In Garner's view, *hereby* clarifies that this is an appointment, not a mere statement. (But then, contrary to Garner, so too would 'I appoint you as my successor', avoiding *hereby*.)
- Francis Bennion, 'Confusion over Plain Language Law' (2007) 16 *Commonwealth Lawyer* 65): 'I [*hereby*] give you my gold pen.' In Bennion's view, *hereby* adds operative effect, making the statement a dispositive act rather than a description. (But then, contrary to Bennion, it is hard to see why 'I give you my gold pen' would be inadequate as a disposition (gift) of the pen.)

Sometimes ambiguous

In some contexts, *hereby* may be ambiguous for failing to indicate where 'here':

> A section in a New Zealand statute gave landowners the right to compensation for loss or damage suffered from 'the exercise of any of the powers *hereby* given'. Did *hereby* mean 'by this

section', or 'by this Part of the Act', or 'by this Act'? Held, it meant 'by this Act': *Superior Lands Ltd v Wellington City Council* [1974] 2 NZLR 251 (CA).

A backstop for lazy drafting?

On occasions, *hereby* may help garner meaning from lazy drafting. This is not to justify the use of *hereby*, but merely to recognise its role as rescuer.

Example

A tenant, having an option to renew a lease, sent the landlord a letter in these terms: 'We would *hereby* like to exercise our option to renew the lease.' Were these words an immediate exercise the option, or did they merely indicate that the tenant intended to exercise the option later, and perhaps more formally? Held, they were an immediate exercise the option. The court considered that *hereby* helped point to that result: *Riltang Pty Ltd v L Pty Ltd* (2002) 11 BPR 20,281, 20,286 [24]. However (to add a comment), did the underlying problem lie in the polite expression 'we *would like to*'—a diffidence inappropriate in the exercise of legal rights? More emphatic wording would have clarified the tenant's purpose, without needing the prop of *hereby*.

See also ***here-* words**; **SIMPLER WORDS AND PHRASES**.

hereditament

Historically, an interest in land that passed on intestacy to the owner's heir (Latin: *heres*): *Woolway v Mazars* [2015] UKSC 53, [4] (Lord Sumption). Because property no longer descends to heirs as such, *hereditament* can no longer carry its literal meaning: Williams and Eastwood, *Real Property*, 25th edn (Sweet & Maxwell, 1933) 80. Indeed, it has lost all connection with its historical derivation, and has come to mean, in essence, 'a self-contained piece of property': *Woolway* (above), [47] (Lord Neuberger). Its inherent archaism is reason enough to avoid it, although it is sometimes still seen in consciously old-fashioned conveyancing documents or wills, drawn by lawyers for whom force of tradition overrides reader-bemusement. That said, *hereditament* survives in some statutory contexts, such as:

- statutory definitions of 'land', where it still carries the traditional meaning of an interest in real property that passes with it and is capable of being inherited—that is, capable of passing on death by will or intestacy (eg, *Law of Property Act 1925*, s 205(1)(ix))
- local government rating statutes, where it means a rateable piece of land: eg, *Local Government Finance Act 1988*, ss 43, 64; *Rossendale Borough Council v Hurstwood Properties (A) Ltd* [2019] EWCA Civ 364; [2019] 1 WLR 4567, [10] (David Richards LJ, although preferring to use 'properties' rather than 'hereditaments'); *Cardtronics Europe Ltd v Sykes* [2020] UKSC 21; [2020] 1 WLR 2184 (sites of fixed ATM machines 'hereditaments').

However (unless compelled by statute), to continue to describe land or interests in land as *hereditaments* is unnecessarily archaic.

See also **corporeal / incorporeal**; **heir**.

herein

A word that strives to add precision, but often misses the mark: where, exactly, herein? In a statute, is *herein* in this Part, in this section, in this subsection? In a document, is *herein* in this clause, in this subclause, in this Schedule? So, avoid the generic *herein*. Instead, specify *where*.

See also ***here-* words**; **SIMPLER WORDS AND PHRASES**.

hereinbefore

An archaic lawyerism for—and supplying no more precision than—*before* or *above*. Thus, 'the document *hereinbefore* mentioned' can mean simply 'the document mentioned *above*' (which still leaves unanswered '*where* above?').

See also ***here-* words**; **SIMPLER WORDS AND PHRASES**.

heretofore

A lawyerism for *before* or *above*. It serves no purpose other than studied archaism; prefer *before* or *above* (and better still, specify exactly *where*).

See also ***here-* words**; **SIMPLER WORDS AND PHRASES**.

hereunder

An archaism, always replaceable by *below*. Also—even when replaced by *below*—it is inherently uncertain: *where* below? Always aim for more specific reference, as shown in this example:

> **Before**: Payments are to be made as specified *hereunder*.
>
> **After**: Payments are to be made as specified in clause [X].

herewith

Always replaceable by *with this*. Sometimes—better still—able to be deleted, with no replacement necessary. Thus: 'I enclose the document ~~herewith~~ [deleted].'

See also ***here-* words**; **SIMPLER WORDS AND PHRASES**.

heritable / inheritable

The meanings are the same—'able to be inherited'; the prefix *in-* is an intensifier, not a negative. In modern usage, *heritable* tends to be used for traits or genetic characteristics, while *inheritable* tends to be used for titles or property.

See also **heir**.

heritage

In Scots legal usage, sometimes used to mean 'land', including in the pairing 'lands and heritages'. Despite its etymology (*heir*), the modern term *land* suffices:

> 'Mr McGregor submitted that at all times the proprietorship of the *heritage* [prefer: *land*] and the tenancy of the head lease had been in different hands.' [*Van Lynden v Gilchrist* [2015] CSOH 147, [10] (Lord Philip)]

hermeneutic circle

The conundrum that understanding the parts of a document is dependent on understanding the larger whole, but that the larger whole can be understood only from the parts: see, eg, *Waugh Hotel Management Pty Ltd v Marrickville Council* [2009] NSWCA 390; (2009) 171 LGERA 112, [33] (Campbell JA). This 'looking ahead and looking back' within the same document is also called the 'hermeneutic spiral': Thomas MJ Möllers, *Legal Methods* (Hart, 2020) 23.

highway

In legal usage, a *highway* is any road or path that members of the public are entitled to use 'as of right'. It may be a 'cartway' (for traversing on foot, or with vehicles or cattle), a 'bridleway' (for traversing on horseback), a 'footway' (for traversing on foot only), or a road. At common law, a navigable river is a 'highway' in this sense.

hinc inde

Latin: on this side; on that side; reciprocal. Given the adequacy of an English translation, to retain the Latin is to be consciously arcane. Prefer a translation. For example:

- 'The other clauses set out the obligations which the parties undertake towards each other *hinc inde* [prefer: *reciprocally*], but the arbitration clause does not impose on one of the parties an obligation in favour of the other.' [*Heyman v Darwins Ltd* [1942] AC 356, 373, (Lord Macmillan)]
- 'Proper consideration was given to the arguments *hinc inde* [prefer: *on both sides*] and this was reflected in the written decision.' [*Pattullo v Inland Revenue Commissioners* [2014] UKFTT 841 (TC), [88]]

hirer

Where property is *hired out*, who is the *hirer*? Is it the owner who hires it out to the user, or the user who takes it on hire from the owner? Usually, context clarifies; but if in doubt, use another word.

See also **ee- / or endings**.

hold (court decision)

See find / hold.

hold and enjoy

A pairing once common in property documents, but now (thankfully) rare. For example, a will might provide: 'I give my house to John to *hold and enjoy* for his lifetime.' But to hold the *house* is to *enjoy* it. Either word would suffice. Better still, use neither word; simply state: 'I give my house to John for his lifetime.'

See also **use and enjoy.**

hold harmless

See **indemnify (variants of)**.

holding company

A company (X) that controls another company (Y) by virtue of share ownership, which gives X effective control over the appointment of Y's directors or control of voting at meetings of Y. While this explanation generally suffices, a statute may define 'holdingness' with more precision for the purposes of that statute. For example, corporations legislation usually specifies four main criteria for X to be the 'holding company' of Y:

(1) X holds a majority of voting rights in Y.
(2) X has the right to appoint or remove a majority of Y's board of directors.
(3) X has the right to exercise a dominant influence over Y.
(4) X is a shareholder in Y and controls, by agreement with other shareholders, a majority of the voting rights in Y.

See, eg, *Companies Act 2006*, s 1162 ('parent undertaking'); *Corporations Act 2001* (Cth), ss 9, 46 (Australia).

Commercial contracts usually contain a similar definition, though pared-down:

> 'A company is a holding company of another company ("the subsidiary company") if it directly or indirectly owns or controls more than [X%] of the shares in the subsidiary company, or if it has the right to appoint or remove a majority of the board of directors of the subsidiary company.'

See also **subsidiary company**.

holograph

A document in the maker's own handwriting; eg, a holograph will.

home in / hone

To *home in* is to move towards; to *hone* is to sharpen. So you *home in* (not *hone in*) on a target, such as your opponent's argument; but you *hone* your skills to rebut the argument.

> 'In chapter 6, the author *hones in* [prefer: *homes in*] on two specific [topics] ...' [Book review, [2020] *Singapore Journal of Legal Studies* 358, 361]

home invasion

A colourful term, with overtones emotive but vague, which has found its way into statutory drafting in some jurisdictions (eg, *Crimes Act 1958* (Vic), s 77A). Unless closely defined, its meaning depends greatly on context—which is never a good omen for those who insist on using it. The problem lies with 'invasion'. In some contexts, 'invasion' implies non-consensual force and hostility (eg, where an 'invading' army enters land); but in other contexts, it implies consensual activity that is benign and beneficial (eg, where a doctor carries out an 'invasive' medical procedure). In the context of 'home' invasion, it more likely reflects the concept of trespass: 'By the laws of England, every invasion of private property, be it ever so minute, is a trespass': *Entick v Carrington* (1765) 19 *Howell's State Trials* 1029, 1066. Because a slight trespass is nevertheless a trespass, even a slight intrusion may be a home 'invasion'—eg, entering an unoccupied house by opening the back door and without causing damage: *Manning v South Australia* [2015] SASC 164; (2015) 124 SASR 76.

homologation

The act of approving, adopting, or ratifying a document which would otherwise be defective. The term seems unique to Scots law and the civil law.

honestly

Whether a person acts 'dishonestly' logically involves two areas of enquiry, one subjective and the other objective: (a) the person's actual state of knowledge or belief about their action; and (b) whether the act is dishonest 'by the standards of ordinary decent people': *Ivey v Genting Casinos (UK)* [2017] UKSC 67; [2018] AC 391, [74]. Depending on the context, the answer may require proof of (a), or proof of (b), or proof of both (a) and (b). Where it requires only proof of (b), then lack of a subjective intent to act dishonestly is irrelevant if reasonable persons would conclude that the conduct is dishonest: *Australian Securities and Investments Commission v Macdonald (No 12)* [2009] NSWSC 714; (2009) 259 ALR 116.

See also **bona fide**; **in good faith**.

honorary bencher

See **bencher**.

HONORIFICS

See **JUDICIAL HONORIFICS**.

hotchpot

Sometimes misspelled *hotchpotch*. The bringing into account of property to ensure equality of division.

Example

> Assume that A dies intestate, and that B is entitled under the intestacy to a share of A's estate. If B had received benefits from A when A was alive, the 'doctrine of hotchpot' may require B to account for ('bring into hotchpot') those benefits when the estate is being distributed.

Wills and settlements of property often contain 'hotchpot clauses', designed to ensure that benefits which a person has already enjoyed from the testator or settlor are brought into account in calculating the beneficiary's share.

In its application to deceased estates, the doctrine of *hotchpot* is regulated by statute, and has been abolished in some jurisdictions.

Further reading

Halsbury's Laws of England, 'Settlements' (vol 91, 2019) [718]–[719] (hotchpot clauses); 'Wills and Intestacy' (vol 102, 2016) [515] (hotchpot following intestacy)

hour (of the day)

See **TIME**.

however

Meaning

However heralds a contrasting statement: eg, 'Yesterday I told you this; *however*, I now tell you something different.' It introduces a qualification or limitation. To use *however* in any other sense confuses readers; it may also lead to litigation over meaning, as in the following example:

> A section of a statute dealt with costs of proceedings before a tribunal. Subsection (1) required applicants to bear their own costs 'unless … the tribunal otherwise orders'. Subsection (2) started with *However* (followed by a comma) and then listed four situations in which the tribunal

could order a party to pay the other party's costs. Held: *However* introduced not a qualification to the general rule that parties bear their own costs, but rather a list of the circumstances—indeed, the *only* circumstances—in which the tribunal could order a party to pay the other party's costs. That is, *However* heralded an explanation, not a qualification: *CIC Australia Ltd v Australian Capital Territory Planning and Land Authority* [2013] ACTSC 96; (2013) 277 FLR 26, [35]–[84].

Starting sentences with *however*

There is no 'rule' against starting a sentence with '*However*, …' Judicial barbs suggesting otherwise—eg, *GM & AM Pearce and Co Pty Ltd v RGM Australia Pty Ltd* (1998) 16 ACLC 429, 432—are misconceived. (Nor is there any rule against starting a sentence with '*But* …' Indeed, being shorter than *However*, *But* introduces the contrast more bluntly and therefore more effectively.)

Comma splices

Ungainly

When placing *however* in midsentence to state a contrast, set it off with commas: eg, 'A knowledge of grammar, *however*, is lacking.' But do not use commas around *however* to 'splice' together two independent clauses (quasi-sentences) that could stand grammatically as separate sentences. To separate the quasi-sentences, insert a semicolon before *however*, not a mere comma. For example, *not* 'He was losing the case, however, his barrister rose to the occasion'; *rather* 'He was losing the case; however, his barrister rose to the occasion.' Even judges (or their stenographers) make this mistake, as the following examples show. Note how the usages (all wrong) vary.

- '[T]he parties could well have been expected to enter into a contract, *however*, although they discussed contractual terms, they had consciously chosen not to do so.' [*Thorner v Major* [2009] UKHL 18; [2009] 1WLR 776, 803 [96] (Lord Neuberger)]
- 'It was common ground that no criminal proceeding resulted from WorkCover's investigation, *however* it was contended this did not preclude the operation of s 69(3)(b).' [*QBE Insurance (Australia) Ltd v CGU Workers Compensation (NSW) Ltd* [2012] NSWSC 377, [64] (Beech-Jones J)]
- 'My provisional view as to costs is that they ought [to] follow the event *however* I will make an order preserving the parties' right to be heard on costs failing agreement between them.' [*Majet v Goggin and Miller* [2015] QSC 38, [43] (Henry J)]

Ambiguous

A comma splice is not merely ungainly. It can also create ambiguity. For example:

> 'The court lists will soon become shorter, however, filing fees will reduce.' Does 'however' qualify the clause before it or the clause after it?

See also **but**.

howsoever

A lawyer's archaism, always replaceable (as in the first three examples below), and sometimes deletable (as in the fourth example).

Examples

- 'You [X], whether by yourself, your employees, agents or *otherwise howsoever* [prefer: *by any other means*] take no steps to bring or continue any legal proceeding in any County

Court …' [Trial judge's order, considered on appeal in *Gopee v London Mercantile Court* [2015] EWCA Civ 944]

- 'There could have been no doubt in the minds of the jury that they had to be sure that the applicant had agreed to join this conspiracy, *howsoever* [prefer: *by whatever means*] that agreement was reached.' [*R v Austin* [2015] EWCA Crim 349, [32] (Fulford LJ)]
- 'A claims "through" B if A has acquired title or rights from B, or from someone who has acquired rights from B, and so on through *howsoever* [prefer: *however*] many intermediary titleholders or holders of rights there might be between A and B.' [*Sahab Holdings Pty Ltd v Registrar-General (No 2)* [2012] NSWCA 42; (2012) 16 BPR 30,353, [28] (Campbell JA and Tobias AJA)]
- 'The [restraint clause in the employment contract] set out the different types of status in which she was to be subject to the restraints which followed, namely "as principal, manager, employee, contractor, consultant, agent or otherwise ~~howsoever~~ [delete]".' [*Tillman v Egon Zehnder Ltd* [2019] UKSC 32; [2020] AC 154, [45] (Lord Wilson, quoting from the restraint clause)]

HUMOUR

Place in legal writing

Humour has a role in legal writing, as in writing generally. Humour can concentrate the mind and reinforce the message. The following two quotations use humour (effectively) to stress the parlous state of legal writing:

- 'There are two things wrong with most legal writing: one is its style, the other is its content. I think that about covers the ground.' [Fred Rodell, 'Goodbye to Law Reviews' (1936) 23 *Virginia Law Review* 38, 38]
- 'Lawyers have two common failings. One is that they do not write well and the other is that they think they do.' [Carl Felsenfeld, 'The Plain English Movement in the United States' (1981–82) 6 *Canadian Business Law Journal* 406, 413]

Humour in court

Humour is often seen in banter between judges, or between bench and bar. In both situations it may be harmless enough—a mere diversion for those involved. It may also help relieve tension and stress. But it must be practised with restraint, lest the litigants feel that their concerns are not being taken seriously—particularly where it is legal 'in-house' humour:

- 'An attempt at judicial sarcasm or humour, directed at a litigant, witness, attorney or law student … has no place in a courtroom. It is deeply resented and inevitably demeans the judge himself.' [*Re Albano* 384 A 2d 144, 146 [2] (1978, NJ)]
- '[T]he bench is not an appropriate place for unseemly levity. … [The litigant's] entire future, or even his life, may be trembling in the balance, and the robed buffoon who makes merry at his expense should be choked with his own wig.' [William Prosser, *The Judicial Humorist* (Little Brown, 1952) vii]

Humour in judgments

Judges sometimes use humour in judgments to help drive home a point, particularly in one or more of the situations in the following examples:

- **To express exasperation with counsel.** 'Judges are not ferrets!' [*Nicholas Acoustics & Specialty Co v H & M Construction Co Inc* 695 F 2d 839, 846–47, 5th Cir, 1983 (Goldberg J, emphasising that it is the task of the claimant's lawyer, not of the court, to disclose material adverse to the claimant's case)]

- **To tell counsel, pointedly, that their case lacks merit.** 'About half the practice of a decent lawyer consists in telling would-be clients that they are damned fools and should stop.' [*Hill v Norfolk and Western Railway Co* 814 F2d 1192, 1202 (7th Cir, 1987) (Posner J)]
- **To gently berate litigants.** '[C]hasing farthings while sovereigns rolled away.' [*Taleb v National Australia Bank Ltd* (2011) 82 NSWLR 489; [2011] NSWSC 1562 [34] (Bryson AJ, chastising a bank which dithered about a minor refund of stamp duty while much greater issues were at stake)]

But humour in judgments can fall flat. It sometimes seems mere self-indulgence, practised on a captive audience. For example:

- 'Inasmuch as this is the penultimate judgment I shall write after 18 years in the Court of Appeal, I am a kindred spirit who has sailed away from the safe harbour of the Royal Courts of Justice, not at all sure how to explore, or what to dream or what I am about to discover.' [*Reeves v Northrop* [2013] EWCA Civ 362; [2013] 1 WLR 2867, [30] (Sir Alan Ward, in a judgment about whether a houseboat was rateable for council tax purposes, and where the houseboat owner had sailed away)]
- 'There is little point in expanding upon these reasons for I am outnumbered, nay outgunned, by the commercial colossi seated either side of me. I prefer the instincts of the youthful Stanley Burnton J before he became corrupted by the arid atmosphere of this Court. It goes to prove what every good old-fashioned county court judge knows: the higher you go, the less the essential oxygen of common sense is available to you.' [*Oceanbulk Shipping and Trading SA v TMT Asia Ltd* [2010] EWCA Civ 79; [2010] 1 WLR 2416, [41] (Ward LJ, dissenting from the other members of the Court of Appeal, including Burnton LJ who earlier (when still a first-instance judge) had taken the same view as Ward LJ took in this case)]
- '[The respondents] together constituted a joint venture engaged in the development of certain land said to be situated at Bossley Park (wherever that is).' [*JPQS Pty Ltd v Comsmarnan Constructions Pty Ltd* [2003] NSWCA 66, [7] (Meagher JA). Sydney lawyers reading the judgment would know that Meagher JA lived in a wealthy Sydney suburb, and that Bossley Park was a poorer Sydney suburb—tainting the humour with elitist overtones. Another judge (Mason P) continued the in-joke by inserting in his judgment a link to a website map, inviting Meagher JA to find his way from his home suburb to Bossley Park: ibid, [1]–[2].]
- In *Funny Cide Ventures LLC v Miami Herald Publishing* Co 955 So 2d 1241 (Fla App 4 Dist 2007), a horse owner alleged that a newspaper's coverage of the horse's wins in the first two races in the Triple Crown had caused the horse to lose the third race. The District Court of Appeal held by majority that the horse owner had failed to prove its case; Farmer J dissented, in a tone that seems excruciatingly flippant.

At other times, attempted humour falls flat because it seems (at least, to modern readers) patronising. An example—perhaps once considered witty, but now dated—is the following, in a judgment concerning a wife's claim on her husband's property:

> '[T]here should be displayed in every conveyancer's office the minatory legend *Cave uxorem*': *Wroth v Tyler* [1974] Ch 30, 64 (Megarry J) [translated: 'beware of wives'].

Another example is likening a deceased's morals to those of a used-car salesman:

> 'The deceased appears to have maintained simultaneous domestic establishments with all three women and their respective children. … This is consistent with his apparent success as a used car salesman.' [*Green v Green* (1989) 17 NSWLR 343, 346 (Gleeson CJ)]

For an egregious example, see *Hampton v North Carolina Pulp Co* 49 F Supp 625 (NC, 1943), a suit for damages for the theft of fish.

Humorous verse

In legal documents

Humorous verse in legal documents is particularly inappropriate. It undermines the solemnity of the transaction and the importance of the document. An example is wills: most lawyers would regard a will as too important to compose in verse. But examples do exist: see, eg, Frank Thomas, *Last Will and Testament* (David & Charles, Newton Abbot, 1972) 74–79; Reginald L Hine, *Confessions of an Un-Common Attorney* (JM Dent & Sons, c 1943) 86–88.

In judgments

Judgments in verse are also found, as in the following examples. Perhaps the judge found it a diverting exercise. But did the litigants feel that their concerns were not being taken seriously?

Examples

1. Where noise complaints were made against a veterinary hospital—*City of Columbus v Becher* 180 NE 2d 836 (Ohio 1962) (Zimmerman J):

   'Dogs will howl and cats will yowl
   When placed in congregation.
   These grating sounds may oft result
   In human aggravation.' [And so on ...]

2. Where a wife sought to set aside a prenuptial agreement on the ground that the husband had represented that the engagement ring was diamond, when in fact it was zirconium—*Porreco v Porreco* 811 A 2d 566, Pa 2002 (Eakin J):

   'A groom must expect matrimonial pandemonium
   when his spouse finds he's given her a cubic zirconium
   instead of a diamond in her engagement band,
   the one he said was worth twenty-one grand.'
   [Then follow six more verses in similar doggerel.]

   (Several other judges in the case rebuked Eakin J for delivering his judgment in verse.)

3. Where a country music star sought to set aside a recording contract on the ground that she was a minor at the time she signed—*Rimes v Curb Records Inc* 129 F Supp 2d 984, ND (Tex, 2001):

   'LeAnn Rimes
   A very rich and famous star
   Wasn't so rich in times afar
   But what a talent she had.'
   [Then follow several pages of similar verse, to be sung to a given tune.]

4. Where the plaintiff sought damages for injury to his tree, which had been struck by the defendant's car—*Fisher v Lowe* 333 NW 2d 67 (Mich App 1983)

   'We thought that we would never see
   A suit to compensate a tree.

   A suit whose claim in tort is prest
   Upon a mangled tree's behest;

   A tree whose battered trunk was prest
   Against a Chevy's crumpled crest;' [And so on ...]

Further reading

- Louise Mailhot and James D Carnwath, *Decisions, Decisions … A Handbook for Judicial Writing* (Les Editions Yvon Blais, 1998) ch 7
- Jack Oatley and Brian Opeskin, 'Banter from the Bench: The Use of Humour in the Exercise of Judicial Functions' (2016) 42 *Australian Bar Review* 82 (arguing that judicial humour can play a variety of useful roles, and that judges should be trusted to 'banter from the bench' in appropriate circumstances)
- George Rose Smith, 'A Critique of Judicial Humor' (1990) 43 *Arkansas Law Review* 1

See also **EXAGGERATION AND HYPERBOLE; SARCASM; TONE.**

HYPERBOLE

See **EXAGGERATION AND HYPERBOLE; HUMOUR; SARCASM.**

HYPHENS

Uses

Single words

Use a hyphen to clarify meaning in single words:

- pre-judicial (*contrast* prejudicial)
- re-lease (*contrast* release)
- re-collect (contrast *recollect*)
- re-sent (*contrast* resent)
- re-sign (*contrast* resign).

Also use a hyphen to help avoid 'letter collision' in single words: *shell-like* (not *shelllike*). But occasions will be rare: eg, *withhold* (*not* with-hold).

Consecutive vowels

Use a hyphen to separate two vowels—but usually only where the vowels are the same: eg, *re-enter, re-examine,* but not *rearrange, reiterate, reorganise, reinforce, reunite.* However, usage is sometimes inconsistent: eg, *cooperate* (now generally replacing *co-operate*), but always *co-opt* (not *coopt*).

A hyphen may also help prevent a miscue—even one that is temporary only: eg, *coworker* (miscue: *co-worker* or *cow-worker*?); *coop* (chicken enclosure or shop?).

Numbers, fractions and time

Use hyphens:

- where compound numbers are spelled out in full: eg, twenty-one years of age, twenty-first day, seventy-five hours, two-thirds majority
- between the elements of a spelled-out fraction: eg, one-half, four-fifths, seven-twentieths
- where the first element in a compound modifier is a number or a time-period: eg, two-sided question; 8-hour day; 21-day notice (but not where the number precedes a possessive noun—21 days' notice).

Preceding capitalised word

By convention (rather than logic), use a hyphen after a prefix that precedes a capitalised word: eg, pre-Bank Holiday weekend, post-Christmas celebration.

Suspended compounds

Hyphenate 'suspended' compounds, where an element common to successive compound adjectives is omitted: eg, *full- and part-time employees*; *three-, five-, or seven-member bench*. If this seems unidiomatic, fill out the words: eg, *full-time employees and part-time employees*; *three-member, five-member, or seven-member bench*.

Modifying phrases

Hyphenate a phrase that functions as an adjective. The hyphen shows the close relationship between the words. This is more than mere convention; it also clarifies whether an adjective attaches to a noun or another adjective. The presence, and location, of the adjective can be crucial:

Original	Hyphenated versions
public housing office	public-housing office / public housing-office
criminal law professor	criminal-law professor / criminal law-professor
small business manager	small-business manager / small business-manager
crude oil merchant	crude-oil merchant / crude oil-merchant
high water mark	high-water mark / high water-mark
common law principle	common-law principle / common law-principle

Some writers, emboldened by style guides, omit hyphens where the first word in a two-word modifier is an adverb (often, but not always, ending in *-ly*). But a hyphen would aid readability: eg, 'heavily-weighted argument' (versus 'heavily weighted argument'), 'publicly-issued securities' (versus 'publicly issued securities'), 'not-too-distant future' (versus 'not too distant future'), 'properly-repaired premises' (versus 'properly repaired premises'). Always preference readability.

Foreign words

Do not use a hyphen in phrases made up of words borrowed from a foreign language, even where they function as a phrasal adjective:

- prima facie case (*not* prima-facie case)
- per diem claim (not per-diem claim)
- quantum meruit defence (*not* quantum-meruit defence)
- respondeat superior argument (*not* respondeat-superior argument).

Multiple hyphen-strings

Despite the advice to hyphenate for readability, a surfeit of hyphens can be distracting. Try to avoid multiple hyphen-strings:

Before	After
judge-made-law analysis	analysis of judge-made law
six-minute-interval-timesheet policy	policy requiring timesheets to record six-minute intervals
no-damages-for-rescission-of-contract rule	rule precluding damages for rescission of contract

The disappearing hyphen

The hyphen is slowly disappearing from legal usage, reflecting its disappearance from usage generally. Thus, *plain-language drafting* is rendered *plain language drafting*; *affirmative-action policy* has become *affirmative action policy*; *money-laundering law* has become *money laundering law* (or more egregiously *anti-money laundering law*, as if the concept were *anti-money*); and *holding-over right* has become *holding over right.* The rationale for this trend is hard to understand. Perhaps hyphen-omitters assume that hyphen-less text looks less cluttered. Perhaps they are right. But a clutter-free appearance is no substitute for efficient, ambiguity-free communication.

Examples

- 'right to buy scheme': *Waaler v Hounslow London Borough Council* [2017] EWCA Civ 45; [2017] 1 WLR 2817, [1] (Lewison LJ)—prefer: 'right-to-buy scheme'
- 'fact sensitive matter': *Project Blue Ltd v Revenue and Customs Commissioners* [2018] 1 WLR 3169, [90] (Lord Hodge JSC)—prefer: 'fact-sensitive matter'
- 'after the event insurance': *Re RBS Rights Issue Litigation* [2019] EWHC 463; [2017] 1 WLR 3539, [1] (Hildyard J)—prefer: 'after-the-event insurance'
- 'third party debt order': Civil Procedure Rules, rule 7.2.3—prefer: 'third-party debt order' or 'third-party-debt order'
- 'off the plan contract': *Conveyancing Act 1919 (NSW)*, s 66P—prefer: 'off-the-plan contract'
- '[umpires] making Indian batsman wicket dismissal deliberations': case note, (2020) 94 *Australian Law Journal* 494—prefer 'Indian-batsman wicket-dismissal deliberations'.

Often, context overcomes the potential ambiguity caused by a missing hyphen. For example:

> A statute prohibited placing placards on 'any house or building or any wall fence lamp post or gate' without the owner's consent. Did 'lamp post' mean two separate things (*lamp* and *post*), or one (*lamp-post*)? Held, it meant lamp-post: *Moore v Hubbard* [1935] VLR 93. This was because the context was a prohibition against placing placards on structures, and a lamp is not usually a structure; and also because when the statute was first enacted (in the 1860s), *lamp-post* was not usually hyphenated.

But even where a missing hyphen does not create ambiguity, it may leave the reader temporarily puzzled. Insert a hyphen to prevent the miscue. For example:

- A short-term lease describes the permitted use of the premises as 'temporary tattoo parlour'. Does this mean 'temporary tattoo-parlour' or 'temporary-tattoo parlour'?
- A contract refers to 'the benefit of insurance and waiver of subrogation clauses'. Does this mean 'the benefit of insurance and waiver-of-subrogation clauses', or 'the benefit of insurance-and-waiver-of-subrogation clauses', or even 'the benefit-of-insurance-and-waiver-of-subrogation clauses'?
- A statute regulates 'serious crime related activity'. Is this 'serious crime-related activity' or 'serious-crime-related activity'? See the (hyphen-less) *Crimes (Serious Crimes Prevention Orders) Act 2016* (NSW).

En dashes vs hyphens

Logically, a link between two expressions each joined by a hyphen is best signalled by an en dash, not another hyphen. For example, a hyphen is used to join *quasi* with words such as *investigative* and *judicial*: ie, *quasi-investigative* and *quasi-judicial*. But to signal a link between those two (compound) terms, an en dash is used: eg, 'I want to emphasise the *quasi-investigative–quasi-judicial* nature of the tribunal.' But while the distinction is logical, it may not be immediately obvious to the eye; in fact, the reader may 'see' a three-hyphen string. A better approach is to rewrite: 'I want to emphasise the tribunal's *quasi-investigative and quasi-judicial* nature.'

See also **DASHES**; **PUNCTUATION**.

hypothecate

In general usage, *to hypothecate* (noun, *hypothecation*) is to earmark money for a specific purpose, or to assign it to a stated purpose. In legal usage, *to hypothecate* means more specifically to pledge property as security, but without passing title or possession. For example, a mortgage of land under the Torrens system of land registration is a *hypothecation*, because it creates a security in the lender's favour but does not pass title or possession to the lender. This legal usage is a term of art, difficult to express briefly in plain language; it may be better explained than replaced.

ibid / id

ibid

Abbreviation for *ibidem* (Latin: in the same place). A rare variant abbreviation is *ib*. A shorthand reference to the same place in the book or work cited in the immediately preceding reference. There is no settled usage about italics: sometimes *ibid*, sometimes ibid.

Example 1

In consecutive footnotes:

1. Peter Smith, *Modern Land Law* (Oxford University Press, 2007) 25.
2. Ibid.

In footnote 2, 'Ibid' incorporates the references to both the book and the specific page.

Example 2

In consecutive footnotes:

1. Peter Smith, *Modern Land Law* (Oxford University Press, 2007) 25.
2. Ibid 27.
3. Ibid.

In footnote 2, 'Ibid' incorporates the reference to the book identified in footnote 1, but to a different page. In footnote 3, 'Ibid' signals the same reference as in footnote 2, ie, page 27.

id

Abbreviation for *idem* (Latin: the same). A shorthand reference to the same book or work cited in the immediately preceding reference, but usually to a different page or numbered paragraph. There is no settled usage about italics: sometimes *id*, sometimes id.

Example 3

1. Peter Smith, *Modern Land Law* (Oxford University Press, 2007) 25.
2. Id 27.

In footnote 2, 'Id' incorporates the reference to the book identified in footnote 1, but to a different page.

Id is also used as a shorthand reference to the same author, where later footnotes refer to a different book by that author.

Example 4

1. RE Megarry, *Miscellany at Law* (Stevens, 1955) 50.
2. Id, *The Rent Acts* (Stevens, 1949) 25.

Particularly punctilious authors use *Ead* for a female author.

In British and wider Commonwealth practice, *ibid* has largely usurped *id*.

id est

Latin: that is; that is to say. In practice, abbreviated to *ie* (no full stops, except in the US, *i.e.*). Usage varies over whether to insert a comma after—'ie,' or simply 'ie'. This book inserts a comma.

To retain the full Latin term is pedantic, but the usage persists:

- 'In the circumstances, neither party could have claimed payment from the second defendant under the first limb of s 61(6), *id est* [prefer: *ie;* or *that is to say*], as executor or administrator …' [*Challaram v Anilkumar* [2005] SLR 625, [6] (Choo Han Teck J)]
- 'But it was implicit in such a result that the defendant had been guilty of negligence, *id est* [prefer: *ie*; or *that is to say*] the tort alleged against him.' [*Curran v Young* (1965) 112 CLR 99, 102 (McTiernan J)]

The purpose of *id est* (or *ie*) is to introduce an explanation. Do not use it to introduce a substantive provision, or to contradict the previous statement, or to enlarge or diminish the previous statement—otherwise, uncertainty may arise over meaning: see, eg, *Stukeley v Butler* (1792) Hobart 168, 171–72; 80 ER 316, 319.

idem

See **ibid / id**.

idiot / lunatic

Historically, the common law distinguished between *idiots* and *lunatics*. *Idiot* denoted a person who 'has understanding, but by disease, grief or other accident has lost the use of his reason'. *Lunatic* denoted a person who 'has lucid intervals, sometimes enjoying his senses, and sometimes not, and that frequently depending upon the change of the moon': William Blackstone, *Commentaries on the Laws of England* (Clarendon, 1765) book 1, 294. Those distinctions have disappeared from modern legal usuage, superseded by references to persons suffering a 'mental disorder' or 'mental illness', or 'of unsound mind'. Indeed, the pejorative overtones in *lunatic* has led some legislatures to abolish the term: eg, *Mental Treatment Act 1930*, s 20(5), (6).

To use *idiot* or *lunatic* today would be both anachronistic and insensitive.

See also **non compos mentis**.

ie / i.e.

Abbreviation for *id est* (that is; that is to say). In modern usage, no full stops (except in the US, *i.e.*). The abbreviation is common in formal writing, and useful as a space-saver. However, in ordinary prose, the full English version ('that is', 'that is to say') helps keep the tone less solemn.

See also **id est**.

IF CLAUSES

See **CONDITIONAL CLAUSES.**

if … then

Where a conditional clause starts with a lengthy introductory '*if* …' statement (or less ideally, a lengthy '*where* …' statement), add a comma after the introductory statement—thus, '*if* …,' (or '*where* …,'). The comma clearly marks off the end of the conditional statement and heralds the start of the substantive statement. Better still, after the comma, add *then*—as if to say 'now comes the substantive provision'. Where the conditional (*If* …) clause is short, perhaps little is gained by adding *then*; but where it is long, much is gained. For example:

- '*If* the court is sitting on Monday, ~~*then*~~ you must report to the registrar.' [Short conditional clause; meaning is clear without *then*.]
- '*If* the court is sitting on the first Monday of next month and public transport is available to get you to the courthouse by 9 am, *then* you must report to the registrar.' [Long '*If* …' introduction; *then* useful.]

See also **CONDITIONAL CLAUSES; then.**

if / when

General

Prefer *when*, not *if*, to introduce a state of affairs with a temporal factor that is likely to occur. For example:

- '*When* [not *If*] Monday comes, the court will sit.'
- '*When* [not *If*] the plaintiff loses, the defendant can seek costs.' [The writer is expressing confidence in the defendant's case.]

When is also the logical starter in two particular situations:

1. Introducing a circumstance relating to time: eg, '*When* [not *Where*; better than *If*] closing the premises, the tenant must …'
2. Avoiding uncertainty or indecisiveness suggested by 'if': eg, '*When* [not *If*] the tribunal comes to a conclusion on the arguments, it must immediately advise the parties.'

'if and when'

In some contexts, a lawyer's needless pairing—either *if* or *when* will suffice; there is no need for both. For example:

> A charterparty provided for a price to be reduced 'if and when' market prices dropped to a stated point. Here, either *if* or *when* would have sufficed. The pairing *if and when* made no difference to the key issue, which was whether the clause applied to a price drop before the date of the charterparty. See *Hansen v Gabriel Wade and English* (1924) 93 LJKB 1089 (HL).

But in other contexts, each of *if* and *when* may carry its own separate meaning. For example:

> A gift to grandchildren was to be paid 'if and when' they attained 21. Held: *when* (used alone) might indicate that the gifts were vested, although with payment postponed until each reached 21; but *if* indicated that the gifts were contingent on each reaching 21. See *Re Kirkley* (1918) 87 LJ Ch 247.

Vesting consequences

If and *when* may produce different consequences when applied to the 'vesting' of interests in property.

Examples

- Property is given to Anne '*if* she attains 25'. The gift is contingent on Anne's attaining 25—until then, she gets nothing.
- Property is given to Anne '*when* she attains 25'. This is usually (there may be exceptions, depending on context) an immediate gift to her. That is, the gift is 'vested' (it is already hers in principle), but it is not to be paid over to her until she attains 25. If she fails to attain 25, the gift will divest (and go to someone else).

See also **CONDITIONAL CLAUSES; if / where; unless and until; vest.**

if / where

Prefer *if* to introduce a contingency that may or may not occur, and *where* to introduce circumstances that are likely to occur. The distinction can be difficult to draw, and sometimes depends on the writer's perspective on the likelihood of the occurrence. For example:

- '*If* a judge makes an order for service, the party must serve the order within 14 days.' [It is not possible to know in advance whether a judge will make the order.]
- '*Where* a judge makes an order for service, the party must serve the order within 14 days.' [The judge will probably make the order.]

In standard prose, writers often fudge the distinction between *if* and *where*, treating them as interchangeable. But the distinction remains useful in legal writing.

See also **CONDITIONAL CLAUSES; if / when.**

if / whether

If introduces a conditional clause: eg, '*If* the tenant pays all rent, then the landlord will grant a right to renew the lease.' *Whether* introduces a choice: eg, '*Whether* the tenant renews the lease or vacates the premises, the landlord is entitled to advertise the premises for sale.'

See also **if … then; whether.**

if [X] thinks fit

The qualification *if [he, she, it] thinks fit* often appears in legal usage. For example: a settlor may be given the power to vary a trust deed 'if he thinks fit'; a court may release an easement 'if it thinks fit'; a landlord may consent to a proposed assignee of the lease 'if it thinks fit'. However, despite regular use, *thinks fit* is inherently vague. 'Thinks' means 'considers'; but 'fit' may mean anything from (in descending order of stringency) 'proper', to 'suitable', to 'appropriate', to merely 'convenient'. Sometimes the vagueness is useful, but at other times more specificity is required. For example:

> 'If a power is given in terms "X *may* if X thinks fit", *may* is strictly superfluous, since both X *may* and *if X thinks fit* give X a discretion whether to exercise the power—*may* emphasises the unfettered nature of the discretion, but does not change the meaning.' [*Julius v Bishop of Oxford* (1880) 5 App Cas 214, 228 (Earl Cairns LC)]

if and only if

When introducing a conditional statement, *if* (alone) is usually sufficient. Sometimes, the stronger *only if* (alone) may help emphasise conditionality. But rarely, if ever, is the pairing *if and only if* required. To explain further:

- Where the meaning is not exclusive, *if* suffices: eg, 'You may wear long trousers *if* you are an adult.' (Leaves open the possibility that children also may wear long trousers.)
- Where the meaning is exclusive, *only if* suffices: eg, 'You may wear long trousers *only if* you are an adult.' (That is, children cannot wear long trousers.) To say '*if and only if* you are an adult' adds nothing.

Examples

- '[An officer] will become a respondent *if, and only if,* [prefer: *if,* or for more emphasis *only if*] he notifies the Registrar that he wishes to participate.' [*Attorney General v National Assembly for Wales Commission* [2012] UKSC 53; [2013] 1 AC 792, [93] (Lord Hope)]
- '[A trustee's act] will be voidable *if, and only if,* [prefer: *if,* or for more emphasis *only if*] it can be shown to have been done in breach of fiduciary duty on the part of the trustees.' [*Pitt v Holt* [2011] EWCA Civ 197; [2012] Ch 132, [127] (Lloyd LJ)]
- 'An enforcement order may extend to a person's conduct outside the United Kingdom *if (and only if)* [prefer: *only if*] he is [one of a specified list of persons].' [*Enterprise Act 2002*, s 86(1)]
- 'The prosecution bears the onus of negativing the existence of a lawful excuse *if, and only if,* [prefer: *only if*] evidence directed to establishing the excuse is first adduced by or on behalf of the defendant.' [*Crimes Act 1900 (NSW)*, s 529(5)]

The variant, *if* ***but*** *only if,* also adds no meaning to *only if.* For example:

- '*If, but only if,* [prefer: *Only if*] error in the relevant sense is found, the second stage arises.' [*Lacey v Attorney-General (Qld)* [2011] HCA 10; (2011) 242 CLR 573, [67], Heydon J]

See also **only if.**

if any

You can often improve the rhythm of a sentence containing *if any*, by deleting *if* and moving *any* to appear immediately before the noun. For example:

- 'You must make your *jury challenges, if any,* [prefer: *any jury challenges*] before the hearing starts.'
- 'The tenant is liable for *storm damage, if any* [prefer: *any storm damage*; or simply *storm damage*] to the premises.'
- 'For prisoners in transit under a production order [the Commission] recommended that *proceedings, if any,* [prefer: *any proceedings*; or simply, *proceedings*] in relation to an escape should be dealt with in the place in which the person was under lawful restraint …' [*Mok v Director of Public Prosecutions (NSW)* [2016] HCA 13, [15] (French CJ and Bell J)]

You may even be able to delete *if any*, as in the following example:

- 'Lord Du Parcq then considered what relevance, ~~*if any*~~, the apparent purpose of the statute had to the question of whether it was binding on the Crown …' [*Secretary of State for Justice v Black* [2016] EWCA Civ 125, [19] (Lord Dyson MR)]

if but only if

See **if and only if.**

if not

Consider avoiding this expression in several contexts, illustrated in the following examples. In example 1, *if not* introduces ambiguity. In examples 2, 3 and 4, *if not* leads to an unnecessarily complex sentence structure—which can be avoided by substituting *unless*.

1. 'He is a competent lawyer, *if not* an excellent one.' Does this mean that he is not an excellent lawyer, but merely a competent one? (Where this is the meaning, then say: 'He is a competent lawyer, but not an excellent one.') Or does it mean that he is at least a competent lawyer, and may even be an excellent one? (In which case, say: 'He is a competent lawyer, perhaps even an excellent one.')
2. '*If* you do *not* sue tomorrow, you will be out of time.' The *if … not* construction is ungainly. By substituting an *unless* construction, you use fewer words (always a benefit) and hint at a positive statement rather than a negative one (also a benefit): '*Unless* you sue tomorrow, you will be out of time.'
3. '[N]o system of law can be workable *if it has not got logic* [prefer: *unless it has logic; without logic*] at the root of it.' [*Hedley Byrne & Co Ltd v Heller & Partners Ltd* [1964] AC 465, 516 (Lord Devlin)]
4. 'A court has *no* jurisdiction to make a declaration concerning a water boundary … *if* … a perceived trend by way of accretion is *not* likely to be indefinitely sustained by natural means.' [*Coastal Protection Act 1979* (NSW), s 55N(2) (repealed)] *Prefer*: 'A court has *no* jurisdiction to make a declaration concerning a water boundary … *unless* a perceived trend by way of accretion is likely to be indefinitely sustained by natural means.' *Or better still* (to capture the intended meaning): 'A court can declare that accretion has altered a water boundary … *only if* the accretion occurs by natural changes that are likely to continue indefinitely.'

ignoramus

Latin: (literally) we do not know. In English usage: a person who knows nothing about the subject matter; an ignorant person; plural *ignoramuses* (not *ignorami*—that would betray ignorance, because the Latin is a verb, not a noun). Historically, *ignoramus* was the response given by a grand jury that considered the evidence of a crime to be insufficient to prosecute: J Chitty, *A Practical Treatise on the Criminal Law* (1816) vol 1, 324 ('ignoramus' meaning 'we know nothing of it').

Ignoramus was the title of a 1615 play by George Ruggle. The play ridiculed the tendency of its main character (Ambidexter Ignoramus) to indulge in the complex legal language of the day, particularly the then-current debased Law French and Law Latin. One commentator described the eponymous Ignoramus as a 'ridiculous pedant, who makes love in the language of the law courts': Edmund BV Christian, *A Short History of Solicitors* (1896) 67.

Further reading

EJF Tucker, 'Ruggle's *Ignoramus* and Humanistic Criticism of the Language of Common Law' (1977) 30 *Renaissance Quarterly* 341

ignorantia juris (legis) neminen (non) excusat

Latin: ignorance of the law excuses no one. The maxim's Latin form, in its various iterations, obscures its inherent vagueness. Any degree of ignorance? No excuses at all? The maxim has come to mean 'everyone is presumed to know the law'—which, taken at face value, is palpably untrue. The use of an English translation would invite scrutiny of the problems hidden by the Latin. Nevertheless, the Latin version is routinely cited, elevating vagueness to imagined precision. For example:

- '[A]lthough it is well known that ignorance of the law excuses nobody (*ignorantia juris neminem excusat*) it is less well known that a corollary of this maxim is that an individual should have access to and be able to determine the laws by which he is governed …' [*Omega Leisure Ltd v Barry* [2012] IEHC 23, [7.2] (Clarke J, citing the English first, followed by the Latin, presumably for the benefit of legal readers)]

- 'The lawfulness or unlawfulness of [the appellant's possession of a prohibited weapon] cannot depend upon whether he knew the provisions of the Order as amended. *Ignorantia juris non excusat* [prefer: *Ignorance of the law is no excuse*]. Accordingly we are satisfied that the conviction is not unsafe.' [*R v McKenzie* [2005] NICA 7, [23] (Nicholson LJ)]
- '[The] *maxim ignorantia juris non excusat* [is] a tag whose dubious utility would have been enhanced, had it gone on to explain who was not excused, and from what. As it stands, it means no more than that ignorance of the general law does not excuse anyone from compliance with it …' [*Pankhania v Hackney LBC* [2002] EWHC 2441 (Ch), [57] (Tedd DHCJ)]

illegal / unlawful

These words are synonymous.

- 'Where issues of *illegality* are raised, the courts have (as it seems to me) to steer a middle course between two unacceptable positions. [One is that … The other is that] it is unacceptable that the court should, on the first indication of *unlawfulness* … refuse all assistance to the plaintiff, no matter how … disproportionate his loss to the *unlawfulness* of his conduct.' [*Saunders v Edwards* [1987] 1WLR 1116, 1134 (Bingham LJ)]
- 'Certainly in equity there is authority for the proposition that where the *unlawful* act has not been carried into effect, the court is able to uphold, despite the attempted *illegality*, an equitable interest.' [*Standard Chartered Bank v Pakistan National Shipping Corporation* [1999] EWCA Civ 3028, [8]; [2000] 1 Lloyd's Rep 218 (Aldous LJ)]

However, in practice, *illegal* is used more in the context of criminal offences, while *unlawful* is a generic word for all breaches of law.

immediately

A term suggesting urgency, but in fact elastic and context-dependent. To require something to be done *immediately* requires more promptness than 'within a reasonable time', and implies 'prompt, vigorous action, without any delay', but does not require the impossible: *Alexiadi v Robinson* (1861) 2 F & F 679, 684; 175 ER 1237, 1240 (Cockburn CJ). The context-dependence appears from the following examples, some of which unhelpfully substitute synonyms or near synonyms—a process that focuses attention on the synonym rather than on *immediately*.

- To do something *immediately* requires that it be done without any substantial lapse of time: *Lister v Forth Dry Dock and Engineering Co Ltd* [1990] 1 AC 546, 569 (Lord Oliver).
- *Immediately* requires 'all reasonable speed considering the circumstances of the case': *Coleman's Depositories Ltd v Life and Health Assurance* [1907] 2 KB 798, 807 (Fletcher Moulton LJ).
- A notice sent by a tax inspector after a delay of 13 days was sent *immediately*: *R v Inspector of Taxes* [1974] QB 220.
- A statute requiring estate agents to pay over a deposit *immediately* on receiving it, meant 'on the same day': *Lumsden v Auctioneers and Agents Committee* [1999] 2 Qd R 599, 606 [49].
- An arrest is made 'immediately after' the commission of an offence where the offence and the arrest, though separated by some time, are part of a single transaction: *R v Jones* [1970] 1 WLR 211; *Wilson v New South Wales* [2010] NSWCA 333; (2010) 278 ALR 74.

As always when dealing with time provisions, if possible avoid uncertainty by specifying particular periods.

See also **as soon as possible / as soon as practicable**; **forthwith**; **promptly**.

immigrate

See **emigrate / immigrate**.

impact

See **affect / effect / impact**.

impanel

See **empanel / impanel**.

impede

A word that carries a breadth of meaning, and so must be used with care. For example, statutes empower courts or tribunals to vary or extinguish land covenants that *impede* the use of the land: eg, *Law of Property Act 1925*, s 84(1)(a)(a). Does *impede* mean 'prevent [completely]', or merely 'hinder'? Is it enough to *impede* economically, or must it be physically (as in *Consett Iron Co Ltd v Clavering Trustees* [1935] 2 KB 42: context required physical impediment)? Courts tend to find synonyms, or near synonyms—creating the risk of diverting attention from the original word to the synonym: eg, *Re Ghey and Galton's Application* [1957] 2 QB 650, 653 (Lord Evershed: hinder 'to a real and sensible degree'). If possible, indicate the degree of intended 'impedance'.

imperative duty / directory duty

See **duty**; **shall / must**.

impertinent

In normal usage, 'rude' or 'unmannerly': eg, 'an impertinent person'. Historically, the legal meaning was '*not* pertinent'—ie, 'irrelevant'. That legal usage is now obsolete. In law, as in normal usage, the meaning is 'rude' or 'unmannerly'.

imply / infer

In general usage, to *imply* means to suggest the truth of something that is not made express, while to *infer* means to deduce (something) from statements, conduct or circumstances. So, 'Your letter *implies* that you like plain English', but 'I *infer* from your letter that you like plain English.' Legal usage generally mirrors these distinctions. However, there is a possible exception in the law governing *implied* terms. Thus, the law speaks of the 'implied' grant of a right of way from certain circumstances, or a landlord's 'implied' obligation to provide quiet enjoyment, or the 'implication' of terms into a contract in accordance with settled principles. In these (and perhaps other) situations, standard English usage would prefer 'inferred'. But these (anomalous) legal usages are well established. The contract law usage has been rationalised by saying that an 'implied' term is one on which the parties did not actually agree but which the law nevertheless *implies* on their behalf; in contrast, an *inferred* term is one on which the parties in fact agreed but which they failed to include in their contract: *The Bell Group Ltd v Westpac Banking Corporation (No 9)* [2008] WASC 239; (2008) 225 FLR 1, [2648].

impotentia excusat legem

Latin: inability (to do something) excuses failure to observe the law. Similarly, *lex non cogit ad impossibilia*—the law does not force a person to do what is impossible (or *nemo tenetur ad impossibilia*—no one is bound to perform impossibilities). These maxims are of venerable antiquity: RH Kersley (ed), *Broom's Legal Maxims*, 10th edn (Sweet & Maxwell, 1939) 163–64. However, like many ancient maxims, their Latin formulation obscures an inherent vagueness. What degree of inability or impossibility is required? Is the 'excusing' absolute or qualified? Nothing is lost by preferring an appropriate English translation or (as in the following examples) adding an explanation.

- 'To hold otherwise … would be a breach of the maxim *impotentia excusat legem*, the law does not punish a person for not doing what they lack the power to do or for being in a situation they are powerless to avoid.' [*Social Security Tribunal Decision* [2004] UKSSCSC CIS 4348, [44], explaining the maxim]
- 'But the principle expressed in the maxim *lex non cogit ad impossibilia*—the law does not compel a man to do that which he cannot possibly perform—is not rendered inapplicable to [the legislation] by anything inherent in [the Act].' [*Dowell Australia Ltd v Archdeacon* (1975) 132 CLR 417, 426 (McTiernan J, supplying his own translation)]

impracticable

Contracts or statutes sometimes excuse a person from performing an obligation that is *impracticable*. The word opens up avenues for dispute: what degree of difficulty makes performance *impracticable*? Clearly, the bar is lower than *impossible*, but how much lower: if an act is possible, though very difficult or very expensive, is it *impracticable?*

When searching for meaning, the temptation is to substitute near-synonyms; but that merely switches attention from the original word to the substitute, and still may not answer the question, as in the following examples:

- An obligation (in the context of a business contract) is *impracticable* 'when it can only be done at an excessive or unreasonable cost': *Moss v Smith* (1850) 9 CB 94, 103; 137 ER 827, 831 (Maule J). But when is cost 'excessive or unreasonable'?
- *Impracticable* 'introduces some degree of reason and involves … some regard for practice': *Jayne v National Coal Board* [1963] 2 All ER 220, 223 (Veale J). But what is 'some'?
- An act is *impracticable* if it is 'not possible', 'not feasible', or 'very much more' than 'not reasonably practical': *Moorcroft v Thomas Powles & Sons Ltd* [1962] 3 All ER 741, 746 (Parker CJ).
- To decide whether something is *impracticable* requires examining the circumstances and asking whether, 'as a practical matter', the obligation can be performed: *Re El Sombrero Ltd* [1958] Ch 900, 904 (Wynn-Parry J). But that seems circular: something that *cannot* be done as a *practical* matter is *im*practicable.

The only practical advice is to try to avoid *impracticable*.

See also **practicable / practical**.

improbative

See **probative**.

improvement (to land)

In general legal usage, an 'improvement' (to land) is any permanent change or addition to the land, such as clearing, adding a building, or installing infrastructure. Often, the work may properly be called an 'improvement' even though it does not in fact 'improve' (ie, increase) the value of the land. In some contexts, however, a requirement of increased value may be implied (eg, where a rating statute requires 'improvements' to be taken into account when valuing the land, or a rental statute requires 'improvements' to be taken into account when assessing the permissible rent).

imputed notice

See **notice / knowledge**.

in a case to which

See **case**.

in absentia

Latin: in absence. Readers may guess the meaning, but that is no reason to retain the Latin in the face of a simple and adequate translation. For example:

- 'One might have expected the United Kingdom legislator … to intend all trials *in absentia* [prefer: *in a person's absence*] to entitle the person affected to a retrial or equivalent.' [*Caldarelli v Court of Naples* [2008] UKHL 51; [2008] 1 WLR 1724, [45] (Lord Mance)]
- 'On 2 July 1996 Ms Johnson was convicted *in absentia* [prefer: *in her absence*].' [*Subramaniam v R* [2004] HCA 51; (2004) 211 ALR 1, [3] (High Court of Australia)]

Compare **in foro**.

in accordance with

In accordance with is commonly seen in legal drafting. Thus, a contract may require something to be done 'in accordance with' a stated criterion; or a statute may require a form to be submitted 'in accordance with' the prescribed form. But inherent uncertainty lurks in many legal phrases, and *in accordance with* is no exception. If something is to be done *in accordance with* a stated criterion, must it be done with undeviating conformity, or is close enough good enough? In the absence of clear direction, the only guide may be context—and context can be a capricious guide. Possible meanings include:

- **exact compliance required**: Where a bankruptcy notice was to be *in accordance* with a statutory form, exact compliance was required: *Re Howes* [1892] 2 QB 628. (Compare *Bendigo Bank Ltd v Williams* [2000] FCA 482; (2000) 98 FCR 377: where a bankruptcy notice was to be *in accordance with* the form prescribed, reasonably strict compliance was sufficient.) Similarly, where an application for an inquiry into a union ballot was to be made '*in accordance with* Form 11', exact compliance was required: *Re La* (1993) 41 FCR 151, 158.
- **substantial compliance enough**: Where a bill of sale was to be *in accordance with* a statutory form, substantial compliance with the form was sufficient: *Ex parte Stanford* (1886) 17 QBD 259, 269–71
- **general harmony enough**: Where a proposed amendment to a town planning scheme was to be *in accordance with* an earlier statement of intent, general harmony with the statement of intent was sufficient, because the key factor was substance not form: *Mount Barker Properties Ltd v Mount Barker District Council* (2001) 80 SASR 449, [24].

Also, in some contexts, *in accordance with* may imply an element of causation. For example, to act *in accordance with* the instructions of another person implies following their instructions. But in other contexts, no element of causation need be involved: eg, *BHP Billiton Ltd v Federal Commissioner of Taxation* [2020] HCA 5; (2020) 94 ALJR 326 (no element of causation required under a statutory provision that defined an associated company to include a company that is accustomed to act, or that may reasonably be expected to act, *in accordance with* the wishes of another company).

See also **in the form of**; **under (and ...)**.

in addition to

Almost always means 'also', or 'as well as'. However, context is crucial, and so (for example) *in addition to* can mean 'apart from' or 'distinct from'. To illustrate:

> Section 15 of a statute empowered the minister to appoint teachers to government schools. Section 9(4) of the same statute empowered the minister to appoint such officers and employees '(*in addition to* the employees of ... the teaching service) as he considers necessary'. Could the minister appoint teachers under s 9(4)? Held, no: s 15 was the only power to appoint teachers. In s 9(4), *in addition to* meant 'apart from'; it gave no power to appoint additional teachers. See *Australian Education Union v Department of Education and Children's Services* [2012] HCA 3; (2012) 248 CLR 1.

If *in addition to* is likely to be ambiguous—as in the above example—clarify.

in all respects

Do the words *in all respects* ever add anything to a statement? For example, does a promise 'to comply *in all respects*' with an obligation differ from a promise merely 'to comply with' the obligation? Does a tenant's promise 'to repair the premises *in all respects*' impose a more onerous obligation than a promise merely 'to repair the premises'? In both examples, the instinctive answer is 'no', making *in all respects* superfluous.

However, *in all respects* may have some work to do in two situations:

1. **For emphasis**, to stress the need for, or breadth of, an obligation. For example:

   > A carpark-ticket condition stated that cars were left at their owners' risk 'in all respects'. Held, these words helped clarify that the carpark owners were free from liability even where they (mistakenly) handed over the car to a thief: *Ashby v Tolhurst* [1937] 2 KB 242, 253 (CA).

2. **To characterise a promise as a condition** (as distinct from a mere warranty, sounding in damages only). By requiring compliance with an obligation 'in all respects', the parties may be taken to have regarded the obligation as a 'condition' in the strict sense that any breach, no matter how slight, will justify termination: *Gumland Property Holdings Pty Ltd v Duffy Bros Fruit Market (Campelltown) Pty Ltd* [2008] HCA 10, [58]; (2008) 234 CLR 237, 259. Or, expressed differently but with the same result, 'in all respects' may indicate that the promise is so important that the parties would not have entered into the contract unless assured of strict or substantial performance: *Tramways Advertising Pty Ltd v Luna Park (NSW) Ltd* (1938) 38 SR (NSW) 632, 641–42 (Jordan CJ).

See also **condition**.

in arguendo

See **arguendo**.

in arrears

See **arrears**.

in bad faith

The opposite of 'in good faith'; often expressed in Latin, *mala fide*—but the plain English is preferable (as with most Latinisms). *Bad faith* is conduct falling short of the standards of acceptable morality, or (in commerce) conduct falling short of the standards of acceptable commercial behaviour. *Bad faith* is said to imply mental awareness of the nature of one's conduct, but that lack of awareness does not excuse a finding of 'bad faith' if reasonable and experienced persons would regard the conduct as falling short of acceptable standards: *Harrison's Trade Mark Application* [2005] FSR 10, [26] (Sir William Aldous). *Bad faith* is also said to be a wider notion than dishonesty or fraud, although it includes both: *DC Comics v Chequot Pty Ltd* [2013] FCA 478; (2013) 299 ALR 110 (Fed Ct of Australia).

See also **bona fide**; **honestly**; **in good faith**.

in banco

Latin: on the bench; variants are *en banc*, *in banc*, *in bank* (rare), or simply *banco*. Legal shorthand for 'in full court', meaning a court comprising three or more judges, usually hearing an appeal from a trial judge. (In some jurisdictions, the appeal court sits in the 'Banco court'.) The term must puzzle non-lawyers. Alternatives such as 'in full court', or 'as an appeal court', would clarify, without loss of meaning:

> 'In *Kops*, the Supreme Court of New South Wales, sitting *in banco* [prefer: *as an appeal court*], held that a trial judge had not erred in telling the jury [certain matters].' [*Azzapardi v R* [2001] HCA 25, [42]; (2001) 205 CLR 50, 66 (Gaudron, Gummow, Kirby and Hayne JJ)]

in camera

Latin: in a room; in a chamber. The term is used in two different contexts: (1) a hearing before a judge in his or her office (chambers); (2) a hearing in closed court, with the public excluded (see discussion in *Clibbery v Allan* [2002] 1 All ER 865, 871–72, Butler-Sloss P). Meaning (2) is now the more common. For meaning (1), the standard term is now 'in chambers'.

The Latin *in camera* is apt to mislead all except those learned in Latin, and can cause miscues: eg, 'The court resolved to hear the claim about CCTV footage *in camera*.' Prefer an appropriate English translation:

> 'The case was examined *in camera* [prefer: *in closed court*] and without the participation of the parties, and the court considered written comments from the prosecutor to which the applicant had no opportunity to respond.' [*R v Parole Board* [2013] 2 WLR 1157, 1179–80 (Lord Reed)]

See also **in chambers**; **in curia**.

in case of / in cases where

See **case**.

in causa

Latin: in the cause (case); in the legal process. Prefer the English translation.

in chambers

In private; often used in relation to a judgment given by, or argument made before, a judge who is sitting in his or her office (chambers) rather than in open court.

See also **in camera**; **in curia**.

in connection with

Meaning

A phrase of unpredictable breadth, with a potential for vagueness that should make drafters think carefully before using it. Judges have said that *in connection with* is a phrase of the 'widest import': *Ashville Investments Ltd v Elmer Contractors Ltd* [1989] QB 488, 503 (Balcombe LJ). It denotes 'any link at all': *Amec Group Ltd v Thames Water Utilities Ltd* [2010] EWHC 419, [29] (Coulson J). It is 'of wide import' and can describe 'a spectrum of relationships ranging from direct and immediate to tenuous or remote': *Director of Public Prosecutions (WA) v White* [2010] WASCA 47; (2010) 41 WAR 249, [33]. However, meaning always depends on context; and so whether in any particular case *in connection with* has the 'widest import' varies with context. The context may, or may not, require a causal connection: *Our Town FM Pty Ltd v Australian Broadcasting Tribunal* [1987] FCA 301; (1987) 16 FCR 465, 479–80.

Where *in connection with* requires a causal connection, how close must the connection be? Cases are difficult to reconcile, as the following examples show:

- A statute imposed a duty of care on persons doing work 'for or *in connection with*' the 'provision of' a dwelling. Held, the statute did not apply to building inspectors. The context indicated that the statute imposed the duty on those who helped create the building (such as builders, architects, and engineers), not on those tasked with ensuring that the work complied with building regulations (such as building inspectors): *Lessees and Management Co of Herons Court v Heronslea Ltd* [2019] EWCA Civ 1423.
- A statute proscribed conduct '*connected with* assistance in a terrorist act'. Held, this encompassed indirect assistance as well as direct assistance: *R v Khazaal* [2012] HCA 26; (2012) 246 CLR 601.
- A statute permitted the Crown to confiscate property used *in connection with* a crime. Held, the connection could be indirect and insubstantial: *Dickfoss v DPP* [2012] NTCA 1; (2012) 31 NTLR 16.
- A statute permitted the Crown to confiscate property obtained by a person *in connection with* the person's criminal conduct. Held, this did not include a landowner who received rent from premises which were unlicensed, in breach of the *Housing Act 2004*: *Sumal & Sons (Properties) Ltd v Newham LBC* [2012] EWCA Crim 1840; [2013] 1 WLR 2078. Importantly, the *Housing Act* did not outlaw the landlord's right to demand rent for unlicensed premises (at [36]).
- A court had jurisdiction to decide 'all questions that may arise *in connection with*' an assessment made under an Act. Held, *in connection with* gave jurisdiction to deal with matters that occurred *before* the actual assessment: *Re Nanaimo Community Hotel Ltd* [1945] 3 DLR 225.
- A contract gave a right to a substantial fee for work done *in connection with* a share offer. Held, *in connection with* included work done *after* the share offer was made, but not work done *before* it was made: *JP Morgan Australia Ltd v Consolidated Minerals Pty Ltd* [2011] NSWCA 3, [51].

Use another term?

Almost always, *in connection with* can be replaced with something simpler, such as *with* or *about*: eg, 'I am writing *in connection with* [prefer: *about*] your case.' These substitutes, too, may be vague—but no more so than *in connection with*.

In rare cases, however, *with* or *about* may be too narrow. For example:

> 'The accused was charged *in connection with* the crime.' To substitute *with*—'The accused was charged *with* the crime'—may be accurate where the accused committed the crime, but not where the accused was involved only tangentially.

See also **in relation to**; **under (and ...)**.

in consequence of

A notoriously imprecise phrase: when is an occurrence *in consequence of* (or *as a consequence of*) another occurrence? Causation is always difficult to prove, even more so where the required degree of connection between cause and effect is unspecified. Unless context requires otherwise, *in consequence of* implies the proximate, effective cause, not a more remote one: *Hall Bros SS Co Ltd v Young* [1939] 1 KB 748, 761–62 (MacKinnon LJ).

See also **by reason of**; **cause (noun, verb)**; **consequential loss**.

in curia

Latin: in court—ie, in open court as distinct from in private ('in camera'). The English translation captures the Latin, so prefer it. For example:

> 'The theory of judicial procedure is that the cogent and binding effect of the order begins immediately from the time when the order is pronounced by the lips of the judge, and [ideally] every order would be completed on the spot, written out by the judicial officer and *in curia* [prefer: *in court*] before the court rises, and delivered to the parties.' [*Re Risca Coal and Iron Co* (1862) 4 De GF and J 456, 460; 45 ER 1261, 1262 (Lord Westbury LC)]

See also **in camera**.

in dubio

Latin: in doubt. There is no reason to doubt the adequacy of the English translation. For example:

- 'In these circumstances, one might think, *in dubio* [prefer: *if in doubt*] the law should favour the claimants.' [*Fairchild v Glenhaven Funeral Services Ltd* [2002] UKHL 22; [2003] 1 AC 32, 112 [155] (Lord Rodger)]
- 'If the question is then left *in dubio* [prefer: *in doubt*] the application must be refused.' [*Re Bali Brassiere Co Inc's Registered Trade Mark* (1968) 118 CLR 128, 137 (Windeyer J)]

in escrow

A term describing a document that is not yet in operation—eg, pending the occurrence of a specified event, or the arrival of a specified date. Such a document is said to be 'held *in escrow*'. This is a loose term, for two reasons: (1) *escrow* is a noun—so a more accurate term would be 'held *as an escrow*'; and (2) in origin, *escrow* is peculiar to deeds, not to documents generally. But the usage is too long-settled to be countermanded by the pull of etymology or history.

See also **escrow**.

in esse / in posse

Latin: *in esse*, in existence; *in posse*, not (yet) in existence. In law, the terms have both a general meaning and a technical meaning.

General meaning

When used in a general and non-technical sense, the terms mean (respectively) 'in existence' or 'not yet in existence'. In such cases, the plain-English translation is adequate—and therefore preferable. For example:

- 'Mere difficulty in ascertaining all the things which are included in a general assignment, whether *in esse* [prefer: *in existence*] or *in posse* [prefer: *coming into existence later*], will not affect the assignee's right to those things which are capable of ascertainment or are identified.' [*Tailby v Official Receiver* (1875) 13 App Cas 523, 533 (Lord Watson)]
- 'Since the infant plaintiff was at the time of the accident [conceived but not yet born] she was not then a person or a human being *in esse* [prefer: *in existence*] and in fact she had no separate existence apart from her mother.' [*Watt v Rama* [1972] VR 353, 355 (Winneke CJ and Pape J)]

Technical meaning

The terms *in esse* and *in posse* were once important in deciding whether the burden of a tenant's covenants would 'run' to bind assignees of the lease. Under the rule in *Spencer's Case* (1583) 5 Co Rep 16a; 77 ER 72, the burden of a tenant's covenant could automatically 'run' where the covenant related to something already in existence (*in esse*), such as a covenant to repair an existing house on the land. But where the covenant related to something not in existence (*in posse*), such as a covenant to build a new house, the covenant would not 'run' unless the lease expressly stated that it bound the original tenant and assignees. Legislation in most jurisdictions has now abolished the distinction between covenants *in esse* and *in posse*: generally speaking, all covenants (regardless of whether *in esse* or *in posse*) that inherently relate to the leased land bind assignees of the lease: see, eg, *Law of Property Act 1925*, s 79; *Conveyancing Act 1919* (NSW), s 70A(1). To distinguish between covenants *in esse* and covenants *in posse* would now be both pretentious and anachronistic.

Further reading

Hill and Redman's Guide to Landlord and Tenant Law (Butterworths, 1999) [4.45]–[4.49]

See also **touch and concern**.

in extenso

Latin: in full; at length. A Latinism that serves no purpose, given its ease of translation. Prefer the translation, eg:

> 'I start my consideration of the issues by saying that I would endorse … the summary of the relevant principles at paragraph 13 of my own judgment in *Gillespie* … and I see no advantage in my repeating them *in extenso* [prefer: *at length*] here.' [*Kalu v Brighton and Essex University Hospitals NHS Trust* [2015] EWCA Civ 897, [17] (Underhill LJ)]

Also, the Latin contains an inherent vagueness. For example, if a passage of text is quoted *in extenso*, is it quoted 'in full' in the sense of word-for-word, or might words be omitted? The Latin may trap the writer into assuming the meaning is unarguable—which is another reason to prefer an English translation.

Examples

- ‘Lewison J gave a short judgment … which is of some importance because it was subsequently incorporated *in extenso* [meaning: *word-for-word*? *at length*?] into the judgment of the judge on the subsequent hearing inter partes.’ [*Abela v Baadarani* [2013] UKSC 44; [2013] 1 WLR 2043, [13] (Lord Clarke)]
- ‘[T]he Court of Appeal quoted *in extenso* [meaning: *at length*? *verbatim*?] a letter sent by the purchasers’ solicitor immediately after the notice of termination was given.’ [*Romanos v Pentagold Investments Pty Ltd* (2013) 217 CLR 367, [46], Kirby J. The decision of the court from which the appeal came indicates that the quotation from the letter was probably in full, except for formal parts: see *Pentagold Investments Pty Ltd v Romanos* [2001] NSWCA 425, [40].]

in extremis

Latin: in the extreme. Usually used in the sense of ‘on the point of dying’ or ‘near death’. The Latin may have become standard English, perhaps because of its euphemistic qualities. However, an English translation is perfectly adequate, even if more pointed. Therefore, prefer the English:

> ‘The evidence shows that this may well be a case in which failures by the ambulance service to provide an ambulance more quickly to a person who was *in extremis* [prefer: *on the point of dying*] was a cause of the death which might have been avoidable if the ambulance had been available earlier.’ [*R v Poplar Coroner* [1993] QB 610, 620 (Tudor Evans J)]

In extremis is also used, more generally, to mean ‘as a last resort’. Here, too, prefer an English translation—particularly one that captures the Latin sense of ‘dying’, as in the second example below:

- ‘The police were prepared to go onto the site *in extremis* [prefer: *if absolutely necessary*; *as a last resort*] but fortunately did not have to do so. The occasion went off more calmly than the previous year.’ [*West Yorkshire Police Authority v Reading Festival Ltd* [2006] 1 WLR 2005, [44] (Scott Baker LJ)]
- ‘Only *in extremis* [prefer: *if nothing can save it*; *as a last resort*] will a statutory provision be construed to be incompatible [with the European Convention on Human Rights].’ [*R v Chief Constable of Dorset Police* [2003] QB 480, [38] (Stanley Burnton J)]

in flagrante delicto

Latin: in blazing wrongdoing; while the crime is ablaze (ie, in the very act of committing the crime). The Latin may exude a certain frisson, but a translation is likely to communicate more immediately to most readers. For example:

- ‘The appellant was informed by his wife that she wished to bring an end to the marriage, that there was another man with whom she was having an affair. She did not seek to boast about it. She did not seek to disparage the appellant. He did not find them *in flagrante delicto* [prefer: *in the very act*].’ [*R v Light* [1995] EWCA Crim J0119-1, 5 (Lord Taylor CJ)]
- ‘If [hazardous conditions] are caused by human agency, the agent, unless detected *in flagrante delicto* [prefer: *in the very act of committing the wrong*], is hardly likely to confess his fault.’ [*Goldman v Hargrave* (1966) 115 CLR 458, 465 (Lord Wilberforce)]

in forma pauperis

Latin: having the status of a poor person; as an impecunious person. This Latin tag goes back at least to a statute of 1495 (11 Hen VII, c 12: *Suing in Forma Pauperis*), allowing a poor person to bring a civil action without payment of court fees, and to have a lawyer appointed to act without payment. In more recent times, court rules and legal-aid statutes regulate proceedings by litigants of limited means. The Latin is now an historical oddity. Where it is used, a translation or explanation is easy to supply:

- 'King's Counsel, except when appearing for a plaintiff *in forma pauperis* [add explanation: *that is, appearing for impecunious plaintiff*], cannot hold a brief for the plaintiff on the trial of a civil cause without a junior ...' [*R v Visitors to Inns of Court* [1993] 3 WLR 287, 323 (Staughton LJ)]
- 'Reference was made to [a decision] which held that a successful plaintiff in an action *in forma pauperis* [add translation: *that is, in the capacity of an impecunious litigant*] was not entitled to recover anything for remuneration from his solicitor or fees to counsel.' [*Angor Pty Ltd v Ilich Motor Co Pty Ltd* [1992] FCA 348; (1992) 37 FCR 65, 73–74 (French J)]

Alternatively, follow the legislative lead taken in Victoria (Australia), in s 12 of the *Crown Proceedings Act 1958* (Vic): the heading uses the Latin ('Persons may defend *in forma pauperis*'), but the text of the section discards the Latin in favour of 'disabled by poverty'.

in foro

Latin: in the forum (court). The English translation *in court* serves perfectly well. Often used as part of a longer phrase, where standard English also serves perfectly well. Examples are:

- *in foro contradictorio* and *in foro contensioso* (prefer: *in a contested action*);
- *in foro conscientiae* (prefer: *in a court of conscience*), usually used in contrast to 'in a forum (tribunal) of law'—ie, in a court. The Latin carries no more meaning than an English translation:

  > 'The basis of the consensual compact [between members of a church concerning the church's institutional structure] must be a willingness to be bound to it because of shared faith, or, in the Latin phrase ... *in foro conscientiae* [prefer: *in a tribunal of conscience*]. Its binding effect does not come from the availability of the secular sanctions of State courts of law.' [*Scandrett v Dowling* (1992) 27 NSWLR 483, 554 (Priestley JA)]

Compare **in absentia**.

in fraudem legis

Latin: in fraud of the law; in deliberate breach of the law. The Latin has no advantage over an English translation:

> '[The appellant] has failed to satisfy the Board that the steps taken by the Government, including the proclamation and the impugned Act, were *in fraudem legis* [prefer: *in deliberate breach of law*] or otherwise unauthorised by the relevant legislation.' [*Ningkan v Government of Malaysia* [1970] AC 379, 390 (PC)]

in futuro

Latin: in the future; sometimes *de futuro* ('for the future'). The meaning of the Latin is guessable, but that is scant justification for preferring the Latin over the plain English. For example:

- '[When s 6(1) is interpreted in this way] no true retrospectivity is involved. Section 6(1) regulates the conduct of appellate courts *de futuro* [prefer: *for the future*].' [*R v Lambert* [2002] 2 AC 545, 567 (Lord Steyn)]
- '[R]elief for misleading and deceptive conduct is not necessarily confined to *in futuro* [prefer: *future*] operation ... [but] orders may be made varying contracts from dates prior to the dates of the orders.' [*O'Brien v Bank of Western Australia Ltd* [2013] NSWCA 71, [12]; (2013) 16 BPR 31,705, 31,712 (Macfarlan JA)]

in good faith

The core meaning is 'honestly'. To do something *in good faith* requires at least honesty: *Central Estates (Belgravia) Ltd v Woolgar* [1972] 1 QB 48, 55 (Lord Denning MR), 57 (Megaw LJ). A person who acts 'honestly blundering and careless' may nevertheless be acting *in good faith*; contrast a person who, though not necessarily intending to defraud, suspects that something is wrong and deliberately chooses not to enquire: *Tatam v Hasler* (1889) 23 QBD 345, 348 (Denman J, applying the distinction drawn by Lord Blackburn in *Jones v Gordon* (1877) 2 App Cas 616, 628–29).

Sometimes, context may give *in good faith* a more nuanced meaning. For example, under whistleblower-protection legislation that protects disclosures made 'in good faith', an honest disclosure might fail the 'good faith' test if motivated by personal gain or other ulterior motive: *Street v Unemployed Workers' Centre* [2004] 4 All ER 839, 841, 853 (Auld LJ).

See also **bona fide**; **honestly**.

in gremio

Latin: in the bosom. A colourful Latinism, but easily translatable into idiomatic English, as the following examples show:

- 'You have a communication issued on a privileged occasion; and *in gremio* [prefer: *in the body*] of that communication are used words which are in themselves defamatory.' [*Adam v Ward* [1917] AC 309, 326–27 (Lord Dunedin)]
- 'In orders that are not final it is unnecessary to make any express reservation of liberty to apply, for all such orders carry with them *in gremio* [prefer: *an inherent*] liberty to apply to the Court.' [*Re Porteous* [1949] VLR 383, 385 (Herring CJ)]

Sometimes *in gremio* is part of longer phrases, also easily translatable into idiomatic English:

- *in gremio judicis*—in the bosom of the judge (in the sense of 'inherently knowable by the judge' under the common-law principle that judges are presumed to know the law)
- *in gremio legis*—in the bosom of the law (in the sense of 'under the protection of the law' or 'under the guidance of the law').

in gross

A description of a right that is enforceable against a parcel of land in the hands of successive owners, but without being 'annexed' or 'attached' to the land. Rights of this kind cannot exist at common law. However, in some countries, statutes grant rights in gross—eg, 'easements in gross' or 'covenants in gross'. An example is the statutory right of an electricity authority to enter land to maintain poles and wires on the land.

Further reading

Kevin Gray and Susan Francis Gray, *Elements of Land Law*, 5th edn (Oxford University Press, 2009) [5.1.22]–[5.1.26]

See also **easements rights and privileges**; **dominant tenement / servient tenement**.

in hoc statu

Latin: in this position; in this situation. A Latinism that is easily translatable into idiomatic English—and therefore should be. It connotes that the matter is being considered in the light of the current situation only, and may require further consideration later. For example:

> [Counsel applied to have evidence excluded as inadmissible] because it was essentially evidence of matters of law. That application was refused *in hoc statu* [prefer: *in the siutation as it then stood; for the time being, pending further argument*].' [*Scottish Widows Plc v Revenue & Customs* [2008] UKSPC 664, [30] (Special Commissioners Reid and Jones)]

in integrum

Latin: entirely; to the fullest extent. Prefer a plain-English translation: eg, 'The plaintif is entitled to ~~*restitutio in integrum*~~ full restitution.'

See **restitutio in integrum**.

in its discretion

When used after *may*, an unnecessary addition: eg, 'The landlord may ~~in its discretion~~ allow the tenant to sublease.' Also unnecessary is the addition to 'discretion' of a qualifying word, such as 'absolute' or 'unfettered': eg, 'The landlord may ~~in its absolute discretion~~ allow the tenant to sublease.'

See also **may**.

in lieu of

This expression may now be part of standard English—but *in place of*, or *instead of*, always suffices. Always avoid the pairing *in lieu and in substitution of*; here too, *in place of* or *instead of* suffices. For example:

> 'I give an annuity of $300 to A, but if A chooses *in lieu and in substitution of* [prefer: *instead of*] the annuity, a lump sum of $20,000.' [Example from the will in *Re Boddington* (1884) 25 Ch D 685 (CA)]

in limine

Latin: at the threshold; at the outset. The Latin term enjoys no advantage in clarity or nuance over the English translation, so prefer the English:

- '[The claims] have been launched and argued on the basis of challenging the Rule *in limine* [prefer: *at the threshold*], and not how it is operated, let alone how it would have been applied in these two cases.' [*R v Secretary of State for the Home Department* [2015] UKSC 68, [95] (Lord Neuberger)]
- 'The respondents submitted that the appeal failed *in limine* [prefer: *at the threshold; at the outset*] because the question … was not justiciable.' [*Yougarla v Western Australia* [2001] HCA 47; (2001) 207 CLR 344, 372–73 [76] (Kirby J)]

in loco parentis

Latin: in the place of a parent; in the role of parent. Thus, a person who, though not the child's parent, takes on the role of parent, is said to stand *in loco parentis*. The English translation is accurate; prefer it. For example:

- 'Asquith LJ regarded membership of the same family as limited to three relationships: that of children, that constituted by way of legitimate marriage and, thirdly, relationships whereby one person *becomes in loco parentis* [prefer: *takes on the role of parent; stands in the place of a parent*] to another.' [*M v Secretary of State for Work and Pensions* [2006] 2 AC 91, [139] (Lord Mance)]

- 'The parents or guardians will have entrusted the children to the school, acting *in loco parentis* [prefer: *in the role of parent*], on the assumption that they will be cared for, not abused.' [*New South Wales v Lepore* [2003] HCA 4; (2003) 77 ALJR 558, [306] (Kirby J)]

in medias res

Latin: into the midst of things; into the thick of it. The Latin has no advantage over an appropriate English translation. For example:

- 'As [the defendant] put it, the moment she saw him she plunged *in medias res* [prefer: *straight in; into the thick of things*].' [*Tharp v Tharp* [1916] 1 Ch 142, 150 (Neville J)]
- 'May I turn then immediately to jump *in medias res* [prefer: *straight to the point*] to [page] 65 of the application book.' (*Ex parte Lam* [2002] HCATrans 315 (Walker SC in argument)]

in nubibus

Latin: in the clouds. The Latin carries the sense of 'up in the air', 'nowhere in particular', 'unresolved'. That sense can be translated into an appropriate English substitute that will mean something to readers untutored in Latin. Examples are:

- 'The title [to land] cannot commence *in nubibus* [prefer: *somewhere vague; in no particular place*] at the exact point of time which is represented by 365 days multiplied by 40.' [*Re Cox & Neve's Contract* [1891] 2 Ch 109, 118 (North J)]
- '[N]o thought was given ... about what was to happen if and when either the defendant or Bartholomew ... were to leave the house for the purpose of living somewhere else. That contingency was left *in nubibus* [prefer: *unresolved*].' [*Lockwood v Lowe* [1954] 2 QB 267, 272 (Romer LJ)]
- 'If a beneficiary under a trust for sale has no interest in the property pending sale where is the equitable fee simple? It is not in the trustees and cannot be *in nubibus* [prefer: *up in the clouds; nowhere in particular*].' [*Cedar Holdings Ltd v Green* [1981] Ch 129, 135 (Millett QC in argument)]

in order for / in order to

In order for is always reducible to *for*:

> '*In order for* [prefer: *For*] the court to sit, a judge must be available.'

In order to is always reducible to *to*:

> '*In order to* [prefer: *To*] answer the summons, you must appear in person.'

in pari casu

Latin: in a similar position; on a par with. No purpose is served by preserving this Latinism, except pedantry. Prefer an English equivalent:

> '[E]ach case must have its own individual form of words, and I doubt whether, except where they are *in pari casu* [prefer: *in a similar position; on a par*], other cases can provide any substantial assistance in determining whether the terms proposed in the particular case are too wide or not wide enough.' [*Webster v Lord Advocate* 1985 SC 173, 186 (Lord Justice Clerk Wheatley)]

in pari delicto potior est conditio defendentis

Latin: where fault is equal, the defendant has the stronger position; where both parties are equally wicked, the defendant's position is the stronger. The Latin encapsulates the principle that, where both plaintiff and defendant are blameworthy, the court will let the loss lie where it falls; or when the right to possession of land is in dispute, the person in possession will not be disturbed: *Bowmakers Ltd v Barnet Instruments Ltd* [1945] KB 65, 72 (CA). Similarly, *in pari delicto melior est conditio possidentis*—where fault is equal, the party in possession has the better position.

Although these are hallowed maxims, the Latin loses nothing in translation:

- 'The maxim is *in pari delicto potior est conditio defendentis*, that is to say, where each party is equally in fault, the law favours the defendant.' [*Commonwealth of Australia v Davis Samuel Pty Ltd (No 7)* [2013] ACTSC 146, [1719]; (2013) 282 FLR 1, 243 (Refshauge J, providing a translation)]
- 'But where both parties are equally privy to the illegality the plaintiff's claim will fail, whether raised in contract or tort, for *potior est condicio* [sic] *defendentis*.' [*Euro-Diam Ltd v Bathurst* [1990] 1 QB 1, 36 (Kerr LJ, beginning with English, then adding the Latin as if to reassure legal readers)]

in pari materia

Latin: in like [similar] material—ie, comparable, equally relevant. Generally used in the sense of 'on the same subject matter', or 'analogous'. The English suffices for the Latin. For example:

- 'Whilst statutes *in pari materia* [prefer: *that deal with comparable matters*] should be construed consistently if possible, a later statute is not a reliable guide to the meaning of an earlier one, especially in a field such as immigration where social and political pressures have led to fast-moving changes in the legislation.' [*R v George* [2014] UKSC 28, [30]; [2014] 1 WLR 1831, 1841 (Lord Hughes)]
- 'The appellant submitted that her case and *Dickson v The Queen* were *in pari materia* [prefer: *comparable*; *analogous*].' [*Momcilovic v R* [2011] HCA 34, [274]; (2011) 245 CLR 1, 121 (Gummow J)]

Further reading

- *Halsbury's Laws of England*, 'Statutes and Legislative Process' (vol 96, 2018) [233] (Acts *in pari materia*)
- Dennis C Pearce and Robert S Geddes, *Statutory Interpretation in Australia*, 9th edn (LexisNexis, 2019) [3.42]–[3.44]

in particular

Where following a general description, *in particular* focuses attention on a specific item or items, but does not usually cut down the width of the general description.

Examples

- 'This licence authorises you to sell provisions, *in particular* meat.' Here, *in particular* introduces an illustration of the general term 'provisions', but it does not cut down the width of that general term. However, a person seeking a licence to sell meat need not show that meat comes within 'provisions'—it is enough that meat comes within the 'in particular' example: *Earl Fitzwilliam's Wentworth Estates Co Ltd v Minister for Housing and Local Government* [1952] AC 362.
- A statute exempted a government official from having to give reasons for a decision in specified situations. One situation was headed 'Decisions relating to the administration of criminal justice, and, *in particular*' [then followed a list of specified decisions]. Held, *in particular* identified specific matters which came within the general class of exempt decisions, but did not limit them: *Pepper v A-G (Qld) [No 2]* [2008] QCA 207, [28]; [2008] 2 Qd R 353.

Sometimes, a statute or document requires a decision-maker to consider a list of specified matters, only one (or more) of which the statute or document tags with *in particular*. The material tagged 'in particular' is a mandatory consideration and carries the most weight. As to the other matters, listed but not tagged 'in particular', the decision-maker is usually free to decide how much importance to attach to them: *R v City of Westminster Housing Benefit Review Board* [2001] 1 WLR 539, 545 (HL).

in perpetuum

Latin: for ever; in perpetuity; without end. The Latin meaning may be guessed, but the English translation is clear, so prefer it. For example:

> '[The] right to such stock is a right to receive an annuity *in perpetuum* [prefer: *for ever; in perpetuity*], subject to an option of redemption on the part of the Government.' [*Re Taylor* [1922] 1 Ch 569, 586 (Peterson J)]

in personam / in rem

Latin: *persona*, person; *res*, thing, property. Hence *in personam* = against the person; *in rem* = against the thing (property). Used in two main contexts:

1. To distinguish a right enforceable against a person (*in personam*) from a right enforceable against property (*in rem*).
2. To distinguish the effect of a judgment binding only the person (*in personam*) [ie, binding only the parties to the litigation] and a judgment binding the property (*in rem*) [ie, binding the property into whosever hands it falls].

Traditionalists may consider that these Latin terms convey a nuance not possible in a plain-English translation, but this is not so. In the first three of the following examples, a translation could easily be given. In examples 4 and 5, the judges themselves proffered explanations that made the Latin redundant.

Examples

1. 'In [making an order against a trustee who acted in breach of trust], courts of equity did not award "damages" but would make an *in personam order* [prefer: *an order against the trustee personally*] for the payment of equitable compensation.' [*AIB Group (UK) plc v Mark Redler & Co Solicitors* [2014] 3 WLR 1367, [30] (Lord Toulson)]
2. '[The principle of indefeasibility of title by registration] in no way denies the right of a plaintiff to bring against a registered proprietor a *claim in personam* [prefer: *a personal claim*] founded in law or in equity, for such relief as a court acting *in personam* [prefer: *against the person*] may grant.' [*Frazer v Walker* [1967] 1 AC 569, 585 (Lord Wilberforce)]
3. 'Jurisdiction is conferred on [certain courts] in respect of proceedings commenced both as actions *in personam* [prefer: *against the person only*] (s 9) and as actions *in rem* [prefer: *against property itself*] (s 10).' [*Laemthong International Lines Co Ltd v BPS Shipping Ltd* (1997) 190 CLR 181, 197 (Gaudron, Gummow and Kirby JJ)]
4. 'A decision on infringement is *in personam*, so it only binds the parties to the action (and their privies), whereas a decision that a patent is invalid (or must be amended) is *in rem*, so it binds the world, just as the patent, so long as it is in force, can be enforced against the world.' [*Virgin Atlantic Airways Ltd v Zodiac Seats UK Ltd* [2014] AC 160, [57] (Lord Neuberger, providing explanations making the Latin redundant)]
5. 'Each category of [property targeted for forfeiture under the Act] is subject to separate forfeiture regimes, reflecting differences between forfeiture *in rem*, attaching to the property connected to an offence, and forfeiture *in personam*, applied to a particular person (here a declared drug trafficker) after criminal proceedings against that person.' [*Attorney-General (NT) v Emmerson* [2014] HCA 13; (2014) 307 ALR 174, [33], providing explanations making the Latin redundant]

in pleno

Latin: in full. There is no reason to prefer the Latin over the English.

in posse

See **in esse / in posse**

in propria persona

Latin: in person. No purpose is served by retaining this scrap of Latin in place of an English translation. For example:

- 'It is difficult to see how a company can sign personally or indeed do any act *in propria persona* [prefer: *personally*]. It can no more seal personally than it can sign personally.' [*Re British Games Ltd* [1938] Ch 240, 244 (Simonds J)]
- 'The notice [of appeal] continued by asserting that the appellant was appearing "*in propria persona*" [prefer: *in person*], unrepresented, but not waiving counsel.' [*Krysiak v Mc Donagh* [2012] WASC 270, [12] (EM Heenan J)]

in pursuance of

See **pursuant to**.

in re

Latin: in the matter of. Usually shortened to *re*. Although a Latinism, the term has become part of business English.

Case names

Case names often begin *In re* (eg, *In re Jones*). However, *Re Jones* suffices, because *In* is implied.

Headings in correspondence

Lawyers conventionally use *In re*, or simply *Re*, and sometimes followed by a colon, to introduce headings to letters or emails. However, *In re* or *Re* are superfluous here. Omit them and get straight to the point. For example:

Not:

Re: your claim against your neighbour [or **In re your claim against your neighbour**]

Instead:

Your claim against your neighbour

in re aliena

Latin: in the property of another person. Used in contrast to *in re propria* (in one's own property). As with many other Latin tags, a plain-English translation suffices. For example:

'[A pledge gives] the pledgee … a power to sell on default … This power is clearly *in re aliena* [prefer: *against the property of another*] and not *in re propria* [prefer: *a matter of personal right only*] because the pledgee has not the general ownership, which has remained in the pledgor.' [Edward Sykes and Sally Walker, *The Law of Securities*, 5th edn (Law Book, 1993) 732]

in re propria

Latin: in one's own affairs; in one's own property. Prefer the English translation.

See **in re aliena**.

in re suam

Latin: on his/her own affairs or business. Prefer the English translation.

Compare **in re propria**.

in relation to

Its reach

A phrase beloved of lawyers and bureaucrats, because of its largely indeterminate reach. It is one of the 'classic phrases of wide connection', which a court has no authority to narrow except in conformity with the purpose of the provision in which it appears: *Attrill v Richmond River Shire Council* (1995) 38 NSWLR 545, 554. It is 'of broad import', requiring 'no more than a relationship, whether direct or indirect, between two subject matters': *O'Grady v Northern Queensland Co Ltd* (1990) 169 CLR 356, 376. For example, an employee corruptly conducting activities as a union shop steward can be acting *in relation to* his employer's affairs: *Morgan v DPP* [1970] 3 All ER 1053. Again, contributions made *in relation to* a de facto relationship can include contributions made before the relationship started: *Harriott v Arena* [2016] FamCAFC 69; [2016] FLC §93-702.

However, the precise reach of *in relation to* depends on the context in which it is used:

> 'The words "in relation to" invariably are words of connection. But there can, in my opinion, be no set meaning as to the ambit and reach of that phrase. It will depend on the particular context, be it statutory or contractual, in which those words appear. As always, context is all.'
> [*Re National Crime Agency* [2020] EWHC 268 (Admin); [2020] 1 WLR 3224, [50] (Davis LJ)]

That creates the spectre of litigation to determine how close or direct a relationship is intended in any particular case. Context may be crucial, and may narrow the normal (and perhaps assumed) reach of *in relation to*. For example, a power of judicial review '*in relation to* a migration decision' allowed judicial review of migration decisions themselves, but not review of collateral aspects of migration proceedings: *Tang v Minister for Immigration and Citizenship* [2013] FCAFC 139; (2013) 305 ALR 547. Again, a statute giving a right to appeal '*in relation to* a question of law only' indicated (by the word 'only') that more was required than a loose connection between a ground of appeal and a question of law: *JFT v Alcohol Mandatory Treatment Tribunal* [2015] NTSC 72; (2015) 35 NTLR 19, [16].

Use a shorter expression

In relation to is inherently wordy. Always consider substituting a single-word alternative such as *about* or *for*. But take care with the substitution, because *about* or *for* may not capture the inherent width of *in relation to*. Thus, a right to make a 'demand *for* a debt' might suggest that the demand must be for the entire debt, but a 'demand *relating to* a debt' may permit a demand for part only of the debt: *Commonwealth Bank of Australia v Garuda Aviation Pty Ltd* [2013] WASCA 61; (2013) 45 WAR 92, [30].

See also **in respect of**; **relating to**; **under (and ...)**.

in rem

See **in personam / in rem**.

in respect of

Indicating a link

In respect of conveys the idea of connection, although in itself does not identify the *nature* of the connection. In that way it is similar to 'in relation to'. Lord Greene MR described *in respect of* as 'colourless': *Cunard's Trustees v Inland Revenue Commissioners* [1946] 1 All ER 159, 164. Its indeterminate reach makes it particularly context-dependent. Australian case law sees its reach as extensive, one judge describing it as having 'the widest possible meaning of any expression intended to convey some connection or relation' between subject matters: *Trustees Executors and Agency Co Ltd v Reilly* [1941] VLR 110, 111 (an assertion later described as 'extravagant' and 'going somewhat too far': *Workers Compensation Board of Queensland v Technical Products Pty Ltd* (1988) 165 CLR 642, 646–47, 653–54). Fowler's recommendation that the phrase be used 'as seldom as possible' has, least one judicial endorsement: *Phonographic Performances (NZ) Ltd v Lion Breweries Ltd* [1979] 2 NZLR 382, 392 (Sir Robin Cooke).

Simpler substitutes: *about*, *for*

Almost always, *about* or *for* are sufficient substitutes for *in respect of*—without sacrificing the hoped-for generality of connection. For example:

- 'The GMC is not empowered to make a decision *in respect of* [prefer: *about*] a section 53 complaint …' [*Michalak v General Medical Council* [2016] EWCA Civ 172, [36] (Ryder LJ)]
- '[T]he proceeding be remitted to a judge of the Federal Court … to determine any pecuniary penalties to be imposed on the first respondent *in respect of* [prefer: *for*] those contraventions.' [*Fair Work Ombudsman v Quest South Perth Holdings Pty Ltd* [2015] HCA 45, terms of Court Order 2B(c) (High Court of Australia)]

If reassurance is needed, several Australian courts have held that *in respect of* merely means *about*, and that sometimes it merely means *for*: see, eg, *Westpac Funds Management Ltd v Chief Commissioner of State Revenue* (2008) 74 NSWLR 566, [59]; *ISS Property Services Pty Ltd v Underwriter Insurance Co Ltd* [2013] SASC 53; (2013) 115 SASR 537, [31]–[34].

However, 'find and replace' substitutions are dangerous. Occasionally (but not always), *in respect of* may have a wider meaning than *about* or *for*. Compare the following two cases:

- Payments made *in respect of* the grant of a lease may not include a payment which a prospective tenant makes to the landlord to purchase the goodwill of a business conducted on the land: *R v Barnet (and area) Rent Tribunal* [1950] 2 KB 506 (CA).
- A right to recover damages *in respect of* personal injury is wider than a right to recover damages *for* personal injury: *Unsworth v Commissioner for Railways* (1958) 101 CLR 73, 87 (Fullagar J).

See also **in relation to**.

in saecula saeculorum

Latin: forever and ever; from age to age; sometimes *per saecula saeculorum*. In days past, when readers of legal texts knew their Vulgate Bible, this phrase may have been a telling alliterative allusion. For most modern readers, it is a pointless artifice. For example:

- 'It is quite clear that it was the intention of the testator that it [a gift to fund a museum at Shakespeare's house] should exist *in saecula saeculorum* [prefer: *for ever*; *in perpetuity*].' [*Thomson v Shakespear* (1860) 1 De GF & J 399, 407; 45 ER 413, 416]

- 'When I use the word "permanent", I mean, of course, permanent so far as is presently foreseeable; I do not suggest that the evidence should prove permanence for ever and ever or, as the Latin has it, *per saecula saeculorum* [delete: the translation has already been given].' [*Re Jupiter House Investments (Cambridge) Ltd* [1985] 1 WLR 975, 979 (Harman J)]

in se

Latin: in itself. There is no good reason to prefer this scrap of Latin over its English translation.

in situ

Latin: in place; in the original place. For some readers, this Latinism may have become part of standard English; but unless readers are in this category, prefer an appropriate English translation. For example:

- 'If a structure can only be enjoyed *in situ* [prefer: *in its place*; *in that location*], and is such that it cannot be removed in whole or in sections to another site, there is at least a strong inference that the purpose of placing the structure on the original site was that it should form part of the realty at that site, and therefore cease to be a chattel.' [*Tristmire Ltd v Mew* [2012] 1 WLR 852, [26] (Patten LJ)]
- 'The area was cordoned off so that the items were not disturbed. They were photographed *in situ* [prefer: *in their location* (ie, *unmoved)*] and those photographs, taken close up and in colour, clearly depict a green baseball cap.' [*Evans v R* [2007] HCA 59; (2007) 235 CLR 521, [257] (Heydon J)]

in so far as

Sometimes four separate words, *in so far as*; sometimes joined, *insofar as* (but never *insofaras*). Modern British English uses both forms:

- '*In so far as* the respondents' activities ... cause no nuisance, they are lawful. ... However, *in so far as* the activities are unlawful, in particular *in so far as* they constitute a nuisance [we must] take those activities into account.' [*Lawrence v Fen Tigers Ltd* [2014] UKSC 13; [2014] AC 822, [66] (Lord Neuberger)]
- 'I am not sure that the evidential differences are of any moment; but, *insofar as* they are and *insofar as* there is evidence in support of this proposition, I do not believe [the witness].' [*R v Hertfordshire County Council* [2016] EWCA Civ 1108; [2017] 1 WLR 2153, [4] (Burnett LJ, quoting from trial judge)]

Each form can usually be shortened to 'so far as': eg, 'We agree *~~in~~ so far as* the evidence allows.'

in solidum

Latin: for the whole; used in the context of liability not only for one's own acts but for the acts of others in the same enterprise; hence the anglicised 'solidary' liability. Examples are:

- co-obligants each liable for the whole of a debt or liability, and not merely for an apportioned part
- tortfeasors each liable for the whole of the damage caused, and not merely for an apportioned part.

Where solidary liability exists, a plaintiff can recover the whole loss from one wrongdoer alone (leaving that wrongdoer to seek contribution from other wrongdoers). This contrasts with proportionate liability, where liability is apportioned to each wrongdoer according to each one's individual responsibility (meaning that the plaintiff must sue all the wrongdoers to recover the total loss).

As with many Latinisms in law, no meaning is lost by preferring a plain-English equivalent, or at least providing an explanation. For example:

- '[I]f held liable *in solidum* [prefer: *each for the whole amount*], solvent defendants ... will often find that they have to pay the whole of the claimant's damages without in fact being able to obtain a contribution from [insolvent defendants].' [*Barker v Corus (UK) Ltd* [2006] UKHL 20, [89]; [2006] 2 AC 572, 607 (Lord Rodger)]
- [At common law] the liability of concurrent tortfeasors causing the same damage was '*in solidum*' each of them being responsible to make good the whole of the damage caused ...' [*Spotless Services Australia Ltd v Herbath* [2009] VSCA 285; (2009) 26 VR 373, [15] (Mandie JA, providing an explanation)]

Compare **singuli in solidum**.

in specie

Latin: in shape; in form; in kind. For example, a will may direct the executor to distribute the estate *in specie*—ie, by transferring assets to the relevant beneficiaries rather than selling the assets and distributing the money.

Whether something exists *in specie* can raise complex issues. Suppose an insurance policy precludes claims for goods that continue to exist *in specie*: does fish that has become rotten, or corn that has become putrid, or pork that has been roasted, continue to exist *in specie* (examples cited in argument in *Duthie v Hilton* (1868) LR 4 CP 138, 141, Mellish QC)?

However, such conundrums apart, this Latin tag is easily recast as idiomatic English—and therefore should be. For example:

- 'If [the plaintiff] succeeds ... the court will treat the defendant as holding the property on a constructive trust for the plaintiff and will order the defendant to transfer it *in specie* [prefer: *in kind*; or rewrite, *transfer the actual property*] to the plaintiff.' [*Boscawen v Bajwa* [1996] 1 WLR 328, 334–35 (Millett LJ)]
- '[The document] did not contemplate the transfer of assets *in specie* [prefer: *in kind*; or rewrite, *transfer of the actual assets*]. It provided for payment in cash.' [*Wellington Capital Ltd v Australian Securities and Investments Commission* [2014] HCA 43; (2014) 254 CLR 288, [36] (French CJ, Crennan, Kiefel and Bell JJ)]

in statu quo

Latin: in the former state; in the original position; unchanged. The Latinism adds nothing to an English translation—so there is no good reason to prefer the Latin over the English. For example:

- 'But it has long been the law that, as a condition of rescission of a voidable contract, the parties must be put *in statu quo* [prefer: *into their original position*].' [*Guinness Plc v Saunders* [1990] 2 AC 663, 697 (Lord Goff)]
- '[T]he issue was whether the form of interlocutory relief granted by Sheppard J was appropriate to keep the matter *in statu quo* [prefer: *unchanged*] pending a determination of the claim to final relief.' [*Jackson v Sterling Industries Ltd* (1987) 162 CLR 612, 616 (Mason CJ)]

in terms of

Prefer a less wordy substitute; the word-saving will improve readability, as in Example 1 below. Additional changes may further improve readability, as in Examples 2 and 3.

Examples

1. **Before**: The new court rules have already proved effective *in terms of* shorter pleadings. (13 words)
   After: The new court rules have already led to shorter pleadings. (10 words)
2. **Before**: 'It is hard to see why, if such a course is appropriate, it would *be beneficial in terms of time or costs* for the issue to be considered by the Court of Appeal.' [*Willers v Joyce (No 2)* [2016] UKSC 44, [18]; [2016] 3 WLR 534 (Lord Neuberger)] (33 words)
   After: 'It is hard to see why, if such a course is appropriate, it would *save time or costs* for the issue to be considered by the Court of Appeal.' (29 words)
3. **Before**: '*In terms of* the primary judge's approach, even though the application his Honour was dealing with was made by the respondent, he directed his initial questions to the appellant.' [*Dennis v Commonwealth Bank of Australia* [2019] FCAFC 231, [36]] (29 words)
   After: 'Even though the primary judge was dealing with the respondent's application, he directed his initial questions to the appellant.' (19 words)

in terrorem

Latin: by way of threat; by way of intimidation. Often used to describe contractual provisions designed to encourage, in a less-than-subtle way, a party to abide by their contractual obligations (eg, by increasing the interest rate on late payment under a mortgage).

The translation 'by way of terror' or 'terrorising', though colourful, may be too strong, because even where a party (eg, the mortgagor) has consented to the provision, a court may protect them against its enforcement: *Bridge v Campbell Discount Co Ltd* [1962] AC 600, 622 (Lord Radcliffe); *Paciocco v Australia and New Zealand Banking Group Ltd* [2016] HCA 28; 258 CLR 525, [17] (Kiefel J). A better translation is 'as a deterrent' or 'as a threat, or 'to coerce' or 'to intimidate', as in the following examples:

- 'The essence of a penalty is a payment of money stipulated *as in terrorem of* [prefer: *to coerce compliance by*; *as a deterrent to*] the offending party …' [*Dunlop Pneumatic Tyre Co Ltd v New Garage and Motor Co Ltd* [1915] AC 79, 80 (Lord Dunedin)]
- 'I do not intend this in any way *in terrorem* [prefer: *as a threat*] or in indicating any concluded view on the matter.' [*Scott-Young v Great* [2001] NSWCA 293, [21] (Mason P)]
- '[The trial judge] found that Bluechip's claim of $2 million was made … *in terrorem in response* [prefer: *as an intimidatory response*] to a claim made by Sunstruct.' [*Central Queensland Development Corporation Pty Ltd v Sunstruct Pty Ltd* [2015] FCAFC 63, [3]; (2015) 106 ACSR 127, 129 (Besanko J)]

See also **penalty**.

in the event that

In the event that simply means *if*. When used to introduce a conditional statement—its most common use—*in the event that* lacks the immediacy of *if*. Always prefer the shorter *if*. For example:

- 'Mr Collier leased his property to his daughter for an illegal purpose, namely to deceive his creditors *in the event that* [prefer: *if*] he became insolvent.' [*Patel v Mirza* [2016] UKSC 42; [2017] AC 467, [238] (Lord Sumption)]
- 'He indicated … that he would seek expedition *in the event that* [prefer: *if*] a stay was granted.' (*Obeid v R* [2016] HCA 9; (2016) 329 ALR 372, [6], Gageler J)

See also **CONDITIONAL CLAUSES**.

in the form of

Statutes or agreements sometimes require notices or forms to follow set templates, using expressions such as 'to the effect of', 'to similar effect', 'in like form', and so on. What departures from the templates does such wording allow? Sometimes, the statute or agreement expressly excuses minor departures. Some general interpretation statutes also allow minor departures: eg, in Australia s 25C of the *Acts Interpretation Act 1901* (Cth) excuses the need for 'strict compliance' with forms and allows 'substantial compliance'. Likewise, a contract may provide that substantial compliance is sufficient for forms under the contract (which appears to be the common-law position in any case: *Hamilton v Minister for Immigration* (1993) 48 FCR 20, 33).

But each case turns on context and the wording of the particular statute or contract. For example, where an electoral law required an electoral nomination notice to be 'in' the form prescribed', reasonably strict compliance was necessary: *Henry v Armitage* (1883) 12 QBD 257. But where a landlord-and-tenant statute required a landlord's notice to a tenant of intention to terminate the lease to be in the prescribed form 'or to a similar effect', an informal notice sufficed as long as the notice brought to the tenant's attention the key contents of the prescribed form: *Fox v Jolly* [1916] 1 AC 1, 17–18; *Ex parte Dalley-Watkins; Re Wilson* (1955) 72 WN (NSW) 454, 456.

In the first two examples below, the court allowed some latitude; in the third, it did not not.

- A regulation required a notice to be '*substantially to the same effect*' as the prescribed form. Held, that formula excused an obvious typographical error: *Pease v Carter* [2020] EWCA Civ 175; [2020] 1 WLR 1459.
- A proxy form was to be '*to the same effect as*' a supplied form. Held, that formula did not require the form to be 'literally followed': *Re Indian Zoedone Co* (1884) 26 Ch 70, 78 (Lord Selborne LC).
- The *Riot Act 1714* required a justice of the peace, seeking to dispel a crowd, to read aloud a prescribed statement 'in these words, *or like in effect*'. A justice of the peace read out the prescribed statement, but omitted the concluding words 'God save the King'. Held, the omission invalidated a prosecution under the Act: *R v Child* (1830) 4 Car & P 442; 172 ER 774.

It is always prudent to state expressly whether strict compliance is required, or whether substantial compliance suffices.

See also **in accordance with**.

in the matter of

A style of reference to certain types of law cases, particularly relator actions: *In the matter of Smith*. Now usually pruned to *In Re Smith*, or better still *Re Smith*.

See also **in re**.

in the process of

Almost always redundant: eg, if something is '*in the process of* occurring', it is 'occurring'. For example:

> 'The arguments ... do not establish that customary international law is not *in the process of evolving* [prefer: *evolving*] to the point where the death penalty as such is a violation of [human rights].' [*R v Secretary of State for the Home Department* [2020] UKSC 10; [2020] 2 WLR 857, [149] (Lord Kerr)]

in totidem verbis

See **totidem verbis**.

in toto

Latin: in the whole; entirely. A mere affectation; an appropriate English translation suffices. For example:

- 'What then is the answer to the question whether the document signed by the deceased gave rise to a contract? One possible answer is that it should be rejected *in toto* [prefer: *entirely*] as a document signed without any intention to create legal relations …' [*Roerig v Valiant Trawlers Ltd* [2002] 1 WLR 2304, 2308 (Waller J)]
- 'The [court] was correct to proceed on the basis that the reference to a "contract" in s 568(1)(f) is to the contract *in toto* [prefer: *in all its aspects*] …' [*Willmott Growers Group Inc v Willmott Forests Ltd* [2013] HCA 51; (2013) 251 CLR 592, [106] (Keane J)]

in transitu

Latin: in transit; in the course of passage. The context is usually (but not always) the right of an unpaid seller of goods to intercept and reclaim goods, still in transit, on news that the buyer is insolvent. The closeness between the Latin and its English translation may be enough to suggest the Latin's meaning; but that of itself is no reason to prefer the Latin over the English. For example:

- '[The] lien on subfreights does not bind third parties. It is merely a personal right to intercept freight before it is paid analogous to a right of stoppage *in transitu* [prefer: *in the course of transit; during passage*].' [*Agnew v Commissioner of Inland Revenue* [2001] 2 AC 710, 728 (Lord Millett)]
- '[The judge had failed to take into account] the fact that the child was here in Australia "merely *in transitu* [prefer: *in transit to another place*]", and had not considered whether there was any sufficient reason why the child's journey should not be continued.' [*Shaw v Ipatoff* (1957) 97 CLR 248, 262 (Dixon CJ, Kitto and Taylor JJ)]

in utero

Latin: in the womb. Unless writing for a medical audience, prefer plain English:

- 'In the event, the baby died *in utero* [prefer: *in the womb; unborn*].' [*Montgomery v Lanarkshire Health Board* [2015] UKSC 11, [64]; [2015] AC 1430, 1456 (Lords Kerr and Reed)]
- 'To abort a child *in utero* [prefer: *in the womb*] is a common law misdemeanour.' [*CES v Superclinics (Australia) Pty Ltd* (1995) 38 NSWLR 47, 86 (Meagher JA)]

in vacuo

Latin: in empty space (in the sense of 'in the abstract', or 'divorced from the surrounding circumstances', or 'isolated'). Sometimes rendered *in vacuuo*. The closeness between the Latin original and the English translation suggests the meaning; but in modern times, when few readers understand Latin, always prefer English.

Examples: in vacuo

- 'Davis J granted leave for that application to be pursued, but rejected it, holding that it was not possible to define the phrase "held for the purposes of journalism" *in vacuo* [prefer: *in the abstract*]. The question was whether the decision … was, on the particular facts, rational and properly open …' [*British Broadcasting Corporation v Sugar* [2008] 1 WLR 2289, [10] (Buxton LJ)]

- 'One does not take an isolated circumstance and say the bales moved, as one circumstance, and treat that *in vacuo* [prefer: *in isolation*], or say was there a rail, and treat that *in vacuo* [prefer: *in isolation*], or was there a blunt hook and treat that *in vacuo* [prefer: *in isolation*], was there a suitable hook being used and treat that *in vacuo* [prefer: *in isolation*]. One has to look at the whole of the circumstances …' [*Foufoulas v FG Strang Pty Ltd* (1970) 123 CLR 168, 177 (McTiernan J, quoting from trial judge)]

Examples: in vacuuo

- '[The appellant's agreement] to the without prejudice principle made *in vacuuo* prefer: *in the abstract*; *in ignorance of the facts*] before any attempt was made to outline what the alleged dispute was[,] nullifies any meaningful agreement to discuss an unknown dispute on a without prejudice basis.' [*McKinstry v Park* [2015] NICA 12 [51] (Gillen LJ)]
- 'The Tribunal did not find that Ms Smalley had a life expectancy of five years *in vacuuo* [prefer: *divorced from the surrounding circumstances*]. Rather, it found that Ms Smalley had a life expectancy of five years from September 2010.' [*Smalley v Secretary, Dept of Health and Ageing* [2011] FCA 302, [67] (Dodds-Streeton J)]

in whole or in part

A pairing commonly found in law, and often unquestioned. Are both limbs of the pairing needed? Sometimes not: if the *whole* of something is affected, every *part* of it is affected. But the reverse may not be true: if *part* of something is affected, the *whole* may not be affected. Care in language may be required.

But there is a larger issue: is the pairing needed at all? For example, leases commonly provide: 'The tenant must not assign the leased premises *in whole or in part*.' Logically, a promise not to assign 'the premises' is broken by an assignment of the *whole* of the premises. But less clear is whether it is broken by an assignment of *part* of the premises: *Cook v Shoesmith* [1951] 1 KB 752; *Norman's Inc v Wise* 747 SW 2d 475 (Tex 1988). Nevertheless, it seems clear that a covenant against assigning '*any* part' of the premises prohibits an assignment of the whole, since a prohibition against dealing with '*any* part' necessarily encompasses a dealing with '*every* part': *Field v Barkworth* [1986] 1 WLR 137, 139. So the wording can at least be pruned to: 'The tenant must not assign *any part* of the leased premises.'

See also **whole or any part of**; **wholly**.

in witness whereof (the parties have signed)

The traditional formulaic lead-in to the signatures at the end of a deed; sometimes called the 'maker's sealing clause'. It appears in various iterations, most of which are extravagantly verbose: eg, 'In witness whereof the parties hereto have hereunto set their hands and seals the day and year first hereinbefore mentioned.' Latin precursors—eg, *in cuius rei testimonium sigillum meum apposui*—can be traced back to the 13th century. While the concept (that the parties have signed and sealed) may still need expressing in some jurisdictions, the archaic formulation has nothing to commend it. A simpler version suffices.

Example

Signed [*Or* 'Signed and sealed', if sealing is necessary] by [name]
Witnessed [if a witness is needed] by [name]
Dated

Or, as some modern deeds state:

Executed as a deed.
Signed by [name]
Witnessed [if a witness is needed] by [name]
Dated

See also **DEED (document)**; **execute (a document)**; **signed, sealed and delivered**.

in writing

See **writing (noun)**.

inalienable / unalienable

Preferred modern usage is *inalienable*: eg, 'property is inalienable', 'human rights are inalienable'. The older form, *unalienable*, is obsolescent, surviving only in historical documents (notably the US *Declaration of Independence*).

Inc

Abbreviation for *Incorporated*, usually part of an entity's name: *Jones Inc.* The usage is common in the US; there it is usually followed by a full stop (*Inc.*) and, where it appears as part of a proper name, is sometimes preceded by a comma (*Jones, Inc.*) In Britain and the wider Commonwealth, *Inc* is rare; the equivalent is *Limited* (abbreviated to *Ltd* [no full stop]).

inchoate / incohate

The meaning is 'incipient', 'in the early stages of development'. Usages include:

- *inchoate instrument*—an instrument (document) which has not yet taken effect (as where registration is required for validity but has not yet occurred)
- *inchoate offence*—a preliminary offence, such as attempt, incitement or conspiracy
- *inchoate property right*—a property right yet to be perfected, such as one which requires court or Ministerial approval before coming into effect.

Inchoate is the more common spelling, although *incohate* is sometimes seen (eg, in *Monarch Steamship Co Ltd v Karlshamns Oljefabriker (A/B)* [1949] AC 196, 218). Examples follow:

- 'In other words the bargain was not absolute, but *inchoate* only ...' [*Roach v Bickle* (1915) 20 CLR 663, 671 (Isaacs and Gavan Duffy JJ)]
- '[T]he assignment of the lease was a conditional undertaking or an *incohate* agreement at best.' [*Wire by Design Ltd v Commercial Factors Ltd* [2015] NZHC 985, [61] (Moore J)]
- '[T]he acceptable minimum posthumous provision for a surviving spouse should correspond as closely as possible to the *incohate* rights enjoyed by that spouse in the deceased's lifetime ...' [*Moody v Stevenson* [1991] EWCA Civ J0712-4, official transcript, 17 (Waite J); but appearing as *inchoate* in the authorised report, [1992] Ch 486, 498.]

See also **choate**.

incidental to

A broad term, always context-dependent. That makes precise meaning doubly difficult to predict, and renders decisions on meaning of limited precedential value. Examples in case law are legion:

- whether a power is 'incidental to' other enumerated powers excisable by a corporation: *Bell Houses Ltd v City Wall Properties Ltd* [1966] 2 QB 656
- whether certain kinds of costs are 'incidental to' court proceedings: *Aiden Shipping Co Ltd v Interbulk Ltd* [1986] AC 965 (HL), reversing [1985] 1 WLR 1222 (CA); *Fifteenth Eestin Nominees Pty Ltd v Rosenberg (No 2)* [2009] VSCA 178; (2009) 24 VR 155
- whether certain expenses are 'incidental to' the birth of a child: *Foy v Brooks* [1977] 1 WLR 160
- whether certain activities are 'incidental to' the use of a dwelling-house: *Emin v Secretary of State for the Environment* (1989) 58 P & CR 416
- whether certain financial transactions are 'incidental to' the powers of local governments: *Hazell v Hammersmith and Fulham LBC* [1991] 2 WLR 372.

If possible, specify the items or powers that are 'incidental to' the subject matter.

inclosed

See **enclosed / inclosed**.

includes

See **means / includes**.

including (but not limited to)

Including is non-exhaustive (in contrast to *means*, which is exhaustive). To add *but not limited to* is tautologous, because *including* imports *is not limited to*. In legal usage, drafters sometimes add the extra words *but not limited to* (sometimes in parenthesis, sometimes not) out of an apparent concern that 'including' alone might in some way limit the generality of the statement that precedes it. But is this concern warranted? For example:

> 'This licence authorises the sale of food and provisions, *including (but not limited to)* fish.' By adding '(but not limited to)', the writer seeks to make crystal clear that 'food and provisions' retains its wide meaning, and is not somehow narrowed-down by the reference to 'fish'—as if only fish-like food and provisions might be covered. But this narrowed-down interpretation seems unlikely. In reality, the formulaic *but not limited to* probably indicates the writer's misunderstanding of the *noscitur a sociis* principle of interpretation, under which the meaning of a word can be controlled by the meaning of nearby words.

A variant is '*including, for example, …*' The aim here too seems to be to ensure that any illustration after *including* does not cut down the width of the preceding words. But is this necessary? For example:

> 'Nothing in this clause affects the tenant's right to trade on public holidays (including, for example, Good Friday).' The words in brackets add nothing.

Unless for some reason (peculiar to the reader) the example will aid the reader's understanding, delete '(including, for example, …)'.

See also **eiusdem generis; in particular; means / includes; noscitur a sociis**.

inclusio unius est exclusio alterius

Latin: the inclusion of one is the exclusion of the other.

See **expressio unius**.

INCLUSIVE LANGUAGE

See **GENDER-NEUTRAL LANGUAGE**.

inclusive (of time)

When indicating a time-span, *inclusive* is almost always unnecessary. In the statement, 'These gardens are open from Tuesday to Thursday *inclusive*' the word *inclusive* adds nothing. (Could anyone seriously argue that the gardens are open only on Wednesday?)

Very ocassionally, though, *inclusive* helps. For example, a lease expressed to run 'from 1 February to 15 December *inclusive*' unarguably includes the starting date and the ending date; without *inclusive*, the meaning could be debatable (noting particularly the effect of *from*, which otherwise might indicate that the lease starts at the first moment of 2 February).

See also **from (a date)**; **TIME**.

INCONSISTENT PROVISIONS

The issue

A provision in a document may conflict with another provision in the same document. The inconsistency may arise from various factors. For example: a 'special' provision may be inconsistent with the regular conditions in an industry-standard form to which the provision is added; or a document may be the work of many drafters, whose respective contributions to the composite product are inconsistent; or a provision in the body of a document may be inconsistent with a provision in a schedule or annexure. How do courts resolve the inconsistency?

Is there an inconsistency?

The first question is always, 'Is there an inconsistency?' It may be more apparent than real. The first step is to read the document as a whole, including all schedules and annexures that are intended to have contractual force. This process may resolve an apparent inconsistency; but if it does not, then courts apply one or more of the following approaches.

Techniques for resolving inconsistency

- Where one of the inconsistent provisions better serves the purpose of the agreement as a whole, prefer it over the one (or more) that does not, on the basis that this is likely to reflect the parties' intentions: *Walker v Giles* (1849) 6 CB 662, 702; 136 ER 1407, 1424 (Wilde CJ).
- Where the inconsistency is between a provision in a standard-form contract and an added 'special condition', prefer the special condition over the standard-form provision, on the basis that this too is likely to reflect the parties' intentions: *Robertson v French*

(1803) 4 East 130, 136; 102 ER 779, 782 (Lord Ellenborough); *Glynn v Margetson & Co* [1893] AC 351, 358 (Earl Halsbury); *Homburg Houtimport BV v Agrosin Private Ltd* [2003] UKHL 12; [2004] 1 AC 715, [11] (Lord Bingham).

Example

> A printed standard-form lease stated that it was granted 'for the term of one year'. Those words remained in place, but the words 'from the 1st day of January, 1944, to the 30th day of June, 1945' were typed onto the standard form. Held, the typed words prevailed over the printed words: *Addis v Burrows* [1948] 1 KB 444.

- Where a handwritten amendment conflicts with a printed form (or with an added 'special condition'), prefer the handwritten amendment, again on the basis that this is likely to reflect the parties' intentions: *Lai v Gong* (1997) 8 BPR 15,837. More difficult is where the handwritten amendment is typed or word-processed into a 'clean' form, obscuring the former visual distinction between the two; on this, see further, **DELETIONS (Make a clean copy)**.
- Apply the *contra proferentem* principle by reading the provisions against the interests of the party who proffered them. But the *contra proferentem* principle can be invoked only where the inconsistency creates an 'ambiguity'. If each inconsistent provision is, in itself, clear (though inconsistent with the other), the principle is not available. Other matters, also, may make the *contra proferentem* principle unavailable. (See discussion under **contra proferentem**.).

Rule of last resort: earlier provision overrides later provision

Where the parties' intentions cannot be deduced by any other method, courts fall back on the expedient of holding that (except in a will) the earlier of the contradictory expressions prevails. The later provision is treated as repugnant to the earlier: *Forbes v Git* [1922] AC 256, 259. The logic is said to be analogous to a principle in the law of deeds: namely, that had the two provisions appeared in consecutive deeds, the grantor's act in dealing with the matter in the first deed would have put it beyond the grantor's power to deal with the matter in the second deed: *Martin v Martin* (1987) 54 P & CR 238, 243–44. The 'earlier overrides later' principle is applied only as a last resort, where the inconsistency cannot be resolved in any other way: *Bush v Watkins* (1851) 14 Beav 425, 432; 51 ER 350, 353; *AMEC Engineering Pty Ltd v Shanks* [2001] SASC 257 (SAFC), [36].

In reality, the principle is entirely arbitrary. It ignores the fact that the parties may have regarded the later clause as their considered view—their 'later and better thoughts': *Durbin v Perpetual Trustee Co Ltd* (1995) NSWConvR §55-725, 55,604 (Kirby P). The principle's arbitrariness led a senior Australian judge to describe it as 'now so unfashionable that one hesitates to mention it': *McGowan v Commissioner of Stamp Duties* [2001] QCA 236; [2002] 2 Qd R 499, [22] (McPherson JA). Nevertheless, it sometimes arises for consideration: eg, *Taylor v Rive Droite Music Ltd* [2004] EWHC 1605 (Ch), [232] (Lewison J, obiter). Several relatively recent antipodean cases have applied it: *Durbin v Perpetual Trustee Co Ltd* (1995) NSWConvR §55-725 (NSWCA); *Missing Link Network Integration Pty Ltd v Olamte Pty Ltd* [2005] NSWSC 430, [68]–[69].

Also, the principle does not apply to wills. In a will, the reverse applies: the later provision overrides the earlier. It has its own Latin maxim: *cum duo inter se pugnantia reperiuntur in testamento, ultimum ratum est* (when two repugnant statements occur in a will, the later prevails). The rationale is that the latest expression of the testator's wishes should prevail: *Re Hammond* [1938] 3 All ER 308; *Thomson v Thomson* [2008] VSC 375, [14]–[16].

Precedence clause

To resolve the potential problem of inconsistent provisions, and to avoid the arbitrariness of the 'earlier overrides the later' principle, some drafters include a 'precedence clause' to direct how conflicts are to be resolved. (See discussion under **PRECEDENCE CLAUSE**.)

See also **contra proferentem; CONSISTENCY OF TERMINOLOGY; DELETIONS; generalia specialibus non derogant; inconsistent (with); Mitsui principle; PRECEDENCE CLAUSE; WORDS AND FIGURES.**

inconsistent (with)

When is A *inconsistent with* B? For example, a statutory provision may apply 'unless *inconsistent with*' another provision; or a contractual provision may apply 'unless *inconsistent with*' another provision. But there may be varying degrees of inconsistency, from minimal to absolute. What degree does the drafter intend?

Courts generally assume that A is not 'inconsistent with' B unless the inconsistency is complete. For example, a section in statute A is not 'inconsistent with' statute B unless the section is 'so at variance' with the machinery and procedure of statute B that, if inserted into statute B, the machinery and procedure 'would not work': *Re Knight and The Tabernacle Permanent Building Society* [1891] 2 QB 63, 69 (Fry LJ). To counter that approach, drafters commonly insert an interpretation clause into contracts to the effect that if a provision ('the former provision') is inconsistent with another provision ('the latter provision'), then the former provision prevails over the latter 'to the extent of the inconsistency'.

See also **INCONSISTENT PROVISIONS; PRECEDENCE CLAUSE.**

incontinent

Historically meaning 'unchaste' or 'subject to lewd desires': eg, priests might be defrocked for '*incontinent* living', or widows might be disinherited if 'found *incontinent*'. Many offences involving *incontinency* fell within the jurisdiction of the ecclesiastical courts; thus, a vicar might be charged with committing 'the foul crime of adultery, fornication, or *incontinency*': *Schultes v Hodgson* (1822) 1 Add 318, 322; 162 ER 111, 113.

incorporeal

Intangible, not physical—usually of interests in property.

See **corporeal / incorporeal; incorporeal hereditament.**

incorporeal hereditament

Originally, an intangible (non-physical) property right that is 'heritable'—ie, capable of passing on death by will or intestacy. Now used more generally to describe an intangible property right that 'runs with' land (ie, passes on transfer of the land), such as an easement.

See **corporeal / incorporeal; hereditament.**

'INCREASED COSTS' CLAUSE

Ideally hyphenated: *increased-costs clause* (because *increased-costs* is a phrasal adjective). A clause allowing a party to an agreement to pass on to another party increases in costs or expenses resulting from changes in the financial or regulatory environment. For example, a lender may include such a clause to pass on to the buyer any increases in the costs of making or maintaining the loan.

See also **HYPHENS**.

incumbrance

A variant of *encumbrance*, so rare these days that readers are likely to regard it as a misspelling (examples include *Care Act 2014*, s 70(6)(a); *Conveyancing Act 1919* (NSW), s 7). Prefer *encumbrance*.

See **encumbrance**.

indebtedness

The state of being indebted. Avoid using *indebtedness* as a wordy substitute for *debt*: 'The bank confirmed that it held unsecured *indebtedness* [prefer: *debts*] from X Co Ltd.'

indefeasibility of title

In the context of registered land, a quality that protects a registered title from being set aside for a defect in a predecessor's title or a defect in the transaction by which the current registered owner acquired title. The quality applies not only to ownership of the land, but also to ownership of lesser interests in the land, such as mortgages and leases; once registered, each is 'indefeasible'. The term is used particularly (but not exclusively) for land under the Torrens system of land registration. There are two variants.

1. *Immediate indefeasibility.* A registered title is indefeasible immediately on registration. For example, if a fraudster forges the signature of the owner (A) on a transfer of the land to a purchaser (B) who is innocent of the fraud, the transfer, of itself, would be void. But on registration of the transfer, B's title becomes indefeasible, despite the fraud; ie, A cannot set it aside.
2. *Deferred indefeasibility.* A registered title, despite registration, is liable to be set aside because of the circumstances in which it was acquired; but if it not set aside, the next holder's title (on its registration) is indefeasible—ie, indefeasibility is 'deferred' until the next holder's registration. To continue the above example of fraud, A *can* set aside B's registered title; but if A does not do so before B transfers the land (or an interest in the land) to an innocent person (C) who becomes registered, C's title is indefeasible—ie, A cannot set aside C's title.

Different land registration systems add different qualifications: eg, has B (in variant 1) or C (in variant 2) paid value? Also (of course), the relevant variant turns on the wording of the land registration statute—which may not be a model of clarity: eg, *Frazer v Walker* [1967] 1 AC 569. Most modern land registration statutes favour immediate indefeasibility.

Further reading

- Kevin Gray and Susan Francis Gray, *Elements of Land Law*, 5th edn (Oxford University Press, 2009) [2.2.16]–[2.2.28]
- Brendan Edgeworth (ed), *Butt's Land Law*, 7th edn (Lawbook, 2017) [12.460]–[12.550] (indefeasibility in Commonwealth jurisdictions)

indemnify (variants of)

To *indemnify* is to make good, or to promise to make good, someone else's loss. *Indemnify* is often encrusted with other words or phrases, which are almost always superfluous, as in the following variants.

'indemnify and hold harmless'

Indemnity derives from *indemnis* = suffering no damage, harmless. So to *indemnify* is to *hold harmless*—making the additional *hold harmless* redundant. An indemnity that does not hold harmless is not a genuine indemnity. The redundancy is a lawyer's reflexive pairing, too familiar to be noticed. But like other redundancies in legal writing, it can be dangerous, given the presumption that all words in a legal document have a purpose. A court faced with interpreting a promise to *indemnify and hold harmless* may well strive to find a purpose in each term, as occurred in a US decision:

> A promise to *indemnify* entitles the promisee to actively sue the promisor to enforce the indemnity (a sword, not a mere shield); but a promise to *hold harmless* gives the promisee a merely defensive right—a right *not to be bothered* by the promisor if the promisor seeks to recover from the promisee. So held in *Queen Villas Homeowners Association v TCB Property Management* 56 Cal Rptr 3d 528 (Cal Ct App, 2007). It seems unlikely that the drafter expected that interpretation.

'indemnify and keep indemnified'

Logically, *keep indemnified* adds nothing to *indemnified*; an indemnity must be a continuing ('keeping') indemnity—otherwise it is not a useful indemnity. Lawyers who favour '*keep* indemnified' may fear that an obligation to *indemnify* might be interpreted as a once-only obligation, spent immediately it is performed for the first time. But no principle of law so holds; nor is it likely that context would compel such a strained implication. Nevertheless, the pairing lives on, and is even encouraged:

> 'Note in [this precedent] the obligation to "keep" indemnified, which makes it clear that the obligation to indemnify is a continuing obligation, so that if an indemnifying event occurs, and then further losses materialise at a later date, the [party] will be indemnified in respect of those later losses as well.' [R Christou, *Boilerplate: Practical Clauses*, 7th edn (Thomson Reuters, 2015) para 5-088]

'full and sufficient indemnity'

In addition to '*keeping* indemnified', some drafters require an indemnity to be '*full* and *sufficient*'. Is this pairing needed? In defence of the pairing, *full* and *sufficient* may not be true synonyms: a *full* indemnity must be a *sufficient* indemnity, but a *sufficient* indemnity might not be a *full* indemnity. But the key question is not whether the words are synonyms, but whether the pairing is needed at all. An *indemnity* must logically be a *full* indemnity (unless deliberately intended as a partial indemnity only); and unless an *indemnity* is a *sufficient* indemnity, it is no indemnity at all. So in almost all cases, it is enough to say: 'A gives B an *indemnity*' (or better, preferring the verb form, 'A *indemnifies* B').

Further reading

Jeffery S Ammon, 'Indemnification: Banish the Word!' (2014) 93 *Michigan Bar Journal* 44 (suggesting replacing *indemnify against* with *pay for*—'A will *indemnify B against* loss suffered by B' becomes 'A will *pay B for* loss suffered by B')

See also **guarantee / indemnity / warranty**; **guarantee (verb)**; **guaranty**.

indemnity

See **guarantee / indemnity / warranty; indemnify (variants of)**.

INDENTING (OF TEXT)

See **CLAUSE STRUCTURE**.

indenture

A deed made between two or more parties, evidencing some act or transaction between them. The name comes from the practice of 'indenting' (Latin: *dentus*, tooth). Originally, when deeds were concise, duplicate originals (one for each party) were written out:

> 'on the same skin or parchment, with some words or letters of the alphabet written between them, through which the parchment was cut in acute angles, *instar dentium*, from which they acquired the name of indentures, or deeds indented, in such a manner as to leave half the word on one part, and half on the other.' (*Cruise's Digest* (1818) vol 4, 'Deed', [23])

This was a protection against forgery; if necessary to prove genuineness, the two halves could later be lined up. When deeds became longer, they would be written on separate parchments, with the parchments then put one on top of the other, and the tops or sides indented identically; here too, the copies could be lined up to verify genuineness. Indenting eventually developed into a necessity for the validity of a deed: *Stile's Case* (1572) 5 Co Rep 20b; 77 ER 80. However, statutes in the mid-19th century dispensed with indenting as a requirement for validity (eg, *Real Property Act 1845*, s 5), and the practice fell into disuse.

See **DEED (document)**; **DEED POLL**.

INDEX

Plural, *indices* or *indexes*. Indexes are rare in legal documents. They were were for a time seen in lengthy UK and Commonwealth statutes, but have now largely fallen out of legislative use. They were (and are) almost never seen in private-sector legal documents. Unless a document is very long, it is doubtful whether an index adds much value over and above a table of contents. And in any case, modern searching tooks usually make it easy for readers to find words or phrases.

See also **TABLE OF CONTENTS**.

indicate

Indicate can be an imprecise word, carrying a range of possible meanings.

1. Most directly, *indicate* can mean *state*—in which case, use *state*.
2. Less directly, *indicate* can mean *point to*, which may indeed be its etymological basis: *Papadopoulos v Goodwin* [1982] 1 NSWLR 413, 417 (Wooten J). An Australian court held that a statutory requirement that an instrument *indicate* certain matters is satisfied if the instrument points to or refers to another instrument in which the matters are stated: *Papadopoulos v Goodwin*, above, and on appeal *Goodwin v Papadopolous* (1985) NSW ConvR 55-256 (Mahoney JA).
3. Less directly again, *indicate* can mean *suggest*: as in 'The judge *indicated* [meaning: *suggested*] that counsel should deal with that argument.'

Many legal writers seem seduced by the apparent formality of *indicate*. But precision is more important than formality. Where the meaning is *state*, or *point to*, or *suggest*, prefer that word over *indicate*.

INDICATIVE (MOOD)

See **SUBJUNCTIVE / INDICATIVE.**

indicia / indicium

Strictly, *indicium* (sign, token) is the Latin singular, and *indicia* the Latin plural. *Indicium* (singular) is occasionally seen:

> 'But it is well established that the most telling *indicium* is the identity of the person who has the right to control the employee's method of work.' [*Shell UK Ltd v Total UK Ltd* [2009] EWHC 540, [207] (David Steel J)]

However, in standard usage, *indicia* is now commonly seen for both singular (eg, 'the title deed was his single *indicia* of ownership') and plural (eg, 'he had three *indicia* of title'). Nevertheless, a careful writer will distinguish:

> 'In the passage quoted above [from a patent application], the phrase "an *indicia*" is used. *Indicia* is a plural noun which should not be preceded by the word "an". This phrase is used throughout the description of the invention and in the claims. It is not immediately clear whether [the applicant] was referring to a single *indicium* or to a group of two or more *indicia*. Later in this judgment when I refer to "an *indicia*", I do so because I am referring to the language used in the body of the specification or the claims.' [*Long v Comptroller General of Patents* [2010] EWHC 2810 (Ch), [6] (Morgan J; italics added)]

Indigenous / indigenous

The conventions are: (1) capital 'I' (*Indigenous*) when referring to a country's first inhabitants; and (2) lower-case 'i' when referring to original inhabitants (of any country) more generally. For example:

> 'We know that *Indigenous* Australians care for their land. They have much to teach *indigenous* peoples everywhere.'

indirect loss

See **consequential loss**.

individual (noun)

In legal usage, a reference to an *individual* is normally a reference to a human being, as distinct from some other legal 'person' such as a corporation. So a statute that allows the appointment of an *individual* as a trustee does not normally allow the appointment of a corporation: *Jasmine Trustees Ltd v Wells & Hind* [2007] 1 All ER 1142. However, meaning always depends on context, and in some contexts *individual* can include a corporation, as in *Société United Docks v Government of Mauritius* [1985] AC 585 ('the [constitutional] right of the *individual* to protection … from deprivation of property without compensation').

Compare **person**.

inducidae

In Scots law, a pause or period of grace in legal proceedings to allow a person to perform an act (eg, pay a debt, or appear in court).

inexpedient

See **expedient**.

infant / minor

Usage

General

In general usage, *infant* is a generic term for very young person. *Minor* (Latin: a smaller person) is particularly appropriate where the context is not merely age but legal capacity—specifically, a person under the age of legal majority (conventionally 21, but now 18 in many jurisdictions). Hence: 'Tom could not make a contract, because he was a *minor*', rather than 'Tom could not make a contract, because he was an *infant*.'

Legal

Traditionally, in legal usage, *infant* means a person who has not attained legal majority (21, or 18). This usage has an eminent pedigree: eg, *Coke's Institute of the Laws of England* (1628) 170–71; Blackstone's *Commentaries on the Laws of England* (1765) book 1, ch 17, 463. The *Australian Constitution* (1901) uses it in the same sense: *King v Jones* (1972) 128 CLR 221, 239 (Barwick CJ).

In more modern times, however, *infant* and *minor* tend to be used interchangeably to denote a person under the age of legal majority:

- 'B was born on 20 May 1969 and accordingly she ceased to be a *minor*, or *infant* to use the quaint language of the law, on 20 May 1987.' [*Re F* [1990] 2 AC 1, 7 (Lord Donaldson)]
- [T]he Crown … had both the power and the duty to protect the persons and property of those unable to do so for themselves, a category which included both *minors* (formerly described as *infants*) …' [*Re F* [1990] 2 AC 1, 57 (Lord Brandon)]
- 'In text books and statutes the words "infant" and "minor" are interchangeable and are used to describe a person who has not come of age.' [Irish Law Reform Commission, *The Law Relating to the Age of Majority, the Age for Marriage and some Connected Subjects*, Working Paper No 2, 1977, [2.1]]

In Scots law (uniquely, it seems), a *minor* is a person who has ceased to be a *pupil* (ie, a boy under 14, or a girl under 12), but has not yet reached 18.

Context

Sometimes, context may make one word more appropriate than another. For example:

> 'The Children's Court of New South Wales focuses on individuals under the age of 18 years, variously described as "minors", "infants", "children" and "young persons" depending on context.' [*P v NSW Trustee and Guardian* [2015] NSWSC 579, [27] (Lindsay J)]

Context may also give *minor* an idiosyncratic meaning. For example:

> A testator directed that income from a property be used to maintain his daughter's children during their *minority*, with the principal to be distributed to them when the youngest attained 25. Held, in the context of the rest of the will, *minority* meant the age of 25: *Milroy v Milroy*

(1844) 14 Sim 48, 54–55; 60 ER 274, 277 (Shadwell V-C, describing the will as 'very strange and bewildering').

See also **nonage**; **pupil**.

infer

See **imply / infer**.

INFINITIVES (SPLITTING)

See **SPLIT INFINITIVES**.

infra

Latin: below; further on (in this discussion). A Latinism sufficiently accepted to be regarded as standard English, although it has no intrinsic advantage over *below*. Often combined with *vide* ('see') to become *vide infra*—which definitely has no advantage over *see below*.

injuria

Latin: a legal wrong, an insult. The Latin loses nothing by translation into English. The Latin term often appears in longer Latin maxims, which also lose nothing by translation into English, as in these examples:

- *injuria non excusat injuriam*: one wrong does not excuse another
- *injuria non praesumitur*: wrong is not presumed
- *volenti non fit injuria*: damage suffered by consent gives no cause of action
- *actus Dei nemini facit injuriam*: an act of God does a wrong to no one.

See also **act of God; damnum sine (absque) injuria; volenti non fit injuria**.

innominate term

A contractual provision, the remedies for breach of which turn not on an initial characterisation as 'condition' or 'warranty' but rather on the consequences of breach. Sometimes called an 'intermediate term'. In some circumstances, breach of an innominate term gives rise to a right in damages only; but if the breach deprives the innocent party of substantially the whole benefit they were to obtain from the contract—or (as it is sometimes put) where the breach goes to the root of the contract—then the innocent party is entitled to terminate the contract: *Hong Kong Fir Shipping Co Ltd v Kawasaki Kisen Kaisha Ltd* [1962] 2 QB 26, 69–70 (Lord Diplock).

Further reading

Halsbury's Laws of England, 'Contract' (vol 22, 2019) [349] (innominate or intermediate terms)

See also **condition / warranty**.

Inns of Chancery

The institutions at which law students who hoped to be admitted to the Bar were trained. The number of Inns of Chancery fluctuated, but by 1500 had settled at nine. Their educational functions virtually ceased in the middle of the 17th century, but they continued to provide accommodation and social facilities for lawyers. They were eventually affiliated to the Inns of Court, and were wound up in Victorian times.

Further reading

- JH Baker, *An Introduction to English Legal History*, 4th edn (Oxford University Press, 2002) 160–61
- Sir Robert Megarry, *Inns Ancient and Modern* (Selden Society Lecture, 1972; Wildy, Simmonds & Hill, 1989) 27–48

See also **Inns of Court**.

Inns of Court

The four institutions through which persons are called to the English Bar. They are Lincoln's Inn, Inner Temple, Middle Temple, and Gray's Inn. By long convention, they are listed in that order.

See also **bencher**.

inquire

See **enquire / inquire**.

inst

Abbreviation for *instant*, used (archaically) to refer to the current month: eg, 'Thank you for your letter of the 25th *inst*.' Contrasted to *ult* (abbrev for *ultimo*), meaning last month, and *prox* (abbrev for *proximo*) meaning next month. All three usages are obsolete.

See also **instant**.

instance

The word *instance*—like the word *case*—can herald an innate wordiness. If it does, prune (and rewrite the sentence as necessary).

- 'In most *instances* juries have 12 members.' [*Prefer*: Most juries have 12 members.]
- 'In this *instance*, he was negligent.' [*Prefer*: This time he was negligent.]
- 'In the first *instance*, …' [*Prefer*: First, …]

See also **case**.

instant

Meaning 'this month'

A lawyer's archaic (and, to modern ears, pretentious) substitute for 'this month':

> 'Thank you for your letter of the 25th *instant*.'

Modern usage prefers 'of this month', or (better still) specifies the month: eg, 'Thank you for your letter of 25 June.' The pretentiousness is heightened by using the abbreviation *inst*:

> 'Thank you for your letter of the 25th *inst*.'

Whether abbreviated or in full, the usage is obsolete.

in the instant case

In the instant case means *in the present case*, or (better, because shorter) *in this case*—so why not say so? Indeed, often it means simply *here*—in which case, say *here*. For example:

- 'In that case, as in this one, the claimant suffered an injury at work … *In the instant case* [prefer: *In this case*; *Here*], the claimant … claimed …' [*Hayward v Zurich Insurance Company plc* [2016] UKSC 48; [2016] 3 WLR 637, [1] (Lord Clarke)]
- 'The [previous decisions] are thus of limited assistance *in the instant case* [prefer: *in this case*; *here*] …' [*Commissioner of Taxation v Anstis* [2010] HCA 40, [34]; (2010) 241 CLR 443, 457 (French CJ, Gummow, Kiefel, and Bell JJ)]

See also **inst**; **proximo**; **ultimo**.

instant case (in the)

See **instant**.

instanter

Latin: immediately; at once. The Latin has no advantage over the English translation. The *Shorter Oxford Dictionary* characterises *instanter* as both 'archaic' and 'jocular'—epithets that may surprise lawyers who persist in using it.

instantly

Instantly carries the same sense as *immediately*. And just as context can colour the apparent urgency of *immediately*, so it can with *instantly*. Thus, a right to require payment '*instantly* on demand' almost always does not require payment then and there, on the spot, but allows time after the demand for the debtor to write a cheque, or if the creditor refuses the cheque, time to obtain cash: *Massey v Sladen* (1868) LR 4 Ex 13, 18 (Kelly CB).

See also **immediately**; **on demand**.

institutional lease

A lease of a kind that will generally be acceptable to an institutional investor, such as a superannuation fund.

instruct

In normal usage, to teach or guide. In legal usage, to appoint a lawyer to act on your behalf, including providing the lawyer with the information on which he or she is to act.

instrument

In its widest sense, any formal legal document—including a contract, deed, will, notice, statute, regulation, or bylaw. Where an *instrument* embodies a contract, legal usage distinguishes between (1) an *instrument under seal*, meaning a deed, and (2) an *instrument under hand*, meaning any signed document other than a deed.

Some statutes widen the meaning of *instrument* beyond the normal concept of a document to include anything on which there is writing, or anything on which there are marks, figures, symbols, or perforations able to be interpreted, or even anything from which sounds, images or writings can be reproduced: see, eg, *Evidence Act 1995* (NSW), Dictionary.

In other contexts, *instrument* clearly means something other than a formal legal document. For example, an 'instrument of crime' is a weapon; in this sense, even land may be an *instrument* where used in the commission of an offence (as in *Director of Public Prosecutions v George* [2008] SASC 330; (2008) 102 SASR 246).

Further reading

'Instrument', in *Law Words* (Centre for Plain Legal Language, University of Sydney 1995) 41; www.clarity-international.net/plain-language-resources/general-resources/

insure / assure

See **assure / ensure / insure**.

intends to ...

Intention is a notoriously difficult concept. For a person to *intend* to do something, how firmly must they be committed to doing it? Must they subjectively (ie, actually) intend to do it, or may they be taken to have intended to do it because reasonable onlookers would have inferred intention from the nature of the act or the reasonably expected outcome?

In the absence of definition, *intends to* generally implies a subjective (ie, actual) intention: *SZTAL v Minister for Immigration and Border Protection* [2017] HCA 34; (2017) 262 CLR 362. However, as a matter of evidence, in some areas of law a person's intent may have to be deduced from the natural and probable consequences of their actions: *R v Moloney* [1985] AC 905, 928–29 (Lord Bridge). As to how far their planning must have progressed: generally, to *intend* to do something requires moving 'out of the zone of contemplation ... into the valley of decision': *Fleet Electrics Ltd v Jacey Investments Ltd* [1956] 3 All ER 99, 102 (Lord Evershed MR). It requires more than mere 'contemplation': *R v Hyam* [1975] AC 55, 73, 74 (Lord Hailsham LC). It requires a resolve that is more than 'embryonic, tentative, provisional, conditional or remote in time', but it need not be 'definite, firm or clear': *Newtown Village No 2 Pty Ltd v Magtio Pty Ltd* [2016] NSWSC 749, [45].

The variability of these factors highlights the need to carefully define the nature of the contemplated *intention.*

INTENSIFIERS

Words or phrases that reinforce the impact of other words or phrases. Most intensifiers seek to heighten a word or phrase: eg, *significantly, definitely, really, highly, extremely.* Some seek to diminish a word or phrase: eg, *barely, relatively, minimally*. While intensifiers have a place in legal writing—'the judgment departed *significantly* from earlier court decisions'—most are best omitted. Instead, let the nouns and verbs do their own work, unadorned. Indeed, intensifiers can be counter-productive. Readers may infer from an intensifier that the writer lacks confidence in the strength of the statement (see *Further reading*, below). An example is the use of *clearly* or *obviously* to bolster an argument: if something is 'true', then to say it is '*clearly* true' or '*obviously* true' usually adds nothing—and may indeed cause the reader to ponder whether it is true.

Further reading

Lance N Long and William F Christiansen, 'When Judges (Subconsciously) Attack: The Theory of Argumentative Threat and the Supreme Court' (2013) 91 *Oregon Law Review* 933 (positing that intensifiers betray the writer's insecurity about a weak argument)

intention

See **intends to ….**

inter alia

Latin: among other things. A Latinism that has probably become part of idiomatic English. Nevertheless, the translation 'among other things' will do just fine. A variant, less commonly seen, is *inter alios* (among other persons, used for both males and females)—or, even less commonly, *inter alias* (among other females, to distinguish from *inter alios* = among other males).

inter apices juris

Latin: among the subtleties of the law: *Tayleur v Wildin* (1869) LR 3 Ex 303, 305 (Kelly CB). Prefer the English translation.

inter partes

Latin: between parties. Used in particular to describe proceedings where two or more parties are represented (compare *ex parte*), or to describe a deed between two or more persons.

See also **ex parte**.

inter se

Latin: between (*or* among) themselves; between (*or* among) persons or things. Like many other Latinisms, this one has no particular legal nuance. To retain the Latin in the face of an adequate English translation is mere pedantry:

- '[T]here is also nothing illogical about a conclusion that each of successive insurers is potentially liable in full, with rights of contribution *inter se* [prefer: *between themselves*].' [*Zurich Insurance PLC UK Branch v International Energy Group Ltd* [2015] UKSC 33; [2016] AC 509, [48] (Lord Mance)]
- '[That case] concerned the content of the fiduciary duties of members of a partnership *inter se* [prefer: *among themselves*].' [*Howard v Commissioner of Taxation* [2014] HCA 21, [34]; (2014) 253 CLR 83, 100 [34] (French CJ and Keane J)]

Sometimes, *inter se* is added out of habit or excessive caution—where in truth it is superfluous. If so, delete it:

> 'But if an airline company makes a contract with a number of other airline companies … for the mutual rendering of services on the terms that no money is to become payable between the various parties ~~*inter se*~~ [delete], I do not think that a liquidator [can ignore the contract].' [*British Eagle International Airlines Ltd v Cie Nationale Air France* [1975] 1 WLR 758, 761 (Lord Morris)]

See also **between**; **FOREIGN (NON-ENGLISH) WORDS AND PHRASES**.

inter vivos

Latin: between living persons. Generally used to describe an instrument or transaction where all parties are alive (such as a conveyance or transfer of land, or the grant of a lease), as distinct from one where the relevant party is dead (such as a will).

Although this Latinism is well entrenched in legal usage, no meaning is lost by an appropriate English translation, as in the following examples.

- 'The [nil rate tax band] was of no possible significance to an *inter vivos gift* [prefer: *a gift from one living person to another*]: it applies only on death.' [*McGraddie v McGraddie* [2013] UKSC 58; [2013] 1 WLR 2477, [25] (Lord Reed)]
- '[In that decision] Windeyer J expressed the view that the method of acquisition [of property by the Commonwealth] might be by "any process known to the law", including by voluntary disposition *inter vivos* [prefer: *while alive*] or [by] testamentary disposition in favour of the Commonwealth.' [*Paliflex Pty Ltd v Chief Commissioner of State Revenue* (NSW) (2003) 219 CLR 325, [44] (plurality)]

Sometimes *inter vivos* can simply be deleted, eg:

- '~~Inter vivos~~ disputes between unmarried cohabiting couples are still governed by the ordinary law.' [*Stack v Dowden* [2007] UKHL 17, [44]; [2007] 2 AC 432, 450 (Baroness Hale).] Delete *Inter vivos*—because persons who are cohabiting must be alive, even if their relationship is not. Alternatively, substitute: '*Except for disputes over wills, disputes between …*'
- 'The Authority must not sell, lease, exchange or otherwise dispose of or deal with property acquired by gift ~~inter vivos~~, devise or bequest …' [*Sydney Harbour Foreshore Authority Act 1998* (NSW), s 25(1)] Delete *inter vivos*—because the provision covers all gifts, by persons alive or dead.

See also **FOREIGN (NON-ENGLISH) WORDS AND PHRASES**.

interact with one another

People who 'interact' do so with one another. Therefore, delete *with one another*. For example:

- 'These [three statutory limitations] clearly interact ~~with one another~~.' [*A-G v News Group Newspapers Ltd* [1987] QB 1, 17 (Parker LJ)]
- 'Where two people reside in the same premises, it does not seem to me to be [unusual] that violence between them occurred in the place where they usually interacted ~~with one another~~.' [*R v Thawer* [2009] NSWCCA 158, [44] (Howie J)]

interest

Meaning

A word of many meanings, depending on context. For example, *interest* can mean:

- the price charged for the use of money
- a type of property right (*interest* in land; *interest* in possession; *interest* in expectancy)
- a requirement that something be considered or evaluated (*interests* of justice).

Make clear to your reader which meaning of 'interest' you intend.

'interested person'

A person with an 'interest' in a state of affairs or litigation. The 'interest' may be intangible or emotional—as where planning statutes allow 'interested' citizens to challenge proposed development. Or it may be tangible and involve actual or hoped-for proprietary or quasi-proprietary ownership—as where probate legislation allows *interested persons* to take proceedings. For example:

- the creditor of a beneficiary under a will has an 'interest' sufficient to challenge the validity of the will (but a creditor of the estate has not): *Randall v Randall* [2016] EWCA Civ 494; [2016] 3 WLR 1217

- a claim to legal professional privilege is not a property 'interest' under insolvency legislation: *Shlosberg v Avonwick Holdings Ltd* [2016] 3 WLR 1330.

See also **person**.

intermeddle

To interfere with, or deliberately take part in, without legal justification. The word is quaint, and plain-language synonyms are hard to find. *Interfere* goes only part of the way, because while all intermeddling involves interference of some kind, not all interference is substantial enough to constitute intermeddling. *Meddling with* might be better, as it carries the sense of doing something without justification.

The act of intermeddling can have significant legal consequences for the intermeddler. Thus, a person who intermeddles in the affairs of a trust may be foisted with the responsibilities of a trustee (a trustee *de son tort*), and a person who intermeddles in the administration of a deceased estate may be foisted with the responsibilities of an executor (an executor *de son tort*).

See also **de son tort**.

intermediate term

See **innominate term**.

interment / internment

An *interment* is a burial; an *internment* is a confinement in a prison or camp, often without trial. Both involve loss of liberty, but an interment makes the loss permanent.

interpretation / construction (of documents)

Some lawyers distinguish *interpretation* (of a document) from *construction* (of a document). In their view:

- *Interpretation* is the process of ascertaining what the parties meant by the expressions they used in the document. The process is restricted to those expressions, although it includes asking what the expressions would mean to a reasonable person possessing the background knowledge reasonably available to the parties at the time of the contract: *Investors Compensation Scheme Limited v West Bromwich Building Society* [1997] UKHL 28; [1998] 1 WLR 896, 913 (Lord Hoffmann).
- *Construction* is a wider process. It takes account (if required) of terms which the parties did not actually use, but which courts can (in accordance with settled principles governing the implication of terms) imply to fill gaps left by the parties. See, eg, *R v Spens* [1991] 1 WLR 624, 630 (Watkins LJ); *Life Insurance Co of Australia Ltd v Phillips* (1925) 36 CLR 60, 78 (Isaacs J); *Sembcorp Marine Ltd v PPL Holdings Pte Ltd* [2013] SGCA 43; [2013] 4 SLR 193, [27]–[33] (Sundaresh Menon CJ). In the context of legislation, *construction* includes ascertaining how parliament would have wished its words to be applied in accordance with settled principles and presumptions: Lord Sales, 'Legislative Intention, Interpretation, and the Principle of Legality' (2018) 40 *Statute Law Review* 53, 57 (giving the example of 'construing' legislation in the light of the presumption that parliament would not have wished its enactment to breach the UK's obligations under international law).

But other lawyers regard the distinction between *interpretation* and *construction* as problematic: eg, *B & B Constructions (Aust) Pty Ltd v Brian A Cheeseman & Associates Pty Ltd* (1994) 35 NSWLR 227, 244–45 (Mahoney JA). They use *construction* and *interpretation* interchangeably:

- '[T]he [Planning Practice Guidance], whilst a potential aid to *construction* could not itself define the meaning in law of the provisions of the 2015 Order. The correct *interpretation* of the 2015 Order is a matter of law for the court.' [*East Hertfordshire District Council v Secretary of State for Communities and Local Government* [2017] EWHC 465 (Admin), [21] (Dove J)]
- 'In the area of statutory *interpretation* and *construction*, courts must be wary of propounding rigid rules.' [*Collector of Customs v Agfa Gevaert Limited* (1996) 186 CLR 389, 410 (Brennan CJ, Dawson, Toohey, Gaudron and McHugh JJ)]

Most text writers eschew any distinction between *interpretation* and *construction*: see, eg, Kim Lewison, *The Interpretation of Contracts*, 6th edn (Sweet & Maxwell, 2015) [2.01]. In line with this approach, a statutory provision headed '*Construction*' of treaties was held to govern the *interpretation* of treaties: *Dotcom v United States of America* [2014] NZSC 24; [2014] 1 NZLR 355, [164] (McGrath and Blanchard JJ).

Assuming that there is no relevant distinction, prefer *interpretation*. Most non-lawyers would instinctively assume that *construction* has to do with the erection of buildings, not the meaning of words.

Further reading

- Edwin W Patterson, 'The Interpretation and Construction of Contracts' (1964) 64 *Columbia Law Review* 833 (arguing for preserving the distinction between 'construction' and 'interpretation')
- JW Carter, *The Construction of Commercial Contracts* (Hart, 2013) [1-05] (discussing the distinction)

See also **CANONS OF CONSTRUCTION (INTERPRETATION)**; **construction**.

interprétation conforme

French: the European Community law principle of interpretation (in English usually called the 'principle of consistent interpretation') under which national courts must interpret a national law consistently with a Community law.

Further reading

Katrine Sawyer, 'The Principle of "Interprétation Conforme": How Far Can Courts Go when Interpreting National Legislation Consistently with European Community Law?" [2007] *Statute Law Review* 165

INTERPRETATION CLAUSES

Function

While definitions specify the meanings of words or phrases used in a document, interpretation clauses give more general directions about how the document is to be interpreted. They often take a standard form, cut-and-pasted into a document without close attention to whether they are relevant to the particular transaction. Sometimes they seek to oust one or more of the general principles of interpretation that would otherwise apply. As with definitions, interpretation clauses are often expressed to be subject to contrary indication in the document.

Standard interpretation clauses cover matters such as those in the following list. (For further discussion of some of the matters, see cross-references in **bold**.)

- The singular includes the plural and vice versa (see **SINGULAR / PLURAL**).
- Headings are for convenience only and do not affect the interpretation of the document (see **HEADINGS**).
- A reference to a document includes any variation or replacement of it (see **TEXTUAL AMENDMENTS**).
- A reference to a clause, annexure, or schedule is a reference to a clause, annexure, or schedule in the document (see **ANNEXURES**).
- A reference to a statute, ordinance, code, or other law includes regulations made under it, and consolidations, amendments, re-enactments, or replacements of them (see **CITATION OF LEGISLATION**).
- The word 'person' includes an individual, a firm, a body corporate, a partnership, a joint venture, an unincorporated body or association, or any authority (see **person**).
- A reference to a particular person includes the person's executors, administrators, successors, substitutes (including persons taking by novation), and assigns (see **heirs, executors, administrators, successors, and assigns**).
- A reference to a body or authority includes a reference to any body or authority that replaces it.
- A right in favour of two or more persons benefits them jointly and each of them individually (see **joint and several**).
- An obligation undertaken by two or more persons binds them jointly and each of them individually (see **joint and several**).
- When introducing an example, the words 'including', 'for example', or 'such as', do not limit the meaning of the words to that example or examples of a similar kind (see **eiusdem generis**).
- This document is not to be interpreted against the interest of the party who drafted it (see **contra proferentem**).
- If something is to be done on a public or bank holiday, it may be done on the next business day (see **business day**).
- If something is to be done by close of business on a day, it must be done by 5 pm on that day (see **TIME**).
- If something is done after 5 pm on a day [business day], it is taken to be done on the next day [business day] (see **TIME**).
- A reference to any thing (including any amount) is a reference to the whole and each part of it (see **whole or any part of**).

Issues with interpretation clauses

Self-evident provisions

Avoid interpretation provisions that are self-evident. For example, the following seems little more than a parody of legal style:

> 'In these Regulations any reference to a Regulation is a reference to a Regulation of these Regulations, any reference in a Regulation to a paragraph is a reference to a paragraph of that Regulation and any reference in a paragraph to a sub-paragraph is a reference to a sub-paragraph of that paragraph.' [*Education (School Governing Bodies) Regulations 1981*, cl 2(3)]

Imposing substantive obligations

Interpretation clauses should 'interpret', not impose substantive obligations. This is not to deny that an interpretation clause *can* impose substantive obligations; rather, that it should not seek to do so. Nevertheless, drafters sometimes ignore this admonition, with sometimes unexpected consequences. In the following example, the 'interpretation' clause effectively made a person liable for another's debts.

> Mr Martin and Mr Gold were in the business of property development together. They jointly owned certain properties, which they jointly mortgaged to a bank as security for loans. The mortgage documents, in the bank's standard form, used the term 'mortgagor' (singular), which it defined as 'the mortgagor named as such on page 1 hereof'. The 'mortgagor' named on page 1 was *both* Mr Martin and Mr Gold. The interpretation clause (clause 1) stated that where 'the mortgagor' included more than one person, it was to be interpreted as referring to all of them, and further (introducing a substantive obligation) that their obligations under the mortgage were to be joint and several. In clause 2, 'the mortgagor' covenanted to repay all moneys which the bank advanced to 'the mortgagor'. Mr Martin separately owned certain properties, which he mortgaged to the bank as security for loans to him personally. Held, the interpretation clause had the effect that 'mortgagor' was to be read distributively, making Mr Gold liable for Mr Martin's debts: *AIB Group (UK) Ltd v Martin* [2001] UKHL 63; [2002] 1 WLR 94.

'subject to contrary intention'

Interpretation clauses are often hedged with the qualification 'subject to contrary intention' or similar. Although lawyers add the qualification more out of habit than forethought, courts must give effect to it. See discussion under '**unless the context otherwise requires**'.

Further reading

Ross Carter, 'Interpretation Acts—Are they, and (how) do they make for, great law?' *The Loophole* (Nov 2020) 2 (the history and purpose of statutory-interpretation Acts)

See also **DEFINITIONS; unless the context otherwise requires**

interpretative / interpretive

Proper usage is *interpretative* (not 'interpretive'), being the adjective formed on the noun 'interpret*ation*'. Perhaps writers favour the shorter word because the longer seems such a mouthful: eg, *R v Secretary of State for the Home Department* [2015] EWCA Civ 1195; [2016] WLR 673, [40], [48], [51] (Sales LJ, referring to '*interpretive* presumptions' and '*interpretive* principles').

See also **preventive / preventative**.

interrogatories

A procedure by which a litigating party serves on another a request for information relating to the matter in dispute between them. In more recent usage, often termed 'requests for further information', following the Woolf Reforms of civil procedure in England and Wales. The purpose is to allow the serving party to obtain information by which to test the strength or weakness of the other party's case; the procedure therefore serves the public purpose of encouraging disputes to be settled before trial. Unless procedural rules compel it, prefer the simpler 'requests for further information'.

See also **WOOLF REFORMS**.

INTERRUPTIVE PHRASES

See **EMBEDDED (NESTED) INFORMATION**.

intestacy / intestate

Intestacy is death without a valid will (either no will at all, or a will that does not comply with the necessary formalities). *Intestate* can be either a noun or an adjective: 'This *intestate*'s name was John. Tragically, he was an *intestate* pauper.'

intra vires

Latin: within power. As with its opposite—*ultra vires*—this Latinism is commonplace in business, bureaucratic and legislative language, and for lawyers can be useful legal shorthand. Nevertheless, an appropriate English translation always suffices. For example:

- '[The issue of shares] was clearly *intra vires* [prefer: *within the legal power of*] the directors. But, *intra vires* [prefer: *within power*] though the issue may have been, the directors' power … may be attacked on the ground that it was not exercised for the purpose for which it was granted.' [*Howard Smith Ltd v Ampol Petroleum Ltd* [1974] AC 821, 834 (Lord Wilberforce)]
- '[An interpretation] of a delegated legislative instrument which is *intra vires* [prefer: *within the power conferred by*] the enabling statute is to be preferred to one which is *ultra vires* [prefer: *beyond the power conferred by*] the enabling statute.' [*Air Services Australia v Canadian Airlines International Ltd* (2000) 202 CLR 133, 216 (McHugh J)]

See also **ultra vires**.

INTRODUCTORY SYMBOLS

See **CITATION SYMBOLS**.

INVECTIVE

See **SARCASM**.

ipse dixit

Latin: he (she) said (in the sense of an assertion that rests only on the speaker's authority); a bare assertion, authoritative only to the extent that its speaker is authoritative. Prefer an appropriate English translation. For example:

- '[T]he bare *ipse dixit* [prefer: *assertion*] of a scientist, however eminent, … will normally carry little weight, for it cannot be tested by cross-examination nor independently appraised …' [*Davie v Magistrates of Edinburgh* 1953 SC 34, 40 (Lord Cooper)]
- 'To accept that claim we would simply be acting on the *ipse dixit* [prefer: *bare assertion*] of counsel.' [*Al Rawi v Security Service* [2011] UKSC 34; [2011] 3 WLR 388, [95] (Lord Kerr)]

ipsissima verba

Latin: the very words (in the sense of the precise words quoted). A lilting Latinism carrying little meaning to modern readers. Prefer the English. For example:

- 'It is worth returning to the *ipsissima verba* [prefer: *very words; actual words*] of Lord Steyn in *Daly*'s case.' [*E v Chief Constable of the Royal Ulster Constabulary* [2009] 1 AC 536, [53] (Lord Carswell, leading into a quotation of Lord Steyn's words in *Daly's* case)]
- 'If a witness can remember [the precise words used in a conversation], evidence should be given of the *ipsissima verba* [prefer: *the precise words*].' [*LMI Australasia Pty Ltd v Baulderstone Hornibrook Pty Ltd* [2001] NSWSC 688; (2001) 53 NSWLR 31, [8] (Barrett J)]

ipso facto

Latin: by that act (in the sense of occurring by that act alone); because of that act. This Latinism may have become accepted English. If so, there is no harm in retaining it. But then, there is no harm in replacing it with an appropriate 'plainer' English expression.

As often happens with Latinisms, the replacement exercise may show that there is no 'one size fits all' translation. For example:

- 'A question arises of whether a corporation which enters into a funding agreement is *ipso facto* [prefer: *by that very act*] a trading corporation within s 51(xx) of the Constitution.' [*Williams v Commonwealth* (2014) 252 CLR 416, 446, in argument]
- '[T]o sleep on particular premises at night, or to have one's meals on them by day, or both, ought not *ipso facto* [prefer: *by those very acts*] ... have the effect in law of making those premises a dwelling-house ...' [*MacMillan & Co Ltd v Rees* [1946] 1 All ER 675, 677, (Evershed J)]
- '[This] only applies to directly effective elections—ie, to elections which *ipso facto* [prefer: *by themselves alone*] result in what the people voted for, and not to ballots which require some further legal step to produce that result.' [*Moohan v Lord Advocate* [2015] 2 WLR 141, [47] (Lord Neuberger)]

In commercial legal practice, an '*ipso facto clause*' is a clause that produces a stated result regardless of a party's actual intention or actions. An example is a clause that specifies that a party to a contract may terminate the contract for default if bankruptcy or insolvency proceedings are started against the other party; the default occurs, and the right to terminate arises, 'by the fact of' the proceedings.

ipso jure

Latin: by the law itself (in the sense of by force of the law alone); by operation of law. To retain the Latin seems pure affectation in the face of an adequate English translation. For example:

- '[A]n English court has no jurisdiction either in a criminal or a civil matter to make orders purporting *ipso jure* [prefer: *by the law itself*; *by mere force of law*] to transfer moveable property situate [sic] abroad.' [*R v Cuthbertson* [1981] AC 470, 485 (Lord Diplock)]
- '[T]he *Gazette* notice operates *ipso jure* [prefer: *by operation of law*] to vest the land in the Commonwealth.' [*WH Blakeley & Co Pty Ltd v Commonwealth* (1953) 87 CLR 501, 519 (High Court of Australia)]

See also **situate at**.

irregardless

An unnecessary variant of *regardless* (perhaps eliding *irrespective* and *regardless*):

> 'I feel bound to inform you there is no word *irregardless* in the English language. The word is *regardless*.' [Renquist CJ, correcting an advocate during oral argument in US Supreme Court; reported in *ABA Journal*, 1 December 1986, 25]

Always prefer *regardless*:

- '[I]t is difficult to see how any allegation concerning the making of a secret profit ... could be sustained *irregardless of* [prefer: *regardless of*] any of the other points raised.' [*Salthill Properties Ltd v Royal Bank of Scotland* [2009] IEHC 207, [4.16] (Clarke J)]
- 'He could have formed the intention to steal *irregardless* [prefer: *regardless*] of whether he had the money to pay or not.' [*Ferooz v Public Defender* [1997] 2 SLR(R) 502, 509 [23] (Yong Pung How CJ)]
- '[I]n some species of constructive trust, equity imposes the trust *irregardless of* [prefer: *regardless of*] any confidence reposed in the trustee.' [*Breen v Williams* (1996) 186 CLR 71, [69] (Gummow J)]

irritancy

In Scots law, the forfeiture of a right, particularly in relation to feudal property or leases. Hence, *irritancy clause*—a clause in an agreement (particularly a lease) governed by Scots law, that the agreement will be void, or able to be avoided, if an obligation is contravened.

is / is being

See **'be' verbs; TENSE**.

is entitled to

Generally carries the sense of *can* or *may*—'you can if you like, but you don't have to'. Where it carries that sense, prefer *can* or *may*: eg, 'The landlord ~~is entitled to~~ *may* enter the premises during normal business hours.' The only exception (probably rare) is where the *entitlement* aspect of the discretion needs emphasis—in which case it is acceptable, and perhaps preferable, to say 'The landlord *is entitled to* [or *has the right to*] enter the premises during normal business hours.'

See also **can**; **may**.

-isation / -ization

See **-ise / -ize**.

-ise / -ize

Verb endings

Conventionally, standard British/Commonwealth usage preferred *-ise* for verb endings: *capitalise, legalise, authorise, radicalise, criticise, penalise*. There was an exception where *-ize* was already part of the word to which the ending is added—thus, *apprize* (*apprizing*), *size* (*sizing*), *seize* (*seizing*).

However, the convention is changing. Some British and Commonwealth dictionaries now allow either ending; or they give the *-ize* ending as the preferred one, with *-ise* as an alternative. The *Oxford English Dictionary* prefers *-ize* endings. The change reflects the gravitational pull of US usage, which prefers *-ize*: *capitalize, legalize, authorize, radicalize, criticize, penalize*. Against this trend, the *Macquarie Dictionary* (Australia) holds out for *-ise* endings.

Noun endings

Similar distinctions between British/Commonwealth usage and US usage were traditionally observed for noun endings, though less universally. The *-ization* ending has long been part of English spelling, particularly for words derived from Greek. Some standard English dictionaries (such as the *Oxford English Dictionary*) still prefer the *-ization* ending, with *-isation* as an alternative; thus, *civilization, democratization, polarization*. The *Macquarie Dictionary* generally prefers *-isation*.

See also **-yse / -yze**.

issue (offspring)

In popular usage, *issue* means children (and perhaps grandchildren). However, in strict legal usage, *issue* means descendants down the generations ad infinitum, not merely children and grandchildren. Thus, in England:

> '[T]he word *issue* is an ambiguous word. In the ordinary parlance of laymen it means children, and only children. When you talk of what issue a man has, or what issue there has been of a marriage, you mean children not grandchildren or great-grandchildren. But in the language of lawyers, and only in that language, it means descendants …' [*Ralph v Carrick* (1879) 11 Ch D 873, 883 (James LJ)]

Similarly, in Australia:

> 'The primary and natural meaning of issue [is] descendants of every degree, not children only …' [*In the Will of Moore* [1963] VR 168, 171 (Adams J). Other decisions to the same effect are *Matthews v Williams* (1941) 65 CLR 639, 650; *Re Matthews* [1960] VR 3, 7.]

However, as with most words, both the popular and legal meanings of *issue* can vary with context. This is particularly (though not exclusively) the case in a will, where courts often interpret *issue* to mean 'children' if that is what the testator clearly meant.

Example

> A testator left property by will to named persons, with a proviso that if one or more should die before the testator, leaving 'issue' surviving them, the 'issue' are to take the share of the deceased parent. Held, the testator's clear intent was that 'issue' meant 'children' of that parent: *Sibley v Perry* (1802) 7 Ves 522; 32 ER 211.

Nevertheless, despite the latitude allowed in the search for the testator's meaning, to use *issue* where 'child' is meant is apt to confuse: always prefer *child*. Indeed, a modern-day lawyer who drafts a document using *issue* to mean *child* may have to pay the costs of litigation needed to clarify the meaning: *Coleman v Orr* [2017] QSC 215 (lawyer allowed only partial reimbursement for his litigation costs, out of estate).

Further reading

Justin Gleeson, 'Spry's Case: Exploring the Limits of Discretionary Trusts' (2010) 84 *Australian Law Journal* 177 (especially at 185–86, on whether *issue* in modern trust deeds includes only children, or includes all descendants, however remote)

See also **child**.

issue estoppel

A principle that precludes relitigating a point (an 'issue') that has already been decided by litigation between the parties. (Unlike *res judicata, issue estoppel* may be raised even though the causes of action were different). The estoppel binds the parties, and all who claim through them, about any issue of fact or law that was legally indispensable to the decision. The requirements for issue estoppel are:

> '(1) that the same question has been decided; (2) that the judicial decision which is said to create the estoppel was final; and, (3) that the parties to the judicial decision or their privies were the same persons as the parties to the proceedings in which the estoppel is raised or their privies.' [*Carl Zeiss Stiftung v Rayner & Keeler Ltd (No 2)* [1967] 1 AC 853, 935]

As with other estoppel terms, *issue estoppel* is a genuine term of art, difficult to encapsulate briefly in plain language. If you feel you must use the term to a non-lawyer, consider adding an explanation: eg, 'You cannot raise this point because you have already litigated it (that is, you are bound by what the law calls 'issue estoppel').'

Further reading

Halsbury's Laws of England, 'Civil Procedure' (vol 12A, 2015) [1623]–[1628]

See also ***Anshun*** **estoppel**; **estoppel**; **res judicata / res adjudicata**.

it is open to

Generally, to say that *it is open to* someone to do something merely means they *may* do it—in which case, simply say they *may* do it. For example:

> '*It is open to the tenant to* end the lease early.' Prefer: '*The tenant may* end the lease early.'

Where the sense is more 'has the power to' do something, then use that formulation; or better still, use 'can'. For example:

> '*It is open to the tenant to* end the lease early.' Prefer: '*The tenant has the power to* [better, because briefer: *The tenant can*] end the lease early.'

See also **can**; **may**.

it is the duty of

Unless emphasising some administrative function or office, rewrite to *must*. '*It is the duty of* the vendor to answer requisitions on title' = 'The vendor *must* answer requisitions on title.'

See also **may**; **shall / must**.

it shall be lawful to

In most contexts, *it shall be lawful to* (do something) means merely *may* or *can* (do something)—and because shorter is better, prefer *may* or *can*: eg, 'If the borrower defaults, ~~*it shall be lawful for the lender to*~~ [prefer: *the lender can*] sell the property.'

However, if the intended emphasis is not so much on the 'lawful-ness' of doing something, as on the 'entitlement' to do it, then a better formulation is *has the right to* or *is entitled to*: eg, 'If the borrower defaults, the lender *has the right to* [or *is entitled to*] sell the property.'

See also **can**; **may**; **shall / must**.

ITALICS

Uses

Italics have four main uses in legal writing:

1. To emphasise a word or selection of text. The convention here is the same as in written text generally, being widely accepted in all forms of English writing. If adding emphasis in a quotation, always insert a parenthetical clause to explain (eg, 'emphasis added', 'my emphasis'.)
2. To indicate the title of a book, journal, or other source.
3. To indicate a foreign word or phrase.
4. To indicate a defined term. But this usage is relatively rare, and may mislead readers who assume that the function of italics is to emphasise, not to define. See further, **DEFINITIONS**.

'Reverse' italics

When italicising text that already includes italics, the convention is to change the italics to roman (ie, non-italic) font, to preserve the contrast:

Original version	Italicised version
The court in *Smith v Jones* decided the case differently.	*The court in* Smith v Jones *decided the case differently.*
The judge emphasised that this was *not* the case.	*The judge emphasised that this was* not *the case.*

See also **CITATIONS; DEFINITIONS; FONTS; FOREIGN (NON-ENGLISH) WORDS AND PHRASES; QUOTATIONS.**

item

Latin: also; likewise. Used to introduce each article in a list or catalogue. From it comes the anglicised noun 'item'.

its / it's

The difference is clear:

- *its* = the possessive form of *it*: 'The court delivered *its* reasons.'
- *it's* = the abbreviated form of *it is*: '*It's* not relevant that the court has delivered *its* reasons.' The apostrophe here indicates omission, not possession.

Never confuse the two, even if esteemed writers in former times were more relaxed about the distinction:

- '[The human species has] opportunities of improving *it's* rational faculties, as well as exerting *it's* natural [faculties].' [Blackstone, *Commentaries on the Laws of England* (1st ed, 1765), vol 2, 8]
- '[A deed] is sometimes called a charter, carta, from *it's* materials …' [Ibid, 295]

ius / jus

Latin: law; right. The prevailing (but not universal) legal usage is *ius* (plural *iura*), reflecting the modern preference for *i* over *j* in Latin terms generally.

ius accrescendi

Latin: the right of increase; the right of survivorship. Often seen as part of a longer Latin expression. But to retain the Latin serves no purpose in the face of an adequate English translation. Examples include:

- *ius accrescendi praefertur oneribus* (the right of survivorship is preferred to encumbrances)—meaning that, generally at least, a surviving joint tenant takes the property free of burdens imposed on it by another joint tenant
- *ius accrescendi inter mercatores locum non habet* (the right of survivorship has no place among merchants)—meaning that merchants (ie, business people) are generally taken to hold property as tenants in common, not as joint tenants
- *ius accrescendi praefertur ultimae voluntati* (the right of survivorship takes preference over the last will)—meaning that a joint tenant cannot, by purporting to devise his or her interest as joint tenant, defeat the right of survivorship of the other joint tenant(s).

See also **common property / joint property**; **joint tenant / tenant in common**.

ius ad rem / ius in rem

Ius ad rem (Latin: right in relation to property): a right which one person (A) has against another person (B) to do something in relation to property—eg, A's right to require B to transfer the property to A because of some act or conduct by B. Such a right is enforceable against B, but no one else.

Ius in rem (Latin: right over property): a proprietary right (ie, a right *in* property, not a mere right *in relation to* property) enforceable against all—eg, an ownership right in property, or a mortgagee's right in property.

The distinction between *ius ad rem* and *ius in rem* is sometimes difficult to draw, especially where a right *in relation to* property is also a right *in* the property—such as the right of a purchaser, who has paid the purchase price, to require the vendor to convey the property.

As with many Latinisms in law, linguistic antiquity obscures the concept to all except readers long-schooled in Latin. There is nothing to lose—and in fact, much to gain—by discarding the Latin *ius ad rem* in favour of *personal right* (or *personal right in relation to property*), and *ius in rem* in favour of *proprietary right*. For example:

- '[I]t is unnecessary to attempt a precise definition of the relation in which a mortgagee … stands to the subjects of his security. It is sufficient … to say that he has, not merely a *ius ad rem* [prefer: *personal right*], but a present interest in and affecting these subjects …' [*Walsh v The Queen* [1894] AC 144, 148 (Lord Watson)]
- '[The former statutory provision regarding the vesting of property in trustees] created a *ius ad rem* (a right *to* the object …) rather than *ius in rem* (a right *in* the object).' [*Re Scottish Environmental Protection Agency* 2014 SC 372, [112] (Lord Carloway, providing his own translation and emphasis)]

ius gentium

Latin: the law of nations (literally: the law of peoples); international law. There seems no reason for preserving this scrap of Latin at the expense of a modern English translation. For example:

> 'A war crime … is not a crime against the law or criminal code of any individual nation, but a crime against the *ius gentium* [prefer: *law of nations*]. The laws and usages of war are of universal application, and do not depend for their existence upon national laws and frontiers.' [*Re Eisentrager (Shanghai, 1947)* 14 Law Reports of Trials of War Criminals 8 (United States Military Commission)]

See also **ius / jus**.

ius quaesitum tertio

Latin: right sought by a third party.

See **ius tertii**; **tertium quid**.

ius tertii

Latin: right of a third person; often *jus tertii*.

Technical use

Behind the Latin lies the ancient principle that a person in possession of land (the defendant), whom a claimant seeks to eject, cannot defeat the claim by invoking the superior right of a third party (*ius tertii*) to possession of the land. Rather, the defendant must establish that his or her right is superior to that of the claimant; a third party's right to possession is relevant only if it demonstrates that the claimant has no right to possession. To some extent, *ius tertii* is a term of art, encapsulating nuances lost in a simple translation. But in all except the most technical of contexts, a plain-English translation suffices. For example:

- 'It is well settled that in an action of trespass a defendant may not set up a *jus tertii* [prefer: *third person's better right*]. He may set up a title in himself, or show that he acted on the authority of the real owner, but he cannot set up a mere *jus tertii* [prefer: *better right in a third party*].' [*Nicholls v Ely Beet Sugar Factory (No 1)* [1931] 2 Ch 84, 86 (Farwell J)]
- '[S]ince *jus tertii* [prefer: *a third person's better right to the land*] is not a defence to an action of nuisance, a person who is in exclusive possession of land may sue even though he cannot prove title to it.' [*Hunter v Canary Wharf Ltd* [1997] AC 655, 688 (Lord Goff)]

General use

Sometimes the Latin is extended, by analogy, to mean simply a higher or better right. Here too, plain English generally suffices. For example:

> 'The [doctors'] invocation of their patients' rights to care and confidentiality was a hollow invocation of *a jus tertii* [prefer: *a higher right*]. The [healthcare organisations] have corresponding duties of care and confidentiality ...' [*Health Services For Men Pty Limited v D'Souza* [2000] NSWCA 56, [6]; (2000) 48 NSWLR 448, 450 (Mason P)]

Further reading

S Bridge, E Cooke and M Dixon (eds), *Megarry & Wade's Law of Real Property*, 9th edn (Sweet & Maxwell, 2019) [7-010]–[7-011] (the technical meaning of *jus tertii*)

See also **tertium quid**.

JARGON

The *Oxford English Dictionary* gives as the original meaning of *jargon* the 'inarticulate utterance of birds, or a vocal sound resembling it; twittering; chattering'. In more modern times it has become a pejorative term to describe professional, bureaucratic, academic, or scientific writing that the non-specialist reader finds unintelligible or meaningless. Sir Ernest Gowers described 'jargon' as 'writing that employs technical words not commonly intelligible': Ernest Gowers, *The Complete Plain Words*, 1st edn (HMSO, 1954) 8(n).

Jargon abounds in legal and quasi-legal documents. It differs from 'legalese', which is more the language that lawyers use out of habit, tradition, or excessive caution (although legal writing often exhibits *both* jargon and legalese). Jargon may perhaps be tolerated in a document prepared by a lawyer to be read solely by other lawyers. But it is inexcusable in a document to be read by non-lawyers; they will find it postured and opaque.

Legal jargon has long been a source of parody. Arthur Symonds famously mocked it in *The Mechanics of Law-Making* (1835). His caricatured version of a lawyer's conveyance of an orange deftly parodies both jargon and legalese:

> 'I give you all and singular, my estate and interest, right, title, claim and advantage of and in that orange, with all its rind, skin, juice, pulp and pips, and all right and advantage therein, with full power to bite, cut, suck, and otherwise eat the same, or give the same away as fully and effectually as I the said [John Smith] am now entitled to bite, cut, suck, or otherwise eat the same orange, or give the same away, with or without its rind, skin, juice, pulp, and pips, anything hereinbefore, or hereinafter, or an in any other deed, or deeds, instrument or instruments of

> what nature or kind soever, to the contrary in any wise, notwithstanding.' [Arthur Symonds, *The Mechanics of Law-Making* (Edward Churton, 1835) 75. As Symonds laments, all the extra words add nothing of legal substance to: 'I give you my orange.']

See also **LEGALESE**.

JJ

Abbreviation for *judges* (plural) when referring to named judges: eg, 'Smith and Jones JJ'. Some jurisdictions (eg, US) retain a full stop after the abbreviation ('JJ.'), but the full stop is fast disappearing in Britain and many Commonwealth countries ('JJ'), in line with the general discarding of full-stops after abbreviations.

joint and several

Terminology

Joint and several (and the adverbial form, *jointly and severally*) is seen mostly in legal language, especially in commercial and banking documents. But it has no legal magic. It simply means *together and separately* or *together and individually*.

Joint liability

Where A and B *jointly* (prefer: *together*) promise to pay $100 to X, there is a single, undivided obligation. X can recover only $100; and if X releases A from the debt, B is also necessarily released.

Several liability

Where A and B *severally* (prefer: *separately*) promise to pay $100 to X, each of A and B is under a separate, independent obligation. X can recover $100 from each of them.

Joint and several liability

Where A and B *jointly and severally* (prefer: *together and separately* or *together and individually*) promise to pay $100 to X, X can recover against both of them collectively or each of them individually: *Georgostathis v General Credits Ltd* (1980) 33 ACTR 21 (vendor able to choose which purchasers to sue). However, the obligations are not cumulative: X can recover only $100.

There is one area of possible uncertainty. Where more than two persons (say, A, B, and C) promise to pay $100 to X *jointly and severally*, doubtless the obligation is by A, B, and C collectively *and* by A, B, and C individually. But what about A and B together, or A and C together? A court would probably hold that these combinations are liable to pay; but to clarify, consider substituting for *jointly and severally* something like *together, separately, or in any combination*.

Presumption

In the absence of an express provision, the law presumes the liability of two or more promisors to be joint, not joint and several.

> '[A] promise is joint when a single promise is made by two or more persons without words indicating that each is to be bound individually as well as jointly. If there are such words, the contract is joint and several. The presumption is that a contract made by two or more persons is joint, express words being necessary to make it joint and several.' [Glanville Williams, *Joint Obligations* (Butterworths, 1949) 35, § 2]

Joint / several duty or power

Where A and B are given a duty or a power *jointly and severally* (prefer: *together and separately* or *together and individually*), the duty or the power can be exercised by both collectively or by either one of them individually. Exceptionally, context may require otherwise; for example, in *Kendle v Melsom* (1998) 72 ALJR 560, the Australian High Court held that receivers appointed 'jointly and severally' had to act together.

Joint / several benefit

Where a promise is made to A and B *jointly and severally* (prefer: *together and separately* or *together and individually*), then A and B can enforce it together or separately (at their option).

More problematic is a promise made to A and B *jointly* (without reference to *severally*). In some jurisdictions, statute allows either of A and B to enforce the obligation, but the precise statutory terms vary from jurisdiction to jurisdiction. For example:

- Section 81 of the *Law of Property Act 1925* converts a 'joint' benefit into a joint and several benefit—ie, either or both of A and B may enforce the promise: *Josselson v Borst* [1938] 1 KB 723, 735–36. It applies only to deeds.
- Section 71 of the *Conveyancing Act 1919* (NSW) requires both A and B to enforce the 'joint' benefit while both are alive, but after the death of one allows the survivor to enforce. It applies to deeds and to covenants implied by the Act.

Therefore, it is prudent in a document to state expressly whether a benefit is a *joint* benefit only, or a *joint and several* benefit—preferring, of course, the more accessible terminology of *together* and *separate* (or *individual*). A boilerplate provision along the following lines is common:

> 'An agreement, covenant, representation or warranty on the part of, or in favour of, two or more people, binds them or benefits them *separately and together*.'

Further reading

- 'Joint and Several', in *Law Words* (Centre for Plain Legal Language, University of Sydney, 1995) 44; www.clarity-international.net/plain-language-resources/general-resources/
- Glanville Williams, *Joint Obligations* (Butterworths, 1949)

joint tenant / tenant in common

Co-owners of land hold (ie, own) under a *joint tenancy* or a *tenancy in common*. In both expressions, *tenant* carries the sense of 'one who holds land as owner' (*not* 'one who has a lease').

Tenancy in common

Under a *tenancy in common*, each co-owner owns a proportionate interest in the land. Their interests are not identifiable in any corporeal sense: one cannot say to another, 'This is my physical portion, and that is yours.' Rather, a tenant in common's share in the land is 'undivided'—meaning that, though distinct in law, it has no separate physical identity from the other shares. Each holder has an 'aliquot' portion of all those rights that together make up ownership of the whole.

The shares need not be equal. They can be of any proportion of the whole. For example, one of two tenants in common may hold a ¼ interest and the other a ¾ interest, or one a 1% interest and the other a 99% interest; one of three tenants in common may hold ½, another ⅓ and another ⅙; and so on.

As a general rule, tenants in common may each deal with their undivided shares without needing the consent or participation of the other(s)—for example, by sale, lease, mortgage, or devise (ie, by will). On death intestate, the deceased's share descends under the normal rules governing intestate succession.

Joint tenancy

Under a *joint tenancy*, each co-owner owns the whole property, along with the other joint tenants. For joint tenants, the notion of 'undivided' shares is inappropriate. Although for some purposes joint tenants have separate 'interests', they do not hold proportionate shares in the property in the same way as tenants in common. Rather, each joint tenant owns *per my et per tout* ('for nothing and for the whole'), meaning that each has a right shared with the others to the whole property but no individual right to any particular share in it: *Murray v Hall* (1849) 7 CB 441, 455n; *Wright v Gibbons* (1949) 78 CLR 313, 330 (Dixon J).

A necessary component ('incident') of a joint tenancy is the 'right of survivorship' (*ius accrescendi*). By this, on the death of a joint tenant, the whole of the land remains with the surviving joint tenants (or joint tenant, if only one survives). It is sometimes said that the deceased's share 'passes' to the surviving joint tenants, but (while a sufficient description for general purposes) this is not strictly correct, because the survivors had it all along. In truth, the property is freed from the control of one of its owners. Eventually, the last surviving joint tenant becomes sole owner.

It follows from this 'right of survivorship' that a joint tenant cannot leave the 'interest' by will. Likewise, a joint tenant who wishes to convey his or her 'interest' to another of the joint tenants has, strictly speaking, nothing to convey, for the other already owns the whole: *Burton v Camden London Borough Council* [2000] 2 AC 399, 404 (Lord Nicholls), 409–10 (Lord Millett; the appropriate way to achieve this end is by a 'release'). However, during his or her lifetime, a joint tenant can defeat the operation of survivorship by converting the interest held as joint tenant into one held as tenant in common. By this process, the joint tenancy is 'severed' as regards that interest. The right to sever is inherent in a joint tenancy.

Drafting dangers

A drafter ignorant of the differences between joint tenancy and tenancy in common is liable to err. For example, where property is held as joint tenant, a direction in a will that the share be sold and the proceeds distributed to beneficiaries is ineffective. A will-drafter who overlooks this reality may be liable in negligence to the disappointed beneficiaries: *Carr-Glynn v Frearsons* [1999] Ch 326 (cf *Vagg v McPhee* [2013] NSWCA 29; (2013) 85 NSWLR 154: on facts, no duty of care).

Further reading

- Kevin Gray and Susan Francis Gray, *Elements of Land Law*, 5th edn (Oxford University Press, 2009) ch 7.4
- S Bridge, E Cooke, and M Dixon (eds), *Megarry & Wade's Law of Real Property*, 9th edn (Sweet & Maxwell, 2019) ch 12

- Brendan Edgeworth (ed), *Butt's Land Law*, 7th edn (Lawbook, 2017) ch 6 (law outside UK)

See also **aliquot**; **common property / joint property**; **ius accrescendi**; **joint tenant / tenant in common**; **seisin / seizin**; **tenant**.

joint venture

A business undertaking (venture) in which two or more parties contribute capital, skills, or knowledge, with the aim of making profits to be shared between them in agreed proportions.

judgment (and variants)

judgment vs judgement

Judgment is the preferred spelling to denote a judicial decision: 'The court's *judgment* favoured the plaintiff.' (In strict theory, the *judgment* is the court's order; the *reasons* for judgment explain how the court reached its order, and may have some force as a precedent, but they are not themselves part of the judgment: *R v Ireland* (1970) 126 CLR 321, 330 (Barwick CJ). But in practice, *judgment* is used to mean the entire text of the court's decision.) In contrast, *judgement* is the general term denoting forming an opinion: 'He made a careful *judgement* before jumping from the train.'

Do not confuse the two terms, even though others sometimes do:

- 'The background history is fully set out in my *judgements* [prefer: *judgments*] in the earlier proceedings ...' [*MA, Re (Judgement* [sic] *Hearing)* [2016] EWFC 46, [3] (Baker J)]
- 'In my *judgement* [correct usage] a defendant is not entitled to resist an application for summary *judgement* [prefer: *judgment*] merely because it raises a set-off or counterclaim.' [*AIS Pipework Ltd v Saxlund International Ltd* [2017] EWHC 1523 (TCC), [12] (Grant J; this decision regularly uses *judgement* in place of the conventional *judgment*)]
- [The local authority may recover unpaid contributions, plus interest 'at the rate at which interest accrues on unpaid *judgements* [prefer: *judgments*] of the Supreme Court.' [*Plantations and Reafforestation Act* 1999 (NSW), s 44(2)]

judgment vs advice

In rare circumstances, a court's judgments are properly termed *advices*. This occurs where the court can merely *advise* another authority of its decision, leaving it to that authority whether to implement the decision. For example, the Privy Council (through its Judicial Committee) merely advises the monarch of its decision on legal matters brought before it; hence, its decisions are *advices*, not *judgments*.

judgment vs ruling / decree / opinion

Ruling often carries the sense of the entire text of the court's decision: eg, 'The court handed down its detailed *ruling* today.' More often though, the *ruling* is the court's conclusion on the issue (eg, 'X is guilty'; 'A must pay B damages'), rather than the reasons for that conclusion.

Decree is an order made by a court, usually requiring someone to do something. Historically, *decree* was particularly appropriate for court orders in equity, probate, divorce, or admiralty. Today, *decree* is used generically to mean court orders in any jurisdiction, including common law.

Opinion is often used interchangeably with *judgment* and *ruling*: eg, 'Judge A delivered her *opinion* [or *judgment*, or *ruling*] today.' In most Commonwealth jurisdictions, *opinion* also means the written reasons of a barrister advising on a case.

JUDICIAL HONORIFICS

Judicial honorifics vary from jurisdiction to jurisdiction. Many court websites give guidance on the proper manner of addressing judicial officers within their jurisdiction. For reasons of space, this discussion covers only superior court judges in Great Britain.

England and Wales

Supreme Court judges are called 'Justices of the Supreme Court'. In court they are addressed as 'My Lord / Lady'. In the law reports, they are referred to as 'Lord / Lady X', or (where appropriate) 'Baron / Baroness X'. Some law reports add the post-nominal letters 'JSC' (eg, 'Lord Oxford JSC / Baroness Cambridge JSC'). The President and Deputy President of the Supreme Court take the post-nominal letters 'PSC' and 'DPSC'.

Court of Appeal judges are called Lords Justice of Appeal, and referred to as 'Lord Justice / Lady Justice X'. They are addressed in court as 'My Lord / Lady' and referred to as 'Your Lordship / Ladyship'. In the law reports and in legal writing generally they are given the post-nominal letters 'LJ' (plural 'LJJ'); for example, 'Hart LJ', 'Hart and Oxford LJJ'.

High Court justices are addressed in court as 'My Lord / Lady' and referred to as 'Your Lordship / Ladyship'. When a Justice of the High Court who is not present is being referred to, the description is 'Mr / Mrs / Ms Justice X.' In judgments and in legal writing, they are given the post-nominal letter 'J': for example, 'Hart J'.

Masters of the High Court are addressed as 'Master'.

Insolvency and Companies Court judges in the High Court are addressed as 'Judge'.

Scotland

Judges in the Court of Session, High Court of Justiciary and the Sheriff Courts are addressed as 'My Lord / Lady' and referred to as 'Your Lordship / Ladyship'.

Northern Ireland

Superior court judges are addressed the same way as those in England and Wales.

Further reading

- Keith Evans, *The Language of Advocacy* (Oxford University Press, 1988) ch 2
- Hon BH McPherson, 'Judicial Honorifics' (2008) 82 *Australian Law Journal* 614

junior counsel

Any barrister who is not Queen's Counsel (QC), King's Counsel (KC), or (in many Commonwealth jurisdictions) Senior Counsel (SC). Even where advanced in years and experienced in practice, a junior counsel remains inferior in rank to a senior counsel who is younger and less experienced. Sometimes shortened to *junior*—as where a senior barrister says to a judge: 'My *junior* will address on that point.'

See also **council / counsel**; **Queen's Counsel**; **silk.**

JURISDICTION CLAUSE

Meaning

A clause by which parties agree that disputes about their contract are to be decided by the courts of a particular jurisdiction. It is usually coupled with a 'choice of law' clause, in which the parties agree that the law of that jurisdiction is to govern their contract. Both clauses follow a familiar pattern, often lifted as 'boilerplate' from standard precedents.

Example

1. This agreement is governed by and construed [*or* interpreted] in accordance with the laws of England.
2. The courts of England have exclusive [*or* non-exclusive] jurisdiction to settle any claim or dispute arising out of or in connection with this agreement or the legal relationship established by this agreement.

Both clause 1 and clause 2 are needed. This is because the parties' choice of the *courts* of a particular jurisdiction does not necessarily imply their choice of the *law* of that jurisdiction: *GDE llc v Anglia Autoflow Ltd* [2020] EWHC 105; [2020] 1 WLR 2381 (choice of jurisdiction, English courts; but Ontario law having the closest connection with the parties' contract).

Exclusive or non-exclusive?

A jurisdiction clause may be exclusive or non-exclusive. Whether it is exclusive or non-exclusive is a matter of interpreting the clause. The parties' use of the word 'exclusive' is an important indicator, but is not determinative: the parties can agree to 'exclusive' jurisdiction despite not using that actual word.

The differences between the two forms of clause are as follows.

1. **Exclusive.** The parties submit to the 'exclusive' jurisdiction of the courts of the specified state or country. This creates a contractual obligation to sue, or be sued, in those courts alone, and the courts hold the parties to their contract. A breach of an exclusive jurisdiction clause is therefore a breach of contract: *Austrian Lloyd Steamship Co v Gresham Life Assurance Society* [1903] 1 KB 249. The breach can give rise to an action in damages, and a threatened breach can be restrained by injunction. A breach is subject to the normal limitation periods that apply to breaches of contract: *AMT Futures Ltd v Boural* [2018] EWHC 750 (Comm); [2018] 3 WLR 358 (breach a 'continuing breach', because the exclusive jurisdiction clause obliged the parties not only not to start proceedings elsewhere, but also not to continue them there once started).

   Despite the contractual agreement, the court retains a discretion to allow proceedings in a jurisdiction *other* than the one agreed; but it will excerise the discretion only where there are 'strong reasons' for doing so—eg, where to enforce the clause would be oppressive or vexatious, or in breach of unfair terms legislation: see, eg, *Dononhue v Armco Ltd* [2001] UKHL 64; [2002] 1 All ER 749, [24] (Lord Bingham), [45] (Lord Hobhouse). The stringency may be relaxed for exclusive jurisdiction clauses in documents such as trust deeds, where beneficiaries have not themselves agreed contractually to the terms of the deeds: *Crociani v Crociani* [2014] UKPC 40.
2. **Non-exclusive.** The parties submit to the 'non-exclusive' jurisdiction of the courts of the specified state or country. This expresses a *preference* for the jurisdiction of

those courts, but it allows a party to litigate in a different court. However, here too, a court will normally hold the parties to their bargain. In England it has been said that the court will not intervene unless the factors relied on for breaching the clause were unforeseeable at the time of making the contract: *Deutsche Bank AG v Highland Crusader Offshore Partners LP* [2009] EWCA Civ 725; [2010] 1 WLR 1023, [61], [64]; *UCP plc v Nectrus Ltd* [2018] EWHC 380 (Comm); [2018] 1 WLR 3409.

Related documents

Where parties enter into multiple documents relating to a series of connected transactions, a prudent drafter will include an identical (or at least similar) jurisdiction clause in each document. However, even if a jurisdiction clause is included in one only of the major documents, a court is likely to presume that the parties intended the same jurisdiction to govern the law applying to all of the documents: *Sebastian Holdings Inc v Deutsche Bank AG* [2010] EWCA Civ 998, [39]–[42] (Thomas LJ); *Etihad Airways PJSC v Flöther* [2019] EWHC 3107 (Comm).

Further reading

James O'Hara, 'Strategies for Avoiding a Jurisdiction Clause in International Litigation' (2020) 94 *Australian Law Journal* 267

See also **boilerplate**; **'CHOICE OF LAW' CLAUSE; GOVERNING LAW**.

juristic person

An entity which, though not a natural person, is treated by the law as having legally enforceable rights and duties.

See also **person**.

jus

Latin: law; right; plural *jura*. Preferred modern spelling is *ius*, in line with the general preference for *i* over *j* in Latin terms.

See **ius / jus**.

JUSTIFIED MARGINS

See **DOCUMENT DESIGN**.

JUSTIFIED TEXT

See **DOCUMENT DESIGN**.

KC

See **Queen's Counsel**.

keep indemnified

See **indemnify (variants of)**.

key-money

Preferably hyphenated, being a composite expression; but sometimes two words, *key money*. Money paid to (or, more widely, any benefit conferred on) a landlord for the grant of a lease; also called a 'premium'. Some statutes prohibit paying or demanding key-money (or premiums) for leases, but the ingenuity of lawyers can make it difficult to know whether a particular payment or benefit is caught: see, eg, *Farrell v Alexander* [1977] AC 59; *Gogos v Christopoulos* (1994) 62 SASR 184; *Gillett v Burke* [1997] 1 VR 81.

Further reading

S Bridge, E Cooke, and M Dixon (eds), *Megarry & Wade's Law of Real Property*, 9th edn (Sweet & Maxwell, 2019) [21-157] (forbidden premiums)

See also **grassum**.

King's Counsel

See **Queen's Counsel.**

know all men by these presents

The traditional salutation in a deed (*these presents* meaning *this document*), and often in upper case: KNOW ALL MEN BY THESE PRESENTS. To use the greeting—whether upper or lower case—in a modern deed is unforgivably archaic and sexist. The general gist is 'Let it be known ....'. However, an opening salutation is not necessary for the validity of a deed, and so can be omitted. The deed can get straight to the point.

See also **presents (document)**.

knowledge

See **notice / knowledge**.

laches and delay

Anglo-Norman *lachés*; 'an old French word for slacknesse [sic] or negligence or not doing': *Partridge v Partridge* [1894] 1 Ch 351, 360 (North J, quoting *Coke on Littleton*). A common legal pairing: a person is said to be prevented by *laches and delay*—or sometimes *laches or delay*—from enforcing a right or taking proceedings. Sometimes the epithet *gross* is added: *gross laches and delay*. The second word in the pairing, *delay*, is probably superfluous, because delay is inherently *laches*.

The defence of laches (or 'laches and delay') applies where a person knows of a wrong which another person has committed against them, but desists or delays in enforcing their rights. If in the circumstances the delay has made it 'inequitable and unreasonable' now to enforce the rights, a court of equity may decline to enforce them: *Erlanger v New Sombrero Phosphate Co* (1878) 3 App Cas 1218, 1279 (Lord Blackburn); *Orr v Ford* (1989) 167 CLR 316, 337–42 (Deane J). The principle reflects the adage that equity aids the vigilant, not the indolent.

The expression is ingrained in law. But in contexts such as legal advices addressed to non-lawyers, prefer a plain-language explanation: eg, 'Unless you take proceedings soon to enforce your claims against X, it may be too late to do so. Your long delay may give X the defence that it is now unjust to enforce the right.' The references in this explanation to 'long delay' and 'unjust' make it clear that minor delay and prejudice do not preclude enforcing rights.

See also **TERMS OF ART**.

lacuna

Latin: gap; oversight; strict Latin plural *lacunae*, but *lacunas* is acceptable (eg, *Project Blue Ltd v Revenue and Customs* [2018] UKSC 30; [2018] 1 WLR 3169, where Lord Hodge uses *lacunas* five times and *lacunae* not at all). Often used in the sense of 'oversight', and implying that the gap should contain something important. When combined with other terms, *lacuna* offers alluring alliteration—*legal lacuna*, *legislative lacuna*, *lacuna in the law*. However, the plain-English translation *gap* or *oversight* is better (though prosaic) for communicating meaning to most readers. For example:

- 'When I first looked at this case, I thought there might be a *lacuna* [prefer: *gap*] in the law in relation to the liability for nuisance of a licensor of residential property.' [*Cocking v Eacott* [2016] EWCA Civ 140, [21]; [2016] 3 WLR 125, 131 (Vos LJ)]
- 'The scope for legislative *lacunae* [prefer: *loopholes* (to capture the alliteration)] is more remote than is commonly believed.' [*New South Wales Bar Association v Meakes* [2006] NSWCA 340, [107] (Basten JA)]

Lady Day

See **quarter days**.

land

In normal usage, real estate as a physical 'thing'. In legal usage, more abstractly, an area of three-dimensional space, its position identified by natural or imaginary points located by reference to the Earth's surface: Stuart S Ball, 'The Jural Nature of Land' (1928) 23 *Illinois Law Review* 45. The three-dimensional space may be below, on or above the Earth's surface, and it may have physical contents or be a void: Kevin Gray, 'Property in Thin Air' [1991] *Cambridge Law Journal* 252. In its legal meaning, *land* includes fixtures on the land.

Legislation often extends the meaning of *land* beyond its ordinary meaning. For example:

> 'Land' includes land of any tenure, and mines and minerals, whether or not held apart from the surface, buildings or parts of buildings (whether the division is horizontal, vertical or made in any other way) and other corporeal hereditaments; also a manor, an advowson, and a rent and other incorporeal hereditaments, and an easement, right, privilege, or benefit in, over, or derived from land …' [*Law of Property Act 1925*, s 205(1)(ix)]

Further reading

Kevin Gray and Susan Francis Gray, *Elements of Land Law*, 5th edn (Oxford University Press, 2009) ch 1.1, 1.2 (the legal concept of 'land')

See also **fixtures and fittings**.

landholder / land-holder

Standard usage is unhyphenated. However, *land-holder* is also seen (eg, *Epic Energy (Pilbara Pipeline) Pty Ltd v Commissioner of State Revenue* [2011] WASCA 228; (2011) 43 WAR 186, discussing a statute which used the hyphenated form).

landlord

In legal usage, a person who stands in the relationship of landlord with the person (tenant) in possession of the land. To illustrate, consider the following set of transactions:

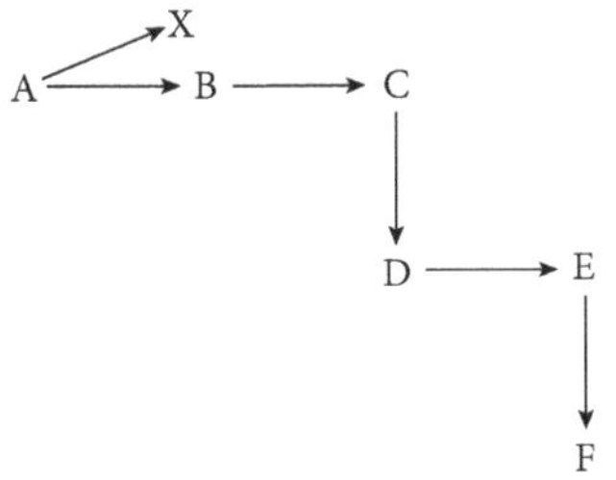

1. The landowner (A) grants a lease to B: A is B's landlord.
2. B later assigns the lease to C: A is C's landlord.
3. C then subleases to D: C is D's landlord.
4. D then assigns the sublease to E: C is E's landlord.
5. E then subleases (ie, sub-subleases) to F: E is F's landlord.
6. If A grants a lease to X (a 'concurrent lease') while the lease to B (or to C, if B has assigned) remains current, X becomes the landlord to B (or to C, if B has assigned) for the duration of the concurrent lease.

See also **concurrent lease**; **lease / sublease**; **lessee**.

lapsus calami

Latin: a slip of the pen. To retain the Latin is an inexcusable lapse into pedantry:

> '[T]he insertion of 6 December 2001 for 25 May 2002 may be an unfortunate *lapsus calami* [prefer: *slip of the pen*] not going to the root of the determination.' [*Adamas Ltd v Cheung* [2011] UKPC 32, [13] (Lord Mance, quoting from the judgment of the Supreme Court of Mauritius)]

lapsus linguae

Latin: a slip of the tongue. The only benefit of the Latin these days is the alliteration—which, though diverting, is a poor substitute for communication. In any case, the alliteration can be captured in translation: eg, *linguistic lapse*. For example:

- 'I am perfectly conscious that I myself, as well as others, have fallen into that *lapsus linguae* [prefer: *slip of the tongue*; *linguistic lapse*]; … The Act of Parliament does not speak of an accident—it speaks of "injury by accident arising out of and in the course of the employment".' [*Warner v Couchman* [1912] AC 35, 38 (Lord Loreburn LC)]
- '[T]here seems nothing inherently improper in a local context in the Sydney office of a "national" partnership conducting litigation in the Federal Court against its Melbourne counterpart, *pace* [despite] Cory J's fears on some *lapsus linguae* [prefer: *slip of the tongue*] at golf revealing all.' [L Aitken, '"Chinese Walls" and Conflicts of Interest' (1992) 18 *Monash University Law Review* 91, 113–14]

LAST-ANTECEDENT RULE

The rule

A 'rule' under which words of relation are taken to refer to the last antecedent. Consider the sentence: 'This is a tree laden with fruit that hasn't been sprayed': *Paul v Cooke* [2013] NSWCA 311; (2013) 85 NSWLR 167, [63] (Leeming JA). What hasn't been sprayed: the tree or the fruit? Read in isolation, it is impossible to tell. Under the last-antecedent rule, 'hasn't been sprayed' is taken to refer to 'fruit'.

English and Commonwealth courts

English and Commonwealth courts sometimes apply the rule: eg, *Ex parte Barnes* [1896] AC 146, 150; *Re Roskrudge* [1947] NZLR 46; *Re Ninnes* [1920] SALR 480, 488; *Campbell v Director of Public Prosecutions* [1995] 2 VR 654. But mostly they see it more as a starting point than a rigid rule of law or grammar, and one that is easily rebuttable: *H Jones & Co Pty Ltd v Kingborough Corp* (1950) 82 CLR 282, 318 (Dixon J); *Minet Australia Ltd v Gemrule Pty Ltd* [1997] NSWSC 636 (Young J). The key question is always: what did the parties intend? For example:

> A partnership agreement required surviving partners to buy out a deceased partner's share by instalments with interest 'thereon' from the date of the balance. Did this require them: (1) to pay interest on each instalment; or (2) when paying each instalment, to pay interest on the outstanding capital amount? The last-antecedent rule would suggest meaning (1), not meaning (2). Held (by majority), meaning (2), since the partnership deed taken as a whole suggested that to be the partners' intention: *John Orr Ewing & Co v Ewing* (1882) 8 App Cas 822.

US courts

US courts commonly apply the last-antecedent rule to resolve ambiguity where a modifying word or phrase could apply to more than one item in a list: 'A pronoun, relative pronoun, or demonstrative adjective generally refers to the nearest reasonable antecedent': Antonin Scalia and Bryan Garner, *Reading Law: The Interpretation of Legal Texts* (West, 2012) 144. Some US authors treat it as a canon of construction (interpretation); Scalia and Garner are in that category. Other US authors are more sanguine, arguing that the best guide to discerning meaning from ambiguity is always context (and, in the case of statutes, legislative history), rather than a fixed rule applied regardless of context (and legislative history): Joseph Kimble, 'The Doctrine of the Last Antecedent, the Example in Barnhart, Why Both Are Weak, and How Textualism Postures' (2015) 16 *Scribes Journal of Legal Writing* 5.

A leading US example is *Lockhart's* case:

> A statute prescribed a mandatory 10-year sentence for a crime, if the accused had been previously convicted of a crime relating to 'aggravated sexual abuse, sexual abuse, or abusive sexual conduct *involving a minor*'. Did 'involving a minor' apply to all the listed crimes or only the last one? Held, it applied only to the last one, under the rule of the last antecedent: *Lockhart v United States* (USSC, 1 March 2016; 135 S Ct 2350; at www. supremecourtreview.com/case/14-8358). (This case is also discussed under **AMBIGUITY**.)

Punctuation

Punctuation—particularly commas—may help clarify meaning, and therefore help clarify whether the last-antecedent rule has a role to play. Compare:

1. 'This new tax applies to transfers and leases of urban land' [ambiguous; apply the rule?]
2. 'This new tax applies to transfers, and leases of urban land' [not ambiguous]
3. 'This new tax applies to transfers, and leases, of urban land' [not ambiguous, but differs from 2].

Further reading

- Joseph Kimble, 'The Puzzle of Trailing Modifiers' (2016) 95 *Michigan Bar Journal* (Jan) 38
- Terri R LeClercq, 'Doctrine of the Last Antecedent: The Mystifying Morass of Ambiguous Modifiers' (2004) 40 *Texas Journal of Business Law* 199; earlier version published in (1996) 2 *Journal of Legal Writing Institute* 81

See also **AMBIGUITY; COMMAS; MODIFIERS; PUNCTUATION; VAGUENESS.**

last will and testament

A formulaic phrase, used ritually in the opening line of a will: eg, 'This is the *last will and testament* of me, John Smith.' The origins of the phrase may lie in the distinctions between real and personal property—*last will* (from the Latin *ultima voluntas*) being the appropriate term for a gift by will (devise) of land, and *testamentum* (Latin: expression of a person's intention) being the appropriate term for a gift by will (bequest) of personal property: Sir E Coke, *Institutes of the Laws of England* (1628) vol 1, folio 11a. The composite term *last will and testament* had become established by at least 1540 (it appears in the *Statute of Wills* of that year). But its continued use today is doubly disingenuous:

1. As used in *last will and testament*, 'last' means merely 'current', not 'final'. This is because the law of wills permits a person to revoke a will and make another (later) one. Indeed, 'last' may be positively misleading: eg, where a testator makes a 'last' will (will 1), then makes a later 'last' will (will 2) revoking will 1, and then makes a codicil reinstating will 1, the 'last' will is in fact the earlier one: *Re Goods of Van Cutsem* (1890) 3 LT (NS) 252.
2. The term *will and testament* is an unnecessary pairing: *will* always suffices.

So the opening flourish can say simply: 'This is my will.'

However, sometimes a little formality goes a long way. In *Re Yu* [2013] QSC 322, a non-lawyer made an effective will by leaving several messages on an iPhone. The court held that the testator had helped clarify his testamentary intent by starting one of the messages with the words 'This is [my] last Will and Testament.'

Further reading

- 'Last Will and Testament', in *Law Words* (Centre for Plain Legal Language, University of Sydney, 1995) 47; www.clarity-international.net/plain-language-resources/general-resources/
- David Mellinkoff, *The Language of the Law* (Little, Brown, 1963) 77–79, tracing the history of *last will and testament*

latent defect

A defect (usually in title to land, or in the condition of goods) that is not observable on a reasonably careful inspection.

Compare **patent defect**.

LATIN

Latin in legal English

Latin has a long history in English law. Latin was for centuries the language of formal records and statutes: Pollock and Maitland, *The History of English Law Before the Time of Edward I*, 2nd edn (Cambridge University Press, 1968) vol 1, 82, 86. It was also the language of scholars, clerics, court writs, and some of the earliest legal textbooks (eg, Glanvill's *Treatise on the Laws and Customs of the Realm of England in the time of Henry II*, 1187–1189). Statutes were in Latin until about 1300: Baugh and Cable, *A History of the English Language*, 5th edn (Routledge, 2002) 153, 154. In 1362 the *Statute of Pleading* (36 Ed III c 15) enacted (in French) that all proceedings should be in English, though they should be enrolled in Latin.

Legal Latin suffered at the hands of lawyers who had not been schooled in classical Latin, earning the rebuke of those who had. This led Sir Edward Coke in 1572 to propose four categories of legal Latin: (1) 'good Latin', accepted by grammarians; (2) words taking a Latin form, and accepted by judges but not by grammarians; (3) words that are not true Latin (ie, 'false Latin') but that could be corrected in writs and pleadings and judgments, and would not vitiate grants or deeds; and (4) words that simply make no sense, and are to be 'utterly rejected': *James Osborn's case* (1572) 10 Co Rep 130a, 133a–133b; 77 ER 1123, 1129.

Legal Latin used abbreviations, making comprehension difficult even for those schooled in Latin. Examples in court records of criminal proceedings included the following:

Latin abbreviation	Full Latin version	English translation
ca null	catalla nulla	no goods / chattels to forfeit
cog ind	cognovit indictamentum	confessed to the indictment
cul	culpabilis	guilty
ign	ignoramus	we do not know (ie, no case to answer)
non cul nec re	non culpabilis nec retraxit	not guilty and did not flee
po se	ponit se super patriam	[the accused] puts himself/herself on the country (ie, opts for jury trial and pleads not guilty)
sus	suspendatur	let him/her be hanged

Latin in modern law

Many modern legal terms reflect Latin origins. Some have been accepted into English: eg, *adjacent*, *frustrate*, *inferior*, *legal*, *quiet*, *solatium*, *subscribe*. But many others have not been anglicised in this way, and remain 'pure' Latin words and phrases—which modern lawyers continue to use, even though Latin has long ceased to be taught in most schools. Latin 'lie[s] in the terraces of English law like scattered fossils of a once dominant linguistic species': Adrian Heyworth-Smith, 'Latin Language and English Law', in *Table Talk of the Seldon Society in Queensland* (Supreme Court Library, Queensland, 2004) 78. This attachment to Latin poses two serious issues.

Will the reader understand?

The first (and main) issue is that Latin fails to communicate to most modern readers. The writer may know the meaning of the Latin word or phrase, but to use it when addressing a reader untutored in Latin is to defeat the purpose of writing—namely, to communicate.

Does Latin suggest false precision?

The second issue is that the use of a Latin word or phrase may suggest (to unwitting readers) a false aura of precision. The Latin may convey a sense of certainty that an English translation would quickly (and rightly) dispel. Lord Wright once said that Latin words or phrases 'distract the mind from the true problem[,] which is to apply the principles of English law to the realities of the case': *Smith, Hogg & Co Ltd v Black Sea and Baltic General Insurance Co Ltd* [1940] AC 997, 1003. Other leading judges have made similar comments. For example:

- 'If that phrase [*res ipsa loquitur*] had not been in Latin, nobody would have called it a principle': *Ballard v North British Railway Co* (1923) SC (HL) 43, 46 (Lord Shaw of Dunfermline).
- The proposition that a person may renounce a right which exists solely for his or her own benefit 'is not improved by legal Latin cant and saying *cuilibet licet* (or *quilibet potest*) *renuntiare* (or *renunciare*) *juri* (or *jure*) *pro se introducto* as have numerous authorities, including the county court judge in the present issue, or the transcriber of his judgment, with varying degrees of deviation from correct Latin grammar and orthography': *Johnson v Moreton* [1980] AC 37, 58 (Lord Hailsham).
- The 'disarming mystique' of Latin is apt to mislead readers: *Kern Corporation Ltd v Walter Reid Trading Pty Ltd* (1987) 163 CLR 164, 192 (Deane J).
- A lawyer's use of Latin may demonstrate an inability to scrutinise the issues in a case—an 'inattention to principle': *Lockrey v Historic Houses Trust of New South Wales* [2012] NSWCA 249, [80] (Barrett JA).

Continued judicial use of Latin

Despite these cautionary observations, many judges and lawyers continue to use Latin words and phrases. Some go quite overboard:

> '*Parens patriae* cannot be *ad fundandam jurisdictionem*. The zoning question is *res inter alios acta*.' [*Mississippi Bluff Motel Inc v County of Rock Island* 420 NE 2d 748, 749 (Ill) (Heiple J). Translated: 'The State's role as guardian cannot be the basis of jurisdiction. The zoning question is a matter between other parties.']

In more recent times, changes to the civil procedure rules (the 'Woolf reforms') sought to expunge Latin from modern court proceedings. Banned words included 'subpoena' (replaced with 'witness summons'), 'ex parte' ('without notice'), 'garnishee order' ('third party debt order'), 'certiorari' ('quashing order'). The move emboldened some judges to lapse into Latin with affected contrition:

- 'The essential features, at the risk of being criticised for using Latin twice in one sentence, are that, as between Mr Maden and Cliffords, the Goodwin action was *res inter alios acta*, and, from the standpoint of the litigation and settlement in the Goodwin action, Cliffords' negligence in 1996 was *novus actus interveniens*.' [*Maden v Clifford Coppock & Carter* [2004] EWCA Civ 1037; [2005] 2 All ER 43, [36] (Neuberger LJ)]

- '[Counsel] referred us to this authority with such enthusiasm and at such length that, but for Lord Woolf's prohibition on resort to Latin, we might have been minded to conclude that he saw this as a *tabula in naufragio*.' [*Vowles v Evans* [2003] EWCA Civ 318; [2003] 1 WLR 1607, [48] (Lord Phillips MR)]
- For other examples, see Roderick Munday, 'Lawyers and Latin' (2004) 168 *Justice of the Peace* 775, 776–77.

Italicise?

Where a Latin word or phrase has become standard English, it is not italicised: eg, 'ad hoc', 'de facto'. But where it has not yet been 'naturalised', it is italicised: eg, *caveat emptor*, *stare decisis*. In borderline cases, either format is acceptable: eg, 'pro bono' or '*pro bono*'.

Abbreviations of Latinisms are not italicised, even if the full term would be italicised: thus, *exempli gratia* becomes 'eg'; *id est* becomes 'ie'.

Latin plurals

In general, Latin words adopted into English take English plurals. However, this practice is not universal: some writers feel duty-bound to preserve the original Latin plural forms, but they are in the minority.

Latin words with English plurals	**Borderline cases**
formula—formulas (*not* formulae)	index—indexes *or* indices
forum—forums (*not* fora)	memorandum—memorandums *or* memoranda
stadium—stadiums (*not* stadia)	referendum—referendums *or* referenda

Four guiding principles

The preferred approach to using Latin in modern law can be summed up in four guiding principles:

1. Where the Latin word or phrase has become accepted in English usage, use it ('bonus', 'data', 'vice versa'). Likewise, where the Latinism has become the standard language of business, use it ('ad hoc', 'inter alia')—although where it might puzzle the particular audience, prefer standard English (not 'ad hoc', but 'temporary'; not 'inter alia', but 'among other things').
2. Where the Latin word or phrase has not become accepted in English usage but can be translated without loss of precision, translate it. To retain the Latin serves no purpose—unless, perhaps, for cadence or alliteration; but you may be able to capture cadence in the translation (eg, *ubi jus ibi remedium* = 'where there is a right, there is a remedy') or alliteration (eg, *de die in diem* = 'from day to day').

   This admonition has judicial support at the highest level:

   > 'Better considered without reference to its original formulation in Latin, which nowadays few people understand, the validity principle proceeds on the premise that the parties to a contract or other instrument will have intended it to be valid. It therefore provides that, in circumstances in which a clause in their contract is … capable of having two meanings, one which would result in its being void and the other which would result in its being valid, the latter should be preferred.' [*Egon Zehnder Ltd v Tillman* [2019] UKSC 32; [2020] AC 154, [38] (Lord Wilson). The Latin, which appears nowhere in the judgement, is *ut res magis valeat quam pereat*.]

3. Where the Latin word or phrase describes a legal concept that is difficult to translate into English without loss of legal precision, nuance, or conciseness, use it—but add an approximate translation. Examples are *res ipsa loquitur* ('it speaks for itself', 'it is self-evident') and *respondeat superior* ('let the employer answer'). For example:

   > '*Expressio unius, exclusio alterius*, as judges were once allowed to say. Put in a more homely way, if a document goes to the trouble of spelling out with apparent specificity what the parcels of a particular piece of land are, it is often not easy (although not necessarily impossible) to interpret it as in fact extending to other land not so specified.' [*Buckley v Tibber* [2015] EWCA Civ 1294; [2016] 2 WLR 963, [92] (Sir Colin Rimer, adding a 'homely' explanation relevant to the facts of the case)]

   However, do not be overly precious about preserving a Latin term. If it is easily translatable, then translate it (without adding an explanation). Take, for example, *solatium* (Latin: solace), a context-dependent term meaning a payment made to a victim as compensation for emotional pain and suffering—such as for trauma following the wrongful death of a relative, or for non-economic losses when the state compulsorily acquires land. Despite its hallowed legal pedigree, *solatium* lends itself to a context-dependent translation. For example, in the context of indigenous land rights, a possible translation is 'cultural loss', to describe non-economic loss suffered by the compulsory taking of indigenous land rights: *Northern Territory v Griffiths* [2019] HCA 7, [53]–[54]; (2019) 93 ALJR 327. In the context of land resumption, a possible translation is 'intangible disadvantages', to describe non-economic loss suffered on the compulsory acquisition of land title: eg, *Lands Acquisition Act 1978* (NT), Sch 2, Rule 9.

4. Where the Latin word or phrase contains an inherent woolliness or ambiguity, avoid it—just as you would avoid a woolly or ambiguous English word or phrase. Instead, find a more precise English expression.

Further reading

- Francis Bennion, 'Confusion over Plain Language Law' (2007) 16 *Commonwealth Lawyer* 61, 65 (arguing that the average lawyer understands basic Latin terms used in law). Compare Mark Adler, 'In Support of Plain Law: An Answer to Francis Bennion' [2008] (August) *Loophole* (Journal of the Commonwealth Association of Legislative Counsel) 15, 27 (taking a more sanguine view of lawyers' knowledge of Latin) (at www.calc.ngo/publications/loopholes#loophole-table-2012)
- Brendan Edgeworth, 'Vale Solatium? (2020) 94 *Australian Law Journal* 323, 323–24 (noting the disappearance of *solatium* and other Latinisms, as part of the process by which 'the language of the law has progressively sidelined Latin.'
- Peter Goodrich, 'Distrust Quotations in Latin' (2003) 29 *Critical Inquiry* 193 (arguing that Latin's rhetorical power is heightened, not diminished, by the declining understanding of Latin in professional and academic circles)
- John Gray, *Lawyers' Latin: A Vade Mecum*, 2nd edn (Crowood Press, 2007) (providing translations of common legal Latinisms, and favouring retaining Latin)
- Michael Kirby, 'How I Learned to Drop Latin and Love Plain Legal Language' [2013] *New South Wales Law Society Journal* (March) 60 (title reflects argument)
- Roderick Munday, 'Does Latin Impede Legal Understanding?' (2000) 164 *Justice of the Peace* 995 (erudite and witty; favouring Latin in law)
- Roderick Munday, 'Lawyers and Latin' (2004) 168 *Justice of the Peace* 775 (favouring Latin in law)
- 'Versus Latinum', *Law Words* (Centre for Plain Legal Language, University of Sydney, 1995) 4; at www.clarity-international.net/plain-language-resources/general-resources/ (generally discouraging Latin in modern law)

See also **FOREIGN (NON-ENGLISH) WORDS AND PHRASES**; **ignoramus**; **LITERARY ALLUSIONS**; **novus actus interveniens**; **res ipsa loquitur**; **respondeat superior**; **tabula in naufragio**; **WOOLF REFORMS**

law agent

The traditional Scots term for a solicitor; often abbreviated to 'agent'. In modern Scottish usage, *solicitor* has become the accepted term (although *law agent* survives in Presbyterian church regulations to mean the lawyer who advises the church).

LAW REPORTS

See **CITATION OF CASES; FICTITIOUS LAW REPORTS.**

lay corporation

A corporation comprised of laypersons (that is, non-ecclesiastics), usually (but not necessarily) established for business or charitable purposes. Contrasted with *ecclesiastical corporation*.

See also **corporation**.

layperson

A lawyer's term for a non-lawyer. The theological allusion ('lay') is accidental, unrelated to delusions of priesthood. Prefer *non-lawyer*.

learned (adjective)

As in 'my learned friend', 'the learned judge'; pronounced *learn-èd* (ie, with two syllables, rather than eliding the second). A term of respect for a judge or an opponent, regardless of their actual learnedness. In most Commonwealth countries, barristers refer to each other as 'my learned friend', but tend not to commend solicitors in the same way.

Further reading

Keith Evans, *The Language of Advocacy* (Oxford University Press, 1988) ch 5

lease / let / rent (verb)

Who is the leasing party?

When premises are *leased* (or *let*, or *rented*), who does the leasing, letting or renting? The words alone can be ambiguous: eg, 'He decided to *lease* the premises'—is 'he' the landlord or the tenant? Context usually resolves the question—but if there is possible doubt, consider changing the word:

- 'The *renter* must pay the land tax.' Is the renter the landlord or the tenant? Change to 'The *landlord* [or *tenant*] must pay the land tax.'
- 'The obligation to pay rates falls on the person who *leases* the premises.' Is this the landlord or the tenant? Change to 'The obligation to pay rates falls on the [*landlord*; or *tenant*].' (Or better still: 'The *landlord* [or *tenant*] must pay the rates.')

Words of demise

In normal usage, the verbs *to lease* and *to let* are synonymous: 'I *lease* my house to you' means the same as 'I *let* my house to you.' However, sometimes it may be necessary to differentiate the words. For example, the common law will imply certain covenants into a lease, where the parties themselves have overlooked including them—eg, the landlord's covenant to provide quiet enjoyment. But for some purposes it may be necessary to draw distinctions. For example, old common-law cases hold that covenants are implied into leases not by the mere relationship of landlord and tenant, but by the use of particular 'words of demise', and that *let* is not one of those words: *Baynes & Co v Lloyd & Sons* [1895] 2 QB 610, 614–15 (Kay LJ); *Jones v Lavington* [1903] 1 KB 253. In some jurisdictions, niceties of this kind have been negated by statutes that imply obligations into leases despite lack of formal language in the grant of the lease; but where such statutes do not exist, *to lease* remains preferable *to let*.

Further reading

S Bridge, E Cooke, and M Dixon (eds), *Megarry & Wade's Law of Real Property*, 9th edn (Sweet & Maxwell, 2019) [16-011], [18-006]

lease / sublease

A *lease* is an interest held from a lessor (landlord). A *sublease* is a lease carved out of a lease. In practice, particularly involving properties held on very long-term leases, *lease* is used to describe what is actually a *sublease*. But this vernacular use of *lease* does not reflect the legal reality. For example, assume that a landlord (L) grants a 300-year lease to A, and A then grants a lease of that lease (ie, a sublease) to B. Because B is in possession, it seems natural to describe B as the *tenant* and B's interest as a *lease*. In legal reality, however, B is the tenant of A and (in the larger picture of the property dealings) is a *subtenant*. For most practical purposes (particularly in a dispute between A and B that does not involve L), no harm is done by describing B's interest as a *lease* and describing B as a *tenant*. But when legal niceties are involved, more precision is required. For example:

- An owner of land (L) leased it to a tenant (T), who in turn subleased it to a subtenant (who went into possession). A statute gave a 'landlord' the right in certain circumstances to serve a notice to quit on the 'occupying tenant'. Held, the person to serve the notice was T, not L: *Kazim v Barrow* [2018] EWCA Civ 2414; [2019] 1 WLR 3168.
- A COVID-relief regulation required 'lessors' to give their 'lessees' a rent moratorium. The owner of the land (L) had leased it to a tenant (T), who had subleased to X. Held, the regulation did not apply as between L and X, because X was the lessee of T, not of L: *First Renewable Pty Ltd v Natevski* [2020] NSWSC 1508.

Some statutes define 'lease' to include 'sublease', either generally or for the purposes of specific provisions. This of course does not conflate the essential differences between leases and subleases—but merely ensures that the statutory provisions dealing with leases apply also to subleases. See, eg, *Law of Property Act 1925*, s 146(5)(a).

Lease (noun and verb) has long lost its Old English meaning of falsehood or lie. No longer would a person say 'Thou shalt destroy them that speak *leasing*' (Psalm 5:6, King James' Version).

See also **landlord**; **sublease / underlease**.

leave

In legal usage, *permission*. Thus, an appeal is lodged *with leave of* [with the permission of] the court. The modern English word *permission* is perfectly adequate, as evidenced by the Woolf Reforms adopting it as a synonym for *leave*.

See also **WOOLF REFORMS**.

legal

In both normal and legal usage, *legal* can mean *lawful*, as in 'This course of action is *legal*.' It can also mean, in a fairly loose and generic sense, *enforceable*—as in 'You are entitled to your *legal* rights.'

In legal usage, however, *legal* also carries an additional (and technical) meaning: *legal* in contrast to *equitable*. Thus, an interest in land might be *legal* (meaning, recognised by the courts of common law) or it might be *equitable* (meaning, recognised by courts of equity); or a remedy might be *legal* (ie, enforceable in the courts of common law—such as by way of damages) or it might be *equitable* (ie, enforceable in courts of equity—such as by way of specific performance). Examples include:

- *legal mortgage*—a mortgage of a legal interest (eg: (1) a mortgage recognised and enforceable in courts of common law, particularly for land under common-law title; or (2) a registered mortgage over land governed by a registration system such as the Torrens system)
- *legal charge*—a charge over a legal interest (ie, one recognised and enforceable in courts of common law)
- *legal estate*—an estate in land recognised by courts of common law, as distinct from an estate recognised by courts of equity
- *legal fraud*—actual fraud of the kind recognised by courts of common law, as distinct from constructive fraud of the kind recognised by courts of equity.

This additional meaning may confuse. For example, if the question is whether an insurance policy has been *legally assigned*, does *legally* mean 'assigned in the way recognised by common-law courts' (as distinct from in the way recognised by equity courts), or does it mean simply (in the popular sense) 'assigned effectually'? See, eg, *Dufaur v Professional Life Assurance Co* (1858) 25 Beav 599, 603–04; ER 766, 767–98 (Romilly MR), where it was held on the facts to mean simply 'assigned effectually'.

LEGAL ADVICE (FORM OF)

See **ADVICE (FORM OF)**.

legal charge

Shorthand for 'a charge by way of legal mortgage over land'. On registration under the *Land Registration Act 2002*, the charge takes effect as if it were a charge by deed by way of legal mortgage: Kevin Gray and Susan Francis Gray, *Elements of Land Law*, 5th edn (Oxford University Press, 2009) [6.1.8].

legal costs

See **costs**.

LEGAL MAXIMS

See **MAXIM**.

legal memory

The extent to which the law remembers something: more archaically, 'the time whereof the memory of men runneth not to the contrary', an expression found in *Littleton's Tenures* (circa 1481). The *Statute of Westminster I* (1275) fixed the extent of 'legal memory' at 3 September 1189, the date of the coronation of Richard I. That date is entirely arbitrary: *Mercer v Denne* [1905] 2 Ch 538, 577 (Vaughan Williams LJ). The concept plays only a limited role in modern law—eg, the time back to which use must be proved under the principles governing the acquisition of rights by prescription at common law.

Further reading

S Bridge, E Cooke, and M Dixon (eds), *Megarry & Wade's Law of Real Property*, 9th edn (Sweet & Maxwell, 2019) [27-059]

See also **time immemorial**.

legal person

A person with legally enforceable rights and duties. The term is normally used to describe legal entities (such as corporations) that are not human beings; but strictly it applies to all 'persons' recognised by the law.

See **person**.

legal representative

In general use, *legal representative* means *lawyer*: eg, 'An accused is entitled to demand the presence of his or her *legal representative*.' In the law of wills and succession, *legal representative* usually means 'executor or administrator': *Re Henderson* (1860) 28 Beav 656, 658; 54 ER 519, 520 (Romilly MR); *Mocatta v Mocatta* (1915) 19 CLR 515, 517 (Griffith CJ). But depending on context, particularly in a will, *legal representative* can carry different meanings, as in these examples:

- *Legal representatives* meant *descendants*: 'I give my house to A; but if A predeceases me, the house is to go to A's personal representatives': *Re Thompson* (1886) 55 LT 85, 87 (Kay J—because the will elsewhere used the term 'executors and administrators', the testator must have intended 'personal representatives' to carry another meaning).
- *Legal representatives* meant children: *Herbert v Forbes* (1831) 1 LJ Ch 118, 120 (Leach MR).

LEGAL UNITS OF MEASUREMENT

Most jurisdictions prescribe legal units of measurement, and the consequences (if any) of failure to use those units in certain transactions. For example, under the *Weights and Measures Act 1985* (UK), a contract for the sale or carriage of goods is not void merely because it contravenes the Act (s 91). In contrast, in Australia, any transaction (except a transaction relating to an interest in land) that fails to use the Australian legal units of measurement is void: *National Measurement Act 1960* (Cth), s 12.

See also **FRACTIONS; NUMBERS; WORDS AND FIGURES.**

LEGALESE

The *Oxford English Dictionary* defines legalese as 'the abstruse and complicated technical language of legal documents'. This might suggest a modicum of justification for legalese—that without it, legal documents might be technically defective. But this of course is not so. In reality, legalese is language that lawyers use out of habit, and that they would not use in ordinary communication (were they not lawyers). Often it is archaic language: eg, 'these presents' (meaning 'this document'), 'herewith', 'therewith', 'herein', 'therein'. Often it is overly formal: eg, 'the same', 'the said', 'hereby'. Often is it pretentious: eg, 'I verily believe'. Often it is simply woolly and wordy: eg, 'to the best of my knowledge, information, and belief' (ie, 'so far as I know'). And often it is set in long, punctuation-free sentences that themselves confound comprehension. A legal writer may consider that words, phrases, and sentence structures of this kind contribute legal 'feel' to legal writing, but they rarely serve any legal purpose. Absent legal purpose, there is no reason for using them.

Legalese often coexists with legal jargon. This can make the writing impenetrable to all but the legally initiated—and even they may be confused.

Example

> A clause in a long-term lease required the tenant to pay increases in maintenance fees:
>
> > '[The tenant agrees] to pay to the Lessor without any deduction in addition to the said rent as a proportionate part of the expenses and outgoings incurred by the Lessor in the repair maintenance renewal and renewal of the facilities of the Estate and the provision of services hereinafter set out the yearly sum of Ninety Pounds and value added tax (if any) for the first Year of the term herby granted *increasing thereafter by Ten Pounds per Hundred for every subsequent year* or part thereof.' [italics added]
>
> Read literally, the italicised words would cause the maintenance fees to increase from £90 to £4,070 over a 40-year period, far outstripping the long-term inflation rate. The legalese, jargon, and sentence length almost certainly confounded the parties (and possibly even the drafter). The Supreme Court upheld the literal reading. In reality, the clause could easily have been drafted, legalese-free: 'The tenant agrees to pay the Lessor maintenance fees of £90 plus VAT for the first year, increasing by 10% each year.' This would have laid the meaning bare. See *Arnold v Britton* [2015] UKSC 36; [2015] AC 1619.

Sometimes the combination of legalese, jargon, and overbearing sentence construction produces drafting that is more than merely difficult to understand. If taken literally, it has consequences so absurd that the parties cannot possibly have intended them. When that stage is reached, the courts can intervene and—without the need for formal rectification—'correct' the drafting to make it reflect what the court perceives the parties to have intended. For example:

> A 20-year lease of bank premises in an Australian country town contained a rent-review clause that bore all the hallmarks of legalese. The purpose was to guarantee the landlord an 8% increase or a CPI increase, whichever was greater. However, as drafted, the CPI-increase provision incorporated an enormous multiplying factor: namely, on each two-yearly review the existing rent was to be increased by the CPI as at the date immediately before the review multiplied by the CPI increase *since the start of the lease*. This compounded the effect of CPI increases alarmingly—so much so that, on one calculation, rent that started at about $70,000 in 1985 would increase to about $40 million in 1999. The sheer complexity of the clause had hidden the meaning from even the drafter. The New South Wales Court of Appeal 'corrected' the drafting to allow the result the parties must have intended: *Westpac Banking Corporation v Tanzone Pty Ltd* [2000] NSWCA 25; (2000) 9 BPR 17,521. For a similar trap in an English rent review clause, see P Kenny, 'Have You Ever Been "Blue Dolphined"?' [2005] *Conveyancer and Property Lawyer* 279.

However, the 'principle of absurdity' can come to a drafter's aid only where the wording produces a result that is absurd, in the sense of 'opposed to reason' or 'irrational'. It is not sufficient that the result is merely commercially unrealistic or commercially disadvantageous to a party: *Miwa Pty Ltd v Siantan Properties Pte Ltd* [2011] NSWCA 297; (2011) 15 BPR 29,545, [13]–[18]. But if the absurdity is obvious on the face of the instrument (and it is clear what correction needs to be made to put it right), the court can correct: *Chartbrook Ltd v Persimmon Homes Ltd* [2009] UKHL 38; [2009] 1 AC 1101, [15]–[25] (Lord Hoffmann, with whom Lords Hope, Rodger, and Walker and Baroness Hale relevantly agreed); *Bank of Queensland Ltd v Chartis Australia Insurance Ltd* [2013] QCA 183.

Further reading

Joseph Kimble, *Lifting the Fog of Legalese: Essays on Plain Language* (Carolina Academic Press, 2006)

See also **CORRECTIONS (BY COURT)**; **JARGON**; **PLAIN LANGUAGE**.

LEGISLATION (REFERENCES TO)

See **CITATION OF LEGISLATION**.

lend / loan (verb)

Do you *lend* money or *loan* money? In US English, and in many Commonwealth countries, *lend / loan* are interchangeable. It is said that UK usage still prefers *lend* as the verb: eg, RD Burchfield (ed), *Fowler's Modern English Usage*, 3rd edn (Oxford University Press, 1998) 466. However, occasional judicial usage seems satisfied with *loan*:

> '[T]he equity [in] the house might persuade Lloyds to *loan* some money (for the purpose of relieving his shortage of funds).' [*Agarwala v Agarwala* [2013] EWCA Civ 1763, [22] (Sullivan LJ)]

less

See **fewer / less**.

less than / more than

Traps can lie in *less than* and *more than*. In particular, does the drafting leave a gap, or produce an impractical result?

Examples

- A section of an Act dealt with 'an interest less than a tenancy from year to year'. Another section dealt with a tenancy 'for a term of two years or upwards'. Held, a tenancy for 18 months was not covered, and the court had no power to fill the gap: *Gladstone v Bower* [1960] 2 QB 384 (CA), the statute being the *Agricultural Holdings Act 1948*.
- A land registration statute allows leases of *less than* 3 years to remain unregistered, but requires leases of *more than* 3 years to be registered. What of leases of *exactly* 3 years?
- A regulation prohibits the importation of bottled water 'unless in bottles of more than 10 litres'. The normal size of water bottles is 10 litres (exactly). Is the result unintended? [Example based on Statutory Instrument No 44 of 2018, Botswana.]

lessee

A *lessee* (or *tenant*) is a person who holds a lease from a landlord. Often, a *lessee* holds directly from the freehold owner of the property. But in law, *lessee* means any person who stands in the relationship of tenant with a landlord. Therefore, a person who holds a sublease can also be termed a *lessee*—namely, a *(sub)lessee* of the lessee. *Lessee* also includes a concurrent lessee; eg, where the landowner (A, the *lessor*) grants a lease to B and then (while the lease to B is current) grants a concurrent lease to B1, B1 is both *lessor* to B and *lessee* of A.

Leasee and *leasor* are always wrong.

See also **concurrent lease; *-ee* / *-or* endings; landlord; lease / sublease.**

lesser of

Grammatically, the proper construction is 'the lesser of A *and* B', as in these two examples:

- The deposit is the lesser of:
  (a) 10% of the purchase price; *and*
  (b) $500,000.
- '[T]he ultimate order [of the court] is always limited to the *lesser of* the proceeds received *and* the amount realisable at the date of the order.' [*R v Briggs-Price* [2009] UKHL 19; [2009] 1 AC 1026, [106] (Lord Mance)]

However, idiomatic usage also allows 'the lesser of A *or* B', and no uncertainty is caused. For example:

> The deposit is the lesser of:
> (a) 10% of the purchase price; *or*
> (b) $500,000.

lessor

See ***-ee* / *-or* endings; landlord.**

lessor / lessee

Where possible, to avoid confusion over words ending in *-ee* / *-or*, prefer *landlord* / *tenant*.

See also ***-ee* / *-or* endings.**

letter of comfort

A letter giving 'comfort' to someone dealing with another person or entity: eg, a letter from a parent company stating that it will honour the financial obligations of a subsidiary company. Depending on its terms and the circumstances in which it was given, a letter of comfort may (or may not) create binding legal obligations: eg, *Kleinwort Benson Ltd v Malaysia Mining Corpn Bhd* [1989] 1 WLR 379 (no); *Anglican Development Fund Diocese of Bathurst v Palmer* [2015] NSWSC 1856; (2015) 336 ALR 372 (yes).

letter of credit

A document (letter) written by a bank or merchant to another bank or merchant, requesting the addressee to give credit or supply goods to a named person (the beneficiary) on stipulated conditions. If acted on, the letter constitutes a binding undertaking by the issuer to meet the amounts drawn or goods ordered by the beneficiary.

LETTER(S) OF INTENT

See **HEADS OF AGREEMENT.**

letters patent

Prerogative instruments that grant Crown offices or franchises, and that are not sealed but open to view—hence, 'patent' (to be distinguished from 'letters close'). The plural form (*letters patent*) is used even for a single document.

LETTER-WRITING TECHNIQUES

See **CORRESPONDENCE (LETTERS AND EMAILS)**.

leverage

The extent of use of borrowed funds for investment purposes, usually expressed as a proportion or percentage. The greater the proportion of borrowings to the value of the investment, the greater the *leverage*. Thus, a 'highly leveraged' borrower is one who has incurred a large amount of debt in relation to equity invested.

lex

General usage

Latin: law. The word is usually part of a longer Latin term. Accurate English translations are always available, as in the following extract. Prefer them over the Latin.

> 'The *lex causae* is a convenient shorthand expression denoting the law (usually but not necessarily foreign) which governs the question. It is used in contradistinction to the *lex fori*, which always means the domestic law of the forum, ie (if the forum is English) English law. The *lex causae* may be more specifically denoted by a variety of expressions, usually in Latin, such as the *lex domicilii* (law of the domicile), *lex patriae* (law of the nationality), *lex loci contractus* (law of the country where a contract is made), *lex loci solutionis* (law of the country where a contract is to be performed or where a debt is to be paid), *lex loci delicti* (law of the country where a tort is committed), *lex situs* (law of the country where a thing is situated), *lex loci celebrationis* (law of the country where a marriage is celebrated), *lex loci actus* (law of the country where a legal act takes place), *lex monetae* (law of the country in whose currency a debt or other legal obligation is expressed). The terms of *lex loci disgraziae* (law of the place where a bill of exchange is dishonoured) and *lex loci stabuli* (law of the place where a motor car is garaged) are used only in jest.' [*Dicey and Morris on the Conflict of Laws*, 13th edn (2000), ed Lawrence Collins, vol 1, 29–30 [1-075], providing translations]

The following discussion considers specific *lex*-related usages.

lex loci

Latin: the law of the place. Often followed by another Latin term to indicate *which* place. As with other *lex*-related Latinisms, prefer plain English:

- 'The Dutch factors were held to be insufficiently significant to displace the *lex loci delicti* [prefer: *the law of the place of the wrong*], which was English.' [*Cox v Ergo Versicherung AG* [2014] UKSC 22; [2014] 1 AC 1379, [30] (Lord Sumption JSC)]
- 'Mr Turner's essential submission is that it is as much incumbent on an applicant to prove a marriage valid or void according to the *lex loci celebrationis* [prefer: *the law of the place where the marriage was solemnised*] as it is to establish that the overseas divorce etc is entitled to be recognised as valid in England and Wales.' [*Shagroon v Sharbatly* [2012] EWCA Civ 1507; [2013] 2 WLR 1255, [27] (Thorpe LJ)]

- 'According to a leading authority in the United States, … the following states continued to apply the *lex loci contractus* [prefer: *the law of the place where the contract was made*] …' [*Wasa International Insurance Co Ltd v Lexington Insurance Co* [2009] UKHL 40; [2010] 1 AC 180, [105] (Lord Collins)]

lex non cogit ad impossibilia

Latin: the law does not compel doing what is impossible. (Similarly, *nemo tenetur ad impossibilia*—no one is bound to perform impossibilities; and *lex non cogit ad inutilia*—the law does not compel doing what is useless.) Although the Latin trips off the tongue, it carries no more meaning than a translation—which can easily be given, as the judges do in the following examples:

- '[The] conclusion in this case can be reached by applying the maxim *lex non cogit ad impossibilia*—the law does not compel people to perform impossibilities.' [*Webber v Carey* [1970] AC 1072, 1090 (Lord Pearson)]
- 'But the principle expressed in the maxim *lex non cogit ad impossibilia*—the law does not compel a man to do that which he cannot possibly perform—is not rendered inapplicable … by anything … in the Act.' [*Dowell Australia Ltd v Archdeacon* (1975) 132 CLR 417, 426 (McTiernan J)]

lex non curat de minimis

Latin: the law is not concerned with minor matters. See **de minimis**.

lex scripta / lex non scripta

Lex scripta (Latin), the written law (often in the sense of statutory law); *lex non scripta* (Latin), the unwritten law (often in the sense of the common law). To retain these Latinisms in the face of adequate English translations is somewhat precious. If, for some reason, you feel compelled to retain the Latin, then at least add a translation, as in the first and second examples below:

1. 'The Appellant's written submissions elaborate the distinction between unwritten law (*lex non scripta*) and written law (*lex scripta*) by reference to Blackstone and other renowned writers.' [*DPP v Devins* [2012] IESC 7 [21] (Supreme Court of Ireland, Fennelly J)]
2. 'Originally enshrined in the memory of judges and legal practitioners, the common law is now located in the pages of law reports and textbooks. Nevertheless it is still called unwritten law or *lex non scripta* whereas legislation (with which common law is nowadays contrasted) is called written law or *lex scripta*.' [Francis Bennion, 'Human Rights: A Threat to Law?' (2003) 26 *University of New South Wales Law Journal* 418, 427–28]
3. '[The Bills of Exchange legislation] … is an attempt to convert a part of the *lex non scripta* [prefer: *unwritten law*; *common law*] into *lex scripta* [prefer: *written law*; *statute*].' [*Stock Motor Ploughs v Forsyth* (1932) 48 CLR 128, 137 (Dixon J)]

lex situs

Latin: the law of the place (usually, where the property is located). See **lex loci**.

Other examples

Other *lex*-related terms include:

- *lex iniusta non est lex*: an unjust law is not law
- *lex loci solutionis*: the law of the place where payment is to be made or performance tendered
- *lex rei situs*: the law of the location of the thing.

liable to

In some contexts, an ambiguous term. *Liable to* can mean (1) 'under an existing obligation to', or (2) 'may/will come under an obligation to' when a situation arises. Thus, under meaning (1) a joint tortfeasor may be legally *liable to* contribute to a damages payout even though no court judgment has declared on liability: eg, *Stott v West Yorkshire Road Car Co Ltd* [1971] 2 QB 651 (departing from an earlier House of Lords decision under a differently worded statute). In contrast, under meaning (2), trustees may be *liable to* expend trust funds, even though they are under no actual obligation to do so until they receive a proper demand (eg, *Re Hill* [1896] 1 Ch 962; *Saunders v Newbold* [1905] 1 Ch 260, 266). Even statutory drafters sometimes fail to draw the distinction. For example, if valuation legislation states that all land is *liable to* rating, does this mean that it is subject to rating (now), or that it may become subject to rating (in the future) when certain procedural steps (such as the issue of a rate notice) are taken (eg, *West Coast Council v Coverdale (No 2)* [2015] TASFC 1, [33])? Context may clarify, but an adept drafter will clarify from the outset.

licence / license

In British and Commonwealth usage, *licence* is the noun, *license* the verb: thus, legislation may *license* a registrar to grant a liquor *licence*. The adjectival form is *licensed* (eg, *licensed* hotel; *licensed* celebrant), and the person who holds a licence is a *licensee* (ie, a 'licensed' person). Thus, a person with a liquor *licence* is a *licensee* of *licensed* premises. In US usage, *license* is the preferred form in all cases.

lien

French, *lien* (from Latin *ligare*, to bind, tie). A right over goods or land to secure the payment of money. *Lien* is an elastic term, applied to rights of different types, sometimes based on possession and sometimes not, and sometimes given by law and sometimes granted by agreement. Variants include the following:

- *banker's lien*—a bank's right to hold securities and negotiable instruments (but not the contents of safety-deposit boxes) lodged by a customer or by someone on the customer's behalf, until the customer's debts to the bank are discharged.
- *carrier's lien*—a carrier's right to retain possession of goods transported, until the owner pays the transportation costs.
- *common law lien*—a lien granted by the common law (ie, a legal lien), and always depending on possession. Cf *equitable lien*.
- *crop lien*—a creditor's lien over growing crops, giving the creditor the right to the crops as security for repayment of a debt.
- *equitable lien*—an equitable right in the nature of a charge, given over real or personal property to protect against an inequitable result or to secure the satisfaction of claims. It may arise independently of contract, and does not depend on possession. Examples are a purchaser's lien (see below), a vendor's lien (see below), and a receiver's lien for expenses properly incurred in the conduct of the receivership.
- *general lien*—a possessory lien (see below) allowing the possessor of goods to hold them, not only as security for the satisfaction of claims arising in relation to the goods, but also for other claims the possessor has against the owner following similar dealings. Cf *particular lien*.
- *innkeeper's lien*—an innkeeper's right to retain a guest's goods until accommodation expenses are paid.
- *maritime lien*—a claim on a ship for service done to it or injury caused by it. The lien travels with the ship into whosever possession it comes, even a purchaser of the ship without

notice of the lien. Subcategories include liens for salvage, seamen's wages, and master's disbursements.

- *mechanic's lien* (or *artisan's lien*)—a possessory lien (see below) to secure payment for work done on property, such as repairs to a car.
- *particular lien (or specific lien)*—a lien allowing the possessor of particular goods to retain them as security for a claim connected with them, as distinct from claims in general against the owner of the goods. Cf *general lien.*
- *partnership lien*—a partner's right to have contributions to partnership assets recognised and (subject to clearing partnership debts) returned on a winding-up of the partnership.
- *possessory lien*—a right to retain possession of goods until a debt or liability is satisfied.
- *purchaser's lien*—a lien in the nature of a charge over land, which courts of equity give to a purchaser who has paid the full purchase price without receiving a transfer of the legal title.
- *solicitor's lien*—a possessory lien that a solicitor has over the client's documents to secure payment of legal fees and disbursements (*Gavin Edmondson Solicitors Ltd v Haven Insurance Co Ltd* [2018] UKSC 21; [2018] 1 WLR 2052).
- *specific lien*. See *particular lien.*
- *vendor's lien*—in relation to land, a lien in the nature of a charge over the land, which courts of equity give to a vendor who has parted with legal title to the land without yet being paid the full purchase price. In relation to goods, a lien to retain possession until the buyer has paid the full price.
- *warehouseman's lien*—a warehouse keeper's right to retain goods deposited for storage until the storage charges are paid.
- *wool lien*—a lien (more in the nature of a charge) over next season's wool clip, given as security for repayment of a debt.

lienee / lienor

The *lienee* is the person with the benefit of a lien. The *lienor* is the person who gives (ie, is burdened by) the lien.

See ***-ee* / *-or* endings**; **lien**.

life estate

Nature of life estate

In the common-law tradition, a life estate is an estate granted to a person for the duration of his or her life. The owner (holder) is the *life tenant*—meaning by *tenant* one who holds (Latin: 'tenere') an estate in land, not one who holds a lease from a landlord. The life tenant is normally entitled to possession of the land and the income from the land. The common law recognises two forms of life estate: an estate for the life of the grantee (an *ordinary* life estate), and an estate for the life of another (a life estate *pur autre vie*). The former is the more common.

In some jurisdictions, life estates can no longer exist as legal estates, but only as equitable interests (eg, *Law of Property Act 1925*, s 1). However, even in those jurisdictions, the terminology of 'life *estate*' survives (and is used in this book).

By its nature, a life estate assumes that the grantee is capable of dying. Thus, a corporation cannot hold a life estate, since corporations do not 'die' as humans do. This is even though corporations may be wound up and, until then, may be said to 'have a life': *Re Dodwell & Co Ltd's Trust* [1979] 1 Ch 301, 308.

In modern law, most life estates are granted by will or under a family settlement, usually to a spouse. A life estate can be qualified to end on a contingency that *may* (not *must*) occur before the life tenant's death—eg, for as long as the holder remains unmarried, or for as long as the holder resides in the house on the land.

Lease for life compared

It is possible to grant a *lease* for a person's lifetime. A '*lease* for life' differs from a 'life estate' because, despite its lifetime-duration, the lease for life remains a lease only. Which kind of right arises is a matter of interpreting the document creating the right. Conventionally, where property is given to a person 'for life', with no obligation to pay for its use, it is likely to be a life estate, particularly if the property is residential: *Re Midland Railway Co's Agreemen*t [1971] Ch 725, 732; *Greco v Swinburne Ltd* [1991] 1 VR 304, 314–16; *Haslam v Money for Living (Aust) Pty Ltd* (2008) 172 FCR 301, [23]. But where the document imposes obligations of the kind commonly found in leases (such as to pay rent, and to repair)—particularly if the property is non-residential—it is likely to be a lease only: *Borambil Pty Ltd v O'Carroll* [1972] 2 NSWLR 302, 305–07, affirmed [1974] 1 WLR 561 (PC).

Further reading

- S Bridge, E Cooke, and M Dixon (eds), *Megarry & Wade's Law of Real Property*, 9th edn (Sweet & Maxwell, 2019) [3-060]–[3-064]
- Kevin Gray and Susan Francis Gray, *Elements of Land Law*, 5th edn (Oxford University Press, 2009) ch 7.5

See also **estate or interest**; **fee simple**; **fee tail**; **tenant**.

life interest

Another term for a life estate.

See **life estate**.

liferent

Liferent (pronounced 'life rent') is a Scots law equivalent of the English and Commonwealth term *life estate*. Although the concepts are similar, the terminology never crosses the jurisdictional divide.

See **life estate**.

like

In legal usage, often combined with other words to produce phrases that seem both quaint and antiquated: eg, '*like* circumstances', '*like* jurisdiction', '*like* nature', '*like* effect', '*like* penalty', '*like* work'. In all such examples, unless the context suggests otherwise, *like* means *similar to*: see, eg, *Re British Concrete Pipe Association's Agreement* [1982] ICR 182, 187–88 (Moccata J). However, *similar to* itself can carry different nuances: eg, 'substantially similar to', 'almost identical to', or 'identical to'. So, if possible, use a more specific term than *like* or *similar to*.

likely to

Likely to—as in 'X is *likely* to happen'—is notoriously imprecise. The general sense is 'prone to' happen, or 'with a propensity to' happen, or 'liable to' happen: *Tillmans Butcheries Pty Ltd v Australasian Meat Industry Employees' Union* (1979) 27 ALR 367, 380 (Deane J). But as the case law shows, that general sense leaves room for doubt about the precise meaning in particular circumstances. For example:

- A court had the statutory power to restrain publication of material in advance of a trial, if the trial was *likely to* establish that publication should be barred. The Court of Appeal unanimously held that *likely* meant 'having a real prospect of success': *Cream Holdings Ltd v Banerjee* [2003] Ch 650. The House of Lords unanimously disagreed, holding that *likely* meant 'will probably succeed', and that sometimes even a lower threshold might suffice: *Cream Holdings Ltd v Banerjee* [2004] UKHL 44; [2005] 1 AC 253.
- A New Zealand review of case law indicated that, depending on context, the meaning of *likely to* can range between possible, distinctly or significantly possible, reasonably probable, probable, and highly probable: *Air New Zealand Ltd v Commerce Commission* [1985] 2 NZLR 338, 342–43 (Davison CJ).
- The Australian High Court viewed *likely* as meaning 'substantial—a real and not remote—chance regardless of whether it is less or more than 50%': *Boughey v R* (1986) 161 CLR 10, 21 (Mason, Wilson, and Deane JJ).

To illustrate from just one Commonwealth country, over a few years only, appellate decisions gave *likely* the following range of meanings:

- a degree of probability at the upper end of the scale, but not necessarily exceeding 50%: *Tillman v Attorney-General (NSW)* [2007] NSWCA 327; (2007) 70 NSWLR 448 (context: whether a convicted person is '*likely* to reoffend')
- more likely than not—ie, more than 50%: *RJE v Department of Justice* [2008] VSCA 265; (2008) 21 VR 526 (context: whether a convicted person is '*likely* to reoffend')
- a realistic possibility: *John R Ring Pty Ltd v Commissioner of Consumer and Business Affairs* [2009] SASC 174; (2009) 104 SASR 163 (context: *likely* price range in property advertisement)
- a substantial likelihood, but without descending to percentages of probability: *R v Hung* [2012] QCA 341; [2013] 2 Qd R 64 (context: whether death or serious harm is *likely* to result from using defensive force)
- more than probable: *R v Crossman* [2011] QCA 126; [2011] 2 Qd R 435 (whether actions are *likely* to case grievous bodily harm)
- a real chance of something eventuating (rather than a greater probability than not of its eventuating): *Australian Competition and Consumer Commission v Metcash Trading Ltd* [2011] FCA 967; (2011) 282 ALR 464 (context: the *likely* effect on competition if a company merger is allowed; result affirmed on appeal, but with reservations about the meaning of *likely*: *Australian Competition and Consumer Commission v Metcash Trading Limited* [2011] FCAFC 151; (2011) 198 FCR 297
- a possibility, rather than a certainty or near certainty: *Retirement Benefits Fund Board v Elmore* [2014] TASFC 1; (2014) 23 Tas R 36 (context: a worker's right to join a pension fund if the worker is *likely* to remain in employment for at least 3 years)
- a real chance or real prospect, not merely more probable than not: *Sinclair v Darwich* [2010] NSWCA 195; (2010) 77 NSWLR 166 (context: whether damages awarded for accident are *likely* to exceed prescribed percentage of allowable maximum).

None of these pronouncements gives cause for confidence in using *likely to*. Think carefully before using so protean a term.

See also **calculated to**; **will**.

limitation period

Legal shorthand for the maximum period allowed for starting court proceedings, as specified by the relevant 'statute of limitations'. For example, in many jurisdictions the limitation period for enforcing a breach of contract is 6 years after the breach, or 12 years for a contract embodied in a deed. Proceedings started beyond the period are 'statute-barred', or 'out of time'.

Limited / Ltd

Use the full version—*Smith Limited*—where the corporation's full title is necessary: eg, in an agreement to which the corporation is a party. However, in case citations it is common to use the abbreviation *Ltd*: eg, *Jones v Smith Ltd* [not *Limited*].

limited partner

A partner whose liability to contribute to the partnership's debts and obligations is limited by the capital that he or she has contributed to the firm.

Compare **general partner**.

limited partnership

A partnership formed under partnership legislation and containing at least one limited partner and at least one general partner.

See **general partner**; **limited partner**.

LINE LENGTH

See **DOCUMENT DESIGN**.

LINE SPACING

See **DOCUMENT DESIGN**.

liquidated

In general usage, *to liquidate* means to put an end to, or wipe out. To some extent, legal usage reflects this general usage: thus, a debt is *liquidated* (paid out, put an end to) and a company is *liquidated* (wound up, dissolved). But in legal usage, *liquidated* bears another meaning also: fixed, ascertained, or (in some contexts) able to be ascertained by a binding process. Thus, a person may claim *liquidated* damages, or make a *liquidated* demand or claim, or sue for a *liquidated* sum or *liquidated* debt. However, despite this settled usage, doubt can exist about the meaning of *liquidated* in some contexts. Recent appellate discussions include *Barnett v Creggy* [2016] EWCA Civ 1004; [2017] 2 WLR 1054 (beneficiary's claim against trustee for equitable compensation is not a *liquidated* claim); *Blavo v Law Society* [2018] EWCA Civ 2250; [2019] 1 WLR 1977 [115] (outstanding legal fees may be a *liquidated* amount).

lis

Latin: a legal proceeding; litigation; court proceedings; controversy. Plural *lites*. A plain-English translation suffices:

> 'The courts are concerned with the practical business of deciding a *lis* [prefer: *court action*; *controversy*].' [*A-G v Prince Ernest Augustus of Hanover* [1957] AC 436, 467 (Lord Normand)]

Lis is used in conjunction with other Latin terms, including the following.

lis alibi pendens

Latin: a suit (proceedings) elsewhere. In practice, usually refers more narrowly to simultaneous proceedings pending in two courts between the same parties and involving the same or similar issues: *Virsagi Management (S) Pte Ltd v Welltech Construction Pte Ltd* [2013] SGCA 50, [26]; [2013] 4 SLR 1097, 1105 (Leong JA). Prefer plain English.

lis pendens

Latin: a pending lawsuit—'pending' in the sense of 'on foot and not yet decided'. A suit is not 'pending' if the moving party is merely considering whether to sue; and an appeal is not pending where, being out of time to appeal, the party has applied to court for an order extending the time to appeal: *Tenaga Nasional Bhd v Frazer-Nash Research Ltd* [2018] EWHC 2970; [2019] 1 WLR 946, [45]–[50]. In some jurisdictions, it is possible to register a *lis pendens* against title to land, binding the title. This warns people planning to acquire an interest in the land—in effect, 'beware: court proceedings are on foot, and any interest you acquire in the land may be subject to the litigant's rights'.

Some commentators regard *lis pendens* as 'a useful Latinism': eg. Bryan A Garner, *Garner's Dictionary of Legal Usage*, 3rd edn (Oxford University Press, 2011) 546. In reality, however, the English translation suffices.

lite pendente

Often rendered *pendente lite*. Latin: pending the suit; with a lawsuit pending; during litigation. 'Pending' here means (as in lis *pendens*) 'on foot' or 'started'; that is, proceedings are under way, not merely anticipated or threatened. Often used in probate law in the context of appointing an administrator or receiver 'pending' litigation about the validity of the will or about the grant of probate or administration; the appointee's duties end when the court case ends. An appropriate English translation removes the justification for retaining the Latin. For example:

- 'However[,] what is clear is that the order made was of the character of an order made *pendente lite* [prefer: *pending the main hearing*] without prejudice to the rights of the parties in the pending litigation.' [*On Demand plc v Michael Gerson plc* [2002] UKHL 13; [2003] 1 AC 368, [6] (Lord Hobhouse)]
- 'When the validity of a notice to quit is in dispute, until that issue is resolved it will not be known whether the tenancy has ended or whether it still exists. The tenancy has a trance-like existence *pendente lite* [prefer: *pending the decision on that point*]; none can assert with assurance whether it is alive or dead.' [*Meadows v Clerical Medical and General Life Assurance Society* [1981] Ch 70, 75 (Megarry V-C)]

See also **FOREIGN (NON-ENGLISH) WORDS AND PHRASES.**

LISTS AND ENUMERATIONS

Usefulness

To *list* is to set out items consecutively; to *enumerate* is to mention items one by one. The verbs overlap, as do their cognate nouns. But the underlying purpose is the same: to enhance readability by dividing information into digestible chunks. This generally involves presenting the information in down-the-page tabular format, rather than running it on in standard sentence format. The tabulated items can be numbered (particularly if they need to be referred to later), or given bullet points, or simply listed without markings. A tabular format diminishes the psychological barrier of dense text. It also brings the items more directly to the reader's attention.

Example

Before: single paragraph

Free from Encumbrances

The Shares and the Shareholder Loans must be transferred free from any Encumbrance and with all rights attached or accruing to them on and from the date of this document. It is expressly agreed that the rights, title and interest of the Seller in and to the Shares to be sold to and purchased by the Buyer hereunder shall include: (i) any shares hereafter issued by the Company by way of stock dividends on the Shares; (ii) any property or cash dividends paid on the Shares from and after Completion Date; (iii) all rights hereafter accruing on the Shares; and (iv) the proceeds of any of the foregoing.

After version 1: tabular format [wording unchanged]

Free from Encumbrances

(a) The Shares and the Shareholder Loans must be transferred free from any Encumbrance and with all rights attached or accruing to them on and from the date of this document.

(b) It is expressly agreed that the rights, title and interest of the Seller in and to the Shares to be sold to and purchased by the Buyer hereunder shall include:

  (i) any shares hereafter issued by the Company by way of stock dividends on the Shares;
  (ii) any property or cash dividends paid on the Shares from and after Completion Date;
  (iii) all rights hereafter accruing on the Shares; and
  (iv) the proceeds of any of the foregoing.

After version 2: better still, improving aspects of drafting

Free from Encumbrances

(a) [X]must transfer the Shares and the Shareholder Loans free from any Encumbrance and with all rights attached or accruing to them on and from the date of this document.

(b) The Seller's rights in the Shares include:

  (i) any shares issued by the Company after the date of this document by way of stock dividends on the Shares;
  (ii) any property or cash dividends paid on the Shares from and after the Completion Date;
  (iii) all rights accruing on the Shares after the date of this document;
  (iv) the proceeds of any of the items in (i), (ii) and (iii).

Punctuation at lead-in to list

Dash or colon?

Good practice is to:

- use a dash (preferably an em dash) immediately after the lead-in, if the listed words flow immediately and naturally as part of the same sentence
- use a colon if the list is the product of the lead-in.

Example

The deputy may exercise all the powers of the principal while—

(a) there is a vacancy in the office of the principal …

[but]

The powers and duties of the principal are these:

(a) to notify the board …

The former common practices of colon + em dash [:—], or colon + en dash [:–], or colon + hyphen [:-], are now rare.

Appositives

Consider ending the lead-in with a word or phrase that suggests more is to come (an appositive), such as 'the following'.

Example

The tenant must do all of the following:

- keep the premises clean
- paint the premises once each year
- keep common passageways clear of obstruction.

Punctuation within items in lists

It is customary to treat the lead-in and the list as part of the same 'sentence'. For that reason, each listed item starts with a lower-case letter (unless the first word is a proper noun), and there is a single full stop at the end of the list (assuming that the sentence does not carry on after the end of the list).

However, practice varies over punctuation at the end of each item in the list. The three options are:

1. use no punctuation
2. use a comma,
3. use a semicolon;

Logically, where the lead-in and the items in the list form a single 'sentence', the appropriate punctuation at the end of each item in the list is a comma (as in option (2) above). This is particularly so where the sentence continues after the last item.

Example 1

A licensee of a supermarket may sell the following items:

(a) fruit,
(b) confectionary,
(c) alcohol, and
(d) stationery,

if holding a current licence.

However, this technique is cumbersome where commas also separate items within subparts of the list. It then makes more sense to use a semicolon at the end of each subpart (except perhaps the last, where the sentence continues to run on).

Example 2

> A licensee of a supermarket may sell the following items:
> (a) fruit, vegetables, and mushrooms;
> (b) confectionary, sweets, and ice-creams;
> (c) beer, wine, and tobacco;
> (d) stationery, gift cards, and SIM cards, [;]
> if holding a current licence.

Better still, in this and the preceding example, remove the 'sandwich' construction by shifting the concluding words up to the lead-in:

> 'A licensee of a supermarket may, if holding a current licence, sell the following items:

What if a second or further sentence begins in the middle of a listed item? Here, most drafters follow a convention peculiar to legal drafting. Within the listed item, they (1) use a full stop at the end of the first sentence, and then (2) start the new sentence within the listed item, but (3) end that sentence with their normal list punctuation style (a comma, a semicolon, or nothing at all). To readers unaccustomed to the convention, this must appear grammatically illogical. Two options to avoid this appearance are:

option (a) recast the offending item to eliminate the illogicality;

option (b) reshape the list into a different type—each item starting with a capital letter and ending with a full stop (preferably making each item a stand-alone sentence, although this is not always possible).

Example

Traditional (grammatically illogical sentence in para 2)	**Recast the offending item [option (a)]**	**Reshape the list [option (b)]**
Before granting a licence, the Department must: 1. ensure that the application form is complete; 2. notify all adjoining owners. *This can be done by mail, fax or email*; 3. verify that the applicant has paid all prescribed fees.	Before granting a licence, the Department must: 1. ensure that the application form is complete; 2. notify all adjoining owners, *by mail, fax or email*; 3. verify that the applicant has paid all prescribed fees.	Before granting a licence, the Department must *take the following steps*: 1. Ensure that the application form is complete. 2. Notify all adjoining owners. *This can be done by mail, fax or email.* 3. Verify that the applicant has paid all prescribed fees.

Linking items in list

Traditional convention

Where items (paragraphs) in a list are to be read conjunctively or disjunctively, the long-standing legal convention is to insert the appropriate linking word ('and' or 'or') between only the second-last and last paragraphs in the list. The reader then implies the same word between earlier items in the list.

Example

Linking word 'and'	**Linking word 'or'**
A notice must be: (a) in writing, (b) in accordance with the prescribed form, (c) printed in duplicate, and (d) served personally.	Service of notices may be: (a) by personal delivery, (b) by post, (c) by email, or (d) by text message.

Repeat the conjunction?

However, that setting-out assumes that readers know the convention—ie, they know to go immediately to the penultimate paragraph, find the linking word ('and' or 'or'), and then imply the same conjunction at the end of each preceding paragraph. Not all readers know that convention. And even if they do, ambiguity can still occur (or be conjured), as in the following example.

> By statute, a landlord could not enforce repairing covenants in a lease unless the landlord could prove:
>
> (a) ...;
> (b) ...;
> (c) ...;
> (d) ...; or
> (e) ....
>
> Undoubtedly, para (e) was an alternative to the prior paras. But if the landlord could not prove (e), did the landlord need to prove *all* of paras (a)–(d), or only *one* of paras (a)–(d). That is, was the word to be implied between paras (a)–(d) 'and' or 'or'? Held, 'or' was to be implied: *Phillips v Price* [1959] Ch 181 (Harman J, stating that the absence of 'or' between the paras was 'a blot on the draftsmanship' and that he was 'at one time inclined' to the view that 'and' was to be implied: at 185–86).

To avoid arguments of this kind, some drafters insert the relevant conjunction ('and' or 'or') after *every* item in a list.

Example

> A notice must be:
>
> (a) in writing, and
> (b) in accordance with the prescribed form, and
> (c) printed in duplicate, and
> (d) served personally.

An advantage of this technique—for the drafter as well as for the reader—is that the repetition avoids the embarrassment that may occur if, in the course of negotiating the document, the penultimate paragraph is deleted, along with the critical 'and' or 'or'.

Avoid the conjunction?

Some drafters consider that the style in the preceding example makes the text appear fussy. It may be possible to avoid repeating the conjunction, by redrafting the lead-in. In Example 1 below, the lead-in clearly implies 'or' between the items in the list. In Example 2, the lead-in sufficiently implies 'and' between the items in the list.

Example 1 (Australian statute)

(2) Without limiting subsection (1), "supply" includes any of these:

(a) a supply of goods;

(b) a supply of services;

[then follow (c)–(h) in the same form]

[Source: *A New Tax System (Goods and Services Tax) Act 1999* (Cth), ss 9–10(2)]

Example 2 (contractual provision)

A notice must be:

(a) in writing,

(b) in accordance with the prescribed form,

(c) printed in duplicate,

(d) served personally.

Parallel structure

In lists and enumerations, always use a parallel structure—one that flows logically and efficiently. That means, for example, not mixing directions, requests, and stand-alone sentences in the same list:

Poor structure	**Parallel structure**
The duties of the directors are:	The duties of directors are to:
1. to attend all board meetings [direction];	1. attend all board meetings [direction];
2. directors must answer all questions from shareholders [stand-alone sentence];	2. answer all questions from shareholders [direction];
3. approval of monthly profit statements [topic heading].	3. approve monthly profit statements [direction].

Consistent flow

Lists and enumerations must flow consistently from the lead-in, without needless variations. The following example (taken from a credit agreement in the 'You/We' style) illustrates the issue.

Example

3.3 Acknowledgement

If a Credit is payable under clause 3.2, You:

(a) *agree* that We can apply the Credit to offset any amounts payable by Us to You;

(b) *acknowledge* that We can elect to waive part or all of a Credit during the term of this Contract;

(c) *acknowledge and agree* that any Credit calculated in accordance with this agreement is reasonable and does not constitute a penalty.

Do the variants *agree*, and *acknowledge*, and *acknowledge and agree*, serve any purpose? Almost certainly not. They are mere habit, or are drawn without analysis from a precedent. Indeed, the repetition could be problematic, given the presumption that a change of wording presumes a change of meaning. In reality, one word—*agree* or *acknowledge*—would suffice, and could be transferred to the lead-in sentence—eg, 'You *agree* that: (a) …'

Also, lists and enumerations must flow grammatically and idiomatically from the lead-in. Breach of these twin requirements may not cause legal uncertainty, but will distract the reader and make the drafter appear careless. In the following 'Before' example (taken from a contract for the sale of shares), the first words in (b) ['must also'] do not follow grammatically from the lead-in. Also, the first word in (c) ['not'], while following grammatically from the lead-in, abruptly and inelegantly reverses the flow of the sentence, from directions (in (a) and (b)) to prohibitions, breaching the ideal of a parallel structure (discussed earlier). Note also the 'orphaned' qualification in the concluding words (highlighted for convenience). The 'After' example cures these defects (though it could also benefit from further editing).

Before	After
Conduct of affairs pending Completion Until Completion the Company must: (a) carry on its affairs in the ordinary course and materially in accordance with the Budget; and (b) must also comply in all respects with the Shareholder Agreement and take all steps to ensure that the Buyer complies with the Shareholder Agreement; and (c) not: (i) incur any capital expenditure (including by way of hire purchase or finance leases) not provided for in the Budget; (ii) enter into any contract not provided for in the Budget; (iii) incur, issue, assume, extend, renew or guarantee any new or additional obligation; (iv) sell, create any Encumbrance on, or otherwise dispose of, or acquire, any of the Company's assets or interests therein, *except with the prior written consent of the Seller.*	**Conduct of affairs pending Completion** (a) Until Completion the Company must: (i) carry on its affairs in the ordinary course and materially in accordance with the Budget; and (ii) comply in all respects with the Shareholder Agreement and take all steps to ensure that the Buyer complies with the Shareholder Agreement. (b) In addition, until Completion the Company must not, *except with the Seller's prior written consent*: (i) incur any capital expenditure (including by way of hire purchase or finance leases) not provided for in the Budget; (ii) enter into any contract not provided for in the Budget; (iii) incur, issue, assume, extend, renew or guarantee any new or additional obligation; (iv) sell, create any Encumbrance on, or otherwise dispose of, or acquire, any of the Company's assets or interests in them.

Undue repetition in enumerated items

As a general rule, avoid repeating the same word or phrase at the beginning of each item in a list or enumeration. Instead, move the word or phrase to the lead-in.

Before (italics added to show repetition)	After
The Bank agrees: (a) *to promptly inform the customer* about interest rate changes; (b) *to promptly inform the customer* about changes in its policies; (c) *to promptly inform the customer* about potential changes in market conditions.	The Bank agrees *to promptly inform the customer* about: (a) interest rate changes; (b) changes in its policies; (c) potential changes in market conditions.

However, the qualification 'as a general rule' is important. Some limited repetition—particularly in the infinitive form of verbs—may help the text flow more easily or add emphasis, as in the following example (italics added to show the repetition):

> The purpose of this action is:
>
> (a) *to* inform …
>
> (b) *to* create …
>
> (c) *to* allow …
>
> *[rather than]*
>
> The purpose of this action is to:
>
> (a) inform …
>
> (b) create …
>
> (c) allow …

Over-fragmentation

Despite the benefits of lists and enumerations, beware of over-fragmenting information. Excessive division into itemised form can make sentences harder to understand, because they force the reader to conceptually re-merge the constituent parts of the sentences. See discussion under **CLAUSE STRUCTURE (Avoid over-division)**.

See also **BULLET POINTS; CLAUSE STRUCTURE; DASHES; DOCUMENT STRUCTURE; PARALLEL STRUCTURE; PUNCTUATION; SEMICOLONS.**

LITERARY ALLUSIONS

Their use

Literary allusions can be a powerful rhetorical tool. They can express ideas powerfully and succinctly—perhaps more powerfully and succinctly than the immediate author's talents allow. They can also help concentrate the reader's mind, by invoking a colorful word, phrase, or usage.

A famous example is Lord Atkin's invocation of *Alice in Wonderland*, in *Liversidge v Anderson* [1942] AC 206, 245. His purpose was to castigate the majority's view in the House of Lords that certain statutory wording permitted the Secretary of State to detain persons based on the Secretary's subjective belief, limited by considerations of good faith but not otherwise testable objectively in court:

> 'I know of only one authority which might justify the suggested method of construction: "When I use a word," Humpty Dumpty said in rather a scornful tone, "it means just what I choose it to mean, neither more nor less." "The question is," said Alice, "whether you can make words mean so many different things." "The question is," said Humpty Dumpty, "which is to be master—that's all".'
>
> [Judicial and societal response to Lord Atkin's reference to *Alice in Wonderland* was mixed: PDT Applegarth, 'Lord Atkin: Principle and Progress' (2016) 90 *Australian Law Journal* 711, 744–49.]

Biblical allusions

Biblical allusions can also be a powerful rhetorical tool. Lord Atkin invoked the 'neighbour principle' in *Donoghue v Stevenson* [1932] AC 562, 580:

> 'The rule that you are to love your neighbour becomes in law, you must not injure your neighbour; and the lawyer's question, Who is my neighbour? receives a restricted reply. You must take reasonable care to avoid acts or omissions which you can reasonably foresee would be likely to injure your neighbour. Who, then, in law is my neighbour? The answer seems to be …'

Limits on usefulness

But there are limits to the usefulness of literary allusions. The key one is audience knowledge. In a lawyer's advice to a client who lacks knowledge of Greek or Latin classics, allusions drawn from Homer or Cicero are likely to serve no purpose—even more so, of course, if a quotation is reproduced in the original Greek or Latin. Similarly, many biblical or Shakespearean allusions are unlikely to communicate to readers unschooled in English-language literary classics: what meaning have camels through needles' eyes, bricks without straw, swords into ploughshares, actors and parts—even, 'who is my neighbour?'

Literary allusions in judgments may have more effect, given that the readership may reasonably be expected to understand them. And so in a judgment a literary allusion may be useful, for example, as an opener to entice readers into the text, or to indicate that the human dilemma posed by the case has exercised writers and thinkers for centuries.

However, overblown allusions are always counter-productive. They distract from the message, impeding rather than enhancing the communication of ideas. In the following extract from an Australian judgment, the mixed biblical and trade allusions become laboured:

> '[In the interpretation of s 260] there were the creationists who believed in the literal interpretation of the section and worked hard and tithed, albeit at 60 cents in the dollar. Dogmatically opposed to these fundamentalists stood the afiscalopalians who regarded s 260 as merely symbolic and neither spun nor toiled. Instead, they believed in the "choice principle" and hitched their wagon to the silk merchants and went forth into the world opening new trade routes and erecting shrines to this art nouveau on exotic islands.
>
> And behold, there came Three Wise Men from the East called Gulland, Watson and Pincus who steered a narrow course between the Scylla of Newton and the Charybdis of Slutzkin with jurisprudential seamanship denied to lesser mariners.' [*Re Taxation Appeals Nos WT85/28* [1988] AATA 264; 19 ATR 3865, [9]–[10] (Deputy President Gerber)]
>
> [To explain: s 260 of the *Income Tax Assessment Act 1936* (Cth) sought to strike down tax-avoidance arrangements. The Three Wise Men were three judges, and *Newton* and *Slutzkin* were court decisions raising s 260 (*Newton* being a decision of the Privy Council, and *Slutzkin* a decision of the High Court of Australia).]

Also counterproductive are 'corny' allusions. An Australian case considered whether, for taxation purposes, a car park for employees was 'in the *vicinity* of' their place of employment. The judge invoked a ditty from *The Pirates of Penzance*: there is 'a doctor of divinity … located in this *vicinity*': *Virgin Blue Airlines Pty Ltd v Federal Commissioner of Taxation* [2010] FCAFC 137; (2010) 190 FCR 150, 164 (Jessup J).

Further reading

- Ken Barlow, 'Alice, Humpty Dumpty and the Law' (2011) 85 *Australian Law Journal* 365 (reviewing case law that quotes Lewis Carroll)
- Elwyn Elms, 'On the use of classical allusions in judgment writing' (2008) *University of NSW Law Journal* 56 (arguing for their use, but restrained)
- Walker Gibson, 'Literary Minds and Judicial Style' (1961) 36 *New York University Law Review* 915
- Michael Kirby, 'Literature in Australian Judicial Reasoning' (2001) 75 *Australian Law Journal* 602
- Michael Meehan, 'The Good, The Bad, and The Ugly: Judicial Literacy and the Australian Cultural Cringe' (1990) 12 *Adelaide Law Review* 432

litigant / litigator

A *litigant* is a party to litigation. A *litigator* is 'one who litigates', but the word is generally used, more narrowly, to mean a person (ie, a lawyer) who conducts litigation on behalf of a *litigant* (the client).

LITIGATED WORDS AND PHRASES

Beware of relying too heavily on the argument that words or phrases are 'safe' because they have been litigated—as if judicial exegesis somehow guarantees certainty. The perceived safety may be misleading, for a number of reasons:

- The words or phrases may have been litigated because they are inherently uncertain—which is a good reason to avoid them.
- They may have been litigated because they are inherently flexible ('reasonable endeavours', 'good faith'), giving no certainty of application in different circumstances—which is a good reason to be careful in their use.
- Almost certainly, the litigation clarified the meaning of the word or phrase in the particular circumstances only. Meaning varies with context. A word or phrase used in one context, or between particular parties, may not carry the same meaning in a different context or between different parties. To adapt Professor Mellinkoff's description, most of the words or phrases are like soldiers who have been 'in the army' but not 'in combat': David Mellinkoff, *The Language of the Law* (Little, Brown & Co, 1963) 375.

Nevertheless, there is a strong principle of interpretation that where a court gives a meaning to a technical word or phrase, it will give the same meaning to that same word or phrase in later cases—particularly (but not exclusively) where the word or phrase is used in a standard-form contract: *Brien v Dwyer* [1976] 2 NSWLR 420, 423–24 (Hutley JA); *The World Symphony* [1991] 2 Lloyd's Rep 251, 257 (Hobhouse J); *Lasermax Engineering Pty Ltd v QBE Insurance (Australia) Ltd* [2005] NSWCA 66 [35]-[37], (2005) 13 ANZ Insurance Cases 61-643 (on the meaning of 'directly caused by' in insurance policies). The law presumes that the parties know how the courts have interpreted the word or phrase, and that they intend their document to be interpreted in that light.

> 'Once a court has put a construction on commercial documents in a standard form, commercial [people] act upon it. It should be followed in all subsequent cases. If the business community is not satisfied with the decision, they should alter the form.' [*The Annefield* [1971] P 168, 183 (Lord Denning MR)]

However, the role of the principle should not be exaggerated. In any given field of law, the percentage of terms with meanings judicially 'settled' in this way is likely to be small. For example, a 1985 survey of property documents put the percentage at not more than 3%: B Barr, G Hathaway, N Omichinski and D Pratt, 'Legalese and the Myth of Case Precedent' (1985) 64 *Michigan Bar Journal* 1136.

Further reading

Mark Adler, 'Tried and Tested: The Myth Behind the Cliché' (1996) 34 *Clarity* 45

See also **CONSISTENCY OF TERMINOLOGY**; **ELEGANT VARIATION**; **INCONSISTENT PROVISIONS**; **Mitsui principle**; **STANDARD FORMS**; **TERMS OF ART**.

live and reside

A lawyer's instinctive pairing. Either *live* or *reside* will suffice:

> '[When] the complainant first occupied the caravan on this piece of land ten years ago, the landlord agreed that he might *live and reside* [prefer: *reside*, because it is used in the following sentences] in that caravan on that land. The premises upon which he was allowed to *reside* are the composite unit of the caravan and the land upon which it stands. ... The land and caravan together are the premises in which the complainant *resided* with the agreement of the defendant.' [*Norton v Knowles* [1969] QB 572, 576 (Salmon LJ)]

LJ

Abbreviation for *Lord Justice*: eg, Rix LJ.

LLB

Abbreviation for *Legum Baccalaureus* (Bachelor of Laws). Often spaced: LL B.

LLM

Abbreviation for *Legum Magister* (Master of Laws). Often spaced: LL M.

loan

See **lend / loan (verb)**.

loan-to-value ratio

For clarity, prefer hyphens (though they are often dropped in practice); abbreviation, *LVR*. The ratio (expressed as a percentage) between the amount advanced under a loan and the value of the property on which it is secured. Thus, a loan of $75,000 secured on a property valued at $100,000 gives a loan-to-value ratio of 75%.

loc cit

Abbreviation for *loco citato* (Latin: in the place cited). In British/Commonwealth usage, no full stops: *loc cit*; but in US usage, *loc. cit.*, in accordance with the US preference for full stops in abbreviations. Indicates that the reference will be found in the place already cited. Some writers prefer *op cit*, which carries a similar meaning.

See also **op cit**.

lockfast place

A place secured by lock or key (eg, premises, a room, a drawer, a box, a car). The term seems unique to Scots law or Scots-trained lawyers. Examples include:

- 'The Lord Ordinary held that ... anyone with half an eye who made use of Macpherson's Close [in Dunfermline] could have seen that the main building of the cinema was no longer *lockfast* and was being regularly entered by unauthorised persons.' [*Smith v Littlewoods Organisation Ltd* [1987] 1 AC 241, 253 (Lord Mackay of Clashfern)]
- 'Nothing in this section authorises any person to enter a dwelling or *lockfast* premises.' [*Nature Conservation (Scotland) Act 2004* (Scot), s 44(4)]

LOCK-UP CLAUSE

A clause, often found in heads of agreement, that attempts to confine a party to taking, or not taking, a particular course of action. They are of two kinds: (1) a *lock-in* clause, in which parties agree to exclusively negotiate with each other towards a commercial end; and (2) a *lock-out* clause, in which a party agrees not to negotiate with others (ie, non-parties). *Lock-in* clauses may be difficult to enforce, being essentially agreements to negotiate: *Walford v Miles* [1992] 2 AC 128. *Lock-out* clauses do not have that failing, and being negative in form may be easier to enforce.

See also **HEADS OF AGREEMENT**.

loco citato

See **loc cit**.

locus

General usage

Latin: place. The word appears in many combinations, none of which are terms of art and all of which can be expressed in plain English. Examples are:

- *locus delicti*: the place where the crime was committed
- *locus in quo*: the place in which (something occurs)
- *locus solutionis*: the place of payment, or the place of performance of an obligation.

A discussion of other usages follows.

locus classicus

Latin: the classic place; the classic source. Often used in the sense of the pre-eminent ('classic') judicial decision, or the pre-eminent statement of a principle. A plain-English translation, varied as required to suit the context, always works:

- 'As it was put in the *locus classicus* [prefer: *classic statement*], *Reg v Eagleton* (1855) …' [*Director of Public Prosecutions (UK) v Stonehouse* [1978] AC 55, 68 (Lord Diplock)]
- '[T]he cases are legion, but the *locus classicus* [prefer: *classic example*] is the judgment of Lord Bingham and Lord Walker in *Sharma v Brown-Antoine*.' [*Wasif v The Secretary of State for the Home Department* [2016] EWCA Civ 82; [2016] 1 WLR 2793, [13] (Underhill LJ)]
- 'Keane J first looked at the *locus classicus* [prefer: *key statement of the rule*] in *Cahill v Sutton* to find the primary rule.' [*Mohan v Ireland* [2018] IECA 13, [47] (Ryan P)]

locus poenitentiae

Latin: the place of (for) repentance—in the sense of an opportunity for reconsideration, a chance to change one's mind before the consequences of an act take effect. The Latinism, though hallowed in legal usage and often masquerading as a term of art, can always be translated into plain English. For example:

- '[A] person who has transferred property for an illegal purpose can nevertheless recover his property provided that he withdraws from the transaction before the illegal purpose has been wholly or partly performed. This is the doctrine of the *locus poenitentiae* [prefer: *opportunity to repent*; *second chance*] and it applies in equity as well as at law …' [*Tribe v Tribe* [1996] Ch 107, 124 (Millett LJ)]

- 'The law does not penalize intention. On the contrary, it recognizes *a locus poenitentiae* [prefer: *an opportunity to repent*] and assumes that the opportunity for repentance may be exercised.' [*Gollan v Nugent* (1988) 166 CLR 18, 48 (Deane, Dawson, Toohey and Gaudron JJ)]

locus sigilli

Latin: the place for [of] the seal. The Latin phrase is no better than the English translation. So, when specifying on a document (usually a deed) where a party's seal is to be affixed, prefer 'place for the seal'.

In practice, this Latinism usually appears in an abbreviated form—*LS*—within a circle, to indicate where the seal is to be affixed. Courts have held that, even if no seal is in fact affixed, the abbreviation 'LS' (whether printed or handwritten) is as effective as an actual seal. For example:

- '[W]hile in 1888 the printed indication of a *locus sigilli* was regarded as being merely the place where a seal was to be affixed, I have no doubt that it is now regarded by most business people and ordinary members of the public as constituting the seal itself.' [*First National Securities Ltd v Jones* [1978] Ch 109, 119, 121 (Sir David Cairns, speaking of 'LS' printed within a circle)]
- '[T]he diplomatic note concluded with the manuscript letters "L.S.", an abbreviation for "*locus sigilli*"—the place of the seal. There is no reason why the trial judge should not have accepted the evidence that … Germany, on occasions, uses the letters "L.S." in diplomatic notes in place of a seal or stamp.' [*Von Arnim v Ellison* [2006] FCAFC 49; (2006) 150 FCR 282, [60] (Young J)]

There is no accepted English counterpart for the Latin 'LS', which may explain the longevity of the Latin abbreviation.

Further reading on locus sigilli

- DC Hoath, 'The Sealing of Documents—Fact or Fiction' (1980) 43 *Modern Law Review* 415
- RJ Vann, 'The Sealing of Deeds by Individuals' (1980) 54 *Australian Law Journal* 46

locus standi

Latin: the place of standing—ie, the right to be heard in court; having a right of audience. The term is always translatable into plain English, the most common substitute being *standing*—as in 'a shareholder has *standing* to sue the company'.

See also **lex** (under **lex loci**).

lodge / register

To *lodge* a document is to deposit it with a person or entity. To *register* a document is to give it formal status by entry on (or digitally, in) an official list (a *register*). The meanings differ but are often conflated. For example, under the Torrens system of land registration, caveats are *lodged*, not *registered*; but judges occasionally speak of caveats being *registered*: eg, *Ginger Development Enterprises Pty Ltd v Crown Developments Australia Ltd* [2003] NSWCA 296; (2003) 12 BPR 22,607, [35] (Davies AJA).

lodgement / lodgment

British and Commonwealth usage prefers *lodgement*. US English prefers *lodgment*.

lodger

See **boarder / lodger**.

LONG DASH

See **DASHES**.

loophole

A drafting gap or oversight, whether accidental or deliberate, able to be exploited to avoid an obligation that the law would otherwise impose. The term is often used pejoratively, but need not carry that nuance. The Commonwealth Association of Legislative Counsel self-deprecatingly calls its newsletter by that name (*The Loophole*: see www.calc.ngo/publications/loopholes).

> '[T]he existence of a *loophole* in the tax legislation would not militate against the interpretation which I favour.' [*Project Blue Ltd v Revenue and Customs* [2018] UKSC 30; [2018] WLR 3169, [37] (Lord Hodge)]

lost modern grant

A quaint label for a legal fiction that attributes a lawful foundation to long-continued use of land. The fiction applies mainly in the law of easements, but in principle applies also to profits à prendre (and to several rarer kinds of interests). To take an example from the law of easements: if a person has for 20 years regularly, peaceably, and openly, walked across a neighbour's land to reach a road, the law presumes that a formal easement (ie, a right of footway) had been granted at some time more than 20 years ago, but that the document granting the easement has since been lost (hence the label—'doctrine of the lost modern grant'). The justification for the fiction is simply that the existing state of affairs is otherwise unexplained: *Clippens Oil Co Ltd v Edinburgh and District Water Trustees* [1904] AC 64, 69; *Hamilton v Joyce* [1984] 3 NSWLR 279, 287. The House of Lords settled many important aspects of the lost-modern-grant doctrine in *Dalton v Angus & Co* (1881) 6 App Cas 740, although some aspects remain open to debate (eg, whether the burdened landowner needs to have 'acquiesced' in the use: *Arcidiacono v Owners Strata Plan No 17719* [2020] NSWCA 269).

Even to lawyers, accustomed to legal fictions, the doctrine seems fanciful. How much more fanciful it must seem to non-lawyers. Lawyers who feel driven to use the label 'lost modern grant' when addressing non-lawyers, should at least provide a plain-language translation.

Example (written advice to a client):

> 'You claim that you have been using the track across your neighbour's land for the past 20 years. By this use (if proven) you may have acquired a right (an easement) to continue to use the track, under the doctrine of the *lost modern grant*. Under this doctrine, the law presumes that long-continued use must have begun legally (even though there is no evidence of any document granting it). As a result, your neighbour may not be able to stop you using the track.'

Further reading

S Bridge, E Cooke, and M Dixon (eds), *Megarry & Wade's Law of Real Property*, 9th edn (Sweet & Maxwell, 2019) [27-062]–[27-065]

See also **nec vi, nec clam, nec precario; prescription / adverse possession**.

LS

Abbreviation for *locus sigilli.*

See **locus** (under **locus sigilli**).

lucri causa

Latin: for the sake of gain. A stilted Latinism; prefer the English:

- 'The common law of larceny does not require the money to be taken *lucri causa* [prefer: *for the sake of gain*], but only to be taken with intent to deprive the owner of it permanently.' [*Leibo v D Buckman Ltd* [1952] 2 All ER 1057, 1066 (Denning LJ)]
- '[B]ut it would be nonsense to suggest that the offences were not committed *lucri causa* [prefer: *for the sake of gain*] and his Honour did not say that. The respondent stood to gain ... at the expense both of the revenue and of honest participants in the industry.' [*DPP (Cth) v Thomas* (unreported, Supreme Court of Victoria, 28 August 1997; [1997] VSC 38 (Callaway JA)]

lunatic

See **idiot / lunatic**.

Magna Carta

Latin: the Great Writing, the Great Parchment; sometimes, *Magna Charta*; usually italicised (*Magna Carta*), following the convention for citing statutes. The date most commonly cited is 1215 (*Magna Carta 1215*). However, the document went through various iterations: there were six versions of *Magna Carta* in the 13th century. The first four were charters; the last two were elevated to statutory status. An extension in 1354 added the famous phrase 'due process of law'. The text usually cited is that of 1225. The practice of dividing the document into chapters was initiated by Blackstone in 1759.

Further reading

Lord Woolf CJ, 'Magna Carta: A Precedent For Recent Constitutional Change' (Magna Carta address, University of London, 15 June 2005)

mainly

An inherently context-dependent word. For example, whether something applies *mainly*, or is used *mainly* to achieve a stated end, necessarily involves questions of degree, on which minds may differ. Its indeterminate reach always raises the possibility of dispute. For example, a requirement that property be used 'exclusively or *mainly*' for a stated purpose may indicate that *mainly* permits only minor departures from that purpose: see, eg, *Royal Commissioners of the Patriotic Fund v Wandsworth Borough Council* (1903) 88 LT 865 and *Pilkington v Ross* [1914] 3 KB 321 (although neither case discussed the permitted degree of departure). Otherwise, *mainly* probably means 'more than half': *Fawcett Properties Ltd v Buckingham County Council* [1961] AC 636, 669 (Lord Morton). An astute drafter will foresee the uncertainty in *mainly* and will draft more precisely.

make provision for

Usually reducible to *provide for*.

See **provision**.

mala in se

See **malum in se**.

mala prohibita

See **malum prohibitum**.

male fide

Latin: in bad faith. As with its opposite (*bona fide*: in good faith), no good reason exists for retaining the Latin, which carries no more precision than the English translation. Thus, 'Ms Jones acted *male fide*' means no more and no less than 'Ms Jones acted in bad faith.'

See also **bona fide; in good faith; in bad faith**.

malfeasance / misfeasance

Malfeasance refers to an unlawful act; *misfeasance* refers to an otherwise lawful act carried out in a wrongful manner (eg, the tort of 'misfeasance in a public office').

malum

An act may be *malum prohibitum* or *malum in se*. *Malum prohibitum* (plural, *mala prohibita*) is an act that is wrong because it is prohibited, usually by statute. For example, smuggling is *malum prohibitum*. In contrast, *malum in se* (plural, *mala in se*) is an act that is wrong because it is inherently evil. Thus, murder is *malum in se*; so also is the deliberate infliction of injury on someone: *R v Lee* [206] NZCA 60, [193] (Glazebrook J).

The distinction is relevant in many areas of law. For example, in the law of wills, where a gift is subject to a condition precedent which requires the donee to perform an act that is *malum prohibitum*, the gift takes effect without the donee having to perform the act; but where the act is *malum in se*, the gift fails: *Re Wolffe's Will Trusts* [1953] 2 All ER 697, 700 (Harman J).

See also **condition precedent / condition subsequent**.

malus animus

Latin: evil intention. The Latin carries no more meaning than the English translation. Thus, unless readers understand Latin, either use plain English, or (as in examples 2 and 3 below) translate or explain:

1. 'The term "malice" [such as is required to prove the tort of malicious prosecution] is not to be considered in the sense of spite or hatred against an individual, but of *malus animus* [prefer: *evil intent*], and as denoting that the party is actuated by improper and indirect motives.' [*Houghton v Chief Constable of Greater Manchester* (1987) 84 Cr App R 319, 327 (Hollings J, quoting from a leading textbook on tort law)]
2. '[B]y 1979 it had become clear that secret trusts may be established in cases where there is no possibility of fraud. By "fraud" [is] clearly meant deliberate and conscious wrongdoing, *malus animus*.' [*Howell v Hyde* (2003) 47 ACSR 230; [2003] NSWSC 732, [44] (Austin J, providing a translation)]

3. 'The malice necessary to be established [in an action for malicious prosecution] is … malice in fact—*malus animus*—indicating that the party was actuated either by spite or ill-will towards an individual, or by indirect or improper motives …' [*Rapley v Rapley* (1930) 30 SR (NSW) 94, 98 (Street CJ, providing an explanation)]

malversation

Corrupt behaviour by a person holding an office of trust. The term is more common in Scots and European law than in English and Commonwealth law. Avoid its archaic quaintness by preferring an appropriate plain-English equivalent. For example:

- 'The plaintiffs allege … that Mr [X] and certain other persons … have been dishonestly plundering the assets of companies … for their own benefit. The plaintiffs say that the London funds, at the commencement of this action, were in imminent danger of such *malversation* [prefer: *corrupt conduct*].' [*Beck v Value Capital Ltd (No 2)* [1975] 1 WLR 6, 11 (Goulding J)
- '[Where] the words spoken impute want of integrity, dishonesty or *malversation* [prefer: *corruption*] to anyone holding a public office whether of profit or not, those words are actionable [for defamation] per se.' [*Gamble v Killingsworth* [1970] VR 161, 163–64 (McInerney J)]

mandamus

Latin: we command. A court order compelling a public official or public authority to perform a public duty or exercise a statutory power. Mandamus is appropriate where there is merely a discretion, not a duty, to act: *Ainsworth v Criminal Justice Commission* (1992) 175 CLR 564.

See also **certiori**; **quash**; **WOOLF REFORMS**.

Mannai principle

The principle (derived from the decision in *Mannai Investment Co Ltd v Eagle Star Life Assurance Co Ltd* [1997] AC 749, HL) that a notice may be valid despite defects in form, if a reasonable recipient of the notice ought reasonably to have understood its purpose. In *Mannai*, the principle saved a landlord's break notice from invalidity. Later cases invoking the *Mannai* principle have saved various kinds of notices: eg, *Atari Corporation (UK) Ltd v Electronic Boutique Stores (UK) Ltd* [1998] 2 WLR 66 (notice of rejection of goods); *Trafford Metropolitan Burough Council v Total Fitness (UK) Ltd* [2002] EWCA Civ 1513; [2003] 2 P & CR 2 (landlord's notice seeking rent review); *MLW Technology Pty Ltd v May* [2005] VSCA 29 (notice enforcing contractual provision); *Etlis v New Age Constructions (NSW) Pty Ltd* [2005] NSWCA 165 (notice triggering right to extension of time); *Pease v Carter* [2020] EWCA Civ 175; [2020] 1 WLR 1459 (landlord's notice of proceedings for possession). While the *Mannai* principle may allow some flexibility in the way in which notices are worded (and therefore interpreted), it does not excuse slipshod drafting. Vague and equivocal notices are rarely salvageable. Also, the principle is subject to an important exception, namely, where by statute or contractual provision the notice must meet strict requirements of form.

Further reading

- Peter Butt, '"Near Enough Is Good Enough" or "We Know What You Mean"' (1997) 71 *Australian Law Journal* 816
- HW Wilkinson, 'Construing Break Notices' [1997] *New Law Journal* 1187

manner in which

Often, a wordy version of 'how' or 'way'. If so, prune:

- 'You have asked for my advice *as the manner in which* [prefer: *how*] you can recover damages.'
- 'Many authors have tips *on the manner in which* [prefer: *how*; *on ways*] you can shorten your sentences.'

mansuetae naturae

See **ferae naturae**.

manufacture

In general usage, to *manufacture* something is to make it (literally, by hand—Latin, *manu*). In legal usage, where context particularly colours meaning, *manufacture* often implies more—namely, the process of producing something different from existing materials: *McNicol v Pinch* [1906] 2 KB 352, 361 (Darling J). This can lead to questions of degree, eg:

- whether fur coats remodelled out of old fur coats are 'manufactured': *Commissioner of Taxation (Cth) v Jack Zinader Pty Ltd* (1949) 78 CLR 336 (answer, yes)
- whether cocaine extracted from cocain-impregnated cloths is 'manufactured': *Beqiri v R* [2013] VSCA 39; (2013) 37 VR 219 (answer, no).

MAPS AND DIAGRAMS

There is no reason to ban maps and diagrams from legal documents. A map or diagram can complement, or even replace, a written description. Judges in former times seemed reluctant to use maps or plans, particularly to describe land parcels. In some law reports, such as *Todrick v Western National Omnibus Co Ltd* [1934] 1 Ch 190, a plan would have shown at a glance how land parcels related to each other, saving pages of verbal description. In another case, Lord Denning lamented: 'This case cannot be properly understood without a map: but I will try to explain it as best I can': *Crabb v Arun District Council* [1976] Ch 179, 183. Perhaps judges were formerly constrained by the practicalities of getting plans into law reports. But modern word-processing options make it easy to incorporate maps or plans directly into documents and judgments. Recent examples in judgments include *Thorpe v Frank* [2019] EWCA Civ 150; [2019] 1 WLR 6217 (plan of area of land claimed by adverse possession); *Fearn v Board of Trustees of Tate Gallery* [2019] EWHC 246; [2019] 2 WLR 1335 (affirmed, plan-less, [2020] EWCA Civ 104; [2020] 2 WLR 1081)

See also **FLOW CHARTS**; **PLANS.**

Mareva injunction

An injunction restraining dissipation of assets in advance of any court judgment on the merits of a claim. It can be sought where there is a danger of the defendant shifting assets out of the jurisdiction to deprive the plaintiff of the benefit of a hoped-for judgment. It takes its name from *Mareva Compania Naviera SA v International Bulkcarriers SA ('The Mareva')* [1980] 1 All ER 213 (decided 23 June 1975). Like many other terms of art, it is meaningless to non-lawyers. So, when addressing them, prefer 'freezing order' (a term now mandated by court rules in some jurisdictions for litigation purposes).

See **freezing order**; **WOOLF REFORMS.**

margin

A word that serves many purposes in law. They include:

1. The difference between the rate at which a lender can borrow and the rate at which it will lend.
2. The difference between the face value of a loan and the market value of the property over which it is secured.
3. In futures trading, a deposit that an investor pays to a broker to protect the broker against losses from securities purchased on credit.
4. In industrial law, the amount paid to an employee over and above the award rate in recognition of the employee's special skills or qualifications.

Make sure that context clarifies the intended meaning—otherwise, explain.

marginal

A multisyllabic substitute for *small*, *slight*, or similar. Prefer the shorter word:

- 'The patient's improvement was *marginal* [prefer: *slight*].'
- 'The chances of persuading the judge are *marginal* [prefer: *small*].'

MARGINAL NOTES

In statutes

Formerly, marginal notes (or sidenotes) were common in statutes. Their purpose was to give an overview (usually brief—no more than a few words) of the provision they accompanied. Being part of the text of the statute, they were relevant to interpreting the text they accompanied, but with two qualifications: (1) brevity necessarily limited their usefulness, and (2) if they contradicted the text, the text prevailed. See, eg, *R v Schildkamp* [1971] AC 1, 28 (Lord Upjohn: 'A side-note is a very brief précis of the section and therefore forms a most unsure guide to the construction of the enacting section'); *Page v Lowther* (1983) 127 Sol J 786; 1983 BTC 394 (Slade LJ).

In modern legislation, marginal notes are rare. Their function is now performed by headings at the start of a provision, and (increasingly frequently) by notes and examples at the end of the provision. However, where marginal notes are still found, modern statutory-interpretation legislation usually diminishes their importance by declaring that they are not part of the formal text of the statute. Despite this, courts have held that marginal notes nevertheless remain part of the 'extrinsic information' relevant to interpreting the text of the statute: *Bushell v Hammond* [1904] 2 KB 563, 567 (Collins MR); *Ombudsman v Moroney* [1983] 1 NSWLR 317, 324–25 (Street CJ).

In other legal documents

Private-sector legal documents rarely used marginal notes. An exception was standard-form documents professionally printed for large-scale use, such as insurance policies, bank mortgages, and leases of government land. In these documents, marginal notes were admissible in interpretation, unless precluded by a provision in the document: *Crown Equipment Pty Ltd v ACN 098 568 702 Pty Ltd* [2013] QSC 24, [33] item 6 (Ann Lyons J), but with the qualifications mentioned earlier about (1) limited usefulness and (2) text contradiction. Nowadays (as with statutes), headings, notes, and examples have taken their place.

See **FOOTNOTES**; **HEADINGS**; **NOTES AND EXAMPLES**.

margin-of-error principle

See **bracket principle**.

MARGINS

See **DOCUMENT DESIGN**.

marketable title

A title that a court will require a purchaser to accept—in most contexts, an unencumbered fee simple. A marketable title need not be 'a mathematical certainty of a good title': *Lyddall v Weston* (1739) 2 Atk 19, 20; 26 ER 409. However, it must be a title so compelling that purchasers will not have an encumbrance enforced against them: *MEPC Ltd v Christian-Edwards* [1979] 3 WLR 713, 720.

marshalling

Meaning

A catch-all term for a number of legal doctrines which, though operating in different contexts, bear the same hallmark: seeking to do justice where a person with a right to payment has the luxury of choosing between several funds. The main doctrines are the following.

1. The principle by which a creditor with the right to satisfy its debt out of two funds must exercise that right in a way that does not prejudice a creditor who has a right to one only of the funds. To illustrate: assume that the owner of two properties, Lots 1 and 2, mortgages both of them to X, and later mortgages Lot 2 to Y. Strictly, X may resort to either Lot 1 or Lot 2; but X's resort to Lot 2 would disadvantage Y. Therefore, under the 'doctrine of marshalling', if X resorts to Lot 2, Y is subrogated to X's rights against Lot 1. In this way, Y may effectively require X to resort first to Lot 1, with resort to Lot 2 restricted to recovering any remaining deficiency.
2. The principle by which, in the administration of deceased estates, assets must ultimately be applied their proper order for paying debts, even though in the actual process of administration they are applied out of proper order. Assume that a will directs that bank funds be used to pay legacies to certain beneficiaries ('legatees') and also directs that debts be paid from real estate. If, in the process of administration, the debts are paid out of the funds from which the legacies were to be paid, the legatees are entitled to have the assets 'marshalled', with payment of their legacies being charged on the real estate.
3. The principle (sometimes called the 'inverse order rule') that if land subject to a mortgage is subdivided, and the mortgagor sells subdivided portions to various purchasers, the mortgagee must look first to the mortgagor's retained land, and only after that to the portions sold (in inverse order to the date of sale): *Sarge Pty Ltd v Cazihaven Homes Pty Ltd* (1994) 34 NSWLR 658, 662; Grant S Nelson and Dale A Whitman, *Real Estate Finance Law*, 2nd edn (West, 1985) §10.10.

Plain-language equivalents

Marshalling—in whichever of the three meanings above—may be a true term of art, difficult to express in a concise plain-language equivalent that captures the legal nuance of the original. In most contexts, however, it is sufficient to add a short explanation. For example:

Solicitor's letter to mortgagee client: 'Because you have access to two funds (Fund 1 and Fund 2), you will need to choose Fund 1, because choosing Fund 2 would unfairly prejudice XYZ Bank, which has access only to Fund 2. In legal parlance, this is the doctrine of 'marshalling'.

Clause in consumer mortgage: 'The Parties agree that, to the greatest extent possible by law, the principle of marshalling is not to apply to the mortgagee's exercise of rights under this mortgage.' [Then in glossary of terms: 'Marshalling: the principle that a mortgagee with rights to claim against two funds must choose the fund that least prejudices another creditor who has access to only one of those funds.']

See also **GLOSSARIES**.

master (of ship)

The person having the command of the vessel. Statutory definitions usually exclude a pilot of the ship. There is as yet no gender-neutral equivalent, except perhaps 'person in command of the ship'.

master and servant

Modern usage prefers *employer and employee*, avoiding the forelock-tugging connotations of *master and servant*. The change in terminology reflects the shift in relationship from social status to contracting parties. The law now recognises the reality that employment gives 'not only a livelihood but an occupation, an identity and a sense of self-esteem': *Johnson v Unisys Ltd* [2001] UKHL 13; [2003] 1 AC 518, [35] (Lord Hoffmann); see also *Commonwealth Bank of Australia v Barker* [2014] HCA 32; (2014) 253 CLR 169, [16] (French CJ, Bell and Keane JJ).

See also **servant**.

material (adjective)

General

A qualifying adjective commonly used in law, but inherently vague. *Material* carries an indeterminate range of meanings, including 'serious', 'significant', substantial', 'important', 'of consequence'. Legal contexts in which *material* (as an adjective) is problematic include:

- deeds: what is a *material* alteration of a deed?
- contract: what is a *material* breach?
- sale of land: when is there a *material* difference between the property as promised, and the property as actually available?
- planning law: what is a *material* consideration in a development application?
- construction law: what is a *material* change to a building in the course of construction?
- insurance law: what is a *material* fact to be disclosed?
- anti-discrimination law: what is a *material* factor permitting discrimination?
- criminal law: what is a *material* irregularity in a trial, justifying a new trial?

Despite its inherent vagueness, the use of *material* in these and other contexts is unlikely to diminish. This is because legal drafters see advantages in its open-ended nature: its indistinct boundaries allow the sense of *substantial* without specifying *how* substantial. But that of course risks dispute over meaning.

material change / material adverse change

An expression commonly found in contracts, allowing a party to rescind or terminate if a *material change*, or *material adverse change*, occurs while the contract is on foot. For example, a contract for the sale of an apartment 'off-the-plan' (ie, before the building is constructed) may state that the purchaser can rescind if a local authority requires a *change* to the plan that is *material* or *materially adverse*. But the terms are inherently vague. What is a *change*—eg, does it relate to floor area, or market value, or the overall number of apartments in the complex? And when is a change *material*—how substantial must it be? The adjective *adverse* is also vague: when is a change, which is already *material*, also *adverse*?

In some respects, it might be best to omit any express statement and leave the parties to their rights under the rule in *Flight v Booth* (1834) 1 Bing NC 370, 377; 131 ER 1160, 1162–63. Under that rule, the purchaser can rescind the contract if the difference between what the vendor promised and what is actually available is sufficiently different that (it may reasonably be supposed) the purchaser, if aware of the difference, would not have entered into the contract. But then, is that any more certain than *material* or *materially adverse*?

Further reading

- *Halsbury's Laws of England*, 'Conveyancing' (vol 23, 2016) [456] (purchaser's remedies for misdescription of property)
- Kenneth A Adams, *A Manual of Style for Contract Drafting*, 4th edn (*American Bar Association*, 2017) ch 9, reviewing US case law
- Peter Butt, *The Standard Contract for Sale of Land in NSW*, 2nd edn (LBC Information Services, 1998) [6.48]–[6.58] reviewing UK and Australian case law on the rule in *Flight v Booth*

matter

In legal practice, a general term referring to circumstances or to a court case. For example:

> **Letter to client**: 'Thank you for your instructions in this *matter* [ie, involving the circumstances in which you find yourself].'
>
> **Barrister to judge**: 'Your Honour, in this *matter* [ie, case, litigation] we are suing for damages.'

However, *matter* has also developed more specific nuances in some contexts. One is where a statute confers jurisdiction on courts to hear *matters*. For example, a power to decide *matters* might not extend to giving a purely advisory opinion on a point of law, because *matter* implies an actual dispute between citizens or between citizen and state (to paraphrase *Re Judiciary and Navigation Acts* (1921) 29 CLR 257, 266). Or legislation may give one court or tribunal jurisdiction to hear *matters*, and another to hear *actions* or *causes*: see, eg, *Re Fawsitt* (1885) 30 Ch D 231; *Johnson v Refuge Association Co Ltd* [1913] 1 KB 259, 263.

MAXIM

A pithy statement, often expressing a legal principle; sometimes called *brocard*. Some legal maxims are vague; some can be countered by one or more contrary maxims; some are maxims of equity; some are maxims of the common law; some are codified by statute (eg, *California Civil Code* §§1597, 3509–48). Treat all maxims with caution:

> 'I detest the attempt to fetter the law with maxims. They are almost always invariably misleading: they are for the most part so large and general in their language that they always include

> something which really is not intended to be included in them.' [*Yarmouth v France* (1887) 19 QBD 647 at 653 (Lord Esher, speaking of the maxim *volenti non fit injuria*: 'Damage suffered by consent gives no cause of action')]

Sir James Stephen was equally unimpressed by maxims:

> 'It seems to me that legal maxims in general are … rather more minims than maxims, for they give not a particularly great but a particularly small amount of information. As often as not, the exceptions and qualifications to them are more important than the so-called rules.' [*A History of the Criminal Law of England* (Macmillan, 1883) vol 2, 94 n 1]

Many legal maxims are Latin fragments, preserved for centuries in the annals of the law and hallowed by judicial citation, but with meanings surprisingly obscure:

> 'The fact that the great majority of legal maxims are clothed in the words of a dead language has had, in some instances, the effect of preventing proper inquiry into their meaning. A phrase couched in Latin seems to some persons invested with "a kind of mysterious halo".' [Jeremiah Smith, 'The Use of Maxims in Jurisprudence' (1895) 9 *Harvard Law Review* 13, 25]

Further reading

- Herbert Broome, *A Selection of Legal Maxims* (Maxwell; first published 1845; multiple editions since)
- RN Graham, 'In Defence of Maxims' (2001) *Statute Law Review* 45

See also **LATIN**; **volenti non fit injuria**.

may

may as discretion

Usually, *may* grants a discretion, in contrast to *must* or *shall*, which impose an obligation:

> 'The tenant *may* assign the lease' gives the tenant a power and right to assign, but not an obligation to do so.

Where *may* bears this meaning, to add *in his* [or *her* or *its*] *discretion* is superfluous:

> 'The landlord *may* ~~in his discretion~~ allow the tenant to assign the lease.'

Some formulations are even more extreme, but equally superfluous:

> 'The landlord *may* ~~in his absolute and unfettered discretion~~ allow the tenant to assign the lease.'

may as entitlement (but still discretion)

Usage

May is also appropriate to express entitlement to do something, while still leaving a discretion whether to do it. Thus:

- 'The tenant *may* assign the lease' indicates the tenant's entitlement (but not obligation) to do so.
- 'The Tribunal *may* order …' gives the Tribunal power to make an order, but not an obligation to do so: *Cain v New South Wales Land and Housing Corporation* [2014] NSWCA 28; (2014) 86 NSWLR 1, [24]–[25].

To emphasise entitlement over mere discretion, some lawyers prefer *is entitled to*: eg, 'The tenant *is entitled to* assign the lease.' There is no harm in that expression, if the change in emphasis is deliberate. More likely, however, use of the longer form (*is entitled to*) is a matter of habit—a wordy phrase where a single word (*may*) would do. Nearly always, *may* suffices to indicate both discretion and entitlement.

Potential for ambiguity

Beware of potential ambiguity in *may be entitled to.*

Example

Assume that a clause in a standard-form building contract requires the builder to provide a security. The purpose is to ensure that funds are available if the landowner (the 'Proprietor') needs to recover money from the builder. The clause states:

> 'Any security provided by the Builder ... shall be available to the Proprietor whenever the Proprietor *may be entitled* to the payment of moneys by the Builder under this Agreement ...'

Do the words 'whenever the Proprietor *may be entitled*' mean: (1) whenever the Proprietor *could possibly be entitled*; or (2) whenever the Proprietor *is entitled*? The ambiguity has divided judges. Some favour the first meaning, others the second meaning: *Bachmann Pty Ltd v Power New Zealand Ltd* [1999] 1 VR 420, [40]–[43]; *Reed Construction Services Pty Ltd v Kheng Seng (Australia) Pty Ltd* (1998) 15 BCL 158, 165–66.

may as entitlement plus duty

In some contexts—rare, but sufficiently encountered to serve as a warning—*may* denotes not merely an *entitlement* to do something, but that that if the circumstances surrounding its possible exercise are satisfied, it *must* (or at a minimum, *should*) be done. This is sometimes seen in statutory provisions stating that a person or body 'may' do something or a court or tribunal 'may' make an order. Courts have held that parliament intended that, on proof of the facts on which exercise of the power depends, the person or body *must* exercise the power. For example:

- A statute provided that a court *may* order a fugitive to be released in certain circumstances. Held, where the circumstances are established, the court *must* order the release: *Re Shuter* [1960] 1 QB 142, 147 (Parker CJ).
- A statute provided that a registration authority *may* register a person to practise their occupation if they are already registered in another jurisdiction. Held, the legislative intent was that the authority *must* register the person: *Victorian Building Authority v Andriotis* [2019] HCA 22; (2019) 93 ALJR 869, [44], [88].
- A statute provided that the Commissioner of Police *may* dismiss a member of the force if satisfied that the member is unsuitable to continue as a member of the force. Held, once the Commissioner is satisfied that the member is unsuitable to continue as a member of the force, the Commissioner *must* dismiss the person: *Shields v Chief Commissioner of Police* [2008] VSC 2; (2008) 19 VR 33.

This implication of compulsion is, however, rare. The normal rule remains that *may*, when creating an entitlement to exercise a power, makes exercise discretionary, not compulsory. For example:

- A statute provided that a court *may* grant an injunction restraining a breach of planning controls. Held, *may* created a discretion to grant an injunction, not an obligation to do so: *South Bucks District Council v Porter* [2003] UKHL 26; [2003] 2 AC 558.
- A statute provided that, if certain conditions were met, a judge *may* issue an order for the production of material related to drug offences. Held, *may* conferred a discretion to issue an order, not a duty to do so: *R v Southwark Crown Court* [1990] 1 QB 650, 661 (Watkins LJ).
- A statute provided that a court *may* order the inspection of the register kept under companies legislation. Held, *may* conferred a discretion to make an order, not an obligation to do so: *O'Brien v Sporting Shooters Association of Australia (Victoria)* [1999] 3 VR 251, 255 (Byrne J); *Pelling v Families Need Fathers* [2002] 2 All ER 440, 446–47 (Mummery LJ).

- A statute provided that a court *may* order the appointment of trustees for sale of co-owned property. Held, *may* conferred a discretion to make an order, not an obligation to do so: *Williams v Legg* (1993) 29 NSWLR 687, 692–93; *Forgeard v Shanahan* (1994) 35 NSWLR 206, 213.

In some jurisdictions, statutory-interpretation legislation removes any implication of compulsion by providing that *may*, when used in legislation to confer a power, indicates that the power may be exercised or not, at discretion: eg, *Interpretation Act 1987* (NSW), s 9(1), discussed in *Council of NSW Bar Association v Li* (2005) 64 NSWLR 603; [2005] NSWCA 415. Provisions of this kind are liable to be undermined by other principles (eg, that a court must give effect to parliament's purpose in the particular statute). But in any case, the solution lies with the drafter: if, in the context, *may* could possibly imply an *obligation* to exercise the power, then clarify whether that is the intended meaning.

may as must

Courts occasionally find that a drafter who used *may* in fact meant *must*. For example:

- A statutory provision that a court *may* make an order where certain requirements are satisfied, can mean that the court *must* make the order where the requirements are satisfied: *Julius v Lord Bishop of Oxford* (1880) 5 App Cas 214, 235; *New South Wales Aboriginal Land Council v The Minister* (1988) 14 NSWLR 685, 692–93; *Leach v The Queen* [2007] HCA 3; (2007) 230 CLR 1, [38].
- A merchant's written instruction to an agent that 'you *may* invest' certain proceeds of sale, meant 'you *must* invest' them: *Entwisle v Dent* (1848) 1 Ex 812; 154 ER 124.

However, because this departs from the usual (discretionary) sense of *may*, judges may well differ. For example:

> A regulation provided that the Director-General of Health *may* cancel a licence to distribute addictive drugs on any one or more of six specified grounds. A three-member Court of Appeal held unanimously that *may* here meant *must*. That is, if one or more of the grounds existed, then the Director-General had no discretion—he or she *had to* cancel the licence. This was despite a provision in the *Interpretation Act* that *may* indicates a discretion. However, on further appeal to the Australian High Court, a five-member Court held unanimously that *may* in the regulation conferred a discretion. There was no *obligation* to cancel the licence even where the specified grounds existed. The arguments from context that had persuaded the Court of Appeal did not persuade the High Court. See *Samad v District Court of New South Wales* (2000) 50 NSWLR 270 (CA); [2002] HCA 24; (2002) 209 CLR 140.

A prudent drafter, foreseeing any possible ambiguity, will clarify the issue—for example, by using *must* (if that is the intended meaning) or by using an expression such as 'may (but is not obliged to)' or 'may (but need not)'.

may as possibility

'may' vs 'might'

The two words *may* and *might* appear to be synonyms, but there is a subtle difference—in some contexts at least. *May* suggests the possibility or likelihood that something could happen: 'the court may sit tomorrow'; 'we may sue the director'. *Might* suggests that the possibility or likelihood is open to some doubt: 'the court might sit tomorrow [but equally, it might not]'; 'we might sue the director [but equally, we might not]'.

'may have a [right]'

This phrase suggests more than mere chance or conjecture.

> A statute gave a claimant the right to inspect documents if the claimant '*may* have a cause of action'. Held, this required more than mere assertion, conjecture or suspicion—although it did not require the claimant to establish positively the existence of a cause of action: *Kelbush Pty Ltd v Australia and New Zealand Banking Group Ltd* [2016] WASCA 14; (2016) 49 WAR 374, [67]–[68].

may as indicating hypothetical state of affairs

Sometimes, *may* is used to introduce a hyphothetical state of affairs, followed by a statement of the consequences if the state of affairs is found to exist. The construction can be ungainly—but the meaning is that *if* or *where* the state of affairs exists, then the stated consequences follow. Usually, a rewrite using *if* or *where* improves the sentence-flow.

Examples

- 'This contract may be in two or more parts or documents. If so, those parts or documents are to be read together as a single contract.' Prefer: '*If* [*Where*] this contract is in two or more parts or documents, those parts or documents are to be read together as a single contract.'
- A land registration statute provided: 'Two or more persons who *may* be registered as joint proprietors [are deemed to be joint tenants]'. The phrase 'who *may* be registered' means that *if* [or *where*] they are registered as joint proprietors, they are treated as if they are joint tenant: *Valverde v Inch* [2018] NSWSC 366, [101] (Lindsay J).

See also **can; if / where; is entitled to; may not; only (may only); shall / must.**

may be (something)

Used as a participiple or adjectival verb, *may be* is ambiguous: does it refer to something that is possibly in existence now, or something that might happen in the future? For example, does a reference to debts that '*may be* due' cover existing debts only, or future debts only, or both existing and future debts? Only context will resolve the uncertainty. Thus, in *Broom v Batchelor* (1856) 9 LJ Ex 299, a guarantee of 'any balance that *may be* due' covered future debts only. But in *Sims v Castiglione* [1905] WN 112 a covenant to insure buildings that '*may be* erected' included buildings currently existing. Draft clearly to avoid the possible uncertainty.

See also **due and payable.**

may not

Given that *may* normally confers a discretion, the logical opposite is *may not*. So, if 'A *may* assign' indicates that 'A may assign, or may choose not to assign', then 'A *may not* assign' should indicate that 'A *need not* assign, but can assign if A wishes.' However, in legal English, *may not* usually means *must not*. So, 'A *may not* assign' means 'A *must not* assign': *R v Secretary of State for the Home Department* [2002] EWHC 2146, [21] (Lightman J); *SGS v Minister for Immigration and Border Protection* [2015] NTSC 62; (2015) 34 NTLR 224, [73] (Hiley J).

Assuming that *may not* is insufficient to express a discretion *not* to do something, a sound substitute would be *need not*. However (for reasons unexplained), *need not* is rarely seen in legal writing—which is a pity, because it would avoid disputes of the kind that arose in the following case:

> A statute provided that the judge *must* explain certain matters to the jury, but that the explanation *may not* take the form of a warning. Did *may not* mean *must not*, or did it mean *need not*?

Two judges held that it meant *must not*. A third judge held that it meant *need not*, in the sense that the judge could choose whether to frame the explanation as a warning. See *R v N* [2012] SASCFC 37; (2012) 112 SASR 399, [34], [147].

Therefore, to more clearly express a discretion *not* to do something, prefer *need not*.

See also **can**; **may**; **need not**; **not required to**; **shall / must**.

may only

See **only**.

mea culpa

Latin: my fault (in the sense of 'I am to blame'). The Latin sometimes hints at dissembling, carrying the sense 'yes, I did it, but it's not such a great wrong'. The plain English—'it's my fault', or 'I am to blame'—seems more sincere. Prefer an apology in plain English:

- '[I]t is no answer to a failure to observe the time rules for solicitors to say: "*Mea culpa*; it is entirely our fault; do not let it redound to the disadvantage of our client."' [*R v Cook* [2003] EWCA Crim 2713, [6] (Hughes J, quoting from Lord Taylor CJ in *R v Burley* (unreported) 7 November 1994), who gives a plain-English version also)]
- 'But quite clearly, my attention to the treatment of [an earlier case] was obviously less than it should have been. I can do no better than plead *mea culpa* [prefer: *I made a mistake*; *I was wrong*].' [*R v Rongonui* [2000] NZCA 273; [2000] 2 NZLR 385, [198] (Thomas J)]

means / includes

Normal usages

The dictionary distinction between *means* and *includes* is clear: *means* implies 'there is no room for anything else', 'this covers the field', or 'this is all'; while *includes* implies 'this is only one instance—there may be more'. Legal usage generally reflects this dictionary distinction.

However, context always plays a key role in word-meaning, a reality to which courts are particularly alert when interpreting *means* and *includes*. This is especially so where *means* and *includes* are used in definition clauses. At least four usages are seen:

'A means B'

This denotes that B is the only possible manifestation of A; A can comprise nothing else. The definition is exhaustive. As a drafting device, this usage promotes certainty and economy of language (to adapt Lord Diplock's description in *Inland Revenue Commissioners v Joiner* [1975] 3 All ER 1050, 1060).

'A includes B'

This denotes that B is one of the possible manifestations of A. There could be others—*include* is a 'word of enlargement': *Mellows v Low* [1923] 1 KB 522, 526 (McCardie J). Thus, A could in fact include B, C and D. *Includes* brings in things that otherwise might not (or sometimes, would not) fall within the normal understanding of the defined term.

Used in definitions, *includes* can have either or both of two functions. One is to extend the ordinary meaning of the term, to bring within its scope something that would not normally be within that scope. The other is to avoid possible misunderstanding about whether something may come within the definition (by stating that it does). See, eg, *Savoy Hotel Co v London County Council* [1900] 1 QB 665, 669 (Channell J). Put simply, the definition is non-exhaustive: *Dilworth v Commissioner of Stamps* [1899] AC 99, 105–06.

Sometimes in this usage, *includes* not only widens but also clarifies, in effect meaning *and*. For example:

> A statute required a valuation of 'all lands … *including* any Crown lands'. Held, given the history of the legislation, *including* encompassed *all* types of Crown lands, including those that might not have come within the common law meaning of 'lands'—as if the statute read 'all lands … *and* any Crown lands': *Coverdale v West Coast Council* [2016] HCA 15; (2016) 259 CLR 164, [41].

'A means and includes B'

At first sight, this seems linguistically incongruous: in ordinary English, *means* (exhaustive) and *includes* (non-exhaustive) contradict each other. Logically, the expression in a definition can have no wider operation than 'A *means* B'. However, as the case law shows, courts do not always adopt this 'logical' approach. This can lead to contrasting results:

- *Includes* (in *means and includes*) clarifies, but does not take the definition any wider than *means*: *Dilworth v Commissioner of Stamps* [1899] AC 99, 106 (Lord Watson). For example:

  > A mortgage defined 'mortgage debt' thus: 'Mortgage Debt *means and includes* …' Then followed a list of four categories of financial obligations. Two of the categories would normally come within the concept of a debt secured by a mortgage, and two would not. Held, the definition was exhaustive of the categories of obligation covered by the definition; to that extent, *includes* did not take the meaning any wider than the four listed categories: *Yazgi v Permanent Custodians Ltd* [2007] NSWCA 240; (2007) 13 BPR 24,567, [31].

- *Includes* takes the meaning wider than *means*. For example:

  > A statute defined 'inclosed lands' to *mean* any land … inclosed or surrounded by a fence, wall or other erection …, *including* … any land occupied or used in connection with the whole or part of any building or structure'. Held, *including* expanded the definition to include land that was open to the public and lacked conventional boundaries: *Director of Public Prosecutions (NSW) v Strang* [2011] NSWSC 259; (2011) 80 NSWLR 412 (department store in shopping mall).

As a drafting device, splitting *means* and *includes* across different paragraphs of the same definition may more easily allow *includes* to travel beyond the limitation of *means*.

Example

> A workers compensation Act defined 'injury' in this way:
>
> **'injury'**—
>
> (a) *means* personal injury arising out of or in the course of employment; [and]
> (b) *includes*—
>   (i) a disease which is contracted by a worker in the course of employment and to which the employment was a contributing factor; and
>   (ii) [omitted]; and
> (c) does *not include* …
>
> Note that para (a) started with *means*, and para (b) started with *includes*. Held: paras (a) and (b) were not mutually exclusive. The drafter intended para (b) to go beyond 'personal

injury' as defined in para (a); ie, para (b) extended the reach of para (a), even though para (a) started with *means*: *Zickar v MGH Plastic Industries Pty Ltd* (1996) 187 CLR 310, 329.

'A means and may include B'

Here, *may* seems superfluous. Almost certainly '*and may include*' introduces items that are merely illustrative, not exhaustive (as in *Cranbrook School v Woollahra Municipal Council* [2006] NSWCA 155; (2006) 66 NSWLR 379, [57] (McColl JA), [91] (Basten JA)).

Where 'includes' means 'means'

When interpreting a legal document, the issue is not the dictionary meaning of words, but what the parties meant when using the words. Thus, the context may indicate that the parties intended *includes* to carry the sense of *means*. This interpretation is rare, but not unknown. It arises particularly where an *includes*-style definition lists items that would normally fall within the defined term's ordinary meaning, implying that the parties intend the list to be exhaustive. For example:

- A statute defined 'security' to *include* bill of sale, mortgage, lien, and charge of any real or personal property, and any assignment, conveyance, transfer, or dealing with any real or personal property to secure the repayment of a loan. Did it include a promissory note? Held (by majority), no. Each of the listed items would fall within the normal meaning of 'security'. This indicated that the drafter intended the list to be exhaustive, despite the introductory *includes*: *YZ Finance Co Pty Ltd v Cummings* (1963) 109 CLR 395.
- A statute defined 'vehicle' to *include* cart, waggon, cab, carriage, aeroplane, motor car, caravan trailer, motor lorry, and bicycle. Did 'vehicle' include bus? Held (by majority), no; the long list of items that would fall within the normal meaning of 'vehicle' suggested that parliament intended the list to be exhaustive, despite the introductory *includes*: *R v McN* [1963] SR (NSW) 186.
- A statute defined 'medical treatment' to *include* treatment by a registered medical practitioner, a registered dentist, a registered physiotherapist, or a masseur. Held, the context indicated that the list was exhaustive, and did not extend to treatment by a chiropractor: *Lamont v Commissioner for Railways* (1963) 80 WN (NSW) 1242.

The principle that these decisions illustrate—that a list of 'included' matters is so extensive that *includes* means *means*—could well apply to detailed statutory definitions, such as the following:

> '***Land** includes* land of any tenure, and mines and minerals, whether or not held apart from the surface, buildings or parts of buildings (whether the division is horizontal, vertical or made in any other way) and other corporeal hereditaments; also a manor, an advowson, and a rent and other incorporeal hereditaments, and an easement, right, privilege, or benefit in, over, or derived from land ...' [*Law of Property Act 1925*, s 205(1)]

'includes but is not limited to'

The formula *includes but is not limited to* is also seen. Linguistically, *but is not limited to* is superfluous, because the sense is already carried by *includes*. But the purpose is clear enough—namely, to oust any possible application of the *eiusdem generis* or *noscitur a sociis* principles of interpretation. For example:

> 'The term "fruit" includes *but is not limited to* oranges, mandarins and limes.' Here, a class or group is discernible from the examples, namely, citrus fruit. Could it be argued that, without the formula *is not limited to*, the *eiusdem generis* principle might limit 'fruit' to fruit that is within the class of citrus fruit? If that argument is open, the words *but is not limited to* serve a useful purpose.

'means but does not include'

Sometimes a definition follows the style *means … but does not include*. Consider a definition: 'The term "fruit" *means* the edible product of a tree *but does not include* bananas.' While this excludes bananas, it says nothing about what else might be excluded (because it is not the edible product of a tree). To illustrate from case law:

> A statute defines 'injury' in these terms: 'injury *means* an injury suffered by an employee, *but does not include* an injury suffered as a result of administrative action'. The expression *but does not include* necessarily excludes injuries suffered from administrative action, but it does not identify other matters that may not be injuries for the purpose of the statute: *Commonwealth Bank of Australia v Reeve* [2012] FCAFC 21; (2012) 199 FCR 463, [26].

'includes … but does not include …'

A definition may take the form: 'X *includes* A *but does not include* B.' There could be several reasons for adding *but does not include*. One is that, without the added words, the issue might be unclear; another is simply to remind readers of the obvious—that the excluded items would fall outside the defined term in any case: see, eg, *Aerotel Ltd v Telco Holdings Ltd* [2006] EWCA Civ 1371, [118]; [2007] 1 All ER 225; *Sojitz Coal Resources Pty Ltd v Commissioner of State Revenue* [2015] QSC 9, [43]. But in the absence of a clear reason, it is unsafe to rely too heavily on '*does* ***not*** *include*' as a guide to what the drafter intended to *include* within the definition: eg, *Corporate Affairs Commission (SA) v Australian Central Credit Union* (1985) 157 CLR 201, 211; *Neumann Dredging Co Ltd v Collector of Customs* (1987) 79 ALR 588, 589.

Further reading

Dennis C Pearce and Robert S Geddes, *Statutory Interpretation in Australia*, 9th edn (LexisNexis, 2019) [6.5]–[6.9] (a comprehensive treatment of *means* and *includes* in statutory definitions)

See also **eiusdem generis**; **noscitur a sociis**.

medium filum aquae

See **ad medium filum**.

medium filum fluminis

See **ad medium filum**.

MEDIUM-NEUTRAL CITATIONS

See **CITATION OF CASES**.

meliorate

A variant of *ameliorate* (to improve); hence *melioration* (improvement). In modern usage, *ameliorate* (*amelioration*) is far more common, but the variant is still seen:

> 'It appears to be settled law that a *mala fide* possessor of another man's property is not entitled to recompense for any *meliorations* he may have made.' [*Trade Development Bank v Warriner & Mason (Scotland) Ltd* 1980 SC 74, 85 (Lord M'Donald)]

See also **waste**.

MEMORANDUM OF ADVICE

See **ADVICE (FORM OF)**.

MEMORANDUM OF AGREEMENT

See **HEADS OF AGREEMENT**.

MEMORANDUM OF UNDERSTANDING

See **HEADS OF AGREEMENT**.

memorandums / memoranda

Either form is acceptable as the plural of *memorandum*.

memorial

In normal use, an object or ceremony that commemorates a person or event. In legal use, a summary ('abstract') of the particulars of a deed. Thus, early registration statutes for land in Middlesex and Yorkshire spoke of registering a 'memorial' of deeds, rather than the complete deeds themselves. This legal use is now obsolete.

mens rea

Latin: evil mind; guilty intent. Used in criminal law to describe the mental element in knowingly doing the act (*actus reus*) that the law prohibits. *Mens rea* is sometimes defined as criminal intention, or knowledge of the wrongfulness of an act: eg, *R v Turnbull* [1944] SR (NSW) 108, 109 (Jordan CJ). But that definition is misleading if it suggests that a criminal intent is always necessary, because crimes of strict or absolute liability require no more than intent to commit the act: *Labour Department v Green* [1973] 1 NZLR 412, 414–15 (McMullin J). So *mens rea* means simply 'the intent to do the prohibited act', regardless of whether the actor knew that act was contrary to law: *Allard v Selfridge & Co Ltd* [1925] 1 KB 129, 138–39 (Shearman J). Both the Latin and the translation (evil mind; guilty intent) fail to tell the whole story.

Further reading

Halsbury's Laws of England, 'Criminal Law' (vol 25, 2016) [8]–[11]

See also **actus reus**.

MERGER CLAUSE

Contract law

In contract law, a clause to the effect that prior agreements and negotiations are 'merged' in the final written contract. Merger clauses of this kind serve the same purpose as 'entire agreement' clauses.

Property law

In property law, a clause to the effect that the doctrine of merger is not to apply to interests in the relevant land (and so more appropriately called a '*non*-merger clause'). By the doctrine of merger, where a lesser estate in land (called a 'particular' estate) becomes vested in a person who also holds a larger estate in the same land, the lesser estate 'merges' in the larger estate and is destroyed. More precisely, in Blackstone's words, 'whenever a greater estate and a less coincide and meet in one and the same person, without any intermediate estate, the less is immediately annihilated; or, in the law phrase, is said to be merged, that is, sunk or drowned in the greater': William Blackstone, *Commentaries on the Laws of England* (Clarendon, 1766) book 2, 177. For example, if a landlord acquires the lease from the tenant, the leasehold estate merges in the reversion and is destroyed: *Rye v Rye* [1962] AC 496, 505, 513.

Merger is a common-law doctrine, and occurs regardless of the parties' intentions. However, courts of equity hold that merger does not occur where the parties do not intend it to occur: *Belaney v Belaney* (1867) LR 2 Ch App 138; *Capital and Counties Bank v Rhodes* [1903] 1 Ch 631. In most jurisdictions, statute adopts the equitable principle: hence the practice of 'no merger' clauses, by which the parties agree that they do not intend the interests to merge.

See also **'ENTIRE AGREEMENT' CLAUSE**.

mesne

Law French: intermediate (in the sense of 'between two things'); pronounced 'main'. A quaint term, now surviving only in law, and always translatable into plain English as 'intermediate' (or similar). Examples are:

- *mesne encumbrance*: an intermediate security—ie, a security ranking between other charges
- *mesne lord*: in feudal terminology, an intermediate-ranking landholder who holds from someone higher and from whom someone lower holds
- *mesne landlord*: a landlord who holds under a lease from a superior landlord
- *mesne process*: a preliminary process taken to ensure that the defendant appears in court
- *mesne profits*: damages that a landlord may recover from a tenant for the period the tenant remains in possession wrongfully after the lease has ended.

messuage

Anglo-Norman: household. *Messuage* was once common in conveyances and leases (as in a conveyance or lease of 'all that *messuage* or dwelling-house'), and in restrictive covenants ('not more than one *messuage* may be built on the land'). The word can mean simply *house*: J Williams and RE Eastwood, *Real Property*, 25th edn (Sweet & Maxwell, 1933) 81. More commonly, it means a house and its outbuildings, gardens, and the adjacent land used with it: *Hill v Grange* (1556) 1 Plowden 164; 75 ER 253; *Royal Sydney Golf Club v Federal Commissioner of Taxation* (1955) 91 CLR 610, 625. The term has been said to be appropriate only for a single household, as distinct from group dwellings or blocks of flats: *Stoops v Frankston CC* [2004] VCAT 591. In practice, though, lawyers conventionally used *messuage* far more generally to mean any kind of premises, with or without accompanying land—eg, houses, flats, offices, hotels, shops, factories.

Regardless of its precise scope, *messuage* today is disappearing from use. True, it still appears in occasional statutory definitions of 'land', which (sadly) are often replete with archaisms:

- 'land includes messuages, tenements, and hereditaments, houses and buildings of any tenure.' [*Taxation of Chargeable Gains Act 1992*, s 288(1)]
- '"land" includes messuages, tenements and hereditaments, corporeal and incorporeal, of any tenure or description, and whatever may be the estate or interest therein.' [*Interpretation Act 1987* (NSW), s 21]

Nevertheless, to use *messuage* in modern drafting is painfully pedantic.

METAPHORS

A metaphor is a non-literal use of words to add colour or meaning to a description of something or someone. It is more subtle than a simile, which uses 'such as' or 'like' (or similar) to introduce a comparison.

A well-turned metaphor can add colour to writing, including legal writing. It allows the writer to express vividly an idea that otherwise might require dry explanation. Notable examples in legal writing include the following from Oliver Wendell Holmes Jr:

- 'A word is not a crystal, transparent and unchanged, it is the skin of a living thought and may vary greatly in color and content according to the circumstances and the time in which it is used.' [*Towne v Eisner* 245 US 418, 425 (1918), punctuation as in original]
- 'We must remember that the machinery of government would not work if it were not allowed a little play in its joints.' [*Bain Peanut Co v Pinson* 282 US 499, 501 (1931)

Examples like these hold the reader's attention. But do not allow metaphors to cloud clarity, by 'elbow[ing] out words perhaps more commonplace but with meanings more precise': Ernest Gower, *The Complete Plain Words*, ed Sidney Greenbaum and Janet Whitcut, 3rd edn (Penguin, 1987) 75. Also, do not let musty metaphors dampen text. As George Orwell famously said: 'Never use a metaphor, simile, or other figure of speech which you are used to seeing in print': 'Politics and the English Language', in George Orwell, *Why I Write* (Penguin, 2004) 119. Above all, avoid metaphors that have become stale. A metaphor may begin life as an arresting turn of phrase, but become so widely used that it becomes a lazy cliché, lacking panache and spontaneity:

- 'In other words the offender must have crossed the Rubicon and burnt his boats.' [*Director of Public Prosecutions (UK) v Stonehouse* [1978] AC 55, 68 (Lord Diplock)]
- '[T]he question was whether [the vendor] could ride off upon a condition to rescind which was obviously not framed with reference to [a case like this one].' [*Re Deighton and Harris's Contract* [1898] 1 Ch 458, 464 (Rigby LJ). The metaphor 'ride off upon a condition to rescind' has been repeated in many later cases in England and Australia, dulling its impact.]

Metaphors are unlikely to be useful in contracts and statutes, both of which favour a style that is blunt and pragmatic.

See also **CLICHÉS**.

metes and bounds

Latin: *meta*, boundary (literally, the point around which chariots turned when racing). A description of the physical dimensions of land, starting from an identifiable point and then tracing each consecutive boundary line by distance and compass-bearing, as if in an unbroken line, eventually ending at the starting point. 'Metes' denotes the sections of the boundary line defined by measurement and compass direction; 'bounds' denotes the location of the boundary line (eg, 'bounded on the west by the River X', or 'bounded on the east by a line bearing north west').

METHOD STATEMENTS

A statement that steps the reader through a process or transaction, as if to say 'This is how it works.' A method statement can be helpful in explaining a complex provision. It begins by stating what the provision aims to do, and then summarises the steps to achieve that aim. The purpose is to ease readers into the detailed text that follows.

Example

(1) This clause sets out how the rent is to be determined on renewal of the lease.
(2) The new rent is to be the current market rent at the time of the renewal.
(3) To determine that rent, the parties must take the following steps.
    Step 1: Each party appoints its valuer to determine the new rent.
    Step 2: The valuers meet to try to agree on the new rent.
    Step 3: If the valuers cannot agree, the parties attempt to agree on the new rent.
    Step 4: If the parties cannot agree, either party can ask the President of the Law Society to appoint a valuer to fix the new rent.
    Step 5: That valuer's decision is binding.

The above example is from a lease. However, statutes now contain many examples: eg, *Social Security Act 1990* (Cth), s 660LE (Australia).

Research shows that some readers find method statements more of a hindrance than a help. Apparently, they find that the deliberate, step-by-step process clouds their general overview: eg, Office of Parliamentary Counsel (Commonwealth of Australia), *Results of the 2010 Legislation Users Survey* (2010), 75.

See also **NOTES AND EXAMPLES; PURPOSE CLAUSE; SIMPLIFIED OUTLINES.**

mezzanine debt

The portion of a loan that exceeds the amount the lender would normally lend. For example, if a lender normally lends 75% of the value of the property, but for a particular transaction the loan equals 90% of the value of the property, the additional 15% is a mezzanine debt. It is often advanced by a different lender.

Michaelmas Day

See **quarter days**.

midnight

Midnight *on* a stated day normally means midnight at the *end* of the day, not at its start. Context may require otherwise—but it would take a strong context to change the standard interpretation. However, if doubt could arise, specify 'midnight at the end of' the stated day.

Midsummer Day

See **quarter days**.

might (auxiliary)

See **may**.

minerals

Minerals generally

The common law offers no single, authoritative definition of *minerals*. Lord Macnaghten said that *minerals* 'probably means every inorganic substance forming part of the crust of the earth other than the layer of soil which sustains vegetable life': *Lord Provost and Magistrates of Glasgow v Farie* (1888) 13 App Cas 657, 689. Courts interpret a Crown grant or reservation of *minerals* to include whatever substances are within the ordinary meaning of that word as used in the mining world, the commercial world, and by landowners, at the time of the grant: *Borys v Canadian Pacific Railway Co* [1953] AC 217, 223; *Minister for Mineral Resources v Brantag Pty Ltd* (1997) 8 BPR 15,815, 15,822 (Mason P).

To clarify potential doubts, legislation often defines *minerals* for the purpose of particular statutes. In Australian jurisdictions, where Crown grants of land invariably exclude rights to *minerals*, the definition is so broad that landowners may not even own the soil on their land: TP Spry, *Freehold and Leasehold Tenancies of Queensland Land* (1946) 86–87.

Royal minerals

Gold and silver are 'royal' minerals. By royal prerogative, they remain the property of the Crown, despite Crown grant of the land in which they lie: *The Case of Mines* (1568) 1 Plowd 310, 336; 75 ER 472, 510. The royal prerogative extends beyond mines of 'pure' gold or silver, to mines where gold or silver is mixed with other metals: *State of NSW v Cadia Holdings Pty Ltd* [2009] NSWCA 174; (2009) 257 ALR 528, [101], [133].

Further reading

Halsbury's Laws of England, 'Mines, Minerals and Quarries' (vol 76, 2019) [10]–[13] (legal meaning of 'minerals')

minor

See **infant / minor**.

minore aetate

See **durante**.

mirror wills / mutual wills

Mirror wills are wills that are made by two or more testators (usually husband and wife) and that contain reciprocal provisions, one will 'mirroring' the other. For example, husband and wife may by their respective wills leave their interest in the matrimonial home to the survivor of them for life, and after the survivor's death, to a third party.

Mutual wills often take the same 'mirror' form of reciprocal provisions, but with the added promise, implied if not expressed, that the one who survives will not revoke his or her will so as to disappoint the expectations of the one who predeceases. The law enforces the promise by imposing a constructive trust on the property taken by the survivor, for the benefit of the intended beneficiary: *Grey v Perpetual Trustee Co Ltd* [1928] AC 391; *Birmingham v Renfrew* (1937) 57 CLR 666, 683 (Dixon J). The term *mutual* does not carry the full nuances of this principle, but no better term yet exists.

misfeasance

See **malfeasance / misfeasance**.

MISPLACED MODIFIERS

See **MODIFIERS**.

misprision of treason

A common-law offence, committed when a person, who knows that treason is being planned or executed, does not report it to the appropriate authorities.

missives

In Scots legal usage, the written communications between prospective seller and prospective buyer that, taken together, constitute the binding contract to sell and buy. In essence, *missives* contain an offer to sell, an acceptance of the offer, and any mutually agreed key conditions. When the final agreement is reached, the missives are concluded and there then exists a legally binding contract. For example:

> 'On 3 August 2004 [the purchaser] concluded *missives* with [the vendor] for the purchase of a plot or area of ground at 152 Dalmellington Road, Ayr.' [*Morris v Rae* [2012] UKSC 50; 2013 3 SCLR 80, [4] (Lord Hope)]

Mitsui principle

A principle to the effect that, the poorer the quality of the drafting, the freer the court is to ignore the grammar, syntax, and inconsistencies, particularly where to apply strict rules would hold the parties to an improbable and unbusinesslike result: *Mitsui Construction Co Ltd v A-G of Hong Kong* (1986) 33 BLR 14. Under this principle, a court searching for the parties' meaning looks beyond grammatical niceties—because when faced with inept drafting, 'fine arguments based upon supposed consistency of language or even thought throughout the document' carry little or no weight: *Oxonica Energy Ltdv Neuftec Ltd* [2009] EWCA Civ 668, [11] (Jacob LJ).

MODIFIERS

Care with placement

Misplaced ('dangling') modifying words or phrases are common causes of ambiguity in legal writing. Sometimes, common sense resolves the ambiguity (after a short chuckle):

- The judge ordered instructions to be sent to jurors *in sealed envelopes*. [What was in sealed envelopes?]
- The police restrained a man with a taser. [Who had the taser?]

At other times, the ambiguity is more stubborn:

- 'I like cats and dogs which are black and fluffy.'

  This could mean: (a) I like all cats, but only dogs that are black and fluffy; *or* (b) I like cats and dogs, but (in each case) only those that are black and fluffy. [Source: *Wood v Sureterm Direct Ltd* [2015] EWCA Civ 839, [37], Clarke LJ]

- 'The judge said *when the jury was discharged* he would rehear the case.' [A 'squinting' modifier, looking both ways.]

  This could mean: (a) when the jury was being discharged, the judge said he would rehear the case; *or* (b) the judge said that, after the jury was discharged, he would rehear the case.

- A company constitution stipulated that documents could be signed by 'a Director or any other person *authorised by the Board*' (emphasis added). Who needed to be authorised by the Board: the Director, or any other person? Did the italicised words modify 'Director'—meaning that a director could not sign unless specifically authorised by the Board? Held, no; syntactically the sentence was ambiguous; but in the context of powers ordinarily given to directors to sign documents on behalf of companies, the parties were unlikely to have intended that a director needed specific authorisation: *Rent Plus Ltd v Sorensen (No 2)* [2013] NSWSC 67, [49] (Garling J).

To reduce the risk of ambiguity, place the modifier as close as possible to the word or phrase it modifies. Readers—and courts—generally expect that location and interpret documents accordingly:

> '[The defendant] quotes a number of textbooks on English grammar in support of its contention that modifiers are intended to refer to the words closest to them in the sentence. That, of course, is the correct rule. … The rule concerning modifiers is:
>
> > "The reader naturally assumes that the parts of a sentence which are placed next to each other are logically related to each other. … The rule which will guide you may be stated in two parts: (1) place all modifiers, whether words, phrases, or clauses, as close as possible to the words they modify; (2) avoid placing these elements near other words they might be taken to modify." '
>
> [*Samano v Sun Oil Co* 621 SW 2d 580, 582 (Tex 1981), quoting Kierzek, The *Macmillan Handbook of English*, 3rd edn (Macmillan, 1954)]

The following example shows how to resolve ambiguity by moving the modifier:

Original (poor)	**Revised (better)**
Landlords … are now prohibited from listing a person who ended their tenancy by giving a domestic violence termination notice on a bad tenant database. [Kellie McDonald, 'New Tenancy Reforms' (2019) 53 *New South Wales Law Society Journal* (March) 78, 79; underlining added for purpose of example]	Landlords … are now prohibited from listing on a bad-tenant database a person who ended their tenancy by giving a domestic violence termination notice.

Omit where superfluous

Always delete superfluous modifiers:

The ~~relevant~~ issues in this case are …

Likewise, delete modifiers that cast doubt on the writer's sincerity:

My ~~frank~~ advice is …

In my ~~honest~~ opinion …

The ~~relevant~~ issues are …

See also **AMBIGUITY; LAST-ANTECEDENT RULE; QUALIFIERS.**

modus operandi

Latin: manner of operation; the way in which a person or entity works (as in the first example below); in particular, a characteristic method of operation which may betray a criminal (as in the second example below). A plain-English translation is never difficult:

- 'The outcome of the appeal could also affect Canwell's modus operandi in its provision of services [prefer: the way Canwell provides services] …' [*Smith Brothers Farms Ltd v The Canwell Estate Co Ltd* [2012] EWCA Civ 237; [2012] 1 WLR 2626, [8] (Mummery LJ)]

- 'The Crown relied on aspects of disguise and concealment as permeating the applicant's overall *modus operandi* [prefer: *method of operation*].' [*Werden v R* [2015] VSCA 72, [35] (Osborn JA)]

Often, *modus operandi* is simply a fancy substitute for *method*. If so, prefer *method*.

moiety

Meaning 'half'

Law French: half; portion. An archaism that is opaque to most readers. In strict legal usage, *moiety* means 'half', and that is its most common usage: *Re Angus' Will Trusts* [1960] 1 WLR 1296, 1300 (Buckley J). But to avoid pedantry and reader-perplexity, prefer the plain-English 'half' or similar:

- 'The testator devised to each of his two sons *a moiety*' [prefer: *a one-half share*] of the estate.'
- 'The partnership agreement allocated each partner *a moiety* [prefer: *an equal share*] of partnership profits.'
- 'If … partition of the property would be more beneficial for the co-owners interested to the extent of upwards of a *moiety* [prefer: *one-half interest*] in value than sale, the court may [order a partition].' [*Conveyancing Act 1919* (NSW), s 66G(4)]

Meaning some other (equal) proportion

Another (less precise) legal usage is 'equal proportion', or 'equal share', or simply 'share'. This usage is rare, but sufficiently encountered to make *moiety* litigation-prone (as occurred, for example, in *Morrow v M'Conville* (1883) 11 LR Ir 236, and in *Re Angus' Will Trusts* [1960] 1 WLR 1296). Again, to avoid pedantry and reader-perplexity, prefer an appropriate (and precise) plain-English substitute. For example:

> 'Under the trust deed, each of the three beneficiaries was entitled to *a moiety* [prefer: *a one-third share*] of the income.'

money

Meaning

A word of wide import, and therefore potentially ambiguous. Courts once limited *money* to the strict sense of 'coin of the realm'. Later, they extended the meaning to encompass such things as money on deposit and 'debts immediately owing', but not such things as stocks or shares, or interests in a deceased estate. Later again, since *Perrin v Morgan* [1943] AC 399 (HL), courts have given *money* a much wider meaning, at least in wills. *Perrin v Morgan* held that a gift of 'all moneys of which I die possessed' included the whole of the testatrix's residuary personal estate (which in turn included investments, dividends received or accrued, rents due before the date of death, income tax refunds, and household effects). Examples in line with this *Perrin v Morgan* extended meaning include:

- A gift by will of *money* included money on deposit, not immediately available: *Re Stonham* [1963] 1 WLR, 245 (Wilberforce J). However, minor variations in wording might change that result: thus, a gift of 'ready money' would not normally pass money on deposit needing substantial prior notice of withdrawal; and a gift of 'cash' would normally pass only ready money, and not money on deposit: ibid.
- A gift by will of *money* included bonds and sums on deposit with banks: *Re Barnes' Will Trusts* [1972] 1 WLR 587 (Goulding J).

Plural

Money is now the preferred plural, superseding *monies* and *moneys*. For example:

- 'The borrower must repay all ~~monies~~ *money* advanced by the bank.'
- 'The [deed] establishes the ADF Super Fund (into which contributions and other *money* are paid).' (*Australian Defence Force Superannuation Act 2015* (Cth), s 6)

However, there are idiomatic exceptions. For example:

'This superannuation fund is a blend of employer and employee *moneys*.'

money laundering

To hyphenate or not? When used as a noun, no hyphen is needed: *money laundering*. When used as a compound adjective, a hyphen is preferred: eg, *money-laundering laws*. However, the modern trend is towards discarding hyphens in all uses: eg, *Money Laundering Regulations* 2007.

See also **anti money laundering**; **HYPHENS**.

money's worth

Meaning

A time-honoured, if quaint, expression meaning 'equivalent to money'; in former times, often hyphenated (*money's-worth*). A thing is 'of money's worth' if a monetary value can be put on it: *Secretan v Hart* [1969] 1 WLR 1599, 1603 (Buckley J). It includes anything that has a material value, including carrying out work (eg, building a wall, to cite the example given by Lord Cranworth LC in argument in *Caledonian and Dumbartonshire Junction Railway Co v Walker* (1856) Paterson 642, 644). But it does not include things or work that have a purely emotional or spiritual value: *Gideon's International Service Mark* [1991] RPC 141. And reflecting the concept of 'consideration' in contract law, an amount or act may be 'money's worth' even though it is well below market equivalence: eg, *Midland Bank Trust Co Ltd v Green* [1981] AC 513.

A suggested substitute

The long history of 'money's worth' makes the term familiar to lawyers, and most non-lawyers would probably guess the meaning. However, 'equivalent to money', or similar, carries the meaning just as well: eg, 'You must pay in money or ~~money's worth~~ something that is equivalent to money.'

See also **consideration**.

month

Possible meanings in law

There are three possible meanings of *month*:

1. Lunar month—a period of 28 days.
2. Calendar month—one of the 12 unequal periods into which the calendar year is divided.
3. Corresponding-date month—the day in a month that corresponds with the corresponding day in an earlier month.

Meaning at common law

General

At common law, *month* meant *lunar month* (except in the ecclesiastical courts, where it meant calendar month), unless context showed that the parties intended calendar month: *Lang v Gale* (1813) 1 M & S 111, 117; 105 ER 42, 45. This common-law interpretation was so contrary to the common understanding of *month* (ie, meaning *calendar month*) that Lord Atkin considered it a 'public disadvantage': *Phipps & Co (Northampton and Towcester Breweries) Ltd v Rogers* [1925] 1 KB 14, 27. But courts continued to apply it: eg, *Development Underwriting (Queensland) Pty Ltd v Weaber* [1971] Qd R 182.

Effect of context

However, context could indicate a different meaning. One such context was mortgages, where (the courts eventually held) parties used *month* to mean *calendar month*: *Schiller v Peterson & Co Ltd* [1924] 1 Ch 394. Another context was mercantile contracts in the City of London, where parties were taken to mean *calendar month*: ibid.

Legislative changes

In most jurisdictions, legislation has overturned the common-law default meaning of lunar *month*. The legislation initially applied to statutes only, but was later extended to contracts and documents generally. In those jurisdictions, and subject to contrary intention in the document, *month* now means *calendar month*: see, eg, *Law of Property Act 1925*, s 61; *Conveyancing Act 1919* (NSW), s 181.

These statutes make superfluous the boilerplate interpretation provision in legal documents that 'month means calendar month'. The only possible reason for including it would be to dispel fears that context might suggest that references to *month* mean lunar month—which seems unlikely.

Calculating 'calendar' month

A calendar month ends at midnight on the day in the ensuing month immediately preceding the day numerically corresponding to the commencing day: *Police v Maindonald* [1971] NZLR 417, 419. So, if on 26 February a person is sentenced to one calendar month's imprisonment, the month expires at midnight on 25/26 March: *Migotti v Colvill* (1879) 4 CPD 233.

Corresponding-date rule

By the corresponding-date rule, a period of '*[x] months of* [or *from*, or *after*]' a stated date ends on the day of the month corresponding with the day on which the period started. So, a period of '2 months from 1 January' expires on 1 March.

See also **corresponding-date rule**.

monthly

A requirement to do something *monthly* can be ambiguous: does it mean (1) at intervals of one month; or (2) once in each month? Different minds may reach different conclusions. Thus, in *Brewarrina Shire Council v Beckaus Civil Pty Ltd* (2003) 56 NSWLR 576, the majority of the court held that a building contractor's obligation to submit payment claims 'monthly' required claims to be submitted on the same day each month (the first being one month after the construction started), while the minority held that claims were to be submitted once in each month (but on any day in that month).

MOOD (OF VERBS)

See **SUBJUNCTIVE / INDICATIVE**.

moot point

A point that is doubtful or open to debate. Also, a point that is of no practical importance: ie, hypothetical or academic. Sometimes it is not clear which meaning the writer intends:

> 'Whether the protection of health and morals encompasses other elements is a moot point.' [*Conway v Secretary of State for Justice* [2018] EWCA Civ 16, [23] (Sir Ernest Ryder, Senior President)—meaning 'arguable', or 'hypothetical'?]

The variant 'mute point' is always wrong:

> 'This may of course be a *mute* [sic: *moot*] point as you will see from the evidence ...' [*R v Cotswold District Council* [2009] EWHC 3702 (Admin), [47], quoting from a letter from the applicant's agent)]

moral turpitude

A phrase that has achieved prominence in Torrens title jurisdictions because of Isaac J's statement that 'fraud', such as deprives a registered title of indefeasibility, means 'actual fraud, moral turpitude': *Butler v Fairclough* (1917) 23 CLR 78, 97. But the term seems overwrought, given that *turpitude* necessarily involves *morality* (or lack of it): *King v Brooks* (1960) 24 DLR (2d) 567 (Monnin J).

moratorium / moratoria

A *moratorium* is a right to delay or postpone an act or obligation, particularly the obligation to repay a debt. Thus, *moratorium legislation* typically suspends liability to pay a debt in times of war or financial hardship. The Latin plural is *moratoria*, but the anglicised *moratoriums* is acceptable and less stilted. For example:

- 'The Ministry of Justice Handbook issued in 1992 states that it can be assumed as a rule that *moratoriums* ... will not be recognised in other countries ...' [*Tchenguiz v Grant Thornton UK LLP* [2015] EWHC 1864 (Comm), [120] (Carr J, citing a departmental handbook)]
- '[T]he court made interim orders ... imposing *moratoria* [prefer: *moratoriums*] on creditors' proceedings ...' [*Narandas-Girdhar v Bradstock* [2016] EWCA Civ 88, [4]; [2016] 1 WLR 2366, 2369 (Briggs LJ)]

more or less

A notoriously imprecise expression. Whether a measurement or quantity is *more or less* is always context-dependent. A boundary shortfall of 10 metres may be within a 'more or less' tolerance on the sale of a large farm, but not on the sale of a mid-city office block. The following British and Commonwealth examples illustrate contexts in which *more or less* gave rise to litigation.

Examples within 'more or less' tolerance

- Dwelling house—stated depth of '217 feet *more or less*' satisfied by actual depth of 204 feet: *Lethbridge v Kirkman* (1855) 25 LJQB 89.

- Orchard—stated area of '24 acres *more or less*' satisfied by actual area of 21 acres, 2 roods, and 26 perches: *Re Oakley and Fitch's Contract* (1915) 12 Tas LR 18.
- Farm—stated area of '200 acres *more or less*' satisfied by actual area of 176 acres: *Follis v Porter* (1865) 11 Grant (Canada) 442.
- Timbered land—stated area 'containing by estimation 200 acres, *more or less*' satisfied by actual area of 162 acres: *Brown v Banks* (1889) 21 NSR 388.
- City property—stated depth of '110 feet *more or less*' satisfied by actual depth of 98 feet 6 inches: *Wilson Lumber Co v Simpson* (1910) 22 OLR 452.

Examples not within 'more or less' tolerance

- Farm—stated area of 321 acres, 2 roods, and 30 perches '*more or less*' not satisfied by actual area of 310 acres, 3 roods, and 18 perches: *Leslie v Tomspon* (1851) 9 Hare 268; 68 ER 503.
- Farm—stated area of '280 acres *more or less*' not satisfied by actual area of 262 acres, 2 roods, and 2 perches: *Belfrage v McNaughton* [1924] VLR 441
- Farm—deficiency in area of 16.5% not covered by *more or* less: Murphy *v Horn* [1929] 4 DLR 693.
- Suburban shop and dwelling—stated frontage of '39 feet 6 inches *more or less*' not satisfied by actual frontage of 39 feet: *Perrin v Reynolds* (1886) 12 VLR 440.
- Town lot with house—stated depth of '172 feet *more or less*' not satisfied by actual depth of 161 feet: *Bouskill v Campea* (1976) 68 DLR (3d) 577.

If possible, strive for a clearer statement of acceptable shortfalls.

See also **WORDS OF APPROXIMATION**.

more suo

Latin: in his/her/its own way; often in the sense of 'in his/her/its own words'. A needless Latinism, given the adequate English translation:

> 'I also note that the actual decision of the Court of Justice is, *more suo* [prefer: *in its own words*], limited to "a situation such as that in the present case" …' [*EBR Attridge LLP v Coleman* UKEAT/71/09; [2010] ICR 242, [15] (Underhill J)]

more than / less than

See **less than / more than**.

more than / over

More than suggests a numerical relationship. For example:

- The court awarded damages of *more than* $100.
- He was *more than* 2 days late in filing the application.

Over generally carries the nuance of a spatial relationship:

- The cow jumped *over* the moon.
- The plane flew *over* the boundary.

However, in practice *more than* and *over* are sometimes used interchangeably. The result can be ambiguous, unless context clarifies. For example:

> 'She was awarded a pay rise of *more than* £10.' This probably means that her pay rose by at least an additional £10 over its current rate. But it could mean (less likely) simply that her pay rose above its current rate of £10.

more than one

This expression is plural in form but singular in meaning, and therefore takes a singular noun or verb. For example:

- More *than one* juror *is* absent today.
- There *is more than one* factor to consider.

mortgage indemnity insurance

Insurance (usually purchased by a one-off premium) to protect the mortgagee against loss if the mortgagor defaults and the proceeds of sale of the mortgaged property turn out to be less than the amount owing under the mortgage. Mortgagees often insist on this insurance where the loan exceeds the mortgagee's normal loan-to-value ratio.

See also **indemnify (variants of)**; **loan-to-value ratio**.

mortgagee / mortgagor

The *mortgagee* is the person in whose favour a mortgage is granted—ie, the lender or creditor. The *mortgagor* is the person who grants a mortgage over property—the borrower or debtor. The words may confuse readers unaccustomed to *-ee* / *-or* endings. Sometimes it is possible to use a substitute word (*lender*, *borrower*). But a substitute word is not appropriate where it would cloud the nature of the transaction ('Is this a mortgage, or merely an unsecured loan?')—in which case, prefer the *-ee* / *-or* word, but perhaps add an explanation.

See also ***-ee* / *-or* endings**; **TERMS OF ART**.

mortis causa

Latin: in case of death; in contemplation of death. Bury the dead Latin; prefer the English.

See **donatio mortis causa**.

mortmain

Law French, *morte main*, dead hand. A grant of land to a monastery or other ecclesiastical institution; called *mortmain* because the land vested in the 'dead hand' of a perpetual body, for ever depriving the superior lord of valuable feudal incidents normally payable on the descent of land to an heir. There is no plain-English equivalent; but none is needed, because the practice was abolished by the *Statute of Mortmain 1279*.

Mother Hubbard clause

A 'cover all' provision, intended to sweep-up things that might not otherwise be caught. The term 'Mother Hubbard clause' is an Americanism, still rare in Britain and most Commonwealth countries; but the concept is familiar.

Examples

- a clause in a mortgage stating that the mortgage secures all debts that the borrower may owe to the lender (an 'all moneys' clause)
- a clause in a will that disposes of all property not otherwise disposed of (a 'residuary clause')

- a request in pleadings that the court make whatever further orders the court considers appropriate ('such other and further relief as the court considers appropriate')
- a provision in a court order to the effect that all relief not expressly granted is denied: eg, *Mafrige v Ross* 866 SW 2d 590 (Texas 1993)
- a clause in an oil and gas lease that ensures access rights over all parcels of land adjoining the main site: eg, *J Hiram Moore Ltd v Greer* 172 SW 3d 609 (Texas 2005).

motu proprio

See **proprio motu**.

movable / moveable

Standard spelling is *movable*. However, legal usage prefers *moveable* (both noun and adjective), a time-hallowed variant that most dictionaries and style guides allow. Moveables are the civil law's counterparts of the common law's chattels; immoveables are the civil law's counterparts of the common law's fixtures. The counterparts are approximate, not exact: eg, the common law—for reasons of history rather than logic—treats leases as *chattels* (*chattels real*), even though they are given over land. Each system of law steadfastly guards its own terminology—and so, for example, the common law courts always prefer *chattels* (not *moveables*) and *fixtures* or *land* (not *immoveable property*).

See also **chattels real; fixtures and fittings; goods and chattels**.

multi / multi-

Standard usage hyphenates *multi-* when followed by a vowel, but not when followed by a consonant. Hence *multi-access, multi-ethnic, multi-utility*; but *multifarious, multigrain, multipartite, multinational*. However, there are some aberrations: *multi-faith, multi-storey, multi-year*.

See also **HYPHENS**.

muniment of title

Latin: *munire*, to fortify. Any document that is necessary to defend (ie, prove) title to land. For example, older forms of contracts for sale required the vendor to hand to the purchaser on completion all 'muniments of title'. (Without them, the purchaser as the new owner might be unable to prove title, and therefore unable to mortgage, lease or sell the land.) The term is now obsolete. Modern contracts use terms such as 'evidences of title'.

See also **title deed**.

must

See **may; shall / must**.

must not

See **may; shall / must**.

mutatis mutandis

Meaning

Latin: changed as the circumstances require; with the necessary changes. Lawyers love this Latinism. Translations include:

- 'varied as required'
- 'with appropriate changes as required by the new context'
- 'with changes to be made so far as relevant to the different transaction [or document]' (example based on *APT Sea Gas Holdings Pty Ltd v ANP SEA Gas Holdings Pty Ltd* [2010] NSWSC 1221, [50], Brereton J)
- 'on terms and conditions that are equivalent to those in [a particular document]' (example based on *Santos Offshore Pty Ltd v Apache Oil Australia Pty Ltd* [2015] WASC 242, [64]–[70], Pritchard J).

An imprecise term

The term's alluring alliteration risks masking the reality that *mutatis mutandis* is no more than a 'vague Latin phrase': *Commissioner for Government Transport (NSW) v Deacon* (1957) 97 CLR 535, 546. Logically, its application requires two steps: first, identify *what* must be changed (the *mutanda*); then, identify *into what* it is to be changed. Neither step is straightforward. Nor is the task of finding a precise translation, because in the context the implications can vary, as the following examples show:

- '[Although] this judgment is concerned particularly with doctors, it is also relevant, *mutatis mutandis* [does this mean *with necessary changes*? or (more vaguely) *with appropriate changes*? or (yet more vaguely) *varied as relevant*?], to other healthcare providers.' [*Montgomery v Larnakshire Health Board* [2015] UKSC 11, [75]; [2015] 2 WLR 768, 789 (Lords Kerr and Reed)]
- 'It will be sufficient for our analysis to focus on the provisions of the *Corporations Act* although our reasoning and conclusions are apt also for the proportionate liability provisions under the *ASIC Act*, *mutatis mutandis* [presumably meaning: *varied as appropriate for the purposes of the ASIC Act*—whatever that may mean].' [*ABN Ambro Bank NV v Bathurst Regional Council* [2014] FCAFC 65; (2014) 309 ALR 445, [1524] (Jacobson, Gilmour and Gordon JJ)]
- '[The tenant claimed that the landlord was bound to offer to renew the Leases] on the same terms and conditions as the existing Leases, or at least on the same terms and conditions *mutatis mutandis* [presumably meaning: *as near as possible*—an invitation to litigation] as the existing Leases.' [*Crown Melbourne Ltd v Cosmopolitan Hotel (Vic) Pty Ltd* [2016] HCA 26; (2016) 260 CLR 1, [206] (Nettle J)]
- 'The provisions of section 12(2)(b) and (5) shall, *mutatis mutandis* [presumably meaning: *with appropriate changes*—an inappropriately vague statement in legislation], apply to [payments] under this section in the same manner as they apply to [payments] under section 12.' [*Mines Subsidence Compensation Act 1961* (NSW), s 12A(3)]

Use another term

Mutatis mutandis has had its day—not merely because it is Latin (in an era when few people understand Latin), but also because the Latin suggests a false sense of precision. Those wishing to preserve the Latin may say: 'The English translation reeks of uncertainty'—to which the obvious response is, 'So too does the Latin.' Where possible, specify *what* changes to make, and *where* to make them. If that is not possible, at least use a plain-English equivalent: eg, 'changed as required', or similar.

See also **FOREIGN (NON-ENGLISH) WORDS AND PHRASES.**

mutual

When using *mutual*, beware of redundancies:

- mutual agreement = agreement
- mutual respect for each other = mutual respect
- mutual benefit of both parties = benefit of both parties
- mutually contradictory = contradictory.

See also **common / mutual**; **mirror wills / mutual wills**.

mutual wills

See **mirror wills / mutual wills.**

namely

Namely is appropriate to explain a previous statement. For example:

- 'You must take immediate steps to remedy the breach: *namely*, …'
- 'The statute penalises certain acts, *namely* …'

Normally, to introduce a list with *namely* indicates that the list is exhaustive (although context may require a different interpretation). In contrast, to introduce a list with a word such as *including* clarifies or expands the description of what went before:

- 'You must take immediate steps to remedy the breach, *including* …'
- 'The statute penalises certain acts, *including* …'

See also **videlicet**.

NAMES (of parties)

In litigation

Where possible, refer to parties by their own names, or by a short name, rather than by the name given to their role in litigation. For example, having identified the plaintiff as Mr Smith, in later references call him 'Mr Smith' (not 'the plaintiff'); likewise, the defendant 'Ms Jones', and (even more so) the sixth cross-defendant 'Ms Lyons'. The naming not only enlivens the prose, but by personalising the parties makes them and their roles easier to remember: who will remember the identity of the sixth cross-defendant without looking it up every time?

Lord Denning was a great exponent of this technique:

> 'I can tell of a judge who is … much respected. In giving judgment he is cold and impassive. … Impersonal and inhuman. He does not call the litigants by their names—John Doe or Richard Roe. But by their *noms de litis*—plaintiff and defendant—appellant or respondent. Quite often he gets them transposed—saying plaintiff when he means defendant—but the shorthand writer puts it right. … It is against that kind of judgment that I set my face. … I try to make my judgment live. … I draw the characters as they truly are—using their true names—so that I never get them mixed up. Never plaintiff or defendant, or appellant and respondent.' [Lord Denning, *The Family Story* (Butterworths, 1981) 206–07]

Short names

Sometimes it is convenient to give a party or entity a short name: 'Jones Trading Co Pty Ltd (**Jones**)'. Here are some tips:

- The shorter the better.
- Make the name obvious and unmistakeable. For example, if there are two parties, Jones Trading Co Pty Ltd and Smith Trading Co Pty Ltd, to call one **Trading Co** will confuse. Similarly, if one party is Burghers of London Ltd (**Burghers**) and the other Burgers and Associated Meat Products Ltd (**Burgers**), the short names may be too similar.
- Beware of short names with unfortunate connotations: eg, Bankers and Debt Collectors Ltd (**Bad**).
- Where a party or entity has its own preferred short name, use it.
- Acronyms can also be useful, but they can also be tiresome.

See also **ABBREVIATIONS**; **ACRONYMS**; **CITATION OF CASES**; **PRONOUNS**; **we / you**.

natural person

A human being, as distinct from an artificial person such as a corporation.

See **person**.

NB

See **nota bene**.

ne plus ultra

Latin: no more beyond; the highest limit (usually in the sense of perfection). Unless your reader understands Latin, prefer an appropriate English translation. For example:

> 'The *ne plus ultra* [prefer: *perfect statement*] of this series [of decisions] is thought to be the decision of the English Court of Appeal in *In re Smith* …' [Matthew Harding, 'Distinguishing Government from Charity in Australian Law' (2009) 31 *Sydney Law Review* 559, 565].

nec vi, nec clam, nec precario

Latin (sometimes with commas, sometimes not): not by force, not by secrecy, and not by permission (or, as translated by Erle J—changing the order of words—not 'clandestine, contentious or by sufferance': *Eaton v The Swansea Waterworks Co* (1851) 17 QB 267, 275; 117 ER 1282, 1285). A trilogy derived from Roman law and imported into the law of easements via the civil law. It states three important conditions for acquiring an easement by prescription. Despite the expression's ancient lineage, prefer modern English, or at least provide a translation, as in the following examples:

- 'It became established that [the use] had to be, in the Latin phrase, *nec vi, nec clam, nec precario*: not by force, nor stealth, nor the licence of the owner.' [*R v Oxfordshire County Council* [2000] AC 335, 350 (Lord Hoffmann)]
- '[The trial judge] found, implicitly at least, that the AJC's user had been "*nec vi nec clam nec precario*" (neither by force, by secrecy, nor by licence or permission), thereby giving rise to the presumption of a grant that had become lost …' [*Williams v State Transit Authority*

of New South Wales [2004] NSWCA 179, [17] (Mason P; the authorised report, (2004) 60 NSWLR 286, omits this para.]

See also **lost modern grant; prescription / adverse possession.**

necessary

A protean word

If a contract or statute requires a person to do 'all things *necessary*' to achieve a stated result, how onerous is the requirement? Is near enough good enough? The cases demonstrate a breadth of meaning, which is sound reason to be more specific:

> '*Necessary* is a somewhat protean word whose meaning depends on the context in which it is used. In some contexts, it means *indispensable* or *essential* ... In *R v Shayler* [2003] 1 AC 247, [23], Lord Bingham of Cornhill said of the word *necessary* ... "*Necessary* has been strongly interpreted: it is not synonymous with *indispensable*, neither has it the flexibility of such expressions as *admissible, ordinary, useful, reasonable* or *desirable*." In some contexts, the word *necessary* has a weaker meaning. But it will usually bear the connotation of some degree of compulsion or exigency. The context will determine where on the spectrum of compulsion or exigency the word *necessary* is placed.' [*Pabari v Secretary of State for Work and Pensions* [2004] EWCA Civ 480, [53]–[55]; [2005] 1 All ER 287, 300 (Dyson LJ)]

Tempered by 'reasonableness'

Unless context requires otherwise, courts generally interpret a requirement to do 'all things *necessary*' as requiring only what can *reasonably* be done in the circumstances. This may dilute the writer's intentions, as possibly occurred in the following examples:

- A liquidator's power to carry on the business of the company so far as *necessary* for its beneficial winding-up, did not require doing what was absolutely necessary but rather what was 'a mercantile necessity', in the sense of being 'highly expedient' under all the circumstances: *Re Wreck Recovery & Salvage Co* (1880) 15 Ch D 353, 362; *Fortress Credit Corp (Australia) Pty Ltd v Fletcher* [2015] NSWCA 85; (2015) 295 FLR 13 (*necessary* = 'anything expedient').
- A tenant's covenant to do 'all things *necessary*' to obtain an easement for water supply to the premises, did not require the tenant to do the impossible (eg, to persuade a recalcitrant adjoining owner to agree) but rather to take all reasonable steps to obtain the water supply: *Skinner v Scott* [1947] NZLR 878, 881–82.
- An obligation to install a *necessary* water main to a new housing estate meant a water main that would carry the quantity of water required to the point or points to which it was practical at reasonable cost to connect the building to the supply: *Royco Homes Ltd v Southern Water Authority* [1979] 1 WLR 1366, 1370 (Viscount Dilhorne).
- A suppression order to prevent the publication of references to criminal proceedings is *necessary* (as prescribed by legislation) when it is 'reasonably appropriate and adapted to achieve its perceived purpose': *Fairfax Digital Australia and New Zealand Pty Ltd v Ibrahim* [2012] NSWCCA 125; (2012) 263 FLR 211, [51].

Statutes sometimes anticipate this approach, by expressly requiring conduct to satisfy a test of *reasonable necessity*. Often, however, the result is merely to shift attention from *necessity* to *reasonable*—a word that poses interpretation issues of its own. A prime example is legislation in several jurisdictions authorising a court to require a landowner to grant an easement over neighbouring land, if the easement is 'reasonably necessary' for the effective use and enjoyment of the neighbour's land. (See case law discussed in Brendan Edgeworth (ed), *Butt's Land Law*, 7th edn (Lawbook, 2017) [16.540].)

'considers necessary'

A right to demand actions that a person *considers necessary* (or *thinks necessary*, or similar formulation) does not authorise demands that are capricious, but only demands that are reasonably required and that are not 'chimerical, capricious, and unjust': *Braunstein v Accidental Death Insurance Company* (1861) 1 B & S 782, 797; 121 ER 904, 910 (Crompton J).

See also **reasonable necessity**.

need / want

To *need* something is to require it because it is essential, or almost essential, regardless of whether it is desirable. To *want* something is to desire it even though it may not be necessary:

> '*Need* is a more flexible word than it might first appear. *In need of* plainly means more than merely *want*, but it falls far short of *cannot survive without*.' [*R v Slough Borough Council* [2008] UKHL 52, [54]; [2008] 1 WLR 1808, 1825 (Lord Neuberger)]

In legal usage, both *need* and *want* are notoriously uncertain. Consider a gift of a house by will 'to X for as long as he *needs* it'. How is X's *need* to be established? Is it purely utilitarian (X has nowhere else to live); is it based on sentimental attachment (X was brought up in the house and would very much like to live there); is it based on financial circumstances (X cannot afford to live elsewhere; or X has no other source of income, making the house a useful income-stream)? The same difficulties arise with a gift of a house 'for as long as X *wants* it'. In both cases, the gift is almost certainly void for uncertainty: *Boettcher v Driscoll* [2014] SASC 86; (2014) 119 SASR 523.

See also **desire**; **need not**.

need not

Need not permits discretion. It therefore differs from *must not*. A direction that a person *need not* do something is not a direction that they *must not* do it. For example, a provision in a lease that the tenant '*need not* clean the drains' is not a prohibition against doing so. And a statutory provision that a husband *need not* be joined as a party in an action by or against his wife does not prevent his being joined if there is good reason to do so: *Seroka v Kattenburg* (1886) 17 QBD 177.

See also **may not**; **need / want**; **not required to**.

negative easement

On first impression, a strange expression (like *negative growth*)—how can an easement be negative? The answer is that legal usage distinguishes between an easement that gives a landowner (A) rights to do something on a property owned by another person (B) (a *positive* easement), and an easement that gives A the right to prevent B from doing something on A's property (a *negative* easement). Examples of *positive* easements are rights of way (A's right to cross B's land) and rights to drain water (A's right to discharge water across B's land). Examples of *negative* easements are rights to receive light for a building (A's right to insist that B not block the light to a building on A's land) and rights to the support of a building (A's right to insist that B not withdraw the support that B's building affords to A's).

NEGATIVE EXPRESSIONS

See **POSITIVES / NEGATIVES.**

negative pledge

A promise (pledge) by a borrower (A) to a lender (B) to refrain from giving security over A's assets to another lender without B's consent.

neighbourhood

A notoriously vague word, though used in many contexts. Examples are found in restraint-of-trade covenants ('not to carry on a similar business in the *neighbourhood*'), liquor-licensing restrictions ('needs of the *neighbourhood*'), and town-planning ordinances ('changes in the character of the *neighbourhood*'). The meaning of *neighbourhood* varies with the circumstances of each case: *Alliance Economic Co v Berton* (1923) 92 LJ (KB) 750, 752–53, 759–60; *Re Miscamble's Application* [1966] VR 596, 602. This makes the use of *neighbourhood* an open invitation to litigation over meaning. Instead of *neighbourhood* in examples such as these, try 'within a radius of [X] miles'.

See also **adjacent**; **adjoining**; **contiguous**; **vicinity**.

neither ... nor

Usage

For parallel negatives, prefer the form '*neither ... nor*'; eg, 'He uses neither punctuation nor plain English.' However, the form '*not ... nor*' is an idiomatic alternative:

- 'Plain English is *not* baby talk, *nor* is it a simplified version of English language.' [Robert Eagleson, *Writing in Plain English* (Australian Government Publication Service, 1991) 4)]
- '[The point] had *not* been argued at the hearing *nor* addressed in the judgments.' [*Alseran v Ministry of Defence* [2017] EWHC 3289; [2018] 3 WLR 95, [64] (Leggatt J)]

Courts readily suffer variants of '*neither ... nor*' if the writer's meaning is clear. For example:

> A testator devised property to a woman in the event of her '*not* intermarrying, *nor* having ... children'. Held, *nor* meant *or not*: *Mackenzie v King* (1848) 17 LJ Ch 448.

However, '*neither ... or*' is unacceptable: 'The judge was *neither* polite *or* [prefer: *nor*] punctual.' Also, take care where a list contains three or more (negative) elements. For example: *not* 'neither A, B, or C', *but* 'not A, B, or C', *or* (acceptable for emphasis) 'neither A, nor B, nor C'.

Singular or plural?

Neither ... nor takes a singular verb in two situations:

1. Where the alternatives are singular:

   'Neither judge nor barrister *is* a clear writer.' [But: 'Neither judges nor barristers *are* clear writers.']

2. Where the second alternative is singular:

   'Neither rules [plural] nor custom [singular] *requires* wigs in court.' [But: 'Neither rules nor customs *require* wigs in court.']

Negatives-string causing ambiguity

Take care when adding further negatives to *neither … nor* or its variants. The placement can introduce uncertainty, as in the following example:

> A tenant covenanted (in a clause devoid of punctuation) *not to* carry on any business except the business of a printer *nor to* hold any sale by auction except with the landlord's consent 'which shall *not* be unreasonably withheld'. Did the qualification '*not* be unreasonably withheld' apply to both limbs of the covenant, or only to the second one? Held, it applied to both limbs: *Killick v Second Covent Garden Property Co Ltd* [1973] 2 All ER 337 (CA).

See also **MODIFIERS.**

Nelsonian knowledge

Knowledge imputed to a person who, though not actually knowing, deliberately abstains from inquiry so as not to learn what he or she suspects to be the case: *Twinsectra Ltd v Yardley* [2002] UKHL 12; [2002] 2 AC 164, [22].

See also **blind-eye knowledge; shut-eye knowledge.**

nem con

See **nemine contradicente / nemine dissentiente.**

nem diss

See **nemine contradicente / nemine dissentiente.**

nemine contradicente / nemine dissentiente

Nemine contradicente (Latin): no one contradicting; no one speaking in opposition; abbreviation, *nem con* (in modern usage, no full stops).

Nemine dissentiente (Latin): no one dissenting; no one speaking in opposition; abbreviation, *nem diss* (in modern usage, no full stops).

Neither Latinism tells the whole story. Both are sometimes translated *unanimous*—but that can be ambiguous. Does *unanimous* mean: (1) everyone voted 'for'; or (2) while not everyone voted 'for', none voted 'against' (ie, some abstained)? For example:

> 'When the adoption of the [Bar] Council's Annual Statement for 1955 was moved, the resolution was carried *nem. con.*' [*Re T (A Barrister)* [1982] QB 430, 435 (Whitford J; full stops in original); does this mean *with no one opposing*, or does it mean *unanimously*?]

It is much better to specify—if it is important—whether the decision was unanimous in the sense that everyone voted for it, or in the sense that while no one voted against it, some abstained. For example:

- 'But it is my duty to say that your Lordships are bound by [*R v Millis*] as much as if it had been pronounced *nemine dissentiente* [prefer: *unanimously*] … [until it is] altered by an Act of Parliament.' [*Beamish v Beamish* (1859) 9 HCL 274, 338; ER 735, 761 (Lord Campbell LC, who had dissented (not abstained) in *R v Millis*, and who still disagreed with the decision in that case, but was bound to treat it as a binding precedent.)]
- 'In fact, it is reasonably clear that what occurred was that the motion [of the local council] was declared to be carried *nemine dissentiente* [prefer: *with no one openly voting against*]. No doubt … no member of the council wished to be seen to be holding his hand in the air or going through a division lobby in favour of it. But the fact is that the council were by

silence accepting this motion. They were thereby voting for it.' [*Ex parte Ewing* [1991] 1 WLR 388, 391 (Lord Donaldson MR)]

- '[O]n October 21, 1977, *nemine contradicente* [prefer: *with no one opposing*], judgment for damages for conspiracy … was entered against her.' [*Midland Bank Trust Co Ltd v Green (No 3)* [1979] 2 WLR 594, 598 (Oliver J)]

nemo dat quod [qui] non habet

Latin: a person cannot give what he or she does not have (or, using *they* as a singular pronoun, 'a person cannot give what they do not have'; or simpler still, 'you can't give what you don't have'). Both usages exist: *nemo dat quod non habet* and *nemo dat qui non habet*. Broome's classic text uses both: RH Kersley (ed), *Broom's Legal Maxims*, 10th edn (Sweet & Maxwell, 1939) 303–05. Both are acceptable. But more acceptable still is an English translation. The Latin may masquerade as a term of art, but in reality expresses a simple idea which requires no Latin prop.

nemo debet bis vexari pro una et eadem causa

Latin: no one should twice be vexed (jeopardised) for one and the same cause. Often shortened to *ne bis in idem*: eg, *Criminal Justice (Mutual Assistance) Act 2008*, s 51B(1)(c))—although somewhat inartfully, given the literal translation 'lest there be twice in the same'. The maxim encapsulates the civil law doctrine of *res judicata* and the criminal law doctrine of *autrefois acquit* or *autrefois convict*. However, although the maxim reflects a fundamental proposition of the common law, its Latin formulation carries no more authority than a plain-English substitute, as the following examples show:

- 'In short he relied upon the general principle that *nemo debet bis vexari pro una et eadem causa*, that is that nobody should be vexed twice in respect of one and the same cause.' [*R v Institute of Chartered Accountants in England and Wales* [2011] UKSC 1, [9]; [2011] 2 AC 146, 152 (Lord Clarke, providing a translation)]
- 'The maxim, *nemo debet bis vexari pro una et eadem causa* (it is the rule of law that a man shall not be twice vexed for one and the same cause), appears in *Sparry's Case* [1589]. … In its application to criminal proceedings, it "has become known as the rule against double jeopardy".' [*Pearce v R* (1998) 194 CLR 610, 625 [54] (Gummow J providing a translation). The 'double jeopardy' quotation is from *Rogers v R* (1994) 181 CLR 251, 277.]

See also **autrefois**; **res judicata / res adjudicata**.

nemo debet esse judex in propria causa

Latin: no one should be a judge in their own cause. (Similarly, *iniquum est aliquem rei sui esse judicem*—it is unjust for a person to be a judge in their own cause.) The maxim expresses a fundamental principle of natural justice. However, none of its significance is lost by using an appropriate English translation, as in these two examples:

- 'One of the cornerstones of our legal system is the impartiality of the tribunals by which justice is administered. In civil litigation the guiding principle is that no one may be a judge in his own cause: *nemo debet esse judex in propria causa*. It is a principle which is applied much more widely than a literal interpretation of the words might suggest.' [*R v Bow Street Magistrate, Ex parte Pinochet (No 2)* [2000] 1 AC 119, 140 (Lord Hope)]
- 'The basic rule is not in doubt. Nor is the rationale of the rule: that if a judge has a personal interest in the outcome of an issue which he is to resolve, he is improperly acting as a judge in his own cause …' [*Locabail (UK) Ltd v Bayfield Properties Ltd* [1999] EWCA Civ 3004; [2000] QB 451, 472 (Lord Bingham CJ, Lord Woolf MR, and Sir Richard Scott V-C)]

nemo judex

See **nemo debet esse judex in propria causa**.

nephew / niece

In strict legal usage, *nephew* and *niece* denote nephews and nieces by blood, not by affinity. So, A's 'nephews and nieces' are the children of A's brothers and sisters, not the children of A's spouse's brothers and sisters: *Wells v Wells* (1874) LR 18 Eq 504; *Trustees Executors and Agency Co Ltd v Johnston* [1970] VR 587, 588. However, that meaning is subject to context—especially in wills, where particular attention is paid to what the testator intended by the words used—and so 'nephews and nieces' can sometimes extend to nephews and nieces by affinity: *Re Daoust* [1944] 1 All ER 443, 446. For example:

> Where a testator had no nephews and nieces by blood, a gift 'to my nephews and nieces' meant a gift to the testator's wife's nephews and nieces: *Sherratt v Mountford* (1873) LR 8 Ch App 928.

NESTED INFORMATION

See **EMBEDDED (NESTED) INFORMATION**.

net-off

See **SET-OFF CLAUSE**.

next-of-kin

Usually hyphenated, though *next of kin* is also acceptable. At common law, *next-of-kin* denotes the nearest blood relations, both ascending and descending; a spouse is excluded. The closest next-of-kin (that is, first degree) are parents (both father and mother) and children. Then follow siblings, grandparents and grandchildren (second degree); then uncles, aunts, nephews and nieces (third degree); and then first cousins (fourth degree). To illustrate:

> A testator devises property 'to my next-of-kin'. The testator is survived by his spouse, his parents, and his children. The testator's parents and children share the gift, to the exclusion of the spouse.

In some jurisdictions, statute decrees that a gift to 'next-of-kin' is interpreted as a gift to those who would take on intestacy (death without a valid will)—which may well alter the devolution.

nexus

Latin: a link, connection. The Latin plural also is *nexus* [not 'nexi']; the English plural is *nexuses*.

> 'There are four possible *nexi* [prefer: *nexuses*] between C and D.' [*Revenue and Customs Comrs v Total Network SL* [2008] AC 1174, 1204 (John Martin QC, in argument)]

nihil ad rem

Latin: not to the point; irrelevant. Nothing is gained by retaining the Latin, except a haughty tone. Prefer straightforward English. For example:

> 'The prisoner locked in the shed is certainly restrained within defined bounds and it is *nihil ad rem* [prefer: *beside the point*; or *irrelevant*] that if he were not locked in the shed, he would be locked in his cell or restrained … in some other part of the prison.' [*Ex parte Hague* [1992] 1 AC 58, 164 (Lord Bridge)]

nihil obstat

Latin: there is no objection. Resist the pedantry of the Latin; prefer an appropriate English translation. For example:

> 'Our courts did not always wait until these [legal developments] had been endorsed by the English Court of Appeal, let alone the House of Lords. Nor did they *await the nihil obstat of the High Court* [prefer: *wait until the High Court raised no objection*].' [*Harris v Digital Pulse Pty Ltd* (2003) 56 NSWLR 298; [2003] NSWCA 10, [221] (Mason P)]

ninety-nine years (lease)

Leases are sometimes for a term of 99 years (or even 999 years). But there is no legal magic in 99 (or 999); that stated duration is mere convention. The term of a lease can be 100 years, or 1,000 years, or any other stated duration.

nisi

Latin: unless; if not; used (for example) in *order nisi* or *decree nisi* to indicate that the order or decree will come into force unless cause is shown why it should not do so, or unless a court-imposed condition remains unsatisfied. An example is a *decree nisi* for divorce: the parties remain married until the decree is made 'absolute'.

nisi prius

Latin: unless sooner. *Nisi prius* was the name of a writ commanding the sheriff to provide a jury at Westminster on a certain day, 'unless before then' (*nisi prius*) the justices of assize visited the county; hence, a 'trial *nisi prius*' came to mean a court-hearing composed of a judge and jury.

'NO ASSIGNMENT' CLAUSE

Meaning

Also: *non-assignability clause*. A clause precluding a party to a contract from assigning their rights under the contract. Sometimes, 'no assignment' clauses are absolute (no assignment at all); sometimes they are qualified (no assignment without consent).

Non-assignability clauses are not contrary to public policy: *Linden Gardens Trust Ltd v Lenesta Sludge Disposals Ltd* [1994] 1 AC 85. However, statute may qualify or limit their terms. For example, a provision against assigning a lease without the landlord's consent is usually subject to a statutory qualification that the landlord cannot unreasonably withhold consent: *Landlord and Tenant Act 1927*, s 19; *Conveyancing Act 1919* (NSW), s 133B.

Limitations

Take care when drafting non-assignability clauses. Courts interpret them narrowly, because the clauses usually seek to restrict what would otherwise be an inherent right to assign.

Examples

- An assignment in breach of a 'no assignment' clause usually remains a valid assignment. The assignment is a breach of contract for which damages lie, but is not itself invalid. Thus, an assignment of a lease in breach of a 'no assignment' clause entitles the landlord to seek damages or (possibly) to terminate the lease, but does not deprive the assignee of the lease (unless the landlord terminates the lease for the breach).
- A 'no assignment' clause does not, of itself, preclude other transactions (eg, in the case of a lease, the grant of a sublease or licence to occupy: *Sweet & Maxwell Ltd v Universal News Service Ltd* [1964] 2 QB 699).
- In commercial contexts, a 'no assignment' clause may, as a matter of interpretation, prohibit only the delegation of performance under the contract (ie, 'you must perform this contract personally'), not the assignment of rights under the contract. This is especially so in the United States: see *Uniform Commercial Code* §2-210(3).
- A 'no assignment' clause, of itself, does not preclude the following transactions, which are not strictly 'assignments':
  - transfers of property by operation of law (eg, on bankruptcy)
  - changes in ownership that result from the operation of legal principles (eg, merger of a lesser interest into a larger one)
  - changes in the control or management of a corporation.

See also **assign / transfer**; **MERGER CLAUSE.**

no earlier than

See **not earlier than.**

no later than

See **not later than.**

'NO MERGER' CLAUSE

See **MERGER CLAUSE.**

'NO ORAL MODIFICATION' CLAUSE

Sometimes abbreviated to 'NOM' clause: eg, *MWB Business Exchange Ltd v Rock Advertising Ltd* [2018] UKSC 24; [2019] AC 119, [20] (Lord Briggs JSC)].

See **'NO VARIATION' CLAUSE'.**

no question but that

Despite this expression's idiomatic use, *but* is superfluous. Delete *but*, as in this example (shown in strikethrough):

> '[I]t is important to remember that there is *no question ~~but~~ that* the local authority exercised reasonable care in placing the Appellant with the foster parents …' [*NA v Nottingham County Council* [2015] EWCA Civ 1139, [48]; [2016] 2 WLR 1455, 1473 (Black LJ)]

'no recourse' loan

Also, *no-recourse loan* (hyphenated), *non-recourse loan* (hyphenated). A loan under which the lender has recourse solely to the borrower's property. If the borrower defaults and the property is not worth enough to recoup the loan, the lender cannot recover the shortfall from the borrower or guarantor personally.

'NO RELIANCE' CLAUSE

A 'no reliance' clause takes one of two forms, each with the same purpose:

1. The parties have made their own enquiries before entering into the contract, and have not relied on any representations, warranties and the like by the other party.
2. All pre-contractual representations, warranties, and the like are superseded by the written terms of the contract, and cannot be relied on by a party to contradict those written terms.

A 'no reliance' clause aims to forestall disputes over what was said, or not said, before entry into a contract or transaction, and thus to forestall lengthy trials—which is said to be 'a reasonable position for each party to be presumed to wish to take and a reasonable aim for them to wish to achieve': *Lloyd v Browning* [2013] EWCA Civ 1637 [34] (Davis LJ). In this, it serves a similar purpose to an 'entire agreement' clause, and is subject to the same limitations as an 'entire agreement' clause. In particular, a 'no reliance' clause:

- does not protect against fraud;
- does not preclude reliance on an estoppel arising from pre-contract negotiations: *Franklins Pty Ltd v Metcash Trading Pty Ltd* [2009] NSWCA 407; (2009) 76 NSWLR 603, [33], [554]; *Caringbah Investments Pty Ltd v Caringbah Business and Sports Club Ltd* [2016] NSWCA 165, [73];
- may be overridden by legislation governing unfair terms or consumer protection (as in *First Tower Trustees Ltd v CDS (Superstores International) Ltd* [2018] EWCA Civ 1396; [2019] 1 WLR 637).

See also **'ENTIRE AGREEMENT' CLAUSE**.

'NO VARIATION' CLAUSE

A 'no variation' clause appears in one of two versions: (1) the parties cannot vary their contract (at all), or (2) a variation is unenforceable unless it satisfies specified requirements (usually that the variation is in writing and signed). The law treats version (1)—a blanket provision that parties cannot vary their contract—as unenforceable.

This is because parties to a contract can always 'unmake' their contract and then re-contract in different terms.

More difficult is how the law treats version (2). Until recently, the preferred (though not universal) view was that version (2) clauses are also unenforceable. The rationale was similar to that for version (1), namely that parties can 'unmake' any part of their contract: *Beatty v Guggenheim Exploration Co* (1919) 225 NY 380, 387 (Cardozo J). This was (and may still be) the view, for example, in Australia (*GEC Marconi Systems Pty Ltd v BHP Information Technology Pty Ltd* (2003) 128 FCR 1; *Cenric Group v TWT Property Group* [2018] NSWSC 1570, [102]–[103]), and in Canada (*Shelanu Inc v Print Three Franchising Corporation* (2003) 226 DLR (4th) 577, [54]). However, despite earlier uncertainty, the current UK view is that 'no variation unless in writing' clauses are enforceable according to their terms: *MWB Business Exchange Ltd v Rock Advertising Ltd* [2018] UKSC 24; [2019] AC 119. They breach no principle of public policy (ibid, [12]), and serve at least three useful purposes (ibid, [12]):

- They prevent attempts to undermine written agreements by informal means.
- They avoid disputes over the meaning of variations—oral discussions may be vague, but written terms are likely to be more precise.
- They allow entities to police their internal rules restricting the authority to agree to variations.

However, 'no variation unless in writing' clauses will be unenforceable where the parties are estopped (prevented) by their words or conduct from denying that they have agreed to vary their contract: *Energy Venture Partners Ltd v Malabu Oil and Gas Ltd* [2013] EWHC 2118 (Comm), [273]–[274] (Gloster J).

See also **'ENTIRE AGREEMENT' CLAUSE.**

'NO WAIVER' CLAUSE

Also, *no-waiver clause* (hyphenated). A clause precluding reliance on the doctrine of waiver, and generally appearing in one of two versions:

1. That specified actions are not to be taken as waiving rights, or that failure to enforce (or delay in enforcing) rights on one occasion is not to be taken as waiving the right to enforce on future occasions. For example, courts usually find that a landlord who accepts rent from a tenant in the knowledge that the tenant has breached a term of the lease, has 'waived' the breach. A 'no waiver' clause in the lease seeks to preclude a finding of waiver.
2. That no waiver of a party's rights is binding unless the waiving party agrees in writing that the conduct amounts to waiver. This goes further than version (1), by indicating the parties' contractual intention that no waiver is to bind until *both* (a) an act of waiver occurs *and* (b) the actor agrees in writing that it is effective to waive rights.

These clauses may provide some comfort to contracting parties, and courts take them into account in deciding whether an act that would normally constitute waiver is to have that effect. Logically, however, 'no-waiver' clauses can never guarantee complete protection, because a party can by conduct waive a contractual right—even a contractual right embodied in a 'no-waiver' clause. This seems well established, although it is of course fact-specific: eg, *Owendale Pty Ltd v Anthony* (1967) 117 CLR 539, 609; *Innercity Businessmen's Club Ltd v James Kirkpatrick Ltd* [1975] 2 NZLR 636, 641–44;

Tele2 International Card SA v Post Office Ltd [2009] EWCA Civ 9; *O'Brien v Bank of Western Australia* [2013] NSWCA 71 at [110]; (2013) 16 BPR 31,705, 31,729.

See also **election**; **estoppel**; **waiver**.

noisome / noisy

Noisome means noxious, smelly, offensive; *noisesome* means making noise (*noisy*). The meanings are distinct, although the terms sometimes appear in combination—as in a restrictive covenant prohibiting the use of land for 'any noisy, noisome, offensive or dangerous trade or calling': *Nussey v Provincial Billposting Co* [1909] 1 Ch 734. Take care to use the correct word:

- '[Words are defamatory if people shun the plaintiff because the words allege that] he suffers from leprosy or the plague or the itch ... or is *noisesome* [sic: *noisome*] and smelly.' [*Berkoff v Burchill* [1997] EMLR 139, 152 (Millett LJ). The spelling *noisesome* is reproduced in Peter Millett, *As in Memory Long* (Wildy, Simmonds & Hill, 2015) 206. However, the All ER uses *noisome*: *Berkoff v Burchill* [1996] 4 All ER 1008, 1019.]
- '[W]hat do we see? Crime, violent crime increasing everywhere; ... pollution, *noisesome* [sic: *noisome*] pollution, increasing everywhere; corruption, corroding corruption, increasing everywhere.' [Lord Denning, Fifth Wilfred Fullagar Memorial Lecture, 'Let Justice be Done' (1975) 2 *Monash University Law Review* 3, 4; the misspelling may be the fault of student editors.]

nolens volens

Latin: whether willing or unwilling. An unnecessary Latinism, given that the English translation is clear. In the first example below, the judge retains the Latin but offers an explanation of the meaning. No similar offer is made in the second example.

- '[I]f the intention of the accused is to have intercourse *nolens volens*—that is[,] recklessly and not caring whether the victim be a consenting party or not—that is equivalent ... to an intent to do the prohibited act without the consent of the victim.' [*R v Morgan* [1976] AC 182, 209 (Lord Hailsham; dashes and comma added)]
- '[T]here may be classes of contract ... where the making of the contract will itself be an illegal act, and where the court would be driven *nolens volens* [prefer: *willing or unwilling*] to hold that the arbitration clause was itself void.' [*Soleimany v Soleimany* [1999] QB 785, 799 (Waller LJ)]

nolle prosequi

Latin: to be unwilling to proceed (usually in the context of a stay of proceedings). *Nolle prosequi* has assumed noun form to indicate an entry in a court record when the plaintiff is unwilling to proceed further against the defendant, or the Crown decides not to continue criminal proceedings. In some jurisdictions, the Latin has been replaced with 'no bill' or 'do not prosecute', reflecting Latin's gradual disappearance from legal language.

'NOM' CLAUSE

Abbreviation for 'no oral modification' clause.

See **'NO VARIATION' CLAUSE**.

nomen juris

Latin: a legal name (in the sense of a legal term carrying a technical meaning). A rare usage in modern times, always replaceable with ordinary English, as in the following examples:

- '"Sale" is, in my opinion, a *nomen juris* [prefer: *term of art*; *technical term*]; it is the name of a particular consensual contract.' [*Kirkness v John Hudson & Co Ltd* [1955] AC 696, 727 (Lord Reid)]
- '[In the notice] no details of the offence are given, other than the *nomen juris* [prefer: *legal description of the offence*] in the case of a common law offence or the statutory provision by which it was constituted.' [*Benichou v Mauritius Commercial Bank* [2007] UKPC 36, [51] (Lord Walker)]

NOMINALISATIONS

See **NOUNS / VERBS**.

Nominate Reports

Published collections of law reports by various reporters from various courts, from the Middle Ages until the 1860s (when the Incorporated Council of Law Reporting began publishing 'official' law reports). They are called 'nominate', because they were published under the reporters' names—unlike the earlier Year Books, which were anonymous. The reporters' names are abbreviated (unless already brief). The quality of the reporting varied greatly. Some reporters were famously incompetent. (For judicial jibes about reporters' failings, see Lord Neuberger, 'Reflections in the ICLR Top Fifteeen Cases' (2015), www.supremecourt.uk/docs/speech-151006.pdf.)

Most of the nominate reports were republished in the *English Reports* (ER). The citation convention is to state first the nominate report, followed by its location in the English Reports, with the two citations separated by a semicolon (or sometimes, a comma). For example:

- *Abraham v Bubb* (1680) 2 Freem Chy [abbr for vol 2 of 'Freeman's Chancery Reports'] 53; 22 ER 1054
- *Barlow v Rhodes* (1833) 1 Cr & M [abbr for vol 1 of 'Crompton and Meeson'] 439; 149 ER 471

Some authors omit the nominate report reference and cite cases only by the *English Reports* reference; but many authors consider that practice to be disrespectful to the nominate reporter. Yet other authors cite only the nominate report (eg, all editions of *Megarry & Wade's Law of Real Property*, including the current 9th edn, 2019)—a practice that is less than helpful to most modern readers, who have access only to the *English Reports*.

See also **Year Books**.

nominatim

Latin: by name. To insist on the Latin in the face of a simple English translation seems eccentric. For example:

- 'Thus there is exempted [by the statute] land owned by the University of Sydney, to which has been added over the years land owned by other new universities in New South Wales *nominatim* [prefer: *by name; separately named*] ...' [*Ashfield Municipal Council v Joyce* [1978] AC 122, 133 (Lord Wilberforce)]

- '[Counsel] did not contend that the statutory right was given to the plaintiffs *nominatim* [prefer: *individually by name*] but asserted that it was given to a discernible group, of whom the plaintiffs were members.' [*Grand Central Car Park Pty Ltd v Tivoli Freeholders* [1969] VR 62, 68 (McInerney J)]

nominee

In law, *nominee* carries at least three different meanings.

1. A person who holds property on behalf of another.
2. A person who, though not a party to an agreement, is entitled to exercise powers under it or to benefit from rights under it—eg, where an option is exercisable 'by A or A's nominee'.
3. A person who is proposed for an office or position.

non / non-

As a prefix

The prefix *non* is variously (1) hyphenated to the word it negates, or (2) joined without a hyphen to the word it negates. Hyphenated forms are more common, but some hyphenless forms remain idiomatic.

Examples—usually hyphenated

non-alcoholic (drink)
non-aligned
non-attendance (at trial)
non-attributable (source)
non-capital (punishment)
non-classified (information)
non-consensual
non-contractual
non-contributory (pension scheme)
non-delegable (duty)
non-delivery (goods)
non-derogation
non-disclosure (information)
non-essential (contractual term)
non-exclusive (jurisdiction)
non-member (of an organisation)
non-monetary (claim)
non-negotiable
non-parties
non-payment
non-performance
non-person
non-profit (organisation)
non-qualified (representative)
non-returnable (deposit)
non-standard (contract term)

Examples—usually joined without a hyphen

noncompliance
nonconformist
nonentity
nonfeasance
nonvoting

As separate word

Sometimes, *non* is separated entirely from the word it negates. While the separation may be idiomatic, it can reduce the immediacy of the negation. For example:

- '[A]pplication for costs order against *non party* [prefer: *non-party*]' [*MG Corrosion Consultants Pty Ltd v Vinciguerra (No 2)* [2011] FCAFC 48 (court-issued catchword; altered to *non-party* in the report at (2011) 276 ALR 319.]
- 'The decision maker made comment as a *non qualified* [prefer: *non-qualified*] person on the condition suffered [by the applicant]' [Ground 3 of claim in *Ali v Minister for Immigration* [2013] FCCA 1702]
- 'An amount is an *eligible non capital* [prefer: *non-capital*] *amount* if it is ...' [Definition in *Income Tax Assessment Act 1936* (Cth), s 159GZZZQ(5); discussed in *Consolidated Media Holdings Ltd v Commissioner of Taxation* [2011] FCA 367, [14], (2011) 82 ACSR 637, 641, where Emmett J instinctively hyphenates the term ('non-capital').]

With adjectives

Using *non* or *non-* with adjectives can be clumsy. Rewriting can often avoid the clumsiness. For example:

Original	**Rewrite**
non-active account	inactive account
non-criminal cases	cases not involving criminal law
non-negligent plaintiff	plaintiff who is not negligent
non-sitting judge	judge who is not sitting

The clumsiness is compounded when using *non* or *non-* with phrasal adjectives. Here too, rewriting is useful:

Original	**Rewrite**
non-income-earning asset	asset that earns no income
non-interest-bearing account	account that bears no interest
non-evidence-based approach	approach that is not evidence-based
non-asset-stripping investment	investment that does not involve asset-stripping

non compos mentis

Latin: not of sound mind; mentally incompetent (eg, to transact legal business). Plural: *non compotes mentis*. In its singular form, this Latinism may well have become part of normal English, perhaps because of its rhythmic ring. Nevertheless, like many Latinisms in law, it has no advantage over a translation (eg, 'of unsound mind'). Prefer a translation.

- 'Until 1939 periods of limitation did not run against infants or against those described ... as *non compos mentis* [prefer: *mentally incapable*], so long as they were under their respective disabilities.' [*Hewer v Bryant* [1970] 1 QB 357, 370 (Sachs LJ)]
- 'The performance of the rites of Christian burial was not authorised on the interment of the remains of a person who had committed suicide, unless, significantly, the deceased was shown to have been *non compos mentis* [prefer: *mentally ill*; *of unsound mind*] at the time. [C]oroners or juries would often add to a verdict that the deceased had killed himself or

herself, words to the effect "whilst of unsound mind" or "whilst the balance of [his or her] mind was disturbed".' [*Stuart v Kirkland-Veenstra* [2009] HCA 15; (2009) 237 CLR 215, [96] (Gummow, Hayne, and Heydon JJ, offering translations).]

See also **idiot / lunatic**.

non constat

Latin: it does not follow [that]; sometimes used less assertively to mean 'it is not clear [that]'. The Latin has no superiority over the plain-English substitute—so prefer the plain English (using the less assertive wording, if intending that nuance). For example:

- 'However, it follows from the foregoing that I cannot agree with Laws LJ's reasoning in the cases of … *Non constat* [prefer: *It does not follow*] however that a purported notice of appeal is a nullity unless accompanied from the outset by grounds.' [*Pomiechowski v District Court of Legnica, Poland* [2012] 1 WLR 1604, [19] (Lord Mance)]
- 'There may be a very high probability that criminal activity causing harm may take place in certain areas of Sydney, but *non constat* [prefer: *it does not follow*; or (if this is the intended nuance) *it is not clear*] that the occupier or adjacent neighbour has a duty of care to those who suffer.' [*WD & HO Wills v State Rail Authority of NSW* (1998) 43 NSWLR 338, 359 (Mason P)]

See also **non sequitur**.

non est factum

Latin: it is not made; often translated 'it is not my deed'. An abbreviation of *scriptum praedictum non est factum*: 'the apparent writing is not of my doing'. A shorthand description for a claim by X that X's apparent signature on a document is a forgery, or that (though not a forgery) X had no understanding of what he or she was signing. The plea normally requires proof of forgery, misrepresentation, or disability.

There is no magic in the Latin. An appropriate translation can carry the sense without loss of legal nuance, and has far more meaning for non-lawyers. For example:

- 'The plea of *non est factum* [prefer: '*it is not my document*'] obviously applies when the person sought to be held liable did not in fact sign the document. But at least since the sixteenth century it has also been held to apply in certain cases so as to enable a person who in fact signed a document to say that it is not his deed.' [*Saunders v Anglia Building Society (Gallie v Lee)* [1971] AC 1004, 1015–16 (Lord Reid; second sentence offering a translation)]
- 'The defence of *non est factum* raised by Mrs Archer before Simos J (that is[,] her defence that there was a radical or fundamental difference between the documents she thought she was signing and the documents she did sign) was rejected by Simos J …' [*Archer v Archer* [2000] NSWCA 314, [8] (Handley JA, providing an explanation more useful than a literal translation)]

non haec in foedera veni

Latin: this was not what I promised to do. Very few readers will understand this Latin expression, so prefer a plain-English substitute. For example:

- 'Frustration [of a contract] occurs whenever the law recognises that without default of either party a contractual obligation has become incapable of being performed because the circumstances in which performance is called for would render it a thing radically different from that which was undertaken by the contract. *Non haec in foedera veni*. It was not this that I promised to do.' [*Davis Contractors Ltd v Fareham Urban District Council* [1956] AC 696, 728–29 (Lord Radcliffe, offering a translation)]

- 'Those who drafted the Constitution … [would] say, if they could examine the authorities on the implied freedom of communication: *Non haec in foedera veni* [Prefer: *This is not what we sought to achieve*].' [*Monis v R* (2013) 249 CLR 92; [2013] HCA 4, [250] (Heydon J, eschewing a translation)]

non liquet

Latin: it is not clear. The English translation is clear, so prefer it:

'[T]he basis for the decision … in *Tate*'s case was that it was inappropriate for a Court to decline to make a declaration concerning the true meaning of a statutory provision on the ground that it was unclear (*non liquet*) or involved a political question.' [*Burrell Demolition Ltd v Burrell* [2002] NZCA 37, [5] (Tipping J, the translation rendering the Latin superfluous)]

non obstante

Latin: notwithstanding; despite; in spite of; even though. There is no good reason to prefer the Latin over the English. This is so whether the Latin is used alone or as part of a longer expression: eg, *non obstante aliquo statuto in contrarium* (despite any statute to the contrary); *non obstante veredicto* (despite the verdict; despite the judgment). For example:

- '[I]t seems difficult to assume that both counsel and both judges [in *Narraway's case*] were unaware of the effect of [*Anderson's case*, which] had certainly been fully reported several months earlier … Thus *Narraway's case* can be taken to have been decided *non obstante* [prefer: *in spite of*; *despite*] *Anderson's case*.' [*Shaw v Groom* [1970] 2 QB 504, 525 (Sachs LJ)]
- 'To use the language of the old practice in this regard, his Honour entered judgment against the tenth and twelfth defendants notwithstanding the verdict of the jury (*non obstante veredicto*).' [*Erglis v Buckley (No 2)* [2005] QCA 404, [4]; [2006] 2 Qd R 407, 410 (McPherson JA—preferring the English but adding the Latin for legal readers needing reassurance)]

non sequitur

Latin: it does not follow (in the sense that the conclusion does not follow logically from the premise). Often used as a noun: 'That proposition is a *non sequitur*'. The Latinism has become common in general as well as legal usage, and for that reason is often not italicised. However, it is no more precise than an English translation. For example:

- 'To say, as counsel submitted, that if material would be disclosed now, it should have been disclosed then, *is a non sequitur* [prefer: *does not logically follow*].' *Macklin v Her Majesty's Advocate* [2015] UKSC 77, [18] (Lord Reed)]
- 'The appellants submit that because [proposition A, then proposition B]. However, the reasoning depends upon a *non sequitur* [prefer: *logical flaw*].' [*Frost v Warner* [2002] HCA 1, [32]; (2002) 209 CLR 509, 519 (Gleeson CJ, Gummow and Callinan JJ)]

Occasionally, *non sequitur* is used to frame a proposition in a way that leaves the reader to unpack the premise. It hints at something following (or not following), but does not state it. While this is not 'wrong', it can be ungainly. For example:

'To compare the judge's activism to that of Lord Denning is a *non sequitur*.' Prefer (unpacked): 'The judge's activism is nothing like Lord Denning's activism.'

See also **non constat**.

nonage

The state of not being of full age (ie, a minor). The word is rare in modern usage—so rare that its use seems consciously stilted. For example:

- 'The three-year [statutory limitation period] is not capable of being extended, except to allow for any time during which the person alleged to have been defamed was under legal disability by reason of *nonage* [prefer: *minority*] or unsoundness of mind.' [*Majrowski v Guy's and St Thomas's NHS Trust* [2007] 1 AC 224, 239 (Lord Hope; *nonage* used in the statute)]
- '[A person comes of full age and capacity in law at the start of the day before the anniversary of his or her birth.] The days of his *nonage* [prefer: *minority*] had at that instant passed.' [*Prowse v McIntyre* (1961) 111 CLR 264, 281 (Windeyer J)]

See also **infant / minor**.

'NON-ASSIGNABILITY' CLAUSE

See **'NO ASSIGNMENT' CLAUSE**.

NON-EXCLUSIVE JURISDICTION CLAUSE

See **JURISDICTION CLAUSE**.

none

None usually takes the singular verb and pronoun, because the sense is 'no single one':

> *None* of the judges [ie, no single judge] *is* available to conduct the trial.

However, the plural verb and pronoun are acceptable where the sense is 'no two or more':

> *None* of the appeal judges *agree* [not *agrees*—because an appeal court has two or more judges] to hearing the appeal, because *none* of the pleadings *have* [not *has*] been filed.

If unsure, rewrite:

- No judge is available to conduct the trial.
- No appeal judge agrees to hear the appeal, because no pleading has been filed.

noscitur a sociis

Latin: known by its associates. A principle of interpretation under which the meaning of a doubtful word or phrase may be ascertained by reference to the meaning of the words or phrases associated with it. The rationale is that the parties are likely to have intended a word in an interrelated, overlapping list to bear a meaning that is consistent with adjoining words: *Lend Lease Real Estate Investments Ltd v GPT RE Ltd* [2006] NSWCA 207, [31] (Spigelman CJ).

Examples

- An insurance policy taken out by a fruit and vegetable importer covered 'physical loss or damage or deterioration' arising out of strikes. A dock strike delayed the arrival of the insured's produce at market. During the delay, market prices fell. Held, 'physical loss or damage or deterioration' did not include fall in market price; each of the three listed misfortunes involved *physical* damage to the produce—*physical* loss, *physical* damage, *physical* deterioration: *Lewis Emanuel & Son Ltd v Hepburn* [1960] 1 Lloyd's Rep 304.

- An insurance policy excluded liability for 'erasure *loss* distortion or corruption of information on computer systems'. Held, *loss* did not include theft of a computer. In the context of the surrounding words, 'loss' connoted loss of information by electronic interference: *Tektrol Ltd v International Insurance Co of Hanover Ltd* [2005] EWCA Civ 845; [2005] 2 Lloyd's Rep 701.
- A statute prohibited bookmaking in any 'house, office, room or *place*'. Held, *place* did not include a public laneway, because the neighbouring words implied *enclosed* spaces: *Prior v Sherwood* (1906) 3 CLR 1054.
- A statute made it an offence in bankruptcy proceedings for the debtor to 'remove, conceal or dispose of' property with intent to defraud creditors. The debtor failed to disclose certain assets to the trustee in bankruptcy. Had he 'concealed' them? Held, no: 'conceal' took its colour from the adjoining words, 'remove' and 'dispose of', each of which connoted a positive act done with the intent of putting assets beyond the reach of creditors; it did not include the mere non-disclosure of assets: *R v Goulis* (1981) 125 DLR (3d) 137 (BCCA).

Further reading

Halsbury's Laws of England, 'Statutes and Legislative Process' (vol 96, 2018) [814] (recognition by associated words)

not … unless / not … until

The double negative form of these expressions complicates understanding. Rephrase in more positive form:

Before	**After**
The Law Society will *not* admit students *unless* they have passed their law exams.	The Law Society will admit students *only if* they have passed their law exams.
The Law Society will *not* admit students *until* they have completed law studies.	The Law Society will admit students *only after* they have completed law studies.

See further **POSITIVES / NEGATIVES**.

not earlier than

Where something is to be done *not earlier than* a stated day, it can be done on that day: *Ward v Berndston* (1889) 8 NZLR 21, 27–28 (Williams J).

See also **from (a date)**.

not later than

not later than = on

As a matter of ordinary English, where something is to be done *not later than* a stated date, it may be done *on* that date: eg, where something is to be done *not later than* 1 January, it can be done *on* 1 January.

not later than … before

It is different where something is to be done *not later than* [a period] *before* a stated date. The force of *before* means that to do it *on* the date is too late. Thus, a payment to be made '*not later than* 3 days *before* 1 February' must be made by midnight on 28/29 January: *Carapanayoti & Co Ltd v Comptoir Commercial Andre & Cie SA* [1972] 1 Lloyd's Rep 139, 142 (Denning MR).

However, other aspects of the calculation can complicate the result, as the following example shows:

> An application to renew a licence needed to be made '*not later than one month before* the expiry of' the licence. The licence expired at the very end (midnight) of 28 November. A renewal application was made on 28 October. Was it too late? All judges agreed that the time-span required a 'clear' month, and that counting started on 29 October. But the court split on whether the application was too late. The majority held that, because the licence expired at midnight on 28 November, the clear month included that day; therefore, the application was made in time. The minority held that the clear month must end *before* the final day of the licence (28 November) began; therefore, the application was too late. See *Forster v Jododex Aust Pty Ltd* (1972) 127 CLR 421.

See also **day**; **not less than (time)**; **TIME**.

not less than (a number)

In line with the general preference for positive formulations over negative ones, try *at least [n]*, or *[n] or more*, as in this example:

> 'A quorum consists of *not less than* [prefer: *at least*] five directors.' However, because five is the minimum, a clearer formulation would be: 'A quorum consists of *five or more* directors.'

See also **POSITIVES / NEGATIVES**.

not less than (time)

General principle

A period of '*not less than* [X] days' means 'not less than X *clear* days': *Re Railway Sleepers Supply Co* (1885) 29 Ch D 204. For example:

- A requirement to give a notice of '*not less than* 14 days' requires 14 clear days: *Moore v Jackson* [1903] 2 KB 163; *R v Turner* [1910] 1 KB 346, 359–60.
- A requirement to give '*not less* than 21 days' notice' of a meeting requires 21 clear days—ie, 21 days exclusive of the day of giving notice and the day of holding the meeting: *Re Hector Whaling Ltd* [1936] 1 Ch 208; *Thompson v Stimpson* [1961] 1 QB 195. (In Scotland, the position may be different: *Neil McLeod & Sons Ltd Petitioners* [1967] SC 16.)

Exceptions

The general principle does not always apply. Context—including perceived statutory purpose—may overturn it. So may other principles, such as the corresponding-date rule. For example:

- A statutory requirement that a landlord give the tenant notice of '*not less than* four weeks' did not require four weeks' clear notice. Rather, the period *excluded* the first day and *included* the last day: *Schnabel v Allard* [1967] 1 QB 627, overruling *Thompson v Stimpson* [1961] 1 QB 195.
- A tenant's statutory right to apply for a new tenancy '*not less than* two months' after being served with a landlord's notice to quit did not require two *clear* months. An application made on the corresponding date exactly two months after service of the notice was not too early. This followed from the corresponding-date rule: *EJ Riley Investments Ltd v Eurostile Holdings Ltd* [1985] 1 WLR 1139.

Prefer positive statements

Not less than hints at the negative. In line with the general preference for positive formulations over negative ones, consider using *at least [x]* or, to avoid possible ambiguity, *[x] or more*. For example:

> 'To recover possession from the tenant requires *not less than* [prefer: *at least*] 10 days' notice.' But beware of potential ambiguity. Would a notice of exactly 10 days suffice? To avoid argument, it may be better to write 'notice of *10 days or more*'.

See also **at least (time); clear day; corresponding-date rule; POSITIVES / NEGATIVES.**

not more than (a number of)

If *not more than* seems to demand mental gymnastics, use *up to*. For example:

> 'The office can accommodate *not more than* [prefer: *up to*] five solicitors.'

See also **not less than (a number); not less than (time); POSITIVES / NEGATIVES.**

not required to

Instead of *[is] not required to*, try *need not*. The meaning is the same, and uses fewer words. For example:

- '[T]he court *is not required to* [prefer: *need not*] give effect to the illegal contract in order to find that Mr Mirza should not be allowed to retain Mr Patel's money.' [*Patel v Mirza* [2016] UKSC 42; [2017] AC 467, [128] (Lord Kerr)]
- 'In such a case the prosecution *is not required to* [prefer: *need not*] prove that the accused intended to transmit the disease to his or her sexual partner.' [*Zaburoni v R* [2016] HCA 12; (2016) 256 CLR 482, [2] (Kiefel, Bell, and Keane JJ)]

See also **may not; need not.**

nota bene

Latin: note well; take notice. More commonly seen in the abbreviation 'NB' (usually capitalised; not italicised).

NOTES and EXAMPLES

Notes and examples can help readers understand the effect of complex provisions. They are not new: for instance, the *Indian Evidence Act* of 1872 used examples to illustrate the effect of its provisions. Modern legislative drafters frequently use notes and examples, often boxed or shaded (or both). However, drafters of private-sector legal documents still seem uncomfortable with them.

Notes

Notes can provide a summary or overview of a particular provision. They can also be useful navigational aids, pointing readers to related provisions. For example, a provision in a statute or document may require a party to give notice before exercising a right; it can be useful to add a note, pointing readers to the provision governing the service of notices.

Examples

Examples can spell out the kinds of situations where a provision may apply. An illustration is s 207 of the *Finance Act 2013*. The section deals with 'tax arrangements' that are 'abusive'. Subss (4) and (5) give examples of tax arrangements that 'might be' abusive. Subs (6) states that the examples given in subss (4) and (5) are not exhaustive.

Also useful are 'worked' examples, demonstrating how a provision is to be applied. For example, a rent-review provision in a lease could contain a worked example of the way in which the valuer is to apply the various factors specified as relevant in calculating the revised rent. A worked example must of course be correct. An example that conflicts with its accompanying text (as in *Whittaker v Comcare* (1998) 28 AAR 55) embarrasses the drafter and confuses the reader.

Location of notes and examples

Notes and examples are best placed at the end of the provision to which they relate. An alternative is to place them alongside the text to which they relate, in a (narrow) dedicated column; this makes them more immediately apparent to the eye.

Cautions in use

Do not overwhelm the text

Do not allow notes and examples to overwhelm the main text. For example, although 'boxing' or 'shading' can be useful to distinguish notes and examples from the main text, the technique can divert attention from that text—which, after all, is the key component. One way to keep notes and examples to their subsidiary role is to use a font smaller than the font for the main text. Another is to cast them as footnotes or endnotes, or put them in a schedule—although these locations can deprive them of immediacy.

Do not state the obvious

Do not use notes and examples to illustrate the operation of provisions that are straightforward. A statement of the obvious insults the reader's intelligence.

Do not use to insert substantive material

Do not use notes and examples to introduce substantive material. While that might be effective legally, it will unsettle the reader (who does not expect examples or notes to fulfil that purpose).

Do not go beyond meaning of the text

Do not allow notes and examples to stretch the ambit of the text they illustrate. This will inevitably allow argument whether an extension of meaning is a legitimate (and effective) purpose of a note or example (as occurred in *Campbells Cash and Carry Pty Ltd v National Union of Workers, New South Wales Branch (No 2)* (2001) 53 NSWLR 393). So also will notes or examples in Explanatory Memorandums which conflict with the text they purport to explain: *Sea Shepherd Ltd v Federal Commissioner of Taxation* [2013] FCAFC 68; (2013) 212 FCR 252, [5].

Some Commonwealth statutory-interpretation legislation expressly allows examples to 'extend' the meaning of the provisions to which they relate: eg, *Interpretation of Legislation Act 1984* (Vic), s 36A(1), and *Electronic Conveyancing (Adoption of National Law) Act 2012* (NSW). But unless readers are alert to this possibility, they may query the usefulness and standing of the example.

Part of text?

Always clarify the status of notes or examples in the document: are they merely for information, or are they an inherent part of the text? Some modern UK legislation clarifies their status by elevating them to substantive provisions: eg, s 7(5) of the *European Union (Withdrawal) Act 2018*, which directs readers to other provisions in the Act about the status of retained EU law.

Failure to indicate the status of a note or example can cause doubt (and litigation) over its precise role.

Examples

- Boxed notes were interspersed between clauses in a banking document, each box carrying a picture of a finger pointing to a clause and introduced with the word 'Important'. Were the boxed notes contractual? Held, yes: *Office of Fair Trading v Abbey National plc* [2008] EWHC 875 (Comm) [137]–[139].
- An insurance policy stated: '**NOTE**: If you knowingly make a false or fraudulent claim, these policies will become void and we will not pay any claims under them.' Did these words have contractual force as a condition of the policy? Held, yes: *Sklavenites v Phoenix Prudential Australia Ltd* (1986) 4 ANZ Insurance Cases 60-745 (NSWCA). This was because: (1) in two other places 'NOTE:' introduced provisions that were clearly contractual, and the drafter is likely to have used the word consistently throughout; and (2) no other provision specified the consequences of making a false or fraudulent claim (and the absence of such a provision would be unusual in insurance policies).

Drafters who give thought to such matters commonly insert a double disclaimer to the effect: (1) notes and examples are for information only, and do not affect the document's interpretation; and (2) if a note or example conflicts with the text to which it relates, the text prevails. Disclaimer (2) is for more abundant caution, because almost certainly where a note conflicts with the relevant text, the text prevails: *Fair Work Ombudsman v Wongtas Pty Ltd* [2011] FCA 633; (2011) 195 FCR 55 [47].

Further reading

- Jeffrey Barnes, 'Shining Examples' [2004] *The Loophole* (June) 8 (examining the different roles of notes and examples in Australian legislation) (at www.calc.ngo/publications/loopholes#loophole-table-2004)
- Francis Bennion, 'Confusion over Plain Language Law' (2007) 16 *Commonwealth Lawyer* 63 (doubting the usefulness of examples, on the basis that a statute's function is to enact the law, not to explain it)
- Ross Carter and Matthew Green, 'The Enactment Is Self-Explanatory … Or Is It? Explanatory Provisions in New Zealand Legislation' (2007) 28 *Statute Law Review* 2
- Ben Piper, 'What, How, When and Why—Making Laws Easier to Understand by Using Examples and Notes' [2007] *The Loophole* (July) 74 (at www.calc.ngo/publications/loopholes#loophole-table-2007)

See also **FOOTNOTES**; **MARGINAL NOTES**; **SIMPLIFIED OUTLINES**.

NOTICE CLAUSE

Purpose

A 'notice clause' governs notices given under a document or legislation. Most notice clauses deal with two basic issues: (1) how a notice is given; and (2) when a notice is received.

Terminology

Notices are variously described as being *served*, *given*, *sent*, *left at* [address], or *posted*. While there are differences in meaning, the key drafting rule is consistency: having chosen the word that best suits your purpose, use it consistently throughout the document. Otherwise, uncertainty may arise. For example, does a notice clause regulating methods of *service* of notices apply to a provision that speaks of notices being *given*, or *sent*, or the like? Again, does a notice clause prescribing that notices *served* by post are deemed to be received two business days later, apply to a notice that a provision of the document requires to be *given* or *sent*?

'Deemed receipt' of notice

Where a notice is served (or given, or similar) by a method of transmission (whether physical or electronic), is it served when it is sent or when it is received? And what if the server initiates the transmission but the notice is never in fact received? Matters of that kind are often dealt with in a 'service of notices' clause. For example, clause 4 (below) treats notices as received—or, in more traditional language, 'deems' them to be received—within a stated period. (Note that the 'deeming' in clause 4 is rebuttable. Some notice clauses make the deeming irrebutable; ie, they make service effective even though the notice is received late, or is never received.)

Example of notice clause

1. **Form of notices**

   All notices under this Agreement must be in writing and must be served by one or more of the following means:
   (a) personally;
   (b) by post;
   (c) by fax;
   (d) by email.

2. **Address for service by post**

   Notices served by post must be served at the addresses for the Parties given in clause [X].

3. **Address for service by email**

   Notices served by email must be served at the email addresses for the Parties given in clause [X]. Each Party must take all reasonable steps to ensure that its email address:
   (a) remains fully operational;
   (b) is checked daily on business days;
   (c) allows unimpeded access to its inbox for the other Party's emails.

4. **Date of receipt of notices**

   Unless the evidence shows otherwise, notices are presumed to be received:
   (a) on the next day after they are posted;
   (b) on the day on which they are transmitted by fax or email (unless the sender receives notification that the transmission was unsuccessful).

5. **Transmission problems with email or fax**
   (a) A Party who receives notification that an email or fax transmission to the other Party's notified address was unsuccessful must make all reasonable efforts to contact the other Party by telephone or mail.
   (b) A Party is not responsible for loss or damage arising out of a failure to notify or communicate with the other Party, if the Party attempting to make the notification or communication has complied with the provisions of clauses 1–5.

See also **deem**; **serve / give / notify**.

notice / knowledge

In general use, *knowledge* and *notice* are often used interchangeably—to have *knowledge of* (ie, to know of) a thing is synonymous with having *notice of* the thing. In legal usage, however, the meanings are different. Specifically, '[t]he word "notice" to a lawyer means something less than full knowledge': *Goodyear Tyre and Rubber Co (Great Britain) Ltd v Lancashire Batteries Ltd* [1958] 3 All ER 7, 12 (Lord Evershed MR). The law is unlikely to treat someone as having *knowledge* of something unless they actually know of it; but it may well treat someone as having *notice* of something without their actually knowing of it.

Legal usage distinguishes three categories of *notice*:

1. **Actual notice**—actual knowledge of facts, from a reliable source: *Barnhart v Greenshields* (1853) 9 Moo PC 18, 36; 14 ER 204, 211.
2. **Constructive notice**—knowledge of matters that a reasonably prudent person would have discovered after making inquiries, or after following up prior information received. An illustration is the so-called rule in *Hunt v Luck* [1902] 1 Ch 428, under which a prospective purchaser or mortgagee, who knows that someone is in possession of the property, is on notice (constructive) of that person's proprietary rights and takes subject to them: *Daniels v Davison* (1809) 16 Ves 249; 33 ER 978; *Barnhart v Greenshields* (1853) 9 Moo PC 18; 14 ER 204.
3. **Imputed notice**—notice which the law regards a principal as having received because the principal's agent has received it. Notice—actual or constructive—received by an agent binds the principal.

These three categories are of *notice* 'received'. In addition, the law often requires notice to be 'given'. For example, notice of assignment of a chose in action must be given to the debtor if the assignee is to enforce the chose in action against the debtor: *Law of Property Act 1925*, s 136. This is usually termed *express notice*—ie, notice for a specific purpose.

Further reading

- *Halsbury's Laws of England*, 'Agency' (vol 1, 2017) [138] (imputed notice)
- *Halsbury's Laws of England*, 'Equitable Jurisdiction' (vol 47, 2014) [130] (actual and constructive notice)
- *Halsbury's Laws of England*, 'Choses in Action' (vol 13, 2017) [80] (express notice under *Law of Property Act 1925*, s 136)
- S Bridge, E Cooke, and M Dixon (eds), *Megarry & Wade's Law of Real Property*, 9th edn (Sweet & Maxwell, 2019) [5-016]–[5-024] ('notice' in property transactions)

notice / prior notice

In the term 'prior notice', is *prior* necessary? Does giving *notice* differ from giving *prior notice*? The answer is, 'it depends'. For example, if a lease requires the tenant (T) to give the landlord (L) *10 days' notice of* intention to exercise an option to renew the lease, the clear implication is that the notice must *precede* exercise of the option; there, *prior* is superfluous. But (to change the example) if a lease requires T to give L *10 days' notice of* changes in T's trading hours, it is less clear whether the notice must be given 10 days before the change, or whether 10 days after will do; thus, if the intent is 10 days before, *prior* is essential.

notice to complete

See **notice to perform / notice to complete**.

notice to perform / notice to complete

Notice to perform

In contract law, a notice given by a contracting party to another contracting party requiring the recipient of the notice to perform contractual obligations. Generally, the notice is not needed to establish a breach (for that has already occurred), but rather to make performance of the obligation 'essential' so as to establish a right for the notice-giver to terminate the contract for the non-performance.

Notice to complete

In conveyancing law, a notice given by one party requiring the other party to complete a contract for the sale of land on a date specified in the notice. The date must allow the recipient a reasonable time in which to get ready to complete (unless the contract specifies an agreed 'reasonable' time). The purpose of the notice is to prepare the ground for the notice-giver to terminate the contract for the recipient's failure to complete. The notice, if valid, makes time for completion 'of the essence', entitling the notice-giver to terminate the contract because of the recipient's repudiation.

Several centuries of case law have honed the requirements for a valid notice to complete. In summary, the requirements are: (1) the notice-recipient must be in sufficient default to justify the notice; (2) the notice-giver must be free of relevant default when giving the notice; (3) the notice-giver must be able, ready, and willing to proceed to completion; (4) the time fixed by the notice must be reasonable in all the circumstances; and (5) the notice must specify what the recipient must do, and the consequences of failure to comply.

In truth, notices to complete are a species of the genus 'notices to perform'—they are notices to perform the obligation to complete. It is therefore inappropriate to give a 'notice to complete' where the breach is of an obligation that logically precedes the obligation to complete. Instead, the proper notice is a notice to perform the particular obligation—unless the recipient's conduct in failing to perform that obligation evidences a general failure to complete the contract as a whole (in which case, a notice to complete is appropriate).

Further reading

- *Halsbury's Laws of England*, 'Conveyancing (vol 23, 2016) [279] (notices to complete)
- Peter Butt, *The Standard Contract for Sale of Land in NSW*, 2nd edn (LBC Information Services, 1998) [4.13]–[4.15], [15.6]–[15.55] (principles of Commonwealth law, settled earlier than UK law)

notice to quit / notice to terminate

Notice to quit

Notice to quit is mainly used to describe two kinds of notice given by a landlord to a tenant: (1) notice to give up possession at the end of a lease; (2) notice of exercise of the landlord's right (if it exists) to end the lease early under a 'break clause' or under a statutory right to end the lease early: *Rene Claro (Haute Coiffure) Ltd v Hallé Concert Society* [1969] 1 WLR 909. Less commonly, *notice to quit* can refer to two kinds of notice given by a tenant to a landlord: (1) notice of intention to give up possession at the end of a lease; (2) notice of exercise of the tenant's right (if it exists) to end the lease early under a 'break clause'.

Notice to terminate

A *notice to terminate* is a notice by one party to the other to terminate the lease for the other's breach of the lease. That kind of notice is also sometimes called a *notice to quit*—but that is to use the term loosely.

notify

Usually, to *notify* someone means simply to *tell* them or *inform* them. If that is the meaning, *notify* inserts an unnecessarily dense tone—prefer *tell* or *inform*. Sometimes, however, a formal process of communication by written notice is intended—as where a contracting party must give written notice to the other party of intention to terminate the contract, or a tenant must give written notice to the landlord of intention to renew the lease. In that context, the more formal *notify* is appropriate—but even there, *tell in writing* or *inform in writing* should suffice.

See also **TONE**.

notwithstanding

Lawyers seem attracted to this word, even though it merely means *despite* (or in some contexts, *even though*)—as if four syllables are better than two. If confirmation were needed, judges have said that *notwithstanding* and *despite* are synonyms: see, eg, *A-G (Commonwealth) v Oates* (1999) 198 CLR 162, 178; *Eddy Lau Constructions Pty Ltd v Transdevelopment Enterprise Pty Ltd* [2004] NSWSC 754, [12]–[14].

But despite this confirmation—and despite the disappearance of *notwithstanding* from the modern legislative lexicon—senior judges still use it. Examples are:

- *R v Maxwell* [2010] UKSC 48; [2011] 1 WLR 1837, [69], [84], [92], [96], [105], [108] (Lord Brown)

- *Assange v Swedish Prosecution Authority* [2012] UKSC 22; [2012] 2 AC 471, [32], [79] (Lord Phillips), [118] (Lord Kerr), [152] (Lord Dyson), [237] (Lord Mance)
- *Electricity Generation Corporation t/as Verve Energy v Woodside Energy Ltd* [2014] HCA 7; (2014) 251 CLR 640, [39], [49] (French CJ, Hayne, Crennan and Kiefel JJ).

Writers who value readability and tone avoid *notwithstanding* and its variants (including the irksome *notwithstanding the fact that*).

Examples

- *Notwithstanding* [prefer: *Despite*] clause 5, the tenant may ....
- *Notwithstanding that* [prefer: *Even though*] a liquor licence had been issued, the tenant failed to open the bar for trade.
- *Notwithstanding the fact that* [prefer: *Even though*] the defendant was guilty, the judge was lenient.
- *Notwithstanding the effect of* [prefer: *Despite*] section 1, the Minister may ...

Further reading

'Notwithstanding', in *Law Words* (Centre for Plain Legal Language, University of Sydney, 1995), 53; www.clarity-international.net/plain-language-resources/general-resources/ (tracing the history of *notwithstanding* in legal usage)

See also **non obstante**.

notwithstanding anything in this agreement to the contrary

See **despite anything in this contract to the contrary**.

NOUN / VERB CORRELATION

See **SUBJECT–VERB AGREEMENT**.

NOUN STRINGS

Noun strings make for difficult reading. Sometimes, they are the product of a lawyer's attempt to be exhaustive—to cover the field and leave no gaps. That attempt can be self-defeating, not merely because the reader switches off, but also because any gaps that remain are taken to be deliberate: see discussion under **expressio unius**.

Sometimes, noun strings result from the writer's attempt to encapsulate a multipartite notion in a single thought. The practice may please the writer, but will usually puzzle the reader, who must unscramble meaning from dense text. Sometimes one or more of the words could be adjectives—it may be hard to tell—further muddying the expression:

- market extension merger model
- workers compensation insurance claim form
- social information processing research study
- Flag Prairie Validation Prescribed Burn Cultural Resource Reconnaissance Report. [See www.core.tdar.org/document/120816/flag-prairie-validation-prescribed-burn-cultural-resource-reconnaissance. I am indebted to Dr Duncan Berry for publicising this example.]

See also **expressio unius**; **WORD STRINGS**.

NOUNS / VERBS

Prefer verbs over nouns

Verbs are *doing* words; nouns identify persons, places or things. Nouns can be turned into verbs, but only by adding words—and a proposition expressed in few words generally communicates more effectively than the same proposition in more words. So, to convert a verb into a noun or a noun phrase slows the process of communication. It also dulls the sentence, often producing a bureaucratic version of something that could be said directly and idiomatically.

The process of converting a verb into a noun or a noun phrase is 'nominalisation'. Notable harbingers of nominalisation are phrases beginning with words such as:

- 'cause': eg, *cause* injury to = injure; *cause* harm to = harm
- 'give': eg, *give* advice to = advise; *give* consideration to = consider; *give* permission for = permit
- 'make': eg, *make* a confession = confess; *make* a finding = find; *make* changes = change; *make* an observation = observe
- 'provide': eg, *provide* a comparison = compare; *provide* assistance to = help; *provide* a summary = summarise; *provide* compensation to = compensate.

Other indicators of the conversion are endings such as *-ance*, *-ence*, *-ity*, *-ing*, *-ment*, *-sation*, *-tion*. Examples follow:

Noun	**Underlying verb**
acceptance	accept
amalgamation	amalgamate
application	apply
assignment	assign
authorisation	authorise
contravention	contravene
deception	deceive
disclosure	disclose
election	elect
enhancement	enhance
occurrence	occur
participation	participate
procurement	procure
promulgation	promulgate
reception	receive
referral	refer
reliance	rely
resolution	resolve
severance	sever
verification	verify

The practice of preferring nouns and noun phrases is not peculiar to legal writing; it also infects bureaucratic and official language. But in legal prose it is ubiquitous. For example, judges do not *decide* a case, but *make a decision*; police do not *assume*, but *make an assumption*; companies do not *resolve*, but *pass a resolution*; landlords do not *consent* to an act, but *give their consent*; co-owners do not *sever* a joint tenancy, but *effect a severance*; and so on.

Some might consider the practice achieves a certain formality of tone; but if so, it is at the expense of effective communication. Try to prune the noun or noun phrase back to its underlying verb. Compare the following examples: in each, the right-hand column (verb) is much crisper.

Noun phrase	**Verb**
assist in the resolution of	help resolve
assist in the reviewing of	help review
assist in the formulation of	help formulate
give a clear indication of	clearly indicate; clearly show
give permission to	permit
has an obligation to	must
has the capacity to	can; is able to
in consideration of the fact that	considering that; because
is dependent upon	depends on
make an argument	argue
make an examination of	examine
make a recommendation	recommend
prior to the commencement of	before commencing; before starting
prior to the gaining of	before gaining; before getting
reach a conclusion	conclude
result in the elimination of	eliminate

The added crispness is particularly evident in lists—as in the following example, where the rewrite in the right-hand column is notably tighter and shorter:

Before	**After**
'The means by which this Act ensures that a person is able to recover a progress payment is by establishing a procedure that involves: (a) *the making of* a payment claim by the person claiming payment; and (b) *the provision of* a payment schedule by the person by whom the payment is payable; and (c) *the referral of* any disputed claim to an adjudicator for determination; and (d) *the payment of* the progress payment so determined.' [Source: *Security of Payment Act 1999* (NSW), s 3(1)]	The means by which this Act ensures that a person is able to recover a progress payment is by establishing a procedure that involves: (a) *making* a payment claim by the person claiming payment; and (b) *providing* a payment schedule by the person by whom the payment is payable; and (c) *referring* any disputed claim to an adjudicator for determination; and (d) *paying* the progress payment so determined. [**Or better, making further changes**:] This Act establishes a procedure for recovering progress payments. The procedure involves: (e) *making* a payment claim; (f) *providing* a payment schedule; (g) *referring* a disputed claim to an adjudicator; (h) *paying* the progress payment so determined.

Caution: do not obscure the legal act

When recasting a noun or noun phrase as a verb, be careful not to obscure the legal act. The recast sentence may be easier to read, but legal precision may suffer. For example:

- *give notice to*: This can be rewritten as *notify*. However, the original may have required a formal notice to be given or served—a distinction which is obscured if 'A must *give notice to* B' becomes 'A must *notify* B'.
- *pass a resolution*: This can be rewritten as *resolve*. However, that might obscure the implication in the original of the need for a formal resolution process.
- *hold an inquiry into*: This can become *inquire into*. However, that may obscure the implication of a formal inquiry.

See also **SIMPLER WORDS AND PHRASES; SUBJECT–VERB AGREEMENT**.

novation / assignment

A *novation* is a transaction by which, with the consent of all parties, a new contract is substituted for an existing contract, thereby discharging the existing contract and usually (but not necessarily) adding a different party to the new contract. In contrast, an *assignment* transfers rights under an existing contract to a third party, but leaves the underlying contract in place. The two concepts are different, and a careful drafter will not confuse them. Novation allows the burden of a contract to be shifted to a new party—sidestepping the general principle that a party cannot assign the burden of a contract.

Novation usually occurs in one of three ways:

1. The existing parties (A and B) agree that C is to replace B as a party to the contract. In the result, (1) a new contract comes into existence between A and C, and (2) B is released from the original contract. As a variant, A and B may agree that, during the life of their contract, A may novate the contract to any person A chooses (and without any further participation by B): *Leveraged Equities Ltd v Goodridge* [2011] FCAFC 3; (2011) 191 FCR 71.
2. The existing parties (A and B) agree to remain contracting parties, but C is to be added, so that the parties are now A, B and C.
3. The existing parties (A and B) agree to change the terms on which they are contracting. If genuinely a novation (ie, substituting a new contract for the old), this discharges the original contract and creates a new contract between the same parties. It differs in principle from a mere variation of contract, where the contract between A and B remains on foot but under different terms. However, the distinction can be difficult to draw: *Hillam v Iacullo* [2015] NSWCA 196, [52]–[53]; (2015) 90 NSWLR 422 (Leeming JA).

novus actus interveniens

Latin: a new act intervening. In the context of causation in law, an event that comes between the initial act and the end result, altering the natural course of events that might otherwise have linked the initial act to the end result. Usually, the English expression 'an independent event' adequately reflects the legal concept. Lord Wright once said that the 'august' phrase *novus actus interveniens* means only that 'there was not such a direct relationship between the act [negligence] and the injury that the one could be treated as flowing directly from the other': *Lord v Pacific Steam Navigation Co* [1943] P 32, 36.

Despite this, at least one senior English judge has questioned the adequacy of that (or any) translation, preferring the Latin. The context was a homicide charge where the fatal shot was fired by a third party reacting to an act of the accused:

> 'We are aware that this time-honoured Latin term [*novus actus interveniens*] has been the subject of criticism. We are also aware that attempts have been made to translate it into English; though no simple translation has proved satisfactory, really because the Latin term has become a term of art which conveys to lawyers the crucial feature that there has not merely been an intervening act of another person, but that that act was so independent of the act of the accused that it should be regarded in law as the cause of the victim's death, to the exclusion of the act of the accused. At the risk of scholarly criticism, we shall for the purposes of this judgment continue to use the Latin term.' [*R v Pagett* (1983) 76 Cr App R 279, 288 (Robert Goff LJ)]

However, for most purposes when addressing non-lawyers, 'an act that breaks the chain of causation' will suffice.

See also **consequence of; cause (noun, verb)**.

now

At the present time. But at what present time? Consider a gift by will of 'all the property I *now* own'. Does this mean the property owned at the date of the will, or the property owned at the date of the testator's death? Either interpretation may be open (see *Halsbury's Laws of England*, 'Wills and Intestacy' (vol 102, 2016) [282] fns 14, 15). Decisions support each interpretation, depending on the circumstances:

'now' = date of will

- 'the house *now* occupied by A': *Hutchinson v Barrow* (1861) 30 LJ Ex 280
- 'the house I *now* live in': *Williams v Owen* (1863) 9 LT (OS) 200
- jewellery and articles '*now* deposited for safe custody': *Re Whitby* [1944] Ch 210.

'now' = date of death

- 'any property I *now* possess': *Re Portal to Lamb* (1884) 27 Ch D 600 (Kay J); reversed, but not on this point (1885) 30 Ch D 50
- 'all copyhold [properties] *now* held by me': *Re Horton* [1920] 2 Ch 1 (Eve J).

A careful writer will be alert to the potential ambiguity.

now this deed witnesseth

The formulaic opening words of the operative part of a deed, following immediately after the recitals. The words can be discarded without affecting the legal efficacy of the deed. Drafters who feel insecure about such a change in habit or tradition can safely substitute the heading 'Operative part'.

See also **DEED (document)**; **RECITALS**.

noxious

In modern usage, both general and legal, *noxious* means poisonous or unhealthy. But in older usage (both general and legal) it carried more the sense of 'unwholesome' or 'rendering the enjoyment of life and property uncomfortable', derived from the Latin *nocivus* (= harmful): *R v White* (1737) 1 Burr 333, 337; 97 ER 338, 340 (Lord Mansfield).

In lease covenants, drafters often combined *noxious* with other terms in an omnibus list seeking to preclude any kind of prejudicial use by the tenant—as in a covenant not to carry on 'any any noisome, noxious, offensive or dangerous trade or business whatsoever':*Reeves v Greenwich Tanning Co* (1864) 2 H & M 54; 71 ER 380.

See also **noisome / noisy**.

nudum pactum

Latin: a bare agreement. Used in two senses: (1) a promise unsupported by consideration (or a 'naked promise') and therefore unenforceable as a contract; (2) more generally, a promise that is contrary to law and therefore unenforceable. Any English translation must pick up those nuances; but as long as it does, there is no benefit in retaining the Latin. For example:

- 'According to English common law a creditor might accept anything in satisfaction of his debt except a less amount of money. He might take a horse, or a canary, or tomtit if he chose, and that was accord and satisfaction; but, by a most extraordinary peculiarity of the English common law he could not take 19 shillings and sixpence in the pound; that was *nudum pactum* [prefer: *an agreement lacking consideration*].' [*Couldery v Bartrum* (1881) 19 Ch D 394, 399 (Jessel MR)]
- 'All contracts or agreements by way of gaming were null and void, *ie*, *nudum pactum* [prefer: *unenforceable*].' [*Ling Yew Kong v Teo Vin Li Richard* [2014] 2 SLR 123; [2014] SGHC 6, [53] (George Wei JC)]

See also **ex nudo pacto non oritur actio**.

nuisance

In general usage, a *nuisance* is an annoyance or inconvenience. In legal usage, *nuisance* carries a stronger and more limited meaning, namely, a substantial and unreasonable interference with another person's rights to use or enjoyment of land. This difference between the general and legal usage can cause ambiguity: which meaning did the parties intend by *nuisance*? Prima facie, in a professionally drawn document, *nuisance* bears its legal meaning, in line with the principle that courts give technical words their technical meaning (as in *Harrison v Good* (1871) LR 11 Eq 338). But context may show that the parties intended the word to carry its (wider) general meaning. For example:

- A tenant covenanted in a lease 'not to cause any annoyance, *nuisance*, grievance or damage'. Held, the collocation of words indicated that *nuisance* carried a sense wider than its strict common-law sense: *Tod-Heatly v Benham* (1888) 40 Ch D 80.
- A statute prohibited tenants from causing '*nuisance* or annoyance' to adjoining owners. Held, the statutory intention was to prevent nuisance in fact, not merely nuisance in law: *Angelo v Kean Clarke Bros* [1950] NZLR 1.

Legal writers should always be careful with their words; *nuisance* is one of them.

null and void

A traditional pairing, using two words where one will suffice. Occasionally the pairing is puffed up to 'absolutely null and void', or even more egregiously to 'absolutely null and void and of no further force or effect whatsoever'. (This intensification has a long pedigree; eg, the *Fraudulent Conveyances Act 1571* declared conveyances intended to defeat creditors to be 'utterly void, frustrate and of none effect'.) The intensifiers rarely add anything: if something is *void*, it is void for all purposes. For example, a court order that an instruction to soldiers is 'null and void and of no effect' means simply that it is 'void', or that is of 'no effect'—the intensifiers add nothing (wording from court order in *Commodore of the Royal Bahamas Defence Force v Laramore* [2017] UKPC 13; [2017] 1 WLR 2752, [33]). To illustrate:

> 'Lawyers speak of statutory provisions as imperative when any want of strict compliance with them means that the resulting act ... is *null and void* [prefer: *void*]. They speak of them as directory when they mean that ... failure to fulfil them does not mean that the resulting act is wholly ineffective, is *null and void* [prefer: *void*; or delete *null and void*, because *ineffective* is sufficient].' [*Clayton v Heffron* (1960) 105 CLR 214, 247 (Dixon CJ, McTiernan, Taylor, and Windeyer JJ)]

A relatively recent substitution is 'null and of no effect'. While this may give a nod to modernity, it still exudes redundancy. If something is 'null' it is 'of no effect'. Perhaps those who use 'null and of no effect' consider 'null' of itself to be unidiomatic; if so, they could try 'of no effect', or 'a nullity':

> '[The Prime Minister's advice to the Queen] was unlawful. It was outside the powers of the Prime Minister to give it. This means that it was *null and of no effect* [prefer: *void; a nullity; of no effect*]. ... It led to the Order in Council which, being founded on unlawful advice, was likewise unlawful, *null and of no effect* [prefer: *void; a nullity; of no effect*] and should be quashed. This led to the actual prorogation. ... It too was unlawful, *null and of no effect* [prefer: *void; a nullity; of no effect*].' [*R v The Prime Minister* [2019] UKSC 41, [69]; [2019] 3 WLR 589]

There may be logic in retaining the pairing in bijural countries such as Canada. Two senior Canadian judges quote a view that a drafter 'mindful of the sensibilities of the two different linguistic audiences, may prefer *null* for civil lawyers and *void* for common lawyers'. See L Mailhot and J D Carnwath, *Decisions, Decisions ... A Handbook for Judicial Writing* (Yvon Blais, 1998) 100 (quoting Susan C Markman, Senior Counsel, Department of Justice, Canada). There may also be logic in retaining the pairing for effect in a parallel construction: 'faith is *null* and the promise is *void*': Romans 4:15 (New Revised Standard Version). But no logic justifies retaining *null and void* as the ritual legal incantation it has become.

Further reading

'Null and Void', in *Law Words* (Centre for Plain Legal Language, University of Sydney, 1995) 58; www.clarity-international.net/plain-language-resources/general-resources/

See also **void / voidable**; **WORD PAIRINGS**.

nulla poena sine lege

Latin: no punishment without a law. Often found in a longer maxim, *nullum crimen nulla poena sine lege* (no crime [and] no punishment without a law; absent a law, there can be neither crime nor punishment). The Latin maxim expresses a noble sentiment—Glanville Williams described it as the 'principle of legality' (in *Criminal Law: The General Part* (Stephen & Sons, 1953) ch 12). But it is no less noble when expressed in plain English. For example:

- 'The starting point is the old rule *nullum crimen, nulla poena sine lege*; only the law can define a crime and prescribe a penalty.' [*R v Rimmington* [2005] UKHL 63; [2006] AC 459, [34] (Lord Bingham, starting with the Latin, then providing a translation)]
- 'Article 7(1) of the Convention [embodies] the principle that only the law can define a crime and prescribe a penalty (*nullum crimen, nulla poena sine lege*). ... [I]t follows from this that an offence must be clearly defined in law.' [*Kokkinakis v Greece* (1993) 17 EHHR 397, 423 [52] (European Court of Human Rights, starting with the English, then providing the Latin)]

NUMBER

See **SINGULAR / PLURAL.**

NUMBERING SYSTEMS

Three main systems

Legal documents use a variety of numbering systems. The table below shows the three main ones in current use: (1) Arabic/Roman; (2) decimal; and (3) a combination of (1) and (2). The choice of numbering system is a matter of personal preference. No one system is best, although many consider the decimal system to be the most logical. (See further, **ADVICE (FORM OF) (Numbered headings)** and **HEADINGS**.) The modern trend in British/Commonwealth legal documents is towards (3), as shown in the right-hand column.

Level	Arabic/Roman	Decimal	Combination
Section/clause	1 [Title] 2 [Title] 3 [Title]	1 [Title] 2 [Title] 3 [Title]	1 [Title] 2 [Title] 3 [Title]
Subsection/subclause	(1) (2) (3)	1.1 1.2 1.3	1.1 1.2 1.3
Paragraph	(a) (b) (c)	1.1.1 1.1.2 1.1.3	1.1(a) 1.1(b) 1.1(c)
Subparagraph	(i) (ii) (iii)	1.1.1.1 1.1.1.2 1.1.1.3	1.1(a)(i) 1.1(a)(ii) 1.1(a)(iii)
Sub-subparagraph	(A) (B) (C)	1.1.1.1.1 1.1.1.1.2 1.1.1.1.3	1.1(a)(i)(A) 1.1(a)(i)(B) 1.1(a)(i)(C)

Indentation

Heading levels are indented progressively. The depth of indent varies, but the structure is typically as follows:

Arabic/Roman	Decimal	Partial combination
1 Title	**1 Title**	**1 Title**
1(1) [text]	1.1 [text]	1.1 [text]
(a) [text]	1.1.1 [text]	(a) [text]
(i) [text]	1.1.1.1 [text]	(i) [text]
(A) [text]	1.1.1.1.1 [text]	(A) [text]

In truth, the decimal system needs no indentation, because the numbering system itself indicates the hierarchy of headings. In practice, however, most drafters indent when using decimal numbering.

The above examples show four levels of indentation (after the Title). Although this degree of subdivision is sometimes seen, it can be too fragmented for ease of reading—and each new indented level reduces available line length. As a practical matter, when subdivision reaches more than three levels, it is time to reconsider the clause structure. See discussion under **HEADINGS (Not too many heading-levels)**.

Renumbering when adding or deleting provisions

When inserting new text between existing consecutive provisions, give it a number that is consistent with the existing numbering system. Normally, when deleting a provision, there is no need to renumber the remaining provisions. (See discussion under **TEXTUAL AMENDMENTS**.)

See also **ADVICE (FORM OF); FONTS; HEADINGS**.

NUMBERS

Cardinal numbers

Standard conventions

- Use Arabic numerals (eg, *25*).
- Where a number contains four digits in total, usage varies: some writers insert a separating comma (*3,000*), some insert a space (*3 000*), and some insert neither (*3000*).
- Where a number comprises one or more groups of three digits, use separating commas (*$987,654,321*).
- Regional variations may exist. For example, on the Indian subcontinent the terms *lakh* (=100,000) and *crore* (=10,000,000) are used to express large numbers. Thus, 120,000 rupees is '1.2 lakh rupees' (written as '1,20,000 rupees'); 50,000,000 (fifty million) rupees is '5 crore rupees' (written as '5,00,00,000 rupees').

Zeros

- Avoid adding a zero-string at the end of numbers, unless precision demands it (*6 pm*, not *6.00 pm*; *$100*, not *$100.00*).
- When referring to quantities of 1 million or greater, use words instead of zero-strings (*$5 million*, not *$5,000,000*).
- Sometimes, *zero* is more idiomatic than *0*: 'less than *zero*', '*zero* annual growth', '*zero* incapacity'; but *0%*, '*0–100* in 5 seconds'.

Number as part of term

Where a number forms part of a term, there is no set usage. Either words or figures can be used: '*2-car* [or *two-car*] pile-up'; '*3-judge* [or *three-judge*] bench'—unless convention has settled on a fixed use: '*five-star* general' [not '*5-star* general'].

Number spans

Number spans are properly indicated with an en dash (ie, a short dash), not an em dash (ie, a long dash), and not a hyphen. However, this is a counsel of perfection, more ignored than honoured in legal documents.

Publishers and legal citation guides generally minimise the number of digits in the second number of a number span. Usually, they retain only the last two digits in the span, unless (exceptionally) clarity requires otherwise. However, these are mere conventions, and a breach does no harm if the meaning is clear. In this book, number spans retain the last two digits, unless clarity requires otherwise. (See also **CITATION OF CASES (Pinpoint references)**.)

Full number span	Convention
11–15	11–15
725–736	725–36
1,725–1,736	1,725–36
1,820–1,980	1,820–980

Words or numbers?

The following conventions are generally observed:

- Use *words* for numbers from one to ten, **except** in:
  - o references to pages, sections, appendices or schedules (page 5; section 7; Appendix 3; Schedule 2)
  - o percentages (5%)
  - o dates (3 January)
  - o numbers that include a decimal point or a fraction (5.5, 5½)
  - o monetary amounts ($5)
  - o sets of numbers ('the numbers of judges retiring in the past three years were 5, 9, and 15')
  - o stating time (5 pm).
- Use *numerals* (figures) for numbers from 11 up (eg, 'ten people played, but they had hoped for 11'). However, some writers make the change at the point when single digit numbers cease, ie, from 10 up ('10 people played'). Yet others, for appearance, prefer numerals for numbers even under 11 (or under 10) if used with other numerals in a series (eg, '9 players are a minimum, but the team performs better with 11').

Use numerals only?

Some writers prefer numerals over words in all cases—regardless of how small or large the number—because numerals strike the eye more clearly than words. For an example, see (2003) 49 *Clarity*, at www.clarity-international.net/clarity-journal/archives/, where all articles in the issue use only numerals for all numbers—including all single-digit numbers.

Starting sentences with numerals?

Conventionally, writers eschew numerals at the start of sentences: '*Twelve* [not *12*] men went to mow a meadow.' However, this convention is changing. Some writers now use numerals to start a sentence, including numbers under 11. Some legislative drafters have adopted this style.

Example

A ***retail shopping centre*** is a cluster of premises having all of the following attributes:

(a) 5 or more of the premises are used wholly or predominantly for carrying on retail businesses;

(b) all the premises—

(i) are owned by the 1 person; or

(ii) have the 1 lessor or head lessor, or, if the premises were leased, would have the 1 lessor or head lessor; …

[*Retail Shop Leases Act 1994* (Qld), definitions]

Parallel constructions—prefer numbers

In parallel constructions, prefer numerals. For example:

- Depending on the seriousness of the case, the court could comprise *4–11* [not *four–11*; not *four–eleven*] judges.
- The committee must have between *5* [not *five*] and *25* members.
- '[The work] would involve a team of several people working over 10 to 12 days, with a further allowance of 2 or 3 days for delays.' [*Agripower Barraba Pty Ltd v Blomfield*; (2015) 317 ALR 202, [51], Sackville AJA; the original at [2015] NSWCA 30 has 'two or three days'.]

Don't mix numerals and words

Avoid mixing numerals and words in the one sentence—and prefer numerals. For example:

> Ideally, the notice period should be *12* months, although *6* months [not *six* months] is acceptable.

Where numbers are very large, then (despite the above exhortation) it may be useful to mix numbers and words when referring to millions, billions, and the like: thus, *$1 million*, not *$1,000,000* (and certainly not *$1,000,000.00*, unless the reference to zero cents is important). This also helps to avoid typographical errors of the kind that occurred in the following case:

> A law firm, intending to certify a debt to be $92,885,000.00, mistakenly certified it to be $92,885.00. This was simply a typographical error, but it led to litigation involving multiple appeals (the end point being *Prudential Insurance Co of America v Dewey, Ballantine, Bushby Palmer & Wood* 605 NE2d 318 (NY 1992)). The law firm could have reduced the risk of error by writing '$92.885 million'.

Pronoun: 'one' or '1'?

Even those who prefer figures over words may feel it unidiomatic to use the numeral '1' as a pronoun in expressions such as 'this is what 1 [ie, *one*] does', or '1 [ie, *one*] should be careful'. Their unease is perhaps heightened by the difficulty in distinguishing between the numeral '1' and the capital letter 'I'.

Ordinal numbers

An ordinal number expresses place in a series (in contrast to a cardinal number, which expresses amount—eg, one, two, three). In line with the convention for cardinal numbers, ordinal numbers are generally written as words up to *ninth* or *tenth*, and then figures: eg, the *second* day of the month; the *11th* day of the month.

There is no settled practice about using superscript (*11th* or 11th). Unless mandated by a relevant style guide or court rules, it is a matter of taste. Superscript may be hard to read if the font size is small.

For dates, the modern convention is to use cardinal numbers (not ordinal numbers): *3 January* [not *3rd January*; not 3rd *January*]; *15 January* [not *15th January*; not 15th *January*].

Numbers with unusual meanings

The content of a number is usually unambiguous. But as with words, custom of the trade or the locality may give a number a meaning that differs from its general meaning. Where the parties to a transaction are shown to have used a number in a special meaning, the courts will implement their intention. For example, a reference in a lease to '10,000 rabbits' meant 12,000 rabbits, because in that county 1,000 rabbits meant 100 dozen rabbits: *Smith v Wilson* (1832) 3 B & Ad 728; 110 ER 266.

Age

When stating an age, use numerals, even where the number is below 10:

- He is 5 years old.

Where an age is expressed as an adjective before a noun, or as a substitute for a noun, use hyphens:

- The book is for 5-year-olds.
- She is a 4-year-old girl.

Doubling-up: words and figures

Formerly, lawyers used both words and numerals (figures) to express a number: eg, 'The deposit is $50,000 (fifty thousand dollars).' The motivation for this doubling-up was twofold: precision, and to guard against fraudulent erasures and interlineations. Now, however, the preferred use is figures alone: eg, 'The deposit is $50,000.' See further, **WORDS AND FIGURES.**

Further reading

- Martin Cutts, *Plain English Lexicon: A Guide to Whether Your Words Will Be Understood* (Plain Language Commission, 2008) Appendix A
- Robert Eagleson, 'Numbers: Figures or Words? A Convention under the Spotlight' (2003) 50 *Clarity* 32; reprinted (2014) 71 *Clarity* 40, at www.clarity-international.net/clarity-journal/archives/
- Robert Eagleson, 'The Doleful Grip of Convention' (2004) 52 *Clarity* 37; reprinted (2014) 71 *Clarity* 44, at www.clarity-international.net/clarity-journal/archives/

See also **DASHES; FRACTIONS; NUMBERING SYSTEMS; WORDS AND FIGURES.**

NUMERALS

See **NUMBERS.**

numerus clausus

Latin: closed list; nothing further may be added. For example, in land law, the '*numerus clausus* principle' asserts that the law cannot accommodate new types of interests. See Kevin Gray and Susan Francis Gray, *Elements of Land Law*, 5th edn (Oxford University Press, 2009) [1.7.12]–[1.7.15].

nunc pro tunc

Latin: now for then. A Latin incantation to the effect that a court order or administrative decision is to operate retrospectively—that is, takes effect from a date earlier than that on which it is made. For example, a court may make an order *nunc pro tunc* to correct a procedural irregularity that does not affect the court's jurisdiction or the parties' rights. In Lord Eldon's words, the court 'is only doing now what the court could have done then': *Donne v Lewis* (1805) 11 Ves Jun 601; 32 ER 1121, 1122. The plain English *retrospectively* captures the meaning, making the Latin redundant.

- '[A]n appeal to the Supreme Court was lodged … seeking to reverse the Governor's decision revoking the licence and to obtain its restoration *nunc pro tunc* [prefer: *retrospectively*] on the ground that he [acted beyond power].' [*Suisse Security Bank Ltd v Central Bank of the Bahamas* [2006] UKPC 11; [2006] 1 WLR 1660, 1662 (Lord Mance)]
- 'ANZ is granted leave *nunc pro tunc* [prefer: *retrospectively*] pursuant to s 500(2) of the *Corporations Act 2001* (Cth) to commence and proceed with its cross-appeal against Nebax.' [*Simic v New South Wales Land and Housing Corp* [2016] HCA 47; (2016) 260 CLR 85, Order 1]
- 'The next question then is whether the Court can give such leave retrospectively, *nunc pro tunc*, and if so, whether it ought to do so.' [*Re Testro Bros Consolidated Ltd* [1965] VR 18, 32 (Sholl J, providing a translation, rendering the Latin superfluous)]

nuncupative

Post-classical Latin *nuncupativus*, declared orally; not written; used especially of an oral will (hence, 'nuncupative will'), which, though unwritten, is valid when made by a mariner, or soldier on active service, if declared before a sufficient number of witnesses. The translation *oral* suffices for almost all purposes, particularly where the context carries the implication 'exempt from the normal formalities for wills'. For example:

- '[T]he courts will examine any case of alleged *donatio mortis causa* and reject it if in truth what is alleged as a *donatio* is an attempt to make a *nuncupative* [prefer: *oral*] will, or a will in other respects not complying with the forms required by the *Wills Act*.' [*Birch v Treasury Solicitor* [1951] Ch 298, 307 (Lord Evershed MR)]
- '[I]n former times … effect might be given to an oral (*nuncupative*) will in certain circumstances. … The concept of a "privileged will" (a *nuncupative* will), able to be made by a soldier or seaman on active service, without formality and whatever the age of the testator, had its origins in the *Statute of Frauds*, s 23.' [*Estate of Scott* [2014] NSWSC 465, [74]–[77] (Lindsay J, preferring English but adding the parenthetical Latin, presumably for the benefit of legal readers)]

See also **donatio mortis causa**.

obiter dictum

Latin: incidental remark, aside; plural: *obiter dicta*. Sometimes shortened to *obiter*, or *dictum*, or *dicta*. A statement made by a judge in the course of a judgment, but not part of the essential reason for the decision (ie, not part of the *ratio decidendi*), and therefore not carrying the binding force of precedent. As with most Latinisms in law, a plain-language translation captures the meaning. For example:

- 'None the less, it is said that the [1936 Law Reform Committee report] accepts the correctness of the *obiter dicta* [prefer: *non-binding propositions*], or at least the *obiter dictum* [prefer: *non-binding proposition*] of Bowen LJ, in *Soar v Ashwell*.' [*Williams v Central Bank of Nigeria* [2014] UKSC 10; [2014] AC 1189, [108] (Lord Neuberger)]
- 'In an impressive analysis of prior authority, [the judge] concluded (para 81) that the *dicta* [prefer: *non-binding statements*] in *Soar v Ashwell* could no longer stand as good law. … A year later [a different judge] expressed his opposite view, albeit *obiter* [prefer: *non-binding*].' [*Williams v Central Bank of Nigeria*, above, [153] (Lord Mance)]

Some texts adopt vaguer meanings of *dicta, obiter dicta*, and related terms. For example, *Halsbury's Laws of England* uses 'dicta' to mean a judge's statements that are not necessary to the decision, that go beyond the occasion, and that lay down a rule that is unnecessary for the purpose in hand (and so are not part of the *ratio decidendi*). It also uses 'dicta' in the narrow sense of a judge's statements about what other judges have said or done in cases that are not reported. Finally, it uses 'judicial dicta' (which, it surmises, may not be precisely the same as 'obiter dicta') to mean a judge's considered opinions ('enunciations') of the law upon some point which does not arise for decision on the facts of the case (and so also is not part of the *ratio decidendi*). (See 'Civil Procedure' (vol 11, 2020) [26].)

See also **dictum**; **ratio decidendi**.

OBJECT CLAUSE

See **PURPOSE CLAUSE.**

obligant

A variant of *obligor*—ie, one who is under an obligation; rare outside Scotland.

See **obligee / obligor**.

obligated (to)

A clumsy substitute for *obliged to* or *bound to*. For example:

Before	**After**
The landlord is *not obligated to* give prior notice.	The landlord is *not obliged to* give prior notice. *Better still*: The landlord *need not* give prior notice.
'[T]he true substance of the dispute was … whether [the employer] was *obligated to the employees in the amounts* which they claimed.' [Source: *Tomlinson v Ramsey Food Processing Pty Ltd* [2015] HCA 28; (2015) 256 CLR 507, [86] (Nettle J)]	The true substance of the dispute was … whether [the employer] was *bound to pay the employees the amounts* which they claimed. *Better still*: The core of the dispute was whether [the employer] was *liable to pay the employees the amounts* they claimed.

obligee / obligor

Like other *-ee* / *-or* words in law, easily confused. The *obligee* is the party benefited by the obligation; the *obligor* is the party burdened by it.

See also ***-ee* / *-or* endings**.

observe and perform

Either word will do

A lawyer's pairing frequently seen in contracts, as where a party promises 'to observe and perform' certain obligations. Are both words needed? The conventional justification for retaining both words invokes the distinction between positive obligations and negative obligations: you *perform* a positive obligation, but you *observe* (ie, do not break) a negative one. For example, if a contract imposes a (negative) obligation not to assign rights without the other party's consent, *observe* is the appropriate term: *Evans v Davis* (1878) 10 Ch D 747, 757 (Fry J, in argument).

However, the trend of modern authority suggests that either word suffices for either kind of obligation. Specifically:

- an obligation to *perform* applies to both positive and negative covenants: *Harman v Ainslie* [1904] 1 KB 698; and
- an obligation to *observe* applies to both positive and negative covenants: *Ayling v Wade* [1961] 2 KB 228, 235 (Danckwerts LJ); *McFarlane v Reffold* (2013) 116 SASR 83; [2013] SASCFC 31, [55]–[60] (Gray J, dissenting).

Based on these decisions, either word will do.

Meaning *indemnify*

At first sight, a promise to *observe and perform* an obligation might seem to be a promise that the promisor personally will observe and perform it. However, context often indicates that it is, rather, not so much a promise to do it as a promise to *indemnify* the promisee if it is not done. Breach then gives rise to a right in damages only. This usage appears in the following examples.

- A tenant assigned its lease. The assignee covenanted to *observe and perform* the tenant's covenants under the lease. Held, this was a covenant to indemnify the assignor against liability if the landlord brought proceedings against the assignor; it was not a promise to personally perform the covenants: *Harris v Boots, Cash Chemists (Southern) Ltd* [1904] 2 Ch 376, 380–81.
- A landlord (L) covenanted in the lease to perform certain obligations in favour of the tenant. While the lease was current, L sold and assigned the premises to a purchaser (P), who covenanted with L to *observe and perform* L's covenants under the lease. Held, P's covenant was to indemnify L against proceedings by the tenant; it was not a covenant that P would itself perform the obligations in favour of the tenant: *Ridgewood Properties Group Ltd v Valero Energy Ltd* [2013] EWHC 98 (Ch); [2013] 3 WLR 327.

If performance in kind is intended, rather than mere indemnity, then make sure the document says so.

See also **guarantee / indemnity / warranty**; **indemnify (variants of)**; **perform and discharge; WORD PAIRINGS.**

obviously

See **clearly / obviously**.

of (as wordy preposition)

To over-use 'of' betrays a wordy style. Eliminating multiple *of*s is usually straightforward—and the process tightens the writing.

Before: 'The decision *of* the judge was a sure indicator *of* an ability to master the complexity *of* the law and the uncertainty *of* the evidence.' [25 words].

After: 'The judge's decision clearly indicated the ability to master complex law and uncertain evidence.' [14 words].

See **POSSESSIVES.**

of even date herewith

A phrase meaning simply 'dated the same date as this document'. Use the simpler phrase.

of which

See **whose / of which**.

offence / offense

See **defence / defense**.

office (position)

Capitalise only when part of an organisation's formal title:

> 'File your stamp duty return with the Internal Revenue *Office* tomorrow.'
>
> **But**
>
> 'Come to the magistrate's *office* tomorrow.'

Whether a person holds an *office* depends on the relationship between the person and the organisation in which the office is said to be held. Normally, *office* assumes a 'permanent, substantive position, which ha[s] an existence independent of the person who fill[s] it, and which [is] filled in succession by successive holders': *Great Western Railway Co v Bater* [1920] 3 KB 266, 274 (Rowlatt J). But that is not an adequate test for all situations. The meaning of *office* is context-dependent, and 'focuses on the substance of the terms upon which a person is engaged—not whether the relevant organisation has attributed a particular label to the engagement—and on the relationship between that engagement and the organisation's performance of its functions': *Commissioner of Taxation v Jayasinghe* [2017] HCA 26; (2017) 260 CLR 400, [37].

off-the-plan

When used as a compound term, preferably hyphenated (as in *sale off-the-plan*; or *off-the-plan contract*). (Contrast: 'Her health having improved, she was taken off the plan'; 'The architect signed off the plans'.) Sadly, however, the compound term is often unhyphenated, reflecting the diminishing use of hyphens in modern writing. For example:

> 'A vendor may rescind an *off the plan contract* [prefer: *off-the-plan contract*] under a sunset clause if ...': *Conveyancing Act 1919* (NSW), s 66ZL(3).

See also **HYPHENS**.

ombudsman

Legal usage prefers *ombudsman* generically to refer to both male and female holders of the office. However, to counter gender-specific implications, *ombudsperson* is sometimes seen. Also seen (eg, in employment awards), but rarer, is *ombud* or *ombuds* (singular and plural, noun and adjective).

See also **GENDER-NEUTRAL LANGUAGE**.

omission

Omission (and its verb *to omit*, and adjective *omitted*) can carry two meanings: (1) left out by error; and (2) simply 'not there'. To illustrate, when considering whether an easement 'omitted' from the register nevertheless binds registered land, Australian case law formerly assumed meaning (1), but more recently law favours meaning (2): Brendan Edgeworth (ed), *Butt's Land Law*, 7th edn (Lawbook, 2017) [12.740]. If doubt could exist, always clarify the intended meaning.

omnia praesumuntur contra spoliatorem

Latin: all things are presumed against the wrongdoer. While the Latin may look (and sound) impressive, it merely reflects a common-sense proposition that where persons destroy evidence it is reasonable to assume that the evidence was against them. That the Latin is unnecessary appears from the Privy Council's statement of the principle:

> 'If any one by a deliberate act destroys a document which, according to what its contents may have been, would have told strongly either for him or against him, the strongest possible presumption arises that if it had been produced it would have told against him …' [*The Ophelia* [1916] 2 AC 206, 229–30]

omnia praesumuntur rite esse acta

Latin: things done are presumed to have been done correctly; often called the 'presumption of regularity'; sometimes abbreviated to *omnia rite esse acta*. A principle of last resort, applied only where it cannot be established whether an act has been done in accordance with requisite formalities, but where it is more probable than not that it was so done—in which case the law presumes that the act was done correctly: *Harris v Knight* (1890) 15 PD 170, 179–80 (Lindley LJ). For lawyers, the legal principle carries more nuance than the mere English translation suggests, making it (possibly) a term of art. Therefore, for non-lawyers, at least offer an explanation, as in the following example:

> 'There is no reason to suppose that [the bye-laws] were not given the publicity required by sections 86 and 87 of the 1847 Act before the Minister confirmed them: *omnia praesumuntur rite esse acta* (the presumption of regularity).' [*R v East Sussex County Council* [2013] EWCA Civ 276; [2014] QB 186, 279 [134] (Lewison LJ)]

on (a date)

Calculating a period

Where a period is stated to begin *on* or *upon* a named day, that day is included: *Sidebotham v Holland* [1895] 1 QB 378. Similarly, *on and from* a day, or *on and after* a day, includes that day: ibid, 384. Thus, a period of one year *starting* (or *commencing*) *on* 1 May ends on the next 30 April; a period of 60 days *starting* (or *commencing*) *on* 1 December expires at midnight on 29/30 next January: *Trow v Inde Coope (West Midlands) Ltd* [1967] 2 QB 899; *Darwin Broadcasters Pty Ltd v Australian Broadcasting Tribunal* (1990) 95 ALR 138.

Nevertheless, where the intention is to include the day, make it specific. For example:

> 'The parties must appoint an arbitrator within three months of notifying a dispute, *starting on* the day of the notification.'

Performing an obligation

Where an obligation is to be performed *on* (or *upon*) a date, it usually must be performed on that very date. Sometimes, though, depending on context, *on* (or *upon*) can be more flexible. Consider: '*On* [the occurrence of an event], A must do X'; depending on context, *on* here could mean *before*, *simultaneously with*, or even *after* the event. For example:

> A grant of option provided that '*Upon* exercise of the option, the grantee must pay the grantor $X.' Held, in the context, *upon* did not require payment simultaneously with exercise of the option: *Bowman v Durham Holdings Pty Ltd* (1973) 131 CLR 8. (Similar cases include *Larter (Inspector of Taxes) v Skone James* [1976] 1 WLR] 607; *R v Fairfield Justices; ex parte Brewster* [1976] QB 600.) The imprecision could be averted by requiring payment to *accompany* exercise of the option—assuming that is the intention.

See also **beginning with / beginning from**; **on or about**.

on / upon

See **upon / on**.

on behalf of

Normally indicates a relationship of agency; thus, if A does an act *on behalf of* B, then A does it as B's agent. If the act is the entry into a contract, then only B can enforce the benefit of the contract and only B is subject to its obligations. However, if A impliedly (and falsely) warrants having B's authority to enter into the contract, A may be liable for breaching that warranty: *Lewis v Nicholson* (1852) 18 QB 503.

In other contexts *on behalf of* can have a wider meaning, such as *in the place of* or *for the benefit of* or *in the interests of*. In such contexts, no agency relationship may be intended: eg, *Plevin v Paragon Personal Finance Ltd* [2014] 1 WLR 4222, [30] (Lord Sumption). A perceptive writer will clarify any possible ambiguity.

on demand

If something must be done *on demand*, must it be done immediately a demand is made? For example, in a transaction under which money is payable *on demand*, must the debtor have cash available for immediate payment, to meet a demand whenever made? Such an interpretation may be open in the circumstances.

More likely, however, the court will follow the general principle that a stipulation to pay a debt *on demand* allows at least some time. Factors in determining exactly how much time include whether the debtor knew of the amount to be demanded, whether the creditor has given the debtor sufficient information to allow the debtor to verify the amount claimed, and the creditor's response to the debtor's prior requests (if any) for time to pay: *Bunbury Foods Pty Ltd v National Bank of Australasia Ltd* (1984) 153 CLR 491, 504. These variables can lead to *on demand* being interpreted flexibly, as in the following cases:

- *On demand* allows the debtor sufficient time to gather the funds, or to implement the mechanics of bank payment: *ANZ Banking Group (NZ) Ltd v Gibson* [1981] 2 NZLR 513, 526.

- *On demand* implies a sense of urgency, but there is no default merely by being unable to pay instantly: *Toms v Wilson* (1862) 32 LJ QB 32; *Brighty v Norton* (1862) 3 B & S 305; 122 ER 116.
- *On demand* does not allow sufficient time to try to borrow the funds: *Bond v Hongkong Bank of Australia Ltd* (1991) 25 NSWLR 286, 295, 316–19.

Given possible argument over the degree of urgency inherent in *on demand*, it is always better to specify a period or date.

See also **immediately**; **instantly**.

on or about

An imprecise formula, of unpredictable flexibility. *On or about* allows some latitude, but the extent depends on context. For example:

- An obligation to deliver substantial farm machinery *on or about* 1 October permitted two or three days' latitude on either side: *Blackett v Clutterbuck Bros (Adelaide) Ltd* [1923] SASR 301, 307.
- A loan to be made *on or about* 1 September was to be made before 7 September: *Edwards v Stocks* [2008] TASSC 12, [25].

Sometimes, the imprecision inherent in *on or about* may be useful. But if not, stipulate a particular date.

See also **on (a date)**.

on the ground that

Prefer the shorter *because*.

See **because**.

on the part of

A wordy substitute for *by*. Prefer *by*. For example:

- 'He saw it as an insult *on the part of* [prefer: *by*] the defendant.'
- 'In truth, these matters point away from the existence of any unreasonableness *on the part of* [prefer: *by*] the respondents.' [*Timbercorp Pty Ltd v Collins* [2016] HCA 44; (2016) 259 CLR 212, [123] (Gordon J)]
- '[The trial judge seemed to suggest] that there has been some kind of "policy decision" *on the part of* [prefer: *by*] the Divisional Court to "a softening of approach" in relation to Article 8. … [But there] is no change of "policy" or "approach" *on the part of* [prefer: *by*] the Divisional Court …' [*Xhelili v Republic of Albania* [2015] EWHC 641 (Admin), [6]–[7] (Aikens LJ)]

one- (fraction)

Hyphenated: *one-half*, *one-third*, *one-tenth*. There is an acceptable exception for large fractions: *one one-hundredth* [not *one-one-hundredth*]. For example:

> 'Mr Shelley has been content to admit that the appropriate proportion is *one one-hundredth* …' [*Ash v Dickie* [1936] Ch 655, 662 (Lord Wright MR)]

See also **FRACTIONS**.

one (pronoun)

Substitutive use

The substitutive use of *one* is a handy word-saving device. For example:

Before	After
The court may appoint an arbitrator with experience in farm disputes if it deems *an arbitrator with experience in farm disputes* to be necessary. [24 words]	The court may appoint an arbitrator with experience in farm disputes if it deems *one* to be necessary. [18 words]
An arbitrator must not decide a dispute between the parties unless the dispute is: (a) *a dispute* relating to rent; (b) *a dispute* that involves less than $1,000; and (c) *a dispute* that has first been referred to mediation. [39 words]	An arbitrator must not decide a dispute between the parties unless it is *one* that: (a) relates to rent; (b) involves less than $1,000; and (c) has first been referred to mediation. [32 words]

one (personal pronoun)

In modern usage, *one* as a personal pronoun seems stilted. It is better to specify who *one* is.

Stilted	Better
One does not like this course of action.	I do not like this course of action.
One should take this course of action.	You should take this course of action.
One does *one's* best to comply.	I try to comply.

one + name

Also stilted is *one* as an adjective before a person's name: '*one* Peter Smith'. Prefer simply 'Peter Smith' (unless, exceptionally, hinting at the unexpected: eg, 'At the table were Lord Neuberger, Lady Arden, and one Peter Smith').

only

Care with placement

A word often placed carelessly, causing ambiguity and occasional bemusement. The carelessness lays bare the writer's lack of attention to detail. Always place *only* as close as possible to the word or phrase it qualifies—preferably immediately before it. Location can change meaning, as in the following examples:

1. Compare:
   - *Only* John could see the accused from the window. [no one else could see the accused]
   - John *only* could see the accused from the window. [no one else could see the accused; John could see but not hear]

- John could *only* see the accused from the window. [John could not also hear the accused]
- John could see *only* the accused from the window. [John could see no one else]
- John could see the accused *only* from the window. [John could see no one else; John could not see from elsewhere]
- John could see the accused from the window *only*. [from nowhere else]

2. '[The] lease *only* conferred a leasehold interest over *part* of the new, amalgamated Lot 1.' [*Mekpine Pty Ltd v Moreton Bay Regional Council* [2014] QCA 317, [12] (McMurdo P). McMurdo P meant: '[The] lease conferred a leasehold interest over *only part* [or less idiomatically, but often seen in legal usage, *part only*] of the new, amalgamated Lot 1.']
3. 'The decision of Lord Coleridge CJ … was *only* reported in a local newspaper.' [*Lynn Shellfish Ltd v Loose* [2016] UKSC 14, [18] (Lords Neuberger and Carnwath). Their Lordships meant: The local newspaper was the only journal to report the decision.]
4. 'In this judgment, it is *only* necessary to refer to one of the four deeds …' [*Marks and Spencer plc v BNB Paribas Securities Services Trust Co (Jersey) Ltd* [2015] UKSC 72; [2015] 3 WLR 1843, [2] (Lord Neuberger). Lord Neuberger meant that it was necessary to refer to *only one* [or *one only*] of the four deeds.]

may only

Take particular care to avoid ambiguity when using *may only* where *only* applies to something other than the verb modified by *may*.

Example 1

'The buyer *may only* claim damages for breach of this clause.' This could mean:

- The buyer may claim *damages*, but not some other remedy (eg, not specific performance). *Or*
- The buyer may claim damages for breach of *this* clause, but no other.

[Source: Paul Clark, 'When Drafting Goes Wrong' (2018) *Conveyancer and Property Lawyer* 109, 112]

Example 2

'The company *may* pay salaries *only* out of annual profits.' This could mean:

- Annual profits can be used to pay salaries, but not to pay anything else. *Or*
- The only source for paying salaries is annual profits (ie, if those profits are not sufficient, the company cannot use other sources).

Avoid the ambiguity by relocating *only*:

- The company *may* pay *only* salaries out of annual profits.
- The company *may* pay salaries out of annual profits *only*.

only if

Only if suggests a narrower focus than *if*. By itself, *if* leaves open other possibilities, but *only if* suggests exclusivity.

Example

Assume that a service-of-notices provision states that a notice 'is served *if* sent by registered post'. Does this mean it is (a) served *only if* sent by registered post, or (b) *sufficiently served if* sent by registered post, but allowing other methods of service also? Context is key—but in the absence of clear contrary indication, courts usually prefer interpretation (b): *Papantoniou v Stonewall Hotel Pty Ltd* [2018] NSWCA 85; (2018) 19 BPR 38. This is in line with the general principle that, unless context requires otherwise, a document is sufficiently served if brought to the attention of the person to be served: *Holloway v Coster* [1897] 1 QB 346, 347; *Re Harris* [1931] 1 Ch 138, 143; *Re A Debtor* [1939] 1 Ch 251, 256.

Hence, for exclusivity, prefer *only if.*

See also **if and only if**.

onus probandi

Latin: burden of proof; the evidentiary burden. The duty of a person to prove a charge or allegation. The English translation carries the legal sense perfectly, although many lawyers seem compelled to keep the Latin. For example:

- 'The burden of proof is on the underwriter to show materiality by satisfying the two tests. … No similar *onus probandi* [prefer: *burden of proof*] should be imposed on a party who makes an inadvertent disclosure …' [*Pan Atlantic Insurance Co Ltd v Pine Top Insurance Co Ltd (No 2)* [1995] 1 AC 501, 505 (counsel's argument)]
- '[T]he *onus probandi* [prefer: *onus of proof*] lies in every case upon the party propounding a will …' [*Barry v Butlin* (1838) 1 Curt 637, 638; 163 ER 223, 223 (Parke B)]

op cit

Abbreviation for *opere citato* (Latin: in the work cited). In British/Commonwealth usage, no full stops: *op cit*; but in US usage, *op. cit.*, reflecting the US preference for retaining full stops after abbreviations. Indicates that the reader will find the reference in the place (book, article) already cited. Some writers prefer *loc cit* (US *loc. cit.*), which carries a similar meaning.

See also **loc cit**.

opere citato

Latin: in the work cited (referred to). Almost always abbreviated to *op cit.*

See **op cit**.

opine (verb)

To express an opinion: 'Judge X *opined* that …' Though reasonably common in legal writing, most non-lawyers probably regard *opine* as pompous or (dare we say?) *opin*ionated. To avoid alienating readers who may consider *opine* to be self-important, prefer 'Judge X *expressed the view* that …' or simply 'Judge X *said* that …'

opinion

See **judgment (and variants)**.

or

The proper use of *or* is to denote disjunction, a choice between alternatives: ie, 'A *or* B' means *only one* of A or B; 'A *or* B *or* C' means *only one* of A, B, and C. However, some usages may be ambiguous.

Example

'A *or* B may sign the document.'

This could mean:

(1) Either A or B may sign, but not both A and B.
(2) A may sign, or B may sign, or both A and B may sign (less likely, but arguable).

Courts have held that context may require *or* to be read as *and*, and *and* to be read as *or* (see further, discussion under **and**).

Further reading

Dennis C Pearce and Robert S Geddes, *Statutory Interpretation in Australia*, 9th edn (LexisNexis, 2019) [2.46]–[2.51] ('or' in statutory interpretation)

See also **and**; **and / or**; **COMMAS**; **CONJUNCTIONS**.

ORAL VARIATION OF DOCUMENTS

See 'NO VARIATION' CLAUSE.

oral / verbal

Strictly *oral* means by mouth, and *verbal* means by use of words (whether written or spoken). When describing a contract formed by words, with no writing, Fowler prefers *verbal*: RD Burchfield (ed), *Fowler's Modern English Usage*, 3rd edn (Oxford University Press, 1998) 820–21. This usage appears in the following example:

> 'The *verbal* contract is made by the consignor tendering the goods and by the carrier accepting them.' [*McCutcheon v David MacBrayne Ltd* [1964] 1 WLR 125, 131 (Lord Guest)]

Logically, when describing the act of speaking, *oral* is the preferred term. For example:

> '[T]here were discrepancies between the appellant's *verbal* [prefer: *oral*] evidence and what he had said to police.' [*Tweed v Shepherd* [2008] WASCA 59, [87]; 49 MVR 470, 483 (Miller JA). That is, there were discrepancies between what the appellant said in court and what he said to the police. However, Fowler (above) prefers '*verbal* evidence'.]

In legal practice, *oral* and *verbal* are often used interchangeably (oral contract, verbal contract; oral evidence, verbal evidence), with no risk to legal certainty.

order nisi

See **nisi**.

ORDINALS

See **NUMBERS**.

ORDINARY SENSE OF WORDS

A 'golden rule' of legal interpretation that requires words to be given their ordinary sense. It reflects a related principle that the meaning of an ordinary English word is a question of fact, not of law: *Cozens v Brutus* [1973] AC 854, 861, Lord Reid.

The key statement of principle comes from Lord Wensleydale's opinion in *Grey v Pearson* (1857) 6 HL Cas 61, 106; ER 1216, 1234 (a case on the interpretation of a will):

> '[I]n all written instruments, the grammatical and ordinary sense of the words is to be adhered to, unless that would lead to some absurdity, or some repugnance or inconsistency with the rest of the instrument, in which case the grammatical and ordinary sense of the words may be modified, so as to avoid that absurdity and inconsistency, but no farther.'

This principle is not easily displaced. The plain and ordinary sense of words is applied, unless to do so would produce a 'commercial absurdity': *Thomson v Goblin Hill Hotels Ltd* [2011] UKPC 8; [2011] 1 BCLC 587, [18]. In finding the plain and ordinary sense of words, the approach is one of common sense and commercial reality, not nit-picking: *Starlight Shipping Co v Allianz Marine & Aviation Versicherungs AG* [2011] EWHC 3381 (Comm); [2012] 1 Lloyds Rep 162, [18].

See also **CONSISTENCY OF TERMINOLOGY; TERMS OF ART.**

ore tenus

Latin: by word of mouth, orally; in particular, describes an application to the court made orally rather than in writing. The Latin is time-hallowed, but the English is fine. For example:

- 'The accused on being arraigned on any indictment may plead the general issue *ore tenus* [prefer: *orally*], or he may in writing demur or plead any matter of law or fact ...' [*Phillip v DPP* [1992] 1 AC 545, 554 (Lord Ackner, quoting from a criminal statute)]
- 'After speaking separately with two duty solicitors at the court, the appellant elected to plead guilty to the charge of basic assault causing harm. The prosecution thereupon pressed an *application ore tenus* [prefer: *an oral application*; better (to convey the sense): *an immediate application*] for breach of the suspended sentence bond.' [*Scott v Police* [2015] SASC 103, [9] (Nicholson J)]

ORGANISATION (STRUCTURE) OF DOCUMENTS

See **DOCUMENT STRUCTURE.**

ORPHANED HEADINGS

See **HEADINGS.**

ORWELL'S PRECEPTS

Legal writers should take to heart George Orwell's precepts on writing, as guidelines to clear, plain writing. The precepts are set out in his essay, 'Politics and the English Language' (1946). They are as relevant today as when first penned:

> 'I think the following rules will cover most cases:
>
> (i) Never use a metaphor, simile or other figure of speech which you are used to seeing in print.
> (ii) Never use a long word where a short one will do.
> (iii) If it is possible to cut a word out, always cut it out.
> (iv) Never use the passive where you can use the active.
> (v) Never use a foreign phrase, a scientific word or a jargon word if you can think of an everyday English equivalent.
> (vi) Break any of these rules sooner than say anything outright barbarous.
>
> These rules sound elementary, and so they are, but they demand a deep change of attitude in anyone who has grown used to writing in the style now fashionable.'
>
> [Source: George Orwell, *Why I Write* [1946] (Penguin, 2004) 119]

Further reading

JD Fischer, 'Why George Orwell's Ideas About Language Still Matter for Lawyers' (2007) 68 *Montana Law Review* 129

See also **ACTIVE VOICE / PASSIVE VOICE; CLICHES; METAPHORS; PLAIN LANGUAGE; SESQUIPEDALIANISM; SIMPLER WORDS AND PHRASES.**

other

See **eiusdem generis**.

otherwise

Meaning

Otherwise is fertile ground for the *eiusdem generis* principle. For example:

> A statute imposed a betterment tax on premises having access to a street through a 'court, passage or *otherwise*'. Held, *otherwise* was to be read *eiusdem generis* to import access along something similar to a court or passage (and not, for example, through a street): *Chatterton v Glanford Rural Council* [1915] 3 KB 707, 713 (Lord Reading CJ).

In some contexts, *otherwise* simply means *or not*. For example:

> A statute allowed the government to recover social security payments paid to a person as a result of misrepresentations made 'fraudulently *or otherwise*'. Held, *or otherwise* meant simply 'or not': *Page v Chief Adjudication Officer* (unreported, England and Wales Court of Appeal, 24 June 1991).

Avoid comma splice

Where using *otherwise* in midsentence as a conjunction linking two constructions that could stand grammatically as separate sentences, it is better to precede *otherwise* with a semicolon or colon, not a mere comma. For example:

> *Not*: 'You should phone today, *otherwise* you will miss me.'
>
> *But*: 'You should phone today; otherwise you will miss me.' (Or better, 'You should phone today *or else* you will miss me.')

Where a colon is used, a comma after *otherwise* may help to emphasise the point being introduced:

> 'You should phone today: otherwise, you will miss me.'

See also **COMMAS; eiusdem generis; however.**

ouster

The act of removing a person from property; often used in the context of co-owners, where one (A) wrongfully excludes another (B) from exercising B's right to possession as co-owner. Ouster may be by actual or threatened violence: eg, *Dennis v McDonald* [1982] Fam 63, 71. It many also be 'constructive' (eg, where one co-owner denies another co-owner's title to the property): *Biviano v Natoli* (1998) 43 NSWLR 695, 703.

outgoings

Regular payments, often for the upkeep of a property. *Outgoings* is a notoriously 'awkward' term (the epithet comes from *Budd v Marshall* (1880) 50 LJ QB 24, 26 (Bramwell LJ), in a passage edited out of the authorised report, (1880) 5 CPD 481). *Outgoings* is often used in commercial documents; for example, a party to a lease may agree to pay the whole or a part of *outgoings*. It is a wide, general term, and has been held to cover at least the following:

- rates and taxes: *R v Shaw* (1848) 12 QB 419, 427; 116 ER 925, 928
- the costs of installing a sewer pipe: *Crosse v Raw* (1874) LR 9 Ex 209
- the costs of street paving: *Aldridge v Ferne* (1886) 17 QBD 212
- the expenses of estate management: *Re Duke of Cleveland's Estate* [1894] 1 Ch 164
- the costs of demolishing a dangerous building: *Tubbs v Wynne* [1897] 1 QB 74.

To leave the word to range at large invites litigation. Where possible, specify which particular *outgoings* the parties have in mind.

OUTLINES

See **SIMPLIFIED OUTLINES**.

outwith

Meaning 'outside' (as in '*outwith* the statute'). Archaic, but still used occasionally in UK decisions, particularly (but not exclusively) by judges with Scottish backgrounds. Examples include:

- 'They are recognised *outwith* [prefer: *outside*; *beyond*] the immigration context ...' [*Ali v Secretary of State for the Home Department* [2016] UKSC 60; [2016] 1 WLR 4799, [169] (Lord Kerr)]
- '[A]n injunction must be framed in sufficiently certain terms that a restrained party can be advised with clarity whether conduct falls within or *outwith* [prefer: *outside*] the terms of the injunction.' [*Emeco International Pty Ltd v O'Shea (No 2)* [2012] WASC 348, [213]; 225 IR 471 (Edelman J)]

over (an age)

See **age**.

over (measurement)

See **more than / over**.

overriding interest

An interest in land that, although not registered, is enforceable against the registered title. In jurisdictions where the Torrens system of registered title applies, the counterpart term is *exception to indefeasibility*.

Further reading

S Bridge, E Cooke, and M Dixon (eds), *Megarry & Wade's Law of Real Property*, 9th edn (Sweet & Maxwell, 2019) [6-028]–[6-030], [6-086]–[6-101]

See also **indefeasibility**.

OVERVIEW

See **EXECUTIVE SUMMARY; SIMPLIFIED OUTLINES.**

owing to the fact that

A wordy substitute for the much shorter *because* or *due to*. The shorter equivalent is always preferable: eg, 'I am doing this *owing to the fact that* [prefer: *because*] I need to.'

owner

The meaning is clear enough in most contexts: ie, the person who 'owns' property, whether real or personal. But that is, of course, self-referential. In fact, 'ownership' is a notoriously slippery concept, its meaning varying enormously with context. In addition, where the context is statute, the first reference point is always the statute's definition of *owner*, which may take the word well beyond its popular meaning.

Further reading

Daniel Greenberg (ed), *Stroud's Judicial Dictionary*, 9th edn (Sweet & Maxwell, 2017)—title 'owner' (myriad cases, all context-dependent)

OXFORD COMMA

See **COMMAS.**

pacta sunt servanda

Latin: agreements are to be observed. Were it not for its rhythmic resonance, nothing would commend this Latin truism over an appropriate English translation. But the English need not lack rhythm. For example:

- 'The rule against penalties is an exception to the general approach of the common law that parties are free to contract as they please and that the courts will enforce their agreements—*pacta sunt servanda* [prefer: *bargains must be kept*].' [*Cavendish Square Holdings BV v Makdessi* [2015] UKSC 67, [257]; [2015] 3 WLR 1373, 1466 (Lord Hodge)]
- 'The fundamental value protected by the law of contract is that *pacta sunt servanda*, bargains are to be kept.' [*Clark v Macourt* [2013] HCA 56, [135]; (2013) 253 CLR 1, 39 (Keane J, providing a translation)]

PAIRINGS

See **WORD PAIRINGS.**

palm tree justice

A pejorative term, referring disdainfully to an approach to judging that prioritises individual fairness over the authority of precedent. The term may have originated in *Newgrosh v Newgrosh* (1950) 100 LJ 525 (Bucknill LJ), but was given wider currency by Evershed MR in *Rimmer v Rimmer* [1953] 1 QB 63, 68. It echoes the earlier *rusticum judicium* (rustic trial; rural justice)—eg, 'It is no answer that magistrates are not the most competent judges, that theirs is a *rusticum judicium*; for the Legislature has appointed them to be the judges in these matters': *The Cuba* (1860) Lush 14, 15; 167 ER 8 at 8 (Dr Lushington).

par in parem non habet imperium

Latin: an equal has no power over an equal. A maxim found particularly in international law and connoting that one state cannot exercise jurisdiction over another state. For example:

> 'Based on the old principle *par in parem non habet imperium*, the rule of international law is not that a state should not exercise over another state a jurisdiction which it has but that (save in cases recognised by international law) a state has no jurisdiction over another state.' [*Jones v Saudi Arabia* [2006] UKHL 26; [2007] 1 AC 270, 283 [14] (Lord Bingham, with an explanation of the Latin)]

The maxim also reflects a principle of local law, that courts cannot bind courts of equal standing in the judicial hierarchy—although the maxim is rarely used in this context. As with most Latin maxims, an appropriate English translation carries the meaning clearly, making the Latin redundant.

para

Abbreviation for *paragraph*. In line with modern conventions, omit the full stop.

paradox

A seeming contradiction; a statement that seems incongruous but which may resolve itself on closer analysis. Thus, *apparent paradox*, though commonly seen, is strictly a redundancy:

> 'While it cannot be denied that Mr Brown's point has force, I think that the *apparent paradox* [prefer: *paradox*] which he identifies is, on analysis[,] readily explicable.' [*Hotak v Southwark London Borough Council* [2015] UKSC 30; [2016] AC 811, [68] (Lord Neuberger)]

PARAGRAPHS

Properly drafted, a paragraph deals with one main point. If it is a single-sentence paragraph, it deals only with that point. If it is a multi-sentence paragraph, all sentences must (or should) relate only to the one main point. A new main point requires a new paragraph.

Topic sentence

A topic sentence (or 'focus sentence' or 'thesis sentence') helps organise the paragraph by providing a pointer to its content. It tells the reader 'in short, this is what this paragraph is about'. For that reason, the ideal topic sentence *starts* the paragraph. Some legal writers find this counter-intuitive, particularly in paragraphs that seek to argue to a conclusion; these writers assume that the paragraph must reflect the reasoning process, arriving at the conclusion only at paragraph-end. But a writer attentive to the reader's needs will revise this order and shift the conclusion up-front, in the form of a topic sentence. The revised order in fact aids the writer's rhetorical purpose, because it gives the reader a context for the reasoning that follows.

Example

> **Poor topic sentence**
>
> The next case is *Jones v Smith*, decided by the Court of Appeal. [Then follow sentences setting out the Court's reasons.] Therefore, the Court ruled that private security officers must act reasonably.

Better topic sentence

In the next case, *Jones v Smith*, the Court of Appeal ruled that private security officers must act reasonably. [Then follow sentences setting out the Court's reasons.]

Transitions

An effective topic sentence shows clearly how the paragraph relates to the paragraph that precedes it. Transition words include:

- for contrast—*however, but, in contrast*
- for comparison—*likewise, similarly*
- for more inforrnation—*moreover, further*
- for next steps—*next, later, afterwards*
- for conclusion—*therefore, to conclude, in summary.*

Paragraph length

A paragraph can be as short or long as necessary to deal with its subject matter. In practice, an unduly long paragraph makes the prose appear denser than its subject matter may require. In Victorian times, paragraphs in law reports sometimes extended over several pages. The modern trend is towards shorter paragraphs. However, while shorter paragraphs are easier to read than longer ones, too many very short paragraphs can make the text appear patronising or infantile. This may require a trade-off between (on the one hand) the exhortation 'one paragraph, one main point' and (on the other) audience empathy.

See also **ADVICE (FORM OF)**; **CLAUSE STRUCTURE (Paragraphing conventions)**; **DOCUMENT DESIGN**; **LISTS AND ENUMERATIONS**; **SENTENCE LENGTH.**

PARALLEL STRUCTURE

A parallel structure heightens the text's order and logic, and therefore helps drive home the writer's message. It is particularly important in bullet points and lists, but it also improves prose more generally. It is achieved by deftly repeating words, sentence parts, or grammatical structures.

A parallel structure can improve even a single sentence, as in Examples 1 and 2. It can also improve the flow of multiple sentences, as in Example 3.

Example 1 (underlining showing lack of parallelism)

Before: In the meeting, we will seek the establishment of a committee, removal of directors, and disallowing staff bonuses.

After: In the meeting, we will seek to establish a committee, to remove directors, and to disallow staff bonuses.

Example 2 (underlining showing lack of parallelism)

Before: All lawyers have a knowledge of law, but only barristers have come to know the benefits of courtroom tactics.

After: All lawyers know the law, but only barristers know the benefits of courtroom tactics.

Example 3

Original	Reorganised in parallel structure
'*There are three great evils* which bedevil probate practice. *The first* and by far the most egregious is homemade wills. *Second there is* the problem occasioned by no will at all and the effects of the blunt instrument that is the *Administration Act 1903* (WA). *Third there are* those cases where there is a will but the testator's circumstances have changed and the will has not been updated. This case is an example of the third category.' [Source: *Sloan v Baldrey* [2018] WASC 206, [1] (Sanderson M); italics added]	*Three great evils* bedevil probate practice. *The first evil is where* the will is homemade; this is by far the most egregious evil. *The second evil is where* there is no will at all, and the effects of the blunt instrument that is the *Administration Act 1903* (WA). *The third evil is where* there is a will but the testator's circumstances have changed and the will has not been updated. This case is an example of the third category. [italics added to show parallel structure]

See **BULLET POINTS; CLAUSE STRUCTURE; LISTS AND ENUMERATIONS; NUMBERS; SENTENCE STRUCTURE (Prefer parallel structure)**.

paraphernalia

In normal usage, personal belongings, with the implication 'of no particular value'. In law, an obsolete term for certain jewels and ornaments that belong to a husband but that pass to his wife on his death. At common law, ownership of a wife's chattels generally passed to her husband on marriage. However, *paraphernalia* were the items he allowed her to wear; and by the common law, on his death, ownership of them passed to her. As Blackstone explained:

> 'Our law uses [the term *paraphernalia*] to signify the apparel and ornaments of the wife, suitable to her rank and degree; which she becomes entitled to at the death of her husband. … Neither can the husband devise by his will such ornaments and jewels of his wife; though during his life perhaps he hath the power (if unkindly inclined to exert it) to sell them or give them away.' [*Commentaries on the Laws of England* (Clarendon, 1766), book 2, 436]

To use the term in this legal sense today would be both obscurantist and misleading.

PARENTHESES

See **BRACKETS**.

pace

Latin: with peace to; ie, with all due respect to; pronounced *pah-chay*. Used to express respectful disagreement with someone: eg, '*pace* Lord Denning'. However, plain English suffices: 'The "deserted wife's equity", *pace* [prefer: *with all due respect to*] Lord Denning, no longer represents the law.'

parens patriae

Latin: the parent of his or her country. A term of art encapsulating the common-law principle under which the courts and the sovereign must help protect those unable to protect themselves (such as people of unsound mind, and children). The Latin's succinctness makes a literal translation unhelpful. Therefore, add an explanation. For example:

- '[T]he jurisdiction … conferred on the Family Court … in proceedings in relation to the custody, guardianship or welfare of a child is a statutory jurisdiction similar to the *parens patriae* jurisdiction [add: *ie, the special protective role*] traditionally exercised by the Court of Chancery.' [*Palmer v Ayres* [2017] HCA 5; (2017) 259 CLR 478, [102] (Gageler J)]
- 'State intervention to prevent suicide may now be seen, at least in part, as the exercise of a *parens patriae* role [add: ie, *a protective role*] and the interest of the State in protecting the life of its own citizens.' [*Stuart v Kirkland-Veenstra* (2009) 237 CLR 215; [2009] HCA 15, [45] (French CJ)]

parent

The ordinary sense is the biological mother or father, but the word is surprisingly context-dependent. For example, depending on the context (and in particular, any relevant statute), *parent* can mean: any lineal ancestor; a person who (though not the birth parent) has adopted the child or assumed parental responsibility; and a foster parent. Conversely, also depending on the context (and statute), *parent* might *not* mean: the natural mother (where the child is adopted); an unmarried mother; or a sperm donor.

Further reading

Daniel Greenberg (ed), *Stroud's Judicial Dictionary*, 9th edn (Sweet & Maxwell, 2017), title 'parent' (case law on meaning of *parent*)

See also **child**.

pari passu

Latin: by equal steps; on an equal footing. Sometimes translated 'equally', but that may not always carry the sense, which is sometimes 'proportionately'. Though hallowed by long legal usage, this Latinism has no advantage over a plain-English translation. For example:

- '[I]n order to achieve a *pari passu distribution* [prefer: *distribution on an equal footing*] between all the company's creditors it would be necessary for there to be a pooling of the company's assets worldwide …' [*Singularis Holdings Ltd v PricewaterhouseCoopers* [2014] UKPC 36; [2015] AC 1675, [58] (Lord Collins)]
- 'To give some unsecured creditors remedies in an insolvency which are denied to others would undermine the basic principle of *pari passu participation* [prefer: *participation on an equal footing*] by creditors.' [*Spies v R* [2000] HCA 43; (2000) 201 CLR 603, [93] (Gaudron, McHugh, Gummow, and Hayne JJ)]

pari ratione

Latin: by the same reasoning; for like reason. A Latinism that may impress but is unlikely to inform. A plain-English translation suffices, as in the following examples:

- 'But there is no conspiracy involved in a lock-out; and the statute under discussion deals with lock-outs *pari ratione* [prefer: *with similar logic*] as with strikes.' [*Toronto Electric Commissioners v Snider* [1925] AC 396, 409 (Viscount Haldane)]
- '[I]n neither case could it be said that the business [of A] had been transferred to the landlord. *Pari ratione* [prefer: *By the same reasoning*], the business [of B] was not transferred to the Government.' [*Barrier Wharf Ltd v Commissioner of Taxes* [1919] SALR 262, 274 (Murray CJ)]

parliament

Lower-case 'p' unless referring to a particular parliament:

- 'The Scottish Parliament passed a similar statute recently.'
- 'A similar statute was recently passed by parliaments around the Commonwealth.'

parol / parole

Oral, by word of mouth—as in *the parol evidence rule* (the rule that evidence cannot be given to contradict the words of a written agreement). Historically, *parol* could also refer to any written agreement not in the form of a deed: *Rann v Hughes* (1778) 7 TR 350n; 101 ER 1014 (Skynner LCB); *Khoury v Khoury* (2006) 66 NSWLR 241, 262 [74] (Bryson JA, quoting Lord Nottingham LC); but that usage is obsolete.

Both spellings—*parol* and *parole*—exist, but *parol* is more common and preferred, because it avoids potential confusion with other meanings of *parole* (eg, 'the prisoner was released on parole'):

- '[I]t is clear that the Lord President was … propounding the long established rule of law that it is impermissible to vary the terms of a written agreement by *parole* [sic; prefer *parol*] evidence as to what one of the parties thought it meant.' [*Alfred McAlpine Construction Ltd v Panatown Ltd* [2000] UKHL 43; [2001] 1 AC 518, 564 (Lord Jauncey)]
- 'I accept that, in proceedings between the applicant and each customer, a tender of the signed document would establish the terms of the agreement between them, subject to the limited exceptions to the *parole* [sic; prefer *parol*] evidence rule.' [*Palgo Holding Pty Ltd v Gowans* [2003] NSWCA 204, [30] (Hodgson JA)]

Part

When denoting a component of an Act, *Part* always took an initial capital; lower-case *part* was never seen. Some style guides now recommend lower case—*part*. But this is not yet the norm. Unless compelled by a style guide, prefer upper-case *Part*.

See also **Division; HEADINGS (Part and Division headings)**.

particeps

General meaning

Latin: partner; accomplice. No magic resides in this Latin word, nor in longer phrases of which it is part—a simple English translation suffices. For example:

- *particeps doli*: partner (accomplice) in crime
- *particeps fraudis*: partner (accomplice) in fraud.

particeps criminis

Latin: partner (accomplice) in crime; plural: *participes criminis*. For readers of Latin, the term has a certain lilt, and those without Latin may well guess its meaning. But an appropriate English translation is better. For example:

> '[Counsel contended that the payment] amounted to a premium unlawfully required under the Rent Restriction legislation, that the [estate agents] committed a criminal offence in demanding it, and that [the prospective tenant] was *particeps criminis* [prefer: *a partner in crime*; *a criminal accomplice*] in paying it …' [*Grace Rymer Investments Ltd v Waite* [1958] Ch 831, 845 (Evershed MR)]

PARTICIPLE PHRASES

See **PARTICIPLES**.

PARTICIPLES

Participles and relative clauses

Brevity always trumps prolixity. One way to reduce word count is to prefer participles over relative clauses.

Before (relative clauses)	**After (participles)**
A consumer contract *that has been regulated* under this section …	A consumer contract *regulated* under this section …
The tenant must produce trading receipts for the year *that ended* [or *that will begin*] on 1 July.	The tenant must produce trading receipts for the year *ending* [or *beginning*] on 1 July.
This clause applies to a consent *that is in force or was in force* before 1 July each year.	This clause applies to a consent *in force* before 1 July each year. [Note that this also removes the need for complex tense constructions.]

Redrafting participle phrases and relative clauses

Traditional legal drafting often uses participle phrases and relative clauses to qualify obligations. This can lead to complex sentence structures. Modern drafting prefers a sparser style, reducing complexity. However, a sparser style that is carelessly expressed can produce unintended changes.

Example

> The traditional form of lease covenant that regulates the tenant's right to assign the lease, uses the following language:
>
> > 'The tenant shall not assign the lease without the landlord's consent, *such consent not to be unreasonably withheld*.' (italics added for illustration)
>
> By long-established case law, the italicised words merely qualify the tenant's right to assign. They are not a covenant by the landlord not to withhold consent unreasonably. If the landlord withholds consent unreasonably, the tenant is free to assign without needing consent—but the landlord is not liable in damages for breach of covenant: *Treloar v Bigge* (1874) LR 9 Ex 151.
>
> A drafter seeking a sparser style might redraft thus:
>
> > 'The tenant must not assign the lease without the landlord's consent, *and the landlord must not withhold consent unreasonably*.' (italics added for illustration)
>
> But this changes both style and substance, for it imposes on the landlord a positive obligation not to withhold consent unreasonably. In doing so, it subjects the landlord to a liability that was absent in the traditional wording: *Ideal Film Renting Co Ltd v Nielson* [1921] 1 Ch 575; *Blake v Official Assignee of Rendell* (1909) 28 NZLR 571.

See also **PROLIXITY**.

PARTIES' NAMES

See **NAMES**.

partus sequitur ventrem

Latin: the offspring follows the dam. A colourful maxim to the effect that the person who owns the mother owns the offspring. The maxim applies to all animals, except swans: Case of Swans (1592) 7 Co Rep 15b, 17a; 77 ER 435, 437. The rationale is said to be that the male is often unknown, that the owner of the female must care for her during pregnancy, and that therefore the loser by the pregnancy should be the gainer by the brood: Sir William Blackstone, *Commentaries on the Laws of England* (Clarendon, 1766) book 2, 390.

party

Main meanings

Party is a generic term, with two main meanings in law.

1. **A person who has engaged in a transaction or entered into a contract.** The *parties* in this sense are usually named at the outset: eg,

   This contract is between A and B ('the Parties').

   Each *party* is a signatory to the document. However, not all signatories are necessarily 'parties' in the strict sense. For example, a guarantor may add his or her signature to a contract signed by the parties, to evidence agreement to guarantee the obligations of a party under the contract; but this of itself does not make the guarantor a party to the contract. Or a company director may sign a contract on behalf of the company, without personally becoming a party.

2. **A person or entity involved in a dispute**. *Party* in this sense can include a person who takes part in legal proceedings, even though not personally on the record: *Law Society of NSW v Jackson* [1981] 1 NSWLR 730, 735; *Knight v FP Special Assets Ltd* (1992) 174 CLR 178, 190.

'third parties'

Persons outside these relationships are often called *third parties*. The usage is incongruous, as they are not *parties* at all; but the usage is common and well understood.

Contracts often attempt to widen the meaning of *party* by a boilerplate provision to the effect that references to a *Party* (capitalised to refer to a defined party) include references to the Party's successors, assigns, or transferees. Provisions of this kind do not always achieve their desired end, because a declaration that outsiders to a contract are parties does not make them parties.

Death of a party

Be alert to the drafting incongruity of giving rights to a 'party' who has died. For example, a contract for the sale of land provided that if a 'party' died, either 'party' could rescind the contract. (This seems counter-intuitive, because a person who has died cannot rescind a contract.) The purpose of the clause may have been to enable the *surviving* party to rescind rather than await the grant of probate of the deceased party's estate. On its face, however, the clause gave each 'party' the right to rescind. In the court's view, the intended meaning was that a party or, if the party had died, the party's legal personal representative (ie, executor or administrator) could rescind: *Deigan v Fussell* [2019] NSWCA 299. The drafter could have avoided the litigation by expressing that meaning more clearly.

See also **heirs, executors, administrators, successors, and assigns**; **person**; **third party**.

party wall

Sometimes hyphenated, *party-wall*. A wall dividing one property from another. While this normal usage seems clear enough and will serve most purposes, the common law discerned four variants of *party wall*. According to *Watson v Gray* (1880) 14 Ch D 192, 194–95 (Fry J), they are:

1. A wall owned by the adjoining owners as tenants in common.
2. A wall divided longitudinally into halves, one half belonging to each of the adjoining owners.
3. A wall belonging entirely to one of the adjoining owners but subject to an easement or right in the other to have it maintained as a dividing wall between the two properties.
4. A wall divided longitudinally into halves, each half belonging to the owner of the land upon which it stands but subject to a cross-easement in favour of the owner of the other.

In England and many Commonwealth jurisdictions, for many years *party wall* generally bore meaning (1). However, legislation now commonly gives *party wall* meaning (4) (eg, *Party Wall Act 1996*; *Conveyancing Act 1919* (NSW), ss 181B and 88BB).

Further reading

Halsbury's Laws of England, 'Boundaries' (vol 4, 2020) [364]–[387] (the law of party walls)

pass and repass

A tautologous pairing often found in the wording of easements—eg, a right to *pass and repass* along a right of way. The single word *pass* suffices, unless it is thought (unrealistically) that a right to pass is exhausted after the first use. A more realistic issue is whether a right to *pass and repass* includes a right to stop and unload, or to stop and park; but the answer (in the UK, probably yes: *Moncrief v Jamieson* [2007] 1 WLR 2620) is unlikely to be affected by whether the right is one to *pass* or one to *pass and repass*.

Further reading

Brendan Edgeworth (ed), *Butt's Land Law*, 7th edn (Lawbook, 2017) [9.680] (British and Commonwealth case law on meaning of a right to *pass and repass*)

See also **WORD PAIRINGS**.

passim

Latin: throughout, everywhere. Used in citations to mean 'in various places', 'in various parts of the chapter (or book)'. It has the benefit of brevity: any English translation is likely to be longer. But brevity is no substitute for intelligibility. For readers unaccustomed to formal texts, plain English serves just as well. For example:

- 'The matter is well put by Dawson J in *Shepherd v The Queen* (1990) 170 CLR 573 (HCA), 579–580 (but also *passim* [prefer: *in other places also*]).' [*JSC BTA Bank v Ablyazov (No 8)* [2012] EWCA Civ 1411; [2013] 1 WLR 1331, [52] (Rix LJ)]
- 'The application of the doctrine of terra nullius to Australia is strongly attacked in Reynolds, *The Law of the Land* (1987), *passim* [prefer: *in various places*].' [*Mabo v Queensland (No 2)* (1992) 175 CLR 1, 181, fn 79 (Toohey J)]

PASSIVE VOICE

See **ACTIVE VOICE / PASSIVE VOICE.**

patent defect

A defect (usually in title to land, or in the condition of goods) that is observable on a reasonably careful inspection.

Compare **latent defect**.

pauperus

Latin: a poor person.

See **in forma pauperis**.

payable on demand

See **on demand.**

penalty

In normal usage, a *penalty* is a punishment for breaking a law or rule (eg, for breaking the criminal law, or breaking a sporting code of conduct).

In contract law, *penalty* has developed the particular meaning of a stipulation that requires a party who breaches a contractual obligation to perform an additional or more onerous obligation—such as by paying a higher rate of interest on default under a mortgage. The *penalty* (ie, additional or more onerous obligation) is unenforceable if (in brief):

1. it is not a genuine pre-estimate of anticipated loss for breach of the obligation: *Dunlop Pneumatic Tyre Co Ltd v New Garage and Motor Co Ltd* [1915] AC 79, 86 (Lord Dunedin); or
2. it is extravagant and unconscionable, in the sense of being out of all proportion to the interests of the innocent party it seeks to protect: *Cavendish Square Holding BV v Makdessi* [2015] UKSC 67; [2016] AC 1172; *Paciocco v Australia and New Zealand Banking Group Ltd* [2016] HCA 28; 258 CLR 525.

Further reading

JGH Stumbles, 'Paciocco in the High Court: Penalties and Late Payment Fees (2017) 91 *Australian Law Journal* 969 (reviewing the law of penalties in the light of recent UK and Australian cases, particularly *Cavendish Square* and *Paciocco*)

See also **debitum in praesenti solvendum in futuro**; **in terrorem**; **liquidated damages**; **TERMS OF ART**.

pendente lite

See **lis.**

people that

To some readers, a barbarism for *people who*. However, *that* referring to people has an impeccable pedigree: 'The people *that* lived in darkness have seen a great light' (Isaiah 9:2, King James Version). Some justify *people that* by analogy with the logic distinguishing *that* and *which* more generally:

- The people *that* lived in darkness have seen a great light. [Some people lived in darkness; others did not.]
- The people, *who* lived in darkness, have seen a great light. [All people lived in darkness.]

But there is no grammatical 'rule' against *people that*. Preference for *people who* is a matter of style, not of grammatical compulsion. Indeed, *people that* is seen at the highest judicial level:

> '[The Order] was bound to have a very real impact on the *people that* were exposed to the restrictions as a result of it.' [*Ahmed v Her Majesty's Treasury* [2010] 2 AC 534, 630 [58] (Lord Hope)]

However, do not allow the conjunction of *people* and *that* to cause a miscue, even if only temporarily:

> 'The impugned provisions of the Act effectively imposed an artificial structure on the electoral activity of the *people that* contradicted direct popular choice of parliamentary representatives.' [*Mulholland v Australian Electoral Commission* [2004] HCA 41, [229]; 220 CLR 181, 259 (Kirby J). The meaning would be clearer if the sentence read: '... of the *people, which* contradicted ...']

See also **that / which**.

peppercorn rent

A rent of a purely nominal kind, not intended to reflect the market value and almost always not intended to be demanded: 'a peppercorn is very seldom handed over except under the stress of a case like this' (*Re Moody and Yates' Contract* (1885) 30 Ch D 344, 346). Hence, the obligation to pay is usually qualified by 'if demanded': eg, 'one peppercorn per year, if demanded'.

per

Meaning 'by' (a judge)

Latin: through; by; according to. In citations, often used to indicate a statement by a particular judge: eg, '[2016] AC 176, 198 per Lord Neuberger'. Modern usage tends to omit *per* in this context, on the basis that a reference to a judge's name at a particular page sufficiently implies that the judge made the statement at that page.

Meaning 'each'

Per is also used in the sense of *each*: 'She works 12 hours *per* [ie, *each*] day.' *Per* may also import an element of averaging. For example, a person who must work 'not less than 2 hours *per* week' to obtain benefits, is not disqualified merely by working for less than 2 hours in a particular week; the question is whether they work on average not less than 2 hours a week: *Stojanovski v Secretary, Department of Social Services* [2014] AATA 466; (2014) 144 ALD 142, [33].

See also **a (indefinite article)**; **CITATION OF CASES**.

per capita

Latin: by the heads; per head. This Latinism has found its way into standard English, making its meaning clear to most readers of legal documents. However, the translation *per head* is precise and can safely replace the Latin:

> 'Iceland is one of the most productive countries *per capita* [prefer: *per head*; *per head of population*] in the world.' [*Joint Administrators of Heritable Bank plc v Winding-Up Board of Landsbanki Islands hf* [2013] UKSC 13; [2013] 1 WLR 725, [1] (Lord Hope)]

Often used in contrast with *per stirpes* (by the stocks of descent; by family).

The singular, *per caput*, is rarely seen; but where it is, *per head* suffices also:

> '[The parties] have pleaded that the *per caput* [prefer: *per head*] consumption of confectionery in the United Kingdom is the highest in the world, and that ... it amounts to over seven oz. *per head* per week ...' [*Re Chocolate and Sugar Confectionery Reference (Foreign Evidence)* [1967] 1 WLR 1129, [1132] (Megaw J, using both Latin and English)]

See also **per stirpes**.

per cent

One word or two?

British/Commonwealth usage conventionally prefers two words—*per cent*, reflecting the two-word Latin source, *per centum* ('by the 100'). However, US usage prefers one word—*percent*—and this US usage is gaining a foothold elsewhere. *Percentage* is always one word.

Percentage symbol

For ease of reading, prefer the symbol (%) over the word, with no space between number and symbol. Thus:

> The deposit is 30% [*not* 30 per cent; *not* 30 %] of the purchase price.

When indicating a range, repeat the symbol:

> The deposit is 10%–20% of the purchase price.

Singular or plural?

Per cent (or %) takes the singular verb when standing alone:

> The judge said that 51% *satisfies* the balance of probabilities.

It also takes the singular verb when a singular word follows an 'of' construction:

> The judge said that 51% likelihood of success *is* enough.

But it takes the plural verb when a plural word follows an 'of' construction:

> The judge said that 90% of the lawyers appearing before him *are* ill-prepared.

'Per year' implied

Where a rate is expressed as 'X per cent', with no mention of the period over which it is calculated, the implication is *per year* (*per annum*). Thus, unless context indicates otherwise, a loan of $X for 2 months 'at 23% per cent' is a loan for 2 months at 23% per year: *London and Harrogate Securities Ltd v Pitts* [1976] 3 All ER 809.

per centum

See **per cent**.

per contra

Latin: on the contrary; on the other hand; conversely. Although an accepted Latinism, it has no advantage over an English translation. For example:

> 'And if he is entitled to unload them he must, *per contra* [prefer: *conversely*], be entitled to load them.' [*Bulstrode v Lambert* [1953] 1 WLR 1064, 1071 (Upjohn J)]

per curiam

Latin: by the court (ie, by the whole court, and not merely by only some of the judges). Although the Latinism is ubiquitous in legal usage, an appropriate English translation always suffices. For example:

- 'In the important case of *Australia and New Zealand Banking Group Ltd v Westpac Banking Corporation* (1988) 78 ALR 187, there are strong indications that the High Court of Australia may be moving towards the same destination (see especially at pp 162 and 168, *per curiam* [prefer: *by the whole court*; *a decision of the whole court*]).' [*Lipkin Gorman v Karpnale Ltd* [1991] 2 AC 548, 580 (Lord Goff)]
- 'See also … a similar statement in *Re Fraser and Public Service Staff Relations Board* … at p 463, *per curiam* [prefer: *by the whole Court*; *by all the judges*].' [*Australian Capital Television Pty Ltd v Commonwealth* (1992) 177 CLR 106, 141, fn 18 (Mason CJ)]

See also **per incuriam**; **per totam curiam**.

per diem

Latin: by the day, daily; similarly, *per diem in diem*, from day to day. Two related Latinisms, but carrying meanings no more precise than their English translations—so prefer the English translations. For example:

- 'If it were otherwise it would have the bizarre consequence that upon summary conviction a fine of £400 *per diem* [prefer: *daily*] could be imposed for each [offence], … whereas for any further offence … a *daily* fine of only £50 could be inflicted.' [*Hodgetts v Chiltern DC* [1983] 2 AC 120, 128 (Lord Roskill, using *per diem* in one place and *daily* in another)]
- 'My Lords, … I think that this was to treat the progress of the damage as creating new causes of action which accrued *per diem in diem* [prefer: *from day to day*].' [*Homburg Houtimport BV v Agrosin Private Ltd* [2003] UKHL 12, [90]; [2004] 1 AC 715 (Lord Hoffmann)]

per incuriam

Latin: by mistake; by error; through want of care. Used especially to indicate that a court made an error because its attention was not drawn to a relevant` binding decision or statutory provision. The meaning is more 'the court overlooked an important point' than 'the court got it wrong' (*Morelle Ltd v Wakeling* [1955] 1 All ER 708, 718, Lord Evershed MR)—though the former may merely be a more polite way of expressing the latter. For some readers, the Latin phrase may be misleading, suggesting the converse of *per curiam* ('by the whole court'). Therefore, prefer the English. For example:

> '[T]his makes it particularly important that we … hold that (i) the decision in *West* was *per incuriam* [prefer: *without the benefit of argument on the point*] so far as it involved holding (or assuming) that article 5(4) was engaged, and (ii) the *obiter dictum* of Lord Brown in *Black*, para 74 is wrong …' [*R v Secretary of State for Justice* [2014] UKSC 39, [46]; [2015] 1 AC 176, 190 (Lord Neuberger, using Latin ('per incuriam') in (i) to criticise the court in *West*, and English ('wrong') in (ii) to criticise Lord Brown)].

See also **per curiam**.

per my [mie] et per tout

Law French: for nothing and for the whole; a term describing the nature of the interests of joint tenants; the equivalent of Bracton's 'totum tenet et nihil tenet': Kevin Gray and Susan Francis Gray, *Elements of Land Law*, 5th edn (Oxford University Press, 2009) [7.4.5], fn 2. Although for some purposes the law treats joint tenants as having separate interests, they do not hold proportionate shares in the property in the same way as tenants in common do. Rather, each joint tenant is said to own *per my* [or *mie*] *et per tout*, meaning that each has a right shared with the others to the whole property but no individual right to any particular share in it: *Murray v Hall* (1849) 7 CB 441, 455n; 137 ER 175, 180n; *Wright v Gibbons* (1949) 78 CLR 313, 330 (Dixon J). No plain-language equivalent exists, and the English translation ('for nothing and for the whole') is opaque; but the phrase is likely to be seen only in textbook explanations of joint tenancies, where readers can expect an explanation.

See also **common property / joint property**.

per procurationem

See **pp**.

per quod consortium [servitium] amisit

Latin: by which he (or she) lost consortium (or services). The traditional formulation of an action for loss of consortium or services. In many jurisdictions, the causes of action for loss of consortium or services have been restricted or eliminated: eg, *Administration of Justice Act 1982*, s 2(c)(i). Regardless, a plain-English translation can capture the sense of the Latin:

> 'The question … is whether [the Act] prevents an employer recovering damages *per actione per quod servitium amisit* for the loss of services of an employee injured as a result of a transport accident …' [*Doughty v Martino Developments Pty Ltd* [2010] VSCA 121; (2010) 27 VR 499, [1] (Nettle JA, providing an immediate translation)]

per se

Latin: through itself; standing alone; as such. Often carrying the sense of 'always' or 'absolutely'—eg, 'juries per se are unpredictable', 'stamp duty per se is not inequitable'. Having been long accepted into standard English, 'per se' needs no italics. Where an English translation is used, commas are added; but when the Latin is used, no commas are added: compare 'Courts, as such, are busy places' and 'Courts per se are busy places.'

per stirpes

Meaning

Latin: by the branches; by the stocks of descent. Used in the law of wills to indicate that a gift is to be distributed by family group rather than by headcount (*per capita*). For example:

- A testator makes a gift *per stirpes* (a 'stirpital gift') 'to the children of A and of B'. Assume that A has 4 children and B has 2 children. The gift will go equally to each group. Therefore, each child of A takes ¼ of one-half; each child of B takes ½ of one-half. In contrast, under a *per capita* gift, each child would take ⅙ of the whole gift.
- A testator (T) has two children (A and B), each of whom also has two children. A predeceases T, and is survived by his two children. B survives T. Distribution of T's estate *per stirpes* will give an equal share to each family. Therefore, A's children take that family's one-half share between them; B takes the whole of his family's share. (Example given by Lord Hope in *Sammut v Manzi* [2008] UKPC 58; [2009] 1 WLR 1834, [28].)

Plain-language equivalent

Per stirpes is 'not an expression that is likely to occur to a testator today when he is telling his lawyer how he wishes his estate to be distributed' (*Sammut v Manzi* [2009] 1 WLR 1834; [2008] UKPC 58, [25], Lord Hope). Therefore (to take up a suggestion by Lord Hope) prefer an alternative expression such as 'by family', or 'by family group'.

Further reading

'Per Stirpes', in *Law Words* (Centre for Plain Legal Language, University of Sydney, 1995) 59; www.clarity-international.net/plain-language-resources/general-resources/ (cautioning care in substituting a plain-language alternative)

See also **FOREIGN (NON-ENGLISH) WORDS AND PHRASES**; **per capita**.

per totam curiam

Latin: by the whole court. Used in law reports to indicate that all the judges agreed on a conclusion. The Latin is no more accurate than the English—so prefer the English.

See also **per curiam.**

percentage

See **per cent**.

PERCENTAGES

Normally expressed using the symbol %, not the word 'percent' (or 'per cent'): eg, '5%' (*not* '5 percent'; *not* '5 per cent').

See also **NUMBERS**; **per cent**.

perform and discharge

A lawyer's pairing, as where a party to a contract promises to *perform and discharge* obligations. *Perform* alone will suffice—and is better than *discharge* alone, because *discharge* carries connotations of bringing a contract to an end under the doctrine of frustration or for breach or repudiation: *McDonald v Dennys Lascelles Ltd* (1933) 48 CLR 457.

See also **observe and perform**.

periculo

Latin: at (someone's) peril. Usages include: *suo periculo* (at his or her peril); *periculo petentis* (at the petitioner's peril; eg, granting leave to appeal at an applicant's peril). Prefer a plain-English translation:

> 'Their Lordships … are clearly of opinion that [leave to appeal] was only granted *periculo petentis* [prefer: *at the petitioner's* (ie, *applicant's*) *peril*], and that the point of whether leave upon a full knowledge of the circumstances should have been granted is still open.' [*Windsor, Essex and Lake Shore Rapid Railway v Nelles* [1915] AC 355, 360 (Lord Dunedin)]

period of time

Sometimes redundant

Period of time is often redundant and can be pruned:

- This can be done in a short ~~period of~~ time.
- This can be done in a short period ~~of time~~.
- The hirer may use the car for ~~a period of~~ 14 days.
- The purchaser is entitled to a reasonable ~~period of~~ time ~~in which~~ to prepare the deed of conveyance.

Note that, even after deleting 'period of', the expression *that period* can be a useful shorthand reference to an earlier period. For example:

> 'The notice must be given within ~~a period of~~ 12 months from the date of the breach. A notice given beyond *that period* is void.' [However, a better second sentence, omitting *period*, would be: 'A notice given any later is void.']

Sometimes useful

Contrast these two sentences:

1. 'You must give notice within 30 days of commencing proceedings.'
2. 'You must give notice *within the period of* 30 days of commencing proceedings.'

Can you give notice *before* the 30 days, or only during the 30-day window?

Version (1) might allow a *before* notice. In effect, '*within* 30 days' could mean '*not later than* 30 days', and 'not later than' logically does not preclude 'earlier than': *Earl of Morton's Trustees v Macdougall* [1944] SC 410.

But version (2) might preclude that argument: *within the period of 30 days* indicates a specific duration, with start date and end date, and may invalidate a notice given *before* the start date. However, an Australian appellate court (by majority) rejected this possible meaning, holding that an action to be taken under a particular statute 'within *the period of* [x] days' did not preclude the action being taken before the start of that period: *St John of God Health Care Inc v Austin* (2014) 46 WAR 208. A later appellate court, in a different Australian jurisdiction, followed this majority view, on the basis that it was not 'plainly wrong': *Woodside Energy Ltd v Zaghloul* [2015] FCAFC 135; (2015) 234 FCR 198, [41], [42].

An indefinite period?

Dictionary meanings of *period* include (to paraphrase) both 'time of indefinite duration' and 'time of defined duration'. Context will determine the intended meaning. For example:

> A statute empowered a judge when releasing a dangerous prisoner from custody to make a supervision order 'for the period stated in the order'. A judge made a supervision order 'until further order by the court'. Held on appeal that an order had to be for a definite period, and that the order in question did not meet this requirement: *Attorney-General v Van Dessel* [2006] QCA 285; [2007] 2 Qd R 1.

See also **within (a period from)**.

perjure[d] / perjurious

In principle, these words can be distinguished: *to perjure* means to lie under oath (hence the adjective *perjured*, as in 'perjured evidence'); *perjurious* means having the tendency to lie under oath. In practice, however, *perjurious* is sometimes used where *perjured* would be more accurate, as in the following two examples. But in any case, prefer the simpler *false* or *lying*.

- 'The only relevantly *perjurious* [sic: *perjured*(?); but prefer: *false*] statement was her claim regarding R's involvement.' [*CTG v R* [2011] VSCA 429, [50] (Maxwell P)]
- '[Would you] consider that to be a *perjurious* statement, a lie?' [Question put to witness in *Gersten v Law Society of New South Wales* (2001) 53 NSWLR 206; [2001] NSWSC 748, [68]. Prefer: 'Would you consider that to be a lie?' Or better still: 'Is that a lie?']

permit (verb)

When does a person *permit* an act? Clearly, actively consenting to someone doing an act is to *permit* it: *Hardcastle v Bielby* [1892] 1 QB 709; *Massey v Morris* [1894] 1 QB 412; *Ferrier v Wilson* (1906) 4 CLR 785. But do you *permit* an act if you stand by and refrain from taking steps within your power to stop it? The answer may depend on the nature of the act. For example, in *Tophams Ltd v Sefton* [1967] 1 AC 50 a restrictive covenant required the owner of land not to *permit* building on the land; the House of Lords held that the owner did not breach the covenant merely by selling the land to a developer.

See also **allow**.

persistently

When is conduct *persistent*? Clearly, it is matter of fact and degree, making the meaning of the word notoriously context-dependent. The concept is of conduct with a degree of repetition—but repeated how many times? To *persistently* fail to discharge parental obligations implies repetition so many times that the conduct is more or less permanent: *Re D* [1973] Fam 209. But to *persistently* make unmeritorious applications to the court may require only three such applications: *CFC 26 Ltd v Brown Shipley & Co Ltd* [2017] EWHC 1594; [2017] 1 WLR 4589. If possible, specify how many times the conduct must be repeated.

person

Meaning

In normal usage, *person* means 'human being'; to describe an inanimate object as a *person* would be unusual. However, legal usage divides *persons* into two categories: (1) *natural persons* (ie, human beings); and (2) *artificial persons* (also called *juristic persons*). An artificial (juristic) person is an entity recognised by the law as being separate from the persons (natural or artificial) who comprise the entity; examples are corporations, courts, tribunals, and some associations.

The common law does not regard an unincorporated association as a *person*, but statute may treat it as one (as in *Worthing Rugby Football Club Trustees v IRC* [1987] 1 WLR 1057). It is unlikely that a 'court' is a *person*, at least in the context of a statute prohibiting a *person* from publishing court decisions that contain proscribed information: *Heath v R* [2014] VSCA 319; (2014) 45 VR 154. Whether the Crown is a *person* varies with the statutory context. For example:

- the Crown is not a *person* for the purposes of taxation legislation: *IRC v Whitworth Park Coal Co Ltd* [1958] Ch 792.
- the Crown is a *person* for the purposes of workers' compensation legislation: *Commissioner for Government Transport v Gumley* [1964–65] NSWR 1564, 1567

Clarifying definitions

Sometimes it is unclear whether a document or statute intends *person* to include an 'artificial' person such as a corporation. It then becomes a question of gleaning meaning from context: is the 'person' required to do acts (eg, drive a car) or suffer consequences of the kind that only individuals can do or suffer (eg, imprisonment)? Viewed this way, 'person' could include a corporation in one provision of a statute but not in another: eg, *Boyd v Croydon Railway Co* (1848) 4 Bing NC 669; 132 ER 946; *Ex parte Sperring* (1890) 11 NSWLR 407.

To clarify doubt over meaning, statutes and documents often define *person*—eg, to include a corporation, partnership, and so on. Some definitions are exhaustive; some are briefer. For example:

- **person** includes any individual, company, corporation, unincorporated association or body (including a partnership, trust, fund, joint venture or consortium), government, state, agency, organisation or other entity, whether or not having separate legal personality.
- **person** includes an individual or a corporation.

In some jurisdictions, statute provides that in deeds, contracts, wills, and other instruments, *person* includes a corporation: see, eg, *Law of Property Act 1925*, s 61; *Conveyancing Act 1919* (NSW), s 181. However, provisions of this kind are not trouble-free, because almost always they contain the qualification 'unless the context requires otherwise' (or similar). The qualification may take an entity out of the definition, as in these examples:

- A provision in tax legislation requiring a *person* to attend and give evidence did not apply to a corporation: *Smorgon v Federal Commissioner of Taxation* (1976) 134 CLR 475 (Stephen J)
- A provision that a *person* could hold an auctioneer's licence did not extend to a corporation: *Gibbs v Clark* [1985] VR 778.

A gender-neutral term

Person is gender-neutral. Nevertheless, some old cases held that, for the purposes of certain legislation, *person* did not include females. For example, the Supreme Court of Canada held that women were not 'persons' entitled to become Canadian Senators: *Edwards v Attorney-General for Canada* [1928] SCR 276 (Sup Ct of Canada); overturned by the Privy Council, [1930] AC 124. Many egregious examples involved the practice of law itself:

- Women were not 'persons' able to sit law qualification exams: *Petition for Admission of a Woman to Law Agents' Examination* (1901) 45 Sol J 673.
- Women could not become barristers, because they were not 'persons' within the legal profession legislation: *Re French* (1912) 1 DLR 80.
- Women could not become solicitors, because they were not 'persons' within the requirements for admission: *Bebb v Law Society* [1914] 1 Ch 286.

Can you lighten-up?

In some contexts, *person* adds unneeded formality. A lighter word (such as *people*) may suffice. If so, prefer the lighter word.

Compare:

- 'This regulation applies to *persons* under 18 years of age.' / 'This regulation applies to *people* under 18 years of age.' / 'This regulation applies to everyone under 18.'
- 'Lifts must have a carrying capacity of 24 persons.' / 'Lifts must be able to carry 24 people.'

See also **artificial person; individual; juristic person; legal person; natural person**.

person aggrieved

A wide-ranging description: the meaning of *aggrieved* could range from 'slightly inconvenienced' to 'seriously injured'. In law, the general sense is of someone whose rights or interests have been affected. So, for example, a tenant or licensee of premises might be a *person aggrieved* by the owner's failure to keep the premises in repair, but a mere 'busybody' would not: *Watkins v Aged Merchant Seamen's Homes Ltd* [2018] EWHC 2410, [41]–[48] (Kerr J).

Further reading

Daniel Greenberg (ed), *Stroud's Judicial Dictionary*, 9th edn (Sweet & Maxwell, 2017), under 'person aggrieved' (case law)

person interested

See **interested person**.

personal estate

Used alone, *estate* can mean land ('real estate') or it can mean property generally (eg, 'all my estate', 'deceased estate'). The addition of *personal* narrows the meaning: *personal estate* is a synonym for *personal property*—ie, property that is *not* real property. However, context may compel a different interpretation, particularly in the law of wills; thus, a devise of 'all my personal estate' can in appropriate circumstances be effective to pass real estate: *Re Cox* [1967] Qd R 173.

See also **estate or interest; personal property; real property**.

personal property

In strict legal usage, *personal* property is property that is not *real* property—ie, property that is not land. However, there are two qualifications. First, for historical reasons, the common law treats leasehold interests in land as personal property, not real property. Second, *personal* can mean simply *my own*—and so, *personal property* can mean *property that I own* (including real property). Thus, a gift by will of 'all my personal property' may be effective to pass real property: see *Re Wass* (1906) 95 LT 758.

See also **personal estate**; **real property**.

personal representative

Usually synonymous with *legal personal representative*—ie, the person appointed as executor or administrator of a deceased estate. However, in certain (limited) contexts, *personal representative* can mean a person's descendants, or even the children of those descendants: *Rainford v Knowles* (1888) 59 LT 359 (Kay J). If doubt is possible about the intended meaning, always clarify.

See also **legal representative**.

personate / impersonate

Of these two synonyms, *impersonate* is the more common; most readers would find *personate* quaint. However, *personate* is still found in legal usage, particularly in some criminal statutes. For modern readers, prefer *impersonate*. For example:

- *Criminal Code* 1985 (Canada), s 403:

  403(1) Everyone commits an offence who fraudulently *personates* [prefer: *impersonates*] another person, living or dead, …

  (c) with intent to cause disadvantage to the person being *personated* [prefer: *impersonated*] or another person; …
- '[T]he applicant asked that a further 34 offences … be taken into account. These [included] 11 offences of fraudulent *personation*, and one count of *impersonating* a police officer.' [*Ryan v R* [2011] NSWCCA 250, [4] (Simpson J, staying faithful to the statutory text for each offence)]

peruse

Historically, meaning 'read closely'; in modern usage, increasingly meaning 'read rapidly' or 'scan'. Now often paired with 'quickly', as if to perfect the departure from the historical meaning:

- 'If, on a *quick perusal* of the material then available, the court thinks that it discloses what might on further consideration turn out to be an arguable case in favour of granting to the applicant the relief claimed, it ought … to give him leave to apply for that relief.' [*R v Inland Revenue Commissioners* [1982] AC 617, 644 (Lord Diplock)]
- 'While some aspects of the juridical nature, origin and incidents of servitudes in Scotland are different from those of easements in England and Wales, there are many aspects of similarity, as can be appreciated even from a *quick perusal* [of two two leading textbooks].' [*Moncrieff v Jamieson* [2007] UKHL 42; [2007] 1 WLR 2620, [111] (Lord Neuberger)]

pessimi exempli

Latin (sometimes *exempli pessimi*): example of the worst kind. In law, often used in the sense of setting a bad precedent. To retain the Latin in the face of an adequate English translation indeed sets a poor example:

- 'It would in my opinion be *pessimi exempli* [prefer: *the worst kind of example*] if, when an employer had exacted a covenant deliberately framed in unreasonably wide terms, the Courts were to come to his assistance …' [*Mason v Providential Clothing & Supply Co Ltd* [1913] AC 724, 745 (Lord Moulton)]
- '[I]t seems to me that it would be *pessimi exempli* [prefer: *setting the worst precedent*] to say that, by the side wind of a very slight alteration … in a consolidating Act, Parliament intended to produce … a very substantial change in the law.' [*Re Dodwell & Co Ltd's Trust* [1979] Ch 301, 310 (Walton J)]
- 'To fail in this would be *exempli pessimi* [prefer: *an example of the worst kind*] in any case, for it would be not law but despotism …' [*R v Hibble* [1920] HCA 83; (1920) 28 CLR 456, 468 (Isaacs and Rich JJ)]

phenomenon

Singular *phenomenon* (not 'phenomena'); plural *phenomena* (not 'phenomenons').

PHRASAL ADJECTIVES

See **HYPHENS**.

piece or parcel [of land]

A lawyer's habitual pairing. The sense is of a separately identifiable portion of land: *Josh v Josh* (1858) 5 CB NS 454, 466; 141 ER 185, 190. Either *piece* or *parcel* will suffice: in this context, the words are synonymous.

PINPOINT REFERENCES

See **CITATION OF BOOKS AND JOURNAL ARTICLES; CITATION OF CASES; CITATION OF LEGISLATION**.

placitum

Latin: a paragraph or division; a principle or maxim; plural: *placita*. Sometimes used to refer to heads of power in a Constitution (as in *Nelungaloo Pty Ltd v Commonwealth of Australia* [1951] AC 34, PC) or, more prosaically, numbered considerations for a court to consider (as in *Police v Siaosi* [2014] SASC 131; (2014) 120 SASR 308—permitted contents of intervention orders).

PLAIN ENGLISH

See **PLAIN LANGUAGE**.

PLAIN LANGUAGE

The term

'Plain language' has come to describe a writing style that is clear, precise, and readily understandable by its intended audience. When the language is English, it is sometimes called 'plain English'. Hazlitt described it as the 'truly English style':

> 'To write a genuine, familiar or truly English style, is to write as any one would speak in common conversation, who had a thorough command and choice of words, or who could discourse with ease, force and perspicuity, setting aside all pedantic and oratorical flourishes': William Hazlitt, *Table-Talk* (Henry Colburn, 1822) Essay VIII, 'On Familiar Style', 185.

The word *plain* might suggest a kindergarten form of communication—an oversimplified language, stripped of vocabulary and deficient in style. But this misunderstands the true nature of 'plain language' and understates its benefits.

Plain language attempts to convey the writer's message in a way that the intended (and moderately interested) reader can understand on a first reading. At the micro-level, it focuses on choice of vocabulary—by using words that are familiar (not rare), concrete (not abstract), and precise (not vague). At the macro-level, it focuses on the way in which material is structured—especially by front-loading key material. And always it focuses on presentation—by using plentiful headings, readable typeface, generous spacing between lines, and thoughtful use of white space to avoid a cramped appearance.

Definitions of 'plain language'

Defining 'plain language' is difficult, because the concept involves many elements. However, most definitions incorporate two key elements: (1) language that is straightforward, direct, concise, and (so far as the subject matter allows) idiomatic; and (2) structure that incorporates thoughtful organisation, helpful layout and design, and (where relevant) aids to comprehension such as notes, examples, and headings. Element (2) shows that plain language goes beyond mere word-use, and extends to the way information is structured for the reader.

Definitions of 'plain language' (or 'plain English') include the following:

Non-judicial definitions

- The 'idiomatic and grammatical use of English that most effectively presents ideas to the reader'. [Bryan A Garner, *Garner's Dictionary of Legal Usage*, 3rd edn (Oxford University Press, 2011), 678]
- Language 'that is clear, direct, and straightforward. It … allows readers to concentrate on the message conveyed, not on the difficulty of the language used. … Plain language uses the right word for the right occasion and does not use unnecessary words. … Communicating in plain language involves careful text presentation. … The result is a text that is well organised with typestyle, layout, page colour, line length, and indentations all designed to communicate the message in the clearest possible way.' [David Elliott, 'A Global Perspective' [1991] *Michigan Bar Journal* (June) 562 (citations and paragraph breaks omitted)]
- A 'flexible and efficient writing style that readers can understand in one reading. It combines clear, concise expression, an effective structure and good document design.' [Plain English Foundation (Australia): plainenglishfoundation.com/index.php/plain-english/whatisplainenglish]
- The 'expression of concepts in clear and direct language and in as simple a manner *as circumstances permit.*' [Michael Hwang, 'Plain English in Commercial Contracts' (1990) 32 *Malaysia Law Review* 296, 297 (emphasis in original)]

- 'A communication is in plain language if its wording, structure, and design are so clear that the intended audience can easily find what they need, understand what they find, and use that information.' [International Plain Language Federation; see plainlanguagenetwork.org/plain-language/what-is-plain-language/]

Judicial definitions

- 'Plain English is, in our view, clear and precise language which is easy to understand and which communicates its message effectively. It is not a simplified form of English. It puts the reader first and avoids archaic words, jargon, unnecessary technical expressions and complex language. Plain English is not just about words. It means using plain language to express ideas so that they make sense to the reader and designing documents so that information is easy to find and understand. ... Using plain English does not mean sacrificing precision.' [*Re Award Simplification Decision* (1997) 75 IR 272, 305]
- 'Clear plain language' in a costs agreement between lawyer and client requires that the 'language of the agreement ... can be understood by the ordinary reader after applying reasonable effort.' [*Russells v McCardel* [2014] VSC 287 [77], Bell J). The judge expanded on the elements in the definition, at [78]–[94]:
  - An agreement can be in 'clear plain language' despite containing some inaccuracies and legal errors.
  - An agreement as a whole can be in clear plain language even though some clauses in it are not. It depends on the relative importance of the clauses that are not in clear plain language.
  - Plain words do not of themselves guarantee plain meaning. The overall meaning of clauses, read in the context of the whole document, must also be clear.]

Statutory definitions

While some statutes mandate 'plain language' for certain types of documents, very few statutes define it. A rare exception is the following:

> '[Information is in "plain language" if] an ordinary consumer of the class of persons for whom the [information] is intended, with average literacy skills and minimal experience as a consumer of the relevant goods or services, could be expected to understand the content, significance and import of the [information] without undue effort, having regard to—
>
> (a) the context, comprehensiveness and consistency of the [information];
>
> (b) the organisation, form and style of the [information];
>
> (c) the vocabulary, usage and sentence structure of the [information]; and
>
> (d) the use of any illustrations, examples, headings or other aids to reading and understanding.'
>
> [*Consumer Protection Act 2008* (South Africa), s 22(2)]

Several US jurisdictions mandate plain language for consumer contracts, and give guidance on meeting plain-language standards. For example, Connecticut requires plain language in consumer contracts, and offers drafters a choice between a formulaic test (prescribing matters such as sentence-length, paragraph-length, line-length, and average number of syllables per word) and an elements test (concentrating on structure, design, and vocabulary): *Connecticut General Statutes*, § 42-152, 'Consumer contract to be written in plain language'. Pennsylvania requires consumer contracts to be 'written, organised and designed so that they are easy to read and understand', and lays out 'language guidelines' and 'visual guidelines': *Plain Language Consumer Contract Act*, Pa Stat Ann Title 73, §§ 2201, 2205.

A new term: 'transparency'

Some modern statutes use a new term, 'transparency'. Perhaps the aim is to avoid connotations of 'simplistic' language sometimes associated (wrongly) with 'plain' language. But whatever the reason, statutes that impose a requirement of 'transparency' in communications are, in effect, mandating 'plain language'. For example:

> **68 Requirement for transparency**
>
> (1) A trader must ensure that a written term of a consumer contract, or a consumer notice in writing, is transparent.
>
> (2) A consumer notice is transparent for the purposes of subsection (1) if it is expressed in plain and intelligible language and it is legible.
>
> [*Consumer Rights Act 2015*, s 68]

Judicial taunts

Some judges, seeking Canute-like to stem the incoming tide of plain language, have offered derisory descriptions of 'plain language'. They include:

- 'the language of the pop songs', with attendant 'vulgarity' and 'obscurity': *GM & AM Pearce and Co Pty Ltd v RGM Australia Pty Ltd* (1986) 16 ACLC 429, 432 (Callaway JA)
- 'grotesque' (speaking of the expression 'must not'): *Halwood Corporation Ltd v Roads Corporation* [1998] 2 VR 439, 445–46 (Tadgell JA)
- 'confused thought and split infinitives': *NRMA Insurance Ltd v Collier* (1996) 9 ANZ Insurance Cases 76,717, 76,721 (Meagher JA).

Also, some judges seem to assume that plain language is necessarily inconsistent with precision. For example, in interpreting a plain-language car insurance policy, Lord Hodge said:

> 'The policy booklet is written in plain language for the benefit of the policyholder and lacks the precision which one might expect from a detailed commercial contract. For example, the statement in clause 1a that [the insurer] will give cover for the insured's liability "if you have an accident in your vehicle" if read strictly would not cover an accident caused by the insured opening his car door and stepping out of the car.' [*R & S Pilling v UK Insurance Ltd* [2019] UKSC 16, [48]; [2019] 2 WLR 1015]

But plain language and precision are not necessarily inconsistent. Plain-language documents need not be unclear or ambiguous. The fault, if any, lies with the drafter, not with the plain-language style.

Judicial support

Published surveys in several countries show that a large majority of judges favour plain language in statutes, contracts, and pleadings. Indeed, many judges themselves have written articles and books extolling the virtues of plain language in law. A number have written specifically about the advantages of plain-language judgments. (See 'Selected publications by judges favouring plain-language judgments', in *Further reading*, below.)

Benefits of plain language

Efficiency

Evidence abounds that plain-language statutes and documents are more 'efficient' than traditionally worded ones. Because they are easier to read, they save time for both lawyers and non-lawyers. These benefits—particularly economic savings—are well documented in studies in the UK, US, Australia and Canada. (See 'Selected studies showing increased efficiency of plain-language documents', in *Further reading*, below.)

Disclosing errors

Plain language helps expose errors. In contrast, the traditional style of legal writing—particularly that 'torrential style' that equates verbosity with precision—tends to hide inconsistencies and ambiguities. Errors are harder to find in dense, convoluted prose. Clear drafting demands clear thinking, requiring drafters to lay bare their ideas—for themselves as well as for their readers.

Image of legal profession

Plain language improves the public image of lawyers. That image has been tarnished by the legal profession's fondness for legalese. Surveys show that readers find legal language largely incomprehensible. These surveys also reveal a widely held public perception that lawyers are indifferent about whether they communicate clearly. (See 'Selected studies of the effects of language on legal profession's image', in *Further reading*, below.)

Difficulties in moving to plain language

Do not underestimate the difficulties involved in moving to plain legal drafting. Here are some:

Cost

It takes time and skill to redraft documents in plain language. Who is going to pay for that work and expertise?

Loss of precedent-value

Long-used legal words or phrases may have the benefit of judicial exegesis. Will it be sacrificed in the rewrite—and is there time to research whether it matters?

Changes in substance

Changes in wording can lead to changes in substance. Will the move to plain language have that result? For example, if the redraft of a lease omits the hallowed term 'exclusive possession', will a mere licence result? If the redraft of a loan agreement omits the word 'mortgage', will some lesser kind of security result? If the default-rate clause in a loan agreement is simplified, will it create a penalty? These are merely some of the myriad examples that may arise. (As to these and similar examples, see **PARTICIPLES (Redrafting participle phrases and relative clauses)**; **TERMS OF ART (Terms of art and key legal concepts)**.)

Closer judicial scrutiny

Being shorn of surplus words, a plain-language document runs the risk that every word will undergo judicial scrutiny—a scrutiny perhaps more intense than that exercised on traditionally drafted documents, where drafters (and their clients) may seek refuge in the sheer weight of verbiage. Shorn of superfluidity, every word in a plain-language document risks close scrutiny (as in Examples 1 and 2, below). On the other hand, a judge might allow a plain-language document more scope for improvisation, given its emphasis on communicating to its intended audience (as in Example 3).

Examples

1. A lease drafted in plain language obliged the landlord to keep the premises in 'good condition and repair'. Held, this wording imposed not one (composite) obligation, but two (separate) obligations. Failure to keep in 'good condition' could be a breach, even though there may have been no failure to 'repair' (which carries a separate—and technical—sense in law): *Welsh v Greenwich Borough Council* [2000] 49 EG 118.
2. A will required the beneficiary of a life estate to keep the property (a house) 'in good repair'. This (the judge considered) required more than merely keeping in 'repair'—otherwise, 'good' would have no work to do. The requirement therefore included work that might result in the property being 'fixed and renewed, or brought up to a standard that is better than the standard which was in existence at the time' the life interest began: *Nomchong v Vey-Cox* [2019] NSWSC 1072, [68]–[70].
3. An AirBnB agreement, drafted in 'commonplace terms' (to quote the judge), specified a 'check out time'. Did 'check out time' sufficiently indicate that the guest's right to occupation expired at that time? Held, yes. When interpreting a document drafted in 'commonplace terms', the court must focus on substance, rather than on the presence or absence of technical language; and 'check out time' was a sufficiently clear indication that the occupant (whether technically a tenant or a mere licensee) must vacate by that time: *Swan v Uecker* [2016] VSC 313, [66] (Croft J)

Going too far?

Plain language serves an important purpose: to allow users to read and understand text as easily and efficiently as possible. But the language of legal documents creates solemn rights and obligations. Readers need to take the document seriously. Does there come a point on the spectrum of simplicity where the language is so casual that readers wonder wheter to take the document seriously?

Example 1: Will

'I leave my property between my children, I hope they will be virtuous and independent, that they will worship God, and not black coats.' (*Nichols v Nichols* (1814) 2 Phill 180; 161 ER 1113; punctuation as in original.)

[The court refused to grant Probate, because the evidence showed that the 'testator' wrote the 'will' in jest, never intending it to be his will, but only to ridicule the tortuous language of lawyers.]

Example 2: Will

'I am John Doe. This is my will. See my signature on this will. See my witnesses' signatures.

I revoke all my other wills and codicils.

See Sam Brown. I want him to be my personal representative. Please court, make him my personal representative. Sam is honest, I hope, and fair, I hope.

Sam won't serve? See Bob Baker. Bob will be personal representative.'

[Opening paragraphs from 'The Plain English Will', in Barbara Child, *Drafting Legal Documents: Principles and Practices*, 2nd edn (West, 1992) 260]

Example 3: Disclaimer

'We don't claim Interactive EasyFlow is good for anything—if you think it is, great, but it's up to you to decide. If Interactive EasyFlow doesn't work, tough. If you lose a million because Interactive EasyFlow messes up it's you that's out a million, not us. If you don't like this disclaimer, tough. We reserve the right to do the absolute minimum provided by law, up to and including nothing.

This is basically the same disclaimer that comes with all software packages; but ours is in plain English and theirs is in legalese.

We didn't really want to include any disclaimer at all, but our lawyers insisted. We tried to ignore them but they threatened us with the attack shark at which point we relented.'

[HavenTree Software Ltd, makers of Interactive EasyFlow; as reproduced in 'Right to the Point', *Canberra Times* (Canberra, Australia, 18 February 1991) 18]

Further reading

Selected judicial surveys showing support for plain language

- R Benson, 'Plain English Comes to Court' (1986) 13 *Litigation* 21
- Bryan Garner, 'Interviews with United States Supreme Court Justices' (2010) 13 *Scribes Journal of Legal Writing* 1–182
- S Harrington and J Kimble, 'Survey: Plain English Wins Every Which Way' (1987) 66 *Michigan Bar Journal* 1024
- J Kimble and J Prokop, 'Strike Three for Legalese', reprinted in J Kimble, *Lifting the Fog of Legalese* (Carolina Academic Press, 2006) 3
- Barbara Child, 'Language Preferences of Judges and Lawyers: A Florida Survey' (1990) 64 *Florida Bar Journal* 32
- Kristen K Robbins Tiscione, 'The Inside Scoop: What Federal Judges Really Think about the Way Lawyers Write' (2002) 8 *Journal of Legal Writing Institute* 257
- S Flammer, 'Writing to Persuade Judges' (2011) 90 *Michigan Bar Journal* 50
- K O'Brien, 'Judicial Attitudes to Plain Language and the Law' (2009) 32 *Australian Bar Review* 204.

Selected publications by judges showing support for plain language

- Kirby J (Australian High Court), 'Ten Commandments for Plain Language in Law' (2010) 33 *Australian Bar Review* 10
- de Jersey CJ (Queensland Supreme Court), Foreword to *Clear and Precise: Writing Skills for Today's Lawyer* (Queensland Law Society, 2000)
- McLachlin CJ (Canadian Supreme Court), 'Preserving Public Confidence in the Courts and the Legal Profession' (2003) 29 *Manitoba Law Journal* 277, 284–85
- Painter J (formerly Ohio 1st District Court of Appeals, later United Nations Appeals Tribunal): *The Legal Writer: 40 Rules for the Art of Legal Writing*, 4th edn (Jarndyce & Jarndyce, 2009)
- Dato' Syed Ahmid Idid (Malaysia), *Writing of Judgments: A Practical Guide for Courts and Tribunals* (LexisNexis 2010).

Selected publications by judges favouring plain-language judgments

- Kirby J (Australia), 'On the Writing of Judgments' (1990) 64 *Australian Law Journal* 691
- Doyle J (Australia), 'Judgment Writing: Are There Needs for Change?' (1999) 73 *Australian Law Journal* 737
- Mailhot and Carnwath JJ (Canada), *Decisions, Decisions … A Handbook for Judicial Decisions* (Éditions Yvon Blais, 1998)
- McLachlin CJ (Canada), 'Legal Writing: Some Tools' (2001) 39 *Alberta Law Review* 695
- Keane J (NZ), 'Decisions that Convince' (2004) 52 *Clarity* 26
- Lord Neuberger (UK), 'Open Justice Unbound?', Judicial Studies Board Annual Lecture 2011, at www.judiciary.gov.uk/Resources/JCO/Documents/Speeches/mr-speech-jsb-lecture-march-2011.pdf
- Laskin J (Canada), 'Teaching Judgment Writing in Canada', *Clarity* 66 (Nov 2011) 17.

US examples are collected in Bryan Garner, 'Judges on Effective Writing' (2005) 84 *Michigan Bar Journal* 44.

Selected studies showing increased 'efficiency' of plain-language documents

- Joseph Kimble, *Writing for Dollars, Writing to Please* (Carolina Academic Press, 2012) part 5, documenting 50 studies
- G Mills and M Duckworth, *The Gains from Clarity: A Research Report on the Effects of Plain-language Documents* (Law Foundation of NSW, 1996)
- Robert Eagleson, 'Plain English—A Boon for Lawyers' [1991] *The Second Draft* (Legal Writing Institute) 12 (time-saving benefits for lawyers)
- J Davis, 'Protecting Consumers from Overdisclosure and Gobbledygook: An Empirical Look at the Simplification of Consumer Credit Contracts' (1977) 63 *Virginia Law Review* 841 (benefits for consumers)
- V Charrow and R Charrow, 'Making Legal Language Understandable: A Pyscholinguistic Study of Jury Instructions' (1979) 79 *Columbia Law Review* 1306 (benefits for potential jurors)
- M Cutts, *Lucid Law* (Plain Language Commission, 1994) 22–26 (law students)
- P Knight, Clearly Better Drafting: A Report to the Plain English Campaign on Testing two versions of the South African Human Rights Commission Act 1995 (UK Plain English Campaign, Feb 1966) (lawyers and non-lawyers)
- Neil James and Greg Moriarty, 'Access starts with the precedent: Evaluating the language of leases' (2020) 81 *Clarity Journal* 34
- Robert Eagleson, 'Efficiency in Legal Drafting', in David St Kelly (ed), *Essays on Legislative Drafting in Honour of JQ Ewens* (Adelaide University Press, 1990).

Contrary findings are reported by R Penman, 'Plain English: Wrong Solution to an Important Problem' (1992) 19 *Australian Journal of Communication* 3 (and see R Penman, 'Unspeakable Acts and Other Deeds: A Critique of Plain Legal Language' (1993) 7 *Information Design Journal* 121; and D Sless, 'The Plain English Problem' (1995) 3(4) *Australian Language Matters* 3). But some have criticised Penman's methods and findings—eg, B Coleman, 'Are Clarity and Precision Compatible Aims in Legal Drafting?' [1998] *Singapore Journal of Legal Studies* 395; 'Replies to Robyn Penman' [1994] *Rapport* (Summer) 8.

Selected studies of the effects of language on legal profession's image

- Ann Abraham, '*Pro Bono Publico*—Revisited' (2001) 4(1) *Legal Ethics* 12 (Ms Abraham was the UK Legal Services Ombudsman)
- Robert Benson, 'The End of Legalese: The Game Is Over' (1984–85) 13 *Review of Law and Social Change* 532
- Plain Language Institute of British Columbia, Preliminary Report, 'Critical Opinions: the Public's View of Legal Documents' (1992) 18, 26

General materials

- Competition and Markets Authority 37: 'Unfair Contract Terms Guidance' (CMA 37, 31 July 2015), [2.42]–[2.61], [3.20]–[3.32] (requirement of 'transparency' in the *Consumer Rights Act 2015*)
- 'Federal Plain Language Guidelines' (being the official guidelines for the *Plain Writing Act*, 2010 (USA)); at www.plainlanguage.gov/guidelines/
- Rabeea Assy, 'Can the Law Speak Directly to its Subjects—The Limitation of Plain Language' (2011) 38 *Journal of Law and Society* 376 (plain language of itself is not sufficient for lay readers to understand complex legal issues)
- Bernard Belink and Christo Botha, 'Aspects of Legislative Drafting: Some South African Realities (or Plain Language Is Not Always Plain Sailing)' (2007) 28 *Statute Law Review* 34 (the many problems in making legislation understandable in South Africa)

- Peter Butt, *Modern Legal Drafting*, 3rd edn (Cambridge University Press, 2013) [3.76]–[3.87] (drafting difficulties inherent in plain language); ch 4 (benefits of drafting in plain language)
- Paul Clark, 'Plain Legal Language' (2019) 83 *Conveyancer and Property Lawyer* 4 (experiences in developing plain-language precedents)
- David Crump, 'Against Plain English: The Case for a Functional Approach to Legal Document Preparation' (2002) 33 *Rutgers Law Journal* 713 (plain language is important in 'persuasion documents' such as briefs, but not so important in 'preservation documents', which record legal rights and are likely to remain unread unless and until an issue arises)
- Adam Feldman, 'Counting on Quality: The Effect of Merits Brief Quality on Supreme Court Opinion Content' (2016) 94 *Denver University Law Review* 43 (statistical evidence that US Supreme Court judgments are more likely to quote verbatim from submissions that are expressed in plain language)
- Jack Stark, 'Plain Language', *The Legislative Lawyer* (June 2012), arguing against using plain language in legislation; at www.ncsl.org/legislators-staff/legislative-staff/research-editorial-legal-and-committee-staff/june-2012-plain-language.aspx. Rejoinder by Joseph Kimble, 'Wrong—Again—About Plain Language', *The Legislative Lawyer* (December 2012) at www.ncsl.org/legislators-staff/legislative-staff/research-editorial-legal-and-committee-staff/lsss-wrong-again-about-plain-language.aspx

See also **ADVICE (FORM OF)**; **AUDIENCE**; **CLAUSE STRUCTURE**; **DOCUMENT STRUCTURE**; **FONTS**; **JARGON**; **LEGALESE**; **penalty**; **READABILITY TESTS**; **REDRAFTING IN PLAIN ENGLISH**; **repair**; **SIMPLER WORDS AND PHRASES**; **TERMS OF ART**.

PLAIN LEGAL LANGUAGE

See **PLAIN LANGUAGE**.

PLANS

Plans can convey information more effectively than words. Legal drafters conventionally use plans to identify land in conveyances, leases, and transfers of part of the land in a registered title. But plans are also suitable for many other kinds of legal documents, including commercial contracts, pleadings, and wills.

Inaccurate plans

Inaccurate plans are a fertile source of litigation. So too are plans that are accurate enough for some purposes, but insufficiently precise for the particular task in hand. Conveyancing plans in England and Wales are often insufficiently accurate to describe the property: Theodore BF Ruoff et al (eds), *Ruoff and Roper on the Law and Practice of Registered Conveyancing* (Sweet & Maxwell, looseleaf, 1996) [4-01]. The English Court of Appeal has warned conveyancers against using plans on a scale too small to warrant precision: *Scarfe v Adams* [1981] 1 All ER 843, 845 (Cumming-Bruce LJ).

Discrepancy between plan and words

In an instrument (such as a conveyance or a lease), where a discrepancy exists between the words describing the property (the 'parcels clause') and a plan describing the property, which prevails: the words or the plan?

The starting point is always the document's terminology. For example:

- Where the words state that the property is 'more particularly described in the plan' (or similar), the plan usually prevails: *Eastwood v Ashton* [1915] AC 900, 920 (HL).
- Where the plan is expressed to be 'for identification purposes only' (or similar), the words usually prevail: *Hopgood v Brown* [1955] 1 WLR 213, 228 (CA); *Neilson v Poole* (1969) 20 P & CR 909; *Wigginton and Milner Ltd v Winster Engineering Ltd* [1978] 1 WLR 1462 (CA); *Johnson v Shaw* [2004] 1 P & CR 10, 133, 138 (CA). However, this assumes that the words describe the property with sufficient certainty. If they do not, the court may be driven back to the plan; and if the plan does not help, then the court may admit extrinsic evidence to identify the property (as in *Wood v Hudson Industrial Services Ltd* [2012] EWCA Civ 599). This evidence may include topographical features: *Alan Wibberley Building Ltd v Insley* [1999] 1 WLR 894, 896 (Lord Hoffmann).

As a practical matter, where the answer is unclear, courts normally hold that the words prevail over the plan: *Druce v Druce* [2004] 1 P & CR 26, 433 (CA).

See also **MAPS AND DIAGRAMS; for the purposes of identification only**.

pleaded / pled

In former times, *pled* was reasonably common, before succumbing to *pleaded*. But *pled* has been making a comeback for some time (particularly among Scots-trained lawyers), as the following examples show:

- '[Counsel] *pled*, and *pled* briefly but strenuously, in favour of a principle of elasticity …' [*Maclaine v Gatty* [1921] 1 AC 376, 393 (Lord Shaw)]
- 'Moreover in light of the way the case was *pled* the Court of Appeal felt that they were not able to take account of any duty which the employer might have had to take care of the children.' [*Lister v Hesley Hall Ltd* [2001] UKHL 22; [2002] 1 AC 215, [49] (Lord Clyde)]
- 'I would have thought it appropriate to allow the claim in contract also to go to proof even if I had had more doubts about whether homologation had been properly *pled*.' [*Hamilton v Ford* [2007] CSOH 15, [19] (Lord Glennie)]
- 'The appellants *pled* not guilty at the first diet, and the case was adjourned for trial.' [*McLean v Procurator Fiscal* [2001] UKPC D3; [2001] 1 WLR 2425, [5] (Lord Hope). Compare Lord Hobhouse, [75]: 'The appellants *pleaded* not guilty at the pleading diet'. The headnote writer at [2001] 1 WLR 2445 also uses *pleaded*.]

plenum

Latin: full; complete. In legal usage, *plenum* and its cognate forms are usually coupled with other Latin words to produce phrases or maxims, all of which can readily be translated into standard English—and which therefore should be so translated in the interests of readability. For example:

- *plena aetas*: full age
- *plena fides*: full faith; full confidence
- *plene administravit*: fully administered (an executor's or administrator's defence, concerning a deceased estate)
- *pleno jure*: with full right
- *plenum dominium*: full ownership
- *plenum rectum*: complete right.

plurality

General meaning

In general usage, *plurality* means simply 'the state of being many', or 'a large number', or 'majority' (ie, greater than one-half). It can also mean, less commonly, holding two or more posts (offices) at the same time. This latter meaning exists in law also: see,eg, *Re Macnamara* (1911) 104 LT 771 (holding two ecclesiastical benefices at the same time).

Legal meaning ('plurality judgment')

A *plurality* judgment is a joint judgment having the greatest number of judges in support of the decison, but not enough to constitute a majority of the court. The *plurality* (noun) is not necessarily the total number of judges who come to the final decision in the case, but rather the most who do so in a joint judgment. For example, in a five-judge court, if A, B, and C write a joint judgment in favour of the final decision, and D and E write separate judgments (or a joint judgment) reaching the same decision, then A, B, and C are the *plurality*. But if D and E dissent, then A, B, and C are the *majority* (not the *plurality*). If only E dissents (but D still writes a separate judgment), then A, B, C, and D together form the *majority*, with A, B, and C forming the *plurality*.

This use of *plurality* is comparatively recent in British case law, possibly first appearing in appellate courts in *Reynolds v Times Newspapers Ltd* [1998] 3 WLR 862, 906 (CA). It borrows from US usage. However, the US usage is slightly different and (it seems) not entirely consistent. Thus, some say that US *plurality* decisions occur when an opinion lacks enough votes to constitute a majority, but receives more votes than any other opinion: *Black's Law Dictionary*, ed Bryan A Garner, 8th edn (West, 2004) 1125. But others say that *plurality* decisions occur when a majority of Justices agree on the result in the case but fail to agree on a uniform rationale in support of the judgment: James F Spriggs and David R Stras, 'Explaining Plurality Decisions' (2011) 99 *Georgetown Law Journal* 515, 517. And yet others say that a *plurality* opinion is:

> 'an opinion announcing the judgment of the Court in a case in which a majority of the Court agrees in the result but there is no majority agreeing with the rationale by which that result is reached *and* in which there are more Members of the Court agreeing with the rationale in the opinion announcing the judgment than with any other rationale (dissenters are not counted in determining whether there is a plurality).' [*The Supreme Court's Style Guide* (ed Jack Metzler (InterAlias, 2016) X-10; emphasis in original]

PLURALS

See **SINGULAR / PLURAL.**

plus quam tolerabile

Latin: more than can reasonably be endured. There is no magic in the Latin, so prefer an English translation. For example:

- 'The critical question is whether what he was exposed to was *plus quam tolerabile* [prefer: *more than could reasonably be endured*] when due weight has been given to all the surrounding circumstances of the offensive conduct and its effects.' [*Watt v Jamieson* 1956 SC 56, 58 (Lord Clyde)]

- '[The textbook says] that the court will not be confined in adjusting the rights of the parties by any artificial rule that the loss must either be total or at least *plus quam tolerabile* [prefer: *more than could reasonably be endured*].' [*Lloyds TSB Foundation for Scotland v Lloyds Banking Group plc* [2013] UKSC 3, [42]; [2013] 1 WLR 366, 381 (Lord Hope)]

POLITENESS

Politeness is usually a virtue, including in legal writing. Most views can be expressed politely, even if strongly. Nor need politeness compromise clarity. Legal writing can be polite yet clear, civil yet unequivocal. That is the case, for example, in advices to clients, letters between adversaries, and pleadings. It is also the case in court judgments—even where a judge feels the need to criticise the views of another judge. A wise judge will temper the criticism—to make it direct but polite—using expressions such as 'with due respect', 'in my view [judge X is wrong]'. Occasionally, however, the desire to criticise overrides the prudence of politeness. Here are some Australian examples:

- 'It is not true, as Kirby J asserts …' [*Al-Kateb v Godwin* [2004] HCA 37, [55]; 219 CLR 562 (McHugh J)]
- 'The reasoning of the Court of Appeal [was] erroneous in parts, exaggerated in other parts, flawed in other ways. … The restitution basis [of the judgment] brought about an abrupt and violent collision with received principles without any assigned justification. [The decision was] unsupported by authority and flew in the face of seriously considered dicta uttered by a majority of this Court.' [*Farah Constructions Pty Ltd v Say-Dee Pty Ltd* [2007] HCA 22; 230 CLR 89, [99], [154], [158] (High Court of Australia). The Court directed these comments at the decision of the New South Wales Court of Appeal, which had sought to introduce into Australian law the doctrine of unjust enrichment.]

See also **HUMOUR; SARCASM.**

poll

See **deed poll**.

POPULAR CASE NAMES

See **CITATION OF CASES.**

portion

In general usage, a part. However, in the law of wills and settlements, a *portion* is a gift intended to set up a child in life or to make substantial provision for the child: *Re Cameron, deceased* [1999] Ch 386, 407 (Lindsay J).

Further reading

Halsbury's Laws of England, 'Settlements' (vol 91, 2019) [528]–[538] ('portions' in property settlements)

positive easement

See **negative easement**.

POSITIVES / NEGATIVES

Accentuate the positive

Prefer positive sentences

Where possible, express sentences in positive form rather than negative form. This is more than a matter of 'tone'—more than 'glass half-full' versus 'glass half-empty'. Almost always, positive-form sentences are easier to take in and understand than negative-form sentences. Compare the following examples:

Negative form	Positive form
You can't reach me until next Monday.	I'm available from next Monday.
Our office remains closed until Friday.	We re-open on Friday.
A person who is not a partner must not sign a letter to a client.	Only partners can sign letters to clients.
We cannot accept majority jury verdicts of 10 or fewer jurors.	We accept majority verdicts of 11 or 12 jurors.
This mortgage approval does not become valid unless signed by the bank manager.	This mortgage approval becomes valid when signed by the bank manager.
The landlord cannot terminate the lease with notice of less than one month.	The landlord can terminate the lease with notice of one month or more.
A court cannot make an order without first considering an expert's report.	Before making an order, a court must consider an expert's report.
Not only judges, *but* barristers and solicitors, must be legally qualified.	Judges, barristers, and solicitors must all be legally qualified.

Prefer positive compound expressions

As with sentences, so with compound expressions within sentences—if possible, recast in positive form.

Before (negative compound)	After
does not have	lacks
not … unless	only if
not … until	when
not accept	reject
not many	few
not often	rarely
not the same	different

Negatives sometimes compulsory

Sometimes (though rarely), the law *requires* a negative form of expression. In that situation, to express the concept in positive form will thwart the intended legal result. For example, in many common-law jurisdictions a covenant controlling land use binds successive owners of the land only if cast as an obligation *not* to do something (hence the term 'restrictive covenant'). It must be cast as a negative; if cast as a positive, the covenant will be unenforceable beyond the original contracting parties. Further, in this area of law 'negativity' is a matter of substance, not mere form: no matter how the covenant is drafted, if in fact it requires money to be spent or work to be done, it is positive: *Haywood v Brunswick Permanent Benefit Society* (1881) 8 QBD 403, 409, 410. For example, a covenant to erect a building on land within six months is positive, but so too is a covenant not to leave land unbuilt-upon for more than six months. On the other hand, a covenant that any building erected on land should cost at least a stipulated sum, or should be used only for certain purposes, is negative—because it can be complied with by not building at all: *Pirie v Registrar-General* (1962) 109 CLR 619, 625–26.

Double negatives

The problem

Double negatives increase sentence complexity, often without good reason. Where possible, rewrite in positive form—as in the following examples.

Before (double negative)	**After**
The finding of trespass did *not disqualify* the claim to title by adverse possession.	The claim to title by adverse possession *survived* the finding of trespass.
In our view, your claim should *not* be *dis*allowed by the court.	In our view, the court should allow your claim.
Documents shall *not* be deemed *not* to be circulars by reason that they are in the form of a periodical publication. [Based on *Prevention of Fraud (Investments) Act 1958*, s 14(4) (repealed)]	Documents may be circulars even though they are in the form of a periodical publication.
'I should *not feel satisfied* that it would be correct to hold that the words used in clause 14 *can have no application* to any request made to a vendor.' [*Godfrey Constructions Pty Ltd v Kanagra Park Pty Ltd* (1972) 128 CLR 529, 543 (Walsh J)]	In my view, the words used in clause 14 could possibly apply to a request made to a vendor.
A false statement will defeat an insurance claim if it would yield 'a *not in*significant improvement' in the insured's chance of success. [*The Aegeon* [2002] EWCA Civ 247; [2003] QB 556, [38] (Mance LJ)]	A false statement will defeat an insurance claim if it would yield 'a *significant* improvement' in the insured's chance of success. [*Versloot Dredging BV v HDI Gerling Industrie Versicherung AG* [2014] EWCA Civ 1349; [2015] 2 WLR 1063, [165] (Christopher Clarke LJ)]

Hedging double negatives—intentional

Sometimes a double negative is used deliberately to hedge a statement—to make a statement that is more nuanced than a blunt positive. For example, 'I am *not un*convinced by the argument' suggests that the writer has some reservations; the proposition is more nuanced than 'I am convinced by the argument.' Again, a statement 'the risk is *not in*significant' is more nuanced than 'the risk is significant.' And to say that something is '*not in*consistent with' a statement is more nuanced than saying it is 'consistent with' the statement.

Hedging double negatives—careless

In contrast to a deliberately hedged double negative, a careless double negative can introduce ambiguity. An adept writer will spot the potential for misunderstanding and clarify.

Example 1

'It is *not uncommon* for courts to award damages for pain and suffering.'

This could mean:

- courts *sometimes* award damages for pain and suffering, or
- courts *commonly* award damages for pain and suffering.

Example 2

'It is *not unimportant* for barristers to be properly attired in court.'

This could mean:

- it is *important* for barristers to be properly attired in court, or
- whether barristers are properly attired in court *can be important*, but it is *not necessarily crucial*.

Example 3

The *Animals Act 1971*, s 2(2)(b) deals with damage caused by non-dangerous species of animals. The provision makes the owner of such an animal liable if the owner knew that the animal possessed characteristics which are '*not normally* found' in animals of that species '*except* in particular circumstances'. The House of Lords found the double negative perplexing:

> '[D]oes one cancel the double negative "not normally ... except" and ask whether what was done in the [particular] circumstances was normal behaviour for the species as a general rule; or is the right approach to ask whether what was done was normal for the species in the particular circumstances even if it will be abnormal in the absence of such circumstances.' [*Mirvahedy v Henley* [2003] 2 AC 491, [54] (Lord Slynn)]

Triple negatives

Even harder to process than double negatives are triple negatives.

- '[The certificate] was *not* a statement in writing the substance of which was *in*consistent with there being *no* proposal ... affecting the land.' [*Copmar Holdings Pty Ltd v Commonwealth* (1988) 4 BPR 9673, 9684 (McHugh JA, wrestling with a triple negative in a regulation)]
- 'It does *not*, however, follow that the parties' agreement is *not* a sine qua *non* of a consent order. Quite the reverse: the court can*not* make a consent order *without* the valid consent of the parties.' [*Sharland v Sharland* [2015] UKSC 60 at [29]; [2016] AC 871 at [29] (Lady Hale, starting with a triple negative, followed by a double negative)]

Usually, triple negatives can be recast in simpler form:

- 'It is *not* the case that a *non-party* who is heard in an interlocutory application is *not* a party to the proceedings before the court.' [2010] ALMD §3789, digest note of *Yirra Pty Ltd v Summerton* [2009] FCAFC 50; (2009) 176 FCR 219.]

  Better: 'A non-party who is heard in an interlocutory application may be a party to the proceedings before the court.'
- '*[N]o* law can be made which will *not* seem *un*just to the loser.' [Sir Frederick Pollock and Frederic William Maitland, *The History of English Law before the Time of Edward I*, ed SFC Milsom, 2nd edn, reissued (Cambridge University Press, 1968) vol 1, xcvii.]

  Better: 'Any law will seem unjust to the loser.'

POSSESSIVES

Practice

Traditional legal writing generally avoided the *'s* form of the possessive, preferring instead to spell out the possessive: eg, 'the decision of the judge' (not 'the judge's decision'), 'the negligence of the surveyor' (not 'the surveyor's negligence'). However, modern legal writing, aiming for crisper expressions, more readily accepts the *'s* form. Common examples are 'landlord's fixtures' (not 'fixtures of the landlord'), 'surveyor's fees' (not 'fees of the surveyor'), 'tenant's covenants', 'claimant's case', 'executor's oath', and so on.

But do not force the *'s* form into situations where it seems unidiomatic or clumsy. This sometimes happens where the *'s* form is used with inanimate nouns:

- The invitee sued after he slipped on the floor of the house [*better than*: 'he slipped on the house's floor'].
- The tenant claimed to rely on severance of the fixtures [*better than*: 'rely on the fixtures' severance'].
- He was unhappy with breach of the contract [*better than*: 'the contract's breach', which might (briefly) puzzle the reader: 'how can a contract cause a breach?'].

Benefits of *'s* form of possessive

Brevity

The *'s* form is always shorter than the spelled-out *of* form: eg, 'the decision of the judge' (5 words) vs 'the judge's decision' (3 words); 'the early recommendation of the Commission' (6 words) vs 'the Commission's early recommendation' (4 words). Thus:

- The aim *of* the lawyers was to explain the reasoning *of* the judge and the role *of* the sheriff. (19 words)
- The *lawyers' aim* was to explain the *judge's reasoning* and the *sheriff's role*. (13 words)

These word-savings might seem modest, but multiplied many times over in a document they can be worthwhile.

Taken to extremes, a string of *of*s is not merely wordy, but cumbersome. The *'s* form can help tighten the sentence. Compare:

- 'The decision *of* the court in relation to the argument *of* the appellant and the evidence *of* the tenant was to to order the removal *of* the fixtures *of* the tenant.' [31 words]
- 'The court's decision in relation to the appellant's argument and the tenant's evidence was to order that the tenant's fixtures be removed.' [Better: 22 words] [Or better still: 'After hearing the appellant's argument and the tenant's evidence, the court ordered the tenant to remove its fixtures.' (18 words)]

Avoiding ambiguity

Sometimes the *'s* form can avoid ambiguity inherent in the *of* form. Compare:

- 'The tipstaff *of* a judge when out of court has no power of arrest.' Who is out of court: the judge or the tipstaff?
- 'The judge's tipstaff when out of court has no power of arrest.' [Better still: 'When out of court, the judge's tipstaff has no power of arrest.']

Taking advantage of stress point in sentence

The *'s* form may facilitate moving a word or phrase to the end of the sentence, where the sentence's natural stress point lies. Compare: 'Termination of the contract is the right of *either party*' with 'Termination of the contract is either party's *right*'. (See further, **SENTENCE STRUCTURE (End sentences forcefully)**.)

Keeping related elements together

The *'s* form can help keep key parts of the sentence together. A spelled-out possessive can divide them.

Example

'The landlord must not delay enforcing the obligation *of* the tenant to remedy breaches.'

The phrase 'to remedy breaches' relates to 'obligation', but is separated from it by 'of the tenant'. The *'s* form of the possessive reunites them:

'The landlord must not delay enforcing the tenant's obligation to remedy breaches.'

Statutory aberrations

Statutes sometimes omit possessives in places where, grammatically, they might be expected. Lawyers then have little choice but to follow the legislative lead, grating though it may seem. For example, some industrial legislation uses *workers compensation* (not *workers' compensation*), and Australian strata title legislation uses *owners corporation* (not *owners' corporation*).

Gerunds

In conventional grammar, a noun that precedes a gerund (ie, a verb ending in *-ing* used as a noun) takes the possessive form: 'delays prejudice the *court's* [or plural, *courts'*] functioning'. The absence of the possessive (creating a fused participle) is unlikely to cause ambiguity—but may cause the reader to ponder the writer's grammatical acuity.

Examples

- *Mortgagors* [prefer: *Mortgagors'*] *defaulting* is a source of constant litigation.
- There is great benefit in *you* [prefer: *your*] *staying away* from the accused.
- Would you mind *me* [prefer: *my*] *citing* that case to the judge?
- The jury did not like the *advocate* [prefer: *advocate's*] *arguing* with the judge. [Without the possessive the meaning is ambiguous: did the jury dislike the advocate or the arguing?]

However, in some contexts the possessive may seem unidiomatic—if so, trust your ear and desist:

- I haven't heard *anyone* [not *anyone's*] *responding* to that argument.
- We do not appreciate Mr *Jones* [not *Jones'* or *Jones's*] taking that point.

Time periods

Use possessives when specifying time periods:

- 1 day's notice; 30 days' notice
- 5 years' experience
- notice of one month's duration [*better*: one month's notice].

See also **GERUNDS**; **GRAMMAR**.

possessory title

See **prescription / adverse possession**.

post hoc ergo propter hoc

Latin: after this; therefore because of this. Used to indicate the fallacy of assuming that because one event follows another, the earlier event must have been a cause of the later. The Latin has a certain rhythm, which is easily captured in English: eg, 'confusing sequence with consequence'. Unless readers are likely to know Latin, prefer an English translation:

'There is always the temptation to fall into the fallacy of *post hoc ergo propter hoc* [prefer: *reasoning that what happens afterwards is caused by what happened before*]; and that is no less a fallacy even if what happens afterwards could have been foreseen before it occurred.' [*Quinn v Burch Bros (Builders) Ltd* [1966] 2 QB 370, 395 (Salmon LJ)]

If for some reason you feel you must retain the Latin, then add a translation or an explanation—or both, as in the following example:

'Perhaps the majority judges below ... fell into the logical fallacy of *post hoc ergo propter hoc*.' [*Melway Publishing Pty Ltd v Robert Hicks Pty Ltd* (2001) 205 CLR 1, 30 (Kirby J; then adding in a footnote both a translation and explanation: '"After it, therefore due to it": the fallacy of confusing consequence with sequence.')]

post obit

Latin: after he or she dies; taking effect after [someone's] death. Sometimes hyphenated: *post-obit*. An example is the description of a bond (a 'post-obit' bond) payable on the death of a named person whose property the borrower expects to inherit. The Latin is pure affectation—always prefer *after death*:

'I do not accept that [the tax statute] includes ... the *post-obit* [prefer: *after-death*] dealings by beneficiaries of the estate.' [*Russell v Inland Revenue Commissioners* [1988] 1 WLR 834, 843 (Knox J)]

postscriptum

Latin: written afterwards; postscript. Sometimes two words, *post scriptum*; usually abbreviated to *PS*. To use the Latin *postscriptum* instead of the vernacular *postscript* or *PS* seems pretentious, although it sometimes appears in judgments. For example:

- 'Post Scriptum' [used as a heading, after 'Conclusion', in *Williams v R* [2014] EWCA Crim 1862 (Fulford LJ)]
- 'Giles JA, after writing his reasons, adopted what Rolfe AJA had said. But ... this *post scriptum* [prefer: *postscript*] ... left in an unsatisfactory state the Court of Appeal's explanation ...' [*Suvaal v Cessnock City Council* [2003] HCA 41, [89]; (2003) 200 ALR 1, 23 (McHugh and Kirby JJ)]

potior (melior) est conditio defendentis

Latin: the position of the defendant is stronger (better).

See **in pari delicto potior est conditio defendentis**.

POWER OF ATTORNEY

Purpose

A document under which a person (the 'principal') authorises another person (the 'attorney') to act on the principal's behalf. The power can be limited to particular acts, or it can be wide-ranging. Legislation in most jurisdictions imposes formal requirements (particularly for powers of attorney that are expressed to remain in force after the principal becomes incapable of cancelling the power, and for powers that authorise withholding medical attention). Legislation may also require powers of attorney to be registered before they can be used to deal with certain types of property (eg, land).

Drafting style

Two drafting styles are seen. One attempts to list the powers exhaustively, sometimes running to several pages of specifics. The problem with this style is the likelihood of 'gaps'. Under the *expressio unius* principle of interpretation, courts presume that a power not included in an apparently exhaustive list is deliberately omitted: see, eg, *Bryant v La Banque du Peuple* [1893] AC 170, 177. This promotes an increasingly exhaustive (and exhausting) style, which logically can never overcome the risk of gaps.

The second style adopts brief, generic language, to the effect: 'I grant all powers that I am legally able to grant.' Many modern-day powers of attorney favour this style. It leaves no room for gaps.

Signing 'under'

The attorney is usually said to sign 'under power of attorney', with no article (definite or indefinite) prefacing 'power of attorney'. For example, 'The son signed under power of attorney from his mother.' There is an exception where it is necessary to identify the *particular* power of attorney: 'The son signed under *the* power of attorney from his mother' (ie, not the power of attorney from his father).

See also **expressio unius**; **WORD STRINGS**.

pp

Abbreviation for *pages*

Indicates more than one page, separately or in a page span: eg, 'pp 3, 10'; 'pp 3–10'. British and Commonwealth usage omits a full stop—eg, 'pp 5–8', *not* 'pp. 5–8'—but US usage retains the full stop ('pp. 5–8').

Abbreviation for *per procurationem*

Latin: *per procurationem*, through the agency of; alternatively, *per procuratorem*, through his (or her) agent. Rarely now with full stops (*pp*, not *p.p.*); sometimes also abbreviated to *per pro*. Indicates that the person signing a document does so on behalf of another. Thus, if Y signs a contract on behalf of X, the formula is 'X *pp* [or *per pro*] Y' (not 'Y pp X'). By signing in this way, Y indicates that he or she is an agent authorised to sign the contract, but is not liable under it—X is the principal who is bound by the contract: *Smith v M'Guire* (1858) 27 LJ Ex 465, 468 (Pollock CB).

practicable / practical

practicable

Practicable means capable of being done, feasible: *Lee v Nursery Furnishings Ltd* [1945] 1 All ER 387, 389 (Lord Goddard). Some cases give *practicable* a wider meaning: eg, in the context of whether it was *practicable* to ask permission to enter premises before requesting a search warrant to do so, *practicable* was wider than 'feasible' or 'physically possible': *R v Leeds Crown Court* [1991] Crim LR 559.

Something may be *practicable* (able to be done) even though it is not 'reasonable' or 'fair'. For example:

> A statute required a court to order a person to pay certain debts to the extent the court considered *practicable*. Held, the court was obliged to order a tenant to pay an amount which it considered *practicable* in the circumstances, even though the landlord received a windfall which the court considered 'unfair': *Re Farquhar* [1943] 2 All ER 781, 783 (Lord Greene MR).

Drafters sometimes hedge *practicable* with qualifications, particularly of 'reasonableness'. For example, to require the police to bring an accused before the courts 'as soon as *reasonably practicable*' allows more time than to do so 'as soon as *practicable*': *R v Governor of Brixton Prison* [2005] EWHC 2405 (Admin); [2006] 1 WLR 1518, 1523 (Scott Baker LJ). But 'reasonably' still demands some rigour: for example, to require an official to make a decision 'as soon as *reasonably practicable*' requires the official to decide without delay (*as soon as*) once it is reasonably practicable to do so: *Snedden v Minister for Justice* [2014] FCAFC 156; (2014) 230 FCR 82, [116].

practical

In contrast, *practical* means actually able to be done. Something may be *practicable* (capable of being done) in a general sense, but not *practical* in the particular circumstances. For example, a lawyer may advise a client that to sue might be *practicable* but not *practical*.

practical completion

In a building contract, the stage at which the construction work to be done under the contract is completed, free from patent defects except those that are trifling: IN Duncan Wallace (ed), *Hudson's Building and Engineering Contracts*, 11th edn (Sweet & Maxwell, 1995) vol 2, para 9-04. To avoid argument over when that stage is reached, standard building contracts define 'practical completion', and declare conclusive an architect's or engineer's certificate that 'practical completion' (as defined) has been achieved.

See also **conclusive certificates**.

praedial

Affecting land. A term unique to Scots law; the common-law equivalent is *proprietary*. Here is a Scottish example:

> 'Certainly, the mere fact that a right equivalent to parking was not recognised as a *praedial* servitude by Roman law would not, of itself, prevent Scots law from recognising such a servitude, just as it has recognised, for instance, a *praedial* servitude to take coal and a *praedial* servitude of fuel, feal and divot, neither of which was recognised by Roman law.' [*Moncrieff v Jamieson* [2007] UKHL 42, [73]; [2007] 1 WLR 2620, 2646 (Lord Rodger). A servitude of fuel, feal, and divot is a right to go on to land to take material such as wood, turf, or peat for heating and fencing.]

praesumptio; praesumitur; praesumuntur

Latin: presumption; it is presumed; they are presumed. The words appear in various Latin maxims, all of which can be translated into standard English without loss of legal accuracy. For example:

- *praesumitur pro legitimatione*: the presumption favours legitimacy (ie, children are presumed to be the offspring of the spouses)

- *omnia praesumuntur*: all things are presumed
- *omnia rite acta praesumuntur*: all things are presumed to have been done correctly
- *omnia praesumuntur contra spoliatorem*: all things are presumed against a wrongdoer
- *omnia praesumuntur rite et solemniter acta esse*: all things are presumed to have been done correctly and with due formality
- *omnia praesumuntur legitime facta donec probetur in contrarium*: all things are presumed to have been done lawfully until the contrary is proved
- *praesumptio juris*: a presumption of law (ie, a rebuttable presumption)
- *praesumptio juris et de jure*: a presumption of law and of right (ie, an irrebuttable presumption)
- *semper praesumitur pro negante*: the presumption favours the person who denies (ie, the onus is on the person who affirms).

prayer

A request to the court for a remedy: the plaintiff 'prays for relief'. Though time-honoured, to non-lawyer litigants the term must seem quaint and obsequious. Unless court rules or procedures require *prayer*, prefer an alternative such as *claim* or *request*. For example:

- 'The Claimant's *prayer* [prefer: *claim*] for relief asked for a declaration that the property … was held on trust for him …' [*Davies v Davies* [2015] EWCA Civ 1008, [8] (Vos LJ)]
- 'The four *prayers* [prefer: *claims*] for relief … are entirely consistent with remedies to be granted after the general accounting had taken place.' [*Friend v Brooker* [2009] HCA 21, [99]; (2009) 239 CLR 129, 99 (Heydon J)]

PRECEDENCE CLAUSE

A provision in a document indicating the order of precedence if clauses are found to be inconsistent. The purpose is to overcome any possible application of the arbitrary principle that where two clauses in a document (other than a will) are inconsistent, the earlier overrides the later. In complex transactions, it may be useful to specify degrees of precedence, as in Example 2.

Example 1 (simple clause)

Precedence

If an inconsistency arises between these standard terms and the product order form signed by the customer, these terms prevail to the extent of the inconsistency.

Example 2 (more complex clause)

Precedence

In interpreting this Agreement, unless expressly stated otherwise, the order of precedence to the extent of any inconsistency, is as follows:

1. the clauses
2. the schedules
3. the technical specifications in the annexures
4. the recitals.

See also **CROSS-REFERENCES; inconsistent(with); INCONSISTENT PROVISIONS; PRIORITY AGREEMENT**.

PRECEDENT

In law, the word *precedent* bears three main senses.

The doctrine of precedent

Under the *doctrine of precedent*, a court's decision on a matter of law binds courts lower in the judicial hierarchy. The doctrine helps ensure predictability in judicial decisions:

> 'Decisions on points of law by more senior courts have to be accepted by more junior courts. Otherwise, the law becomes anarchic, and it loses coherence[,] clarity and predictability.' [*Willers v Joyce* (No 2) [2016] UKSC 44, [4]; [2016] 3 WLR 534, 538 (Lord Neuberger)]

The doctrine of precedent operates top-down. Courts are not bound by decisions of other courts on the same level in the judicial hierarchy, although they tend to follow them for reasons of comity.

Some judges take a robust approach to precedent: there is, after all, a first time for everything. Lord Denning was an exemplar:

> 'Let it not be thought … that I am against the doctrine of precedent. I am not. It is the foundation of our system of case law. This has evolved by broadening down from precedent to precedent. By standing by previous decisions, we have kept the common law on a good course. All that I am against is its too rigid application—a rigidity which insists that a bad precedent must necessarily be followed. I would treat it as you would a path through the woods. You must follow it certainly so as to reach your end. But you must not let the path become too overgrown. You must cut out the dead wood and trim off the side branches, else you will find yourself lost in thickets and brambles. My plea is simply to keep the path to justice clear of obstructions which would impede it.' [Lord Denning, *The Discipline of Law* (1979), 314]

Also, some judges have a higher reputation than others in particular areas of law. This makes their decisions in those areas more persuasive than decisions of other judges in that area. The following exchange took place in a 1973 case:

> '*Lord Diplock*: Could you tell me this, because I am not so familiar with the reputation of the Chancery Judges. Where does Neville J rank in the hierarchy between Eve J and Kekewich J?
>
> *Counsel*: I am bound to say: at the Kekewich end of the scale. But although Neville J's general reputation is not enormously high, he in fact did do quite a lot of trade mark work.' [*GE Trade Mark* [1973] RPC 297, 306, in argument]
>
> [To explain: Chancery judges held Eve J in high regard. They considered Kekewich J less sound, partly because his judgments were appealed against 'with uncomplimentary frequency': *National Dictionary of Biography* (1912) vol 2, 386. A kinder assessment points out that Kekewich J's success rate on appeal was 50% (at least, in the period 1901–02), a result comparable with that of his fellow judges: Sir Robert Megarry, *A New Miscellany-at-Law*, ed Bryan A Garner (Hart, 2005) 36.]

Legal forms

A *precedent* is also a model legal form—a template—which can be used for multiple transactions of the same kind. Most law firms have their own in-house precedents; and published books of precedents are readily available in hard copy and online.

Properly used, precedents save time, effort and cost, because they avoid the need to create a document afresh for each new transaction. But they can also detrimentally affect style, for two main reasons:

1. They tend to preserve the archaic language of earlier precedents, which in turn tend to preserve the archaic language of yet earlier precedents. Current users of the

precedents may be unwilling to update the language. This is partly because they fear that they may unwittingly change substance. But this fear is (or should be) largely unfounded, because competent drafters can update language without changing substance. It is also partly because they fear that they may lose the benefit of judicial decisions on the language of the existing precedent. But this fear also is (or should be) largely unfounded, because the proportion of judicially defined terms in any given document is likely to be low. And in any case, meaning is always context-dependent; judicial decisions are based, not on the immutable meaning of words, but on their meaning in the context of the particular document and the admissible surrounding circumstances. (See discussion under **TERMS OF ART**.)

2. They encourage prolixity. While documents may start life as the product of a sole author, they are often supplemented and refined by later lawyers, all eager to add their contributions. Collective authorship rarely promotes brevity. While in principle it should be as easy to delete as to add, in practice lawyers are reluctant to cull material from 'settled' precedents (just in case the material might prove to be legally important).

Conditions 'precedent'

A condition *precedent* is a provision under which a contract does not come into existence, or a right or obligation does not arise, unless a stipulated event occurs. It is contrasted with a condition *subsequent*, under which a contract comes to an end, or rights or obligations cease, if a stipulated event occurs.

See also **condition precedent**; **condition subsequent**; **PROLIXITY**; **TERMS OF ART**.

precondition

Condition is usually sufficient: 'pre' is implied. For example, 'consent is a *precondition* of assignment' means 'consent is a *condition* of assignment'. The only possible qualification is where the writer feels the need to emphasise the element of 'prior'—eg (to return to the example), to make it abundantly clear that *post*-assignment consent never suffices. But in such a case, a better formulation would be: 'prior consent is a condition of assignment'.

predecessor in title

A person who formerly held title to (ie, owned) the same interest in the land as the current owner holds. Strictly speaking, the interests must correspond precisely; if they do not, the previous owner may be a 'predecessor', but is not a *predecessor in title*. However, context may allow a looser meaning: for example, a statute may use *predecessor in title* in the more general sense of 'earlier owner' even though their interests do not match precisely.

See further **successor in title**.

pre-empt / preempt

The hyphen allows the meaning more easily to be sensed (*pre-*, before). In US usage, usually spelled as one word without a hyphen, *preempt*. In British and Commonwealth usage, still generally hyphenated, although the usage is changing in line with the modern trend towards hyphen-less usage generally. For example:

- '[The borrowers] in effect agreed to *preempt* a forced sale by effecting a sale of the property themselves …' [*Paulin v Paulin* [2009] EWCA Civ 221; [2010] 1 WLR 1057, 1064 [15] (Wilson LJ)]

- In *Momcilovic v R* [2011] HCA 34, [219]; (2011) 245 CLR 1, 104, Gummow J quite properly retained the original US spelling when quoting from the US Supreme Court—which (inconsistently) used both hyphenated and unhyphenated forms—while preferring the hyphenated form in his own writing:

  > 'The decisions of the United States Supreme Court speak of the power of the Congress to "*pre-empt*" State law. ... When delivering the Opinion of the Court ... Souter J ... said that "[e]ven without an express provision for *preemption*", State law must yield to an Act of the Congress [where] "state law is naturally *preempted* to the extent of any conflict with a federal statute". ... His Honour added that the categories of *pre-emption* were not rigidly distinct and also said: "We will find *preemption* where it is impossible for a private party to comply with both state and federal law ...".'

See also **HYPHENS**; **right of first refusal**.

pre-exist / preexist

In British and Commonwealth usage, hyphenated; in US usage, usually spelled as one word without a hyphen, *preexist*.

See **HYPHENS**.

preliminary to

A verbose substitute for 'before'. Prefer 'before':

> 'I shall set out the argument on the second point *preliminary to* [prefer: *before*] considering whether [A's] actions were sufficiently closely connected to his discharge of the functions assigned to him.' [*Various Claimants v Wm Morrison Supermarkets plc* [2017] EWHC 3113; [2019] QB 772, [148] (Langstaff J)]

premises

A word with varying uses in law, historically traceable one from another. These legal uses differ from the common meaning of *premise*—or *premiss*—as an assertion or hypothesis that forms the basis of a proposition or theory. The following discussion considers only the legal uses of the word.

That which has gone before

Historically and etymologically, *premises* means 'that which has been mentioned before' (Latin *praemissa*; *praemittere* = to send or set before). This was its initial legal meaning: *Metropolitan Water Board v Paine* [1907] 1 KB 285, 297 (Ridley J). In line with this meaning, conventionally drawn pleadings may set out arguments and conclude, 'therefore, *in the premises*, we assert ...'—meaning simply, 'therefore, following from what we have said, we assert ...' Or again, a conventionally drawn deed or contract may recite certain facts, and continue 'in consideration *of the premises*'—meaning simply 'in the light of *what has been mentioned above*': see, eg, *Bell v Welch* (1850) 9 CB 154, 159, 170; 137 ER 851, 853, 857; *Unidare PLC v Cohen* [2005] EWHC 1410 (Ch); [2006] 2 WLR 974.

This meaning of *premises* has long disappeared from normal usage. To continue it in legal usage is consciously archaic. There is no reason to perpetuate it. Always prefer a plain-language alternative. For example:

> '*In the premises* [prefer: *For the reasons given above*] the discretion exercised by his Honour and the order made was [sic] well open to him ...' [*Meridien Airlie Beach Pty Ltd v Karamist Pty Ltd* [2015] QCA 192, [66] (North J)]

The parts of a deed that precede the habendum

From the sense of 'that which has been mentioned before' comes the meaning found in traditional deeds of conveyance: *premises* means those parts of the deed that precede the habendum (the habendum being the description of the estate or interest being conveyed): Sir William Blackstone, *Commentaries on the Laws of England* (Clarendon, 1766) book 2, 298; *Cruise's Digest* (Butterworths, London, 1804) vol 4, 431. Those preceding parts were: the nature of the document (eg, 'Deed of Conveyance'), the date, the names of the parties, the recitals, the amount of the consideration, and a 'metes and bounds' description of the property being conveyed.

Land or buildings

Meaning

In turn, from the location in the *premises* of the 'metes and bounds' description of the property (as discussed above) comes the modern meaning of *premises*, ie, land and buildings:

> 'How [*premises*] originally became applied to property is, I think, generally known. It was from the habit of conveyancers when they were drawing deeds of conveyance referring to property and speaking of "parcels". They set out the parcels in the early part of the deed, and later they would refer to "the said premises," meaning strictly that which had gone before, and gradually by common acceptance "premises" became applied, as it generally is now, to houses, land, shops, or whatever it may be, so that the word has come to mean generally real property of one sort or another.' [*Gardiner v Sevenoaks Rural District Council* [1950] 2 All ER 84, 85 (Lord Goddard CJ)]

This normal meaning of *premises* in modern law—'land', 'buildings', or 'land with buildings'—can be coloured by context. *Premises* is a 'chameleon-like word which takes its meaning from its context ... [and] can mean almost anything': *Spring House (Freehold) Ltd v Mount Cook Land Ltd* [2001] EWCA Civ 1833; [2002] 2 All ER 822, [28] (Ward and Rix LJJ). Examples of different kinds of *premises* in this sense include:

- a cave used as a storeroom: *Gardiner v Sevenoaks Rural District Council* [1950] 2 All ER 84
- an outbuilding ancillary to a house: *Wolf v Crutchley* [1971] 1 All ER 520
- a room used as an office within a larger building: *Frost v Caslon* [1929] 2 KB 138
- gallops (training ground for racehorses): *Bracey v Read* [1963] Ch 88
- a holiday camp with chalets and facilities: *Phonographic Performance Ltd v Pontin's Ltd* [1968] Ch 290
- a permanent caravan and the site on which it stands: *Norton v Knowles* [1969] 1 QB 572
- a ski field: *Ruapehu Alpine Lifts Ltd v State Insurance Ltd* (1998) ANZ Insurance Cases §61-404.

However (in landlord and tenant legislation), *premises* did not include:

- farmland: *Maunsell v Olins* [1975] AC 373
- 1.25 acres of unbuilt-on land: *Turner v York Motors Pty Ltd* (1951) 85 CLR 55.

Plural form

Conventionally, *premises* takes the plural form, with a plural verb, even where the reference is to a single property or a single part of a single property: eg, 'The *premises* known as flat 1.' This can sometimes leave unclear whether in the context *premises* refers to a single property or to a number of properties (as in *Ninety Broomfield Road RTM Co Ltd v Triplerose Ltd* [2016] 1 WLR 275, where the Court of Appeal interpreted a statutory reference to *premises* as limited to a single self-contained building). Some legal writers have taken up the neologisms 'a premise' or 'a premises' (in each case with a singular verb) to refer to a single property: eg, 'the lease was of a premises'. To many readers, however, these usages remain unidiomatic—and they are easily avoided, as in the following examples:

- 'The difference ... was the difference between acquiring *a premises* [prefer: *a property*] and business being lawfully run, and acquiring *a premises* [prefer: *a property*] and business being unlawfully run.' [*D'Agostino v Anderson* [2012] NSWCA 443, [11] (Bathurst CJ)]
- 'Until early 2014, the Premises *was* [prefer: *were*] owned by [A]. ... In early 2014, the Premises *was* [prefer: *were*] sold to [B], and pursuant to a sale and leaseback arrangement, the Premises *was* [prefer: *were*] leased to [C].' [*Impact Funds Management Pty Ltd v Roy Morgan Research Ltd* [2016] VSC 221, [7] (Croft J; the defined term 'Premises' referred to a single building only)]

See also **habendum**; **metes and bounds**; **presents**.

PREPOSITIONS

At sentence-end

There is no grammatical rule against ending a sentence with a preposition. Even the best writers do so: 'The peculiarities of legal English are often used as a stick to beat the [government] official with' (Ernest Gowers, *The Complete Plain Words*, 1st ed (HMSO, 1954) 8). However, a sentence that ends with a preposition may be a weak sentence, because it fails to capitalise on the emphasis that falls naturally at sentence-end. For example, a sentence that ends with a preposition such as *about*, *for*, *to*, *on*, or similar, peters out without punch. The remedy is to recast the sentence to take advantage of the natural stress point.

Before	**After**
Do not use a preposition to end a sentence *with*.	Do not end a sentence with a *preposition*.
You cannot exercise the option unless you can find the landlord to serve the notice *on*.	You cannot exercise the option unless you can find and serve notice on the *landlord*.

However, take care in recasting the sentence not to appear foppish. For example: 'He could not find anyone to turn to', versus 'He could not find anyone to whom to turn'. Also, choosing a more relaxed tone (eg, in an email to a regular client) may help propel the preposition to sentence-end. For example, a letter to a client may quite naturally say: 'This accident was not related to the injury *that* you complained *of*' (compare: 'This accident was not related to the injury *of which* you complained').

Repeating after conjunction

Sometimes, clarity demands a repeated preposition, particularly after *and* or *or*. For example:

> A US statute empowered the following persons to transfer actions to the District Court: 'Any officer of the United States or any agency thereof'. Did this mean: (1) Any officer of [the United States or any agency of the United States]; or (2) Any [officer of the United States] or any [agency of the United States]? Held, it meant (1): *International Primate Protection League v Tulane Educational Fund* 111 Sup Ct 1700 (1991). The ambiguity could have been avoided by repeating the preposition *of*: 'Any officer *of* the United States or *of* any agency thereof'.

Wordy compound prepositions

Avoid wordy compound prepositions. Prefer shorter substitutes that mean the same. For example:

Original	Prefer
as a consequence of	because of
by means of	by, with, using
by virtue of	by, under
for the purpose of	to
for the reason that	because
in accordance with	by, under
in addition to	besides
inasmuch as	since, because
in association with	with
in case of	if
in excess of	more than, over
in favour of	for
in order to	to
in the absence of	without
in the course of	during
in the event that, in the event of	if
in the nature of	like
in the neighbourhood of	near
in the vicinity of	near
in view of	because of
on the grounds of	because of
on the part of	by
prior to	before
subsequent to	after
with a view to	to
with the exception of	except

Wordy *of* phrases

Of phrases are essential parts of English, but their overuse promotes wordiness. The remedy is to eliminate as many as possible. One technique is to use the possessive (see **POSSESSIVES**). Another technique is to change a prepositional phrase to an adjective or an adjectival phrase. The examples below use both techniques.

Before	After
The notice *of* appeal must be lodged by the solicitor *of* the plaintiff at the office *of* the court no later than 10 am *of* the morning *of* the trial. [30 words]	The plaintiff's solicitor must lodge the appeal notice at the court office by 10 am on the trial day. [19 words]
Nothing in this section limits the *powers of the council* to order the *demolition of the building* if in the *opinion of the council* the *circumstances of the case* require it. [31 words]	Nothing in this section limits the *council's building-demolition powers* if the council considers that demolition is required. [17 words]

Yet another technique is to convert nouns or noun phrases to their underlying verb form—which in any case is a sound way to tighten writing: *not* 'it was the recommendation *of* the Board', *but* 'the Board recommended'; *not* 'this conduct is in breach *of* the contract', *but* 'this conduct breaches the contract'.

See also **NOUNS / VERBS; POSSESSIVES; SENTENCE STRUCTURE; SIMPLER WORDS AND PHRASES.**

prescribe / proscribe

To *prescribe* (noun, *prescription*) means to regulate or lay down a rule; to *proscribe* (noun, *proscription*) means to prohibit. The possibility for confusion is apparent, as in the following extract:

> '[In the witness's affidavit] I think "prescribed" is a slip for "proscribed," and "prescribed re-organisation" should be "proscribed organisation".' [*John v Rees* [1969] 2 WLR 1294, 1327 (Megarry J)]

When writing for a general audience, unless necessity requires the use of *prescribe* or *proscribe* (eg, where discussing the wording of a statutory provision), consider an alternative. For *prescribe*, try *give*, *fix*, *set out*; for *proscribe*, try *forbid*, *prohibit*. For example:

- The regulations *prescribe* [prefer: *set out*, *specify*] the lodgement fees.
- The regulations *proscribe* [prefer: *prohibit*] speeding in residential areas.

Prescribed as an adjective can also be legal shorthand for *prescribed in the regulations*. For readers unfamiliar with the shorthand, consider a different formulation:

> **Original**: In this section, 'residential premises' means premises of a *prescribed* kind.
>
> **Rewrite**: Regulations made under this Act set out the meaning of 'residential premises'.

prescription / adverse possession

British and Commonwealth usage

Prescription

A process recognising the acquisition of rights over land by long-term use. For example, a landowner (A) who for at least 20 years regularly crosses the land of a neighbour (B) to reach the street may acquire by 'prescription' a right of way over the land, entitling A and future owners to continue to cross the land by the same path (even after B has on-sold). The law recognises the right on the basis that long-continued exercise of an apparent right presumes an actual right; and it endeavours to find a lawful origin for the right, such as by means of the fiction that the right had been granted by a document that is now lost (the doctrine of the 'lost modern grant'): *Attorney-General v Simpson* [1901] 2 Ch 671, 698; *Bakewell Management Ltd v Brandwood* [2004] 2 AC 519, [9], [27], [49] (HL).

Adverse possession

A process by which title to land is extinguished by long possession adverse to the title of the owner. Unlike prescription, which is an acquisitive process (burdening the owner's title with a right, but leaving the underlying title otherwise intact), adverse possession is an extinctive process, extinguishing the title of the (former) owner. That is, if continued for a statutory period (varying between jurisdictions, but often 12 years), adverse possession makes the adverse possessor the owner. The possessor is said to have gained a *possessory title* (or, in the vernacular, a *squatter's title*).

US usage

In US legal usage, *prescription* is sometimes used to indicate both processes—the acquisition of interests such as rights of way, and the extinction of title by *adverse possession*. This conflates the distinctions drawn in British and Commonwealth usage.

Further reading

- Kevin Gray and Susan Francis Gray, *Elements of Land Law*, 5th edn (Oxford University Press, 2009) [9.1.43]–[9.1.74] (UK law of adverse possession)
- Brendan Edgeworth (ed), *Butt's Land Law*, 7th edn (Lawbook, 2017) [16.30]–[16.480] (Commonwealth law of prescription and adverse possession)
- Jon W Bruce and James W Ely Jr, *The Law of Easements and Licences in Land* (Thomson Reuters, 2019) §5.1—US courts' attitudes to the relationship between adverse possession and prescription

See also **lost modern grant**; **nec vi nec clam nec precario**.

PRESENT TENSE

See **TENSE**.

present time (at the)

A verbose variant of *now* or *at present*. Prefer the shorter version.

> '[T]here is another reason why an interruption in the enjoyment of light *at the present time* [prefer: *at present*; *now*] might be or grow to the damage etc of the freeholder. If there is no interruption *at the present time* [prefer: *at present*; *now*] and the light continues to be enjoyed until the head lease ends [then certain consequences follow].' [*Metropolitan Housing Trust Ltd v RMC FH Co Ltd* [2017] EWHC 2609; [2018] Ch 195, [45] (Morgan J)]

presents (document)

Latin: *presens scriptum* (literally, present writing), later shortened to *presens*, and finding its way into English as *presents*, meaning 'writing'. For example:

> A clause in a mortgage of land allowed the mortgagee (a solicitor) to charge for his work 'in or about these *presents*'. Held, this allowed him to charge for drawing up the deed of mortgage (ie, the document), but not for other work he had done in relation to the mortgaged property after the date of the mortgage: *Field v Hopkins* (1890) 44 Ch D 524.

This usage is now obsolescent. It is still echoed in phrases such as 'know all men *by these presents*'—meaning *by this writing* [ie, *by this document*], a usage traceable back to at least 1389: John Toulmin Smith and Lucy Toulmin Smith, *English Gilds* (Oxford University Press, 1870) 48.

Nowadays, to use *presents* to mean 'document' would be consciously obscurantist. Prefer 'document'.

See also **know all men by these presents**; **premises**.

presume

See **assume / presume**.

PRESUMPTIONS

Their nature

A *presumption* is something that can be taken for granted. In law, there are two categories of presumptions: *rebuttable* and *irrebuttable*. Most standard legal presumptions are *rebuttable*—ie, they can be disproved by evidence, for example:

- presumption of undue influence—that in transactions between persons in close relationships (typically parent and child, solicitor and client, and trustee and beneficiary), the more powerful is presumed to have taken advantage of the weaker
- presumption of innocence—that persons are presumed innocent until proven guilty
- presumption against intestacy—that a testator does not intend to die without leaving a valid will
- presumption of advancement—that where a person transfers property to a spouse, the transfer was intended as a gift
- presumption of survivorship—that where two persons die at the same time, the younger is presumed to have survived the elder.

However, some legal presumptions are *irrebuttable*. Statutes and other legal documents sometimes elevate presumptions to this status. Examples are provisions regulating 'service of notices', which are often declared to be irrebuttable—eg, by stating that a notice sent by post is *irrebuttably* presumed to have been received [X] days later. The irrebuttability is usually stated expressly; but it can also be implied (eg, by declaring inadmissible any evidence conflicting with the presumption).

Drafting considerations

Before creating presumptions, always consider the 'fairness' of the result. This is obvious for irrebuttable presumptions—is it fair to preclude evidence to contradict the presumption? But it is also important for presumptions that are rebuttable, because the presumption effectively reverses the onus of proof. To return to the example of a notice sent by post:

- If the presumption is irrebuttable, is it fair that the addressee may never in fact have received the notice?
- If the presumption is rebuttable, is it fair to cast on the addressee the onus of proving that the notice was never received?

See also **deem**.

preventive / preventative

Prefer *preventive* (not 'preventative'), being based on the noun 'prevent'. Compare *interpretative* (not 'interpretive'), being based on the noun 'interpretation'.

See also **interpretative / interpretive**.

previous to

Prefer the less pretentious 'before'. (Likewise, prefer 'after' for 'subsequent to'.)

See also **prior to**.

prima facie

Prefer English

Latin: at first glance; on first impressions. (Formerly, sometimes hyphenated: *prima-facie*.) Used as an adjective in familiar terms such as *prima facie case*, *prima facie evidence*, and *prima facie presumption*. For many lawyers, *prima facie* is plain Latin, its meaning known; but it is easily translatable into plain English—and for most readers plain English is better than plain Latin:

> 'So I return to the facts of this case. *On the face of things* [sic: much better than *Prima facie*], Bocardo is the paper title owner ...' [*Bocardo SA v Star Energy Onshore Ltd* [2009] EWCA Civ 579; [2010] Ch 100, 124 [68] (Aikens LJ)]

Inherent complexity?

As with some other Latin terms used in law, *prima facie* may imply more than a literal translation suggests—more than *at first glance* or *on first impressions*. It can mask an inherent complexity, which surfaces only when scrutinised in its legal context. For example, to paraphrase Lord Atkin's words, a *prima facie case* requires evidence showing a greater probability than not that the claimant's allegation is more correct than not: *McGowan v Stott* (1923) 99 LJKB 357n, 360. Or, in the Australian High Court's view, a *prima facie case* is a serious case (as opposed to a speculative case), having a real possibility of ultimate success: *Beecham Group Ltd v Bristol Laboratories Pty Ltd* (1968) 118 CLR 618. Analyses like these demonstrate the dangers of assuming that a simple Latin term has a simple legal meaning.

primo loco

Latin: in the first place (then: *secundo loco*, and so on). This Latinism still appears, especially in Scots legal usage, but seems impossible to justify on any ground except conscious affectation. For example:

> 'Reliability of witnesses was a matter *primo loco* [prefer: *in the first place*] for the panel.' [*Garner v General Teaching Council for Scotland* [2015] CSIH 34, [54] (Lady Paton)]

primus inter pares / prima inter pares

Latin: first among equals; *primus* (masculine); *prima* (feminine). There seems little justification for retaining the Latinism in the face of an easy, and gender-neutral, translation. For example:

- 'It is a lay committee in every sense. ... The legal member is only *primus inter pares* [prefer: *first among equals*].' [Argument before the court in *Metropolitan Properties Co (FGC) Ltd v Lannon* [1969] 1 QB 577, 590]
- 'In the light of the evidence before him, Bell DCJ found that the applicant's role was more that of *primus inter pares* [prefer: *first among equals*] than ringleader.' [*R v Taylor* [2005] NSWCCA 242, [16] (Grove J)]

principal / principle

In legal usage, as in standard usage, the meanings differ. A *principal* is a person who heads an organisation (such as a school or college), or a person for whom another acts (as in the principal–agency relationship). A *principle* is a fundamental rule or proposition. Using the two terms close to each other may cause a temporary miscue, hindering communication. For example:

- 'In *principle* a *principal* can allow his agent to ...' [*Galaxy Aviation v Sayegh Group Aviation FZE* [2015] EWHC 3478 (Comm), [104] (Smith J)]
- [O]n grounds of practicality, policy and *principle*, a *principal* should be beneficially entitled to a bribe or secret commission received by his agent ...' [*FHR European Ventures LLP v Cedar Capital Partners LLC* [2014] UKSC 45, [11]; [2015] AC 250, 263 (Lord Neuberger)]

prior [est] tempore potior [est] jure

Latin: the earlier in time has the better right. As with many Latin phrases in law, this one's time-hallowed nature does not preclude accurate translation into standard English.

See **qui prior est tempore, potior est jure; tempus / tempore / temporis**.

prior notice

See **notice / prior notice**.

prior to

Prefer *before* (unless for parallelism you prefer the ungainly antonym *posterior to*). As Gowers said, 'There is no good reason to use *prior to* as a preposition instead of *before*. *Before* is simpler, better known and more natural, and therefore preferable': Sir Ernest Gowers, *The Complete Plain Words*, ed Sydney Greenbaum and Janet Whircut (HMSO, rev edn, 1986) 110.

Also prefer *before* over longer constructions containing *prior to*: eg, *prior to the time when* and *prior to the time at which*. In all these cases, *before* not only reduces word-count, but also simplifies sentence-construction (eg, by changing noun-formations to verbs). For example, '*prior to ... the commencement of* the Act' (7 words), can be recast: '*before* the Act *commenced*' (4 words). Other examples are:

- 'Second, and also *prior to the making of the confiscation order* [prefer: *before the confiscation order was made*], Mr Maye suffered the unpleasant indignity of false imprisonment ...' [*Re Maye* [2008] UKHL 9, [4]; [2008] 1 WLR 315, [4] (Lord Scott)]
- 'It was not possible for the AWU to distribute the notice *at a time prior to the time* [prefer: *before*] it was required to prepare its content.' [*Esso Australia Pty Ltd v The Australian Workers' Union* [2016] FCAFC 72; (2016) 258 IR 396, [361] Bromberg J)]

See also **NOMINALISATIONS; previous to; subsequent to.**

PRIORITY AGREEMENT

An agreement that regulates the ranking of charges or mortgages over property. (To be distinguished from a 'precedence clause', which seeks to resolve conflicts between clauses in a document.) For example, Lender A and Lender B may each have charges over the same property. If A's charge was created earlier than B's, normally A's would prevail. But A and B may agree (usually in a 'Priority Deed') that B's charge is to prevail over A's.

See also **PRECEDENCE CLAUSE.**

privilege

Formerly *priviledge* (see, eg, *Statute of Monopolies 1623*, s 6), a spelling now obsolete. In general usage, a *privilege* is a special right or advantage. In legal usage, a *privilege* was originally a right granted to an office (eg, a mayor's 'privileges of office') or to a town (eg, the right to hold a fair). Later it came to mean also an advantage of some kind enjoyed by an individual or group of individuals, as distinct from an advantage enjoyed by all: *Le Strange v Pettefar* (1939) 161 LT 300, 301 (Luxmoore LJ). In modern legal usage, *privilege* is often folded into a word-string with no separate role of its own—in which case, discard it. An example is the omnibus expression 'rights and *privileges*'—in modern law, *privileges* here adds nothing to 'rights', so discard it.

privity / privy

privity

Privity denotes a legal relationship between persons on opposite sides of a transaction. For example, persons who are parties to the same contract are in *privity of contract*, and persons who have reciprocal interests in the same estate in the land are in *privity of estate* (such as in the relationship of landlord and tenant). Persons may be in both privity of contract and privity of estate. For example, on the grant of a lease, landlord and tenant are in both privity of contract and privity of estate. But (to continue the example) later events may break one or both of the privities. Thus, if the tenant assigns the lease, the landlord and the assignee are in privity of estate, but no longer in privity of contract—and the landlord and the original tenant remain in privity of contract but not in privity of estate. *Privity* in these senses is a term of art, difficult to express concisely in plain English; so when addressing a non-lawyer audience, it is better explained than replaced.

privy

Parties are *privies* if they have a mutual interest in the same action or thing. For a party (B) to be a *privy* of another party (A), B must claim under or through A. Where the parties are privies, then an estoppel that binds A binds also B: *Timbercorp Finance Pty Ltd* v *Collins* [2016] HCA 44; (2016) 259 CLR 212, [54]. Even more than *privity, privy* is a term of art, difficult to express in plain English. And given its vernacular overtones, when addressing non-lawyers it needs explaining.

Further reading

S Bridge, E Cooke, and M Dixon (eds), *Megarry & Wade's Law of Real Property*, 9th edn (Sweet & Maxwell, 2019) [19-003]–[19-008] (privity of contract and privity of estate in the law of leases)

See also **estate or interest**; **estoppel**.

pro bono

Latin: for good; abbreviation of *pro bono publico* (for the public good). In legal usage, legal work done for free (or at reduced rates) for those otherwise unable to afford it, or for charities whose resources would otherwise be depleted by legal costs.

The term is not well-understood by non-lawyers (see *Further reading*, below); so prefer a plain-language alternative. For example:

- 'On the appeal, Mr Darby appeared for Mr Turner, acting *pro bono* [prefer: *for no fee*].' [*Turner v Secretary of State for Communities and Local Government* [2015] EWCA Civ 583; [2015] 1 WLR 5085, [5] (Sales LJ)]
- 'In this Court, the applicant refused the offer of senior counsel to appear *pro bono* [prefer: *for no fee*] on his behalf and argued his own case.' [*Gassy v R* [2008] HCA 18; (2008) 236 CLR 293, [9] (Gummow and Hayne JJ)]

Further reading

'Pro Bono' in *Law Words*, Centre for Plain Legal Language, University of Sydney, 1995) 63; www.clarity-international.net/plain-language-resources/general-resources/. (The Centre's survey showed that only half of those surveyed knew the meaning of *pro bono*. The Centre suggested substituting 'free legal work' or 'public interest legal work'.)

pro forma

Latin: as a matter of form; occasionally hyphenated (*pro-forma*), but more commonly two separate words. Often used to describe a document in standard form (eg, a *pro forma* contract)—indeed, 'standard form' is the preferred substitute (hyphenated if used as an adjective). For example:

- 'The justices used the same formulation in the *pro forma* [prefer: *standard-form*] document that recorded the reasons for their decision.' [*Re B (a child)* [2009] UKSC 5, [14]; [2009] 1 WLR 2496, 2499 (Lord Kerr)]
- '[The statutory criteria] are not to be satisfied by *pro forma* [prefer: *standard-form*] affidavits containing conclusionary statements.' [*Condon v Pompano Pty Ltd* [2013] HCA 7, [75]; (2013) 252 CLR 38, 74 (French CJ)]

pro hac vice

Latin: for this occasion; on this occasion. The English translation echoes the Latin perfectly—so prefer the English. For example:

- 'If however the hirers intervene to give directions as to how to drive which they have no authority to give, and the driver *pro hac vice* [prefer: *on this occasion*] complies with them, … the hirers may be liable as joint tort-feasors.' [*Mersey Docks and Harbour Board v Coggins & Griffith (Liverpool) Ltd* [1947] AC 1, 11 (Viscount Simon)]
- '[The appellant sought to argue that the respondent] was his employer *pro hac vice* [prefer: *for this occasion*] in respect of the task the appellant was performing at the time of his injury.' [*Conray v Scotts Refrigerated Freightways Pty Ltd* [2008] NSWCA 60, [50] (McColl JA)]

pro loco et tempore

Latin: for the place and time; for now. For example, under Scots law, the Crown may desert (withdraw) criminal proceedings *pro loco et tempore*, reserving the right to reinstate them later. In all except the most technical contexts, 'for now' suffices.

pro non scripto

Latin: as if not written (eg, where the court disregards part of a text on grounds such as illegality). Prefer an appropriate English equivalent. For example:

- 'I am driven to the conclusion that the parties never intended that clause 16 should operate and that it was mere dressing up in an endeavour to clothe the agreement with a legal character which it would not otherwise have possessed. It follows that it should be treated *pro non scripto* [prefer: *as if it were not in the document*].' [*AG Securities Ltd v Vaughan* [1990] 1 AC 417, 477 (Lord Jauncey)]

- 'If it is impossible, on construction of the condition, to reach a conclusion as to what was in the draftsman's mind, the condition is meaningless and must be read as *pro non scripto* [prefer: *as if not in the document*; *as if not present*].' [*Fawcett Properties Ltd v Buckingham County Council* [1961] AC 636, 670 (Lord Keith)]

pro rata

Latin: in proportion; at the rate of. A Latinism that has become part of standard English and so is not italicised. The verb *to prorate* (= to divide pro rata) is chiefly a US usage, and to British and Commonwealth readers may seem a studied affectation. The longer phrase *on a pro rata basis* simply means *pro rata*—so prefer *pro rata*.

pro re nata

Latin: for a special emergency. There seems no justification for retaining the Latin, given the adequacy of the English translation. For example:

- 'Such duty [of care] arises only *pro re nata* [prefer: *in a special emergency*] and cannot be stated as a universally present obligation.' [*Browne v Central SMT Co Ltd* 1949 SC 9, 15, (Lord Mackay)]
- 'The ***chemical restraint*** of a resident of a residential facility is the use of medication prescribed by a medical practitioner, including a fixed daily dose and *pro re nata* [prefer: *emergency*] medication, for the purpose of controlling the resident's behaviour.' [*Disability Services Amendment Act 2012* (NSW), s 34, definition]

pro tanto

Latin: for so much; for as far as it goes; proportionately. A Latinism that for some users has become standard English; but the standard English translation nevertheless works just fine.

pro tempore

Latin: for the time being; abbreviated to *pro tem*. Although the Latin (both fuller and abbreviated) hints at the meaning, a context-appropriate English translation is better for most readers. For example:

- '[T]he argument would entail that even in respect of those contracts which the company ultimately fulfilled by delivery the moneys were *pro tempore* [prefer: *for that time*; *temporarily*] subject to a trust which would have prevented the company from lawfully treating them as its own.' [*Re Goldcorp Exchange Ltd* [1995] 1 AC 74, 102 (Lord Mustill)]
- 'If a matter be referred by a State Parliament, that matter becomes, either permanently or *pro tempore* [prefer: *temporarily*; *for a period*], one with respect to which the Commonwealth Parliament may under the Constitution make laws.' [*Airlines of NSW Pty Ltd v New South Wales* (1964) 113 CLR 1, 53 (Windeyer J)]

probable

A notoriously open-ended word, yet found in key statements in leading cases. For example, in the law of nuisance: was the damage 'a natural or *probable* or foreseeable result of the nuisance?': *Overseas Tankship (UK) Ltd v Miller Steamship Co Pty Ltd (The Wagon Mound) (No 2)* [1967] 1 AC 617, 634 (PC). Or in contract law: did the parties contemplate the damage suffered 'as *the probable* result of the breach?': *Hadley v Baxendale* (1854) 9 Ex 341, 354; 156 ER 145, 151 (Alderson B).

Despite its prevalence, *probable* is imprecise. It can carry a range of meanings, including:

- 'liable to result': *Konfos v C Czarnikow Ltd (The Heron II)* [1969] 1 AC 350, 410–11 (Lord Hodson)
- 'likely to happen': *Goldman v Thai Airways International Ltd* [1983] 3 All ER 693, 700 (Eveleigh LJ)
- anything on a spectrum that includes 'more probable than not', 'likely but not very likely', 'anything more than a bare possibility' (to paraphrase Lord Reid in *Overseas Tankship (UK) Ltd*, 634–35).

If possible, be more precise.

probative

Tending to prove; having the ability to prove or show. Antonym: *improbative*. In Scots law, *probative* is used of a deed or document that appears to be signed and attested in accordance with the necessary formalities, and therefore is taken to be authentic. For example:

> 'It would, in my humble opinion, be ludicrous, as well as dangerous, to permit law Courts to turn an *improbative* into a *probative* deed, [merely] because they were of opinion that the granter meant the one to be as good as the other.' [*Walker v Whitwell* 1916 SC (HL) 75, 92 (Lord Shaw of Dunfermline)]

PROCEDURAL TAGS

See **CITATION OF CASES.**

proceedings

When denoting court action, *proceedings* traditionally takes the plural form, even where referring to only one court action. Thus, 'We will take *proceedings* against you to recover the debt.' However, the singular form is now becoming more common: thus, 'We will seek to have the *proceeding* transferred from the tribunal to a court' is now acceptable.

process

See **in the process of**.

procure (that something be done)

A familiar lawyerism, reeking of archaism. It simply means 'see to it': *Re Royal Victoria Pavilion, Ramsgate* [1961] Ch 581, 587 (Pennycuick J). If *see to it* seems too colloquial, try *ensure*. For example, 'the tenant must *procure that* all insurances are kept current', means simply 'the tenant must *see to it* [or *ensure*] that all insurances are kept current' (or better still, because simpler, 'the tenant must *keep* all insurances current').

See **ensure (that something be done)**

professes to

Usually means no more than *purports to*—ie, intends to, or seems or appears to. Thus, a provision exonerating trustees from liability for acts done 'in the *professed* exercise of their powers as trustees' means 'in the *purported* exercise of their powers as trustees'. The question is how the trustees' acts appeared to the outside world, not what was the trustees' subjective state of mind when carrying out the act: *Barnsley v Noble* [2016] EWCA Civ 799; [2017] 2 WLR 1231, [33] (Sales LJ).

profit à prendre

Law French: a right to take [from land]; sometimes shortened to *profit*; plural, *profits à prendre*. A *profit à prendre* is a right to enter another person's land and take away part of the soil or the natural produce of the soil: *Australian Softwood Forests Pty Ltd v Attorney-General (NSW)* (1981) 148 CLR 121, 130–32. Because of the complex law regulating profits à prendre, the term may be an example (rare in practice) of a foreign-language term that is impossible to translate into plain English without sacrificing legal nuance.

Examples of *profits à prendre*

- rabbits: *Mason v Clarke* [1955] AC 778
- wild animals such as birds and game: *Fuller v Kitzing* [2017] EWHC 810 (Ch); [2017] 3 WLR 615
- crops, timber, soil, minerals: *Nicholls v Lovell* [1923] SASR 542 (salt); *Ex parte Henry* [1963] SR (NSW) 298 (minerals)
- pine trees: *Corporate Affairs Commission v ASC Timber Pty Ltd* (1989) 18 NSWLR 577
- stone, gravel, timber: *Bayview Properties Pty Ltd v A-G* [1960] VR 214
- slate: *Mills v Stokman* (1967) 116 CLR 61.

Profits à prendre are proprietary rights, not mere contractual rights. This distinguishes them from, for example:

- rights to enter land under a contract for the sale of items which, although the produce of the land, are sold as chattels: *Marshall v Green* (1875) LR 1 CPD 35, 44 (sale of standing timber to be felled and taken away); *Ashgrove v Deputy Commissioner of Taxation* (1994) 124 ALR 315
- licences to enter land for a specific purpose: *Beach v Trims Investments Ltd* [1960] SASR 5 (agreement for sheep agistment not a profit à prendre); *Permanent Trustee Australia Ltd v Shand* (1992) 27 NSWLR 426, 431–32 (mere right to cultivate not a profit à prendre).

Further reading

S Bridge, E Cooke, and M Dixon (eds), *Megarry & Wade's Law of Real Property*, 9th edn (Sweet & Maxwell, 2019) [26-055]–[26-068] (the law of profits à prendre)

profit à rendre

Law French: a right to put [on land]; plural: *profits à rendre*. Historically, an obligation on the owner of the burdened (servient) land to make a payment to the owner of benefited (dominant) land—such as an obligation to pay tithes or rents. In modern times, *profits à rendre* have experienced a resurgence in the guise of a right or obligation to enter land to place there or do something of benefit to the land: *Fuller v Kitzing* [2017] EWHC 810; [2017] Ch 485, [44] (following Australian cases such as *Clos Farming Estates Pty Ltd v Easton* (2002) 11 BPR 20,605, [59], and *Permanent Trustee Australia Ltd v Shand* (1992) 27 NSWLR 426, 431). As with profits à prendre, profits à rendre are proprietary rights, differing from mere contractual rights (which do not 'run with' the land). Whether a right to put or do something on someone else's land creates a proprietary right or a mere contractual right is a matter of interpreting the agreement that creates the right: *Commissioner of State Revenue (Vic) v Pioneer Concrete (Vic) Pty Ltd* (2002) 209 CLR 651 (right to tip materials on land a contractual right only).

Further reading

Brendan Edgeworth (ed), *Butt's Land Law*, 7th edn (Lawbook, 2017) [9.870] (rediscovering profits à rendre)

See also **profit à prendre**.

PROLIXITY

The problem

Prolixity abounds in legal writing. It casts unnecessary burdens on readers, who must unravel meaning from verbosity, duplication, and redundancy. It is found in contracts, deeds, wills, corporate constitutions, regulations, bylaws, and statutes that have not yet moved to a modern, plain style. Readers have long complained of it:

> Who dares presume to pen a deed,
> Unless you [ie, lawyers] are fee'd?
> 'Tis drawn; and, to augment the cost,
> In dull prolixity engross'd.
>
> [John Gay, 'Fables—The Dog and the Fox', from *Poems of John Gay* (The British Poets, 1822) vol 32, 104]

Prolixity is also found in court pleadings. This often attracts judicial opprobrium:

> '[Acceptable pleadings practice] does not extend to planting a forest of forensic contingencies and waiting until final address or perhaps even an appeal hearing to map a path through it. In this case, there were hundreds, if not thousands, of alternative and cumulative combinations of allegations.' [*Forrest v Australian Securities and Investments Commission* [2012] HCA 39; (2012) 247 CLR 486, [27]]

Sometimes the approbrium hits hard:

> In an old case, the court ordered a prolix pleader to be fined, imprisoned, and paraded around the courts of Westminster with his head thrust through the offending document, as punishment for drafting pleadings that ran to 120 pages, when (according to the judge) 16 pages should have sufficed: *Milward v Welden* (1596) Tothill 102; 21 ER 136 (reported more fully in George Spence, *Equitable Jurisdiction* (Stevens, 1846) 376–77).

Prolix pleadings can also have implications for the conduct of litigation more generally. Examples are:

Prolix pleadings can be struck out

- *Hague Plant Ltd v Hague* [2014] EWCA Civ 1609, [23]: pleadings a source of 'bewilderment and confusion', and 'a rambling narrative of the supposed twists and turns of the defendants' case ... serving no apparent purpose, and obscuring, rather than clarifying, the claimant's own case.'
- *Tchenguiz v Grant Thornton UK LLP* [2015] EWHC 405 (Comm); [2015] 1 All ER (Comm) 961: 94-page statement of case in breach of the Commercial Court's limit of 25 pages; statement of case struck out, and costs of redrafting disallowed.

Costs can be disallowed

- Excessive prolixity in pleadings can deprive the victorious party of the costs of preparing the pleadings. For warnings and punishment, see, eg, *Khader v Aziz* [2010] EWCA Civ 716, [35]–[37], [50]–[52]; [2010] 1 WLR 2673; *Standard Chartered Bank Plc v Via Mat International Ltd* [2013] EWCA Civ 490, [26]; [2013] 2 All ER (Comm) 1222; *In player Ltd v Thorogood* [2014] EWCA Civ 1511, [57]); *Tchenguiz v Thornton UK LLP* [2015] EWHC 405, [16]–[17]; [2015] 1 All ER (Comm) 961.

The reasons

There are several explanations—but not justifications—for prolixity in law. One is the power of precedent. Lawyers adopt precedents (ie, document templates) from the past to fulfil a need of the present. The practice is not peculiar to litigation: lawyers in all fields of practice adopt (and adapt) precedents. There are sound reasons for this. But precedents from the past use the language from the past, which (in law) was often tortuous, verbose and repetitive. (See further, **PRECEDENT, Legal forms.**)

Another explanation (but not justification) for prolixity is the writer's lack of understanding of the subject matter. Lawyers who know their subject matter have the confidence to be succinct. But those unfamiliar with their subject matter may be tempted to waffle, as if to camouflage insecurity beneath a torrent of words:

> Words are like leaves; and where they most abound,
> Much fruit of sense beneath is rarely found:
> False eloquence, like the prismatic glass,
> Its gaudy colours spreads on ev'ry place.
>
> (Alexander Pope, *Essay on Criticism*, part 2, lines 309–12)

Lack of familiarity with subject matter may explain the blitzkrieg of operative words formerly found in deeds of conveyance: 'The vendor doth hereby *grant, bargain, sell, release, enfeoff and confirm* unto the purchaser and his heirs ...' (emphasis added). This verbosity prompted the eminent conveyancer Davidson to comment:

> 'This multiplication of useless expressions probably owed its origin to the want of knowledge of the true meaning and due application of each word, and a consequent apprehension, that if one word alone were used, a wrong one might be adopted and the right one omitted; and to this something must be added for carelessness and the general disposition of the [legal] profession to seek safety in verbosity rather than in discrimination of language.' [*Davidson's Conveyancing Precedents*, 3rd edn (William Maxwell, 1860) vol 1, 67]

Yet another explanation (but not justification) for prolixity may be the writer's wish to soften a hard message, or to create 'distance' between writer and reader. This the writer achieves by 'padding'. But these ends can be achieved, padding-free, by prose that is concise and direct:

> ' "Padding" ... comes partly from a feeling that wordiness is an ingredient of politeness, and blunt statement is crude, if not rude. There is an element of truth in this: an over-staccato style is as irritating as an over-sostenuto one. But it is a matter of degree; and official prose is of the sort that calls for plainness rather than elegance. Moreover the habit of 'padding' springs partly from less meritorious notions—that the dignity of an official's calling demands a certain verbosity, and that naked truth is indecent and should be clothed in wrappings of woolly words.' [Ernest Gower, *The Complete Plain Words*, ed Sidney Greenbaum and Janet Whitcut, 3rd edn (Penguin, 1987) 65–66, dealing with bureaucratic writing]

The cure

The chief cure for prolixity is to prune—ruthlessly. If something can be expressed in prose that is brief, crisp, and clear, always express it that way.

Sometimes the pruning process simply requires deleting words. Example 1, below, is such a case; the marked-up version shows the deletions.

At other times, it is necessary not merely to delete but also to reorganise. Example 2, below, is such a case: the pruning reveals the need to reverse the original order of provisions.

At yet other times, the inherent problem lies in the power of precedent, particularly in areas of law that require deep learning. The document has been used for so long, and the concepts are so time-honoured, that both terminology and structure have become sacrosanct. Then, salvation may lie only in asking 'What is this document trying to achieve?' and starting afresh. This requires a bold and competent drafter—but the results can be startling, as with Example 3.

Example 1

Before

Any and all persons operating motor vehicles of any type or kind whatsoever in the [Territory] shall obtain third party insurance. [21 words]

After

Marked-up version

~~Any and all~~ Persons operating motor vehicles ~~of any type or kind whatsoever~~ in the [Territory] shall obtain third party insurance.

Clean version (with minor further refinement)

Persons operating motor vehicles in the [Territory] must obtain third party insurance. [12 words]

[Source: Robert D Eagleson, 'The Commonsense of Plain English', *Current Affairs Bulletin* (Centre for Continuing Education, University of Sydney, Jan 1985), 19]

Example 2

Before

(1) The Commission may, on application made by an offeror before the time by which the consideration specified in the relevant take-over offer is required by the terms of the offer to be paid or provided, fix a later time as the time by which that consideration is to be paid or provided and, where a later time is so fixed, the offer or, if the offer has been accepted, the contract that resulted from the acceptance shall be deemed to be varied accordingly. [83 words]

(2) An offeror shall ensure that the consideration specified in the relevant take-over offer is paid or provided not later than the time by which that consideration is required by the terms of that take-over offer to be paid or provided or, if a later time has been fixed under subsection (1), not later than the time so fixed. [58 words]

[*Companies (Acquisition of Shares) Act 1980 (Cth)*, s 19 (Australia)]

After

(1) An offeror must ensure that the consideration specified in an accepted offer is provided on time. [16 words]

(2) The Commission may extend the time for paying the consideration if the offeror applies for an extension before the consideration is due. [22 words]

[Rewrite by Robert D Eagleson, in 'Efficiency in Legal Drafting', *Essays on Legislative Drafting in Honour of JQ Evans*, ed David St L Kelly (University of Adelaide Press, 1990) 13, 23. Professor Eagleson adds: 'Nothing more needs to be said. In particular, "on time" encapsulates all the prolixity of [the original] subsection (2).']

Example 3

[*Introductory note*. This example is a 'further assurance covenant', one of four covenants for title implied for centuries into conveyances of unregistered land. The wording of the covenants, once enshrined in statute, has been described as a 'jungle of verbiage': *Meek v Clarke* (Slade LJ, unreported, 7 July 1982). The covenants are no longer used in the UK, but are still used for conveyances of unregistered land in many common-law countries. Where they survive, their wording remains virtually unchanged from Sir Orlando Bridgman's 1660s precedent: see Charles Harpum (1995) *Clarity 33*, 24 (at www.clarity-international.net/clarity-journal/archives/)]

Before (italics added to show key elements)

'And further, that *the person therein expressed to convey as beneficial owner*, and any person therein expressed to be conveying by his direction, and every other person having or rightfully claiming any estate or interest in the subject-matter of the conveyance, other than an estate or interest subject whereto the conveyance is expressly made, by, through, under, or in trust for the person therein expressed to convey as beneficial owner, or by, through, or under any person therein expressed to be conveying by his direction, or by, through, or under any one through whom the person therein expressed to convey as beneficial owner derives title, otherwise than by purchase for value, *will from time to time* and at all times after the date of the conveyance, on the request and at the cost of any person to whom the conveyance is expressed to be made, or of any person deriving title under him, *execute and do all such lawful assurances and things for further or more perfectly assuring the subject-matter of the conveyance to the person to whom the conveyance is expressed to be made*, and to those deriving title under him, subject as, if so expressed, and in the manner in which, the conveyance is expressed to be made, as by him or them, or any of them, shall be reasonably required.'

[Source: *Law of Property Act 1925*, s 76 and Sched II (repealed); italics added to indicate key parts of sentence; 223 words]

After

'[Vendor] will, at the request and the expense of [purchaser], execute all documents, and do all other acts, for the better assuring of the title to the estate or interest, as [purchaser] may from time to time reasonably require.'

[Source: *Law of Property Act 2007* (NZ), s 284 and Schedule 4; 42 words. We might be tempted to improve it a little more, along these lines: 'If the Purchaser asks, the Vendor will, at the Purchaser's expense, do whatever is reasonably necessary (including executing documents) to better assure the title to the Purchaser.' (27 words)]

For more examples, some demanding more sophisticated responses, see **REDRAFTING IN PLAIN ENGLISH**.

See also **EDITING; PLAIN LANGUAGE; PRECEDENTS; REDRAFTING TECHNIQUES; SIMPLER WORDS AND PHRASES; TERMS OF ART; THROAT-CLEARING PHRASES; WORD STRINGS**.

promissory estoppel

See **estoppel**.

promptly

As with other words relating to time, *promptly* is inherently vague and must take its meaning from context. It could mean 'without any delay' or it could mean 'as soon as reasonably possible in the circumstances'. Judicial exegesis includes:

- more speed than 'within a reasonable time': *Burton v Police* (2004) 88 SASR 152; [2004] SASC 85, [28] (Gray J)
- a 'little more expedition than a reasonable time': *Nichols Global Enterprises Pty Ltd v Biviano* (2000) 10 BPR 18,303; [2000] NSWSC 956, [18] (Young J, citing US cases).

For more precision, specify a period: eg, 'within 2 hours', 'within 2 days'.

See also **as soon as possible / as soon as practicable; forthwith; immediately**.

PRONOUNS

Use them

Traditionally, legal writing eschewed personal pronouns. Instead of repeating the parties' names or using pronouns, drafters preferred terms such as *the said* or *the aforesaid*, rather than *he*, *she*, *it*, or *they*. This archaic practice continues in some legal quarters. But it stultifies the writing and depersonalises the parties. It is much better to use personal pronouns: they lighten the prose and humanise the parties.

We / You

The increasing acceptance of personal pronouns in legal documents is evidenced in the increasingly popular *we / you* style of drafting, particularly in consumer documents. (See separate entry, **we / you**.)

Pronouns for collective ('group') nouns

In legal writing, as in writing generally, a singular noun takes a singular pronoun: eg, 'The *house* rested firmly on *its* foundations.' A plural noun takes a plural pronoun: eg, 'The *foundations* remained firmly in *their* original position.' In each case, the pronoun agrees in number with its antecedent.

But group nouns pose more difficulties. The general rule is: where the group acts as a single entity, use a singular pronoun; and where its members act separately, use a plural pronoun. Sometimes, either single or plural will do, as in the following legal examples.

Singular	Plural
The *judiciary* meets each month to consider *its* response to recent legal developments.	The *judiciary* [ie, the *judges*] meet each month to consider *their* response to recent legal developments.
The *jury* retired to consider *its* verdict.	The *jury* [ie, the *jurors*] retired to consider *their* verdict.
The *board* reviewed *its* priorities.	The *board* [ie, the board members] reviewed *their* priorities. (However, that could introduce ambiguity. Better: The board *members* reviewed *the company's* priorities.)
The *sheep* [singular] cannot be sued for *its* trespass.	The *sheep* [plural] cannot be sued for *their* trespass.

Relative pronouns

Take care to keep a relative pronoun (*that, which, who, whose*, etc) as close as possible to the noun it modifies. Too wide a gap promotes obscurity.

Examples

- 'The decision of the court *that* [or *which*] I was discussing yesterday made no sense.' What were you discussing—the decision or the court? Better: 'The court decision that [which] I was discussing yesterday made no sense.' Or 'I was discussing the court yesterday; its decision made no sense.'
- 'The court ordered the tenant to vacate the leased property and the adjoining property, *whose* owner had let it fall into disrepair.' Which property was in disrepair?
- 'The court conducted a Facebook advertising campaign encouraging the use of computer-generated drafting, *which* it hopes will appeal to all young lawyers.' What will appeal to young lawyers—the advertising campaign or computer-generated drafting?

See also **GENDER-NEUTRAL LANGUAGE; NAMES; SINGULAR / PLURAL; SUBJECT–VERB AGREEMENT; that / which; we / you.**

PROOFREADING

The need

Proofreading is a key element of any writing project, including legal writing. Even experienced lawyers, practised in the art of drafting and skilled in their area of law, make the kinds of mistakes that careful proofreading should avoid.

Most legal writers understand the benefits of proofreading—as an ideal. But practical considerations get in the way: 'I know the document well', 'I don't have the time', 'Who will pay for my time?' Yet the practical effect on the client of failure to proofread may be important: 'Doesn't my lawyer care?', or even 'Is my lawyer incompetent?' And of course there is an even more important practical effect: an error left uncorrected may give rise to a legal issue, which in turn may give rise to liability for professional negligence. The error may be so insignificant as an errant *and*:

> A lessor instructed its solicitor to prepare a lease, which was to include a provision excluding the value of the tenant's fixtures when calculating rent. The solicitor's version of the rent clause began: '[T]he value of the following fixtures and fittings are to be ignored', followed by a list of tenant's fixtures. However, that list ended at the foot of the page with the word 'and'. Over the page there followed immediately a list of the *landlord's* fixtures. Held, the effect was to exclude from the rent calculations *both* the tenant's fixtures *and* the landlord's fixtures, which produced a significantly lower rent than if only the tenant's fixtures were excluded. Held, the solicitor was liable in negligence for the lessor's loss (exceeding $Aus 1 million): *The Stuart Park (D580060) Reserve Trust v Peedoms Lawyers Pty Ltd* [2012] NSWSC 1133.

The techniques

Techniques for proofreading vary, and most who practise it have their own methods. However, the following techniques should suit most legal writers.

- Ideally, allow time between the initial writing and the proofreading. Time allows writers to come to the document with fresh eyes (attuned to what is actually written, rather than what was meant to be written).
- Do not let attention to detail distract from the need also to step back and view the larger picture. Proofreading scrutinises the text for such matters as spelling mistakes, omitted words, punctuation errors, grammar lapses, misspelled case names, and incorrect citations. Attention to the larger picture (which we may call, loosely, 'editing') looks to larger matters such as style, tone, paragraph structure, sentence structure, sentence length, preference for active voice, and excessive verbiage.
- If time is short, do not spend it on proofreading alone. Time spent in editing (more generally) may greatly improve readability.
- If time and budgets allow, adopt a 'buddy system' under which each drafter reviews another's draft.
- Print the document in a different font before reviewing. The changed typeface (and line-endings) may bring fresh attention to the task.
- Beware of auto-correction functions in word-processing programs.
- Beware of undue reliance on spell-checkers. They will not pick up 'wrong' words that are correctly spelled; nor will they pick up words or lines omitted, or (probably) tense confusions.

Proofreaders' marks

By convention, proofreaders use standardised marks to indicate corrections. Key ones follow:

[Source: *Chicago Manual of Style*, 16th edn (University of Chicago Press, 2010) para 2.116, figure 2.6]

In modern times, the importance of these standard marks is diminishing. In legal offices, for example, corrections are more likely to be made using word-processing mark-up or revision functions, entered directly into the text electronically.

Further reading

- Neil James, *Writing at Work* (Allen & Unwin, 2007) ch 17
- Timothy Perrin, *Better Writing for Lawyers* (Law Society of Upper Canada, 1990) ch 14 ('Grammar, Spelling and Punctuation')

See further **CONSISTENCY OF TERMINOLOGY; CORRECTIONS (BY COURT); EDITING; ELEGANT VARIATION; INCONSISTENT PROVISIONS.**

proportion (of / as)

Provisions requiring the calculation of 'proportions'—eg, proportionate contributions, or proportionate liability—can be complex. If words prove difficult, try a formula. For example:

Before (words)	**After (formula)**
The Tenant must pay as outgoings an amount that bears the *same proportion* of the total outgoings for the Centre *as* the floor area of the Tenant's premises bears to the floor area of the Centre.	$\text{Proportion of outgoings} = \dfrac{\text{Tenant's floor area}}{\text{Centre's floor area}}$

See also **FORMULAS.**

proprio motu

Latin: by his (her) own motion; on his (her) initiative; of his (her) own accord. Sometimes rendered *de proprio motu*, or *ex proprio motu*; but however rendered, these days an affectation. Prefer an English translation. For example:

- '[The section] provides that the Chief Justice may, either *proprio motu* [prefer: *on his [or her] own initiative*] or on application by any party, direct that any case shall be heard by two or more judges.' [*Lesage v The Mauritius Commercial Bank Ltd* [2012] UKPC 41, [5] (Lord Kerr)]
- 'But to prevent those rules being used oppressively the Court will intervene *proprio motu* [prefer: *of its own accord*] if necessary.' [*New Zealand Social Credit Political League Inc v O'Brien* [1984] 1 NZLR 84, 95 (Somers J)]

proprio vigore

Latin: by its (his, her, their) own force. Prefer standard English:

> '[B]y virtue of the legal supremacy of the United Kingdom Parliament certain Imperial statutes operate *proprio vigore* [prefer: *by their own force*] in this country …' [*Kirmani v Captain Cook Cruises Pty Ltd (No 1)* (1985) 159 CLR 351, 380 (Mason J)]

proscribe

See **prescribe / proscribe.**

prospectus

Latin: view, prospect—hence, a brochure or document giving details. The Latin plural is also *prospectus*; hence, the appropriate English plural is *prospectuses* (not *prospecti*). For example:

> 'Universities publish more conventional course material, *prospecti* [amend: *prospectuses*], charters and teaching plans that may have the same legal effect as more obvious marketing material ...' [J Stephen Kos and Russell McVeagh, 'The View from the Bottom of the Cliff: Enforcement of Legal Rights between Student and University' (1999) 4 *Australian and New Zealand Journal of Law and Education* 18, 28]

protected person

A person whose affairs are controlled under guardianship, court order, or similar legal administration.

See also **person**.

provided / provided that

See **PROVISOS**.

provision

Meaning (1): part of a document

A *provision* is any part of a document that 'provides for' something. Thus, *provision* can mean a clause, or paragraph, or part-clause or part-paragraph: *Berkeley v Berkeley* [1946] AC 555, 580 (Lord Simonds). It can also mean a fragment of information, such as a mere phrase—although in practice only if the phrase 'provides for' something (eg, by way of a stipulation or condition). In one English case, the 'provisions of this Act' included regulations made under the Act: *Willingale v Norris* [1909] 1 KB 57.

The High Court of Australia has held that where a statute renders void a 'provision' of a contract, it does not necessarily render void the entire clause, but only the part or parts necessary to fulfil the statutory command (for otherwise, drafters could manipulate the effect of the statute by the way they divide their clauses): *Zurich Australian Insurance Ltd v Metals & Minerals Insurance Pte Ltd* [2009] HCA 50; 240 CLR 391, [31].

Provisions in this sense can be superfluous. If so, delete it:

- Subject to ~~any other provisions of~~ this contract, ...
- According to ~~the provisions of~~ s 5, the punishment is life imprisonment.
- Under ~~the provisions of~~ this agreement, damages are not payable for negligence.

Meaning (2): benefits 'provided by' a document

In an appropriate context, *provision* can mean the benefits provided by the document: *Berkeley v Berkeley* [1946] AC 555, 580 (Lord Simonds)—eg, a will makes *provision* for (ie, 'provides for') the beneficiaries. Sometimes, the two meanings of *provision* appear in the one document, eg: 'The *provisions* of this will make *provision* for my children' (better drafted as: 'This will *provides* for my children'). Which of the two meanings applies is not always clear: *Saunders v Inland Revenue Commissioners* [1956] Ch 283, 288–89 (Wynn-Parry J).

Variant: 'make provision for'

The expression *make provision for* (or more simply, *provide for*) is often used generically to refer to something done—as in 'the regulations *make provision for* …' As with other generic expressions, it is better (and briefer) to specify *what* is to be done, as in the following example:

Before	After
The Rules of the Shopping Centre may contain *provisions for* any of the following: (a) *provisions for* authorising persons to enter the Shopping Centre after-hours; (b) *provisions for* ensuring common passageways are kept clear of obstructions; (c) *provisions for* regulating use of the car park; (d) *provisions for* procedures for amending the Rules from time to time.	The Rules of the Shopping Centre may: (a) *authorise* persons to enter the Shopping Centre after-hours; (b) *ensure* that common passageways are kept clear of obstructions; (c) *regulate* use of the car park; (d) *set out procedures* for amending the Rules from time to time.

PROVISOS

Origins

A proviso adds a qualification to a legal proposition, usually introduced with the formulaic 'provided that', or 'provided however that'—and often with an initial capital, 'Provided that', and sometimes all capitals, 'PROVIDED THAT' (as if to shout from the page).

Provisos have a long legislative history. For centuries, statutes in England used 'provided' or 'provided that' as a contraction of the enacting formula 'It is provided [that]' to introduce substantive provisions. This use has long ceased, but the expression 'provided' or 'provided that' has survived into the modern era. With its usage now divorced from its historical foundations, the expression has degenerated to a 'legal incantation … an all-purpose conjunction, invented by lawyers but not known to or understood by grammarians': E Driedger, *The Composition of Legislation*, 2nd edn (Edmond Cloutier, 1976) 96.

As long ago as 1845, Coode railed against the inconsistent and illogical use of provisos:

> 'It is indeed a question whether there is ever a real necessity for a proviso. At present the abuse of the formula [*provided that*] is universal. … [What] doctrines of interpretation can possibly be applied to the innumerable provisoes [sic] used in our statutes only as formulae for heaping together matter wholly unconnected?' [George Coode, *On Legislative Expression* (William Benning & Co, 1845) 50–51]

The proper role of provisos

Nevertheless, provisos have a proper role in legal drafting. Correctly used, a proviso limits or qualifies what has gone before: *Re Barker* (1890) 25 QBD 285, 292 (Lord Esher MR). It indicates an exception or limitation to a preceding statement: *Emmerton v Federal Land Tax Commissioner* (1916) 22 CLR 40, 49. In this usage, a proviso needs no particular introductory formula—and certainly not the formulaic 'provided that' or 'provided however that'. Provisos can serve their purpose perfectly well with plain introductory words such as 'if', 'but' or 'however'.

Example 1: proviso in will

A traditionally drafted will might say:

'I give my property to my children *provided that* they marry.'

The drafter could substitute 'if' or 'when'. Indeed, it would be better to do so, because the existing wording leaves unclear whether the proviso introduces a condition precedent or a condition subsequent. Specifically, is the gift: (1) initially contingent, with marriage being a condition precedent to vesting, or (2) initially vested, but subject to divesting in the case of children who do not marry? (See *Re Cohn* [1974] 3 All ER 928 (CA); *Nicholls v Public Trustee (South Australia)* (1945) 72 CLR 86.) A perceptive drafter would use 'if' to introduce a contingent gift, or 'to be paid over when' to introduce a vested gift (eg, 'to be paid over to them when they marry'): see *Hume v Perpetual Trustees Executors and Agency Co of Tasmania* (1939) 62 CLR 242; FV Hawkins and EC Ryder, *The Construction of Wills* (Sweet & Maxwell, 1965) 303–08.

Example 2: proviso in statute

Original (containing formal provisos)

'A mortgagor is entitled to redeem the mortgaged property although the time appointed for redemption has not arrived; *but in such case* the mortgagor shall pay to the mortgagee, in addition to any other moneys then owing under the mortgage, interest on the principal sum secured thereby for the unexpired portion of the term of the mortgage: *Provided that* redemption under this subsection shall not prejudice the right of the mortgagee to any collateral benefit, or to enforce any burden or restriction to the extent to which the mortgagee would be entitled under the mortgage or otherwise if the mortgage were paid off at the due date.' [*Conveyancing Act 1919* (NSW), s 93(1), emphasis added]

[One sentence, 107 words. Notice the twin provisos—the first introduced by *but*, and the second by *Provided that*. The first is a genuine proviso. The second would be better as a stand-alone provision.]

Suggested redraft (removing formal provisos but retaining concept)

(1) A mortgagor is entitled to redeem the mortgaged property although the time appointed for redemption has not arrived.

(2) *To do so*, the mortgagor shall pay to the mortgagee, in addition to any other moneys then owing under the mortgage, interest on the principal sum secured thereby for the unexpired portion of the term of the mortgage.

(3) *However*, redemption under this subsection shall not prejudice the right of the mortgagee to any collateral benefit, or to enforce any burden or restriction to the extent to which the mortgagee would be entitled under the mortgage or otherwise if the mortgage were paid off at the due date.

[105 words; emphasis added to show links]

Better still (other aspects improved)

(1) A mortgagor may redeem the mortgaged property before the due date for redemption.

(2) To do so, the mortgagor must pay to the mortgagee, in addition to any other money then owing under the mortgage, interest on the principal sum for the unexpired term of the mortgage.

(3) Early redemption under this section does not affect the mortgagee's right:

  (a) to any collateral benefit, or

  (b) to enforce any obligation to the extent to which the mortgagee could have enforced it if the mortgage were paid off on the due date.

[89 words]

The misuse of provisos

A genuine proviso qualifies or limits what has gone before. In practice, however, a (self-styled) 'proviso' sometimes introduces information that is of equal force, and that should have appeared in a stand-alone clause. Perhaps the drafter needed to add fresh material late in the drafting process, when renumbering provisions was difficult; or perhaps the negotiation process required last-minute changes, also when renumbering provisions was difficult. In either case, the drafter adds the material by way of 'proviso', tacked onto an existing clause.

While understandable, this 'afterthought' use of the proviso is problematic. The reader is uncertain whether the proviso limits the preceding provision (its proper function) or introduces a separate, stand-alone provision. This can lead to litigation over the precise 'status' of the proviso: see, eg, *Minister of State for the Army v Dalziel* (1944) 68 CLR 261, 274–75; *Commissioner of Stamp Duties v Atwill* [1973] AC 558, 561.

Sometimes, judges disagree over the purpose of a purported 'proviso'. For example, the Privy Council interpreted a 'Provided that ...' provision as introducing new, stand-alone material, not as a proviso qualifying a preceding statement: *Commissioner of Stamp Duties v Atwill* [1973] AC 558, 561. In doing so, it reversed the decision of the Australian High Court, which had treated the words as a genuine proviso, qualifying a preceding statement. The lesson is clear: where the purpose is to introduce new material, resist the temptation to use the formulaic *provided that*, or *provided however that*, and instead start a new sentence (as shown in the following example).

Example

Before

All fixtures installed during the term of the lease by the tenant become the property of the landlord upon the expiry of the term *provided that* the tenant may remove its fixtures at the end of the term.

[Source: based on Robert C Dick, *Legal Drafting*, 3rd edn (Carswell, 1995) 104]

After

All fixtures installed during the term of the lease by the tenant become the property of the landlord upon the expiry of the term. *However*, the tenant may remove its fixtures at the end of the term.

Comment

Note that the **Before** example reflects a legal misconception, which the **After** redraft perpetuates—namely, that items affixed by the tenant belong to the tenant during the lease. But the common law regards fixtures attached by the tenant as the *landlord's* property, subject to the tenant's right to remove them at or before the end of the lease. So a better redraft would be:

1. The tenant may remove its fixtures at the end of the lease.
2. Fixtures not so removed remain the landlord's property.

Cascading provisos

Provisos become doubly perplexing when used in series—one proviso following on the heels of another. Does the second proviso qualify the first proviso, or does it qualify the original statement? For example:

Assume that a lease contains the following clause:

> 'The tenant must keep the premises in good repair, *provided that* the tenant need not repair damage by fire and *provided further that* the tenant need not repair damage by water.'

Does the second proviso introduce a total exemption from any obligation to repair water damage, or merely an exemption for water damage caused when extinguishing a fire?

Provisos and the burden of proof

A party (X) who wishes to prove a case against another party (Y) normally bears the onus of proof. If X discharges that onus, but Y then seeks the protection of a proviso, the onus shifts to Y to prove that the facts come within the proviso. This shift is often legislated (eg, *Magistrates' Courts Act 1980*, s 101; *Gatland v Metropolitan Police Commissioner* [1968] 2 QB 279). But even in the absence of statutory provision, the common law requires the same result: *Vines v Djordjevitch* (1955) 91 CLR 512, 520. Where proof of facts is difficult, the issue of who bears the onus of proof becomes crucial.

Example

> A lease requires the tenant to keep the premises in repair, with a proviso (ie, exemption) for reasonable wear and tear. This compels a two-step process: (1) proving that the premises are in disrepair; and (2) proving that the disrepair is due to reasonable wear and tear. The landlord bears the onus of proving step (1), and the tenant then bears the onus of proving step (2): *Haskell v Marlow* [1928] 2 KB 45, 59; *Brown v Davies* [1958] 1 QB 117, 127; *Wicks Farming Pty Ltd v Waraluck Mining Pty Ltd* [1996] 1 Qd R 99, 103).

However, this shifting of the onus of proof assumes that the proviso is a 'genuine' one. Where, despite its form as a proviso, the clause in substance is a stand-alone provision which introduces new material, the court will treat it as such and there will be no occasion to shift the burden of proof: *Commissioner of Stamp Duties v Atwill* [1973] AC 558, 561; *Minister of State for the Army v Dalziel* (1944) 68 CLR 261, 274–75.

Provisos and interpretation

Although a proviso serves a primarily qualifying role, it is part of the provision in which it appears. It is therefore relevant in interpreting the meaning of that provision, because a provision is interpreted as a whole, with 'each portion throwing light, if need be, on the rest': *Jennings v Kelly* [1940] AC 206, 229 (Lord Wright).

Where a proviso follows a number of provisions, it may be unclear whether it relates to all of the provisions, or only to the last. A prudent drafter will clarify the possible ambiguity.

Example

> A schedule to an Act set out material in listed paragraphs, the last of which was (h). Para (h) ended with a colon (not a full stop), and was followed immediately by a proviso introduced by 'Provided that ...' Parliament later substituted a new para (h), which ended with a full stop and did not include the proviso. Did the proviso survive the repeal of para (h)? Held, yes: the legislative history showed that Parliament intended the proviso to apply to all the preceding paras, not merely to para (h), and so the proviso was unaffected by the repeal and substitution of para (h): *Piper v Harvey* [1958] 1 QB 439 (CA).

Further reading

- Elmer A Driedger, *The Composition of Legislation*, 2nd edn (Edmond Cloutier, 1976) ch 9 ('The Proviso')
- Mark Duckworth and Arthur Spyrou (eds), *Law Words* (Centre for Plain Legal Language, University of Sydney, 1995) 67 ('Provided that'); at www.clarity-international.net/plain-language-resources/general-resources/

proximity

See **close proximity**.

proximo / prox

Latin: in the next; shorthand for *proximo mense*, 'in the next month'; usually abbreviated to *prox*. Thus, a notice might require a tenant to vacate the premises 'on the 10th proximo [*or* prox]', meaning 'on the 10th of next month'. Whether abbreviated or in full, the usage is obsolete; modern usage prefers 'next month'.

See also **ultimo**.

PS

See **postscriptum**.

public domain

Known publicly; available to the public at large. The term often appears in confidentiality agreements, and in copyright and defamation law. It has become a legal buzzword; but it is not a true term of art, and for most purposes a more general, vernacular, expression such as 'publicly available' or 'publicly known' suffices. For example:

- 'Sometimes the conduct was notorious and thus *in the public domain* [prefer: *publicly known*].' [*Spiller v Joseph* [2010] UKSC 53; [2011] 1 AC 852, [87] (Lord Phillips)]
- 'This company disclosed a substantial quantity of material consisting of or based on *documents in the public domain* [prefer: *publicly available documents*].' [*Baker v Quantum Clothing Group Ltd* [2011] UKSC 17; [2011] 1 WLR 1003, Appendix para [3] (Lord Mance)]

public holiday

Meaning

A day fixed by legislation as a holiday for members of the public in the particular jurisdiction: *Ophel v Yarra City Council* (1998) 80 IR 183; *Cabal v Minister for Immigration and Multicultural Affairs (No 1)* [1999] FCA 13, [20]; (1999) 91 FCR 309, 312.

Performance of obligation on public holiday

The law does not defer a contractual obligation to perform merely because performance falls due on a public holiday. Rather, the party must perform on a day before the public holiday, unless contrary intention or settled commercial practice allows otherwise: *Mardorf Peach & Co Ltd v Attica Sea Carriers Corp of Liberia (The Laconia)* [1977] AC 850. To overcome the inconvenience of this principle, commercial contracts commonly provide that if the day on which something falls to be done is a public holiday (or a bank holiday), it may be done on the next business day. Because public holidays can vary across a country, the provision is often expressed to apply to public holidays in the place where performance is to occur—ie, regional holidays. This may allow a party to postpone performance even though it may be possible to perform at places outside the region: *Magic Mountain Developments Pty Ltd v Laureate Australia Pty Ltd* [1991] 2 Qd R 570.

See also **bank holiday**; **business day**.

puisne

Junior; of lower ranking; pronounced 'puny'. Thus, a *puisne* mortgage is a mortgage ranking below others. Although found in standard dictionaries, *puisne* is peculiarly legal, and is likely to confound even the most well-read non-lawyer (and even many well-read lawyers). Prefer an equivalent term, such as *junior*; *subsidiary*; *lower-ranking*. For example:

> '[Where] a senior mortgagee exercises a power of sale and a surplus is generated after the senior mortgagee's secured debt has been discharged in full, the surplus belongs to the next *puisne* [prefer: *ranking*] mortgagee, to the extent of the amount secured by that ~~*puisne*~~ [delete] mortgagee's mortgage.' [*Australia and New Zealand Banking Group Ltd v Fairfield City Council* [2016] NSWSC 668, [30] (Emmett AJA)]

Another usage is '*puisne* judge'—ie, a judge of a court below the highest court in the land. But take care with your chosen plain-English equivalent: eg, a *puisne* judge may be unimpressed with the description 'junior' judge, particularly if he or she sits in an intermediate appellate court.

punctual

Punctual usually means 'strictly on time'. So, an obligation to make a payment *punctually* generally allows no latitude for delay: *Agricultural and Rural Finance Pty Ltd v Gardiner* [2008] HCA 57, [116]–[117]; (2008) 238 CLR 570, 609–11 (Kirby J). If a debt is to be repaid *punctually* on a stated day, it must be paid on that day; otherwise, a requirement to pay *punctually* on 1 June would allow payment on 2 June: *Maclaine v Gatty* [1921] 1 AC 376, 383. By extension, where a contract requires payment into a bank account *punctually* on a day that turns out to be a bank holiday, then it must be paid on an earlier day, not a later day: *Mardorf Peach & Co Ltd v Attica Sea Carriers Corp of Liberia* [1977] AC 850. Nevertheless, because words take their meaning from context, *punctual* can lose the connotation of urgency, allowing room for argument over the degree of required punctuality. Therefore, where possible, specify a precise date, rather than leave rights or liabilities to turn on the vagaries of *punctual*.

PUNCTUATION

Traditional legal view: avoid punctuation

Traditional legal drafting omitted punctuation. As late as 1881, Kelly wrote in the introductory notes to his highly regarded conveyancing precedents:

> 'Punctuation is not used in legal instruments, for no one would wish the title to his estates to depend on the insertion of a comma or a semicolon. The commencement of sentences, and now and then some few important words, which serve as landmarks, are rendered conspicuous by capitals: by the aid of these the practised eye at once collects the sense; whilst, at the same time, the absence of stops renders it next to impossible materially to alter the meaning of a deed without the forgery being discovered.' [J Henry Kelly, *The Draftsman*, 2nd edn (Butterworths, 1881) 3–4]

This approach reflected the judicially-endorsed principle that punctuation played little or no part in interpreting legal documents. For example, in 1816 Sir William Grant MR said that the sense of legal writing should be gathered from the words of the document and their context, rather than from punctuation: *Sandford v Raikes* (1816) 1 Mer 646, 651; 35 ER 808, 810. Earlier judges had expressed the same view, most notably Lord Kenyon CJ in *Doe d Willis v Martin* (1790) 4 TR 39, 65, 66; 100 ER 882, 897.

The same view was repeated as late as 1920 in a Canadian case (*City of Medicine Hat v Howson* (1920) 53 DLR 264 (Alberta CA)), and as late as 1959 in an Australian case (*Deputy Federal Commissioner of Taxation v Carpenter* [1959] VR 470, 471).

Modern legal view: use normal punctuation

But that is no longer the prevalent view. The modern style of legal drafting uses punctuation for the same reason as any other carefully written prose uses punctuation—to elucidate meaning. Judges have endorsed that approach (despite occasional waverings) for at least a century. In 1918, Lord Shaw pointed out that punctuation is part of the composition of language, and is sometimes 'quite significantly employed', and he saw no reason to deprive legal documents of the significance that other forms of writing attach to punctuation: *Houston v Burns* [1918] AC 337, 348.

Normal punctuation techniques, then, apply as much to legal writing as they do to normal prose. Properly employed, punctuation is an aid to comprehension. Judges now pay close attention to the drafter's punctuation (eg, *Re Steel* [1979] Ch 218, interpreting a will) or lack of punctuation (eg, *Coffill v Lagudi Holdings Pty Ltd* [2016] NSWSC 1764, [38], interpreting an easement). For example, senior Australian judges have given effect to commas in the text of statutes to indicate the drafter's (or Parliament's) intention: see, eg, *Ryde Municipal Council v Macquarie University* (1978) 139 CLR 633, 636 (Gibbs ACJ); *N & D Ridolfo Pty Ltd v Mayer* (1974) 7 SASR 530 (Bray CJ).

Punctuation does not necessarily reflect pauses in speech. The purpose is to clarify meaning for (silent) readers, rather than give speakers time to pause. So, in the following sentence, a speaker might well pause after *covered*, but it would be inappropriate to insert a comma there: 'An issue still to be covered concerns the award of damages.' Conversely, in the following sentence a speaker might not pause after *that*, but readers might welcome a comma as an aid to meaning: 'The judge decided that, because damages had now been assessed, the claim should be dismissed.'

Punctuation and the judge

Judicial recourse to punctuation comes with an important qualification: judges may ignore punctuation, or the lack of it, if (in their view) that approach better discerns the drafter's meaning. For example, Sir Robert Megarry famously said: 'Punctuation is the servant and not the master of substance and meaning': *Marshall v Cottingham* [1982] 1 Ch 82, 88. The US Supreme Court has said, in the context of interpreting statutes, that punctuation cannot control the true meaning of a statute: eg, *United States v Shreveport Grain & Elevator Co* 287 US 77, 82-2 (1932); *United States National Bank of Oregon v Independent Insurance Agents of America Inc* 508 US 439, 454 (1993). Other US courts have said the same:

> 'In construing statutes, we will not indulge in quibbles over minute points of punctuation; they are among the atomies of grammar. At best, the so-called grammatical stops are widely misunderstood and applied even among average and reasonably well-educated laymen, including legislators and, mirabile dictu, even judges.' [*Hill v Conway*, 463 A 2d 232, 234 (Vermont, 1983)]

In similar vein, Australian judges have said that a court may take notice of punctuation but is not to be controlled by it where the context requires otherwise (eg, *Committee of Direction of Fruit Marketing v Collins* (1925) 36 CLR 410, 421 (Isaacs J); *Chew v The Queen* (1992) 173 CLR 626, 639 (Dawson J)).

In particular, punctuation is not a useful guide where the drafter's style displays ignorance of punctuation and grammatical conventions:

> '[A] prerequisite to relying on punctuation is being satisfied that it has been used consciously and not haphazardly. … I am not satisfied, in a clause which is littered with grammatical errors and which does not pay regard to defined terms, and which plainly was copied verbatim from [a superseded document], that the commas are a meaningful guide to its grammatical, let alone legal, meaning.' [*Mainteck Services Pty Ltd v Stein Heurtey SA* [2014] NSWCA 184; (2014) 89 NSWLR 633, [105]–[106] (Leeming JA)]

The following cases illustrate the modern judicial approach to punctuation, particularly the freedom to ignore or discount punctuation where (in the court's view) that best reflects the parties' purpose. The cases are listed under various punctuation conventions.

Commas

- Sir Robert Megarry added a comma to a clause in a will, because that better reflected the intention of a testator who was semi-literate and unfamiliar with the role of commas: *Re Steel* [1979] Ch 218.
- An Australian judge disregarded a comma in a statute where it served no apparent purpose and the provision made sense by ignoring it: *Transport Accident Commission v Hipwell* [1995] 1 VR 582, 590.
- A Canadian appellate court disregarded a comma in a statute where the comma would 'destroy the reasonable inference to be deduced from the language of the whole clause': *Re Winding-up Act and Gibson Mining Co Ltd* [1923] 3 DLR 1052, BCCA).
- An Australian appellate court treated as inconsequential the absence of a comma in an exclusion clause in a motor vehicle insurance policy, where the document was poorly punctuated, and where to place undue importance on correct grammar would undermine the legislative policy behind documents of this kind: *Zhang v ROC Services (NSW) Pty Ltd* [2016] NSWCA 370.

Semicolons

- The Privy Council discounted a semicolon in a will, where a testator left a 25% share of his estate to: '(a) my cousins [A, P, W and J]; [note semicolon] and (b) my ex-spouse [R].' The Privy Council held that the context showed this to be a share of 5% to each of the five named persons, not 12.5% to the four persons in (a) and 12.5% to the ex-spouse in (b): *Sammut v Manzi* [2008] UKPC 58; [2009] 1 WLR 1834, [12].
- A Canadian court ignored a semicolon in a statutory provision, so as to make the meaning (and punctuation) consistent with an earlier provision on which the present provision was based: *Smart Hardware Co Ltd v Town of Melfort* (1917) 32 DLR 552.
- An Australian court treated a semicolon that separated two clauses (therefore suggesting grammatically independent clauses) as if it were a comma: *Minister for Immigration and Multicultural Affairs v Savvin* (2000) 61 ALD 107.
- An Australian court treated a sentence divided in the middle by a semicolon as if it were two separate sentences divided by a full stop: *Carlton Shire Council v Ruse* (1912) 14 CLR 220, especially at 225.

Full stops

- A US court ignored a full stop where the sense showed that the sentence was meant to run on, not stop: *Richter v Commonwealth Casualty Co* (93 Pa Super 28, Pa 1928).

Paragraph breaks

- An Australian judge ignored the paragraphing of a statutory provision and preferred instead the paragraphing of the English precedent from which the local statute was drawn: *Re AB* [1950] VLR 1, 3–4 (Barry J).

- Another Australian judge rewrote the paragraphing of a statutory provision to reflect what he saw to be the legislator's intent: *Strahan Marine Board v Kirkpatrick* [1967] Tas SR 179, 184 (Crisp J).

Quotation marks

- The US Supreme Court 'moved' quotation marks in an amending Act to correct 'a scrivener's error'. If left where they appeared, the quotation marks would have inserted an amendment into an Act that had been repealed. The Court 'moved' the quotation marks so as to insert the amendment into an Act that remained in force. See *United States National Bank v Independent Insurance Agents of America, Inc* 508 US 439, 455 (1993).

Spacing following punctuation

In typewriter times, lawyers inserted two spaces after a full stop, colon, or semicolon. But with modern word-processing programs and printers, the trend is towards a single space only. The only likely issue with this trend occurs where a sentence starts with a word or phrase that might, at first glance, be a continuation from the preceding sentence. A temporary miscue might result, as in the following examples:

- The court convened on the beach, under a palm tree. Justice is not easily dispensed from there.
- These words should not be split. Infinitives are another issue.
- Matthew kept looking for John St. Andrew went to church instead.
- 'The answer must be No. I accept the arguments of counsel.' [based on *Allied Dunbar Assurance plc v Fowle* [1994] BCC 422, 433 (Garland J)]

But these occasions are rare, and in any case a perceptive writer can avoid the miscue by changing the sentence structure.

Consistency with punctuation

Careful writers are consistent with their punctuation usage, just as they are consistent with their terminology. Sometimes, however, even the finest writers (or their editors) slip up.

Example

No 1 West India Quay Ltd v East Tower Apartments Ltd [2018] EWCA Civ 250; [2018] 1 WLR 5682:

- colon used instead of semicolon [19]
- commas used between multi-word items in run-on list, where semicolons preferable ([26])
- no punctuation before last item in run-on list, where semicolon conventional ([26])
- comma after 'fourth', but not after 'first' or 'second' or 'third' ([26])
- no punctuation before or after 'ie' ([28]).

See also **ABBREVIATIONS; APOSTROPHES; BRACKETS; BULLET POINTS; COLONS; COMMAS; CONSISTENCY OF TERMINOLOGY; DASHES; EXCLAMATION MARKS; FORWARD SLASH; HYPHENS; LAST-ANTECEDENT RULE; LISTS AND ENUMERATIONS; POSSESSIVES; QUESTION MARKS; QUOTATIONS; SEMICOLONS.**

pupil

In Scots law, a prepubescent child, defined as a boy under 14 years or a girl under 12 years; hence, *pupillarity*—the status of a pupil.

More generally in legal usage, a person undertaking a course of instruction and reading to become a barrister. The British and Commonwealth preferred spelling is *pupillage*; US spelling is *pupilage*. However, as increasingly happens, the gravitational pull of US spelling is felt in the UK also: eg, *Doegar v The Bar Standards Board* [2009] EWHC 2231 (Admin) (Sullivan LJ), where both spellings are used ('pupillage' 5 times, 'pupilage' 8 times).

See also **infant / minor**.

pur autre vie

Norman French: for the life of another [person]—used especially in the context of the grant of a life estate.

See **life estate**.

purchaser

In legal usage, as in normal usage, a person who buys land or goods. However, the legal usage has for centuries extended more widely to include any person who, for value, acquires any interest in property: *Goodright d Humphreys v Moses* (1774) 2 Wm Bl 1019, 1022; 96 ER 599, 600. In this sense, *purchaser* includes, for example, mortgagees and lessees. This breadth of meaning is reflected in the definition of 'purchaser' in property law legislation: eg, '*Purchaser* means a purchaser in good faith for valuable consideration and includes a lessee, mortgagee or other person who for valuable consideration acquires an interest in property ...': *Law of Property Act 1925*, s 205(1)(xxi).

purports to

In general usage, *to purport to* do something is to intend to do it, or to seem or appear to do it. In legal usage, *to purport to* do something normally implies that the act has been done, but that it is unsuccessful on one or both of two grounds.

1. **Lack of legal power to do the act.** For example:
   - A person *purports* to enter into a contract as agent for a principal, but in fact has no authority to act.
   - A landlord *purports* to evict a tenant, but the eviction is ineffective because the tenant has statutory protection.
2. **Failure to comply with the legal requirements for the act to be effective.** For example:
   - A person (with testamentary capacity) *purports to* make a will, but fails to have it signed by the necessary witnesses.
   - A person (with contractual capacity) *purports to* execute a deed, but fails to 'deliver' the deed as required by the law of deeds.

See also **professes to**; **purpose**.

purpose

In some legal contexts, references to a person's *purpose* are to 'subjective' purpose (ie, what the person actually intended). In other legal contexts, references to a person's *purpose* are to 'objective' purpose (ie, what observers would have assumed the intention to be). Which meaning of *purpose* a statute or contract intends in particular contexts is the stuff of litigation: see, eg, the many cases cited in Daniel Greenberg (ed), *Stroud's Judicial Dictionary*, 9th edn (Sweet & Maxwell, 2017) title 'purpose'. To add to *Stroud's* examples:

- in the context of tax evasion, a person's *purpose* in entering into a transaction is usually tested subjectively: eg, *Federal Commissioner of Taxation v Starr* [2007] FCAFC 204; (2007) 164 FCR 436
- but in the context of crimes legislation, a person's purpose in engaging in conduct is often tested objectively: eg, *Ex parte Attorney-General (WA)* [2011] WASCA 129.

However, these are no more than generalities; context is everything.

PURPOSE CLAUSE

A clause (sometimes called an 'objects clause') that sets out the purpose of a document. In a contract, it sets out the parties' purpose in entering into the contract; in a statute, it sets out the objectives of the legislation. If a provision in a contract or statute is ambiguous, courts search for the document's purpose to help resolve the ambiguity. A purpose clause facilitates that search by stating the purpose or purposes (eg, *Lynn v State of New South Wales* (2016) 91 NSWLR 636, 647).

Purpose clauses have limitations. For example:

- Strictly, a purpose clause should state only the purpose (object) of the document. It should not, for example, explain the document's effect, or how its stated purpose is to be achieved.
- A purpose clause is diminished if the purposes are expressed in weasel words ('an exercise in apologetics'): *Russo v Aiello* (2003) 215 CLR 643, 645 (Gleeson CJ, speaking of a statute).
- A purpose clause is unlikely to be of much use if expressed in colloquialisms: eg, where the stated purpose is to ensure 'a fair go all round' to parties to an employment dispute (as in the Australian *Workplace Relations Act 1996* (Cth), s 635(2), repealed).
- A purpose clause expressed with a high level of generality is unlikely to be of much use in interpreting particular provisions: *Shannongrove Pty Ltd v Environment Protection Authority* [2013] NSWCA 179; (2013) 84 NSWLR 668, [19].
- A purpose clause containing multiple statements that lack a harmonious theme is unlikely to be helpful.
- A purpose clause is part of the whole document, and is interpreted as part of that larger whole. Thus, if a provision of the document clearly extends beyond a purpose as stated in the purpose clause, a court is unlikely to allow the stated purpose to limit the provision: *Cappello v Roads and Maritime Services* [2019] NSWCA 227, [39]–[43].

Further reading

- Jeffrey Barnes, 'Statutory Objects Provisions: How Cogent Is the Research and Commentary?' (2013) 34 *Statute Law Review* 12 (reviewing the limited empirical research on the utility of purpose clauses)
- Duncan Berry, 'Purpose Sections: Why They Are a Good Idea for Drafters and Users' *The Loophole* (May 2011) 49 (arguing that purpose sections in statutes help drafters to focus on the aims of the legislation, and help readers to understand what the legislation seeks to achieve); at www.calc.ngo/publications/loopholes#loophole-table-2011

pursuant to

Meaning *under*, *by*

Usually, *pursuant to* is an habitual legalism, meaning simply *under* or *by*—in which case, prefer *under* or *by*. For example:

- 'A person with a right to possession *pursuant to* [prefer: *under*] a lease, must …'
- 'An officer authorised *pursuant to* [prefer: *by*] a warrant may …'

Potential ambiguity

Some uses of *pursuant to* are ambiguous. For example, if a person does something *pursuant to* a power, do they do it *by authority of* the power or *in [purported] exercise of* the power? The uncritical substitution of *under* or *by* may not, of itself, clarify the ambiguity. To illustrate:

> A regulation sets prices for goods. In addition, the regulation authorises an agency to set prices. A reference to a price set *pursuant to* the regulation could mean (1) a price set *by* the regulation itself, or (2) a price set by the agency: *Ex parte Zietsch* (1944) 44 SR (NSW) 360. If *pursuant to* obscures the distinction, so too will *under* or *by*.

More subtle meanings

Like some other habitual legalisms, *pursuant to* can obscure subtlety of meaning. A plainer alternative may help bring the subtleties to the surface. But this may require a more nuanced alternative than *under* or *by*. Possibilities may be 'by the authority of' or 'complying with' (or 'in conformity with').

'by the authority of'

- 'The Court acts *pursuant to* [prefer: *by the authority given by*; *under authority from*] section 5 of the Act.'
- 'The Minister issues the licence *pursuant to* [prefer: *by the authority of*] s 5.'
- 'The vendor can rescind *pursuant to* [prefer: *under the power given by*] the legislation.'

'complying with' / 'in conformity with'

- 'A mortgage *pursuant to* [prefer: *complying with*; *that satisfies the requirements of*] s 55 confers a power of sale.' [To explain: s 55 requires mortgages to be registered.]
- 'A licence *issued pursuant to* [prefer: *issued in conformity with*; *that complies with*] s 10 gives a right of entry onto the land.'

See also **under**.

pursuer

In Scottish legal usage, the person who initiates a civil action. In English legal usage, called the *plaintiff*.

put option

An agreement between parties (A and B) that entitles one party (B) who owns property to require the other party (A) to enter into a specified transaction in relation to that property—eg, that A buy the property from B, or take a lease of the property from B.

Often coupled with a call option (hence, 'put and call option') to ensure complete control over the disposition of property. Thus (to continue the example), B may grant A a call option, entitling (but not requiring) A to buy the property from B, but coupled with a put option so that, if A fails to exercise the call option, B can 'put' the property to A, compelling A to buy.

Compare **call option**.

QC

See **Queen's Counsel**.

qua

Latin: in the capacity of; in the role of. A Latin scrap, meaning (in plain English) 'in the capacity as' or, even more simply, 'as'. Prefer the plain English: eg, 'The solicitor signed the deed *qua* [prefer: *in the capacity of*; *as*] solicitor, not *qua* [prefer: *in the capacity of*; *as*] trustee.'

> '[T]he fact that Mr Johnson was claiming, as it were, *qua* [prefer: *as*] employee, rather than *qua* [prefer: *as*] shareholder, made no difference. I can see no basis whatever in logic or principle as to why, if a claim *qua* [prefer: *as*] employee is barred by the rule, a claim made *qua* [prefer: *as*] creditor is not similarly so barred.' [*Gardner v Parker* [2004] 2 BCLC 554, [70] (Neuberger LJ)]

quaere

Latin: to query; to inquire (hence *quaeritur*: it is questioned). *Quaere* still finds its way regularly into legal usage, despite a perfectly adequate English translation. To retain it serves no purpose but pedantry.

- '[The] issue between those parties … [was] whether the owner assured was entitled to be paid for a total loss (*quaere* [prefer: *query*] whether actual or constructive) or only for a partial loss …' [*Masefield AG v Amlim Corporate Member Ltd* [2011] EWCA Civ 24, [27]; [2011] 1 WLR 2012, 2020 (Rix LJ)]
- 'If one [joint tenant] can grant a licence—*as to which, quaere* [prefer: *question whether this is so*; or *this might or not be so*]—then, surely, the other can revoke the licence.' [*Robson-Paul v Farrugia* (1969) 20 FCR 820, 825 (Davies LJ)]

See also **sed quaere**.

QUALIFIERS

Always question whether you need qualifiers such as 'probably', 'likely', 'maybe'. Sometimes, of course, you may need to qualify a statement. But too often legal writers add qualifiers out of habit, introducing an unnecessary hesitancy into what could be a clear and unequivocal proposition.

See also **MODIFIERS**.

QUALIFYING PHRASES

See **MODIFIERS**.

quantum meruit

Latin: as much as deserved—usually in the sense of 'as much money as is reasonably deserved'. For example, a builder may claim *quantum meruit* for partial performance under a building contract (eg, to be paid for materials supplied or work done). Some may regard *quantum meruit* as an indispensable term of art—and so it may be in, for example, court pleadings. But in many contexts a translation or explanation will suffice.

- 'An unjust enrichment claim may … take the form of a claim for recompense for benefits provided by one party to the other (a *quantum meruit* claim). [*Patel v Mirza* [2016] UKSC 42; [2017] AC 467, [43] (Lord Toulson, adding the Latin as if to reassure legal readers about the basis for the claim)]
- 'The appellants' first ground of appeal raises for consideration the correctness of the proposition that a claim for *quantum meruit—that is, for the reasonable value of the work performed*—may be made at the election of the innocent party [in place of claim for damages post-termination for repudiation].' [*Mann v Paterson Constructions Pty Ltd* [2019] HCA 32; (2019) 93 ALJR 1164, [5], supplying a translation; emphasis added]

quantum sufficit

Latin: as much as suffices; sufficient. An English translation suffices. For example:

> 'It was not made clear to me whether the plaintiff's proposition depended upon all the eggs of all its hens being sent to Victoria, or whether the same argument would be available, *quantum sufficit* [prefer: *as much as suffices; to the extent needed*], if some of the eggs of all the hens, or all the eggs of some of the hens, were sent there.' [*Damjanovic & Sons Pty Ltd v Commonwealth* (1968) 117 CLR 390, 405 (Windeyer J)]

quarter day

Literally, the day at the end of a quarter of the year; as a noun, sometimes hyphenated (*quarter-day*), as an adjective preferably always hyphenated ('*quarter-day* dates'). In legal usage in England and Ireland, *quarter days* are the four ecclesiastical feast days, namely:

- Lady Day (25 March)
- Midsummer Day (24 June)
- Michaelmas (29 September)
- Christmas Day (25 December).

In Scotland, the *quarter days* are Candlemas (2 February), Whitsunday (15 May), Lammas (1 August), and Martinmas (11 November).

Quarter days were specified in leases as the standard dates for taking up possession and paying rent. Most modern leases use conventional dates.

In the United States, *quarter days* are the days at the beginning of each quarter, being 1 January, 1 April, 1 July, and 1 October.

In some jurisdictions, statute fixes *quarter days*: eg, in Australia, 31 March, 30 June, 30 September, and 31 December: *Corporations Act 2001* (Cth), s 9.

See also **day**; **Whitsunday**.

quash

To annul, put an end to, declare invalid, stop. A word used now almost exclusively in law: eg, to *quash* proceedings, to *quash* the decision of an official or tribunal. To non-lawyers the term must seem quaint, suggesting *squash*. Plain-English alternatives are easy to find, as in the following example.

Original	Alternatives
The court *quashed* the Minister's decision.	The court *overturned* the Minister's decision. The court *set aside* the Minister's decision. The court *annulled* the Minister's decision. The court *declared* the Minister's decision *to be void*.

Purists might argue that these alternatives do not completely capture the nuance of 'rendering the decision as if it had never been made': *Grafton Group (UK) plc v Secretary of State for Transport* [2017] 1 WLR 373, 381 (Laws LJ). But except in the most technical of contexts, they are sufficient.

See also **certiorari**.

quasi-

Latin: as if. Used as a prefix, *quasi-* (preferably hyphenated) indicates that a thing is 'sort of' like another thing, but is not actually that other thing. Examples are *quasi-contract*, *quasi-criminal*, *quasi-easement*, *quasi-judicial*.

Queen's Counsel

Abbrev QC; singular and plural forms are the same. In times when the monarch is male, called *King's Counsel* (KC); in some Commonwealth countries now called *Senior Counsel* (SC). A formal title bestowed on senior barristers; occasionally bestowed on Attorneys-General and senior parliamentary drafters. Historically, chosen by the government on recommendation of the Attorney-General; but in many jurisdictions now chosen more transparently by a selection panel. Queen's Counsel wear a gown of silk (in reality, sometimes wool, or silk–wool mix, or artificial silk)—hence the description of Queen's Counsel as 'silks' and the process of appointment as 'taking silk'. Traditionally, Queen's Counsel could not draft pleadings, or appear in court, without a junior (ie, a non-QC); but in most jurisdictions that rule has now been relaxed.

See also **council / counsel**; **junior counsel**.

question whether

Prune to *whether*. For example:

- 'The first proviso emphasises that *the question whether* [prefer: *whether*] a term is implied is to be judged at the date the contract is made.' [*Marks and Spencer plc v BNP Paribas Securities Services Trust Co* [2015] UKSC 72; [2016] AC 742, [23] (Lord Neuberger)]
- '*The question whether* [prefer: *Whether*] a contract has been made depends on whether there has been a *consensus ad idem* ...' [*Oceanic Sun Line Special Shipping Co Inc v Fay* (1988) 165 CLR 197, 225 (Brennan J)]

Similarly, prune the variants 'the question *of* whether' and 'the question *about* whether':

- '*[T]he question of whether* [prefer: *Whether*] permission to amend should be given must be considered in the light of the need to conduct litigation fairly and justly and at proportionate cost.' [*Elite Property Holdings Ltd and another v Barclays Bank plc* [2019] EWCA Civ 204, [40] (Asplin LJ)]

- 'I can turn now to deal with *the question of whether* [prefer: *whether*] the judge was right to answer the second preliminary issue in the negative.' [*Energy Solutions EU Ltd v Nuclear Decommissioning Authority* [2015] EWCA Civ 1262, [47] (Vos LJ)]
- '[The quoted passage] … deals with *the question about whether* [prefer: *whether*] at review the prime rental values in Glasgow city centre should be ascertained by reference to the "headline" rents, or *whether* [preferred usage] those "headline" rents should be adjusted for the effect of *grassum*, reverse premiums, etc.' [*Legal Services Centre Ltd v Peter Samuel LLP* [2009] CSOH 141, [162] (Lord Glinnie)]

Even more so, prune *the question whether or not*:

> 'He was clearly engaging with *the question whether or not* [prefer: *whether*] an extended sentence would be adequate for the purpose of protecting the public …' [*Gray v R* [2016] EWCA Crim 1034, [33] (Lang J)]

See also **whether**.

QUESTIONS

Direct / indirect questions

Some legal writers, perhaps striving for a formal tone, prefer to cast questions indirectly: eg, 'The question is whether these facts give rise to a duty of care.' But a more effective (and shorter) sentence gets straight to the point: 'Do these facts give rise to a duty of care?'

Question marks

Direct questions need question marks: 'Have you answered the question?' Indirect questions do not need question marks: 'I am asking you whether you answered the question.'

For the proper location of question marks when quoting material, see **QUOTATIONS**.

See also **QUOTATIONS**.

qui facit per alium facit per se

Latin: a person who acts through another is regarded as acting through himself or herself. The maxim reflects the rationale behind the doctrine of vicarious liability, under which an employer (or principal) is responsible for damage caused by an employee's (or agent's) negligent acts committed within the scope of the employment (or agency): *Stevens v Brodribb Sawmilling Co Pty Ltd* (1986) 160 CLR 16. The maxim is easily translated—so use a translation:

> 'The principle that a person who acts through an agent does the act himself (*qui facit per alium facit per se*) would apply.' [*Forde and McHugh Ltd* v *Revenue and Customs Commissioners* [2012] 3 All ER 1256; [2012] EWCA Civ 692, [116] (Arden LJ, expressing the principle in English and then adding the Latin in parentheses, as if to reassure legal readers)]

qui prior est tempore[,] potior est jure

Latin: the person earlier in time has the stronger claim. A maxim for resolving claims between competing equitable interests in property (usually land), namely, that an earlier-created interest prevails over a later-created one. As with many Latin maxims, the meaning is lost on English readers—which is a good reason to translate it for them.

Also, the Latin obscures a major qualification. Rather than automatically applying the 'first in time' maxim, courts usually search for the 'better equity'—and that can postpone the earlier interest to the later. An example is where the earlier interest holder's conduct led the later interest holder to assume that the earlier interest did not exist; the maxim is then displaced and priority is given to the later interest: *Farrand v Yorkshire Banking Co* (1888) 40 Ch D 182; *Taylor v Russell* [1892] AC 244; *Latec Investments v Hotel Terrigal Pty Ltd* (1965) 113 CLR 265, 276. Indeed, in reality, courts often seek to determine the parties' respective merits by considering all the circumstances of the case, including the nature of the competing interests, the manner of their acquisition, and the parties' entire conduct. Only if—after that exercise—the merits remain equal and no other sufficient ground exists for preferring one interest over the other, do the courts invoke the 'first in time' principle: *Rice v Rice* (1853) 2 Drew 73, 78; 61 ER 646, 648. This makes the maxim a principle of last resort, not of first resort.

As with many legal Latinisms, nothing is lost in translation. For example:

- '[T]he general rule as to the priority of equitable charges is *qui prior est tempore potior est jure* [prefer: *an earlier charge prevails over a later one*].' [*Mortgage Corp Ltd v Nationwide Credit Corp Ltd* [1994] Ch 49, 54 (Dillon LJ)]
- 'If the merits are equal, priority in time of creation is considered to give the better equity. This is the true meaning of the maxim *qui prior est tempore potior est jure*.' [*Latec Investments Pty Ltd v Hotel Terrigal Pty Ltd* (1965) 113 CLR 265, 276 (Kitto J, offering a translation)]

Further reading

- S Bridge, E Cooke, and M Dixon (eds), *Megarry & Wade's Law of Real Property*, 9th edn (Sweet & Maxwell, 2019) [25-014]
- Brendan Edgeworth (ed), *Butt's Land Law*, 7th edn (Lawbook, 2017) [12.1160] (Commonwealth case law)

quia timet

Latin: because he or she fears. Hence, *quia timet injunction*—an injunction to restrain wrongful acts that are threatened but not yet commenced. A term of art, with a meaning more hinted-at than expressed, and difficult to translate into a one- or two-word English equivalent.

quicquid plantatur solo, solo cedit

Latin: whatever is affixed to the soil, becomes part of the soil. The maxim encapsulates the law of fixtures:

> 'The meaning of "real property" in law … includes certain physical objects which are treated as part of the land itself. The general rule is "*quicquid plantatur solo, solo cedit*" ("whatever is attached to the soil becomes part of it"). Thus if a building is erected on land and objects are permanently attached to the building, then the soil, the building and the objects affixed to it are all in law "land", ie, they are real property, not chattels.' [S Bridge, E Cooke, and M Dixon (eds), *Megarry & Wade's Law of Real Property*, 9th edn (Sweet & Maxwell, 2019) [22-001].]

However, taken alone, the Latin oversimplifies that law, because not all things affixed are, in law, fixtures.

Although the maxim may impress some readers, it loses nothing in translation. Nor do its variants:

- *aedificatum solo, solo cedit*—whatever is built on the soil, becomes part of the soil
- *omne quod solo inaedificatur solo cedit*—everything built on the soil passes with the soil; everything built on land becomes part of the land.

See also **fixtures and fittings**.

quid pro quo

Latin: this for that, usually in the context of something offered in return for something else. So, a purchaser of property offers a *quid pro quo*—namely, the purchase price in return for a transfer of the title. The most logical plural is *quid pro quos* (not *quids pro quo*). Although a Latinism, most readers probably understand its meaning—and the closest plain-English substitute is 'one thing in return for another', which lacks the Latin's brevity and rhythm.

quiet enjoyment

Enjoyment (possession) free from interference. Commonly found in leases in the 'covenant for quiet enjoyment', under which the landlord covenants (ie, promises) that the tenant will enjoy possession of the premises without interruption by the landlord or persons claiming through the landlord: *Kenny v Preen* [1963] 1 QB 499, 511. *Quiet* here means 'free from interruption', not 'free from noise'. The covenant is implied wherever the relationship of landlord and tenant exists, including where the lease is informal: *Budd-Scott v Daniell* [1902] 2 KB 351, 356, 358, 361; *Markham v Paget* [1908] 1 Ch 697, 715–16.

Further reading

- S Bridge, E Cooke, and M Dixon (eds), *Megarry & Wade's Law of Real Property*, 9th edn (Sweet & Maxwell, 2019) [18-006]–[18-009]
- Brendan Edgeworth (ed), *Butt's Land Law*, 7th edn (Lawbook, 2017) [7.510]–[7.550] (Commonwealth case law)

quilibet potest renunciare juri pro se introducto

Latin: a person may renounce the benefit of a stipulation or right introduced for his or her own benefit: see RH Kersley (ed), *Broom's Legal Maxims*, 10th edn (Sweet & Maxwell, 1939) 477. The maxim applies only to a benefit for the person's *sole* benefit: *Heron Garage Ltd v Moss* [1974] 1 WLR 148. No magic resides in the Latin. Prefer an appropriate English translation that captures the essence of the maxim: eg, 'a person may waive a clause that is for their sole benefit'.

quit

In legal usage, *quit* has two distinct meanings.

1. As an adjective: exempt, free from. For example, in colonial times Crown grants of land reserved a *quit rent* (sometimes hyphenated, *quit-rent*) in place of other tenurial services: Enid Campbell, 'The Quit Rent System in Colonial New South Wales' (2009) 35 *Monash University Law Review* 32.
2. As a verb: to leave. For example, a *notice to quit* is a landlord's notice requiring the tenant to vacate the premises.

quo animo

Latin: by (with) what intention. A Latinism beloved by lawyers, but lacking any particular legal nuance. Prefer the English translation:

> 'Lord Mansfield CJ held that it depended upon the answer to the question, *quo animo* [prefer: *with what intention*] the rent was accepted.' [*Oliver Ashworth (Holdings) Ltd v Ballard (Kent) Ltd* [2000] Ch 12, 39 (Laws LJ)]

quoad hoc

Latin: in this respect; so far as it goes. In modern legal usage, a needless Latinism. Prefer a context-appropriate English translation, as in the following examples:

- 'If the company itself attempted to [exclude interest on investments from its account sheet], it would *quoad hoc* [prefer: *to that extent*] sterilise that portion of the account …' [*Liverpool and London and Globe Insurance Co v Bennett* [1913] AC 610, 617 (Lord Shaw of Dunfermline)]
- '[W]hen an employee is sent by his employer to do work for another, it is a question of fact whether he becomes *quoad hoc* [prefer: *in this respect*] the employee of the person for whom he is, for the time being, working, or whether he remains in all respects the employee of his ordinary employer.' [*Waterside Workers' Federation of Australia v Gilchrist, Watt & Sanderson Ltd* (1924) 34 CLR 482, 546 (Starke J)]

quod erat demonstrandum

Latin: which was the thing to be proved. Abbreviation: QED. Although this Latinism appears often in technical and scientific writing, non-technical audiences may find it pretentious—in which case, prefer an appropriate plain-English translation. For example:

> 'The case for the Crown's claim therefore fails. *Quod erat demonstrandum* [prefer: *The issue is settled;* or, *Case closed*].' [*Attorney-General v Luncheon and Sports Club Ltd* [1929] AC 400, 406 (Viscount Dunedin). A more literal translation—'That was the point to be established'—would miss the sense.]

Non-technical readers may also find the variants pretentious: *quod erat faciendum* (which was the thing to be done; abbreviation QEF) and *quod erat inveniendum* (which was the thing to be found; abbreviation QEI). Here too, prefer plain English.

quod vide

Latin: see which thing (in the sense of 'look to the discussion elsewhere'). Usually abbreviated: *qv* (or in US usage, *q.v.*). A Latinism common in formal texts, including legal texts, but easily rendered in standard English: *see*, or *see that discussion*.

quondam

Latin: former; once; that which was formerly. A Latinism that has found its way into English—but is hardly standard English. Prefer a plain-English substitute. For example:

> 'In this connection there was a submission, ultimately I think withdrawn, made by Michael Harvey QC. … In my judgment therefore I think that Mr Harvey's *quondam* [prefer: *former; one-time*] submission is an impossible one.' [*HLB Kidsons v Lloyd's Underwriters* [2008] EWCA Civ 1206, [125]; [2009] Bus LR 759 (Rix LJ)]

quorum

Plural: *quorums* (not *quora*). Some 'quorum' requirements are poorly drafted. For example: 'A director may be elected *on* a vote of 75% of members.' Does this impose a quorum of 75% of members, or does it merely indicate the majority vote needed for election? See *Theard v Briede* 52 So 2d 568 (La 1951; held, imposed a quorum).

QUOTATION MARKS

See **QUOTATIONS**.

QUOTATIONS

Formatting conventions

Lead-in punctuation

Where a quotation is incorporated into a sentence, it may need no lead-in punctuation; you may be able to introduce it seamlessly. For example:

> I must say, as did the judge, that 'this is a most frustrating case'.

Where a quotation is longer and is set on a new line—a 'block quotation' (see further, below)—standard usage is to insert an introductory colon. For example:

> Then the parties said:
>
> > 'We are most unhappy with the judge's decision. Also, we did not appreciate the barrister's tone. Furthermore … [continue with quotation].'

Notice that in this example the quoted material does not run-on as part of the lead-in sentence. Where the quoted material grammatically continues the lead-in sentence, but is still best reproduced as a block quotation, omit the colon. Thus:

> Then the parties said they were
>
> > 'most unhappy with the judge's decision [and they] did not appreciate the barrister's tone.'

Capitalisation at start of quotations

Where the quotation is of a complete sentence, capitalise the first letter (as in the original). Where the (complete) sentence would run more idiomatically with a lower-case first letter for the quoted material, let it do so, but use square brackets to indicate a change from the original punctuation.

- As the judge said, 'This is a most unusual case.'
- As the judge said, '[t]his is a most unusual case.'

Where the quotation is part only of a sentence, there is no need to capitalise the first letter, unless it is useful to warn your reader that you are omitting an earlier part of the quoted material.

- The judge made her views clear: 'this is a most unusual case.' [Judge's original statement: 'I would like to make it clear that this is a most unusual case.']
- The judge made her views clear: '[T]his is a most unusual case.' [indicating omission of part of quoted sentence]

Quotation marks: single or double?

Two usages are found:

1. double quotation marks, with single marks for quotations within quotations; or
2. single quotation marks, with double marks for quotations within quotations.

Usage (1) is the more traditional, and remains favoured in some office-drawn legal documents. However, the modern trend is towards usage (2), because of its crisper appearance. Legal publishers in British and Commonwealth countries now favour (2), although many US publishers still prefer (1).

Quotation marks for block quotations

Historically, lengthy quotations were enclosed with quotation marks. Where the quotation ran for many paragraphs, each paragraph would begin with opening quotation marks, but closing quotation marks were used only for the final paragraph. In modern times, this technique is so rare that it seems eccentric—but it is sometimes still used: see, eg, *Roundlistic Ltd v Jones* [2018] EWCA Civ 2284; [2019] 1 WLR 4461, [4] (Sir Andrew McFarlane P, quoting verbatim 18 paragraphs from the trial judge).

More commonly now, quotations that run for more than one or two sentences are simply set in 'block form'. They start on a new line, are indented, and are sometimes set in smaller font to mark them off clearly from the main text. Modern usage increasingly omits both opening and closing quotation marks for block quotations.

Punctuation marks: inside or outside quotation marks?

1. Where the quotation is a stand-alone sentence, the punctuation marks should reproduce the original precisely, and so should remain inside the quotation marks:
   - 'The laws of precedent must be followed.' All lawyers quote that sentence.
   - The lawyer then quoted from the law report: 'The laws of precedent must be followed.'
2. Where the quotation is a complete sentence, but is inserted into another sentence, British/Commonwealth usage traditionally places punctuation marks outside the quotation marks. More modern British/Commonwealth usage follows US usage and places them inside the quotation marks.
   - The principle in these situations is said to be that 'The laws of precedent must be followed'. [traditional British/Commonwealth]
   - The principle in these situations is said to be that 'The laws of precedent must be followed.' [US and more modern British/Commonwealth]
3. Where part only of a sentence is quoted, British/Commonwealth usage places punctuation marks outside the quotation marks, while US usage places them inside the quotation marks.
   - The advocate quoted the judge's statement that the laws of precedent 'must be followed', and then attempted to limit the width of that statement. [British/Commonwealth]
   - The advocate quoted the judge's statement that the laws of precedent 'must be followed,' and then attempted to limit the width of that statement. [US]

Emphasis and omissions

Explaining altered emphasis

When altering or adding emphasis to a word or phrase in a quotation, point it out to the reader by a parenthetical statement after the quotation. The following conventions are common:

Parenthetical statement	Meaning
(emphasis added)	Original text contained no emphasis at that point.
(my emphasis)	Original text contained no emphasis at that point.
(emphasis altered)	Emphasis in original text altered or removed.
(emphasis in original)	Emphasis in original text unchanged.

The parenthetical statements in the above table use round brackets: (...). Some publishers use square brackets: [...].

Omitting citations from quotations

Sometimes it is convenient to omit citations from a quotation—eg, to save space, or because their inclusion detracts from the flow of the text. In that case, indicate the omission by a parenthetical statement such as '(citations omitted)'.

Ellipses in quotations

Start of sentence

An ellipsis (…) is unnecessary to indicate words omitted at the start of a quoted sentence. Instead, start the first word of the quotation with an initial capital letter within square brackets, to indicate a deletion from the original. Thus:

> '[T]he house caught on fire.' [Original statement: 'Despite their best efforts, the house caught on fire.']

Midsentence

Where an ellipsis indicates words omitted from within a quoted sentence, omit punctuation marks that appeared on either side of the omitted material (unless to retain them aids readability or understanding). For example:

- 'Unless you do this … I will dismiss the jury.' [Original: 'Unless you do this, exactly as I instruct you, I will dismiss the jury.']
- 'When adjourning the case, … the judge said that the barristers needed to do more research.' [Original: 'When adjourning the case, much earlier than normal, the judge said that the barristers needed to do more research.']

End of sentence

Where an ellipsis indicates words omitted from the end of a quoted sentence, practice differs. Two variants are possible:

1. After the ellipsis, add a full stop (but with no space between the ellipsis and the full stop), then the closing quotation mark. Proponents of this style include *Garner's Modern English Usage*, 4th edn (Oxford University Press, 2016), 'Punctuation' F; and 'Quotations' E), and the *Redbook*, 2nd edn (2006), [1.44], [1.45]. The logic (unexpressed) seems to be that the reader will be expecting a full stop to end the sentence, so a mere ellipsis is not enough.
2. After the ellipsis, immediately insert the closing quotation mark, omitting any space or full stop. This book adopts that practice. The ellipsis sufficiently indicates that part of the omitted material is the full stop.

A further variant is to omit the ellipsis entirely, proceeding immediately to the closing quotation mark. The proponents of this style include the *Chicago Manual of Style* (online edn, accessed August 2020) [13.55], *New Oxford Style Manual* (2012) [9.3.3], and the *Australian Guide to Legal Citations*, (3rd edn, 2010), [1.5.6]. The reader must simply accept that the original sentence may have continued after the closing quotation mark.

Lengthy quotations

Do you need them?

Always consider whether you need to quote at length. Legal writers tend to over-quote. Practising lawyers quote large slabs of text in their advices and memos. Judges quote large slabs of earlier judgments (perhaps out of homage to the principle of precedent). Modern word-processing programs, with easy cut-and-paste facilities, encourage the practice.

The practice is sometimes the product of laziness. But it also reflects the writer's failure to appreciate that the crucial element in a quoted passage is often not the precise words but the point being made. That point can usually be summarised, saving the reader the need to read the original text. And in reality lengthy quotations can be pointless, because busy readers skip them and go straight to the next part of the main text.

This is not to deny that, sometimes, lengthy quotations are useful—for example, to capture tone or cadence, or to reproduce faithfully the fine reasoning of a complex argument. But even in such cases, it is wise to explain to your readers *why* you are quoting at length—and therefore *why* they should persevere in reading the quotation at length. This is best done by explaining the gist of the quotation before starting it. In that way, the writer asserts the proposition and the quotation affirms it.

Example

> '[The Court in *Stingel's* case] left no doubt that it was drawing a distinction between the fact and effect of the provocation and the standard of self-control:
>
> > '[T]he fact that the particular accused lacks the power of self-control of an ordinary person by reason of some attribute or characteristic which must be taken into account in identifying the content or gravity of the particular wrongful act or insult will not affect the reference point of the objective test, namely, the power of self-control of a hypothetical "ordinary person".'
>
> [*Green v R* (1997) 191 CLR 334, 404 (Kirby J, prefacing the block quotation by explaining its purport)]

Cascading quotations

Avoid cascading quotations. Judges often use them to emphasise that a proposition is hallowed by precedent. Thus, Judge A quotes at length from Judge B, and in that quote Judge B quotes at length from Judge C, who in turn quotes at length from Judge D, and so on. But readers are almost certain to skip to the first available post-quotation material—so what then was the point of including the cascading quotations? Perhaps each judge was impressed with the material he or she quoted; but there is no need to impose the accumulated weight on readers.

See also **ELLIPSES**; **PUNCTUATION**.

qv

See **quod vide**.

rack rent / rack-rent / rackrent

The full market rent for a property: *Compton Group v Estates Gazette* (1978) 36 P & CR 148, 154, 161, 162. Traditionally hyphenated—*rack-rent*: eg, William Blackstone, *Commentaries on the Laws of England* (Clarendon, 1766) book 2, 43; *Rawlance v Croydon Corporation* [1952] 2 QB 803. Sometimes a single (unhyphenated) word—*rackrent*: eg, *Linpac Mouldings Ltd v Aviva Life and Pensions UK Ltd* [2010] EWCA Civ 395, [60] (Sedley LJ). But in modern British and Commonwealth usage, usually two words—*rack rent*. For example:

- '[The] lessee or tenant enjoys a recognisable species of property right, in return for payment, either in the form of a premium, a *rack rent* or a fair rent.' [*Moorjani v Durban Estates Ltd* [2016] 1 WLR 2265, [31] (Briggs LJ)]

- '[T]he taxpayer would be required by its co-subsidiary to pay a *rack rent* for premises in respect of which it had already paid the value in fee simple.' [*Federal Commissioner of Taxation v South Australian Battery Makers Pty Ltd* (1978) 140 CLR 645, 669 (Jacobs J)]

ransom strip

A colourful, if non-technical description, of a strip of land which serves no purpose except to enable its owner to extract a fee for selling it or giving rights of access over it. For example, a vendor of land may retain a 'ransom strip', or a developer of a subdivision may retain one or more 'ransom strips', for the sole purpose of precluding consolidation of 'adjoining' parcels of land, or precluding access to a road or lane—except at a price.

RATCHET CLAUSE

A clause by which a fluctuating amount (such as a price or rent) is not to fall back below its former amount.

See also **ESCALATION CLAUSE**.

rateable

So spelled in British and Commonwealth usage. US usage prefers *ratable*.

ratio decidendi

Latin: the reason for the decision. A Latinism that carries a nuance not immediately apparent in the bare English translation. The *ratio decidendi* is that part of the decision that can bind later courts under the doctrine of precedent:

> 'What constitutes binding precedent is the *ratio decidendi*, and this is almost always to be ascertained by an analysis of the material facts of the case. … The concrete decision alone is binding between the parties to it, but it is the abstract *ratio decidendi*, as ascertained on a consideration of the judgment in relation to the subject matter of the decision, which alone has the force of law and which … is binding.' [*Halsbury's Laws of England*, 'Civil Procedure' (vol 11, 2015) [25], fns omitted]

However, almost certainly non-lawyers will find the Latin term meaningless, so offer them an explanation. For most purposes, 'the essential legal reasoning' or 'the core reasoning', will suffice:

- 'Only the *ratio decidendi* of Smith's case [prefer: *the essential legal reasoning of Smith's case*], not findings on the evidence, binds later courts.'
- 'The *ratio decidendi* of Smith's case [prefer: *The core reasoning in Smith's case*] is that trespass requires entry on to the land.'

See also **obiter dictum**.

re

See **in re**.

READABILITY TESTS

Purpose

Readability tests (or 'readability formulas') may help assess a legal document's 'readability'. Most readability tests focus on word complexity and sentence length, the assumption being that shorter words and shorter sentences make writing easier to read. Five popular tests are:

- *Flesch Reading Ease Formula*: counts the number of syllables and the number of words per 100-word sample. (See further, below.) Scores range from 0 to 100.
- *Flesch–Kincaid Grade Level Formula*: takes the same variables as the Flesch Reading Ease Formula, and then converts them to a US school grade-level. In the UK, add five to get the UK reading age: eg, US level 8 = UK reading level 13 (8 + 5).
- *SMOG Formula* ('Simple Measure of Gobbledegook'): counts the number of words of three or more syllables, and averages them over three 10-sentence samples (from the start, middle, and end of the document); takes the resulting number, calculates its square root, and adds three (for US grade level) or eight (for UK age level). Most people will understand a document with a result of 10 or lower.
- *Fog Index* (or *Gunning Fog Index*): calculates the reading grade by three steps: (1) takes the average number of words per sentence; (2) adds the percentage of words of three or more syllables (with some adjustment for words that reach three syllables because of *-ing* or *-ed* endings); and (3) multiplies the result by 0.4. The test gives the number of years of education the reader will need to understand the document. If a document scores 7 or 8, most people will understand it; if it scores 12 or more, most people will find it difficult to understand.
- *Fry Readability Formula*: averages the number of sentences in three 100-word samples from the text (start, middle, end), and averages the number of syllables in those 100-word samples, then plots the results on a graph which is correlated to US grade reading levels.

Of these, the *Flesch Reading Ease Formula* seems the most influential, following its adoption by Microsoft Word. It produces a score from 0 to 100—the higher the score, the easier the reading. The formula is:

$$\text{Reading Ease} = 206.835 - (1.015 \times \text{ASL}) - (84.6 \times \text{ASW})$$

where

ASL = average number of words per sentence, and

ASW = average number of syllables per word.

A score of 90–100 means that the writing should be understood by an average 11-year-old; a score of 60–70 means the writing should be understood by 13- to 15-year-olds (and therefore is suitable for most adult audiences); and a score of 0–30 means the writing is suited best for college or university graduates.

Example

The following example applies two readability tests—the Flesch Reading Ease Formula and Flesch–Kincaid Grade Level Formula—to illustrate the results.

Before (text of original statute)

> All the amounts and sums authorised by this Act and the other Act mentioned in Schedule 1 to this Act, for the service of the year that ended with 31st March 2007 and of the year ending with 31st March 2008, totalling, as is shown in the said Schedule, £22,441,622,000 in amounts of resources authorised for use and £15,099,258,000 in sums authorised for issue from the Consolidated Fund, are appropriated, and shall be deemed to have been appropriated as from the date of the passing of the Acts mentioned in the said Schedule 1, for the services and purposes specified in Schedule 2 to this Act. [Source: *Appropriation Act 2008*, s 4(1)]

Results of readability tests:

- Flesch Reading Ease Formula (on scale from 0–100) = –27 (ie, exceptionally difficult)
- Flesch–Kincaid Grade Level Formula = US school grade 46.3 (impossibly high).

After (plain English revision)

For the purposes listed in schedule 2, this Act appropriates the money authorised by:

(a) the Consolidated Fund Act 2007, with effect from the date of that Act; and

(b) this Act, with immediate effect.

Results of readability tests [assuming three 'sentences']:

- Flesch Reading Ease Formula = 58
- Flesch-Kincaid Grade Level Formula = US school grade 8 (ie, 13- or 14-year-olds).

[Based on Mark Adler, 'Legalese and Plain Language', *The Loophole* (Jan 2010) 74.]

Court use

Readability tests are becoming more widely used to assess the readability of legal documents, particularly consumer documents. In the following case, evidence was tendered of a SMOG test of a statutory notice:

> A driver received a departmental notice advising that his licence would be cancelled. The driver challenged the validity of the notice on the ground that it breached his due process rights. An amicus curiae brief used the SMOG Formula to assess the readability of the notice. It found that the text required literacy skills far exceeding those of the average US high school graduate. The brief also cited research findings that almost two-thirds of adults could not read at high school graduate level. [*Johnson v Jessup*, Case No 1:18-c-v00467; amicus curiae brief filed 26 August 2019]

Limits on usefulness

Readability formulas have some limits, well-documented in the research literature. For example:

- They ignore structure, organisation, presentation, font, or graphic aids (tables, flow charts, and the like).
- They ignore the reader's motivation, skill, or pre-existing knowledge of subject matter.
- They ignore the inherent complexity of ideas. To illustrate:

  > The sentence 'Jack hit John' scores well on the Flesch–Kincaid Grade Level Formula (= grade 6, easily understandable by 11- or 12-year-olds). But so does the conceptually complex sentence 'I think therefore I am' (= grade 8, easily understandable by 13- or 14-year-olds). So too does the legally complex sentence 'A fee tail must vest within a life in being plus 21 years' (= grade 8, easily understandable by 13- or 14-year-olds).

- They underestimate the difficulty of measuring 'reading grade' levels.
- They are prone to manipulation by writers who 'write to the formula', giving a false impression of readability. For example, a text made up entirely of very short sentences will rate well, even though the excessive division may hinder the flow of ideas.

Nevertheless, provided the limitations are recognised, readability formulas remain a useful starting point. They encourage attention on the needs of the 'audience'. And they can produce uncomfortable results, which at least point up the need for the writer to try harder. For example, a readability test showed that to understand part of the Australian taxation legislation required 27 years' education (12 years of schooling, plus 15 years of university education): *Australian Financial Review*, 27 September 1991, 19 (test conducted by Victorian Law Reform Commission).

Further reading

- Bertram Bruce et al, 'Why Readability Formulas Fail' (1981), at www.ideals.illinois.edu/bitstream/handle/2142/15490/why-rf-fail.html?sequence=3
- Annetta Cheek, 'Defining Plain Language' (2010) 64 *Clarity* 5 (discussing strengths and weaknesses of various readability formulas); at www.clarity-international.net/clarity-journal/archives/
- Martin Cutts, 'Writing by Numbers: Are Readability Formulas to Clarity what Karaoke Is to Song?' (2008), available from Plain Language Commission, at www.clearest.co.uk
- William H Dubay, *The Principles of Readability* (2004), at www.impact-information.com/impactinfo/readability02.pdf
- William H Dubay, *Working with Plain Language* (2008), at www.impact-information.com/Resources/working.pdf
- Rudolph Flesch, *How to Write Plain English: A Book for Lawyers and Consumers* (Barnes & Noble, 1979) ch 2
- Edward Fry, 'A Readability Formula That Saves Time' (1968) 11 *Journal of Reading* 513–16 (part 1), 575–78 (part 2)
- Edward Fry, 'Readability versus Leveling' (2002) 56 *Reading Teacher* 286 (comparing readability and grade-level calculations)
- M Hochhauser, 'Why Patients Won't Understand Their HIPAA Privacy Notices' (2003), at www.privacyrights.org/ar/HIPAA-Readability.htm (using the Flesch Reading Ease Formula to analyse medical privacy forms)
- Lance N Long and William F Christensen, 'Does the Readability of Your Brief Affect Your Chance of Winning an Appeal?' (2011) 12 *Journal of Appellate Practice and Process* 145 (answer: statistically, no; the authors explore the various reasons for the answer. The article also analyses various readability formulas.)
- Thomas Oakland and Holly B Lane, 'Language, Reading and Readability Formulas: Implications for Developing and Adapting Tests' (2004) 4 *International Journal of Testing* 239, 250
- KA Schriver, *Dynamics in Document Design: Creating Texts for Readers* (Wiley, 1997)
- KA Schriver, 'Readability Formulas in the New Millenium: What's the Use?' (2001) 24 *ACM Journal of Computer Documentation* 138.

See also **AUDIENCE; DOCUMENT TESTING.**

ready and willing

See **ready, able, and willing**.

ready, able, and willing

A legal trilogy, familiar to property and commercial lawyers; ideally with the serial comma (*ready, able, and willing*), but more often not (*ready, able and willing*). At first glance the expression seems at least partly tautologous, because a person cannot be *ready* (to do something) unless they are *able* (to do it)—'When a man is incapable of doing a certain act, it may be safely concluded that he is not ready to do it': *Lawrence v Knowles* (1839) 8 LJ CP 210, 217 (Bosanquet J). But at least some recent authorities hold that each word has a separate meaning and a separate role to play—in which case, each is justifiable:

> '[A real estate agent was contractually entitled to commission on introducing a person *ready, able and willing* to buy the property.] These words do not mean a person ready, able and willing "to make an offer," or even "to enter into a contract": they mean a person ready, able and willing "to purchase", that is, to complete the purchase. He must be a person who is "able" at the proper time to complete; that is, he must then have the necessary financial resources. He must also be "ready"; that is, he must have made all necessary preparations by having the cash or a banker's draft ready to hand over. He must also be "willing"; that is, he must be willing to hand over the money in return for the conveyance.' [*Dennis Reed Ltd v Goody* [1950] 2 KB 277, 287 (Denning LJ)]

Further reading

Halsbury's Laws of England, 'Conveyancing' (vol 23, 2016) [279]

real property

In legal usage, *real* generally means *relating to land*. Its etymological derivation is *res* (Latin: the thing itself), as reflected in the medieval '*real* actions', which facilitated recovery of the land itself (as distinct from damages for loss, which was the sole remedy for deprivation of most other forms of property). Property recoverable by the real actions came to be called 'real' property. Other legal terms reflecting this historical connection include *realty*, *real* estate, *real* burden.

See also **personal property**.

realty

From the Latin: *res*—thing: used in the sense of 'real estate'. If *realty* seems stilted or unidiomatic, prefer *real estate* or *land*.

See also **real property**.

reasonable

Issues

The law often applies a standard of *reasonableness*. It is seen in expressions such as *reasonable* person, *reasonable* time, *reasonable* care, *reasonable* precautions, *reasonable* necessity, *reasonable* endeavours, *reasonable* excuse, *reasonable* price, *reasonable* doubt, *reasonable* cause, *reasonable* detail. In itself, *reasonable* is not ambiguous—*reasonable* means *reasonable*. However, its content is elastic, varying with the circumstances: what is *reasonable* depends on the circumstances. As a result, *reasonable* is inherently litigation-prone.

And there is always the question: '*reasonable* to whom?' Is *reasonableness* tested objectively (ie, how a hypothetically reasonable bystander would approach the matter) or subjectively (ie, how the actor personally approached the matter)?

Examples

- A local authority served a statutory notice on landowners requiring them to carry out improvement works on their property. The landowners could appeal where it was not practical to comply with the notice 'at reasonable expense'. Held, 'reasonable expense' meant reasonable to those called on to bear it: *Harrington v Croydon Corporation* [1968] 1 QB 856 (CA).

- The amount of statutory housing benefit payable to a tenant depended (in part) on whether the tenant's rent under the lease was 'unreasonably high' compared to the rent payable for suitable alternative accommodation. Held, 'unreasonably high' was viewed from the tenant's standpoint, in the light of the tenant's financial and other circumstances, not from the landlord's standpoint: *S v Birmingham City Council* [2016] EWCA Civ 1211; [2017] 1 WLR 2251.

Prefer certainty

For these reasons, where possible, always specify *what* is required to be done and *when* it is to be done, rather than allow scope for argument about what is *reasonable* in the circumstances. For example, merely to specify that a notice must contain '*reasonable* details about a claim' is an invitation to litigation (see, eg, cases discussed in *ROK plc v S Harrison Group Ltd* [2011] All ER (D) 02 (Mar), [61]–[72]). So too is a provision allowing a landlord to recover 'reasonable' service charges from a tenant: *Avon Ground Rents Ltd v Cowley* [2019] EWCA Civ 1827; [2020] 1 WLR 1337.

See also **best endeavours / reasonable endeavours**; **reasonable grounds / belief (etc)**; **reasonable time**.

reasonable grounds / belief (etc)

Terms importing concepts of 'reasonableness' into a person's decision-making processes are familiar in legal usage. They include:

- *reasonable grounds* (eg, 'the landlord may refuse consent to assignment on *reasonable grounds*')
- *reasonable belief* ('X may do [something] if X has a *reasonable belief* that …')
- *reasonable suspicion* ('the police may arrest on *reasonable suspicion* of a crime').

Despite their familiarity, such formulas leave unstated whether the criterion of *reasonableness* is subjective or objective. The answer depends on the context and the circumstances: *R v A-G* [2014] EWCA Civ 254; [2014] QB 855, 916, [36]–[37] (Lord Dyson MR). Sometimes, context and circumstance make the answer tolerably clear. For example, whether a person has '*reasonable* excuse' for carrying a gun in public suggests an objective test—as indeed the court held in *Bryan v Mott* (1975) 62 Cr App R 71, 73 (Lord Widgery CJ). Again, whether a person receiving property should *reasonably suspect* that it is the proceeds of crime, suggests an objective test (as the court held in *Lordianto v Commissioner of the Australian Federal Police* [2019] HCA 39, [89], [90], [92]; (2019) 93 ALJR 1282). But often the answer is not so clear, and may require fine distinctions. The answer may even be 'partly subjective and partly objective'—ie, an enquiry into what the person actually knew (subjective) and whether that knowledge should have raised an (objectively) reasonable response. For example:

- A statute created the offence of supplying money with '*reasonable* cause to suspect' that it may be used to commit a terrorist offence. Held, this required focus, first, on what the accused actually knew (subjective), and then on whether a person possessing that knowledge would reasonably suspect (objective) that the money might be used for terrorism: *R v Lane* [2018] UKSC 36; [2018] 1 WLR 3647, [24].
- A statutory defence of duress was available where a person's response to a threat was a '*reasonable* response … in the circumstances as the person *believes* them to be'. Held, the expression '*reasonable* response' connoted an objectively reasonable response, and the expression 'as the person believes them to be' connoted a subjective belief. That is, the statute imposed a test that was objective, but viewed through a subjective lens: *Marchesano v Western Australia* [2017] WASCA 177; (2017) 52 WAR 176, [124] (Buss P).

Where possible, clarify whether the intended test is objective or subjective. For example:

> **Subjective test intended**: 'The tenant may assign the lease if the tenant considers that the assignee has relevant commercial experience (regardless of whether that belief is reasonable).'
>
> **Objective test intended**: 'The tenant may assign the lease if there are reasonable grounds to believe that the assignee has relevant commercial experience.'

See also **best endeavours / reasonable endeavours**; **reasonable**.

reasonable doubt

See **beyond reasonable doubt**.

reasonable endeavours

See **best endeavours / reasonable endeavours**.

reasonable necessity

A term often seen, though oxymoronic: 'necessity' implies absoluteness—something is either necessary or it is not. How then can 'necessity' be tempered by notions of 'reasonableness'?

> '[The phrase "reasonable necessity" … does not begin to be expressed in the King's English. The words "reasonably necessary", used as a phrase in which the adverb is designed to qualify the adjective, are meaningless. A thing is necessary or it is not necessary. … As it stands, the phrase, to me, is a contradiction in terms.' [Re *Naylor Benzon Mining Co Ltd* [1950] Ch 567, 575 (Wynn-Parry J)]

Nevertheless, *reasonable necessity* is hallowed by legal usage. Where it is used, courts must give it a meaning. For example, statutes in some jurisdictions authorise the compulsory grant of easements that are 'reasonably necessary' for the use and development of land. Courts have held that, in this context, 'reasonable necessity', while not requiring absolute necessity, requires more than mere desirability or convenience—the test is closer to 'necessity' than to 'convenience'. (For authorities, see Brendan Edgeworth (ed), *Butt's Land Law*, 7th edn (Thomson Reuters, 2017) [16.540]; *Gordon v Lever (No 2)* [2019] NSWCA 275.)

See also **necessary**.

reasonable time

Whether a period is a '*reasonable time*' in which to do something is always context-dependent.

To illustrate, factors in determining what is a *reasonable time* for a purchaser to complete a contract for the sale of land include:

- whether the contract imposes obligations over and above those that are 'normal' in sales of land
- whether, at the date of contract, the seller knew that the buyer needed time to arrange finance
- whether the transaction occurs in a holiday period, when the parties' lawyers' offices will be closed
- the time that is needed to make standard searches and enquiries.

These kinds of factors make *reasonable time* an open-ended concept in commercial contracts—not so open-ended as to be void for uncertainty, but sufficiently open-ended to risk litigation. It is much better, if possible, to specify a fixed time. That is why, for example, contracts for the sale of land now commonly require the purchaser to complete within a stated time, not merely within a *reasonable time*.

Further reading

Peter Butt, *The Standard Contract for Sale of Land in New South Wales*, 2nd edn (LBC Information Services, 1998) [15.13], [15.23]–[15.28]

reasonable wear and tear

See **wear and tear**.

rebut / refute

To *rebut* is to *contradict* or *argue the opposite*; to *refute* is to *defeat* (an opposing argument). The two words are often used interchangeably, but the distinction is useful. For example:

> 'The defendant sought to *refute* the plaintiff's claim, by *rebutting* the many arguments of plaintiff's counsel'.

Hence, the law speaks (correctly) of '*rebuttable* presumptions', not '*refutable* presumptions'.

RECITALS

Nature of recitals

Recitals give the background to a legal document. They are easily identified, particularly when heralded by the ubiquitous *Whereas*.

Recitals can serve a number of purposes (see below, **Uses of recitals**). But some recitals seem to be inserted out of habit, with no thought to whether they serve a purpose in the document. For example, a recital at the start of a contract for the sale of goods may state that the vendor has agreed to sell, and the purchaser has agreed to buy, the goods specified in the agreement, on the terms specified in the agreement. Such a recital serves no purpose. Where a recital serves no purpose, discard it.

Some documents expressly incorporate the recitals into the agreement: 'The recitals are incorporated in this agreement', or 'The recitals form part of this agreement'. But this seems otiose. The recitals *are* part of the agreement. True, they are not part of the *substantive* provisions of the agreement—but then, as discussed below (See **Abuses of recitals**), recitals should not contain substantive provisions anyway.

Terminology of recitals

Whereas

There is no need to introduce recitals with the formulaic *Whereas*. Choose instead one of the following substitutes:

- *Recitals*. This is the obvious replacement for *Whereas*.
- *Introduction*. This substitute is effective to invoke the law about the operation of recitals: *Lewis v Nortex Pty Ltd* [2001] NSWSC 511, [36].

- *Background*. This is becoming an increasingly common substitute for *Whereas*. It appears to effectively invoke the law about the operation of recitals—or at least, that has been assumed in a number of appellate decisions in Australia, where the substitute *Background* has become standard: see, eg, *Sunland Waterfront (BVI) Ltd v Prudentia Investments Pty Ltd* [2013] VSCA 237; *BB Retail Capital Pty Ltd v Alexandria Landfill Pty Ltd* [2015] NSWCA 319 (dispelling any doubts that might be suggested by *400 George Street (Qld) Pty Ltd v BG International Ltd* [2010] QSC 66; [2010] Q Conv R 54-731).

Recital 'of / to' this agreement

The preferred formula is 'Recital [X] *to* this agreement', not 'Recital [X] *of* this agreement'; but no misunderstanding results from *of*.

Uses of recitals

To provide an easy way into the document

Recitals can ease both drafter and reader into a complex document. For the drafter, preparing recitals usually requires stating in broad terms the background to the document, which then helps frame a logical structure for the document. For the reader, the recited background explains why the document was created, and that in turn eases the way into the document's complexities.

Recitals may also be useful for non-parties who, though not involved directly, must for some reason read the document. For example, a party's auditors may need to read the document to understand their client's exposure; or a party's accountant may need to read the document for taxation purposes; or a lawyer in a transaction years later may need to read the document for 'due diligence' purposes.

To help interpret the document

Recitals may be invoked to help interpret a document. The main principles are:

1. Where a document contains two inconsistent operative provisions (A and B), and the recitals are consistent with A but not with B, the court may regard A as more likely to reflect the parties' intentions.
2. Where the operative part of a document is ambiguous and the recitals are clear, the recitals may help clarify the ambiguity. (For example, a recital may help clarify that the parties intended their arrangement to constitute a mere licence rather than a formal lease.)
3. Where the recitals are ambiguous and the operative part is clear, the operative part prevails.
4. Where both the operative part and the recitals are clear but inconsistent with each other, the operative part prevails.

(For these principles, see, eg, *Leggott v Barrett* (1880) 15 Ch D 306, 311; *Ex parte Dawes* (1886) 17 QBD 275, 286; *Rutter (Inspector of Taxes) v Charles Sharpe & Co Ltd* [1979] 1 WLR 1429; *Bolton v Weige* (1981) 2 BPR 97123; *O'Loughlin v Mount* (1998) 71 SASR 206, 217–18; *Franklins Pty Ltd v Metcash Trading Ltd* [2009] NSWCA 407; (2009) 76 NSWLR 603, [385]–[388].)

The limitations in propositions (3) and (4) reflect the reality that recitals, though part of the document, are not themselves operative terms: *Bath and Mountague's Case* (1693) 3 Chan Cas 55, 101; 22 ER 963, 991; *Franklins Pty Ltd v Metcash Trading Ltd*, above, [380 (2)].

To set up an estoppel

A recital can create an estoppel, precluding the party who made the statement from later denying the truth of the matter recited: *Bensley v Burdon* (1830) 8 LJ (OS) Ch 85; *Heath v Crealock* (1874) LR 10 Ch App 22; *Grant v John Grant & Sons Pty Ltd* (1954) 91 CLR 112. This is seen in the following example:

> A clause in a deed between a creditor (C) and a debtor (D) stated that, if D defaulted in performing an obligation under the deed, C could demand immediate repayment of the full amount outstanding. D claimed that the clause was unenforceable as a 'penalty'. Recitals in the deed indicated that the debt was an existing debt, presently owing in full. Held, the recitals precluded (estopped) D from claiming that the clause was a 'penalty'. They showed that the clause fell within an exception to the 'penalty' doctrine—namely, that a creditor's act in calling in the full debt is merely withdrawing a concession that the creditor will not demand payment in full as long as the obligations continue to be performed: *Lachlan v HP Mercantile Pty Ltd* [2015] NSWCA 130; (2015) 89 NSWLR 198; *Auzcare Pty Ltd v Idameneo (No 123) Pty Ltd* [2015] NSWCA 412; (2015) 91 NSWLR 581.

The estoppel applies even where the reciting party knew at the time that the statement was false: having made it, the party is bound by it: *Prime Site Ltd v Lavarello* [2013] UKPC 22; [2014] AC 436.

However, the use of recitals to set up an estoppel has limitations. They include the following:

- The recital must be a distinct statement of a particular fact, not a mere statement in general terms. To illustrate: a general statement in a deed of conveyance that the vendor was 'seised or otherwise well and sufficiently entitled to' the fee simple did not preclude the vendor from later denying the truth of the statement: *Heath v Crealock* (1874) LR 10 Ch App 22.
- The estoppel applies only in an action based on the document, as distinct from a collateral action: *Carter v Carter* (1857) 3 K & J 617, 645; 69 ER 1256, 1268.
- Where a recital is intended as a statement by all parties to a deed, it binds them all: *Stroughill v Buck* (1850) 14 QB 781, 787; 117 ER 301, 303. But if it is intended as the statement of one party only, it binds only that party, not other persons merely because they are parties to the deed: *Discount & Finance Ltd v Gehrig's Wines Ltd* (1940) 57 WN (NSW) 226, 227–28 (Jordan CJ).
- The benefit and burden of an estoppel passes to persons who are 'privy' to the estoppel: *Richards v Jenkins* (1887) 18 QBD 451; *Partridge v McIntosh and Sons Ltd* (1933) 49 CLR 453, 462–63, 465, 466–67. Otherwise, though, non-parties to the deed cannot enforce it: eg, *Commissioner of Taxes (Qld) v Ford Motor Co Pty Ltd* (1942) 66 CLR 261 (taxation authority unable to enforce recital against the reciting party).
- It may be that an estoppel arises only where the recital is in a *deed*—ie, that the principle does not apply to documents that are not deeds. This follows from the solemnity which the common law accords to deeds, above other forms of writing. If this view is correct, a recital in a non-deed may still found an estoppel, but it will be a different category of estoppel (eg, estoppel by convention), and may require different elements to establish it: see, eg, *Labracon Pty Ltd v Cuturich* [2013] NSWSC 97, [125], [127], [131], [153]; (2013) 17 BPR 32,497.

- Estoppel by deed is a common-law doctrine, 'founded on the principle that a solemn and unambiguous statement or engagement in a deed must be taken as binding between parties and privies and therefore as not admitting any contradictory proof': *Greer v Kettle* [1938] AC 156, 171 (Lord Maugham). In a court of equity, however, an equitable remedy may be available to negate it—eg, where the recital was included by mutual mistake, or where the the deed is amendable to rectification (ibid).

To pass title to land

By the doctrine of 'feeding the estoppel', a recital can operate to pass title to land. This typically occurs where a vendor, although having no title to land which he or she is purporting to convey, recites in the deed of conveyance that he or she has title. If the vendor later acquires title to the land, the vendor is 'estopped' from denying the truth of the recital, the effect of which is to pass title to the purchaser without the need for any further deed of conveyance: *Re Bridgewater's Settlement* [1910] 2 Ch 342. However, the recital must be clear and unambiguous; an unclear recital cannot fill the vendor's title: *Right v Bucknell* (1831) 2 B & Ad 278, 281; 109 ER 1146, 1147; *Heath v Crealock* (1874) LR 10 Ch App 22.

To obtain statutory presumption of truth of statement

In vendor and purchaser transactions, recitals of facts in documents at least 20 years old at the date of the contract for sale are presumed to be correct: *Law of Property Act 1925*, ss 44, 45. A similar provision exists in other Commonwealth jurisdictions: eg, *Conveyancing Act* 1919 (NSW), s 53(2)(a); *Property Law Act* 1974 (Qld), s 238(6); *Property Law Act* 1958 (Vic), s 45(6). In some jurisdictions the period is different; eg, in Hong Kong it is 15 years: *Conveyancing and Property Ordinance* Cap 219, s 13(4).

To preserve a party's rights

Recitals may help preserve a party's rights, as in the following examples.

- In a deed of settlement of a legal dispute, a party recites that, although agreeing to settle the dispute, they do not concede that their case was inferior. The recital precludes argument that the settlement was a concession.
- In a commercial contract, a party (A) recites that if the other party (B) were to breach the contract, A would suffer specified losses. The purpose is to ensure that the losses are recoverable under the 'second limb' of *Hadley v Baxendale* (1854) 9 Exch 341; 156 ER 145. Under that 'second limb', a party may recover such damages as the parties may reasonably have contemplated at the time of the contract as flowing from the breach. The recital ensures that specific heads of damage are within their contemplation. (See ***Hadley v Baxendale* ('limbs' of)**.)

To facilitate the implication of terms

In appropriate cases, a recital may facilitate the implication of a term into a contract. For example, a recital that a party has agreed to carry out a particular action can support the implication of a term requiring the party to carry it out (*Ansett Transport Industries (Operations) Pty Ltd v Commonwealth of Australia* (1977) 139 CLR 54, 72; *Franklins Pty Ltd v Metcash Trading Ltd* (2009) 76 NSWLR 603, [380]). In effect, the recital may cure the drafter's oversight in omitting the actual term, as in the following case:

> A lease recited that the tenant had agreed to pull down a building on the land and replace it with a larger one. The operative part of the lease contained no express obligation on the tenant to pull down and rebuild, but did require the tenant to keep the new building in repair. Held, the recital, coupled with the obligation to keep in repair, amounted to a covenant to erect the

building: *Sampson v Easterby* (1829) 9 B & C 505; 109 ER 188; affirmed on appeal, (1830) 6 Bing 644; 130 ER 1429.

Again, a recital that the reciting party intends to do something may, taken with what follows in the substantive part of the document, amount to a covenant or warranty by the reciting party that it will be done: eg, *Lay v Mottram* (1865) 19 CB 479; 144 ER 874; *Milne v Municipal Council of Sydney* (1912) 14 CLR 54, 72 (Isaacs J).

However, these consequences do not apply unless the parties have reached agreement that one or both of them will take some action. For example, a recital that the parties *intend* to do something cannot overcome an absence of *actual* agreement: *Australian Securities and Investment Commission v Fortescue Metals Group Ltd* [2011] FCAFC 19, [155]–[163] (reversed on other grounds, *Forrest v Australian Securities and Investments Commission* [2012] HCA 39; (2012) 247 CLR 486).

Abuses of recitals

Recitals containing substantive obligations

Recitals should not contain substantive provisions. By their nature, recitals are background statements, not operative provisions. Where a document is lawyer-drawn, courts assume that the drafter understood the distinction, making it 'inherently unlikely' that parties intended recitals to give rise to substantive obligations: *Fairstate Ltd v General Enterprise & Management Ltd* [2010] EWHC 3072, [74].

This is not to deny the validity of substantive obligations that are in fact contained in recitals—rather, that they should not be there. Where the parties clearly intended a substantive obligation, it will be given effect to despite appearing only in a recital. See, eg, *Aged Care Services Pty Ltd v Kanning Services Pty Ltd* [2012] NSWSC 531, [47] (not challenged on appeal, [2013] NSWCA 393, [26]); *Ivory Land Developments v Goorigubba* [2015] NSWSC 224, [15]–[16].

Recitals and notice

Recitals can put readers on notice of matters they would prefer not to know. A careful drafter will ensure that a recital does not have this unwanted result. For example, a deed of conveyance usually recites that the vendor is the owner of ('seised of') the land. Ideally, the recital should simply state that proposition, and not refer to the particular documents (eg, conveyances, wills, grants of probate) through which the vendor acquired ownership. Reference to particular documents will put the purchaser (and later purchasers) on notice of their contents—notice which a purchaser may prefer not to have, because it may preclude reliance on the doctrine of bona fide purchaser of the legal estate *without notice* of earlier equitable interests. Hence the conventional conveyancing wisdom that a recital should recite events, not documents: C Davidson, TC Wright and J Waley (eds), *Davidson's Precedents and Forms in Conveyancing*, 3rd edn (William Maxwell, 1860) 54.

Definitions in recitals

Recitals conventionally appear at the start of a document, before the definitions clause. This poses a practical problem where the recitals use one or more of the defined terms: readers will not yet have met the definitions. For experienced readers, the problem is more imagined than real, because they will know where to find the definitions. But readers unaccustomed to legal documents may be puzzled; and so it may be useful, when first using a defined term in the recitals, to add '(as defined in clause [X])'.

Also problematical is the practice, sometimes seen, of recitals themselves defining terms as they are first used, rather than postponing the definitions until the main definitions clause. Readers who go first to the definitions clause may not realise that terms missing from that clause are defined in the recitals. A better technique may be not to include the full definition in the recitals, and instead state on first use of the defined term in the recitals: '(as defined in clause [X])', or similar.

Recitals and supplemental instruments

As a word-saving device, legislation in most common-law jurisdictions allows the text of an instrument (the earlier instrument) to be read into a later instrument if the later instrument is expressed to be 'supplemental to' the earlier: see, eg, *Law of Property Act 1925*, s 58; *Conveyancing Act 1919* (NSW), s 36D. The text of the later instrument is then taken to contain a 'full recital' of the earlier.

See also **DEFINITIONS**; **estoppel**; **notice**; **privy**; **supplemental to**; **whereas**.

reckless

In normal usage, foolhardy, negligent. In legal usage, *reckless* can carry the additional nuance of 'indifferent to the result'. So, for example:

- an offender may have foreseen that certain consequences would follow planned conduct, but goes ahead anyway '*reckless* of' (ie, indifferent to) the consequences: *R v Cunningham* [1957] 2 QB 396;
- a vendor may have entered into a contract for sale *recklessly* in the sense of 'indifferent to' the likelihood of being able to make title to the land: *Selkirk v Romar Investments Ltd* [1963] 1 WLR 1415.

If doubt is possible about the intended meaning, clarify.

recognizance

So spelled traditionally in British English, although some dictionaries now prefer *recognisance* (including the *Macquarie Dictionary*, used widely in Australia). US English prefers *recognisance*. A recognizance is an acknowledgement by a person that he or she owes a debt to the state, to be extinguished if a stipulated event occurs (eg, the person appears in court, or remains of good behaviour for a specified period). See *Re Nottingham Corporation* [1897] 2 QB 502, 515 (Ridley J).

Further reading

'Recognizance', in *Law Words* (Centre for Plain Legal Language, University of Sydney, 1995) 69; www.clarity-international.net/plain-language-resources/general-resources/ (tracing the history of *recognizance* in law)

rectification

In ordinary use, a correction. In legal usage, more specifically, a correction to give effect to the intent of the parties to a document. In its legal usage, *rectification* may be a term of art, because the plain English 'correction' (alone) does not carry the full legal nuance. For example, in the context of *rectification* of a written contract, the word does not mean merely correcting a typographical slip (though that may be included), but rather varying the written terms to overcome a common mistake, namely that the document the parties signed did not accurately record the terms of their agreement: *FSHC Group Holdings Ltd v GLAS Trust Corp Ltd* [2019] EWCA Civ 1361; [2020] 2 WLR 429 (reviewing recent UK and Commonwealth law on rectification). Again, in the context of *rectification* of a will, the word does not mean merely correcting a clerical error (though that may be included), but rather varying the written terms so that the will carries out the testator's intentions: *Administration of Justice Act 1982*, s 20(1).

In many contexts, 'correction' may suffice as a substitute for rectification: eg, in a lawyer's advice to a client, 'We recommend an application to the court to *correct* the terms of the contract.' But in submissions to the court, the technical term would be required: 'Your honour, this is an application to *rectify* the terms of the contract.'

Further reading

- *Halsbury's Laws of England*, 'Mistake' (vol 77, 2016) [53]–[57] (rectification of contracts)
- *Halsbury's Laws of England*, 'Wills and Intestacy' (vol 102, 2016) [187] (rectification of wills)

recuse

To disqualify oneself from deciding a case or dispute, or to seek the disqualification of someone from deciding a case or dispute, usually on the ground of apprehended bias or conflict of interest: 'I recuse myself from this case.' / 'Your honour should recuse yourself from this case.'

red tape

Rigid and complex bureaucratic procedures; excessive bureaucracy—'These tax-refund claims require too much red tape.' The term derives from the pink ribbon which, until relatively recently, lawyers and government officials used to tie their papers together.

reddendo singula singulis

Latin: referring each to each. A principle of interpretation stating that where two or more subjects are qualified by two or more matters, the matters attach to the subjects in the order in which they appear; sometimes called the principle of 'distributive construction'.

Lord Millett, in *AIB Group UK Plc v Martin* [2002] 1 All ER 353, 357–58; [2001] UKHL 63, [15]–[16], explained:

> 'A distributive construction is commonly adopted when a plural subject is followed by a plural predicate and the plurals are broken down into their component singulars. An example from everyday speech would be to say: "A and B took their children to school". Prima facie the word "their" means "belonging to both of them". But this is not its only possible meaning, and if A and B are not married it is obviously not its meaning. In that case the word "their" means "of each of them". But this means that A and B took their respective children to school, not each other's children. The children are distributed to the relevant parent. And it goes further than that. Although the word "school" is in the singular, it may conceal a plural. If necessary, the sentence means that A and B took the children to their respective schools.'

The principle is rebuttable if the result appears contrary to the parties' intentions. While a useful backstop, the principle suffers from the obvious flaw that the writer may not have had it in mind, and so its application can be arbitrary.

Further reading

Halsbury's Laws of England, 'Statutes and Legislative Process' (vol 96, 2018), [816] ('render each to each')

redeem

Literally, to *buy back*. The term appears particularly in the law of mortgages: eg, the *right to redeem* (the mortgagor's right to repay the mortgage and recover the property) and the *equity of redemption* (the mortgagor's interest remaining in the property after granting the mortgage).

REDRAFTING IN PLAIN ENGLISH

What is the best way to redraft traditionally worded documents into plain English? Techniques vary, depending on the complexity of the original. One or more of the techniques discussed below, with illustrative examples, should work for most documents. The examples start with simple, one-step, procedures that are adequate for many documents. As the examples become more complex, so too do the procedures, often requiring a number of steps for documents that suffer from the twin vices of poor structure and complex language.

So as not to distract from the techniques themselves, the following examples deliberately avoid the question: what to do with terms of art? For that topic, see **TERMS OF ART**.

Prune superfluous words and phrases

Sometimes, to redraft in plain English requires little more than pruning superfluous words and phrases. The following Examples 1 and 2, with marking-up, show the process and the benefits.

Example 1 (deed of indemnity)

Before

The Owner covenants and agrees that it will indemnify and keep indemnified Council, its officers, servants, agents, workmen and contractors from and against all costs, expenses, losses or damages which Council, its officers, servants, agents, workman and contractors may sustain, incur or suffer or be or become liable for or claim brought by any person arising from or referable to the obligations stated in this Agreement. [66 words]

After

Marked-up version (showing deletions)

The Owner ~~covenants and~~ agrees that it will indemnify ~~and keep indemnified~~ Council, ~~its officers, servants, agents, workmen and contractors from and~~ against all ~~costs, expenses, losses or~~ damages which Council~~, its officers, servants, agents, workman and contractors~~ may ~~sustain, incur or~~ suffer ~~or be or become liable for or claim~~ brought by any person arising from ~~or referable to~~ the obligations ~~stated~~ in this Agreement. [25 words remaining]

Clean version (with further refinement)

The Owner agrees to indemnify Council against all damage Council may suffer arising from breach of obligations in this Agreement. [20 words]

Example 2 (pleadings)

Before

Plaintiffs, ZACHARY BELLI, BENJAMIN PETERSON, ERIC KINSLEY, and LARRY JOHNSON, (hereinafter referred to as "Plaintiffs"), individually and on behalf of all others similarly situated ("Class members"), by and through the undersigned counsel and pursuant to the Fair Labor Standards Act of 1938, (the "FLSA"), 29 U.S.C. § 216(b) files this motion seeking an order (1) conditionally certifying this case as a collective class action; (2) requiring the Defendant, HEDDEN ENTERPRISES, INC. d/b/a INFINITY TECHNOLOGY SOLUTIONS (hereinafter "Defendant"), to produce and disclose all of the names and last known addresses and telephone numbers of the potential Class Members so that notice may be implemented; and (3) authorizing notice by U.S. First Class mail to all similarly situated persons employed by Defendant within the past three (3) years to inform them of the pendency of this suit and to inform them of their right to opt-in to this lawsuit. In support of this Motion, Plaintiffs sets forth the following facts and provides this Court with a Memorandum of Law in support of the Motion, and asserts as follows: [176 words]

After

Marked-up version (showing deletions)

Plaintiffs~~, ZACHARY BELLI, BENJAMIN PETERSON, ERIC KINSLEY, and LARRY JOHNSON, (hereinafter referred to as "Plaintiffs"), individually and on behalf of all others similarly situated ("Class members"), by and through the undersigned counsel and pursuant to the Fair Labor Standards Act of 1938, (the "FLSA"), 29 U.S.C. § 216(b) files this motion seeking an order~~ [move] (1) [to] conditionally certify~~ing this case as~~ a collective ~~class~~ action; (2) [to] requir[e]~~ing~~ the Defendant~~, HEDDEN ENTERPRISES, INC. d/b/a INFINITY TECHNOLOGY SOLUTIONS (hereinafter "Defendant"),~~ to produce ~~and disclose~~ ~~all of~~ the names[,] ~~and last known~~ address~~es~~[,] and telephone number~~s~~ of the [each] potential ~~C~~[c]lass ~~M~~[m]ember~~s so that notice may be implemented~~; and (3) [to] authoriz[e]~~ing~~ notice ~~by U.S. First Class mail to all~~ [of this action to each] similarly situated person~~s~~ employed by Defendant within ~~the past~~ three ~~(3)~~ years[.] ~~to inform them of the pendency of this suit and to inform them of their right to opt-in to this lawsuit. In support of this Motion, Plaintiffs sets forth the following facts and provides this Court with a Memorandum of Law in support of the Motion, and asserts as follows:~~

After

Clean version

Plaintiffs move (1) to conditionally certify a collective action; (2) to require Defendant to produce the name, address, and telephone number of each potential class member; and (3) to authorize notice of this action to each similarly situated person employed by Defendant within three years. [45 words]

[Source: *Belli v Hedden Enterprises Inc* (Case No: 8:12-cv-1001-T-23MAP; USDC, Florida; noted by Joseph Kimble, [2013] *Michigan Bar Journal* (Jan) 48; marking-up and amendments by the judge (Judge Merryday)]

Choose simpler words and phrases

Sometimes the problem lies not so much with an over-abundance of words as with word-choice—in particular, using words that are too complex for the intended audience. It then becomes necessary not so much to prune as to recast in simpler terms. The following Example 3 redrafts a statutory notice to make it more accessible to the intended readership.

Example 3 (statutory notice)

[Introduction: US drivers brought proceedings to set aside the cancellation of their driving licences. They argued that the government notice warning drivers of the pending licence cancellation was beyond the average citizen's reading ability and therefore violated their constitutional right to due process. Several plain-language experts lodged an amicus curiae ('friend of the court') brief, which discussed readability research and then redrafted part of the notice in plain language, to demonstrate how to improve its readability. The following is an extract from the brief.]

Original (all in capitals)	**Rewritten in plain language**
WE REGRET TO INFORM YOU	We're sorry,
THAT EFFECTIVE 12.01 AM, 31/11/2018,	but on 03/11/2018 (the "effective date")
YOUR NC DRIVING PRIVILEGE	your North Carolina license
IS SCHEDULED FOR INDEFINITE SUSPENSION	will be suspended
IN ACCORDANCE WITH GENERAL STATUTE 20-24.1	[Incomprehensible to non-lawyer readers who don't know what a Statute is or where to access it]
FOR FAILURE TO PAY FINE	because you didn't pay your fine.
PLEASE COMPLY WITH THIS CITATION	You need to take the following steps
PRIOR TO THE EFFECTIVE DATE.	before 03/11/2018
IN ORDER TO STOP THIS SUSPENSION	to stop your license from being suspended.

[Source: Amicus curiae brief (p 21), filed in *Johnson v Jessup* (Case No 1:18-c-v00467), 26 August 2019, WL 4196740 (CA 4)]

Improve structure

Sometimes the problem lies not merely in words (too many, or audience-inappropriate), but with poor structure. The combination of words and structure then makes the document appear far more complex—inscrutable, even—than it needs to be. It is then necessary to recast both language and structure. This is shown in Example 4, taken from a contract for the sale of land.

Example 4 (contract for sale of land)

Before (italics added to show key elements)

1. It is especially agreed between the parties hereto that *in circumstances requiring the issue of a notice to complete* this matter that any such notice to complete providing for *settlement at the expiry period of fourteen (14) days* from the date of the said notice *shall be deemed to be reasonable and sufficient notice* for this purpose.
2. *Completion shall take place within forty two (42) days from the date hereof* and the parties hereby agree that *such time shall be and be deemed to be a reasonable time* within which to settle. *Should settlement not be effected within such aforesaid time, then either party hereto shall be at liberty to serve a Notice to Complete* on the other party, requiring completion within fourteen (14) days of service of such Notice *and such Notice shall make* and be deemed to have made *time of the essence of this Agreement.*

[Total 150 words. Source: special conditions of sale (clause numbers changed, but clause order and punctuation retained), taken from *Doyle v Howey* (1990) 6 BPR 13,401 (Cohen J)]

Step 1: Reorganise structure and carry out initial (basic) pruning

Logically, the order of these two conditions should be reversed. The key concepts are in clause 2; clause 1 is ancillary to those concepts. So the first step is to reverse the order. Next, it would be helpful to separate the component parts of the reorganised text, to better show the logical flow of events. In the process, we can prune obvious wordiness (shown below in strike-through). The result should be something along these lines (for now, retaining the italics to show the key elements):

1. *Completion shall take place within ~~forty two (42)~~ days from the date hereof.*
2. The parties ~~hereby~~ agree that *such time shall be ~~and be deemed to be~~ a reasonable time* within which to settle.
3. *Should settlement not be effected within such aforesaid time, then either party [may] ~~hereto shall be at liberty to~~ serve a Notice to Complete* on the other party, requiring completion within ~~fourteen (~~14~~)~~ days of service of such Notice.

4. *Such Notice shall make* ~~and be deemed to have made~~ *time of the essence of this Agreement.*
5. ~~It is especially agreed between the parties hereto that~~ *in circumstances requiring the issue of a notice to complete* ~~this matter that~~ any such notice to complete providing for *settlement at the expiry period of* ~~*fourteen (*~~*14*~~*)*~~ *days* from the date of the said notice *shall be deemed to be reasonable and sufficient notice* for this purpose.

Step 2: Further prune, using plain English

Having reorganised the text and carried out an initial pruning, we can work more closely on what remains. This will include eliminating more archaisms and redundancies:

1. *Completion* ~~*shall*~~ *must take place within 42 days from the date hereof.*
2. ~~The parties hereby agree that~~ [no need for this – it is obvious] *such time shall be* ~~*and be deemed to be*~~ *a reasonable time* within which to settle.
3. *Should settlement not be effected within such aforesaid time, then either party [may]* ~~*hereto shall be at liberty to*~~ *serve a Notice to Complete* on the other party, requiring completion within 14 days of service of such Notice.
4. *Such Notice shall make* ~~and be deemed to have made~~ *time of the essence of this* ~~*Agreement*~~ *contract.*
5. ~~It is especially agreed between the parties hereto that~~ *in circumstances requiring the issue of a notice to complete* ~~this matter that~~ any such notice to complete providing for *settlement at the expiry period of 14 days* from the date of the said notice *shall be deemed to be reasonable and sufficient notice* for this purpose.

Step 3: Remove redundancies and archaisms

We can now improve the plain-language redraft. The aim is to retain the legal efficacy of the original, while improving structure and readability, and reducing word-count. This stage should produce something like this:

1. The parties must complete within 42 days from the date of this contract.
2. The parties agree that 42 days is a reasonable time within which to complete.
3. If completion does not occur within 42 days, either party may serve a notice to complete requiring completion within 14 days from the date of service.
4. The parties agree that 14 days is a reasonable and sufficient period for the notice to complete.
5. The notice to complete makes time of the essence of this contract.

Step 4: Polish

We can now finalise the plain-language redraft, cleaning up the structure to prevent unnecessary repetition. The final result should look something like this:

1. The parties must complete the contract within 42 days from the date of the contract.
2. The parties agree that:
   (a) 42 days is a reasonable time within which to complete; and
   (b) if completion does not occur within 42 days, either party may serve a notice to complete requiring completion within 14 days from the date of service; and
   (c) 14 days is a reasonable and sufficient period for the notice to complete; and
   (d) the notice to complete makes time of the essence of this contract.

[Total 89 words; original was 150 words]

'Sense-bites' approach

The final two examples (Examples 5 and 6) start with a 'sense-bites' approach. That is, they first break the original text into 'sense bites', to help draw out the ideas in the original. Only then do they reorganise the structure, prune, and polish.

Example 5 (company constitution)

Before

Where a member or any person assisting the Board or a committee of the Board is present at a meeting of the Board or a committee of the Board, at which meeting a matter which is the subject of consideration is one in which he or she is directly or indirectly interested in a private capacity, the member or the person shall, immediately upon the commencement of the meeting, disclose such interest and shall not take part in any consideration or discussion of, or vote on any question concerning that matter.

[Source: Article 16 of company constitution; 92 words]

Step 1: Break into 'sense bites' (with minimal changes in wording)

This article applies where:

- a member or any person assisting the Board or a committee of the Board is present at a meeting of the Board or a committee of the Board; and
- at the meeting a matter which is the subject of consideration is one in which he or she is directly or indirectly interested in a private capacity.

The member or person shall:

- immediately upon the commencement of the meeting, disclose such interest; and
- shall not take part in any consideration or discussion of, or vote on any question concerning that matter.

Step 2: prune and polish (strikeouts indicate deletions; underlining indicates new words)

(1) This article applies where:

(a) a Board member or ~~any~~ a person assisting the Board or a committee of the Board is present at a meeting of the Board or ~~a~~ committee ~~of the Board~~; and

(b) ~~at which~~ the meeting ~~a matter which is the subject of consideration is one~~ considers a matter in which he or she is directly or indirectly interested in a private capacity.

(2) The member or person ~~shall~~ must:

(a) immediately ~~upon the commencement of the meeting~~ at the start of the meeting, disclose ~~such~~ the interest; and

(b) ~~shall not, take part~~ take no part in any consideration or discussion of the matter, or vote on any question ~~concerning that matter~~ about it.

Step 3: final clean copy

(1) This article applies where:

(a) a Board member, or a person assisting the Board or a committee of the Board, is present at a Board or committee meeting; and

(b) the meeting considers [*better*: is to consider?] a matter in which that member or person is directly or indirectly interested in a private capacity.

(2) The member or person must:

(a) at the [very] start of the meeting, disclose the interest; and

(b) take no part in any discussion of the matter, or vote on any question about it.

[89 words. Reduction in word-count is small, but the structure and language make the rewrite much easier to read than the original. Note use of 'narrative' style in subs (1)—see further, **DEFINITIONS (Narrative definitions)**.]

Example 6 (tenant's covenant not to alter leased premises)

Before

The Lessee shall not make or cause or suffer to be made any alterations, additions, or improvements to the premises, or install or cause or suffer to be installed therein, or thereon any trade fixtures exterior signs, floor coverings, partitions, interior or exterior lighting, plumbing, fixtures, shades or awnings, or drive nails or screws into the premises or any part thereof or in any way damage or deface ceilings walls, partitions, floors, wood, stone, concrete or ironwork thereof during the said term, without first obtaining the written approval of the Lessor. The Lessee shall present to the Lessor plans and specifications for such work at the time approval is sought. The Lessor shall be entitled to obtain the advice of its architects in respect thereof, and any fees payable by the Lessor to such architects shall be paid by the Lessee to the Lessor on demand.

[Source: lease covenant; 145 words]

Step 1: Break into 'sense bites' (no changes to wording at this stage)

The Lessee shall not

- make or cause or suffer to be made any alterations, additions, or improvements to the premises,
- or install or cause or suffer to be installed therein, or thereon any trade fixtures exterior signs, floor coverings, partitions, interior or exterior lighting, plumbing, fixtures, shades or awnings,
- or drive nails or screws into the premises or any part thereof
- or in any way damage or deface ceilings walls, partitions, floors, wood, stone, concrete or ironwork thereof during the said term,

without first obtaining the written approval of the Lessor.

The Lessee shall present to the Lessor plans and specifications for such work at the time approval is sought.

The Lessor shall be entitled to obtain the advice of its architects in respect thereof, and any fees payable by the Lessor to such architects shall be paid by the Lessee to the Lessor on demand.

Step 2: prune (underlined words to be pruned later, at step 3)

The Lessee shall not

- make ~~or cause or suffer to be made~~ any alterations, additions, ~~or improvements~~ to the premises, or
- install ~~or cause or suffer to be installed therein, or thereon~~ any trade fixtures, exterior signs, floor coverings, partitions, interior or exterior lighting, plumbing, fixtures, shades or awnings, or
- drive nails or screws into the premises ~~or any part thereof~~, or
- ~~in any way~~ damage ~~or deface~~ ceilings, walls, partitions, floors, wood, stone, concrete or ironwork thereof ~~during the said term~~,

without first obtaining the written approval of the Lessor.

The Lessee shall present to the Lessor plans and specifications for such work at the time approval is sought.

The Lessor shall be entitled to obtain the advice of its architects in respect thereof, and any fees payable by the Lessor to such architects shall be paid by the Lessee to the Lessor on demand.

Step 3: polish further (underlined words still to be pruned)

[Tasks include: replacing nouns with verbs; using the possessive; preferring active voice over passive; removing archaisms (eg, 'shall'); removing 'sandwich' constructions.]

The Lessee must not do any of the following work without the Lessor's prior written approval:

- alter or add to the premises;
- install any fixtures, exterior signs, floor coverings, partitions, interior or exterior lighting, plumbing, shades or awnings;
- drive nails or screws into the premises;
- damage ~~any part of~~ the premises.

When seeking approval, the Lessee must give the Lessor plans and specifications for the proposed work.

The Lessor may seek its architects' advice about the proposed work. If the Lessor asks, the Lessee must pay the architects' fees.

Step 4: final clean copy

(1) The Lessee must not do any of the following without the Lessor's prior written approval:
   (a) alter or add to the premises;
   (b) install items in or outside the premises;
   (c) drive nails or screws into the premises;
   (d) damage the premises.

(2) When seeking approval, the Lessee must give the Lessor plans and specifications for the proposed work.

(3) The Lessor may seek its architects' advice about the proposed work. If the Lessor asks, the Lessee must pay the architects' fees.

[83 words]

Further reading

Joseph Kimble, *Seeing Through Legalese: More Essays on Plain Language* (Carolina Academic Press, 2017) 21–132 (essays on redrafting US court rules, by a master of the art)

See also **CLAUSE STRUCTURE; 'FURTHER ASSURANCE' CLAUSE; PROLIXITY; PLAIN LANGUAGE.**

REDUNDANCIES

The issue

A redundancy repeats what has already been said. Its very nature makes it unnecessary. Occasionally—very occasionally—a redundancy may be justified for emphasis or rhetorical flourish; but most redundancies are the product of habit or oversight. Examples abound in legal writing:

actual facts	true facts	actual experience
final conclusion	final outcome	advance warning
harmful injuries	live witness	knowledgeable expert
basic fundamentals	closely scrutinise	few in number
free gift	new innovation	completely full
refer back	surrounded on all sides	interact with each other

Redundancies often surface in lawyers' habitual word pairings and word strings: eg, 'cease and desist', 'each and every', 'advice and guidance', 'right, title and interest', 'will and testament'.

Redundancies in legal writing pose two main issues. First, courts assume that each word in a legal document serves a deliberate purpose; redundant words or phrases severely test that principle. (See **SURPLUSAGE (PRESUMPTION AGAINST)**.) Second (less legal), redundancies may irritate busy readers, who may feel that the writer is indifferent to demands on readers' time—why else would the writer take so many words to say something that could be said in just a few?

Removing redundancies

Redundancies are easily removed. The problem is to spot them.

- 'In addition to the facts set out in the *short synopsis* [prefer: *synopsis*] in this judgment in paragraph 5 …' [*AB v Leeds Teaching Hospital NHS Trust* [2004] EWHC 644; [2005] QB 506, [27] (Gage J)]
- 'Pleadings arguments have occurred over a *period of time* [prefer: *period*] and these have now been *narrowed down* [prefer: *narrowed*] to the issue which is the subject of *the present* [prefer: *this*] application for permission to appeal.' [*Susu Pty Ltd v M Marinos Pty Ltd* [2008] SASC 227, [9] (Full Court)]
- '*Earlier in time* [prefer: *Earlier*] the deceased had told her brother that she had informed the appellant of her wish to be divorced.' [*Bayram v R* [2012] VSCA 6, [14] (Warren CJ)]
- '[T]here was a fairly general *consensus of opinion* [prefer: *consensus*] amongst the many medical practitioners whom he had consulted … that he was suffering from schizophrenia.' [*Pappas v Neil-Smith* [2003] NSWCA 197, [8] (Brownie AJA)]
- 'At this stage *a brief overview* [prefer: *an overview*] of the scheme … will suffice.' [*Kumar v R* [2010] NSWCCA 138, [6] (Simpson J]

See also **AMBIGUITY; PROLIXITY; SURPLUSAGE (PRESUMPTION AGAINST); TAUTOLOGIES; WORD PAIRINGS; WORD STRINGS**.

REFERENCES TO DOCUMENT CLAUSES

See **CLAUSE STRUCTURE**.

REFERENCES TO LEGISLATION

See **CITATION OF LEGISLATION**.

referendum / referenda

The Latin plural of *referendum* is *referenda*. In modern usage, however, the anglicised plural *referendums* is acceptable.

refute

See **rebut / refute**.

Register / Registrar

A *Register* (or lower case, *register*) is an official record, such as a register of title. A *Registrar* is a person who manages a Register.

registrable / registerable

The correct spelling is *registrable*. However, even experienced judges (or editors of the law reports) sometimes slide into *registerable*:

- '*registerable* charge': *FG Wilson (Engineering) Ltd v John Holt & Co (Liverpool) Ltd* [2014] 1 WLR 2365, [28] (Longmore LJ)
- '*registerable* transfer': *Registrar-General v Behn* (1981) 148 CLR 562, 569 (Murphy, Aickin and Brennan JJ)
- '*registerable* title': *Quarmby v Keating* [2008] TasSC 71, [2] (Slicer J)
- Other examples: *National Starch Manufacturing Company v Munn's Patent Maizena and Starch Co* [1894] AC 275, 279, 281 (PC); *Sharp v Coates* [1949] 1 KB 285, 293 (Lord Goddard CJ); *Eastbourne Town Radio Cars Association v Customs and Excise Commissioners* [2001] 1 WLR 794 (Lord Slynn).

Registrar-General

Plural: *Registrars-General*. Historically, always hyphenated; in modern times, often hyphen-less: eg, 'The Registrar General [no hyphen] is a corporation sole by the name of the Registrar General [no hyphen] for England and Wales': *Registration Service Act 1953*, s 1(2).' Even where statute hyphenates the term, Registrars themselves sometimes omit it: eg, *Conveyancing Rules Version 1, 2016*, issued by the New South Wales *Registrar General*.

regulation

Abbreviation *reg* (plural, *regs*); not capitalised (ie, *reg*, not *Reg*), following the convention for *section*.

See further **CITATION OF LEGISLATION**.

rehearing

Do you need a hyphen: *re-hearing*? Probably not; but where a statute uses a hyphen, it is conventional to follow suit when citing the provision. (See, eg, *Boland v Boxall* [2016] TASSC 30; (2016) Tas R 444, [8], discussing *Legal Profession Act 2007* (Tas), s 458(3), which uses 're-hearing'. Notably, on appeal the Full Court omitted the hyphen: *Boland v Boxall* [2018] TASFC 11, [11].)

relating to

General meaning

A term that is inherently vague: is the 'relationship' it envisages close or loose, strong or tenuous, direct or indirect? Clearly, the nature of the relationship will depend on the context. There is no prima facie presumption that *relating to* means '*directly* relating to'; the phrase can embrace both a direct and an indirect connection: *Lownie v Information Commissioner* [2020] UKUT 32 (AAC); [2020] 1 WLR 3319, [59], [62]–[64]. This makes *relating to* similar to other open-ended relational terms, such as *in connection with* or *in respect of*. A prudent legal writer, with a nose to avoid potential litigation, may wish to define with care the degree of relationship intended.

Special meaning: land law

In the law of restrictive covenants, '*relating to* land' has a technical meaning. Covenants 'relate to' land if they 'touch and concern' the land. The concept is of a covenant that inherently affects the way in which the land can be occupied or used, or directly affects its value: *Rogers v Hosegood* [1900] 2 Ch 389, 395. This meaning is far removed from the general meaning discussed above. It has statutory recognition in s 78(1) of the *Law of Property Act 1925*.

Further reading

S Bridge, E Cooke, and M Dixon (eds), *Megarry & Wade's Law of Real Property*, 9th edn (Sweet & Maxwell, 2019) [31-013], [31-058], [31-063] (on covenants that 'relate to' land)

See also **in relation to; in respect of; touch and concern.**

RELATIVE CLAUSES

See **PARTICIPLES.**

RELATIVE PRONOUNS

See **PARTICIPLES; PRONOUNS; that / which.**

release / re-lease

To *release* is to let go; to *re-lease* is to grant another lease. The hyphen makes all the difference.

See also **HYPHENS.**

relict

In former usage, a wife who survives a deceased husband (ie, a widow); hence, probate or letters of administration might be granted to the deceased's widow as 'relict of the testator': *Re Forster* (1919) 20 SR (NSW) 156, 157. Also, but more rarely, a husband who survives a deceased wife. Scots law recognised the *jus relictae* (the right of a widow to a proportion of her deceased husband's property), and the *jus relicti* (the widower's similar right).

In modern times to describe a surviving spouse as a *relict* would be offensive. Prefer *widow* (or *widower*).

remainder / reversion

remainder

In normal usage, *remainder* is what is left after part of something has been given away or taken away ('I gave away part of my lottery winnings and kept the *remainder*'). In strict legal usage, a *remainder* is an interest in property that arises where an owner of property (the 'grantor') disposes of their whole interest in the property in two or more 'slices of time' to take effect consecutively. The second and subsequent slices are *remainder* interests (or simply *remainders*), because they 'remain away' from the grantor after the first 'slice' expires. For example:

> A owns the freehold ('fee simple') in a parcel of land. A carves up that fee simple into two slices to take effect consecutively, by conveying a life estate to B and the rest of the fee simple to C. C's interest is a *remainder*, because on B's death the land 'remains away' from A.

reversion

A *reversion* is an interest that remains in a property owner who has disposed of less than the whole of their interest. The most common example is the interest left in a landlord who has granted a lease—the landlord retains the *reversion*. But other examples exist:

> A owns the freehold ('fee simple') in a parcel of land. A conveys a life estate to B but nothing further to anyone else. Logically, since a life estate is 'less than' a fee simple, portion of the fee simple remains in A. That portion is called—confusingly, perhaps—not a *remainder* but a *reversion*.

Further reading

S Bridge, E Cooke, and M Dixon (eds), *Megarry & Wade's Law of Real Property*, 9th edn (Sweet & Maxwell, 2019) [3-009], [8-008]

See also **remainderman**; **reversioner**.

remainderman

A person who holds a *remainder* interest in property (usually land). The *-man* suffix may seem unsatisfactory to modern readers accustomed to gender-neutral language: eg, 'The daughter … claims to be entitled as remainderman under the testator's will …': *Ritchie v Magree* (1964) 114 CLR 173, 180 (Kitto J). But no generally accepted gender-neutral term has yet emerged. Very occasionally, *remainderperson* is seen (as in the examples below), but the word seems ungainly. At present, the best substitute is 'holder of a remainder interest'.

- 'The plaintiff was favoured in the defendant's will as life income beneficiary, and three of his four children as *remaindermen* (or perhaps the more modern term, *remainderpersons*).' [*Hall v SG Hall Pty Ltd* [2010] NSWSC 573, [4] (Bergin CJ in Eq)]
- '*Remainderperson* or reversioner may be registered as such' [Heading to *Land Titles Act 1925* (ACT), s 56. Notably, *remainderperson* appears in the heading only; the body of the section uses 'person entitled in remainder'.]

See also **GENDER-NEUTRAL LANGUAGE**; **remainder / reversion**.

remediate

To redress, to repair, or (in the context of environmental action) to restore to the previous, unpolluted condition. Often used to mean simply *remedy* or *fix*—in which case, prefer *remedy* or *fix*. For example:

- 'This treatment did not *remediate* [prefer: *remedy*] any of the aspects of his illness.' [*Melham v R* [2011] NSWCCA 121, [35] (Garling J)]
- '[He had a duty] to ensure that the Company either remitted the [tax payments] or took other steps … to *remediate* [prefer: *remedy*] the situation.' [*Deputy Commissioner of Taxation v Dick* [2007] NSWCA 190; (2007) 242 ALR 152, [69] (Santow JA)]

re-mediate

To mediate again. The hyphen clarifies the meaning: compare *remediate.*

remise

To give up, surrender. An archaism, formerly common in deeds of release, where the releasor would '*remise*, release and for ever quit-claim': William Blackstone, *Commentaries on the Laws of England* (Clarendon, 1766) book 2, 324. In a modern, plain-language deed of release, *release* is sufficient.

rent

The income from property, usually land. The meaning of *rent* has evolved over the centuries. Medieval law regarded *rent* as 'reserved or arising out of' the land itself, as an 'incident' of the landlord's reversion: S Bridge, E Cooke and M Dixon (eds), *Megarry & Wade's Law of Real Property*, 9th edn (Sweet & Maxwell, 2019) [18-081], n 378. It was a 'thing', as capable of possession and dispossession as the land itself, and was therefore recoverable by the 'real' actions: Holdsworth, *History of English Law*, 2nd edn (Sweet & Maxwell, 1937) vol VII, 262. Because rent issued out of the land, its payment was secured by the land itself; the landlord could seize the land for unpaid rent and hold it until the rent was paid. Also, rent could be reserved in favour of the landlord only, not in favour of a stranger to the lease: *Oates v Frith* (1615) Hob 130; 80 ER 280; *Applerly v Federal Commissioner of Land Tax* (1914) 17 CLR 535, 546.

The modern concept of *rent* is somewhat different, reflecting more the influence of contract law than medieval property law. In modern law, *rent* is not so much a 'thing' issuing from the land, as a payment the tenant is contractually bound to make to the landlord for the use of the land: *Property Holding Co Ltd v Clark* [1948] KB 630, 648; *United Scientific Holdings Ltd v Burnley Borough Council* [1978] AC 904, 935, 947, 963; *Booker Industries Pty Ltd v Wilson Parking (Qld) Pty Ltd* (1982) 149 CLR 600, 610–11.

Despite this development in meaning, many property statutes continue to give *rent* a meaning that harks back to its medieval sense of 'a payment issuing out of land'. For example:

> '"Rent" includes a rent service or a rentcharge, or other rent, toll, duty, royalty, or annual or periodical payment in money or money's worth, reserved or issuing out of or charged upon land, but does not include mortgage interest ...' [*Law of Property Act 1925*, s 205(1)(xxiii)]

Except in the most technical contexts, these extended meanings are unlikely to occur to, or be relevant to, most modern users of *rent.*

rents and profits (of land)

A compendious term meaning *income* (from land). So, a beneficiary entitled for life to the *rents and profits* of land is entitled to such items as rents, proceeds of sale of crops or other income-generating activity, and royalties from mines (as to mines, see *Greville-Nugent v Mackenzie* [1900] AC 83). *Income* suffices as a plain-language alternative.

RENUMBERING

See **NUMBERING SYSTEMS**.

renumerate

To renumber. However, more usually found as a misspelling for 'remunerate' (pay). For example:

- '[The appellant] asked … whether she could work and was told that, since her *renumeration* [sic: *remuneration*] was small, she could.' [*Bennett v Secretary of State for Work and Pensions* [2012] EWHC 371 (Admin), [3] (Cranston J)]
- '[It] was pleaded that Goodyear had failed to *renumerate* [sic: *remunerate*] Mr Andrade at the level … of pay prescribed … under the Retail Award …' [*Andrade v Goodyear & Dunlop Tyres (Aust) Pty Ltd* [2016] FCCA 238, [2] (Barnes J)]

repair

In normal usage, *to repair* means to fix, to make good. In legal usage, it carries the same general sense, but with nuances developed in the case law—particularly in the areas of landlord and tenant (covenants to 'repair') and taxation (deductions for 'repairs'). When used in a professionally drawn document, the courts give *repair* its nuanced, case-law meaning, in line with the principle that those who use legal terms intend to give them their legal meaning (see **LITIGATED WORDS AND PHRASES**).

Examples of nuanced meaning of *repair* in landlord and tenant law

1. 'Repair' requires only replacing subsidiary parts of the premises. It does not extend to renewing or reconstructing the whole or substantially the whole of the premises: *Lurcott v Wakely & Wheeler* [1911] 1 KB 905, 924; *Weatherhead v Deka New Zealand Ltd (No 2)* [1999] 1 NZLR 453. Therefore, a drafter intending to impose an obligation to renew or rebuild the whole or substantially the whole, must go further than requiring mere *repair*: *Norwich Union Life Insurance Society v British Railways Board* (1987) 283 EG 846.
2. 'Repair' does not extend to putting the premises into mint condition, but only into the condition that (having regard to their age, character and locality) would make them 'reasonably fit for the occupation of a reasonably-minded tenant of the class who would be likely to take [them]': *Proudfoot v Hart* (1890) 25 QBD 42, 52, 55. Therefore, a drafter intending to impose a more stringent requirement must do so expressly or by necessary implication. The precise wording may be important:
    - to keep in 'good and substantial repair' may impose a higher standard than simply to keep in 'good tenantable repair': *Alcatel Australia Ltd v Scarcella* (1998) 44 NSWLR 349;
    - to maintain in 'good condition and repair' may impose a higher standard than simply to keep in 'repair', since 'good condition' may be a separate concept from, and add significantly to, 'repair': *Welsh v Greenwich London Borough Council* [2000] 49 EG 118 (CA), as interpreted in *Lee v Leeds City Council* [2002] EWCA Civ 6; [2002] 1 WLR 1488, [61].
3. Where premises are in disrepair at the start of a lease, a covenant to 'keep' the premises in repair will (unless expressly or impliedly qualified by reference to their condition at the start of the lease) require the tenant to put the premises into repair. This is because, as a matter of ordinary English, premises cannot be 'kept' in repair unless they are first put into repair: *Payne v Haine* (1847) 16 M & W 541; 153 ER 1304; *Busby v Joseph* (1868) 7 SCR (NSW) 200, 207–08; *Puhi Maihi v McLeod* [1920] NZLR 372.

Further reading

- S Bridge, E Cooke, and M Dixon (eds), *Megarry & Wade's Law of Real Property*, 9th edn (Sweet & Maxwell, 2019) [18-056]–[18-062]
- Antra Hood, 'The Extent of the Modern Covenant to Repair in Commercial Leases' (1997) 5 *Australian Property Law Journal* 53

replace

A word with various meanings, shading into ambiguity. Context may resolve the ambiguity; but unless this is so, a better approach is to avoid it. For example:

> 'The tenant must *replace* all worn carpets in the premises.' Does this mean: (1) take up all worn carpets and substitute new carpets; or (2) take up all worn carpets and substitute different carpets, which must not be worn but need not be new? Presumably, meaning (1) is intended; but if both meanings are open, clarify.

See also **repair**.

represents and warrants

See **warrants and represents**.

repudiation

In general usage, to *repudiate* (noun, *repudiation*) usually means to reject: 'X *repudiated* the deal' or 'Labour *repudiated* the Conservative policy on education'. However, in law, *repudiation* carries several narrower, more nuanced meanings:

1. Conduct that evinces an unwillingness or an inability to render substantial performance of a contract. More specifically, conduct that evinces an intention no longer to be bound by the contract, or to perform it in a manner substantially inconsistent with one's obligations: *Heyman v Darwins Ltd* [1942] AC 356, 397 (using the term 'renunciation'); *Koompahtoo Local Aboriginal Land Council v Sanpine Pty Ltd* [2007] HCA 61; (2007) 233 CLR 115, [44].
2. A breach of contract that justifies termination by the other party: *Koompahtoo Local Aboriginal Land Council v Sanpine Pty Ltd* (above, [44]).
3. Termination of the performance of a contract: eg, *Hongkong Fir Shipping Co Ltd v Kawasaki Kisen Kaisha Ltd* [1962] 2 QB 26; *Luna Park (NSW) Ltd v Tramways Advertising Pty Ltd* (1938) 61 CLR 286, 305 (Latham CJ). However, this usage does not represent current use, and is best avoided.

In line with the general principle of interpretation that courts give technical terms their technical meaning, courts are likely to assume that, in formal legal documents, parties intended one or more of the nuanced legal meanings of *repudiation*.

Further reading

Halsbury's Laws of England, 'Contract' (vol 22, 2019) [351]–[354]

See also **TERMS OF ART**.

require

Meaning

To *require* someone to do something, or to *require* something to be done, can have a range of meanings. They vary from (at one end of the range) a mere *request* (with no legal consequences for non-compliance), to (at the other end) a *demand* (with a legal obligation to comply). In the absence of a more precise indication, context will be crucial to the intended meaning, and even then will not necessarily produce a clear answer (as in *Arnesto v Hickman* (2016) 26 Tas R 409, 418–20).

Wordiness

Require, in its various forms (including the negative *is not required to*) often leads to wordy constructions. Rewrite, as in these examples:

Before	After
Your attendance *is required in* court today.	You *must* attend court today.
Your attendance *is not required* in court today.	You *need not* attend court today.

requisitions

In general usage, questions or enquiries, usually requiring some action in response. In legal conveyancing usage, questions which purchasers 'raise' with vendors about the property being sold, and requiring answers or action. They are usually called 'requisitions *on title*'—a loose term, in that not all strictly relate to 'title'. There are four categories:

1. requisitions on title (strictly so called): questions about the title to the property
2. requisitions as to conveyance: questions about the form that the conveyance (or transfer) will take
3. general enquiries about the property, not falling into either of the above categories
4. reminders to the vendor of the vendor's obligations under the contract.

The law relating to each category is complex. In addition, the terms of standard contracts for sale often circumscribe the purchaser's common-law rights to ask ('raise') requisitions.

Further reading

- *Halsbury's Laws of England*, 'Conveyancing' (vol 23, 2016) [199]–[201]
- Peter Butt, *The Standard Contract for Sale of Land in NSW*, 2nd edn (LBC Information Services, 1998) ch 5 (Commonwealth law on requisitions on title)

res

Latin: thing (singular), things (plural).

See **real property**.

res gestae

Latin: things done. Singular: *res gesta*. Usually denotes things so close in time or space to the matter in question as to be inseparable from it—and therefore admissible in proving that it occurred. They are 'part of the thing done'; ie, part of the event itself. The sense of the Latin may be clear to lawyers, but to translate it into standard English is notoriously difficult. Indeed, even for lawyers, the Latin may be somewhat vague—as witness

Lord Wilberforce's statement that *res gestae*, 'like many Latin phrases, is often used to cover situations insufficiently analysed in clear English terms': *Ratten v R* [1972] AC 378, 388. For non-lawyers, an approximate, context-appropriate translation may suffice; if not, add an explanation. For example:

- '[T]hough you cannot give in evidence a declaration *per se*, yet when there is an act accompanied by a statement which is so mixed up with it as to become part of *the res gestae* [prefer: *the elements of the crime*], evidence of such statement may be given.' [*Howe v Malkin* (1879) 40 LTR 196, 198 (Grove J)]
- '[F]or identification purposes in a criminal trial[,] the event with which the words sought to be proved must be so connected as to form part of *the res gestae* [prefer: *the critical facts*], is the commission of the crime itself, the throwing of the stone, the striking of the blow, the setting fire to the building or whatever the criminal act may be.' [*Teper v R* [1952] AC 480, 488 (Lord Norman)]
- '[T]he findings of the judge are part of *the res gestae of the proceedings* [prefer: *an integral part of the proceedings*]. They are, as it were, writings on the wall, and would need to be considered ... in any subsequent proceedings ... and at trial, by the same judge or by any other judge.' [*JSC BTA Bank v Ablyazov (No 9)* [2012] EWCA Civ 1551; [2013] 1 WLR 1845, [69] (Rix LJ)]

Further reading

- S Odgers, 'Res Gestae Regurgitated' (1989) 12 *University of New South Wales Law Journal* 262
- Julius Stone, 'Res Gesta Reagitata' (1939) 55 *Law Quarterly Review* 66

res integra

Latin: a matter untouched (specifically, a point of law not previously decided). Always a needless Latinism; prefer an appropriate English translation. Thus:

- 'The matter is not, however, *res integra* [prefer: *novel*; *previously unconsidered by a court*], as examination of the Strasbourg jurisprudence shows, for the European Court of Human Rights has approached it by reference to the individual articles of the Convention.' [*R (Ullah) v Special Adjudicator* [2004] UKHL 26; [2004] 2 AC 323, [66] (Lord Carswell)]
- 'If the matter had been *res integra* [prefer: *without binding precedent*; *something that had not been considered previously*] it might have been thought to be a nice question whether a statute requiring an act to be done "not later than" or "at least" or "not less than" so many days before a given event meant that the act must be done so many clear days before that event.' [*Forster v Jododex Australia Pty Ltd* (1972) 127 CLR 421, 444–45 (Gibbs J)]

res inter alios

Latin: a thing (ie, a matter) between others (in the sense of 'that is a matter between other people'). Hence, *res inter alios acta*: the acts of strangers, or of third parties. Also in the longer maxim, *res inter alios acta alteri nocere non debet*—something done (or agreed) between certain persons ought not to harm another. As with many Latinisms in law, the meaning can be given in plain English. Unless the reader can reasonably be expected to understand the Latin, offer a translation or (as in the second example below) an explanation. For example:

- 'As between Mr Makdessi and the company, the right of Cavendish to a price reduction cannot affect the measure or recoverability of the company's loss. It is *res inter alios acta* [prefer: *a matter between strangers*].' [*Cavendish Square Holdings BV v Makdessi* [2015] UKSC 67, [76]; [2015] 3 WLR 1373, 1406 (Lords Neuberger and Sumption)]

- 'This approach can be explained in terms of one of the maxims traditionally recognised by English law: "*Res inter alios acta alteri nocere non debet*". This holds that a transaction between strangers ought not to injure another party.' [*Imbree v McNeilly* [2008] HCA 40, [146]; (2008) 236 CLR 510, 554 (Kirby J, providing a translation/explanation)]

res ipsa loquitur

Meaning

Latin: the reason is self-evident; it speaks for itself (literally: the thing itself speaks). This Latinism surfaces particularly in tort law, expressing compactly the notion that a court may hold a person liable in negligence without evidence of a particular negligent act or omission, if the circumstances show that the act or omission could not have happened without negligence. See, eg: *George v Eagle Air Services Ltd* [2009] 1 WLR 2133 (in the absence of negligence, modern aircraft do not normally crash); *SJ Weir Ltd v Bijok* (2011) 112 SASR 127; [2011] SASCFC 165 (in the absence of negligence, buildings do not normally subside into adjoining excavation sites).

Prefer plain English

The doctrine of *res ipsa loquitur* may have originated in a casual remark by Baron Pollock during argument in *Byrne v Boadle* (1863) 2 H & C 722, 725; 159 ER 299, 300, to the effect that in some cases the mere fact of an accident is evidence of negligence. But regardless of its origins, the doctrine's complexities do not require continued adherence to the Latin. The plain-English equivalents 'it speaks for itself' or 'the reason is self-evident', are perfectly adequate and carry the same legal nuance as the Latin:

- '[This] convenient and succinct formula [*res ipsa loquitur*] possesses no magic qualities: nor has it any added virtue, other than that of brevity, merely because it is expressed in Latin.' [*Roe v Minister of Health* [1954] 2 QB 66, 87–88 (Morris LJ)]
- 'The doctrine of *res ipsa loquitur* ("the thing speaks for itself") is not one of the greatest sources of pride for the common law. When an established doctrine continues to be described in Latin or in French, there is sometimes cause to suspect that the reason for this is because of a lack of clarity in the doctrine itself. What is the "thing" that is speaking? Why does the "thing speak for itself"?' [*Swick Nominees Pty Ltd v LeRoi International Inc (No 2)* [2015] WASCA 35; (2015) 48 WAR 376, [446] (Murphy JA and Edelman J)]

See also **FOREIGN (NON-ENGLISH) WORDS AND PHRASES; LATIN.**

res judicata / res adjudicata

Latin: a matter decided (in the sense of finally decided by a court); a matter finally determined. The usual form is *res judicata*; the variant *res adjudicata*, once common, is now rare. The Latin encapsulates a principle that parties cannot relitigate a matter in dispute between them (the *res*) once a court has decided the matter: *Ord v Ord* [1923] 2 KB 432, 439 (Lush J); *Carl-Zeiss-Stiftung v Rayner & Keeler Ltd (No 2)* [1967] 1 AC 853, 933 (Lord Guest). By extension, nor can a party set up facts which, had they been set up in the earlier litigation, could have affected the decision: *Robinson v Robinson* [1943] P 43, 44 (Henn-Collins J; more commonly called *issue estoppel*).

Res judicata is a term of art, with a meaning not necessarily filled out in a translation such as 'binding judgment'. It is (in Lord Sumption's words) a 'portmanteau term' that describes a number of different legal principles with different juridical origins: *Virgin Atlantic Airways Ltd v Zodiac Seats UK Ltd* [2013] UKSC 46; [2014] AC 160, [17] (adding that 'the label tends to distract from the contents of the bottle'). However, in contexts such as legal advices, *res judicata* is explained easily enough with a sentence such as: 'You cannot litigate this issue, because a court has already decided it against you. In legal terms, the matter is *res judicata*.' Perhaps unhelpfully, most judges use the Latin alone—sometimes explaining the principle by invoking yet more Latin:

> 'The doctrine of *res judicata* [prefer: *binding litigation*] rests on the twin principles which cannot be better expressed than in terms of the two Latin maxims *interest reipublicae ut sit finis litium* [prefer: *the public has an interest in putting an end to litigation*] and *nemo debet bis vexari pro una et eadem causa* [prefer: *nobody should be subjected to litigation twice for the same matter*]. These principles are of such fundamental importance that they cannot be confined in their application to litigation in the private law field. They certainly have their place in criminal law. In principle they must apply equally to adjudications in the field of public law.' [*Thrasyvoulou v Environment Secretary* [1990] 2 AC 273, 289 (Lord Bridge)]

Further reading

Halsbury's Laws of England, 'Civil Procedure' (vol 12A, 2015) [1634]–[1641]

res nullius

Latin: a thing belonging to no one; no one's property. A Latinism carrying no more legal meaning than an idiomatic English translation. (The same can be said of *terra nullius* (land of no one; land with no owner), despite its passing into the vernacular in the law of indigenous title to land.) Prefer idiomatic English:

- '[T]he Court has the right and the duty to direct [the liquidator] how to distribute all the assets. No part of them can remain undistributed as *res nullius* [prefer: *ownerless property*].' [*Sinclair v Brougham* [1914] AC 398, 458 (Lord Sumner)]
- 'A riparian owner does not have a right to the ownership of the water, *which is res nullius* [prefer: *which no one owns*].' [*British Waterways Board v Severn Trent Water Ltd* [2001] Ch 32, 52 (Arden J)]

rescind / terminate / end

'rescind' vs 'terminate'

'rescind'

Rescind (noun, *rescission*) is the appropriate verb to describe bringing a contract to an end for some vitiating element in its formation, such as fraud, duress, misrepresentation, or mistake. It is also appropriate to describe bringing a contract to an end in exercise of an express contractual right to do so, not involving default by either party. A contract that is *rescinded* in either of these senses is treated as if it had never come into existence. The parties are restored, so far as possible, to their former position—hence the term *rescission ab initio* (rescission from the beginning).

'terminate'

Terminate (noun, *termination*) is the appropriate verb to describe the act of one party in bringing the contract to an end for the other party's breach. If valid, the termination puts an end to prospective duties and liabilities of both parties under the contract, but does not discharge the offending party from liability for breaches of obligations which had accrued due for performance before the termination: *McDonald v Dennys Lacelles Ltd* (1933) 48 CLR 457, 476–77; *Johnson v Agnew* [1980] AC 367, 393.

Imprecise uses

Despite the clear technical differences between *rescind* and *terminate*, some lawyers confuse or conflate them. In particular, they use 'rescind' when they mean 'terminate'. This is even though eminent judges have criticised this use of *rescission*: eg, *Photo Production Ltd v Securicor Transport Ltd* [1980] AC 827, 844 (Lord Wilberforce; Lords Salmon, Keith, and Scarman agreeing). Nevertheless, so common is the confusion that courts often overlook drafters' use of the 'wrong' term and give effect to what the parties must have *intended*. For example:

- Where a contract for the sale of land provided for *rescission* in certain circumstances, but with rights to damages for default, *rescission* meant *termination*, because that was the legal consequence the parties intended: *Horsler v Zorro* [1975] Ch 302, 311–12.
- Where a clause in an insurance policy allowed the insurer to *terminate* the policy at the request of the insured, *terminate* meant *rescind* (by mutual consent or agreement), because that was what the parties intended: *Willcocks v New Zealand Insurance Co* [1926] NZLR 805, 810. (The court gave the same meaning to *cancel*.)

Indeed, judges themselves sometimes use the 'wrong' term, perpetuating the confusion. For example:

- '[Repudiation includes] where a party evinces an intention no longer to be bound and the other party accepts the repudiation and *rescinds* [prefer: *terminates*] the contract.' [*Heyman v Darwins Ltd* [1942] AC 356, 379 (Lord Wright)]
- 'If a party to a contract repudiates it[,] the effect of that repudiation … is that the other party may elect to *rescind* [prefer: *terminate*] and on so doing the contract is at an end.' [*Neeta (Epping) Pty Ltd v Phillips* (1974) 131 CLR 286, 297 (Barwick CJ and Jacobs J)]

'end'

End has a role to play in some legal contexts. For example, *end* is an appropriate verb to describe the process of a landlord or tenant bringing their lease to an early 'end' under a 'break clause' in the lease: see, eg, *Bevan v Chambers* (1896) 12 TLR 417 (CA). But as a general principle, *end* is not an adequate substitute for *rescind* or *terminate* (even though shorter words are usually better than longer words). The substitution prejudices precision. For example, if a contract states that a party may *end* the contract in certain circumstances, does this imply *rescind* (an 'ending' from the start, with limited rights to damages) or *terminate* (an 'ending' from that time forwards, with substantial rights damages for unperformed obligations)? Or if a contract states that it will be 'at an *end*' if a condition is not fulfilled within 30 days, does the contract come to an end automatically on non-fulfillment, or must a party to take active steps to put an end to it? (It seems they must take active steps: *Donaldson v Bexton* [2006] QCA 559; [2007] 1 Qd R 525.) Where precision requires a clear demarcation between remedies, prefer *rescind* or *terminate* (as appropriate).

See also **TERMS OF ART**.

reservation/exception

See **excepting and reserving**.

respective

Respective (and *respectively*) complicate a sentence, often needlessly. The reader must go backwards and forwards to correlate what relates to what. If the meaning is clear without *respective* (or *respectively*), delete it. For example:

- 'Both plaintiff and defendant then outlined their ~~respective~~ arguments.'
- 'The present appeals concern claims for damages by two individuals in respect of their allegedly wrongful detention by British forces in ~~respectively~~ Iraq and Afghanistan. I have had the benefit of reading in draft three of the other judgments which have been prepared, by ~~respectively~~ Lord Sumption, Lord Wilson and Lord Reed JJSC.' [*Al-Waheed v Ministry of Defence* [2017] UKSC 2; [2017] 2 WLR 327, [145] (Lord Mance)]
- 'Divisions 2A and 2B, containing ss 218A–218CA and ss 218D–218F ~~respectively~~ govern, relevantly, how areas are amalgamated …' [*Woollahra Municipal Council v Minister for Local Government* [2016] NSWCA 380, [68] (Beazley P)]

Where a clear indication is needed of what relates to what, recast the sentence to avoid the instinctive prop of *respectively*:

- 'A and B must sue C and D *respectively*.' **Rewrite**: 'A must sue C, and B must sue D.'
- 'Hassell and the Club should bear 25% and 75% *respectively* of Mr Turner's costs.' [*Harrington Estates (NSW) Pty Ltd v Turner* [2016] NSWCA 369, [73] (Leeming JA)]. **Rewrite**: 'Hassall should bear 25% of Mr Turner's costs, and the Club 75%.'

respondeat superior

Latin: let the superior answer. A Latinism reflecting a principle of somewhat indeterminate reach, by which some 'superiors' are legally responsible for the actions of those they engage. Its generality makes it difficult to translate into standard English; but to retain the Latin risks not only failing to communicate but also implying a certainty that the underlying principle lacks. One option is to retain the Latin for more abundant caution, but add an explanation. For example:

- 'So far as conduct within the scope of the employee's employment is concerned, the doctrine *respondeat superior* [add: *ie, let the employer answer*; or more idiomatically, *ie, the employer is responsible*] applies irrespective of whether the duty the employee has breached was laid on him by the common law or by statute.' [*Majrowski v Guy's and St Thomas's NHS Trust* [2006] UKHL 34, [58]; [2007] 1 AC 224, 242 (Lord Hope)]
- 'But in carrying out the duty of keeping the peace, e.g. in making an arrest, [police officers] do not attract the maxim *respondeat superior* [add: *under which superiors may have to answer for the actions of their subordinates*].' [*R v Tween* [1965] VR 687, 697 (Sholl J)]
- 'The common law applied the maxim *respondeat superior* [add: *ie, let the employer be responsible*] when a [ship's pilot] was voluntarily taken on board[,] because he was selected by or on behalf of the owners and there was between them and the pilot a contractual relationship of master and servant …' [*Oceanic Crest Shipping Co v Pilbara Harbour Services Pty Ltd* (1986) 160 CLR 626, 683 (Dawson J)]

See also **LATIN; TERMS OF ART**.

rest, residue and remainder

A trilogy common in wills: eg, 'I give the *rest, residue, and remainder* of my estate to X'. Ideally with the serial comma (ie, two commas in total) to clearly delineate the three terms; but often with one only—*rest, residue and remainder*; and sometimes with none—*rest residue and remainder*. It is a ritual incantation, always tautologous. The expression may carry a certain ponderous alliteration, but that is no justification for retaining three words where one will do. Any one of the three words sufficiently indicates the meaning—ie, 'everything else'. Perhaps centuries ago *remainder* was the more appropriate word for 'all the rest of' real estate, and *residue* for 'all the rest of' personal estate (*Hogan v Jackson* (1775) 1 Cowp 308; 98 ER 1096), but that is no longer the case. For over a century, any one of the three words has effectively covered any type of property: *Re Mason* [1901] 1 Ch 619, 625. Because the simplest of the three is *rest*, prune the trilogy to: 'I give the *rest* of my estate to X'. Another one-word equivalent is *balance*—'I give the *balance* of my estate to X': *Re Duffel* [1926] VLR 489, 491).

Further reading

'Rest, Residue and Remainder', in *Law Words* (Centre for Plain Legal Language, University of Sydney, 1995) 73; www.clarity-international.net/plain-language-resources/general-resources/

See also **remainder**; **WORD PAIRINGS**.

restitutio in integrum

Latin: restoration to the unchanged; restoration to the former position; complete restitution. The Latinism appears particularly (but not exclusively) in two common-law principles: (1) that on rescission of a contract, the parties are to be restored, as far as possible, to their pre-contract positions; and (2) that on a claim for damages in tort or contract, the injured party is to be put in the same position, as far as possible, that he or she would have enjoyed had the tort or breach of contract not occurred. The Latin loses nothing by a context-dependent translation or explanation. For example:

- 'The principle of *restitutio in integrum* [prefer: *complete restoration*] applies comparatively straightforwardly in non-discrimination cases: the claimant is prima facie entitled to recover whatever financial loss he can prove was directly consequent on the violation of his rights.' [*R v Commissioners of Inland Revenue* [2005] UKHL 30, [44]; [2005] 1 WLR 1718, 1728 [44] (Lord Brown)]
- 'The fundamental principle for the assessment of damages in cases of breach of contract … is the principle of *restitutio in integrum* [prefer: *restoration to the pre-contract position*] within the limits expressed in *Hadley v Baxendale*.' [*Bunge SA v Nidera BV* [2015] UKSC 43, [76]; [2015] 3 All ER 1082, 1105 (Lord Toulson)]
- 'Where the breach of duty was in a solicitor acting for a client in a transaction in which the solicitor had a personal interest, the court may order the solicitor "to replace property improperly acquired from the client" and achieve this by an order for rescission, unless it be shown that *restitutio in integrum* [prefer: *unwinding the transaction*] is no longer possible.' [*Maguire v Makaronis* (1997) 188 CLR 449, 467 (Brennan CJ, Gaudron, McHugh and Gummow JJ, citations omitted)]

See also **in integrum**; **rescind / terminate / end**.

restore / re-store

To *restore* is to make new; to *re-store* is to put back into storage. For example:

> 'The gallery director decided to *re-store* the *restored* painting.'

restricted entail

A fee tail that descended only to a particular class of lineal descendants, such as a fee tail male, a fee tail female, or a special tail.

See **fee tail.**

result of

When is event B the 'result of' event A? Clearly, a causal link of some kind is implied, but how close? Must the 'result' be direct, or may it be indirect? Must it be immediate, or is lapse of time permitted? The answers turn on the context in which 'result of' is used. In this, similar considerations apply as with other expressions suggesting a causal link, such as 'in consequence of' (see discussion under **consequence of**). For example, an employee's disease may be a 'result of' an employer's actions if those actions are *a* cause of the disease, even though not the only cause, and even though exacerbated by other factors: *Comcare v Martin* [2016] HCA 43, [42], [45]; (2016) 258 CLR 467. But other contexts may indicate that the 'result' must follow directly from one act alone.

The lesson for drafters using the expression is to be as specific as possible about the nature of causation contemplated.

See also **consequence of**.

retention of title

See **Romalpa clause**.

retroactive / retrospective

Used particularly to describe statutes that take away accrued rights—such a statute is said to apply *retroactively* or *retrospectively*. The 'backwards' operation may be because the statute states that it is deemed to have commenced at a time already past, or (more commonly) because it takes away rights accrued under other statutes or sets aside transactions already entered into.

The two words are not true synonyms: *retrospective* denotes *looking* backwards, while *retroactive* denotes *operating* backwards. A statute that is deemed to be already in operation, or that affects accrued rights, does not merely *look* backwards but *operates* backwards—and so the more appropriate word is *retroactive*. In practice, however, *retrospective* is more common for this purpose: eg, *Jazztel plc v Revenue and Customs Commissioners* [2017] EWHC 677 (Ch); [2017] 1 WLR 3869, [87]–[98] (Marcus Smith J).

See also **deem**.

rev'd

Abbreviation for *reversed*—denoting that the appeal court overturned the decision being referred to.

reversion

See **remainder / reversion; reversionary**.

reversionary

The adjectival form of *reversion*. When used in the term *reversionary interest*, it can mean three different (though related) things:

1. The *reversion* itself. For example, a freehold owner (A) who grants a life estate, retains a 'reversionary interest' (ie, the actual reversion, namely, the freehold subject to the life estate). Similarly, a freehold owner (A) who grants a lease to a tenant (T) retains a 'reversionary interest' (ie, the actual reversion, namely, the freehold subject to the lease).
2. An *interest in* the reversion (but not the whole of that reversion). For example (to continue the above illustrations):
   a if A, having granted a life estate or lease, then grants a mortgage over the reversion, the mortgagee has a 'reversionary interest' (ie, an interest *in* the reversion); or
   b if A, having granted the lease to T, grants a lease of the same property to X, expressed to commence when the lease to T expires, then X holds a 'reversionary lease' (again, an interest *in* the reversion): *Green v Bowes-Lyon* [1960] 1 WLR 176, 181.
3. To change the lease example slightly, if A grants a lease to a tenant (T) and then, while that lease is current, grants another lease over the same property to Y, to take effect immediately, Y's lease gives Y an interest *in* A's reversion. (However, although sometimes called a 'reversionary lease', this is better called a 'concurrent' lease, because it runs concurrently with T's lease: see discussion under **concurrent lease**.)

See also **remainder / reversion**.

reversionary interest

See **remainder / reversion; reversionary**.

reversioner

A person who holds a *reversion*, or *reversionary interest*, in property (usually land). It is conveniently gender-neutral, unlike its kindred term *remainderman*.

See **remainder / reversion; remainderman; reversionary**.

revert back (to)

Here, *back* is superfluous. Always delete it. Where else could someone (or something) revert to? For example:

- 'The court must therefore take a "broad and practical approach" to the question of when the land is no longer used for the purposes of section 2 of the 1841 Act and beneficial ownership *reverts* ~~*back*~~ …' [*Rittson-Thomas v Oxfordshire County Council* [2019] Ch 435 (counsel, in argument)]

- '[T]he paramedic could *revert* ~~*back*~~ to operational paramedic work at the conclusion of the secondment.' [*State of New South Wales v Chapman-Davis* [2016] NSWCA 237, [24] (Gleeson JA)]

Revert has also come to mean *reply*—'let me *revert* to you later'. Here too, *back* is superfluous.

REVISING TEXT

See **EDITING; REWRITING IN PLAIN ENGLISH**.

revolving warranty

A warranty, common in the sale of goods, that extends also to any later repair or replacement of the original goods. The warranty continues indefinitely until repaired or replacement items survive the warranty period.

RHETORICAL QUESTIONS

A rhetorical question expects no answer, usually because the answer is self-evident. Rhetorical questions have a place in persuasive legal prose. Why would they not?

> 'I find these submissions [of counsel] quite astonishing. Given that his client and her daughter were the principal parties to these transactions, why on earth should the court be expected to draw "inferences" as to what was in their minds? Why should we speculate as to the extent of any "historic shortfalls", when she presumably has access to the actual accounts, and has resisted the lessees' requests for disclosure? What evidence is there that by 2000 anyone was seriously concerned about an imminent risk of return to double-digit inflation? Finally, what possible reason would these lessees have had for wishing to "compensate" the lessor for the past or future financial consequences of imperfections in leases for which they were not responsible?' [*Arnold v Britton* [2015] UKSC 36; [2015] 2 WLR 1593, [152] (Lord Carnwath JSC)]

However, because rhetorical questions may also invite the reader to find reasons *against* the answer being implied, use them with care. To avoid the risk of reader dissent, it may be useful to answer the rhetorical question. Thus, a judge may entice readers into an issue and then, having captured their attention, posit the preferred answer, as in the following example:

> 'Why was so much trouble taken at the hearing before Judge Downs to prove the authenticity of the transcript before the Commission? If inference is to be given full rein, why not simply tender the transcript, point to its seeming authenticity and suggest that it was hardly likely that the Commission would tamper with its own record? Why, for proof of judicial proceedings, was special legislation deemed necessary? The answer to these questions is that, at least until now, strict proof of the elements of an offence has meant just that.' [*Cassell v R* [2000] HCA 8; (2000) 201 CLR 189, [60] (Kirby J)]

right (as of)

In normal usage, to speak of an act exercised *as of right* means that the exercise is legally enforceable. In legal usage, the same meanings are seen: eg, 'the mortgagee exercised the power of sale *as of right*'; 'the police entered the premises *as of right*'.

However, in some areas of law *as of right* connotes rather that the act is exercised openly and without hindrance, and therefore has the outward appearance (though not necessarily the legal reality) of being exercised legally. A more precise expression might be 'as *if* of right': *Cumbernauld and Kilsyth DC v Dollar Land (Cumbernauld) Ltd* [1992] SLT 1035, 1043. Illustrations exist in the law of commons registration and the law of prescriptive easements. For example, to acquire a right of way over neighbouring land by long use (prescription), the claimant must show (among other things) that he or she exercised the use openly, without having received actual permission (and so not *by* right), *as though* entitled to do so as an incident of ownership of the benefited land—ie, as *if* of right: *R v North Yorkshire County Council* [2014] UKSC 31; [2015] AC 195, [14] (Lord Neuberger).

Further reading

S Bridge, E Cooke, and M Dixon (eds), *Megarry & Wade's Law of Real Property*, 9th edn (Sweet & Maxwell, 2019) [27-048]–[27-049]

See also **lost modern grant**; **nec vi nec clam nec precario**.

right and liberty

A pairing often introducing a list of appurtenant rights. For example: a lease may give the tenant 'full right and liberty' to use the access ways to the property; or a right of way may give the benefited owner 'full right and liberty' to pass along the way. Strictly, a *right* differs from a *liberty*. However, most legal drafters use the pairing uncritically, when in almost all cases either word will do. Prefer *right*, being the more idiomatic.

See also **WORD PAIRINGS**.

right of first refusal

Also called *right of pre-emption*. A right to buy property (usually land) ahead of anyone else, if and when the owner decides to sell it, usually on terms similar to those the owner may offer to another person. In itself it imposes no obligation on the owner to sell—rather, that *if* the owner decides to sell, then the holder of the right of first refusal is entitled to receive the first offer, which he or she can freely accept or reject. It is not a technical term. Indeed, it is an inept term, because what the potential offeree wants is an opportunity of *accepting* an offer rather than an opportunity of refusing an offer: *Woodroffe v Box* (1954) 92 CLR 245, 257.

See also **pre-empt / preempt**.

right of pre-emption

See **right of first refusal**.

right of way

Plural: *rights of way* (not 'right of ways'); formerly, often hyphenated (*right-of-way*), but now generally unhyphenated. A right to pass over land, satisfying the legal requirements for an easement (ie, a proprietary right, not a mere contractual right). A 'private' right of way gives the right to pass over a parcel of land (the 'servient tenement'—ie, the burdened land) to access another parcel of land (the 'dominant tenement'—ie, the benefited land). A 'public right of way' is the public's right to use highways.

See also **easements rights and privileges**; **dominant tenement / servient tenement**; **highway**.

right, title and interest

Usually with one comma, 'right, title and interest', though logically (and better) two (ie, using the serial comma) to more clearly delineate the terms—'right, title, and interest'; but often punctuation-less: 'right title and interest'. A traditional triplet, needlessly repetitive. Purists may argue that each word in the trilogy has a separate meaning. In this, they are correct:

- *right* means a benefit or claim entitling a person to act, or be treated, in a particular way: eg, a *right* of way; a *right* to remain silent; a *human* right
- *title* means ownership (usually of property): eg, land *title*; freehold *title*
- *interest* means an enforceable claim over, or advantage in relation to, something (again, usually of property): eg, freehold *interest*; equitable *interest*.

However, the issue is not what each word means, taken in isolation. Rather, the issue is whether all three are needed? The answer is no; one word will suffice, and that word is usually *interest*. So 'I convey to you my *right, title and interest* in' a parcel of land, becomes 'I convey to you my *interest* in' the land. (It would also be effective, though less idiomatic, to write, 'I convey to you my *title to*' the land, or 'I convey to you my *rights in*' the land; or more radically and simply, 'I convey to you my *land*'.) Always prune this trilogy.

Further reading

'Right, Title and Interest', in *Law Words* (Centre for Plain Legal Language, University of Sydney, 1995) 77; www.clarity-international.net/plain-language-resources/general-resources/

See also **WORD PAIRINGS.**

Romalpa clause

A clause under which the seller of goods retains title to them, even though delivery has occurred, until a specified condition (usually, payment) is fulfilled. European law has long recognised the enforceability of such clauses. British law first recognised their enforceability in *Aluminium Industrie Vaassen BV v Romalpa Aluminium Ltd* [1976] 2 All ER 552 (CA), a case followed in many Commonwealth jurisdictions. A *Romalpa* clause is particularly useful if the buyer becomes insolvent, because it allows the seller to recover the goods rather than merely to claim for the price along with other ordinary creditors.

root of title

See **good root of title**.

ROUND BRACKETS

See **BRACKETS**.

roup

A Scots law term meaning 'auction' (as in *public roup*). English and Commonwealth usage is *auction*.

Royal minerals

See **minerals**.

ruat caelum

Latin: let the heavens fall.

See **fiat justitia ruat caelum**.

rule

A principle or regulation governing conduct, action, or procedure. Whether statements are 'rules', and what effect is to be given to 'rules', depends on text and context. For example, the 'rules' of an association included both its constitution and its by-laws: *Rush v WA Amateur Football League (Inc)* [2007] WASCA 190; (2007) 35 WAR 101, [60]. However, a statement of the 'objects' of an industrial organisation (to improve the conditions and protect the interests of its members) was not a 'rule' enforceable in an industrial court: *Oddy v Transport Salaried Staffs Association* [1973] 3 All ER 610, 614.

See also **rule of thumb**.

Rule in [X's case]

A shorthand way of referring to a principle established by a decision—eg, 'the Rule in *Shelley's Case*'. Stylistic conventions vary: 'Rule' may take an upper-case *R* or lower-case *r*; 'Case' may take an upper-case *C* or lower-case *c*; and the italics may extend to 'case' or they may not. So, variants include:

> the Rule [or rule] in *Shelley's Case* [or *Shelley's case*] [or *Shelley's* case]

Of course, mere reference to 'the Rule in [X's case]' is meaningless for readers who do not know the rule—or if they do know it, glimpse its subtleties only dimly. Therefore, include an explanation of the rule or its effect, as in the following statutory provision.

> **184 Abolition of Rule in Pigot's Case**
>
> (1) The rule of law known as the Rule in *Pigot's Case* is abolished.
>
> (2) Accordingly, a material alteration to a deed does not, by itself, invalidate the deed or render it voidable, or otherwise affect any obligation under the deed.
>
> [*Conveyancing Act 1919* (NSW), s 184]

rule of thumb

An expression that may be sufficiently precise in standard prose, but rarely in statutes or contracts. For example, are *rules of thumb* to be applied rigorously, or are they merely a guide, and can one or more be ignored if the circumstances warrant?

See further, **guidelines**.

rulemaking

Should it be *rule making*, *rule-making*, or *rulemaking*? All three variants are seen. If preferring *rule making* (separate words), remember to hyphenate when using as a compound adjective: *rule-making power*, *rule-making function*, *rule-making administrator*; eg, '*Rule making* is exercised under *rule-making* powers.'

See also **HYPHENS**.

ruling

See **judgment (and variants)**.

said

A lawyer's empty formalism for 'the' or 'that' when referring to something previously mentioned: eg, 'the *said* document'. Apart from heralding an archaic tone, *said* may have other failings.

1. ***Said* may be superfluous**. For example, a will may provide: 'I appoint my mother as my executor, and I give all my property to my *said* mother.' Delete *said*; how many mothers can one have?
2. ***Said* may not link to any particular referent**. For example, *said* may refer generically to matters mentioned before, but not necessarily to any particular one (as in *Product Management Group Pty Ltd v Blue Gentian LLC* [2015] FCAFC 179, involving a *said*-sprinkled patent application). In one case, a reference to my '*said* sons or daughters' was meaningless, because there was no earlier reference to 'sons or daughters': *Giles v Giles* (1837) 8 Sim 360; 59 ER 143.
3. ***Said* may link to a number of referents whose descriptions differ**. For example, if a lease refers, apparently indiscriminately, to 'the said premises', 'the said demised premises', and 'the said premises hereby demised' (as in *Spring House (Freehold) Ltd v Mount Cook Land Ltd* [2002] 2 All ER 822), is it referring to the same thing?

If it is unclear to which of a number of earlier referents *said* applies, does it prima facie apply to the nearest previous referent? The answer is usually yes, because this is likely to follow the writer's thought-sequence: *R v Hinckley* (1818) 1 B & A 273; 106 ER 101; *Shepherd's Trustees v Shepherd* 1945 SC 60. (The same applies to the use of *such*.) However, this result is never more than a presumption, liable to be ousted by context. For example, in *R v Countesthorpe* (1831) 2 B & Ad 487; 109 ER 1224 a deed mentioned county A and later county B, followed by a reference to '*such* county'; the court held that *such* referred to county A, not county B.

If it is necessary to refer to a previous thing, do so unambiguously, and prefer (instead of *said*) *the*, *that*, *as previously mentioned*, or similar.

See also **aforesaid**; **LAST-ANTECEDENT RULE**.

SALUTATIONS

See **CORRESPONDENCE (LETTERS AND EMAILS)**.

same

Same, as a pronoun, is one of the hallmarks of legalese. Lawyers use *same*, or *the same*, instead of *it*, or *that*, or some similar referent. Perhaps they consider that *same* adds gravity and precision. If so, they are mistaken. *Same* throws up three main problems:

1. **Pretentiousness**. To the modern ear, *same* is pretentious and conveys an air of archaism. HW Fowler wrote that *same* 'is avoided by all who have any skill in

writing' and that those who use it seem 'bent on giving the worst possible impression' of themselves: *Modern English Usage*, 1st edn (Oxford University Press, 1926) 511. Substitute a modern, plain-language equivalent: *it*, *the*, or similar. For example:

> 'If the tenants wish to exercise their rights under the deed of option, they must sign *same* [prefer: *it*] and return *same* [prefer: *it*] to the landlord.'

2. **Ambiguity of referent**. *Same* is ambiguous where there are two or more possible referents: the *same* what? For example:

   Article II, § 1 of the US Constitution formerly provided:

   > 'In case of the removal of the President from office, or of his death, resignation, or inability to discharge the powers and duties of the said office, the *same* shall devolve on the Vice-President.'

   What devolved on the Vice-President: the powers and duties of the office of President, or the office (of President) itself? That is, did the Vice-President actually become President, or did the Vice-President merely assume the President's 'powers and duties'? This remained unclear until clarified by constitutional amendment in 1967: David P Currie, 'His Accidency', 5 *Green Bag* [2d series] 151 (2002).

3. **Ambiguity of meaning**. Depending on context, *same* can mean *identical*, or it can mean merely *similar to* or *corresponding with*. For example:
   - A taxation statute allowed a taxpayer to claim certain deductions if it carried on the '*same* business' before and after a change in its ownership. Held, *same* meant 'identical with', not merely 'similar to': *Avondale Motors (Parts) Pty Ltd v Commissioner of Taxation* (1971) 124 CLR 97.
   - A deed of settlement contained two gifts. The first gave property to A for life and after A's death, to A's children subject to specified conditions. The second gave property to B for life, and after B's death 'to the *same* uses' (ie, on the same terms) as the gift to A's children. Held: *same* meant 'similar' or 'analogous', not 'identical'. After B's death, her share went to *her* children on conditions similar to those in the gift to A's children; it did not go to A's children: *Kingsbury v Martin* (1901) 1 SR (NSW) 272.

sanction

A word with contrasting meanings: (1) to approve or permit; (2) to punish. For example:

- Meaning *approve*: 'The judge *sanctioned* the accused's act in refusing to answer counsel's badgering questions.'
- Meaning *punish*: 'The judge *sanctioned* the accused for violent behaviour towards the witness.'

Usually, context indicates the intended meaning (as in the above examples); but if not, clarify.

SANDWICH CONSTRUCTIONS

See **CLAUSE STRUCTURE**.

SARCASM

'Sarcasm, a form of speech not often used by honest men for honest purposes; a word of grim and sinister meaning': FAA Russell, *Essays and Excursions in Law* (Law Book Co, 1929) 18. While gentle wit has a place in legal writing, sarcasm does not.

Sarcasm vs wit

Sometimes, the dividing line between sarcasm and wit—between deliberate nastiness and gentle humour—is hard to draw. To illustrate:

- Was Darling J being witty or sarcastic when, speaking of the trades disputes legislation that freed unions from liability for certain torts, he said that the legislation had relieved registered trade unions '[f]rom the humiliating position of being on a level with other lawful associations of his Majesty's subjects' and that they were '*super legem* [above the law], just as the Emperor was *super grammaticam* [above grammar].' See *Bussy v Amalgamated Society of Railway Servants* (1908) 24 TLR 437, 437. The reference is to Emperor Sigismund's response to a cardinal who presumed to correct Sigismund's grammar.
- Was Lord Macnaghten being witty or sarcastic (or offensive) when saying that he found 'difficulty in believing that a gap in a roadside fence is a strange and unusual spectacle in any part of Ireland': *Cooke v Midland Great Western Railway of Ireland* [1909] AC 229, 233, in a case where a child was injured after entering land through a gap in a fence.
- Was Joske J being witty or sarcastic (or merely of strong conviction) when, declining to endorse standard professional practice in a comparable jurisdiction, he asserted that 'the practice stems from a statute that has been superseded, from a headnote which is erroneous, from a judicial assertion which quite evidently is unfounded, since it is evident that it goes far beyond the judgments which it relies on, and from an alleged acceptance by the legal profession which is treated as justification for departing from the ordinary meaning of the statutory language': *Gasiunas v Meinhold* (1964) 8 FLR 182, 186.

Sarcasm in court

Sarcasm has no place in court. American courts have said that lawyers who resort to sarcasm in pleadings or argument display at best a lack of professionalism and at worst a lack of confidence in their case: *State v Union Electric Co* 312 SW 2d 151, 154 (Mo App 1958). Professionalism and civility are required of all who practise law:

- 'Professionalism and civility are not optional behaviors to be displayed only when one is having a good day. Professionalism and civility are the mainstays of our profession and the foundations upon which lawyers practice law. The public expects it. Fellow lawyers expect it. Our profession demands it.' [*Wisner v Laney* 984 NE 2d 1201, 1203 (Ind 2012)]
- '[L]awyers who know how to think but have not learned how to behave are a menace and a liability ... to the administration of justice. ... [T]he necessity for civility is relevant to lawyers because they are ... living exemplars—and thus teachers—every day in every case and in every court; and their worst conduct will be emulated ... more readily than their best.' [*Bettencourt v Bettencourt* 909 P 2d 553, 557–58 (1995, Haw), where the appellant's opening brief 'substitut[ed] personal attacks for legal and factual analysis', contained 'vituperative sniping', and was 'an egregious example of the substitution of rancorous rhetoric for legal and factual analysis'. The court referred the offending lawyer for disciplinary proceedings.]

Despite these admonitions, American judges themselves occasionally resort to sarcasm, particularly to excoriate lawyers for lack of research or inferior pleadings (as in the first two extracts below), and even to criticise their own colleagues (as in the third extract).

- 'The ostrich is a noble animal, but not a proper model for an appellate advocate.' [*Gonzalez-Servin v Ford Motor Company* 662 F 3d 931, 934 (7th Cir, 2011) (Posner J), condemning lawyers for failing to cite several strong precedents which were contrary to their client's position. Posner J included in his judgment two photographs—one of an ostrich head-in-sand, the other of a man (presumably a lawyer) also head-in-sand.]
- '[The pleadings are] some of the most amateurish ... ever to cross the causeway into Galveston. ... [The drafters have] obviously entered into a secret pact—complete with hats, handshakes and cryptic words—to draft their pleadings entirely in crayon on the back sides

of gravy-stained paper place mats, in the hope that the Court would be so charmed by their child-like efforts that their utter dearth of legal authorities in their briefing would go unnoticed.' [*Bradshaw v Unity Marine Corp Inc* 147 F Supp 2d 668, 670 (US District Ct, Galveston). This sarcasm has been widely castigated: see, eg, Steven Lubet, 'Bullying from the Bench' (2001) 5 *Green Bag* 11, 12; Richard H Underwood, 'What Gets Judges into Trouble?' (2003) 23 *Journal of the National Association of Administrative Law Judges* 101, 130; Alifya Curtin and Lisa Solomon, 'Ethical Judicial Opinion Writing' (2008) 21 *Georgetown Journal of Legal Ethics* 237, 281–82.]

- '[The opinion of the majority] is couched in a style that is as pretentious as its content is egotistic. … [T]he opinion's showy profundities are often profoundly incoherent. [The majority] has descended from the disciplined legal reasoning of John Marshall and Joseph Story to the mystical aphorisms of the fortune cookie.' [*Obergefell v Hodges* 135 S Ct 2584 (2015), 2630 (Scalia J, excoriating the majority decision)]

An Australian appellate court set aside the judgment of a trial judge who had constantly interrupted the arguments for one party with sarcastic and snide remarks ('hectoring, insulting, belittling, sarcastic and rude'). The appellate court held that the trial judge's interruptions showed apprehended bias and denied the party a fair trial, and ordered a retrial by another judge: *Adacot & Sowle* [2020] FamCAFC 215.

Sarcasm directed at legislative drafters

Judges sometimes use sarcasm to condemn legislative drafting. This is poor style. The sarcasm might provide an outlet for the judge's exasperation, and may even amuse the lawyers and litigants in the case; but it is a gratuitous insult to the drafter, who has no chance to be heard. Examples include:

- 'To reach a conclusion on this matter involved the court in wading through a monstrous legislative morass, staggering from stone to stone and ignoring the marsh gas exhaling from the forest of schedules lining the way on each side. I regarded it at one time, I must confess, as a Slough of Despond through which the court would never drag its feet, but I have by leaping from tussock to tussock as best I might, eventually, pale and exhausted, reached the other side.' [*Davy v Leeds Corporation* [1964] 3 All ER 390, 394 (Harman LJ), speaking of the *Housing Act 1957*.]
- 'The luxuriant growth of this legislative jungle abounds in ambiguities, inconsistencies, incoherences and lacunae and it is too much to hope that every judge who has had to consider these proceedings would choose to enter the jungle at the same point, still less to emerge from it by the same route.' [*City of Marion v Becker* (1973) 6 SASR 13, 29 (Bray CJ), speaking of planning laws and regulations.]

More justified, perhaps, is criticism of the *legislature*, which has ultimate responsibility for the wording and scope of the legislation it enacts. An example is Lord Westbury's censure of Parliament for having enacted a consolidating tax Act 'so slovenly and so unintelligible that it is impossible satisfactorily to ascertain and declare its meaning', and that if only Parliament had the time ('which it has not') it could produce tax legislation with an 'intelligible meaning': *Great Western Railway Co v Bater* [1922] 2 AC 1, 30–31.

Further reading

- Marvin E Aspen, 'A Response to the Civility Naysayers' (1998) 28 *Stetson Law Review* (arguing from US surveys and case law that civility and fearlessly arguing a client's case are not incompatible aims)
- Philip Sales, 'The Contribution of Legislative Drafting to the Rule of Law' (2018) 77 *Cambridge Law Journal* 630 (in praise of legislative drafters)

See also **EXAGGERATION AND HYPERBOLE**; **HUMOUR**; **TONE**.

save / save for / save and except for

These words and expressions exude archaism, and add no legal worth. Prefer modern standard English equivalents, as follows:

- save = except
- save for = except for
- save and except for = except [or, except for]
- save and except for the fact that = except that.

Examples

- 'There is no support for that proposition in any domestic authority *save and except for* [prefer: *except*] perhaps *In re K*.' [*Birmingham City Council v D* [2016] EWCOP 8, [99] (Keehan J)]
- 'There is nothing remarkable as to the circumstances in which the offending occurred, *save and except for the fact that* [prefer: *except that*] the appellant has not seen fit to obtain a driver's licence.' [*Stewart v Police* [2007] SASC 148, [11] (Debelle J)]

SC

Abbreviation for *Senior Counsel.*

See **Queen's Counsel**.

sc

See **scilicet**.

SCHEDULES

Purposes

Schedules are useful receptacles for at least three types of information:

1. *In standard-form documents*: for information that is transaction-specific. For example, residential leases are often in standard form. A schedule to the standard form might list key variables such as the description of the premises, the tenant's name, the rent, the duration of the lease, and special conditions. This allows the body of the standard form to remain unamended; readers (including lawyers) familiar with the form need not scrutinise it afresh each time they use it.
2. *In commercial documents*: for information that is ancillary to the main deal and that, while important, would clutter the document's main structure. Examples include detailed product specifications, boilerplate terms and conditions, and meeting procedures.
3. *In all documents*: for information that is repeated in different parts of the document. The information can be collected in a schedule, with the different parts of the document then cross-referring to the schedule.

Terminology

The preferred formula is 'Schedule [X] *to* this agreement', not 'Schedule [X] *of* this agreement'.

Divisions within a schedule are usually called *Parts*—thus, 'Part A', 'Part B'; or 'Part 1', 'Part 2' (increasingly preferred to Roman capitals, 'Part I', 'Part II'). Divisions of text within schedules are usually called *clauses* (not *sections* or *paragraphs*)—thus, 'Schedule 1, clause 5.2'.

Linking schedules to main document

Schedules are a substantive part of the document, and so strictly need no clause incorporating them into the document. Nevertheless, most private-sector drafters include a provision in the main agreement to the effect that schedules are part of the agreement. Statutory drafters generally use a shorthand statement such as 'Schedule 5 applies'.

For reader-convenience, it is useful to cross-refer items in a schedule to the provision to which they relate: eg, 'Item 2 (clause 10)'. Where an entire schedule relates to a single provision, include the cross-reference in the schedule heading: eg, 'Schedule 5 (clause 20)'.

Interpretation

Being part of the document, schedules are not legally 'inferior' to the main body of the document. And so, for example, a provision in a schedule to an agreement can lawfully extend the operation of a provision in the body of the agreement; and a provision in a schedule to an Act can lawfully extend the operation of a section in the Act. But actual instances are rare—and would surprise most readers (and their legal advisers), who would not expect the body of the document to be amended by a side wind in this way. A drafter who does not want a schedule to operate in this way can expressly preclude the possibility: *Inland Revenue Commissioners v Gittus* [1920] 1 KB 563, 576 (Lord Sterndale MR); *Re Foley* (1952) 53 SR (NSW) 31, 36 (Roper CJ in Eq).

Signatures—before or after schedules?

Practice varies over the place for the parties' signatures where a document contains one or more schedules. Some English law firms favour signing after the schedules. Some Australian and US law firms favour signing at the end of the main provisions and before the schedules. Either practice is acceptable.

See also **ANNEXURES**.

scienter

Latin: knowingly; used particularly in 'the *scienter rule*' (literally, 'the knowing rule'), which is legal shorthand for the common-law rule that the owner of an animal of a kind not ordinarily dangerous is not liable for injury caused by the animal unless the owner knew that the animal had a dangerous disposition. Purists may retort that to use 'the knowing rule' as a plain-language equivalent says nothing about the content of the rule—but then, nor does 'the *scienter rule*'. The shorthand '*knowing rule*' suffices in most contexts. For example:

> 'The [*Animals Act 1971*] addressed … the rule imposing strict liability on the keeper of an animal mansuetae naturae, ie tame, for damage caused by the animal attributable to a vicious, mischievous or fierce propensity which the keeper knew the animal possessed (the so-called *scienter rule* [prefer: *knowing rule*]) …' [*Mirvahedy v Henley* [2003] 2 AC 491, 519 [82] (Lord Scott)]

scilicet

Latin: namely; that is to say. Sometimes abbreviated to *sc* (or US, *sc.*) or *scil* (or US, *scil.*). A pedantic Latinism now falling into disuse. Prefer alternatives such as *namely* or *that is to say*. For example:

- 'The proposal form [required] the proposer to confirm that neither he, nor any other member of his family living with him, had made a claim (*scilicet* [prefer: *that is to say*] a claim under a household insurance policy) within the last five years.' [*Bate v Aviva Insurance UK Ltd* [2014] EWCA Civ 334, [16] (Tomlinson LJ)]
- 'By additional cl 4.13(b), the Purchaser acknowledged that it was not entitled to make any "Obligation" (*sic*; *scilicet* "objection") or rescind or terminate or refuse to complete the contract because of the works by the Vendor.' [*Raphael Shin Enterprises Pty Ltd v Waterpoint Shepherds Bay Pty Ltd* [2015] NSWCA 406, [33] (Emmett JA). Here, the judge uses *sic* to indicate that the original used 'Obligation', and *scilicet* to introduce the correction.]

See also **sic**.

scintilla

General meaning

Latin: a spark (ie, the smallest part, a mere speck, a scrap). This Latinism may have become anglicised; but for readers unlikely to understand it, prefer a more prosaic English equivalent. For example:

- '[T]he judge, after considering the CHIS report, concluded that there was not a *scintilla* [prefer: *scrap*] of evidence which lent support to the proposition ...' [*R v Gjikokaj* [2014] EWCA Crim 386, [64] (Lord Thomas CJ)]
- 'But [that fact] ... cannot reflect upon the outcome of this appeal which, at all times, has been without a *scintilla* [prefer: *scrap*; *hint*] of merit.' [*Ferella v Official Trustee in Bankruptcy* [2015] NSWCA 411, [53] (Tobias AJA)]

See also **scintilla juris**; **scintilla temporis**.

scintilla juris

Latin: a spark or fragment of a legal right. The term is used in two main situations:

1. A person bringing a case that has no merit is said to have not even a *scintilla juris*. While colourful, unless your reader will understand it (which is unlikely), prefer 'no hope of success' or similar—effective communication trumps colour.
2. In real property law, *scintilla juris* carries the meaning 'spark of title'. This usage goes back to case law developed under the *Statute of Uses* 1535. By the operation of that statue, a trustee (technically, a 'feoffee to uses') retained a *scintilla juris* ('spark of title') in the land sufficient to allow the legal estate to shift over to, or spring up in, a different beneficiary if a stipulated contingency occurred (eg, if that beneficiary married): see, eg, W Holdsworth, *History of English Law*, 2nd edn, reissued (Sweet & Maxwell, 1968) vol VII, 138–40. Most jurisdictions have abolished this real-property-law meaning of *scintilla juris*, making the term obsolete except in technical or historical discussions of land law.

See also **shifting / springing interest**.

scintilla temporis

Latin: a spark of time (ie, a brief moment, a split second). Plural: *scintillae temporis*. Lawyers use this expression in two different senses.

Non-technical use

Occasionally, lawyers use *scintilla temporis* to mean 'very briefly' or 'for a very short time'. But the Latin expresses no technical nuance, and to retain the Latin is pure affectation. The plain English is perfectly adequate, as in the following examples:

- 'On the premise that the loss by fire was only separated from the loss by sinking by a *scintilla temporis* [prefer: *very short time*], [counsel] disputed the judge's finding of separate losses and separate casualties as wholly artificial.' [*Kastor Navigation Co Ltd v AXA Global Risks (UK) Ltd* [2004] EWCA Civ 277; [2005] 2 All ER (Comm) 720, [30] (Rix LJ)]
- '[The taxpayer argued that] the creditor's rights were transferred to the Issuer even if only for a *scintilla temporis* [prefer: *fraction of time*; *split second*]. [The Revenue Commissioner] characterised this argument as "angels dancing on pinheads". I agree. I do not believe that the [proper] approach to interpretation of taxing statutes … with its insistence on a realistic view of the facts leaves any scope for angels, pinheads or *scintillae temporis* [prefer: *fractions of time*].' [*DMWSHNZ Ltd v Commissioners for Revenue and Customs* [2015] EWCA Civ 1036, [50] (Lewison LJ)]

Technical use

The technical use of *scintilla temporis* involves the situation where a purchaser borrows money on mortgage to buy a property. In conveyancing reality, there is a necessary interval of time between when the purchaser acquires the legal title (from the vendor) and when the purchaser grants the mortgage (to the lender). The interval may be very short, but (logically) during that interval, the purchaser could grant to third parties interests that would take priority over the mortgage, because they would precede the mortgage, even if only by a few seconds. However, courts take the view that, in commercial reality, the purchaser acquires the property subject to the mortgage. The purchaser's acquisition of the title and grant of the promised mortgage are treated as a single, indivisible transaction. It is as if there were no interval between them. So even if the purchaser in fact grants an interest to a third party during that short interval, it is treated as if granted subject to the mortgage, and the mortgage retains priority: *Abbey National Building Society v Cann* [1991] 1 AC 56; *Mortgage Business plc v O'Shaughnessy* (alternatively titled *Southern Pacific Mortgages Ltd v Scott*) [2015] AC 385. The doctrine can be explained in plain-English expressions such as 'moment in time' or 'gap in time'. For example:

> 'Were there to be a *scintilla temporis* [prefer: *moment in time*] between the conveyance [to the purchaser] and the grant of the mortgage, the [other interest would override the mortgage]. But it has … been accepted that, at least in the standard case where completion and mortgage take place virtually simultaneously and the mortgage is granted to secure borrowings without which the purchase would not have taken place, completion and mortgage are one indivisible transaction and there is no *scintilla temporis* [prefer: *gap in time*] between them.' [*Southern Pacific Mortgages Ltd v Scott* [2014] UKSC 52; [2015] AC 385, 426 [114] (Baroness Hale)]

SCOPING PROVISION

A statement in a document or statute that sets out its area of application: eg, 'This agreement [statute] applies if / to …' The scoping provision can relate to the entire document or statute, or a part only. It helps readers by identifying the provision's coverage—and therefore what parts (if any) they need to read.

See also **EXECUTIVE SUMMARY; SIMPLIFIED OUTLINES.**

scot-free

In origin, to be free from the medieval 'scot', a tax payable by a feudal tenant to his or her lord or ruler. Now meaning more generally 'without being punished', or 'without suffering injury or harm'—eg, 'he got away scot-free'. Never 'scott-free':

> 'As far as the second judicial review claim goes, the criticisms that I made about the decision-making process apply to that and it is not right that the defendant local authority should emerge *scott-free* [prefer: *scot-free*] from the making of such criticisms.' [*R v London Borough of Barnet* [2013] EWHC 523 (Admin), [92] (Mitting J)]

seal

See **signed, sealed and delivered.**

section

Abbreviation *s* (no full stop—except in US usage: *s.*); plural, *ss* (no full stop); not italicised or capitalised. The US symbol § is rare in British and Commonwealth usage.

See further **CITATION OF LEGISLATION.**

SECTIONS (REFERENCES TO)

See **CITATION OF LEGISLATION.**

secundum

Latin: according to. Usually in combination with other Latin words. Whether alone or in combination, today it is a needless Latinism. Prefer an appropriate English translation, as in the following:

- *secundum artem*: artificially, skilfully
- *secundum naturam*: naturally, not artificially
- *secundum quid*: in respect only, with limitations
- *secundum ordinem*: in order
- *secundum subjectam materiam*: according to (ie, in the context of) the subject matter.

sed quaere

Latin: but query; but ask; but question. Used to express doubt on the correctness of a statement and to imply that it needs reconsidering. As with the stand-alone *quaere*, this term is easily translatable into standard English. To retain it in modern legal usage is pedantic. For example:

- '*Sed quaere* [prefer: *But query whether this is correct*]: certainly the ground of frustration was expressly rejected …' [*Metall Market OOO v Vitorio Shipping Co Ltd (The Lehmann Timber)* [2013] EWCA Civ 650; [2014] QB 760, 819, fn 7 (Rix LJ, having quoted from a statement of Lord Sumption in an earlier case)]

- 'Independently of any lien granted by the charterparty the owner may also be entitled to demand that freight due to a charterer or sub-charterer under an owners' bill of lading should in fact be paid directly to the owner—*sed quaere* [prefer: *but question*] whether he can do so in the absence of a default by the immediate time charterer.' [*Scrutton on Charterparties and Bills of Lading*, 23rd edn (Sweet & Maxwell, 2015) [17-015]]

See also **quaere**.

seisin / seizin

Seisin is the right to possession of a freehold estate in land (ie, a life estate, a fee tail, or a fee simple). Although derived from the Old French *seisine* (to seize), in law *seisin* (noun) and *seise* (transitive verb) carry no implications of taking by violence. Indeed, quite the contrary—*seisin* implies the right to quiet, uninterrupted possession. To medieval lawyers, a person put in *seisin* of land was 'set' there, and had the right to continue to 'sit' there. The preferred spelling is *seisin*, although *seizin* is also seen (mostly pre-19th century). There is no precise plain-language equivalent, but for all practical purposes 'own' is sufficient; ie, the traditional formula 'A *is seised of an estate in fee simple in* Blackacre' means 'A *owns* Blackacre.'

Further reading

S Bridge, E Cooke, and M Dixon (eds), *Megarry & Wade's Law of Real Property*, 9th edn (Sweet & Maxwell, 2019) [A-002]–[A-004]

See also **estate**; **fee simple**.

semble

Law French: it seems; it appears.

Normal use: 'it seems'

Generally, *semble* indicates that a legal proposition is undecided or doubtful. However, it carries no particular legal nuance, and so is a pointless affectation. Prefer 'it seems [that]' or 'it appears [that]'. For example:

- '*Semble* [prefer: *It appears that*] … in the absence of special circumstances … there is no legal duty on the replying bank [giving a credit-worthiness reference] beyond that of giving an honest answer …' [*Hedley Byrne & Co Ltd v Heller & Partners Ltd* [1963] 2 All ER 575, 576 (Headnote)]
- '[T]he respondents submitted that the applicants were within the class of persons whom the Parliament was entitled to consider aliens because, *semble* [prefer: *it seems*], they were not born in Australia to Australian parents.' [*Koroitamana v Commonwealth* [2006] HCA 28; 227 ALR 406, [36] (Gummow, Hayne, and Crennan JJ)]

Occasional use: indicating apparent error in original

Sometimes, *semble* indicates an apparent error in text being quoted—serving the same purpose as *sic*.

- 'Kitchin J concluded: "[I]t is more likely than not that the expression BAU was used in the course of the discussion but I do not accept that it was used proscriptively [*semble* prescriptively] to limit the scope of the project".' [*Liffe Administration and Management v Pinkava* [2007] EWCA Civ 217, [19]; [2007] 4 All ER 981, 990 (Sir Andrew Morritt C, using *semble* to indicate a mistake in the original)]

- '"[T]he accusation ... is evidence before you in reputation [*semble* repudiation] of the Accused's claim that he is a person of good character".' [*BRS v R* (1997) 191 CLR 275, 281 (Brennan CJ, quoting from, and correcting an apparent error in, a court reporter's transcript)]

See also **sic**.

semi-

Half; partial. Hyphenation of *semi-* in British English is irregular; sometimes a hyphen is used, sometimes not (*semi-final* vs *semifinal*). Examples follow:

Hyphen	No hyphen	Hyphen	No hyphen
semi-annual	semicolon	semi-professional	semibreve
semi-apparent	semibold	semi-permanent	semimetal
semi-automatic	semicircle	semi-conscious	semiquaver
semi-final	semifinal	semi-detached	semitone
semi-monthly	semiconductor	semi-darkness	semivowel

SEMICOLONS

Sometimes hyphenated ('semi-colon'), but less often in modern writing, which prefers more open punctuation. Semicolons are 'stronger' than commas but 'weaker' than full stops. This makes them useful punctuation tools. Their main uses are the following.

To link sentences

Semicolons link sentences that could stand alone—divided by a full stop—but that are better shown as having related subject matters.

Examples

- 'To err is human; to forgive, divine.'
- 'Some lawyers use full stops; others prefer semicolons.'

In each case, the writer could have used independent sentences, separated by a full stop. The semicolon, however, more accurately reflects the closeness between the ideas.

To group related items in list

The conventional tool for separating items in a run-on list is the *comma*. But commas offer little opportunity for subtlety—they merely separate. Semicolons afford some sophistication by allowing items in a list to be 'grouped'—eg, by subject matter or relative importance. This makes semicolons a 'hierarchically superior punctuation mark': *Minister for Immigration and Multicultural Affairs v Savvin* (2000) 98 FCR 168, 184–85 (Katz J).

Examples

- 'The Courts will presume that Parliament did not intend a statute to have consequences which are objectionable or undesirable; or absurd; or unworkable or impracticable; or merely inconvenient; or anomalous or illogical; or futile or pointless.' [*R v Central Valuation Officer* [2003] UKHL 20; [2003] 4 All ER 209, [116] (Lord Millett)]

- A lease provides:

  > 'The tenant may use the premises to sell the following items: coffee and tea; sandwiches, sweets and cakes; fruit and vegetables; newspapers and magazines.'

  The drafter could have used commas throughout, but the semicolons indicate a more nuanced division of subject matter.

  An alternative would be a vertical list, but this would take more space:

  > 'The tenant may use the premises to sell:
  > - coffee and tea
  > - sandwiches, sweets and cake
  > - fruit and vegetables
  > - newspapers and magazines.'

To encourage closer focus on items in list

Semicolons also encourage closer focus on individual items in a run-on list. Being stronger than commas, they suggest a more deliberate break between items—focusing attention on each item; slowing the reader; encouraging attention; discouraging skimming. For example:

> 'In my view, the "ordinary person" in Australian society today is not so homophobic as to respond [by murder or serious violence] to a non-violent sexual advance by a homosexual person. … He or she might, depending on the circumstances, be embarrassed; treat it at first as a bad joke; be hurt; insulted. He or she might react with the strong language of protest; might use as much physical force as was necessary to effect an escape; and where absolutely necessary assault the persistent perpetrator to secure escape.' [*Green v R* (1997) 191 CLR 334, 408–09 (Kirby J)]

See also **COMMAS**; **LISTS AND ENUMERATIONS**; **PUNCTUATION**.

Senior Counsel

Abbreviation: SC.

See **Queen's Counsel**.

sensu stricto

See **stricto sensu**.

SENTENCE LENGTH

The problem

Some legal sentences go on and on, and on. Examples abound in lawyers' letters and advices to clients, in judgments, and in contracts, deeds, wills, and statutes. Some older-style commercial documents contain sentences of hundreds of words, with no paragraphing and minimal punctuation.

Even experienced legal readers, accustomed to long sentences, find them frustrating.

> Lawyer-drawn pleadings included sentences of 291, 345, and 385 words. At least 23 sentences contained more than 100 words each. Many sentences contained 'rampant grammatical, syntactical, and typographical errors'. The court described the pleadings as 'unintelligible'; they

required the reader to 'try to fish a gold coin from a bucket of mud'. The court ordered the drafter to show cause why he should not be suspended from practice: *Stanard v Nygren* 658 F 3d 792 (US Court of Appeals, 7th Cir, 2011).

The ideal: maximum 20–25 words

Most writing texts recommend that sentences not exceed 20 or 25 words. Some allow an occasional longer sentence, as long as the *average* is 20–25 words. See, for example:

- Bryan A Garner, *Guidelines for Drafting and Editing Court Rules* (Administrative Office of the United States Courts, Washington DC) 13
- *Guidelines for Document Designers* (American Institutes for Research, 1981) 41–43
- Law Reform Commission of Victoria (Australia), *Plain English and the Law* (1987, Appendix 1) 33.

These recommendations reflect research that sentences longer than 20–25 words put unnecessary demands on the reader's short-term memory.

Of course, skillful writers can produce sentences that exceed 25 words yet flow with elegance and grace. They lead the reader along, with skill and artistry—not 'a sea-serpent, with half of its arches under the water, [but] a torchlight procession': Mark Twain, 'Reply to the Editor of "The Art of Authorship"', in Mark Twain, *Tales, Speeches, Essays, and Sketches* (Penguin, 1994) 360. But most legal writers lack those skills, and in any case are engaged in a task that is largely prosaic: to communicate to busy readers information that may be pedestrian and technical. That task is best performed by using sentences that are short, and that keep subject, verb, and object close together.

The exhortation to keep sentences reasonably short must be viewed in context. For example, a clause in a legal contract may be divided into paragraphs and subparagraphs, clauses and subclauses, each starting on a separate line; or information may be set out in a long bullet-point list. Grammatically, the parts may comprise one sentence. But to treat the entire provision as a single sentence would miss the point; the readability issue is the number of words in each 'bite'.

Techniques for shortening sentences

Older-style documents broke up the boredom of long slabs of text by inserting words or phrases in capital letters in places where, in normal prose, readers would expect to find full stops. This gave the appearance (though not the grammatical reality) of shorter sentences. Common insertions included:

NOW THIS DEED WITNESSETH

ALL THAT

TO HOLD

PROVIDED THAT

AND IT IS HEREBY AGREED AND DECLARED

IN WITNESS

That technique is now rarely seen. But in any case, it is a sleight of hand. Other, more thoughtful, techniques are better. The following discussion considers three of them: (1) using lists; (2) dividing sentences into shorter sentences; and (3) removing embedded information.

(1) Use lists

Where a sentence is excessively long because it contains a long list of information, consider dividing the list into individual items, each starting on a new line. Although grammatically still a single sentence, the breakup helps the reader digest the information. The items can be listed by bullet points, or (to make it easier to cross-refer to items in the list) by numbered paragraphs.

Example

Before

'The power to make regulations providing for discipline and punishments shall include and be deemed always to have included power to make regulations providing for appropriate tribunals to inquire into disciplinary offences by police officers other than gazetted police officers, for suspension of punishment awarded, for the review of an appeal from the findings and awards of such tribunals, for appeals against the award of the Commissioner, for limiting the powers of punishment exercisable by any appropriate tribunal, for the seizure and detention of any property reasonably suspected to be the property of a police officer which is required or likely to be required for the purposes of investigating a disciplinary offence and for the subsequent disposal, whether by sale or otherwise, of any property so seized and detained, for the forfeiture of any property admitted as an exhibit in any disciplinary proceedings and for the subsequent disposal, whether by sale or otherwise, of any property so admitted and generally for the procedure to be followed in cases where a police officer other than a gazetted police officer is alleged to have committed any of the disciplinary offences specified in the regulations.'

[Source: *Police Force Ordinance* (Hong Kong) cap 232, s 45(2). I am indebted to Dr Duncan Berry for drawing this provision to my attention.]

After

The power to make regulations providing for discipline and punishments shall include and be deemed always to have included power to make regulations providing:

(a) for appropriate tribunals to inquire into disciplinary offences by police officers other than gazetted police officers,
(b) for suspension of punishment awarded,
(c) for the review of an appeal from the findings and awards of such tribunals,
(d) for appeals against the award of the Commissioner,
(e) for limiting the powers of punishment exercisable by any appropriate tribunal,
(f) for the seizure and detention of any property reasonably suspected to be the property of a police officer which is required or likely to be required for the purposes of investigating a disciplinary offence, and for the subsequent disposal, whether by sale or otherwise, of any property so seized and detained,
(g) for the forfeiture of any property admitted as an exhibit in any disciplinary proceedings and for the subsequent disposal, whether by sale or otherwise, of any property so admitted, and
(h) for the procedure to be followed in cases where a police officer other than a gazetted police officer is alleged to have committed any of the disciplinary offences specified in the regulations.

Ideally, we could make other drafting improvements; but the simple act of creating a list would improve readability.

(2) Divide sentence into shorter sentences

Consider dividing a long sentence into two or more shorter ones.

Before	After
'A notice is not unequivocal, in the sense in which such notices are required to be unequivocal in relation to their essential contents, if a reasonable person, having considered the notice as a whole, fairly and properly, might entertain a doubt as to its meaning in relation to some essential matter, even though he would form in his mind a preference for one view, rather than the other of what the notice was intended to convey.' [76 words; 1 sentence. Source: *Catley v Watson* (1981) V ConvR 54-003 at 62,115 (Brooking J)]	Whether a notice is unequivocal about an essential matter depends on how a reasonable person would understand it. If a reasonable person, having considered the notice, fairly and properly, might be in doubt about what it means when it refers to the matter, the notice is equivocal. This is even though the person might consider that the drafter more likely intended one interpretation than another. [65 words; 3 sentences; average = 22 words]
'This basic concept, that parties to a contract have complete freedom by further agreement to "unbind" themselves as to their future conduct, is in principle applicable not merely to their substantive mutual obligations, but also to any procedural restraints upon which they may agree, including restraints as to how they may vary their existing contractual relationship.' [56 words, 1 sentence. Source: *MWB Business Exchange Ltd v Rock Advertising Ltd* [2018] UKSC 24; [2019] AC 119, [23] (Lord Briggs JSC)]	This basic concept—that parties to a contract have complete freedom by further agreement to 'unbind' themselves as to their future conduct—is in principle applicable not merely to their substantive mutual obligations. It is also applicable to any procedural restraints upon which they may agree, including restraints as to how they may vary their existing contractual relationship. [58 words, 2 sentences. Note that dashes replace commas in stating the 'basic concept' in the first sentence; this helps separate (and highlight) that concept.] **Or** (further edited): The basic concept is that parties to a contract have complete freedom by further agreement to 'unbind' themselves about their future conduct. In principle, this concept applies not merely to their substantive mutual obligations. It applies also to any procedural restraints upon which they may agree, including restraints about how they may vary their existing contractual relationship. [57 words, 3 sentences]

The division has the added benefit of rhetorical effect, because by increasing the number of sentences it increases the number of emphasis points (which lie at sentence-end—see **SENTENCE STRUCTURE (End sentences forcefully)**).

Sometimes, rewriting requires more effort than mere sentence-division, because it is necessary first to identify the main idea (or ideas). Once that is done, the rewriting usually becomes relatively easy, as in Example 1 below. But the process may highlight organisational difficulties in the original, requiring more extensive recasting, as in Example 2.

Example 1

Before	After
In the event of the tenant wishing to take a renewal of the lease for a further term, he shall prior to the expiration of the term hereby granted give to the landlord or his agent not more than six (6) months and not less than three (3) months previous notice in writing of his intention to do so and provided he has duly and punctually paid the rent reserved by this lease at the times therein appointed for payment therefore and shall have duly performed and observed all the covenants and agreements contained in this lease up to expiration of the term hereby granted on his part to be performed and observed, then the landlord will at the cost to the tenant grant to him a further term at a rent payable by him which would at such time be current market rental of the premises. [1 sentence, 147 words] [*Note* that this sentence contains four main ideas: 1. what the tenant must do to renew 2. the conditions for renewal 3. the costs of renewal 4. the new rent. A rewrite should reflect this division of subject matter.]	**Version 1: run-on sentences** The tenant can renew the lease by giving the landlord or agent written notice between 3 and 6 months before the current lease expires. The tenant must pay the costs of the new lease. The rent will be the current market rental at the time of the new lease. However, there is no right to renew unless the tenant has performed all its obligations under this lease (including paying all rent on time) up to the time the lease expires. [4 sentences, 80 words] **Version 2: each sentence a numbered clause (more readable)** 1. The tenant can renew the lease by giving the landlord or agent written notice between 3 and 6 months before the current lease expires. 2. The tenant must pay the costs of the new lease. 3. The rent will be the current market rental at the time of the new lease. 4. However, there is no right to renew unless the tenant has performed all its obligations under this lease (including paying all rent on time) up to the time the lease expires. [4 sentences, 84 words]

Example 2

Before	After
'The usual form of order and the sanction it prescribes of a stay until security is given and ultimately either an "unless" order or (in the Commercial Court) a hearing to put the paying party to their election whether to offer security or have the claim be dismissed (see *CPR 25.12.10*) serves to re-emphasise that an order for security is intended, not to stifle claims, but to give a claimant a choice as to whether to put up security and continue with their action or withdraw the claim (see *CPR 25.12.8*).' [1 sentence, 91 words] [Source: *Re RBS Rights Issue Litigation* [2017] EWHC 463, [52] (Hildyard J). The report at [2017] 1 WLR 3551, [52] expands the abbreviation *CPR*, making the sentence appear even longer.]	The usual form of order and the sanction it prescribes serves to re-emphasise the purpose of an order for security. That purpose is not to stifle claims, but to give a claimant a choice whether to put up security and continue with their action or withdraw the claim (see *CPR 25.12.8*). The order and sanction prescribe a stay until security is given and ultimately one of two events occurs. One is an 'unless' order. The other (in the Commercial Court) is a hearing to put the paying party to their election whether to offer security or have the claim dismissed (see *CPR 25.12.10*). [5 sentences, 103 words; sentences 3, 4 and 5 clarify the meaning of the original]

Caution: do not lose the links

Take care when breaking a long sentence into several shorter ones not to sever the relationship that existed between the various parts of the original sentence. For example, breaking a long sentence into three shorter sentences may fracture the link that once existed between what are now the first and third sentences; and allocating separate clause or paragraph numbers to the new sentences may further fracture the link. The following example illustrates the issue:

> A statute divided a section into paragraphs (a), (b), and (c). The court considered that the division created the risk that readers might focus on one paragraph only and neglect the remaining paragraphs, thereby missing the relationship between them. In the court's view, Parliament's intention would be more clearly discerned by reading the provision as if the separate parts constituted a single whole. The Court accordingly 'redrafted' the provision as a single run-on sentence, which was both clearer (because not broken up) and shorter (50 words instead of 71 words): *PJ v R* [2012] VSCA 146, [35]–[37]; (2012) 36 VR 402.

(3) Remove embedded information

Embedded (nested) information interrupts the *subject–verb–object* relationship. Remove the embedded information and shift it to a separate sentence. The 'After' version of the immediately preceding Example 2, above (ie, based on *Re RBS Rights Issue Litigation*) illustrates the technique. So do the following examples.

Before	**After**
The plaintiff, *who was a lawyer of some professional standing, but clearly lacked sufficient practical wisdom to understand the consequences of his actions*, had neglected to warn his client about the folly of litigating a matter such as this. [1 sentence, 39 words; italics indicate embedded information]	The plaintiff had neglected to warn his client about the folly of litigating a matter such as this. He was a lawyer of some professional standing, but clearly lacked sufficient practical wisdom to understand the consequences of his actions. [2 sentences; average 19 words] [**Or, better:** The plaintiff was a lawyer of some professional standing. Yet he had neglected to warn his client about the folly of litigating a matter such as this. He lacked sufficient practical wisdom to understand the consequences of his actions. [3 sentences; average 13 words]
'With the retreat of Empire, the emergence of Australia as an independent nation in world affairs and the unshackling of Commonwealth legislative competence from Imperial oversight through the enactment of the *Statute of Westminster Adoption Act 1942* (Cth), s 51(xix) provided ample power for Australia to respond to the invitation contained in the resolution of the Imperial Conference of 1937 that, together	The Imperial Conference resolution of 1937 invited Australia to determine whom it should recognize as members of its community. It extended the same invitation to other former British colonies by then recognised as 'autonomous Communities' within the Commonwealth of Nations. This was the time of retreat of Empire, the emergence of Australia as an independent nation in world

(continued)

(Continued)

Before	After
with other former British colonies which had by then become recognised as "autonomous Communities" within what had by then become known as the Commonwealth of Nations, it determine "which persons have with it that definite connexion ... which would enable it to recognize them as members of its community".' [Source: *Love v Commonwealth of Australia* [2020] HCA 3, [97] (Gageler J), citations omitted] [1 sentence, 111 words]	affairs, and the unshackling of Commonwealth legislative competence from Imperial oversight through the *Statute of Westminster Adoption Act 1942* (Cth). Section 51(xix) provided ample power for Australia to respond to that invitation. [4 sentences, average 22.5 words; minor tweaking]

Further improvements

Two other techniques can further improve the effectiveness of sentences.

(1) Vary sentence lengths

Do not use *only* short sentences. Short sentences always improve readability. But a surfeit of short sentences becomes wearisome, like sea-chop, offering the reader no variety. They also deny the writer the rhetorical punch of a short sentence that follows several longer ones.

An acknowledged master of short sentences was Lord Denning. His staccato sentences breathed fresh air into the traditional style of judgment-writing. But did even his style become wearisome in long passages?

> 'She was born in Ethiopia. Her name was Sophia Abrahim. In 1975 she was 19 years of age. She had a baby son, David, aged 2. An Englishman then came to Addis Ababa. He was Alan Streeting. He was aged 45. He asked Sophia to marry him. He told her he was divorced. They were united in marriage in Addis Ababa on May 17, 1975. ... It then transpired that he had not been divorced at all. His wife was still alive in England. So his marriage to Sophia was a bigamous marriage. It was a nullity. But his company took pity on her. They arranged for her to go back to Greece to sort out her affairs there. They paid her fare. But when she arrived at Athens airport, she was not allowed to enter: on the ground that she had not a valid residency permit. So she returned to England. That was on May 25, 1979.' [*R v Hillingdon Borough Council* [1980] 1 WLR 1425, 1431 (Lord Denning MR)]

The better technique is to use a mix of sentence lengths—some very short, some short, some mid-length, some 20–25 words, some even (rarely) exceeding 25 words. The mix provides variety, which helps keep the reader interested. It also allows the writer to harness the power of a very short sentence, especially to stress a point. The following two extracts illustrate the power of short sentences in general, and the power of a very short sentence in particular.

- 'No judge's decisions are beyond criticism. In a democracy, criticism is healthy. Most judges of my acquaintance welcome and reflect upon public criticisms of their reasoning. The High Court's decisions themselves uphold a high measure of free speech in this country. But epithets like "ranting and raving" and "basket weavers" deserve nothing but contempt from the people. The message should go out clearly. Criticise decisions. Object to reasoning. Propound alternatives. Suggest lessons from other places. But leave off the personal attacks and common name calling. Otherwise this conduct becomes cumulative. It debases our polity. It encourages others to join in the verbal and personal abuse.' [Hon Michael Kirby, *The Sydney Morning Herald*, 16 August 1997, p 5]

  [Average sentence length, 7.5 words; longest sentence, 16 words; key sentences of 2 or 3 words.]

- 'Plaintiff was standing on a platform of defendant's railroad after buying a ticket to go to Rockaway Beach. A train stopped at the station, bound for another place. Two men ran forward to catch it. One of the men reached the platform of the car without mishap, though the train was already moving. The other man, carrying a package, jumped aboard the car, but seemed unsteady as if about to fall. A guard on the car, who had held the door open, reached forward to help him in, and another guard on the platform pushed him from behind. In this act, the package was dislodged, and fell upon the rails. It was a package of small size, about fifteen inches long, and was covered by a newspaper. In fact, it contained fireworks, but there was nothing in its appearance to give notice of its content. The fireworks when they fell exploded. The shock of the explosion threw down some scales at the other end of the platform many feet away. The scales struck the plaintiff, causing injuries for which she sues.' [*Palsgraf v Long Island Railway Co* 162 NE 99, 99 (NY 1928) (Cardozo J)]

  [Average sentence length, 15 words; longest sentence, 27 words; shortest sentence, 6 words. Note the unusual arrangement of the shortest sentence—'The fireworks when they fell exploded.'—deliberately placing the most forceful word at sentence-end.]

(2) For emphatic conclusion, use a short sentence

State your conclusion in a short sentence. Even where the writer has been drawing readers along with a mix of sentence lengths, and with an average of no more than 20–25 words, the conclusion will hit home harder in a shorter sentence than in a longer one. 'No.' 'I do not agree.' 'This is not so.' 'You're fired.' The following two examples from senior judges illustrate the technique.

- 'The question of whether a term should be implied, and if so what, almost inevitably arises after a crisis has been reached in the performance of the contract. So the court comes to the task of implication with the benefit of hindsight, and it is tempting for the court then to fashion a term which will reflect the merits of the situation as they then appear. Tempting, but wrong.' [*Philips Electronique Grand Public SA v British Sky Broadcasting Ltd* [1995] EMLR 472, 482 (Sir Thomas Bingham MR)]

  [Average sentence length until final sentence, 33 words; final 'sentence', 3 words—providing a natural emphasis.]

- 'In truth, [those] judicial statements, made in the context of a different issue from that with which we are concerned, are of little assistance. But they serve to reinforce the point that, on the defendant's argument, the claimant's capacity would depend on whether she had received good advice, bad advice or no advice at all. If she had received good advice or if she had received no advice at all but brought her claim as a litigant in person, then she would lack the capacity to make the decisions which her claim required of her. But if, as in this case, she received bad advice, she possessed the capacity to make the decisions required of her as a result of that bad advice. This cannot be right.' [*Dunhill v Burgin* [2014] 1WLR 933, 941 [17] (Lady Hale)]

  [Average sentence length, until final sentence, 34 words; final sentence, 4 words.]

See also **EMBEDDED (NESTED) INFORMATION; SENTENCE STRUCTURE.**

SENTENCE STRUCTURE

Subject-verb-object

A readable sentence usually follows the pattern *subject-verb-object*. Inserting too many words between these key elements fractures the pattern, interrupting the sentence-flow and making the sentence harder to read. In legal writing, this fracturing often occurs where information is embedded ('nested') between the key elements. It should be moved elsewhere in the sentence, or (sometimes better) given its own sentence.

Often the embedded information is in the form of one or more conditions that qualify the main proposition. If, for some reason, you simply *must* retain the conditions in the same sentence as the main proposition, at least put the main proposition first, ahead of the conditions. Refrain from inserting the condition between subject and verb.

Poor (key elements shown in italics)	**Better (key elements shown in italics)**
The Court may, if it considers that the applicant has satisfied the requirements of the section, *award compensation.*	*The Court may award compensation* if it considers that the applicant has satisfied the requirements of the section.
The arbitrator's decision, appearing to have been signed by the arbitrator, stating that he or she has considered all the arguments raised by the parties, and lodged with the court within 21 days of the completion of the arbitration, *is binding on the parties.*	*The arbitrator's decision is binding on the parties* if it appears to have been signed by the arbitrator, states that he or she has considered all the arguments raised by the parties, and is lodged with the court within 21 days of the completion of the arbitration. **Better still** *The arbitrator's decision binds the parties* if it: • appears to have been signed by the arbitrator; and • states that the arbitrator has considered all the arguments raised by the parties; and • is lodged with the court within 21 days after the arbitration ends.
This conclusion makes it unnecessary to consider whether the respondent's concession, that if the verdicts in relation to the offences charged in the first incident are unreasonable or cannot be supported by the evidence then it follows that the same conclusion should be reached in relation to the verdict concerning the offence charged in the second incident, *amounts to a mode of reasoning that contravenes ss 44F and 44G of the Jury Directions Act.* [Source: *Pell v R* [2020] HCA 12; (2020) 94 ALJR 394, [128] (High Court of Australia)]	*Our conclusion makes it unnecessary to consider whether a concession by the respondent amounts to a mode of reasoning that contravenes ss 44F and 44G of the Jury Directions Act.* The concession was that, if the verdicts in relation to the offences charged in the first incident are unreasonable or cannot be supported by the evidence, then it follows that the same conclusion should be reached in relation to the verdict concerning the offence charged in the second incident.

Sometimes the problem lies in a qualifying phrase that is too far from the (main) phrase that it qualifies. If so, move it closer to the main phrase. Consider the following example (italics indicate the main phrase).

Original (poor)	**Revised (better)**
Landlords are now prohibited from listing a person who ended their tenancy by giving a domestic violence termination notice *on a bad tenant database.* [Source: Kellie McDonald, 'New tenancy reforms' (2019) 53 *New South Wales Law Society Journal* (March) 78, 79]	*Landlords are now prohibited from listing on a bad tenant database a person* who ended their tenancy by giving a domestic violence termination notice.

Put general information before specific

To hold your reader's attention, put general information before specific information. The general gives context to the specific. To start with the specific information deprives the reader of a framework to process it.

Poor (specific first)	**Better (general first)**
A good knowledge of language, a mastery of legal principle, and an ability to think clearly, are all *requisites of effective legal writing.*	*Effective legal writing requires* a good knowledge of language, a mastery of legal principle, and an ability to think clearly.

Change adverbial clauses to adjectival clauses

You can sometimes improve sentence structure by replacing adverbial clauses with adjectival clauses. The substitution can help the sentence get to the main point sooner.

Before	**After**
If a party considers that the other party has breached a term of this agreement, the first party may require the second party to participate in mediation.	*A party who considers that* the other party has breached a term of this agreement may require the other party to participate in mediation.
If a judge decides that the accused is guilty beyond reasonable doubt, he may direct the jury to convict.	*A judge who decides that* the accused is guilty beyond reasonable doubt may direct the jury to convict. [Note that this construction also avoids the gender-specific *he*.]

Consider subordination

Many writers join part sentences with *and*—a co-ordinated structure which, while grammatically correct, suggests that each part is of equal importance. But if you intend one part to be less important than the other(s), a subordinate structure will more readily bring that out. For example:

> 'The court adjourned at noon and that allowed all parties to go to the races.'

The coordinating *and* reduces the impact of the sentence. Much better would be:

> 'Because the court adjourned at noon, all parties could go to the races.'

Or, to shift the emphasis,

> 'All parties could go to the races, because the court adjourned at noon.'

Or yet again,

> 'By adjourning at noon, the court allowed all parties to go the races.'

End sentences forcefully

Put the most important word or phrase at the end of the sentence. That is the sentence's natural stress point. In the English language,

> '[T]he most emphatic place in a clause or sentence is the end. This is the climax; and, during the momentary pause that follows, that last word continues, as it were, to reverberate in the reader's mind. It has, in fact, the last word. One should therefore think twice about what one puts at sentence-end.' [FL Lucas, *Style*, 2nd edn (Cassell, 1955) 39–40]

Of course, you can emphasise a word or phrase by using formatting techniques—eg, **bold**, *italics*. But you may also be able to achieve emphasis by adept sentence-order, without needing the prop of formatting. Compare the following:

- There is always freedom after a prison-term.
- After a prison-term there is always freedom.

Because the natural stress point is at the end, try to avoid ending a sentence with a preposition—you waste a strong place on a weak word:

- This is the kind of advice I will never put up with.
- I will never put up with this kind of advice.

See also discussion under **PREPOSITIONS**.

Prefer parallel structure

In consecutive sentences, a parallel structure communicates more effectively than a haphazard one.

Before	After
The trial judge directed the jury to acquit the accused. [*sentence in active voice*] However, a point was then taken by the prosecution that some of the evidence was inadmissible. [*sentence in passive voice*] An appeal lies for inadmissible evidence, the prosecution reminded the court. [*prosecution, as actor, placed near sentence-end; 'court' replaces 'judge'*]	The trial judge directed the jury to acquit the accused. However, the prosecution then took the point that some of the evidence was inadmissible. The prosecution reminded the judge that an appeal lies for inadmissible evidence.
Please arrange for both copies of the lease to be executed where indicated. The signatories must sign and write their full names. Blue or black ink must be used. The annexure pages must also be signed.	Please arrange for the signatories to execute both copies of the lease where indicated. The signatories must sign and write their full names, using blue or black ink. They must also sign the annexure pages. [Note: some lack of parallelism remains: *execute* vs *sign*. Unless the writer intended a distinction—which is unlikely—prefer *sign*. Also, a 'bullet point' approach would be clearer:] Please arrange for the signatories to sign both copies of the lease where indicated. They must: • use blue or black ink • sign, and write their full names • also sign the annexure pages.

Link consecutive sentences

A good writer 'links' sentences in ways that make them flow easily and logically from one to the next. Techniques include the following.

1. Use linking words such as *and, but, even though, next, finally.*
2. Introduce important information with clear hints: *crucially, most importantly, strictly speaking.*

3. When moving on to a related idea, use helpful transitions such as: *in that case, this means that, on the other hand, in addition.*
4. Start successive sentences with a word or phrase that appeared at or near the end of the preceding sentence ('anadiplosis').

   'Interpretation of a legal document requires context. Establishing context requires research. Research requires time. And time is money.'

   However, do not overdo the technique. If the number of sentences in the series exceeds about four, the resulting predictability may become wearisome.
5. To ease the reader gently into new material, start the sentence with a hint of what has gone before—a reference to content already encountered or a word or phrase already seen. That is, use a sentence structure that moves from the familiar to the new. The adage is 'old information first, new information later', or 'given→new'. This avoids the jolt of strangeness when meeting new information: 'how does this relate to what I've just read?'

   Example 1

   [*First sentence*] When considering how best to make sentences flow, try a linking technique. [*Second sentence*] Using a familiar word or phrase, before introducing new information, is a good linking technique.

   These sentences are poorly linked. A reader must work through most of the second sentence before discovering its relationship with the first sentence—'Ah, it's giving me examples.' A better formulation would be:

   Better (old and new in italics)

   [*First sentence*] When considering how best to make sentences flow, *try a linking technique.* [*Second sentence*] *A good linking technique* is to start the second sentence with a familiar word or phrase before introducing new information.

   Example 2

   [*First sentence*] Our law firm offers the country's best expertise in property law. [*Second sentence*] If you catch the train to Temple Station, then walk along the Embankment, up along Middle Temple Lane to Fleet Street, then turn right and walk 100 yards, you will find our office.

   Better (old and new in italics)

   [*First sentence*] *Our law firm* offers the country's best expertise in property law. [*Second sentence*] *To find our law firm's office*, catch the train to Temple Station, then walk along the Embankment, up along Middle Temple Lane to Fleet Street, then turn right and walk 100 yards.

Further reading

- Duncan Berry, 'Reducing the complexity of legislative sentences', *The Loophole* (January 2009) 38–77
- Herbert H Clark and Susan E Haviland, 'Comprehension and the Given-New Contract' in Roy O Freedle (ed), *Discourse Production and Comprehension* (Ablex Publishing, 1977) 1–40
- Stanley Fish, *How to Write a Sentence* (Harper, 2012) (inspirational instruction from a professor of law)

See also **CLAUSE STRUCTURE; EMBEDDED (NESTED) INFORMATION; PARALLEL STRUCTURE; PREPOSITIONS; PROLIXITY; SENTENCE LENGTH.**

separatim

Latin: separately, independently (of something else); often in combination with *et* (= and): *et separatim*. A Latinism that has survived in Scots legal usage, but seems largely to have disappeared from legal usage elsewhere. There is no magic in the Latin. Prefer standard English:

> '[The pursuers] alleged that this advice was negligent *et separatim* [prefer: *and additionally*; *and was also*] in breach of contract.' [*Gilchrist v McClure Naismith LLP* [2015] CSOH 134, [2] (Lord Bannatyne)]

seq

Abbreviation for Latin *sequens* (plural, *sequentia*), 'following'; usually in the expression *et seq*, 'and the following'. In British and Commonwealth usage, no full stop (*seq*); US usage prefers a full stop (*seq.*).

See **et seq.**

sergeant / serjeant

General meanings

A *sergeant* is a person of military rank; a *serjeant* is the holder of a legal or quasi-legal office (*serjeant-at-arms, serjeant-at-law*).

serjeant-at-law

Formerly, the highest rank of counsel at the English bar, with the exclusive right of audience in the Court of Common Pleas when sitting *en banc* (ie, in full court), and the same right of audience as barristers in all other courts. As Sir Robert Megarry explained:

> 'Serjeants were appointed by writ under the Great Seal, a far more formal document than the letters patent that a QC receives. The appointment was made by the Crown on the advice of the Lord Chancellor, though he acted only on the advice of the Chief Justice of the Court of Common Pleas; and even in the relaxed conditions of the nineteenth century, none of less than seven years' standing at the Bar need apply. When appointed, "Mr Jones" was transmuted into "Mr Serjeant Jones". There would be much ceremonial, including feasting and the distribution of gold rings engraved with a suitable motto of the serjeant's choice; and nearly always the serjeant, after having been formally made a bencher of his Inn of Court for his short remaining period there, would ceremonially leave his Inn for Serjeant's Inn, the bell of his former Inn being tolled as for one dead.' [*Inns Ancient and Modern* (Selden Society lecture series, Selden Society, 1972) 16]

Serjeants-at-law are no longer appointed. The last British serjeant-at-law was Lord Lindley (appointed 1875, died 1921). Ireland also used the title *serjeant*, but the system was different. The last Irish-appointed serjeant was Serjeant Sullivan QC, who practised in London and was best known for his (unsuccessful) defence of Sir Roger Casement: see AM Sullivan, *The Last Serjeant* (Macdonald, 1952).

Serjeants-at-law had their own Inn of Court, Serjeants' Inn. Membership of the Inn was usual for serjeants-at-law, but not compulsory: RE Megarry (above) 23–26.

See also **Inns of Court**.

SERIAL COMMA

See **COMMAS**.

seriatim

Latin: in a series; one after another. Favoured by lawyers, but easily translatable into plain English when writing for readers unimpressed by pedantry. For example:

- 'This exercise in judgment does not require the judge to reach a specific conclusion in relation to each listed factor *seriatim* [prefer: *one by one*; *one after the other*]; rather it requires him to exercise his overall judgment in the light of them ...' [*Misick v R* [2015] UKPC 31; [2015] 1 WLR 3215, [40] (Lord Hughes)]
- 'Beazley JA listed eight issues and proceeded *seriatim* [prefer: *one by one*] to decide them all.' [*New South Wales v Amery* [2006] HCA 14; (2006) 226 ALR 196, [97] (Kirby J)]

serious

A word with shades of meaning, the appropriate colour supplied by the context in which it appears. 'What may be serious for one purpose may not be serious for another': *AH (Algeria) v Secretary of State for the Home Department* [2012] EWCA Civ 395, [52]; [2012] 1 WLR 3469 (Ward LJ). For example:

> A refugee convention disqualified claimants from protection where there existed '*serious* reasons' for considering that the claimant had committed a '*serious* non-political crime' outside the United Kingdom. Was 'serious' to be qualified in some way, such as 'substantially'? Held, no: *AH (Algeria) v Secretary of State for the Home Department (No 2)* [2015] EWCA Civ 1003; [2016] 1 WLR 2071 (CA); leave to appeal refused, [2016] 1 WLR 2449, SC(E).

The potential for ambiguity makes it prudent, if possible, to clarify the intended degree of *serious*ness.

servant

In general usage, when referring to a person who works in return for payment, *servant* (with its overtones of servility) is obsolescent; modern usage prefers *employee*. Similarly in this context, *master* is obsolescent; modern usage prefers *employer*.

In legal usage, however, *servant* survives in expressions such as 'civil *servant*' and '*servant* of the Crown'. But except where (for some reason) you must use administrative jargon, prefer *employee*.

> '[T]he Commonwealth asserted the right by its *servants* [prefer: *employees*] or agents to assault detainees and physically restrain them.' [*Plaintiff M68-2015 v Minister for Immigration and Border Protection* [2016] HCA 1, [354] (Gordon J)]

See also **master and servant**.

serve / give (notices)

Meanings

These two words—*serve*, *give*—describe ways in which notices are communicated. In normal usage, *serve* suggests more formality than *give*: a person may *give* notice to another by informal means, but to *serve* notice implies compliance with prescribed formalities. In legal usage, however, 'service' clauses in contracts or statutes often deliberately conflate the terms by stating that a notice may be 'served or given' by certain means, imposing the same formalities on both *giving* and *serving* notices. This reflects the case law, which generally draws no distinction between *serving* a notice and *giving* a notice: *Kinch v Bullard* [1999] 1 WLR 423, 426G.

Ideally, do not switch between *serve* and *give*. To do so invites uncertainty. For example, if clause 1 of a lease says that a tenant may renew the lease by *giving* notice to the landlord, and clause 2 regulates the methods of *serving* notices under the lease, does clause 2 apply to a notice given under clause 1? And if clause 2 also states that a notice *served* in the prescribed way is deemed to be effective even though it was not received, does it apply to a notice *given* under clause 1? The uncertainty is increased if yet another term is introduced, such as *notify*: is *notifying* to be equated with *giving* or *serving*? The answers may require interpreting the document as a whole, not merely the particular clauses (as in *FAI General Insurance Co Ltd v Parras* (2002) 55 NSWLR 498; [2002] NSWCA 334).

Receipt of notice

Normally, a notice is not *served* or *given* unless it is received: *Sun Alliance & London Assurance Co Ltd v Hayman* [1975] 1 WLR 177, 185 (Lord Salmon). However, this is subject to contrary intention, express or implied, in the relevant statute or document. So, for example, under court rules a claim form is 'served' if put into the post before midnight on the day on which time for service expires (as in *Oran Environmental Solutions Ltd v QBE Insurance (Europe) Ltd* [2020] EWHC 1271 (Comm); [2020] 1 WLR 327). Even when not in the context of court rules, a reference (eg, in a contract) to 'service' of documents may carry the meaning of service in the manner laid down in the court rules then in force: *T & L Sugars Ltd v Tate & Lyle Industries Ltd* [2014] EWHC 1066, [16] (Flaux J). Some interpretation clauses specify that a notice *served* or *given* in the manner specified is 'deemed' to have been received within the ordinary course of post, or (more specifically) within a stated number of days afterwards. As a matter of interpretation, the 'deeming' may be rebuttable, or it may be conclusive. If it is conclusive, a party is taken to have been served despite never receiving the document: see, eg, *Galinski v McHugh* (1988) 57 P & CR 359, 365.

Service formalities

Normally, service methods prescribed in a contract or statute are regarded as facultative, not mandatory. That allows some leniency in the service process. For example:

- Even where the prescribed service method is not followed, service may be effective as long as the person-to-be-served in fact receives the notice: *UKI (Kingsway) Ltd v Westminster City Council* [2018] UKSC 67; [2019] 1 WLR 104.
- *Service* does not necessarily require personal service on the recipient. For example, it may be enough to send the relevant document by post, or by email, or to leave it with a responsible person for handing on to the person-to-be-served: *UKI (Kingsway) Ltd*, above (service effective where document left with a third party who was not authorised to accept receipt, but who emailed a scanned copy to the person-to-be-served).
- Where a service-of-notice clause requires service at a person's 'last known place of address', it usually means last known to the sender; so a notice sent to that address is effective even though the intended recipient has moved: *Austin Rover Group Ltd v Crouch Butler Savage Associates* [1986] 1 WLR 1102, 1111.

However, these more lenient consequences do not always apply. In particular, a service-of-notice clause may state or imply that the prescribed service methods are mandatory. In that case, service by any other means is ineffective. Even minor departures will invalidate the service, even though the notice is actually received: *Capital Land Holdings Ltd v Secretary of State for the Environment* 1997 SC 109 (service at place of business not service at 'registered office'); *FAI General Insurance Co Ltd v Parras* (2002) 55 NSWLR 498. Lord Hoffmann once said that if a service-of-notice clause requires a notice to be on blue paper, a notice on green paper would be ineffective: *Mannai Investment Co Ltd v Eagle Star Life Assurance Co Ltd* [1997] AC 749, 776.

Further reading

Russell Hewitson, 'Sit Up and Take Notice' (2019) 83 *Conveyancing and Property Lawyer* 93 (case law on aspects of serving notices)

See also **deem**; **NOTICE CLAUSE**.

service selfie

A photograph taken by camera or mobile phone to prove service of a document. The language is jocular but the purpose serious. For example, the photograph or video clip might show the server handing the document to the recipient, or placing it a post box (with the address and the postage on the envelope visible), or leaving it at identified premises.

Further reading

Robert Angyal, 'Can a Notice that Never Arrived Be Properly Served?' (2015) 89 *Australian Law Journal* 439

servient tenement

See **dominant tenement / servient tenement**.

servitude

Latin: *servitus*, meaning *subjection*. A term derived from the civil law, and used in Scotland (but not in most other Commonwealth countries) to denote a right or obligation attached to land. The law divides servitudes into positive and negative servitudes. A 'positive servitude' allows a landowner to exercise rights over another's land—eg, to cross it, or to take crops from it, or to drain water across it. A 'negative servitude' allows a landowner to restrict the use to which another owner puts his or her land—eg, by limiting the height of buildings, or prohibiting certain types of activities. The approximate equivalent in England and most Commonwealth countries is *easement*.

See also **easement**.

SESQUIPEDALIANISM

A disease afflicting lawyers addicted to *sesquipedalia verba* (Latin: words a foot and a half long). Writers who prefer long words over shorter words perhaps assume that long words impress readers. But studies show the opposite: in readers' estimations, writers who use long words are less intelligent than writers who use shorter words (see study by Oppenheimber, in *Further reading*, below).

So, resist the urge to use long words. Instead, follow George Orwell's advice: 'Never use a long word where a short one will do.': 'Politics and the English Language' (1946), reprinted in George Orwell, *Why I Write* (Penguin, 2004) 119. Likewise, follow Lord Denning's exhortation:

> '[The first principle is] "Don't use long words", unless you are sure your hearers or readers understand them. ... If your hearer says to himself, "That is a word I've never heard before. What does it mean?", you have failed. If your reader says, "I must look it up in a dictionary", again you have failed. You have not conveyed your meaning to him.
>
> A lot of speakers and writers do not appreciate that simple truth. They use long words so as to "show off". ... By doing so, they go wrong.' [Lord Denning, *The Closing Chapter* (Butterworths, 1983) 59–60. Lord Denning goes on to criticise Lord Diplock's use of 'synallagmatic'; see quotation under **synallagmatic**.]

Further reading

- JD Fischer, 'Why George Orwell's Ideas About Language Still Matter for Lawyers' (2007) 68 *Montana Law Review* 129
- DM Oppenheimer, 'Consequences of Erudite Vernacular Utilized Irrespective of Necessity: Problems with Using Long Words Needlessly' (2006) 20 *Applied Cognitive Psychology* 139 (describes intelligence ratings that readers give to writers who use complex styles and high-level vocabularies); see at www.psych.utoronto.ca/users/psy3001/files/simple%20writing.pdf

See also **SIMPLER WORDS AND PHRASES**.

set-off / set off

Settled practice is to hyphenate the noun (*set-off*) and adjective ('*set-off* principles'), but not the verb (*to set off*). For example:

- 'Therefore, [the party] is in my judgment entitled to *set off* its counterclaim, even if I am wrong to think that it fell within the scope of equitable *set-off*.' [*Geldof Metaalconstructie NV v Simon Carves Ltd* [2010] EWCA Civ 667, [54]; [2010] 4 All ER 847 (Rix LJ)]
- 'In our opinion, however, the *set-off* cases ... are not relevantly distinguishable. ... Any payment which satisfies par (n) would be ... *set off* against damages for personal injury.' [*Commissioner of Taxation v Scully* [2000] HCA 6, [38]; 201 CLR 148, [38] (Gaudron ACJ, McHugh, Gummow and Callinan JJ)]

See also **SET-OFF CLAUSE**.

SET-OFF CLAUSE

Meaning

A clause that seeks to regulate a party's right to 'set off' a debt or obligation against a debt or obligation owed by or to another party. It would be better termed a 'no set-off' clause, because it usually seeks to *preclude* a party from exercising a right of set-off. For example, a lease may require the landlord to keep the building in repair; and then, to prevent the tenant withholding rent if the landlord breaches that obligation, the lease may stipulate that the tenant must pay rent 'without set-off'. Or a deed of guarantee may require the guarantor to pay the guaranteed sum 'without set-off'. In both cases, the aim is to preclude delay in payment based on a possible claim the payer may have against the recipient.

Drafting

General considerations

'Set-off' is probably a genuine term of art, difficult to express plainly without adding many words. So, prudence suggests that the drafter of a set-off clause might use the technical term *set-off*, but add a definition or glossary for the benefit of non-technical readers.

Some drafters—perhaps seeking a plainer style, or perhaps wishing to cast a wider net—use a more general term than 'set-off'. For example, they provide that the amount must be paid 'without deduction', or 'clear of all deductions', or similar. Does such wording encompass the technical aspects of the law of 'set-off'? There are two contrasting views:

1. **It does not encompass set-off.** Parties are presumed not to intend to exclude valuable rights, such as set-off, except by clear words—and 'without deduction' (or similar) is not a sufficiently clear reference to 'set-off'. This view has support in England and New Zealand: *Connaught Restaurants Ltd v Indoor Leisure Ltd* [1994] 1 WLR 501; *Grant v New Zealand Motor Corporation* [1988] NZCA 135; [1989] 1 NZLR 8.
2. **It does encompass set-off.** Expressions are to be given their plain meaning. An expression such as 'deduction' sufficiently encompasses set-off. The current trend of Australian authority favours this view: *Batiste v Lenin* 10 BPR 19,441; [2002] NSWSC 233 (but left open on appeal, [2002] NSWCA 316; (2002) 11 BPR 20,403); *Sandbank Holdings Pty Ltd v Durkan* [2010] WASCA 122, [35]; *Norman v FEA Plantations Ltd* [2011] FCAFC 99; (2011) 195 FCR 97. Indeed, the logic of this view has been taken further, to hold that a clause that requires full payment of outstanding money (but without expressly referring to set-off), is effective to exclude set-off where the parties must have known when entering into their contract that they might have unresolved claims: *Smith v Acquire Asia Pacific Philippines Inc* [2016] NSWSC 1084, [92].

Given this difference of approach, it may be prudent (when seeking to exclude set-off claims) to use the specific term *set-off*, rather than a more general term such as 'deduction'.

Further, set-off operates differently at common law and in equity. Therefore, it may be prudent expressly to exclude both 'common-law set-off' and 'equitable set-off', to avoid argument over whether *set-off*, without more, encompasses only common-law set-off. This, though, seems a counsel of perfection, because it is tolerably clear (at least in some jurisdictions) that a clause precluding 'set-off' (without more) precludes both legal and equitable set-off: *O'Brien v Bank of Western Australia* [2013] NSWCA 71; (2013) 16 BPR 31,705; *Palaniappan v Westpac Banking Corp Ltd* [2016] WASCA 72 [76], [156]–[158]; *Ozton Pty Ltd v Cromwell Seven Hills Pty Ltd* [2016] NSWSC 1339.

Qualified clauses

In practice, 'no set-off' clauses are sometimes qualified. Common qualifications are:

- The party claiming the right of set-off must bring proceedings, within a stated period, to establish the right—otherwise, the amount must be paid without set-off.
- The amount claimed as a set-off must be paid to a stakeholder while a court decides whether there is a right of set-off.

'Set-off' versus 'net-off'

Under a 'net-off' agreement, the amounts due from each party to the other are totalled, and then the net balance due to one party only is calculated. In essence, each party agrees that neither owes any amount to the other until the respective debts have been 'squared off' (to use the vernacular), leaving one party entitled to payment of the net debt from the other party. (Insolvency and bankruptcy legislation often impose this regime.) A *net-off* does not necesarily equate with a *set-off*. Whether an agreement provides for *net-off* or *set-off* is a matter of interpretation of the agreement; but it will be difficult for a party to circumvent a 'no set-off' provision by claiming that their true agreement was for a less technical (and probably more generous) 'net-off': eg, *Hammersley Iron Pty Ltd v Forge Group Power Pty Ltd* [2017] WASC 152, [136]–[143]; (2017) 52 WAR 90 (reversed on a matter of statutory interpretation, *Hammersley Iron Pty Ltd v Forge Group Power Pty Ltd* [2018] WASCA 163).

Other issues

Set-off claims may give rise to other issues, which an effective 'no set-off' clause may need to cover:

- Can a present debt be set off against a future liability (and if so, should the future liability be discounted, and at what rate)?
- Can a contingent liability (eg, a liability under a guarantee where the principal debtor has not defaulted) be set off?
- Can an amount payable in one currency be set off against an amount payable in another currency, and if so, at what exchange rate?

'Set-off' rights may intrude into other calculations also. For example, when calculating an amount that is *due and payable*, credit may have to be given for offsets, leaving only the net amount due and payable. Thus, a court invalidated a landlord's notice to quit for failing to credit against 'rent *due*' an amount that the tenant was entitled to set off against the outstanding rent: *Secretary of State for Defence v Spencer* [2019] EWHC 1526 (Ch); [2019] 1 WLR 6065.

See also **set-off / set off**; **TERMS OF ART**.

settler / settlor

A *settler* is a person who settles in a new country or a new area of country. A *settlor* is a person who establishes a settlement or trust of property—ie, who 'settles' property on someone. Even leading lawyers sometimes confuse the two:

> 'In *In re Detmold*, a *settlor* made a marriage settlement settling income on himself for life or until [bankruptcy]. A judgment creditor obtained the appointment of a receiver [and] the *settler* [substitute: *settlor*] was adjudicated bankrupt.' [*Perpetual Trustee Co Ltd v BNY Ltd* [2012] 1 AC 383, 436 [155] (Lord Mance)]

SEVERABILITY CLAUSE

A contractual clause to the effect that if a provision of the contract is found to be void, or unenforceable, or illegal, it is to be severed (ie, deleted) from the contract. The purpose is to ensure that, where at all possible, the rest of the contract takes effect.

Example

> **Severability**
>
> If a provision in this contract is or becomes illegal, invalid or unenforceable, that does not affect the legality, validity or enforceability of any other provision.

The clause in the above example is basic. Some severability clauses go further and seek to clarify the parties' post-severance positions, particularly if severance could alter the essential nature of their contract. Other clauses go yet further, to deal with whether courts in the jurisdiction adopt a 'blue pencil' rule or a 'reasonableness' rule. In 'blue pencil' jurisdictions, the courts delete the offending provision; in 'reasonableness' jurisdictions, they trim the offending provision until it becomes acceptable. In either case, the result may upset the parties' expectations—hence the need for severability clauses to seek to cover those kinds of matters.

severable

Able to be severed; in law, chiefly in relation to a provision that is able to be deleted ('severed') without affecting the validity of the rest of the document.

See **SEVERABILITY CLAUSE**.

several

Indicating separateness

In its strict legal usage, *several* means 'separate' or 'individual'. For example:

- A and B have *several* liability to C for a debt—ie, C can sue each of them for the entire debt.
- A gift 'to A and B *severally*' was a gift to A and B as tenants in common, not as joint tenants: *Sheppard v Gibbons* (1742) 2 Atk 441; 26 ER 666. *Severally* indicated separateness, rebutting the notion of a joint tenancy (under which A and B would own the whole property indivisibly, not in separate shares).
- A testator bequeathed property to his four daughters 'for their respective lives', and 'from and after the *several* deceases of my said daughters ... to the respective children of my respective daughters ... ' Held, this was a gift taking effect on the death of each daughter in turn—ie, on the death of a daughter, that daughter's children took their share immediately: *Woodstock v Shillito* (1833) 6 Sim 416, 419; 58 ER 650, 651.

This meaning of *several* is rare in common usage—which is good reason to avoid it in legal usage if the reader is unlikely to understand the meaning. Prefer instead 'separate' or 'individual'.

Indicating numbers

When indicating numbers, *several* can be vague. For example, the general sense of '*several* people' is 'more than two or three, but not very many'. Context might make precise delineation unnecessary; but if in doubt, indicate a specific number, to avoid arguments of the kind in the following case:

> A planning policy applied to a site affected by aircraft noise, if the number of flights exceeded '*several* times' per hour. Held, *several* did not mean two; rather, it meant more than two, but less than 'many': *Clowes Development (UK) Ltd v Secretary of State for the Environment* [1996] EWHC Admin 126; [1996] EG (CS) 163.

Meaning 'respectively'

In older cases, *several* could mean 'respectively'. (An example is the gift in *Woodstock v Shillito*, above, where the testator used 'several' and 'respectively' as synonyms.) However, this usage is archaic and courts are unlikely now to apply it:

> A building contractor undertook to carry out an itemised list of building works, and to remedy defects discovered within 3 months of completing the '*several* works'. Held: *several*

did not mean 'respective'. The 3-month period ran from completion of the entire building project, and not from the time of completion of each individual item: *Cunliffe v Hampton Wick Local Board* (1893) 9 TLR 378; affirmed 2 Dec 1892 (CA, 2 Hudson's BC (4th edn) 250, (10th edn) 393).

Meaning 'sole' or 'exclusive'

Certain rights, such as profits à prendre, may exist 'in common' (ie, exercisable in common with others) or they may exist 'in severalty' (ie, exercisable to the exclusion of others). 'Several' here means 'sole' or 'exclusive'. Whether a profit à prendre is in common (a 'right of common') or exclusive (a 'right in severalty', or a 'several profit') turns on the interpretation of the instrument granting the profit à prendre: *Robinson v Duleep Singh* (1879) 11 Ch D 798; *Reid v Moreland Timber Co Pty Ltd* (1946) 73 CLR 1; *Ellison v Vukicevic* (1986) 7 NSWLR 104.

See also **joint / several**; **profit à prendre**.

severalty

See **several**.

sewer / sewage / sewerage

A *sewer* is a drain (from *sew*, to drain); *sewage* is effluent (eg, waste water or refuse from a factory or a house) passing through drains; and *sewerage* is the removal of sewage by means of sewers, or by a system of pipes and sewers for sewage removal. The meanings are frequently conflated, but the distinction remains important in some contexts. For example, an easement for *sewer* differs from an easement for *sewage*. To prevent confusion, it may be prudent to use more modern terms, such as 'easement to drain water' and 'easement to drain sewage'.

shall / must

shall as legalese

In almost all non-legal writing, *shall* as a word of obligation has yielded to *must*. For some reason, however, *shall* lives on as a word of obligation in legal writing. But *shall* reeks of legalese. Perhaps modern lawyers who insist on *shall* consider that it gives their writing precision, authenticity, and a sense of formality that is not possible with substitutes such as *must*, or *agrees to*, or *is to*. If so, they are wrong. *Shall* has no innate superiority over *must*; quite the contrary, *shall* (unlike *must*) gives legal writing an air of pretentious archaism. *Shall* has had its day.

The confusing uses of *shall*

A key issue with *shall* in legal writing—apart from its archaism—is its use for multiple purposes. This creates the potential for uncertainty. Which use of *shall* does the writer intend? By replacing *shall* with a more targeted, standard-English word, the meaning is instantly clarified.

Examples: the many uses of *shall*

Use of 'shall'	**Example of usage**
To impose obligation	The tenant *shall* [ie, must] keep the premises in good condition and repair.
To grant a right	The tenant *shall be entitled to* [ie, can; may] break the lease after 12 months.
To give a direction	The tenant *shall* [ie, is to] pay the rent to the landlord's agent. [This directs *how* to pay the rent. The *obligation* to pay rent will be set out elsewhere.]
To impose a condition precedent	If the tenant *shall give* [ie, gives] notice to the landlord of intention to renew the lease, the landlord *shall* [ie, must] grant a renewal. [The first *shall* imposes a condition precedent to the renewal of the lease; the second *shall* imposes an obligation.]
To add a condition subsequent	The tenant's right to remove fixtures ceases if the tenant *shall not have* [ie, has not] paid all rent up to the date of exercise of the right. [The right to remove fixtures—an accrued right—will be lost if the tenant fails to pay rent.]
To state a fact or assumption	The fixtures in the premises at the start of the lease *shall be deemed to be* [ie, are] tenants' fixtures.
To denote futurity	The right to remove fixtures *shall terminate* [ie, will terminate; terminates] at the end of the lease.

This list of possible uses of *shall* is not exhaustive. But it demonstrates the potential for misunderstanding. To repeat the earlier question: which use of *shall* does the writer intend? Here are two more examples, one from a company's constitution and the other from a statute:

Company's governing document

'The CFO of the company *shall be* one of the directors of the company.'

This could have three meanings:

1. The CFO must be selected from the directors.
2. The CFO need not be a director when appointed, but becomes one on appointment.
3. The CFO must be a director when appointed, and must remain one (ie, a CFO who ceases to be a director, ceases to be the CFO).

[Example based on Robert C Dick, *Legal Drafting in Plain Language*, 3rd edn (Carswell, 1995) 95]

Statutory example

Article 160 of Hong Kong's *Basic Law* stated:

> 'Upon the establishment of the Hong Kong Special Administrative Region, the laws previously in force in Hong Kong *shall be adopted* as the laws of the Region …' (italics added)

Did the italicised words mean that: (1) a positive act of adoption was required before the previous laws became the laws of the Region (no such act had occurred); or (2) the laws previously in force in Hong Kong *are* the laws of the Region, without the need for a positive act of adoption? Held: meaning (2). That is, *shall* bore a present, declaratory sense, not a sense of requiring future action: *HKSAR v Ma Wai-kwan* [1997] 2 HKC315; [1997] 2 HKC 315, 326–28, 347.

shall as triggering event

Shall is also problematical when used to introduce a triggering event that gives rise to rights or obligations. Here are two examples:

Lease

> A lease states: 'If the tenant *shall* become bankrupt, the landlord may terminate the lease.' Can the landlord terminate the lease on the ground that the tenant was already bankrupt at the date of the lease? Or does *shall* indicate a bankruptcy occurring only *after* the date of entry into the lease? The decided cases conflict. One line of cases (typified by *Re Walker* [1930] 1 Ch 469) holds that *shall* necessarily implies futurity—ie, a *shall* provision relates only to the period after the document's date. But another line of cases (based on *Loring v Thomas* (1861) 30 LJ Ch 789) holds that a *shall* provision merely describes a state of affairs, whenever occurring—ie, something that has already happened before the document's date can be a triggering event.

Will

> A testator left property by will to her children. The will provided (in a so-called 'substitutional provision'): 'If any of my children … *shall predecease me* leaving children him or her surviving, [then] such children shall take … the share to which [their] parent would have been entitled had [the parent] survived me.' At the date of the will, a child of the testator had already died, leaving a child (ie, a grandchild of the testator) alive at the testator's death. Did the grandchild take his parent's share? Held, no: *shall predecease me* meant *predecease me in the future*; the words excluded grandchildren whose parents died before the date of the will. The words looked to the future, and their 'natural and ordinary sense' excluded a child already dead when the will was made: *Re McPherson* [1968] VR 368.

shall meaning *may*

Interpretation

Shall-users must confront the reality that courts have long held that, in appropriate circumstances, *shall* can mean *may*. More precisely, courts have held that, in the context of the document as a whole, the drafter used *shall* to mean *may*—ie, to grant a discretion, not to impose an obligation.

Examples

- A contract for the sale of a leasehold interest was subject to a condition that, if the landlord refused consent to the sale, the purchaser *shall* vacate the premises. Held, this meant that the purchaser *shall be entitled to*, or *may*, vacate, not must vacate: *Balabel v Mehmet* [1990] 1 EGLR 220 (CA).
- A statute provided that, if a certain body approved a person as fit and proper to become a barrister, the court *shall* admit the person as a barrister. Did this: (1) compel the court to admit the person, or (2) leave the court with a discretion to refuse admission? The issue split the High Court of Australia. One judge held that *shall* compelled the Court to admit the person—*shall* meant *must*. Three other judges held that *shall* meant *may*—the court was free to refuse admission for any reason it considered sufficient. See *Re Davis* (1947) 75 CLR 409.

Both examples demonstrate that *shall* is 'a notoriously slippery word that careful drafters avoid': *McCready v White* 417 F 3d 700, 702 (7th Cir 2005) (holding that *shall* in the statute in question meant *may*).

'shall and may' (combined term)

Formerly, statutes or documents sometimes combined *shall* and *may* into a composite expression: 'A *shall and may* do X.' This collocation is puzzling: does it impose an obligation (*shall*) or confer a discretion (*may*)? Conclusions have differed, depending on context: see, eg, *R v Eye Corporation* (1822) 1 B & C 85; 107 ER 32 (discretion); *Crump v Adney* (1833) 1 Cr & M 355; 149 ER 436 (obligation). No self-respecting modern drafter would use the combination *shall and may*.

Prefer *must* over *shall*

A new general rule

Instead of *shall*, prefer *must* as the legal word of obligation. That *must* is effective to impose obligation is beyond argument, as the following cases show:

- *must* 'is clearly intended to carry a mandatory requirement': *Re Federated Furnishing Society* (1993) 113 ALR 137, [19]
- *must* 'denotes a mandatory obligation': *Surveyor-General v Seychell* (2002) 81 SASR 277, 286
- *must* has a 'normal, mandatory sense': *Mikhman v Royal Victorian Aero Club* [2012] VSC 42, [24]
- *must* is 'stronger' than *shall*: *Churnin v Pilot Developments Pty Ltd* [2003] NSWCA 391; (2003) 11 BPR 21,603, [54] (Santow JA). (But that is probably an exaggeration—unless Santow JA merely meant that *must* seems starker than *shall*.)

Most legal writing experts now recommend *must* as the universal word to impose obligation. Indeed, most would go further and banish *shall* completely from legal writing. A few, however, resist wholesale banishment, and recommend retaining *shall* for expressing obligations that carry consequences for breach. That is, they retain *shall* where the sense is 'you have a duty to—or else you will be liable'. (For references for both views, see *Further reading* at the end of this entry.) However, this limited retention of *shall* requires fine distinctions, likely to be overlooked by busy lawyers and misunderstood by busy readers. For that reason, a simpler approach is preferable: use *must* in all instances of obligation.

Specify the consequences of breach

When using *must* for obligation, it is still necessary (as it was with *shall*) to specify the consequences of failure to comply. The mere use of *must* does not fill the gap.

Example (rent review clause in a lease):

> 'If the landlord and the tenant cannot agree on the new rent, then either party may appoint a valuer who *must* fix the new rent.' Because the valuer is not a party to the lease, neither landlord nor tenant can compel the valuer to fix the new rent. *Must* indicates no more than a hope or expectation. The only element of compulsion (implied, not expressed) is that a party who appoints a valuer must instruct the valuer to asses the new rent.

can 'must' mean 'may'?

A word of caution when using *must*: just as courts can hold that in context *shall* means *may*, so also they can hold that in context *must* means *may*. Hopefully the occasions will be rare—and certainly there is as yet no settled body of case law about *must/may* as there is about *shall/may*. But already on occasions courts have interpreted *must* to mean *may*: see, eg, *DPP v George* (2008) 102 SASR 246; [2008] SASC 330; *Howie v Youth Justice Court* (2010) 27 NTLR 132; [2010] NTSC 32. So, care is still needed.

'must' as facultative, not mandatory (directory)

Further, context may show that *must* is used in a *facultative* sense—ie, *allowing* something to be done in a particular way, but not *mandating* it as the only way. For example:

- Patent legislation specified that a patent specification *must* end with a distinct statement of the invention. Held, *must* was not obligatory, but merely directory—ie, failure to comply did not render the patent void: *Siddell v Vickers, Sons & Co Ltd* (1888) 39 Ch D 92, CA; affirmed *Vickers, Sons & Co Ltd v Siddell* (1890) 15 App Cas 496.
- A takeover offer specified that an acceptance form 'must' be posted to the company secretary. Instead of posting the acceptance form, a shareholder handed it personally to the company secretary. Held, in the context of the takeover document as a whole (and despite the use of 'must'), acceptance by post was facultative, not mandatory, and that personal delivery was a valid method of acceptance: *George Hudson Holdings Ltd v Rudder* (1973) 128 CLR 387, 394–95.
- Legislation governing powers of attorney provided that an instrument signed by the attorney *must* be signed in a way that shows that the attorney signed it as attorney for the principal. Held: *must* did not prescribe that method of signing as the *only* effective method. A power of attorney would still be effective if signed in any other way that the common law accepts as showing that the attorney signs as attorney for the principal. See *Nielsen v Capital Finance Australia Ltd* [2014] QCA 139, [26], [76]–[80], [87].

A softer tone: 'is to', 'agrees to'

Some legal writers, though willing to banish *shall*, find *must* too harsh. They prefer softer-toned alternatives such as *is to* and *agrees to*:

- 'The tenant *is to* [*agrees to*] keep the premises in repair'
- 'The landlord *is to* [*agrees to*] provide a set a keys'.

There is no risk (in these examples) that *is to* means merely *may*: *Smithton Ltd v Naggar* [2015] 1 WLR 189, [110] (Arden LJ). A cautious drafter might add an interpretation provision that *is to* is mandatory (as some interpretation statutes do: eg, *Acts Interpretation Act 1931* (Tas), s 10A); but that seems unnecessarily cautious.

must / will

Is *will* a substitute for *must*? In most contexts, yes. Where used consistently to denote obligation, *will* causes no ambiguity: 'The tenant *will* do X' = 'The tenant *must* do X'. For example, *will* meant *shall* [ie, *must*] in a company's articles which provided that 'every member who intends to transfer shares *shall* inform the directors, who *will* [ie, *must*] take the said shares' at a fair value: *Rayfield v Hands* [1960] Ch 1.

However, here too, context may cloud whether *will* imposes an obligation. For example:

> The *Civil Procedure Rules* stated that in considering applications a court '*will* consider' certain listed matters. Did this impose an obligation to consider the matters, or was it merely an exhortation to do so? Held (somewhat ambivalently), *will* did not impose a duty to consider every one of the listed matters, but that judges *should* still consider each one of them, lest an appeal court overturn their decision for failing to consider all material considerations: *Woodhouse v Consignia* [2002] EWCA Civ 275; [2002] 2 All ER 737, [36], [41].

Presumably to overcome any uncertainty on this point, the *Civil Procedure Rules* have since 2014 preferred *must* over *will* when stipulating an action to be done by the court:

> 'From and including 1 October 2014 … where an amendment … to these Rules … provides for an action to be done by the court, the Rules will generally provide that the court *must* do the action, rather than *will*. This is to make it clearer where an obligation lies with the court to do something. Occasionally in the future, it may still be appropriate to use the word *will*,

for example in a statement of future intent, and on those occasions, *will* will be used.' [*Practice Direction 2D*—'References in the Rules to Actions Done by the Court']

Some legislatures use *will* when addressing a court ('the court *will* do something'), but *must* when addressing a party ('a party *must* do something'). This difference in terminology may reflect a degree of deference to the courts, for whom a polite nod should suffice. But some other legislatures are less circumspect, specifying that judges *must* do something: eg, 'Before making an order ..., the court *must* have regard to [certain listed matters]' (*Evidence (Document Unavailability) Act 2006* (Vic), s 89C).

Also, context may give *will* a potential for ambiguity about futurity. Where an agreement provides that 'A *will* do something', does it require A to do it now or in the future? If *will* creates ambiguity, prefer *must*.

must / should

Is *should* an appropriate word for obligation? Almost certainly, no. In ordinary English usage, *should* implies *ought to*—a course of action that is morally or ethically appropriate, but not necessarily legally binding. In legal English, also, *should* generally carries this less-than-legally-binding sense of *ought to*. But it does not always carry that sense. Context can give *should* different shades of meaning. For example:

1. **Should means 'may'**
   - A requirement that beneficiaries *should* allow land to devolve on their children in a certain way meant that they had a choice whether to do so—ie, *should* meant *may*, not *must*: *Kanayson v Rasiah* [1968] AC 746, 764
   - A statutory provision that a magistrate *should* impose certain bail conditions if the Crown consented gave *a discretion* whether to impose bail conditions: *R v Cooke* [2003] SASC 403.

2. **Should means 'ought to' (but not 'must')**
   - A statutory provision that criminal proceedings *should not* be commenced against a child except by way of a court attendance notice was an exhortation but not an obligation: *PM v R* [2007] HCA 49; (2007) 232 CLR 370.
   - A requirement that an order for spousal support *should* have certain aims meant '*ought to, but need not*': *Re Santosuosso* (1997) 32 OR (3d) 143, [28].
   - A statutory provision that a court *should* award exemplary damages against an employer for knowingly exposing a worker to asbestos allowed a residual discretion but implied that normally the court '*ought to*' award exemplary damages once the criteria were met: *BHP Billiton Ltd v Parker* [2012] SASCFC 73, [228]–[230]; (2012) 113 SASR 206. (An earlier provision in the statute stated that the court *may* do certain things; a later provision stated that the court *must* do certain things.)

3. **Should means 'must'**
   - A statutory provision that a manor '*should* have power and authority' to decide disputes imposed an *obligation* to decide disputes: *R v Havering Atte Bower* (1822) 5 B and Ad 691; 106 ER 1343.
   - A statutory provision that an order for child support *should* recognise certain matters meant that the order *must* recognise those matters: *Re Morrison-Pelletier* (1993) 108 DLR (4th) 358 (O'Brien J); (1997) 143 DLR (4th) 766 (Ont CA).

However, these last two cases are the exception, not the rule. In most contexts, *should* does not impose an obligation. Nevertheless, these variant meanings provide good reason to shun *should* in legal writing. Instead, for obligation prefer *must*, and for discretion prefer *may*.

Be consistent

Having chosen a word to impose obligation, use it consistently. To mix *must* and other words of obligation (such as *is to*) in the one document is liable to create uncertainty, given the presumption that a change in terminology heralds a possible change in meaning. (See **CONSISTENCY OF TERMINOLOGY**.) Even statutory drafters sometimes overlook this:

> **135D Requirements for application**
>
> (1) An application for a boundary determination …:
>
> (a) *is to* be made in a form approved …, and
>
> (b) *is to* be accompanied by such information …, and
>
> (c) *is to* be accompanied by the prescribed application fee.
>
> (2) The Registrar-General *must* refuse to make the determination unless satisfied …
>
> (3) The Registrar-General *is to* give notice to an applicant …
>
> (*Real Property Act 1900* (NSW), s 135D)
>
> Is there an intended difference between *is to* and *must*? Presumably not, but the inconsistency is ungainly and invites argument.

Negatives—*shall not / must not / may not*

Terminology

If lawyers prefer *must* over *shall* for obligation, then logically they should prefer the parallel *must not* over *shall not* for prohibition. So, 'The tenant *shall not* damage the premises' becomes 'The tenant *must not* damage the premises.'

In fact, some statutory drafters have been using *must not* for decades:

- *Norfolk and Suffolk Broads Act 1988*, s 13(9): 'the period specified … *must not* be less than twenty-eight days' (although the same section also uses 'shall not').
- *Proceeds of Crime Act 2002* (NI), s 160A: the court '*must not* exercise the power' without giving the parties the opportunity to be heard (discussed in *R v McLaughlin* [2018] NICA 5, [62]).
- *Animal Welfare Act 1993* (Tas), ss 7, 8: a person *must* not cause pain or suffering to an animal: *Mitchell v Marshall* [2014] TASSC 43; (2014) Tas R 1. (The court held that *must not* indicated so strong a prohibition that an offender could be prosecuted for breach even in the absence of a 'guilty mind'—ie, the wording created an offence of strict liability, at [36].)

However, other legal writers seem to shrink from the directness of *must not*. They prefer *may not*. For example:

- 'The tenant *may not* damage the premises.'
- 'A circus operator *may not* use a wild animal in a travelling circus in England': *Wild Animals in Circuses Act 2019*, s 1(1).

Examples like these should create no uncertainty. The meaning is clear enough—the person *must not* do it. (See further discussion under keyword **may not**.) Logically, however, where a document uses *must* to impose obligation, it is hard to argue against the parallel *must not* for prohibition—despite an Australian judge's description of *must not* as 'grotesque': *Halwood Corporation Ltd v Roads Corporation* [1998] 2 VR 439, 445–46 (Tadgell JA).

Consequences of breach?

Must not shares a common issue with *shall not*: what are the consequences of disobeying the direction? For example, assume that legislation stipulates that a body *must not* (or *shall not*) take specified action without giving prior notice to affected parties. If the body takes the action without giving prior notice, is the action invalid? The answer is simply (and not always helpfully) that it is a question of interpretation whether the legislation intends the action to be invalid in the circumstances: *Montreal Street Railway Company v Normandin* [1917] AC 170, 175; *Victoria v The Commonwealth and Connor* (1975) 134 CLR 81, 161–62, 178–79; *2 Elizabeth Bay Road Pty Ltd v The Owners—Strata Plan No 73943* [2014] NSWCA 409; (2014) 88 NSWLR 488, [34]–[35] (Barrett JA).

shall denoting simple future tense in correspondence

In correspondence it remains appropriate to retain *shall* with the first person to denote the simple future tense (or *will* with the second and third persons). For example:

- 'I/We *shall* terminate the contract tomorrow.' (Sometimes also: 'I/We *will* terminate the contract tomorrow.')
- 'The vendor *will* terminate the contract tomorrow.'

Further reading

On *shall* generally

- *Australian Law Journal*: Correspondence (1989) 63 ALJ 75–78, 522–25, 726–28; (1990) 64 ALJ 168–69
- Jeffrey Barnes, 'Duties and Discretions: How have "Plain English" legislative drafting techniques fared in Administrative Law?' (2016) 83 *Australian Institute of Administrative Law Forum* 36
- Peter Butt, *Modern Legal Drafting*, 3rd edn (Cambridge University Press, 2013) 262–27
- Giuliana Garzonem 'Variation in the Use of Modality in Legislative Texts: Focus on *Shall*' (2013) 57 *Journal of Pragmatics* 68 (tracing the declining use of *shall* in UK legislation)
- New Zealand Law Commission, *Legislation Manual* (Wellington, 1996) [171]–[173]
- Dennis C Pearce and Robert S Geddes, *Statutory Interpretation in Australia*, 9th edn (LexisNexis, 2019) ch 11 ('Obligatory and Discretionary Provisions')
- *Stroud's Judicial Dictionary* (Sweet & Maxwell, 5th edn, 1986) 2403–11; (6th edn, 2000), 2428–30; (9th edn, 2017) title 'shall'
- A Watson-Brown, 'Shall Revisited' (1995) 25 *Queensland Law Society Journal* (June) 263
- A Watson-Brown, 'Do We Still Need "Shall"?' [1998] *Hong Kong Law Journal* 29

On abolishing *shall* completely

- Michèle Asprey, *Plain Language for Lawyers*, 4th edn (Federation Press, 2010) 205–18
- Bryan A Garner, *Dictionary of Legal Usage*, 3rd edn (Oxford University Press, 2011) 952–54
- Joseph Kimble, *Lifting the Fog of Legalese* (Carolina Academic Press, 2006) 159–60
- Office of Parliamentary Counsel, *Drafting Guidance* (2020) [1.2.9]

On retaining *shall* for actions that carry consequences for breach

- Kenneth A Adams, *A Manual of Style for Contract Drafting*, 4th edn (American Bar Association, 2017) [3.87]–[3.103]
- Kenneth A Adams, 'Banishing *Shall* from Business Contracts: Throwing the Baby Out with the Bathwater' (2014) 24(3) *Australian Corporate Lawyer* 12
- Robert C Dick, *Legal Drafting in Plain Language*, 3rd edn (Carswell, 1995) 93
- Reed Dickerson, *Fundamentals of Legal Drafting*, 2nd edn (Little, Brown & Co, 1986) 214
- Editorial, 'In Honour of the Moribund *Shall*' (2014) 35(2) *Statute Law Review* v–vi
- RW Ramage, 'Will or Shall?' (1970) 120 *New Law Journal* 402
- Stanley Robinson, *Drafting* (Butterworths, 1973) 40

See also **can**; **duty**; **has a duty to**; **may**; **may not**.

shall be lawful for

Usually means simply *may* or *can*: eg, 'It *shall be lawful for* the tenant to open during business hours' means 'The tenant *may* [or *can*] open during business hours.' Where that is the intended meaning, prefer *may* or *can*—a simpler formulation trumps a complex one.

However, sometimes the sense is not so much discretion (*may*) or ability (*can*) as *legal entitlement*. In that case (and avoiding the archaic *shall*), prefer *has the right to*—or even stronger, *has the legal right to*. Thus, 'It *shall be lawful for* ambulance drivers to ignore traffic lights in an emergency' becomes 'Ambulance drivers *have the* [*legal*] *right* to ignore traffic lights in an emergency.'

See also **can**; **may**; **shall / must.**

shall be the duty of …

A lawyer's verbose substitute for *must*. For example: 'It *shall be the duty of* the employee to report all thefts' means simply 'The employee *must* report all thefts.' Always prefer the simpler wording.

See also **has a duty to**; **shall / must**.

shall not

See **shall / must**.

sham

In ordinary English, a sham is a pretence. This usage is reflected in law also, although in law *sham* often means, more narrowly, a transaction that parties deliberately cast in a particular form to obscure its true legal effect. That is, the transaction professes to be one thing but is in fact something different: *WT Ramsay v Inland Revenue Commissioners* [1982] AC 300, 323 (Lord Wilberforce); *Equuscorp Pty Ltd v Glengallum Investments Pty Ltd* (2004) 218 CLR 471, [46].

The classic example is a lease drafted in the form of a licence. The purpose is to deny the 'licensee' the right to exclusive possession, without which an occupant lacks many of the rights that belong to tenants: *Radaich v Smith* (1959) 101 CLR 209; *Street v Mountford*

[1985] AC 809; *Bruton v London & Quadrant Housing* [2000] 1 AC 406. Courts commonly disregard 'smoke-screens' of this kind: *Hadjiloucas v Crean* [1987] 3 All ER 1008, 1014 (Purchas LJ).

Further reading

Kevin Gray and Susan Francis Gray, *Elements of Land Law*, 5th edn (Oxford University Press, 2009) [4.1.111]–[4.1.114]

share and share alike

An archaic expression for 'in equal shares'. A gift 'to A and B *share and share alike*' is a gift 'to A and B in equal shares'. There is no benefit in preserving *share and share alike*. Prefer 'in equal shares'.

See also **several**.

shifting interest / springing interest

These terms (*shifting interest*, *springing interest*), though colourful, express concepts that are dry and technical. A *shifting interest* is that one moves (shifts) from one person to another if a stipulated event occurs—as where land is conveyed to A on terms that ownership is to move (shift) from A to B if B marries. In contrast, a *springing interest* is one that arises (springs up) for the first time if a stipulated event occurs—as where ownership springs up in A 'if A should marry'. Both kinds of interest developed under the *Statute of Uses 1535*, initially as 'shifting uses' and 'springing uses'. In modern law, the context in which *shifting interest* and *springing interest* appear usually makes their meanings self-evident.

Further reading

AWB Simpson, *A History of the Land Law*, 2nd edn (Oxford University Press, 1986) 196–98

SHORT DASH

See **DASHES**.

SHORT NAMES

See **NAMES (of parties)**.

SHORT TITLE

The 'authorised' short version of the title of a statute (or regulation, or bylaw)—'authorised' because it is sanctioned by the statute (or regulation, or bylaw) itself. Initially, the *Short Titles Act* 1896 bestowed short titles on certain specified Acts. Now, each Act supplies its own short title, by which the Act is then known: 'This Act *may be cited as* the [short title].' In some other jurisdictions (eg, various Australian jurisdictions), the statute states more plainly: 'This Act *is* the [short title]'.

shortly after

See **after (a date)**.

shortly after (a date)

See **after (a date)**.

should

See **shall / must**.

shut-eye knowledge

Knowledge imputed to a person who suspects that certain facts exist but chooses not to look. The expression is less common than its counterpart, *blind-eye knowledge*, but is sometimes used: see, eg, *Swain v Natui Ram Puri* [1996] PIQR 442, 448; *Milne v Express Newspapers* [2003] 1 WLR 927, 935.

See also **Nelsonian knowledge**; **blind-eye knowledge**.

sic

Latin: thus, so; abbreviation for *sic erat scriptum*, thus it was written. It is added (in brackets) after a word or phrase in a quoted passage to indicate that the quotation is accurate even though it may appear incorrect or absurd—ie, that the error or absurdity is in the original. Given that quotations should always faithfully reproduce the original, *sic* should be superfluous; but the insertion helps to reassure attentive readers.

Brackets enclosing *sic* may be round or square; but convention favours square, because square also conventionally indicates inserted material. For example:

- '"So it is not enough for a worker merely to establish that they are [sic] a member of the relevant group".' [*Home Office (UK Border Agency) v Shafic Essop* [2015] EWCA Civ 609, [47] (Sir Colin Rimer, quoting from a Code of Practice—but perhaps (with respect) missing the point that the drafter consciously used the plural for gender-neutrality)]
- '"I will have to make a decision as to whether to waiver [sic] my privilege and right to silence".' [*Commissioner of Australian Federal Police v Zhao* (2015) 255 CLR 46; [2015] HCA 5, [9] (High Court of Australia, quoting from a litigant's affidavit)]
- '[Counsel's] submission appears to have been that matters to which objection were taken would "breach the parole (sic) evidence rule being a pre-contractual negotiation".' [*Hardinge v Schidor* [2002] NSWCA 277, [11] (Powell JA, using round brackets, noting the departure from the normal spelling, *parol*)]

See also **BRACKETS**.

sic utere tuo ut alienum non laedas

Latin: use your property so as not to interfere with another's. A long-established Latin maxim, expressing a basic principle of the law of nuisance. Despite its pedigree, it is eminently translatable into standard English without loss of legal nuance, as in the first quotation below. If for some reason you feel you must retain the Latin, then provide a translation (as suggested in the second quotation).

- '[T]he true legal justification for the right of support is the legal principle encapsulated in the Latin maxim *sic utere tuo ut alienum non laedas*, which translates in English to: use your own property in such a manner as not to injure that of another.' [*Xpress Print Pte Ltd v Monocrafts Pte Ltd* [2000] 2 SLR(R) 614, 633 [48] (Yong Pung How CJ, providing a translation)]

- 'The law of nuisance is concerned with balancing the conflicting interests of adjoining owners. It is often said to be encapsulated in the Latin maxim *sic utere tuo ut alienum non laedas* [suggest add: *that is, use your property so as not to interfere with another's*].' [*Southwark London Borough Council v Tanner* [2001] 1 AC 1, 20 (Lord Millett)]

side deal

Commercial shorthand for a collateral contract—ie, a contract made 'alongside' the main contract. A 'side deal' or 'side agreement' of this kind is not enforceable unless consistent with the main contract, because the main contract is the key expression of the parties' agreement: *Maybury v Atlantic Union Oil Co Ltd* (1953) 89 CLR 507, 517 (Dixon CJ). But where it is consistent with the main contract, and where the evidence shows that the parties did not intend the main contract to exhaustively cover their agreement, then the side agreement can stand: *Hoyt's Pty Ltd v Spencer* (1919) 27 CLR 133; *B & R Stevens Transport Pty Ltd v Burkitt* [2016] NSWCA 259.

See also **collateral contract**.

SIDE NOTES

See **MARGINAL NOTES**.

sign / signature

To *sign* is to authenticate one's agreement to a document by adding a signature or identifying mark. The precise requirements for a valid signature may depend on the context. For example:

- allowing one's name to be added in typed capitals at the end of a document, but without some further marking to confirm authentication, is probably not a signature: *Goodman v J Eban Ltd* [1954] 1 QB 550, 555, 561; *Firstpost Homes Ltd v Johnson* [1995] 1 WLR 1567, 1577
- writing one's name in capital letters may be signature: *Payne v Payne* [2018] EWCA Civ 985; [2018] 1 WLR 3761 (witness to a will).

The law of 'signing' has had to take account of modern communication practices: for example, typing one's name at the end of an email may suffice as a signature: *J Pereira Fernandes SA v Metha* [2006] EWHC 813, [26]–[28]. Legislation governing electronic transactions now commonly allows for 'digital signatures'.

Further reading

Brian Sloan, 'Testing Times for Attestation' (2019) 83 *Conveyancer and Property Lawyer* 182 (discussing *Payne v Payne*, above)

See also **execute**.

SIGNAL WORDS

See **CITATION SYMBOLS**.

signed, sealed and delivered

A formulaic trilogy associated with the execution of deeds. Usually, with one comma only: 'signed, sealed and delivered'. Ideally, though, with the serial (Oxford) comma—'signed, sealed, and delivered'—because it contains three separate concepts.

signing and sealing

Historically, the first word in the trilogy (*signed*) was strictly unnecessary, because the common law required deeds to be *sealed*, a more practical requirement than signing in times before universal literacy. The sealing could be a formal wax seal, or a wafer (ie, an embossed gummed sticker), or an impression marked on the page—in fact, anything to indicate the party's consent. Case law in the 19th and 20th centuries relaxed the requirement of sealing somewhat by treating a document as 'sealed' if it contained an analogous indication of authenticity, such as a ribbon attached to the document (*Re Sandilands* (1871) LR 6 CP 411), or even a printed circle containing the letters 'LS' (ie, 'locus siggili'—the place for the seal): *First National Securities v Jones* [1978] Ch 109. Modern legislation now generally removes altogether the requirement for 'sealing' of deeds executed by individuals, substituting *signing* rather than sealing: eg, *Property Law (Miscellaneous Provisions) Act 1989*. Some jurisdictions take a midcourse: while not strictly dispensing with the need for sealing, their legislation states that a deed that is *signed* is deemed also to be *sealed*: eg, *Conveyancing Act 1919* (NSW), s 38(3).

For corporations, the requirement of sealing survived for longer, because corporations could contract only under their common seal. But that has changed also in many jurisdictions, where legislation allows individuals to sign to bind corporations without needing the formality of 'sealing' with the company's common seal.

delivery

In most jurisdictions *delivery* remains essential for a valid deed. Until 'delivery', a deed cannot become effective. *Delivery* requires some words or conduct showing that the party executing the deed regards it as 'presently binding': *Xenos v Wickham* (1867) LR 2 HL 296, 312 (Blackburn J). Whether a deed has been 'delivered' is a question of fact in all the circumstances of the case: *Xenos v Wickham* (1867) LR 2 HL 296, 309; *Scook v Premier Building Solutions Pty Ltd* (2003) 28 WAR 124, 133. Ultimately, 'delivery' is an act showing 'an intention to be bound' by the deed: *Vincent v Premo Enterprises (Voucher Sales) Ltd* [1969] 2 QB 609, 619 (Lord Denning MR). That act is often the physical handing over of the deed. However, it may be some other conduct, or words—eg, faxing a copy of the deed to a third party, even though the original document remains with the deed-maker (as in *Segboer v A J Richardson Properties Pty Ltd* [2012] NSWCA 253; (2012) 16 BPR 31,235).

Delivery must be the final formality, chronologically, in executing a deed: *Goddard's* case (1584) 2 Co Rep 4b, 5a; 76 ER 396, 399–400. A deed cannot be delivered until it has first been signed and sealed: *Lift Capital Partners Pty Ltd v Merrill Lynch International* [2009] NSWSC 7, [74]. If the signing and sealing occur *after* a purported delivery, the deed must be delivered again to become effective: *Tupper v Foulkes* (1861) 9 CB (NS) 797; 142 ER 314; *Powell v London and Provincial Bank* [1893] 2 Ch 555.

Delivery of a deed can be 'conditional'. A deed delivered conditionally is an *escrow*.

'Executed as a deed'

Executed as a deed is becoming a popular substitute for *signed, sealed and delivered.* It has the benefit of non-technical language (although *Executed* may seem quaint to those unaccustomed to legal terminology). Those who use *Executed* assume (probably correctly) that it carries the meaning of 'doing whatever is necessary to bring the deed into effect'—ie, signing, sealing (where necessary), and delivering.

Further reading

- Nicholas Seddon, *Seddon on Deeds* (Federation Press, 2015) chs 2 and 3
- 'Signed, Sealed and Delivered', in *Law Words* (Centre for Plain Legal Language, University of Sydney, 1995) 83; www.clarity-international.net/plain-language-resources/general-resources/ (suggesting 'signed [or made] by [name] as a deed and taking effect on [date]')

See also **COMMAS; DEED (document); escrow; execute (a document); in witness whereof (the parties have signed); sign / signature.**

SIGN-OFFS

See **CORRESPONDENCE (LETTERS AND EMAILS).**

signpost definition

A 'definition' that merely refers to the reader to the relevant part of the document where the full definition is contained: eg, '*registrable instrument*'—see clause 10' [clause 10 sets out the definition in full].

See **DEFINITIONS.**

silk

A person who has been appointed Queen's Counsel (QC), King's Counsel (KC), or senior counsel (SC). The term derives from the conventional entitlement to wear a silk gown (hence 'taking silk').

See also **junior counsel; Queen's Counsel; Senior Counsel.**

SIMILES

See **METAPHORS.**

simony

Sometimes capitalised, *Simony*, because named after Simon Magus (see Acts 8:18–19). Strictly, the buying or selling of holy orders or ecclesiastical benefices (a practice declared void by the *Simony Act* 1588); more broadly, trafficking in sacred things.

SIMPLER WORDS AND PHRASES

Use them

For clarity and readability, always prefer simpler words and phrases over more complex ones, and shorter words over longer words. Many lawyers ignore this advice, instinctively preferring complex, longer words and phrases. Perhaps they hope that readers will be impressed; but the opposite is true. Surveys show that readers are more impressed by writers who use shorter, simpler words than by writers who use longer, more complex words—indeed, readers regard writers who use long and complex words as comparatively unintelligent (see study by Oppenheimer, in *Further reading*, below). Worryingly for lawyers, surveys also show that readers (and clients) have less trust in lawyers who use complex language (see, eg, Neil James and Greg Moriarty, 'Access starts with the precedent: Evaluating the language of leases' (2020) 81 *Clarity Journal* 34). And surveys of judges show that judges are more impressed by lawyers who use plain words than by those who use long words and legalese (see too, *Further reading*, below).

Simpler substitutes

Some law firms encourage a simpler style by supplying lists of 'unsatisfactory' words and phrases, with suggested alternatives. The following is a list of that kind, compiled from many sources. It includes not only longer words and multi-word phrases, but also wordy prepositions and redundant pairings.

However, the list comes with important qualifications:

- Writing styles, and readers' tastes, vary.
- There is always a role for technical or specialist words (though few of the words and phrases in the list fit that role).
- 'Tone' is important. Readers should not feel patronised or 'talked down to'.
- Not every 'Try' suggestion will work in every situation. Context is always key. A blanket 'find and replace' may be problematic.

In general, however, writing is more compelling when it uses a shorter word in place of a longer one, a single word in place of a word string, and a concrete word in place of an abstract one.

An asterisk denotes that the term (or a variant) or its preferred alternative (or a variant), has a separate entry in this book.

Do not use	**Try**
ab initio*	from the beginning
abate [as in: *abate* a nuisance]*	reduce, lessen
abeyance [as in: *abeyance of* seisin]*	gap in [the title]
abeyance [as in: hold in *abeyance*]*	wait, postpone
above-mentioned	above*, mentioned above
above-stated	above*
absolute and unfettered discretion	discretion [better still: may*]
absolutely essential	essential
absolutely nothing	nothing
abut*	adjoin, touch
accede to	agree, allow
accompanied by	with
accorded, afforded	given
according to the law	legally
accrue	add, gain
acknowledge receipt of [as in: 'I acknowledge receipt of your letter']	thank you for [your letter]

(continued)

(Continued)

Do not use	**Try**
acquaint [yourself] with	find out about, read
acquiesce in	agree to
acquire	get
actual experience	experience
ad hoc*	for this case only, occasionally
add an additional	add
add the point that	add
additional	more
adequate enough	adequate, enough [but not both]
adequate number of	enough
adjacent to*	next to
admeasurement*	measurement
admit of	allow
admix*	mix
adumbrate*	list, outline, foreshadow
advance planning	planning
advantageous	helpful, useful
affix [your] signature to	sign
afford an opportunity	let, allow
afforded	given
aforementioned	[omit], above, already described, these
aforesaid*, said*	[omit], the, already described
aggregate	total
all and any*	all, any [but not both]
all and every*	all
all and singular*	each, every [but not both]
all of*	all
alleviate	ease, reduce
alter or change	alter, change [but not both]
ameliorate	improve, help
antecedent	previous
any and all*	any, all [but not both]
any and each	any
any one of the two	either
apparent*	clear, obvious; likely

(continued)

(Continued)

Do not use	**Try**
appears to be the case that	seems
appertaining to*	relating to, about
appreciate it if [as in 'I would appreciate it if you [did something]']	please [do something]
apprise	tell, inform
approximately*	about, roughly
arguendo*	in (the course of) argument
as a consequence of	because of
as of now	now
as of the date of	from [better still, specify the date]
as of this date	today
as prescribed by	under
as regards	about
as well as	and
as you may or may not know	as you may know
ascertain*	find out
ask a question	ask
assist	help
assist in the resolution of	help resolve
assistance	help
assuming that	if
at a later date	later
at an earlier date	earlier
at an early date	soon
at hand	here
at its discretion	can, may
at present / at the present time	now
at regular intervals	regularly
at that particular time	then
at that point in [of] time	then
at that time	then
at the conclusion of	after
at the moment	now
at the time / at the time when	when
at this point in [of] time	now
at this time	now

(continued)

(Continued)

Do not use	Try
at which time	when
attached hereto	attached
attains the age of [x] years	reaches [x] years
authorised and empowered	authorised
aware of the fact that	know
be grateful if [as in 'I would be grateful if you …']	please [do something]
beforementioned	above, mentioned earlier
belated	late
beyond a shadow of a doubt	doubtless
biannual*	twice a year, every six months
biennial*	two-yearly, each two years
binding upon	binds
bona fide*	in good faith
by and under	by, under [but not both]
by and with	by, with [but not both]
by means of	by, with, using
by reason of*	because of
by the use of	by
by virtue of	by, under
by way of illustration	for example, eg
carte blanche	unconditional authority
cause [something] to be done*	have [something] done, do it
cease	stop
cease and desist*	stop
cestui que trust*	beneficiary
chattels*	goods*
circa [abbreviation = c]*	about
circle around	circle
circumvent	get around, skirt, avoid
close proximity*	close
cognisant	aware
cognisant of	know, aware of
collateral*	security [for a loan]
combine together	combine
come to an agreement	agree

(continued)

(Continued)

Do not use	Try
come to an end	end
commence*	start, begin
commingle	mingle
communicate	talk, write, email, fax [be specific]
complete [verb]	finish
completely destroy	destroy
comprises*	is made up of, consists of, includes
compulsory [as in 'it is compulsory']	you must
concur	agree
condition*	requirement, condition [unless condition is meant to suggest essentiality—in which case, take care]
confidential nature	confidential
conflagration	fire
connect together	connect
consensus ad idem*	agreement
consequently	so
construe*	interpret*
contiguous to*	next to
correspondence	letter, email, fax [be specific]
costs the sum of	costs
costs the amount of	costs
covenant [noun]*	legally binding promise
covenant [verb]*	agree
covenant and agree*	agree
currently	now
custom and usage	custom, usage [but not both]
de facto*	in reality, existing (but unofficial)
de minimis	miniscule, minor
deem*	is, considered to be, taken as
deleterious	harmful
delineate	mark out, describe accurately
demise [noun]*	lease*, death
demise [verb]*	lease*
despite the fact that	although
determine*	decide, end

(continued)

(Continued)

Do not use	Try
disclose	show, tell
discrete [adjective]	separate
divers [archaic adjective]	different, several, many
does not operate to	does not
due to the fact that*	because
duly*	properly [or omit]
duly incorporated	incorporated
duly signed	signed
duly witnessed	witnessed
during such time as	while
during the course of	during
during which time / during the time which / during the time that	while
each and all	each, all [but not both]
each and every*	each, every [but not both]
earlier in time*	earlier
effected	done
effectuate	carry out, do
elucidate	make clear, explain, expand on
enclosed [as in 'please find enclosed']	I/we enclose
enclosed herewith	enclosed
endeavour [verb]	try
enter into a contract with	contract with
entitled [as in 'is entitled']	named, called
entitled to [as in 'is entitled to']	can*
equitable	fair [unless used in the technical sense of an 'equitable' principle; or unless used in the context of 'inequitable' conduct, where 'unfair' is not a synonym for 'inequitable']
equivalent to; the equivalent of	equals
erroneous	wrong
estate or interest*	interest
et al*	and others
et alia	and other things
et alios	and other people
et seq	and following
evaluate	test, check

(continued)

(Continued)

Do not use	Try
evident	clear
evince [eg, evince an intention to be bound]	make evident, show
ex officio*	because of [his or her] office
ex post facto*	after the event
execute [a document]*	sign
exhibit a tendency to	tend to
expedite	speed up, hurry up
expeditiously	quickly, as quickly as possible [but always better to state a time limit]
expended	spent
expenditure of a capital nature	capital expenditure
expiration*	end
extant	current, in force
facilitate	help, ease, make easier
facsimile*	fax
failed to*	did not [unless wanting to allocate blame, in which case 'failed to' is better]
falls within the responsibility of [X]	[X] is responsible for
few in number	few
filled to capacity	filled
final and conclusive*	final, conclusive [but not both]
fixtures and fittings*	fixtures
for a period of	for
for the avoidance of doubt	to avoid doubt, to clarify
for and on behalf of	for, on behalf of [but not both]
for the duration of	while, during
for the purpose of*	for, to
for the reason that*	because
force and effect	effect
foregoing [adjective]*	preceding [or simply: the, that, those]
forgo [verb]*	give up, do without
forthwith*	immediately, promptly, as soon as possible [better to name a time limit]
forward	send
free and clear*	free
free and uninterrupted*	unhindered

(continued)

(Continued)

Do not use	Try
from the point of view of [X]	for [X], in [X's] opinion
full and complete	full, complete [but not both]
full force and effect (in)*	in effect, in force [but not both]
furnish*	give, send
furthermore	also
gainful employment	paid work
give an indication of	indicate, show
give consideration to	consider, think about
give recognition to	recognise
give, devise[,] and bequeath*	give
going forward	[omit]
good and effectual	good, effective [but not both]
goods and chattels*	goods
grateful for [as in 'I am grateful for your letter']	thank you for [your letter]
has no bearing (on)	is irrelevant (to)
have a responsibility to	must
have an obligation to	must
have and hold	have, hold [but not both]
have the right to	may
have regard to*	consider ['have regard to the evidence in this case'], give
henceforth / henceforward	from now on
hereafter*	after, afterwards
hereby*	[omit]
herein*	in this [agreement, deed, clause, etc]
hereinafter*	below [in this agreement, deed, clause, etc]
hereinbefore*	before, above [in this agreement, deed, clause, etc]
hereof	of this [agreement, deed, clause, etc]
hereon	on this [date]
hereto	to this [agreement, deed clause, etc]
heretofore*	until now, before [in this agreement, deed clause, etc]
hereunder*	under, below, under this [agreement, deed clause, etc]
hereunto	[omit]
herewith*	with this [letter, etc] [or omit]

(continued)

(Continued)

Do not use	**Try**
hitherto	until now
hold and enjoy	hold, enjoy [but not both]
howsoever*	in whatever way
id est	ie
if and when*	if, when [but not both]
if that were the case	if so
impacted upon	affected
implement	do, carry out, put into effect
in a position to [do something]	may, is able to
in accordance with*	by, under, because of
in addition to*	also, besides
in all likelihood	probably
in an effort to	to
in as much as, inasmuch as	because, since
in association with	with
in case of*	if
in circumstances where	where
in close proximity to	close to, near
in conjunction with	with
in connection with*	about, with, for
in consideration of the fact that	because
in excess of	more than, over
in extenso	in full, at length
in favour of	for
in lieu of*	instead of, in place of
in light of the fact that	because
in many cases	often
in order for*	for
in order that	so that
in order to*	to
in receipt of [as in 'we are in receipt of your letter']	have received
in relation to*	about, regarding, concerning, with
in respect of*	about, for
in so far as*	to the extent that
in some instances	sometimes

(continued)

(Continued)

Do not use	Try
in the absence of	without
in the amount of [$X]	of [$X], for [$X]
in case of*	in, for, by, if
in the course of	while, during
in the event of / in the event that*	if
in the first place	first
in the interest of	for
in the majority of cases / instances	mostly, usually
in the nature of	like
in the neighbourhood of	about
in the near future	soon
in the preceding section	in section [x]
in the process of*	during, while
in the proximity of	near, nearby, about
in the second place	second [in preference to secondly]
in the State of	in [name of State]
in the third place	third [in preference to thirdly]
in the vicinity of	near, around
in toto*	completely, as a whole
in view of	because
in view of the fact that	because, given that
including but not limited to*	including
inclusive [eg, 'ss 25–30 inclusive']*	[omit: ie, 'ss 25–30']
incumbent upon	must [it is incumbent upon you to pay rent = you must pay rent]
indict	charge with offence
inequitable	unfair
inform	tell
infra*	below
initiate [verb]	start, begin
is in accord with	agrees with
insomuch as	to the extent that
instanter*	instantly
institute [verb]	start, begin
instrument*	document
inter alia*	among other things

(continued)

(Continued)

Do not use	**Try**
interrogate	question, ask
ipso facto*	by the fact itself, therefore
irrespective of	even if, despite
is able to	can, may
is applicable to	applies to
is authorised to	can, may
is binding upon	binds
is deficient in	lacks
is dependent on	depends on
is empowered to	can, may
is entitled [name]	is called
is entitled to*	can, may
is of the opinion of	thinks, considers, believes
is of the view that	thinks, considers
is unable to	cannot
issue	child, children
it is anticipated that this [will help]	this should [help]
it is appropriate that [you do something]	you should [do something]
it is open to [do something]*	can [do something]
it is the duty of [X]*	[X] must
it shall be lawful to*	may
it would appear that	it appears that
jeopardise	risk, threaten
jointly and severally*	together and separately
keep and maintain	keep, maintain [but not both]
know all men by these presents	[omit]
known and described as	known as, described as [but not both]
last of all	last
last will and testament*	will
lessee*	tenant
lessor *	landlord
liable to*	must
made and entered into	made
magnitude	size
majority of / vast majority of	most / nearly all

(continued)

(Continued)

Do not use	Try
make a determination	determine
make a recommendation	recommend
make a valuation	value
make an application	apply
make an investigation	investigate
make payment	pay
mandate	compel, require
mandatory [as in 'it is mandatory that you …']	compulsory, you must
manner	way
manner in which	how
marginal	small, slight
master and servant*	employer and employee
material*	relevant
materialise	occur, happen
may at all times	may*
may at any time	may*
may in its discretion*	may*
means and includes*	means, includes [but not both]
mens rea*	state of mind
Messrs A and B	Mr A and Mr B
mingle together	mingle
money / monies*	money
moreover	and, also, as well
mortgagee*	lender [unless it is crucial to specify the legal nature of the transaction as a mortgage]
mortgagor*	borrower [unless it is crucial to specify the legal nature of the transaction as a mortgage]
mutatis mutandis*	varied as the circumstances require, with the necessary changes
mutual co-operation	co-operation
necessary requisite	requirement
necessitate	require, demand
new innovation	innovation
non compos mentis*	of unsound mind, mentally incompetent [to enter into an agreement]
non constat*	it does not follow [that]

(continued)

(Continued)

Do not use	**Try**
no later than*	by
not required to*	need not
notify*	tell [except in formal sense of giving notice]
notwithstanding*	although
notwithstanding the fact that	even if, even though, despite
now the parties agree and acknowledge	the parties agree
now this deed witnesseth*	[omit]
null and void*	void, of no legal effect
[a] number of	some, many (or the precise number)
numerous	many [better still, say how many]
obligated to [as in 'you are obligated to']*	must
obliged to [as in 'you are obliged to']	must
occasioned by	caused by
of the one / other part	[nothing is needed, unless you really need to distinguish one party from another]
on a daily / weekly / monthly / quarterly basis	daily / weekly / monthly / quarterly
on behalf of*	for
on each occasion	every time
on numerous occasions	often
on request [as in 'we will send it to you on request']	if you ask
on the grounds of / on the ground that*	because
on the part of*	by, among
on two different occasions	twice
only difference being that	except that
opine*	give an opinion, consider
optimum	best, ideal
order and direct [verbs]	order, direct [but not both]
otherwise (than)*	except (for)
over and above	over, above [but not both]
owing to the fact that*	because
paradigm	model, example, pattern, fundamental [paradigm shift]
pari passu*	equally, in equal amounts
part and parcel	part
partially	partly

(continued)

(Continued)

Do not use	Try
particulars	details
Party of the first part (second part, etc)	[use Party's name]
passim*	throughout, from place to place
past history	history
peer	equal, person of the same standing
penultimate	next to last, second last
per*	each, a [eg, per year], by, through
per annum	yearly, a year
per diem*	daily
per incuriam*	by mistake
per se	in itself
perform and discharge*	do, carry out
period of several days / weeks / months / years	several days / weeks / months / years
period (of time)*	period, time [but not both]
persons [eg, 'corporations are legal persons']*	people, legal entities
pertaining to	about
peruse*	[in strict usage] read closely; [in common usage] scan, skim-read
please be advised that	[omit]
possess	have
post hoc	after this
postpone until later	postpone
précis	summary
predominant	main
premises* [in the sense of 'material already referred to']	[omit]
prescribe*	fix, set [unless used in the precise legal sense of something imposed by regulation, in which case retain 'prescribe']
preserve	keep
prima facie case	a case to answer
prima facie*	at face value, at first appearance
principal*	main [helps distinguish from 'principle']
prior to*	before
pro bono*	free, without charge [literally, 'for the public good']
pro rata*	in proportion to, proportionately

(continued)

(Continued)

Do not use	Try
pro tempore [abbreviation, pro tem]*	for the time being, temporarily
proceed to [verb]	[use verb by itself]
procure*	get, obtain, arrange
prolong [verb]	delay, drag out
prolonged [adjective]	long
promptly*	quickly, at once [better still, specify when]
provide	give
provide guidance for	guide
provided that*	but, if, however
provision [of law]	law
proximity [*see also* 'in the proximity of']	closeness
purchase / purchaser*	buy / buyer
purports to (rely)*	relies
pursuant to*	under, because of, in line with
quantum	amount
question whether*	whether
question at issue	question, issue [but not both]
quinquennial	5-yearly, every 5 years
quondam	former
read and construed as	read as, interpreted as
recur again	recur
referred to as	called
regardless of the fact that	although
relating to*	about
remainder*	the rest, what is remaining [unless it is crucial to specify the precise legal nature of the interest of a person who holds a 'remainder' interest in property]
remunerate	pay
render [in the sense of 'cause to be']	make
render [in the sense of 'give']	give
request	ask
require [in the sense of 'need to do']*	need
rest, residue[,] and remainder*	rest, all other property
retain	keep
revert back	revert

(continued)

(Continued)

Do not use	Try
right and liberty [to do something]*	right [to do something]
right, title[,] and interest*	[use any one of the three], interest
said / the said*	the, that, those
same / the same [as substitute for 'it', 'she', 'he']*	it, she, he [or repeat the person's name]
save and except*	except
seldom if ever	seldom, rarely
separate and apart	apart
separate and distinct	separate, distinct [but not both]
seriatim*	one after another, in series
shall*	must
shall be lawful to [do something]*	can, may, is entitled to [do something]
share and share alike	in equal shares
signed, sealed[,] and delivered*	executed as a deed
situate at [address]*	at [address]
sole and exclusive*	sole, exclusive [but not both]
subject to*	under, depending on
submit	send, give
subsequent to*	after
subsequently	later
such*	the, that, those [or use another pronoun]
suffer*	allow
suffer and [or] permit*	allow, permit [but not both]
sufficient	enough
sufficient number of	enough
sui juris*	of full legal capacity
supra*	above
surround on all sides	surround
surrounding circumstances	circumstances
take into consideration	consider
take(s) the position that	argue(s)
terminate*	end, finish [unless need to distinguish between 'terminate' and 'rescind']
terms and conditions*	terms [unless need to draw legal distinction between a term and a condition]
that being the case	if so, and so

(continued)

(Continued)

Do not use	**Try**
that is to say*	that is
the manner in which	how
there is no doubt but that	doubtless, no doubt
thereafter*	after, afterwards,
thereat	at that place, on that account
thereby*	by that means, by the [document, agreement, deed, etc]
therefor*	for that purpose
therefore*	so
therefrom	from [she left therefrom], after [six weeks therefrom]
therein	in that place, in [the document, agreement, deed, etc], in that matter
thereinafter*	in it [the document] specified later
thereinbefore*	in it [the document] specified earlier
thereof*	of it
thereon	on it, on [that land, that place, etc]
thereto*	to it [or omit]
thereunder	under it, under [the document, agreement, deed, etc]
thereupon	immediately after
therewith	with it
these presents*	this deed, this agreement
to the effect that	so [that]
to wit*	namely
transmit*	send
true and correct	true, correct [but not both]
true copy*	copy
true fact	fact
truly believe	believe
type and kind	type, kind [but not both]
ultra vires*	outside (or beyond) the (legal) authority of
under the provision(s) of	under
undernoted	stated below, the following
undersigned [the]	I, we, the person signing
undertake and agree	undertake, agree [but not both]

(continued)

(Continued)

Do not use	Try
unilateral	one-sided
unless and until*	unless, until [but not both, unless deliberately intended]
unoccupied	empty
until such time as*	until
upon*	on
utilisation	use
utilise*	use
vacillate	waver
vary or modify*	vary, modify [but not both]
vendor	seller
veracious	true
verbatim*	word for word
verily believe	believe
vide*	see
vis-a-vis	about, concerning,
viz*	namely
ways and means	ways, means [but not both]
well and truly*	very, completely
whatsoever*	whatever, what [or omit]
whensoever	when, whenever
whereas*	but, while
whereby*	under which, by which
wherein	in which
whereof	of that
whereon	on which
wheresoever	wherever
whereupon	at, after, then, when
whether or not*	whether
whilst*	while
whosoever	whoever
with a view to*	to
with certain knowledge that	knowing
with effect from	from
with immediate effect	immediately, straight away
with reference to*	about, for

(continued)

(Continued)

Do not use	Try
with regard to	about, regarding, for
with respect to*	about, for
with the exception of	except, except for
with the object of	to
with the result that	so that
within named	[omit]
within the realm of possibility	possibly, possible
without prejudice*	not to be used as evidence in court
without prejudice to*	without affecting
witnesseth	witness, attests [to]

Further reading

- *Bad Language: The Use and Abuse of Official Language*, HC 17 (First Report of House of Commons Public Administration Select Committee, Nov 2009)
- RW Benson and JB Kessler, 'Legalese v Plain English: An Empirical Study of Persuasion and Credibility in Appellate Brief Writing' (1987) 20 *Loyola of Los Angeles Law Review* 301, 312
- Martin Cutts, *Plain English Lexicon: A Guide to Whether Your Words Will Be Understood* (Plain Language Commission, 2008)
- JD Fischer, 'Why George Orwell's Ideas About Language Still Matter for Lawyers' (2007) 68 *Montana Law Review* 129
- K O'Brien, 'Judicial Attitudes to Plain Language and the Law' (2009) 32 *Australian Bar Review* 204
- DM Oppenheimer, 'Consequences of Erudite Vernacular Utilized Irrespective of Necessity: Problems with Using Long Words Needlessly' (2006) 20 *Applied Cognitive Psychology* 139 (discussing intelligence ratings that readers give to writers who use complex styles and high-level vocabularies); see at www.psych.utoronto.ca/users/psy3001/files/simple%20writing.pdf
- Irving Younger, 'In Praise of Simplicity' [1984] *New Zealand Law Journal* 277

See also **'be' verbs**; **BREVITY**; **PROLIXITY**; **SESQUIPEDALIANISM**; **WORD PAIRINGS**.

simpliciter

Latin: absolutely; without limitation; simply (in the sense of 'alone' or 'with nothing else'). Ideally, replace this Latinism with an appropriate English translation. However, some lawyers and judges find this exhortation difficult. For example, in *Independent Assessor v O'Brien* [2004] EWCA Civ 1035 Auld LJ used *simpliciter* 13 times (though, to be fair, sometimes in quotations from other judges.) Other judicial examples include:

- 'Lord Phillips MR's emphasis ... was not so much upon the presence or absence of control *simpliciter* [prefer: *alone*; *by itself*], but on the importance of the question whether in these cases the institution had itself undertaken the care of the claimant.' [*Woodland v Swimming Teachers Association* [2012] EWCA Civ 239, [29] (Laws LJ)]

- 'Statutory developments … created new offences relating to reckless, dangerous and negligent driving *simpliciter* [prefer: *as stand-alone offences*] and culpable, reckless or dangerous driving causing death.' [*King v R* [2012] HCA 24; (2012) 245 CLR 588, [30] (French CJ, Crennan and Kiefel JJ)]

SIMPLIFIED OUTLINES

The concept

A *simplified outline* gives the reader a snapshot of what is to follow in a piece of writing. Unlike an *introduction* (which merely sets the scene), or an *executive summary* (which crystallises the main arguments and conclusion), a *simplified outline* seeks merely to give an overview—an easy lead-in to what may be a complex document or statute.

In legislation

Legislative drafters in some jurisdictions have been using simplified outlines for years. Often the outline is of the whole Act, but it may be of a Part or Division only, or of a section only. The simplified outline is usually part of the text of the Act, not a mere ancillary comment. Courts have found them useful in discerning meaning from the provisions they sketch: see, eg, *Allan v Transurban City Link Ltd* [2001] HCA 58, [22]; (2001) 208 CLR 167, 175–76; *Hudson v Minister for Immigration and Citizenship* (2010) 188 FCR 393, [88]; *Gheko Holdings Pty Ltd v Chief Executive Medicare* [2013] FCA 164, [30].

Example (Australian statute)

3 Simplified outline

The following is a simplified outline of this Act:

- This Act sets out the entitlements of holders of a Life Gold Pass.
- The basic rules are as follows:
  - (a) a former Prime Minister is entitled to a maximum of 40 domestic return trips per year;
  - (b) other pass holders are entitled to a maximum of 25 domestic return trips per year.
- This Act also deals with travel by:
  - (a) spouses of pass holders; and
  - (b) the widows and widowers of deceased pass holders; and
  - (c) the spouses of sitting members who have satisfied the qualifying period for the issue of a Life Gold Pass.
- If a superannuation order is made under the Crimes (Superannuation Benefits) Act 1989 in relation to a person convicted of a corruption offence, the person is disqualified from Life Gold Pass travel and severance travel.

[Source: *Members of Parliament (Life Gold Pass) Act* 2002 (Cth), s 3 (repealed).]

The outline gives the reader a bird's-eye view of the document, introducing in summary form the main points and key concepts. And by 'boxing' the outline (as in the statute itself), the drafter clearly distinguishes the outline from the substantive provisions.

In the past, legislative drafters sometimes used the *concept* of a simplified outline without calling it such. The following is an example from 1943: the Departmental

Explanatory Note at the end fulfills the same purpose as a simplified outline, though taking the more conventional form of an explanatory note.

Example (Statutory Order)

> 'The Control of Tins Cans Kegs Drums and Packaging Pails (No. 5) Order, 1942([b]), as varied by the Control of Tins Cans Kegs Drums and Packaging Pails (No. 6) Order, 1942([c]), the Control of Tins Cans Kegs Drums and Packaging Pails (No. 7) Order, 1942([d]), the Control of Tins Cans Kegs Drums and Packaging Pails (No. 8) Order, 1942([e]), and the Control of Tins Cans Kegs Drums and Packaging Pails (No. 9) Order, 1942([f]), is hereby further varied in the Third Schedule thereto (which is printed at p 2 of the printed (No. 6) Order), in "Part II. Commodities other than Food", by substituting for the reference "2A" therein, the reference "2A(1)"; and by deleting therefrom the reference "2B".' [Source: *Statutory Rules and Orders 1943* No 1216, 19 August 1943; punctuation as in original; superscript letters ([b]), ([c]), etc, direct readers to volume and page references for the Orders.]
>
> **Departmental Explanatory Note** (printed at foot of Order): 'The above Order enables tinplate to be used for tobacco and snuff tins other than cutter-lid tobacco tins.' This is remarkably like a modern 'simplified outline'.

In private-sector legal documents

Simplified outlines are still rare in private-sector legal documents. But they can be useful in any document of length or complexity—including deeds, contracts, wills, and legal advices. They can be outlines of the whole document, or a part of it, or a specific clause in it; and their use for one part of the document does not compel their use in all parts. The aim is to help readers, not to impose uniformity for its own sake.

Example (mortgage)

Simplified Outline

This is a mortgage over your property at 1 Smith Street, Jonesville. In simplied form, these are its main provisions.

- It is an 'interest only' mortgage, and lasts for 5 years. That means that your payments cover interest only. At the end of the 5 years, you must repay the full amount you borrowed (plus any unpaid interest).
- Your payments are due on the first day of each month.
- The initial interest rate is 8% per annum. We can vary that rate at any time. If you pay your interest instalments on time, we will accept interest at a rate 2% below the interest otherwise payable at that time.
- If you fail to pay interest instalments on time, or if you fail to repay the full amount owing at the end of the 5 years, we can sell the property to recover what you owe (plus legal and other expenses). If the sale does not cover what you owe, you must still pay us the balance. Our right to sell is regulated by legislation.
- During the 5 years, you must keep the property in good repair. You must also pay all property rates and taxes, and you must keep the property insured.
- You cannot grant any other mortgage or right over the property without our prior consent.

This Simplified Outline is not intended to be an exhaustive statement. You should read the whole mortgage document.

Content of simplified outline

To be useful, a simplified outline should contain more than a list of the document's headings or topics; that role is for an index or a table of contents. Rather, a simplified outline should indicate the *substance* of the provisions. Where the provisions contain exceptions, the simplified outline should warn of them, but without encumbering the reader with detail; one technique is to use language such as 'generally' or 'with some exceptions', or similar.

The language of a simplified outline can be lighter in tone than the language of the substantive text of the document, since the outline does not presume to impose rights or obligations. However (because it is part of the document), where a simplified outline uses terms that are defined in the document, it should use them in their defined sense.

If a simplified outline conflicts with the substantive provisions, the substantive provisions prevail. The descriptions 'simplified' and 'outline' necessitate that conclusion: *Hudson v Minister for Immigration and Citizenship* [2010] FCAFC 119, [89]).

Further reading

- Office of Parliamentary Counsel, *Drafting Guidance* (June 2020), 3.2 ('Overview')
- Office of Parliamentary Counsel (Commonwealth of Australia), *Drafting Manual*, 'Simplified Outlines' (edn 3.2, July 2019), [138]–[139]

See also **METHOD STATEMENTS**; **PURPOSE CLAUSES**.

since

When denoting cause, prefer *because*, which carries more punch. For example:

> 'The judge had to follow the higher court's decision *since* [prefer: *because*] the rules of precedent required it.'

Also, *since* may have connotations of time, which can create ambiguity. For example:

> 'He was unable to attend court to give evidence *since* he was in hospital.' Does this mean '*because* he was in hospital', or '*after* he was in hospital'?

See also **because**.

sine

Latin: without. Found in many Latin-based legal expressions, all of which can be translated into standard English without loss of meaning.

See also **causa sine qua non**; **damnum sine (absque) injuria**; **nulla poena sine lege**; **sine die**; **sine qua non**.

sine die

Latin: without a (fixed) day; ie, postponed indefinitely. Often used in the context of court proceedings: an adjournment *sine die* is an adjournment without a resumption date yet being fixed. While useful legal shorthand, the continued use of the Latin is difficult to justify, because an appropriate (and more meaningful) English translation always suffices. For example:

- '[A] litigant is not entitled as of right to an adjournment simply because he is unable to attend. [I will not] adjourn the hearing of the application in effect *sine die* [prefer: *to an open-ended date*]. If a litigant is unable to attend a hearing himself, he can instruct lawyers to represent him. [*Bank of Beirut SAL v Prince Adel El-Hashemite* [2015] EWHC 1451 (Ch), [41]; [2016] Ch 1, 14 (Nugee J)]

- 'The question of costs is adjourned *sine die* [prefer: *to a date to be fixed*].' [*Bowesco Pty Ltd v Zohar* (2007) 156 FCR 129 (terms of court order)]

sine qua non

Latin: without which not; indispensable for achieving some purpose; a necessary condition. In legal usage, often denotes an indispensable condition or a fundamental requirement. For some readers, the Latinism may have become an accepted English idiom; for others, it will be as incomprehensible as many other Latinisms. For readers in the latter category, prefer standard English. For example:

- 'It does not, however, follow that the parties' agreement is not a *sine qua non* [prefer: *fundamental requirement*; *indispensable requirement*] of a consent order. Quite the reverse: the court cannot make a consent order without the valid consent of the parties.' [*Sharland v Sharland* [2015] UKSC 60, [29]; [2016] AC 871, [29] (Lady Hale)]
- 'She points out that her injury was a *causa sine qua non* [prefer: *a fundamental cause*] of her inability to work. That being so, her injury was a *sine qua non* [prefer: *a fundamental cause*] of the payment to her.' [*Commissioner of Taxation v Scully* [2000] HCA 6, [37]; (2000) 201 CLR 148, 170 (Gaudron ACJ, McHugh, Gummow and Callinan JJ). *Suggest rewrite*: 'She points out that the injury was a fundamental reason why she could not work. That being so, the injury was a fundamental reason why she was paid.']

See also **causa sine qua non**.

SINGULAR / PLURAL

Prefer the singular

Many legal sentences can be cast in either the singular or the plural: for example, 'Contracts for sale must be in writing' / 'A contract for sale must be in writing'. In such an example, it is merely a matter of drafting preference; no ambiguity arises either way. However, experienced drafters usually prefer to draft in the singular, if at all possible, because the singular speaks more 'personally' to the reader.

Plural	Singular (preferred)
Applicants must file appeal papers within 14 days.	An applicant must file appeal papers within 14 days.
Decisions must be given within 30 days of conclusion of argument.	A decision must be given within 30 days of conclusion of argument.
Vendors who enter into contracts for sale must first get the consent of their mortgagees.	A vendor who enters into a contract for sale must first get the consent of the vendor's mortgagee. [*or better*: Before entering into a contract for sale, a vendor must get their mortgagee's consent.]
The builder must issue certificates at the specified completion stages.	The builder must issue a certificate at each specified completion stage. [Unless the intended meaning is that the builder must issue certificates (plural) at each completion stage.]

Mix of singular and plural

If you choose to draft in the singular, keep to the singular. Do not mix the singular and the plural (unless grammatically essential). To illustrate: the following statutory provision is directed at '*a* local education authority' (singular) but uses plural pronouns (*their*, *them*). The mix of singular and plural is incongruous:

> 'A local education authority shall (so far as *their* [prefer: *its*] powers enable *them* [prefer: *it*] to do so) contribute towards the spiritual, moral, mental and physical development of the community by securing that efficient primary education, secondary education and further education are available to meet the needs of the population of *their* [prefer: *its*] area. [Source: *Education Act 1996*, s 13(1)]

That said, very occasionally a mix of singular and plural can improve sentence-flow.

Before (plural)	**After (mix of singular and plural)**
Public holidays are days that are proclaimed as public holidays, but do not include weekends or religious festivals.	A public holiday is a day proclaimed as a public holiday, excluding weekends or religious festivals.

Avoid parenthetical plurals

However, avoid singular/plural forms ('parenthetical plurals'), not because they are ambiguous but because they are ungainly: not 'borrower(s) must pay on time, but 'a borrower must pay on time', or 'borrowers must pay on time'.

Beware of ambiguity

Beware of ambiguity when recasting the plural to the singular. For example: 'The directors [plural] may appoint a proxy' can be redrafted 'A director may appoint a proxy'. But is the meaning the same? Does the original require *all* directors acting together to appoint a proxy? If so, the redraft is not adequate.

'Singular includes plural' (and vice versa)

The clause

A standard interpretation clause states that, unless the context requires otherwise, the singular includes the plural and the plural includes the singular. Most commercial documents include such a provision; so too do many statutes: eg, *Law of Property Act 1925*, s 61.

Example

> A statute declared that 'trustees or personal representatives' (plural) had certain powers over property vested in them. Certain property was vested in one person only (being the personal representative of the last to die of several trustees). Held, under the 'plural includes the singular' interpretation provision, the statute applied to that person: *Re Myhill* [1928] 1 Ch 100.

Indeed, this kind of provision is so common that a court may perhaps infer from its absence that the parties intended the singular *not* to include the plural (as in *Phoenix Enterprises Pty Ltd v City of Canada Bay Council* [2010] NSWCA 64, [210]). Likewise, a court may perhaps infer from its absence that the plural does not include the singular. Blackstone notes a case where a statute denying benefit of clergy for a person convicted of stealing *horses* (plural) did not apply to a person who stole one *horse* (singular): *Commentaries on the Laws of England* (1756) book 1, 88. (But that seems an unlikely interpretation in modern times, and was roundly criticised by Jeremy Bentham as 'scrupulousness carried to the extreme': *A Commentary on the Commentaries and A Fragment on Government*, ed JH Burns and HLA Hart (Oxford, Clarendon Press, 1977, rev edn 2008) 141.)

'Subject to context'

Normally, the standard interpretation clause is expressed to be 'subject to context' or 'subject to contrary intention' (or similar wording). Therefore, readers cannot safely assume that the singular *always* includes the plural and vice versa. Close scrutiny may be required, as the following cases show:

- A clause in a partnership deed between three partners empowered 'the other partners [plural]' to expel a partner. Held, this did not allow *one* partner acting alone to expel a partner: *Re A Solicitors' Arbitration* [1962] 1 All ER 772.
- A statute provided for property to vest in 'trustees' (plural) of a settlement 'as joint tenants'. Held, 'trustees' could not be read as 'trustee' (singular), because one person cannot hold property as 'joint tenants': *Re Price* [1929] 2 Ch 400.
- A health and safety regulation prohibited 'a person' from lifting an object exceeding a prescribed weight. Clearly, *person* could be read as *persons*. But was the prescribed weight also to be correspondingly 'pluralised'—ie, multiplied—according to the number of lifters? Held, no; the question was whether each person's share of the weight exceeded the (basic) prescribed total: *Medved v Dunlop Olympic Ltd* ((1990) 21 NSWLR 288.
- A statute awarded compensation where a person suffered mental harm as a result of witnessing an injury to 'another person'. The plaintiff witnessed injuries to many people (in a train crash). Held, 'another person' was to be read as meaning 'another person or persons (as the case requires)': *Wicks v State Rail Authority (NSW)* [2010] HCA 22; (2010) 241 CLR 60, [54].

Further reading

Dennis C Pearce and Robert S Geddes, *Statutory Interpretation in Australia*, 8th edn (LexisNexis, 2014) [6.39]–[6.41]

See also **DEFINITIONS; GENDER-NEUTRAL LANGUAGE; PRONOUNS; SUBJECT-VERB AGREEMENT; unless the context requires otherwise.**

singular includes plural

See **SINGULAR / PLURAL.**

singuli in solidum

Latin: each (is liable) for the whole. The Latin has no advantage over a plain-English translation—so prefer plain English:

> 'Many of these cases concerned a standard form of clause along the lines that trustees should "not be liable for omissions, neglect, or diligence of any kind, nor *singuli in solidum* [prefer: *each for the defaults of all*], but each only for his own intromission"—intromission here being used in the sense of positive intervention or intermeddling.' [*Spread Trustee Co Ltd v Hutcheson* [2011] UKPC 13, [89]; [2012] 2 AC 194, 231 (Lord Mance). Here, 'diligence' presumably means 'lack of diligence'.]

See also **in solidum; jointly and severally.**

situate at

A quaint archaism, describing the location of a property: eg, '*situate at* 21 Smith Street'. Idiomatic English expects 'situated at'. But in either case, *situate[d] at* means simply *at*—so delete *situate[d]* and simply say '*at* 21 Smith Street'.

skeleton argument

A summary of a party's argument. The purpose is to put the argument succinctly, honing the issues and saving court time. Court rules usually limit the number of words or pages (or both) for skeleton arguments. An unnecessarily long skeleton argument may obscure (rather than clarify) the points germane to the case: see, eg, *Tchenguiz v Director of Serious Fraud Office* [2014] EWCA Civ 1333 (Sharp LJ).

SLASH

See **FORWARD SLASH.**

SMOG FORMULA

SMOG = Simple Measure of Gobbledegook. A readability tool that measures the number of words of more than two syllables in a sample of 30 words.

See **READABILITY TESTS.**

so as to

Almost always reducible to one word, *to*. If so, prune: eg, 'The rent must be reviewed each year ~~*so as*~~ *to* ensure consistency with market increases.' Some may fear that the pruning blunts the forward-propelling sense of 'with the aim of [achieving a result]' or 'for the purpose of [achieving a result]'. But in fact the sense still comes through, as in these examples:

- '[I]n case of doubt, the Act should be read ~~*so as*~~ *to* promote, not ~~*so as*~~ *to* defeat or impair, its central purpose.' [*R (Al-Skeini) v Secretary of State for Defence* [2007] UKHL 26; [2008] AC 153, [57] (Lord Rodger)]
- 'The rules … were set out … with sufficient clarity and with sufficient safeguards ~~*so as*~~ *to* avoid arbitrary interference and ~~*so as*~~ *to* render the statutory scheme compatible with article 8 of the Convention.' [*R v Secretary of State for the Home Department* [2019] WLR(D) 443 (Headnote)]

so long as

A phrase with two (different) connotations: (1) the passage of time ('*so long as* the sun shines'—better, '*for as long as* the sun shines'), or (2) a qualification '(A applies *so long as* B applies'). Context will determine the particular meaning. Meaning (2) can give rise to uncertainty. For example, the formula 'A applies *so long as* B applies' could mean:

1. A applies 'to the extent that' B applies (ie, A may have partial application only),

   or

2. A applies only if B applies (ie, to use the more traditional formula, 'A applies provided that B applies').

See, eg, *Motor Cycling Events Group Australia Pty Ltd v Kelly* [2013] NSWCA 361; (2013) 86 NSWLR 55, [15]–[16], [116]–[117], in the context favouring meaning (2).

See also **PROVISOS.**

socius / socii

Latin: partner; associate; plural *socii*. The word often appears in longer Latin expressions, all hallowed by legal usage but all easily translatable into standard English without loss of legal nuance. Examples are: *noscitur a sociis* (known by its associates; known by the company it keeps); *socius criminis* (an accomplice in crime).

See also **noscitur a sociis.**

sole and exclusive

A common pairing, in which each word often covers the same ground; if so, prune one. For example, if A grants B 'sole and exclusive' access to A's land, either *sole* or *exclusive* suffices. If the access to the land is *exclusive*, no one else can use it; and if the access is *sole*, no one else can use it.

Occasionally, however, context may justify keeping both words. For example, a franchisor may give a franchisee 'sole and exclusive' rights to exploit a product. Here, *sole* indicates that the franchisor will not license any one else to exploit the product, but may retain the right itself to exploit the product; *exclusive* indicates that the franchisee is the only person who may exploit the product, with no right even for the franchisor to do so.

SOLIDUS

See **FORWARD SLASH.**

sovran

An archaism for 'sovereign'. As an adjective, a term applied to Imperial statutes in force in a British colony either by express provision or necessary implication. This usage appears in, eg, HB Bignold, *Imperial Statutes in Force in New South Wales* (Law Book, 1913) vol 1, 9–10.

SPACING

See **DASHES; DOCUMENT DESIGN; ELLIPSES; FONTS; PUNCTUATION.**

special circumstances

A term with an inherently malleable meaning: when are circumstances sufficiently noteworthy to be 'special'? Occasionally, vague expressions such as *special circumstances* have a useful role. For example, parliament may wish to give police a discretion to excuse breaches of the criminal law 'in special circumstances'. But (if possible) specify the *precise* circumstances in which breaches are to be excused—otherwise, you leave readers in doubt.

Judges called upon to decide whether 'special circumstances' exist inevitably reason by analogy from similar expressions. However, that technique carries the risk of diverting attention away from the actual expression ('special circumstances') to the analogue. Analogous expressions include:

- circumstances that are 'so outside a run of the mill case ... as to justify departing from' [the normal solicitors' costs rules], but not necessarily being 'exceptional circumstances': *Bentine v Bentine* [2015] EWCA Civ 1168; [2016] 2 WLR 1035, [67]–[69]

- a state of affairs that is 'continually repeated or so often repeated as to be specially liable' [to cause workplace accidents, and so require permanent protection for workers]: *Harris v Rugby Portland Cement Co* [1955] 1 WLR 648, 651
- circumstances that are 'uncommon or out of the ordinary' [to justify not giving unions prior notice of workers' redundancies]: *Clarks of Hove Ltd v Bakers' Union* [1978] 1 WLR 1207, 1215–16.

As a matter of ordinary English, circumstances that apply to all people within the relevant class cannot be 'special' circumstances: *United Mexican States v Cabal* [2001] HCA 60; (2001) 209 CLR 165, [61].

special loss

See **consequential loss.**

special tail

A fee tail restricted to heirs descended from a specified spouse: as in a fee tail 'to A and the heirs of his body born from Mary'.

See **fee tail**.

specialty

Sometimes misspelled *speciality*. Used in at least three senses in law:

1. In its widest sense, a document executed by sealing (ie, for most practical purposes, a deed).
2. More commonly (and more precisely), a deed that evidences a debt or secures an obligation to pay money: hence, *specialty debt*.
3. A debt due from the Crown, or a debt arising under statute: *Collin v Duke of Westminster* [1985] QB 581, 603 (Oliver LJ).

In jurisdictions where sealing is no longer necessary for a deed—eg, under s 1 of the *Law of Property (Miscellaneous Provisions) Act* 1989—a document that bears no seal can be a specialty as long as the parties executed it intending it to be a deed: *Liberty Partnership Ltd v Tancred* [2018] EWHC 2707 (Comm); [2019] QB 903.

See also **DEED (document); signed, sealed and delivered**.

specie

See **in specie**.

specify

To *specify* something means to state it clearly, to designate it, to point it out distinctly; ie, to identify something with particularity. So, if a document or statute requires a notice to *specify* certain things, the notice must mention those things particularly and not leave them to implication; it must state the various items 'in explicit terms': *Jolly v Yorktown District Council* (1968) 119 CLR 347, 351 (Barwick CJ and Owen J). However, because words take their meaning from context, *specify* may sometimes mean *indicate generally* rather than *indicate particularly*; but that would be a departure from the normal meaning, which connotes unambiguous precision: *Gantry Acquisition Corp v Parker & Parsley Petroleum Australia Pty Ltd* (1994) 51 FCR 554, 569F (Burchett J).

See also **indicate**.

specious / spurious

Specious means 'superficially attractive, but actually wrong'; *spurious* means 'false' or 'fake'. The meanings can overlap when applied to legal arguments. A *specious* argument seems attractive until countered; a *spurious* argument seems valid until unmasked. Sometimes, using both terms is justified:

> 'The landlord's] intentions under section 30(1)(f) must be genuine and not *spurious* or *specious*, and they must be to do what the words of the section describe, and to do it at the time denoted.' [*Fisher v Taylors Furnishing Stores Ltd* [1956] 2 QB 78, 90 (Morris LJ)]

spes successionis

Latin: hope of succeeding, particularly in the context of a hope or expectation of inheriting property. Being a hope or expectation only—a bare expectation—a *spes successionis* is not an actual interest in property, and so cannot be conveyed or dealt with: it is even too ephemeral to come under the umbrella of legislative provisions that allow contingent claims to be dealt with: *Law of Property Act 1925*, s 4; *Re Ellenborough* [1903] 1 Ch 697.

As with many Latinisms hallowed in law, *spes successionis* is eminently translatable into modern English. For example:

- '[No one] can have any estate or interest ... in the property of a living person to which he hopes to succeed as heir-at-law or next-of-kin of such living person. During the life of such person no one can have more than a *spes successionis*, an expectation or hope of succeeding to his property.' [*Re Parsons* (1890) 45 Ch D 51, 55 (Kay J, supplying a translation)]
- '[T]he only interest that the intended beneficiary had in the bequest was an expectation, a *spes successionis* [prefer: *a mere hope of inheriting*]. There was no enforceable right or interest.' [*Hill v van Erp* (1997) 188 CLR 159, 179 (Dawson J)]

spinster

An unmarried woman, especially one advancing in years, usually childless. The term was formerly added after a woman's name in documents such as conveyances and wills, as if it were her proper legal designation. It occasionally surfaces still when courts have to consider the continuing provisions of historic wills or trusts. But *spinster* is rare in modern legal documents; indeed, most legal drafters would now instinctively recoil from using it: cf *J v C* [2006] EWCA Civ 551; [2007] Fam 1, [9] (Wall LJ).

SPLIT INFINITIVES

The issue

To split or not to split? The infinitive is the tenseless form of the verb, preceded by *to*—eg, 'to run', 'to decide'. The former 'rule' against splitting infinitives forbade inserting a word (usually an adverb) between *to* and the verb: eg, 'to quickly run', 'to promptly decide'. However, the 'rule' never had much to recommend it. Some asserted that it derived from Latin usage; but in Latin, as in Old English, infinitives were written as a single word, inherently unsplittable. At best, the 'rule' was a matter of style.

To modern readers, a 'no-split' style can draw attention to itself, impeding communcation:

> '[The lawyer] prepared a form *to sever unilaterally* the joint tenancy.' [*McCoy v Caelli* [2010] NSWSC 1233, [10], straining to avoid the split.]

Indeed, it can even produce ambiguity:

> 'The barrister *failed completely to address* the relevant issue.' The writer seems to have been determined to avoid a split infinitive, but in doing so has missed an inherent ambiguity. Does the sentence mean (1) the barrister did not address the issue at all (ie, *completely failed* to address it), or (2) the barrister *failed to address the issue completely* (ie, addressed it partly, but not sufficiently)?

The solution: split where idiomatic

Modern writers split infinitives freely and readers rarely notice. The only guide—admittedly a loose one—is to be idiomatic: 'to boldly go', 'to specifically enforce', 'to strongly recommend'. But if in doubt, sidestep the issue by rewriting:

Before (split)	**After**
The court declined *to* specifically *enforce* the contract.	The court declined *to enforce* the contract specifically. (Or simply: The court declined *to enforce* the contract.)
The corporation used its market dominance *to* aggressively *destroy* its competitors.	Using its market dominance, the corporation aggressively destroyed its competitors.

However, even those who unhesitatingly split should avoid excessive splitting, as in this cascading example from Gowers' *Complete Plain Words*, 3rd edn (Penguin, 1987) 145:

> The tenant hereby agrees:
>
> (i) *to pay* the said rent;
>
> (ii) *to* properly *clean* all the windows;
>
> (iii) *to* at all times properly *empty* all closets;
>
> (iv) *to* immediately any litter or disorder shall have been made by him or for his purpose on the staircase or landings or any other part of the said building or garden *remove* the same.

sponte sua

See **sua sponte**.

springing interest

See **shifting / springing interest**.

spurious

See **specious / spurious**.

SQUARE BRACKETS

See **BRACKETS**.

squatter's title

A colourful term for a title acquired by adverse possession. To an extent, all squatters acquire *some* title to the land they occupy, in the sense of a right to possession good against everyone except those with a better title (such as the genuine owner). But *squatter's title* has become synonymous with a title gained by a person who originally entered the land as a trespasser and who has remained there openly and for a sufficient time to extinguish the ownership of the documentary owner. For example:

> 'In 1997 Michael Graham registered cautions at the Land Registry against Pye's title on the grounds that he had obtained "squatter's title" by adverse possession.' [*Pye (Oxford) Ltd v Graham* [2003] 1 AC 419, 430 [22] (Lord Browne-Wilkinson)]

See **prescription / adverse possession**.

SQUINTING MODIFIERS

See **MODIFIERS**.

stakeholder

In standard English, a *stakeholder* is a person who is directly *interested* in something; thus, politicians consult *stakeholders* before making a decision that may affect the stakeholders' interests. In law, however, a *stakeholder* is a person who holds property or money *disinterestedly*—ie, independently of the parties who lay claim to it. For example, under a contract for the sale of land an estate agent holds the deposit (the 'stake') independently of the seller and buyer, until it is known which party is ultimately entitled to it.

STANDARD FORMS

Standard forms exist for many kinds of legal transactions. Some forms are published by professional bodies, legal stationers, or book publishers; others are developed and used by commercial entities such as banks, insurance companies, and internet providers; and yet others are produced in-house by law firms for their own use.

Advantages and disadvantages

Standard forms reduce the time needed to prepare documents; this in turn reduces costs. Where forms are industry-standard, readers in the industry can take them 'as read', saving time and money. Standard forms also encourage a consistency of practice; this too can save time and money. These are significant advantages.

However, standard forms also have disadvantages. One is prolixity: once a clause or phrase finds its way into a standard form, it tends to remain, even though later changes in law or practice make it irrelevant. Human nature, modern technology, and the power of legal precedent, conspire to make it easier to add than expunge. Again, a standard form may be 'generic', designed for several kinds of transactions which, though of a similar kind, require added specific provisions. For example, a standard-form lease may cater for different kinds of premises—commercial, retail, and industrial—all with similar core provisions but each needing additional provisions for its own kind; the additions (particularly if poorly integrated) can add greatly to the document's overall length and complexity. Or (to vary the example) a standard-form lease may provide alternative forms of rent review (cost-of-living increases, market review by a valuer, fixed-amount increases), and leave it to the parties to choose which one is to apply to their transaction; this too adds length and complexity to the standard form.

Standard interpretation

Courts presume that parties who choose a standard form also choose to govern their relationship based on the law and practice that has evolved in the use of that form: *Dunlop & Sons v Balfour Williams & Co* [1892] 1 QB 507, 518 (CA, Lord Esher MR); *The Nema* [1982] AC 724, 737 (HL, Lord Diplock); *Legal & General Insurance Australia Ltd v Eather* (1986) 6 NSWLR 390, 394 (Kirby P). '[W]here a settled construction has been given to a particular form of words, courts will recognise that other commercial parties are entitled to rely and act on it': *Caresse Navigation Ltd v Office National de l'Electricité* [2014] EWCA Civ 1366, [19]; [2015] 2 WLR 43 (Beatson LJ).

Further, when a new standard form supersedes an old one, courts tend to interpret words and phrases in the new form in the same way as they interpreted similar words and phrases in the old form. Courts presume that the drafter knew how the courts have interpreted earlier versions of the form, and that he or she (and therefore the parties) intended to carry the judicial exegesis across to the new form: *Brien v Dwyer* [1976] 2 NSWLR 420, 423–24 (Hutley JA).

Nevertheless, courts retain the power to declare that a settled interpretation of a standard form, even though accepted and acted upon for many years, is wrong. They may be reluctant to declare it wrong—but they have the power to do so, and those who have acted on the accepted understanding will be taken to have been aware of that possibility (as in *Re Spectrum Ltd* [2005] 2 AC 680, overturning the long-settled interpretation of a debenture).

See also **AMENDING TEXT; CONSISTENCY OF TERMINOLOGY; DOCUMENT STRUCTURE; PRECEDENT (Legal forms); SURPLUSAGE (PRESUMPTION AGAINST); TERMS OF ART**.

stare decisis

Latin: to stand by decisions; in legal usage, to abide by precedent. Although encapsulating an important legal doctrine, the Latin is readily translated into standard English. Purists may object that the translation reflects none of the complexity of the doctrine; but then, nor does mere recitation of the Latin—so prefer the standard English. For example:

- 'I consider that the decisions of the Court of Appeal in [two cases] were wrongly decided, although I can see how it might be said that they were justified on the basis of *stare decisis* [prefer: *the doctrine of precedent*].' [*Re Nortel GmbH* [2013] UKSC 52, [91]; [2014] AC 209, 241 (Lord Neuberger)]
- 'This appeal does not involve any question of *stare decisis* [prefer: *the binding force of precedent*]. The only sense in which this Court is "bound" by any decision is that it will not lightly overrule one of its own.' [*Australian Crime Commission v Stoddart* [2011] HCA 47, [56]; (2011) 244 CLR 554, 574 (Heydon J)]

See also **PRECEDENT**.

starting with / starting from

See **beginning with / beginning from**.

State / state

The convention is to capitalise the first letter when referring to a particular state ('the State of New South Wales'), but not otherwise (eg, 'all states are part of the federation').

status quo

Latin: the state in which; the position in which.

See **status quo ante**.

status quo ante

Latin: the previous position; the state of affairs before (the change occurred). A needless Latinism, given the clarity of the English translation, but one which lawyers seem loath to discard. For example:

- '[R]ather than regulating the consequences of an illegal act (for example by restoring the parties *to the status quo ante* [prefer: *to their previous position*], in the same way as upon the rescission of a contract) the courts withhold judicial remedies, leaving the loss to lie where it falls.' [*Les Laboratoires Servier v Apotex Inc* [2014] UKSC 55; [2015] AC 430, [23] (Lord Sumption)]
- 'The purpose of a reinstatement order is to ensure that the employee in question is placed in the *status quo ante* [prefer: *previous position*; *position before the order was made*].' [*Blackadder v Ramsay Butchering Services Pty Ltd* [2005] HCA 22; (2005) 221 CLR 539, [34] (Kirby J)]

statute-barred

A description of the effect of the statute of limitations on rights or remedies left too long unenforced (sometimes called 'stale claims'): they are *statute-barred*. Preferably hyphenated, particularly when used as a compound adjective (a 'statute-barred remedy'), but *statute barred* (two words, no hyphen) is also seen.

See **limitation period**.

statutes general

English statutes in force in British colonies because they are applicable to the circumstances of the colony, either at the time of colonisation or at some other date fixed by statute. The usage appears in HB Bignold, *Imperial Statutes in Force in New South Wales* (Law Book, 1913) vol 1, 9–10.

See also **sovran**.

STATUTES (REFERENCES TO)

See **CITATION OF LEGISLATION**.

stet

Latin: let it stand (in its original form). A direction that something which has been deleted or altered in a manuscript or proof is to remain uncorrected—as if to say, 'on reflection, I made a mistake in correcting this; let the original stand'.

See further **PROOFREADING (Proofreaders' marks)**.

stillicide

See **eavesdrop**.

storey / storeys

In British English, modern spellings are *storey* (singular) and *storeys* (plural); in older British usage (and in current US usage), *story* and *storeys*. The concept is of one or more levels of a single building, each above the other. Normally, the levels are on top of each other, but context may allow it sufficient that each be merely higher than the other. For example, in planning law, a building stepped-back into a rising slope, with ten 'steps' incorporated in the structure, was a 10-storey building: *Leichhardt Municipal Council v Daniel Callaghan Pty Ltd* (1981) 46 LGRA 29, 37 (Samuels JA). Again, in building regulations, a room enclosed on three sides by vertical walls and on the fourth by a sloping roof was a top storey: *Foot v Hodgson* (1890) 25 QBD 160 (the report uses 'story').

When used as part of a compound adjective, prefer a hyphen: eg, 'a six-storey building'; compare, 'a building of six storeys'. For example:

- 'The Property … consists of a large *five storey* [prefer: *five-storey*] house in West London' [*BMC Properties & Management Ltd v Jackson* [2015] EWCA Civ 1306, [3] (Patten LJ)]
- 'The serviced apartments were incorporated in levels one to nine of a *twenty-two storey* [prefer: *22-storey*] development.' [*Brookfield Multiplex Ltd v Owners Corporation SP 61288* [2014] HCA 36, [1]; 254 CLR 185, 192 (French CJ)]

strata / stratum

One *stratum*; two or more *strata*. In legal usage, *strata* title is a form of high-rise title invented in Australia. As originally enacted, *strata* title legislation was true to its etymological foundations and applied only to buildings containing more than one stratum; later, however, its scope was widened to include certain single-storey buildings. The equivalent in England is 'commonhold'.

In some jurisdictions, legislation also allows the subdivision of a floor within a high-rise, non-strata title building, called in those jurisdictions *stratum* title.

Further reading

- *Halsbury's Laws of England*, 'Real Property and Registration' (vol 87, 2017) [1103]–[1162] (commonhold)
- Brendan Edgeworth (ed), *Butt's Land Law*, 7th edn (Lawbook, 2017) ch 13 (Commonwealth strata title law)

stricken / struck

Both *stricken* and *struck* are past participles of 'strike'. The more idiomatic choice in modern English is *struck*—though *stricken* still appears in compounds such as 'grief-stricken', 'poverty-stricken', and 'conscience-stricken'. In law, *stricken* is seen in 'stricken from the record', a US usage which has seeped into other jurisdictions. But 'struck from the record' would do just as well—and, being idiomatic, should be preferred in non-US jurisdictions. For example:

- 'Accordingly, I will order that the pleadings in this case be *stricken* [prefer: *struck*] from the record.' [*Riordan v Hamilton* [2000] IEHC 189, [18] (Smyth J)]
- 'His pleadings were *stricken* in their entirety and judgment was granted in default to the plaintiffs …' [*Masters v Leaver*, Times Law Reports, 5 August 1999 (Morritt LJ, speaking of proceedings in Texas)]
- 'When I read [the material] over the weekend the thought occurred to me it ought to be *stricken* [prefer: *struck*] from our record. It is totally irrelevant.' [*Re Australian Bishops Conference* [2001] HCATrans 410 (McHugh J)]

stricti juris

Latin: according to strict right (law). Prefer a plain-English translation. For example:

- 'What the sheriff did was to grant the "ford" route not the "bridge" route. What he granted and what the plan showed must be construed *stricti juris* [prefer: *according to strict law*; better still: *strictly*] and if ambiguous then in a way least burdensome to the [land].' [*Bell v Cambell* [2004] ScotCS 14, [162] (Lord McEwan)]
- 'This means that the Tribunal is not bound, *strictly* speaking, to decide proceedings *stricti juris* [prefer: *according to strict law*].' ['Commercial Tribunal Decisions', Editor (1993) 15 *Adelaide Law Review* 241, 253; ungainly repetition]

stricto sensu

Latin: in strict sense (literally: in tightened sense, in compressed sense); strictly speaking. Often rendered *sensu stricto*, and occasionally (but incorrectly) *strictu sensu*. Readers untutored in Latin may well guess the meaning; but an appropriate English translation can capture both the meaning and rhythm of the original, making the Latin redundant. Examples include:

- 'In this court's view … the principled solution to a case such as this would be to [leave] the detailed provisions of Chapter 1 … to deal with sickness benefits *stricto sensu* [prefer: *in the strict sense of that term*].' [*Secretary of State for Work and Pensions v Tolley* [2015] UKSC 55, [24]; [2016] 1 All ER 40, 48 (Lady Hale)]
- 'Lord Lyndhurst declined to confine [legal professional privilege] to the lawyer's work *stricto sensu* [prefer: *in the strict sense*] of drawing the agreements, investigating the title and preparing the conveyance.' [*Three Rivers District Council v Bank of England (No 6)* [2005] 1 AC 610, [91] (Lord Carswell)]
- 'It was thought by at least one writer that … there was a "less exacting test" for the admissibility of "relationship evidence" than there was for similar fact evidence *strictu sensu* [sic: *stricto sensu*; prefer: *strictly speaking*; *in the strict sense of that term*].' [*HML v R* [2008] HCA 16, [465]; (2008) 235 CLR 334, 48 (Crennan J)]

STRUCTURE

See **DOCUMENT STRUCTURE**.

structure / structural

A *structure* is something that is 'constructed' (*Mills & Rockleys v Leicester City Council* [1946] 1 All ER 424, 427 (Lord Goddard CJ); not included in authorised report, [1946] KB 315, 319), or something that has been 'built together, constructed' from different items put together to make a whole (*Hobday v Nicol* [1944] 1 All ER 302, 303–04). But these definitions are unhelpful, because they invoke a compound of the word being defined: con*structed*. A better definition is: *structure* means 'those elements of the overall [building] which give it its essential appearance, stability and shape' (*Irvine v Moran* (1990) 24 HLR 1, 5). For example, the main walls and roof of a building are *structural* (*Granada Theatres Ltd v Freehold Investments (Leytonstone) Ltd* [1959] Ch 592), as are large plate glass windows forming the frontage of the walls of a building (*Boswell v Crucible Steel Co* [1924] 1 KB 119); but standard wooden-framed windows are not a *structure* (*Holiday Fellowship Ltd v Hereford* [1959] 1 WLR 211).

Of course, *structure* and *structural* take their meaning from context. The issue is not what *structure* means in the abstract, but what it means in the particular context. For example:

- In various statutory contexts, a suspended concrete terrace attached to a house was a 'building or *structure*' (*Heaton v Lobday* (1959) 60 SR (NSW) 332), as was a road (*Black & Shaw & Official Receiver* (1913) 33 NZLR 194, 196) and an airstrip (*Carter v Mid-Murray Council* [2007] SASC 145; (2007) 97 SASR 462).
- In a landlord's covenant to repair the '*structure*' of the premises, internal plasterwork was part of the structure: *Grand v Gill* [2011] 1 WLR 2253 (CA).

See also **building**.

sua sponte

Latin (sometimes *sponte sua*): voluntarily; without prompting; of one's own free will. A Latinism with no mysterious legal meaning. Prefer an English translation that captures the sense. For example:

- '[If] the tenant is allowed to remain until he is turned out under the Act, owing to the [lessor] requiring personal residence, he has a statutory remedy in damages; but if he is turned out by the lessor *sua sponte* [prefer: *unprompted*; *independently*] on the ground that the lease is void ab initio he has no remedy.' [*Rickard v Graham* [1910] 1 Ch 722, 726 (Swinfen Eady J in argument)]
- 'The Grievance Committee had commenced an investigation, *sua sponte* [prefer: *of its own motion*], concerning whether the applicant attorney was in breach of a rule requiring disclosure of an attorney's name and address [in an advertisement].' [*Toal v Honorable Society of Kings Inn Barristers Disciplinary Tribunal* [2015] IEHC 512, [24] (Keane J)]

sub

Latin: under. Used in combination with other Latinisms, all of which are readily translatable into standard English. Examples are *sub judice* (under consideration in court; currently before the court); *sub nomine* (under the name of); *sub poena* (under a penalty); *sub voce* (under the voice, ie quietly).

See also **sub judice; sub modo; sub nom**.

sub judice

Latin: under a judge—ie, before a court (or tribunal) for consideration. (More fully, *lis sub judice*: a case before the judge.) Preferred usage is two words: *sub judice*; but *subjudice* is seen, as is (very rarely) *sub-judice*. The translation 'before the court' is usually sufficient, eg:

> 'Once a matter *becomes sub judice* [prefer: *comes before the court*], and while it remains *sub judice* [prefer: *before the court*], comment that could influence judgment is unlawful.' [*James v Robinson* (1963) 109 CLR 593, 615 (Windeyer J)]

Sometimes, however, a translation requires more nuance. For example, a journalist may decline to report a crime 'because it is *sub judice*'—meaning not merely that the case is before the court, but that to report it would be a contempt of court. But here too, an appropriate English translation will carry sufficient meaning. For example:

> '[F]or many years Parliament and the courts have each been astute to respect the sphere of action and the privileges of the other—Parliament, for example, by its *sub judice rule*

[prefer: *rule not to comment on matters currently before the courts*], the courts by taking care to exclude evidence which might amount to infringement of parliamentary privilege.' [*British Railways Board v Pickin* [1974] AC 765, 799 (Lord Simon of Glaisdale)]

See also **contempt**.

sub modo

Latin: under condition; under restriction. In some contexts, this Latinism is difficult to translate, because its context is technical and its reach is broad. However, for clearer communication, it is always worth the try. For example:

- 'These duties and rights [of a purchaser] arise from the contract of sale and it is because of their existence that the vendor is said to be a constructive trustee, or *a trustee sub modo* [prefer: *a trustee for that purpose; a trustee to a limited extent*], of the estate for the purchaser from the time when the contract is constituted.' [*Berkely v Poulett* [1977] 1 EGLR 86, 93 (Stamp LJ)]
- 'If the letter of 26 June were an election not to rescind, it was *an election sub modo* [prefer: *an election to a limited extent; a qualified election*], conditional upon the Trust's ability to complete the transfer at that time.' [*Immer (No 145) Pty Ltd v Uniting Church in Australia Property Trust* (NSW) (1993) 182 CLR 26, 30 (Brennan J)]

sub nom

Abbreviation for *sub nomine*—Latin: under the name; usually italicised. Refers to an earlier decision involving the same parties but cited differently (eg, by inverting the order of names, or using different names): eg, *Jones v Smith* (2017), *sub nom Smith v Jones* (2016). Modern British and Commonwealth usage generally omits the full stop after *nom*; US usage generally retains it (*sub nom.*). Rarely seen is the full term *sub nomine*; and hopefully never seen is *sub nominee* (cf *Pegasus Gold Australia Ltd v Metso Minerals (Australia) Ltd* [2003] NTCA 3, [6]; (2003) 16 NTLR 54).

As with many Latin abbreviations, mystique is easily dispelled by using a plain-English translation—eg, 'under the name of', or 'reported as', or (where grammatical construction allows it) 'as'. For example:

- 'In *R (Reynolds) v Secretary of State for Work and Pensions* (reported *sub nom.* [prefer: *under the name of; as*] *R (Carson) v Secretary of State for Work and Pensions* [2006] 1 AC 173) … Lord Hoffmann … put the point very clearly …' [*R v Secretary of State for Business, Innovation and Skills* [2015] 1 WLR 3820; [2015] UKSC 57, [98] (Lords Sumption and Reed). The transcript at UKSC 57 inserts a full stop after *nom*; the report at [2015] AC 57 omits it.]
- '*Baird v Wallace-James* (1916) 85 LJ PC 193, 198 (also reported *sub nom* [prefer: *under the name of; as*] *James v Baird* 1916 SC (HL) 158, 163–64).' [*Papaconstuntinos v Holmes à Court* [2012] HCA 53; (2012) 249 CLR 534, [77] (Heydon J, footnote)]

sub nomine

See **sub nom**.

subject matter

Usually two words, not hyphenated: eg, 'The *subject matter* was contract.'

subject to [a provision]

Indicating priority

When one provision (clause A) is expressed to be *subject to* another (clause B), the implication is that clauses A and B conflict, or have different emphases, and that clause B is to prevail over clause A. To the extent of the conflict or difference in emphasis, clause B is the 'master' provision: *C & J Clark Ltd v Inland Revenue Commissioners* [1973] 2 All ER 513, 520 (Megarry J). Or, putting it another way, to the extent of the inconsistency, clause B 'swallows up' or 'negates' clause A: *Benge v Guardian Assurance Co Ltd* (1914) 34 NZLR 81, 86 (Stout CJ; held, where an insurance policy provided coverage *subject to* stated conditions, the conditions negated the coverage).

It has been said that *subject to* 'throws no light on whether there would in truth be a conflict without' those words: *Harding v Coburn* [1976] 2 NZLR 577, 582 (Cooke J). However, this runs counter to the presumption against surplusage—otherwise, why include *subject to*? Therefore, it seems logical to view a *subject to* statement as reflecting the parties' intent that a conflict or issue of priority would otherwise exist.

Indicating limitation

In some contexts, *subject to* introduces a mere limitation. For example, a statute may confer jurisdiction on a court to make certain orders, *subject to* rules of court: here, the rules of court regulate the exercise of the jurisdiction, but do not negate it: *Omerod v Todmorden Joint Stock Mill Co Ltd* (1882) 8 QBD 664, 676 (Brett LJ); *Vitzdamm-Jones v Vitzdamm-Jones* (1981) 55 ALJR 192, 196 (Barwick CJ).

Complex interactions

More complex interactions are sometimes seen. For example, clause 1 may be expressed to be *subject to* a number of provisions—eg, 'subject to clauses 10–20', or 'subject to the provisions of Part 5'. Then, logically clause 1 is subject to all of those clauses or provisions. The superficial intent is clear enough, but the practical working-out may be complex. The complexity is heightened if those clauses or provisions are themselves *subject to* yet other clauses or provisions; the range of potential interactions may then become unworkably intricate.

See also **CROSS-REFERENCES; INCONSISTENT PROVISIONS; SURPLUSAGE (PRESUMPTION AGAINST); subject to this Agreement**.

subject to contract

Meaning

A formulaic expression indicating that an offer, or the acceptance of an offer, is not binding until: (1) a formal contract is drawn up and signed, and (2) the parties have carried out any formal ceremony conventionally signifying a binding contract (such as exchange of signed counterpart contracts for the sale of land): *Keppel v Wheeler* [1927] 1 KB 577, 584 (Bankes LJ).

Variants

Although the concept of 'subject to contract' is familiar, the formula itself may vary. Any words are sufficient if they clearly indicate that the negotiations are not legally binding until the usual formalities for that kind of transaction are concluded. For example, in a shipping contract, the expression '*SUBJS DETAILS*' was the maritime equivalent of *subject to contract* and signified that the parties did not intend to be bound until they had agreed on all its main terms: *Transfield Shipping Inc v Chiping Xinfa Huaya Alumina Co Ltd* [2009] EWHC 3642 (Comm), [60] (Clarke J).

Conduct of the parties

Despite using the formula *subject to contract* (or similar), the parties' later conduct may show that they have waived the conditional nature implicit in the words and have in fact entered into a binding contract. As Lord Clarke explained:

> '[I]t is possible for an agreement "subject to contract" or "subject to written contract" to become legally binding if the parties later agree to waive that condition, for they are in effect making a firm contract by reference to the terms of the earlier agreement. Put another way, they are waiving the "subject to [written] contract" term or understanding.' [*RTS Flexible Systems Ltd v Molkerei Alois Müller Gmbh & Co KG* [2010] UKSC 14; [2010] 1WLR 753, [55]]

Further reading

Halsbury's Laws of England, 'Contract' (vol 22, 2019) [72] (sales of land 'subject to contract')

subject to finance

A formula indicating that, although the parties have entered into a binding contract, performance is conditional on a party obtaining the finance needed to complete the transaction. Sometimes the formula is expressly qualified (eg, 'subject to *suitable* finance being arranged', or 'subject to finance on *terms suitable to the [party]*'). Even if not expressly qualified, courts usually imply a qualification to that effect: *Meehan v Jones* (1982) 149 CLR 571, 588 (Mason J).

Further reading

JW Carter, *Carter on Contract* (online, LexisNexis) ch 5, pt 3 ('Subject to finance')

subject to this Agreement

Although often seen, this qualifying phrase is too general to be of much use. The implication is that if a provision qualified in this way is inconsistent with other parts of the agreement, then the other parts take priority. But what other parts take priority? Perhaps even the drafter is unsure (which might explain the generality of the 'subject to' provision). It is worse still if the agreement contains more than one 'subject to this Agreement'—how is a reader to make sense of these irreconcilable statements?

See also **INCONSISTENT PROVISIONS**; **subject to [a provision]**.

SUBJECT-VERB AGREEMENT

Conventions

Singular nouns take the singular form of verbs. Plural nouns take the plural form of verbs. The principle is easy to state, but can be difficult to apply. The following conventions are standard.

- Nouns that are plural in form, but singular in concept, take the plural verb: eg, 'the premises *were* old' (even though only one building); 'the works *were* completed' (even though only one activity).

- Collective nouns (eg, committee, board) normally take the singular verb, unless the emphasis is on the individual members: eg, 'the committee *resolves to* …'; but 'the board *vote* according to their consciences'.
- A plural subject takes a singular verb where the subject signifies a single entity, such as a country or a measure: eg, 'the UK *decides* this year whether to leave Europe'; '12 months *is* sufficient notice'.
- Two nouns (whether both singular or both plural, or a combination of singular and plural) linked by *and* normally take a plural verb: eg, 'judge and jury *are* agreed on the verdict'), unless the two nouns form a single composite concept (eg, 'law and order *has* been restored').
- Where *each* is the subject of the sentence, the verb is singular (eg, 'each *has* the right to a fair trial'); but where a plural pronoun or noun is the subject with *each* in apposition, the verb is plural (eg, 'they *each* have the right to a fair trial'; 'the defendants each *have* the right to a fair trial').
- Corporations and associations are singular (eg, 'X Pty Ltd *is* going into liquidation'), while law firms and partnerships are plural (eg, 'Smith and Jones *are* having financial difficulties')—but these conventions are not universally followed.
- The following words are singular, and therefore take a singular verb:

anyone	no one	one
anybody	nobody	each
everyone	someone	either
everybody	somebody	neither

Relevance in case law

The principles of subject–verb agreement can help determine the meaning of provisions. Two US cases illustrate the point.

Examples

- A statute prohibited 'visible emissions' of asbestos. It defined 'visible emissions' as 'emissions containing particulate asbestos material that *are* visually detectable without the aid of instruments'. Held, the plural *are* indicated that what must be visually detectable were the *emissions*, not the particulate asbestos material: *United States v Midwest Suspension & Brake* 49 F 3d 1197 (6th Cir 1995).
- Under a contract for the sale of land, the buyer could sue the seller if, within 5 years of completion of the sale, the buyer provided the seller with 'the results of a survey which discloses' a shortfall in the property's stated area. The buyer obtained a survey which showed a shortfall. Within 5 years, the buyer provided the seller with the results of the survey, but not the survey itself. Held, the singular verb (*discloses*) referred to the (singular) *survey*; and therefore what needed to be provided within 5 years were the (plural) *results* of the survey, not the survey itself: *Davis v Pletcher* 727 SW 2d 29 (Tex App 1987).

Mistakes

In the above two cases, the courts assumed that the drafters knew their 'subject–verb' principles and had drafted accordingly. Sometimes, however, the drafter has clearly made a subject–verb mistake. In such cases, subject–verb disagreement does not undermine legal efficacy unless it creates ambiguity or absurdity. Usually, it creates only embarrassment. For example, a US appeal court declined to strike down a referendum question for subject–verb disagreement, where (in the court's view) the grammatical lapse caused no ambiguity: *Stickler v Ashcroft* 359 SW 3d 702 (Mo App WD, 2017). The decision reflects other US decisions in which courts have refused to strike down instruments for grammatical errors (ibid, [8]).

See also **GENDER-NEUTRAL LANGUAGE**; **premises**; **PRONOUNS**; **SINGULAR / PLURAL**.

subjudice

See **sub judice**.

SUBJUNCTIVE / INDICATIVE

Usage

Writing in 1952, HW Fowler described the subjunctive mood as 'moribund': *Modern English Usage* (OUP, 1952) 574. Yet it survives, and remains useful for at least the following purposes:

- *To express a wish*: eg, 'If only my husband *were* on time' (implying that he is late).
- *To point to a state of affairs that is hypothetical* rather than real: eg, 'If I *were* you …' (implying that I am not).
- *To make a suggestion or proposal*: eg, 'I move that new directors *be appointed*'; 'The judge suggested that counsel *check* her instructions.'

Whether to insist on the subjunctive in these situations may be a matter of audience. If the reader is likely to find the subjunctive strained, unidiomatic, or pompous, drawing attention to itself and diverting attention from the message, then it might be better to avoid it and use the indicative—unless of course the result *were* to be ambiguous (which is unlikely). The above examples would then read:

- 'If only my husband *was* on time.'
- 'If I *was* you …'
- 'I move that new directors are *appointed*'; 'The judge suggested that counsel *checks* her instructions.'

Potential for ambiguity

Using the subjunctive where you mean the indicative may create ambiguity—at least, to readers familiar with the distinction.

Example

> A clause in a building contract requires the builder to provide a security, to ensure that funds are available if the landowner (the 'Proprietor') needs to sue the builder for breach of contract. The clause states:
>
> > 'Any security provided by the Builder shall be available to the Proprietor whenever the Proprietor *may be entitled* to the payment of moneys by the Builder under this Agreement' [emphasis added].
>
> Do the words 'whenever the Proprietor *may be entitled*' mean: (1) whenever the Proprietor *could possibly be entitled*; or (2) whenever the Proprietor *is entitled*? The potential ambiguity has divided judges. Some favour meaning (1), others favour meaning (2). See, eg, *Bachmann Pty Ltd v Power New Zealand Ltd* [1999] 1 VR 420, [40]–[43]; *Reed Construction Services Pty Ltd v Kheng Seng (Australia) Pty Ltd* (1998) 15 BCL 158, 165–66.

Further reading

Robert C Farrell, 'Why Grammar Matters: Conjugating Verbs in Modern Legal Opinions' (2008) 40 *Loyola University Chicago Law Journal* 1, 4–13 (reviewing US cases on the importance of mood—indicative, subjunctive, imperative)

See also **TENSE**.

sublease / assignment

See **assignment / sublease; lease / sublease**.

sublease / sub-lease

Both forms are used, but *sublease* (hyphen-less) is preferred; similarly preferred are *sublessor* (not *sub-lessor*) and *sublessee* (not *sub-lessee*). However, usage is not consistent; even judges in the same case can differ: see, eg, *Meridien Airlie Beach Pty Ltd v Karamist* [2015] QCA 192, [4] (Ann Lyons J: *sublessors, subleases*), [61] (North J: *sub-lessee, sub-leases*).

sublease / underlease

Strictly, these terms are synonymous—each denotes a lease granted out of a lease. However, in practice *underlease* more commonly refers to a sublease granted (ie, 'carved') out of a long-term lease (the 'headlease'). In theory, any number of subleases (or underleases) can be carved out of a headlease: eg, the landlord may grant a headlease to A, out of which A grants a sublease (underlease) to B, out of which B grants a sub-sublease (sub-underlease) to C, out of which C grants a sub-sub-sublease (sub-sub-underlease) to D, and so on.

See also **assignment / sublease; lease / sublease**.

submortgage

Usually not hyphenated. Where a *submortgage* is itself mortgaged, then *sub-submortgage*.

subordinate legislation

Regulations, bylaws, rules, and the like, that are not themselves Acts of Parliament but are made under an Act of Parliament.

subpoena

An order to attend court, under penalty (Latin: *sub poena*) of punishment for failure to comply. The proper plural is *subpoenas*; the plural *subpoenae* is sometimes seen, but is based on the misconception that *subpoena* is a Latin singular noun—in fact, it is a Latin expression (*sub poena*) which has been anglicised. Historically, a subpoena to attend court was called *subpoena ad test*, being an abbreviation for *subpoena ad testificandum*, meaning subpoena 'to give evidence'; and a subpoena to produce documents in court was called *subpoena duces tecum*, meaning subpoena 'to bring with you'. Unless court rules require otherwise, there is no need to continue using the Latin terms.

subprime

In relation to a loan or mortgage—risky; with less than ideal recovery prospects (hence, 'subprime loan'). *Subprime* is not a legal term of art, but merely finance-industry jargon.

subscribe

To subscribe usually means *to pay money*: so you *subscribe* to a service, or *subscribe* for shares. It can also mean *sign* (literally, 'write under'); but that usage is obsolescent, and most would regard it as archaic.

SUBSECTIONS (REFERENCES TO)

See **CITATION OF LEGISLATION**.

subsequent to

Prefer *after*—a shorter word is better than a longer word, and one word is better than two. For example:

- 'The appellant was extradited to the US *subsequent to* [prefer: *after*] the original SIAC hearing. He was prosecuted in the US .... In 2016, *subsequent to* [prefer: *after*] the decision of the Supreme Court, by a plea bargain he pleaded guilty to three counts.' [*Pham v Secretary of State for the Home Department* [2018] EWCA Civ 2064; [2019] 1 WLR 2070, [6] (Arden LJ)]
- 'This special case concerns benefits conferred by legislation on Commonwealth Parliamentarians *after* [note: not *subsequent to*] their retirement. The four plaintiffs are retired [parliamentarians] who were, *subsequent to* [prefer: *after*] their retirement, receiving retirement benefits. ... The third and fourth plaintiffs were, *subsequent to* [prefer: *after*] their retirement, also receiving travel benefits.' [*Cunningham v Commonwealth of Australia* [2016] HCA 39; (2016) 90 ALJR 1138, [197] (Nettle J)]

subsidiary company

A company that is controlled by another company by virtue of share ownership and control over the appointment of directors. Legal documents often incorporate a statutory definition or a bespoke definition for the purposes of the document. For example:

Statutory definition [*Companies Act 2006*, s 1159(1)]

> 'A company is a "subsidiary" of another company, its "holding company", if that other company—
>
> (a) holds a majority of the voting rights in it, or
>
> (b) is a member of it and has the right to appoint or remove a majority of its board of directors, or
>
> (c) is a member of it and controls alone, pursuant to an agreement with other members, a majority of the voting rights in it,
>
> or if it is a subsidiary of a company that is itself a subsidiary of that other company.'

Bespoke definition

> 'A company is a subsidiary of another company ("the holding company") if more than [X%] of its shares is directly or indirectly controlled by the holding company.'

See also **holding company**.

subsist

See **exist / subsist**.

substantially

A word of degree, inviting litigation: eg, whether A is '*substantially* the same as' B is open to debate. *Substantially* implies *some* degree of permissible variance, but the actual degree depends on the circumstances. Also open to debate are formulations such as whether a form is completed '*substantially* as required by' a statute, or whether building works have been '*substantially* commenced' within a prescribed time.

In seeking to discern the meaning of words or phrases, courts sometimes reason from analogous words or phrases. Thus, *substantial* can mean:

- 'real' or 'weighty or serious': *Superior Overseas Development Corp v British Gas Corp* [1982] 1 Lloyd's Rep 262, 266, 269
- 'worthy of consideration': *R v Monopolies and Mergers Commission* [1993] 1 WLR 23, 29, 32
- 'considerable': *Calder v Simpson* 1994 SLT 32, 36
- 'more than trivial': *R v Golds* [2016] UKSC 61; [2016] 1 WLR 5231, [41]–[43].

However, to discern meaning by analogy may focus attention more on the analogue than on the original. Also, any meaning thus discerned applies chiefly to the case at hand—rarely does it provide a definitive precedent for all future cases. The only way to avoid argument is to indicate more precisely the degree of variance envisaged by 'substantially'.

successor in title

Strict usage

A person who acquires (ie, 'succeeds to') the same interest in the property as their predecessor ('the predecessor in title') once held. For example, when land is transferred, the purchaser becomes the vendor's *successor in title*; when a lease is assigned, the assignee becomes the assignor's *successor in title*. However, the interests must correspond precisely. If they do not, the later holder may be a 'successor', but is not strictly a *successor in title*.

Examples

- A statute provides that a resuming authority that compulsorily acquires land takes the land free of any lease that bound the land in the hands of the person from whom the land is acquired. The authority is not a *successor in title*, because the interest acquired (freehold, free of the lease) differs from the interest held by the former landowner (freehold, subject to the lease): *Leichhardt Municipal Council v N H Bowers & Leard Pty Ltd* (1944) 62 WN (NSW) 85, 85–86.
- A statute entitles a tenant's family members to remain in possession of the property after the tenant's death. The family members are not *successors in title*, because (properly interpreted) their statutory right is a mere personal right to occupy; they do not acquire the deceased's leasehold interest in the land: *Shaw v Kadwell* [1960] NSWR 689, 691–92.
- A land registration statute provides that a registered purchaser acquires the land free from an unregistered lease that bound the land in the hands of the vendor. The purchaser is not a *successor in title*, because the interest acquired (freehold, free of the lease) differs from the interest held by the vendor (freehold, subject to the lease): *Cambridge Acceptance Ltd v Fetherston* [1965] NSWR 1513, 1515; *R v Kontos* [1966] 2 NSWR 38, 45.

Imprecise usage

Sometimes, *successor in title* is used in the vernacular sense of anyone whose ownership follows on from another's. For example, where a tenant grants a sublease, the subtenant may be called (loosely) the tenant's 'successor in title'. But this is a legally imprecise use of the term, because the sublease is not the same interest as that held (formerly) by the tenant; rather, it is an interest carved out of it (the tenant still holding a reversion in the lease out of which it is carved).

Sometimes this loose use appears in statutes also. For example, under s 78 of the *Law of Property Act 1925*, for the purpose of enforcing covenants over land, 'successors in title' expressly includes occupiers of the land. This widens the notion of *successor in title* beyond the common-law understanding, although only for the purpose of the statute. Likewise (but under a different statute), a long-term ground tenant was a 'successor in title' of the freehold owner and could therefore claim under building insurance available to the freehold owner's 'successors in title': *Owners Strata Plan No 91322 v Trustees of the Roman Catholic Church for the Archdiocese of Sydney* [2019] NSWCA 89.

See also **predecessor in title; remainder / reversion**.

such

Such as a referent

Generally unnecessary

When used to refer to something already mentioned, *such* is an unnecessary legalism. Perhaps legal writers use *such* out of a desire for precision—if so, the desire is misplaced, for *such* is easily replaced with words that preserve precision but avoid legalism: eg, *the*, *that*, or similar. For example:

- An applicant must give *such information as is* [prefer: *the information*] required by the Director.
- The information must in *such form as may be* [prefer: *the form*; *a form*] specified by the Director.
- You must submit an application *and in such application give* [prefer: *and in the application give*; or *and in it give*; or simply *giving*] your details.
- I appoint my wife as my executor, and I give all of my property to *such* [prefer: *my*] wife.

Good legal writers have long avoided the legalistic *such*.

An exception?

Some plain-language advocates would banish *such* completely, on the ground that it always smacks of legalism. But in limited contexts *such* remains useful as a word-saving referent. In the example that follows, it would be possible to write-out *such*, but only by using more words—in which case, anti-*such* zeal would trump brevity.

Example [letter from tenant to landlord]

> 'Before you can terminate the lease, statute requires you to give me one month's notice in writing, specifying the breach you allege that I have committed, the circumstances in which you allege I have breached it, and giving me a reasonable time in which to remedy the breach. I have received no *such* notice.' [*Such* in the final sentence catches up all the detail of the preceding sentence.]

Potential ambiguity

Such is ambiguous where it may possibly refer to a number of previous matters. Which one is intended? As a starting point, a court presumes that *such* points to the immediately preceding referent: *Ex parte Barnes* [1896] AC 146, 150, Lord Halsbury LC; *Re Ninnes* [1920] SASR 480, 488 (Poole J). But that is a starting point only. It can be rebutted by the circumstances, leaving the operation of *such* potentially uncertain. For example:

- An obligation in a bank guarantee to pay 'all *such* sums' was ambiguous where *such* could refer to one or other of several sums: *Rainy Sky SA v Kookmin Bank* [2011] UKSC 50; [2011] 1 WLR 2900.
- A statutory provision stated that failure to register a security interest under Act A did not invalidate the security interest if it was registered under Act B, and that Act B applied to 'any *such* security interest'. *Such* was ambiguous, because it could refer to (1) securities that had not been registered under Act A, or (2) securities that had been registered under Act B. Held (by majority of the Ontario Court of Appeal), interpretation (2): *Euroclean Canada Inc v Forest Glade Investments Ltd* (1985) 16 DLR (4th) 289.

Such meaning *any*

Sometimes, *such* is used to mean *any* or *whatever*, particularly where a discretion is conferred. Prefer *any* or *whatever*—which will also help lay bare the breadth of the discretion. For example:

> The court may take into account *such other factors as* [prefer: *any other factors*; *whatever else*] it considers relevant.

Such in series

When used in series, *such* can become particularly 'legalistic'. Consider the following extract:

> 'A judge … shall deposit … to the credit of the retirement fund, an amount equal to 3.5 percent of the judge's pay. … Each *such* judge may elect to make *such* deposits in installments during *the* judge's period of service in *such* amount and under *such* conditions as may be determined … by the chief judge. Notwithstanding the failure of a judge to make *such* deposit, … credit shall be allowed for *the* service rendered, but the annual annuity of the surviving spouse of *such* judge shall be reduced by … 10 percent of the amount of *such* deposit, computed as of the date of the death of *such* judge, unless *the* surviving spouse elects to eliminate *such* service entirely from credit …' [38 US Code §7297, on judicial annuities. Note the occasional *the*, suggesting that even the drafter had trouble sustaining the *such*-torrent.]

Also, when used in series, *such* may carry different meanings. While this does not necessarily introduce ambiguity, it is better to choose the appropriate word or phrase for each different meaning. In the following examples, sufficient replacement words are indicated in underlined italics.

Example (lease)

> If the tenant requests a new lease, the landlord's management committee will consider ~~*such*~~ *the* request, and for that purpose may:
>
> (a) convene ~~*such meetings as may be required*~~ *any meetings required* to consider ~~*such*~~ the request;
>
> (b) require the tenant to produce ~~*such books of account as may be required*~~ *any books of account* required to be considered at ~~*such*~~ *the* meetings; and
>
> (c) at ~~*any such*~~ *the* meetings, require the tenant to explain any entries in ~~*such*~~ *those* books of account; and
>
> (d) make ~~*such*~~ *any* other enquiries as it considers necessary in relation to ~~*such*~~ *those* entries.

Such in wordy expressions

Such often appears in composite expressions. Almost always, they are unnecessarily wordy. Two common instances are *such … (if any)* and *such … as*.

'such … (if any)'

Such … (if any) simply means *any*. Perhaps the writer considers that *such … (if any)* hints at a lesser degree of choice, or a less idiosyncratic degree of choice, than the blunter *any*; but this is not so—the meaning is the same. For example:

- 'The court may make *such order (if any)* as it considers appropriate.' This means simply: 'The court may make *any order* it considers appropriate' (including making no order at all).
- 'The auditors may recommend *such changes (if any)* to the accounts as they consider necessary.' This means simply: 'The auditors may recommend *any changes* to the accounts they consider necessary' (including recommending no changes at all).

'such … as' / 'such as'

The wordy *such … as* can often be replaced with idiomatic (and less legalistic) English, or even deleted, without affecting meaning. For example:

- The court may make ~~such~~[substitute: *the*] orders ~~as~~ it considers appropriate.
- The judge may make ~~such~~ [substitute: *all*] orders ~~as are~~ necessary to finalise the dispute.
- 'Mr Masri would only be able to bring ~~such~~ claims against the defendants … ~~as~~ [substitute: *that*] were not time barred …' [*Masri v Consolidated Contractors International Company SAL* [2011] EWHC 1024 (Comm), [23] (Clarke J)]
- 'Whether there was extinguishment can only be determined by reference to ~~such~~ [substitute: *any*] particular rights and interests ~~as may be~~ asserted and established.' [*Wik Peoples v Queensland* (1996) 187 CLR 1, 133 (Toohey J)]

However, contrast the use of *such as* to introduce an example. That use is acceptable: eg, 'This regulation prohibits parking by vehicles, *such as* cars and buses.' Here, *such as* denotes that the example is non-exhaustive: *Franklins Pty Ltd v Metcash Trading Ltd* (2009) 76 NSWLR 603, [353].

suffer

Meaning *allow*

Suffer is an archaism for *allow*. To *suffer* something to be done (or not to be done) is to *allow* it to be done (or not to be done). Prefer *allow*. It is true that *allow* may sometimes be ambiguous; eg, do you *allow* something to occur where you have no power to stop it occurring? But it is no worse than *suffer*—which may range in meaning from *permit*, to *fail to prevent*, or to *endure*: *Roffey v Bent* (1867) LR 3 Eq 759, 761.

In word pairings

'suffer or allow'

To *suffer* something to be done is to *allow* it to be done, so *suffer or allow* is a needless pairing. And because *suffer* in this sense is archaic, prefer *allow*, eg:

> 'The tenant must not ~~*suffer or*~~ *allow* trespassers to enter the property.'

'suffer or permit'

Similarly, *suffer or permit* is a needless pairing. To *suffer* something to occur is to *permit* it to occur. *Suffer* means *permit*, and *permit* means *suffer*; all dictionaries agree, and so do the courts: see, eg, *Ex parte Eyston* (1877) 7 Ch D 145, 149 (James LJ). Here too, because *suffer* in this sense is archaic, prefer *permit*.

'suffer or incur'

In most contexts, this pairing is unnecessary: either *suffer* or *incur* alone suffices. However, sometimes (though rarely) it may be useful to retain the distinction. For example, it might be useful to distinguish between *suffering* a liability and *incurring* a liability: the first connotes passively permitting the liability to arise, while the second connotes some positive act causing it to arise.

See also **allow**; **cause (to be done)**; **permit**; **WORD PAIRINGS**.

sufferance

So spelled in modern English (in medieval English, sometimes *suffrance*). In legal usage, as in normal usage, *sufferance* connotes the absence of objection rather than the granting of approval. Thus, a 'tenant at sufferance' is a tenant whose initial lease has expired but who remains in possession without the landlord's assent or dissent: *Remon v City of London Real Property Co Ltd* [1921] 1 KB 49, 58; *Anderson v Bowles* (1951) 84 CLR 310, 319.

suggestio falsi

Latin: the suggestion of what is false; a suggestion of untruth; a misrepresentation; the deliberate misrepresentation of something without actually lying. Usually found in tandem with *suppressio veri* (suppression of the truth) as part of the longer expression. *suppressio veri suggestio est falsi*:

> 'That is the worst of our mortgage deed—owing to the action of equity, it is one long *suppressio veri* and *suggestio falsi*. It does not in the least explain the rights of the parties; it suggests that they are other than they really are.' [FW Maitland, *Lectures on Equity* (Cambridge University Press, 1910) 269]

When FW Maitland used these expressions over a century ago, his audience (Cambridge law students) would have understood the Latin and relished the alliteration. But modern audiences, untutored in Latin, need plain-English translations—which, happily, are easily supplied without loss of legal meaning. For example:

- '[I]n my opinion the principle that a party to a general release cannot take advantage of a *suggestio falsi* [prefer: *misrepresentation*] or *suppressio veri* [prefer: *falsehood*], in other words, of what would ordinarily be regarded as sharp practice, is sufficient to deal with any unfairness which may be caused by such releases.' [*Bank of Credit and Commerce International SA v Ali* [2001] UKHL 8, [71]; [2002] 1 AC 251, 279 (Lord Hoffmann)]
- 'By implying that the plaintiff had served a sentence, the article added *suggestio falsi to suppressio veri* [prefer: *misrepresentation to untruth*].' [*Howden v Truth & Sportsman Ltd* (1937) 58 CLR 416, 426 (Evatt J)]

sui juris

Latin: in one's own right. Used in law to mean 'legally competent', 'with full legal capacity'. The Latinism is a handy shorthand for lawyers, but a stumbling block for non-lawyers. It is eminently translatable into standard and context-appropriate English, as in the following examples:

- 'The principle [in *Saunders v Vautier*] recognises the rights of beneficiaries, *who are sui juris* [prefer: *who have full legal capacity*] and together absolutely entitled to the trust property, to exercise their proprietary rights to overbear and defeat the intention of a testator or settlor …' [*Goulding v James* [1997] 2 All ER 239, 247 (Mummery LJ)]

- 'The interests of the children were vested and *all were sui juris* [prefer: *all had full legal capacity; all were entitled to exercise legal control over their affairs*].' [*Chief Commissioner of Stamp Duties (NSW) v Buckle* (1998) 192 CLR 226, 241 (High Court of Australia)]

suitable

A protean word, taking its meaning from context. This makes it notoriously vague, yet examples in law are common: '*suitable* accommodation' (for homeless person), '*suitable* container' (for blood specimens), '*suitable* safety precautions' (for factory workers). Where possible, specify requirements rather than leave them to the vagaries of *suitable*. As Lord Hoffmann observed:

> 'The word "suitable" is an empty vessel which is filled with meaning by context and background.' [*R v Human Fertilisation and Embryology Authority* [2005] 2 AC 561, 573 [33] (speaking of a statutory reference to 'practices designed to secure that embryos are in a *suitable* condition to be placed in a woman or to determine whether embryos are *suitable* for that purpose')]

sum of (money)

Superfluous?

In references to money, *the sum of* (money) is almost always superfluous. For example, 'I promise to pay you *the sum of* £100' means simply 'I promise to pay you £100'—so strike out 'the sum of'.

However, in the law of wills it has been said that a gift 'of' a stated amount may differ from a gift of '*the sum of*' a stated amount. For example (it has been said): 'I give to A £100 in my handbag' could be a specific gift of the actual cash in the handbag, but 'I give to A *the sum* of £100 in my handbag' could be a gift of money generally, to be paid out of the estate as a whole but preferably out of the money in the handbag: see *Re Pratt* [1894] 3 Ch 491, 494 (North J). But the distinction seems exceedingly fine, and in any case depends on the meaning of the particular will in the light of the particular testator's intentions.

Prefer *amount*

When referring to money, idiomatic English prefers *amount* over *sum*. Follow this preference in legal writing also: *amount* means the same, and softens the legal 'feel' of *sum*: eg, 'I owe you *an amount* [not *a sum*] of money.' (Or better still, of course: 'I owe you money.') However, *sum* remains appropriate where the concept is of accumulated amounts—eg, 'the *sum* of all the creditor's debts'.

SUMMARY

See **EXECUTIVE SUMMARY**.

summon / summons

To *summon* someone is to beckon or call them. To *summons* someone means to beckon or call them by means of a *summons* (or similar procedure) to appear in court. Both words derive from the same Latin root (*summonere*: in earlier Latin, to give a hint to; in medieval Latin, to call or summon).

Some writers seem to find the verb *to summons*—ie, to require someone to attend court—aesthetically unpleasing, and prefer *to summon*. For example:

- 'The horrible expression "summonsed for an offence" (turning the noun "summons" into a verb) has now become accepted usage, but "summoned" remains not only allowable but preferable.' [Glanville Williams, *Learning the Law*, 11th edn (Stevens and Sons, 1982) 15, fn 28]
- 'Two criteria must be satisfied before a court is to *summon* a person under s 596A for examination … First, … Second, the court must be satisfied that the person to be *summoned* is …' [*Palmer v Ayres* [2017] HCA 5, [12] (Kiefel, Keane, Nettle, and Gordon JJ)]

But other writers, favouring convention over aesthetics, prefer *summons*. For example:

- '[H]e was *summonsed* to attend the correction facility on 28 July 2008 …' [*Goluchowski v District Court in Elbag* [2016] UKSC 36; [2016] 1 WLR 2665, [15] (Lord Neuberger)]
- 'In September 2003, the appellant was *summonsed* to attend the Commission …' [*Z v New South Wales Crime Commission* (2007) 233 ALR 17; [2007] HCA 7, [25] (Hayne and Crennan JJ)]

The only guiding principle is to be inwardly consistent:

- 'There was a dispute between the parties about the production of *summonsed* documents. Briefly, documents were *summoned* returnable on 11 August 2004.' [*Robichaux v Curry* [2004] NSWTTT 788; inconsistent use]

sunset

As an adjective, describing a clause in a statute or contract that sets an end-date (*sunset clause, sunset provision*). For example:

> '*Sunsetting* transitional provisions assists in avoiding unnecessary clutter in the statute book. … [T]hese *sunsetted* transitional provisions can be readily located …' [*Statute Law Amendment Act 2006* (ACT) Sch 2, cl [2.6] (Explanatory note)]

In recent times, this use has spawned the cumbersome verb *to sunset* or (yet more cumbersome) *to be sunsetted*. If this neologism seems a step too far, it is easily recast:

> 'We propose that … each authority *should be sunsetted so that it expires* [prefer: *each authority should automatically cease to exist*] after five years.' [New Zealand Law Commission, *Review of the Privacy Act 1993* (Issues Paper No 17, March 2010), 244]

SUNSET CLAUSE

So-named because it contemplates an end-time for the whole or part of the document in which the clause appears. There are two main kinds of sunset clauses:

1. A contractual provision specifying that the contract (or part of it) is to come to an end, or authorising a party to bring the contract (or part of it) to an end, unless a stated event occurs within a stated time. Examples are:
   - a provision in an insurance policy specifying an end-date after which the insurer will no accept claims for incidents that took place while the policy was in force
   - a clause in a contract for the sale of land in a yet-to-be-registed subdivision specifying that a party may rescind the contract unless the subdivision is registered by a stated date.
2. A statutory provision specifying that an Act (or a regulation or ordinance) will expire on a stated date or after a stated period. The purpose is usually to allow legislation with a limited purpose expire automatically at the specified time without needing

the additional step of formal repeal. In the case of regulations, sunset provisions help declutter the statute book, by removing regulations that have outlived their usefulness; if Parliament or the Executive considers that the regulations remain relevant, they can be re-enacted.

Further reading

Sofia Ranchordás, 'Sunset clauses and experimental regulations: blessing or curse for legal certainty?' (2015) 36 *Statute Law Review* 28 (exploring the rationale for, and the literature about, sunset clauses in legislation)

See also **sunset**.

sup cit

See **supra citatum**.

SUPERFLUOUS MATERIAL

Delete it

Delete all superfluous material. A legal document should contain only material relevant to the subject matter. This is so regardless of the type of document—whether a legal advice, a statute, a contract, a deed, or a judgment.

Deciding what is superfluous can be difficult and may require research. However—though a hard reality—uncertainty over whether material is necessary is no excuse for retaining it. If drafters do not understand why they include material, then readers are even less likely to. Every sentence, every word, should serve a purpose.

Some words or phrases are superfluous because they necessarily follow from other provisions or from the law. For example:

- In a conveyance of land to A and B 'as tenants in common', it is superfluous to add 'and not as joint tenants', because ownership as tenants in common necessarily precludes ownership as joint tenants.
- In a provision in company's constitution regulating voting by directors, it is superfluous to add that, on a tied vote, the chairperson does *not* have an additional casting vote, because the common law already provides that on a tied vote the chairperson has no additional casting vote (unless conferred by statute or by the company's constitution): *Nell v Longbottom* [1894] 1 QB 767, 771.
- In a trust deed that intends to give trustees only those powers given by law, it is superfluous to specify the trustees' actual powers, because trustee legislation does so anyway.

Qualification

Despite the admonition to omit superfluous material, there may be audience-related exceptions. It is sometimes helpful to spell out information that necessarily follows from what has already been said, or that is implied by law, to help the parties understand their rights and obligations. Thus, in the second of the above examples, it may be helpful to add a provision about the chairperson's lack of a casting vote; and in the third, it may be useful to add a provision listing the trustees' powers; because in both cases, the expected readership is unlikely to know the legal principles.

See also **SURPLUSAGE (PRESUMPTION AGAINST)**.

supersede / supercede

Supersede is correct; *supercede* is a common misspelling:

- '[The judge] acceded to the father's application for an expert opinion as to the law of Romania, presumably either to clarify or to *supercede* [prefer: *supersede*] the judgment of the court.' [*Re D (a child)* [2006] EWCA Civ 830, [4] (Thorpe LJ)]
- 'I do not agree that that *supercedes* [prefer: *supersedes*] clause 6 of the constitution.' [*Cody v Live Board Holdings Ltd* [2014] NSWSC 78, [21]; (2014) 97 ACSR 606, 612 (Brereton J)]

supplemental to

It is sometimes necessary or useful to make a document 'supplemental to' another document—as where parties enter into a document (Doc 1), and later find it necessary to enter into an ancillary document (Doc 2). By a convenient statutory shorthand, if Doc 2 is expressed to be 'supplemental to' Doc 1, the contents of Doc 1 are treated as if recited in full in Doc 2: *Law of Property Act 1925*, s 58. This allows recourse to Doc 1 when interpreting Doc 2: *Plumrose Ltd v Real and Leasehold Estate Investment Society Ltd* [1970] 1 WLR 52, 55–56.

Importantly, Doc 1 is read into Doc 2 as a recital only, not as an operative provision. This may have several consequences:

1. If the documents conflict, Doc 1 (having the subsidiary role of a recital) may be interpreted as subject to Doc 2.
2. If Doc 1 has expired or been terminated, its status as a recital in Doc 2 does not, of itself, revive it: *Fattal v Walbrook Trustees (Jersey) Ltd* [2010] EWHC 2767 (Ch), [102] (Lewison J).

See also **RECITALS**.

suppressio veri

Latin: suppression of the truth.

See **suggestio falsi**.

supra

Latin: above. As with its opposite (*infra*, below), although the Latin has become standard English, it has no intrinsic advantage over *above*. Often combined with *vide* ('see') to form *vide supra*—which also has no advantage over *see above*.

See also **vide**.

supra citatum

Latin: above cited; abbreviation *sup cit* (in US usage, with full stops, *sup. cit.*). Indicates a matter already referred to. The English translation is always sufficient.

SURPLUSAGE (PRESUMPTION AGAINST)

The presumption

The 'presumption against surplusage' asserts that the drafter intends every word or phrase in a statute or legal document to serve a purpose. Courts approach the task of interpretation on the basis that all the expressions have a purpose, and that the court's task is to discern that purpose. For example, where legislation imposes taxation on rights to use land 'conferred on or acquired by' a person, 'conferred on' is assumed to have a purpose (and meaning) separate from 'acquired by': *Chief Commissioner of State Revenue v Pacific National (ACT) Ltd* [2007] NSWCA 325, [45]–[46]; (2007) 70 NSWLR 544.

Sometimes, the presumption may give a word or phrase a wider operation than the drafter intended. For example, many contracts use the expression 'successors and *permitted* assigns [ie, assignees]'. The word 'permitted' may well be a mere formulaic addition, with little or no thought given to its meaning. However, the presumption against surplusage treats it as intentional, not superfluous. A Queensland court held it means 'authorised', so that *permitted* assigns were persons in whose favour an assignment has been authorised: *Parmalat Australia Ltd v Norco Co-operative Ltd* [2006] QCA 129.

It follows from the presumption against surplusage that where two interpretations are open, one requiring *all* words to have meaning and the other requiring *some* words to be ignored, the former is favoured: *AMP Inc v Utilux Pty Ltd* [1972] RPC 103, 109 (Lord Reid); *Minister of State for Resources v Dover Fisheries Pty Ltd* (1993) 43 FCR 565, 574 (Gummow J).

Limitations

The presumption against surplusage is unreliable in three situations:

1. **The drafter's style is consistently prolix or tautologous**. The court may then have to discount, or even ignore, surplus words. In commercial contracts, for example, tautology 'is not unknown' and is often coupled with 'a degree of verbal exuberance': *Wood v Sureterm Direct Ltd* [2015] EWCA Civ 839, [49] (Clarke LJ). In such situations, 'little weight is to be given to considerations based on surplusage': *Taheri v Vitek* [2014] NSWCA 209, [121]; (2014) 87 NSWLR 403 (Leeming JA). Or as Lord Hoffmann observed, 'the argument from redundancy is seldom an entirely secure one [because] people often use superfluous words': *Beaufort Developments (NI) Ltd v Gilbert-Ash (NI) Ltd* [1999] 1 AC 266, 274.
2. **The material, though strictly superfluous, is consistent with the contract's commercial purpose**. This is particularly so where the superfluous words appear in boilerplate clauses, or have been added out of more abundant caution: *Centennial Mandalong Pty Ltd v Delta Electricity* [2013] NSWSC 1505, [67] (McDougall J). For example, landlords' repairing covenants commonly state, 'the landlord must *well and sufficiently repair*' the leased premises. Courts have long held that the obligation is defined by the word *repair*, with *well and sufficiently* adding nothing to the meaning or content of the obligation: *Anstruther-Gough-Calthorpe v McOscar* [1924] 1 KB 716, 729 (Scrutton LJ).
3. **The drafter is a non-lawyer, untutored in legal niceties**. Such drafters sometimes assume that they must copy old-fashioned legal words and phrases despite the inherent wordiness. For this reason (amongst others), courts may 'go easier' on (for example) testators who draft their own wills (*Re Will of Masci* [2014] QSC 281, [7]) and local sporting clubs who draft their own by-laws (*Echunga Football Club Inc v Hills Football League Inc* [2014] SASC 201; (2014) 121 SASR 449, [18]).

See also **boilerplate**; **HENDIADYS**; **PROLIXITY**; **REDUNDANCIES**; **SUPERFLUOUS MATERIAL**; **TORRENTIAL STYLE (OF DRAFTING)**; **WORD STRINGS**; **WORD PAIRINGS.**

survivorship (right of)

See **joint tenant / tenant in common**.

suspects (verb)

See **believes / suspects**.

SYMBOLS

See **CITATION SYMBOLS; FORMULAS; FRACTIONS; NUMBERS.**

synallagmatic

From Greek: imposing mutual obligations. A *synallagmatic* contract is one imposing reciprocal obligations on the parties. The adjective was first used in English law by Lord Diplock in *Hongkong Fir Shipping Co Ltd v Kawaski Kisen Kaisha Ltd* [1962] 2 QB 26, 65. It was soon criticised for its obscurity. One critic was Lord Denning:

> 'A little while ago I heard of a contract being a "synallagmatic" contract. I had never heard of such a contract before. Nor had any other lawyer of my acquaintance. Nor had the textbook writers. At any rate, their books did not contain the word. I have since looked it up in the dictionary. I believe it means a two-sided contract; but I am not quite sure about it.' [Lord Denning, *The Closing Chapter* (Butterworths, 1983) 60]

Lord Diplock was unrepentant:

> 'In *Hongkong Fir Shipping* … I was careful to restrict my own observations to synallagmatic contracts. The insertion of this qualifying adjective was widely thought to be a typical example of gratuitous philological exhibitionism; but the present appeal does turn upon the difference in legal character between contracts which are synallagmatic (a term which I prefer to bilateral, for there may be more than two parties), and contracts which are not synallagmatic but only unilateral, an expression which, like synallagmatic, I have borrowed from French law.' [*United Dominions Trust (Commercial) Ltd v Eagle Aircraft Services Ltd* [1968] 1 WLR 74, 82]

Unless writing for the legal cognoscenti, prefer the simpler 'imposing reciprocal obligations'.

See also **SIMPLER WORDS AND PHRASES.**

SYNONYM STRINGS

See **WORD PAIRINGS; WORD STRINGS.**

SYNTACTIC AMBIGUITY

See **AMBIGUITY.**

TABLE OF CONTENTS

Usefulness

In a document of any length, add a table of contents. A table of contents eases the reader's path by providing an overview of the document. It also helps the writer ensure a logical grouping of topics. Most modern legislation includes a table of contents (even for short statutes), and court rules sometimes mandate one in submissions (eg, *California Rules of Court 2019*, Rule 8.204). Private-sector documents could do well to follow these leads.

Grouping topics in table

A table of contents is improved if clause headings are not merely listed one after another (eg, clauses 1–30), but are 'grouped' by topic under Part or Division headings. The grouping helps the writer ensure a logical organisation, and gives the reader an easier overview of the document's structure. The following example compares an 'ungrouped' table of contents against a 'grouped' table.

Table of contents (not grouped)	Table of contents (grouped under Parts)
1. Definitions 2. Interpretation 3. Landlord grants lease 4. Landlord to obtain mortgagee's consent to lease 5. Payment of bond 6. Payment of rent 7. Rent-free holiday 8. Payment of outgoings 9. Payment of stamp duty and landlord's legal costs 10. Tenant to repair 11. Provision of bank guarantee 12. Quiet enjoyment 13. Warranty as to fitness of premises 14. Dispute resolution procedures 15. Right to terminate on default 16. Release and indemnities 17. Notices 18. No waiver 19. Entire agreement 20. Law of contract 21. Joint and several liability 22. Counterparts	**Part 1: Introductory** 1. Definitions 2. Interpretation **Part 2: Grant of lease** 3. Landlord grants lease 4. Landlord to obtain mortgagee's consent to lease **Part 3: Tenant's obligations** 5. Payment of bond 6. Payment of rent 7. Exception for rent-free holiday 8. Payment of outgoings 9. Payment of stamp duty and landlord's legal costs 10. Tenant to repair 11. Provision of bank guarantee **Part 4: Landlord's obligations** 12. Quiet enjoyment 13. Warranty as to fitness of premises **Part 5: Default** 14. Dispute resolution procedures 15. Right to terminate on default **Part 6: General** 16. Release and indemnities 17. Notices 18. No waiver 19. Entire agreement 20. Law of contract 21. Joint and several liability 22. Counterparts

See also **DOCUMENT STRUCTURE; INDEX.**

TABLES

Purpose

Tables are valuable tools for displaying complex material in digestible form. Modern legal drafters increasingly use tables to help present information. Judges, too, sometimes use them: see, eg, *Forge v Australian Securities and Investment Commission* (2006) 228 CLR 45, 97–109 (Kirby J).

Tables can also be useful to illustrate the order of steps in a transaction, or to set clauses side-by-side for easy comparison, or to show lists of figures. The following two examples demonstrate their usefulness.

Example 1

Before

Hours of operation

Hours of operation will be limited to 7 am to 6 pm, Monday to Friday inclusive and 7 am to 1 pm on Saturdays, provided that operations may continue until 8 pm on Monday to Friday inclusive on condition that between 6 pm and 8 pm there will be no movement of vehicles or loaders on site associated with the drying plant operation save as required for essential plant maintenance. No operations are permitted on a Sunday or Public Holiday.

[Source: Agreement under *Planning and Environment Act 1987* (Vic), s 173]

After

Hours of operation

Monday to Friday	**Saturdays**	**Sundays and Public Holidays**
• 7 am–6 pm • 6 pm–8 pm, but only if no movement of vehicles or loaders on site associated with the drying plant operation, unless required for essential plant maintenance.	7 am–1 pm	No operations permitted

Example 2

Before

New York County Lawyers Association
House and Library Rules

The Office of the Association shall be open on weekdays, other than Saturdays and holidays, from 9 a.m. to 5 p.m. The building of the Association and its library and reading rooms shall be open from 9 a.m. to 10 p.m. on weekdays, other than on Saturdays; and on Saturdays the library shall be open from 9 a.m. to 6 p.m.; excepting that on weekdays in July and August it shall close at 6 p.m. with the exception of Wednesday when it shall be open until 10 p.m. and be closed on Saturdays; and it shall be closed entirely on all Sundays and holidays, exception Columbus Day, Lincoln's Birthday, Veteran's Day and Election Day, other than presidential elections, when it shall be open from 9 a.m. to 6 p.m., and on Christmas Eve and New Year's Eve it shall close at 4 p.m.

[Source: Professor Reed Dickerson, seminar exercise, Plain English Campaign conference, Madingley, UK, 1990]

After

Office hours

Weekdays	9 am–5 pm
Saturday, Sunday and public holidays	Closed

Building and Library hours

Normal opening hours	Monday–Friday: 9 am–10 pm Saturday: 9 am–6 pm Sunday: closed Christmas Eve: early closing (4 pm) New Year's Eve: early closing (4 pm)
July and August	Monday: 9 am–6 pm Tuesday: 9 am–6 pm Wednesday: 9 am–10 pm Thursday: 9 am–6 pm Thursday: 9 am–6 pm Saturday and Sunday: closed
Public holidays	Closed **Except** the following days • Columbus Day (open 9 am–6 pm) • Lincoln's Birthday (open 9 am–6 pm) • Veteran's Day (open 9 am–6 pm) • Election Day (open 9 am–6 pm). **Note**: Presidential Election Day – normal opening hours

Table 'lines'

Avoid thick vertical lines ('rules') in tables; either replace them with subtle lines, or eliminate them. It may also be possible to eliminate horizontal lines, using instead alternate white and grey (or similar) rows. The eye is then drawn to the contents of the table, not to its grid structure.

tabula in naufragio

Latin: plank in a shipwreck.

Technical use

A colourful label for a complex doctrine, under which an inferior interest in land may 'tack' onto a superior interest in the land and gain the priority enjoyed by that superior interest. In its classic form, the doctrine operates where land is mortgaged first to A (legal mortgage), second to B (equitable mortgage), and third to C (equitable mortgage). Normally, priority would be determined by the dates on which the respective mortgages were created: A comes first, followed by B, followed by C. But under the *tabula in naufragio* doctrine: (i) *if* C made his or her loan without notice of B's equitable mortgage; and (ii) *if* C acquires the legal estate from A; then (iii) C can 'tack' the third (equitable) mortgage to the first (legal) mortgage and become entitled to be repaid the amount owing under both mortgages in priority to B (*Taylor v Russell* [1892] AC 244). In Hanbury's words, 'The legal estate [held by A] was regarded as *tabula in naufragio*, a plank in a shipwreck, to be scrambled for by drowning equitable mortgagees': RH Maudsley (ed), *Hanbury's Modern Equity*, 9th edn (Stevens & Sons, 1969) 583.

Some may regard the Latin as a term of art, indispensable to understanding the doctrine. But in reality it is merely a Latin tag for a settled principle. Of itself, the Latin says nothing about the detail of *how* the doctrine operates. Nor of course does the English translation 'plank in a shipwreck'—but the English remains adequate for most purposes:

> '[T]he acquisition of the mortgage by assignment is similar to tacking pursuant to the doctrine of *tabula in naufragio* [prefer: *plank in a shipwreck*].' [*Olympic Holdings Pty Ltd v Windslow Corp Pty Ltd* [2008] WASCA 80; (2008) 36 WAR 342, [116] (EM Heenan AJA)]

Non-technical use

Sometimes, the Latin tag is used in a more general sense of 'life-saving device'. Here, the Latin is mere flourish—which (unless the reader understands Latin) misses the mark because it fails to communicate. Prefer a context-appropriate plain-English alternative or, as in the first example below, add a translation.

- '[Counsel] submitted that the Defendants' allegations of breach of duty are inappropriate because they are in the nature of a *tabula in naufragio* (a plank in a shipwreck) in the sense that, as Slade LJ explained [in a case], they are put forward on "rather slender grounds, as representing substantially the only hope of obtaining the discharge of injunctions in cases where [the merits are weak]".' [*PJSC Tatneft v Bogolyubov* [2016] EWHC 2816 (Comm), [123] (Picken J, adding a translation)]
- 'But to my mind this argument is not only incorrect, but also exposes another fallacy which underlies the respondent's reliance on s 4(2) as a jurisdictional *tabula in naufragio* [prefer: *life raft*].' [*Leech v Deputy Governor of Parkhurst Prison* [1988] AC 533, 564 (Lord Bridge)]
- '[That case] has for more than half a century justifiably remained one of those submerged cases which lawyers in general have tacitly accepted as being a total loss, until it was dredged up in the course of the hearing of the instant case in your Lordships' House to provide … a *tabula in naufragio* [prefer: *lifeboat*] for the buyers.' [*Berger & Co Inc v Gill & Duffus SA* [1984] AC 382, 392 (Lord Diplock)]

Further reading

S Bridge, E Cooke, and M Dixon (eds), *Megarry & Wade's Law of Real Property*, 9th edn (Sweet & Maxwell, 2019) [25-051]–[25-053]

tabula rasa

Latin: scraped tablet; clean slate; a blank surface ready to receive new impressions. Hence, a legal issue which the court can decide as it sees appropriate, unfettered by precedent. Unless readers can be expected to know the Latin, prefer the plainer English. For example:

- '[T]he question at the heart of this case is whether the statutory language, properly construed, means that … the revocation [of the deportation order] has given rise to a *tabula rasa* [prefer: *clean slate*; *clean sheet*] awaiting inscription by the Secretary of State as she considers appropriate …' [*R v Secretary of State for Home Department* [2013] 1 WLR 1319; [2012] EWCA Civ 1362, [39] (Kay LJ)]

- '[W]e cannot interpret [the Code's] general provisions concerning such basic principles as if they were written on a *tabula rasa* [prefer: *clean slate*], with all that used to be there removed and forgotten.' [*Vallance v R* (1961) 108 CLR 56, 75 (Windeyer J)]

take effect

A lawyer's legalistic euphemism for 'occur' or 'come into operation'. Prefer a less legalistic expression: eg, 'This contract ~~takes effect~~ *comes into operation* [or *starts*] on 1 January.'

Also, beware of potential ambiguity when using *take effect* in the context of an interest in property coming into existence. For example:

> A testator devises property 'To my son X, to *take effect* when X attains 25.' When the testator dies, X is 20. Does the gift to X 'vest' immediately on the testator's death, subject to divesting if X fails to attain 25? Or is it contingent on X's attaining 25 (so that, until then, X gets nothing)? The expression *take effect* leaves the issue open. It is true that the law generally favours 'early vesting', under which the gift would vest when the testator dies, subject to divesting if X fails to attain 25: *Bickersteth v Shanu* [1936] AC 290. But an alert drafter would not leave the issue to chance.

See also **vest**.

TAUTOLOGIES

Tautologies are problematical in legal writing, for two main reasons. The first is that they lay bare the writer's lack of self-awareness. For example, to say that something is 'absolutely void' is tautologous: if something is void it must necessarily be absolutely void. Again, 'actual facts' is tautologous: if something is a fact, it must be an actual fact. And 'solitary isolation' is tautologous, because isolation is necessarily solitary. The second reason is that tautologies transgress the 'presumption against surplusage'—which assumes that drafters intend every word to have a purpose.

Nevertheless, courts may be prepared to overlook tautologies where to do so better reflects the writer's assumed purpose. This is particularly the case where the writer is untutored in law (and so cannot be expected to know the presumption), or where the writer is 'given to flamboyance and tautologies' (as in some home-drawn wills: eg, *Marshall v Tasmanian Perpetual Trustees Ltd* [2015] TASFC 2; (2015) 26 Tas R 120, [8]).

See also **AMBIGUITY; PROLIXITY; REDUNDANCIES; SURPLUSAGE (PRESUMPTION AGAINST); WORD PAIRINGS; WORD STRINGS.**

tax

Latin: *taxare*, to compute, assess the value of. The meaning of *tax* is notoriously imprecise. For example, if a lease of premises in a shopping centre requires the tenant to pay a proportion of 'landlord's *taxes*' on the property, does it include land tax (which in most jurisdictions is levied on the landlord's total property holdings, not merely the shopping centre)? Or if a statute exempts a landowner from liability for 'taxation', does it include an exemption from 'rates': *Orthodox Patriarchate of Jerusalem v Municipal Corpn of Jerusalem* [1944] AC 1 (PC) (answer, after much litigation, yes).

The meaning of *tax*, as with most other words, is context-dependent. The only general criteria seem to be that a *tax* is: (1) an exaction for public purposes, not for services rendered (*Lower Mainland Dairy Products Sales Adjustment Committee v Crystal Dairy Ltd* [1933] AC 168, 175); and (2) a liability imposed on the general body of subjects or citizens, as distinguished from isolated levies on individuals (*Leake v Commissioner of*

Taxation (State) (1934) 36 WALR 66, 67). If context or these general criteria are unhelpful, always clarify—and preferably list—what obligations are intended by *tax*.

taxation (of costs)

When used of costs, *taxation* means the adjudication, usually by a court official, on whether a lawyer is entitled to be paid the amount claimed in a bill of costs. In modern legal systems, sometimes called *detailed assessment* (of costs), following the Woolf Reforms to civil procedure in England and Wales. Historically, to *tax* a lawyer's bill of costs involved going through each item one-by-one, either allowing it or disallowing it: *Re Grant, Bulcraig & Co* [1906] 1 Ch 124, 128 (Farwell J). In modern practice, however, legal costs are often taxed on a global basis, not on an item-by-item basis.

See also **WOOLF REFORMS**.

TECHNICAL TERMS

See **TERMS OF ART**.

tempus / tempore / temporis

Latin: time / in time / of time. *Tempus* (or its grammatical variants) often appears as part of a Latin maxim, always translatable into standard English without loss of meaning. Examples (with translations) include:

- *post tantum temporis*: after so long a time
- *prior tempore potior [est] jure*: the first in time has the stronger right
- *punctum temporis*: a point of (in) time
- *scintilla temporis*: a spark of time (ie, a brief moment of time)
- *nullum tempus occurrit regi*: time does not run against the Crown
- *tempus continuum*: time running on, without interruption.

Unless your reader knows the meaning of the Latin, translate. If for some reason you feel compelled to retain the Latin, give an explanation.

See also **prior [est] tempore potior [est] jure**; **scintilla temporis**.

tenancy for a term of years

A *tenancy for a term of years* (or a tenancy for a 'fixed term of years') is a tenancy that, from the outset, is fixed to expire at an agreed, certain time. The description 'term of *years*' (though common in legal usage) is apt to mislead, because the tenancy (ie, lease) may be:

- for any fixed period, no matter how short (eg, one day, one week, one month) or long (eg, one year, three years, one thousand years), or
- for discontinuous periods (eg, three successive bank holidays: *Smallwood v Sheppards* [1895] 2 QB 627), or for one week a year for 80 years (eg, time-share holiday premises: *Cottage Holiday Associates Ltd v Customs and Excise Commissioners* [1983] QB 735).

Further reading

S Bridge, E Cooke, and M Dixon (eds), *Megarry & Wade's Law of Real Property*, 9th edn (Sweet & Maxwell, 2019) [16-075] ('fixed term' tenancies)

tenant

One who holds an interest in land (from the Latin: *tenere*, to hold). The word can mean:

1. a *tenant* (in the landlord–tenant sense); or
2. an *owner* (reflecting the feudal doctrine of a person *holding* land from the Crown—as in *tenant in fee simple*, or *joint tenant*, or *tenant in common*).

Meaning (1) reflects standard English; meaning (2) assumes an understanding of the feudal origins of modern land law. If readers are likely to be puzzled by *tenant* in meaning (2), avoid the term and use instead *freehold owner*, or simply *owner*.

See also **fee simple**; **freehold**; **joint tenant / tenant in common**.

tenant for years

A tenant under any fixed-term tenancy—even one for less than a year (to that extent, a misleading label).

See **tenancy for a term of years**.

tenant in common

See **joint tenant / tenant in common**.

tenant-like manner

A circular (but settled) description of the nature of a tenant's obligation when using the leased premises. To use premises in a *tenant-like manner* is to use them as a reasonably careful tenant would use them, taking reasonable care of them, and not damaging them deliberately or carelessly. In Lord Denning's memorable (if quaint) exposition: a *tenant-like manner* requires the tenant to 'do the little jobs about the place which a reasonable tenant would do', including unblocking the sink, cleaning the chimneys, and, if going away for the winter, turning off the water and emptying the boiler: *Warren v Keen* [1954] 1 KB 15, 20.

Further reading

S Bridge, E Cooke, and M Dixon (eds), *Megarry & Wade's Law of Real Property*, 9th edn (Sweet & Maxwell, 2019) [18-053]

tenement

In normal usage, a *tenement* is a dwelling, often a flat or an apartment, or a house in a row of joined-up houses (a 'tenement row'). Legal usage is wider. In law, *tenement* retains the sense of its Latin root, *tenere*, to hold. Land was (and in most common-law jurisdictions, still is) governed by the feudal doctrine of *tenure*; and historically, a *tenement* was any holding of land, with no particular reference to the specific nature of the holder's interest: Sir Frederick Pollock and Frederic William Maitland, *The History of English Law before the Time of Edward I*, ed SFC Milsom, 2nd edn, reissued (Cambridge University Press, 1968) vol 2, 146–48. That is, any land *held* under a tenure was a *tenement*: William Blackstone, *Commentaries on the Laws of England* (Clarendon, 1766) book 2, 16–17. In later times, *tenement* in law also acquired the normal meaning of *house*: Joshua Williams and RA Eastwood, *Real Property*, 25th edn (Sweet & Maxwell, 1933) 81; *Re Lehrer and the Real Property Act 1900* [1960] NSWR 570, 575 (Jacobs J)—a meaning it still bears, with studied archaism, in the lawyerly *lands and tenements*.

See also **dominant tenement / servient tenement; tenant.**

tenor

General sense or meaning; purport; effect. In legal usage, seen in the expression 'according to the *tenor* of' a document (often a statute), and usually meaning 'according to the actual words of the document': *Good v Walker* (1892) 61 LJQB 736 (payment of a promissory note 'according to its tenor' required payment in accordance with its precise terms). Thus, Lord Kerr spoke of '[t]he *tenor* of the provision, looked at from a purely textual perspective': *R v Secretary of State for Home Deparment* [2016] UKSC 37; [2016] 1 WLR 2814, [25]. But sometimes *tenor* means, not so much the actual words of a document, but its spirit. Thus, Lindblom LJ spoke of certain paragraphs of a document fitting in with 'the general *tenor* of' other paragraphs: *Birmingham City Council v SS* [2016] EWCA Civ 1211, [39].

If readers could be in doubt about your intended meaning of *tenor*—the actual words or the general spirit?—then be more precise.

TENSE

Prefer the present tense

For documents that speak continuously

Once a legal document comes into operation, it usually 'speaks continuously'—ie, its provisions continue in operation for as long as the document itself continues in operation. For that reason, the present tense is appropriate for most legal documents. There may be an inclination to use the future tense, particularly where (at the drafting stage) the document has not yet come into being. But the drafting should anticipate the time when the document comes into being—hence, prefer the present tense.

For simplicity

Not only is the present tense appropriate for a document that speaks continuously, but it also helps sidestep some of the complex tense constructions seen in legal drafting. These complex constructions are often the product of the lawyer's striving for absolute precision. But that effort is usually misplaced: the much simpler present tense usually suffices.

Avoid	Prefer (simpler, and accurate)
The penalty for littering *is to be* …	The penalty for littering *is* …
If the Registrar *shall have determined* that the caveat is in proper form, the Registrar may …	If the Registrar *determines* that the caveat is in proper form, the Registrar may …
This agreement *will come* into force on …	This agreement *comes* into force on …
The committee *to be established* by this deed *will consist of* 10 members.	The committee *established* by this deed *consists of* [better: *has*] 10 members.

(continued)

(Continued)

Avoid	**Prefer (simpler, and accurate)**
If the purchaser *shall fail* to pay the deposit, then …	If the purchaser *fails* to pay the deposit, then …
If the purchaser *should fail* to pay the deposit, then …	If the purchaser *fails* to pay the deposit, then …
If the purchaser *shall have failed* to pay the deposit, then …	If the purchaser *fails* to pay the deposit, then …

However, take care that the present tense does not frustrate readers, by forcing the document into a 'tenses strait-jacket'—sometimes, indeed, subverting the simplicity it seeks to achieve. In a notable example, a court considered that the widespread use of the present tense in a document made interpretation difficult and 'represent[ed] a triumph of form over substance': *Anglian Water Services Ltd v Laing O'Rourke Ltd* [2010] EWHC 1529 (TCC), [28].

And of course, take care to ensure that the present tense does not cause ambiguity. For example:

> A statute protected trade unions from prosecution for industrial action, but on condition that the unions 'must not have contravened any orders that *apply* [present tense] to them and relate to' the industrial action. Held, this included contraventions of orders that had *ceased* to apply at the time of the industrial action: *Esso Australia Pty Ltd v Australian Workers Union* [2017] HCA 54; (2017) 263 CLR 551. The court criticised the combining of tenses ['contravened … apply'] as 'potentially ambiguous', because the combination 'could be taken to mean either that a person must not have contravened an order which applied to the person at the time of contravention or, alternatively, that a person must not have contravened an order which continues to apply to the person' (at [29]). To resolve the ambiguity, the court considered the history and context of the legislation, including the Second Reading Speech.

Consistency in use

Having chosen the appropriate tense, be consistent. Do not change the tense unless clarity or context requires it. Even experienced drafters sometimes overlook this admonition.

> 'Where either the Landlord or the Tenant *has* [present tense] the right to … stipulate or vary any matter or thing under this Lease, that right *will be* [future tense: prefer *is*] subject to a condition that it *will be* [future tense: prefer *is*, or subjunctive *be*] exercised reasonably and properly …' [British Property Federation, 'Lease of Whole of Office Building' (version 1.4a, 7 June 2019) cl 2.10; see www.modelcommerciallease.co.uk/leases/mcl-office-01/]

Judicial approach to tense

Prudent dafters choose tenses with care, just as they choose words with care. But judges, in seeking to discern the intended meaning of a document, may consider that the drafter's choice of tense was poor, and may prefer to interpret the document as if it used another tense. The drafter's only bulwark against this judicial intervention is to make it clear beyond argument that the chosen tense genuinely reflects the parties' (or, for statutes, Parliament's) purpose. But as the following two groups of examples show, that is a difficult task. In the first group, judges ignored the tenses used by legislative drafters, to reach a conclusion that the judges considered better reflected the legislative policy. In the second group, judges strictly observed the tense used by legislative drafters, even though this arguably subverted the legislative policy.

Examples (1): tense ignored

- A statute allowed subtenants to remain in possession after the head lease came to an end, where the premises '*have been* lawfully sub-let'. Held, this meant *are being* [present tense] lawfully sublet; past unlawful subletting was irrelevant if the current subletting was lawful: *Norman v Simpson* [1946] KB 158.
- A statute empowered the Minister to decide whether a person '*is* or *is not* a hospital patient'. Held, the power extended to people who *had been* hospital patients but were no longer so: *Public Trustee v McKay* [1969] NZLR 995, NZCA.
- A statute authorised a court to make a care order for a child who '*is* suffering, or *is likely to* suffer' harm. Held, the authority extended to a child who *had* suffered harm in the recent past but (for the moment) was out of harm's way: *Re M (a minor)* [1994] 3 All ER 298 (HL).
- A statute entitled a tenant to give a notice requesting a renewal of the tenancy; the landlord could reply with a counter-notice refusing the request. One ground for a counter-notice was that the landlord '*intends to*' [present tense] reconstruct the premises. Did this require the landlord to have the intention to reconstruct: (1) at the (present) time of giving the counter-notice, or (2) at the (future) time of the hearing of any dispute about the matter? Held, (2), despite parliament's use of the present tense: *Hough v Greathall Ltd* [2015] EWCA Civ 23; [2015] 3 WLR 587.
- A statute regulated debt collectors who collected 'debts *owed*' to another person. Held, *owed* included debts currently *owing* [ie, present tense]. But held also that debt collectors who purchased debts and then sought to recover them in their own name, were not recovering debts owed [ie, owing] to *another* person: *Henson v Santander Consumer USA Inc* 137 S Ct 1718 (2019).

Examples (2): tense strictly observed

- A statute empowered landlords to evict tenants who '*endanger*' [present tense] the safety of neighbours. Held, the present tense implied that the tenant must be *presently* endangering the safety of neighbours; therefore, a landlord could not evict a tenant for *past* endangering, now ceased: *Director of Housing v Pavletic* [2002] VSC 438; (2003) V ConvR 54-668.
- A statute made it harder for a defendant to obtain bail 'if the defendant *is* [present tense] a participant in a criminal organisation'. Held, this required the defendant to be *presently* participating in a criminal organisation: *Da Silva v DPP* [2013] QSC 316.
- A statute made it unlawful to a person '*to receive* any firearm or ammunition *which has been shipped or transported* in interstate … commerce'. The accused purchased from a shop a firearm that had been shipped from interstate. The accused claimed that the statute was directed at interstate gun trafficking, not at gun shop sales. Held, the accused was guilty. Congress had used the present tense (*receive*) to denote a present act, and the present perfect tense (*has been shipped or transported*) to denote an act that has been completed—which fitted the facts here: *Barrett v United States* 423 US 212 (1976).

Further reading

Robert C Farrell, 'Why Grammar Matters: Conjugating Verbs in Modern Legal Opinions' (2008) 40 *Loyola University Chicago Law Journal* 1, 19–25 (reviewing US cases on the relevance of tense)

See also **SUBJUNCTIVE / INDICATIVE**.

term

This carries three different meanings in law:

1. a provision in an agreement;
2. a prison sentence;
3. a period for which a lease is held ('a lease for a *term of 5 years*').

Meanings (1) and (2) are common. Meaning (3) is rarer. Do no confuse your readers by drafting a lease provision along these lines: 'Under the *terms* of this lease, the lease *term* is 5 years.'

See also **condition; term (of lease); terms and conditions.**

term (of lease)

The *term* of a lease may denote three things:

1. A provision in the lease (eg, 'the lease is granted on the following *terms*').
2. The duration of the lease (eg, 'a *term* of 3 years').
3. The leasehold interest itself ('the lease *term*'). Meaning (3) comes from the Latin *terminus*, because '[a lease's] duration or continuance is bounded, limited, and determined; for every such estate must have a certain beginning, and certain end': Sir William Blackstone, *Commentaries on the Laws of England* (Clarendon, 1766) book 2, 143.

Non-lawyers may find these three meanings confusing. If so, change your *term*inology:

Before	After
Meaning (1) 'Take particular note of the key *term* of this lease.'	Take particular note of the key *condition* of this lease. Take particular note of the key *provision in* this lease.
Meaning (2) 'The *term* of this lease is 3 years.'	This lease *is for* 3 years. This lease *lasts for* 3 years. The *duration* [or *length*] of this lease is 3 years.
Meaning (3) 'Take care that you do not lose the *term* by failing to pay rent.'	Take care that you do not lose the *lease* by failing to pay rent.

See also **fixed term; term; terminus.**

terminate

See **rescind / terminate / end.**

terminate by notice of [stated period]

A provision in a contract allowing a party to 'terminate by notice [of a stated period]' can be ambiguous. Does the termination occur: (1) immediately the notice is given, or (2) not until the period stated in the notice expires? Usually, the meaning is (2). However, sometimes the answer may not be so clear. For example:

> Assume that a contract (which is to run for some years) allows a party to terminate 'within the first 2 years of the contract by giving 12 months' notice' to the other party. Does this mean: (a) that the 12 months' notice must *expire* within the first 2 years (which would effectively preclude a notice being given in year 2); or (b) merely that the notice must be *given* within the first 2 years (regardless of when the 12-month period expires)?

See also **automatically.**

termination 'for convenience'

A ground for termination sometimes seen in contracts: eg, 'Party A may terminate this contract *for convenience* at any time without prior notice.' The meaning is that A can terminate ['rescind' would be a better term] at any time for any reason, or for no reason, with immediate effect. *For convenience* seems a feeble expression for such a powerful right. Consider using a starker statement along these lines: 'Party A may terminate [rescind] this contract at any time for any reason.'

See also **rescind / terminate / end**.

TERMINOLOGY (CONSISTENCY OF)

See **CONSISTENCY OF TERMINOLOGY**.

terminus

Latin: boundary mark; extremity. Used in the sense of 'place' or 'point' at which something begins or ends (as in the English 'terminal'). It appears in composite legal terms such as *terminus a quo* (the 'place from which') and *terminus ad quem* (the 'place to which'). An appropriate English translation can fully capture the meaning of these Latin expressions. So unless your reader understands the Latin, prefer English, or at least add an explanation. For example:

- 'There is no doubt that the words 'a right of access' from a *terminus a quo*, ie, the beginning of the way, to a *terminus ad quem*, ie, the end of the way, do not as a matter of ordinary language carry with them a right to park a motor vehicle at or near the latter terminus.' [*Moncrieff v Jamieson* [2007] UKHL 42; [2007] 1 WLR 2620, [107] (Lord Neuberger, providing a translation)]
- 'Every lawful [right of way] must be capable of identification; it must have a *terminus a quo* [prefer: *starting point*], and a *terminus ad quem* [prefer: *end point*]. But it is not essential to a way that there shall be a beaten track between its *termini* [prefer: *points*].' [*Geraghty v M'Cann* [1905] 1 IR 181, 184 (FitzGibbon LJ)]

termor

A person holding a term of years—ie, a tenant.

See **term (of lease)**.

terms and conditions

Though a common pairing, *terms and conditions* is a loose expression, showing the writer's lack of legal acumen. The expression is 'traditional rather than appropriate': *Property and Bloodstock Ltd v Emerton* [1968] Ch 94, 118. *Term* bears a generic meaning, namely, any provision of a contract, whether important or not, and whether giving rise on breach to a right to terminate or a mere right to damages. In contrast, *condition* bears a specific meaning, namely, a contractual term any breach of which, however slight, entitles the other party to terminate the contract. In contract law, all *conditions* are *terms*, but not all *terms* are *conditions*.

Despite the technical distinction between the two words, the composite, catch-all *terms and conditions* usually means only the generic *terms*. So, eg, 'This contract is subject to the *terms and conditions* set out in the annexure' can be rewritten, without loss of meaning or precision, as 'This contract is subject to the *terms* set out in the annexure.'

See also **condition**; **condition / warranty**.

TERMS OF ART

Meaning

Definition and examples

A term of art is an expression 'used by persons skilled in some particular profession, art or science, and which the practitioners clearly understand even if the uninitiated do not': *Skerrits of Nottingham Ltd v Secretary of State for the Environment, Transport and the Regions* [2000] 3 WLR 511, 518 (Robert Walker LJ, holding that *curtilage* is not a term of art). More simply, a term of art is a term with a fixed technical meaning, unmodified by context, and difficult to express in any other way. Law, like other professions, uses terms of art.

Examples of legal terms of art are:

- *bailment* (the delivery of property on terms that the recipient will redeliver it or deal with it in a stipulated way)
- *beneficial ownership* (ownership for the holder's sole benefit, not for the benefit of others)
- *certiorari* (as in an 'order of certiorari')
- *charitable* (a purpose within the accepted categories established in case law in the context of the *Statute of Charitable Uses 1601*)
- *chose in action* (a personal right of property that can be claimed or enforced only by action, and not by taking physical possession)
- *consideration* (value given in return for a promise)
- *easement* (a landowner's right to use another person's land for a limited purpose—eg, a right of way)
- *escrow* (a deed delivered on a condition)
- *fee simple* (the greatest ownership interest possible in land)
- *joint tenancy* and *tenancy in common* (two methods of co-owning property)
- *profit à prendre* (a right to take something from someone else's land)
- *requisitions on title* (questions which a purchaser may ask in a conveyancing transaction).

Lord Coke, writing in 1628, described many Law-French terms as terms of art (*vocabula artis*). He considered them 'so apt and significant to express the true sense of the laws, and … so woven in the laws themselves, as it is in a manner impossible to change them, neither ought legal terms to be changed': Preface to *Coke on Littleton* (1628) 8 (in original edition, pages unnumbered; English modernised). But while many legal terms in modern use have a French heritage, modern legal style does not seek to preserve remnants of Law French for their own sake—in the same way as it does not seek to preserve remnants of Latin for their own sake.

Pseudo terms of art

Although many legal terms *appear* to be terms of art, in fact they are not. They can be replaced by everyday English words without risking legal precision or efficacy. Examples are *moiety* ('half'), *dwelling-house* ('house'), *premises* ('property'), and *will and testament* ('will').

Also, many words and phrases used in law have meanings hallowed by custom and usage, particularly in commercial law, property law, and the law of wills. (Evidence is admissible to show their meanings: *Halsbury's Laws of England*, 'Custom and Usage' (vol 32, 2019) [69].) But long use in law does not, of itself, make them legal terms of art, even though their meanings will escape many non-lawyers.

Terms of art with ordinary meanings

Some terms used by lawyers as terms of art also carry standard, non-legal meanings. These can cause difficulties for non-lawyers who, unfamiliar with the legal meaning, naturally assume the ordinary meaning. For example:

Term	**Ordinary meaning**	**Technical meaning**
action	activity; undertaking	court proceeding
charitable trust	a fund set up to help those in need	a fund set up for relieving poverty, advancing education or religion, or for purposes beneficial to the community, within the spirit of the Preamble to the *Charitable Uses Act 1601*
consideration	thoughtfulness	something of value given in return for a promise
demise	death	lease
determine	decide; make up one's mind	put an end to
discovery (of documents)	finding; locating	disclosing
execute	put to death	sign
instrument	implement for doing something; apparatus for making music	document
licence	written authority to do something (eg, driver's licence, restaurant licence)	a right to use another's land for a particular purpose, but not granting a proprietary interest in that land
recital	musical performance	preliminary provision in a document
time immemorial	for longer than anyone can remember	dating back to at least the accession of Richard I (3 September 1189)
without prejudice (as heading to correspondence)	unbiased	cannot later be used in court

Interpreting terms of art

General rule

In interpreting legal documents, courts give terms of art their technical meaning, unless to do so would produce absurdity, repugnance, or uncertainty: *Lalit Mohun Singh Roy v Chukkun Lal Roy* (1897) LR 24 Ind App 76, 85 (PC); *Phoenix Commercial Enterprises Pty Ltd v City of Canada Bay Council* [2010] NSWCA 64, [174]. This promotes predictability of interpretation, since both drafter and court can safely assume that the meaning commonly attributed to the term is the meaning the parties intended: *Falkiner v Commissioner of Stamp Duties (NSW)* [1973] AC 565, 577 (PC); *Sydall v Castings Ltd* [1967] 1 QB 302, 313 (Diplock LJ). Where the drafter has used a composite expression—some words being terms of art, others being ordinary words—there is no difficulty (in principle) in giving the ordinary words their ordinary meanings: *Collector of Customs v Agfa-Gevaert Ltd* (1996) 186 CLR 389, 402.

Examples (interpreting terms of art)

- An agreement exempted a person from the consequences of 'actual knowledge' of certain matters. Held, 'actual knowledge' is a term of art, to be interpreted in its technical meaning (and so in contradistinction to other legal categories of knowledge such as 'constructive knowledge' or 'imputed knowledge'): *Infiniteland Ltd v Artisan Contracting Ltd* [2005] EWCA Civ 758.
- A deed of settlement authorised trustees to settle funds on specified categories of persons, including persons as-yet-unborn, in ways 'as shall not infringe the rule against perpetuities'. It was clear from the deed as a whole that the drafter misunderstood the effect of the rule against perpetuities. Held, the court must apply the 'rule against perpetuities' in its technical, term-of-art meaning, not in the drafter's (misunderstood) meaning: *Inland Revenue Commissioners v Williams* [1969] 1 WLR 1197.
- A life insurance policy was expressed to benefit the deceased's 'descendants'. The deceased was survived by an illegitimate child. Held, the legal term of art 'descendants' included only children fathered in wedlock, not illegitimate children: *Sydall v Castings Ltd* [1967] 1 QB 302 (CA, by majority).

Exceptions

However, there are exceptions to the general principle that technical terms carry their technical meanings:

1. Where context shows that the drafter used the technical term in a non-technical sense. On this basis, a court held that the word *equity*—which carries the technical meaning of the body of law developed by the courts of Chancery—bore its non-technical sense of 'fairness': *Estate of Rangi Kerehoma* [1924] NZLR 1007. Similarly, a court held that the word *consideration*—which carries the technical meaning of something of value given in return for a promise—bore the non-technical sense of 'a payment made': *Brooks v Commissioner of Taxation* (2000) 100 FCR 117, [36].
2. Where the document drafter (often, but not necessarily, a non-lawyer) was ignorant of the technical meaning and therefore could not be assumed to intend the technical meaning: *Sydall v Castings Ltd* [1967] 1 QB 302, 314, Diplock LJ.
3. Possibly, where the document was self-evidently drafted in plain English for non-lawyers who could not be expected to understand technical terms: *Homeowners Insurance Pty Ltd v Job* (1993) 2 ANZ Insurance Cases 60-535, 78,102 (Hutley JA, dissenting). That is, the court may go easier on the drafter, making allowances for the purpose behind the drafting style.

How to deal with terms of art

The problem with terms of art, of course, is that many readers will not understand them. Some lawyers might not rate this problem highly; they see their priority as 'getting the law right', on the premise that parties are generally bound by what they sign regardless of whether they understand it. To some extent, they are right: difficulty of understanding is not usually a defence: *L'Estrange v F Graucob Ltd* [1934] 2 KB 394; *Toll (FGCT) Pty Ltd v Alphapharm Pty Ltd* [2004] HCA 52; (2004) 219 CLR 165; *Stack v Dowden* [2007] UKHL 17, [2007] 2 AC 432, [67] (Baroness Hale). And so these lawyers prefer to retain the terms of art and do nothing, despite the reader's lack of understanding. Perhaps they justify this approach by asserting (correctly) that the proportion of terms of art in any given document is likely to be small—so that the problem should not be exaggerated.

But other lawyers reject that response. They argue that a key purpose of all writing, including legal writing, is to communicate, and that terms of art thwart that purpose for many readers.

Hence the question: what techniques are available for legal writers who prize precision but fear that readers will not understand terms of art?

At least four techniques exist. Each has advantages and disadvantages.

1. Replace term with plain-language equivalent

This approach replaces the term of art with a plain-language equivalent. Proponents of this approach place a premium on comprehension: if the reader will not understand the term, then it is better to find an equivalent that the reader will understand. This casts great responsibility on the drafter, because the substitute term must capture the legal nuances of the original.

2. Retain term, but explain it

This approach retains the term of art, but then adds an explanation of what the term means. It is a 'best of both worlds' approach. For example:

> 'A and B are liable jointly and severally (that is, they are liable together and separately).'

Alternatively, the drafter uses a plain-language term and then adds the legal term of art intended to be invoked, as in the following examples:

- 'A and B are liable separately and together (known as 'joint and several liability').'
- 'If the borrower fails to pay, the bank can seek court authority for the bank to take over ownership of the property (known as 'foreclosure').'
- 'If the borrower fails to pay, the bank can foreclose (ie, take over ownership of the property after obtaining a court order authorising that action).'

3. Explain term in glossary or note

This approach retains the term of art, but explains its meaning in a 'glossary' of technical terms, or in a note on the page where the term appears. The glossary or note is not a definition (and should not pose as one)—merely an explanation. For example:

> A clause in a contract for the sale of land states:
>
> > 'The purchaser must complete on 1 December 2012, time of the essence.'
>
> The reader is unlikely to understand the implications of 'time of the essence'. So a glossary could explain:
>
> > '*Time of the essence*: if the date for completion is stated to be 'time of the essence', no delay past that date is allowed. If the purchaser fails to complete on that date, the contract allows the vendor to terminate the contract and keep the deposit, and then either (a) resell the property and recover any loss on resale, or (b) keep the property and sue for damages.'

4. Use term in heading, but plain language in text

This approach uses the term in the heading to a provision, but uses a plain-language substitute in the text of the provision. For example:

> **Force majeure**
>
> Either party may terminate this contract by immediate notice to the other party if performance of the contract becomes impossible through circumstances beyond the control of the terminating party.

However, this technique is somewhat opaque. The non-lawyer reader, puzzled by the heading, may not realise that the text of the clause contains a plain-language statement of the heading's legal effect.

Terms of art and overall purpose of document

Lawyers use terms of art not merely to ensure precision in choice of words, but also to ensure that the document gives effect to an intended legal result. The words or phrases help bring about that intended result. Plain-language drafters, attuned to readers' needs, may be tempted to substitute ordinary English words for terms of art. But does that prejudice the planned legal purpose? The issue can arise in a number of legal areas, including the following.

Leases

1. An intended lease must give the tenant the right to exclusive possession, otherwise a mere licence results. This is not to suggest that the drafter must use the exact term *exclusive possession*. However, it may well be prudent to use it. At least one judge has said that in discerning whether a document creates a lease or a licence, a general imprecision of language can point to a licence rather than to a lease; so too can the labels the parties use (eg, *agreement* rather than *lease*, and whether payments are described as *rent*); and—significantly for plain-language drafters—so too can the absence of technical words of grant: *National Outdoor Advertising Pty Ltd v Wavon* (1988) 4 BPR 973.
2. A lease (granted now) differs from an agreement to grant a lease (in the future). To grant a lease (now), the document preferably uses a formula such as 'I lease' or (more arcanely) 'I demise'. The case law shows that other words will suffice to grant a lease (now), but they must show an intention to give (now) exclusive possession: *Bicknell v Hood* (1839) 5 M & W 104, 108; 151 ER 45, 47. A plain-language drafter, untutored in these niceties and meaning to grant a (present) lease, may unwittingly create a mere agreement to grant a lease: *Truro Diocesan Board of Finance v Foley* [2009] 1 WLR 2218.
3. The law distinguishes between an *assignment* of a lease and the grant of a *sublease*. Both are terms of art, and both are usually given their technical meaning. Thus, a tenant who covenants not to *assign* the lease may still be free to grant a *sublease*, and vice versa: *Church v Brown* (1808) 15 Ves Jun 258, 265; 33 ER 752, 755; *Russell v Beecham* [1924] 1 KB 525; *Sweet & Maxwell Ltd v Universal News Service Ltd* [1964] 2 QB 699. There are no accepted plain-language substitutes for these terms of art, and so a drafter who dispenses with them runs the risk of not achieving the desired aim.

Mortgages

1. A mortgage over land gives the mortgagee the power to sell the land if the mortgagor defaults. A plain-language lawyer, knowing that non-lawyers often confuse the words *mortgagor* and *mortgagee*, may prefer *borrower* and *lender*, and may even be tempted to drop the foundational word *mortgage*. But the risk is that some lesser security may result, perhaps a mere charge.
2. A mortgagee cannot stipulate for a collateral advantage as 'part and parcel' of the mortgage transaction, if the advantage will continue to benefit the mortgagee even after the loan is repaid (for that would make the mortgage 'irredeemable'): *Bradley v Carritt* [1903] AC 253; *Kreglinger v New Patagonia Meat and Cold Storage Co Ltd* [1914] AC 25. However, the principle does not strike down advantages that are

independent of the mortgage: *Noakes & Co Ltd v Rice* [1902] AC 24. This has led to much ingenious drafting, seeking to ensure that a collateral advantage is not 'part and parcel' of the mortgage transaction, but rather a separate (ie, 'independent') transaction. A plain-language drafter, ignorant of the niceties of mortgage law, may unwittingly blur the distinctions, and create a collateral advantage that the court will not enforce.

Easements and restrictive covenants

1. To create an easement or restrictive covenant, the language must create a proprietary right that 'runs with' the land, not a mere contractual right that binds only the immediate parties. This is usually done by a formula along the lines that the easement or covenant binds the original contracting parties and their 'successors in title'. If the drafter, aiming for simplicity, omits the term of art 'successors in title', the easement or covenant may bind the original parties only; if one or more of them on-sells, the easement or covenant may cease to bind the land. The drafter may have failed to make the intended interest 'run'. See *City Inn (Jersey) Ltd v Ten Trinity Square Ltd* [2008] EWCA Civ 156; for a similar result in Australia, see *Palm Beach Lands Pty Ltd v Marshall* (1988) NSW ConvR 55-411.
2. In many common-law countries, a covenant can 'run' with land only if it is 'negative' (hence the description 'restrictive covenant'). A plain-language drafter, aware that an expression in positive form is often easier to understand than one in negative form, may seek to cast the covenant in positive form. But this will thwart the intended legal result. For example, a covenant by a purchaser of land in a subdivision '*not to build* on the land within the first six months' is valid to bind successors in title, but a covenant '*to build* on the land after the first six months' will not bind successors in title. See *Haywood v Brunswick Permanent Benefit Society* (1881) 8 QBD 403, 409, 410.

Penalties

1. A provision in a loan agreement or mortgage that stipulates an agreed interest rate (say, 10%), but then stipulates an increased rate (say, 20%) on late payments, is generally unenforceable, because the law regards the increase as a 'penalty': *Dunlop Pneumatic Tyre Co Ltd v New Garage and Motor Co Ltd* [1915] AC 79, 86. To bypass that consequence, experienced drafters instead stipulate the higher interest rate (20%) with a proviso that the lender will accept the lower rate (10%) if paid on time. By long-settled law, this format avoids the risk of penalty; the rationale is that 10% is a concession for prompt payment, and there is no 'penalty' in withdrawing a concession on default. A plain-language drafter, wishing to simplify but unaware of this settled sophistry, may end up drafting a clause that is unenforceable as a penalty.
2. Also unenforceable as a 'penalty' is a provision that if the mortgagor breaches a term of the mortgage, the mortgagee can immediately demand payment—not merely of the outstanding principal and interest to date, but also of all interest to the end of the period of the mortgage (perhaps stretching many years into the future). However, the courts allow the provision (an 'acceleration' provision) to stand if the mortgagee can show that it is a genuine pre-estimate of the mortgagee's expected loss on default. Much ingenuity goes into crafting the acceleration provision as a genuine pre-estimate of the mortgagee's expected loss. One (successful) method is by requiring the mortgagor to pay up-front, as an aggregated amount, all of the principal and interest for the entire period of the mortgage, but then stipulating that, for as long as the mortgagor does not default, the mortgagee will accept payment by regular

(eg, monthly) instalments throughout the term: *Protector Endowment Loan and Annuity Co v Grice* (1880) 5 QBD 592, 596 (Brett LJ); *O'Dea v Allstates Leasing System (WA) Pty Ltd* (1983) 152 CLR 359, 368 (Gibbs CJ), 382–83 (Wilson J), 386–87 (Brennan J),403–04 (Deane J). A plain-language drafter, unfamiliar with these niceties and wishing to simplify what seems an unnecessarily complex provision, may end up creating an unenforceable penalty.

Further reading

- *Halsbury's Laws of England*, 'Statutes and Legislative Process' (2018) vol 96, [812] (interpretation of technical terms)
- Dennis C Pearce and Robert S Geddes, *Statutory Interpretation in Australia*, 9th edn (LexisNexis, 2019) [4.21]–[4.22], [4.26]–[4.27] (interpretation of technical terms)
- Roy Goode, 'Penalties in Finance Leases' (1988) 104 *Law Quarterly Review* 25

See also **CONSISTENCY OF TERMINOLOGY; LATIN; LITIGATED WORDS AND PHRASES; penalty; POSITIVES / NEGATIVES.**

terra nullius

See **res nullius.**

Territory / territory

The convention is to capitalise the first letter when referring to a particular territory (eg, 'the Northern Territory'), but not otherwise (eg, 'all territories lack self-government').

See also **State / state.**

tertium quid

Latin: a third something (ie, something between two other things; something related to two things but distinct from them; an intermediate between two things). This Latinism is easily translated into plain English—so prefer plain English. Similarly, *ius quaesitum tertio*—right sought by a third party; *ius tertii*—right of a third person. For example:

- 'If the choice, and the antithesis, is between a gratuitous promise, and a promise for consideration, as it must be in the absence of a *tertium quid* [prefer: *third way*; *third option*], there can be little doubt which, in commercial reality, this is.' [*The Eurymedon* [1975] AC 154, 167 (Lord Wilberforce)]
- 'This means that the Contract is neither a cost plus contract nor a fixed price contract but some kind of *tertium quid* [prefer: *halfway house*].' [*OneSteel Manufacturing Pty Ltd v United KG Pty Ltd* (2006) 94 SASR 376, 379; [2006] SASC 119, [4] (Debelle J)]

See also **ius tertii.**

test case

Test case carries two related meanings:

1. A case that raises ('tests') a point not raised before; or, if raised before in a lower court, is now taken to a higher court, which is not bound by the lower court's decision.
2. A case used as a vehicle to test the operation of a statute or legal principle, and where the outcome may be more important for the broader principle it will establish than for

the parties to the litigation: see, eg, *Vriend v Alberta* (1996) 141 DLR (4th) 44, 53; *Jacka v Australian Capital Territory* [2015] ACTSC 239, [32]. Where a case falls within this more specific meaning, a court may be reluctant to order a losing party who has been 'dragged into' the case to pay the winning party's costs.

testator / testatrix

The form *testatrix* (a female will-maker) is falling out of use, in favour of the more gender-neutral *testator*. Some modern lawyers retain *testatrix* to distinguish between a particular female will-maker and will-makers in general, or between a particular female will-maker and a particular male will-maker. For example:

- 'In the present case the question must be whether the *testator* and *testatrix* intended that the [beneficiaries] should be only those persons who had been born in wedlock ...' [*Wright's Trustees v Callender* 1993 SC (HL) 13; 1993 SLT 556 (Lord Jauncey of Tullichettle)]
- 'The issue in [*Hughes*' case], relevantly, was whether a statement made by a *testatrix* about the misconduct of her son, an applicant for *testator's* family maintenance, was admissible ... as proof of the truth of what the *testatrix* said or believed.' [*Robert Bax & Associates v Cavenham Pty Ltd* [2012] QCA 177, [31]; [2013] 1 Qd R 476, 484 (Muir JA)]

However, even in those circumstances, many modern drafters prefer the gender-neutral *testator*, in line with the modern move to gender-neutral writing more generally.

See also **executor / executrix; GENDER-NEUTRAL LANGUAGE**.

testatum

The operative part of a deed. Traditionally, it began with the formula: 'Now this deed witnesseth ...' Modern deeds do not use that formula—or at least, *should* not use that formula. The modern equivalent is 'The parties agree [covenant] as follows: ...'

See also **DEED (document)**; **execute**; **INDENTURE**; **signed, sealed and delivered**; **testimonium**.

testimonium

The part of a deed stating that the parties have 'signed, sealed and delivered' the deed in the presence of witnesses, who also have signed. Modern drafters often shorten 'signed, sealed and delivered' to 'Executed as a deed'.

See also **attestation clause**; **DEED (document)**; **execute**; **INDENTURE**; **signed, sealed and delivered**; **testatum**.

TESTING

See **DOCUMENT TESTING**; **READABILITY TESTS**.

TESTING CLAUSE

In Scots legal usage, the place in a document for recording the signatures and details of the witnesses, and (commonly) other information about the signing process, such as where and when it took place. (In English legal usage, called the *attestation clause*.) It usually appears at the end of the document, just above the parties' signatures. In modern practice, the more formal testing clause is sometimes replaced with a signature block or box, which contains the same information but in tabular form.

See also **attest**; **ATTESTATION CLAUSE**.

TEXTUAL AMENDMENTS

Techniques

There is an art to amending legal documents. Different techniques suit different circumstances.

Piecemeal amendment ('textual' amendment)

This is the conventional technique for amending legal documents; it is sometimes called 'textual' amendment. It lists each amendment in turn, directing the reader to delete or vary a specified word, phrase or provision. It could be used, for example at the negotiation stage of a proposed contract, setting out suggested changes to a draft document; or it could be used in a special condition in a signed document, setting out agreed changes to be made to existing clauses (and therefore avoiding the need to make changes to the body of the document).

Example

> The parties to a proposed contract for the sale of land agree to use a standard form, with changes to be tailored to their particular transaction. Rather than change the printed form itself, the parties add a special condition to this effect:
>
> - In clause 27, delete 'agent' and insert 'stakeholder'.
> - In clause 35, delete 'rescission' where first appearing, and insert 'termination'.
> - In clause 47, after 'notified' insert 'in writing', and delete 'not' where thirdly appearing.
> - Throughout, delete 'solicitor' and insert 'conveyancer'.

However, where there are many amendments, this technique can be cumbersome. Thus (to return to the example), the reader must go backwards and forwards between the standard form and the special condition, collating fragmented information.

Amendment by strike-out

By this method, the writer uses the 'mark-up' facility of a word-processing program to strike out text and substitute new text. The reader can easily see what is to be deleted and what is to be added.

For readability, some prefer to strike out whole words, rather than individual letters, and to underline the new text. Some prefer to place the old (struck-through) text before the new (underlined) text, so the reader knows what is removed before what replaces it.

Poor	**Better**
The ~~c~~Court sat today.	The ~~court~~ Court sat today.
$4~~3~~,500	$~~3~~4,500 **Better still**: re-do the whole number: ~~$43,500~~ $4,500
The landlord must carry out all structural repairs. ~~The landlord is responsible for attending to all structural repairs.~~	~~The landlord is responsible for attending to all structural repairs~~. The landlord must carry out all structural repairs.

Amendment by schedule

This technique states the broad effect of the amendments, and then sets out the detailed textual amendments in a schedule. It is useful where many amendments are to be made to a complex document. For example:

> Mortgagor and mortgagee are the parties to an existing complex mortgage over a large commercial site. They agree to vary aspects of the mortgage: specifically, the mortgagee will release part of the site from the mortgage, in return for an increased interest rate and increased powers on default. This will be done by a deed of variation. The parties *could* set out piecemeal the changes to be made to the various clauses of the mortgage. But a better technique would be to outline the general effect of the new arrangements in the body of the deed of variation, and then set out the textual amendments in a schedule.

Substituting entire provision

Where a clause requires many amendments, it is often best to delete the whole clause and substitute the new one, as an entire provision.

Renumbering provisions

It may be necessary to insert entire new provisions or delete entire existing provisions. How are the additions or deletions to fit into the existing numbering scheme?

Inserting provisions: statutes

Conventions for numbering additional provisions in statutes vary between jurisdictions. However, most are along the following lines:

- New sections inserted between section 1 and section 2—numbered 1A, 1B, 1C, and so on.
- New sections inserted between section 1A and 1B—numbered 1AA, 1AB, 1AC, and so on.
- New sections inserted between 1AA and 1AB—numbered 1AAA, 1AAB, and so on. However, once this stage is reached, it is time to consider recasting to avoid such confusing numbering. (For example, the Australian *Income Tax Assessment Act 1936* (Cth) includes ss 159FZZZZG and 160ZZRAAA.)
- New paragraphs inserted between paragraphs (a) and (b)—numbered (aa), (ab), (ac), and so on.
- New subparagraphs inserted between subparagraphs (i) and (ii)—numbered (ia), (ib), (ic), and so on.

Inserting provisions: documents other than statutes

Private-sector drafters generally follow conventions similar to those of statutory drafters:

- New clauses inserted between clauses 1 and 2—numbered 1A, 1B, 1C, and so on.
- New clauses inserted between clause 1A and 1B—numbered 1AA, 1AB, 1AC, and so on.
- New paragraphs inserted between paragraphs (a) and (b)—numbered (aa), (ab), (ac), and so on.
- New subparagraphs inserted between subparagraphs (i) and (ii)—numbered (ia), (ib), (ic), and so on.

Deleting numbers: statutes

When deleting a provision from a statute, do you renumber the subsequent provisions to cover the gap? For example, if you delete section 2, do you renumber section 3 as section 2 (and then renumber all subsequent sections accordingly)? To leave gaps may confuse non-lawyers ('Why is there no section 2?'), but to renumber may confuse readers familiar with the text (and numbering) of the existing statute. In practice, the convention is *not* to renumber. Readers who want to know what was removed can research the statutory history.

Deleting numbers: documents other than statutes

Similarly when deleting a provision from private-sector legal documents (non-statutes), the convention is *not* to renumber the remaining provisions. This applies especially for industry-standard forms in common use. However, it is common (and useful) to add a statement 'Clause deleted' or similar, to confirm that the gap is not an error.

In summary, the conventions are:

Statute (section 26 deleted)	Legal document (clause 26 deleted)
25	25
27	26 (Clause deleted)
[No reference to deleted 26]	27

Reusing numbers

For both statutes and private-sector legal documents, dangers lie in reusing 'spare' numbers. Assume that a section (statute) or clause (private-sector legal document) has been deleted, leaving a spare number. Assume now that the drafter needs to insert a new section or clause somewhere in the document. Should the new provision take the freed-up number? Best practice asks whether the subject matter of the new provision is similar to the subject matter of the deleted provision:

- *Similar subject matter*: the new provision takes the freed-up number.
- *Different subject matter*: the new provision does not take the freed-up number. To give it the freed-up number will confuse readers familiar with the document, because they assume that a continuing number implies a continuing subject matter.

Amending headings to reflect amended content

Where an amendment changes a provision's substance, the heading also may need amending. This is particularly so where headings are relevant to interpretation (a rare circumstance, given the common provision negating this possibility).

Etiquette and the 'style' of amendments

Sometimes, a lawyer may have to insist on amending another lawyer's draft: eg, to protect a client's interest, or to rectify errors of substance, or to correct typographical or grammatical errors that may cause ambiguity. But such matters aside, professional etiquette frowns on amending merely to 'improve' another drafter's style:

> 'The duty of counsel (the observation applies equally to solicitors) in perusing a draft drawn or settled for the other side, is merely and exclusively to protect the interest of the client on whose

behalf he is consulted. He is not justified, therefore, in altering the structure or language of a draft merely because it is not such as he himself would have adopted or approved of if he had been advising on the other side.' [Henry Dart, *Dart's Treatise on the Law and Practice Relating to Vendors and Purchasers of Real Estate*, 8th edn (Stevens & Sons, 1929) 510. For an Australian observation to similar effect, see RC Teece, *Law and Conduct of the Legal Profession in NSW*, 2nd edn (Law Book, 1963) 87.]

Consistency of style

Modern legislative drafters, when amending older-style statutes, usually keep to the style of the original, for consistency. Modern private-sector drafters, when amending traditionally worded documents, should do the same, also for consistency—even if the style goes against their plain-language instincts. For example:

> Amendments are to be made to a ground lease, signed many years ago but still current. The original document uses the old-fashioned *shall* to impose obligation, and uses the word-string *right title and interest* to describe the nature of the right granted. The temptation when amending is to update these terms with the plainer *must* and *interest*. But the change could pose problems of interpretation under the 'consistency of terminology' principle: does a change in language herald a change in meaning? The lesser evil is to continue with the original terminology.

A deed to amend a deed?

At common law, a deed can be amended only by another deed: *West v Blakeway* (1841) 2 Man & G 751; 133 ER 940. However, if valuable consideration is given for the amendment, that principle can be overcome by recourse to equity. Equity has the power to specifically enforce a (non-deed) contract to amend a deed, or at least preclude the parties from denying that they have amended their deed: *ING Funds Management Ltd v ANZ Nominees Ltd* [2009] NSWSC 243, [72]–[77]).

See also **CONSISTENCY OF TERMINOLOGY; DEED (document); DELETIONS; HEADINGS; INCONSISTENT PROVISIONS; NUMBERING SYSTEMS.**

that / which

In modern prose, few writers discriminate between *that* and *which*. The modern trend is towards *that* as a universal substitute. However, grammarians distinguish the roles of the two words, and those different roles can be important to precise meaning—particularly in legal writing, where precision should be prized.

that

That is the restrictive, or defining, relative pronoun. It sets off a restrictive clause—ie, a clause that is necessary to the sentence—and is used without commas. For example:

- 'Titles *that* are registered are indefeasible.' [The implication is that some titles are registered and some are unregistered; but only registered ones are indefeasible.]
- 'The tribunals *that* hear cases quickly rate well in surveys.' [Some tribunals hear cases quickly and some hear cases slowly; only the quick ones rate well.]
- 'The courts *that* sit in London hear criminal cases.' [Courts that sit elsewhere may or may not hear criminal cases; but the ones in London do hear criminal cases.]

which

Which is the non-restrictive, or non-defining, pronoun. It sets off a non-restrictive clause—ie, a clause that is not essential to the sentence—and is generally set off with commas (because the commas indicate a kind of parenthesis). The sentence could stand grammatically without *which*. For example:

- 'Titles, *which* are registered, are indefeasible.' [All titles are registered, and therefore all are indefeasible.]
- 'The courts, *which* sit in London, hear criminal cases.' [The courts sit only in London, and they hear criminal cases.]
- 'The tribunals, *which* hear cases quickly, rate well in surveys.' [All tribunals hear cases quickly—hence they rate well.]

Many writers would omit the commas in the above sentences (eg, 'Titles which are registered are indefeasible'). But the sense is more clearly expressed with commas.

Does the 'that/which' distinction matter?

Yes

The choice of the appropriate word—*that* or *which*—can be crucial to eliminate any possibility of misunderstanding about whether the clause that follows is restrictive or non-restrictive. Consider the following road regulation, where penalties apply for breach:

> 'Large trucks *which* require registration must be under the control of qualified drivers.'
>
> The comma-less *which* is ambiguous. Do *all* large trucks require registration? A careful writer would, depending on intended meaning, insert commas around the *which* clause or change *which* to *that*.

An exception?

In one situation, it may be useful to substitute *that* for *which* in the interests of a cleaner style—namely, where a *that* sentence would end with a preposition. To illustrate, compare:

- 'The buyer may return any goods *that* this section applies *to*.'
- 'The buyer may return any goods *to which* this section applies.'

The first version is grammatically correct—*that* is the correct choice—but the sentence ends with a preposition. While no 'rule' prohibits ending a sentence with a preposition (see **PREPOSITIONS**), some readers find it ungainly. The second version avoids that construction, but needs 'to *which*', because English offers no option of 'to *that*'.

Two further 'that' issues

1. Keep *that* close to its noun

Avoid separating the relative pronoun *that* from the noun to which it refers. Failure to do so may not create ambiguity, but it always increases sentence complexity.

Example 1

> **Before**: 'The vendor must provide a *completion statement* to the purchaser *that* adjusts all rates and taxes as of the completion date.'
>
> **After**: 'The vendor must provide the purchaser with [*better*: give the purchaser] a *completion statement that* adjusts all rates and taxes as of the completion date.'

Example 2

Before: 'In making *regulations*, even when acting in haste, *that* affect human rights, Parliament must act ethically.'

After:

- 'In making *regulations that* affect human rights, even when it acts in haste, Parliament must act ethically.'
- 'Even when it acts in haste, Parliament must act ethically in making *regulations that* affect human rights.'
- 'In making *regulations that* affect human rights, Parliament must act ethically, even when it acts in haste.' (Here, however, the emphasis may appear to be on *haste* rather than on *ethically*.)

2. *that*-deletion

Some writers favour deleting *that* wherever possible, in the interests of a cleaner text. But a deleted *that* can cause readers to miscue, and can even create ambiguity:

- 'Following comments from counsel, the judge decided *that* the issue needed further consideration.' To delete *that* might invite the miscue (even if only for a moment) that the judge decided the issue.
- 'He said today *that* he was suing for negligence.' To delete *that* would create an ambiguity: did he say it today, or was he suing today?

Further reading

Douglas Laycock, 'That and Which' (1991) 2 *Scribes Journal of Legal Writing* 37

See also **PARTICIPLES; PREPOSITIONS; PRONOUNS.**

that / who

Conventionally, *that* refers to things, *who* refers to people. However, the contemporary vernacular often uses *that* for both.

See **people that**.

that is to say

See **id est**.

the

The definite article, signifying an exclusive reference—*the* man, as distinct from *a* man or *any* man. But context or drafting infelicity may require *the* to be read as *a* or *any*—as in *Coast Brick & Tile Works Ltd v Raichand* [1967] 1 AC 192, 202 ('*the* security' read as '*a* security').

British and Commonwealth usage includes the definite article when referring to litigation-party descriptors: eg, '*The* appellant argues that *the* defendant was at fault.' US legal usage generally omits it: eg, 'Appellant argues that defendant was at fault.' (Or even, 'Appellant argues defendant was at fault.')

See also **a (indefinite article)**; **NAMES (of parties)**

the provisions of

See **provision**.

the question (of) whether

See **question whether**.

then

Even small, simple words can create ambiguity. *Then* is no exception. It can mean 'at that time' or 'in that case', as the following cases illustrate:

- 'But if the above trusts in this will fail, *then* [= *in that event*] my trustees are to hold the property on trust for those of my next-of-kin who would *then* [= *at that time*] be entitled to it as my next-of-kin.' [Example based on *Bullock v Downes* (1860) 9 HL Cas 1; 11 ER 627; context, gift by will.]
- 'If the trust fund fails to vest, *then* [= *in that event*] on trust for my next-of-kin.' [Example based on *Falkiner v Commissioner of Stamp Duties* [1973] AC 565, 582–83 (PC); context, clause in settlement deed.]
- '[I give my property to] A and B for life, and after their deaths to apply the income for their children until they attain 21, and upon the youngest child attaining 21 *then* [= at that time] to transfer the property to the children equally, and if there is only one such child *then* [= in that case] to transfer the property to that child, but if no child attains that age *then* [= in that case] to my next of kin *then* [= at that time] surviving.' [Example based on *Re Anders* [1924] SASR 34, Poole J; but differing from Poole J on the meaning of the third *then*; context, gift by will.]

See also **if ... then**.

thenceforth

In modern legal writing, a conscious archaism, serving no useful purpose. Prefer 'from that moment', 'from that time', or similar. If authority is needed for such an obvious substitution, see *Farrer v Billing* (1818) 2 B & A 171, 177; 106 ER 329, 332 (holding that *thenceforth* means 'from and after' a specified event).

there is / there are

A sentence that contains the construction '*there is* ...' or '*there are* ...' is likely to be cumbersome and wordy. Rewrite to eliminate the construction—and in the process you will find yourself eliminating other needless words. Sometimes, '*there is* ...' or '*there are* ...' starts the sentence (as in the first three examples below); sometimes, it appears in midsentence (as in the last two examples). Regardless of the location, the sentence is shorter and better without it.

Before	**After**
'*There are* three reasons why you should do this.' [9 words]	You should do this for three reasons. [7 words]
'*There are* some laws which can be set out by way of a few simple propositions.' [Office of Scottish Parliamentary Counsel, *Plain Language and Legislation* (2008) 9; 16 words]	Some laws can be set out by way of a few simple propositions. [13 words]

(continued)

(Continued)

Before	**After**
'*There is* no indication in the Lord Chancellor's Department's transposition note or elsewhere that anything was intended other than …' [*Moreno v The Motor Insurers' Bureau* [2016] UKSC 52; [2016] 1 WLR 3059, [15] (Lord Mance); 19 words]	Nothing in the Lord Chancellor's Department's transposition note or elsewhere indicates that anything was intended other than … [17 words]
'The result … is that *there are* elements of the framework *which* do not fit easily … within the overall structure.' [*Blavo v Law Society* [2018] EWCA Civ 2250; [2019] 1 WLR 1977, [50] (Moylan LJ); 21 words]	The result … is that elements of the framework do not fit easily … within the overall structure. [18 words]
'To date, *there have only been* a small number of native title claims *that have been* determined by the Federal Court to hold native title, however *there is* a large number of native title claims *that have been* registered by the National Native Title Tribunal and attract native title procedural rights. [*Investing Down Under: A Guide for Real Estate Investors* (King & Wood Mallesons, 2016) 40; 51 words; punctuation and grammar in original]	To date, only a small number of native title claims *have been* determined by the Federal Court to hold native title. However, a large number of native title claims *have been* registered by the National Native Title Tribunal and attract native title procedural rights. [44 words] **Better still** (further tightening, and avoiding passives): To date, the Federal Court has determined only a few native title claims to native title. However, the National Native Title Tribunal has registered many native title claims, and these attract native title procedural rights. [35 words]

there- words

Most *there-* words—like most *here-* words—are archaic. Examples include:

- thereby
- therefrom
- therein
- thereon
- thereinafter
- thereinbefore
- thereof
- thereto
- theretofore
- thereunto
- thereupon
- therewith

Always substitute a modern equivalent.

See also ***here-* words**; **SIMPLER WORDS AND PHRASES**; **thereafter**; **thereby**; **thereinafter / thereinbefore**; **thereof**; **thereto**; **theretofore**; **therewith**.

thereabouts

A word of approximation, with a meaning that changes with context. The variability of context makes *thereabouts* a target for litigation, as the following British and Commonwealth examples show. The issue in each was whether the qualification *thereabouts* excused a discrepancy between a property's stated dimensions and its actual dimensions.

Discrepancy excused by *thereabouts*:

- Cottage and small farm—area 'by estimation' of 3 acres *or thereabouts* satisfied by actual area of 2 acres, 1 rood, and 12 perches: *Joliffe v Baker* (1883) 11 QBD 255.
- Farm—stated area of 137 acres *or thereabouts* satisfied by actual area of 134 acres: *Nixon v Lofts* (1928) 29 SR (NSW) 9.

Discrepancy not excused by *thereabouts*:

- Houses with workshops—stated area of 753 square yards *or thereabouts* not satisfied by actual area of 573 square yards: *Whittemore v Whittemore* (1869) LR 8 Eq 603.
- Lakeside property in Australian outback—stated area of 500 acres *or thereabouts* not extending to actual area of 520 acres: *Southern Centre of Theosophy Inc v South Australia* (1979) 21 SASR 399 (reversed on other grounds, [1982] AC 706, PC).
- Farm—stated area of 349 acres '*or thereabouts*, be the same more or less' not satisfied where deficiency was about 100 acres: *Portman v Mill* (1826) 2 Russ 570; 38 ER 449.

Where possible, specify the precise permissible variation.

See also **about**; **approximately**; **WORDS OF APPROXIMATION**.

thereafter

An archaism, meaning simply 'after that'. Depending on context, substitute 'then', 'next', 'afterwards', 'later', or the like.

> 'The prior charge ... was discharged on or about 12 September 1991. *Thereafter* [prefer: *Later*; *Next*], the charge over the Leeds property was executed by the applicant and it was dated 29 August 1991. ... No steps were taken at that time, or *thereafter* [prefer: *later*] formally to discharge the charge over the Bury property. ... *Thereafter* [prefer: *Later*; *Next*], the facility was extended and increased ... Mrs Butterworth succeeded Mr Cooper as manager of the branch in or about July 1993. *Thereafter* [prefer: *After that*] the facility was progressively reduced over the Bury property. ... [I]mmediately *thereafter* [prefer: *after that*], the applicant took steps towards lodging an appeal. ... *Thereafter it took* [prefer: *It then took*] until 29 November 2000 for legal aid to become available.' [*Sarwar v Royal Bank of Scotland Plc* [2001] EWCA Civ 252, [4]–[19] (Chadwick LJ), *passim*]

Sometimes, a series of *thereafter*s is not merely archaic, but ambiguous:

> A clause in an oil and gas lease specified the duration of the lease: '[T]his lease shall remain in force for a term of ten years from this date, called primary term, *and* as long *thereafter* as oil, gas or other mineral is produced from said land, *or* as long *thereafter* as Lessee shall conduct drilling or re-working operations thereon ...' (emphasis added). Broken into its component subclauses, this contemplated three periods: (1) 10 years (the primary term); *and* (2) *thereafter*, for as long as oil, gas or other mineral was produced from the land; *or* (3) *thereafter* for as long as the lessee conducted operations on the land. Did the second *thereafter* refer to the period in (1) or (2), or both? Held, by majority, it applied to both: *Samano v Sun Oil Co* 621 SW 2d 580 (Tex 1981). The dissenting judge held that it applied only to (1)—for him, a key factor was the introductory *or* before period (3).

thereby

As with most *there-* words, a conscious archaism, serving little purpose in modern legal writing. Sometimes, *thereby* can be deleted; at other times a less archaic word may need to take its place. For example:

> 'The government will resume the land. If any person loses out *thereby* [prefer: *as a result*; or delete], compensation is payable.'

See also **hereby**.

therefore / therefor

Therefore means 'for that reason', or 'so'; it points to a conclusion. *Therefor* means 'for that' or 'for it'; it is a statement. *Therefor* is stilted and prone to confusion with *therefore*—so it is best avoided.

> '[T]he judge *therefore* declined to grant permission for the challenge ... However, the judge required [the appellant] to issue a fresh claim form ... and pay the fee *therefor* [prefer: *for it*].' [*R v Secretary of Justice* [2017] 1 WLR 761; [2016] EWCA Civ 1111, [11] (Sales LJ)]

When using *therefore*, watch for two points:

1. In long sentences, use commas to set off *therefore*. But in short sentences, resist that temptation—the commas may interrupt the rhythm. Compare:
   - 'The judge[,] therefore[,] rejected the claim.' (No need for commas, unless intentionally to slow the reader.)
   - 'The judge, therefore, having considered all the evidence and heard all the legal arguments, rejected the claim.'
2. Beware of a comma splice. For example:

   'The barrister refused to stand up when addressing the court, *therefore*, the judge fined him for contempt of court.' Replace the first comma with a semicolon or a full stop.

thereinafter / thereinbefore

Consciously archaic lawyerisms for 'later' or 'earlier'. Rewrite, making necessary changes to indicate *where* later or earlier.

Before	After
'The beneficiary under a will takes subject to any terms and conditions *thereinafter* [or *thereinbefore*] *specified*.'	'The beneficiary under a will takes subject to any terms and conditions *later* [or *earlier*] *specified in the will*.' [Better:] 'The beneficiary under a will takes subject to any terms and conditions *specified in it*.'

thereof

A lawyerism for *of it*. Rewrite, omitting the lawyerism, as in these examples:

- 'This is subject to the contract for sale and *the terms thereof* [prefer: *its terms*]'.
- 'A declaration should be made that [A owns the items] ... and is entitled to immediate possession *thereof* [prefer: *of them*].' [*Agripower Barraba Pty Ltd v Blomfield*; [2015] NSWCA 30, [108]; (2015) 317 ALR 202, 222 (Sackville AJA)]

thereto

An archaism, always replaceable with *to it* or similar. Some lawyers use *thereto* out of habit. Some use it for perceived precision—but as the following example shows, *thereto* is not always precise, particularly where it can refer to several items previously mentioned:

> A tribunal had jurisdiction 'to hear and determine all applications made under [a certain Act] and any matters *related thereto*'. What was the meaning of *related thereto*? Two options were open. It could mean: (1) related (only) to *hearing and determining* applications; or (2) related to *matters about hearing and determining* applications generally. If meaning (2) applied, the

jurisdiction would not terminate when the application was heard and determined, but would continue to cover such matters as enforcing orders made under the application. Held, meaning (2): *Chrysler Canada Ltd v Canada (Competition Tribunal)* (1992) 92 DLR (4th) 609, 618 (Supreme Court of Canada).

theretofore

An unforgivable archaism for 'before that time'—unforgivable not merely for its studied archaism, but for its potential for ambiguity, as in the following examples:

- A statute required landowners to contribute to the cost of street-paving, if the street had not '*theretofore* been well and sufficiently paved'. Did *theretofore* mean: (1) before the statute was passed (1857); or (2) when the street was last paved (1879)? Held, it meant (2): *Portsmouth Corporation v Smith* (1885) 10 App Cas 364.
- A statute permitted existing liquor licences to be transferred to persons 'intending to keep inns *theretofore* kept by other persons'. Did *theretofore* mean: (1) at any time before; or (2) immediately before? Held, it meant (2): *R v Cotham* [1898] 1 QB 802.

Using a modern plain-language substitute for *theretofore* will help identify potential ambiguities like these.

therewith

A lawyerism meaning *with it*. Prefer *with it*.

> 'The argument that one must start with the express terms of article 5 of the Convention, and read [Security Council Resolution] 1546 consistently *therewith* [prefer: *with it*] is not in my opinion sustainable.' [*Al-Waheed v Ministry of Defence* [2017] UKSC 2; [2017] AC 821, [161] (Lord Mance)]

these presents

An archaism for 'this deed', 'this document'.

See **presents**.

they (singular pronoun)

See **GENDER-NEUTRAL LANGUAGE**.

thinks fit

An expression meaning simply 'considers appropriate'. Although commonly used, it reeks of legalism, and has no advantage over the less strained 'considers appropriate'. Notably, neither 'thinks fit' nor 'considers appropriate' allows unfettered arbitrariness, free from restraints of good faith and (perhaps) reasonableness, as the following examples show.

- A power in trustees to invest in 'such stocks … as they shall *think fit*' does not allow the trustees to make investments they know to be wrong: *Re Smith* [1896] 1 Ch 71.
- An administrator's 'absolute power' to dispose of a person's property as '*shall seem fit*' to the administrator, requires the administrator to act reasonably, properly, and in good faith: *Carr v Anderson* [1903] 1 Ch 90, 94–95.
- A company's power to charge 'such reasonable sum as the company *may think fit*' does not give power to fix an arbitrary sum, but only a reasonable sum: *Midland Railway Co v Myers, Rose & Co Ltd* [1909] AC 13.

Thinks, in *thinks fit* and similar expressions ('*thinks* proper', '*thinks* necessary'), means 'forms an opinion in the exercise of a proper legal discretion': *Wilover Nominees Ltd v Inland Revenue Commissioners* [1973] 1 WLR 1393, 1396 (Goulding J; affirmed on a different point, *Wilover Nominees Ltd v Inland Revenue Commissioners* [1974] 1 WLR 1342).

third party

A somewhat misleading term, with a meaning always context-dependent. In some contexts, a *third party* is not a 'party' at all, but rather an outsider to a transaction, event, or court proceedings—in reality, a *non*-party. So, under an insurance policy, the insurer is one party, the insured is another party, and a person who causes loss for which the insured claims under the policy, is a *third party*: *Digby v General Accident Fire & Life Assurance Corp Ltd* [1943] AC 121, 127 (Lord Simon LC). Statute also often calls a non-party a *third party*:

> Subject to the provisions of this Act, a person who is not a party to a contract (a 'third party') may ... enforce a term of the contract if ...' [*Contracts (Rights of Third Parties) Act 1999*, s 1(1)]

A more meaningful term could be *non-party*, or *stranger*, or similar. For example:

- '[The trial judge rejected the speculative argument that] a trial in the open would have led to either the named gangsters or *any third party* [prefer: *anyone else*; or *any other person with knowledge of the crime*] coming forward.' [*R v Central Criminal Court* [2015] UKSC 76, [15] (Lord Mance)]
- '[A]n express term in [a] contract that one *party* is to hold property on "trust" for another *party*, or for a *third party* [meaning: *non-party*], will be recognised and enforced in equity as a trust.' [*Korda v Australian Executor Trustees (SA) Ltd* [2015] HCA 6, [109] (Gageler J)]
- 'Mr Dunstan might have suffered devastating injury or been killed, perhaps due to a *third party's* [meaning: *stranger's*] negligence, before the ingested asbestos fibre triggered the manifestation of his disease ...' [*Orica Ltd v CGU Insurance Ltd* (2003) 59 NSWLR 14, 28 (Mason P)]

If *third party* could be ambiguous, always clarify your meaning.

See also **party**.

THROAT-CLEARING PHRASES

Introductory meanderings ('throat-clearing') may be acceptable padding in verbal communications, to give the speaker time to 'think into' the content. But they are generally inexcusable in written communications, such as legal advices and legal documents. To start a sentence, 'It is to be noted that ...', or 'It is interesting to note that ...', or 'You should note that ...', usually adds nothing to what is about to be said. Perhaps an occasional 'Please note that ...' is excusable for intentional emphasis—the meaning is: 'I really do want you to take note of this'; but it serves no purpose when added as a rote opener, prompted by reflex not reflection. There are many examples; some are listed below. Always excise them—and in any case, readers will probably skip them.

In documents: avoid—

- It is hereby agreed and declared ...
- The parties hereby expressly agree and declare ...

In correspondence: avoid—

• As you know ... • As you are aware ... • Of course, ... • It is important to point out that ... • I would point out that ... • It should be noted that ... • It should be appreciated that ...	• We note that ... / We further note that ... • It goes without saying that ... • In the final analysis ... • To all intents and purposes ... • The fact that ... (As in '*The fact that* A has defaulted means that B can rescind.' Rewrite: 'Because A has defaulted, B can rescind.')

See also **PROLIXITY**; **SIMPLER WORDS AND PHRASES**; **'be' verbs**; **WORD PAIRINGS**.

ticket cases

Legal shorthand for the case law on whether a party to a contract (A) is bound by terms which A has not actually read but which were available for A to read: are they taken to have been within A's knowledge or means of knowledge? The description comes from early cases involving the issue, in which the terms were written on the back of a ticket, such as a bus ticket or entrance ticket.

Further reading

JW Carter, *Carter on Contract* (online, LexisNexis) [10-170]

timber

In normal usage, *timber* means 'wood' or 'trees' generally. But in older legal usage, *timber* acquired a special meaning, particularly (but not exclusively) in the principles governing the use that life tenants could make of timber. *Timber* (or 'timber trees') became a term of art, generally (with some variation from county to county) encompassing oak, elm, and ash at least 20 years old and containing a reasonable quantity of usable wood 'sufficient to make a good post' (*Honywood v Honywood* (1874) LR 18 Eq 306, 309)—that is, timber which custom or usage regarded as suitable for constructing and repairing houses, as distinct from suitable only for temporary or makeshift buildings, fences, and the like: *Cruise's Digest*, 4th edn (Saunders & Benning, 1835) vol 1, 116; *Chapman v Strawbridge* [1910] SALR 118, 125–33. Unless the land was cultivated as a timber estate (where growing timber was part of the natural produce of the land), the law treated these 'timber trees' as part of the remainderman's inheritance, not for the life tenant's use. For the life tenant to cut them down was 'waste'.

All this of course is far removed from the meaning of *timber* or *trees* in other contexts—eg, whether a seedling or a sapling is a *tree* for the purposes of a statutory notice requiring a landowner to replace 'trees' clear-felled from the land: *Distinctive Properties (Ascot) Ltd v Secretary for State for Communities and Local Government* [2015] EWCA Civ 1250; [2016] 1 WLR 1839 (answer, yes).

Further reading

S Bridge, E Cooke, and M Dixon (eds), *Megarry & Wade's Law of Real Property*, 9th edn (Sweet & Maxwell, 2019) [3-070], [3-073]–[3-078]

See also **life estate**; **waste**.

TIME

Vagueness of expression

Many expressions of time in legal writing are vague or uncertain. Their use is fraught with difficulty. Chitty J once said:

> 'Probably no question has more exercised the minds of Judges in former times than the question as to the proper mode of computing time. ... It is no wonder to my mind that persons who do not read statutes with care and have not legal knowledge at their finger's [sic] ends should make a mistake ...' [*Re Railway Sleepers Supply Co* (1885) 29 Ch D 204, 208]

The following table illustrates some of the issues.

Original	Difficulty	Suggested redraft(s)
You must do X *by* 1 January.	Is performance *on* 1 January sufficient?	You must do X *on or before* 1 January.
You must do X within 5 days *from* 1 January.	When do you start counting?	You must do X within 5 days *after* 1 January. You must do X within 5 days *from and excluding* 1 January.
You have *until* 1 January to complete the contract.	When do you stop counting?	You have *up to and including* 1 January to complete the contract. You have *up to but excluding* 1 January to complete the contract.
You may do this at any time *between* 1 and 8 January.	Can you do it *on* 1 January or 8 January?	You may do this at any time *between* 1 and 8 January inclusive. [To add 'inclusive' may seem pedantic, but it aids precision.]
You may do this *either before or after* the date of this agreement.	Can you do it *on* the date of the agreement?	You may do this *before, on, or after* the date of this agreement.
You must do this within six months *of* 1 January.	Do you have to do it within six months *before* 1 January or within six months *after* 1 January?	You must do this within six months *before (and including)* 1 January. You must do this within six months *after (and including)* 1 January.

This book considers various time expressions under individual headings. See, eg, **after**; **as soon as possible / as soon as practicable**; **at any time**; **at least (time)**; **at once**; **before**; **between**; **by**; **corresponding-date rule**; **day**; **forthwith**; **from**; **immediately**; **month**; **not later than**; **on**; **on or about**; **reasonable time**; **shortly after**; **until**; **week**; **within**; **year**.

Presumption of local time

Where a contract or statute requires something to be done at or by a stated time, the time is presumed to be local time—ie, the time at the place where the act is to be done. For example:

> A company based in the UK owned land in New South Wales, Australia. The New South Wales government offered to purchase the land, the offer remaining open for acceptance by '30th June 1902'. Held, this meant 30 June New South Wales time. Therefore, an acceptance despatched by cable from London at 3.55 pm Greenwich Mean Time on 30 June (Sydney time: 1.55 am on 1 July) was too late: *White Cliffs Opal Mines Ltd v Miller* (1904) 4 SR (NSW) 150.

Interpretation clauses often circumvent potential misunderstandings by stating that a reference to time is a reference to that time in a specific place (such as London, or New york).

Fractions of day

The law normally takes no account of fractions of a day. In the absence of express provision or commercial convention, the time 'within' which something is to be done does not start running until the end of the starting day and does not expire until the end of the finishing day: *Lester v Garland* (1808) 15 Ves 248; 33 ER 748.

Hour of day

Under old case law, an obligation to be performed at a specified hour may be performed at any time between that hour and the next. On this basis, an obligation to pay a mortgage instalment 'at 3 pm' allowed payment until 4 pm: *Knox v Simmons* (1793) 4 Bro CC 433; 29 ER 975; *Bernard v Norton* (1864) 10 LT 18.

However, this may not reflect modern commercial expectations—and if commercial expectations have changed, the law may no longer condone such apparent flexibility. In any case, parties can preclude flexibility by expressly or impliedly requiring performance to be timely (or, in the quaint language of the law, 'timeous'). An example is by stating that the specified time is 'of the essence'. For example, if a modern commercial contract were to require payment 'at 3 pm, time of the essence', this would almost certainly require payment at 3 pm precisely—even a few minutes late may be too late: see, eg, *Union Eagle Ltd v Golden Achievement Ltd* [1997] 2 WLR 341 (PC); *Re Ronin Pty Ltd* [1999] 2 Qd R 172 (QCA). (However, the lateness would not necessarily preclude relief against forfeiture if strict insistence on the time were inequitable, even—the Supreme Court has held—in some cases involving non-proprietary interests: *Vauxhall Motors Ltd v Manchester Ship Canal Co Ltd* [2019] UKSC 46; [2019] 3 WLR 852.)

See also **day**; **time of the essence**; **timeous**.

time immemorial

In common usage, 'from time immemorial' is a quaint version of 'for longer than anyone can remember'. In legal usage, however, 'from time immemorial' normally means 'dating back at least as far as 3 September 1189' (being the date of accession of Richard I). For example, it carries that legal meaning in the doctrine of prescription under the *Prescription Act 1832*. The qualification 'normally' is needed because in recent times 'from time immemorial' is used in the legal context of indigenous land title to mean, in effect, 'for millenia, way back before colonisation': eg, *Re Southern Rhodesia* [1919] AC 211, 232 (PC); *Mabo v Queensland (No 2)* (1992) 175 CLR 1, 176 (Toohey J).

A related term is 'time out of mind', or (more fully) 'time whereof the memory of man runneth not to the contrary'. Both short and long forms appear in the Preamble to the *Prescription Act 1832*. But both have little place in modern law, except to explain the operation of that Act (and its colonial counterparts) and the common-law doctrine of prescription. Unless explaining to readers (versed in archaic terminology) the technical context of prescription, prefer the more modern (if prosaic) 'for longer than anyone can remember'.

See also **legal memory**; **lost modern grant**.

time of the essence

Two meanings

Lawyers use *time of the essence* in two senses, one non-technical and the other technical. The non-technical use generally relates to exercising rights; the technical relates to performing contractual obligations.

Non-technical meaning: a deadline (but no breach of contract involved)

Here, *time of the essence* means simply: 'This is a deadline [for exercise of this right]—if you are late, the right ceases.' Non-exercise of the right, or purported late exercise of the right, entails loss of the right but creates no liability. This non-technical sense probably reflects the general understanding that *time of the essence* means 'deadline'. For example, in jurisdictions where the practice is for purchasers of land to send requisitions on title to the vendor, contracts for sale commonly state that the purchaser must send the requisitions 'within [X] days of entry into the contract, *time of the essence*'. The stated period is a deadline; after then the right ceases, but the only consequence is loss of the right: *Oakden v Pike* (1895) 34 LJ Ch 620; *Shenston v Hewson* (1927) 28 SR (NSW) 53; E Walford, *Contracts and Conditions of Sale of Land*, 2nd edn (Sweet & Maxwell, 1957) 48. Indeed, in this context, *time of the essence* is unnecessary: *Dart on Vendors and Purchasers*, 8th edn (Sweet & Maxwell, 1929) 158.

Technical meaning: conferring right to terminate for breach

Here, *time of the essence* is a legal term of art, carrying a meaning deeper than its words might suggest to non-lawyers. A contractual provision that requires a party to perform an obligation on a specified date *time of the essence* means more than 'time is important' or even 'this deadline is critical'. Rather, it means that failure to perform on the specified date is a fundamental breach of contract, entitling the innocent party to terminate the contract and sue for damages: *Steedman v Drinkle* [1916] 1 AC 275; *Hoad v Swan* (1920) 28 CLR 258, 263; *Lombard North Central Plc v Butterworth* [1987] 1 QB 527. This is generally so even where the parties inserted *time of the essence* as a mere formality, unaware of its true effect. The presence of the formula 'is compelling and leaves a court ... with no option but to give effect to it': *Mehmet v Benson* (1965) 113 CLR 295, 303 (Barwick CJ). That draconian consequence is subject only to the court's power—exercised only in exceptional circumstances—to relieve a defaulting party against forfeiture: *Shiloh Spinners* Ltd *v Harding* [1973] AC 691; *Legione v Hateley* (1983) 152 CLR 406.

Use another term?

Few non-legal readers are likely to understand *time of the essence*. Is there another suitable, compact, term? The short answer is: none has yet become accepted. Certainly, the precise formula *time of the essence* is not necessary. Any formula will do, as long as it makes clear, expressly or by necessary implication, that on-time performance of the obligation is an essential term of the contract: *Scandinavian Trading Tanker Co AB v Flota Petrolera Ecuatoriana* [1983] 2 AC 694, 703 (Lord Diplock, all other Law Lords agreeing). The formula must show that the time limit 'is obligatory and means what it says': *Touche Ross & Co v Secretary of State for the Environment* (1982) 46 P & CR 187, 190. Despite these guidelines, no settled substitute has surfaced.

Add an explanation?

Given that no settled substitute is available, most lawyers are reluctant to give up *time of the essence*. They feel the force of Lord Diplock's admonition that terms of art are useful to avoid interpretation being dictated by personal idiosyncrasies: *Sydall v Castings Ltd* [1967] 1 QB 302, 313–14. But some lawyers also realise that their clients will not understand the full force of *time of the essence*. A practical solution may be to use *time of the essence* in the relevant clause, and then add a non-binding explanation of its meaning. The explanation need not be a definition—to draft which might cause even the most confident to quail—but more akin to a glossary. For example:

> 'The purchaser must complete this contract by 30 June 2021, time of the essence'.
>
> (Explanatory note for Parties: *time of the essence* is a legal term of art. It makes 30 June 2021 the absolute deadline. If the purchaser fails to complete by that date, the vendor may be able to terminate the contract, keep the deposit, and sue for damages.)

Further reading

- Kenneth A Adams, *A Manual of Style for Contract Drafting*, 4th edn (American Bar Association, 2017) [13.829]–[13.840], on US usage, and suggesting that US courts are more ready to relax the strict enforcement of 'time of the essence' provisions if the parties were ignorant of the term's draconian effect
- Jeffrey S Ammon, 'Time Is of the Essence (to Banish That Phrase from Your Contracts)!' (2016) 95 *Michigan Bar Journal* (Feb) 40, arguing against retaining the term
- K E Lindgren, *Time in the Performance of Contracts*, 2nd edn (Butterworths, 1982) ch 3
- 'Time Is of the Essence', in *Law Words* (Centre for Plain Legal Language, University of Sydney, 1995) 86; www.clarity-international.net/plain-language-resources/general-resources/, arguing against continued use of *time of the essence*

See also **GLOSSARIES; TERMS OF ART**.

time out of mind

See **time immemorial.**

time whereof the memory of man runneth not to the contrary

See **time immemorial.**

timeous

A quaint archaism for 'within the time allowed' or 'not late'. While not strictly a legal term, its use in modern times is largely limited to legal writing. Replace it with a vernacular equivalent, such as *timely*, *promptly*, *within the time allowed*. For example:

- '[The court decided that] a failure to mount a *timeous legal challenge* [prefer: *a legal challenge within the prescribed time*] to the screening opinion was no bar to a challenge to a subsequent permission on the same grounds.' [*R v North Norfolk District Council* [2015] UKSC 52; [2015] 1 WLR 3710, [63] (Lord Carnwath)]
- 'More than a mere failure in *timeous* [prefer: *on-time*] performance is necessary to warrant an inference of repudiation …' [*Laurinda Pty Ltd v Capalaba Park Shopping Centre Pty Ltd* (1989) 166 CLR 623, 643 (Brennan J)]
- '[T]here remains the public interest in the effective, efficient and *timeous* [prefer: *prompt*; *timely*] disposal of litigation.' [*Damjanovic v Maley* (2002) 55 NSWLR 149, 160 (Stein JA)]

title deeds

Documents indicating ownership, usually of land. The word *deed* in 'title *deed*' reflects the historical common-law principle that title to land passed only under a *deed*. However, title 'deeds' include all documents relevant to the passing of title—including non-deeds such as wills and grants of probate.

Under most modern land registration systems, title passes by the act of registration, not by deed. The registered title is then evidenced by a 'certificate of title' (or similar description), which is not in the form of a deed. Nevertheless, the language of 'title deed' is so ingrained that it remains common practice to call the certificate of title the 'title deed' to the property.

See also **DEED (document)**.

to avoid doubt

See **for the avoidance of doubt**.

to be

See **'be' verbs**.

to like effect

See **like**.

to the same effect as

See **in the form of**.

to wit

An archaism for *that is to say*, *ie*, *namely*, or similar. To retain *to wit* in modern legal usage is to be consciously pedantic. Prefer a vernacular expression (as suggested in the first example below) or delete it as superfluous (as in the second example):

- '[T]here is likely to be available to [a mortgagor] a wide choice of sources of information, *to wit* [prefer: *namely*; *such as*], independent valuers to whom he can resort ...' [*Smith v Eric S Bush* [1990] 1 AC 830, 872 (Lord Jauncey)]
- 'It appears to me that the law as so stated is recognized in an Act of the year 1932 to which I must now refer: *to wit* [delete] the *Rights of Way Act, 1932*.' [*British Transport Commission v Westmorland County Council* [1956] 2 QB 214, 247 (Singleton LJ)]

See also **videlicet**.

TONE

Meaning

'Tone' is the way in which the author addresses the reader. It includes choice of words (formal/informal, long/short), style (dense/relaxed), and attitude to the subject matter (serious/light-hearted). Tone is important in all writing, including legal writing. Some lawyers instinctively strive for a 'legalistic' tone, imperious and lofty, which can confound the reader. Others strive for a 'chatty' tone, familiar and condescending, which can patronise the reader. The task is to find the right tone for the particular reader. Relevant questions include: is the tone stuffy; is it patronising; is it sexist; is it approachable yet professional?

Aim for 'formal yet friendly'

For most legal writing, the ideal tone is 'formal yet friendly': 'formal' because the context requires a serious, considered approach to the task at hand, and 'friendly' because the writing needs to be approachable and immediate, without being patronising. The following table shows some of the key differences between a tone that is purely 'formal' and one that is 'formal yet friendly':

Formal	**Formal yet friendly**
long sentences	short sentences
long words	short words
abstract words and phrases	concrete words and phrases
nouns and noun phrases	verbs
passive voice	active voice
third person	we / you
buzzwords / jargon	plain language
small font / long lines	readable font / wide margins
no 'signposts' for readers	headings / subheadings / notes and examples / executive summaries
run-on lists	bullet points

Avoid polemics

In legal writing, a polemical tone is almost always counter-productive. Say what you want to say—briefly, crisply, and directly—but avoid snide remarks, exaggerated accusations, and personal name-callings. This is particularly the case in pleadings: not only will polemical pleadings attract the court's ire, but they may lead to striking-out and adverse costs orders. For example:

> Particulars of claim were exceptionally long (94 pages, where court rules prescribed a maximum of 25 pages). According to the judge, they included 'background facts, evidence and polemic' in a way that complicated the issues; their phrasing was 'not just contentious but tendentious' and 'liberally interspersed with assertions of fraud, falsity, dishonesty and improper motive'; they defined the defendants as 'the Conspirators'; and they used headings such as 'the plot' and 'the plot evolves'. The style 'has no place in English civil procedure'. The judge struck out the particulars of claim, disallowed costs for drafting them, and ordered the party to lodge new particulars: *Tchenguiz v Thornton UK LLP* [2015] EWHC 405 (Comm).

Difficulties in lightening tone

Sometimes, attaining a tone that is 'formal yet friendly' is relatively easy: it merely requires avoiding long words, long sentences, archaic words, and passive constructions. At other times, however, it is more difficult, especially when dealing with complex concepts and terms of art. The issue then is whether, in seeking a lighter tone, the drafter must sacrifice legal certainty.

To illustrate, consider the following redrafts of a clause from an employment contract. Each iteration lightens the tone slightly more than its predecessor. The original is clearly too heavy. But at what stage in the redrafting process does the writer start to sacrifice legal precision in the interests of readability? Is the final redraft (Version 5) too simple to be taken seriously?

Tone	Successive redrafts
Version 1 (original): Legalese	[Underlining indicates text that particularly needs simplifying.] A person who, being an employee, wishes to make a claim for reimbursement for expenses incurred in the course of his or her employment, must keep, retain and maintain in readable condition any receipt, document, or other evidence of such expenditure, in the absence of which no reimbursement shall be allowed, permitted or acknowledged in favour of the said employee.
Version 2: Formal	[Underlining indicates text that still needs simplifying.] A person, being an employee, who wishes to claim reimbursement for an expense incurred in their employment, must keep a permanent record of such expenditure by way of a receipt.
Version 3: Formal yet friendly	[Underlining indicates text that could be further simplified.] An employee who seeks reimbursement for a work expense must keep a receipt of the expense.
Version 4: Too light?	To be reimbursed for work expenses, you must keep a receipt.
Version 5: Far too light?	No receipt, no reimbursement!

Further reading

Kelly vanBuskirk and Matthew R Letson, 'An IBM Watson Tone Analysis of Selected Judicial Decisions' (2020) 19 *Scribes Journal of Legal Writing* 25 (analysing the 'tone' of selected Canadian judgments)

See also **PROLIXITY; PLAIN LANGUAGE; REDRAFTING IN PLAIN ENGLISH; SENTENCE LENGTH; SIMPLER WORDS AND PHRASES.**

TORRENTIAL STYLE OF DRAFTING

Lord Hoffmann castigated as 'torrential' the drafting style that uses lists of synonyms or near-synonyms to cover the field as exhaustively as possible, as if to guarantee precision by sheer weight of words: *Norwich Union Life Insurance Society v British Railways Board* [1987] 2 EGLR 137, 138. The lease covenant that provoked Lord Hoffmann's epithet was as follows:

> '[The tenant covenants] to keep the demised premises in good and substantial repair and condition and when necessary to rebuild, reconstruct or replace the same and in such repair and condition to yield up the same at the expiration or sooner determination of the said lease.'

A torrential style alienates readers. It can also be self-defeating for the drafter, for two main reasons. One is that a court may assume that words omitted from the torrent were intentionally omitted, leading to a gap in the coverage (the 'expressio unius' principle). The other is that a court may assume that every word plays a part, calling for distinctions finer than the drafter anticipated. For example:

> A landlord covenanted 'to maintain repair amend renew cleanse repaint and redecorate and otherwise keep in good and tenantable condition'. The court gave the word *renew*, though merely one word in the verb-chain, its own meaning—namely, requiring the landlord to remedy a defect going beyond mere 'repair'. See *Credit Suisse v Beegas Nominees Ltd* [1994] 4 All ER 803.

See also **expressio unius; SURPLUSAGE (PRESUMPTION AGAINST); WORD PAIRINGS; WORD STRINGS.**

tortious / tortuous / torturous

Tortious means involving a tort: 'His conduct was *tortious*.' *Tortuous* means full of twists and turns: 'His argument was *tortuous*.' *Torturous* means exhibiting torture: 'The army engaged in *torturous* conduct.'

totidem verbis

Latin: in so many words (sometimes, *in totidem verbis*). Rarely seen nowadays—and unnecessary, given the ready availability of a plain-English translation. For example:

- '[When a lease granted a right of renewal 'on the same terms as' the existing lease], the courts refused to give literal effect to that language, which if taken literally would mean that the second lease would contain the same covenant (or option) to renew, *totidem verbis* [prefer: *in so many words*; *in those exact words*], and so on perpetually.' [*Caerphilly Concrete Ltd v Owen* [1972] 1 WLR 372, 374 (Russell LJ)]
- 'It seems clear enough having regard particularly to s 43 that every successor is liable for duty, though curiously enough the statute nowhere says so directly and *totidem verbis* [prefer: *in so many words*].' [*Livingston v Commissioner of Stamp Duties (Qld)* (1960) 107 CLR 411, 427 (Dixon CJ)]

toties quoties

Latin: as often as; for each time; repeatedly. A Latinism that in modern times is commended only by its rhythm—which is a poor substitute for communication. Prefer an appropriate English translation. Alternatively, add an explanation (as in the third example, below).

- 'If the result of the act is that one damage is done today and another subsequently, there is nothing to prevent a fresh action *toties quoties* [prefer: *each time*; *on each occasion*] fresh damage is inflicted.' [*Earl of Harrington v Derby Corporation* [1905] 1 Ch 205, 227 (Buckley J)]
- 'The mortgages subsequent to the legal mortgage are inoperative at law, but in equity they operate *toties quoties* [prefer: *on each occasion*] as mortgages of the mortgagor's equity of redemption.' [WB Rayner and RH McLaren (eds), *Falconbridge on Mortgages*, 8th edn (Carswell, 1977) 82]
- [T]here is always a difficulty … in holding that a covenant to renew [a lease] on the same conditions implies a *toties quoties* covenant—namely, that the covenant itself to renew shall be included in the document which is to contain the same conditions.' [*Sherwood v Tucker* [1924] 2 Ch 440, 449 (Sargant LJ)]

See also **FOREIGN (NON-ENGLISH) WORDS AND PHRASES**.

touch and concern

A term of art that is difficult to express in plain English. It encapsulates, in language both archaic and opaque, a key requirement for covenants to 'run with' land. The concept is of a covenant that inherently affects the way the land can be occupied or directly affects its value: *Rogers v Hosegood* [1900] 2 Ch 389, 395. A covenant that 'touches and concerns' land can transcend the limits of contract law.

Example

Lots 1 and 2 are adjoining parcels of land. Lot 1 is owned by A; Lot 2 is owned by B. B contracts ('covenants') with A that he (B) will not use his land for certain purposes—eg, that B will not open a shop on Lot 2. A can enforce the covenant against B under contract law. But if B later sells lot 2 to C, there is no contractual nexus between between A and C: ie, under *contract law*, A cannot prevent C from opening a shop. Similarly, if A sells lot 1 to D, there is no contractual nexus between D and C, so D cannot prevent C from opening a shop. However, if the covenant meets certain *property law* requirements, each of the benefit and the burden of the covenant 'runs' with ownership of the benefited and burdened lots, so that successive owners of the benefited land can enforce the benefit of the covenant, and successive owners of the burdened land are bound by it (with some exceptions). One of those requirements is that the covenant *touch and concern* the benefited land (lot 1). In essence, this requires that the covenant benefit the land (lot 1) itself, either by reference to its value or the way it is used and enjoyed, and not merely benefit its owner personally: *Rogers v Hosegood* [1900] 2 Ch 389, 395; *McGuigan Investments Pty Ltd v Dalwood Vineyards Pty Ltd* [1970] 1 NSWR 686, 690.

An analogous requirement, using the same archaic and opaque terminology, applies to determine whether each of the benefit and the burden of a covenant in a lease 'runs' to bind successors of the landlord and the tenant. Specifically, a covenant *touches and concerns* leased land if it inherently relates to the land or to the way in which the land is used, or if it affects the landlord in his or her capacity as such and the tenant in his or her capacity as such: *Breams Property Investment Co Ltd v Strougler* [1948] 2 KB 1, 7.

In both instances (freehold and leasehold), the law throws up complex issues that the language of *touch and concern* fails to illuminate. However, there should be little need to agonise over a plain-English substitute for non-lawyers, because the term is found only in textbooks. Drafters have no need to use it in documents to be signed by clients, because whether a covenant *touches and concerns* land is a question of fact, which is not answered merely by asserting in the document that the covenant *touches and concerns* the land.

Further reading

- S Bridge, E Cooke, and M Dixon (eds), *Megarry & Wade's Law of Real Property*, 9th edn (Sweet & Maxwell, 2019) [31-013], [31-058], [31-063] (on covenants that 'touch and concern' land)
- Brendan Edgeworth (ed), *Butt's Land Law*, 7th edn (Lawbook, 2017) [7.1290]–[7.1300] (Commonwealth law on covenants that 'touch and concern' land)

See also in **esse / in posse**; **relating to**.

toward / towards

Usage

Most writers prefer *towards* over *toward*, when meaning 'in the direction of'; but usage is not consistent. For example:

- 'But the Government decided that it would move *towards* this goal over a period of time.' [*R v Secretary of State for the Home Department* [2015] UKSC 68, [8]; [2015] 1 WLR 5055, 5062 (Baroness Hale)]
- '[T]he Government may need to take further steps *toward* providing opportunities for spouses and partners to meet the requirement …' [ibid, 5076 [61] (Lord Hodge)]

Wordy substitute for *to*

Often, *toward / towards* is a wordy substitute for *to*. If so, prefer the shorter word, eg:

> 'Lawyers have duties *towards* [prefer: *to*] their clients.'

tracing

The process by which a wronged plaintiff may (instead of recovering damages) recover the property into which the wrongdoer has 'invested' the plaintiff's property: PW Young, C Croft, and ML Smith, *On Equity* (Lawbook, 2009) [12.820]. Unlike 'following', which pursues the same asset as it moves from hand to hand, 'tracing' identifies a new asset as a substitute for the original asset: *Foskett v McKeown* [2001] 1 AC 102, 127 (Lord Millett).

Further reading

Halsbury's Laws of England, 'Equitable Jurisdiction' (vol 47, 2014) [238] (following and tracing assets)

transaction

In legal usage, *transaction* often implies a degree of formality: thus, 'legal transactions', 'mortgage transactions', 'share transactions'. However, case law shows that *transaction* is a wide term, and that even an informal arrangement can be a *transaction*. For example:

- A non-binding verbal arrangement was a *transaction* for the purposes of a regulation: *R v Dairy Quota Tribunal for England and Wales* (1988) 27 EG 79; subsequent proceedings on a different point, [1990] 2 AC 738.
- Where land was held under a trust, the unilateral, voluntary (ie, without payment) act of resettling the land under a different trust, was a *transaction* for the purposes of legislation governing settlements of land: *Hambro v Duke of Marlborough* [1994] Ch 158.

If the inherent width of *transaction* makes the term broader than needed, or could introduce uncertainty, then either qualify its operation or choose a different term.

transfer (noun)

The act by which a person passes ownership of property to another. It can also mean the document which passes the ownership (eg, 'I will sign the *transfer*'). It is the appropriate term when passing ownership of registered land. For unregistered land (ie, land under old system—common law—title), the appropriate term is *convey* (verb) or *conveyance* (noun).

Seee also **assign / transfer (verb)**; **conveyance**.

transfer (verb)

See **assign / transfer (verb)**.

transfer and assign

See **assign / transfer (verb)**.

transferable development right

The right, granted by some planning codes, for the owner of land with unused development potential to transfer that potential to another site. Most commonly, this occurs where a planning code precludes the owner of an historic building from developing the site, while giving the owner the opportunity to recoup the lost potential by transferring the unusable development rights to another site. Transferable development rights are not 'land', but they are a form of 'property': *Uniting Church in Australia Property Trust (NSW) v Immer (No 45) Ltd* (1991) 24 NSWLR 510, 511.

transmit

In most contexts, a fancy alternative for *send*; if so, prefer *send*. But if the meaning is 'send electronically', *transmit* may be the better word.

TRANSPARENCY

See **PLAIN LANGUAGE.**

treasure trove

Hidden or lost treasure, whose owner is unknown, and which becomes the property of the Crown. Old authorities hyphenated the term—*treasure-trove* (see, eg, William Blackstone, *Commentaries on the Laws of England* (Clarendon, 1765) book 1, 285). However, the hyphen had disappeared from the term in British and Commonwealth law reports by at least the mid-19th century. It still appears in some US legal sources: see, eg, William S Anderson (ed), *Ballentine's Law Dictionary*, 3rd edn (Lawyers Co-operative Co, 1969) 1297.

In law, for an item to become the property of the Crown as *treasure trove*, three conditions apply:

- it must be of gold or silver: *Attorney-General of Duchy of Lancaster v G E Overton (Farms) Ltd* [1982] Ch 277, 291–92 (Lord Denning MR: the percentage of gold or silver must be 'substantial', probably at least 50%); and
- its true owner must be unknown; and
- it must have been hidden rather than lost: Sir William Blackstone, *Commentaries on the Laws of England* (Clarendon, 1765) book 1, ch 8, § XIII; *Attorney-General v Trustees of the British Museum* [1903] 2 Ch 598, 608–09.

Gold or silver abandoned at sea is not treasure trove. It becomes the property of the finder: *Robinson v Western Australian Museum* (1977) 138 CLR 283, 338 (Jacobs J).

trespassers will be prosecuted

A legal falsehood in most jurisdictions, because (with some exceptions) trespass is a tort, not a crime.

trifle

'trifling'

Whether something is *trifling* involves questions of degree, making *trifling* an inherently uncertain word. For example, in criminal law, whether an offence is 'of so *trifling* a nature' as to excuse punishment, is context-dependent: *Phillips v Evans* [1896] 1 QB 305. It is 'probably impossible and certainly unwise for the courts to lay down any hard and fast rules as to what is meant by an offence of a *trifling* nature': *Police v Ludlow* [2008] SASC 43, [13] (White J). Contemporary attitudes will play a part: for example, exceeding the blood alcohol limit, even by a very small amount, is unlikely to be a 'trifling' breach of drink-driving laws (*Police v Berry* [2014] SASC 33; (2014) 119 SASR 200); nor is reckless driving (*Speake v Police* [2008] SASC 314). An intriguing issue arises where a person commits a series of offences, each of which is trifling; can the cumulative effect mean that the last in the series is no longer *trifling*? (The answer, it seems, is no: *Vinters v Freedman* (1902) 71 LJ KB 48, involving successive offences of baking bread on Sundays.)

A careful writer will find another, more certain term than *trifling*, or will set an objective standard by which to judge questions of degree.

'trifle with'

Trifle appears also in a legal maxim: 'the law will not allow itself to be *trifled with*'. The meaning is that the law does not allow fine distinctions to defeat its overall objective. For example, a person who, having knocked on the door of a house as if to seek permission to enter, then rushes in and robs the house, commits a burglary even though no breaking occurred, 'for the law will not suffer itself to be *trifled with* by such evasions': TR Fitzwalter Butler and M Garsia (eds), *Archbold: Pleading, Evidence and Practice in Criminal Cases*, 36th edn (Sweet & Maxwell, 1966) 658 (last edition of that text before the *Theft Act* did away with 'breaking').

See also **de minimis**.

TRIPLETS

See **WORD PAIRINGS**.

true copy

A copy can be a *true copy* despite containing some deviation from the original. Just how mcuh deviation depends on the context:

> Bills of sale legislation required registration of a 'true copy' of a bill of sale. Held: a 'true copy' need not be an exact copy. Clerical errors or blanks could be excused, if the missing information was trivial or could be deduced from elsewhere in the original bill or the supporting documents filed with it. However, a failure to insert 'per annum' into the clause relating to payment of interest was more important, and denied the copy the status of a 'true copy': *Burchell v Thompson* [1920] 2 KB 80.

The overriding principle is that the copy must be sufficiently accurate as not to mislead a person relying on it: *Burchell v Thompson* [1920] 2 KB 80, 103 (Scrutton LJ).

trustee de son tort

Law French: trustee 'by his own wrongdoing'. A person who, though not actually appointed as a trustee, nevertheless purports to act as one. Despite the terminology of 'wrong', there need be no conscious wrongdoing. For example, a person who acts as trustee, unaware that a formal defect in the appointment process has vitiated his or her appointment, may become a *trustee de son tort*.

As with many other Law French terms, the meaning may be guessable; but it is always better to provide a translation. For example:

> '[The] responsibility [of a properly appointed trustee] may no doubt be extended in equity to others who are not properly trustees, if they are found either making themselves trustees *de son tort* [prefer: *by their own unauthorised conduct*] or actually participating in any fraudulent conduct of the trustee to the injury of the [beneficiary].' [*Barnes v Addy* (1874) 9 Ch App 244, 251 (Lord Selborne LC)]

See also **de son tort**.

truster

In Scots legal usage, a person who establishes a trust over property; in other jurisdictions, *settlor*.

See also **settler / settlor**.

turnover rent

Rent calculated in accordance with business turnover. For example, a retail lease may require the tenant to pay *turnover rent* in addition to base rent.

tutor / tutrix

A person appointed by the court to represent a minor or other person legally incapable of conducting their own litigation. *Tutor* is gender-neutral. The female variant—*tutrix*—is rare. (For an exception, see *George v Eagle Air Services Ltd* [2009] 1 WLR 2133, on appeal from the Eastern Caribbean Court of Appeal, where the Privy Council used *tutrix*, presumably reflecting Caribbean usage.)

TYPOGRAPHY

See **CAPITALS; DOCUMENT DESIGN; FONTS; PUNCTUATION.**

uberrimae fidei

Latin: of the utmost good faith; from *uberrima fides* (utmost good faith). A Latinism which, though hallowed in law, carries no more meaning than its English translation. Prefer the English translation. For example:

- 'It is well established that a guarantee is not, as such, a contract *uberrimae fidei* [prefer: *of the utmost good faith*]. Consequently the creditor is not obliged to disclose all matters relevant to a decision of the surety whether or not to enter into the guarantee.' [*North Shore Ventures Ltd v Anstead Holdings Inc* [2012] Ch 31, 45; [2011] EWCA Civ 230, [29] (Sir Andrew Morritt C)]
- 'An insurance contract is a contract requiring the utmost good faith (*uberrimae fidei*) of both parties and it was the law for centuries that a person seeking insurance had a duty to make full disclosure of all material circumstances.' [*CGU Insurance Ltd v Porthouse* (2008) 235 CLR 103, 117; [2008] HCA 30, [49], preferring the English but adding the Latin as if to reassure legal readers.]

ubi jus [ius] ibi remedium

Latin: where there is a right [literally, law], there is a remedy. A Latinism expressing a fine sentiment in fine rhythm, but inherently vague (what rights? what remedies?) and having no advantage over an English translation with similar sentiment and rhythm.

- '[T]he common law enables the judges, when faced with a situation where a right recognised by law is not adequately protected, either to extend existing principles to cover the situation or to apply an existing remedy to redress the injustice. There is here no novelty; but merely the application of the principle *ubi jus ibi remedium* [prefer: *where there is a right, there is a remedy*].' [*Sidaway v Bethlem Royal Hospital* [1985] AC 871, 884 (Lord Scarman)]
- '[The applicants] sought to place reliance upon the much vaguer principle that rights should not be without remedies (*ubi jus ibi remedium*). A principle at that level of generality is apt to invite, rather than answer, questions as to who enjoys the right, against whom and by whom is it to be enforced?' [*Li v Zhou* [2014] NSWCA 176, [35]; (2014) 87 NSWLR 20 (Basten JA, providing an explanation)]

ult

Abbreviation for *ultimo* (Latin: in the last), an archaism referring to the previous month: eg, 'Thank you for your letter of 25th *ult*.'

See **ultimo**.

ultimata

The Latin plural of *ultimatum*. Prefer the anglicised *ultimatums*:

- 'Although Mr Bailey was forever sending *ultimata* [prefer: *ultimatums*] to [X], his various negotiating ploys were markedly unsuccessful.' [*Elvanite Full Circle Ltd v Amec Earth & Environmental (UK) Ltd* [2013] EWHC 1191 (TCC); [2013] 148 Con LR 127, [156] (Coulson J)]
- 'The appellant issued three *ultimata* [prefer: *ultimatums*] at 8h30, 10h30 and 15h30 calling on the employees to return to work. The third and final *ultimatum* concluded with the following: ...' [*Chevron Engineering (Pty) Ltd v Nkambule* [2003] ZASCA 150, [4]; [2004] 1 All SA 137, [4] (Mlambo AJA)]

ultimo

Latin: in the last; in the preceding. Generally used as shorthand for *ultimo mense*, 'in the last (ie, previous) month', and further abbreviated to *ult*. Both long form and abbreviation are obsolescent. To continue to use them is pure pedantry. Modern usage prefers 'last month', or (better still) specifies the month. Thus, *not*: 'Thank you for your letter of 25th *ultimo* [or *ult*]', *but* 'Thank you for your letter of 25 May.'

See also **proximo**.

ultra vires

Latin: beyond power. This Latinism has passed into business, bureaucratic, and legislative language. It is used in two contexts:

1. where a person or entity has no power to do the impugned act;
2. where a person or entity has the power to do the act, but fails to follow the procedures prescribed for doing it.

Context (1) is more common: *Rolled Steel Products (Holdings) Ltd v British Steel Corp* [1986] Ch 246, 303 (Browne-Wilkinson LJ). But regardless of the context, a plain-English translation captures both the literal meaning and the legal nuance of the Latin—so prefer the plain English. For example:

- 'Any payment out of the consolidated fund made without Parliamentary authority is simply illegal and *ultra vires* [prefer: *beyond power*], and may be recovered by the Government if it can, as here, be traced.' [*Auckland Harbour Board v R* [1924] AC 318, 327 (Viscount Haldane)]
- 'As such [it was argued], the taking order is *ultra vires* [prefer: *beyond power*], invalid and of no effect.' [*Mandurah Enterprises Pty Ltd v Western Australia Planning Commission* [2010] HCA 2; (2010) 240 CLR 409, [46] (plurality of High Court of Australia)]

See also **intra vires**.

unclean hands

A colourful description of a principle under which courts of equity may refuse relief if they consider that the applicant's conduct in the circumstances surrounding the transaction or proceedings has been improper or inequitable. Hence the maxim: 'A person who comes to equity must come with clean hands.'

Further reading

Halsbury's Laws of England, 'Equitable Jurisdiction' (vol 47, 2014) [112]

unconscionable

In normal usage, usually meaning simply 'very unfair' or perhaps even merely 'unfair'. But in legal use, *unconscionable* carries the stronger sense of 'against good conscience'. Hence, in this stronger sense, a court of equity will restrain a person from exercising property or contractual rights where it would be 'unconscionable' for them to do so. Again in this stronger sense, *unconscionable* conduct includes taking advantage of someone who is under a special disability because of factors such as age, illness, ignorance, impaired faculties, or financial need. Consumer legislation often uses wider expressions, such as 'unjust', or 'unfair'. For example, UK consumer legislation uses 'unfair': a contract is 'unfair' if, contrary to the requirement of good faith, it causes a significant imbalance in the parties' rights and obligations to the detriment of the consumer: *Consumer Rights Act 2015*, s 62(4).

Further reading

Halsbury's Laws of England, 'Consumer Protection' (vol 21, 2016) [422] (unfair commercial practices), 'Contract' (vol 22, 2019) [98] (unconscionable contracts)

under

When is something done *under* a statute or other authorising document? The answer is not always clear. For example, whether something is done *under* a statute is open to two interpretations: (1) it is expressly or impliedly required or authorised by the statute (ie, in the time-honoured term, it is done 'pursuant to' the statute); or (2) it derives from the statute (ie, it is done 'by virtue of' the statute). For example:

> A statute created a drug offence. Police charged a person, not with the offence but with conspiracy to commit the offence—a common-law crime. Held, the person was charged *under* (ie, by virtue of) the statute, not 'pursuant to' the statute—because the statute itself did not make conspiracy an offence: *R v Kemp* (1979) 69 Cr App R 330.

If doubt could arise, clarify which meaning of *under* is intended.

See also **pursuant to**.

under (and ...)

Some legal writers seem unable to let *under* stand alone; they feel compelled to add extra words. For them, nothing is ever done *under* a contract, but rather *under and in connection with* a contract, or *under and arising out of* a contract, or even *under or in connection with or arising out of* a contract. But is the expansion necessary? Often not: while the extra words may give the undiscriminating drafter satisfaction for having so perspicaciously covered the field, the prolixity may irritate the reader and cause a court to question whether the drafter intended different meanings for each added word or phrase.

under / in accordance with

Often found as a pairing—*under and in accordance with*—but without sufficient attention to whether both 'limbs' are needed. For example, to do something *under* a statutory provision usually means to exercise the authority given by that provision; and to do something *in accordance with* a statutory provision usually means to do it in the way required by (in compliance with) that provision. While in principle there is a difference between these two statements, the practical issue is whether both are needed in the particular case under consideration. If they are, use both; but if (as is more likely) one will do, then choose the relevant one and omit the other.

under / in connection with

Is there a difference between something arising *under* a contract or statute, and something arising *in connection with* a contract or statute? Generally, yes: in ordinary English, *under* is not as broad as *in connection with*: *Heyman v Darwins* [1942] AC 356, 383, 399. Thus, a dispute arising *under* an agreement is a narrower concept than a dispute arising *in connection with* an agreement (or, for that matter, a dispute arising *out of* an agreement): *Samick Lines Co Ltd v Owners of the Antonis P Lemos* [1985] AC 711, 727 (Lord Brandon); *Reinhart v Welker* [2012] NSWCA 95, [123]–[145] (Bathurst CJ). The distinctions could be relevant, for example, in interpreting arbitration clauses: a clause giving an arbitrator power to determine disputes arising *under* the contract confers a narrower remit than power to determine disputes arising *in connection with* the contract.

However, these distinctions do not justify mere wordiness. In particular, they do not justify always pairing *under* with such phrases as *in connection with*. If, in the particular case, *under* (alone) is wide enough to cover the intended meaning, then omit *and in connection with*; and if you need the extra reach of *in connection with*, choose that expression but omit *under*. For example:

- Misrepresentations made before entry into a contract were not made *under* the contract, because logically they preceded the contract: *Paper Products Pty Ltd v Tomlinsons (Rochdale) Ltd* (1993) 43 FCR 439. But they can be said to have been made *in connection with* the contract: *QH Tours Ltd v Ship Design & Management (Aust) Pty Ltd* (1991) 33 FCR 227.
- A claim for rectification of an agreement was not a dispute arising *under* the agreement: *Printing Machinery Co Ltd v Linotype and Machinery Ltd* [1912] 1 Ch 566, 572–73 (Warrington J). An expression such as 'in connection with' may be needed: *Dowell Australia Ltd v Triden Contractors Pty Ltd* [1982] 1 NSWLR 508.
- However, in an agreement aimed at quelling numerous complex commercial disputes between the parties, a clause requiring disputes '*under* this deed' to be referred to arbitration included disputes about the validity of the deed: *Rinehart v Hancock Prospecting Pty Ltd* [2019] HCA 13; (2019) 93 ALJR 582. (That is, there was no need for the wider '*under or in connection with*' this deed.)

See also **arising from / out of / under**; **in connection with**; **in relation to**.

under hand

As a single word (*underhand*), denoting fraud or sharp practice; as two words (*under hand*), denoting 'signing by hand' as distinct from 'signing under seal'—ie, signed, as distinct from 'signed, sealed and delivered'. Where, for purposes of solemnity or authenticity, both signing and sealing are required, the double-barrelled formula *under hand*

and seal is sometimes seen: eg, *Electronic Rentals Pty Ltd v Anderson* (1971) 124 CLR 27, 42–43 (Windeyer J).

In rare contexts, *under hand* might denote an instrument that is *un*signed:

> For stamp duty purposes, an unsigned document embodying an agreement to lease a house was an 'agreement *under hand only*': *Chadwick v Clarke* (1845) 14 LJCP 233.

Usually, however, *under hand* connotes *signed.* For example:

> For the purposes of Scottish succession law, a testatrix's unsigned direction to trustees to dispose of her property in a particular way was not 'an informal writing *under my hand*': *Cameron v Whyte* 1943 SC 369.

See also **signed, sealed and delivered**; **under seal**.

under seal

A term indicating executing a document by sealing (as distinct from by mere signing), particularly a deed: eg, 'A and B executed the deed *under seal*.'

See also **execute (a document)**; **EXECUTION CLAUSE**; **under hand**.

underlease

See **sublease / underlease**.

undertaking

1. A promise, usually with at least a modicum of formality and with contractual intent—as where parties enter into 'mutually enforceable *undertakings*'. Whether an *undertaking* is binding legally depends on general principles of contract law, including whether the law prescribes formalities for entry into binding obligations (eg, that contracts for the sale of land must be in writing and signed). Some *undertakings* lacking contractual status are legally enforceable—eg, lawyers' undertakings, which are enforceable under a court's supervisory jurisdiction over its officers: *Re a Solicitor* [1966] 1 WLR 1604; *Re C (a solicitor)* [1982] 1 NZLR 137; *Wade v Licardy* (1993) 33 NSWLR 1, 7–9.
2. An entity that carries on business. Depending on context, the *undertaking* may be the whole of that entity, or (if the entity is divided into business units) part of that entity: *Re Memco-Med Ltd's Patent* [1992] RPC 403, 414 (Aldous J).

unencumbered

See **encumbrance**.

uninterested

See **disinterested / uninterested**.

United Kingdom

In strict legal usage, the combined areas of Great Britain (ie, England, Wales, and Scotland) and Northern Ireland: *Interpretation Act 1978*, s 5, Sched 1. This usage does not include the Channel Islands or the Isle of Man; thus, an insurance policy covering acts in the United Kingdom does not cover acts in the Channel Islands, in the absence of contrary intention: *Navigators and General Insurance Co v Ringrose* [1962] 1 All ER 97. However, strict meaning may yield to different usage—eg, where the parties to a contract clearly intend a meaning that differs from the strict legal definition.

Compare **Great Britain**.

UNITS OF MEASUREMENT

See **FRACTIONS; LEGAL UNITS OF MEASUREMENT; NUMBERS; WORDS AND FIGURES.**

unlawful

See **illegal / unlawful**.

unless

A seemingly harmless word, meaning *if not*. But because *unless* implies a negative, its meaning can be less than clear. For example:

- A tenant covenants not to do an act *unless* he or she makes a stipulated payment to the landlord. Does that give the tenant automatic permission to do the act on making the payment? Answer, yes, because it is a single, composite covenant: *Legh v Lillie* (1860) LJ Ex 27.
- A statute provides that a person is not eligible to become a local councillor '*unless* he is a local resident, or *unless* he owns land worth at least $X'. Does this require the person to *both* reside locally *and* own land worth at least $X, or is it enough to satisfy one only of the requirements? The uncertainty arises from the second *unless*. If meaning one only of the requirements, it would be clearer to write, '*unless* he is a local resident *or* owns land worth at least $X' (hypothetical example from *Re Sommerville* (1889) 7 NZLR 400, 416–17).

See also **POSITIVES / NEGATIVES.**

unless and until

A lawyer's common pairing. A pedant may seek to justify it by arguing that each word serves a separate purpose—*unless* introduces a condition, and *until* introduces a time limit. This may be true in principle, but in most actual contexts one word would suffice. Make the appropriate choice—ie, *unless* (alone) to introduce a condition, or *until* (alone) to introduce a time limit.

See also **if and when**.

unless the context otherwise requires

Definition clauses

Definition clauses often add the cautionary qualification that a word or phrase bears its defined meaning 'unless the context otherwise requires', or 'where the context so admits', or similar. But in principle a defined term should *always* bear its defined meaning. Therefore, the only logical purpose of such a provision is to spare the drafter the embarrassment—and perhaps the legal consequences—of having 'overlooked a differential usage somewhere in [the] text': *M v Secretary of State for Work and Pensions* [2006] QB 380, 407 [84] (Sedley LJ). Drafters confident in their skills do not need an 'unless the context …' let-out. Some may even put their skills to the test with a clause to the effect that defined meanings apply *'for all purposes'*: *Anglo Continental Educational Group (GB) Ltd v Capital Homes (Southern) Ltd* [2009] EWCA Civ 218, [5] (Arden LJ).

A number of comments may be made about an 'unless the context …' qualification:

1. The qualification should be unnecessary. A careful drafter always uses a defined term in its defined sense. Word-processing 'search' functions can help ensure this result.
2. The law implies the qualification anyway. The meaning of a word or phrase always yields to its context. The absence of the provision does not preclude a judge from finding that the drafter used a defined word in a non-defined sense. Authoritative judicial statements to that effect are legion: eg, *Knightsbridge Estates Trust, Limited v Byrne* [1940] AC 613, 621; *Alcan (NT) Alumina Pty Ltd v Commissioner of Territory Revenue* [2009] HCA 41; (2009) 239 CLR 27, [6] (French CJ); *Lisbeth Enterprises Ltd v Mandy Luk* [2006] 9 HKCFAR 131; [2006] HKCFA 29, [16] (Bokhary PJ).
3. It does not necessarily preclude litigation over meaning, because it still leaves open whether the context in fact 'requires' or 'admits' (or whatever word is used) a meaning different from the defined meaning: eg, *Blue Metal Industries Ltd v Dilley* [1970] AC 827 (PC); *Floor v Davis* [1980] AC 695 (PC).
4. It may even encourage litigation over meaning. This is because the drafter has 'made it clear that it is possible that different contexts may give rise to different meanings': *Onixa Energy Ltd v Neuftec Ltd* [2009] EWCA Civ 668, [14] (Jacobs LJ).
5. Courts start with the presumption that the drafter used defined words in their defined sense. The 'deliberate use of defined words is not to be lightly passed over', even if the definition clause allows for the possibility of another meaning for a defined term: *BHP Petroleum (Australia) Pty Ltd v Sagasco South East Inc* [2001] WASCA 159, [24].
6. The onus of proving that the qualification applies is on the person asserting it: *Anti-Doping Rule Violation Panel v XZTT* [2013] FCAFC 95; (2013) 214 FCR 40, [92].
7. A finding that the qualification applies in one instance does not necessarily flow through to all instances where it is used: *Duperouzel v Cameron* [1973] WAR 181. However, because a document must be read as a whole, whether the qualification applies in any particular instance may require considering *all* instances: *Official Trustee in Bankruptcy v Buffier* [2005] NSWSC 839; (2005) 54 ACSR 767, [29]–[30].
8. The precise formula is important. Some formulas are 'stronger' than others. For example, the formula 'unless the context otherwise *requires*' may mean that the context must *demand* it; ie, it must be *necessary*, rather than merely sensible or reasonable: *Hammonds v Jones* [2009] EWCA Civ 1400, [32]. But the variant formula 'unless a contrary intention *appears*' may allow easier departure from the defined meaning: *Thompson v Ludwig* (1991) 37 IR 437, [17]. So too may the formula 'where the context so *admits*': *Franklins Pty Ltd v Metcash Trading Ltd* [2009] NSWCA 407; (2009) 76 NSWLR 603, [343], [344].
9. Some formulas widen the qualification beyond 'context' to 'subject matter'. A formula such as 'unless context or *subject matter* otherwise requires' may allow 'a more flexible approach' than other formulas: *Conde v Gilfoyle* [2010] QCA 109, [20].
10. What is the *context* ('unless the *context* otherwise requires')? In a document, is it the particular clause in the document, or is it the document as whole, or is it the matrix of facts out of which the document arose? In a statute, the New Zealand Supreme Court has held that the 'context' includes the immediate provision, the surrounding provisions, the statute's purpose, and even the policy considerations reflected in the statute and its legislative history: *AFFCO New Zealand Ltd v New Zealand Meat*

Workers and Related Trade Unions Inc [2017] NZSC 135; [2018] 1 NZLR 212, [65]. This casts the net wide.

11. The qualification casts unreasonable burdens on the reader. It says to the reader: 'Somewhere in this document, I may have used the term in its undefined sense, or I may not have; I am not telling; work it out for yourself.'
12. The qualification may cast doubt on the drafter's skill or interest. If the drafter needs this protection against inconsistency in the use of definitions, how reliable is the rest of the document?

Interpretation clauses

The qualification 'unless the context otherwise requires' (or variants of it) appears also in interpretation clauses. Unlike a definitions clause (which defines specific words or phrases), an interpretation clause controls the interpretation of an entire document. Similar issues as those considered above apply to an '*unless the context* …' qualification in interpretation clauses.

See also **DEFINITIONS; INTERPRETATION CLAUSES.**

until (a date)

As a matter of ordinary English, if a state of affairs continues *until* a stated day, it continues for the whole of that day. For example:

- A fire insurance policy expressed to continue '*until* 14 August' extends to loss by fire *on* 14 August: *Isaacs v Royal Assurance Co* (1870) LR 5 Ex 296.
- Protection against bankruptcy proceedings *until* a stated date extends for the *whole of* that date: *Backhouse v Mellor* (1859) 28 LJ Ex 141.
- A stay of execution granted '*until* May 1 next' does not prevent issue *on* that day: *Rogers v Davis* (1845) 8 Ir LR 399.

If in doubt in any particular case, consider expanding the expression:

- '*until and including* 1 May'; or
- '*until but not including* 1 May' (ie, if 1 May is not to be included).

See also **from (time)**.

until such time as

Always reducible to *until*: eg, 'The hirer may use the car *until* ~~*such time as*~~ the owner demands it back.'

unwilling

A term rarely left to operate without a qualification of 'reasonableness'. For example, a party may have a right to rescind a contract if *unwilling* to perform a specified obligation; but a court is likely to circumscribe the party's exercise of the right with a requirement of 'reasonableness'. Thus, contracts for the sale of land commonly allow the vendor to rescind if the purchaser insists on an objection or requisition on title with which the vendor is *unwilling* to comply. However, the vendor can invoke this clause only if acting reasonably and honestly: see, eg, *Selkirk v Romar Investments Ltd* [1963] 1 WLR 1415, 1422–23 (PC); *Gardiner v Orchard* (1910) 10 CLR 722, 738–40. Or, more bluntly, the vendor cannot rescind by invoking *unwillingness* 'at his sweet will': *Hurley v Roy* (1921) 64 DLR 375, 377.

unwritten law

A euphemism for 'non-statute law'—ie, the law laid down by the courts, as distinct from the law laid down by parliament. Modern statutes often use *unwritten law* in this sense, but the use can be traced back much earlier: eg, *Bristol Tramways & Carriage Co Ltd v Fiat Motors Ltd* [1910] 2 KB 831, 838 (Cozens-Hardy MR, characterising the aim of the *Sale of Goods Act 1893* as being 'to codify the unwritten law applicable to the sale of goods'). The euphemism ignores the reality that the law laid down by the courts is in fact mostly *written*, in that superior court judges almost always deliver their judgments in writing.

up to

up to (a date)

Unless context requires otherwise, an obligation to be performed, or a right to be exercised, *up to* a date can be performed or exercised *on* that date: *Simmons v Associated Furnishers Ltd* [1931] 1 Ch 379.

up to (an amount)

A gift of money *up to* a stated amount might seem vague—the maximum is clear enough, but what about the minimum? Yet in context, even such an expression may be unambiguous: eg, in a will, the context may make it clear that a gift *up to* a stated amount means a gift of that maximum amount unless reduced under other provisions of the will: *Re Hely* [2018] VSC 614.

upon / on

Prefer *on*

Upon is a needless variant of *on*. A shorter word is always better than a longer one, if the meaning is the same—as it is here. True, an occasional extra syllable does no harm. More likely, though, the writer who employs additional syllables does so out of habit—thus, '*Upon* [prefer: *on*] entering the courtroom, and *upon* [prefer: *on*] hearing the argument of counsel, the judge gave her views *upon* [prefer: *on*] the meaning of the contract.' The cumulative effect then deadens the prose. So, prune to *on*. For example:

- 'There is no route map … which focuses the minds of the parties and the court *upon* [prefer: *on*] the issues which are likely to bear *upon* [prefer: *on*] whether [an] order should or should not be granted.' [*Re a child* [2016] EWCA Civ 572; [2016] 4 WLR 111, [38] (Black LJ)]
- 'The judge adopted the two stage approach urged *upon* [prefer: *on*] him by [the respondents]. … He held that, *upon* [prefer: *on*] a purely domestic interpretation of s 37(1), the court had jurisdiction to make the orders sought [and that] even if the court did not have the power to make the orders *upon* [prefer: *on*] a purely domestic interpretation of s 37(1), the section could and should be construed [in a certain way].' [*Cartier International AG v British Sky Broadcasting Ltd* [2016] EWCA Civ 658, [34] (Kitchin LJ)]

Exceptions?

There may be several (rare) exceptions to this preference for *on*:

- **Cadence or rhythm**: 'like a painted ship *upon* a painted ocean'. But while cadence and rhythm have a place in legal writing, they rarely require *upon*.
- **Greater sense of urgency**: in limited contexts, some might argue that *upon* imports a sense of greater urgency than *on*. For example: 'The court may order the prisoner to

be taken to the cells *upon* conviction.' The sense is of making the order *immediately* after conviction. But in truth, the distinction is very fine (if it exists at all), and *on* does just as well: 'The court may order the prisoner to be taken to the cells *on* conviction.'

- **To introduce a condition**: some consider *upon* preferable when introducing a condition or event, where the sense is of meeting a qualification. For example: '*Upon* lodging the pleadings, you will get a hearing date.' Or, 'I give my house to my son *upon* his attaining 25 years.' But here too, *on* does just as well.

Possible ambiguity

Upon and *on* can be ambiguous.

Denoting causation or time?

Depending on context, *upon* [or *on*] can denote either causation or time. Which is meant? For example, a will may state: 'I give my house to A, effective *upon* [or *on*] the death of B.' This could mean: (1) nothing vests in A until B dies (ie, *upon* connotes causation); or (2) the house vests in A immediately, but with possession postponed until B dies (ie, *upon* denotes time).

Denoting unclear time

When referring to time, *upon* can mean (depending on context) 'before', or 'at the same time as', or even 'after': *R v Arkwright* (1848) 12 QB 960, 970; 116 ER 1130, 1134. Context is everything. So, where a tax statute deemed a disposal of assets to occur *on* a taxpayer's death, the court held that this could mean before the death, or simultaneously with the death, or after the death: *Larter v Skone James* [1976] 2 All ER 615, 618 (Walton J). Again, where a statute authorised justices of the peace to issue a summons *upon* an information being laid before them, the court held that *upon* included *after*, so that a summons issued 6 months later was within time: *R v Fairford Justices* [1976] QB 600, 604 (Lord Widgery CJ).

See also **vest**.

upon the expiration of

Usually a wordy substitute for *at the end of*—in which case, prefer *at the end of*. For example:

> 'The tenant must vacate the premises *upon the expiration of* [prefer: *at the end of*] the lease.' [Or better still: 'The tenant must vacate the premises *when the lease ends*.']

use (verb)

Uncertainty can lurk in the simplest words—and *use* is an example. When does a person *use* something? The question arises in different areas of law, and always the answer is context-dependent. For example:

1. **Land**. When does a person 'use' land? Depending on context, the answer may be (for example) 'when they reside on it' or 'when they occupy it for business purposes' or (in the case of a farm) 'when they cultivate it'. But the answer is not always so predictable. For example, in some cases land may be 'used' although it is vacant:
    - a hospital 'uses' land that it deliberately leaves vacant to provide patients with clear air, room for exercise, and solitude: *Newcastle City Council v Royal Newcastle Hospital* [1959] AC 248

- a brickworks 'uses' land that it leaves vacant in anticipation of future quarrying: *Parramatta City Council v Brickworks Ltd* (1972) 128 CLR 1.

2. **Motor vehicles**. When does a person *use* a motor vehicle? Clearly, they *use* it when they *drive* it. But can they *use* it when they are not driving it? Here too, the answer varies with the context. For example: do they *use* it:
   - when, having run out of petrol, they leave it to seek help from a friend? (Answer, yes: *Dunthorne v Bentley* [1996] RTR 428)
   - when they park it by the roadside for some months, during which time it deteriorates to the extent that it needs towing? (Answer, yes: *Elliot v Grey* [1960] 1 QB 367; *Brown v Roberts* [1965] 1 QB 1)
   - when, having immobilised it by removing the battery, they repair it in an employer's loading bay? (Answer, no: *R & S Pilling v UK Insurance Ltd* [2019] UKSC 16; [2019] 2 WLR 1015)
   - when they sleep in it? (Answer, probably yes: *Dodd v Brown* [2012] NTSC 102)
3. **Animals**. When does a person *use* an animal? For example: does a police-dog handler 'use' the dog when taking it for a walk, unconnected with policing activities? (Answer, no: *R v PY* [2019] EWCA Crim 17; [2019] 1 WLR 3249, in the context of an exemption from liability for injury caused by a police dog 'being *used* for a lawful purpose'.)

These examples show the critical importance of context, even for a simple word such as *use*. An adept drafter, alert to the possibility of uncertainty and the vagaries of context, will seek to clarify.

use and enjoy

A lawyer's habitual pairing—eg, a lease gives a tenant the right to 'use and enjoy' the property. As with some other familiar legal pairings, the etymology helps explain the redundancy: each word derives from a different language stock. Thus, *use* derives from Latin (*usus*); *enjoyment* derives from Old French (*enjoier*: to give joy to), or perhaps from the Latin *fruor*, denoting the exercise and use of a right: see *Kenny v Preen* [1963] 1 QB 499 (Pearson LJ). In a legal context, however, to *enjoy* something (usually property) almost always means simply to *use* it. Nor does *enjoy* here carry any connotation of pleasure, happiness or recreation. So, almost always, the two words are synonyms. Choose one—preferably *use*, being more idiomatic.

See also **WORD PAIRINGS**.

user

In standard English, *user* means 'a person who uses'. In legal English, however, *user* can also mean 'the act of using', as in 'a restriction on *user*' (ie, an obligation restricting *use* of land). This legal usage is not a term of art, but mere habit. Prefer the more idiomatic *use*.

Before	**After**
The land is subject to a *restriction as to user*.	The land is subject to a *restriction on use*.
The *permitted user* under this lease is the sale of meat.	The *permitted use* under this lease is the sale of meat.
The purchaser must enter into a *covenant against user* for retail purposes.	The purchaser must enter into a *covenant against use* for retail purposes.

Sometimes, *use* and *user* are used interchangeably in the same sentence, causing careful readers to ponder whether the author intends a change in meaning, or has merely overlooked a typographical error:

> '[It was irrelevant that the rights amounted to] exclusive *user* of the part of the servient tenement affected by the easement and that as a result the servient owner was deprived of the whole beneficial *use* of the land ...' [*Jea Holdings (Aust) Pty Ltd v Registrar-General of NSW* [2013] NSWSC 587, [36] (Windeyer AJ)]

usque ad coelum et ad inferos

Latin: from the heavens to the centre of the earth. A fanciful maxim said to describe the extent of legal ownership above and below the surface of land: the surface owner is said to own *usque ad coelum et ad inferos*. Modern law places more sensible limits on upwards and downwards ownership. (See Kevin Gray and Susan Frances Gray, *Elements of Land Law*, 5th edn (Oxford University Press, 2009) [1.2.15], [1.2.31]–[1.2.41].)

See also **cuius est solum**.

usque ad filum aquae / viae

Latin: up to the middle line (thread) of the water / road. A common-law principle that a person's title to land bounded by a road or river extends up to the middle line of the road or river. Statutes have much reduced the ambit of the principle by vesting ownership of roads and rivers in state or local authorities. The Latin obscures a number of complexities in the principle (including when it is rebutted), so nothing is lost by substituting a plain-English expression such as 'the middle-line rule'.

Further reading

- Kevin Gray and Susan Francis Gray, *Elements of Land Law*, 5th edn (Oxford University Press, 2009) [1.2.4]
- Brendan Edgeworth (ed), *Butt's Land Law*, 7th edn (Lawbook, 2017) [2.510]–[2.540] (Commonwealth case law, including the effect of land registration statutes)

usual (terms)

Parties to a contract may be content to agree that 'the *usual terms* will apply to our transaction'. But lawyers know that such a formula invites litigation: what is 'usual', and who is to determine it? In only one area does the law supply some time-settled certainty, namely, in the law of leases. Where a lease states that the 'usual' covenants (ie, terms) are to apply, the common law implies into the lease the covenants (terms) that the courts have settled as 'usual' in leases of that kind of property. If a lease contains no express covenants (terms) between landlord and tenant, the common law implies into the lease the covenants that are 'usual' in leases of that kind of property.

Conventionally, the *usual* covenants in leases are:

by the tenant:

(i) to pay rent, with a proviso allowing the landlord to re-enter and terminate the lease for non-payment (but not for breach of any other covenant)

(ii) to pay taxes imposed on the land, except those expressly payable by the landlord

(iii) to keep and deliver up the premises in repair

(iv) to allow the landlord to enter and view the state of repair.

by the landlord:

(v) for quiet enjoyment, protecting the tenant's possession against interference by the landlord and persons claiming through the landlord.

See *Hampshire v Wickens* (1878) 7 Ch D 555.

But even here, uncertainty can intrude. This is because the *usual* covenants are not frozen in time, but vary from time to time and according to the type and location of the premises: *Flexman v Corbett* [1930] 1 Ch 672, 678; *Charalambous v Ktori* [1972] 1 WLR 951, 953. This makes the character of 'usualness' unpredictable. Indeed, whether a particular lease covenant is a *usual* covenant is a question of fact (which can lead to argument):

> 'If it is established that (to put a strong case) in nine cases out of ten the covenant would be found in a lease of premises of that nature for that purpose and in that district, I think that the court is bound to hold that the covenant is *usual*.' [*Flexman v Corbett* [1930] 1 Ch 672, 677 (Maugham J)]

In establishing the 'nine cases out of ten', courts commonly look to the practice of conveyancers and the established texts on conveyancing precedents: *Hampshire v Wickens* (1878) 7 Ch D 555, 561–62. One consequence is that the *usual* covenants in one common-law jurisdiction are not necessarily *usual* in others. Another is that the *usual* covenants may vary from one generation to the next.

Further reading

Kevin Gray and Susan Francis Gray, *Elements of Land Law*, 5th edn (Oxford, Oxford University Press, 2009) [4.3.90]

See also **quiet enjoyment**.

ut infra

Latin: as below. Little purpose, except academic pedantry, favours the Latin over the English translation. Prefer *as below*.

See also **ut supra**.

ut res magis valeat quam pereat

Meaning

Latin: in order that the thing may succeed rather than perish; sometimes rendered *ut res valeat potius quam pereat*. Its fuller version is usually given as *verba ita sunt intelligenda ut res magis valeat quam pereat*: 'words should be interpreted so as to make the thing valid rather than ineffective': *Lancashire County Council v Municipal Mutual Insurance Ltd* [1996] 3 All ER 545, 557 (Staughton LJ). Expressed more bluntly, 'validate if possible': *Pavilion Property Trustees Ltd v Permira Advisers LLP* [2014] EWHC 145, [20] (Morgan J).

The maxim reflects a principle of interpretation under which a court will, if possible, prefer an interpretation that renders a document or a provision valid rather than one that strikes it down. For that reason, some call it 'the validity principle'. The principle usually seeks to uphold legislative instruments as within power rather than *ultra vires*. But it applies also to private documents: *Brown v Gould* [1972] Ch 53, 56–58 (Megarry J); *Sheffield City Council v Jackson* [1998] 1 WLR 1591. One area in particular is the law of wills—it is better to favour an interpretation that preserves testamentary dispositions rather than destroys them: *Langston v Langston* (1834) 2 Cl & Fin 194, 243; 6 ER 1128, 1147; *Fell v Fell* (1921) 31 CLR 268. Other contexts include:

- to find a transfer by one joint tenant to another joint tenant to be effective: *Wright v Gibbons* (1949) 78 CLR 313

- to find a notice to quit to be valid: *Harihar Banerji v Ramsashi Roy* (1918) LR 45 Ind App 22; *Burnham v Carroll Musgrove Theatres Ltd* (1928) 41 CLR 540, 553
- to find a contract of guarantee to be valid (by holding that the consideration was executory and therefore effective, rather than past and therefore ineffective): *Breusch v Watts Development Division Pty Ltd* (1987) 10 NSWLR 311, 314.

As with other maxims of interpretation, this maxim is applied only where ambiguity exists. Where meaning is so clearly expressed that no alternative interpretation is open, there is no scope for adopting an interpretation that favours validity over invalidity or certainty over uncertainty: *IRC v Williams* [1969] 1 WLR 1197, 1201 (Megarry J). For example, a clause may impose a restraint of trade that is invalid because it is too widely cast; if the clause is unambiguous, a court cannot save it by invoking this maxim to reduce its ambit: *Eastes v Russ* [1914] Ch 468 (CA); *Konski v Peet Ltd* [1915] Ch 530, 538.

Avoid the Latin

As with most Latin maxims, this one can be expressed in plain English without loss of meaning or nuance. The encouragement to do so has high-level support:

> 'Better considered without reference to its original formulation in Latin, which nowadays few people understand, the validity principle proceeds on the premise that the parties to a contract or other instrument will have intended it to be valid. It therefore provides that, in circumstances in which a clause in their contract is … capable of having two meanings, one which would result in its being void and the other which would result in its being valid, the latter should be preferred.' [*Egon Zehnder Ltd v Tillman* [2019] UKSC 32; [2020] AC 154, [38] (Lord Wilson)]

See also **verba ita sunt intelligenda ut res magis valeat quam pereat**.

ut supra

Latin: as above. As with its counterpart *ut infra* ('as above'), to retain the Latin in the face of the English translation serves no purpose but pedantry.

utilise

The *Oxford English Dictionary* also allows *utilize*; in US English, *utilize*. But regardless of its spelling, always prefer *use*—it is shorter, less pretentious, and means exactly the same:

- 'The majority of the loan was repaid by *utilising* [prefer: *using*] money lent to the borrower by the owner of the lending company.' [*Swynson Ltd v Lowick Rose llp* [2015] EWCA Civ 629; [2016] 1 WLR 1045, [1] (Longmore LJ)]
- 'The appellant was … entitled therefore to *utilize* [prefer: *use*] the plans without falling into any breach of any copyright …' [*Concrete Pty Ltd v Parramatta Design and Developments Pty Ltd* [2006] HCA 55, [170] (Callinan J; the authorised report, (2006) 229 CLR 577, [170] uses *utilise*)]

utter

In normal usage, to speak. In legal usage, to put forward a document or object, often a forgery, with intent to pass it off as genuine.

v (abbreviation)

Abbreviation for *versus* (Latin: against). Used in case names to identify who is suing whom: *Jones v Smith* (the current convention being to italicise the names and the *v*).

British and Commonwealth usage omits the full stop after *v*; US usage generally inserts it (*v.*). When a case name is spoken aloud, the word *and* generally replaces *versus* and the abbreviation *v*; thus, *Jones v* [or *versus*] *Smith* is spoken '*Jones and Smith*'.

See also **CITATION OF CASES.**

vacant possession

Generally used in real-estate law to mean 'free of tenants and occupants'; eg, a vendor who promises *vacant possession* must hand over the property empty of all tenants and occupants. For general purposes, that meaning is sufficient. However, in truth the legal meaning is more refined. In the classic exposition, a promise to give *vacant possession* requires that the property be free of any 'physical impediment which substantially prevents or interferes with the enjoyment of the right of possession of a substantial part of the property': *Cumberland Consolidated Holdings Pty Ltd v Ireland* [1946] KB 264, 271. That is, the impediment must be substantial, not minor. Depending on context, therefore, 'vacant possession' can mean:

- free of a substantial amount of rubbish: *Cumberland Consolidated Holdings*, above
- free of chattels that hinder enjoyment of a substantial part of the property: *NYK Logistics (UK) Ltd v Ibrend Estates BV* [2011] EWCA Civ 683, [44]
- legally able to be occupied: *Topfell Ltd v Galley Properties Ltd* [1979] 1 WLR 446 (no *vacant possession* where council regulations precluded occupation of part of the property).

VAGUENESS

The issue

A concept or description is 'vague' if its meaning is doubtful, inconclusive, or open-ended. Vagueness is not always inappropriate in legal writing. For example, a vague answer may be appropriate for a vague question; or the subject matter may justify vagueness (eg, some international treaties); or vagueness may be appropriate simply because nothing more precise is available. And because the law must deal with words, precision of meaning cannot always be guaranteed: 'Condemned to the use of words, we can never expect mathematical certainty from our language': *Grayned v City of Rockford* 408 US 102, 110 (1972). The real danger lies not so much with vagueness as with *ambiguity*—namely, where a word or phrase carries several inconsistent meanings and it is impossible to tell from text or context which meaning is intended.

Examples of 'vague' terms in law include: *reasonable, reasonable time, as soon as possible, as soon as practicable, immediately, whenever, reputable, satisfactory, usual, material, fair, proper, trifling.* The meaning of these and similar words and phrases necessarily varies with context.

The following examples illustrate that vagueness does not necessarily result in unenforceability.

- '*Abnormal occurrence*'. Whether damage to a ship was caused by an 'abnormal occurrence' within the meaning of a time charter may raise contested issues of fact and degree (what is 'abnormal'?), but the term is not void for uncertainty: *Gard Marine and Energy Ltd v China National Chartering Co* [2017] UKSC 35; [2017] 1 WLR 1793.
- '*With all convenient speed*'. An obligation to do something 'with all convenient speed' is 'intractably indeterminate', but the term is not void for uncertainty. Whether the obligation is satisfied is a question of fact, turning on the particular circumstances: *Registrar of Motor Vehicles v Vu* [2013] SASCFC 10, [19].

- *'Efficient'*. An obligation to maintain a ship or vehicle in 'efficient condition' is not too vague to be enforceable. The required degree of maintenance will vary with the circumstances: *Hogarth v Miller, Brother & Co* [1891] AC 48 (ship); *McInnes v National Motor & Accident Insurance Union Ltd* (1963) Ll R 415 (motor vehicle).

Tread carefully

Despite the above illustrations, some contexts demand more precision than others. For example, vagueness is inappropriate in lawyers' undertakings, because an undertaking must be susceptible to judicial enforcement as part of the court's supervisory jurisdiction over its officers: *Re a Solicitor* [1966] 1 WLR 1604; *Wade v Licardy* (1993) 33 NSWLR 1, 7–9; *Re C (a solicitor)* [1982] 1 NZLR 137.

Also, beware of deliberately using vagueness to obscure the full implications of a clause: see, eg, Michael Hwang, 'Plain English in Commercial Contracts' (1990) 32 *Malaya Law Review* 296, 306. Quite apart from ethical implications, consumer law and the *contra proferentem* principle of interpretation may make the tactic legally problematic.

See also **AMBIGUITY; contra proferentem; GENERALITY.**

valid and binding

A lawyer's habitual pairing, the product more of reflex than reflection. Usually, either word will do. Occasionally, both words *might* be needed. For example, a contract could be *valid* but not *binding* (eg, where it complies with all legal formalities [valid], but is liable to be set aside for duress [not binding]). But that is rare—and always a contract that is *binding* is necessarily *valid.*

valuable / invaluable

Two words with similar meanings—the prefix *in-* here being an intensifier, not a negative.

valuable consideration

See **consideration.**

VARIATION OF DOCUMENTS

See **'NO VARIATION' CLAUSE.**

vary or modify

Synonyms

A lawyer's unnecessary pairing; the meaning of each word being the same, either word will do. For example, land obligations (easements or covenants) commonly confer on one or both parties the right to *vary or modify* the obligation; either *vary* or *modify* is sufficient.

Extent of variation or modification

In themselves, *vary* and *modify* do not imply that the permissible change must be minor or within narrow limits: thus, unless context requires otherwise, a planning tribunal's power to *vary* an approval is not limited to slight changes only: *Nairm v Metro-Central*

Joint Development Assessment Panel [2018] WASCA 18; (2018) 55 WAR 20, [116]–[119]. But does a power to *vary* or *modify* extend to *extinguish* or *revoke*? For example, if a statute gives a court the power to *vary* or to *modify* a contract or obligation, does it authorise extinguishing it entirely, or (even further) substituting something in its place? The answer seems to be 'yes', according to the following cases:

- A power to *vary* a trust included the power to revoke the trust and substitute a new one: *Re Holt's Settlement* [1969] 1 Ch 100.
- A power to *vary* the decision of an industrial magistrate (who had rejected an employee's claim for wrongful dismissal) included the power to quash the decision and order the employee to be reinstated: *R v Industrial Court* (1982) 30 SASR 504.

However, *vary* and *modify* take their meaning from context, and context may require a different answer. For that reason, a careful writer will indicate whether a power to *vary* or *modify* permits extinguishment or substitution of a new thing.

venire de novo

Latin: to come afresh. A court order requiring a new trial where the original trial was so affected by procedural irregularity as to be a mistrial; originally a writ (*venire facias de novo juratores*) addressed to the sheriff, ordering him to cause new jurors to try the case afresh. In most circumstances, *new trial* or *retrial* will suffice as a translation—and will make much more sense to most readers. For example:

- 'The main issue which has been argued before this court has ... been whether the court should order a *venire de novo* [prefer: *retrial*] or exercise its discretion that the appellant should not be tried again.' [*R v Gowans* [2015] EWCA Crim 952, [10] (Leveson P)]
- 'We are satisfied for all the reason[s] we have given that an application for *an order to issue a writ of venire de novo* [prefer: *an order for a retrial*] cannot be made as a free-standing application to this Court. The *issue of such a writ* [prefer: *making of such an order*] is a remedy available to this court upon an appeal against conviction, subject to the ordinary rules relating to time limits and leave.' [*R v Stromberg* [2018] EWCA Crim 561; [2018] 3 WLR 812, [34] (Lord Burnett of Maldon CJ; by way of exoneration, most of the decision was taken up with the history and role of the *writ of venire de novo*, and so the intended readership might be expected to know the Latin.)]

verba accipienda sunt secundum subjectam materiam

Latin: words are to be accepted (interpreted) according to their subject matter—ie, words are to be understood in context. A Latin maxim expressing a fundamental principle of interpretation—but carrying no more meaning than the English translation. Therefore, prefer the English; but if you feel you must use the Latin, add a translation or explanation:

> 'The ancient maxim *verba accipienda sunt secundum subjectam materiam* (words are to be understood according to the subject matter with which they deal) provides the best guide to the meaning that should be given to what Lord Brown said in this paragraph [of a decision].' [*R v Secretary of State for the Home Department* [2012] UKSC 12, [38]; [2012] 2 AC 135, 153 (Lord Hope, supplying a translation)]

verba chartarum fortius accipiuntur contra proferentem

Latin: the words of an instrument are taken most strongly against the party employing them.

See **contra proferentem**.

verba ita sunt intelligenda ut res magis valeat quam pereat

Latin: words are to be understood thus, that the matter [*res*] may be effective rather than be struck down. A variant is *verba debent intelligi cum effectu ut res magis valeat quam pereat* (words should be understood as of some effect, so that the matter may succeed rather than fail). A maxim of interpretation, designed to help something succeed rather than fail. However, the maxim cannot prevail where a legal principle makes it impossible for the thing to be effective. Unless your reader understands Latin, offer a translation or explanation.

See **ut res magis valeat quam pereat**.

verbal

See **oral / verbal**.

VERBAL AWARENESS (LACK OF)

Take care lest words placed near each other produce incongruity or unintended humour. Judicial lapses include the following (italics added in some quotations to show incongruity):

- 'I have myself a *very grave doubt* whether any right is conferred in *cemeteries* ... to do anything more than to [bury persons].' [*Hoskins-Abrahall v Paignton Urban District Council* [1929] 1 Ch 375, 386 (Greer LJ)]
- '[T]he children of this union were unaware that their parents had not married until after their father's death.' [*Public Trustee v Bellotti* (1986) 4 BPR 9196, 9197 (Cohen J); a posthumous marriage?]
- 'Although the rule ... was held not to be applicable to the circumstances of *The Albazero* where the breach of a charterparty resulted in a *total loss of cargo* [the judge] refused to accept counsel's invitation *to jettison* it.' [*Alfred McAlpine Construction Ltd v Panatown Ltd* [2001] 1 AC 518, 563–64 (Lord Jauncey)]
- 'A person of unsound mind is *non compos mentis in Latin*.' [*Wan Chon v Chua Ka Bu* [1990] 1 SLR(R) 473, 477 [8] (Chan Sek Keong J). What the judge meant was: 'In Latin, a person of unsound mind is termed *non compos mentis*.']
- '[M]uch of this area of the law is *virgin territory* ...' [*R(TT) v Registrar General for England and Wales* [2019] 3 WLR 1195; [2019] EWHC 2384 (Fam), [138] (Sir Andrew McFarlane P), in a decision about whether a person, who was born a woman but had transitioned to live as a male, and who later gave birth to a child, could be registered as the child's father.]
- 'I am satisfied not only that the respondent has committed adultery, but that she was actually *committing adultery while she was denying it in the witness-box*.' [Draft judgment of Lord Denning, as quoted in Sir Robert Megarry, *A New Miscellany-at-Law*, ed Bryan A Garner (Hart, 2005), 271]

Occasionally, the need to use specific words, phrases, or titles, makes humour impossible to avoid, as in the Australian court order that the Clock Company of Australia Pty Ltd 'be wound up': *Commonwealth of Australia Gazette*, 1 October 1985, p 3767.

verbatim

Latin: word for word; more fully, *verbatim et literatim* (word for word and letter for letter). A Latinism that has found its way into standard English, but is no more precise than its standard English translation. If readers are unlikely to understand *verbatim*, prefer *word for word*. For example:

- '[R]egulation 14(2)(b) reproduces *verbatim* [prefer: *word for word*] article 9(1)(b) of the Directive ...' [*R v Legal Services Board* [2015] UKSC 41, [6] (Lords Reed and Toulson)]

- 'In 1934 that passage was repeated *verbatim* [prefer: *word for word*] in the second edition with the same citation.' [*Australian Crime Commission v Stoddart* [2011] HCA 47; (2011) 244 CLR 554, [111] (Heydon J)]

VERBS

See **NOUNS / VERBS; SUBJECT–VERB AGREEMENT**.

versus

Latin: against.

See **v (abbreviation)**.

vest

Meaning

Interests in property are either *vested* or *not vested* (ie, 'contingent'). *Vested* is a Latin-derived metaphor meaning 'clothed'. But although now a legal term of art, *vested* has not shed 'the inherent imprecision of metaphor': *Fairbairn v Vavaressos* [2010] NSWCA 234; (2010) 78 NSWLR 577, [35] (Campbell JA). It carries the sense of 'owned'. But a person can 'own' an interest in property without having the present right to physically enjoy the property or its income. For example, ownership of land can be divided into consecutive interests, as where it is given to A for life and thereafter to B in fee simple. The life estate *vested* in A gives A (for life) the right to possess the land and receive its income. The remainder *vested* in B, while a presently existing interest, gives no right to physical possession or income until A dies. To reflect this situation, legal terminology divides *vested* into two categories—*vested in possession* (ie, both owned and currently enjoyed) and *vested in interest* (ie, owned but not currently enjoyed). In our example, A's life estate is vested in both interest and possession, and (until A dies) B's remainder is vested in interest only.

Preference in favour of vesting

Where it is unclear whether an interest is *vested* or contingent, where possible the law leans towards holding it to be vested. This has long been a general principle: eg, *Duffield v Duffield* (1829) 3 Bligh (NS) 260; 4 ER 1334; *Hicklin v Fair* [1899] AC 15, 27. The rationale is that the law prefers interests to succeed rather than fail. For example:

> Assume that property is given 'to A if A attains 25, but if A fails to attain 25, then to B'. The law prefers to hold A's interest to be vested immediately, subject to divesting in favour of B if A fails to attain 25. This is the so-called 'Rule in *Phipps v Ackers*' (1842) 9 Cl & Fin 583; 8 ER 539. The alternative would be to treat A's interest as contingent on attaining 25—meaning that A gets nothing until A attains 25. But that would pose the risk of the gift to A failing.

Where an interest is described merely as *vested*, the law leans towards treating it as *vested in interest*. This leaning is rebuttable depending on the terms of the document and the admissible surrounding circumstances.

See also **remainder / reversion**.

vi et armis

Latin: with force and arms; with violence; violently. Historically, a formula used in the writ of trespass (*trespass vi et armis*). In modern law, where the phraseology of the writ of trespass has passed into history and most readers are unschooled in medieval forms of action, prefer an English translation:

- '[In this case] a foot was interposed between the door post and the door itself. In the other two cases arms were thrust in, but it is perfectly clear that whilst in those cases some force was used, in neither of them was entrance being sought *vi et armis* [prefer: *by violence*; *violently*].' [*Vaughan v Mckenzie* [1969] 1 QB 557, 563 (Winn LJ); was Winn LJ playing on words—*arms* vs *armis*?]
- 'One should have thought that the death of an Aboriginal person who died whilst being watched and guarded by police, acting *vi et armis* [prefer: *violently*; *with violence*], was likely to be a proper subject matter for inquiry by the Royal Commissioner.' [*Re Eatts* (1990) 21 FCR 166, 179 (Morling and Gummow JJ)]

See also **nec vi, nec clam, nec precario**.

via media

Latin: middle course (often in the sense of a course between two extremes). The Latin has become part of formal written English, but is no more precise than its English translation—so prefer the English. For example:

- 'There is no third choice, as a sort of *via media* [prefer: *middle course*], to affirm the contract and yet to be absolved from tendering further performance unless and until A gives reasonable notice that he is once again able and willing to perform.' [*Fercometal SARL v Mediterranean Shipping Co SA* [1989] AC 788, 805 (Lord Ackner)]
- 'In order to avoid this consequence, ... [counsel] offered a *via media* [prefer: *middle path*] by which the obligation to serve a notice [was to be understood].' [*Scottish & Newcastle plc v Raguz* [2008] UKHL 65; [2008] 1 WLR 2494, [11] (Lord Hoffmann)]

vicinity

To describe something as being *in the vicinity of* something else is notoriously imprecise—so imprecise that, for example, an order that a person not be 'in the *vicinity* of' premises was void for uncertainty: *Police v Siaosi* [2014] SASC 131; (2014) 120 SASR 308. Even if not void for uncertainty, references to *vicinity* may require litigation to clarify, and the meaning will necessarily vary with context. For example, an outer airport car park was not 'in the *vicinity* of' the airport terminal, because the context—taxation legislation—envisaged 'close spatial proximity': *Virgin Blue Airlines Pty Ltd v FCT* [2010] FCAFC 137, [36]; (2010) 190 FCR 150. And merely to substitute synonyms such as *near*, *proximate*, or *close to* may not help, because those words also are context-dependent.

See also **neighbourhood**.

vide

Latin: see. An instruction to readers, but no more precise than its English translation—which is therefore better where the reader is unlikely to know the Latin. Often found in combination with other Latin words—also no more precise than their English translations. Examples are: *vide ante* ('see before'; 'see previously'); *vide infra* ('see below'); *vide post* ('see after this'; 'see the following'); *vide supra* ('see above'); *vide ut supra* ('see as [stated] above').

videlicet

Latin: that is to say, namely; usually abbreviated to *viz*. Prefer plain English over *videlicet* and *viz*.

By prefacing a word or phrase with *namely*, *that is to say*, or similar, the writer indicates that the word or phrase explains an earlier statement. For example:

> 'This is a contract for the sale of headwear, *namely*, hats, beanies, and caps.' The list (after *namely*) explains the earlier reference to headwear. There is also an implication that the list of headwear is exhaustive.

However, context may require a different interpretation. For example:

> An exemption clause in a charterparty stated: 'Should the vessel be detained by causes over which the charterers have no control, *viz.*, quarantine, ice, hurricanes, blockade, clearing the steamer after the last cargo is taken over, *etc.*, no demurrage is to be charged and lay days do not count.' Held, although *videlicet* (*viz*) normally introduced an exhaustive list, the additional *etc* negated this normal meaning, freeing the exemption clause to apply to 'any causes over which the charterers have no control': *Ambatielos v Anton Jurgens Margarine Works* [1923] AC 175.

vinculum

Latin: chain; bond. The Latin, though time-honoured in law, is easily translated into standard English:

> [T]he parties … must have understood … that the Legislature had power to dissolve the contract, to undo the *vinculum* [prefer: *bond*; *tie*] which its own law created …' [*Delaney v Great Western Milling Co Ltd* (1916) 22 CLR 150, 168 (Isaacs J)]

Likewise, terms that incorporate *vinculum* are easily translated into standard English: eg, *vinculum juris* (bond of the law); *vinculum matrimonii* (bond of marriage).

The meaning of 'chain' or 'bond' carries over into surveying practice: a surveyor's *vinculum* is a wavy line on a plan indicating that two areas are part of a single whole:

> 'The only indications the draft plan of the ground level gives about anything other than the external boundaries … are a north point which fixes orientation and a surveyor's *vinculum* joining two parts of the whole divided by a line.' [*Higgins v Statewide Developments Pty Ltd* [2010] NSWSC 183, [27] (Barrett J)]

VIRGULE

See **FORWARD SLASH**.

vis major

See **force majeure**.

vitiate

In normal usage: to spoil, mar, impair. In legal usage, more specifically: to invalidate. For example, a court's wrongful assumption of jurisdiction *vitiates* the decision; or a tribunal's consideration of irrelevant factors may *vitiate* its ruling. Often used to describe the effect on a contract of fraud, undue influence, or mistake: thus, 'Fraud *vitiates* a contract' (often in the passive, 'A contract is *vitiated* by fraud'), or 'X was entitled to *vitiate* [ie, *rescind*, *set aside*] the contract because he was induced by misrepresentation.'

viz

That is to say; abbreviation for *videlicet*.

See **videlicet**.

VOICE

See **ACTIVE VOICE / PASSIVE VOICE; TONE.**

void / voidable

The distinction

Void means 'of no effect'; thus, a 'void marriage' is not a marriage at all (and therefore, logically, cannot be set aside: *Akhter v Khan* [2020] EWCA Civ 122; [2020] 2 WLR 1183, [46]). *Voidable* means 'able to be made void' or 'liable to be made void'. For example, if the parties' signatures to a contract are forged, the contract is said to be *void*; and if the parties have never reached agreement on the key terms of their bargain, the contract is said to be *void*. In each case, *void* is a solecism for 'there is no contract at all'. However, if a party's signature to a contract is genuine, but the party has been induced by misrepresentation to enter the contract, the contract is *voidable* (ie, liable to be set aside, but valid until then).

Fine distinctions are sometimes needed. To deal first with *void*: a statute may declare a contract *void* for all purposes; or *void* for some purposes only; or *void* as against some persons (eg, an income tax authority) and not against others (eg, creditors); or *void* as against a particular person or class, but by implication valid against others: *Young v Billiter* (1860) 8 HLC 682; 11 ER 596; *Davies v Rees* (1886) 17 QBD 408.

Then as to *voidable*: a statute may declare a transaction *voidable* by some persons (eg, consumers) but not others (eg, retailers); or *voidable* by one party but by implication not *voidable* by the other party (eg, *Sale of Land Act 1958* (Vic), s 29N, declaring a contract for the sale of land voidable by the purchaser, but by implication not by the vendor).

Void meaning *voidable*

Drafters sometimes confuse *void* and *voidable*, declaring a transaction *void* when they mean *voidable*. For example:

- A statute declared certain sales of land *void* as against a mortgagee of the land. Held, this meant *voidable* at the option of the mortgagee: *Amatruda v Roberts* [1938] VLR 154.
- Bankruptcy legislation made certain preferences *void*. Held, this meant *voidable*: *Valoutin Pty Ltd v Furst* (1998) 154 ALR 119, 148–49.

Also, a contract may state that if a certain event happens or fails to happen, the contract is to become *void*. But under the principle that the law does not allow a party to benefit from their own wrong, if the event happens or fails to happen because of a party's own failure to perform, then in effect the contract is *voidable* at the innocent party's option: *New Zealand Shipping Co Ltd v Société des Ateliers et Chantiers de France* [1919] AC 1.

absolutely void

If something is void, it is necessarily '*absolutely* void'; *absolutely* is superfluous. Despite this, *absolutely void* is occasionally seen in statutes: eg, *Colonial Laws Validity Act 1865*, s 2; *Electoral Act 1907* (Tas) (the Supreme Court may declare some elections *void* and others *absolutely void*). The distinction is rather between *void* and *voidable*, as discussed above.

See also **null and void**.

volens

Latin: willing. Usually seen in the maxim *volenti non fit injuria* (no wrong is done to a person who consents), which is often shortened to 'the *volens* defence'.

See **volenti non fit injuria**.

volenti non fit injuria

Latin: no wrong is done to a person who consents; there can be no injury to the willing. The maxim reflects the rationale for the defence of 'voluntary assumption of risk' in negligence actions. As with many legal maxims, the Latin formulation falsely implies clarity and precision. In reality, the Latin carries no more meaning or precision than the English translation, which is more accessible to non-legal readers. Therefore—for non-legal readers at least—prefer the English. Thus:

- '[The judge] … rather thought that [each party] would have consented to the risk as regards themselves and that each would have a defence of *volenti non fit injuria* [prefer: *willing consent to damage*].' [*Coope v Ward* [2015] EWCA Civ 30, [41]; [2015] 1 WLR 4081, 4090 (Christopher Clarke LJ)]
- '[No one previously] ever suggested the possibility that a police constable might be excluded from recovery on the basis of negligence by reference to the notion of voluntary assumption of risk (*volenti*).' [*New South Wales v Fahy* [2007] HCA 20, [88]; (2007) 232 CLR 486, 514 (Kirby J, explaining the principle and adding a shorthand reference to the Latin)]
- **37—Injured persons presumed to be aware of obvious risk**

  (1) If, in an action for damages for negligence, a defence of voluntary assumption of risk (*volenti non fit injuria*) is raised by the defendant and the risk is an obvious risk …'

  [*Civil Liability Act 1936* (SA), s 37—adding the Latin as if to reassure legal readers]

voluntary / volunteer

In both standard English and legal English, a *voluntary* act is something freely done; it is an act to which the actor directs his or her will: *DPP for Northern Ireland v Lynch* [1975] AC 653, 689 (Lord Simon). If made under force or duress, it is not *voluntary* in this sense—for example, a payment is not *voluntary* if made under compulsion: *Strachan v Barton* (1856) 11 Exch 647, 650; 156 ER 990, 991 (Alderson B).

In legal usage, however, *voluntary* takes the additional meaning of 'without receiving payment'. Thus, a *voluntary* transfer of property is a transfer made without payment in return ('consideration'). Similarly, a *volunteer* is a person who receives property or some other benefit without giving consideration in return.

Context should clarify which sense of *voluntary / volunteer* the writer intends. However, sometimes sufficient doubt exists to provoke litigation. For example, in *A-G v Ellis* [1895] 2 QB 466, 470, Lord Russell CJ held that *voluntarily* as used in certain revenue legislation meant 'freely, without compulsion', not 'without consideration'.

See also **consideration**.

wager

A promise to give money or another benefit if a particular event happens; a gamble or bet. The common law allowed parties to enforce wagers given for consideration, unless against public policy. Statute now usually determines whether wagers are enforceable.

A *wager policy* (or *wagering policy*) is a policy of insurance in which the insured has no interest and no expectation of acquiring one. In most jurisdictions, such contracts are void by statute.

See also **gaming and wagering**.

waifs

From the Latin: *bona waviata*, meaning 'goods to which claims are waived'. In normal usage, *waifs* means 'street urchins' or similar. In legal usage, *waifs* means goods found but unclaimed by anyone; more specifically, stolen goods discarded by a thief in flight, in fear of apprehension. According to Sir William Blackstone, the law forfeits such goods to the Crown, to punish the owner for not pursuing the thief and reclaiming them: *Commentaries on the Laws of England* (Clarendon, 1765) book 1, 286–87.

wait and see / wait-and-see

In standard English, *to wait and see* (verb) is unhyphenated. But as an adjective, it is hyphenated: eg, in context of the rule against perpetuities, the '*wait-and-see* rule'. This may require hyphenated and unhyphenated use in the same sentence: 'Under the *wait-and-see* rule, you do not test the validity of an interest from the outset but rather *wait and see* whether it vests within the perpetuity period.'

See also **HYPHENS**.

waiver

Meaning

To *waive* a right is to give it up or choose not to enforce it. It is an intentional act, either done expressly or implied from words or conduct, and inconsistent with the continuance of the right. A common example occurs in the law of leases. A landlord may have the right to terminate the lease for the tenant's breach; but if the landlord, despite knowing of the breach, accepts rent, the landlord *waives* the right to enforce the breach: *Matthews v Smallwood* [1901] 1 Ch 777; *Segal Securities Ltd v Thoseby* [1963] 1 QB 887; *Thirunavukkrasu v Brar* [2019] EWCA Civ 2032; [2020] 2 WLR 841. The rationale is that the landlord had two courses of action: (1) to terminate the lease, or (2) to allow the lease to continue. By accepting rent, the landlord has chosen (2).

The noun *waiver* describes the effect of the act of waiving, eg: 'Her conduct amounted to a *waiver* of her rights.' There is as yet no single-word noun to describe the person who waives—*waiver* being the act, not the actor.

Confused usage

Rosco Pound described *waiver* as 'a slippery word worn smooth with overuse': Foreword to John S Ewatt, *Waiver Distributed* (Harvard University Press, 1917) vi. It is a 'vague term used in many senses': *Ross T Smyth & Co v TD Bailey Son & Co* [1940] 3 All ER 60, 70 (Lord Wright). In both ordinary and legal usage, *waiver* is sometimes used to describe the effect of what are, in truth, different principles. Two such principles are *election* and *estoppel*. *Election* occurs where a party chooses between inconsistent rights (such as to affirm or rescind a contract); having chosen one, the party cannot later choose the other. *Estoppel* occurs where a party is prevented (estopped) by their words or conduct from enforcing a right they otherwise would have had. According to the preferred view, *waiver* is not a stand-alone principle but rather describes the effect of these two principles (and several others, including variation of contract). Yet *waiver* 'remains firmly embedded in the lawyer's lexicon': *Agricultural and Rural Finance Pty Ltd v Gardiner* [2008] HCA 57; (2008) 238 CLR 570, 587 (Gummow, Hayne and Kiefel JJ).

Further reading

- *Halsbury's Laws of England*, 'Equitable Jurisdiction' (vol 47, 2014) [250]
- JW Carter, *Carter on Contract* (online, LexisNexis) [07-180]–[07-210]
- Jeremy Stoljar, 'The categories of waiver' (2013) 87 *Australian Law Journal* 482 (identifying 11 different categories of waiver)

See also **approbate and reprobate; election; estoppel; 'NO WAIVER' CLAUSE**.

want

See **need / want**.

ward of court

A minor who is under the care of a court-appointed guardian.

See also **infant / minor**.

warrants and represents

This pairing appears often in contracts: 'X *warrants and represents* that …' Are both words needed? It is true that a *warranty* is a contractual statement, having contractual force; in contrast, a *representation* may or may not have contractual force. However, where a representation is incorporated into a contract ('X *represents* that …'), *represents* acquires contractual force, and if breached confers a right in damages just as much as *warrants* does. So the pairing ('warrants *and* represents') is then unnecessary. One word will do.

Further reading

- Kenneth A Adams, *A Manual of Style for Contract Drafting*, 4th edn (American Bar Association, 2017) [3.374]–[3.419] (US usage; recommending *represents* or (preferably) *states*)
- Kenneth A Adams, 'Eliminating the Phrase *Represents and Warrants* from Contracts' (2015) 16 *Tennessee Journal of Business Law* 203
- JW Carter, *Carter on Contract* (online, LexisNexis) [10-040]–[10-090] (representations), [14-040] (warranties)

See also **condition / warranty; guarantee / indemnity / warranty; WORD PAIRINGS**.

warranty

See **condition / warranty; guarantee / indemnity / warranty**.

warranty of authority

A warranty (ie, a promise sounding in damages) that a person has the authority to enter into an agreement on behalf of the party he or she purports to represent. The warranty cannot overcome a lack of actual authority, but renders the warrantor liable in damages.

Further reading

Halsbury's Laws of England, 'Agency' (vol 1, 2017) [161]–[162]

warranty of good standing

Legal shorthand for a warranty (ie, a promise sounding in damages) that a company is registered and is not the subject of an action to have it deregistered.

was

The past tense of the verb *to be*. Tense can be as crucial in legal writing as in writing generally. Legal rights can depend on precise use of tense (for case law, see discussion under **TENSE**). This can include the use of *was*:

> A statute compensated property owners whose rights had been extinguished. The compensation amount turned on whether the property '*was* free from rates'. Held, in using the past tense, the statute meant property that was free from rates *before* the statute was enacted, not after it was enacted: *Tithe Redemption Commissioners v Governors of Queen Anne's Bounty* [1946] 1 All ER 148, 154, 157 (Romer J).

See also **'be' verbs**; **TENSE**.

waste

Terminology

In normal usage, *waste* (noun) means 'rubbish', and *to waste* (verb) means 'to throw away' (as in *to waste* an opportunity) or 'to destroy' (as in *to lay waste to*). That normal usage applies in legal usage also, subject to two qualifications:

1. Context or definition may require a different meaning. For example, environmental legislation may define 'waste' by considerations of whether the owner has any further use for the material, not its inherent value or ability to be recycled: *Shannongrove Pty Ltd v Environment Protection Authority* [2013] NSWCCA 179; (2013) 84 NSWLR 668.
2. In land law, *waste* carries the technical meaning of an act that permanently alters land: *West Ham Central Charity Board v East London Waterworks Co* [1900] 1 Ch 624, 635, 636. In particular, the 'doctrine' of waste imposes obligations on life tenants (and, to a lesser degree, ordinary tenants) in the way they use the land. The rationale is that life tenants (and ordinary tenants) have interests of limited duration only, and so must not use the land in a way that unduly prejudices the rights of those with later rights to possession.

The law has no word for the person who commits waste. *Waster* might seem logical, but it has not achieved currency, perhaps it too readily evokes *wastrel* (an idle, good-for-nothing person), which carries unnecessarily odious connotations.

Land law: the four categories of waste

Permissive waste

Passively allowing property to fall into disrepair; failure to keep in repair or good working order. A life tenant is not liable for permissive waste, unless the instrument creating the life tenancy imposes the obligation to repair: *Powys v Blagrave* (1854) 4 De G M & G 448; 43 ER 582. For example, in the absence of such an obligation to repair, a life tenant is not accountable if a house falls into a dilapidated condition through long years of neglect: *Re Cartwright* (1889) 41 Ch D 532, 536; *McDonald v Ellis* (2007) 72 NSWLR 605, [17].

Voluntary waste

A deliberate act of injury to property. An example is demolishing internal walls and fittings: *Marsden v Edward Heyes Ltd* [1927] 2 KB 1, 8. A life tenant is liable for voluntary waste, unless the instrument conferring the interest exempts liability for voluntary waste.

Equitable waste

Waste that a court of equity will restrain. Specifically, equitable waste occurs where a life tenant with a right to commit waste at common law (ie, the instrument conferring the interest exempts liability for voluntary waste) engages or threatens to engage in wanton or flagrant acts of harm to the property—for that is not to use the legal right, but to abuse it: *Turner v Wright* (1860) 2 De GF & J 234, 243–44, 247; 45 ER 612, 615, 616; *Baker v Sebright* (1879) 13 Ch D 179, 186. Examples include:

- wantonly felling trees that provide ornament and shelter to a house: *Packington's Case* (1744) 3 Atk 215; 26 ER 925; *Marker v Marker* (1851) 9 Hare 1, 17; 68 ER 389, 396; *Turner v Jackson* (1856) 1 VLT 127; *Weld-Blundell v Wolseley* [1903] 2 Ch 664
- wantonly stripping lead, iron, glass, doors, and timber from a house (on the facts, a castle): *Vane v Lord Barnard* (1716) 2 Vern 738; 23 ER 1082.

Statutes in most jurisdictions allow the instrument conferring the life estate to exempt a life tenant from liability even for equitable waste: eg, *Law of Property Act 1925*, s 135.

Ameliorating waste

Acts that improve property. The concept of 'waste' that 'improves' may seem counter-intuitive, and indeed early cases held that unless the act reduced the value of the property, courts would not intervene: *Doherty v Allman* (1878) 3 App Cas 709, 724. Later cases allow the possibility of court intervention, although instances are rare. Examples include:

- erecting a lead smelter in ornamental gardens: *Hunt v Hodges* (1849) 1 Ir Jur 33 (improving the market value of the land but destroying its amenity)
- demolishing a house of significant historical interest and replacing it with an apartment block: *Brokaw v Fairchild* 237 NY Supp 6 (1929), affirmed 245 NY Supp 402 (1930), further affirmed 256 NY 186 (1931) (ie, increasing the market value of the property by doing work that augments its value but destroys its character).

Further reading

S Bridge, E Cooke, and M Dixon (eds), *Megarry & Wade's Law of Real Property*, 9th edn (Sweet & Maxwell, 2019) [3-066]–[3-071]

See also **life estate**.

waste land

In standard English, generally one word: *wasteland*, a waterless or treeless region, a desert. In legal usage, generally two words (*waste land*) meaning:

- land that lies uncultivated and unoccupied: *A-G v Hanmer* (1858) 27 LJ Ch 837, 840 (eg, land between high and low watermarks is *waste land*); or
- land that has never been granted—as in 'waste land of the manor', or the colonial law term 'waste land of the Crown'.

wasted costs order

To hyphenate or not? Given that compound adjectives ought to be hyphenated, preferred usage is *wasted-costs order*. However, in line with the seemingly inexorable demise of hyphens, it is usually rendered as *wasted costs order*: eg, *Practice Direction (Criminal Proceedings: Costs)* [2010] 1 WLR 2351, rule 4.6.1.

See **HYPHENS**.

wayleave / way-leave

A *wayleave* was originally a form of right of way, usually for carrying away the produce of a mine. Later, statute extended its meaning to a route across land for electricity transmission. The extended meaning first appeared in the side note to s 22 of the *Electricity Supply Act 1919*.

Preferred usage is unhyphenated (*wayleave*):

> '[W]hat is being negotiated is a fair price for the *wayleave*.' [*Bocardo SA v Star Energy UK Onshore Ltd* [2010] UKSC 35, [139]; [2011] 1 AC 380, 427 (Lord Clarke)]

However, the hyphenated form (*way-leave*) is sometimes seen:

> '[The principle] originated in the *way-leave* cases, where the defendant trespassed by carrying coals along an underground way through the plaintiff's mine. [The plaintiff] recovered damages equivalent to what he would have received if he had been paid for a *way-leave*.' [*Stoke-on-Trent City Council v J & W Wass Ltd* [1988] 1 WLR 1406, 1410–11 (Nourse LJ)]

we / you

Increasing use of *we / you*

The *we/you* style of drafting is increasingly seen, particularly in consumer-related documents and statutes. It is also used, for example, in Australian taxation legislation, spelling out consequences if 'you' acquire goods: see, eg, *A New Tax System (Goods and Services Tax) Act* 1999 (Cth), s 66.5.

Response to the increasing use of *we/you* is mixed. A leading tax lawyer described the style in statutes as 'condescending': AH Slater, 'Tax in Australian Society: An 80 Year Perspective' (2007) 81 *Australian Law Journal* 681, 696. An Australian judge decried it as a 'happy chappy' approach, and another described it as 'almost offensive': K O'Brien, 'Judicial Attitudes to Plain Language and the Law' (2009) *Australian Bar Review* 204, 236. While these responses might appear out of touch with community feelings, research in fact shows a mixed response to *we/you*, even at general readership level. For example, a 2010 survey of readers of legislation found high levels of dissatisfaction with the *we/you* style in Australian legislation: Office of Parliamentary Counsel (Commonwealth of Australia), *Results of the 2010 Legislation Users Survey* (2010) 79–80. Responses included: feeling patronised; difficulties with *you* when referring to corporations and deceased estates; and a sense of dumbing-down. However, on the positive side, many readers considered that the *we/you* style made legislation plainer and easier to understand.

Capitalising *we / you*?

When defining the parties, follow the convention of initial capital letters ('***We*** means …', '***You*** means …'). But after that, consider using lower-case *we/you* for the rest of the document (except at the start of a sentence). Although this departs from the convention of initial capitals whenever using defined terms, there can be no confusion about meaning—there is only one possible *you* and only one possible *we*—and the text looks leaner. To illustrate:

Before	**After**
You acknowledge that You perform Your obligations under this contract as an independent contractor, and nothing in this contract constitutes You or any of Your personnel as an employee, agent, partner or joint venturer of or to Us or confers on You any authority to bind Us in any way.	You acknowledge that you perform your obligations under this contract as an independent contractor, and nothing in this contract constitutes you or any of your personnel as an employee, agent, partner or joint venturer of or to us or confers on you any authority to bind us in any way.

Plural *you*

Beware of ambiguity where *you* consists of more than one person. The English language lacks an acceptable plural form of *you*. Careless use of a plural-intended *you* may require litigation to clarify, as in the following cases:

- A member of a newly formed multi-person partnership completed an insurance proposal form on behalf of the partnership. The form asked, 'Have *you* ever sustained a loss?' Did this mean: (1) 'Have you as individuals ever sustained a loss?', or (2) 'Have you as a partnership ever sustained a loss?' Held, meaning (2): *Becker v Marshall* [1922] Lloyd's LL Rep 114.
- Co-owners of a house took out an insurance policy which referred to them as *you*. The policy allowed the insurer to refuse a claim if *you* have made a false disclosure. Could the insurer refuse to pay a claim where one only of the co-owners made a false disclosure? Held, yes, because a false disclosure 'by you' meant 'by either of you': *Advance (NSW) Insurance Agencies Pty Ltd v Matthews* (1989) 116 CLR 606.

Extended *you*

Also be careful when defining *you* to include a person who is not a party to the document. This can lead to unexpected results:

> A lease required the tenant to take out insurance against damage to the premises, in the name of both the tenant and the landlord. The tenant took out the insurance. The policy named the tenant as *you*, and defined *you* as including anyone for whom the tenant was obliged to provide insurance; that is, the tenant's cover effectively included the landlord as a co-insured. In the policy, the insurer waived any right of subrogation against 'any co-insured'. The tenant suffered loss because the landlord breached its obligation to keep the premises in repair. The insurer paid out the tenant's claim and then sought to recover from the landlord, exercising a right of subrogation. Held, the definition of *you* made the landlord a co-insured, and so the insurer had waived any right to recover from the landlord: *Standard Publishing House v Chen* [2012] NSWSC 1544.

Joint promises

'We' as promisors

At common law, a promise made *by* two or more persons ('we promise to') is a joint promise, not a several (ie, separate or individual) promise, unless the words used or the context shows that the promisors were promising jointly and severally: *White v Tyndall* (1888) 13 App Cas 263, 269 (Lord Halsbury LC). And because a joint promise creates only one obligation, usually all promisors must be joined as defendants in any claim to enforce the promise.

'We' as promisees

At common law, a promise made *to* two (or more) persons is a joint promise. The two (or more) are entitled collectively to its performance, and since the promise is made to them jointly, all must join in an action to enforce it: *Chaplin v Leslie Frewen (Publishers) Ltd* [1966] Ch 71 (CA). Section 81(1) of the *Law of Property Act 1925* now provides that a covenant (promise) made with two or more persons jointly is treated as also being made with each of them separately. Similar provisions exist in most other Commonwealth jurisdictions—although the wording varies, and some analogues of s 81 do not so obviously convert a joint covenant into a several (ie, individual) one.

Boilerplate provision

To avoid doubt over the joint or individual nature of covenants made to or with a number of persons, commercial contracts often include a boilerplate provision clarifying the parties' intentions:

> 'An agreement, covenant, representation or warranty on the part of, or in favour of, two or more people, binds them or benefits them separately and together.'

See also **DEFINITIONS; joint and several; NAMES (of parties); PRONOUNS.**

wear and tear

Legal usage

In land law, separate terms: *wear* = deterioration caused by use of premises; *tear* = deterioration to premises caused by the forces of nature. In other contexts (such as insurance law), drafters sometimes conflate *wear and tear* to a composite concept of 'damage due to, or sustained during, ordinary usage': *JSM Management Pty Ltd v QBE Insurance (Australia) Ltd* [2011] VSC 339, [24] (Osborn J).

The pairing is often qualified, as in the familiar '*reasonable*' *wear and tear* and '*fair*' *wear and tear*. On their face, such expressions are syntactically ambiguous: does the qualification '*reasonable*' (or '*fair*') qualify only *wear* or does it also qualify *tear*? That is, does the expression mean: (1) *reasonable wear and [any kind of] tear*, or (2) *reasonable wear and reasonable tear*? In tenancy law, some authorities favour meaning (1) and some favour (2): compare *Taylor v Webb* [1937] 2 KB 283, 303–04; *Haskell v Marlow* [1928] 2 KB 45, 59. Most lawyers, at ease with the expression, probably do not notice the ambiguity—but if they do, they can easily clarify it: eg, 'The tenant must repair the premises, except for damage caused by reasonable use of the premises and by the ordinary operation of the weather.'

Plain language: warnings

Beware of two qualifications to a *reasonable* (*fair*) *wear and tear* exemption, particularly in leases. Plain language may obscure them, just as legalese does.

1. The person seeking to invoke the exemption—usually the tenant—bears the onus of proof. That is, although the landlord bears the initial onus of proving that the premises need repairing, the onus then shifts to the tenant to bring the facts within the exemption for *reasonable* (*fair*) *wear and tear*: *Brown v Davies* [1958] 1 QB 117, 127; *Wicks Farming Pty Ltd v Waraluck Mining Pty Ltd* [1996] 1 Qd R 99, 103.
2. The exemption applies only to deterioration due *directly* to reasonable (fair) wear and tear. It does not exempt the relevant party from liability to repair damage that

flows *consequentially* from reasonable (fair) wear and tear. To cite the classic example: if a tile blows off the roof in a storm, the tenant is not liable to replace it under a repairing covenant that contains a 'reasonable (fair) wear and tear' exception. But if the tenant does nothing and in consequence water gets in and damages the carpets, the tenant cannot say that the water damage is reasonable wear and tear—in truth, it is the result of the tenant's failure 'to prevent what was originally caused by wear and tear from producing results altogether beyond what was so caused': *Haskell v Marlow* [1928] 2 KB 45, 59. The tenant should replace the tile to prevent the consequential damage: *Regis Property Co Ltd v Dudley* [1959] AC 370, 410.

Further reading

Hill and Redman's Guide to Landlord and Tenant Law (Butterworths, 1999) [10.18], [10.59]

See also **AMBIGUITY**.

WEBSITES

When referring to websites, it is now common practice to start with *www*, omitting *http://* (or *https://*). Exceptionally, some website addresses do not contain *www*, in which case the *http://* (or *https://*) is retained.

Some styles guides use angle brackets: <www.london.edu.uk>; others omit them.

Wednesbury reasonableness

The principle of administrative law that courts can quash the decision of a tribunal or person exercising a statutory discretion, if the decision is so unreasonable or irrational that no reasonable person could have reached it: *Associated Provincial Picture Houses Ltd v Wednesbury Corporation* [1948] 1 KB 223. The decision must be so unreasonable 'that it might almost be described as being done in bad faith' or 'so absurd that no sensible person could ever dream that it lay within the powers of' the decision-maker (ibid, 229)—in short, so unreasonable that it was irrational (*Council of Civil Service Unions v Minister for the Civil Service* [1985] AC 374, 410, 415) or was 'beyond the range of responses open to a reasonable decision-maker' (*R v Ministry of Defence* [1996] QB 517, 554).

Further reading

Halsbury's Laws of England, 'Judicial Review' (vol 61A, 2018) [18] ('manifest unreasonableness')

See also **quash**.

week

Meaning

Normally, the calendar period beginning on Sunday (the first day of the week) and ending on the following Saturday: *Bazalgette v Lowe* (1855) LJ Ch 368, 416; *Aberdeen City v Watt* (1901) 3 F 787, 790. However, like all words, *week* takes its meaning from context—and that meaning can vary. For example, it can mean any consecutive period of 7 days, or the week for wages calculation, or simply Monday to Friday: *Dunlop Perdriau Rubber Co Ltd v Federated Rubber Workers Union of Australia* (1931) 46 CLR 329, 341 (Dixon J.

week's notice

Unless context requires otherwise, a *week's notice* is a period starting from one day in the week and continuing to the end of the same day in the next week. So, a *week's notice* given on Monday expires at the end of the following Monday. This is not because a *week's notice* requires 7 clear days, but because (under the normal rules for computing time) a notice period excludes the day on which the notice is given, and allows the whole of the day on which the notice expires: *Newman v Slade* [1926] 2 KB 328, 329–30 (Salter J). Also (unless context requires otherwise), in computing a *week's notice*, no allowance is made for weekends or public holidays. Thus, *four weeks' notice* means 4 calendar weeks, even where the weeks bridge Christmas holidays and fairness might suggest 4 weeks of actual working days: *Benton v Sanderson Kayser Ltd* [1989] ICR 136, 140.

See also **clear day**; **TIME**; **week**.

well and truly

In general usage, an expression with varying meanings, depending on context. For example: 'this theory is *well and truly* [ie, *very*] settled'; 'these funds are *well and truly* [ie, *completely*] mingled'. In law, often found in formal contexts to connote 'doing one's honest best', with *well* meaning 'properly' and *truly* meaning 'honestly': *Mayor etc of Kingston-upon-Thames v Harding* [1892] 2 QB 494, 504 (Lord Esher MR), 509 (AL Smith LJ). A plainer substitute sacrifices no meaning:

- 'I promise that I will *well and truly* [ie, *do my best honestly to*] serve the Queen.'
- 'I promise that I will *well and truly* [ie, *properly and honestly*] administer the estate.'

whatever / whatsoever

Needed?

Whatever, being shorter, is usually better than *whatsoever*. But the larger question is whether either word is needed. For example, does 'We accept no liability *whatever* [or *whatsoever*]' mean any more than 'We accept no liability'? Or does 'We release you from all claims *whatever* [or *whatsoever*]' mean any more than 'We release you from all claims'? A sceptic may say 'no', citing cases such as *Norman v FEA Plantations Ltd* [2011] FCAFC 99, [199]–[200]; (2011) 195 FCR 97, 119, where 'without any deduction *whatsoever*' meant simply 'without any deduction'. On the other hand, 'whatsoever' can serve to emphasise the point, as if the drafter means to say: 'yes, I really mean that'. That is its purpose in some Australian legislation: eg, *A New Tax System (Goods and Services Tax) Act 1999* (Cth), s 9-10: 'A "supply" is any form of supply *whatsoever*.'

Euisdem generis?

A line of case law holds that *whatever* or *whatsoever* can serve at least one purpose, namely to thwart the *eiusdem generis* principle, by casting the genus as widely as possible. For example:

- A reservation in a conveyance of 'all mines of coal culm iron and other mines and minerals *whatsoever*' was not limited by the *eiusdem generis* principle to exclude brick clay: *Jersey v Guardians of the Poor of Neath* (1889) 22 QBD 555, 566 (Fry LJ).
- An exception in a charterparty exempting parties from liability for 'frosts floods strikes … [and] any other unavoidable accidents or hindrances of *what kind soever* beyond their control' was not limited by the *eiusdem generis* principle to exclude delays caused by a backlog of ships at the loading port: *Larsen v Sylvester & Co* [1908] AC 295.

- The expression 'or by any other cause *whatsoever*' in a standard-form charterparty was limited by the *eiusdem generis* principle: *The Apollo* [1978] 1 Lloyd's Rep 200 (even more so where *whatsoever* was a typed addition).

However, the case law is not entirely consistent. For example, in *Hughes v Winter* [1955] SASR 238 the court held that a list of prohibited actions ('speaking, shouting, singing, playing upon, operating or sounding any musical or noisy instrument *or doing anything whatsoever*') was limited to the genus of actions that generate noise. It seems that *whatsoever* was ineffective to cast the net wider.

Hence, a drafter seeking a foolproof way of ousting the *eiusdem generis* principle will need a more nuanced approach than simply adding *whatever* or *whatsoever*.

See also **eiusdem generis**.

when

In some contexts, *when* can leave important issues unanswered. For example, a gift of a sum of money 'to A *when* he attains 25' can mean either: (1) the gift is conditional on A attaining 25—ie, *when* introduces a condition precedent to the gift vesting in A, so that A gets nothing unless and until he or she reaches 25; or (2) the gift to A takes effect immediately, with time of payment postponed until A reaches 25—ie, *when* introduces a condition subsequent, under which the gift (initially vested) divests if A fails to reach 25. Unless words or context supply the intended meaning, about the only guidance is the last-ditch presumption that courts prefer to treat gifts as vested rather than contingent: *Hume v Perpetual Trustees Executors and Agency Company of Tasmania Ltd* (1939) 62 CLR 242.

See also **if / when**; **upon / on**; **vest**; **where / when**.

whenever

Often seen in the expression '*whenever* it appears that …' But the expression can be ambiguous: does it mean (1) 'as often as it appears that' (ie, on any number of occasions), or (2) 'at the time it appears that' (ie, on the one occasion)? An adept drafter will clarify—avoiding the need to litigate. For example:

- Property was appointed 'for the children of A and B who attain 21, *whenever born*'. Held, meaning (1)—*whenever born* meant as often as children are born; the class of children was to stay open until no further children could be born, and was not to close (as would otherwise happen under the class-closing rules) as soon as the first child attained 21: *Re Edmondson's Will Trusts* [1972] 1 WLR 183.
- A regulation empowered the Board of Works to require the owner of a building to carry out work on a building '*whenever* it appears to the Board' that work was required. Held, meaning (2)—*whenever* meant *at whatever time, once and for all*, and not *so often as*. Therefore, having in the past ordered work to be done, the Board could not later require additional work: *St James's Hall Co v London County Council* [1901] 2 KB 250.

where

See **if / where**; **where / when**.

where / when

Different usages?

Legal writers tend to use these two words interchangeably, particularly for introducing the circumstances in which a provision is to apply. However, in his renowned text on legislative drafting, Gareth Thornton urged a more discriminating practice. He recommended *where* as the general term for this purpose, and *when* for cases involving a single or rare event: GC Thornton, *Legislative Drafting*, 3rd edn (Butterworths, 1987) 93. Thornton gave these examples:

- *Where* a notice of cancellation is given under section 7, the purchaser shall deliver to the vendor …
- *When* the amount of compensation payable to any person under subsection (1) is determined, the Minister for Finance shall …

But the battle may be lost. The editor of the latest edition of Thornton's work omits this advice: GC Thornton, *Legislative Drafting*, ed Helen Xanthaki, 5th edn (Bloomsbury, 2013). The omission probably reflects the reality that the distinction is difficult to draw and overlooked in practice. In the examples above, modern usage would allow either *where* or *when*—and in an example directed to a particular person, would prefer *if*.

Ambiguous *where*?

Occasionally, *where* can be ambiguous, meaning either *if* or *at that place*. Usually context will resolve any doubt. For example, a tax statute expressed to apply '*where* a company has a tax deficit' did not refer to a place, but meant *if* or *whenever*: *Davies Jenkins & Co Ltd v Davies* [1968] AC 1097, 1118 (Lord Morris). However, if your reader could be puzzled, always clarify.

See also **CONDITIONAL CLAUSES**; **if / where**; **if / when**; **when**.

whereas

In both normal usage and legal usage, *whereas* means 'but on the contrary': eg, 'The judge appears at 10 am, *whereas* [ie, *but*] the jurors must arrive by 9 am.' This use is idiomatic, even if now somewhat old-fashioned.

Lawyers also use *whereas* to introduce a statement—'*Whereas* …' This is an archetypal legalism, habitually prefacing a recital or series of recitals—a ritual throat-clearing to get a document under way (Martin Cutts, *Making Sense of English in the Law* (Chambers, 1992) 241). The use of *whereas* may stem from a belief that *whereas* in a recital prevents ('estops') the person making the recited statement from later denying it: see, eg, *Bowman v Taylor* (1834) 4 LJ KB 58. That estoppel arises may be true; but it is not because of the introductory *whereas*. Rather, estoppel flows from the nature of and effect of recitals (particularly in deeds), not the *whereas* that precedes them.

Modern drafters increasingly reject *whereas* as a way of introducing recitals or other prefatory statements. Instead, they prefer *Recitals* or *Background*. A rare exception is for some public documents, where *whereas* adds an aura of deliberate solemnity; examples are international treaties, and documents that seek to protect national or cultural interests.

Further reading

'Whereas', in *Law Words* (Centre for Plain Legal Language, University of Sydney, 1995) 92; www.clarity-international.net/plain-language-resources/general-resources/

See also **RECITALS**.

whereby

Whereby means 'by which', or 'owing to which', or 'as a result of'. For example, a power to declare void a contract 'whereby' a person performs work, means 'as a result of which' or 'in consequence of which' a person performs work: *Stevenson v Barham* (1977) 12 ALR 175, 177 (Stephen J). But to retain *whereby* in such a sentence preserves an unnecessarily archaic tone. This is even more so where the writing is aimed at the general public: eg, 'This statute sets aside unfair contracts *whereby* [prefer: *under which*; *by which*] consumers purchase goods online.'

The reality is that lawyers who use *whereby* do so out of habit. Almost always, a more modern expression will suffice:

> 'In our system, the inquest is the normal means *whereby* [prefer: *by which*] an obligation to investigate will be fulfilled. In certain circumstances, a satisfactory system *whereby* [prefer: *by which*] the death can be properly investigated by civil, criminal, disciplinary or other procedures or a combination of them may suffice.' [*R v Oxfordshire Assistant Deputy Coroner* [2008] EWHC 694; [2008] 3 WLR 1284, [28] (Collins J)]

whether

Many *whether* expressions are prolix. Prune them. Examples follow.

'as to whether'

In this expression, *as to* is always superfluous. Indeed, for some critics, 'superfluous' may be too mild a condemnation:

> 'The *as to* [in *as to whether*] is not incorrect, but merely repulsive.' [*State v Heslop* 639 A 2d 1100, 1111 (NJ, 1994) (Clifford J, quoting *Fowler's Modern English Usage*)]

Prefer simply *whether*. For example:

- 'There will, however, be rare occasions where this court has concerns *as to whether* [prefer: *whether*] a decision of the Strasbourg Court sufficiently appreciates or accommodates particular aspects of our domestic process.' [*Horncastle v R* [2009] UKSC 14; [2010] 2 AC 373, [11] (Lord Phillips)]
- 'The claimant then amended its claim to seek a determination … *as to whether* [prefer: *whether*] there was a valid arbitration agreement. … The defendant counterclaimed for a preliminary ruling *as to whether* [prefer: *whether*] an arbitration agreement had been concluded …' [*AES Ust-Kamenogorsk Hydropower Plant LLP v Ust-Kamenogorsk Hydropower Plant JSC* [2011] EWCA Civ 647; [2012] 1 WLR 920, [67] (Rix LJ)]

'of whether'

Of is redundant; strike it out. For example:

- the issue ~~of~~ whether
- the question ~~of~~ whether (or better still: ~~the question of~~ whether).

'whether or not'

The *or not* is superfluous—delete it. For example:

- The jury could not decide *whether ~~or not~~* the defendant was guilty.
- '*Whether ~~or not~~* the Minister had the power to include members' clubs in the Order depends on the proper interpretation [of the Act].' [*Hotel and Catering Industry Training Board v Automobile Pty Ltd* [1969] 1 WLR 697, 699 (Lord Reid)]
- '[It] makes no difference *whether ~~or not~~* the consumer possesses the goods.' [*Consumer Rights Act 2015*, s 5(3)]

Even more so, delete double *or nots*:

> 'But there is a nice question … whether "true evidence" … means "objectively true evidence" or "the evidence that a witness truly believes and would give under oath", *whether or not that evidence is objectively true or not* [prefer: *regardless of whether that evidence is objectively true*].' [*Vasilevski v R* [2019] NSWCCA 277, [101]]

If for some reason you feel compelled to retain *or not*, at least place it as close as possible to *whether*—unlike the following example:

> 'The offence of attempt to commit a crime may be committed … *whether* under the circumstances it was possible to commit such a crime *or not*.' [*Criminal Code* (Tas), s 2(2)]

'as to whether or not'

Prune to *whether*. For example:

> '[T]his court must consider the matter again and exercise its own discretion ~~*as to*~~ *whether* ~~*or not*~~ *to* set aside each of the default judgment and the order …' [*Gentry v Miller* [2016] EWCA Civ 141, [22] (Vos LJ)]

See also **question whether**.

which / that

See **that / which**.

whichever is the less

Since this expression posits a comparison between two items, prefer *whichever is the lesser*, or (better, because shorter) *whichever is less* (not *whichever is lesser*).

while

Temporal or causative?

While (or the archaic *whilst*) can be used in a temporal sense (*when*) or a causative sense (*because; caused by*). Sometimes the distinction is clear enough—even if after a temporary miscue:

> '*While* I am a director, I have no interest in company reconstruction'. The meaning is 'for as long as', not 'because'.

But at other times the distinction is less clear. For example:

> An insurance policy precludes claims for injury sustained *while* (or *whilst*) driving under the influence of alcohol. Does it preclude claims: (1) for injury suffered *when* driving under the influence of alcohol (ie, a mere temporal link is sufficient); or (2) for injury *caused by* driving under the influence of alcohol (ie, a causal link is required)? Compare:
>
> - *Loudon v British Merchants Insurance Co Ltd* [1961] 1 All ER 705, 706 (temporal link sufficient)
> - *Cassidy v State Government Insurance Office* [1965] WAR 81 (temporal link sufficient)
> - *R v O'Callaghan* [1985] 1 NZLR 198 (causal link required, under a criminal statute penalising drivers who cause injury while under the influence of alcohol).

Meaning *although*

Where the intended meaning of *while* is *although*, for clarity prefer *although* (or *but*, or similar conjunction). For example:

> 'The plaintiff gave evidence in Cantonese *while* [prefer: *although*] the defendant gave evidence in Japanese.' [Example from GC Thornton, *Legislative Drafting*, 3rd edn (Butterworths, 1987) 94]

whilst

An archaism for *while*. To retain *whilst* serves no purpose but pedantry.

See **while**.

WHITE SPACE

See **DOCUMENT DESIGN.**

Whitsunday

The seventh Sunday after Easter. In Scottish landlord and tenant law, one of the 'quarter days' for payment of rent, notionally 15 May, regardless of when Whitsunday actually falls. (Idiosyncratically, the *Removal Terms (Scotland) Act 1886* provides that entry to and removal from a house, agreed to take place on Whitsunday, takes place at noon on 28 May.)

See also **quarter days**.

who / whom / whose

Usage guides differ on the 'correct' uses of *who*, *whom*, and *whose*. Despite the differences, generally speaking modern usage has settled into the following basic principles (drawn from RD Burchfield (ed), *Fowler's Modern English Usage*, 3rd edn (Oxford University Press, 1998), with added legal examples).

who

Who (not *whom*) is used:

- as a relative pronoun with a person as antecedent: eg, 'The judge was a tyrant *who* was known for his constant interruptions of counsel.'
- as an interrogative pronoun: eg, '*Who* do you think should go?'
- where introducing an indirect question: eg, 'This raised the obvious question about *who* would act for the defendant.'
- where leaving a preposition stranded: eg, '*Who* do you think you are talking to?'

whom

Whom is only ever used as an object (not the subject) in a sentence:

- after a preposition: eg, 'There were judges before *whom* no litigant wanted to appear.'
- in a relative clause: eg, 'Was there anyone *whom* she could approach for legal advice?'

Examples

- '[T]he answer depended on … the parties between *whom* the issue was raised. In an action against the company by a third party *who* had been defrauded, the company was responsible.' [*Bilta (UK) Ltd v Nazir (No 2)* [2015] UKSC 23; [2015] 2 WLR 1168, [84] (Lord Sumption)]
- 'The [housing authority] … would have to provide accommodation to someone about *whom* it had made an [adverse decision] and to *whom* it had already given a reasonable opportunity to obtain alternative accommodation. … [This] may deprive other applicants *who* may have priority need of suitable accommodation …' [*R v Lewisham London Borough Council* [2014] UKSC 62; [2014] 3 WLR 1548, [35] (Lord Hodge)]
- 'An employer, *who* has discriminated unlawfully in employing his workforce, is not placed under a duty to engage in further unlawful discrimination in the selection of the employees *whom* he will dismiss.' [*Australian Iron & Steel Pty Ltd v Banovic* (1989) 168 CLR 165, 172 (Brennan J)]

whose

Formerly, grammarians limited *whose* to animate objects: 'I prefer directors *whose* reputations are respected', but not 'I prefer companies *whose* directors are respected'. But this can produce ungainly sentences—'I prefer companies the directors *of which* are respected'—and modern usage is content with *whose* for inanimate objects.]

See also **whose / of which**.

WHOLE DOCUMENT (PRINCIPLE OF INTERPRETATION)

A principle that requires a document to be interpreted as a whole. Under the principle, the meaning of part of a document must be viewed in the context of all other parts: *Re Sigma Finance Corporation* [2009] UKSC 2; [2010] 1 All ER 571, [12] (Lord Mance), [35] (Lord Collins).

A variant of the principle applies where a transaction is embodied in a series of documents: the documents may be read together to clarify the meaning of part of one of them, at least where they are executed contemporaneously or within a short time of each other: *Smith v Chadwick* (1882) 20 Ch D 27, 62; *EDWF Holdings 1 Pty Ltd v EDWF Holdings 2 Pty Ltd* [2010] WASCA 78; (2010) 41 WAR 23, [104]. The logic is that the parties intended the documents to be read 'back-to-back', as part of the one transaction: *Lexington Insurance Co v AGF Insurance Ltd* [2010] 1 AC 180, [111] (Lord Collins). Thus, if a provision in one of the documents is ambiguous, but a relevant provision in another is clear, the clear may be invoked to clarify the ambiguous: *Maye v Colonial Mutual Life Assurance Society Ltd* (1924) 35 CLR 14, 23 (Isaacs J).

See also **CONSISTENCY OF TERMINOLOGY**.

'WHOLE AGREEMENT' CLAUSE

See **'ENTIRE AGREEMENT' CLAUSE**.

whole or any part of

A phrase often seen, as where a lease requires the tenant to repair *the whole or any part of* the property. But are both 'limbs' of the phrase needed—*whole* and *any part*? Logically, no: because the sum of the parts is the whole, it should be enough to require repair of *any part* of the property. However, to overcome any possibility of argument—particularly (even if unlikely) that the obligation to repair might be discharged by a one-off repair of a single part—rewrite as follows: 'The tenant must repair *every part* of the property' (or, more simply, 'The tenant must repair the property').

See also **in whole or in part**; **wholly**.

wholly

A word often found in familiar pairings, exuding redundancy. Almost always, prune or rewrite. For example:

- 'If the purchaser fails to pay *the deposit wholly or partially* [prefer: *any part of the deposit*], the vendor may terminate the contract.' [Better still: '… fails to pay *the deposit* …', because failure to pay any part of the deposit is a failure to pay *the* deposit.]
- 'The taxpayer can claim a deduction for premises used *wholly or mainly* [prefer: *mainly*, since that is the minimum requirement for deductibility] for the purposes of trade.'
- 'Partners can claim credit for contributions they make *wholly and exclusively* [prefer: either *wholly* or *exclusively*; one word will suffice] for the benefit of the partnership.'

See also **in whole or in part**.

whom

See **who / whom / whose**.

whomever / whomsoever

Whomsoever is an archaic intensifier for *whomever*; prefer *whomever*. But do you even need *whomever*—or, for that matter, *whoever*? In many contexts, no: the plainer *anyone at all*, or similar, suffices. 'This applies to any person *whomever*' = 'This applies to *anyone at all*'. (Better still in some contexts: 'This applies to *everyone*.')

However, occasionally *whoever* (or similar) can be useful for emphasis—and emphasis can be important in interpretation. For example:

- A landlord's covenant (ie, promise) for quiet enjoyment normally protects tenants against interference only by those authorised by, or claiming through, the landlord. But a covenant for quiet enjoyment 'without interruption by any person *at all*' (or similar) widens the covenant to protect tenants against interference even by those not authorised by, or not claiming through, the landlord: *Kenny v Preen* [1963] 1 QB 499.
- A statute established an investigatory committee. Section 5 empowered the committee to compel certain named officers to produce certain information. Section 7 empowered the committee to compel certain persons 'and any other persons *whomsoever*' to appear before the committee. Held, *whomsoever* was to be taken at face value and was not limited to those persons already named in s 5: *R v Doubleday* (1861) 3 El & El 501; 121 ER 530.

whose

See **who / whom / whose**.

whose / of which

Conventionally, *whose* is preferred when referring to animate objects, and *of which* is preferred when referring to inanimate objects. Thus, 'He abandoned the car, the engine *of which* had failed', not 'He abandoned the car, *whose* engine had failed.' But *of which* requires a more complex sentence construction, and so good writers have long used *whose* for both animate and inanimate objects.

Conventional ('of which')	**Acceptable ('whose')**
A landlord may evict a corporate tenant the trading records *of which* show an inability to pay rent on time.	A landlord may evict a corporate tenant *whose* trading records show an inability to pay rent on time.
'Article 3(a) [of the Convention] provides that it modifies pro tanto the Inter-Bureaux Agreement, *the terms of which* otherwise remain in force.' [*Moreno v The Motor Insurers' Bureau* [2016] UKSC 52; [2016] 1 WLR 3194, [6] (Lord Mance)]	Article 3(a) [of the Convention] provides that it modifies pro tanto the Inter-Bureaux Agreement, *whose terms* otherwise remain in force.

Judicial examples of 'whose '(for inanimate objects)

- '[T]here may be fundamental principles … *whose* abrogation Parliament neither contemplated nor authorised.' [*Abd Ali Hameed Al-Waheed v Ministry of Defence* [2017] UKSC 2, [48] (Lord Sumption)]
- '[T]he order granted the respondent summary judgement [sic] on the issue of confidentiality, subject to reservations *whose* effect was necessarily uncertain.' [*DSM SFG Group Holdings Ltd v Kelly* [2019] EWCA Civ 2256, [30] (Simon LJ)]
- 'To obtain those certificates from the Inland Revenue the company granted a bond in respect of past tax liabilities of an associated company, *whose* business had been transferred to the company …' [*MacDonald v Carnbroe Estates Ltd (Scotland)* [2019] UKSC 57, [35] (Lord Hodge)

whosever / whosever's

While the apostrophe is commonly seen (and pronounced), it is strictly incorrect, because *whosever* already implies the possessive. The first example below is correct usage; the second (though perhaps idiomatic) is strictly incorrect.

- 'But, *whosever* interpretation is correct, [certain things follow]' [*Arnold v Britton* [2015] UKSC 36; [2015] AC 1619, [46] (Lord Neuberger)]
- 'In my judgment, *whosever's* [prefer: *whosever*] numbers are right, the differences are appreciable.' [*Basf Se v Sipcam (UK) Ltd* [2013] EWHC 2863 (Pat), [18] (Birss J)]

wilful

Meaning

Historically, in law as in general usage, *wilful* connoted perverse or wrongful intent. Something done *wilfully* was done with dishonest purpose, or at least wantonly or without good cause. For example:

- A tanner did not *wilfully* discharge waste into a watercourse, when he discharged it while carrying on his lawful business: *Smith v Barnham* (1876) 1 Ex D 419, 423–24 (Bramwell B).
- A surveyor was not guilty of *wilfully* demanding more money than he was entitled to, when he was acting honestly but mistakenly: *R v Badger* (1856) 6 El & Bl 137, 171; 119 ER 816, 828 (Lord Campbell CJ).

However, in more modern usage, *wilful* can also carry the ethically neutral sense of something that is done in the knowledge that it is being done—done as an act of will, intentionally or deliberately—but not necessarily with wrongful intent. It is simply an act 'freely done', in the sense that the person knows what he or she is doing and intends to do it, as a free agent: *Re Young & Harston's Contract* (1885) 31 Ch D 168, 174–75 (Bowen LJ). For example, this is the meaning when statutes create the offence of *wilfully* making a false statement (*R v Millward* [1985] 2 WLR 532), or *wilfully* pretending to be a solicitor (*Hall v Jordan* [1947] 1 All ER 826, 827, Goddard CJ).

In combination with other terms

Wilful often appears in familiar combinations: eg, *wilful default, wilful neglect.* The nuance varies with the context.

'wilful default'

Default that is deliberate, as distinct from merely careless or inadvertent. For example, in the context of an exclusion clause exempting trustees from liability:

> '[The term *wilful default*] means a deliberate breach of trust. ... Nothing less than conscious and wilful misconduct is sufficient. ... A trustee who is guilty of such conduct either consciously takes a risk that loss will result, or is recklessly indifferent whether it will or not.' [*Armitage v Nurse* [1998] Ch 241, 254 (Millett LJ)].

'wilful neglect'

Neglect that is intentional, or recklessly indifferent to the consequences, and not merely inadvertent. In the context of a statute allowing the Commissioner to assess tax after the normal cut-off date where a taxpayer was guilty of 'fraud or wilful neglect':

> '[The meaning of *wilful neglect*] may vary according to the context but generally [means] that there has been an intentional or purposive omission to do something that the person in question knows he has a duty to do.' [*de Maroussem v Commissioner of Income Tax* [2004] 1 WLR 2865, 2876 (PC)]

'wilful misconduct'

Misconduct that is deliberate, not merely careless:

> '[*Wilful misconduct* means] deliberately doing something which is wrong knowing it to be wrong or with reckless indifference to whether it is wrong or not.' [*Graham v Teesdale* (1981) 81 LGR 117, 123 (Webster J); approved in *Porter v Magill* [2002] 2 AC 357, 464 (Lord Bingham)]

'wilful wrongdoing'

A trustee acts with 'wilful wrongdoing' by acting in 'knowing and deliberate breach of duty or reckless indifference' to the possibility of such breach: *Armitage v Nurse* [1998] 1 Ch 241, 252 (Millett LJ), applied in *Barnsley v Noble* [2016] EWCA Civ 799; [2017] 2 WLR 1231, [36]–[37] (Sales LJ).

wilful default

See **wilful**.

wilful misconduct

See **wilful**.

wilful neglect

See **wilful**.

will

Indicating obligation

Some legal writers use *will* to indicate obligation, as a softer-toned substitute for *shall* or *must*. But this usage is not ideal. Although the meaning of compulsion is probably clear enough, *will* may also imply 'futurity'. This can create doubt about whether the act must be done now, or whether future compliance will suffice. Therefore, prefer *must* (or one of the substitutes discussed under **shall / must**).

Pointing to future event

When used to indicate a future event (ie, 'something *will* happen'), the meaning of *will* can range between 'is likely to', 'is highly probable to', and 'is certain to'. This creates potential for ambiguity. Unless the context requires otherwise, a court will probably ascribe the meaning 'is certain to' or 'is almost certain to'. For example:

> A life insurance policy provided for a payout before death, if the insured was suffering an illness that '*will* result in death' within 12 months. Held, *will result in* meant more than 'merely likely' or even 'highly likely', but rather having a 'very high probability, approaching certainty': *Galaxy Homes Pty Ltd v National Mutual Life Association of Australasia Ltd* [2013] SASCFC 34; (2013) 116 SASR 41, [49].

If the range of possible meanings of *will* is uncertain, clarify the intended meaning.

See also **calculated to**; **likely to**; **shall / must**; **TENSE**; **would**.

windfall

An unexpected bonus; unexpected good fortune. In land law, the term has long carried the literal meaning of things blown down by the wind (eg, trees or fruit), which the holder of a life estate (a 'life tenant') can keep in certain circumstances. But more generally, *windfall* simply means any good fortune that is 'unearned' (ie, not derived through personal effort or initiative). This use of the word appears in various areas of modern law. For example:

- A vendor who validly forfeits (ie, keeps) the purchaser's deposit following the purchaser's failure to pay the balance of the purchase price, is said to gain a *windfall*. The vendor may have to repay it.
- A landlord who terminates the lease for the tenant's default may receive the *windfall* of improvements the tenant has made to the property. The landlord may have to pay for them.
- A partner in a business that has failed may, on dissolution of the partnership, receive a *windfall* from the financial or other contributions of other partners. The partner may have to repay the windfall. Likewise, a person in a business relationship analogous to a partnership who receives similar benefits may have to repay them, under the doctrine of the so-called '*windfall* equity': *Henderson v Miles (No 2)* [2005] NSWSC 867; (2005) 12 BPR 23,579, [19] (Young CJ in Eq).

Further reading

Halsbury's Laws of England, 'Settlements' (vol 91, 2019) [780] ('windfalls' in context of life estates)

WIT

See **HUMOUR; SARCASM; to wit.**

with a view to

A common phrase in legal and bureaucratic writing. The general meaning is 'with the object or purpose of': *Bacon v Salamane* (1965) 112 CLR 85, 91 (Owen J). For example, a criminal statute may prohibit certain acts if done '*with a view to* obtaining a benefit', or a partnership agreement may state that prospective partners wish to carry on business together '*with a view to* profit'.

Distinguish between 'with *a* view to' and 'with *the* view to'. To illustrate: action taken with '***a** view to*' an end implies that other ends might be countenanced, but action taken with '***the** view to*' to an end suggests a sole end in mind. For example:

- A statute made it an offence to take a child out of the country 'with *a* view to' adoption. Held, 'with *a* view to' was a 'broad and comprehensive' expression and included taking a child out of the country where the purpose was not to seek immediate adoption but was one step in a larger process with adoption as its end aim: *Re M* [1973] 2 WLR 515, 519.
- A trade mark statute made it an offence to be in possession of goods 'with *a* view to' breaching a registered trade mark. Held, 'with *a* view to' required the doer to have in mind *an* end that might realistically occur, but not necessarily *the* planned or hoped-for end: *R v Zaman* [2002] EWCA Crim 1862, [12], [18]. In support of this interpretation, the court pointed out that under the statute it was an offence to do certain acts '*with a view to*' or '*with intent to*'; having used these two different terms, Parliament must have intended to give them different meanings.

with cause

A lawyer's shorthand for 'with justification' or 'for a valid reason', as distinct from *without cause* (needing no justification, needing no reason).

See also **without cause**.

with reference to

Almost always, a wordy substitute for *about*: eg, 'I am writing to you *with reference to* [prefer: *about*] your claim.' But there may be nuances—sometimes, *with reference to* may carry a consciously wider meaning than *about*. See, eg, *R v Noble* [1974] 2 All ER 811, 814, where a statutory reference to offences committed '*with reference to*' persons or their property was held to be broader than offences committed '*against*' persons or their property.

with respect to

A wordy prepositional phrase, overused in legal writing—as in writing generally. *With respect to* suggests connection; but connection is better expressed with a shorter word or phrase—such as *about*, *concerning*, *for*, or similar:

- 'However, the policy and its wording only govern the parties' relationship *in and with respect to* [prefer: *for*] the policy periods and risks arising during such periods.' [*Zurich Insurance PLC UK Branch v International Energy Group Ltd* [2015] UKSC 33, [24] (Lord Mance)]
- 'The Commission sought to challenge the finding of McDougall J *with respect to* [prefer: *about*; *on*] s 184(1) by way of notices of contention *in relation to* [prefer: *about*] Mr Duncan and others, but as the central ground of its proposed appeal *with respect to* [prefer: *about*;

concerning] Mr Kinghorn.' [*Independent Commission Against Corruption v Kinghorn* [2015] NSWCA 342, [25]]

- 'The regulations may establish schemes *for or with respect to* [prefer: *about*] the interment industry ...' [*Cemeteries and Crematoria Act 2013* (NSW), s 31(1)]

However, always think before substituting *for*. In some contexts, *with respect to* may sweep up a broader range of connections than the bare alternative *for*: see, eg, *Paull v Munday* (1975) 11 SASR 346, 348–49 (Bray CJ).

See also **PROLIXITY**.

within [a period] from

Calculating the period

When an act is to be done *within* a stated period *from* (or *of*, or *after*) an event, counting begins on the day after the event, and the period extends to the end of the last day. This method of calculation is settled by a myriad of cases, from as early as *Lester v Garland* (1808) 15 Ves 248; 33 ER 748 and continuing to the present day. For example:

- Where a complaint must be filed '*within* one calendar month of' an event (which occurred on 30 May), a complaint filed on June 30 was within time: *Radcliffe v Bartholomew* [1892] 1 QB 161.
- Where a document must be filed '*within* 21 days from' the execution of goods, and the execution occurred on 9 December, filing on 30 December was within time: *Williams v Burgess* (1840) 12 Ad & E 635; 113 ER 955.
- Where a contractual condition must be fulfilled '*within* 14 days *of* this agreement', the first counting-day is the day after the date of the contract: *Mission Corporation Ltd v Telecom Auckland Ltd* [1994] 2 NZLR 357.
- Where money must be paid '*within* 14 days *from* 1 June', the 14-day period starts on 2 June, then runs for the next 14 days, and expires at the end of 15 June: *Morton v Hampson* [1962] VR 364, 365–66.

If counting is to *include* the day of the event, prefer 'within X days *beginning with*' the day of the event.

Performance up until last moment

Where something is to be done *within* a stated period *of* or *from* a date, it can be done at any time up until the end of that period. For example:

- Where a court order is made on Tuesday 18 June, an application to be made 'within 6 weeks' of the court order can be made up until midnight on Tuesday 30 July: *Okolo v Secretary of State for the Environment* [1997] 2 All ER 911.
- An application to be made within three months of 31 December can be made at any time up until the end of 31 March: *Ex parte Toohey's Ltd* (1934) 34 SR (NSW) 277.
- A notice to be filed within six months of 22 December can be filed at any time up until the end of 22 June: *Re Gray* (1993) 115 ALR 638.
- A notice to complete requiring completion 'within 14 days from the date of the notice' must allow the whole of the 14th day (effectively, until the start of the 15th day): *Kalamen v Al Aubodi* [2010] NSWSC 544; (2010) 15 BPR 28,357.

Too early?

Normally, where something is to be done '*within* X days *from* 1 March', the *earliest* day on which it can be done is 1 March. That is, *from* means *starting from*; and to do it *before* 1 March is not to do it 'within X days *[starting] from* 1 March': *Zaghloul v Woodside Energy Ltd (No 5)* [2014] FCA 1042.

However, context may allow an interpretation that the act can also be done any time *before* (say) 1 March; ie, the prohibition is against doing the act too late, not against doing it too early: *Plumor Pty Ltd v Handley* (1996) 41 NSWLR 30, 34 (where the shortness of the time-span and the importance of the matter to be done aided such an interpretation). For example:

> A contract of life insurance specified that an insured who intended to exercise an option must do so '*within* 30 days *of*' 16 June. (Note: not 'within 30 days *after*' 16 June.) The insured exercised the option *before* 16 June. Was exercise *before* 16 June exercise *within 30 days of* 16 June? Held, yes. The provision specified the *last* day for exercising the option; exercise *before* that date would suffice; in short, 'within 30 days of 16 June' did not mean merely 'starting from 16 June and up until 30 days after 16 June': *Dowsley v Westpac Life Insurance Services Ltd* [2013] NSWSC 1208.

See also **period (of time)**; **TIME**; **within (a period from)**.

without affecting / limiting the generality of

The words *the generality of* are superfluous. Strike them out:

- 'Without affecting ~~the generality of~~ clause 5, …'
- 'Without limiting ~~the generality of~~ clause 5, …'

without cause

A quaint lawyerism for 'freely', 'unrestrictedly', in the sense of 'without having to justify the action'. The expression has the benefit of conciseness; but conciseness rarely trumps effective communication. Non-lawyers may assume *without cause* means 'without justification'; but actually (of course) it means 'without having to justify the decision'—ie, 'without having to give a reason'. When writing for non-lawyers, prefer an alternative that better communicates the intended meaning. For example:

> '[T]he very nature of a power to dismiss *without cause* [prefer: *without needing any reason*] was that its exercise did not have to be justified and there was no room for the argument that the right … was in such circumstances qualified by [an] implied term of trust and confidence …' [*Reda v Flag Ltd* [2002] UKPC 38, [42] (Lord Millett)]

See also **termination 'for convenience'**; **with cause**.

without prejudice

Technical meaning

In correspondence offering to settle potential or actual litigation, the term *without prejudice*—invariably inserted as a heading—seeks to invoke a form of privilege to ensure that the offer cannot be introduced as evidence in court if the attempted settlement fails. It is legal shorthand for 'without prejudice to the position of the writer of the letter if the negotiations … propose[d] are not accepted': *Walker v Wilsher* (1889) 23 QBD 335, 337 (Lindley LJ). By enforcing the privilege, courts give effect to an underlying public policy that the law should encourage parties to settle their disputes without resort to litigation or, if litigation has started, should encourage them to discontinue it: *Rush & Tomkins Ltd v Greater London Council* [1989] AC 1280, 1299.

This principle does not depend on using the precise term *without prejudice*. Any phrase indicating the intent will suffice. Indeed, no phrase at all is needed if the negotiations have begun and there is a genuine attempt at settlement: *Re Daintry* [1893] 2 QB 116;

Sternberg Reed Solicitors v Harrison [2019] EWHC 2065; [2020] 2 WLR 176, [27]–[37]. However, the term is so familiar in law that lawyers are unlikely to give it up. Indeed, its use is so closely associated with legal jargon that a non-lawyer who used it was more readily convicted of unlawfully posing as a solicitor: *Hall v Jordan* [1947] 1 All ER 826.

Conversely, using the term *without prejudice* does not necessarily keep negotiations away from judicial gaze. For example, when interpreting a settlement agreement, the court can look to the parties' *without prejudice* negotiations as part of the factual matrix relevant to discerning the meaning of their agreed terms: *Oceanbulk Shipping and Trading SA v TMS Asia Ltd* [2010] UKSC 44; [2011] 1 AC 662.

A misunderstood term

Research indicates that many non-lawyers misunderstand *without prejudice*. Their (mis) conceptions range from believing that a binding contract cannot arise from accepting the terms of a *without prejudice* letter, to believing that a lawyer writing a letter headed 'Without prejudice' is acting impartially. (See survey reported in Mark Adler, 'Bamboozling the Public' [1991] *New Law Journal* 1032.) Of course, no misunderstanding should occur where a lawyer uses *without prejudice* in correspondence with another lawyer—lawyers should know its meaning. But to use the term in correspondence to non-lawyers is apt to mislead. A writer insistent on using it for a non-legal audience should at least consider adding an explanation, perhaps along these lines:

> 'All admissions or offers we may make in these negotiations are *without prejudice*. This means that you cannot use them in court in evidence against us if this case does not settle.'

Further reading

- Lee Aitken, '*Without Prejudice* Revealed' (2011) 34 *Australian Bar Review* 296
- *Halsbury's Laws of England*, 'Civil Procedure' (vol 12, 2015) [663] (communications 'without prejudice')
- 'Without Prejudice', in *Law Words* (Centre for Plain Legal Language, University of Sydney, 1995) 95; www.clarity-international.net/plain-language-resources/general-resources/ (This article is the basis of the suggested explanation of *without prejudice* when writing to non-lawyers.)

See also **without prejudice to**.

without prejudice to

The expression *without prejudice to* appears in two main contexts.

To preserve existing rights or offers

Usage

Here, *without prejudice to* connotes that an act, statement, or offer is made without affecting existing rights or offers. That is, existing rights or offers are to remain, preserved and unaltered: *Turner v Haji Goolam Mahomed Azam* [1904] AC 826, 837 (PC). This differs from *without prejudice* in the litigation context, where the purpose is to keep material from being used in court.

Sometimes it is not clear which meaning the writer intends. It then is a matter of interpreting the document in which the expression appears. Where *without prejudice* appears in the body of the document, rather than as a heading, it is more likely to carry the meaning of 'without affecting existing offers or rights' and therefore be admissible in court. For example, in *Peterborough Council v Manchester Developments Ltd* [1996] 2 CLY 3713 (also reported as *Peterborough City Council v Mancetter Developments Ltd* [1996] EGCS 50), the Court of Appeal considered that the location of *without prejudice* in the body of a letter, rather than as a heading, indicated that it meant 'without affecting our other rights against you'.

Effectiveness

Regardless of wording and location, whether an attempt to reserve rights succeeds is a different issue. The attempt may be no more than 'a pious but ineffective wish': *Alleyn v Thurecht* [1983] 2 Qd R 706, 718 (Thomas J). Or, more likely, principles of waiver or estoppel may nullify the attempt. This is because a person who has moved to exercise one of a number of alternative rights is generally bound by the choice, even though they purport to act 'without prejudice'. A person, 'having eaten his cake, does not still have it, even though he professed to eat it without prejudice': *Haynes v Hirst* (1927) 27 SR (NSW) 480, 489 (Long Innes J). For example:

- A landlord may add a 'without prejudice' qualification when accepting rent after learning of the tenant's default. The purpose is to preserve the right to terminate for the tenant's default. However, the purpose will almost certainly fail, because the law regards acceptance of rent (even 'without prejudice') after notice of the breach as waiving the breach: *Segal Securities Ltd v Thoseby* [1963] 1 QB 887.
- A vendor may add a 'without prejudice' qualification when answering the purchaser's out-of-time requisitions on title. Being out-of-time, the vendor need not have answered them. But by answering them, even 'without prejudice', the vendor may be held to the answers: *Cutts v Thodey* (1842) 6 Jur 1027; *McNally v Waitzer* (unreported, Supreme Court of New South Wales, McLelland J, 12 December 1980; affirmed on different grounds, [1981] 1 NSWLR 294). The qualification '*may* be held to the answers' is added, because some decisions have allowed vendors in this situation to invoke their *without prejudice* qualification: eg, *Oakden v Pike* (1865) LJ Ch 620; *Saben Developments Ltd v Dutchmen Homes Ltd* (1977) 84 DLR (3d) 95, 109–11.

A plainer-language alternative

When used in the sense of 'without affecting existing rights or offers', there is no magic in the precise formula *without prejudice to*. A plainer-English expression—eg, *without affecting [our rights]*, or *without limiting [our rights]*—captures the meaning.

To preserve the force of a provision against a contrasting or overlapping provision

Here, *without prejudice to* means simply *despite* or *without limiting* or similar—in which case, prefer the simpler expression. For example:

- *Without prejudice to* [prefer: *Despite*] clause 5, the purchaser may take possession before completion.
- *Without prejudice to* [prefer: *Without limiting*; *Without affecting*] rights under clause X, the purchaser may terminate this contract.

However, this meaning assumes that the two clauses in fact conflict. If they do not, then the formula has no work to do; it is meaningless (as in *Dooba Developments Ltd v McLagan Investments Ltd* [2016] EWHC 2944 (Ch) [35]).

See also **estoppel; waiver; without prejudice**.

without prejudice to the generality of

A needlessly wordy expression. Prune it. For example, instead of '*without prejudice to the generality of clause X*', say '*without limiting clause X*' or even '*despite clause X*'.

WOOLF REFORMS

A compendious term for the many changes to the rules of civil procedure introduced under the *Civil Procedure Rules 1998*. The reforms are named after Lord Woolf CJ, whose report *Access to Justice* (1996) recommended a new, simpler procedural code for civil litigation in England and Wales.

A key reform was to 'update' many well-known words and phrases used in litigation. Examples were *writ* (becoming *claim form*), *subpoena* (becoming *witness summons*), *ex parte* (becoming *without notice*), *garnishee order* (becoming *third-party debt order*), *mandamus* (becoming *mandatory order*), and *certiorari* (becoming *quashing order*). Many of the old terms were Latin; replacing them was part of a broader aim to reduce the incidence of Latin in the language of litigation.

Further reading

Access to Justice, Final Report (Lord Woolf CJ; 1996), at https://webarchive.nationalarchives.gov.uk/20060213223540/http://www.dca.gov.uk/civil/final/contents.htm

See also **FOREIGN (NON-ENGLISH) WORDS AND PHRASES; LATIN**.

WORD ORDER

Avoid word orders that are eccentric or unidiomatic. Their capriciousness invites attention, diverting readers from the message. Legal writing provides copious examples:

Eccentric	**Revised**
I revoke all wills by me heretofore made.	I revoke all previous wills.
The lessee shall not assign without the landlord's consent first had and obtained.	The lessee must not assign without the landlord's prior consent.
The lessee shall repair, fair wear and tear and damage by storm and tempest only excepted.	The lessee must repair, except for fair wear and tear and storm damage.
She died, leaving four children her surviving.	She died, leaving four surviving children.
In witness whereof the parties hereto have hereunto set their hands and seals on the day and year first hereinbefore mentioned.	Signed and sealed on … [date].

WORD PAIRINGS

The use of two words where one should suffice; sometimes called *doublets* (a term better reserved for medieval gentlemen's jackets). Examples are legion in legal writing; for some discussed in this book, see **null and void**; **observe and perform**; **right and liberty**; **use and enjoyment**. More extreme is word-*tripling*: using three words where one should suffice; examples discussed in this book include **give, devise and bequeath**, and **right, title and interest**.

Word pairings are sometimes explained on the basis that English law endured successive language changes—from Old English to Norman French, to Latin, and finally to modern English. As each new language became accepted, lawyers retained an equivalent word from the superseded language, in that way accreting lists of synonyms or near-synonyms. This may conveniently explain some common pairings from different language stocks—*null* [Latin] and *void* [French]; *observe* [Latin] and *perform* [Old French]; *right* [Old English] and *liberty* [Latin]—but it seems unlikely for many, if not most, pairings. In any case, historical origins do not justify continuing the practice into modern times.

The modern plain-language approach is to use one word only, if it is sufficient to cover the field.

Word pairing or tripling	Sufficient single word
cease and desist	stop
due and payable	due; payable
freely and voluntarily	freely
goods and chattels	goods
null and void	void
pass and repass	pass
terms and conditions	terms
true and correct	correct
will and testament	will
right, title and interest	interest
give, devise and bequeath	give

See also **expressio unius**; **pass and repass**; **PROLIXITY**; **WORD STRINGS.**

WORD STRINGS

The problem

Word strings are prevalent in legal writing. No area of law is immune. They exist in statutory drafting and in private-sector legal drafting. Taken to extremes, they self-parody the excesses of traditional legal drafting. Two examples follow.

Example 1: statutory drafting

Section 50.10 Trees, shrubs, plants, grass and other vegetation.

General injury. No person shall prune, cut, carry away, pull up, dig, fell, bore, chop, saw, chip, pick, move, sever, climb, molest, take, break, deface, destroy, set fire to, burn, scorch, carve, paint, mark, or in any manner interfere with, tamper, mutilate, misuse, disturb or damage any tree, shrub, plant, grass, flower, or part thereof, nor shall any person permit any chemical, whether solid, fluid, or gaseous, to seep, drip, drain or be emptied, sprayed, dusted or injected upon, about or into any tree, shrub, plant, grass, flower, or part thereof, except when specifically authorized by competent authority; nor shall any person build fires, or station, or use any tar kettle, heater, road roller or other engine within an area covered by this part in such a manner that the vapour, fumes or heat therefrom may injure any tree or other vegetation.'

[Code of Federal Regulations, Title 36 (Parks, Forests, and Memorials), Chapter 1, reg 50.10 (text as of 1 January, 1967); since repealed]

Example 2: lease

'[The tenant covenants] when where and so often as occasion requires well and sufficiently to repair renew rebuild uphold support sustain maintain pave purge scour cleanse glaze empty amend and keep the premises and every part thereof (including all fixtures and additions thereto) and all floors walls columns roofs canopies lifts and escalators (including all motors and machinery therefor) shafts stairways fences pavements forecourts drains sewers ducts flues conduits wires cables gutters soil and other pipes tanks cisterns pumps and other water and sanitary apparatus thereon with all needful and necessary amendments whatsoever ...'

[Extract of lease, from *Ravenseft Properties Ltd v Davstone (Holdings) Ltd* [1979] 1 All ER 929. It is easy to pick holes in this drafting. For example:

- There is a 15-verb string after 'repair'; did the drafter intend each verb as a synonym or near-synonym for 'repair', or was the aim to widen the obligation beyond 'repair'?

- An expression such as 'in repair' needs to follow 'to keep'.
- Why list some parts of the premises but not others? Does not the reference to 'the premises and every part thereof' suffice? (The case involved leaking windows and faulty cladding—which do not appear in the list.)
- There is no punctuation.]

Lord Hoffmann called this drafting technique 'torrential': *Norwich Union Life Insurance Society v British Railways Board* [1987] 2 EGLR 137, 138. Rudolf Flesch called it the 'shotgun principle' of legal drafting: Flesch, *How to Write Plain English* (1979) 41. The style confirms Charles Davidson's critique that the legal profession's general disposition is 'to seek safety in verbosity rather than in discrimination of language': C Davidson, TC Wright and J Waley (eds), *Davidson's Conveyancing Precedents*, 3rd edn (William Maxwell, 1860) vol 1, 67.

The excuses

At least three excuses are given for the ubiquity of word strings in legal writing. None seems persuasive.

1. *Exhaustiveness*. The drafter aims to cover every possible eventuality, no matter how unlikely to arise. As Lord Hoffmann said:

   > 'The draftsmen [of leases] traditionally employ linguistic overkill and try to obliterate the conceptual target by using a number of words or phrases expressing more or less the same idea.' [*Tea Trade Properties Ltd v CIN Properties Ltd* [1990] 1 EGLR 155, 158]

   This approach may be client-motivated, to protect the client's interests in all conceivable circumstances; but the aim can be achieved in a more reader-friendly way.
2. *Inertia*. The drafter uses an existing precedent, and has neither time nor inclination to prune out the words that are not needed for the particular transaction. Words are always 'easier to copy than expunge': *Osborne to Rowlett* (1880) 13 Ch D 774, 786.
3. *Ignorance*. The drafter does not know why all the words are in the precedent, and assumes (wrongly) that because they have always been there, they must be relevant.

A thoughtful drafter avoids unnecessary word strings, preferring instead (where possible) one or two generic words in place of lists of specifics.

The dangers

Risk of gaps

A list of specifics, no matter how carefully compiled, may leave gaps. Under the principle of interpretation known as *expressio unius*, a court may consider the gaps to be intentional. Examples are found in cases interpreting older-style powers of attorney. These documents usually included long lists of powers, perhaps running to several pages. Courts assumed that a power not included in a seemingly exhaustive list was deliberately omitted: see, eg, *Bryant v La Banque du Peuple* [1893] AC 170, 177. By comparison, many modern-day powers of attorney use generic language: 'I grant all powers that I am legally able to grant' (or similar). That leaves no room for gaps.

Reader switch-off

Lists of specifics make for boring reading. Readers switch off. That of itself is no reason to avoid lists of specifics where they are essential to legal validity—but unless they are essential, it is better to lighten up by using generic terms. In extreme cases, lists of specifics can be a sad self-parody of legal style, as in the following deed of settlement between a litigant (X) and a bank (ABC Bank).

> 'In consideration of [amount] and for other good and valuable consideration, receipt of which is hereby acknowledged, [X] remises, releases, and forever discharges [ABC Bank] and each of the Lenders, and each of their respective present and former officers, directors, attorneys, agents, parents, subsidiaries, affiliates, predecessors, successors, assigns and employees, and their respective administrators, executors, affiliates, parents, subsidiaries, predecessors, successors and assigns, including without limitation, [ABC Bank] acting both as agent and individually, from any action, cause of action, suit, debt, dues, sum of money, account, reckoning, bond, bill, specialty, covenant, contract, controversy, agreement, promise, variance, trespass, damage, judgment, extent, execution, claim or demand whatsoever, in law, admiralty or equity, whether accrued or unaccrued, liquidated or contingent, which it may now or hereafter own, hold, have or claim to have by reason of any matter, cause or thing whatsoever *from the beginning of the world* to the day of the date of this Settlement Agreement, including, but not limited to, any claims which are, were or could have been asserted in the Lawsuit.' (173 words, 1 sentence; emphasis added)
>
> [Source: a UK bank's standard-form deed of release. The release of claims *from the beginning of the world* is a nonsensical notion in the context of modern statutes of limitation, but it has a long pedigree. The wording can be traced back to precedents from the 17th century (and perhaps earlier). See, eg, deed of release (quitclaim) dated 20 February 1690 by which Renatus Harris released the Honourable Society of the Inner Temple from all claims 'from the beginning of the world unto the day of the date of these presents': *Records of the Inner Temple*, vol 2, fol 71. The term 'extent', meaning a writ to seize land in payment of a debt, is long obsolete.]

Much to be preferred is Professor Dickerson's 'lowest common denominator' approach, under which the drafter selects a word or words to cover the particular group or activity intended, but no more: Reed Dickerson, *Fundamentals of Legal Drafting*, 2nd edn (Little, Brown & Co, 1986) 18.

See also **DEED OF RELEASE**; **expressio unius**; **NOUN STRINGS**; **PROLIXITY**; **SYNONYMS**; **WORD PAIRINGS**.

WORDINESS

See **PROLIXITY**; **SYNONYMS**; **WORD PAIRINGS**; **WORD STRINGS**.

WORDS AND FIGURES

Historical convention: double-up

Formerly, lawyers used both words and numerals (figures) to express numbers: 'The rent is one thousand dollars ($1000) per month.' They did so more out of habit than reason; but on those rare occasions when they applied reason, their logic was twofold: (1) to ensure precision ('how can you doubt a number twice-written?'); and (2) to guard against later fraudulent alterations. But the doubling-up caused grave doubt where the words and figures differed: which prevailed? (For the answer, see below.)

Modern convention: figures alone

Practice is changing. While some drafters still use both words and figures, most now use words alone, or figures alone—and of those, most prefer figures alone because figures appear crisper on the page than words.

Resolving conflicts between words and figures

Where a document uses both words and figures, and they conflict, which prevail? The answer depends on the nature of the document:

Commercial documents

Where words and figures conflict in a commercial document, prima facie the words prevail: *Saunderson v Piper* (1839) 5 Bing (NC) 425; 132 ER 1163 (involving a discrepancy between words and figures in a bill of exchange, but pre-dating the legislation by which words prevail over figures in negotiable instruments); *Coote v Borland* (1904) 35 SCR (Can) 282, 284.

Example

> The landlord served on the tenants a rent review notice, specifying the new market rent as '£8,850 (Eight thousand seven hundred and fifty pounds)'. The tenants argued that the discrepancy of £100 rendered the notice void. The Court of Appeal disagreed, on the basis that the notice would not have misled the tenants. The tenants 'would naturally go by the words', and would regard the notice as meaning that 'they had to pay anyhow £8,750—at least that': *Durham City Estates Ltd v Felicetti* [1990] 1 EGLR 143, 146 (Croom-Johnson LJ).

The rule that the words prevail seems premised on the assumption that words take longer to write than figures, and are therefore more deliberately considered: *Bankstown Airport Ltd v Noor Al Houda Islamic College Pty Ltd* (2003) NSW Conv R 56–108, [27]. However, the rule presumably does not apply where internal factors indicate the contrary. For example:

> Assume that a contract for the sale of land states (in words and figures) each of the purchase price, the deposit, and the balance payable on completion. Assume also that the words and figures for the deposit conflict internally—the figures reflect the 'normal' convention of 10% of the purchase price, but the words state a different amount. If the figures for the deposit, plus the stated balance payable on completion, total the stated purchase price, that indicates that the parties intended the normal 10% deposit. The figures would prevail.

Wills

In wills, the rule is reversed. The courts assume that where words and figures conflict, the latter of the two expressions prevails (whether words or figures), in line with the general assumption that in a will containing contradictory provisions the later provision better reflects the testator's considered intention.

Example

> A testator made a series of gifts:
>
> > 'I bequeath to [A] the sum of five hundred pounds (£500), to [B] the sum of five hundred pounds (£500), to [C] the sum of one hundred pounds (£500), to [D] the sum of five hundred pounds (£500).'
>
> Held, the rule and the context showed that the testator intended C to receive £500: *Re Hammond* [1938] 3 All ER 308.

See also **INCONSISTENT PROVISIONS; NUMBERS.**

WORDS AND PHRASES (LITIGATED)

See **LITIGATED WORDS AND PHRASES.**

WORDS OF APPROXIMATION

It is often necessary—or at least convenient—to introduce into a description the qualification 'approximately' or similar: eg, 'The property being sold is 100 hectares *approximately*.' Some 'words of approximation' may suggest more certainty than others: eg, *approximately* might suggest more precision and less wiggle room than *about* or *more or less*. But in fact all words of approximation are interpreted in the context of the circumstances of the particular case, and all are susceptible to litigation over meaning. If possible, state precisely the permitted variation, rather than leave it to the guesswork of the parties or the vagaries of the courts.

Some common words of approximation are considered separately in this book. See **about**; **approximately**; **more or less**; **thereabouts**.

words of limitation

The words that mark out (or 'delimit') the nature of an estate in land. For example, historically a freehold grant or conveyance of land to A used the formula 'to A and his heirs'; in this formula, the words 'and his heirs' were words of limitation, denoting that A took a fee simple. Or a fee tail used the formula 'to A and the heirs of his body'; the words 'and the heirs of his body' were words of limitation, denoting that A took a fee tail. Modern statutes have all but dispensed with the need for precise words of limitation: see, eg, *Law of Property Act 1925*, s 60(1).

Further reading

S Bridge, E Cooke, and M Dixon (eds), *Megarry & Wade's Law of Real Property*, 9th edn (Sweet & Maxwell, 2019) [A-005]–[A-012]

See also **fee simple**; **fee tail**; **words of purchase**.

words of procreation

The words in a grant of a fee tail that confined 'heirs' to the heirs of the grantee. Thus, in a grant 'to A and the heirs of his body', the words 'of his body' were words of procreation. The concept is now of historical interest only, because fees tail have been abolished in most common-law jurisdictions.

Further reading

S Bridge, E Cooke, and M Dixon (eds), *Megarry & Wade's Law of Real Property*, 9th edn (Sweet & Maxwell, 2019) [A-014]

See also **fee tail**.

words of purchase

The words that mark out the person who takes property under a grant or conveyance of land. For example, in the formula 'to A and his heirs', the words 'to A' identify A as the person who takes under the grant, while the words 'and his heirs' denote the nature of A's interest (a fee simple).

See also **fee simple**; **words of limitation.**

working day

See **business day**.

works (noun)

The noun *works* is plural, and takes a plural verb. However, in building contracts, *works* is often a defined term (*Works*) and takes a singular verb if referring to a (single) building activity. For example:

Defined term: **'Works'** *means* [ie, singular] the repair of the roof.

Clause: The Works *are* [ie, plural noun] to be completed within 6 weeks.

See also **SUBJECT–VERB AGREEMENT**; **premises.**

would

A dangerously vague word, with a range of meanings, not all easily discernible from context. The range extends from 'might possibly' to 'almost certainly'. Which is meant? The vagueness makes the word inherently litigation-prone. For example:

- A statute penalised arson carried out with disregard about whether property *would* be damaged and about whether a person's life *would* be thereby endangered. Held, *would* meant *might foreseeably*, not the stronger *will*; it was enough that a prudent bystander would have 'perceived an obvious risk' that the act of setting fire to chairs in a flat could damage the flat and thereby endanger life: *R v Sangha* [1988] 1 WLR 519, 525.
- A property interest was forfeitable if the holder did anything 'by which the income *would* become vested in' another person. Did '*would* become vested' mean *might* become vested or *will* become vested? Held, it meant *will* become vested: *Ex parte Dawes, Re Moon* (1886) 17 QBD 275, 282.
- A tax statute authorised the revenue authorities to apply to a claimant's taxation arrangements the reasoning from existing court rulings about similar arrangements, if to do so *would* deny the claimant the tax advantage from its arrangements. Did '*would* deny' mean (1) 'more likely than not deny' (ie, a 51% likelihood would suffice), or (2) 'a substantial degree of confidence in the outcome'? Held, it meant (2): *R v Revenue and Customs Commissioners* [2019] EWCA Civ 747; [2019] 1 WLR 4723, [36]–[37].

Given the almost indeterminate meaning of *would*, prefer an alternative word that conveys the precise intended meaning.

See also **will.**

writing (noun)

Writing signifies something that is *written*, and *written* historically means marked on a surface with a pen or pencil or similar. However, meaning varies with context, which can include social realities. Hence, an email message is almost certainly 'writing', at least to the extent necessary to satisfy a requirement that a notice be 'in writing': *Kavia Holdings Pty Ltd v Suntrack Holdings Pty Ltd* [2011] NSWSC 716, [33]; *UKI (Kingsway) Ltd v Westminster City Council* [2018] UKSC 67; [2019] 1 WLR 104 (service by email effective).

Definitions in statutes or legal documents often extend the meaning of *writing* to include other means of representing or reproducing words in visible form, including by electronic means. For example: '*Writing* includes typing, printing, lithography, photography and other modes of representing or reproducing words in a visible form, and expressions referring to writing are construed accordingly': *Interpretation Act 1978*, Sched 1.

Of course, definitions such as this are no wider than their terms allow. For example, a similar provision did not include a message contained on a USB stick, because a USB stick does not of itself represent or reproduce words in a visible form: *Parkview Constructions Pty Ltd v Total Lifestyle Windows Pty Ltd* [2017] NSWSC 194, [78]—'Looking at [a USB stick] one sees only a small piece of plastic, perhaps with some circuitry on it' (Hammerschlag J). To avoid argument, commercial contracts often contain a boilerplate provision along the following lines:

> 'For the purpose of this agreement, an electronic communication is treated as being in writing.'

Also, context may demand that *in writing* means not merely printed but also signed: eg, *Profit Investment Sim SpA v Ossi* [2016] 1 WLR 3822 (ECJ) (requirement that a jurisdiction clause be 'in writing' not satisfied by being printed in a prospectus, unless the contract signed by the parties acknowledges their acceptance of the clause or refers to the prospectus).

WRITTEN ADVICE (FORM OF)

See **ADVICE (FORM OF)**.

wrongous

An obsolescent Scots law term for *wrongful*. To use *wrongous* today would be consciously archaic.

year

Year can carry different meanings, depending on context. They include:

- calendar year (starting 1 January)
- financial year (the starting date being the statutory or commercial norm in the jurisdiction)
- a continuous period of 365 days (or, in a leap year, 366 days)
- by custom, a number of time periods within a year (eg, a contract to pay an actor 'for three *years* at £X per week' meant, in the theatre trade, payment only for the weeks the theatre was open during those years: *Grant v Maddox* (1846) 15 M &W 737, 745; 153 ER 1048, 1051)
- a year and continuing afterwards until determined at any time on reasonable notice: *Duff v Kyle* (1901) 20 NZLR 706 (contract for supply of milk from a dairy farm 'all the year round').

Further (but unusually), the meaning of *year* can vary within the same document:

> A taxpayer entered into a deed on 5 May 1953. Two provisions of the deed used the term *year*: (1) the taxpayer covenanted to pay a stated sum of money on May 1 'in each *year*'; and (2) the covenant was to last for 8 *years* from the date of the deed. Held, *year* meant in (1) calendar year, but in (2) the period of 12 months from the date of the deed: *IRC v Hobhouse* [1956] 1 WLR 1393.

If doubt is possible over the intended meaning of *year*, clarify.

Year Books

A collection of notes about medieval English cases, dating from about 1270 and continuing to 1535. Manuscript versions organised the cases by topic; later printed collections (known as the *black-letter books*) organised them by regnal year. The notes concentrate more on the debates between lawyer and judge about the legal points in issue, rather than the court's decision. Their purpose was:

> 'to record the intellectual aspect of litigation: to circulate and preserve for future learning, both by students and by their practising elders, the possible moves in the recondite games of legal chess played by the pleaders in open court': JH Baker, *An Introduction to English Legal History*, 4th edn (Oxford University Press, 2002) 179.

More succinctly, Maitland considered that the Year Books were not intended to be law reports, but to provide instruction: 'made by learners for learners, by apprentices for apprentices': FW Maitland, 'Introduction', *Year Books Series, 1 & 2 Ed II* (Selden Society, 1903) vol 17, xiii. Their inaccuracy is legendary: WC Bolland, *The Year Books* (Cambridge University Press, 1921) 37–40.

See also **black-letter books**.

you

See **we / you**.

your Honour

The conventional way in many Commonwealth countries of addressing a presiding judge. Elsewhere, the usage is 'my Lord', 'my Lady'.

See **JUDICIAL HONORIFICS**.

-yse / -yze

British and Commonwealth dictionaries generally prefer *-yse* endings: *analyse, paralyse* (see, eg, *Oxford English Dictionary*; *Macquarie Dictionary*). US English prefers *-yze* endings: *analyze, paralyze*.

See also **-ise / -ize**.

ZERO

In standard English, *zero* is gradually replacing *nought*. Thus, 'string of *noughts*' is now usually expressed 'string of *zeros*'.

See also **NUMBERS**.

www.ingramcontent.com/pod-product-compliance
Ingram Content Group UK Ltd.
Pitfield, Milton Keynes, MK11 3LW, UK
UKHW051416150926
475561UK00005B/202

9 781509 936243